Handbook of

CENTURY PSYCHOLOGY SERIES

Behavior Modification and Behavior Therapy

HAROLD LEITENBERG, editor

PRENTICE-HALL, INC., Englewood Cliffs, New Jersey

Library of Congress Cataloging in Publication Data

Main Entry Under Title:

Handbook of Behavior Modification and Behavior.

(Century Psychology Series)
Includes Bibliographies and Index.
1. Behavior Therapy. 2. Behavior Modification.
I. Leitenberg, Harold. [DNLM: 1. Behavior Therapy.
WM420 H231]
RC489.B4H36   616.8′914   75–44435
ISBN 0–13–372508–1

© 1976 by Prentice-Hall, Inc., Englewood Cliffs, New Jersey

10   9   8   7   6   5   4   3

Printed in the United States of America

Prentice-Hall International, Inc., *London*
Prentice-Hall of Australia Pty. Limited, *Sydney*
Prentice-Hall of Canada, Ltd., *Toronto*
Prentice-Hall of India Private Limited, *New Delhi*
Prentice-Hall of Japan, Inc., *Tokyo*
Prentice-Hall of Southeast Asia Pte. Ltd., *Singapore*

**This book is dedicated
to my family and students.**

Authors

W. Stewart Agras, M.D.
Professor
Department of Psychiatry
Stanford University

Jay S. Birnbrauer, Ph.D.
Associate Professor
Department of Psychology
University of Western Australia

John D. Burchard, Ph.D.
Professor
Department of Psychology
University of Vermont

William J. DeRisi, Ph.D.
Research Specialist
California Department of Health

Paul T. Harig, Ph.D.
Psychology Consultant
Academy of Health Sciences
Fort Sam Houston, Texas

Hyman Hops, Ph.D.
Program Director
Center at Oregon for Research in the
    Behavioral Education of the Handicapped
University of Oregon

Larry W. King, Ph.D.
Assistant Research Psychologist
UCLA School of Medicine
Camarillo–NPI Research Program

David C. Klein, Ph.D.
Psychologist
Norwich Hospital

Leonard Krasner, Ph.D.
Professor
Department of Psychology
State University of New York at Stony
    Brook

Harold Leitenberg, Ph.D.
Professor
Department of Psychology
University of Vermont

Robert Liberman, M.D.
Associate Research Psychiatrist
UCLA School of Medicine
Camarillo–NPI Research Program

O. Ivar Lovaas, Ph.D.
Professor
Department of Psychology
UCLA

Michael J. Mahoney, Ph.D.
Associate Professor
Department of Psychology
Pennsylvania State University

Isaac M. Marks, M.D.
Reader in Experimental Psychopathology
    and Consultant Psychiatrist
Institute of Psychiatry
Maudsley and Bethlehem Royal Hospitals,
London

William A. Miller, Ph.D.
Director of Research
Division of Family Study
Marriage Council of Philadelphia

Peter E. Nathan, Ph.D.
Professor and Director
Alcohol Behavior Research Laboratory
Rutgers University

Crighton D. Newsom, Ph.D.
Experimental Psychologist
Children's Learning Laboratory
Camarillo State Hospital

K. Daniel O'Leary, Ph.D.
Professor
Department of Psychology
State University of New York at
    Stony Brook

Susan G. O'Leary, Ph.D.
Assistant Professor
Department of Psychology
State University of New York at
    Stony Brook

Gerald R. Patterson, Ph.D.
Research Associate
Oregon Research Institute

Todd R. Risley, Ph.D.
Professor
Department of Human Development
University of Kansas

Robert L. Schwitzgebel, Ed.D., Ph.D.
Associate Professor
Department of Psychology
Claremont Graduate School

Martin E. P. Seligman, Ph.D.
Associate Professor
Department of Psychology
University of Pennsylvania

David Shapiro, Ph.D.
Professor
Department of Psychiatry
UCLA School of Medicine

John R. Stahl, Ph.D.
Psychologist
Regional Educational Assessment and
    Diagnostic Services
Lakeville Hospital

Albert J. Stunkard, M.D.
Professor
Department of Psychiatry
Stanford University School of Medicine

Richard S. Surwit, Ph.D.
Instructor
Department of Psychiatry
Harvard Medical School

Sandra Twardosz, Ph.D.
Assistant Professor
Department of Child Development and
    Family Relationships
University of Tennessee

Robert G. Wahler, Ph.D.
Professor
Child Behavior Institute
University of Tennessee

Robert L. Weiss, Ph.D.
Professor
Department of Psychology
University of Oregon

Contents

CHILDREN AND YOUTH

Preface

The idea for this handbook was conceived in the spring of 1972. I wanted to put together a text on behavioral research and mental health (for the most part, on operant conditioning as applied to treatment and prevention of behavior disorders in adults and children) comparable in style, depth, authority, and sophistication to Honig's 1966 edited volume on basic research in operant conditioning.

The number of clinical applications of behavioral procedures and principles has greatly increased during the last decade. Journal articles describing and evaluating these applications are mushrooming. As a result of this publication pressure, there are now four professional journals devoted exclusively to the behavior therapy/modification area. The major professional journal outlets in psychology and psychiatry such as the *Journal of Abnormal Psychology, Journal of Consulting and Clinical Psychology, Archives of General Psychiatry, American Journal of Psychiatry*, and the *British Journal of Psychiatry* are devoting more and more space to this topic. Obviously this vast literature needs to be integrated and critically reviewed.

None of the broader introductory texts and books of readings in behavior modification has provided a detailed and thorough review of the applied operant research literature in the mental health area. This leaves an unfortunate vacuum that needs to be filled for students *and* mental health professionals who want to become familiar with clinical research developments in this vital new field.

Leading researchers in the field were willing to write original, up-to-date, and comprehensive chapters which would critically review and integrate the literature that has been accumulating in diverse publications. The chapters emphasize, wherever possible, empirical evaluation of therapy components and outcomes rather than simple description of techniques. The major purpose is to provide detailed examination of research on the use of behavioral strategies for treatment of specific behavior disorders in a variety of clinical settings. Some traditional psychiatric disorders (e.g., suicide, manic depressive psychosis) are excluded simply because not enough research on behavioral treatment exists to make a review worthwhile. Of course, the amount of work in the areas that are included still varies considerably. For example, even though less has been done in marital conflict or depression than in mental retardation or neuroses, the former topics are included because some beginnings have been made and some perspective on what has transpired and what still needs to be done can be provided. There is no fixed outline or page limit for every chapter because the size and nature of the topics are so variable.

In a venture like this, it is noteworthy that we lost only one of the original contributors. I will be eternally grateful to the authors for their hard work, perseverance, cooperation, and toward the end, tolerance of some of my editorial suggestions and proddings. Several contributors swore, "Never again—this is the last chapter I'll ever write." I know how they feel.

I sincerely hope this will be a useful text for advanced undergraduate and graduate courses in behavior modification and behavior therapy and that professionals and students of the various mental health disciplines, including psychology, psychiatry, social work, and psychiatric nursing will find the handbook a valuable resource. The rapid pace of research in behavior modification and behavior therapy shows little sign of abatement. Hence, there will be new developments. This book cannot be the final word, but it can serve as a relatively complete reference for what has been achieved so far; we hope it will also be an influential guide for the future.

HAROLD LEITENBERG

Adults

Alcoholism

1

PETER E. NATHAN

Historical Perspectives on Alcohol and Alcoholics

Alcohol and alcoholics have been part of man's history ever since man learned that fermented grain or fruit yields an intoxicating substance whose effects on mood and conviviality are pleasant and hence reinforcing.

Noah may have been mankind's first recorded inebriate. At least the Old Testament Bible says of him, somewhat ruefully: "And Noah the husbandman began, and planted a vineyard. And he drank of the wine, and was drunken; and he was uncovered within his tent [Genesis, 9: 20, 21]." The authors of the Book of Proverbs condemn the social drinker just as emphatically: "Look not upon the wine when it is red, when it sparkleth in the cup, when it goeth down smoothly; at the last it biteth like a serpent and stingeth like an adder [Proverbs 23: 31, 32]."

The use of alcohol has waxed and waned through the ages. It waxed under the Greeks and Romans and waned in those lands controlled by Islam during the Dark Ages. In more recent times, it waxed during the lusty hedonism of the Elizabethan era and waned

as efficiency and productivity became by-words during the Industrial Revolution. To this end, ardent tracts condemning the effects of alcohol appeared at the beginning of the industrial era in support of efforts to make more widely known the dangers of alcohol to life and morals. In response to these persuasive documents, groups formed in England and the United States to take up the cause of Temperance. The most notable of these groups in the United States was Carrie Nation's Women's Christian Temperance Union (WCTU). The WCTU was most influential in creating Prohibition—the "experiment noble in purpose" as President Hoover called it—which began in 1920 and ended in 1932.

The end of Prohibition marked the beginning of a more scientific approach to alcoholism, brought on in large part by recognition of Prohibition's dismal failure to legislate public morality. A variety of more empirical approaches to alcoholism began around that time, fostered by the founding of the Yale Center of Alcohol Studies and its *Quarterly Journal of Studies on Alcohol*. At the same time, the advent of the "vitamin age" led to research which strongly suggested that many diseases that had been considered "alcoholic diseases" were actually products of malnutrition and vitamin deficiency. Alcoholics Anonymous also came into being around this same time. Though contemporary research, especially from the behavioral point of view, will be reviewed below, it is interesting in this context to point out that AA's continuing objective approach to alcoholism has recently resulted in legislation defining alcoholism as a medical disease rather than a criminal offense. Whether this new attempt to legislate public opinion about alcohol will be more successful than Prohibition, however, remains to be seen.

Who Is an Alcoholic?

Although there is no single definition of alcoholism, several behavioral criteria taken together enable us to judge the severity of a drinking problem. Among these criteria are: (1) the person reports a "loss of control" of his drinking behavior; (2) he "needs a drink" to get going in the morning, to keep going during the day, or to prepare himself for stressful events; he has become psychologically dependent upon alcohol; (3) he has lost job(s), family, or friends because of his drinking; (4) he has experienced "blackouts," increasing tolerance for alcohol, or both with continued drinking; (5) he reports withdrawal symptoms when he stops drinking; he is physically dependent upon alcohol.

Psychological dependence describes a strong, sometimes overwhelming need for a drug. *Physical dependence* refers to a need for a drug that is accompanied by painful symptoms of physiological withdrawal (for example, restlessness, nausea, vomiting) when the drug is no longer ingested. After a fixed dose of a drug has been ingested at regular and frequent intervals, certain of its effects progressively decrease in intensity. This phenomenon, *drug tolerance*, necessitates ingestion of larger and larger doses of the drug to produce the desired effect.

Blackouts are characteristic short-term memory deficits that appear after a person has been a heavy drug user for a long period of time. These terms, of course, describe effects that are common to all drugs, not just to alcohol.

The Varieties of Alcoholism

The two most commonly used formal systems for categorizing problem drinkers and/or alcoholics are those put forth by Jellinek (1960) and the *Diagnostic and Statistical Manual* (American Psychiatric Association, 1968). Jellinek categorizes the varieties of alcoholism as follows: (1) *Alpha alcoholism* represents reliance upon alcohol to relieve bodily or emotional pain that does not lead to loss of control. The major damage is to interpersonal relationships. This alcoholic is often termed the "problem drinker." (2) *Beta alcoholism* is associated with physical complaints such as gastritis or cirrhosis of the liver. It does not involve either physical or psychological dependence upon alcohol. (3) *Gamma alcoholism* refers to increased tissue tolerance to alcohol, withdrawal symptoms upon cessation of drinking, psychological dependence upon alcohol, and loss of control of drinking. Most "skid row" alcoholics are of this type. (4) *Delta alcoholism* differs from gamma alcoholism in one way: delta alcoholics cannot abstain from drinking while gamma alcoholics, though they have lost control of their drinking, are nonetheless capable of periods of sobriety.

The *Diagnostic and Statistical Manual* (1968) categorizes three separate physical and psychological concomitants of alcoholism. The brain damage that is caused by heavy, prolonged drinking is grouped with other "organic psychoses." Simple drunkenness that does not involve psychotic-like behavior is listed separately as "nonpsychosis of physical origin." The largest group of alcohol-related problems is included within the broad "personality disorder" category. Within this grouping are four separate entities: *episodic excessive drinking, habitual excessive drinking, alcohol addiction,* and *other alcoholism.* Though a more objective and hence more verifiable categorization system than Jellinek's, this "official" schema—essentially a static one—may accord less with the actual behavior of alcoholics, whose patterns of alcoholism often change as time and circumstances change, than Jellinek's system. This point will become more clear when we review empirical data on the drinking behavior of alcoholics.

The ultimate utility of either classification system, however, is limited by the bugaboo which confronts all systematizers of psychopathologic behavior—that their diagnostic efforts have no real value beyond the *pro forma* exercise of classification itself. In this case, affixing diagnostic labels to persons who abuse alcohol does not prevent others from falling prey to that behavioral excess; more important, the label finally applied fails to point to effective treatment for the alcoholic's abuse of alcohol.

The Etiologies of Alcoholism

No definitive etiology of alcoholism has been established.

BIOPHYSIOLOGICAL THEORIES

A variety of biophysiological theories of alcoholism have been proposed. One of the first and most persistent hypothesizes that alcoholics and nonalcoholics differ in the rate at which they metabolize alcohol. If it could be demonstrated, this difference would have profound etiologic significance. However, a number of recent studies have concluded that the rate of ethanol metabolism between groups of alcoholics and nonalcoholics does not differ (Mendelson, 1968; Truitt, 1971.) Efforts to establish differences between alcoholics and nonalcoholics in terms of cellular adaptation

to ethanol, or adrenal medullary and adrenergic mechanisms (which influence tolerance phenomena) have also failed. These mechanisms clearly depend upon alcohol consumption and nutritional variables rather than on innate or acquired differences in bodily function between alcoholics and nonalcoholics (Mendelson, 1970).

Although no physical basis for alcoholism has yet been found, research into biophysiological determinants of alcoholism continues. Lately this effort has focused on the possible role of genetic factors in alcoholism. Support for a genetic view of the disorder comes from human twin studies (Kaij, 1960) which indicate that monozygotic twins have a higher concordance rate for alcoholism than dizygotic twins; from animal research yielding strains of inbred mice that prefer alcohol (Rodgers & McClearn, 1962); and from adoption studies suggesting that adopted children with a natural parent who was alcoholic have higher rates of alcoholism as adults than adopted children whose natural parents were not alcoholic (Goodwin, 1973).

SOCIOCULTURAL THEORIES

Strongest support for the sociocultural approach to alcoholism comes from research showing the profound impact that cultural drinking patterns have on rates of alcoholism. First generation Italian Americans and Jewish Americans, both from cultures in which drinking takes place in a family and/or religious context, drink frequently but have low rates of alcoholism (Cahalan, Cisin, & Crossley, 1969; Lolli, Serianni, Golder, & Luzzatto-Fegiz, 1958). The Irish, whose drinking takes place in public houses outside the family context, have lower consumption rates but higher alcoholism rates than the other cultural groups. It is interesting to note that as these groups acculturate within the American "melting pot," their rates of alcoholism come closer and closer to each other. Thus, recent data indicate that second and third generation American Jews, have significantly higher rates of alcoholism than first generation Jews, while the reverse seems true of Irish Americans (Department of Health, Education, and Welfare, 1971).

Although cultural factors can predispose to alcoholism, social variables play a major role in translating that predisposition to addiction. They can also pressure an alcoholic to keep drinking despite strong pressures from other sources in the direction of abstinence. In this regard, Braucht, Brakarsh, Follingstad, and Berry (1973) conclude, on the basis of a thorough review of the literature, that peer pressure plays an especially important role in the development of deviant drinking patterns among adolescents. Pointing especially to work by Jessor, Collins, and Jessor (1972), which most clearly documents this etiologic model of alcohol abuse, Braucht and his colleagues summarize their review by noting that "peer influences on adolescent attitudes toward drinking and drinking behavior are substantial [1973, p. 93]." Of relevance to the behavioral model of alcoholism, these observations by nonbehaviorists strongly suggest that modelling may well play an important role in the etiology of alcoholism.

PSYCHOANALYTIC THEORIES

Alcoholism, like most other behavioral disorders, has also been explained by psychoanalytic theory. Psychoanalysts variously see the alcoholic as fundamentally suicidal in his efforts to destroy a "bad, depriving mother" with whom he has identified; as "defending" himself against an underlying depression by drinking to oblivion; or as drinking in defense against overwhelming anxiety (deVito, Flaherty, & Mozdzierz, 1970). Critics of the psychoanalytic approach to alcoholism (e.g., Franks, 1970) point to the absence of empirical data in support of psychoanalytic hypotheses about the disorder, and apparent failure of the method to help most alcoholics who seek psychoanalytic treatment.

BEHAVIORAL THEORIES

The behavioral view of alcoholism has not been especially well articulated. Thus, most current behavioral theories are variations on the basic theme first developed in the animal laboratory (Conger, 1951, 1956) that drinking is a learned means of reducing conditioned anxiety. Variations on this basic theme derive largely from disagreement over the precise mechanisms responsible for the presense of the conditioned anxiety. Franks (1970) offers a detailed historical treatment of this body of research and the resultant conflict over its interpretation.

Implicit in the hypothesis that drinking alcohol is a tension reducing event is the assumption that alcohol eases prevailing high levels of anxiety in alcoholics. However, a recent study comparing alcoholics and matched nonalcoholics on a variety of behavioral dimensions (Nathan & O'Brien, 1971) reported that alcohol actually *increases* levels of anxiety and depression in alcoholics, following an initial 12- to 24-hour period of drinking during which levels of anxiety do decrease modestly. Another recent behavioral study (Okulitch & Marlatt, 1972), drawing the same conclusion, speculates that alcohol may come to act as a discriminative stimulus which has both positive and negative properties for the alcoholic. An excellent review of the animal literature on tension reduction and alcohol was recently published by Cappell and Herman (1972); research in this area with humans has been carefully reviewed by Mello (1972).

Assessment Methods

TRADITIONAL ASSESSMENT PROCEDURES AND ASSUMPTIONS

For every study that proclaims the alcoholic an "oral character," "dependent," "masochistic," or a "masked depressive" on the basis of projective test results or "depth" interviewing, another three admit their inability to find such distinguishing characteristics (Tremper, 1972; Zucker & Van Horn, 1972).

Objective tests, however, have identified what seem to be reliable behavioral differences between alcoholics and nonalcoholics. For example, Scale 4 of the Minnesota Multiphasic Personality Inventory (MMPI), the "Psychopathic Deviant" subscale, differentiates alcoholics and nonalcoholics (MacAndrew, 1965) and is also sensitive to treatment changes in hospitalized alcoholics (Rohan, 1972). Other MMPI scales that tap levels of depression and anxiety also appear to be sensitive to individual differences in the severity and intensity of alcoholism among a range of drinkers (Overall & Patrick, 1972).

Perusal of the items from Scale 4 which differentiate drinkers from nondrinkers reveals that the sensitivity of this scale to "alcoholic behavior" is largely a consequence of just three items: those which ask whether the subject has ever used alcohol to excess, has ever been in trouble with the law, or feels that he has not lived the right kind of life. Given this finding, one must ask whether it might not be much simpler to ask these three questions of all suspected alcoholics!

Other self-report questionnaires designed specifically to enable assessment of incidence and severity of alcoholism have also been developed. The two best known, the Manson Evaluation Test (Manson, 1948a) and the Alcadd Test (Manson, 1948b), have neither successfully identified alcoholics in mixed populations of alcoholics and nonalcoholics nor assessed the severity of the problem in individual alcoholics. In large part, this failure reflects the difficulty everyone has in differentiating alcoholics from problem or heavy drinkers, especially when neither group is convinced that it has a serious problem with alcohol. More recently, Lanyon (1974) described a self-report measure that shows promise in this regard,

largely because it contains a variety of discriminating items that are also sufficiently nonthreatening that they are readily answered truthfully by suspicious patients.

BEHAVIORAL ASSESSMENT TECHNIQUES

Concerted efforts to develop behavioral assessment instruments for use specifically with alcoholics have recently been made in recognition of the well known unreliability of alcoholics' self-reports of their own drinking (Summers, 1970). In addition, traditional assessment methods fail to specify the kind and severity of a given person's immoderate drinking for purposes of treatment planning (Franks, 1970), and are often inappropriate for the pre- and posttreatment assessments that are necessary components of all behavioral treatment efforts (P. M. Miller, 1973).

Approaches to the assessment of alcoholic behavior by behaviorists have taken a variety of forms. Included among them have been the adaption of standard behavioral instruments (e.g., the Reinforcement Survey Schedule, the Fear Survey Schedule) for use by alcoholics; observation of the behavior of alcoholics during free drinking periods in controlled laboratory settings employing the operant paradigm; "choice" situations in which alcoholics choose among a variety of alcoholic and nonalcoholic beverages, again in a laboratory setting; and experimental bar settings in which the precise nature of the drinking sequence can be recorded objectively by observers.

In a study designed to evaluate the utility of the Reinforcement Survey Schedule (RSS) for use specifically with alcoholics, Keehn, Bloomfield, and Hug (1970) administered the RSS to 40 hospitalized alcoholics. Contrary to expectation, these subjects responded to the scale very much like a student population first given the scale by its developers. In particular, the alcoholic subjects did not consider alcohol to be a powerful reinforcer, preferring "occupational success," "loving intimacy," and "pleasure from nature" in that order. Although Keehn and his colleagues took these results to indicate that behavioral treatment of alcoholics might well be directed toward making the preferred reinforcers attainable by means other than drinking, the RSS might also validly reflect changes in the value of specific environmental reinforcers as a function of blood alcohol level, length of a drinking episode, and stresses associated with prolonged drinking.

Controlled studies of the behavioral concomitants of drinking by alcoholics have been possible only within the past ten years, largely because giving alcohol to alcoholics even for this purpose met with virtually universal disapproval from large segments of lay society until the potential benefits of such studies had been demonstrated. Studies involving the acute administration of alcohol to alcoholics and nonalcoholics were begun before chronic studies were undertaken; for the most part, they focused on the effects of measured doses of alcohol on physiological, metabolic, and behavioral functioning of alcoholics as compared to nonalcoholics. To this end, Docter and Bernal (1964) found that acute ingestion of alcohol by alcoholics leads to increases in heart rate, rapid eye movements during sleep, and EEG alpha activity. The same investigators reported that maximum increases in EEG activity were induced by very light alcohol dosages and that performance on a task demanding continuous attention to an auditory signal did not worsen after the alcoholic subjects had begun to drink. This finding, like those of Talland and his coworkers (1964) and others, suggested that even relatively large amounts of alcohol do not interfere with some perceptual and motor performances by alcoholics. Some investigators (cf. Mello, 1972, for review) have actually observed an *increase* in the ability to perform these and other tasks when alcoholics are drinking at moderate levels, though others (Talland & Kasschau, 1965) have reported the reverse.

Acute drinking studies cannot accurately portray the drinking behavior of chronic alcoholics as they usually drink. For this reason the work of Mendelson and Mello, the first investigators to study prolonged drinking by alcoholics in an operant laboratory setting, is worthy of more detailed overview here. Their early studies (Mello & Mendelson, 1965; Mendelson & Mello, 1966) were done on a research ward at the Boston City Hospital, an appropriate research site in view of Boston's distinction as the city with the second highest per capita incidence of alcoholism in the United States (Efron & Keller, 1970). (San Francisco claims national honors, by the way).

Among the most important findings of this first set of studies of prolonged drinking under ad lib conditions were the following: (1) Tolerance (behavioral adaption to alcohol) was exhibited by most subjects; it was reflected by altered performance on a number of perceptual-cognitive and visual-motor coordination tasks as drinking continued. (2) A change in cardiac function associated with both alcohol ingestion and alcohol withdrawal was identified. (3) "Craving" for alcohol, a phenomenon thought to "doom" the recovered alcoholic who takes as much as a single drink after a period of sobriety, was not observed even when subjects were given a drink after a period of sobriety; in fact, craving failed to appear until large quantities of alcohol had been consumed over a period of many days. (4) Observation of relationships among alcohol ingestion, spontaneous cessation of drinking, and onset of alcoholic gastritis (irritation of the stomach lining intense enough to cause vomiting) suggested that gastrointestinal tolerance might be one of the major determinants of the drinking patterns of many alcoholics.

Since this first set of laboratory studies, Mendelson and Mello's efforts have been joined by those of Nathan and his coworkers in independent research designed to illuminate the physiological and psychological effects of prolonged drinking by alcoholics.

Both groups of researchers have demonstrated that certain behaviors associated with prolonged drinking—including the characteristic, often dramatic, increase in levels of depression and anxiety that occurs shortly after drinking begins, and the equally common cycle of "spree" and "maintenance" phases within a single prolonged drinking episode—appear to be relatively unaffected by psychological or social factors (McNamee, Mello, & Mendelson, 1968; Nathan, Titler, Lowenstein, Solomon, & Rossi, 1970).

Research comparing the social, affective, and drinking behavior of skid row alcoholics and nonalcoholics (Nathan & O'Brien, 1971) brought two groups of subjects to a research ward at the Boston City Hospital. A group of four alcoholics and a group of four nonalcoholics were admitted to the ward for successive 33-day studies. Major results of the study were: (1) Though both alcoholics and nonalcoholics reached the same high blood alcohol levels early in drinking, the alcoholics remained at these levels longer and returned to them more frequently. Hence, they drank almost twice as much as the nonalcoholics. (2) Alcoholics began drinking with a six- to eight-day "spree," followed by a longer "maintenance" drinking period; nonalcoholics were only maintenance drinkers. (3) Unlike nonalcoholics, alcoholics were social isolates before, during, and after drinking. (4) Alcoholics became significantly more depressed and less active and demonstrated significantly more psychopathology (e.g., anxiety, manic behavior, paranoia, and the neurotic behaviors of phobia and compulsions) than nonalcoholics once drinking began.

The results of this study, like those from other studies by Mello, Mendelson, and Nathan, suggest—contrary to widespread belief—that the alcoholic may not be an "all or-none" drinker and may not drink largely to reduce high levels of depression and anxiety. In this way these findings tend to refute with fervor prior conclusions derived from anecdote and theory. These data also suggest that the uncontrolled drinking behavior of the alcoholic—rather than a set of distinguishing personality characteristics— may be his most relevant identifying feature. This conclusion, in turn, leads naturally to a behavioral (as opposed to a dynamic) approach to therapy for alcoholism, an approach detailed below.

Behavioral assessment of alcoholic patients in "choice" situations may be a promising alternative to assessment by means of more prolonged, more expensive observational methods. To this end, some investigators (e.g., Chapman, Burt, & Smith, 1972; Moroski & Baer, 1970) have given alcoholic patients the opportunity to choose among a number of alcoholic and nonalcoholic beverages before, during, and after treatment, in the effort specifically to assess treatment efficacy. Though these studies tried to disguise the intent of this procedure, both clearly permitted perceptive subjects to "see through" the disguise. For this reason, other investigators (Marlatt, 1973; Miller & Hersen, 1972) have attempted to disguise the assessment by announcing it to be a "taste experiment" akin to the model employed successfully by Schachter, Goldman, and Gordon (1968) to disguise interest in the consummatory behavior of obese people.

Acknowledging that a related shortcoming of both behavioral and nonbehavioral assessment of alcoholism is validity (the degree to which such assessments accurately reflect actual drinking behavior outside the laboratory setting), Marlatt's studies employed a "nonobtrusive" assessment method whose true purposes were cleverly masked. The intent of the first study using Marlatt's "taste-rating task" (Marlatt, Demming, & Reid, 1973) was to determine whether it is the actual presence of alcohol or merely the alcoholic's expectancy of alcohol in the drinks he consumes that affects consequent drinking rates. This test of the crucial "loss of control" hypothesis—that one drink of alcohol by an alcoholic sets off an inexorable chain of events leading to an alcoholic spree—employed a 2×2 factorial design in which subjects were told either that they would be testing an alcoholic beverage or a nonalcoholic one when, in fact, alcohol or no alcohol was varied as an independent variable. Telling subjects that they were participants in a study designed to produce comparative taste ratings for either three varieties of vodka mixed with tonic or three varieties of tonic water (depending on the expectancy condition), the experimenters then conducted 15-minute taste-rating sessions, complete with suitable additional deception devices (taste-rating adjectives). Subjects were permitted to drink as much of three sample beverages as they wished in the time allotted to the study. The results of this study encouraged Marlatt to continue to hold a behavioral view of alcoholism, since the only significant determinant of amount of alcohol consumed was the subject's expectation of what he was drinking (rather than actual beverage consumed or an interaction between expectancy and actual beverage.) Marlatt has used the "taste-rating task" in three other studies, all designed to investigate additional behavioral determinants of alcohol consumption. To this end, Higgins and Marlatt (1973) found that being fearful or under stress did not increase alcohol consumption by either alcoholics or nonalcoholics; Higgins (1973) reported that an impending threat of interpersonal evaluation did increase levels of wine consumption by heavy drinkers; and Marlatt and Kosturn (1973) observed that heavy drinkers who were angered by insulting remarks but who were not allowed to retaliate against their persecutor drank significantly more than insulted subjects who could retaliate; the latter, in fact, drank less than subjects who were not insulted to begin with.

Development of this assessment paradigm, in our view, represents a methodological advance that permits rapid, valid, and relatively inexpensive assessment of drinking behavior as a direct function of treatment intervention. Although research

has yet to establish the precise nature of relationships between drinking by alcoholics in a "taste test" and "on the street," Marlatt's preliminary reports encourage the expectation that these relationships will be consistent.

Although a bar setting was part of the controlled operant studies undertaken by Nathan and his coworkers, it was used only to maximize the degree to which the laboratory setting resembled the *in vivo* drinking settings chosen by many of their alcoholic subjects. Model bars have also been used, however, as the setting for behavioral assessment, most notably by Schaefer, Sobell, and Mills (1971). After a prolonged period of behavioral observation of 16 male alcoholics and 15 male social drinkers, Schaefer and his colleagues concluded that the drinking behavior of their alcoholic subjects differed from that of the social drinkers in at least three important ways: (1) alcoholics preferred straight rather than mixed drinks; (2) alcoholics consumed their drinks by gulping more often than by sipping; (3) alcoholics continued to drink beyond the stage of intoxication at which the social drinkers stopped. Though these findings have not been confirmed independently, the assessment method itself was of value in a study by the same group designed to pilot a new behavioral treatment for alcoholics (Mills, Sobell, & Schaefer, 1971). Nonetheless, replication of this assessment procedure would appear necessary before it is used again as a therapy outcome measure.

We believe that behavioral approaches to the assessment of alcoholism are probably more sophisticated in terms of methodology, more sensitive to the specifics of the maladaptive behaviors in question, and, most important, more reliable than the behavioral methods that have been developed to assess most other behavioral disorders. This promising "state of the art" reflects the length of time alcoholism has troubled society; the degree to which alcoholics are "visible" and hence troublesome; and the fact that the maladaptive behavior that lies at the center of alcoholism —excessive drinking—is more susceptible to quantification than the hallucinations of the schizophrenic patient or the obsessions of the obsessive-compulsive neurotic patient. It is also important to note that one or more of the behavioral assessment methods used for alcoholism might be useful in assessing other behavior disorders; as a pre- and posttreatment assessment method (e.g., Marlatt's model); as a means of targeting behavior for behavioral treatment (as the Schaefer paradigm permits); or as a procedure for identifying concurrent behavioral differences between patients and nonpatients (as in the Nathan and the Mello & Mendelson operant models).

Treatment Approaches to Alcoholism

DRUGS

Although no drug exists which by itself prevents uncontrolled drinking, the history of two drugs formerly thought to be "magic bullets" for alcoholism is of interest. Flagyl (metronidazole), a drug of proven utility in the treatment of vaginal fungi (Krupp, Chatton, & Margen, 1971), recently attracted a good deal of attention following the observation that women alcoholics treated with the drug for this physical disorder sharply reduced their alcohol intake. As a result, Flagyl quickly attracted a host of supporters claiming its therapeutic efficacy in treating alcoholism. It was only after careful, controlled clinical trials on large numbers of alcoholics that the supposed utility of the drug in this connection was finally disproved (Penick, Carrier, & Sheldon, 1969).

The second drug, Antabuse (disulfiram), interferes with the metabolism of alcohol so dramatically that its presence in the bloodstream in even trace amounts causes dramatic, prolonged, and extremely unpleasant effects when alcohol is ingested.

These effects include precipitous nausea, vomiting, dramatically increased heartbeat and respiration, and cold sweats. Though initially embraced by many as a panacea for alcoholism, Antabuse must now be viewed more realistically. When taken as directed on waking in the morning—before the impulse to drink strikes—it is an effective deterrent to drinking for two or three days. On the other hand, when "the mood to drink" does strike, Antabuse can easily be avoided, thus permitting the alcoholic to resume drinking. To this end, a recent study (Lubetkin, Rivers, & Rosenberg, 1971) reported that less than 1% of all patients receiving maintenance doses of Antabuse under optimal conditions in the hospital continued to take it on their release. The authors of this study conclude that Antabuse can serve the useful function of protecting the recovered alcoholic from occasional "reversion impulses" only if he is well motivated.

ALCOHOLICS ANONYMOUS

The history of Alcoholics Anonymous—AA to its worldwide coterie of members and friends—began in May 1935, when Bill W. and Dr. Robert S. (both alcoholics) met to discuss formation of an alcoholic-centered milieu free from the medical and moral domination that then characterized alcoholism treatment.

The latest edition of AA's *World Directory* (1974) provides a glimpse of the phenomenal growth of the organization over the first 37 years of its existence. From the initial two-man group have come over 7,500 autonomous AA groups holding over 10,000 weekly meetings throughout the United States, the District of Columbia, the Canal Zone, and Puerto Rico. Though firm figures are not available, it is likely that there are well over 250,000 active AA members in the United States. The *World Directory* also lists over 1,000 AA groups in Canada and close to 200 other groups scattered through the rest of the world.

Though objective data on the therapeutic efficacy of AA are hard to come by, many professionals familiar with the movement believe that it represents the most effective current treatment for alcoholism. For this reason, it is striking that AA's "cure" rate seems to be only 30 to 35% (Ditman, 1967), a rate of treatment success that would be roundly condemned as grossly inadequate for any other major social problem.

THE DYNAMIC THERAPIES

Although Sigmund Freud only occasionally referred to treatment of the alcoholic patient, dynamically based individual and group treatment probably remains the predominant mode of professional treatment of alcoholics. This is so even though Freud himself was dubious about the utility of psychoanalysis for "character neuroses," of which alcoholism is one. The results of a recent careful review of 49 papers published between 1952 and 1963 which reported on studies of psychotherapy with alcoholics draws the unhappy conclusion that the authors were "unable to form a conclusive opinion as to the value of psychotherapeutic methods in the treatment of alcoholism [Hill & Blaine, 1967]."

Others, however, have claimed success with alcoholics using psychoanalytically oriented psychotherapy (Silber, 1970), psychoanalysis (Shentaub & Mijolla, 1968) and dynamically oriented group therapy (Smith, 1969). Unfortunately, these selected claims of success are unaccompanied by empirical research data which forces us to conclude that the utility of psychotherapy for alcoholics, despite its widespread use, remains to be established.

BEHAVIORAL APPROACHES TO THE TREATMENT OF ALCOHOLISM

Alcoholism has become a central target of behavioral attempts to modify maladaptive human behavior for a number of reasons: alcoholism is one of the country's major public health problems; many nonbehavioral mental health workers have acknowledged the ineffectiveness of their procedures with alcoholics; productive early basic research on alcoholism was undertaken by behaviorally oriented researchers; and alcoholism is defined by a single quantifiable target behavior whose modification would represent undoubted behavioral success.

Behaviorally trained clinicians chose first to design treatment strategies whose final therapeutic aim was abstinence. They were motivated, in part, by the widespread belief—instilled by Alcoholics Anonymous in every new recruit—that the "one drink, one drunk" concept is valid. Also they saw alcoholism as the consequence of inevitable loss-of-control set off by the reintroduction of alcohol into a physiological system which reacted violently and maladaptively to its introduction. Another reason was widespread acceptance of the validity of the anxiety reduction model of alcohol addiction since cessation of drinking, according to that model, would necessarily eliminate the reinforcing consequences of drinking. This latter assumption fails to take into account other reinforcing consequences of drinking—such as increased conviviality, more relaxed social intercourse, sedation—that are also lost when abstinence is imposed.

BEHAVIORAL EFFORTS TO INDUCE ABSTINENCE. Though by now a full range of behavioral methods (including systematic desensitization, covert sensitization, and broad-spectrum approaches) have been applied to the alcoholic, his treatment by behaviorists for many years was confined largely to the aversive conditioning therapies, most often with electric shock. These early behavioral approaches to alcoholism will be reviewed here first.

Aversive conditioning: Electric shock. More than 45 years ago Russian physician N. V. Kantorovich treated 20 Russian alcoholics by pairing the sight, smell, and taste of a variety of alcoholic beverages with repeated electric shock (1930) . Follow-up of this dramatic new treatment lasted from 3 weeks to 20 months and revealed that 70% of the patients so treated had remained abstinent during that time. These were extremely encouraging data, especially since Kantorovich, unlike many contemporary alcoholism researchers, made provision for follow-up of a control group of 10 alcoholics given "standard treatment" (either hypnotic suggestion or medication) who returned to alcohol within a few days of their release from the hospital.

Despite the positive nature of Kantorovich's findings, it was not until the 1960s that electrical aversion was reintroduced as a prime behavioral treatment for alcoholism (although chemical aversion methods to punish alcohol consumption were widely used in the 1940s). The resurgence of interest in electrical aversion (as opposed to chemical aversion) for treating a variety of disorders may have resulted from theoretical papers by Eysenck (1960) and Rachman (1961). Rachman pointed out, for example, that chemicals are difficult to administer reliably, cause unpleasantness for both patient and therapist, and generate "aggressiveness and hostility on the part of the patient [p. 237]." Contrasting these negative features of chemical aversion with electrical aversion, Rachman stated that (1) the long history of aversive conditioning with animals and humans guaranteed better research on therapeutic outcome; (2) the nature of electrical stimulus permits its reliable and accurate administration; and (3) electrical stimulation also enables use of portable apparatus for delivery of shock to humans, another decided plus. These views, along with similar conclusions by others in favor of electrical aversion, accounted at least in part for the recent primacy of the electrical aversion model, despite encouraging data from a large-scale study of chemical aversion conditioning with alcoholics (discussed below) that had

been reported earlier (Voegtlin, 1940, 1947; Lemere & Voegtlin, 1950).

At about the same time these theoretical papers were written, McGuire and Vallance (1964) reported their initial attempts to treat alcoholism by electrical aversion. They used their approach—straight-forward aversive (classical) conditioning—on both alcoholics and nonalcoholics (e.g., a fetishist, an obsessional ruminator, a heavy smoker, a victim of writer's cramp). They concluded that alcoholism responded less well than heavy smoking or fetishism to this treatment method.

One of the most extensive series of electrical aversion studies was conducted shortly thereafter by Blake at the Crichton Royal Hospital, Scotland (1965, 1967). A more sophisticated application of behavioral principles than McGuire and Vallance's project, Blake's paradigm combined training in progressive relaxation with electrical aversion conditioning. This multimodal attack on behaviors associated with chronic alcoholism anticipated similar present day approaches to this disorder. By defining alcoholism as "the result of a learned habit of uncontrollable drinking which is used by the individual in an effort to reduce a disturbance in psychological homeostasis," Blake (1965, p. 77) made clear that he accepted the anxiety reduction hypothesis in its virtual entirety. He went on to justify his choice of seemingly incompatible treatment methods by noting that electrical aversion is less than a permanent solution to alcoholism in that the maladaptive behavior it confronts (uncontrolled drinking) is itself the consequence of other behaviors (heightened fear and anxiety) with which it does not deal directly. As a result, electrical aversion must be employed in conjunction with training in relaxation which would deal specifically with the fear and anxiety he felt to be at the center of alcoholism.

In the initial report on this method (Blake, 1965), the treatment of a single group of 37 alcoholics was described. Sub-

TABLE 1–1a   6-month follow-up of 37 cases treated by relaxation-aversion therapy

Outcome	Number of cases			Percent of total
	Male	*Female*	*Total*	
1. Sober	15	5*	20	54
2. Relapsed	9	5	14	38
3. No information or opted out of therapy	3	—	3	8
Total	27	10	37	100

SOURCE: Blake, 1965, p. 81.
* Includes one case relapsed, readmitted for further aversion training and has remained sober since.

jects were in their middle 40s, had been drawn from higher socioeconomic classes, and suffered from what seems to have been only moderate alcoholism. All subjects received relaxation training (averaging about 12 sessions); "motivational arousal" (designed to increase subjects' motivation for treatment by forcing them to dwell repeatedly on the consequences of their alcohol abuse); and aversion conditioning (lasting about 15 sessions, in which shock was begun when a sip of alcohol was taken and terminated when it was spit out—technically, this method was aversion relief).

Follow-up data reported in the same paper were gathered when subjects returned to the hospital at 1-, 3-, 6-, 9- and 12-month intervals. Tables 1–1a and 1–1b summarize 6- and 12-month follow-up data from this study; they suggest that about half the patients identified at followup had remained abstinent. An additional followup of the same patients (Blake, 1967) described a comparison of a new treated group of 25 alcoholic subjects with the original 37 aversion-relaxation subjects. Matched with the original 37 subjects for age, sex, socioeconomic status, chronicity of alcoholism, previous hospitalization, concurrent psychiatric diagnosis, and intelligence, the new 25 subjects received electrical aversion (aversion relief) therapy alone. Tables 1–2a and 1–2b, which summarize the 12-month follow-up data for both groups, show that

TABLE 1–1b   12-month follow-up of 25 cases treated by relaxation-aversion therapy

Outcome	Number of cases			Percent of total
	Male	*Female*	*Total*	
1. Abstinent	8	5*	13	52
2. Relapsed	7	2	9	36
3. No information or opted out of therapy	3	—	3	12
Total	18	7	25	100

SOURCE: Blake, 1965, p. 81.
* Includes one case relapsed, readmitted for further aversion training and has remained sober since.

TABLE 1–2a   12-month follow-up of 37 cases treated by relaxation-aversion therapy

Outcome	Number of cases			Percent of total
	Male	*Female*	*Total*	
1. Abstinent	12	5	17*	46
2. Improved	3	2	5*	13
3. Relapsed	8	3	11	30
4. Others	4	—	4	11
Total	27	10	37	100

SOURCE: Blake, 1967, p. 91.
* Includes three subjects (one male, two female) relapsed, readmitted for further relaxation-aversion therapy and have been abstinent or improved for 12 months since last discharge.

alcoholics receiving both relaxation training and aversion therapy (Table 1–2a) were more apt to be judged either abstinent or improved than those given electrical aversion therapy alone (Table 1–2b). However, since Blake dealt with neither "time-in treatment," the reliability of the follow-up data, nor the comparability of his two groups of subjects in his report, and since he failed to employ an untreated control group for comparative purposes, we believe that his results—though they encourage treatment of alcoholism that is multimodal rather than unimodal—must nonetheless be viewed cautiously.

In a study designed to establish the overall efficacy of an aversion relief paradigm similar to Blake's, McCulloch, Feldman, Orford, and MacCulloch (1966) applied the "technique of anticipatory avoidance learning" to a group of four alcoholics. They had previously used this procedure successfully with homosexual subjects. These alcoholic subjects, it is clear, were not as highly motivated for treatment, were of greater chronicity, and were of lower socioeconomic status than Blake's—all factors which by themselves militated against positive outcome. MacCulloch and his colleagues described the alcohol-related stimuli used in their method as follows:

Subjects are presented with a range of photographs of beer and "spirits," the sight of an actual bottle of alcohol (stoppered), the sight of an open bottle of alcohol, and alcohol in a glass. We also use a tape recording which consists of a repeated invitation to have a

TABLE 1–2b   12-month follow-up of 22 cases treated by electrical-aversion therapy alone

Outcome	Number of cases			Percent of total
	Male	*Female*	*Total*	
1. Abstinent	3	2	5	23
2. Improved	6	—	6*	27
3. Relapsed	4	2	6	27
4. Others	5	—	5	23
Total	18	4	22	100

SOURCE: Blake, 1967, p. 91.
* Includes one subject readmitted for booster treatment during follow-up.

drink of whatever alcohol is the patient's preferred choice [1966, pp. 187–188].

Slides of orange squash were counterposed as relief stimuli. The complete battery of alcohol-related and nonalcohol-related stimuli was shown randomly to each subject; when an alcohol-related stimulus was presented, it was followed eight seconds later by a shock unless switched off by the subject, at which point the aversion relief stimulus would appear. This treatment design was thought to promote an increase in the reinforcement value of nonalcohol-related stimuli and a concomitant decrease in the reinforcement value of alcohol-related stimuli within the context of a combined operant-classical paradigm.

In reporting their essentially negative findings—all four subjects returned to drinking within relatively short periods of time—the authors of the study observed that three of the four subjects had consistently failed to avoid shock during conditioning in that they failed to switch off alcohol-related stimuli (in other words, they failed in large part to permit themselves to be conditioned). They observed further that the unknown role of biochemical factors in alcoholism might have played a role in determining these negative results in view of the method's apparent success with homosexuals. Finally, they felt that social factors implicit in the maintenance of uncontrolled drinking may have been stronger maintainers of that behavior than like factors in the environments of homosexuals. Parenthetically, it is important to point out that the role of social factors in the maintenance of alcoholism has proved significant in behavioral treatment efforts, as the work of a number of investigators reviewed below strongly suggests.

Though other investigators (Hallam, Rachman, & Falkowski, 1972; Hsu, 1965; Miller & Hersen, 1972; Sandler, 1969) have also reported on the use of electrical aversion conditioning with alcoholics— some with and some without the aversion relief option—only one additional direct clinical trial of electrical aversion conditioning with chronic alcoholics will be discussed here. That study (Vogler, Lunde, Johnson, & Martin, 1970) will be considered here because of its sophisticated design and methodology, the apparent care with which follow-up was conducted, and, less positively, because its encouraging findings are marred by what may have been a central conceptual-methodological error.

Vogler's study was designed to build on Hsu's and Blake's encouraging data by adding the appropriate control groups which most earlier studies using electrical aversion conditioning with chronic alcoholics did not provide. Vogler's study also programmed reconditioning (booster) sessions in response to suggestions by behavioral theorists (e.g., Ullmann and Krasner, 1969; Rachman, 1961) that the efficacy of aversive conditioning and other behavioral procedures might be extended beyond the immediate posttreatment period in this way. Subjects in the Vogler study were 73 male chronic alcoholics who met a variety of criteria designed to guarantee that they were alcoholics in good physical and mental health. Subjects were randomly assigned to one of four groups: (1) *Booster*—subjects to whom both in-patient aversion relief conditioning and out-patient reconditioning were offered. Shock was delivered when a sip of alcohol was taken and terminated when the sip was spit out. Subjects took at least 20 sips per conditioning session. Twenty conditioning sessions were programmed during a two-week period. Booster sessions averaging three in number were arranged on the subjects' release from the hospital. (2) *Conditioning only*—subjects to whom aversion relief conditioning was administered only when they were in-patients. These subjects did not return for booster reconditioning sessions. (3) *Pseudo-conditioning*—control subjects who sipped alcohol as the booster and conditioning only subjects had, but then received shocks randomly rather than contingently upon sipping. (4) *Sham conditioning*—control subjects who received the same treatment as had subjects in the booster and conditioning only groups except that they were administered no shocks. These subjects were told before the sham conditioning sessions began that they might be shocked when alcohol was in their mouths but they never were. A *ward control group* which received only "routine hospital treatment," was later added to the study.

An extensive series of follow-up contacts with all subjects was planned when the study was initiated in order to guarantee that accurate data on posttreatment drinking behavior would be available and to ensure that long-term follow-up for treatment would be maintained.

Vogler's booster group maintained abstinence longer than did any of the other groups at an eight-month follow-up, a difference significant beyond the .002 level. Unfortunately, these results are deceptive unless one looks carefully at the data on which the significance level was computed. Those data reveal that 13 booster and conditioning only subjects and 1 pseudoconditioning subject dropped out of treatment early; 1 pseudoconditioning and 7 ward control subjects were lost to follow-up. If one views these 14 subjects as the treatment failures they likely were, the apparent efficacy of the behavioral treatment employed by Vogler and his colleagues is significantly attenuated. Despite the fact that the authors do call their readers' attention to this attrition in the results section of their report, they discuss their results almost as though the loss of subjects had not occurred:

> The electrical aversion conditioning method used in this study significantly reduced drinking behavior when compared with the control methods used, that is, pseudoconditioning,

sham conditioning, and ward controls. Relapse took significantly longer for both booster and conditioning-only subjects than for control subjects . . . [Vogler et al., 1970, p. 306].

The additional fact that a certain unspecified number of subjects in the conditioning only group were actually booster group subjects who had failed to report back to the hospital for booster sessions further dilutes the support that this study provides for the electrical aversion conditioning model.

A one-year follow-up of the same subjects (Vogler, Lunde, & Martin, 1971) revealed that the initial follow-up data encouraging the authors to believe that their electrical aversion method was efficacious (at least when coupled with booster sessions) had become less positive at the one-year mark. Specifically, these data showed that the two groups of conditioning subjects did not differ from the pseudo-conditioning subjects on any rehospitalization criteria (the measure employed at this follow-up to reflect treatment efficacy). Both groups of conditioning subjects did do better, according to these criteria, than did the sham conditioning subjects.

With others, we remain unconvinced that electrical aversion conditioning, at least as it has been employed until now, constitutes a definitive behavioral treatment for alcoholism. Like Franks (1966), we are convinced that electrical aversion methods that aim solely to punish drinking without also focusing on concurrent development of behaviors incompatible with drinking (e.g., enhance social functioning, anxiety and/or fear reduction, greater resistance to stress) are doomed to failure. A recent study by Wilson in our own laboratory (Wilson, Leaf, & Nathan, 1975), demonstrating the resistance of drinking by chronic alcoholics to concurrent electric shock, speaks directly to this point as does the thoughtful paper by Wilson and Davison (1969). These studies make the convincing point that consideration of the topography of the stimuli and responses most closely associated with uncontrolled drinking by alcoholics would lead to a choice of other than electrical shock (e.g., chemical agents) as the most appropriate aversive consequence for drinking. Further, we would suggest on the basis of our own experience that *any* unidimensional approach to a maladaptive behavior as complex as alcoholism is bound to fail. Finally, we would reemphasize the importance of periodic reconditioning (booster) sessions, whether devoted to aversive reconditioning or maintenance of other behavioral programs, in the successful behavioral treatment of alcoholism. This point will be made again when we consider some of the behavioral treatment approaches aiming at controlled drinking which programmed regular booster sessions during follow-up periods.

Aversive conditioning: Chemicals. The earliest reported use of chemical aversion conditioning with alcoholics (Lemere & Voegtlin, 1950; Voegtlin, 1940, 1947) also represents the most comprehensive program of aversion therapy with alcohol abusers up to our own time. The method Voegtlin and his associates developed at Shadel Sanatorium in Seattle in the late 1930s involves the use of Emetine, an emetic drug, as the aversive agent; this method is still in use at the present time at Shadel, as well as at a few other small private hospitals. Shortly after Emetine (or Apomorphine, another emetic drug) is ingested or injected, the patient receiving chemical aversion conditioning is instructed either to ingest an ounce of his favorite alcoholic beverage or to sip but not swallow the beverage; in either case ingestion of the beverage is timed to coincide with the prolonged extensive vomiting that invariably follows Emetine injection. Two or three such trials per 45-minute treatment session are programmed. Typically, treatment takes place every other day, up to the usual four to six sessions during the patient's hospital stay.

Lemere and Voegtlin (1950) reported on an extensive follow-up 10 to 13 years after treatment of over 4,000 patients given chemical aversion conditioning at the Shadel Sanatorium. Overall, 60% of patients so treated were abstinent after one year and about 50% were abstinent at the 13-year follow-up, but because these figures include patients who relapsed but were successfully retreated, their comparability to outcome data generated by other behavioral methods is uncertain.

Although no other investigators employing nausea-producing substances to establish conditioned aversion to alcohol have been able to follow up their patients as extensively as did the Shadel group, some have also reported promising findings. Thimann, for example, used Emetine approximately as did Voegtlin and Lemere to treat 245 alcoholic patients (1949). At a four-year follow-up, he reported that 51% of these patients had remained abstinent, though his forced reliance on self-report detracts from the overall reliability of these encouraging data. Similarly, Raymond (1964) reported positive outcome data in the context of a choice situation in which patients could choose either alcoholic or nonalcoholic beverages as a behavioral measure of response to chemical aversion conditioning.

"Expectancy," belief that a therapeutic method will work, seems to have played an important role in the apparent success of the Shadel/Voegtlin treatment paradigm. Building on a lengthy history of seeming treatment success, Voegtlin, Lemere, and those who came after them at Shadel "built in" the expectation in their patients that chemical aversion is a proven treatment method. And, in fact, when combined with in-patient group therapy conducted along Alcoholics Anonymous lines and the group comraderie generated by the fact that all are sharing an intense and unique experience, chemical aversion within the Shadel treatment model does appear to be quite effective. The specific role of chemical aversion in this model is, however, unknown since an experimental analysis of the separate components of the method has not been undertaken. Further, since most Shadel patients are relatively better motivated and of higher educational and socioeconomic level than patients offered other forms of behavioral treatment, the efficacy of the total Shadel method as compared to other treatment methods is similarly uncertain. Research designed to explore these areas seems long overdue.

Another chemical aversion procedure (utilizing succinylcholine chloride dehydrate, or Scoline to induce total apneic [respiratory] paralysis) has not yielded outcome data as promising as those from aversion conditioning with emetics. The most often cited study employing this method of aversive control was done by Sanderson, Campbell, and Laverty (1962, 1963). Laverty (1966) describes the method used in this research as follows:

After initial ascertainment of fitness for treatment, the fasting subject was presented with beverage alcohol using the beverage with which he was most familiar or for which he had the most preference. Two presentations of this beverage were given, the subject being asked to take the bottle or glass from the experimenter, raise it up, look at it, put it to his nose and smell it, put it to his lips and taste it, and then hand it back to the experimenter. This insured a sequence of drinking behavior which lasted from about 6 to 10 seconds. The anesthetist then carried out the injection of succinylcholine, unknown to the patient, through a long polyethylene tube. The injection itself took about 3–4 sec. Initial signs of scoline action were demonstrated in a sudden change in GSR (also seen in the appearance of fine fasciculation in the facial muscles and a general reaction in the patient, for whom the experience usually presented as a tremulousness and twitching in certain muscles, followed by inability to move or breathe) appearing between 9 and 12 seconds after the injection had been completed. . . . Some 40–60 sec. were allowed to elapse, depending on the condition of the patient. If respiration had not returned at this time,

complete pulmonary ventilation or respiratory assistance was given using a respirator. Patients initially treated were then offered the beverage alcohol again some 5 min. after the traumatic experience had passed. Many patients showed strong behavioral reactions toward the re-presentation of alcohol [pp. 653–654].

Alcoholic subjects treated by this technique were followed up at three-month, six-month, and one-year intervals. Three groups of 15 patients each were followed. Group 1 received three presentations of alcohol without Scoline and then received a fourth presentation of alcohol accompanied by Scoline; Group 2 received three presentations of alcohol unaccompanied by Scoline and then received Scoline unaccompanied by alcohol; Group 3 received four presentations of alcohol in each case unaccompanied by Scoline. All patients were offered three posttreatment presentations of alcohol which were, however, refused by some.

Follow-up of these patients revealed that during the first three months of posttreatment, many experienced both physical symptoms (dizziness, feelings of suffocation, headache) and emotional symptoms (crying spells, agitation, feelings of guilt and fear about alcohol). Patients in Group 1 experienced these symptoms more often than patients in either of the other two groups. Table 1–3 summarizes data on posttreatment reactions to alcohol at initial follow-up. It shows that significantly more patients in the two groups which received Scoline (Groups 1 and 2) reported aversive reactions to alcohol. Unfortunately, despite these reactions, "the appearance of such reactions in the face of alcohol did not prevent the majority of patients in the treated groups from experimenting with alcohol again [Laverty, 1966, p. 659]." Many of these experiments, though, caused unpleasant enough reactions that drinking by several subjects again ceased. This sequence took place with 12 of the 30 patients in Groups 1 and 2.

TABLE 1–3   Responses in relation to alcoholic beverages

Reaction	Group 1	Group 2	Group 3
Physical symptoms on approaching alcohol	6	15	4
Affective change on approaching alcohol	9	8	2
No craving or enjoyment	10	12	5
Reexperience of treatment sensations	2	1	0
Aversion	4	7	1
Slowness, delay, and voluntary stopping of drinking	13	11	5
Change of beverage	6	8	4
Exaggerated reaction to continued drinking	6	6	1
Total	56	68	22

SOURCE: Laverty, 1966, p. 658.

Self-reports elicited one year after treatment revealed that "many patients had either discontinued drinking or were drinking in a similar pattern, although usually less than before [Laverty, 1966, p. 660]." Data presented in support of this conclusion are shown in Table 1–4. They reveal that all three groups of alcoholics significantly reduced alcohol intake and significantly increased periods of abstinence after treatment. While these gains were greater for Groups 1 and 2 (the groups receiving Scoline), clear differences between Group 1 (which received contingent Scoline) and Group 2 (which received it noncontingently) were not revealed.

We must conclude—along with others who have employed apneic paralysis as an aversive conditioning agent for alcohol abuse (e.g., Farrar, Powell, & Martin, 1968) —that despite the undoubted impact and drama of Scoline conditioning, its power to effect permanent change in drinking patterns remains unproved. Whether things would have been different if these Scoline experimenters had made provision for regular booster sessions, had tried to teach subjects new behaviors to compete with or take the place of drinking, and had directly attacked the anxiety and depression that often accompany the alcoholic way of life cannot of course be known at this time. It seems best to view Scoline as simply an interesting way station along the road to

TABLE 1–4   Longest period of abstinence following treatment (one-year follow-up)

	Weeks of Abstinence	
	One Year, Pretreatment	*One Year, Posttreatment*
Group 1 (15 subjects)	4.66	23.10
Group 2 (15 subjects)	5.53	23.00
Group 3 (12 subjects)	3.92	14.30

	Median Gain (weeks)	*Median Difference*	*Median Significance**
Group 1	+13		
		+2 (p < .42)	
Group 2	+11		+8 (p < .07)
		+6 (p < .19)	
Group 3	+5		

SOURCE: Laverty, 1966, p. 663.
* In weeks of abstinence, all groups showed a significant gain.

newer, more successful behavioral treatment of alcoholism.

Aversion conditioning: Imagery. Covert sensitization is an aversive conditioning method utilizing images instead of shocks or chemicals. It has been put forth by Cautela, its creator, as a promising treatment approach for such disparate conditions as obesity, smoking, obsessions and compulsions, stealing, homosexuality, and alcoholism, (1966, 1967, 1970). For an alcoholic, Cautela suggests combining covert sensitization with standard relaxation training and systematic desensitization in order to treat the anxiety component of the patient's drinking behavior as well as the specifics of that behavior itself.

Cautela suggests telling the alcoholic patient that he will be unable to stop drinking in excess until he can learn to eliminate this "faulty habit" by associating it with an unpleasant stimulus. To this end, the patient is instructed to close his eyes and imagine that he is about to drink some alcoholic beverage. He is then brought in his imagination to experience the sensations of nausea and vomiting. Repeated often enough, the association between sight, smell, and taste of alcohol and nausea is presumed to establish a conditioned aversion to alcohol.

Central to the covert sensitization procedure are the aversive scenes the therapist provides the patient. Cautela gives the following example of such a scene:

> You are walking into a bar. You decide to have a glass of beer. You are now walking toward the bar. As you are approaching the bar you have a funny feeling in the pit of your stomach. Your stomach feels all queasy and nauseous. Some liquid comes up your throat and it is very sour. You try to swallow it back down, but as you do this, food particles start coming up your throat to your mouth. You are now reaching the bar and you order a beer. As the bartender is pouring the beer, puke comes into your mouth... As soon as your hand touches the glass, you can't hold it down any longer. You have to open your mouth and you puke. It goes all over your hand; all over the glass and the beer. You can see it floating around in the beer... [1970, p. 87].

On both theoretical and practical bases, covert sensitization offers advantages over either chemical or electrical aversion. It permits patient and therapist to adjust the topographical properties of the aversive imagery to the specifics of the patient's problem behavior, it permits direct (imaginal) association between the aversive image and the full range of behaviors associated with drinking (including the people and places with which it is associated), and it is sufficiently mobile that it can be employed by the patient himself in tempting situations.

Despite these advantages of covert sensitization, it is still not widely used to treat alcoholics. One reason for this may be that outcome data documenting the efficacy of the procedure have been questioned. Thus, although Cautela (1967) reported that a 29-year-old female alcoholic given covert sensitization remained abstinent at an eight-month follow-up, and Anant (1967) reported that 96% of his 26 patients given similar treatment were abstinent at post-treatment periods ranging from 8 to 15 months, neither investigator employed appropriate control groups that would have enabled assessment of the differential efficacy of the several components of the treatment method or comparison of the natural history of untreated subjects with those given covert sensitization.

The aversive procedures in perspective. We can conclude that none of the aversive conditioning procedures reviewed above has proven itself to be definitive for the treatment of alcoholism. In this regard, we are impressed by accumulating research data to the effect that the electrical aversion procedures, despite the numbers of studies which have employed them as a unimodal treatment method, are not by themselves of much value in bringing about abstinence in chronic alcoholics. However when it is combined with other treatment methods (which may include systematic desensitization, positive reconditioning, and environmental manipulation), electrical aversion may well enable some alcoholics to achieve and maintain abstinence and others to attain the goal of controlled drinking. These latter uses of electrical aversion will be considered below. We believe that essentially the same conclusions can be drawn from the covert sensitization literature—though it is not nearly as extensive as that involving electrical aversion.

Largely as a function of the impressive amount of follow-up data accumulated by those who have used chemical aversion with alcoholics, as well as the fact that nausea as an aversive agent seems more central to the drinking sequence than electric shock, we believe that chemical aversion may be more useful by itself than either electrical aversion or covert sensitization. We would add, however, that Voegtlin and Lemere employed chemical aversion in the context of a multifaceted attack on the behavior of their alcoholic patients, a treatment approach we have consistently espoused through this review. In fact, chemical aversion involving nausea has not to our knowledge been used in isolation; the Voegtlin and Lemere data suggest that there is very likely no advantage to doing so.

Systematic desensitization: Clinical and experimental applications. Systematic desensitization, the "treatment of choice" by many behavior therapists for many of the neurotic behaviors, has not been employed extensively as the sole component of a program for the behavioral treatment of alcoholism. In fact, only Kraft and Al-Issa (1967) and Kraft (1969) have reported on the use of systematic desensitization by itself to induce abstinence. Both of their clinical case reports described the successful use of systematic desensitization to attenuate the social anxiety which characterized many of the social interactions of a group

of young alcoholics. Of eight alcoholic patients so treated, all were judged improved in social functioning and more moderate in their use of alcohol.

In a recent study of the relationships of drinking behavior, muscle tension level, and subjective response to relaxation—all of which are foci of the clinical use of systematic desensitization with alcoholics—Steffen (1974) and Steffen, Taylor, and Nathan (1974) explored the effects of a feedback-induced relaxation training procedure upon the drinking behavior of four male chronic alcoholics.

The study began with a 12-day baseline drinking period, during which subjects were given free access to beverage alcohol. Concurrent measurements of blood alcohol level (BAL), electromyographic tension level from the *frontalis* muscle (EMG), and subjective discomfort were made every other hour during each 16-hour drinking day. At the conclusion of this baseline period, two subjects received six days of electromyographically induced relaxation training while the other two subjects received a placebo training condition. Subjects did not have access to alcohol during this training period. Afterwards, they were permitted free access to beverage alcohol for four days. Conditions were then reversed during a second six-day training period, with those subjects who had received placebo training receiving EMG feedback training and *vice versa*. Subjects were given free access to beverage alcohol again following the second training period.

The most notable finding from this study was that subjects reached significantly lower blood alcohol and muscle tension levels and reported significantly less subjective discomfort during drinking periods following electromyographically induced relaxation training than during drinking periods following placebo training. This finding suggests that EMG feedback may represent a potential addition to behavioral treatment methods for alcoholics. It also indicates that state of muscle tension and level of reported discomfort could be correlates of changes in drinking behavior, a possibility that warrants further intensive exploration. Another major finding from this research was that blood alcohol level and state of muscle tension correlated positively and significantly, while blood alcohol level and reports of subjective disturbance correlated negatively and significantly. This suggests that an unequivocal assumption of correlation between tension level and subjective disturbance in drinking alcoholics cannot be made. Instead, it may be that some alcoholics associate decreased tension accompanying intoxication with aversive events that took place during earlier periods of intoxication, with the result that lowered tension serves as a discriminative stimulus for discomfort, anxiety, and/or panic.

Broad-spectrum and multimodal approaches to abstinence. An early report on a behavioral approach to alcoholism that combined systematic desensitization with other behavioral techniques (Lazarus, 1965) marked the first use of the term "broad-spectrum" to describe a multimodal-multitechnique therapeutic strategy. Praised by some, denounced by others, Lazarus' broad-spectrum behavior therapy is nonetheless now firmly accepted as a legitimate behavioral treatment paradigm by many behavior therapists. In the 1965 report, Lazarus listed the following five components of his behavioral approach to alcoholism: (1) medical care to return the patient to physical well-being; (2) aversion therapy and anxiety relief conditioning to attack directly the patient's uncontrolled drinking behavior; (3) tests and interviews to identify "specific stimulus antecedents of anxiety" in the patient's environment as an aid in constructing anxiety hierarchies for subsequent systematic desensitization; (4) systematic desensitization, assertive training, behavioral rehearsal, and hypnosis, all to countercondition "anxiety-response habits;" (5) development of a cooperative relationship with the patient's spouse, even

to the extent of providing the spouse with the behavior therapy necessary to alter the patient's living situation in such a way as to reduce or eliminate another of the major determinants of his excessive drinking. Lazarus' early commitment to a multimodal approach foreshadows the development of his "multimodal therapy" (Lazarus, 1973), designed specifically to focus on seven key areas of human psychological malfunctioning.

Miller, Stanford, and Hemphill (1974) describe a roughly similar multifaceted approach to alcoholism that is now used in a 15-bed alcoholism ward at the Veterans Administration Center, Jackson, Mississippi. Although they provide no data on the efficacy of their treatment methods—largely because the unit had been open only a short time when the paper was written—Miller and his coworkers present a coherent behavioral rationale for their three-fold behavioral approach to treatment. Therapeutic strategies include: (1) techniques "to decrease the immediate reinforcing properties of alcohol" (including aversion conditioning with electric shock, use of emesis drugs, and covert sensitization); (2) development of "new ways of coping with life . . . incompatible with alcohol abuse" (involving instruction in more appropriate ways of dealing with stressful situations); (3) alteration of the social and vocational environment so that the patient "receives increased satisfactions from life" (these include family treatment and vocational counseling).

One of the few controlled studies of a multifaceted approach to alcoholism with abstinence as its goal was reported recently by Lanyon, Primo, Terrell, and Wener (1972). In that study, 21 male alcoholics with a median age of 40 and median education of 11.5 years were randomly assigned to one of the following three groups: (1) "interpersonal aversion" in which subject watched his own videotaped drinking "confessions" while being systematically excoriated by two therapists; this was immediately followed by 30 minutes of systematic desensitization to "drinking-related anxieties;" (2) interpersonal aversion (the same as group 1) but followed by a control procedure involving friendly interactions that also lasted 30 minutes; (3) group discussion lasting for 60 minutes.

A six- to nine-month follow-up of Lanyon's subjects, conducted by mail, revealed that five of the seven traceable patients in the aversion-desensitization group (eight were originally in the group) had remained abstinent. In addition, one of seven patients in the aversion-counseling group, and one of four of the traceable patients in the group discussion control group had remained abstinent during the follow-up period. The small number of subjects in this study, the relatively brief and inadequately designed follow-up period, and the choice of skid row alcoholics as subjects all make this study an imperfect one. The study does suggest, however, that controlled research that directly compares unimodal approaches to the behavioral treatment of alcoholism is possible.

Most commentators on the behavioral treatment of alcoholism stress the importance of establishing some kind of formal link between the treatment facility and the patient's home community in order to ensure generalization of behavioral change from the consulting room or hospital to the patient's living situation. However, few investigators have addressed themselves to just how behavioral control of drinking can be extended to the community. The "community-reinforcement approach to alcoholism" described by Hunt and Azrin (1973) is directed toward this goal. To test out assumptions implicit in this novel approach, the authors selected for a pilot study 16 alcoholics who were being treated at the Anna (Illinois) State Hospital. The 16 subjects were divided into equal-sized groups matched for age, education, number of previous hospitalizations, marital status, and vocational status. One of the two groups then received "community reinforce-

ment counseling;" the other group participated in a standard hospital ward-milieu therapy program.

The community reinforcement program was designed above all to alter the alcoholic's natural reinforcers—vocational, familial, and social—in such a way that time out from them would occur whenever he began to drink. In order to do this, efforts were made to develop subjects' job acquisition and maintenance skills to enable them to find suitable jobs. In addition, subjects received training in marital and family skills so that they could function as responsible husbands and/or fathers, and in social skills so that relationships with persons other than alcoholics would be possible. In all three target areas, modelling, role playing, exhortation, verbal reinforcement, and identification of competing responses were employed to bring about specified behavioral changes.

While they were hospitalized, both groups of subjects received additional counseling and education about the hazards to health and well-being of continued drinking, along with information on Alcoholics Anonymous. During the first month after their release from the hospital, subjects in both groups were visited weekly by a counselor in an effort to maintain their commitment to the improved social, familial, and vocational functioning they had attained in the hospital and also as a follow-up procedure. These visits continued twice a month after the first posttreatment month, then decreased to once a month for the six-month follow-up period.

Data gathered at the six-month follow-up revealed that mean time spent drinking, unemployed, away from home, or institutionalized was more than twice as high for the control group as for the "community-reinforcement" group. Six of eight community-reinforcement subjects spent less time drinking than their matched controls.

As encouraging as these initial data are, we must note two cautions. First, it seems clear that alcoholics in the community reinforcement group received not just *different* but *much more* therapy in the form of time spent reintegrating them into the community from which they had come. Second, it is well known that alcoholics who possess family, vocational, and social ties to the community have better prognoses for successful recovery (regardless of the kind of treatment accorded them) than alcoholics who have lost such ties. It is necessary to point out that the clear difference in outcome in favor of the community reinforcement group may have been due to this factor, which had nothing to do with the operant thrust of the project. For these reasons, Hunt and Azrin's explicit assumption that the threat of time out from effective vocational, social, and marital adjustment for drinking accounted for their positive findings is not convincing.

BEHAVIORAL EFFORTS TO TEACH CONTROLLED DRINKING. Several investigators (Bolman, 1965; Davies, 1962; Pattison, 1968) have described alcoholics who later became social drinkers. Their reports countered the prevailing view strongly fostered by Alcoholics Anonymous and the medically oriented therapies that alcoholics can never became controlled drinkers, and led to a series of controlled studies of the "loss of control" phenomenon thought to be responsible for the inability of alcoholics to resume normal drinking habits. Data from these studies question the loss of control thesis, and encourage behavioral efforts to train alcoholics explicitly to become social drinkers.

Assumptions about craving for alcohol and its role in maintaining uncontrolled drinking by alcoholics have been tested in both acute and chronic drinking studies. Merry (1966) and Williams (1970) reported that single doses of alcohol surreptitiously given to abstinent alcoholics did not increase their craving for alcohol. Cutter, Schwab, and Nathan (1970) found that drinking alcoholics were no more likely than social drinkers to consume alcohol when

they were primed with 44 ml of alcohol. McNamee, Mello, and Mendelson (1968) similarly failed to find evidence for craving and loss of control, even in alcoholics who had been drinking for several days. Elsewhere, Mello (1968) has reported that alcoholics sometimes stop drinking voluntarily after several days of heavy drinking, a finding also reported by Nathan, O'Brien, and Lowenstein (1971), and Gottheil, Corbett, Grasberger, and Cornelison (1972).

As a result of these reports, controlled drinking by alcoholics has become a viable treatment goal. One of the first teams of behavioral researchers to report on work in this area (Lovibond & Caddy, 1970) detailed an interesting treatment procedure by which alcoholics are first taught to discriminate their own blood alcohol levels (supposedly from visceral cues) and are then instructed on how to use this discrimination training to modulate consequent drinking behavior.

Blood alcohol level discrimination and controlled drinking. Twenty-eight of 31 alcoholic subjects had completed Lovibond and Caddy's prescribed treatment program at the time of their 1970 article. All completed the following sequence: (1) *Discrimination training*—at the beginning of this first segment of therapy, subjects were given a general idea of the behavioral effects of different blood alcohol levels. They were then asked to drink some alcohol mixed with fruit juice in order to observe their consequent subjective experiences. For two hours afterwards, blood alcohol level (BAL) readings were taken every 15 to 20 minutes after each subject gave an estimate of his blood alcohol level; after BAL measurement, subject received feedback on his actual blood alcohol level. One of these discrimination training sessions was given to each subject before the second phase of the therapy program. (2) *Control conditioning*—subjects were required to drink their favorite alcoholic beverage within one and a half hours to a blood alcohol level of 65 mg/% (a moderate level). Subjects gave concurrent BAL estimates every

TABLE 1–5   Outcome of completed treatment of 28 experimental subjects

Category	Definition	Number of cases
Complete success	Drinking in controlled fashion exceeding 70 mg/% only rarely	21
Considerably improved	Drinking less but exceeding 70 mg/% once or twice per week	3
Slightly improved	Drinking only slightly less	4

SOURCE: Lovibond & Caddy, 1970, p. 440.

15 to 20 minutes of this drinking period, followed by feedback on the accuracy of their estimations. (A blood alcohol level of 65 mg/% results from approximately two highballs.) As soon as the "target" BAL of 65 mg/% was reached, subjects were shocked intermittently (via chin electrodes) as they continued to drink beyond the target level (which they were required to do). Shock frequency, intensity, and duration were varied, as was the point in the drinking sequence at which shock was imposed, all in the effort to maximize generalization of conditioning.

The first three such conditioning sessions were held five to seven days apart; between 8 and 10 shocks were administered at each session. Later conditioning sessions were spaced farther apart and the number of shocks delivered was reduced to 3 to 4. After 6 to 12 conditioning sessions and 30 to 70 shocks, treatment was discontinued for all subjects.

Lovibond and Caddy also had a control group of 13 subjects who were given treatment identical to that given the 31 experimental subjects except that the control subjects received random, noncontingent shocks before and after their BAL reached 65 mg/%.

Accepting the validity of prior data attesting to the apparent ability of both alcoholics and nonalcoholics to learn to estimate BAL with a high degree of accuracy (Lovibond, 1970), Lovibond and Caddy devoted little space in their 1970 report to a discussion of the process of discrimination training or training in control;

instead, the bulk of their discussion centered on analysis of treatment outcome data. To this end, Table 1–5 shows that of the 28 experimental subjects completing treatment, 21 were "regarded tentatively as complete successes in that they were drinking in a controlled fashion, exceeding the 70 mg/% BAL only rarely" four or more months after treatment. Figure 1–1 shows, in line with these data, that during conditioning, experimental and control subjects differed in alcohol intake, presumably as a function of the differential treatments accorded members of these groups.

In view of its promising results (albeit generated in the context of a research design that raised important questions) Silverstein, Nathan, and Taylor (1974) designed a project both to replicate and to extend the Lovibond and Caddy paradigm. Above all, the new study was designed to permit an experimental analysis of the discrete components of BAL discrimination training as well as the determinants of subsequent controlled drinking by the alcoholic subjects chosen for the study.

The overall design of the Silverstein, Nathan, and Taylor study is summarized in Tables 1–6a and b. The goals of Phase 1 of the study, which lasted 10 days, was to train subjects to estimate BAL accurately (see Table 1–6a). Target behavior in this context was defined as 75% of all of a subject's BAL estimations falling within 20 mg/ 100 cc (20 mg/%) of his actual BAL. Throughout Phase 1, drinking was programmed in two-day cycles to cause subjects' BALs to rise slowly to 150 mg/100 cc

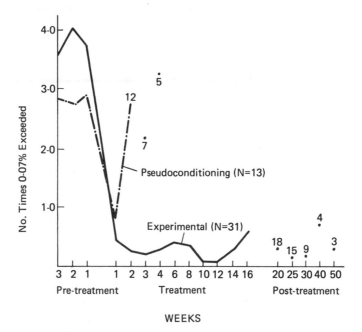

FIGURE 1–1   During conditioning, experimental and pseudoconditioning, subjects differed in number of times they exceeded a moderate blood alcohol level (Lovibond & Caddy, 1970).

during the first day, to remain at approximately that level overnight, and then to fall through the next day to a zero BAL. The first two days of Phase 1 constituted a baseline period (B1) during which subjects estimated BAL without being provided feedback of actual BAL and with minimal instructions for converting their subjective feelings of intoxication into a BAL estimate. The next three two-day cycles (T1, T2, T3) were devoted to training in BAL estimation. The first training period (T1) differed from the baseline period in that feedback of subjects' actual BALs was provided after each of their own BAL estimates. During the second training cycle (T2), feedback was given intermittently on a random schedule averaging 50% of trials. This change permitted direct comparison of accuracy on trials following feedback versus those unaccompanied by feedback. The third cycle (T3) marked the first time reinforcement (delivered as points con-

vertible into subsequent alcohol or money) was made contingent upon accurate BAL estimation; points previously had been awarded noncontingently. Intermittent feedback on BAL continued to be given during T3, although now yoked with point contingency. The final two days of the estimation phase (B2) replicated the first baseline cycle (B1); point reinforcement for accuracy, feedback on BAL, and attention to physical and emotional correlates of BAL were all withdrawn at the beginning of B2 in order to reestablish the experimental conditions of B1.

The goal of Phase 2 (which lasted 26 days) was to train subjects to use their BAL estimates as discriminative stimuli for controlling their own drinking behavior (see Table 1–6b). Control was ultimately defined as the ability to maintain a BAL at the target of 80 mg/100 cc. The core of the control training (periods C1, C2, and C3) employed three converging behavioral con-

TABLE 1–6a   Phase 1: Estimation training

	B1 (Estimation baseline period)	T1	T2 (Training cycles)	T3	B2 (Estimation baseline period)
Feedback	none	continuous	intermittent	intermittent & contingent	none
Reinforcement	none	none	none	variable	none
Days	1–2	3–4	5–6	7–8	9–10

TABLE 1–6b   Phase 2: Control training

	BC1 (Control baseline period)	RS (Reinforcement sampling)	C1	C2 (Control training)	C3	BC2 (Control baseline period)	G (Target generalization)
Type of drinking	ad lib	programmed	partially programmed	ad lib	ad lib	ad lib	ad lib
Feedback	none	variable	variable	variable	fade out	none	none
Reinforcement	none	variable	variable	variable	fade out	none	none
Target	80 mg/100 cc	80 mg/100 cc	80 mg/100 cc	80 mg/100 cc	80 mg/100 cc	80 mg/100 cc	variable
Days	11–13	14–15	16–22	23–25	26–28	29–34	35–36

trol procedures: (1) the locus of control over drinking was gradually shifted from completely external (that is, programmed by the experimenter [E] to completely self-controlled; (2) the range of positively reinforced BALs estimations was successively narrowed closer and closer to the BAL target of 80 mg/%; (3) all reinforcers and BAL feedback were gradually faded out. The prevailing experimental conditions during BC2 (ad lib drinking, no feedback, and no reinforcement for drinking at or around the target BAL of 80 mg/%) replicated exactly those in BC1, the pretraining Phase 2 baseline.

To assess drinking behavior subsequent to the project, each subject was given 40 postcards to be returned at the rate of one each day. The cards were designed to provide specific information about self-control of drinking and the amount of alcohol consumed. Data to corroborate the postcard information was sought from each subjects' closest family member or friend. At the 10-week follow-up, personal interviews were arranged with each subject for the same purpose.

Figure 1–2 shows that while all subjects were unable to estimate BAL accurately during the Phase I baseline (B1), three of the four markedly increased the accuracy of their BAL estimates as soon as BAL feedback was introduced on the first day of T1. No additional gain in estimation accuracy was observed for any of these three subjects after this first day of estimation training. By contrast, subject 4's estimation accuracy continued to improve to the end of T2, though it never attained the levels of estimation proficiency reached by the other three subjects. On the day after baseline conditions were reinstated, all subjects' estimation accuracy deteriorated. Though subjects 1, 2 and 3 still remained largely accurate, with discrepancies averaging only 30 mg/100 cc, subject 4's estimates became essentially random and averaged 257 mg/100 cc from actual BAL. Accuracy of

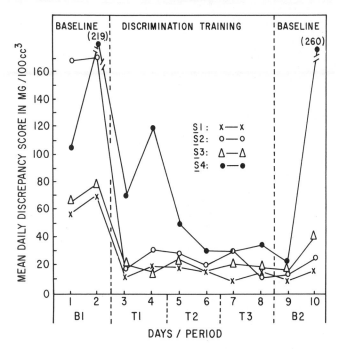

FIGURE 1–2   Although all four subjects were unable to estimate BAL accurately during baseline, three of the four immediately achieved accurate estimation levels once feedback was provided during discrimination training. Accuracy broke down, however, when feedback was removed during the second baseline period (Silverstein, Nathan, & Taylor, 1974).

BAL estimation remained high during those portions of Phase 2 that provided subjects continued feedback on BAL.

Figure 1–3 shows that subjects did not successfully "target in on" the 80 mg/100 cc criterion during the first two days of the Phase 2 baseline (BC1) when reinforcement for doing so was not available. During the first segment of control training itself (C1), reinforcement contingencies were successfully narrowed to bring subjects' drinking closer and closer to the ultimate BAL target of 70 to 90 mg/%. Figure 1–3 shows that subjects' drinking responded to these changing demands. By the last three days of this period (days 20–22), all subjects were demonstrating controlled drinking in that all mean daily discrepancy scores were within 20 mg/100 cc the the target level of 90 mg/100 cc.

During the remaining periods of the study (C2, C3, BC2, and G), subjects assumed increasing responsibility for scheduling times and amount of alcohol intake (up to 150 mg/100 cc). During C2, and C3, BAL feedback and reinforcement were still provided all subjects; during that time, drinking behavior remained close to the target BAL. As Figure 1–3 shows, however, this high degree of control disappeared when reinforcement contingencies and feedback were removed during BC2.

Of the three subjects who completed the study, two (subjects 2 and 3) returned daily post cards for 40 days after discharge. The same two subjects also were interviewed after 80 days. Corroborative data from members of their families were also obtained. Subject 1, who returned only one

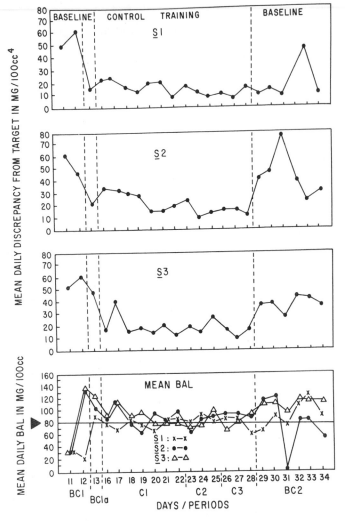

FIGURE 1–3 Once feedback and reinforcement for controlled drinking were instituted all three subjects moderated their levels of alcohol consumption (Silverstein, Nathan, & Taylor, 1974).

postcard, was also unavailable for the follow-up interview. It was known, though, that he had resided at the local Salvation Army shelter for all but 3 of the 80 post-study days, permitting an adequate follow-up of his drinking to take place.

Summary follow-up data revealed that one subject had been able to maintain a controlled pattern of drinking through the follow-up period, another had remained abstinent during much of the period by virtue of his residence at a Salvation Army Shelter, and the third had spent much of his posttreatment time drinking heavily, without control.

This study provided additional evidence to support prior findings that alcoholics can, under certain circumstances, learn to control their drinking. It also reaffirmed Lovibond and Caddy's findings that alcoholics can learn to make accurate estimations of blood alcohol level, although the authors of the new study concluded that it required a good deal longer than the two hours reported by Lovibond and Caddy. The Silverstein, Nathan, Taylor study also found that feedback on blood alcohol level, whether intermittent or continuous, whether accompanied by explicit reinforcement or not, appeared to be the controlling stimulus for accurate BAL estimation by their subjects, contrary to Lovibond and Caddy's belief that their subjects had depended upon visceral cues for this purpose. Finally, Silverstein and his colleagues questioned the determinants of Lovibond and Caddy's positive data (21 of 28 alcoholics drinking socially on follow-up), positing this outcome to have depended as much on undefined expectancy or demand variables as on BAL discrimination training. The basis for questioning the prior findings was the fact that the ability of Lovibond and Caddy's subjects to estimate BAL accurately was not tested once it was first established during the two-hour discrimination training period.

A multimodal approach to controlled drinking. One of the most extensive continuing applications of behavior modification to alcoholism has been the work of M. B. Sobell, Schaefer, and L. C. Sobell and their colleagues at the Patton (California) State Hospital. Their work, which is aimed at developing techniques to train controlled drinking in chronic alcoholics, emphasizes accurate specification of the parameters of the target behaviors associated with alcoholism, development of methods designed to enhance the reliability of treatment follow-up studies, explicit training in social skills to take the place of the maladaptive behaviors the alcoholic will have to forsake, and development of methods permitting relatively large groups of subjects to be treated simultaneously.

An early report (Schaefer, Sobell, & Mills, 1971) comprised a baseline study of differences in drinking behavior between alcoholics and nonalcoholics. Though Nathan & O'Brien (1971) had compared the amounts and temporal distribution of drinking by alcoholics and matched nonalcoholics (as well as their differences in social interaction and the affective consequences of drinking), they did not directly compare the topographies of drinking by these two groups as did Schaefer and his colleagues. This latter effort was a useful one in that the subsequent efforts by Schaefer, Sobell and their colleagues to modify uncontrolled drinking depended on accurate data on the manner and quantity of drinking by alcoholics. To this end, Schaefer, Sobell and Mills (1971) studied drink preferences, magnitude of sips, amount of time to consume a drink, and amount of time between sips in 42 male chronic alcoholic in-patients and 38 male social drinkers from the community surrounding the Patton State Hospital. All test sessions took place in a simulated bar located on the alcoholism treatment ward of the hospital. Groups of three alcoholics or three to six social drinkers were observed concurrently.

When a six-ounce limit was placed on ingestion during a three- to four-hour test session, alcoholics and nonalcoholics did not differ in number of drinks ordered. At a 16-ounce limit, however, the groups differed significantly: alcoholics averaged 15.27 drinks while nonalcoholics ordered only 6.65 drinks. At both ingestion limits, alcoholics preferred straight over mixed drinks, a preference social drinkers reversed. Social drinkers and alcoholics also differed in terms of the magnitude of the sips they took: regardless of kind of alcoholic beverage ordered, alcoholics took larger sips (they were often gulps) than did social drinkers. As a result, alcoholics usually finished a drink in two to three sips while social drinkers took upwards of nine sips to do so.

The next step in the Patton project was design and implementation of a comprehensive behavior modification program for teaching chronic alcoholics to become controlled drinkers. The separate components of this program, as outlined by Mills, Sobell, and Schaefer (1971) and Sobell and Sobell (1973 a & b), were included in a 17-session treatment plan which "dealt directly with the inappropriate behavior of excessive drinking and emphasized a patient's learning alternative [and] more appropriate responses to stimulus conditions which had previously functioned as setting events for heavy drinking [Sobell & Sobell, 1973, p. 53]." This treatment model also permitted controlled outcome research in that it provided for concurrent treatment of alcoholics who aimed for controlled drinking, alcoholics who aimed for abstinence, and control subjects whose therapeutic goals were either controlled drinking or abstinence.

Though individually tailored to take into account each patient's prior treatment, the treatment program at Patton State Hospital took the following general form:

Sessions 1 and 2 (videotaping): Subjects were permitted to drink to drunkenness. In that state, they engaged in intensive discussions with the staff about the determinants of their drinking, their behavior during intoxication, and their concerns about the study. Videotapes of these sessions were made.

Session 3 (treatment plan): The treatment plan was explained in detail to all subjects. In addition, subjects whose therapeutic goal was controlled drinking were trained to recognize and identify the separate components of mixed drinks, a skill in which most alcoholics are deficient.

Sessions 4 and 5 (videotape replay): The videotapes of drunken behavior previously recorded were replayed to demonstrate to subjects how inappropriate and maladaptive their behavior often was during these times and to serve as a means of increasing motivation for treatment (as prior research had suggested it might).

Session 6 (failure experience): Twenty minutes before the session began, subjects attempted to complete a series of tasks that were in fact impossible to complete. The therapy session which followed focused then on subjects' maladaptive responses to this and prior stresses because these responses were likely part of their chain of alcoholism.

Sessions 7 through 16 (stimulus control): Controlled drinker subjects were shocked for emitting behaviors characteristic of uncontrolled drinkers and reinforced with alcohol (up to a limit) for drinking like social drinkers; abstinence subjects were shocked whenever they drank at all. In most cases, a variable ratio (VR2) schedule was employed. Control subjects received random shock at the intensity and frequency given treatment subjects. During other portions of these sessions, emphasis was placed on helping subjects identify the crucial stimulus variables associated with their decision to drink; they were also helped to evolve a set of possibly effective alternative responses to those situations. Modelling and role playing such responses then followed. During "probe" sessions (8, 12, and 16), noncontingent drinking was programmed in order to enable assessment of the effectiveness of treatment insofar as ad lib drinking behavior was concerned.

Session 17 (summary; videotape contrast): Selected replays of drunken behavior from Sessions 1 and 2 were contrasted with videotapes of sober behavior taken during Session 16. Progress during therapy was discussed and the subject was given a wallet-sized list of "dos" and "dont's" specific to his own drinking history and response to treatment. Discharge from the hospital usually followed completion of this program by no more than two weeks.

In the most extensive trial of the utility of this multifaceted behavioral treatment program (Sobell & Sobell, 1973a, 1973b), 70 male gamma alcoholic patients (see p. 00) at the Patton State Hospital completed the full treatment regimen; their drinking behavior during midtreatment probe sessions was assessed in order to provide an index of treatment response in midstream. Follow-up assessment of their drinking, social, personal, and vocational behavior then took place at six-week, six-month, one-year, and two-year intervals. Before treatment began, the original 70 patients were assigned to one of two treatment groups on the basis of history: 40 patients were assigned to a group whose treatment goal was controlled drinking; 30 patients were assigned to a group whose goal was abstinence. Subjects in these two groups were further divided into experimental and control groups to yield a study with four groups in all: controlled drinker, experimental (CD-E); controlled drinker, control (CD-C); nondrinker, experimental (ND-E); nondrinker, control (ND-C).

Figure 1–4 shows that shortly after con-ditioning began in Session 7, the non-drinker (abstinence) experimental subjects stopped drinking, a demonstration of the powerful effects of conditioning on drinking; however, when contingent shock for drinking was removed during the probe sessions, drinking rate returned to baseline levels. Essentially the same phenomenon took place with the controlled drinker experimental subjects: the rate at which they emitted inappropriate drinking behavior (ordering drinks less than 20 minutes apart, ordering more than three drinks in a single session, gulping drinks) decreased once conditioning began, except when non-shock probe sessions intervened.

Follow-up data gathered at six weeks and six months, summarized in Table 1–7, show that subjects in all four groups did

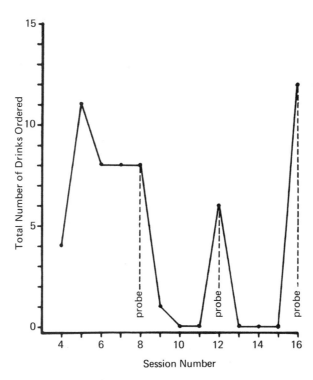

FIGURE 1–4   Shortly after conditioning began in Session 7, these subjects stopped ordering drinks. When contingent shock for drinking was removed during the three "probe" sessions, drinking returned to baseline levels (Sobell & Sobell, 1973a).

TABLE 1–7   Mean percentage of days spent in different drinking dispositions by subjects in four experimental groups for 6-week and 6-month follow-up intervals

A. Follow-up Months 13–18

Drinking dispositions	Experimental condition			
	CD-E	CD-C	ND-E	ND-C
Six-week follow-up				
Controlled drinking	41.80	10.70	7.20	12.93
Abstinent, not incarcerated	30.95	39.32	60.33	42.13
Drunk	17.55	42.70	23.20	41.60
Incarcerated, alcohol-related:				
Hospital	9.15	2.00	6.94	3.20
Jail	0.55	5.35	2.33	0.44
Total	100.00	100.00	100.00	100.00
Six-month follow-up				
Controlled drinking	27.33	9.10	2.87	14.54
Abstinent, not incarcerated	37.89	29.40	62.63	16.55
Drunk	20.33	50.50	19.38	40.91
Incarcerated, alcohol-related:				
Hospital	12.12	4.10	12.25	8.09
Jail	2.33	6.90	2.87	19.91
Total	100.00	100.00	100.00	100.00

SOURCE: Sobell & Sobell, 1973a, p. 65.

better (i.e., were abstinent or were drinking in a controlled fashion) at six weeks than at six months. In addition, the two experimental (treatment) groups adhered better to their respective treatment goals (abstinence or controlled drinking) than did the control groups. Finally, the two experimental groups of subjects had significantly better "drinking dispositions" at both followup intervals (were either abstinent or drinking in controlled fashion) than the two control groups. Concomitant evaluation of the vocational status and general adjustment of these same 70 subjects revealed that the experimental (treatment) groups were again doing better than the group of control subjects.

Eighteen-month and two-year follow-up data on these subjects are shown in Table 1–8. They confirm observations made from six-week and six-month data that experimental subjects remain either abstinent or controlled in their drinking at higher rates than control subjects. These data also show that subjects in the experimental (treatment) controlled drinker group spent fewer drunk days, days in hospital, or days in jail and more abstinent or controlled drinking days than the experimental (treatment) abstinence group. In other words, behavioral treatment aiming at controlled drinking appeared to have been more efficacious than behavioral treatment aiming at abstinence.

Because these outcome data are so much more positive than those reported by any other alcoholism therapy researchers, they are exciting—but they are also disturbing. They are exciting because after implementation of a multifaceted, coherent, controlled behavioral treatment program with a large group of alcoholics and a lengthy, extensive, carefully planned follow-up, the data suggest that experimental treatment subjects both drank less and drank less often than control subjects. As a consequence, this research encourages the view that controlled drinking may well be a viable treatment goal for some alcoholics. Unfortunately, Sobell and Sobell's data are disturbing because important design and data analysis problems prevent their unequivocal interpretation. Among these problems are the following: (1) Why did the experimental procedures effect change on follow-up and not during treatment? Specifically, why did subjects drink in maladaptive (uncontrolled) ways during the nonshock probe periods but then, on release from hospital, modify their drinking patterns to embrace abstinence or controlled drinking? (2) Which of the many components of the treatment paradigm was or were responsible for the treatment gains reported? Since this behavioral model employed a wide range of treatment methods designed to focus on different components of the behavior of the alcoholic subjects treated, it would have been important to identify the most active of these methods (e.g., aversive conditioning, training in social skills, videotape replay) as well as to assess the extent to which a lengthy follow-up period which called for repeated examination of consequent drinking be-

havior contributed to the positive results that were reported. (3) Follow-up data were largely collated from self-reports of drinking behavior, a form of follow-up notoriously susceptible to experimenter bias and subject unreliability. Data on vocational adjustment, general adjustment, and occupational status are more objective and reliable and, for that reason, may have been more acceptable. (4) All follow-up data were gathered by a single person who was, in fact, one of the two experimenters. While intentional bias on this person's part can, of course, be ruled out, unintentional bias cannot. This fact, of serious potential significance to the future widespread implementation of the behavioral program outlined by Sobell and Sobell, is fortunately in the process of being confronted. Two independent teams of investigators are now following up the 70 patients on whom follow-up data has been reported by the Sobells in an effort to provide independent

TABLE 1–8 Mean percentage of days spent in different drinking dispositions by subjects in four experimental groups displayed separately for the third and fourth six-month (183-day) follow-up intervals.

A. Follow-up Months 13–18

Drinking dispositions	Experimental condition			
	CD-E	CD-C	ND-E	ND-C
	(N=20)	(N=18)	(N=14)	(N=14)
Abstinent, not incarcerated (X %)	61.56	37.10	59.41	41.02
Controlled drinking (X %)	21.58	4.25	2.89	1.13
Drunk (X %)	12.81	51.49	19.75	35.95
Incarcerated in hospital (X %)	2.71	2.16	6.40*	10.81*
Incarcerated in jail (X %)	1.34	5.00	11.55*	11.09*
Total	100.00	100.00	100.00	100.00

B. Follow-up Months 19–24

Drinking dispositions	CD-E	CD-C	ND-E	ND-C
	(N=19)	(N=18)	(N=14)	(N=14)
Abstinent, not incarcerated (X %)	66.98	36.70	62.84	46.21
Controlled drinking (X %)	24.79	8.02	3.53	1.99
Drunk (X %)	7.08	46.12	19.72	35.87
Incarcerated in hospital (X %)	0.49	2.12	6.22*	6.05*
Incarcerated in jail (X %)	0.66	7.04	7.69*	9.88*
Total	100.00	100.00	100.00	100.00

SOURCE: Sobell & Sobell, 1973b, p. HO-9.
* Nondrinker incarceration data overrepresents extreme scores of a few individuals.

validation for the reported findings. Until then, of course, these data must be considered promising but tentative. (5) The format within which the Sobells reported follow-up data (in terms of percentage of controlled drinking and abstinent days) makes real sense; on the other hand, because this format is a new one, previous outcome data are not strictly comparable. As a result, it is impossible to know whether the Sobells' patients actually did much better in posttreatment as the data suggest they did, just as it is impossible to compare the Sobells' success rate with that achieved by earlier researchers.

Environmental manipulation of determinants of controlled drinking. A final group of behavioral researchers, working at the Baltimore City Hospitals and the Johns Hopkins Medical School, recently explored important environmental determinants of drinking by alcoholics in a series of studies more frankly experimental than the treatment-oriented studies already reviewed above. One of the first of these projects (Cohen, Liebson, Faillace, & Allen, 1971) conceptualized excessive drinking as an operant that is reinforced by a vast array of the consequences of drinking, and attempted to determine under what environmental conditions alcoholics could be brought to moderate drinking.

Five alcoholic subjects participated in two studies described in the 1971 report. All were skid row alcoholics in good physical and psychological health who, during the time of the studies, lived on a research ward of the Baltimore City Hospital in a six-bed self-contained unit. The goal of the first five-week study was to determine whether alcoholics would maintain moderate drinking, defined as no more than five ounces of beverage alcohol a day, when doing so resulted in an enriched living environment and not doing so produced an impoverished environment. The enriched environment was designed to permit subjects to work in the hospital laundry four hours a day for one dollar an hour, to use a private telephone, to enjoy a fully-equipped recreation room, to participate in daily group therapy, to eat a regular diet, to have a bedside chair, and to receive visitors. The impoverished environment allowed none of these "extras." Resultant data on drinking behavior during the five-week study showed that during the weeks (one, three and five) that the subjects could live in the enriched environment if they drank less than five ounces of beverage alcohol a day, they rarely exceeded that moderate level. By contrast, during the two weeks that the subjects had to live in the impoverished environment regardless of how much they drank, subjects almost always consumed the full 24 ounces available to them.

Four of the five subjects who participated in this first study remained on the ward for a second study designed to test the hypothesis that they had drunk immoderately during weeks two and four of the first study simply because they were living in an impoverished environment. Accordingly, the design of the second study was changed so that subjects could remain in the enriched environment during weeks 2 and 4 whether or not they drank moderately, while they had to drink moderately to remain during weeks 1, 3, and 5. Despite this change, subjects behaved essentially as before: when they had to choose between drinking moderately and living in the enriched environment or drinking immoderately and living in the impoverished environment, they chose the former course. When, however, the adequacy of their living situation was not contingent on drinking moderately, they drank up to the limit of 24 ounces.

Additional research by the Johns Hopkins group centering on the controllability of alcoholic drinking by explicitly scheduled behavioral consequences (Bigelow, Liebson, & Griffiths, 1973) has more recently revealed that brief (10-minute) isolation contingent upon the ingestion of small amounts of beverage alcohol effectively suppresses drinking by alcoholics by about one-half. It has showed, in addition, that moderate drinking (less than five ounces a day) can be maintained by contingent reinforcement in the form of the opportunity to leave the hospital for visits with a girlfriend (Figure 1–5), and that alcoholics given access to a greater total quantity of alcohol during a two-day period contingent on stopping drinking on the first day of the period did so.

Though all the Johns Hopkins studies were demonstrations—in that relatively small numbers of subjects were included in brief ABA studies designed to demonstrate the power of one or another environmental manipulation to moderate alcoholic drinking—they do reinforce the view that controlled drinking by alcoholics is possible; they also suggest a range of contingencies of potential value for this purpose as well as temporal sequences within which these contingencies would appear to be operative.

Behavioral efforts to teach controlled drinking in perspective. The studies reviewed in this section demonstrate that chronic alcoholics can moderate their drinking behavior under certain circumstances. These circumstances include: (1) adequately powerful reinforcement for drinking moderately and/or punishment for drinking immoderately and reasonable time expectancy for duration of moderation in drinking; (2) occasional feedback on BAL and patient belief that BAL discrimination training is of potential value to him; (3) a broad-spectrum, multimodal treatment program, combining aversive, modeling, and educative components, implemented by clinicians who believe the program to be a helpful one.

Does the fact that some alcoholics have returned to controlled, social drinking of their own accord (Bolman, 1965; Davies, 1962) while others maintain controlled drinking for moderate periods of time after behavior modification mean that controlled

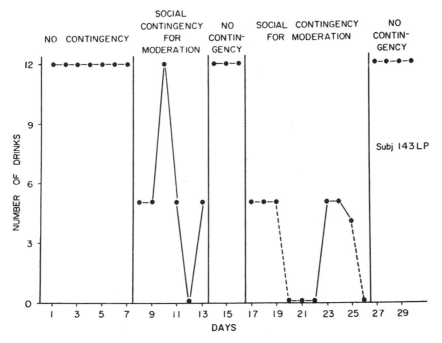

FIGURE 1–5   When moderate drinking was associated with the chance to leave the hospital to be with his girlfriend, this subject moderated his drinking (Bigelow, Liebson, & Griffiths, 1973).

drinking is a viable goal for some alcoholics? On this all important point, unfortunately, enough data are clearly not yet in, largely because only two studies of controlled drinking (Lovibond & Caddy, 1970; Sobell & Sobell, 1973a, 1973b) made systematic provision for follow-up. And neither of these studies can stand without significant criticism or question.

It is also clear that the narrow range of reported studies of controlled drinking is so restrictive that valid generalizations about the form therapy ought to take cannot be made. Based on our own clinical experience, however, and on the more extensive literature in the abstinence area, we are convinced that multimodal therapy —therapy designed to attack simultaneously a range of behavioral excesses and deficits (such as uncontrolled drinking, social anxiety, interpersonal deficits, and vocational shortcomings)—will probably be more effective in this regard than therapy directed at excessive drinking alone. We believe, as a result, that this feature of the Sobells' paradigm is one of its major strengths, even while we wish that these investigators had attempted to "sort out" on an experimental basis the active components of their regimen to permit rearrangement or reemphasis when and as appropriate.

In summary, is controlled drinking a viable goal for some alcoholics? Perhaps. Is research on controlled drinking an appropriate research emphasis for behavior modifiers? Absolutely. Is development of behavioral approaches to controlled drinking far enough along to justify direct application of these procedures to the clinical setting? Yes, given that such applications continue to combine research *and* practice in the effort to enable continued development of new behavioral approaches and refinement of existing ones.

BEHAVIORAL RESEARCH ON TREATMENT OF ALCOHOLICS: WHERE HAVE WE BEEN?

WHERE ARE WE GOING?   Despite the plethora of behavioral research on the treatment of alcoholism reviewed in this chapter, it seems both possible and desirable to try to summarize the central findings of this body of research in this concluding section:

1. Aversive conditioning alone has proven itself to be largely ineffective in treating alcoholics. Thus, electrical aversion, whether presented in the context of noncontingent aversion, escape (aversion relief), or avoidance, is clearly not of major therapeutic significance by itself. Similarly, though chemical aversion therapy with emetic agents may be somewhat more effective, the fact that its effectiveness in isolation from other concomitant behavioral and nonbehavioral treatments has not been established prevents direct comparison of its efficacy vis-à-vis electrical aversion. Finally, covert methods for aversion conditioning have not been employed with sufficient controls to enable assessment of their ultimate utility.

2. Behavioral approaches to alcoholism aimed at inducing abstinence, including systematic desensitization, assertive training, and broad-spectrum behavior therapy methods, have similarly not been studied with the controls necessary to enable objective assessment of their efficacy. Despite this, it does seem clear that systematic desensitization used alone to reduce the heightened anxiety that often accompanies alcoholism does not comprise a definitive treatment for alcoholism since, like aversion conditioning, it confronts but a segment of the disordered behavior. In contrast, the broad-spectrum approaches employ a variety of concurrent methods to deal with a range of behavioral deficits and excesses associated with alcoholism. When they include explicit efforts to train alcoholics in deficient social, familial, and vocational skills, they would appear to hold real promise—though objective data attesting to that promise have not yet been reported.

3. Controlled drinking by alcoholics

may well be a viable treatment goal for an unknown, probably relatively small, group of chronic alcoholics. As with behavioral efforts to induce abstinence, training in controlled drinking may be most successful when it attacks several problem behaviors simultaneously. It is not known now, however, what combination of these methods is best for this purpose. That is, what grouping of blood alcohol level estimation and subsequent control training, training in social skills, identification of environmental stimuli most closely associated with drinking onset, aversive conditioning of behaviors associated with immoderate drinking, and selection and contingency control of reinforcers in the environment will enable longest-term maintenance of controlled drinking by alcoholics.

Given these three conclusions, it is also possible to anticipate some directions of future research on behavioral treatment for alcoholism.

1. *Experimental analysis of those components of a multimodal approach to abstinence which contribute most to long-term abstinence.* One such study would compare three multimodal programs for inducing abstinence that would differ from each other only in the aversion component each employed (either electrical aversion, chemical aversion, or covert aversion).

2. *Examination of psychophysiological correlates of successful and unsuccessful behavioral treatment.* Research would determine whether changes in the character of physical tolerance must accompany short-term changes in drinking behavior for these changes to be permanent.

3. *Experimental analysis of those components of a multimodal approach to controlled drinking which contribute to* *long-term abstinence.* Such research would include alcoholics who did not believe in controlled drinking as a viable treatment goal since all studies of controlled drinking to this time have employed only alcoholics who failed to achieve abstinence and, for that reason, believed that controlled drinking might be a more appropriate goal for them.

4. *Identification of objective correlates of adaptive change in drinking behavior.* This would enable immediate prediction of the long-term outlook for a given patient's alcoholism. Such a correlate might be drinking behavior during a standard ad lib period immediately following a course of behavioral treatment.

5. *Determination of the most appropriate follow-up procedures and periods to assess the outcome of behavioral treatment for alcoholism.* At present researchers use such a variety of follow-up procedures employed over such a range of follow-up periods that direct comparison of the treatment efficacy of different methods over time is impossible. The development of standard behavioral procedures for followup (rather than reliance on test scores or self-reports on drinking behavior) to be given at systematic intervals during posttreatment would enable this direct comparison. Cost effectiveness studies of intensive versus intermittent follow-up and prolonged versus short-term follow-up are also needed. They would answer important questions like whether five years of follow-up predict permanency of change in drinking behavior more validly than a two-year follow-up or whether four different behavioral outcome measures at six months versus one or two measures at two years are most predictive of final treatment status.

References

ALCOHOLICS ANONYMOUS. *World directory.* New York: Alcoholics Anonymous, 1974.

AMERICAN PSYCHIATRIC ASSOCIATION. *Diagnostic and statistical manual of mental disorders.* (2nd ed.) Washington, D.C.: American Psychiatric Association, 1968.

ANANT, S. S. A note on the treatment of alcoholics by a verbal aversion technique. *Canadian Psychologist*, 1967, **1**, 19–22.

BIGELOW, G., LIEBSON, I., & GRIFFITHS, R. Experimental analysis of alcoholic drinking. Paper presented at the meeting of the American Psychological Association, August 1973.

BLAKE, B. G. The application of behavior therapy to the treatment of alcoholism. *Behaviour Research and Therapy*, 1965, **3**, 75–85.

BLAKE, B. G. A follow-up of alcoholics treated by behavior therapy. *Behaviour Research and Therapy*, 1967, **5**, 89–94.

BOLMAN, W. M. Abstinence versus permissiveness in the psychotherapy of alcoholics. *Archives of General Psychiatry*, 1965, **12**, 456–463.

BRAUCHT, G. N., BRAKARSH, D., FOLLINGSTAD, D., & BERRY, K. L. Deviant drug use in adolescence. *Psychological Bulletin*, 1973, **79**, 92–106.

CAHALAN, D., CISIN, I. H., & CROSSLEY, H. M. *American drinking practices*. New Brunswick, N.J.: Rutgers Center of Alcohol Studies, 1969.

CAPPELL, H., & HERMAN, C. P. Alcohol and tension reduction: a review. *Quarterly Journal of Studies on Alcohol*, 1972, **33**, 33–64.

CAUTELA, J. R. Treatment of compulsive behavior by covert sensitization. *Psychological Record*, 1966, **16**, 33–41.

CAUTELA, J. R. Covert sensitization. *Psychological Reports*, 1967, **20**, 459–468.

CAUTELA, J. R. The treatment of alcoholism by covert sensitization. *Psychotherapy: Theory, Research and Practice*, 1970, **7**, 86–90.

CHAPMAN, R. F., BURT, D. W., & SMITH, J. W. Electrical aversion conditioning to alcohol: individual measurement. Paper presented at the Western Psychological Association Convention, April 1972.

COHEN, M., LIEBSON, I. A., FAILLACE, L. A., & ALLEN, R. P. Moderate drinking by chronic alcoholics. *Journal of Nervous and Mental Disease*, 1971, **153**, 434–444.

CONGER, J. J. The effects of alcohol on conflict behavior in the albino rat. *Quarterly Journal of Studies on Alcohol*, 1951, **12**, 1–29.

CONGER, J. J. Alcoholism: theory, problem and challenge. II. Reinforcement theory and the dynamics of alcoholism. *Quarterly Journal of Studies on Alcohol*, 1956, **17**, 291–324.

CUTTER, H. S. G., SCHWAB, E. L., & NATHAN, P. E. Effects of alcohol on its utility for alcoholics. *Quarterly Journal of Studies on Alcohol*, 1970, **30**, 369–378.

DAVIES, D. L. Normal drinking by recovered alcohol addicts. *Quarterly Journal of Studies on Alcohol*, 1962, **23**, 94–104.

DEPARTMENT OF HEALTH, EDUCATION, AND WELFARE. *Alcohol and Health*. Washington, D.C.: HSMHA, NIMH, NIAAA, 1971.

deVITO, R. A., FLAHERTY, L. A., & MOZDZIERZ, G. J. Toward a psychodynamic theory of alcoholism. *Diseases of the Nervous System*, 1970, **31**, 43–49.

DITMAN, K. S. A controlled experiment on the use of court probation for drunk arrests. *American Journal of Psychiatry*, 1967, **124**, 160–163.

DOCTER, R. F., & BERNAL, M.E. Immediate and prolonged psychophysiological effects of sustained alcohol intake in alcoholics. *Quarterly Journal of Studies on Alcohol*, 1964, **25**, 438–450.

EFRON, V., & KELLER, M. *Selected statistics on consumption of alcohol (1850–1968) and on alcoholism (1930–1968)*. New Brunswick, N.J.: Rutgers Center of Alcohol Studies, 1970.

EYSENCK, H. J. (Ed.). *Behavior therapy and the neuroses*. London: Pergamon Press, 1960.

FARRAR, C. H., POWELL, B. J., & MARTIN, L. K. Punishment of alcohol consumption by apneic paralysis. *Behavior Research and Therapy*, 1968, **6**, 13–16.

FRANKS, C. M. Conditioning and conditioned aversion therapies in the treatment of the alcoholic. *International Journal of the Addictions*, 1966, **1**, 61–98.

FRANKS, C. M. Alcoholism. In C. G. Costello (Ed.), *Symptoms of Psychopathology*. New York: John Wiley, 1970.

GOODWIN, D. Is alcoholism inherited? Paper presented at the 3rd Annual NIAAA Conference on Alcoholism, June, 1973.

GOTTHEIL, E., CORBETT, L. O., GRASBERGER, J. C., & CORNELISON, F. S. Fixed-interval drinking decisions. *Quarterly Journal of Studies on Alcohol*, 1972, **33**, 311–324.

HALLAM, R., RACHMAN, S., & FALKOWSKI, W. Subjective attitudinal and physiological effects of electrical aversion therapy. *Behaviour Research and Therapy*, 1972, **10**, 1–14.

HIGGINS, R. L. Manipulation of social evaluative anxiety as a determinant of alcohol consumption. Unpublished doctoral dissertation, University of Wisconsin, 1973.

HIGGINS, R. L., & MARLATT, G. A. The effects of anxiety arousal upon the consumption of alcohol by alcoholics and social drinkers. *Journal of Consulting and Clinical Psychology,* 1973, **41,** 426–433.

HILL, M. J., & BLAINE, H. T. Evaluation of psychotherapy with alcoholics: a critical review. *Quarterly Journal of Studies on Alcohol,* 1967, **28,** 76–104.

HSU, J. J. Electroconditioning therapy of alcoholics. A preliminary report. *Quarterly Journal of Studies on Alcohol,* 1965, **26,** 449–459.

HUNT, G. M., & AZRIN, N. H. The community-reinforcement approach to alcoholism. *Behaviour Research and Therapy,* 1973, **11,** 91–104.

JELLINEK, E. M. *The disease concept of alcoholism.* New Haven: College and University Press, 1960.

JESSOR, R., COLLINS, M. I., & JESSOR, S. L. On becoming a drinker: social-psychological aspects of an adolescent transition. *Annals of the New York Academy of Sciences,* 1972, **197,** 199–213.

KAIJ, L. *Alcoholism in twins.* Stockholm: Almquist & Wiksell, 1960.

KANTOROVICH, N. V. An attempt at associative-reflex therapy in alcoholism. *Psychological Abstracts,* 1930, **4,** 493.

KEEHN, J. D., BLOOMFIELD, F. F., & HUG, M. A. Use of the reinforcement survey schedule with alcoholics. *Quarterly Journal of Studies on Alcohol,* 1970, **31,** 602–615.

KRAFT, T. Alcoholism treated by systematic desensitization: a follow-up of eight cases. *Journal of the Royal College of General Practice,* 1969, **18,** 336–340.

KRAFT, T., & AL-ISSA, I. Alcoholism treated by desensitization: a case study. *Behaviour Research and Therapy,* 1967, **5,** 69–70.

KRUPP, M. A., CHATTON, M. J., & MARGEN, S. *Current diagnosis and treatment.* Los Altos, Calif.: Lange Medical Publications, 1971.

LANYON, R. I. The assessment of problem drinking in males. Unpublished manuscript, Northeastern University, 1974.

LANYON, R. I., PRIMO, R. V., TERRELL, F., & WENER, A. An aversion-desensitization treatment for alcoholism. *Journal of Consulting and Clinical Psychology,* 1972, **38,** 394–398.

LAVERTY, S. G. Aversion therapies in the treatment of alcoholism. *Psychosomatic Medicine,* 1966, **28,** 651–666.

LAZARUS, A. A. Towards the understanding and effective treatment of alcoholism. *South African Medical Journal,* 1965, **39,** 736–741.

LAZARUS, A. A. Multimodal behavior therapy: treating the "basic id." *Journal of Nervous and Mental Disease,* 1973, **156,** 404–11.

LEMERE, F., & VOEGTLIN, W. L. An evaluation of the aversion treatment of alcoholism. *Quarterly Journal of Studies on Alcohol.* 1950, **11,** 199–204.

LEMERE, F., VOEGTLIN, W. L., BROZ, W. R., & O'HALLAREN, P. Conditioned reflex treatment of alcohol addiction. V. Type of patient suitable for this treatment. *Northwestern Medicine,* 1942, **4,** 88–89.

LISMAN, S. A. Alcoholic "blackout": state-dependent learning? *Archives of General Psychiatry,* 1974, **30,** 46–53.

LOLLI, G., SERIANNI, E., GOLDER, G. M., & LUZZATTO-FEGIZ, P. *Alcohol in Italian culture.* New Brunswick, N.J.: Rutgers Center of Alcohol Studies, 1958.

LOVIBOND, S. H. Pure and applied psychology: towards a significant interaction. *Australian Psychologist,* 1970, **5,** 120–140.

LOVIBOND, S. H., & CADDY, G. Discriminated aversive control in the moderation of alcoholics' drinking behavior. *Behavior Therapy,* 1970, **1,** 437–444.

LUBETKIN, B. S., RIVERS, P. C., & ROSENBERG, C. M. Difficulties of disulfiram therapy with alcoholics. *Quarterly Journal of Studies on Alcohol,* 1971, **32,** 168–171.

MACANDREW, C. The differentiation of male alcoholic outpatients from nonalcoholic psychiatric outpatients by means of the MMPI. *Quarterly Journal of Studies on Alcohol,* 1965, **26,** 238–246.

MACCULLOCH, M. J., FELDMAN, M. P., ORFORD, J. F., & MACCULLOCH, M. L. Anticipatory avoidance learning in the treatment of alcoholism: a record of therapeutic failure. *Behaviour Research and Therapy,* 1966, **4,** 187–196.

MANSON, M. P. A psychometric differentiation of alcoholics from nonalcoholics. *Quarterly Journal of Studies on Alcohol,* 1948, **9,** 175–205. (a)

MANSON, M. P. The Alcadd Test. Beverly Hills, Calif.: Western Psychological Service, 1948. (b)

MARLATT, G. A. Determinants of alcohol consumption in a laboratory taste-rating task: implications for controlled drinking. Paper presented at the meeting of the American Psychological Association, August 1973.

MARLATT, G. A., DEMMING, B., & REID, J. B. Loss of control drinking in alcoholics: an experimental analogue. *Journal of Abnormal Psychology,* 1973, **81,** 233–241.

MARLATT, G. A., & KOSTURN, C. F. Elicitation of anger and opportunity for retaliation as determinants of alcohol consumption. Unpublished manuscript, University of Washington, 1973.

MCGUIRE, R. J., & VALLANCE, M. Aversion therapy by electric shock, a simple technique. *British Medical Journal,* 1964, **1,** 151–152.

MCNAMEE, H. B., MELLO, N. K., & MENDELSON, J. H. Experimental analysis of drinking patterns of alcoholics. Concurrent psychiatric observations. *American Journal of Psychiatry,* 1968, **124,** 1063–1069.

MELLO, N. K. Psychopharmacology of alcoholism. In D. Efron (Ed.), *Psychopharmacology: a review of progress 1957–1967.* Washington, D.C.: U.S. Government Printing Office, 1968.

MELLO, N. K. Behavioral studies of alcoholism. In B. Kissin & H. Begleiter (Eds.), The biology of alcoholism. New York: Plenum Press, 1972.

MELLO, N. K., & MENDELSON, J. H. Operant analysis of drinking patterns of chronic alcoholics, *Nature,* 1965, **206,** 43–46.

MENDELSON, J. H. Ethanol-1-C^{14} metabolism in alcoholics and nonalcoholics, *Science,* 1968, **159,** 319–320.

MENDLESON, J. H. Biologic concomitants of alcoholism. *New England Journal of Medicine,* 1970, **283,** 24–32.

MENDELSON, J. H., & MELLO, N. K. Experimental analysis of drinking behavior of chronic alcoholics. *Annals of the New York Academy of Sciences,* 1966, **133,** 828–845.

MERRY, J. The "loss of control" myth. *Lancet,* 1966, **1,** 1267–1268.

MILLER, N. E. Autonomic learning: clinical and physiological implications. In M. Hammer, K. Salzinger, & S. Sutton (Eds.), *Psychopathology: contributions from the social, behavioral, and biological sciences.* New York: Wiley-Interscience, 1973.

MILLER, P. M. Behavioral assessment in alcoholism research and treatment: current techniques. *International Journal of the Addictions,* 1973, **8,** 831–837.

MILLER, P. M., & HERSEN, M. Quantitative changes in alcohol consumption as a function of electrical aversive conditioning. *Journal of Clinical Psychology,* 1972, **28,** 590–593.

MILLER, P. M., STANFORD, A. G., & HEMPHILL, D. P. A comprehensive social learning approach to alcoholism treatment. *Social Casework,* in press.

MILLS, K. C., SOBELL, M. B., & SCHAEFER, H. H. Training social drinking as an alternative to abstinence for alcoholics. *Behavior Therapy,* 1971, **2,** 18–27.

MOROSKI, T. E., & BAER, P. E. Avoidance conditioning of alcoholics. In R. Ulrich, T. Stachnich, & J. Mabry (Eds.) *Control of human behavior.* Vol. 2. Glenview, Ill.: Scott, Foresman, 1970.

NATHAN, P. E., GOLDMAN, M. S., LISMAN, S. A., & TAYLOR, H. A. Alcohol and alcoholics: a behavioral approach. *Transactions of the New York Academy of Sciences,* 1972, **34,** 602–627.

NATHAN, P. E., & O'BRIEN, J. S. An experimental analysis of the behavior of alcoholics and nonalcoholics during prolonged experimental drinking. *Behavior Therapy,* 1971, **2,** 455–476.

NATHAN, P. E., O'BRIEN, J. S., & LOWENSTEIN, L. M. Operant studies of chronic alcoholism: interaction of alcohol and alcoholics. In P. J. Creaven & M. K. Roach (Eds.), *Biological aspects of alcohol.* Austin: University of Texas Press, 1971.

NATHAN, P. E., TITLER, N. A., LOWENSTEIN, L. M., SOLOMON, P., & ROSSI, A. M. Behavioral analysis of chronic alcoholism. *Archives of General Psychiatry,* 1970, **22,** 419–430.

OKULITCH, P. V., & MARLATT, G. A. Effects of varied extinction conditions with alcoholics and social drinkers. *Journal of Abnormal Psychology,* 1972, **79,** 205–211.

OVERALL, J. E., & PATRICK, J. H. Unitary alcoholism factor and its personality correlates. *Journal of Abnormal Psychology,* 1972, **79,** 303–309.

PATTISON, E. M. A critique of abstinence criteria in the treatment of alcoholism. *International Journal of Social Psychiatry,* 1968, **14,** 268–276.

PENICK, S. B., CARRIER, R. N., & SHELDON, J. B.

Metronidazole in the treatment of alcoholism. *American Journal of Psychiatry*, 1969, **125**, 1063–1066.

RACHMAN, S. Sexual disorders and behavior therapy. *American Journal of Psychiatry*, 1961, **118**, 235–240.

RAYMOND, M. J. The treatment of addiction by aversion conditioning with apomorphine. *Behaviour Research and Therapy*, 1964, **1**, 287–291.

RODGERS, D. A., & McCLEARN, G. E. Mouse strain differences in preference for various concentrations of alcohol. *Quarterly Journal of Studies on Alcohol*, 1962, **23**, 26–33.

ROHAN, W. P. MMPI changes in hospitalized alcoholics: a second study. *Quarterly Journal of Studies on Alcohol*, 1972, **33**, 65–76.

SANDERSON, R. E., CAMPBELL, D., & LAVERTY, S. G. Traumatically conditioned responses acquired during respiratory paralysis. *Nature*, 1962, **196**, 1235–1236.

SANDERSON, R. E., CAMPBELL, D., & LAVERTY, S. G. An investigation of a new aversive conditioning treatment for alcoholism. *Quarterly Journal of Studies on Alcohol*, 1963, **24**, 261–275.

SANDLER, J. Three aversive control procedures with alcoholics: a preliminary report. Paper presented at the meeting of the Southeastern Psychological Association, April 1969.

SCHACHTER, S., GOLDMAN, R., & GORDON, A. Effects of fear, food deprivation, and obesity on eating. *Journal of Personality and Social Psychology*, 1968, **10**, 91–97.

SCHAEFER, H. H., SOBELL, M. B., & MILLS, K. C. Baseline drinking behaviors in alcoholics and social drinkers: kinds of drinks and sip magnitude. *Behaviour Research and Therapy*, 1971, **9**, 23–27.

SHENTAUB, S. A., & MIJOLLA, A. Note sur la particularité de "l'agir" dans la relation psychoanalytique avec la patient alcoolique chronique. *Revue France Psychoanalytique*, 1968, **32**, 1049–1053.

SILBER, A. An addendum to the technique of psychotherapy with alcoholics. *Journal of Nervous and Mental Disease*, 1970, **150**, 423–437.

SILVERSTEIN, S. J., NATHAN, P. E., & TAYLOR, H. A. Blood alcohol level estimation and controlled drinking by chronic alcoholics. *Behavior Therapy*, 1974, **5**, 1–15.

SMITH, C. G. Alcoholics: their treatment and their wives. *British Journal of Psychiatry*, 1969, **115**, 1039–1042.

SOBELL, M. B., & SOBELL, L. C. Individualized behavior therapy for alcoholics. *Behavior Therapy*, 1973, **4**, 49–72. (a)

SOBELL, M. B., & SOBELL, L. C. Evidence of controlled drinking by former alcoholics: a second year evaluation of individualized behavior therapy. Paper presented at the meeting of the American Psychological Association, August 1973. (b)

STEFFEN, J. J. Electromyographically induced relaxation in the treatment of chronic alcohol abuse. *Journal of Consulting and Clinical Psychology*, 1975, **43**, 275.

STEFFEN, J. J., TAYLOR, H. A., & NATHAN, P. E. Tension-reducing effects of alcohol: further evidence and some methodological considerations. *Journal of Abnormal Psychology*, 1974, **83**, 542–547.

SUMMERS, T. Validity of alcoholics' self-reported drinking history. *Quarterly Journal of Studies on Alcohol*, 1970, **31**, 972–974.

TALLAND, G. A., & KASSCHAU, R. Practice and alcohol effects on motor skill and attention: a supplementary report on an experiment in chronic intoxication and withdrawal. *Quarterly Journal of Studies on Alcohol*, 1965, **26**, 393–401.

TALLAND, G. A., MENDELSON, J. H., & RYACK, P. Tests of motor skills. In J. H. Mendelson (Ed.), Experimentally induced chronic intoxication and withdrawal in alcoholics. (Supplement #2) *Quarterly Journal of Studies on Alcohol*, May 1964.

THIMANN, J. Conditioned reflex treatment of alcoholism. II. The risks of its application, its indications, contraindications, and psychotherapeutic aspects. *New England Journal of Medicine*, 1949, **241**, 408–410.

TRAVIS, N. Observations of blackouts and other alcohol-induced memory impairments. Unpublished doctoral dissertation, Rutgers University, 1973.

TREMPER, M. Dependency in alcoholics: a sociological view. *Quarterly Journal of Studies on Alcohol*, 1972, **33**, 186–190.

TRUITT, E. B. Blood acetaldehyde levels after alcohol consumption by alcoholic and nonalcoholic subjects. In M. K. Roach, W. M. McIsaac, & P. J. Creaven (Eds.), *Biological aspects of alcohol*. Austin: University of Texas Press, 1971.

ULLMAN, L. P., & KRASNER, L. *A psychological approach to abnormal behavior.* Englewood Cliffs, N.J.: Prentice-Hall, 1969.

VOEGTLIN, W. L. The treatment of alcoholism by establishing a conditioned reflex. *American Journal of Medical Science,* 1940, **199**, 802–809.

VOEGTLIN, W. L. Conditioned reflex therapy of chronic alcoholism: ten years' experience with the method. *Rocky Mountain Medical Journal,* 1947, 44, 807–812.

VOGLER, R. E., LUNDE, S. E., JOHNSON, G. R., & MARTIN, P. L. Electrical aversion conditioning with chronic alcoholics. *Journal of Consulting and Clinical Psychology,* 1970, **34**, 302–307.

VOGLER, R. E., LUNDE, S. E., & MARTIN, P. L. Electrical aversion conditioning with chronic alcoholics: follow-up and suggestions for research. *Journal of Consulting and Clinical Psychology,* 1971, **36**, 450.

WILLIAMS, T. K. The ethanol-induced loss of control concept in alcoholism. Doctoral dissertation, Western Michigan University, 1970.

WILSON, G. T., & DAVISON, G. C. Aversion techniques in behavior therapy: some theoretical and metatheoretical considerations. *Journal of Consulting and Clinical Psychology,* 1969, **33**, 327–329.

WILSON, G. T., LEAF, R., & NATHAN, P. E. The aversive control of excessive drinking by chronic alcoholics in the laboratory setting. *Journal of Applied Behaviour Analysis,* 1975, **8**, 13–26.

ZUCKER, R. A., & VAN HORN, H. Sibling social structure and oral behavior: drinking and smoking in adolescence. *Quarterly Journal of Studies on Alcohol,* 1972, **33**, 193–197.

Behavioral Treatment of the Eating Disorders

2

ALBERT J. STUNKARD
MICHAEL J. MAHONEY

The application of behavioral methods to eating disorders during the past eight years has resulted in what may be the most significant advances that have yet been made in treating these refractory and baffling conditions. An account of these developments is instructive, not only for their contributions to therapy, but also for the light they shed on the development of theory involving such a vital life process as eating.

This account concerns behavioral methods of treating the pathological extremes of nutrition: obesity and anorexia nervosa. These disorders, and particularly their treatment, have much in common, as we shall see. Of the two, however, anorexia nervosa seems to be a more homogeneous disorder and one readily encompassed by a learning theory framework. Furthermore, it was the first of the two disorders which was found to respond to behavioral methods of management, and this responsiveness has played a considerable role in encouraging behavioral analysis of eating behavior in obesity, as well as in anorexia nervosa. We will therefore consider first the behavioral treatment of anorexia nervosa.

Anorexia Nervosa

Anorexia nervosa is a rare disorder characterized by voluntary restriction of food intake, weight loss, and amenorrhea (Stunkard, 1975). It may vary from a mild, transitory, and even unrecognized state to a severe, chronic illness lasting many years and ending in death. It occurs primarily among females, and puberty is the most frequent time of onset. The term "anorexia" is a misnomer, since patients are probably not without appetite until late in the illness. "Weight phobia" may more accurately reflect the central problem (Crisp, 1970).

In striking contrast to obesity, current evidence suggests that genetic influences in anorexia nervosa are far less important than are familial, presumably learned, ones. There is a very high incidence of anorexia nervosa among sisters; two studies have reported that 7% of the sisters of probands also suffered from the disorder. As might be expected, there have been isolated reports of monozygotic twins concordant for anorexia nervosa. Of probably greater significance is Crisp's (1970) finding that three of four monozygotic twin pairs were *dis*cordant, a particularly striking finding in light of the high concordance among sisters. Furthermore, Crisp has reported the interesting occurrence of anorexia nervosa in two adopted girls unrelated to each other or to the couple raising them.

Treatment of anorexia nervosa may be divided into two quite distinct phases: short-term intervention to restore body weight and save life, and long-term therapy to ameliorate the often long-standing and pervasive difficulties. To date, behavioral programs have been largely confined to the first phase.

Two general kinds of behavioral approaches to anorexia nervosa have been employed; systematic desensitization and operant reinforcement. Strong evidence that a central problem in anorexia nervosa is a phobia of being overweight, which can reach delusional intensity, makes a desensitization procedure eminently reasonable. Such a procedure was described in individual case reports by Lang (1965) and by Hallsten (1965). Each author reported increased eating and weight gain through desensitization directed toward the eating behavior itself, rather than toward the phobia of increased body weight or obesity. Despite this promising start, desensitization procedures have since been reported only infrequently in the treatment of anorexia nervosa (Schnurer, Rubin, and Roy, 1973; Crisp and Toms, 1972). Instead, operant reinforcement procedures have been increasingly utilized (e.g., Ayllon & Haughton, 1962; Ayllon, Haughton, & Osmond, 1964; Azerrad & Stafford, 1969; Stumphauzer, 1969).

Bachrach, Erwin, and Mohr reported one of the first attempts to use an operant reinforcement approach in their 1965 case report of a 37-year-old woman whose weight had fallen from 118 to 47 pounds over a seven-year period. The patient was initially required to eat all meals in her room with the experimenters who used verbal reinforcement to shape her eating responses. Access to other reinforcers, such as watching television and walks with other patients and visitors, was made contingent on eating progressively larger meals. The patient's initial response was favorable and she gained 16 pounds. When her weight did not rise past 63 pounds, however, the authors concluded that she had begun to vomit secretly. At this point they made reinforcement contingent upon weight gain rather than on eating. This procedure resulted in additional weight gain sufficient to warrant discharge from the hospital. Eighteen months after hospitalization, in the absence of continuing treatment, the patient's weight had fallen to 72 pounds.

In 1968, Leitenberg, Agras, and Thomson reported the successful treatment of two patients by means of an operant reinforcement paradigm similar to that of the previous study, with rewarding consequences such as praise and ward privileges attached to eating and weight gain. Very rapid weight gain—four and four and a half pounds per week—was produced, and the patients were discharged from the hospital in good condition. The authors further attempted to assess the specificity of the reinforcement procedures by control periods during which praise and tangible reinforcers were withheld. These results were equivocal and prompted a further study reported below.

Two studies from the University of Pennsylvania added a significant number of patients to those already successfully treated by operant reinforcement procedures. Further, they identified a particularly potent reinforcer which proved valuable in managing these patients whose behavioral repertoire is so often severely depleted. By means of pedometers, Blinder, Freeman, and Stunkard (1970) showed that anorexic patients in the hospital walked an average of 6.8 miles per day, compared with the 4.9 miles per day for women of normal weight living in the community, and far lesser levels for other hospitalized patients. This marked hyperactivity suggested that access to physical activity might serve as a reinforcer. It not only served as a reinforcer but proved to be so potent in this regard that the first three patients gained over four pounds a week on a program whose sole contingency was making access to physical activity dependent upon a weight gain of half a pound a day. Similarly favorable outcomes were reported for three other patients in whom additional or other reinforcement contingencies were utilized. One of these was based upon the patient's strenuous dislike of chlorpromazine, and consisted of making the daily dosage of the medication contingent upon the amount of weight gained during the previous day (Stunkard, 1972). The patient received 400 mg if there were no weight gain, 300 mg if she gained one-quarter of a pound, 200 mg if she gained one-half pound, 100 mg of she gained three-quarters of a pound, and no chlorpromazine if she gained at least one pound.

Most of the six patients in this series received chlorpromazine in addition to the reinforcement contingencies, and one patient who had failed to gain weight with the behavioral paradigm alone showed prompt weight gain with institution of chlorpromazine. It is of interest that these patients showed considerable improvement in their personal relationships and heightened feelings of well-being in addition to their weight gain. Although two of the patients were reported in good condition one year after discharge, two others died—one by suicide a month after discharge and one by inanition following recurrence of the disorder five years later.

Brady and Rieger (1972) greatly extended the findings of the previous study in their report of 16 consecutive patients successfully treated by operant measures. Their report demonstrates that the behavioral treatment of anorexia nervosa, heretofore an experimental measure, is sufficiently well understood that it can become a standard method of in-hospital treatment.

During the first four or five days in the hospital the patient's weight was recorded and her behavior observed for the purpose of discerning suitable reinforcers. Hyper-

activity was observed in nine of the 16 patients. For them the principal contingency in each case was access to physical activity—specifically a six-hour pass to leave the ward on any day on which the patient had gained at least half a pound. Three patients, who were not hyperactive but who spent much of the observation period in social activity with other patients, were put on a schedule in which permission to socialize was made contingent upon weight gain. In other patients, more highly individualized measures were used. Twelve patients received concurrent phenothiazines, usually chlorpromazine in a dose of 200 mg to 500 mg per day. Six received tricyclic antidepressants, either in combination with phenothiazines or alone, and two patients received no medication.

The median length of hospitalization was six weeks, during which the patients gained an average of four pounds a week. Most of the patients were referred to the program from outside the Philadelphia area. They returned home for continuing care, and most, therefore, did not receive continuing behavioral management. At follow-up an average of two years later, the adjustment of five patients was rated as "good," five "fair," and two "poor." Two were dead and two lost to follow-up.

Anorexia nervosa, as it appears in academic medical centers, at the end of a long referral chain, is clearly a most serious chronic condition. In-hospital treatment designed to restore weight and decrease the threat to life is only the first stage in treatment. There is a great need for study of the application of behavioral measures to long-term management of the condition.

The most recent report of "Behavior Modification in Anorexia Nervosa" provides the most systematic analysis to date of the effectiveness of the different therapeutic variables which have been utilized in behavioral approaches to anorexia nervosa (Agras, Barlow, Chapin, Abel, & Leitenberg, 1974). In this report, Agras and his co-workers describe a series of related single-case experiments of nine patients treated for anorexia nervosa. They were stimulated by the puzzling results of their earlier attempt at a controlled analysis of the effects of positive reinforcement (Leitenberg, Agras, & Thomson, 1968). That attempt showed that when various reinforcers were made contingent upon weight gain, caloric intake and weight increased as compared with a baseline period in which no such increases were noted. When reinforcement was stopped, however, caloric intake was maintained and weight gain continued. This sequence raised the question of whether the weight gains reported by themselves, and by other authors, were indeed due to the positive reinforcement, or whether other variables were responsible for the therapeutic effect.

In an elegant series of experiments, four different variables which had been combined in all previous operant reinforcement approaches, were separately analyzed. They were: positive reinforcement, negative reinforcement, informational feedback, and the size of the meal. The authors demonstrated that all four variables contributed to increased food intake and weight increase but that their relative effectiveness varied considerably. The most potent variable appeared to be feedback of information as to weight and caloric intake. Without such feedback, positive reinforcement, to which all previous authors had attributed the major influence, appeared to be relatively ineffective. Further, the authors distinguished for the first time between positive and negative reinforcement, which had been inextricably linked in all previous programs. They were impressed by patients' statements that they wanted to leave the hospital as quickly as possible, and knew that the only way to do this was to gain weight. They concluded that such a contingency constituted negative reinforcement. Patients were apparently working (eating more and gaining weight) to terminate an unpleasant event (being in the hospital), rather than for the positive re-

inforcement of praise and access to activity. To separate such negative reinforcement from positive reinforcement, the authors contracted with the patient and her parents for a 12-week stay "for research purposes, whether or not the patient gained weight." Isolation of the influence of negative reinforcement by this means revealed that it had an influence upon the patient, but, like positive reinforcement, was not as potent as feedback regarding weight gain and caloric intake. Finally, the authors found that meal size exerted a small but significant influence on caloric intake: patients ate more when larger meals were served, even when the meals were so large that they could not finish them.

In the brief span of seven years we have seen the introduction of operant reinforcement measures for treating the rare and refractory condition of anorexia nervosa, and their development in two directions. First, the procedures have been sufficiently standardized that they can now be used with the expectation of success by trained hospital personnel. Second, the effective elements of the behavioral package are beginning to be isolated and progress is being made in defining their relative potency.

So far behavioral approaches to anorexia nervosa have been confined to treating severely ill, hospitalized patients. Their effectiveness in this life-threatening stage of the illness is a major therapeutic advance. Behavioral principles have not yet been applied to the adjustment of these patients in the period after they leave the hospital and return to often very difficult family situations. The long-term results of the treatment of anorexia nervosa are sufficiently poor that there is sore need for such application.

Obesity

When we turn from anorexia nervosa to obesity, we move from a rare condition of little public health importance to one of the nation's major health problems. Obesity may affect as many as one-quarter of American adults, and it may contribute to their poorer health and higher death rates. Obesity is, furthermore, a condition of vastly greater complexity than anorexia nervosa. In distinction to the unequivocal role of learning in anorexia nervosa, obesity is a disorder of multiple origins, all of them poorly understood.

It seems important, in a volume on behavior modification, to consider in some detail these multiple origins of obesity. For the rapidly growing literature of behavior modification of obesity is already producing the kind of unjustified claims which, 70 years before, helped to herald the diversion of psychoanalysis into expensive and unprofitable theorizing. These claims assert that, because we can change behavior, we can thereby explain its origins. More specifically, we are now beginning to hear with increasing frequency the proposition that, because food intake can be controlled by behavioral techniques, it follows that obesity is the result of inappropriate and maladaptive eating habits.

A homely example may illustrate the problem. Persons who do not, or cannot, write can be taught to do so by appropriate behavioral techniques. What does this say about the relationship of the techniques to the origins of the behavior? Four possible examples come to mind.

1. A person does not write because of inappropriately learned behavior, ineffective study habits, and inadequate reinforcement. By applying the appropriate contingencies such a person may be taught to write. This sequence may, indeed, tell us a great deal about the origins of the disorder.

2. A schizophrenic may not write. Here, again, arrangement of the appropriate contingencies can induce him to write. What does this tell us about the origins of his behavioral deficits?

3. A person with minimal brain damage and a hyperkinetic syndrome has never learned to write. Behavioral methods may help him to

write; this outcome explains at best only a small part of his problem.

4. A right-handed person loses his arm in an accident and cannot write. Learning techniques help him to write with his left arm. The new learning tells us nothing about the origins of the deficit.

Such a schema is relevant to a consideration of the role of behavior modification in treating obesity. For, at the present time, obesity is a disorder of unknown and almost certainly diverse origins, lying anywhere on the spectrum from one to four. Weight loss of an obese person through behavior modification may or may not help to explain the origins of his obesity.

THE BIOLOGY OF BODY WEIGHT

Let us consider now the biology of body weight. What are the biological constraints within which behavior modification programs must operate? What causes obesity? In one sense the answer is quite simple— eating more calories than are expended as energy. In another sense the answer still eludes us. We do not know why some people eat more calories than they expend. But we are making progress. For example, we no longer expect to find *the* cause of obesity, and we are increasingly aware of the many factors involved in regulating body weight, for with behavior modification we are intervening in a complex regulatory process. What do we know about the regulation of body weight?

An average nonobese man stores fat to the extent of about 15% of his body weight, enough to provide for all his caloric needs for nearly a month. This same man consumes approximately one million calories a year. His body fat stores remain quantitatively unchanged during this time, because he expends an equal number of calories. An error of no more than 10% in either intake or output would lead to a 30-pound change in body weight within the year. Clearly, body weight in persons of normal weight is regulated with remarkable precision.

Even when persons of normal weight are experimentally subjected to very large changes in weight, they show a remarkable ability to return to their original body weight. The most detailed exploration of the effects of caloric restriction in man were the classic studies of Keys et al. (1950) during World War II. They restricted 36 young male volunteers to low-calorie diets which produced a deficit of 1600 calories per day for a period of six months. Subjects lost 25% of their body weight while developing severe behavioral disorders subsumed under the designation "semistarvation neurosis." When they were provided free access to food, all the subjects promptly began to restore their lost body weight and within three months were maintaining it at pre-starvation levels.

The studies of Sims et al. (1968) provide even more dramatic evidence of the stability of regulation of body weight. When normal-weight volunteers ate a diet containing 8,000 calories a day, all gained weight. The average gain, however, consisted of no more than a 25% increase in body weight, which asymptoted below 220 pounds in all subjects. When they were released from these pressures and allowed to self-select their food, all subjects returned promptly and without effort to their previous weight.

Numerous studies on experimental animals of normal weight amply confirm the remarkable stability of the regulation of body weight. More recent work shows a surprisingly similar stability of regulation also in obese animals. Although the body weights of hereditary-obese hyperglycemic mice and of hypothalamic obese rats were double and even triple that of their non-obese littermates, once they reached their maximum weight, fluctuations about this level were not greater, percentage-wise, than those of the nonobese rats. In experimentally obese animals, therefore, it appears that the regulation of body weight may be in-tact. What is altered is the set-point around which this regulation occurs.

What do we know about the factors influencing the set-point for body weight?

GENETICS. The existence of numerous forms of inherited obesity in animals, and the ease with which adiposity can be produced by selective breeding, make it clear that genetic factors can play a determining role in obesity (Mayer, 1965, 1968). These factors must also be presumed to be important in human obesity, although clearcut evidence of genetic transmission has been obtained only in such rare conditions as the Laurence-Moon-Biedl syndrome.

A number of studies have confirmed the layman's impression that obesity "runs in families." In one study, obesity was reported in the offspring of approximately 80% of obese–obese matings, in 40% of obese–non-obese matings, and in more than 10% of nonobese–nonobese matings (Mayer, 1957). In another series, Davenport reported that among 51 children of slender parents none was of more than average weight and most were slender; among 37 children of obese parents, on the other hand, none was slender, all were of at least average weight, and a third were obese (Davenport, 1923). But such figures inevitably confuse genetic and environmental influences. Although there have been efforts to separate these influences—by studies of twins and adopted children—none has elucidated the mechanism of transmission nor provided more than rough estimates of the relative contribution of inheritance (Withers, 1964). Because so many nongenetic factors can influence body weight, it is generally agreed that overweight per se is an unsatisfactory phenotype for the study of the genetics of human obesity.

Interest is now shifting to the transmission of somatotypes. Their relevance is clear from Seltzer and Mayer's (1964) demonstration that obesity occurs with much greater frequency in some physical types than others. Obese adolescent girls, for example, show extremely low ratings for ectomorphy; the presence of even a moderate degree of ectomorphy appeared to protect against obesity. It has been estimated that two-thirds of women in the general population may be sufficiently ectomorphic to receive significant protection against obesity. Preliminary studies by Withers (1964) suggest that somatypes are heritable, particularly father-daughter transmission of mesomorphy and mother-son transmission of endomorphy. Further investigations of the inheritance of body types, and of their relation to obesity are sorely needed.

OBESITY IN CHILDHOOD.   The obesity of persons who became obese in childhood—the so-called "juvenile-onset obese"—differs from that of persons who became obese as adults. Juvenile-onset obesity tends to be more severe, more resistant to treatment, and more likely to be associated with emotional disturbances.

Obesity that begins in childhood shows a very strong tendency to persist. Long-term prospective studies in Hagerstown, Maryland have revealed the remarkable degree to which obese children become obese adults. In the first such study, 86% of a group of overweight boys became overweight men, as compared to only 42% of boys of average weight (Abraham & Nordsieck, 1960). Even more striking differences in adult weight status were found among girls: 80% of overweight girls became overweight women, as compared to only 18% of average weight girls. A later study showed that the few overweight children who reduced successfully had done so by the end of adolescence. The odds against an overweight child becoming a normal weight adult, which were 4 to 1 at age 12, rose to 28 to 1 for those who did not reduce during adolescence (Stunkard & Burt, 1967).

An even more recent study, which used a longer time interval (35 years) and unfortunately, different (more rigid) criteria

for obesity, found the difference in adult weight status continuing to grow: 63% of obese boys became obese men, as compared to only 10% of average weight boys (Abraham, Collins, & Nordsieck, 1971).

A brilliant series of studies of adipose tissue has recently helped explain the remarkable persistence of juvenile-onset obesity. Many obese persons, particularly those with juvenile-onset obesity, show a marked increase in total number of adipocytes in subcutaneous tissue and in other depots (Hirsch & Knittle, 1971). Whereas the average nonobese person has a total of $25-30 \times 10^9$ fat cells, obese persons may have five times this number. The average fat content of the fat cells of normal weight and obese persons varies to a far smaller degree: 0.7 micrograms for the nonobese and 1.0 micrograms for the obese.

With weight reduction, individual cells shrink greatly, but the total fat cell number remains constant. A number of animal studies suggest that early in life adipose tissue grows both by increasing cell size and increasing cell number. If feeding patterns are changed during the first three weeks of a rat's life there will be marked changes in cell number (Knittle & Hirsch, 1968). But when the animal is made obese in adult life, he grows no new fat cells; the ones he has simply enlarge.

These studies of cellularity in obesity focus attention on the influence early feeding patterns have on the later development of obesity. Fat cell size and number may be another factor that influences hypothalamic activity and feeding behavior. Obese persons who have lost weight, but whose increased number of fat cells persists, tend to overeat and thus refill these extra cells. We have no biochemical data as yet to indicate the nature of the signal from adipose tissue to the hypothalamus.

METABOLISM.   In man, gross metabolic abnormalities, like gross genetic ones, are rarely the cause of obesity. But two kinds

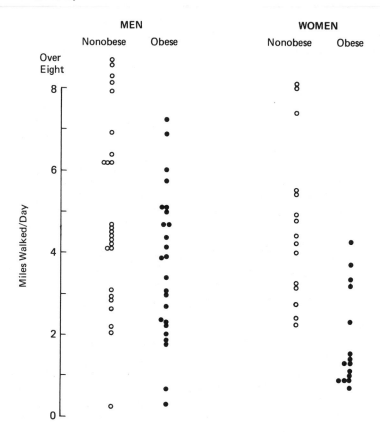

FIGURE 2–1   Daily activity pattern of obese and nonobese men and women (Chirico & Stunkard, 1960). Reprinted by permission from *The New England Journal of Medicine*, 1960, *263*, pp. 935–46.

of endocrine disorders are sufficiently closely related to obesity that they can be considered at least partial causes: hypothyroidism and the adrenocortical dysfunction of Cushing's syndrome.

Recent metabolic research has shown that the more common, garden variety of obesity may also have genetic determinants. The body weights of Sims' (1968) subjects leveled off at 220 pounds despite the continuing ingestion of 8,000 calories a day. Clearly the usually accepted figure of 3,500 calories as the caloric equivalent of a pound of fat did not apply in these subjects when their weights became stable.

Passmore et al. (1955, 1963) have provided further evidence of the uncertain

relationship between calories of food intake and gain and loss of body weight, evidence that obese persons can gain weight on fewer calories than that required by nonobese persons. Weight gains of five pounds required 20,000 excess calories in each of three thin subjects, fairly close to the usually accepted caloric equivalent of fat. A similar weight gain required only 10,000 excess calories in two obese women. In this, as in other similar studies, differences in sex and possible differences in physical activity and fluid retention may have played some role in the unexpected findings.

Does this mean that "calories don't count," in the words of an old best-seller? Hardly. Calories do count, but perhaps they use different number systems under different conditions and in different persons.

PHYSICAL ACTIVITY. The only component on the energy expenditure side of the caloric ledger that both fluctuates and is under voluntary control is physical activity. As such, it is a vital factor in the regulation of body weight. Indeed, the marked decrease in physical activity in affluent societies seems to be the major factor in the recent rise of obesity as a public health problem. Obesity is a rarity in most underdeveloped nations, and not solely because of lack of food. In some rural areas, high levels of physical activity are at least as important in preventing obesity. Such levels of physical activity are the exception in this country. And if the trend exemplified by automatic can openers and mechanized swizzle sticks continues, we may succeed in reducing our energy expenditure to near basal limits. Among many obese women, the trend is already far advanced.

Figure 2–1 shows marked reduction of physical activity of a group of Philadelphia housewives; this reduction is so great as to account almost entirely for their excess weight. But such low levels of physical activity are not present among all obese persons. Figure 2–1 shows that the differences in physical activity among the men were so small that the additional energy expended by obese subjects in moving their heavier bodies produced a caloric expenditure equal to that of nonobese men.

Until quite recently, physical inactivity was considered to cause obesity primarily via its restriction of energy expenditure. There is now good evidence that inactivity may contribute also to an increased food intake. Although food intake increases with increasing energy expenditure over a wide range of energy demands, intake does not decrease proportionately when physical activity falls below a certain minimum level, as shown in Figure 2–2. In fact, restricting physical activity may actually

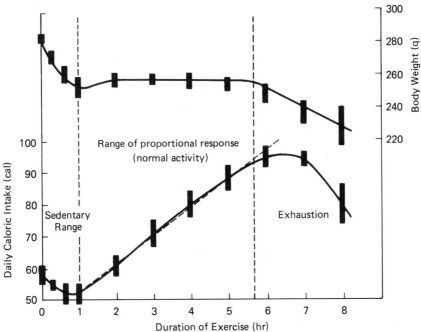

FIGURE 2–2   The relationship between energy expenditure and daily caloric intake (Mayer & Thomas, 1967). Copyright 1967 by the American Association for the Advancement of Science.

increase food intake! Conversely, when sedentary persons increase physical activity, their food intake may decrease. The mechanisms involved in this intriguing control are still unclear, but its great therapeutic potential makes it worthy of careful study.

These studies convey some idea of the complexity of factors involved in regulating body weight. They indicate why a behavior modification program which is successful in reducing body weight and body fat may *not* be simply a matter of unlearning maladaptive eating habits and learning more appropriate ones. Such a program may instead have helped a person who biologically *should be* obese to maintain a statistically normal, but biologically abnormally low, body weight. It may, in short, have simply helped him to live in a state of semistarvation.

Such a feat in no way impunes the power of the behavioral technique. Indeed, effecting chronic semistarvation may be an even greater tribute to its power than would be a simple learning—or relearning—of appropriate eating habits. But this power of the technique should not blind us to what we may be doing. And in the current state of our knowledge of the biology of body weight we will not usually know which of the two we are doing with any particular patient.

This possibility puts into bold relief the proposition that the ability to modify behavior does not necessarily tell us anything about the causes, or origins, of that behavior. And it emphasizes the stake that we all have in better understanding *all* the factors which influence the behaviors to be modified—genetic, metabolic, developmental—as well as those defined by the more immediate contingencies.

BEHAVIORAL TREATMENT APPROACHES

Until quite recently uncertainty as to the origins of obesity was accompanied by ineffectiveness in its treatment. The "state of the art" could be summarized in 1958 as follows: "Most obese persons will not re-

main in treatment. Of those who do remain in treatment, most will not lose much weight, and of those who do lose weight, most will regain it" (Stunkard, 1958). This situation was radically changed in 1967 by the appearance of Stuart's landmark paper on "Behavioral Control of Overeating." The ensuing years have seen a veritable explosion of research applying behavioral techniques to the treatment of obesity. In an unprecedentedly short time those techniques have been shown to be superior to all other treatment modalities for managing mild to moderate obesity (Stunkard, 1972; Abramson, 1973; Hall & Hall, 1974).

The actual techniques used in the behavior modification of obesity have varied from one researcher to the next. Underlying each inquiry, however, has been the assumption that overeating (and underexercising) can be directly influenced to produce a change in body weight. Current research is increasingly directed toward identifying the effective treatment variables in behavior modification programs (Mahoney, 1972b). In addition to therapist contact, participation in an "experiment," and frequent weigh-ins, most behavioral programs have employed one or more of the following components: (1) self-monitoring of body weight and/or food intake; (2) implicit or explicit goalsetting; (3) nutritional, exercise, and health counseling; (4) tangible operant consequences (reward and punishment); (5) aversion therapy; (6) social reinforcement in the form of either therapist, group, or family support; (7) covert conditioning and cognitive restructuring strategies; (8) self-presented consequences (self-reward, self-punishment); and (9) stimulus control procedures. The contribution of each of these components has yet to receive extensive controlled research. However, some tentative generalizations seem justified at the present time.

SELF-MONITORING.   The role of self-recording in the management of obesity has received recent experimental attention. Research in other areas of self-regulation has suggested that simply recording a behavior may influence its occurrence (Kazdin, 1974). This reactive effect has been generally found to be both variable and transient, however (Thoresen & Mahoney, 1974). The effects of self-monitoring on body weight and food intake have been evaluated by several researchers. Stollak (1967), for example, conducted a study in which two control and four experimental groups were employed. In one experimental group subjects were given a food diary and asked to return in eight weeks with daily records of the amount and timing of their eating. A second self-monitoring group met with a therapist weekly and received social praise for moderate food intake. The effects of electrical aversion were explored in two different conditions, both of which also involved self-monitoring of food consumption. In a "non-specific shock group," painful electric shocks were administered to subjects at predetermined times during their discussion of weekly food intake. Shock presentation in this procedure was unrelated to subjects' verbalizations. In the second aversion group, however, shock was presented contingent on subjects' imagining one of their favorite fattening foods. At the end of eight weeks only the self-monitoring plus social praise group had lost a significant amount of weight (8.5 pounds). This superiority disappeared, however, during an 8-10 week follow-up in which all groups gained weight. The importance of social reinforcement as a supplement to self-monitoring is noteworthy (Thoresen & Mahoney, 1974). This need for supplementary influences has also been noted by other researchers. Stuart (1971), for example, reported that clients who self-monitored their food intake and body-weight for five baseline weeks displayed dramatic rates of weight loss during the first few weeks but then began to stabilize or regress. These findings were replicated by Mahoney (1974a) who asked obese adults to self-record their eating habits and body-weight for two baseline weeks. Subjects received standardized weight loss and habit improvement goals during a subsequent six-week treatment period. After dramatic but variable reductions during baseline, subjects who continued self-monitoring, attended weekly weigh-ins, and received standardized goals failed to show significant weight reductions. These findings also replicate those of an earlier study by Mahoney, Moura, and Wade (1973) who found that subjects who attended frequent weigh-ins and self-monitored their eating habits and body weight failed to display any more improvement than information control subjects. Recent research by Romanczyk and his colleagues has suggested that self-monitoring of caloric intake may enhance initial treatment effects, although its capacity to singularly maintain significant losses over a long time interval is questionable (Romanczyk, 1974; Romanczyk, Tracey, Wilson, & Thorpe, 1973).

In combination with other treatment variables, self-observation may provide an important source of influence as well as data. Bellack, Rozensky, and Schwartz (1974) combined stimulus control procedures with either prerecording (dietary planning) or postrecording of food intake. They found that prerecording was superior to both postrecording and control procedures. It should be noted that self-monitored data may provide an invaluable base for ongoing treatment evaluation. Thus, although it may not be singularly sufficient for successful weight reduction, self-recording can play a very important role when supplemented with other strategies.

GOAL SETTING. Although many behavioral researchers have specified explicit weight loss and habit change goals for clients, few efforts have been directed toward the evaluation of this treatment component. The established goals have frequently been part of an operant contingency for reduction (e.g., Mann, 1972, 1973; Upper & Newton, 1971). Mahoney (1974a) found that goal setting did not substantially enhance the impact of simple self-monitoring for most subjects. For specific individuals, however, the establishment of explicit performance goals may increase the likelihood of self-evaluation and performance improvement (Locke, Cartledge, & Koeppel, 1968; Bandura, 1971). Indeed, a frequent phenomenon in weight control research is the adoption of unrealistically high goals by program participants. The clinical implication of this is that explicit short-term goals may offer a therapeutic component in stimulating positive self-evaluations. The reasonableness of this goal setting may be extremely important with regard to continued motivation and performance maintenance.

NUTRITION AND EXERCISE COUNSELING. The provision of information on calories, exercise, and basic nutritional principles has been a frequent and commendable component in several of the more successful behavioral reduction programs. Weight losses which are obtained at the expense of essential nutrients may seriously jeopardize the individual's health. For example, the total exclusion of major food groups may result in medical complications ranging from ketosis and retarded weight loss rate to serious infection susceptibility and lean mass atrophy. Along a similar vein, exercise management is an extremely important aspect of successful weight control and one which is often underemphasized (Mayer, 1968). Evaluations of the impact of nutritional counseling and exercise management by themselves, however, have generally shown them to be important but insufficient factors for enduring significant loss (e.g., Jongmans, 1969, 1970; Stuart, 1971; Levitz & Stunkard, 1972; Harris & Hallbauer, 1973). It is worth noting that several researchers have emphasized a relatively flexible nutritional exchange strategy rather than restrictive dieting (e.g., Stuart & Davis, 1972; Mahoney & Mahoney, 1975). One possible reason for this emphasis is the fact that going "on" a diet implies that the individual will eventually go "off" the diet and return to the eating patterns which created the

problem in the first place. A non-restrictive nutrition exchange strategy avoids "forbidden fruits" and allows the individual to establish reasonable long-term eating patterns.

It is possible, of course, that individuals who lose substantial amounts of weight in behavioral treatment programs do so at the expense of sound nutrition. This possibility was examined by Mahoney and Mahoney (1975) through intermittent analyses of participants' Mean Adequacy Ratios. This nutritional measure evaluates the adequacy of individual calcium, protein, iron, vitamin A, thiamin, riboflavin, and ascorbic acid intake. Statistical analysis revealed not only an absence of general nutritional deterioration, but some evidence for individual improvements on specific nutrients (Welles, 1973). Thus, it appears that behavioral treatment programs can produce substantial weight reductions without endangering adequate nutritional intake.

OPERANT CONSEQUENCES. One technique which has been frequently employed deals with the operant consequences (reinforcement and punishment) of changes in body weight and/or food intake. Bernard (1968), for example, reported a case study in which a grossly obese (407-pound) mental patient lost 102 pounds during a six-month period in which she received token reinforcement for her progress. In another case study Steffy (1968) found that contingency contracting and operant reinforcement were successful in producing a 96-pound weight loss in a hospitalized female. The effectiveness of these strategies has been replicated by several researchers using very diverse populations (e.g., Mann, 1972; Dinoff, Rickard, & Colwick, 1972; Harris & Bruner, 1971; Harmatz & Lapuc, 1968). One concern, however, has been that brief and unrealistic modifications of response consequences may produce short-lived successes which do not generalize or maintain. In a program which employed contracting and operant consequences, Mann (1972) reported that subjects frequently used extreme measures (e.g., laxatives, total fasts, diuretics, etc.) to earn their weight-loss-contingent reinforcers. Since these dramatic maneuvers are difficult and dangerous to continue over long periods of time, substantial relapse is to be expected (Harris & Bruner, 1971). In an experiment which combined self-presented rewards with other weight control strategies, Mahoney (1974a) found that reinforcement for habit change produced larger and more lasting weight losses than reinforcement for pounds shed. The use of naturally available reinforcers (e.g., programmed familial praise) and symbolic self-reward may likewise enhance maintenance after termination of a formal treatment program.

AVERSION THERAPY. Several investigators have used real or symbolic aversive consequences paired with food stimuli and/or thoughts about food. Electric shock, for example, has been employed in classical conditioning paradigms which were aimed at producing a conditioned avoidance response to certain types of food (Wolpe, 1954; Meyer & Crisp, 1964; Stollak, 1967). Aversion relief procedures have likewise been used (e.g., Thorpe, Schmidt, Brown, & Castell, 1964). The effectiveness data in these studies has not been uniform. While some individuals responded very well to therapy, others terminated or reported no improvement. The rate of attrition in aversion therapy for obesity appears to be a major clinical concern. Some investigators have employed aversive stimuli which are more portable and physiologically relevant than electric shock. Kennedy and Foreyt (1968, 1971), for example, have reported successful results using a conditioning procedure which paired smells of favorite foods with very aversive odors (e.g., butyric acid). The use of olfactory and gastrointestinal stimuli in alimentary conditioning may increase both its effectiveness and its generalization.

SOCIAL REINFORCEMENT. Implicitly or explicitly, social reinforcement has been employed in the large majority of behavioral programs for obesity (e.g., Moore & Crum, 1969; Penick, et al., 1971; Jeffrey & Christensen, 1972; Jeffrey, Christensen, & Pappas, 1972; Abrahms & Allen, 1974; Bellack, Schwartz, & Rozensky, 1974). Attempts to evaluate its contribution have been relatively rare, however. In a study involving 79 obese subjects, Wollersheim (1970) demonstrated that group social reinforcement could produce dramatic reductions when focused on individuals' progress in behavior change. Hagen (1970) replicated these results in an experiment which evaluated the role of therapist and group support in successful reduction. Using behavioral treatment manuals, Hagen found no differences among subjects who received or did not receive therapist contact. The manual employed, however, recommended self-reinforcement as an alternative means of maintaining motivation. Further examination of behavioral bibliotherapy has been reported by Jongmans (1969, 1970) in a series of experiments at the University of Amsterdam.

In a subsequent study, Fernan (1973) used Hagen's treatment manual and distributed it with or without therapist contact and either unit-by-unit or in its entirety. He found the unit plus contact group to be most effective. Similar evidence favoring social reinforcement was reported by Abrahms and Allen (1974). Thus, the nature and extent of social reinforcement would appear to be important. Simply self-monitoring, receiving instructions, and weighing in in front of a therapist may not be sufficient for improvement (Mahoney, Moura, & Wade, 1973). On the other hand, group and therapist support may offer an important motivational component for specific individuals. One of the clinical problems with heavy reliance on social reinforcement from a therapist or group is that it may jeopardize subsequent maintenance after a formal treatment program has ended. Since the therapist or group will not be around indefinitely to provide support, an individual may be doomed to relapse if his major motivation has come from these sources. An alternative to this is to establish environmental social reinforcement during the treatment program itself. For example, Mahoney and Mahoney (1975) trained participants' families in social reinforcement to enhance naturalistic maintenance conditions. They found that degree of family support correlated strongly with participants' success in their program.

COVERT CONDITIONING AND COGNITIVE RE-STRUCTURING STRATEGIES.   In 1966, Cautela reported the successful use of a procedure called covert sensitization in the treatment of obesity. This clinical technique involves the pairing of problematic behaviors with unpleasant (e.g., nauseous) scenes in imagination. Cautela's client lost 66 pounds and demonstrated perfect maintenance at a seven-month follow-up. This case study prompted several other researchers to employ covert sensitization and other cognitive strategies in weight control therapy. Stuart (1967), for example, used covert sensitization with two of his subjects. Harris (1969) and Wollersheim (1970) also employed this strategy. Efforts toward a controlled replication of Cautela's results, however, have been rare (Mahoney, 1974b). In a group study comprised of 41 subjects, Manno and Marston (1972) compared the relative effectiveness of covert sensitization and covert positive reinforcement. The former involved imagined scenes of food approach followed by nausea and relief after escape. Covert positive reinforcement utilized imaginary appropriate performances followed by rewarding consequences. After four treatment weeks subjects in the covert sensitization and covert positive reinforcement groups had lost 4.1 and 5.1 pounds respectively, as compared with 0.8 pounds for a control group. A three-month follow-up revealed continuing losses on the part of all three groups (8.9, 8.9, and 5.2 cumulative pounds lost, respectively). Although one other research study has supported the clinical promise of covert conditioning

(Janda & Rimm, 1972), a number of researchers have failed to find it effective (Lick & Bootzin, 1971; Foreyt & Hagen, 1973; Wilson, 1974; Balters, 1974). Moreover, the processes operative in covert sensitization are in dire need of controlled scrutiny (Mahoney, 1974b).

The relevance of thoughts and self-statements to significant daily behaviors was emphasized by Homme (1965) in a classic paper entreating behavioral researchers to deal with "coverants"—the covert operants of the mind. Homme outlined a treatment strategy for the modification of specific thought patterns and recommended that investigators pursue these private events as important influences in self-regulation problems. Although controlled research on Homme's paradigm has been sparse (Mahoney, 1970, 1972a, 1974b) , several investigators have employed variants of it in the treatment of obesity. Tyler and Straughan (1970) compared coverant control to a breath-holding (self-punishment) strategy and relaxation training. Losses in all three groups during a nine-week program were very minimal. Horan and Johnson (1971), however, reported a significant amount of weight loss (5.66 pounds in eight weeks) on the part of coverant control subjects. In a subsequent study, Horan and his colleagues (1975) replicated the finding that coverant control strategies offer some promise as weight reduction aids. Individuals who rewarded thoughts about the benefits of reducing lost an average of 11.1 pounds in eight treatment weeks.

Cognitive strategies have been used as a device for maintaining motivation as well as prompting and consequating behaviors. In several experiments subjects have been asked to monitor their covert monologues and to alter weight relevant thought patterns (Mahoney, Moura, & Wade, 1973). A more extensive program for the improvement of "cognitive ecology" (cleaning up what you say to yourself) was reported by Mahoney and Mahoney (1975). They classified weight relevant thoughts into five categories with appropriate and inappropriate responses in each: (1) thoughts about pounds lost (e.g., "I've starved myself and haven't lost a thing,"); (2) thoughts about capabilities (e.g., "I just don't have the will-power,"); (3) excuses (e.g., "If it weren't for my busy schedule, I could lose weight,"); (4) standard setting (e.g., "Well I blew it with that doughnut. My day is shot,"); and (5) thoughts about actual food items. Subjects reported that their cognitive restructuring was an invaluable component in their weight reduction success.

The contribution of cognitive and covert conditioning strategies in the treatment of obesity requires further controlled investigation. However, based on preliminary results and the significant role of cognitive influences in other complex human behaviors (Mahoney, 1974b; Meichenbaum & Cameron, 1974), the clinical promise of these strategies appears to be impressive.

SELF-PRESENTED CONSEQUENCES. One of the more recent trends in the treatment of obesity has been that of training the individual to rearrange the consequences of his weight relevant behaviors. These strategies have involved either self-reinforcement or self-punishment (e.g., Harris, 1969; Penick et al., 1971; Wollersheim, 1970; Hagen, 1970). In a comparison of the relative effects of self-reward and self-punishment, Mahoney, Moura, and Wade (1973) asked obese subjects to either present or fine themselves specified amounts of money for progress (or lack of progress) in their reduction. They found self-reward to be superior as a treatment strategy. A later study (Mahoney, 1974a) found that self-reward for habit improvement was significantly more effective than self-reward for actual weight loss. Individuals who reinforced their changes in eating patterns not only lost more weight but exhibited superior maintenance at a one-year follow-up. Jeffrey (1973) has replicated this superiority on the part of subjects trained in self-reward procedures.

In one of the few overwhelmingly successful applications of aversion therapy to the treatment of obesity, Morganstern (1974) reported a weight loss of 53 pounds over 24 weeks in a case involving self-regulated aversion. The subject used aversive cigarette smoke as the negative stimulus paired with the fattening foods.

In addition to the economical advantages which accrue when a subject becomes his own therapist, self-regulated consequences provide a strategy which can be maintained long after termination of a formal treatment program. Indeed, the data cited above suggest that self-reward strategies in particular may enhance long-term maintenance of appropriate weight control. For this reason, their inclusion in a treatment program seems amply justified.

STIMULUS CONTROL. Perhaps more than any other treatment strategy, the procedures labeled "stimulus control" have shown themselves to be a very powerful component in the successful regulation of obesity. These techniques were previewed by Ferster, Nurnberger, and Levitt (1962) who analyzed the extent to which naturalistic cues come to elicit and control eating responses. A room frequently associated with eating, a clock indicating mealtime, and a bountiful display of snacks are all stimuli which may be followed by food consumption. These stimuli may come to control eating in the same manner that the behavior of laboratory animals comes under the control of prereinforcement cues. Ferster and his colleagues recommended several specific strategies for the alteration of cues associated with eating. For example:

1. *Separate eating from all other activities.* Eat in a specified room at designated times. Do not engage in any other activities while you are eating—no television viewing, studying, pleasure reading, etc. Limit the times and places you eat.

2. *Make high-calorie foods unavailable, inconspicuous, or hard to prepare.* Do not buy high calorie foods. Always buy groceries on a full stomach.

3. *Alter food portions.* Use shallow bowls and small diameter plates. Put surplus food away before you eat.

4. *Eat slowly.* Swallow one bite before putting the next one on the fork. Put food utensils down between bites. Toward the end of a meal, interrupt eating for several minutes. Delay second helpings.

5. *Avoid waste eating.* Do not eat something simply because it has been paid for or would otherwise be thrown out. Set aside small portions of each food item at the beginning of the meal and leave these to be thrown out (i.e., do not "clean" your plate).

The goal of each of these techniques, of course, is to progressively restrict both the range and frequency of cues associated with eating.

Stuart (1967), in what must be called *the* classic study on the behavioral control of obesity, utilized these stimulus control procedures with eight obese women. His results were unprecedented in the obesity literature. Stuart's *least* successful subject lost 26 pounds! The remaining seven ranged up to a 47-pound loss at the end of the year. These impressive results stimulated a host of studies which incorporated stimulus control strategies (e.g., Harris, 1969; Wollersheim, 1970; Hagen, 1970; Hall, 1972).

In 1971, Stuart replicated his earlier findings with six obese women in a single subject crossover design. After a five-week baseline of self monitoring body weight and food intake, three of the subjects were given nutrition and exercise information. The other three subjects received instruction in the behavioral management of food intake and energy expenditure. After 15 weeks, the first three women were likewise given behavior modification training. Follow-up assessments continued up until one year after initial contact. All six subjects lost an average of 28 pounds. The immediate treatment group was somewhat more successful than the delayed (mean = 35 versus 21 pounds, respectively). Psychometric assessment showed no negative personality changes during this time. The latter finding

was cited as evidence against psychodynamic "symptom substitution."

A replication of the effects of a program emphasizing stimulus control was reported by Kerbauy (1972) in a study conducted at the University of São Paulo. Subjects receiving individualized behavioral counseling lost an average of 18.8 pounds and demonstrated commendable maintenance.

In an ambitious study involving 260 subjects and 16 different TOPS (Take Off Pounds Sensibly) groups, Levitz and Stunkard (1974) evaluated the impact of professional versus nonprofessional leadership in a behavior modification program emphasizing stimulus control. Four treatment groups each comprised of four TOPS chapters were employed. The two experimental treatments consisted of presentation of behavior modification techniques by either a professional therapist or a TOPS chapter leader who had been given brief training. A third treatment consisted of the usual TOPS program with the addition of nutrition education provided by TOPS chapter leaders. In an effort to control for nonspecific effects of training and attention, these leaders received the same amount of training in nutrition education as the other leaders had received in behavior modification. The final treatment simply involved the continuation of standard TOPS self-help techniques—weekly weigh-ins, announcement of weight change, singing, and group discussion (cf. Stunkard, Levine & Fox, 1970). Treatment of all 16 chapters was carried out over a period of 12 weeks.

The first major finding was that far fewer subjects dropped out of the behavior modification treatments: 38 and 41%, compared to 55% for the nutrition education and 67% for the standard TOPS program. Secondly, despite the bias against the behavior modification treatments as a result of the higher attrition rates (of presumably poorer losers) in the other treatments, behavior modification produced greater weight losses than either of the two control treatments. Professionally led chapters lost a mean of 4.2 pounds compared to the loss of 1.9 in the TOPS led chapters. The non-specific training group lost only 0.2 pounds and the group without additional intervention actually gained 0.7 pounds. These differences were highly significant.

The relative superiority of the behavioral groups further increased at one-year follow-up assessment. The groups which had had professional leadership continued to show lower attrition rates and to lose weight, to a mean 5.8 pounds. The initial weight loss of subjects in the behavior modification program conducted by TOPS leaders was not maintained during follow-up, and their weight returned to its pre-treatment level. These behaviorally treated subjects, however, did better than the nutrition-education and standard TOPS programs. Subjects in these latter two conditions actually gained weight (2.8 and 4.0 pounds) during the year after treatment.

Virtually every study that has employed stimulus control strategies has reported an average weight loss of at least one pound per week. Thus, in terms of treatment consistency, the techniques developed by Ferster et al. and refined by Stuart have shown themselves to be somewhat superior to other procedures. However, data on the *sufficiency* of these procedures is somewhat equivocal. Mahoney, Moura, and Wade (1973) found that the provision of basic stimulus control information was not sufficient to produce weight loss in the absence of other treatment variables. On the other hand, Jongmans (1969, 1970), Hagen (1970), and Fernan (1973) have shown that some individuals can achieve substantial reductions by simply receiving a treatment manual which describes stimulus control strategies. In Fernan's study, however, the most effective group was that which received therapist contact along with technical information. Moreover, the manual employed in two of these studies recommended the use of self-reward so that the contribution of stimulus control procedures alone was not evaluated. At the

present time, it would appear that the highest prognosis for clinical success can be obtained when stimulus control procedures are supplemented by other self-regulatory strategies (Mahoney, 1972a).

The foregoing review has discussed the behavioral treatment of obesity from several different technical perspectives. An outline of the existing research in this area is provided in Table 2–1. As illustrated in the table, the results of behavior modification for obesity have been relatively consistent and positive. Although the processes and active components in behavioral treatments have yet to be identified, there can be little doubt that obesity can be profitably viewed as a modifiable aspect of human behavior (Stunkard, 1972).

EVALUATION

When compared with contemporary treatment alternatives, behavioral techniques appear to offer the most promising and pragmatic approach to weight control. However, at least three major issues remain to be answered in the exploration and application of these innovative techniques.

First, the effective components of behavioral treatment programs need to be isolated. To what extent are the observed improvements attributable to stimulus control and other self-regulatory strategies rather than to frequent weigh-ins, therapist contacts, group support, and so on?

Second, given that behavioral techniques are effective in the treatment of obesity, what measures can be taken to optimize their consistent application and maintenance? The latter half of this question is particularly important. Most motivated patients will initially implement a new diet or weight control strategy provided that sufficient instructions and encouragement are provided (traditionally supplied either by group recognition or by therapist approval). However, once the active treatment program has terminated and encour-

TABLE 2-1

Study	N	Results*	Comments
Ferster, Nurnberger, & Levitt (1962)	10	modal loss of 10 lbs. (range = 5–20); treatment duration unspecified	employed stimulus control techniques plus self-monitoring
Meyer & Crisp (1964)	2	loss of 20 lbs. during 6 treatment weeks in one client with a cumulative loss of 72 lbs. at 20-month follow-up; second client lost 13 and 7 lbs. during two brief treatment series (5 and 4 weeks) but had relapsed to 25 lbs. above initial weight at one year follow-up	aversion therapy (electrical)
Cautela (1966)	1	66-lb. loss; unspecified treatment duration; complete maintenance at 7-month follow-up	covert sensitization plus self-monitoring
Stollak (1967)	138	mean loss (self-monitoring plus contact) of 8.5 lbs. during 8-week treatment; relapses to 4.5 lbs. at 8–10-week follow-up	compared unmotivated and no contact control groups to (1) self-monitoring, (2) number 1 plus contact, (3) number 2 plus electric shock aversion to favorite foods, and (4) number 2 plus shock aversion to irrelevant verbalizations
Stuart (1967)	10	mean loss of 37.75 lbs. over 12 months (range = 26–47); two dropouts	employed stimulus control, covert sensitization, and self-monitoring
Bernard (1968)	1	102-lb. loss over 6 months	token reinforcement
Harmatz & Lapuc (1968)	21	mean loss (behavior modification) of about 7.4 lbs. during 6 treatment weeks; 12.7 at 4-week follow-up	compared 1,800 calorie diet to diet plus group therapy and diet plus behavior modification (operant reinforcement and punishment)
Kennedy and Foreyt (1968)	1	loss of 30 lbs. over 22 treatment weeks	aversion therapy (butyric acid)
Steffy (1968)	1	96-lb. loss over 12 months	contingency contracting (tokens)
Harris (1969)	21	mean loss (treatment group) of 8.25 lbs. in 2.5-month program; 11.25 at 4-month follow-up	compared no contact control to treatment comprised of stimulus control, self-monitoring, self-reward, and covert sensitization
Jongmans (1969, 1970)	49, 56, 60	demonstrated equivalence of therapist contact behavioral counseling and behavioral bibliotherapy; self-reinforcement equally effective as external (mean maintained loss of 8.03 and 8.25 lbs. respectively at 6 months following 4 weeks of treatment)	three experiments examined the relative effects of dietary counseling, stimulus control, therapist contact versus bibliotherapy, covert sensitization, and self- versus external reinforcement (non-directive and no treatment control groups were employed)
Moore & Crum (1969)	1	loss of 35 lbs. over 26 weeks	public charting and social reinforcement
Hagen (1970)	89	mean loss (manual plus contact) of 15.0 lbs. over 11 weeks with very slight relapse at 4-week follow-up	compared no treatment control to behavior modification manual, manual plus therapist contact, and contact only; all treatments superior to control and did not differ from one another

Study	N	Results	Description
Kunzelman (1970)	1	loss of 31 lbs. in 13 weeks with total loss of 60 lbs. at follow-up (interval unspecified)	subject (author) monitored and reduced number of bites per minute
Shipman (1970)	20	mean loss (behavior therapy) of 11.8 lbs. over 10 treatment weeks (range = +4–24 lbs.); cumulative loss of 16.2 lbs. at 3-month follow-up	compared group therapy with behavioral (self-monitoring, stimulus control, dietary counseling)
Tyler & Straughan (1970)	57	mean loss (coverant control) of 0.75 lbs. over 9 treatment weeks	compared coverant control, breath-holding, and relaxation training
Wollersheim (1970)	79	mean loss of 10.33 lbs. in 12 weeks (behavioral group) with maintained loss of 8.66 lbs. at 8-week follow-up	after 18 week baseline, compared no contact control, social pressure and nonspecific therapy to behavioral (stimulus control, self-monitoring, self-reward, covert sensitization, and social reinforcement)
Foreyt & Kennedy (1971)	12	mean loss of 13.3 lbs. over 9 weeks (range = 5–19); maintenance at 9.2 lbs. at 48 weeks	compared aversion therapy (olfactory) to TOPS control group
Harris & Bruner (1971)	32, 18	study 1: mean loss (contract) = 13.4 lbs. over 12 weeks, relapse 2 + 2.75 lbs. at 10-month follow-up; study 2: (self-control) loss of 1.75 lbs. during 16 weeks	compared contingency contracting, self-reward, and stimulus control to control procedures; significant attendance and attrition problems
Horan & Johnson (1971)	96	mean loss (reinforced coverants) of 5.66 lbs. after 8 weeks (range = +8.5–19.25)	compared delayed control and information control (nutrition) to scheduled versus reinforced coverant (thought) control
Penick, Filion, Fox, & Stunkard (1971)	32	median loss (behavior modification) of 18.5 lbs. during 3 treatment months with additional losses at 3- to 6-month follow-up	compared supportive group therapy to behavior modification (stimulus control, self-monitoring, self-reward, social reinforcement)
Stuart (1971)	6	mean loss of 28.0 lbs. at week 52 following 15 to 20 weeks of treatment	stimulus control, self-monitoring, exercise and nutritional counseling
Upper & Newton (1971)	2	losses of 63 and 31 lbs. in 28 and 26 weeks	token reinforcement
Hall (1972, 1973)	10	after 26 treatment weeks, mean loss (all subjects) = 8.3 lbs. with maintenance at 10.4 lbs. after 2 years	compared stimulus control to external monetary reinforcement (crossover design)
Janda & Rimm (1972)	18	mean loss (covert sensitization) of 9.5 lbs. in 6 weeks; maintenance at 11.7 lbs. after 6 weeks	compared covert sensitization to no treatment and attention control groups
Jeffrey & Christensen (1972)	43	mean loss (behavior therapy) of 16.3 lbs. in 18 weeks (range = +10–30); maintenance at 18-week follow-up	compared "will power" and control conditions to behavior therapy (stimulus control, self-monitoring, social praise and monetary reinforcement)
Jeffrey, Christensen, & Pappas (1972)	4	mean loss of 27 lbs. in 24 weeks (range = 20–32); 1 relapse and 1 partial relapse at 6 months	self-monitoring, contingency contracting, and social reinforcement
Kerbauy (1972)	15	mean losses (individual and group behavior modification) of 18.8 and 13.7 lbs. (combined range = +5.5–47.7); mean of 32.2 sessions, 6.5 months	compared individual and group behavior modification (self-monitoring, stimulus control, coverant control, nutrition and exercise counseling)

TABLE 2-1 Continued

Study	N	Results*	Comments
Levitz & Stunkard (1972)	260	mean loss (behavior modification, TOPS leader) of 4.2 lbs. in 12 weeks; maintenance at 24 weeks and 1 year	compared control and nutritional counseling to behavior modification (self-monitoring, stimulus control) taught by professional therapist or trained TOPS leader
Mann (1972)	8	losses reported for only 2 subjects; 58 lbs. in 200 days and 40 lbs. in 400 days	contingency contracting
Manno & Marston (1972)	41	mean loss (both covert groups) of 8.9 lbs. in 4 weeks with maintenance at 3 months	compared control group to covert sensitization and covert reinforcement groups
Bellack, Rozensky, & Schwartz (1974)	37	mean loss (premonitoring) of approximately 6 lbs. in 6 weeks plus additional 2.5 loss at 6-week follow-up	compared waiting control group to non-monitoring, premonitoring, and postmonitoring of food intake
Bornstein & Sipprelle (1973)	40	mean loss (induced anxiety) of 12 lbs. over 8 weeks; maintenance at 3 and 6 months	compared induced anxiety and relaxation procedures to nonspecific and control groups
Fernan (1973)	65	mean loss (contact plus lessons) of 11.8 lbs. in 10 weeks; maintenance at 7.4 lbs. at 4.5 months	compared no treatment control to behavioral treatment manual given in its entirety or lesson-by-lesson and with or without therapist contact
Jeffrey (1973)	62	mean loss (complete self-control) of about 6 lbs. over 7 weeks with maintenance at week 14	compared external contingency management to partial and complete self-control (monetary reward)
Mahoney & Mahoney (1975)	12	mean loss of 9.0 lbs. during 10 treatment weeks (range = +1.5–22.5) with additional losses to mean of 18.1 lbs. at 2 years	self-monitoring, stimulus control, nutrition and exercise counseling, thought management, relaxation, family instruction, and self reward; faded follow-up contacts using progressive intervals
Mahoney, Moura, & Wade (1973)	53	mean loss (self-reward) of 6.4 lbs. in 4 weeks with improvement to 11.5 lbs. at 4-month follow-up	compared stimulus control information only, self-monitoring, self-reward, self-punishment, and self-reward plus self-punishment
Mann (1973)	1	loss of about 25 lbs. during successive treatment and reversal conditions (BABABA) over 7 months	employed contingency contracting to effect maintenance; final contact reflected partial relapse
Martin & Sachs (1973)	1	loss of 15 lbs. in 4.5 treatment weeks with cumulative loss of 18 lbs. at 14 months	self-monitoring, stimulus control, self-reward, and contingency contracting
Romanczyk (1974)	70	mean loss of 8 lbs. over 4 weeks by group 5 subjects with a maintained loss of 13.1 lbs. at week 23	compared the relative effects of (1) no treatment, (2) self-monitoring of weight, (3) self-monitoring of weight and calories, (4) a behavioral package comprised of stimulus control, covert sensitization, relaxation, and dietary and exercise counseling, and (5) number 4 plus self-monitoring of weight and calories

Reference	N	Results	Description
Romanczyk, Tracey, Wilson, & Thorpe (1973)	102, 60	study 1: group 6 subjects lost 8.2 lbs. in 4 weeks; maintenance at 8 weeks; this same package was superior in study 2 (mean loss of 8.1 lbs. in 4 weeks; 8.8 lbs. at 12-week follow-up)	study 1 compared (1) no treatment, (2) weight self-monitoring, (3) calorie and weight self-monitoring, (4) number 3 plus covert sensitization, (5) number 4 plus relaxation, (6) number 5 plus stimulus control, and (7) number 6 plus contingency contracting; study 2 examined maintenance effects of weight and calorie self-monitoring plus relaxation and technical information versus behavioral package (number 6, study 1)
Weisenberg & Fray (1974)	24	mean loss of 16.1 lbs. in 16 weeks by supportive group subjects (range = 5–42.)	compared minimal contact with (1) stimulus control and (2) supportive group condition (dietary and exercise counseling; social reinforcement); 3 groups were widely discrepant in degree of obesity
Wijesinghe (1973)	2	loss of 25 lbs. over 6 months in one subject (data not reported for second subject)	aversion therapy (electrical)
Horan, Baker, Hoffman, & Shute (1975)	40	mean loss of 11.1 lbs. in 8 weeks by group counseling subjects who used positive coverants (range = 7.75–13.5)	evaluated parameters of coverant control therapy with a $2 \times 2 \times 2$ design (group versus individual, positive versus negative coverants, eating versus noneating rewards; basic stimulus control information was provided
Mahoney (1974a)	49	median loss (SR–Habit) or 8.3 lbs. in 8 weeks; 70% maintenance or improvement at 1 year follow-up	compared self-monitoring, self-reward for weight loss, and self-reward for habit change to delay treatment control; stimulus control information was given
Morganstern (1974)	1	41-lb. loss in 18 weeks; 53 lbs. at week 24	self-managed aversion (cigarette smoke)
Sachs & Ingram (1972)	10	measured only self-reported intake of selected foods; found that both forward and backward covert sensitization reduced food intake relative to baseline	compared forward and backward covert sensitization
Foreyt & Hagen (1973)	39	mean loss of 8.5 lbs. during 9 treatment weeks by the placebo condition with maintenance at 7.1 lbs. during 9 subsequent follow-up weeks	compared covert sensitization, no treatment, and a placebo modeled after covert sensitization but using positive rather than aversive imagery
Harris & Hallbauer (1973)	50	mean loss of 9.1 lbs. during 12 treatment weeks by an exercise group, with maintenance of 13.1 lbs. at 7 months	compared treatments emphasizing behavioral approaches to eating versus exercise plus an attention-placebo; combined emphasis was most successful at follow-up
Balch & Ross (1974)	45	full treatment subjects lost an average of 10.6 lbs. during 9 treatment weeks with additional losses averaging 3.3 lbs. during a 6-week follow-up	compared the success of subjects who completed a full treatment package (modeled after Stuart & Davis, 1972) with that of partial participants and controls

TABLE 2-1 Continued

Study	N	Results*	Comments
Bellack, Schwartz, & Rozensky (1974)	20	mean losses of 3.0 and 3.3 lbs. during 8 weeks by the direct contact and mail groups	using self-monitoring and stimulus control procedures, compared direct (therapist) contact with mail and no contact
Abrahms & Allen (1974)	49	after a 6-week baseline, subjects receiving behavioral programming plus social reinforcement lost an average of 12.2 lbs. during 8 treatment weeks with no additional change at an 8-week follow-up	compared a no-treatment control to social reinforcement, behavioral programming plus social reinforcement, and behavioral programming with monetary reward
Hall, Hall, Hanson, & Borden (1974)	94	during 10 treatment weeks, subjects in the combined self-management group lost 6.6% of their bodyweight as compared with 5.7, 0.5, and +0.9 for the other groups; pounds lost were 11.9 and 10.3 for the first 2 groups; follow-ups at 3 and 6 months suggested relapse	compared a combined self-management package (stimulus control, self-monitoring, etc.) with a simple bite-reduction strategy, relaxation training, and no treatment

* In most successful group (where appropriate)

agement from the group or therapist is no longer available, what is to insure that patients will continue appropriate weight control efforts? This problem is one which has plagued the field of obesity for many years—i.e., maintenance of improvement after the cessation of formal treatment. It is often presumed that the rewards of improved health, social attention, and better physical appearance are sufficient to maintain patient's post-treatment self-control endeavors. However, as the records of all too many obesity researchers will attest, this assumption is sorely unjustified (Stunkard, 1958; Stuart & Davis, 1972). Therefore, behavioral researchers need to address the issue of developing effective means for maintaining weight loss improvements long after patients have left a formal therapy program.

A third major issue has to do with the wide individual variations in responsiveness to behavioral treatment programs. In terms of group averages, these techniques have shown themselves to be superior to traditional obesity treatments. However, patients exhibit great variability in the magnitude of improvement they display while employing behavioral techniques. Research is needed to isolate effective predictor variables which will inform therapists of success probabilities in specific clinical circumstances.

These three issues have received very little empirical attention. Based on preliminary findings, however, the following tentative generalizations are offered.

COMPONENT ANALYSIS. As mentioned earlier, at least nine specifiable components have been used in the behavioral treatment of obesity. Of these, very few have been evaluated with regard to their individual contribution to a program's effects. Self-monitoring, explicit goal setting, frequent weigh-ins, and nutrition and exercise counseling have shown themselves to be insufficient as single treatment influences for the production of long-term weight re-

duction. This, however, does not mean that they do not offer significant assistance when combined with other therapeutic variables. Likewise, group and therapist support have been shown to lack sufficient power in weight control, although they can be used advantageously to both focus upon and socially reinforce appropriate behavior. The contribution of the remaining treatment components is much more difficult to evaluate. Successful studies have been reported which have both included and excluded stimulus control, aversion therapy, self-presented consequences, covert/cognitive strategies, and operant procedures. Given that each of these factors has been a relatively frequent component in some of the more successful programs, their combined use may enhance the probabilities of therapeutic success. Based on the above evidence and geared toward an adult out-patient volunteer population, the existing data would seem to recommend the following components for a maximally effective program (Mahoney & Mahoney, 1976):

1. A simple and portable self-monitoring system which emphasizes actual *behaviors* rather than *weight* (e.g., eating habits, exercise, food relevant thoughts, etc.).

2. Basic information on nutrition with an emphasis on the development of sound long-term eating patterns which permit weight control without jeopardizing essential nutrient intake (i.e., no crash dieting, no totally restricted foods, etc.).

3. Instruction in exercise management outlining the physiological assets of exercise and encouraging increases in daily energy output (activity patterns) which are more likely to be maintained than effortful calisthenics.

4. Guided instruction in the many facets of stimulus control as a means of regulating food intake.

5. Initial provision of therapist or group support with the magnitude and frequency of this reinforcement gradually withdrawn as the individual continues progressing.

6. Training of spouses and other family members in social reinforcement strategies in order to maintain program-induced improvements.

7. Training in the modification of self-defeating thought patterns and unrealistic performance standards.

8. Training in the development of broad problem-solving skills and the establishment of self-regulated incentive systems (e.g., tangible self-reward, self-praise) to enhance maintenance.

MAINTENANCE OF WEIGHT LOSS. The second major issue in behavioral weight control—and one toward which many of the above components are geared—is maintenance. Because weight reduction via habit alteration is usually more gradual than that produced by short-lived and drastic dietary means, the reward of seeing pounds "melt away" is often more delayed than many would anticipate. In order to bridge the motivational gap between initiation of a weight control program and ultimately impressive weight loss, several motivational influences can be employed. As was mentioned earlier, the provision of group or therapist support for the initial implementation of and adherence to a self-control regimen has already been shown to be effective. However, the eventual withdrawal of these influences may result in unfortunate relapse, particularly when they have supplied the major motivational force in an individual's reduction efforts. The importance of maintenance considerations in the behavioral treatment of obesity is highlighted in a report by Jeffrey, Christensen, and Pappas (1972). Four obese subjects participated in a program involving stimulus control, contingency contracting, self-recording, and reinforcement procedures. After 24 treatment weeks, the participants had lost an average of 27 pounds each (range = 20 to 32). However, follow-up assessments at week 52 indicated that one subject had returned to his initial weight and another had partially relapsed. It is interesting to note that these two individuals had experienced the most difficulty in altering their eating habits.

At least four factors have been cited as possible influences in successful weight maintenance: (1) the provision of "booster" contacts, (2) emphasis on the establishment of long-term eating habits, (3) training in problem-solving and self-regulated incentive systems, and (4) cultivation of family support. Booster contacts, of course, provide technical feedback as well as social reinforcement and ongoing evaluation. The emphasis on habit change as a maintenance-enhancing strategy was demonstrated in Mahoney's (1974a) study. Subjects' weight losses were significantly related to their eating habit improvements. Moreover, at a one-year follow-up subjects who had focused on establishing appropriate eating habits were much more successful in their maintenance.

Self-regulated incentive systems, particularly self-reward, have likewise demonstrated some promise as maintenance-enhancing factors. Given that reinforcers are effective regardless of whether the patient or therapist administers them, training as a personal behavioral engineer is not only warranted but therapeutically prescribed. By acquiring skill as a self-reinforcing agent, the individual may be capable of overriding temporary inadequacies in environmental contingencies. Development of independent problem solving skills may likewise provide invaluable assistance.

The final maintenance strategy is that of cultivating family support during the treatment program itself. The most influential factor in a participant's continued progress may very well be the environment to which he returns after termination of formal treatment. If his family and friends are critical, caustic, or unconcerned about his weight management, its continuation is unlikely. For this reason, several researchers have begun to work with obese couples and have incorporated techniques to modify marital interactions which might influence successful weight control. Mahoney and Mahoney (1975), for example, have described a program in which participants' spouses and family members were given direct training in the alteration of weight-related interactions. Data from that program suggested a positive correlation between degrees of family support and successful weight management.

INDIVIDUAL VARIABILITY. Marked variability in responsiveness to behavioral weight control techniques has been reported by several researchers (e.g., Penick et al., 1971; Horan & Johnson, 1971; Mahoney, 1974a). The source of these variations has yet to be identified. Stuart and Davis (1972) comment that idiosyncratic eating patterns may account for some of this diversity. Two other possibilities are that the techniques themselves are variable in their effects or that subjects may vary in their actual use of the suggested techniques.

Until very recently, some of the basic assumptions in the behavioral treatment of obesity has remained virtually unexamined. For example, the conscientious adoption of therapist suggestions was presumed to be more extensive in successful rather than unsuccessful clients. This use of a dependent variable to infer an independent variable is a dangerous research strategy. Moreover, a series of recent studies on the "obese eating style" have questioned some of the fundamental premises in weight control therapies (Mahoney, in press). They do not, of course, challenge the outcome of behavioral treatment, but rather its process. Continuing investigations in this area will hopefully lend clarification and refinement to the clinical treatment of obesity.

References

ABRAHAM, S., COLLINS, G., & NORDSIECK, M. Relationship of childhood weight status to morbidity in adults. *HSMA Health Reports*, 1971, **86**, 273–284.

ABRAHAM, S., & NORDSIECK, M. Relationship of excess weight in children and adults. *Public Health Reports*, 1960, **75**, 263–273.

ABRAHMS, J. L., & ALLEN, G. J. Comparative effectiveness of situational programming, financial pay-offs and group pressure in weight reduction. *Behavior Therapy*, 1974, **5**, 391–400.

ABRAMSON, E. E. A review of behavioral approaches to weight control. *Behavioral Research and Therapy*, 1973, **11**, 547–556.

AGRAS, W. S., BARLOW, T. H., CHAPIN, H. N., ABEL, G. G., & LEITENBERG, H. Behavior modification of anorexia nervosa. *Archives of General Psychiatry*, 1974, **30**, 279–286.

AYLLON, T., & HAUGHTON, E. Control of the behavior of schizophrenic patients by food. *Journal of the Experimental Analysis of Behavior*, 1962, **5**, 343–352.

AYLLON, T., HAUGHTON, E., & OSMOND, H. O. Chronic anorexia: a behavior problem. *Canadian Psychiatric Association Journal*, 1964, **9**, 147–154.

AZERRAD, J., & STAFFORD, R. L. Restoration of eating behavior in anorexia nervosa through operant conditioning and environmental manipulation. *Behaviour Research and Therapy*, 1969, **7**, 165–171.

BACHRACH, A. J., ERWIN, W. J., & MOHR, J. P. The control of eating behavior in an anorexic by operant conditioning techniques. In L. P. Ullmann & L. Krasner (Eds.), *Case studies in behavior modification*. New York: Holt, Rinehart & Winston, 1965.

BALCH, P., & ROSS, A. W. A behaviorally oriented didactic-group treatment of obesity: an exploratory study. *Journal of Behavior Therapy and Experimental Psychiatry*, 1974, **5**, 239–243.

BALTERS, H. L. The effects of age of obesity onset, aversive and non-aversive weight reduction techniques, and length of instructional time on weight reduction measures. Unpublished doctoral dissertation, University of Nebraska, 1974.

BANDURA, A. Vicarious and self-reinforcement processes. In R. Glaser (Ed.), *The nature of reinforcement*. New York: Academic Press, 1971.

BELLACK, A. S. ROZENSKY, R., & SCHWARTZ, J. Self-monitoring as an adjunct to a behavioral weight reduction program. *Behavior Therapy*, 1974, **5**, 523–530.

BELLACK, A. S., SCHWARTZ, J. & ROZENSKY, R. H. The contribution of external control to self-control in a weight reduction program. *Journal of Behavior Therapy and Experimental Psychiatry*, 1974, **5**, 245–249.

BERNARD, J. L. Rapid treatment of gross obesity by operant techniques. *Psychological Reports,* 1968, **23,** 663–666.

BLINDER, B. J., FREEMAN, D. M., & STUNKARD, A. J. Behavior therapy of anorexia nervosa: effectiveness of activity as a reinforcer of weight gain. *American Journal of Psychiatry,* 1970, **126,** 1093–1098.

BORNSTEIN, P. H., & SIPPRELLE, C. N. Group treatment of obesity by induced anxiety. *Behaviour Research and Therapy,* 1973, **11,** 339–341.

BRADY, J. P., & RIEGER, W. Behavioral treatment of anorexia nervosa. Paper presented at the International Symposium on Behavior Modification, Minneapolis, October 1972.

CAUTELA, J. R. Treatment of compulsive behavior by covert sensitization. *Psychological Record,* 1966, **16,** 33–41.

CHIRICO, A. M., & STUNKARD, A. J. Physical activity and human obesity. *New England Journal of Medicine,* 1960, **263,** 935–946.

CRISP, A. H. Anorexia nervosa: feeding disorder, nervous malnutrition or weight phobia? *World Review of Nutrition and Dietetics,* 1970, **12,** 452–504.

CRISP, A. M., & TOMS, D. A. Primary anorexia nervosa or weight phobia in the male: report on 13 cases. *British Medical Journal,* 1972, **1,** 334–338.

DAVENPORT, C. B. Body build and its inheritance. Carnegie Institute of Washington, Publication No. 329, 1923.

DINOFF, M., RICKARD, H. C., & COLWICK, J. Weight reduction through successive contracts. *American Journal of Orthopsychiatry,* 1972, **42,** 110–113.

FERNAN, W. The role of experimenter contact in behavioral bibliotherapy of obesity. Unpublished master's thesis, Pennsylvania State University, 1973.

FERSTER, C. B., NURNBERGER, J. I., & LEVITT, E. B. The control of eating. *Journal of Mathetics,* 1962, **1,** 87–109.

FOREYT, J. P., & HAGEN, R. L. Covert sensitization: conditioning or suggestion? *Journal of Abnormal Psychology,* 1973, **82,** 17–23.

FOREYT, J. P. & KENNEDY, W. A. Treatment of overweight by aversion therapy. *Behaviour Research and Therapy,* 1971, **9,** 29–34.

HAGEN, R. L. Group therapy versus bibliotherapy in weight reduction. *Behavior Therapy,* 1974, **5,** 222–234.

HALL, S. M. Self-control and therapist control in the behavioral treatment of overweight women. *Behaviour Research and Therapy,* 1972, **10,** 59–68.

HALL, S. M. Behavioral treatment of obesity: a two-year follow-up. *Behaviour Research and Therapy,* 1973, **11,** 647–648.

HALL, S. M., & HALL, R. G. Outcome and methodological considerations in behavioral treatment of obesity. *Behavior Therapy,* 1974, **5,** 352–364.

HALL, S. M., HALL, R. G., HANSON, R. W., & BORDEN, B. L. Permanence of two self-managed treatments of overweight in university and community populations. *Journal of Consulting and Clinical Psychology,* 1974, **42,** 781–786.

HALLSTEN, E. A., Jr. Adolescent anorexia nervosa treated by desensitization. *Behaviour Research and Therapy,* 1965, **3,** 87–92.

HARMATZ, M. G., & LAPUC, P. Behavior modification of overeating in a psychiatric population. *Journal of Consulting and Clinical Psychology,* 1968, **32,** 583–587.

HARRIS, M. B. Self-directed program for weight control: a pilot study. *Journal of Abnormal Psychology,* 1969, **74,** 263–270.

HARRIS, M. B., & BRUNER, C. G. A comparison of a self-control and a contract procedure for weight control. *Behaviour Research and Therapy,* 1971, **9,** 347–354.

HARRIS, M. B., & HALLBAUER, E. S. Self-directed weight control through eating and exercise. *Behaviour Research and Therapy,* 1973, **11,** 523–529.

HIRSCH, J., & KNITTLE, J. L. Cellularity of obese and nonobese human adipose tissue. *Federation Proceedings,* 1971, **29,** 1516–1521.

HOMME, L. E. Perspectives in psychology. XXIV. Control of coverants, the operants of the mind. *Psychological Record,* 1965, **15,** 501–511.

HORAN, J. J., BAKER, S. B., HOFFMAN, A. M., & SHUTE, R. E. Weight loss through variations in the coverant control paradigm. *Journal of Consulting and Clinical Psychology,* 1975, **43,** 68–72.

HORAN, J. J., & JOHNSON, R. G. Coverant conditioning through a self-management application of the Premack principle: its effect on weight reduction. *Journal of Behavior Therapy and Experimental Psychiatry,* 1971, **2,** 243–249.

JANDA, L. H., & RIMM, D. C. Covert sensitization in the treatment of obesity. *Journal of Abnormal Psychology*, 1972, **80**, 37–42.

JEFFREY, D. B. Self-control versus external control in the modification and maintenance of weight loss. In R. C. Katz & S. I. Zluntnick (Eds.), *Applications of behavior therapy to health care*. New York: Pergamon, 1973.

JEFFREY, D. B., & CHRISTENSEN, E. R. The relative efficacy of behavior therapy, will power, and no-treatment control procedures for weight loss. Paper presented at the Sixth Annual Meeting of the Association for the Advancement of Behavior Therapy, New York, October 1972.

JEFFREY, D. B., CHRISTENSEN, E. R. & PAPPAS, J. P. A case study report of a behavioral modification weight reduction group: treatment and follow-up. Paper presented at the meeting of the Rocky Mountain Psychological Association, Albuquerque, 1972.

JONGMANS, J. G. Vermagerings-Therapieen. Unpublished doctoral dissertation, Psychological Laboratory of the University of Amsterdam, 1969.

JONGMANS, J. G. Een ontwerp voor een vermageringsmodel. Unpublished manuscript, Psychological Laboratory of the University of Amsterdam, 1970.

KAZDIN, A. E. Self-monitoring and behavior change. In M. J. Mahoney & C. E. Thoresen (Eds.), *Self-control: power to the person*. Monterey, Calif.: Brooks/Cole, 1974.

KENNEDY, W. A., & FOREYT, J. Control of eating behavior in an obese patient by avoidance conditioning. *Psychological Reports,* 1968, **22**, 571–576.

KERBAUY, R. R. Autocontrole: Manipulacão de condicoes antecedentes e consequentes do compartamento alimetar. Unpublished doctoral dissertation, University of São Paulo, Brazil, 1972.

KEYS, A., BROZEK, J., HENSCHEL, A., MICKELSON, O. & TAYLOR, H. L. *The biology of human starvation*. Minneapolis: University of Minnesota Press, 1950. 2 vols.

KNITTLE, J. L., & HIRSCH, J. Effect of early nutrition on the development of the rat epididymal fat pads: cellularity and metabolism. *Journal of Clinical Investigation*, 1968, **47**, 2091–2098.

KUNZELMAN, H P. (Ed.) *Precision teaching.* Seattle: Special Child Publications, 1970.

LANG, P. J. Behavior therapy with a case of nervous anorexia. In L. P. Ullman & L. Krasner (Eds.), *Case studies in behavior modification.* New York: Holt, Rinehart & Winston, 1965.

LEITENBERG, H., AGRAS, W. S., & THOMSON, L. E. A sequential analysis of the effect of selective positive reinforcement in modifying anorexia nervosa. *Behaviour Research and Therapy,* 1968, **6**, 211–218.

LEVITZ, L. S., & STUNKARD, A. J. A therapeutic coalition for obesity: behavior modification and patient self-help. *American Journal of Psychiatry*, 1974, **131**, 423–427.

LICK, J., & BOOTZIN, R. Covert sensitization for the treatment of obesity. Paper presented at the Midwestern Psychological Association, Detroit, 1971.

LOCKE, E. Q., CARTLEDGE, N., & KOEPPEL, J. Motivational effects of knowledge of results: a goal-setting phenomenon? *Psychological Bulletin,* 1968, **70**, 474–485.

MAHONEY, M. J. Toward an experimental analysis of coverant control. *Behavior Therapy*, 1970, **1**, 510–521.

MAHONEY, M. J. Research issues in self-management. *Behavior Therapy*, 1972, **3**, 45–63. (a)

MAHONEY, M. J. Self-control strategies in weight loss, Paper presented at the Sixth Annual Meeting of the Association for the Advancement of Behavior Therapy, New York, October 1972. (b)

MAHONEY, M. J. Clinical issues in self-control training. Paper presented at the meeting of the American Psychological Association, Montreal, August 1973.

MAHONEY, M. J. Self-reward and self-monitoring techniques for weight control. *Behavior Therapy*, 1974, **5**, 48–57. (a)

MAHONEY, M. J. *Cognition and behavior modification*. Cambridge, Mass: Ballinger, 1974. (b)

MAHONEY, M. J. The obese eating style: Bites, beliefs, and behavior modification. *Addictive Behaviors,* in press.

MAHONEY, M. J., & MAHONEY, K. Treatment of obesity: a clinical exploration. In B. J. Williams et al., *Obesity: Behavioral approaches to dietary management*. New York: Brunner/Mazel, 1975.

MAHONEY, M. J., & MAHONEY, K. *Permanent weight control*. New York: W. W. Norton, 1976.

MAHONEY, M. J., MOURA, N. G. M., & WADE, T. C. The relative efficacy of self-reward, self-punishment, and self-monitoring techniques for weight loss. *Journal of Consulting and Clinical Psychology*, 1973, **40**, 404–407.

MANN, R. A. The behavior-therapeutic use of contingency contracting to control an adult behavior problem: weight control. *Journal of Applied Behavior Analysis*, 1972, **5**, 99–109.

MANN, R. A. The use of contingency contracting to facilitate durability of behavior change: weight loss maintenance. Paper presented at the meeting of the American Psychological Association, Montreal, August 1973.

MANNO, B., & MARSTON, A. R. Weight reduction as a function of negative covert reinforcement (sensitization) versus positive covert reinforcement. *Behaviour Research and Therapy*, 1972, **10**, 201–207.

MARTIN, J. E., & SACHS, D. A. The effects of a self-control weight loss program on an obese woman. *Journal of Behavior Therapy and Experimental Psychiatry*, 1973, **4**, 155–159.

MAYER, J. Correlation between metabolism and feeding behavior and multiple etiology of obesity. *Bulletin of the New York Academy of Medicine*, 1957, **22**, 744–761.

MAYER, J. Genetic factors in obesity. *Annals of the New York Academy of Sciences*, 1965, **131**, 412–421.

MAYER, J. *Overweight: causes, cost, and control.* Englewood Cliffs, N.J.: Prentice-Hall, 1968.

MAYER, J., & THOMAS, D. W. Regulation of food intake and obesity. *Science*, 1967, **156**, 328–337.

MEICHENBAUM, D., & CAMERON, R. The clinical potential of modifying what clients say to themselves. In M. J. Mahoney and C. E. Thoresen (Eds.), *Self-control: power to the person.* Monterey, Calif.: Brooks/Cole, 1974.

MEYER, V., & CRISP, A. H. Aversion therapy in two cases of obesity. *Behaviour Research and Therapy*, 1964, **2**, 143–147.

MOORE, C. H., & CRUM, B. C. Weight reduction in a chronic schizophrenic by means of operant conditioning procedures: a case study. *Behaviour Research and Therapy*, 1969, **7**, 129–131.

MORGANSTERN, K. P. Cigarette smoke as a noxious stimulus in self-managed aversion therapy for compulsive eating. *Behavior Therapy*, 1974, **5**, 255–260.

PASSMORE, R., MEIKLEJOHN, A. P., DEWAR, A. D., & THOW, R. K. Energy utilization in overfed thin young man. *British Journal of Nutrition*, 1955, **9**, 20.

PASSMORE, R., STRONG, A., SWINDELLS, Y. E., & EL DIN, N. The effect of overfeeding on two fat young women. *British Journal of Nutrition*, 1963, **17**, 373.

PENICK, S. B. FILION, R., FOX, S., & STUNKARD, A. J. Behavior modification in the treatment of obesity. *Psychosomatic Medicine*, 1971, **33**, 49–55.

ROMANCZYK, R. G. Self-monitoring in the treatment of obesity: parameters of reactivity. *Behavior Therapy*, 1974, **5**, 531–540.

ROMANCZYK, R. G., TRACEY, D. A., WILSON, G. T., & THORPE, G. L. Behavioral techniques in the treatment of obesity: a comparative analysis. *Behaviour Research and Therapy*, 1973, **11**, 629–640.

SCHNURER, A. T., RUBIN, R. R., & ROY, A. Systematic desensitization of anorexia nervosa seen as a weight phobia. *Journal of Behavior Therapy and Experimental Psychiatry*, 1973, **4**, 149–153.

SELTZER, C. C., & MAYER, J. Body build and obesity—who are the obese? *Journal of the American Medical Association*, 1964, **189**, 677–684.

SHIPMAN, W. Behavior therapy with obese dieters. *Annual Report of the Institute for Psychosomatic and Psychiatric Research and Training.* Chicago: Michael Reese Hospital and Medical Center, 1970.

SIMS, E. A., GOLDMAN, R. F., GLUCK, C. M., HORTON, E. S., KELLEHER, P. C., & ROWE, D. W. Experimental obesity in man. *Transactions of the Association of American Physicians*, 1968, **81**, 153–170.

STEFFY, R. A. Service applications: psychotic adolescents and adults. Paper presented at the meeting of the American Psychological Association, San Francisco, September 1968.

STOLLAK, G. E. Weight loss obtained under different experimental procedures. *Psychotherapy: Theory, Research and Practice*, 1967, **4**, 61:64.

STUART, R. B. Behavioral control of overeating. *Behaviour Research and Therapy*, 1967, **5**, 357–365.

STUART, R. B. A three-dimensional program for the treatment of obesity. *Behaviour Research and Therapy*, 1971, **9**, 177–186.

STUART, R. B., & DAVIS, B. *Slim chance in a fat world: behavioral control of obesity.* Champaign, Ill.: Research Press, 1972.

STUMPHAUZER, J. S. Application of reinforcement

contingencies with a 23-yr. old anorexic patient. *Psychological Reports,* 1969, **24,** 109–110.

STUNKARD, A. J. The management of obesity. *New York Journal of Medicine,* 1958, **58,** 79–87.

STUNKARD, A. J. New therapies for the eating disorders: behavior modification of obesity and anorexia nervosa. *Archives of General Psychiatry,* 1972, **26,** 391–398.

STUNKARD, A. J. Anorexia nervosa. In J. P. Sanford (Ed.), *The science and practice of clinical medicine.* New York: Grune & Stratton, 1975.

STUNKARD, A. J., & BURT, V. Obesity and the body image. II. Age at onset of disturbances in the body image. *American Journal of Psychiatry,* 1967, **123,** 1443–1447.

STUNKARD, A. J., LEVINE, H., & FOX, S. The management of obesity: patient self-help and medical treatment. *Archives of Internal Medicine,* 1970, **125,** 1067–1072.

THORESEN, C. E., & MAHONEY, M. J. *Behavioral self-control.* New York: Holt, Rinehart & Winston, 1974.

THORPE, J. G., SCHMIDT, E., BROWN, P. T., & CASTELL, D. Aversion-relief therapy: a new method for general application. *Behaviour Research and Therapy,* 1964, **2,** 71–82.

TYLER, V. O., & STRAUGHAN, J. H. Coverant control and breath holding as techniques for the treatment of obesity. *Psychological Record,* 1970, **20,** 473–478.

UPPER, D., & NEWTON, J. G. A weight-reduction program for schizophrenic patients on a token economy unit: two case studies. *Journal of Behavior Therapy and Experimental Psychiatry,* 1971, **2,** 113–115.

WEISENBERG, M., & FRAY, E. What's missing in the treatment of obesity by behavior modification? *Journal of the American Dietetic Association,* 1974, **65,** 410–414.

WELLES, S. L. Nutritive intake of members of weight reduction programs. Unpublished master's thesis, Department of Nutrition, Pennsylvania State University, 1973.

WIJESINGHE, B. Massed electrical aversion treatment of compulsive eating. *Journal of Behavior Therapy and Experimental Psychiatry,* 1973, **4,** 133–135.

WILSON, G. T. Behavior therapy in adults. Paper presented at the American Psychopathological Association, Boston, March 1974.

WITHERS, R. F. L. Problems in the genetics of human obesity. *Eugenics Review,* 1964, **56,** 81–90.

WOLLERSHEIM, J. P. The effectiveness of group therapy based upon learning principles in the treatment of overweight women. *Journal of Abnormal Psychology,* 1970, **76,** 462–474.

WOLPE, J. Reciprocal inhibition as the main basis of psychotherapeutic effects. *Archives of Neurology and Psychiatry,* 1954, **72,** 205–226.

Learned Control of Physiological Function and Disease

3

DAVID SHAPIRO
RICHARD S. SURWIT

This chapter concerns itself with the application of learning techniques to the remediation of disease. Although the idea of teaching people to control their physiology can be traced back to antiquity, learned control of visceral responses and other involuntary functions has only recently come under systematic investigation by psychologists. This research has developed techniques which, for the first time, have enabled therapists to place the physiological activity of the body under the control of environmental contingencies, in much the same way as has been done with other types of behavior. In essence, it now seems feasible to extend the scope of behavior modification into the domain of medicine.

Traditionally, the area of overlap between medicine and psychology involving the psychological treatment of physical diseases is known as *psychosomatic medicine* (Dunbar, 1943). This field has generally concerned itself with the relationship be-

tween emotion and illness, and has relied mainly on the *personality* of the patient as both the prognosticator and focus of therapy (Alexander & Flagg, 1965). The psychosomatic approach to disease is essentially the same as psychodynamic methods of dealing with behavioral disorders and falls prey to the numerous criticisms that have been leveled at the latter (e.g., Bandura, 1969). In brief, such formulations invoke unnecessary hypothetical constructs between the stimuli confronting the patient and the behavior in question. This results in a treatment plan aimed more at a *hypothetical cause* than at the presenting problem itself. Therapy may therefore be slow and inefficient with the presenting symptoms largely neglected. In contrast to the approach of psychosomatic medicine, a behavioral model employing learning techniques would see as its target for therapy the environment of the individual rather than his or her personality. For this reason, Birk (1973) has proposed calling this new area of research and treatment *behavioral medicine.*

Although the application of learning techniques to behavioral disorders followed nearly half a century of animal and human

Supported by National Institute of Mental Health Grants K5-MH-20, 476, MH-08853, and MH-08934; Office of Naval Research Contract N00014-67-A-0298-0024, NR 101-052. We thank J. Alan Herd for his advice.

74

laboratory experimentation, the clinical applications of biofeedback and autonomic instrumental conditioning have been dovetailed in less than 10 years of basic research. In many areas, clinical application has preceded systematic research and is therefore hard to evaluate. Consequently, this chapter has been organized to provide the reader with a grasp of the experimental background upon which each treatment application is based. The following section presents an overview of the evaluation of the basic research on instrumental autonomic learning in animals and man. Further sections are ordered with respect to the amount of research done in each area. Each contains a brief review of the physiology of the disorder, the documented ability of the relevant systems to be brought under learned control, and clinical experiments and/or case studies exploring the effectiveness of biofeedback and instrumental learning techniques in the treatment of the disorder. The final sections of the chapter are devoted to a discussion of theoretical, methodological, and clinical issues in the learned control of physiological functions and its application to disease.

Review of Experimental Foundations

The earliest research on the instrumental modification of autonomically mediated behaviors was carried out in human subjects. Although this research involved numerous complications of subject cooperation and motivation, individual differences, and reward definition, it is of historical interest that much of it preceded the more systematic and highly controlled animal work to follow.

One of the most promising functions from the standpoint of instrumental conditioning was electrodermal activity, which is under sympathetic nervous system innervation. Early in the 1960s, a number of laboratories independently reported that the human electrodermal response, either

measured as a skin resistance or skin potential change, could be relatively increased or decreased in frequency by contingent reinforcement (Fowler & Kimmel, 1962; Johnson, 1963; Shapiro, Crider, & Tursky, 1964). The electrodermal response is typically considered a reflexive, automatic, or "involuntary" response, and there is an enormous body of research showing how it relates to attentional, emotional, and motivational variables (see Edelberg, 1972). The electrodermal response also occurs spontaneously, without being correlated with external stimuli, and it can thus be classified as an unelicited or emitted response. The spontaneous electrodermal response is relatively discrete in nature, and it occurs intermittently. Unlike continuously varying biological functions such as heart rate or skin temperature, the fact that the electrodermal response is discrete lends it still further to operant analysis and experimentation. It is akin to a simple response of the skeletal muscles and can be analyzed by the traditional methods of operant conditioning.

One study in this series (Shapiro et al., 1964) is highlighted because it contains within it many of the critical issues that have preoccupied basic researchers in the field. In this study, a spontaneous fluctuation of palmar skin potential of a given amplitude was selected as the response to be brought under control by means of operant conditioning (Figure 3-1). One group of subjects was given a reward each time the response occurred, and a second group was given the same number of rewards but at times when the response was absent. All subjects were given the same instructions, that the purpose of the experiment was to study the effectiveness of various devices for measuring thought processes and that their task was to think actively about emotional experiences. The subjects were instructed that each time the apparatus detected an "emotional thought" they would hear a tone and earn a five-cent bonus. As a result of the reinforcement con-

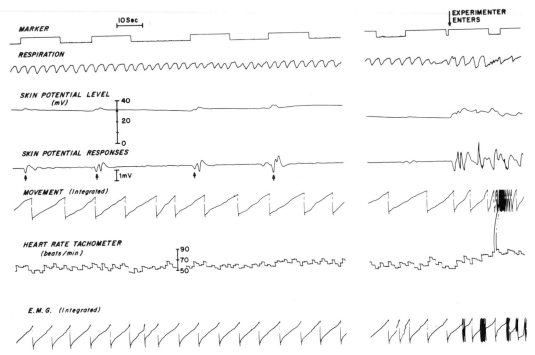

FIGURE 3–1   Portion of a typical record of a subject reinforced for criterion spontaneous skin potential responses (panel on left). Arrows indicate reinforced responses. Marker indicates onset of a 1.5-second
tone followed by a "time-out" period. Tone is cue to subject of a monetary bonus. Note that polarity of
"skin potential responses" channel (AC recording with 1-second time constant) is opposite from polarity
of "skin potential level" channel (DC recording). Panel on right indicates reaction of subject to experimenter
opening subject room door and talking with subject (Crider et al., 1966. Copyright 1966 by the American
Psychological Association. Reprinted by permission).

tingency, the first group showed increases
in response rate relative to the second
group which showed a decrement in response rate over time. That the same reward
could be used either to enhance *or* to diminish the autonomic behavior eliminated the
explanation that the eliciting effect of the
reinforcer itself could account for the observed differences. In subsequent research,
even aversive stimuli such as very loud tones
were found to have differential effects on
electrodermal responding depending on
their relation in time to the occurrence of
the response (Crider, Schwartz, & Shapiro,
1970; Johnson & Schwartz, 1967). That is,
the contingent presentation of a punishing
stimulus suppressed the electrodermal response, while pairing the aversive stimulus

with the absence of or randomly with the
response resulted in sustained electrodermal
activity, as would be expected.

A more significant result emerged from
the Shapiro et al. study. Learned variations
in electrodermal response rate were found
not to be associated with such physiologically related functions as skin potential
level and heart rate. Nor were the variations
obviously associated with differences in
breathing rate or breathing irregularities.
Moreover, cognitive factors, to the extent
they could be detected by blind ratings of
recorded post-session interviews, were not
relevant to the observed effects. Response
contingent and nonresponse contingent subjects reported the same moderate relationship between the reinforcer (tone indicating

bonus) and their thoughts or ideation; the level of involvement in the task was also about the same for the two groups.

The apparent capability of an operant procedure to have a selective effect on an autonomically mediated behavior such as the skin potential response made a convincing argument for the value of exploring autonomic regulation with operant conditioning methods. The methods also provided a means of investigating the extent to which an autonomic response can be differentiated from other autonomic and somatic behaviors. The association between learned electrodermal responding and somatomotor responses was explored in further research (Birk, Crider, Shapiro, & Tursky, 1966; Crider, Shapiro, & Tursky, 1966). From these and other related studies (Rice, 1966; Van Twyver & Kimmel, 1966), it could be seen that the role of somatomotor activity was not entirely consistent. As Birk et al. concluded, "Whether these variables [somatomotor] are to be classified as 'mediating' phenomena cannot be decided until such questions are phrased in terms of known physiological mechanisms or testable hypotheses [p. 166]." Critical experiments on these mechanisms could best be carried out in animal subjects using drugs and surgical procedures.

The fact that a given autonomic function could be increased or decreased while other presumably related functions (somatomotor, autonomic, cortical) did not co-vary was to be given a more comprehensive interpretation in later research. It was reasoned that if the other concurrent functions were in reality *independent* of or only slightly interrelated with the function to be learned, under natural or nonexperimental conditions, then the dissociation of one from the others through conditioning would not be surprising. This line of reasoning was followed closely in research on the operant control of human blood pressure and its association with heart rate. It had been reported that subjects rewarded for increases or decreases in systolic blood pressure showed relative pressure changes in the appropriate direction without differential changes in heart rate (Shapiro, Tursky, Gershon, & Stern, 1969; Shapiro, Tursky, & Schwartz, 1970b). Similarly, subjects could learn to increase or decrease their heart rate without corresponding changes in systolic blood pressure (Shapiro et al., 1970b). Starting with these reports, Schwartz (1972) developed a model for research and theory on the control of "multi-autonomic" functions, a model that explained specificity of learning in the autonomic nervous system. He hypothesized that if two functions such as heart rate and blood pressure are very highly correlated, then when one is reinforced and shows learning, the other should do the same. If they are not correlated, however, then reinforcing one should result in learned changes in that function but not in the other. As a further implication, if you give feedback and reward for a given function and it shows learning, the degree to which other concurrent functions also show learning is informative about the natural interrelations of the functions to begin with. This model of autonomic learning is based on the measurement and analysis of the commonality of responses comprising a complex set of functions. In an empirical test of the model, Schwartz developed an on-line procedure for assessing the simultaneous pattern of systolic blood pressure and heart rate at each beat of the heart. Thus, when subjects were reinforced for a *pattern* of simultaneous change in *both* heart rate and blood pressure, these two functions could either be deliberately associated (both going in the *same* direction) or deliberately dissociated (going in *opposite* directions). The degree of association or dissociation was further limited by certain biological and adaptive constraints. The relative independence of heart rate and systolic blood pressure, established in the context of autonomic learning, was also confirmed by their relative independence under preconditioning resting conditions.

In a further test, it was observed that

under resting conditions diastolic blood pressure and heart rate tended to co-vary in large measure. In this case, conditioning one system (diastolic pressure) resulted in associated changes in the other (heart rate), a finding that was clearly predictable on the basis of the commonality model (Shapiro, Schwartz, & Tursky, 1972b). Furthermore, it was found difficult, if not impossible, to make these two highly integrated functions go in opposite directions by reinforcing differential patterns (Schwartz, Shapiro, & Tursky, 1972).

These basic data obtained in systematic human experiments provide a framework for extending the principles of instrumental learning to visceral and glandular responses and for examining the associated mechanisms involved in the learning process. Through the analysis of concurrent changes in multiple response systems and the study of autonomic pattern learning, a simple predictive model of concurrent changes during visceral learning can be stated. The degree of commonality of the separate responses occurring in contiguity with the feedback and reinforcement determines the degree to which the responses remain associated or become dissociated as a result of the conditioning procedure. With this model, the study of "mediational" processes in visceral learning can be given further precision.

While emphasis above has been given to heart rate, blood pressure, and electrodermal activity, the phenomenon of learned physiological self-regulation in man has also been demonstrated for electrical activity of the brain (Beatty, 1971; Kamiya, 1969; Nowlis & Kamiya, 1970; Rosenfeld, Rudell, & Fox, 1969), peripheral vasomotor activity (Lisina, 1958; Snyder & Noble, 1968), single motor unit activity (Basmajian, 1963; Hefferline & Keenan, 1961), skin temperature (Roberts, Kewman, & Macdonald, 1973), and muscle tone (Budzynski, Stoyva, & Adler, 1970). Specific therapeutic applications of biofeedback techniques to abnormal

response processes and additional basic studies will be reviewed in later sections of this chapter.

So far, we have focused entirely on research with human subjects. A great deal of systematic research has been published indicating that a wide variety of functions can be modified in a number of other species. Examples of physiological responses studied in nonparalyzed animals are: salivation in dogs (Miller & Carmona, 1967), heart rate in monkeys (Engel & Gottlieb, 1970), blood pressure in monkeys (Benson, Herd, Morse, & Kelleher, 1969), blood pressure in baboons (Harris, Gilliam, Findley, & Brady, 1973), and the cortical sensorimotor rhythm in cats (Sterman, Howe, & Macdonald, 1970; Wyrwicka & Sterman, 1968).

A large number of studies have also been carried out in rats paralyzed by curare in which the reward is either electrical brain stimulation or shock escape and avoidance; for example, heart rate (DiCara & Miller, 1968a; Trowill, 1967), blood pressure (DiCara & Miller, 1968b), intestinal contractions (Miller & Banuazizi, 1968), peripheral vasomotor activity (DiCara & Miller, 1968c), amount of blood in the stomach wall (Carmona, Miller, & Demierre, 1974), and kidney urine formation (Miller & DiCara, 1968). Black, Young, and Batenchuck (1970) found that dogs paralyzed by Flaxidil could learn to control their hippocampal theta waves. The point of these experiments on paralyzed animals is that they rule out the effects of purely peripheral aspects of respiratory changes and skeletal muscle activity. That rather large changes could be achieved in relatively short periods of time without the aid of peripheral muscular activity suggested that paralysis might even *facilitate* visceral learning (Miller, 1969). Moreover, a high degree of specificity of learning was often observed. For example, rewarding differential vasomotor responses in the two ears of the rat, vasodilation was observed in one ear and either no change or vasoconstriction in the other (DiCara & Miller, 1968c).

Recently, however, the significance of the curare research has been called into question by the reported difficulties in reproducing results of experiments on heart rate control (Brener, Eissenberg, & Middaugh, 1974; Miller & Dworkin, 1974). This failure to replicate has been discussed in terms of certain undesired peripheral autonomic and central nervous system effects of curare and of difficulties in maintaining a stable animal preparation with artificial respiration (Hahn, 1974; Roberts, 1974). Moreover, curare does not affect the central nervous system linkage between cardiovascular or other autonomically mediated behaviors and somatomotor behaviors. That is, central somatomotor activity may initiate peripheral autonomic and skeletal motor activity, but the latter cannot be observed because the muscles are paralyzed. With respect to this central linkage, therefore, the use of curare cannot provide a *critical* experimental test of the role of central somatomotor processes in learned visceral control (Obrist, Howard, Lawler, Galosy, Meyers, & Gaebelein, 1974). Nevertheless, experiments with animals in both paralyzed and nonparalyzed states provide data on some of the limiting conditions of visceral learning. Basic research in animals along these lines using surgical lesions, paralytic and various biochemical agents should help further elucidate physiological mechanisms of visceral learning.

This review of experimental evidence has touched on some of the major studies and trends in an area of research that has grown rapidly over the past 10 to 15 years. Hundreds of studies have been published, and many are reprinted in a series of annuals and a reader (Barber, DiCara, Kamiya, Miller, Shapiro, & Stoyva, 1971; Kamiya, Barber, DiCara, Miller, Shapiro, & Stoyva, 1971; Miller, Barber, DiCara, Kamiya, Shapiro & Stoyva, 1974; Shapiro, Barber, DiCara, Kamiya, Miller, & Stoyva, 1973; Stoyva, Barber, DiCara, Kamiya, Miller, & Shapiro, 1972). A number of major reviews and position papers have also recently been published (Blanchard & Young, 1973; Brener, 1974; Miller, 1975; Schwartz, 1973).

Clinical Applications

HYPERTENSION

Hypertension is a disorder that has interested researchers concerned with behavioral physiology. It is an illness that poses a major public health problem in the United States, and methods that can augment those already in common medical practice are obviously important. The prevalence of hypertension is estimated to be about 5 to 10% of the general population, and high levels of arterial blood pressure increase the risk of other life-threatening disorders such as coronary artery disease, atherosclerosis, and nephrosclerosis (Kannel, Gordon, & Schwartz, 1971). Even occasional large increases in resting levels of pulse and blood pressure are thought to be associated with a shortening of the life span (Merrill, 1966).

A vast proportion of all cases of hypertension is classified as "essential." These are cases in which a specific endocrine or renal disorder cannot be found. With no known physical etiology, essential hypertension is defined solely by the presence of a chronic elevation in blood pressure. While medical investigators are not in agreement about the significance of psychological factors in hypertension, there is evidence that the disorder is related to and can be aggravated by behavioral, social, and environmental conditions (Gutmann & Benson, 1971). Hyperreactivity of the sympathetic nervous system may be a major factor in the elevation of blood pressure, particularly in the early stages of the illness, as evidenced by increased heart rate, high cardiac output, and increased cardiac contractility. This hyperreactivity may occur in individuals who are particularly susceptible by reason of genetic, constitutional, and other factors such as obesity, smoking, or particular personality and emotional patterns.

In view of the assumed environmental, personality, and autonomic nervous system components of essential hypertension, a method of psychophysiological relearning such as biofeedback could offer a nonsurgical, nonpharmacologic means of lowering pressure. It is important to point out that current medical practice advocates drug treatment, especially where there is any reason to suspect that the illness is becoming more severe. "Since various effective hypotensive agents exist, it is now justifiable to utilize mild forms of therapy (including reassurance) for mild forms of hypertension, . . . [Merrill, 1966, p. 711].

Although the measurement of blood pressure posed many technical problems, particularly for purposes of providing continuous feedback, the relation between blood pressure and the illness itself seemed simple and direct to researchers. The course of action was clear. By obtaining a continuous measure of blood pressure, providing feedback to subjects, and rewarding the appropriate decreases, blood pressure could presumably be lowered, and the illness thereby brought under control. Furthermore, basic research on blood pressure regulation in normal human and animal subjects using operant conditioning techniques provided ample evidence for the extension of the techniques into a therapeutic setting. In the curarized rat, instrumental conditioning of systolic blood pressure was demonstrated using a shock escape and avoidance procedure (DiCara & Miller, 1968b). The learned changes were about 20% of baseline in both increase and decrease directions, and they were not associated with heart rate or rectal temperature. In a subsequent study in noncurarized rats, the changes obtained were much smaller— about 5%—and the learning was found not to transfer to the curarized state (Pappas, DiCara, & Miller, 1970). Elevations in diastolic pressure of large magnitude were obtained in the rhesus monkey using a shock avoidance procedure in which the elevations functioned as the avoidance response (Plumlee, 1969). Benson et al. (1969) reported more modest elevations of mean arterial pressure in the squirrel monkey using similar procedures. In the dog-faced baboon, substantial elevations in blood pressure were established by an operant conditioning procedure that provided for food delivery and shock avoidance contingent upon increases in diastolic pressure (Harris, Findley, & Brady, 1971, Harris et al., 1973). In their recent work, these investigators produced sustained increases of about 20 mmHg in both systolic and diastolic blood pressure with the additional significant finding that the increases in blood pressure were associated with elevated but progressively decreasing heart rates.

An experimental animal with behaviorally induced hypertension is of great significance, particularly if the high blood pressure can be maintained for long periods of time. It suggests that the illness can in fact be learned in this fashion, and it provides a means of applying and exploring the value of different relearning procedures. Benson et al. (1969) put squirrel monkeys on a work schedule in which they were required to press a key in order to avoid electric shock, and the schedule resulted in increases in mean arterial blood pressure. The shock avoidance keys were then removed, and an increase in blood pressure was made the instrumental response required to avoid shock. Prolonged elevations in pressure were maintained in this way. When the schedule was reversed, and decreases in pressure became the criterion for shock avoidance, pressures were shown to decline 10 to 20 mmHg. However, there is no certainty that in this experiment stable elevations in pressure were achieved. The capacity to reduce blood pressure using an operant procedure may be related to the length of time that the high level is present (Teplitz, 1971).

Turning to research in normotensive

humans, Brener and Kleinman (1970) used a finger cuff method of following systolic pressure. In an experimental group, subjects were instructed to decrease their blood pressure with the aid of pressure feedback. In a control group, subjects were instructed to observe the feedback, but they were not informed about its meaning. Differences of about 20 to 30 mmHg were obtained between the two groups after about 30 minutes of training, and the differences were not associated with heart rate. Inasmuch as blood pressure values obtained with a finger cuff are different from those obtained with an arm cuff, it is difficult to compare these results with the smaller effects (4 mmHg) reported earlier by Shapiro et al. (1969) using a constant cuff technique (see below). The differences may be greater in the Brener and Kleinman study as a result of giving the experimental subjects specific instructions to lower pressure. No blood pressure instructions were employed in the Shapiro et al. experiment. Subjects were merely informed to increase the feedback which signified some undefined physiological response.

Inasmuch as most of the normal human data on blood pressure control follow the procedures first described by Shapiro et al. (1969), a brief description of the measuring technique will exemplify the development of a feedback technology. A method had to be devised to obtain a measure of blood pressure on each beat of the heart so as to be able to provide as complete information as possible to the subject. Intermittent measurements (once or twice a minute) using an ordinary pressure cuff provide information on only 2 to 3% of the changes. They are also inadequate because of the inherent variability of blood pressure. A single determination of systolic or diastolic pressure every half minute can be as much as 20 to 30 mmHg off from the average measurement. For example, in a single minute's direct recording of pressure via a catheter in a given patient, two successive cuff blood pressure measurements in that

period would have yielded 124/90 and 144/60 mmHg, while the median value for the 50-odd pressure waves was actually 128/68 mmHg (Tursky, Shapiro, & Schwartz, 1972). Direct arterial catheterization is not feasible for routine repetitive training.

The automatic procedure designated the "constant cuff" method is as follows. A blood pressure cuff is wrapped around the upper arm and a crystal microphone is placed over the brachial artery under the distal end of the cuff. If the cuff is inflated to about the average systolic pressure and held constant at that level, whenever systolic pressure rises and exceeds the occluding cuff pressure, a Korotkoff sound can be detected from the microphone. When the systolic level is less than the occluding pressure, no Korotkoff sound is detected. Using a regulated low-pressure source, logic and programming apparatus, it is possible to find the constant cuff pressure at which 50% of the heart beats yield Korotkoff sounds. This pressure level is by definition *median* systolic pressure. Inasmuch as the time between the R-wave in the electrocardiogram and the occurrence of the Korotkoff sound is approximately 300 msec, it is also possible to detect either the presence of the Korotkoff sound (high pressure relative to the median) *or* its absence (low pressure relative to the median). In this way, the system provides information about directional changes in pressure relative to the median on each successive heart beat. Typically, the cuff is inflated for 50 heart beats and deflated for about 30 seconds to allow recirculation of the blood. Depending on the percentage of Korotkoff sounds in a single 50-beat trial, the constant pressure in the next trial can be changed by a small amount (±2 mmHg) to return to the subject's median. Thus, the system can provide blood pressure feedback on each heart beat and can also track median pressure from trial to trial. This system has been evaluated against simultaneous data obtained using a direct arterial recording, and a close correspondence has been obtained for all of its essential features (Tursky et al., 1972). Comparable procedures can be used to determine the diastolic values. Typically, subjects are provided with binary (yes–no) feedback of either relatively high or low pressure on each heart beat. After a prescribed number of feedback stimuli, rewarding slides are presented. Figures 3-2 and 3-3 illustrate the procedures.

The initial studies attempted to determine whether normal volunteer subjects could learn to modify their systolic or diastolic blood pressure. Complete details may be found in Schwartz (1972), Schwartz, Shapiro, & Tursky (1971), Shapiro et al. (1969), Shapiro, Tursky, & Schwartz (1970a), Shapiro et al. (1970b), and Shapiro et al. (1972b). In these studies, subjects were simply told to make the feedback occur as much as possible and to earn as many rewards as possible. They were not told that the feedback was being given for changes in blood pressure; nor were they told in what direction it was to change. This con-

FIGURE 3–2   Subject in blood pressure study. Light at right is turned on with cuff inflation and cues subject that trial period has begun. Light at left flashes for 100 msec with correct pressure change (feedback). Simultaneously, brief tone is presented. Slides (correlated with monetary bonus) are projected either for criterion number of feedback stimuli or predetermined change in median pressure.

trolled for any complications due to the natural ability of subjects to control pressure "voluntarily," and tested the pure effects of feedback and reward contingency. Current research in this area is concerned with the ability of subjects to modify their blood pressure with instructions only and with the effects of combining feedback with instructions (Shapiro, 1973; see also Brener, 1974). "Pure" voluntary control of blood pressure and other changes in circulation has been reported in unusual individual cases (Ogden & Shock, 1939) and may be more widespread than previously believed.

Using the above procedures, subjects could learn to modify their blood pressure with feedback and reward. Average differences in systolic pressure between increase and decrease conditions for groups of subjects at the end of a single session of training varied from 3 to 10% of baseline. The best results were obtained for diastolic pressure (Shapiro et al., 1972b) with individual subjects showing increases up to 25% and decreases up to 15% of baseline values. Heart rate was found to be clearly independent of the learned changes in systolic but not of the changes in diastolic pressure. In a related study, systolic pressure was not associated with the learned changes in heart rate.

Although the average curves indicated that it was easier to obtain reductions rather than increases in pressure (in a single session), further data under conditions of random reinforcement suggested a tendency for baseline values to adapt over time. Increases in pressure over baseline values are probably more likely (Shapiro et al., 1970a). This is a common interpretation of findings in heart rate and other autonomic biofeedback studies (see Engel, 1972). Moreover, as in the case of heart rate, the processes involved in increasing blood pressure may be completely different from those involved in decreasing pressure (see Lang & Twentyman, 1974). In normal subjects, typical resting pressures are close to

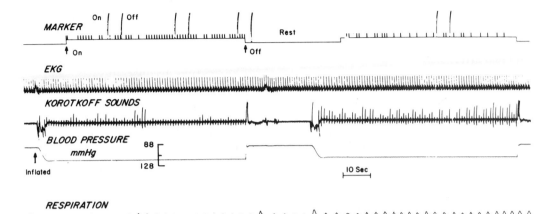

FIGURE 3–3   Segment of polygraph record of a subject in a *decrease* systolic blood pressure condition in which subject is reinforced for lowering his pressure. Two trials are shown. Marker channel indicates onset of trial with presentation of blue light as cue (first arrow), feedback (small marks), and slide presentations (large spikes). Rest period begins when blue light is turned off. For this subject in a decrease condition, feedback was administered when Korotkoff sounds were below critical amplitude. Blood pressure channel shows cuff inflation and deflation. Applied pressure was 116 mm on first trial shown. During this trial there was 76% success. On second trial shown, applied pressure was changed to 114, making task more difficult. Note reduction in success rate to 37% on this trial (Shapiro et al., 1969. Copyright 1969 by the American Association for the Advancement of Science.)

minimal values, but there is a potential for large increases above baseline, depending upon motor activity, emotionality, and so on. For individuals who already have significantly elevated pressure levels, significant decreases are more likely.

By and large, normal subjects could not report whether they were in fact learning to raise or lower their pressure; nor did they reveal the consistent use of specific thoughts, images, or physical strategies such as respiratory maneuvers, as far as could be detected.

To explain the conditions under which specificity of conditioning would occur, Schwartz (1972) hypothesized that when feedback is given for one response, simultaneous learning of other responses will depend on the degree to which these other responses are directly associated with the response for which feedback is given as well as on other homeostatic mechanisms. Schwartz developed an on-line procedure for tracking both phasic and tonic patterns of blood pressure and heart rate in real

time and for showing that subjects could in fact learn to control patterns of simultaneous changes in *both* functions. Subjects could readily learn to integrate systolic blood pressure and heart rate (i.e., make both increase or both decrease simultaneously) and to some extent learn to differentiate both functions (i.e., make one increase and the other decrease simultaneously). Further analysis of the patterning of both functions over time and of natural tonic reactivity in this situation made it possible to predict the extent and time course of pattern learning in the different conditions. Subjective reports of a "relaxed" state were associated with learned reduction in *both* systolic pressure and heart rate.

These basic data in animals and man provided the foundations for the clinical use of biofeedback techniques in hypertension. Using the constant cuff method, Benson, Shapiro, Tursky, and Schwartz (1971) investigated the application of operant feedback techniques to the lowering of systolic blood pressure in seven hypertensive patients, five of whom had essential hypertension. Of the other two, one did not have elevated systolic pressure and the other had renal artery stenosis. The latter patients showed little or no decrease in systolic pressure as a result of the conditioning procedure. The five patients responding positively showed decreases of 34, 29, 16, 16, and 17 mmHg with 33, 22, 34, 31, and 12 sessions of training, respectively. No reliable pressure readings were taken outside the laboratory so the general effectiveness of the training could not be determined.

The average amount of in-session decrease in systolic pressure for the patients was about 5 mmHg, about the same as in normal studies. In resting control conditions, no such reductions were observed in the patients. Although the lowered pressure tended to carry over from one session to the next, the trends were not always consistent. The individual curves suggested a pattern of successive cycles of decreasing pressure, followed by an increase, and then a new lowering trend. Apparently, certain events in the life of the patient, or other factors not presently understood, disturbed the decremental process and the pressure bounced back, although not necessarily to the original level. The data suggested a possible process of successive habituation interrupted by periods of dehabituation. It may be hypothesized that the feedback reward technique facilitates the process of habituation. It is not known whether random feedback, attempts at voluntary control without feedback, muscular relaxation, or simply sitting in the laboratory would achieve the same results. The latter possibility seems remote, inasmuch as little or no reduction in pressure was observed after as many as 15 control sessions under resting conditions with no feedback or rewards. Nonspecific placebo effects have to be considered, in addition to simple adaptation to the laboratory situation, as an alternative explanation of the observed reductions. The patients studied had been in treatment for

hypertension for long periods of time, and no changes in their drug treatment were made. However, the innovation of "biofeedback" as a new technique involving unusual instrumentation, feedback displays, and the idea of self-control may have served a placebo function.

Using essentially the same feedback procedure, Kleinman and Goldman (1974) recently reported maximum decreases of 18% in systolic and diastolic pressure in seven patients with average baseline values of 167/109 mmHg. Those patients showing the greatest maximum decreases in both systolic and diastolic pressure during biofeedback training also showed the greatest improvement on a Category Test of the Reitan Neuropsychological Test Battery for Adults. As this test is related to cognitive dysfunctioning, the results of the study imply that biofeedback may be useful not only in lowering pressure but also in overcoming a cognitive impairment associated with hypertension. Neither Benson et al. (1971) nor Kleinman and Goldman (1974) has provided data on the persistence of training effects outside the laboratory. The cognitive improvement reported by Kleinman and Goldman, however, suggests that the training may not be entirely laboratory specific.

Miller (1975) reported on unpublished research in his laboratory in which he attempted to train 28 patients with essential hypertension to reduce their diastolic blood pressure. A few patients appeared to reduce their blood pressure, but after reaching a plateau the pressure drifted up again. One patient showed excellent results, and was trained to alternate in increasing and decreasing her pressure. Over a period of three months, this patient acquired the ability to change pressure over a range of 30 mmHg. Her baseline pressure decreased from 97 to 76 mmHg, and similar decreases were observed on the ward. Later on, she lost voluntary control and was put back on drugs as a result of emotional stresses. Miller reported that this patient came back to training two and a half years later and rapidly regained a large measure of control.

An instructive quote from Miller's paper underscores the role of environmental events in controlling a function such as blood pressure. "The question raised sharply by this patient, however, is whether she is merely using her voluntary control to produce a spuriously low measure in clinical tests while failing to transfer it to crucial parts of her daily life and thus conceivably misleading her physician about her need for antihypertensive medication." The need for continuous recording of blood pressure in daily life situations is apparent, and techniques are now being developed to make this possible.

The above clinical trials attempted direct control of blood pressure with biofeedback. An alternative indirect approach has been employed by Moeller and Love (personal communication). In their view, by teaching subjects to relax their muscles, it may be possible to reduce blood pressure which they assume to be associated with muscle tension. According to these investigators, this procedure has an added advantage in that patients are more likely to be able to "sense" and control their muscles and thereby possibly develop a means of self-control of blood pressure outside the laboratory. A sample of six patients with average baseline pressures of 153/100 mmHg was given exercises which included muscle feedback and autogenic training as a means of facilitating general bodily relaxation. The training covered a period of 17 weeks. Moeller and Love reported that both systolic and diastolic pressure were reduced by 13% in this program.

A number of other indirect behavioral methods of lowering blood pressure, not involving the use of feedback, need to be mentioned in this context. These include progressive relaxation (Jacobson, 1938), meditation (Benson, Rosner, Marzetta, & Klemchuk, 1974), yoga practices (Datey,

Deshmukh, Dalvi, & Vinekar, 1969), and autogenic training (Luthe & Schultz, 1969). An innovative approach to relaxation training was utilized with some success in lowering pressure in patients with essential hypertension, as discussed in a recent preliminary report by Brady, Luborsky, and Kron (1974). It is called "metronome-conditioned relaxation" (see Brady, 1973) and requires that the patient lie down for one-half hour with eyes closed and listen to a tape recording. The recording consists of instructions to relax the muscles, and it includes suggestions to "let-go" and "re-lax" the muscles, paced with rhythmic beats of an auditory metronome set at 60 beats per minute. With repeated training, several patients showed significant reductions in pressure. Two patients who used the tape recording at home for a protracted period showed further reductions in pressure.

These indirect behavioral procedures have all been shown to be effective in reducing high blood pressure to some degree. Comparative studies are needed to determine their relative effectiveness. It would appear from the studies reported so far that the various procedures discussed, including biofeedback, have more or less similar effects. This suggests that a relaxation or low-arousal state may be a common factor (see Benson, Beary, & Carol, 1974; Stoyva & Budzynski, 1974). This state may well be facilitated if the patient is confident that he is able in fact to exert control over his own blood pressure. While the different behavioral procedures do not seem to affect blood pressure to different degrees, it is reasonable to expect that detailed analysis of the results of extended training will show differences in extent, degree, and persistence of achieved self-control and in the physiological patterns associated with this control.

The problem of transfer of training outside the laboratory may be illustrated by observation of a single case studied in our laboratories at the Massachusetts Mental Health Center. The patient was a 35-year-old mental health worker who was highly motivated and cooperative. He was diagnosed as having essential hypertension with a pressure of 160/110 mmHg taken during a routine medical examination. The patient was given feedback for reductions in diastolic pressure after six resting control sessions in which he fluctuated from 80 to 105 mmHg diastolic. Over nine training sessions, he steadily reduced his pressure from over 100 to about 85 mmHg. A variety of other procedures were then tried, including autogenic phrases and progressive relaxation in addition to feedback, and the patient began oscillating in diastolic pressure between 85 and 95 mmHg. His systolic pressure, recorded in a final session, ranged from 135 to 130 mmHg over a 35-minute period. Following these sessions, he returned to his physician for a second examination, and he was recorded again at 160/110 mmHg (see Shapiro, 1974).

Although it is hazardous to draw any conclusions, this patient, in the laboratory, seemed to show reduction in pressure with the aid of feedback, although nonspecific factors cannot be ruled out. Was he unable to transfer this learning to other relevant situations, or was his hyperreactivity confined to the medical examination? The latter could be a classically conditioned response unique to the physician taking his pressure. It seems likely, however, that other stressors in the patient's environment would have also yielded abnormal responses.

Several approaches to the problem of transfer of training in the case of hypertension are suggested: (1) More extensive long-term training may be needed. Then, periods of training without feedback could be instituted as a means of enhancing self-control and effecting permanent reductions. (2) In cases exhibiting hyperreactivity that appears to be situation specific, some combination of a desensitization procedure and biofeedback could be used to facilitate adaptation to real life situations (see Sirota, Schwartz, & Shapiro, 1974). (3) Feedback training could be instituted in a stimulating or a mildly stressful environment (produced by noise or distracting tasks) as a means of possibly building up resistance to and reducing abnormal physiological responses to stress in general, and possibly to specific stressful events. (4) Other behavioral procedures (meditation, relaxation, autogenic training, yoga exercises) could also be combined with feedback procedures to facilitate more effective behavioral control.

Finally, diastolic pressure is thought to be more critical in certain later stages of hypertension because of its closer relationship to peripheral resistance (Merrill, 1966). Initial studies at the Thorndike Memorial and Channing Laboratories of the Boston City Hospital in collaboration with Dr. Herbert Benson indicated that it is difficult to reduce abnormally high diastolic levels. Part of the problem may be related to some unreliability in obtaining consistent diastolic values over repeated sessions. Learned control of diastolic pressure was observed in a single-session study of normal subjects with consistent changes occurring in most subjects (Shapiro et al., 1972b). However, systolic pressure by itself may be a meaningful prognostic index of future disease. Comprehensive data have been obtained in the Framingham Study on the contribution of various indices of blood pressure to the risk of coronary heart disease (Kannel et al., 1971). It was concluded that "... the association between antecedent blood pressure and the incidence of coronary heart disease is actually stronger for systolic than for diastolic pressure [p. 340]." For these reasons, one possible strategy is to work with early cases of illness and to concentrate on reductions in the systolic level, which is most reliably measured and easiest to work with. Additional case material and further discussion of the clinical data and the problems of clinical management in hypertension may be found in Schwartz (1973), Schwartz and Shapiro (1973), and Shapiro (1974).

In conclusion, the major trends in this

research on hypertension may be summarized as follows:

1. Biofeedback techniques are effective in controlling normal blood pressure levels in a laboratory situation, and further research is needed to determine whether larger changes can be achieved with more refined feedback and reward techniques, relevant instructions, and long-term training. The degree to which the training persists over time and carries over to other situations needs to be investigated.

2. Both direct and indirect feedback methods appear to be useful as a means of reducing blood pressure in patients with essential hypertension. By and large, the clinical studies have not employed adequate controls for placebo and other nonspecific effects. Such controls are needed to distinguish between those effects that are unique to the use of feedback itself and those that are related to the novelty of this method of treatment, enthusiasm of the clinician, or attitudes of the patient.

3. The simplified notion of direct symptom treatment (blood pressure training per se) may be inadequate, and alternative biofeedback strategies should be considered, e.g., giving feedback for a pattern of reduced pressure and heart rate, giving feedback for reductions in overall sympathetic activity or cardiac output as general functions of importance in the lowering of pressure (particularly in early or labile phase of hypertension), or giving feedback for combined decreases in muscle tension and blood pressure. The choice of feedback strategy depends upon an understanding of the dynamics of the cardiovascular system (see below) and of the mechanisms of hypertension. These are complex issues under extensive investigation by scientists in physiology, medicine, and other disciplines. Moreover, the physiological processes in hypertension are probably not uniform from case to case and may depend upon many factors. In our view, further interdisciplinary research on the part of behavioral, physiological, and medical scientists will enhance the potential of biofeedback and other behavioral methods in research and treatment of hypertension.

CARDIAC ARRHYTHMIAS

"A cardiac arrhythmia is defined as any abnormality in the site of impulse formation, in the spread of impulses through the conduction system, in the rate at which the heart beats, or in the rhythm with which the heart beats (Engel & Bleecker, 1974, p. 457)." Certain arrhythmias occur in the absence of structural disease of the heart, e.g., sinus arrhythmias, bradycardia or tachycardia of sinus origin, atrial and ventricular premature beats, milder forms of first degree heart block, and paroxysmal atrial tachycardia. Disorders of these rhythms may be associated with specific eliciting factors such as tobacco or coffee, but they generally occur in the absence of structural heart disease. Other arrhythmias occur in persons with organic heart disease. These arrhythmias include fibrillation and tachycardia of the ventricles, atrial flutter and fibrillation, and advanced degrees of atrioventricular block (Eddleman, Resnik, & Harrison, 1966).

A rationale for the use of operant conditioning and biofeedback techniques in bringing cardiac arrhythmias under control is summarized by Engel:

By the time we began our experiments, we already had carried out three cardiac conditioning studies with normal subjects (Engel & Chism, 1967; Engel & Hansen, 1966; Levene, Engel, & Pearson, 1968), and Miller and his colleagues had shown that it was possible to operantly condition heart rate in the rat (Miller, 1969). Furthermore, there was extensive literature that showed that the nervous system could play a major role in modulating the prevalence of cardiac arrhythmias (Scherf & Schott, 1953), and that showed that temperamental variables affected the prevalence of many arrhythmias (Stevenson, Duncan, Wolf, Ripley, & Wolff, 1949). These data indicated that the nervous system exercised a significant role in cardiac function, and that at least some aspects of this nervous control were associated with volitional behavior [1973, p. 433].

Engel and his associates applied operant training procedures in a number of different arrhythmias—premature ventricular contractions (Weiss & Engel, 1971), atrial fibrillation (Bleecker & Engel, 1973b), and Wolff-Parkinson-White syndrome (Bleecker & Engel, 1973a). In the most up-to-date summary, results with other arrhythmias are cited (Engel & Bleecker, 1974). These included sinus tachycardia, supraventricular tachycardia, paroxysmal atrial tachycardia, and third degree heart block.

A variety of training procedures were employed in these studies. In most cases, the patients were trained both to increase and to decrease their heart rate, and the training procedures were found to be coupled with variations in the prevalence of their arrhythmias. Typically, the patient was provided with a display consisting of lights and a meter. A green light was a cue to the patient to speed up his heart rate, and a red light was a cue to slow it down. Whenever the patient met the heart rate performance criterion, a yellow light was turned on indicating success in the task. A meter ran whenever the patient was performing successfully and indicated the percentage of time he was successful during the session. One important training innovation involved the use of a kind of intermittent reinforcement, in this case variable periods of practice without feedback but with specific instructions to continue attempting control.

In the most extensive clinical study in this series (Weiss & Engel, 1971), eight patients with premature ventricular contractions were trained to increase, decrease, alternately increase and decrease, or maintain their heart rate within a certain range. Variations in the heart rate training procedure were associated with different frequencies of this arrhythmia. Five patients showed significant decreases in frequency of the premature contractions, and four of them persisted in this control for periods up to 21 months. One patient has since been followed over a five-year period, and her arrhythmia continued at a very low rate (Engel & Bleecker, 1974).

During the 21-month period, one of the patients had no reported myocardial infarctions as compared with three in the 11 months prior to training. Weiss and Engel (1971) conjectured that this consequence may be related to the diminished prevalence of the arrhythmia. Premature ventricular contractions are associated with diminished coronary artery and cerebral blood flow (Corday, Gold, DeVera, Williams, & Fields, 1959; Corday & Irving, 1960) and with an increased probability of sudden death (Chiang, Perlman, Ostander, & Epstein, 1969; Lown & Wolf, 1971). Biofeedback and reward techniques provide a specific behavioral means of direct symptom control in cardiac arrhythmias and an indirect influence on related cardiovascular disorders.

Using autonomic nervous system drugs, Weiss and Engel (1971) were able to distinguish at least two different physiological mechanisms involved in the diminution of premature ventricular beats. In one patient, drug-induced diminished sympathetic tone resulted in fewer premature beats; and, in another, the mechanism involved an increase in vagal tone. In both these cases, a decrease in heart rate could be associated with *either* physiological process. In other patients, increases in heart rate, reflecting different underlying physiological processes, could also be associated with a reduced frequency of premature beats. Weiss and Engel argue that it is not the heart rate per se that determines the presence or absence of premature beats, but rather the degree to which such a change reflects the critical underlying physiological process. For example, in the patient for whom reduced sympathetic tone to the heart was responsible for the decreased incidence of premature beats, increases in heart rate induced by isoproterenol were associated with premature beats, whereas similar heart rate increases induced by atropine were not. If this patient were to reduce heart rate by means of an increase in vagal tone, no reduction in the symptom would be observed.

It is apparent in this research that the relations between feedback training procedure, actual heart rate change, symptom frequency, and the critical underlying physiological mechanisms are not unambiguous. Although Weiss and Engel concluded that operant conditioning can be used to alter pathologic conditions mediated by different physiological mechanisms, the choice of an appropriate feedback strategy is also not clear. If sympathetic nervous function is critical in the particular case, there may be other responses aside from heart rate that, if altered, could serve to alter the function in the required direction. That is, other indices of sympathetic function could be equally effective for feedback training purposes. As in other disorders, the issues in this research are quite complex. There is no question that wisdom and judgment have to be exercised in the choice of a feedback training method. In the final analysis, the clinical value of the method must be empirically tested to determine its efficacy. As Weiss and Engel suggest, extensive, short-term experimental drug studies are useful in clarifying the mechanisms of the cardiac symptoms in different patients and, therefore, in suggesting a feedback strategy.

Miller (1975) reported on attempts to replicate Engel's research on premature ventricular contractions. In Miller's laboratory, T. Pickering succeeded in training two patients to control their arrhythmia with data supporting Engel's findings that patients can voluntarily suppress or control the responses. The lasting therapeutic value of this more recent work has not been determined.

Weiss and Engel (1971) proposed six factors that are important in learning to control frequency of premature ventricular contractions: (1) Peripheral receptors are stimulated by the arrhythmia and provide the possibility of the patient learning to recognize and control the abnormal response. This process is facilitated by external feedback in the early stages of training. (2) Afferent nerves carry the information to the central nervous system. (3) Central nervous system processes enable the patient to recognize information about the arrhythmia and provide the necessary motivation to facilitate learning and sustained change in performance. (4) Efferent nerves bring about the desired change in cardiac functioning. (5) The heart must be able to beat more regularly, that is, not be too diseased. (6) The patient's homeostatic system must be able to tolerate a more normal heart function.

All together, the findings of Engel and his associates are among the most remarkable of the clinical applications of biofeedback and operant conditioning techniques to date. Some reasons for this success may be isolated. First, cardiac arrhythmias are circumscribed disorders in which the symptom is quite specific and the physiological rationale for the specific training procedure more or less straightforward. Second, the training sessions were extensive and comprehensive in design. As many as 50 to 60 sessions of different contingencies were conducted in individual cases. Third, patients were trained *both* to increase as well as decrease the frequency of the abnormal rhythm, and it was thought that this experience enhanced self-control. Fourth, Engel used periods of self-control without feedback, the goal of which is summed up as follows:

> Our purpose in including this procedure was to wean the patient from the gadgetry, be-depended on the subject being able to per-cause the clinical value of the conditioning form successfully in nonlaboratory environments. Apparently this technique was successful, since the patients report that their ability to perform without feedback is strong evidence *to them* that they have developed

their own intrinsic cues, and that they "know" when their hearts are beating normally *and* abnormally, and that they "know" how to change the rhythm in either direction [Engel & Bleecker, 1974 p. 473].

EPILEPSY

"Epilepsy is an intermittent disorder of the nervous system due presumably to a sudden, excessive, disorderly discharge of cerebral neurones. . . . This discharge results in an almost instantaneous disturbance of sensation, loss of consciousness, convulsive movements, or some combination thereof [Adams, 1966, p. 245]." It has been estimated that half of all epileptic patients have generalized convulsions, 8% have minor or petit mal seizures, and 1% have psychic or psychomotor seizures. Psychomotor epilepsy is the most prominent remaining type of epilepsy, in which there is no distinct loss of control of thoughts and actions, and the behavior pattern is said to be automatic (Adams, 1966). The electroencephalogram (EEG) is one source of diagnostic information about the disorder in addition to a variety of other clinical and behavioral observations.

A biofeedback approach to epilepsy revolves around attempts to modify characteristics of the EEG. Control of certain normal EEG rhythms has been widely studied, and also widely publicized because of the presumed association of pleasurable subjective states with the production of alpha waves (8–12 Hz) (Brown, 1970; Kamiya, 1969; Nowlis & Kamiya, 1970). Systematic findings supporting the operant control of alpha and beta waves have been reported (Beatty, 1971; Beatty & Kornfeld, 1972), and a few attempts have been made to examine mechanisms of such control and the extent to which unusual or persistent alterations of brain wave rhythms are possible (Lynch & Paskewitz, 1971; Mulholland, 1968; Paskewitz & Orne, 1973).

Few relations of significance have been established between operantly regulated

cortical activity and human behavior, normal or abnormal. Operant suppression of theta activity (3–7 Hz) was found to enhance efficiency (vigilance) in a radar monitoring task, while operant theta enhancement degraded performance in the task (Beatty, Greenberg, Deiblen, & O'Hanlon, 1974). Numerous speculations and case studies have been offered to support the therapeutic application of EEG feedback training in psychiatry, but few systematic data are available. Discussion of some potential applications may be found in Budzynski (1973) and Green, Green, & Walters (1971). Aside from the human experimentation, numerous studies of infrahuman subjects have demonstrated the operant modification of central nervous system electrical activity, including single cell, "spontaneous" EEG, and evoked cortical potentials. Black (1972) published a comprehensive review of operant neural conditioning research in both man and animals, including a consideration of the many behavioral and theoretical issues involved.

Sterman and his associates pioneered in applying operant EEG techniques to epilepsy (Sterman, 1973). The work started with the recording of a 12–14 Hz rhythm appearing over sensorimotor cortex in cats, a rhythm which appears during the voluntary suppression of movement. This electrical activity is termed the sensorimotor rhythm (SMR). Cats trained by operant conditioning to produce SMR assumed stereotyped motionless postures, and the SMR was associated with a sustained decrease in tonic motor discharge and heart rate along with very regular respiration. As another result of SMR training, sleep EEG spindles were enhanced, motor disturbances during sleep were diminished, and the overall amount of time spent sleeping was reduced. The observation of greatest interest for epilepsy research was that SMR-trained cats showed a surprising resistance to drug-induced seizures.

These observations led Sterman and his group to view EEG biofeedback as a neural process, rather than a problem of learning or somatic mediation. In the case of SMR training, the apparent increase in seizure threshold could be seen as resulting from the activation of motor inhibitory pathways which has in some way modified connectivity of these pathways. The investigators hypothesized that "... *overuse* might produce opposite changes in synaptic organization leading to decreased excitability and greater signal specificity [p. 511]." *Disuse* or denervation of neural components appears to result in increased excitability and less signal resolution. This hypothesis led them to pose the following question: "Could EEG biofeedback provide a means of selectively overstimulating discrete neural networks and thereby decrease excitability in the mechanisms that they subserved [p. 511]?" Thus was the stage set for testing the efficacy of SMR feedback in epileptic patients.

The physiological recording techniques were similar in principle to those used in cats. Cortical electrical activity was obtained via cup or needle electrodes in the area of the central cortex, and an active frequency filter was sharply tuned to respond to 12–14 Hz activity or the SMR. The feedback display consisted of two rows of 10 lamps. Each criterion SMR change rang a chime and advanced illumination of the top row of lamps. After 10 such feedbacks, a double chime occurred, and the bottom lamps advanced, thus providing a decimal count of total feedback accumulation. Other feedback modalities were added at successive phases of the research. One was a lamp which varied directly in intensity with the total amount of appropriate EEG activity. A rather ingenious reinforcement procedure was also devised. The SMR output operated a slide projector which presented pictures consisting of sequences depicting nature scenes or providing for completion of picture puzzles. Chains of attention holding, novel stimuli would appear to be ideal reinforcers in human learning studies.

Four epileptic patients were studied, one with a mixed seizure disorder (major motor and petit mal variant), a second with a major motor disorder (focal), a third with a mixed seizure disorder (petit mal variant), and a fourth with adult petit mal. Training sessions of 20 to 40 minutes with SMR feedback were repeated three times a week. With training, patients showed clinical improvement with fewer manifestations of grand mal and petit mal seizures than they had ever shown during their illness. As to the EEG, a progressive sustained decrease in abnormal low frequency discharge was observed. The patients showed a central cortical alpha rhythm (6–8 Hz) which diminished with training. When training was discontinued for a nine-week period, in three of the patients seizure activity returned within six weeks to the level prior to training. When training was recommenced, however, the patients improved rapidly. Aside from the direct clinical benefits of the training, Sterman reported positive behavioral side effects as well—increased general awareness, an improved ability to sustain attention, and better sleep.

Sterman has summarized some of the issues that need to be clarified in further research. For one, the SMR is difficult to observe in some subjects and occurs at much lower voltages in man than in cats. Is it in fact a meaningful EEG rhythm? Second, is it possible that factors other than the feedback account for the clinical improvement, such as sustained periods of relaxation, or a placebo effect facilitated by a positive doctor-patient relationship? Third, Sterman's hypothesis of neuronal reorganization implies that the training effects could be long-lasting, yet the return of the symptoms after discontinuation of training is not supportive. Kaplan (1973) described an unpublished study in which epileptic patients were rewarded for their dominant frequency within a range of 6–12 Hz with indications of marked improvement. Kaplan attributed the success to learned relaxation, rather than to learning of a specific EEG rhythm (see Miller, 1975). To settle some of these questions, additional studies are needed in which other EEG rhythms are fed back and reinforced or other behavioral procedures such as relaxation training are used as an alternative to SMR training. Neuropsychological testing procedures can be employed to help differentiate specific and nonspecific neural effects of training.

TENSION HEADACHE

One extremely common form of headache, tension headache, results from sustained contraction of the muscles in the face, scalp, and neck (Ostfeld, 1962). Although skeletal muscle tension is a voluntary response, patients suffering from tension headaches show a higher resting level of electromyographic activity of the frontalis than people not suffering from this problem (Sainsbury & Gibson, 1954). Consequently, Budzynski, Stoyva, Adler, and Mullaney (1973) reasoned that an EMG feedback-aided training procedure for frontalis activity might be useful in the management of this painful and common disorder. To test their hypothesis, these investigators designed and executed one of the most complete clinical studies on the application of biofeedback existing to date.

Eighteen patients complaining of frequent tension headaches were selected from a pool of volunteers after being screened for other physical and psychological disorders. These patients then underwent a two-week baseline period during which time daily self-report headache evaluations were kept and two EMG baselines were taken. All patients were then randomly assigned to one of three treatment conditions. The first group received EMG feedback for frontalis activity twice a week for eight weeks. In between sessions, patients in this group were encouraged to practice at home what they were learning in the laboratory. Patients in the second group were also seen twice a week. However, instead of receiving EMG feedback training, they were simply encouraged to relax during "treatment ses-

sions." In addition, they were presented with the taped auditory feedback of the patients in the first treatment group. This auditory stimulation was not presented as feedback, but rather as an aid to keep out intrusive thoughts during relaxation. As in the first condition, these patients were encouraged to practice relaxation at least every day in between sessions. The third group of patients served as a no-treatment control; these patients did not receive treatment of any sort but, like the other two groups, were simply asked to record daily headache activity. Data from the eight weeks of treatment and from a three-month follow-up confirm the hypothesis of the investigators. Patients receiving EMG training lowered their basal EMG below that of controls and showed a significantly reduced level of headache activity both during treatment and follow-up. An 18-month follow-up on a sample of these patients suggests that the EMG feedback training had a permanent therapeutic effect.

Despite the fact that this is one of the most well controlled of the clinical biofeedback studies, several difficulties typical of the problems encountered in biofeedback research are present in this work. The question of a proper control group is paramount. Budzynski et al. used two kinds of control groups, a no-treatment control and a sham feedback control. As the authors point out, true sham feedback could not be given because it would have easily been detected. As a compromise, subjects in the sham group were just told to listen to the feedback of other subjects because the clicking sound of the feedback "would be relaxing." It seems obvious that such a procedure would have no more credibility than telling the subjects that the feedback of others was their own. If indeed there is a placebo component to biofeedback treatment as Stroebel and Glueck (1973) have suggested, then perhaps giving feedback for an irrelevant response such as finger EMG, or, better still, frontalis increase instead of decrease, would serve as a more adequate control. This is certainly a difficult problem and will be discussed in greater detail later on.

In addition to this research, there are several other less systematic investigations which add some support to the notion that frontalis EMG feedback is useful in the treatment of tension headache. Raskin, Johnson, and Rondestvedt (1973) reported that after frontalis EMG training for chronic anxiety, patients who also had tension headaches reported that EMG training was of benefit to their headaches as well. Wickramasekera (1972) has also reported that the clinical use of EMG training is useful in the remediation of tension headaches.

MIGRAINE HEADACHE

Not to be confused with tension headaches, the migraine headache is an extremely debilitating disorder of complex, if not vague, etiology. The complete syndrome not only includes a severe, throbbing, often unilateral headache, but also various combinations of emotional irritability, nausea, photophobia, vomiting, constipation, and diarrhea (Beeson & McDermott, 1967). It is thought to be of vascular origin with pain resulting from extreme dilation of the cranial arteries (Schumacher & Wolff, 1941). However, the exact mechanism mediating the disturbance is unknown (Wolff, 1963). Biochemically, serotonin appears to be implicated in the syndrome in that blood levels of this substance, which acts as a vasoconstrictor, appear to drop immediately before an attack (Anthony, Hinterberger, & Lance, 1967). However, given the well known ability of emotional stimuli to trigger attacks, a more central, perhaps hypothalamic, mechanism is thought to be involved in the initiation of a migraine response (Herburg, 1967).

Against this rather confusing etiological background, it is not immediately apparent how biofeedback could be integrated into a treatment program for migraine. Sargent, Walters, and Green (1973) devised a be-havioral method based on digital skin temperature feedback using the following rationale. First, there have been numerous clinical reports of successful applications of autogenic exercises involving imagery of warmth in the limbs in relief of migraine headaches. Second, peripheral vasoconstriction is associated with sympathetic arousal, and an increase in peripheral blood flow as measured by increased digital skin temperature should reflect a decrease in sympathetic activity.

To test their hypothesis, Sargent et al. tried to assess the clinical efficacy of a temperature training procedure. Seventy-five patients suffering from migraine and other "mixed" disorders were asked to complete an extensive daily self-rating one month prior to the start of treatment. Each patient was then supplied with a "temperature trainer" which consisted of two thermistors, a bridge circuit, and a visual meter display. One thermistor was attached to midforehead and the other to the right index finger. Patients were also provided with a type-written list of autogenic phrases which they were to recite to themselves during training to facilitate learning. All patients were first seen at weekly intervals until they had learned to raise hand temperature, relative to forehead temperature, as displayed on the meter. After temperature control had been established, the temperature trainer was gradually withdrawn, and patients were encouraged to practice on their own without equipment. All patients kept their own records of headache frequency, severity, subjective ability to "feel warm," and "objective" temperature change. After 150 days, about 80% of the "true" migraine patients (42 out of the 75 had true migraine headaches) achieved some subjective measure of relief from their headaches. No group data are reported on the relationship between the ability to thermoregulate and the effectiveness of treatment.

Although there exist other reports of the efficacy of digital hyperthermia training in the treatment of migraine (Budzynski, 1974), unfortunately, there are no more systematic studies than that of Sargent et al. to evaluate the validity of the numerous clinical claims made for this technique. While the number of patients treated by these investigators is impressive, their study lacks the necessary controls for it to be a true experiment, and consequently must be evaluated as a collection of case studies.

Several important questions remain in the evaluation of digital thermoregulation techniques as a treatment of migraine. The hypothesis put forward by Sargent et al. is too vague to be tested by their study. The use of differential feedback between the hand and the forehead also needs further rationalization. To our knowledge, there is no systematic data on hand temperature during a migraine attack. Some data exists on forehead skin temperature, however. Lance and Anthony (1971) have demonstrated that in many migraine patients forehead skin temperature decreases on the affected side (about $1° C$) during the attack. Injections of serotonin were found to relieve the attack with forehead temperature returning to normal about 30 minutes after the pain began to ease. In light of this, it becomes increasingly unclear as to what is being accomplished by differential temperature feedback.

If the therapeutic effect of handwarming on migraine is merely some sort of reduction of general autonomic arousal, it is not at all clear why feedback for the difference between head and hand temperature should be the method of choice in achieving that goal. Other techniques, such as relaxation training, should prove equally effective if this were true. No systematic data exist on this point. Further, it must be noted that even the efficacy of handwarming per se remains to be demonstrated. Since no effort has been made to relate the ability to thermoregulate with treatment success, it is quite possible that the reported treatment effects can be attributed to the autogenic instructions used. In fact, Schultz and Luthe (1969) report that autogenic training alone

is effective in alleviating migraine. More careful investigations are required in order to separate fact from fiction in the evaluation of biofeedback procedures as a viable, novel treatment alternative for the problem of migraine headaches.

RAYNAUD'S DISEASE

Raynaud's *disease,* like essential hypertension, is a functional disorder of the cardiovascular system involving no observable organic pathology in its early stages. Its symptoms consist of intermittent, bilateral vasospasms of the hands, feet, and, rarely, the face, which can be elicited by cold stimulation and/or emotional stress. During an attack, the affected area usually goes through a three-stage color change, first blanching, then turning cyanotic blue, and finally becoming bright red as the spasm is relieved and reactive hyperemia sets in. When this syndrome results secondarily from an identifiable pathological process, it is known as Raynaud's *phenomenon* (Fairbairn, Juergens, & Spittell, 1972).

The first modern-day report of voluntary vasomotor control came from the USSR, where Lisina (1958) was able to demonstrate that subjects could learn to increase the blood flow in their arms if allowed to watch their plethysmographic record. Snyder and Noble (1968), using a dichtomous feedback procedure, were able to train subjects in vasoconstriction of the fingers independent of changes in heart rate, finger movement, muscle tension, or respiration. Volow and Hein (1972), using analogue and discrete feedback, trained subjects both to increase and decrease blood flow in their fingers. They reported, however, that constriction seemed to be easier to learn than dilation. Taub and Emurian (1972) trained subjects to increase or decrease the skin temperature of their hands by an analogue feedback method, while Roberts, Schuler, Bacon, and Zimmerman (1974) have been able to train subjects to differentially raise and lower skin temperature in the two hands. Despite these encouraging data, there have been some recent unpublished reports of negative results. Surwit and Shapiro (1974) did not find significant skin temperature learning both with and without autogenic-like instruction in a one-session study, while Lynch, Hama, Kohn, and Miller (1974) have been unable to replicate the work of either Roberts or Taub and Emurian. Lynch, however, has found reason to believe that skin temperature learning is possible in some subjects but points out that the exact variables necessary to reliably reproduce this phenomenon are not known.

Surwit (1973) recently reviewed four cases in which biofeedback was successfully employed as the major mode of treatment of Raynaud's disease or Raynaud's phenomenon. Although these four reports involve the implementation of somewhat different methods and are probably not all dealing with Raynaud's disease per se, they have in common one essential point; in each case, patients reported achieving control of a Raynaud's symptom they previously thought to be involuntary. The first of these cases involved a patient treated for over a year at the Allen Memorial Institute of McGill University. Upon referral, the patient, a 21-year-old female, had been suffering from Raynaud's disease for about five years and had both cervical and lumbar sympathectomies. Training consisted of a temperature feedback procedure. A sensitive thermistor was mounted on the patient's left hand. If there was a net increase in temperature in excess of 0.1° C, the patient was given feedback. This consisted of a bell, a flashing light, and an increment in a cumulative graph displayed on a videoscope. The therapist would then verbally reinforce the patient for her success. Each session consisted of three 10-minute trials separated by 5- or 10-minute rest periods. Fourteen sessions were administered over a three-week period after which time the patient stopped treatment for one month to go on vacation. Upon her return, sessions were administered twice a week and consisted of two 10-minute

trials for each hand. This mode of therapy lasted for four months and was supplemented by counseling and assertive training (Wolpe, 1958) for family problems. All therapy was then discontinued for one month after which feedback training was resumed at weekly intervals for the next six months. Since the beginning of training, this patient managed to increase her basal hand temperature (both hands) from an average of 23° C to 26.6° C. She no longer required elaborate protective garments for the Montreal winter and markedly decreased the number of Raynaud's attacks she experienced.

Two other investigators employed temperature feedback in the treatment of Raynaud's phenomenon or Raynaud's disease. Peper (personal communication) reported treating a 50-year-old woman who suffered from what appeared to be Raynaud's disease for about 30 years. As in the previous case report, this patient was first instructed in relaxation and autogenic techniques before the onset of biofeedback training. Biofeedback training, however, followed a different procedure. Thermistors were placed on both the temporal artery and on the finger of one hand. The net difference between the readings of these two thermistors was used to drive an analogue auditory feedback system. That is, the patient received an auditory signal which varied directly with the temperature difference between the reference thermistor placed on the temporal artery and the thermistor on her finger. The patient was instructed in the use of the auditory feedback device and was told to practice with it twice a day for 10 minutes. After a month of training, the patient's basal skin temperature, as measured on the finger tip, increased from 75° to 85° F. In addition, she reported that for the first time in 30 years she could hold on to the cold steering wheel of her car without gloves. No systematic follow-up data are available.

Working with a similar technique, Jacobson, Hackett, Surman, and Silverberg (1973) have reported success in the alleviation of Raynaud's-like symptoms· in a 31-year-old male. The patient experienced these symptoms for four years and claimed they were increasing in severity during the year preceding treatment. The patient was first trained in autohypnosis for relaxation and then given four sessions of differential temperature feedback like that employed by Peper. After this brief treatment, the patient was able to voluntarily produce increases in skin temperature of up to 4.2° C, even outside the feedback situation. Corresponding color changes, suggesting increased blood flow, were also observed. As in the case reported by Peper, the patient reported that for the first time in years he was able to grasp very cold objects without triggering a vasospasmodic attack. Seven and a half months after treatment, the patient reported continued relief from Raynaud's symptoms.

Finally, Shapiro and Schwartz (1972) reported the successful application of biofeedback for a related circulatory problem. Their patient was a 60-year-old man who complained of chronic sensations of cold in his hands and feet for two years. Although no signs of vascular disease or specific reaction to cold were found by the examining physician, this patient did complain of increased difficulty in winter months as found in Raynaud's disease. A treatment procedure was devised by using a measure of digital blood volume, the DC component of a photoplethysmograph, for feedback. A photoplethysmograph transducer was attached to the patient's large toe of each foot. Feedback training was conducted for 30-minute sessions four times a week for three weeks. At first, feedback was given for increases in blood volume in the left toe (where he experienced the most severe discomfort), and later training was done for increases in blood volume in the right toe. One month later, five additional sessions were administered following the same procedure. Although the patient was given no direct autogenic instructions, he reported that he experienced the most success in increasing his blood flow while imagining experiencing warmth. Through the surreptitiously

arrived at strategy, this patient obtained much relief and showed control of his symptoms for approximately a year. Recently he has requested some further training because he felt he was losing the control he experienced earlier. Unfortunately, the same procedure failed to produce positive results with a second patient. This woman had more severe manifestations of vasospasms and was very ambivalent about this mode of treatment. Upon mutual agreement, treatment was terminated after approximately 10 sessions because of lack of progress and sufficient motivation. More recently, Taub, Emurian, and Howell (1974) reported that several Raynaud's patients have been able to demonstrate the same amount of skin temperature control as is found in normals.

Persuasive though these reports are, it would be premature to conclude that biofeedback was the sole therapeutic agent responsible for improvement. In each case, relaxation and/or autogenic imagery were used by or suggested to the subject in the process of training. In addition, the large amount of attention given to each patient coupled with the enthusiasm of the therapists for this new treatment may have given these procedures considerable placebo value. It is noteworthy, however, that in two cases (Jacobson et al., 1973; Surwit, 1973) patients specifically reported that they first had to abandon relaxation and autogenic strategies in order to control the feedback. As in many biofeedback studies of physiological systems, these patients could not verbalize what, if any, strategy they used to control blood flow. Nevertheless, it is clear that carefully controlled investigations must precede any conclusion about the exact contribution biofeedback can provide in the treatment of Raynaud's disease and other peripheral vascular disorders.

The optimal physiological measures to use in a biofeedback treatment for Raynaud's disease would, of course, depend upon the precise physiological mechanism involved in the disorder. Unfortunately, Raynaud's disease, like essential hypertension, is by definition of unknown etiology. Though it is known that during a spasm blood is initially absent in the capillaries (Lewis, 1949), it is not known whether the spasm occurs at the arterial, arteriolar, or capillary level (Willerson, Thompson, Hookman, Herdt, & Decker, 1970). Langer and Croccel (1960) have suggested that arteriovenous anastomoses might play a central role in Raynaud's disease, shunting the blood away from the outermost layers of the skin during an attack. If indeed this is true, then skin temperature would not be the measure of choice in a biofeedback treatment procedure. Rapid flow through the arteriovenous anastomoses might heat the finger but leave the affected layers deprived of blood. Indeed, one of the patients discussed in Surwit (1973) reported persistent pain even after her temperature had risen to normal ranges, confirming the earlier observations of Mittlemann and Wolff (1939). If arteriovenous shunting is involved in the production of Raynaud's disease, then a photoplethysmographic measure of surface blood volume might be a better response for feedback than skin temperature in the treatment of this vascular problem.

In evaluating the place of biofeedback in the treatment of Raynaud's disease, one must consider the record of conventional treatments now available. Medical-pharmacological remedies have not been particularly effective in relieving this disorder (Fairbairn et al., 1972). Sympathectomy seems to have been equally unreliable, having the added disadvantage of permanent side effects (Ruch, Patton, Woodbury, & Towe, 1965). It might therefore be preferable to attempt biofeedback in lieu of surgery when more conservative techniques have failed.

MUSCULAR REHABILITATION

Although striate muscle is normally considered to be under "voluntary" control, there are instances when, through accident,

disease, or spasm, responses in this type of muscle seem as difficult for a subject to control as those of smooth muscles. The need for certain people to have to learn to relax perhaps best illustrates this point. Jacobson (1964) has developed a variety of techniques designed for each specific muscle group in order to treat "anxiety and tension." Modifications of this technique (e.g., Wolpe & Lazarus, 1966) are commonly employed in behavior therapy treatments. Electromyograph feedback has been shown useful in training patients with tension headaches to relax their scalp muscles (Budzynski et al., 1973). Hefferline (1962) demonstrated that subjects could learn to control extremely small muscle groups with the aid of feedback and reinforcement, even if the subject himself was not aware that learning was taking place! Through the use of small implanted wire electrodes, Basmajian (1972) has trained normal subjects to control *single motor units*. Within a relatively short period of time, most normal subjects are reported to achieve excellent control of both frequency and intensity of motor unit activity, while some talented subjects even demonstrate rhythm in trained units.

However, as is often the case, clinical application of this technique seems to have preceded much of the basic research. As early as 1955, Alberto Marinacci had reported that direct electromyographic feedback was a useful technique in muscular rehabilitation following poliomyelitis. More recently, Marinacci (1973) has suggested that EMG training might be useful in a range of cases where some anatomical transmission pathways are available but not being used. This might occur in paralysis resulting from trauma causing temporary dysfunction, temporary blocking of pathways due to local edema, severe pain resulting in long-lasting immobility and muscle atrophy, nerve lesions where regeneration has taken place but function is still absent, cases in which temporary dysfunction has led to substitution of function by adjacent muscle groups which continues after function returns in the afflicted area, or excessive neuromuscular transmission leading to hypertonia. In cases of paresis and paralysis, Marinacci (1973) describes the following procedure, Needle electrodes are inserted into a healthy muscle, and the patient is asked to voluntarily flex it. The patient's attention is then drawn to an audio analogue (clicks) of the EMG which varies with the force of voluntary movement. Following this, the procedure is repeated in disabled muscle. Training progresses from a complete failure of the muscle to transmit impulses, to the emission of reflexive impulses, to the gradual establishment of full voluntary control.

Electromyographic feedback has also proven useful in training muscles in spasm to relax. Jacobs and Felton (1969) carried out a controlled study to assess the utility of EMG feedback in reducing injury-induced muscle tension. Fourteen normal women and 14 women with injuries of the trapezius muscle served as subjects. The first 10 subjects in each group received instruction to relax followed by visual EMG feedback trials. All subjects showed a marked reduction of EMG activity only after feedback. The injured subjects took slightly longer to learn to relax, but eventually reached the same level of relaxation as did the normal subjects. To control for practice incurred in the no-feedback condition, the remaining four normal and four injured subjects were given only feedback training. They learned to relax the trapezius muscle to the same degree as was evidenced in the first two groups.

Recently, Brudny, Grynbaum, and Korein (1974) successfully employed EMG feedback in treating patients with spastic torticollis. Their treatment consisted of two stages. First, patients were trained, using EMG feedback to relax the spasm. As treatment progressed, training was also instituted to *increase* the tension in the atrophied muscle group on the side contralateral to the spasm. As practice resulted

in a normal neck position, training visits were gradually phased out. Brudny et al. also reported EMG feedback as useful in the treatment of spastic paralysis resulting from strokes. Marinacci and Horande (1960) and Amato, Hermsmeyer, and Kleinman (1973) have also found EMG feedback useful in the treatment of hypertonia.

Another problem involving excessive muscle tension is that of bruxism, or chronic teeth clenching. Bruxism is stress related, often occurs without the patient being aware of it, and can cause severe oral problems if left untreated (Thomas, Tiber, & Schireson, 1973; Yemm, 1969a; Yemm, 1969b). Solberg and Rugh (1972) developed a small portable EMG feedback device which could be worn during the day by patients to signal periods of excessive masseter muscle tension. Rugh and Solberg (1974) reported that 10 out of 15 patients suffering from temperomandibular joint pain resulting from bruxing showed significant improvement after wearing the device from four to seven days. These patients reported an increased awareness of clenching and were able to identify more clearly the stimulus situation which provoked bruxing for them.

ASTHMA

Asthma is a disorder in which the mucous membranes of the trachea and/or bronchi swell up and restrict the flow of air to the lungs. This response can come in reaction to a variety of allergens and can be exacerbated by emotional and physical stress. Using an allergen as an unconditioned stimulus, it has been demonstrated that the asthmatic reaction can be conditioned to occur to once-neutral stimuli following a simple classical conditioning procedure (Ottenberg, Stein, Lewis, & Hamilton, 1958). In light of this ability of the reaction to be learned, there is good reason to assume the possibility of behavioral components in the development of some asthmatic conditions. Nevertheless, as in the case of other disorders, a behavioral etiology is not necessary in devising a successful behavioral treatment.

Perhaps because asthmatic attacks are commonly thought to be emotion-related (Dunbar, 1943) and can be objectively measured, the behavioral literature contains a variety of conventional behavior therapy approaches to this problem as well as more recent methods employing biofeedback. The first report of a successful behavioral treatment of an asthmatic was by Walton (1960). Working empirically, Walton successfully used assertive training (Wolpe, 1958) for a patient whose asthmatic reactions seemed to occur most frequently when the patient had difficulty expressing aggression. Moore (1965) carried out a controlled study in which she compared systematic desensitization (Wolpe, 1958) with relaxation and suggestion and relaxation alone using subjects as their own controls. She found that while all methods produced subjective reports of improvement, only systematic desensitization produced objective improvement in respiratory function. Sargeant and Yorkston (1969) also reported the successful application of systematic desensitization in the treatment of bronchial asthma.

More recent evidence seems to suggest that, contrary to Moore's findings, relaxation training alone is effective in treating asthma. Alexander, Miklich and Hershkoff (1972) demonstrated that peak expiratory flow rates were increased in children trained in progressive relaxation as compared to children who were asked to sit quietly for a comparable period of time. In a second study, Alexander (1972) replicated the results of Alexander et al., and through the use of a questionnaire technique concluded that anxiety changes were not mediating the therapeutic effect. It was found, however, that subjects whose asthmatic attacks tended to be emotionally related benefited more from relaxation

training than other treated children. Although the overall treatment effect was about a 10% increase in peak expiratory flow rate, the effect reached about 35% in the top third of the sample. Alexander concluded that relaxation could therefore be a clinically useful technique if patients were carefully screened by an interview for emotional asthma precipitating factors. Sirota and Mahoney (1974) also found relaxation training to be of benefit in the treatment of asthma. They described a case in which a patient was taught to abort her asthma attacks and decrease her use of a portable nebulizer by relaxing on cue.

In addition to the promising results obtained with conventional behavioral techniques, there are some indications that direct biofeedback for respiratory resistance can also be used to control asthma. Levenson, Manuck, Strupp, Blackwood, and Snell (1974) devised a technique in which respiratory resistance is measured on each breath, quantified, and fed back to the subject via a digital display. Preliminary data indicate that learned control of airway resistance established in this manner can be of therapeutic benefit in the treatment of asthma.

PAIN

Pain is an extremely complex and interesting sensory phenomenon. It can occur in the absence of apparent stimulation, and it can fail to occur even after extensive tissue damage (Melzack, 1973). In that pain seems to be extremely susceptible to attentional shifts and expectancies (Barber, 1970), it seems reasonable that any technique which could influence attention might be beneficial for people experiencing severe pain.

Gannon and Sternbach (1971) reasoned that since meditative states have been shown to coincide with increased EEG alpha activity, and that since alpha activity could be increased with feedback (Kamiya,

1969), feedback training for alpha enhancement might be useful in the treatment of pain. They reported treating one patient who suffered from headaches resulting from an injury. After teaching the patient to increase occipital alpha activity with eyes open and closed, the patient reported that he was able to prevent some headache from occurring by inducing alpha, but was not able to abort pain once the headache began.

Melzack and Perry (personal communication) explored the use of alpha feedback training more systematically. Patients suffering from severe clinical pain received one of three treatments: alpha feedback training, hypnotic suggestion, and alpha feedback and hypnosis in combination. Only the group receiving both alpha feedback and hypnosis together showed a significant reduction in pain as measured by the McGill pain questionnaire. These authors concluded that suggestion plays a major role in determining whether or not alpha training will have an ameliorative effect on pain.

Control of EEG is not the only method in which biofeedback has been shown to be useful in affecting the perception of pain. Sirota et al. (1974) attempted to control directly the visceral components of emotional reactions to pain by manipulating heart rate through feedback. These investigators hypothesized that since heart rate control seems to affect fear in animals (DiCara & Weiss, 1969) and heart rate is closely associated with human fear (Lang, Rice, & Sternbach, 1972), learned control of heart rate should affect human performance in an experimental fear situation. Twenty female subjects were given feedback and reward for either heart rate increases or decreases. Half of the 72 15-second training trials were followed by an electric shock. Warning lights allowed the subjects to differentiate shock from non-shock trials. Voluntary reduction of heart rate was found to lead to a relative reduction in the perceived aversiveness of the shock, particularly for those subjects who reported experiencing cardiac reactions to fear situations in daily life. This novel application of biofeedback has provided a mechanism through which the old James-Lange (James, 1890) theory of emotion might be employed for therapeutic benefit.

MALE SEXUAL RESPONSE

Penile tumescence is normally thought to be a reflexive spinal response produced by innervation of the parasympathetic vasodilator fibers emanating from the sacral cord (Weiss, 1972). However, as has been the case with the other autonomic responses discussed so far, recent evidence has suggested that penile tumescence can be brought under the control of both external contingencies and the "volition" of the subject. Laws and Rubin (1969) demonstrated that subjects could voluntarily partially suppress erections to an erotic film and produce partial erections on demand without external stimulation or manipulation. Henson and Rubin (1971) replicated the suppression results using taped verbal erotic stimuli which minimized the possibility that subjects were using antagonistic cognitive strategies to suppress erections.

More recently, Rosen (1973) has demonstrated that direct feedback for penile tumescence was more effective than instructions alone in suppressing erections elicited by tape recorded erotic stimuli. It is therefore apparent that aversion therapy techniques (e.g., Bancroft, 1966; Bancroft, 1971; Rachman & Teasdale, 1969) are not necessary in erection suppression paradigms for the treatment of deviant sexual responses.

Feedback and reinforcement have also been found to be useful in the production of erection. Quinn, Harbison, and McAllister (1970) used iced lime to reinforce heterosexually stimulated penile tumescence in a patient who had been water deprived for 18 hours. Although this patient had been given prior aversion training for homosexual arousal, he showed no response to female stimuli before training. Interestingly, increases in penile tumescence in response to female nude pictures were accompanied by verbal expression of increased heterosexual interest. A controlled study on feedback-induced tumescence was carried out by Rosen, Shapiro, and Schwartz (1974). These investigators gave normal subjects instructions to develop erections without external stimulation during cued periods. A variable intensity light provided half of the subjects with analogue feedback of tumescence while the other half received no feedback. All subjects received monetary bonuses for increase in tumescence. While all subjects showed substantial ability to increase tumescence, analogue feedback seemed to increase performance. Despite these promising results, Rosen (1974) cautions against therapists using biofeedback in lieu of couples counselling for treatment of sexual dysfunctions because most cases of erectile failure seem to involve crucial relationship factors.

CONTRACEPTION

French, Leeb, and Fahrion (1974) have explored a novel method of contraception using biofeedback. Several male subjects, first trained in hand temperature control, were then trained in producing scrotal hyperthermia utilizing temperature feedback from the scrotal sac. Regular training sessions were found to produce a marked reduction in viable sperm production which was reversible when training was discontinued. Scrotal hyperthermia training without prior hand temperature training, however, was not found to be effective in reducing sperm output. While this application of biofeedback technology is dramatic, the data available to date are preliminary and cannot be used as a basis for application as a means of contraception. Data need to be collected on the long-term effect of

such training in order to assure that the procedure is both safe and practical.

Limitations and Pitfalls of Clinical Application

The preceding review has suggested that it now seems possible to consider using behavioral techniques in the treatment of a wide variety of physiological disorders. Specifically, there is tentative evidence that direct biofeedback can help in the remediation of physical problems once treatable only by somatic therapy. Much research needs to be done before biofeedback can be advocated as a viable treatment for any disorder. In addition to the question of efficacy there are a host of practical issues which need to be dealt with in evaluating the possible place of biofeedback in the treatment of disease.

The first and perhaps most obvious question of practical concern in the evaluation of biofeedback as a clinical tool is the question of economy. How much time and effort, on the part of both the patient and the practitioner, is needed to obtain a clinically useful result? Even if biofeedback techniques can be shown to be therapeutically effective, what patient would opt for a costly time consuming training course if equal therapeutic benefit could be obtained from a pill? It is true that there are no medications which are completely effective for Raynaud's disease, tension headache, and cardiac arrythmias. However, in many cases medication can be a simple, effective, and painless way to remedy hypertension, epilepsy, and migraine headaches. Unless the side effects of the medication are serious or the efficacy of biofeedback is shown to be superior to that of medication, it seems unlikely that biofeedback will be considered as a treatment of choice.

A related issue has to do with patient motivation. Several articles (e.g., Schwartz, 1973; Schwartz & Shapiro, 1973; Shapiro & Schwartz, 1972; Surwit, 1973) have commented on the importance of patient motivation in any biofeedback treatment program. It is not sufficient to assume that feedback indicating therapeutic improvement will, in and of itself, act as reinforcer and maintain the persistent practice required to gain therapeutic benefit. Indeed, those who have used biofeedback clinically have noted this problem. In one case, Surwit (1973) reported that a patient who had made a long trip to receive biofeedback training complained of being bored during the training sessions and made no progress.

One of the reasons for this problem has been elaborated by Shapiro and Schwartz (1972). Many of the disorders to which biofeedback might be applied have no short-term aversive consequences. Hypertension works its insidious destruction within the cardiovascular system without causing any serious discomfort to the patient. By the time a painful heart attack occurs it is often too late to correct the damage. It is only the knowledge that the patient has hypertension in conjunction with the knowledge that this disorder is not good for him that provides motivation to undergo treatment. However, in light of the fact that most hypertensive patients will not even take their medication regularly, it becomes rather doubtful if biofeedback training requiring long periods of practice will prove useful for most patients. Similar problems can be seen for any disorder in which the practice of biofeedback is not immediately reinforcing. Conversely, one might expect biofeedback treatments to be most appropriate for disorders such as tension headaches where training can lead to immediate relief from pain. Unfortunately, no data exist on the comparative effectiveness of biofeedback in treating disorders such as hypertension as opposed to tension headache.

A second motivational problem encountered in the clinical application of biofeedback is that the symptom itself may be reinforcing for the patient. In other words, the disorder may have secondary gain. A striking example of this was reported by Surwit (1973). A patient who was involved in intensive biofeedback treatment for Raynaud's disease spontaneously expressed her ambivalence of "giving up" her illness because she did not know how to relate to people without it. She was aware of using her Raynaud's disease as an excuse for a poor social life and dependent relationship with her mother. In this case social training was carried out to attempt to remedy the problem. Patients suffering from psychosomatic illnesses often use their well known sensitivity to emotional situations to manipulate others (Lachman, 1972). A therapy based on "voluntary control" would tend to undermine their manipulations and consequently might not be seen as desirable by the patient. Although early models of behavior therapy tended to ignore the more subtle contingencies implicit in some behavioral problems, more recent writers are taking them into account (e.g., Kraft, 1972; Lazarus, 1971). In that some of these contingencies might not be known to the patient explicitly, they may be considered unconscious. A behavioral therapy designed to treat a disorder supported by secondary gain would therefore have to include techniques aimed at making up any social deficit left by the removal of the symptom. These might include setting up family contingencies and/or working on alternative means of social interaction. When the patient himself does not see the need for such additional procedures, an insight-oriented approach may be called for as a first step.

A third possible area of motivational difficulty may arise from other behaviors strongly entrenched in the patient's repertoire which are in conflict with the aim of therapy. This is best illustrated in a case discussed by Schwartz (1973). A patient was treated for essential hypertension and a week of treatment would lower his blood pressure by as much as 20 mmHg. Over the weekend his pressure would become elevated again. The difficulty turned out to be that the patient liked to gamble at the race track on weekends and persisted in doing so despite the fact that such activities were countertherapeutic. This last point is extremely important. There is good evidence that certain schedules of reinforcement can induce ulcers and hypertension in normal animals (Benson et al., 1969; Benson, Herd, Morse, & Kelleher, 1970; Brady, 1958; Harris et al., 1973). It would seem futile to attempt to treat a disorder by biofeedback unless work were also done on analyzing and correcting contingencies that may be aggravating the problem.

An issue closely related to motivation and equally important in the successful application of biofeedback techniques is transfer of training. It is often all too easy to forget, even for psychologists, that learning techniques cannot be administered the way most medical treatments can. There is no reason to believe that biofeedback, like radiation therapy and diathermy, can be expected to produce sustained effects outside the treatment session. It is completely logical that a patient may show perfect control over his problem during a feedback session and no control at home. In basic research in normal subjects, some investigators have explored the use of intermittent reinforcement schedules as an aid to generalization (Greene, 1966; Shapiro & Crider, 1967; Shapiro and Watanabe, 1971), but the evidence is too scanty to conclude that partial reinforcement increases resistance to extinction in the case of visceral responses. Weiss and Engel (1971) in their study of the control of premature ventricular contractions phased the feedback out gradually, making it available all the time at first, then one minute on and one minute off, then one on and three off, and finally one on and seven off. The purpose of the procedure was to wean the patient from the feedback and also enable the patient to become more aware of his arrhythmia through his own sensations rather than through the feedback. Hefferline and Bruno (1971) de-

scribed a similar technique of slowly fading out the feedback as a means of transferring external to internal control. There is also evidence for the short-term maintenance of learned control of diastolic pressure (Shapiro et al., 1972b), but the need is great for comprehensive research on extinction processes and on self-control without feedback in autonomic learning.

A related but more complex issue concerns the need of patients to control their reactivity to stressful stimuli or situations. In most cases, biofeedback procedures are applied in resting, nonstimulating laboratory settings. Will the patient be able to transfer this training to the relevant situations in everyday life? Sirota et al. (1974) attempted to explore the effects of feedback assisted voluntary control of heart rate to facilitate adaptation to noxious events. An earlier study (Shapiro, Schwartz, Nelson, Shnidman, & Silverman, 1972) combined skin resistance feedback and reinforcement with a variant of desensitization procedure in attempting to facilitate adaptation of phobic subjects to the feared stimuli (snakes). The methodology of this research follows from several studies indicating that discrete electrodermal responses to stimuli in human subjects can be relatively increased or decreased by means of reinforcement for the appropriate response, and that these changes may have consequences for performance related to these stimuli (Kimmel, Pendergrass, & Kimmel, 1967; Shnidman, 1969; Shnidman, 1970; Shnidman & Shapiro, 1971).

In the Sirota study, in anticipation of receiving noxious electrical stimulation, subjects learned to control their heart rate when provided with external heart rate feedback and reward for appropriate changes. In this study, subjects were also informed about the actual physiological response required for reward. The results showed that voluntary slowing of heart rate led to a relative reduction in the perceived aversiveness of the noxious stimuli, particularly for those subjects who reported experiencing cardiac reactions to fear situations in their daily life. Sirota et al. concluded:

> Taken together, the results support the general conclusion that direct feedback control of autonomic functions which are appropriate for given subjects in terms of their normal fear responding and/or whose relevance for fear has been instructionally induced may possibly be used in systematic desensitization to inhibit anxiety from occurring in response to phobic stimuli and as an adjunct to other therapeutic techniques for the prevention and reduction of anxiety and fear reactions [1974, p. 266].

Procedures such as these should be studied to increase the potential of transfer of learned control to relevant situations for the individual. In the case of different psychosomatic disorders, to the extent that they involve behavioral and physiological reaction patterns specific to certain types of eliciting stimuli or situations, a physiological desensitization procedure can be designed accordingly.

In addition to motivation, Shapiro and Schwartz (1972) have pointed out that patient characteristics must also be considered in determining the feasibility of biofeedback as a treatment. Because most clinical and experimental work on biofeedback has been done with highly educated, motivated individuals, it is presently unclear how the variables of intelligence, socioeconomic status, and overall adjustment are related to treatment outcome. Until more data shed light on these questions, therapists should be cognizant of the particular characteristics of the population from which successful behavior therapy patients have been drawn.

Because biofeedback involves the treatment of disease, it is one area of psychological practice where the medical model of illness cannot be dismissed. Although many physical disorders can be exacerbated by emotional and environmental variables, most of them have a distinct physical etiology and may represent the "symptom" of a more profound physiological dysfunction. Also, certain disorders which have resulted in permanent destruction and/or alteration of tissue may not be amenable to a behavioral treatment. In many cases, it is conceivable that medication should be used as a valuable concomitant to biofeedback. Engel and Bleecker (1974) have recently argued that one can treat cardiac arrhythmias as isolated symptoms. However, it is probably wise to employ an eclectic strategy in determining the treatment of any physiological disorder. As Pinkerton (1973) aptly remarked, ". . . no single factor is of overriding importance in symptom production [in psychosomatic illness]. The clinical outcome is always determined by a composite etiological sequence, so that the key to successful management lies in correctly evaluating each factor's importance in any given case [p. 462]."

In any event it is clearly not up to the psychologist alone to decide how biofeedback will contribute to the treatment of a physical problem. Consequently, biofeedback should be used clinically only after a competent medical diagnosis has been made and the examining physician has decided that biofeedback may be valuable. Patients coming directly to psychologists for biofeedback or other behavioral treatments of a physical disorder should be referred first to a medical specialist for a thorough examination and work-up. The need for medical participation in any biofeedback case is both an ethical and legal responsibility of the psychological practitioner. Conversely, it is also the ethical responsibility of a physician who wishes to employ biofeedback in treatment to consult with a psychologist for the behavioral aspects of the proposed therapy. Medical training usually does not provide the in-depth knowledge of behavioral variables of which the practitioner must be cognizant in order for training to be successful. Therefore, the use of biofeedback in therapy for various physiological disorders should be a collaborative endeavor involving both medical and behavioral specialists.

Theoretical and Research Issues

FEEDBACK VERSUS REWARD

Early reports of learned voluntary control of visceral responses did not distinguish between operant conditioning and biofeedback in the development of autonomic learning (e.g., Crider et al., 1966; Engel & Hansen, 1966; Shapiro et al., 1969). Though the term biofeedback seems to be taking priority in describing human studies in this area, the two terms are still often used interchangeably (Shapiro et al., 1972). That the label of biofeedback is restricted to human experiments often implies a qualitative difference between the human and animal work on the control of autonomic functions. Lang (1974) has suggested that the greater intellectual capacities of the human subject and the loosely controlled situations in which he is tested change the learning situation to such an extent that the operant conditioning paradigm is no longer an adequate description of how human visceral learning takes place. He sees the theoretical models developed for human skills learning (e.g., Bilodeau, 1969) as perhaps more appropriate. In such models, feedback is seen more as information than reinforcement, and motivation due to instructional set is considered more important than some deprivation-induced drive. What then is the best way to conceptualize biofeedback training? Unfortunately, a direct answer to this question demands specific investigations designed to separate the relative reward components from the information gained from biofeedback training. With the exception of a few studies (Brener, 1974; Lang, 1974), such data do not exist. However, there are data from both human and animal experiments which may help shed light on this issue.

According to Annett (1969), Thorndike (1933) was perhaps the first to deal with the distinction between reward and information. His argument was that feedback, while not an appetitive reinforcer, triggered off an "OK reaction" which was the mental equivalent of a physical reinforcer. After all, information only has meaning insofar as it relates to the goal at hand. This concept was formally extended by Hull (1951) who postulated the existence of secondary reinforcers. In his behavioral scheme, secondary reinforcers were those stimuli whose power came from a close association with primary drive reduction. Those who follow a strictly instrumental model of automatic learning consider feedback a secondary reinforcer. This position, combined with the Skinnerian rule of defining reinforcement operationally, makes it seem futile to try to distinguish the reinforcing from the informative value of a stimulus.

However, research on information feedback in human skills learning has uncovered certain very distinct differences between the operation of feedback and reinforcement. Bilodeau (1969), in listing key variables in the effects of feedback upon behavior, has pointed out that the optimal timing relationship between feedback and response is just opposite from what we would expect if feedback were acting as a reinforcer. While reinforcement is most effective the closer it occurs in time to the preceding response, feedback operates best the closer it occurs to the next response. That is, in the feedback information conception, the delay from feedback to the next response is more crucial than the delay from response to feedback (reinforcer).

Although this appears to be the most irreconcilable point between feedback and reinforcement formulations, other differences in the two schemes occur. Whereas the efficacy of reinforcement can be seen as dependent upon the schedule with which it is applied, Bilodeau sees frequency as the overriding variable affecting the potency of feedback. In addition to absolute frequency of feedback, the *scale grain* or detail of feedback is also considered a crucial variable in the learning of skills. This last, perhaps more than any other, points out one essential conceptual difference between feedback and reinforcement; that is, feedback contains *information* which provides response-correcting properties as well as confirmation of correct performance. The importance of the cuelike nature of biological feedback was suggested in one of the earliest studies (Lisina, 1958) in which it was found that avoidance conditioning of vasodilation was effective only when subjects were able to see their own polygraph tracings. More recently, Brener (1974) showed that subjects allowed to listen passively to their own analog heart rate feedback did better than controls who listened to someone else's feedback when later tested on a heart rate control task. Lang and Twentyman (1974) demonstrated that subjects receiving detailed analog feedback for heart rate did better in controlling heart rate than those receiving simple binary right-wrong information, although Shapiro et al. (1970b) found no differences between auditory analog and auditory binary heart rate feedback.

The notion that feedback and reinforcement differ in the functions they serve can be further elucidated by studies which have directly attempted to manipulate reward independent of feedback. The earliest of these studies (Bunch, 1928) dealt with a problem of human motor learning. In this investigation, it was shown that subjects shocked for entering a blind alley learned a Carr stylus maze faster than unshocked subjects. Bernard and Gilbert (1941) in a similar study, though not finding a difference in learning rate, did show a decrease of errors in a shocked group. Bahrick, Fitts, and Rankin (1952) demonstrated that the knowledge of contingent reward improved the performance of subjects on perceptual tasks.

Research on hyperactive children also sheds some light on this issue. Hyperactive children, like normals, show an increased difficulty in learning concept attainment tasks when reinforcement is given on a partial schedule. However, for hyperactive children the difficulty is more severe. In order to determine whether this deficit is due to reduced informational versus motivational properties of partial reinforcement conditions, Parry (1973) placed a sample of hyperactive children in one of three reinforcement conditions. The first group received a black marble (which could be exchanged for money) for correct responses in a concept attainment task. The second group was told that they would receive a marble for every correct response but only half of the marbles (the black ones) were exchangeable for money. The last group received black marbles on a partial schedule (all exchangeable for money). Subjects in groups 2 and 3 did significantly poorer than those in group 1, demonstrating that reinforcement was more important than feedback in this concept attainment task.

From this brief summary, it would appear that there are two competing models of learning, the reinforcement or instrumental model and the feedback or informational model. In comparing the two, Annett (1969) concluded that the feedback model is the more powerful of the two and ultimately can be used to explain all behavior. However, feedback and reinforcement do not appear to be mutually exclusive explanations, nor must they be viewed as totally independent phenomena. Rather, feedback seems to be necessary for a subtle response to be learned, while reinforcement affects performance. It appears as though those working in the area of feedback and information have concentrated most of their attention on *habit development*, while those interested in reinforcement and motivation have concerned themselves mainly with *habit maintenance*. Operant conditioners studying reinforcement and schedule effects have normally employed responses already in the subject's repertoire. These responses, being usually skeletal responses, provide so much interoceptive feedback that additional feedback is not required or employed in training. Shaping or developing the response is normally only a technical consideration, whereas for the feedback researchers it is the main focus of their attention.

At this point, let us integrate the feedback and reinforcement models as applied to autonomic response learning. Autonomic and other so-called involuntary responses normally provide little in the way of obvious or conscious interoceptive stimulation and control of these responses is not normally within the repertoire of the subject. Consequently, they have been considered as "involuntary," and their interaction with external stimulation is considered weak at best. It has, therefore, been difficult to classify them as operants manipulable by schedules of reinforcement. It would appear that biofeedback provides a prosthetic learning capability by which autonomic responses may be shaped into operants. Brener (1974) has proposed that during feedback training subjects learn to calibrate existing interoceptive sensation with the feedback signal. In this fashion they learn to utilize existing sensation to "voluntarily" control what was previously beyond their control. This type of learning seems more analogous to the tasks described by Bilodeau in his elaboration of the feedback model (1969) than it does to an operant paradigm. Once the response has been learned to a given criterion, it could then be treated as an operant by supplying appropriate contingent reinforcement. Thus, it is proposed that two distinct stages may be isolated in autonomic response learning. The first stage is one of response development during which time feedback is utilized much like the feedback in skills learning. In the second stage, when the autonomic response can be emitted with

high probability and can therefore be considered as operant, reinforcements can be applied contingently and the response brought under the control of schedules.

Most studies on human biofeedback training have concentrated their attention on demonstrating that a so-called involuntary response can be made voluntary. That is, they have focused their attention on making a certain physiological response into a possible operant. For clinical problems, such a process, according to the present model, would only constitute the first stage of a successful therapeutic intervention. This newly created operant must then be brought under appropriate stimulus control in order for any useful long term change to be effected. The task of bringing behaviors under stimulus control is the main concern of behavior modification approaches (Bandura, 1969). Unfortunately, there has been little or no research on applying the principles of clinical behavior change to physiological malfunctions. It is not surprising, therefore, that some studies on the clinical utility of biofeedback procedures which have focused solely on developing physiological responses into operants have had limited long-term success (e.g., Benson et al., 1971). Although Budzynski et al. (1973) attempted to maximize generalization of trained EMG responses with the use of structured at home practice with tape recorded instructions and Weiss and Engel (1971) tried to increase generalization by fading out feedback, there have been no attempts at instituting the type of social contingencies which have been so effective in other forms of behavior modification (e.g., Patterson, 1971; Stuart & Davis, 1972). In these programs, family and other significant people in the patient's life space are encouraged to use their interaction with the patient as contingent reinforcement as long as the patient is meeting the criteria of behavior change developed with the therapist. When a physiological response is the target behavior, the response must be first made observable so that social contingencies can be exercised. For example, a man with hypertension could be provided with his own sphygmomanometer after feedback training has taught him to control his pressure voluntarily. His wife could then be taught how to measure blood pressure and be asked to take her husband's pressure several times a day. In this way, blood pressure becomes an operant at least partially under the control of the patient's wife's responses. Or, groups of hypertensive patients could meet regularly, as do Weight Watchers, publically recording their pressure and exposing themselves to the social consequences. Needless to say, many different plans could be designed. Their essential common point is that they provide situations in which the physiological response in question is put under the control of social contingencies. Without this second step, there is no reason to believe that biofeedback training alone will lead to meaningful, long-term therapeutic improvement.

EFFECTS OF BIOFEEDBACK ON COMPLEX PHYSIOLOGICAL SYSTEMS

In applying biofeedback or instrumental learning techniques to the control of any disorder, it must be remembered that one is dealing with an extremely complex physiological system and not one simple response. Often, the response one chooses to modify is the end product of many interacting processes, all of which might be measurable and trainable, in and of themselves. Optimal therapeutic manipulation of a system may therefore be achieved by manipulating underlying physiological processes directly rather than the gross response which constitutes the target behavior. This is probably best illustrated by the case of essential hypertension. Figure 3–4 is a schematic diagram summarizing the basic physiological processes which affect arterial blood pressure. As can be seen, mean arterial pressure is determined by cardiac output and total peripheral resistance. Though cardiac output and peripheral resistance are somewhat interrelated functions, they can also be seen to be independent in the etiology of hypertension. For instance, patients suffering from sustained hypertension are known to have increased peripheral resistance but normal cardiac output while patients displaying labile hypertension show increased cardiac output and normal peripheral resistance. In deciding to use biofeedback for treating hypertension, different procedures might be indicated depending upon the stage of hypertension. For example, since heart rate is one component of cardiac output, labile hypertensives might benefit more from a combination of blood pressure and heart rate feedback than fixed hypertensives, since high cardiac output is one characteristic of their disorder. Heart rate feedback, however, would not be indicated for fixed hypertensives, since their cardiac output is normal. For them, some combination of pressure and muscle tension might be useful.

Those conducting research on the application of biofeedback to hypertension should be cognizant of the multitude of ways in which pressure can be reduced—some of which may not be particularly therapeutic. Since instrumental control of urine formation may be possible (Miller & DiCara, 1968), one might want to check that patients were not decreasing their blood pressure by reducing their volume. Such laboratory induced changes would be transient, lasting only until the patient had a drink of water. It is also possible that patients could learn to control cardiac output through manipulation of respiration and intrathoracic pressure. Again, such changes are unlikely to be generalized to outside the laboratory. Longer lasting changes *might* be achieved through training aspects of peripheral resistance or cardiac output.

Research suggests that the most useful method of control of blood pressure might

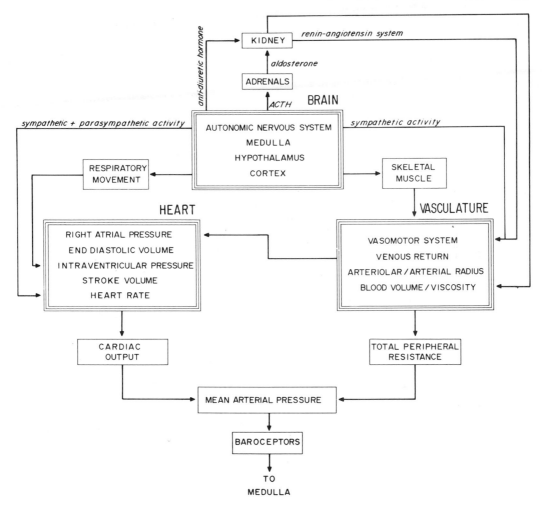

FIGURE 3-4   Schematic diagram summarizing the physiological mechanisms involved in the regulation of arterial blood pressure. The diagram oversimplifies the processes involved in order to provide a general overview of mechanisms most relevant to behavioral manipulation. Boxes labeled heart, brain, and vasculature each contain a subset of relevant systems and functions. While these are not necessarily temporally or functionally related in the order presented, the outside arrows indicate the site at which other systems exert their influence on the system described in the box. Note the numerous and diverse pathways through which behavioral control over blood pressure could be exerted. For example, relaxation techniques acting on the muscles could have their main effect on the vasculature, producing a decrease in peripheral resistance. Yogic exercises emphasizing breath control might have their main effect on cardiac output by changing intraventricular pressure. Although the diagram suggests that a feedback approach including both cardiac and vascular parameters would be most efficacious, it illustrates how verbal instruction acting on the cortex might also be seen to affect blood pressure.

be decrease of sympathetic activity. It may be hypothesized that *general* physiological functions such as sympathetic activity are more readily subject to control because they involve a number of common nervous pathways that are integrated at higher levels of the nervous system. Thus, Schwartz (1972) found larger decreases (or increases) in heart rate *and* systolic blood pressure when feedback and rewards were given for the simultaneous occurrence of decreases (or increases) in *both*, as compared to earlier results when only one or the other function was reinforced (Shapiro et al., 1970b).

On the other hand, modifying a global pattern of activity means that some unwanted accompanying change may be augmented. While unpublished data (Schwartz et al., 1972) suggest that it is difficult to dissociate such closely integrated responses as diastolic pressure and heart rate with a small amount of training, such response discrimination is theoretically possible unless there are rigid constraints of anatomy or physiology. The strategy of training would be to go from the general to the specific, at first utilizing as many common response tendencies and then selectively controlling the specific response independently of the others.

Kimble and Perlmuter (1970) describe the process of acquiring voluntary control over involuntary responses as one that is

> . . . always accomplished with the aid of supporting responses already under voluntary control. The desired response is elicited initially as a part of a larger pattern of reactions. With practice the supporting responses gradually drop out, an accomplishment that required a careful paying of attention to the desired behavior and a simultaneous ignoring of the others. With still further practice the now voluntary reaction becomes capable of being performed without deliberate intent. What was once involuntary and later became voluntary is now involuntary again, in the sense of being out of awareness and free of previous motivational control [p. 382].

These authors cite an old study by Bair in 1901 to exemplify the process of developing voluntary control of ear movement. Bair elicited the movement by electrical stimulation of the retrahens muscle in order to provide subjects with the sensations accompanying this movement. The electrical stimulation was not effective in and of itself, and subjects needed to practice by making large facial contortions, lifting their brows, and grimacing at first, then detecting the desired movement, and subsequently differentiating it out from the massive reaction. Kimble and Perlmuter point out that it was important for subjects to focus attention on the responses to be performed and to ignore the unwanted elements of the behavior. They add, ". . . the subjects specifically stated that this did *not* mean trying to inhibit these other responses and that when they did try to do so it only made the responses occur more vigorously [p. 375]." The methods described by Schwartz et al. (1971) and Schwartz (1972) for measuring ongoing complex patterns of autonomic (or other) responses can be applied in examining such processes of differentiation as may operate in physiological control. Whether the Kimble-Perlmuter model of voluntary control pertains equally to visceral response patterns as to somato-motor responses is a problem for further research.

FEEDBACK AND MEASUREMENT PROBLEMS

The transformation of physiological information into sensory analogues is a basic psychophysical and psychophysiological problem. Some investigators prefer to maximize information by continuously changing displays which closely match the physiological dimensions, while others prefer to categorize the information into a small number of groupings. In normal heart rate control, a few studies have addressed themselves to the differential effectiveness of varying amounts of feedback (Brener, Kleinman, & Goesling, 1969; Shapiro et al., 1970b,) and a number of investigators are currently pursuing this question. Lang (1974) compared the effectiveness of beat by beat feedback with summary information about longer series of beats (5 or 10) and concluded that the more information the better, but only for speeding heart rate, not for slowing.

The mathematical transformation of physiological dimensions into feedback is an issue that has received little formal investigation. Heart period, which is the inverse of heart rate, may be the more significant function from a physiological standpoint, and could be more effective in autonomic learning (see Khachaturian, Kerr, Kruger, & Schachter, 1972). Similar questions can be raised about the most suitable transformation of blood pressure, although the limitations of measuring techniques have restricted most of the research to the use of binary feedback. Moreover, in blood pressure work, a decision has to be made as to whether the measure should be systolic, diastolic, or mean pressure. This decision rests on the availability of instruments for detecting the different indices of pressure and for providing feedback. In hypertension, medical and physiological considerations as to the stage and variety of the illness, its duration and severity, have a bearing on this decision. Further questions arise concerning the time course and amplitude of the response that is fed back or reinforced. Consider the fact that successive changes in pressure are often directly linked with changes in respiration and heart rate. Should these phasic changes be reinforced or is it desirable to insist on fluctuations going beyond respiratory induced values?

Finally, the pros and cons of using one sensory modality or another depend on such factors as ease of discrimination of stimulus change and the type of matching of such changes with the physiological phenomenon. Application of these methods of psychophysics in crosschecking physiological and sensory dimensions could provide answers to some of these questions (see Stevens, 1966).

AUTONOMIC AWARENESS

Although autonomic responses seem to be directly manipulable by feedback, some investigators feel that the development of the autonomic awareness is a necessary precondition for voluntary physiological control. A theoretical question of present concern is whether the effects of biofeedback are mediated by the development of heightened autonomic awareness. There has been little research on the role of interoception in the regulation of visceral functions (see Bykov, 1957; Razran, 1961; Slucki, Ádám, & Porter, 1965). Some studies suggest that humans can learn to discriminate internal stimuli (Ádám, 1967; Baron, 1966). Moreover, it has been reported that when subjects learned to identify variations in their pulse prior to biofeedback training, subsequent heart rate control was facilitated (Brener, 1974).

Research on autonomic awareness poses complex methodological problems. This is reflected in inconsistent findings on the role of individual differences in autonomic perception and on the effects of providing specific instructions to subjects regarding the response to be controlled (see Bergman & Johnson, 1972; Blanchard & Young, 1973; Blanchard, Young, & McLeod, 1972; Engel & Hansen, 1966). Some authors imply that it is better to inform subjects about the response to be controlled because it facilitates awareness and learning, but others have come to an opposite conclusion. In the latter view, it may be that information about the response serves to limit exploratory behavior as a result of some misconception about the behavioral or cognitive significance of the physiological activity.

The necessity of awareness has been questioned by Kimble and Perlmuter (1970) in their analysis of the problem of volition. They noted that the elimination, reduction, or distortion of kinesthetic feedback interferes with but does not prevent voluntary behavior. They emphasized the importance of centrally located feedback loops or "images" in the production of voluntary action. The role of central imagery in developing voluntary control of the viscera is under investigation (Bell &

Schwartz, personal communication). Such central nervous processes may be effective in fostering autonomic control independently of sensations arising directly from the viscera.

INSTRUMENTAL CONDITIONING AND PSYCHOSOMATIC ETIOLOGY

Little research has been done on the possible role of instrumental learning in the etiology of psychosomatic illness. Miller (1969) argued that the evidence on visceral learning removes the major basis for assuming that psychosomatic symptoms that are autonomically mediated are fundamentally different from so-called hysterical symptoms that derive from somatomotor and central nervous system processes. Concerning the etiology of psychosomatic disorders, theorists have emphasized one or some combination of such causative factors as constitutional vulnerability, organ response learning, stimulus situation, emotional reaction pattern, and personality profile (Lachman, 1972). However, no really systematic extension of instrumental learning concepts to specific psychosomatic disorders has been attempted to explain the selective differentiation of symptoms through reinforcement. Miller gave an example of a child who is reinforced by being kept at home from school on the basis of a particular physiological symptom and who thereby avoids an important examination for which he is not prepared. Depending upon particular parental concerns, the child may be reinforced for gastric distress, headache, skin rash, respiratory symptoms, cardiovascular changes, muscle tension, or other potential symptoms. With repetitive reinforcement, and the possible generalization of the learned reactions to other situations, a workable model of learned psychosomatic symptom formation might be constructed.

As to evidence of the experimental induction of psychosomatic symptoms in animals by instrumental conditioning methods, this critical research has as yet achieved only limited attention (Benson et al., 1969; Harris et al., 1973). Benson et al. (1970) reported on changes in mean arterial pressure associated with operant conditioning schedules in monkeys. The animals were trained to press a key on a fixed ratio schedule to avoid electric shocks. This schedule exerted strong control over their behavior and resulted in increases in mean pressure of more than 20 to 30 mmHg during the training sessions. Subsequently, pressure measured for 24-hour periods remained more than 10 mmHg above pretraining baselines. Of the five monkeys studied, four exhibited no gross renal pathology or changes of the renal arteries. One monkey had petechial hemorrhages in the renal cortex and focally proliferative, obliterative changes of the renal arteries. The degree to which work schedules such as these can yield organic pathology is a problem meriting further study. Laboratory studies on the physiological consequences in humans of avoidance schedules such as those used by Benson et al. may be fruitful in assessing their pathological potential. In many respects, these schedules resemble the high-pressure conditions of many work situations, and it would be useful to develop this laboratory model further.

Conclusion

This chapter has reviewed research on the behavioral regulation of visceral, somatomotor, and neural processes by means of biofeedback and operant conditioning techniques. Considering the newness of the field and that its major push came such a short time ago with Neal Miller's review in *Science* (1969) on the powerful effects obtained in curarized animals, it is surprising that scores of basic empirical studies have been published. This attests to the recognition by behavioral scientists and psychophysiologists that the approach represents the most significant advance since Pavlov in systematic theory and method for the study of learned modifications of visceral and neural activities. The studies have largely been demonstrative in nature—to show that a wide variety of responses in different species can be altered and to evaluate to some degree concurrent changes in related physiological processes. Although there have been difficulties in reproducing the findings in curarized rats, the human experiments have yielded relatively consistent and convincing data. Experiments on the control of electrodermal activity, heart rate, blood pressure, and brain waves have been repeated successfully in the same and independent laboratories.

Now investigators are turning their attention to more incisive questions of a theoretical and practical nature: (1) What are some of the biological, behavioral, and environmental mechanisms of learned physiological control? How is the learning constrained by other forces within and outside the individual? (2) What can be said about the extent and persistence of learning brought about by the techniques? Can they bring about a *true* "altered" state of physiology? Of consciousness? (3) How do the effects achieved by these techniques compare with other factors, perhaps less well defined, known to influence physiological functioning, e.g., stress, anxiety, emotion, and attitudinal dispositions of the individual? (4) What is the practical value of this new development in research? Can the techniques and concepts be used to enhance potentialities for human growth and development? Can abnormal physiological processes be altered significantly? What are the possibilities for nonmedical use of the techniques, e.g., in education or recreation?

We have focused our attention on clinical application, reflecting the wide interest and enthusiasm for biofeedback as a corrective therapy, as evidenced by its exten-

sive coverage in the media, the founding of "biofeedback clinics," and the advertising, sometimes misleading or distorted, of feedback devices for individual use. In a short period of time, the Biofeedback Research Society has grown to a membership of more than 400, and many members are in the hot pursuit of clinical goals. Yet, while the clinical work we have reported is extensive, its scientific quality is not up to par. The stage has been one, for both scientists and clinicians, of finding therapeutic effects as rapidly as possible. This has meant the short-circuiting of time, effort, and money involved in long-term, controlled clinical trials. This has also meant that there is *not one* well controlled scientific study of the effectiveness of biofeedback and operant conditioning in treating a particular physiological disorder. The clinical data and case studies described are convincing in some instances, not at all in others. The most substantial work has been done where medical and physiological factors in the illness are given precise definition, where symptoms are shown to vary as the treatment conditions are varied, and where long-term and follow-up data are reported. As yet, the lack of controls for placebo and other nonspecific effects leaves open the question of what is unique to biofeedback training methods and what is not. Carefully controlled and evaluated clinical trials are obviously difficult, but they are vital before biofeedback methods will take their place along side other established practices in medicine.

In his 1973 overview entitled "Biofeedback as Therapy: Some Theoretical and Practical Issues," Schwartz introduced a note of pessimism about the application of biofeedback techniques to chronic physical disease, particularly in the absence of other therapeutic procedures. He opposed the simplistic use of the feedback method without regard for a thorough appraisal of the interaction of biological and environmental factors in any particular disorder or patient. He advocated a combined "behavioral-biological" approach that stresses three broad factors: (1) the natural interrelations of responses (pattern of interaction among various concurrent physiological responses), (2) the exact manner in which the feedback and reward is presented, and (3) the role of biological, cognitive, and environmental constraints. This is a tall order, yet an important acknowledgement that biofeedback is neither panacea nor magic pill, that most symptoms do not exist in a vacuum, that a *comprehensive* approach to treatment is required utilizing as many positive forces within and outside the individual as necessary. The mindless application of biofeedback training is no more sensible than the mindless taking of pills or patent medicines.

The power of the biofeedback concept and method, it seems to us, lies in its preciseness. Unlike other disciplines such as various forms of yoga and meditation practice, which are only recently beginning to be defined in terms of specific associated physiological and behavioral processes (see Benson et al., 1974), the focus of biofeedback is on specific responses or patterns of responses and its potential to bring these under specific control. In disorders with circumscribed, isolated, or well defined symptoms, this precision is of enormous significance from a behavioral standpoint. In disorders in which the symptomatology is less well defined or the critical responses or response patterns are not readily accessible to peripheral measurement or available feedback techniques, the precision of biofeedback is to less avail, although feedback for global patterns of response such as in total relaxation has its place. As research on the physiological and behavioral concomitants of the different disorders progresses, the potential value of biofeedback as a treatment will improve.

We must also highlight the apparent split-focus that exists in this area of research and clinical application. The feedback concept appears to emphasize internal processes, internal regulation and awareness, and self-control. The operant or instrumental concept appears to emphasize external forces, reinforcers in the environment that shape behavior *and* physiology. While feedback and reinforcement may be seen as separate but interdependent processes, the techniques themselves are essentially the same. However, when viewed as separate techniques, the implications for their effective application in therapy may be sufficiently different to call attention to them. In some respects, the feedback concept, ignoring reinforcement and motivation, would seem to put the onus on the individual—on *his* turning off his maladaptive responses and on *his* developing a general attitude toward the environment (for example, a passive unreactive stance). The instrumental concept would seem to give greater emphasis to external events or reinforcers, to environmental contingencies acting in relation to the individual's behavior and physiological responses. In this perspective, the onus is not on the individual per se but on the interaction of his behavior with environmental events, usually social reinforcers. It is the link between behavior and reinforcement that needs to be altered. Of course, what is external becomes internal; both forces come together, and both must be recognized and accounted for in any effective application. Both the individual *and* the environment must be involved in any corrective therapy.

Finally, the translation of biofeedback into a form of "behavioral medicine" (Birk, 1973) calls attention to the importance of man's adaptive and coping mechanisms, both internal and external, in illness and in health. With this, we see an important renewed emphasis in medicine on *behavioral* approaches, not only in treatment but also in prevention of illness and maintenance of good health. We hope that the clinical and research potentials of biofeedback and instrumental learning will provide further means of integrating behavioral sciences, biology, and medicine.

References

ÁDÁM, G. *Interoception and behavior*. Budapest: Akademiai Kiado, 1967.

ADAMS, R. D. Recurrent convulsions. In J. V. Harrison, R. D. Adams, I. L. Bennett, W. H. Resnik, G. W. Thorn, & M. M. Wintrobe (Eds.), *Principles of internal medicine*. New York: McGraw-Hill, 1966.

ALEXANDER, A. B. Systematic relaxation and flow rates in asthmatic children: relationship to emotional precipitants and anxiety. *Journal of Psychosomatic Research*, 1972, **16**, 405–410.

ALEXANDER, A. B., MIKLICH, D. R., & HERSHKOFF, H. The immediate effects of systematic relaxation training on peak expiratory flow rates in asthmatic children. *Psychosomatic Medicine*, 1972, **34**, 388–394.

ALEXANDER, F., & FLAGG, G. W. The psychosomatic approach. In B. B. Wolman (Ed.), *Handbook of clinical psychology*. New York: McGraw-Hill, 1965.

AMATO, A., HERMSMEYER, C. A., & KLEINMAN, K. M. Use of electromyographic feedback to increase inhibitory control of spastic muscles. *Physical Therapy*, 1973, **53**, 1063–1066.

ANNETT, J. *Feedback and human behavior*. Baltimore: Penguin Books, 1969.

ANTHONY, M., HINTERBERGER, H., & LANCE, J. W. Plasma serotonin in migraine and stress. *Archives of Neurology*, 1967, **16**, 544–552.

BAHRICK, H. P., FITTS, P. M., & RANKIN, R. E. Effect of incentives upon reaction to peripheral stimuli. *Journal of Experimental Psychology*, 1952, **44**, 400–406.

BAIR, J. H. Development of voluntary control. *Psychological Review*, 1901, **8**, 474–510.

BANCROFT, J. The application of psychophysiological measures to the assessment and modification of sexual behavior. *Behaviour Research and Therapy*, 1971, **9**, 119–130.

BANCROFT, J. H. J. Aversion therapy. Unpublished dissertation for Diploma, Psychological Medicine, University of London, 1966. (Reported in S. Rachman & J. Teasdale, 1969.)

BANDURA, A. *Principles of behavior modification*. New York: Holt, Rinehart & Winston, 1969.

BARBER, T. X. *LSD, marihuana, yoga, and hypnosis*. Chicago: Aldine, 1970.

BARBER, T. X., DiCARA, L. V., KAMIYA, J., MILLER, N. E., SHAPIRO, D., & STOYVA, J. (Eds.)

Biofeedback and self-control 1970: an Aldine Annual on the regulation of bodily processes and consciousness. Chicago: Aldine-Atherton, 1971.

BARON, J. An EEG correlate of autonomic discrimination. *Psychonomic Science*, 1966, **4**, 255–256.

BASMAJIAN, J. V. Control and training of individual motor units. *Science*, 1963, **141**, 440–441.

BASMAJIAN, J. V. Electromyography comes of age. *Science*, 1972, **176**, 603–609.

BEATTY, J. Effects of initial alpha wave abundance and operant training procedures on occipital alpha and beta wave activity. *Psychonomic Science*, 1971, **23**, 197–199.

BEATTY, J., GREENBERG, A., DEIBLEN, W. P., & O'HANLON, J. F. Operant control of occipital theta rhythm affects performance in a radar monitoring task. *Science*, 1974, **183**, 871–873.

BEATTY, J., & KORNFELD, C. Relative independence of conditioned EEG changes from cardiac and respiratory activity. *Physiology and Behavior*, 1972, **9**, 733–736.

BEESON, P. B., & McDERMOTT, W. (Eds.) *Cecil-Loeb textbook of medicine*. (12th ed.) Philadelphia: W. B. Saunders, 1967.

BENSON, H., BEARY, J. F., & CAROL, M. P. The relaxation response. *Psychiatry*, 1974, **37**, 37–46.

BENSON, H., HERD, J. A., MORSE, W. H., & KELLEHER, R. T. Behavioral induction of arterial hypertension and its reversal. *American Journal of Physiology*, 1969, **217**, 30–34.

BENSON, H., HERD, J. A., MORSE, W. H., & KELLEHER, R. T. Behaviorally induced hypertension in the squirrel monkey. *Circulation Research* (Supplement 1), 1970, **26–27**, 21–26..

BENSON, H., ROSNER, B. A., MARZETTA, B. R., & KLEMCHUK, H. M. Decreased blood-pressure in pharmacologically treated hypertensive patients who regularly elicited the relaxation response. *Lancet*, 1974, **7852**, 289–291.

BENSON, H., SHAPIRO, D., TURSKY, B., & SCHWARTZ, G. E. Decreased systolic blood pressure through operant conditioning techniques in patients with essential hypertension. *Science*, 1971, **173**, 740–742.

BERGMAN, J. S., & JOHNSON, H. J. Sources of information which affect training and raising of heart rate. *Psychophysiology*, 1972, **9**, 30–39.

BERNARD, J., & GILBERT, R. W. The specificity of the effect of shock per error in a maze learning experiment with human subjects. *Journal of Experimental Psychology*, 1941, **28**, 178–186.

BILODEAU, I. McD. Information feedback. In E. A. Bilodeau & I. McD. Bilodeau (Eds.), *Principles of skill acquisition*. New York: Academic Press, 1969.

BIRK, L. (Ed.) *Biofeedback: behavioral medicine*. New York: Grune & Stratton, 1973.

BIRK, L., CRIDER, A., SHAPIRO, D., & TURSKY, B. Operant electrodermal conditioning under partial curarization. *Journal of Comparative and Physiological Psychology*, 1966, **62**, 165–166.

BLACK, A. H. The operant conditioning of central nervous system electrical activity. In G. H. Bower (Ed.), *The psychology of learning and motivation: advances in research and theory*. New York: Academic Press, 1972.

BLACK, A. H., YOUNG, G. A., & BATENCHUCK, C. Avoidance training of hippocampal theta waves in Flaxedilized dogs and its relation to skeletal movement. *Journal of Comparative and Physiological Psychology*, 1970, **70**, 15–24.

BLANCHARD, E. B., & YOUNG, L. D. Self-control of cardiac functioning: a promise as yet unfulfilled. *Psychological Bulletin*, 1973, **79**, 145–163.

BLANCHARD, E. B., YOUNG, L. D., & McLEOD, P. G. Awareness of heart activity and self-control of heart rate. *Psychophysiology*, 1972, **9**, 63–68.

BLEECKER, E. R., & ENGEL, B. T. Learned control of cardiac rate and cardiac conduction in the Wolff-Parkinson-White syndrome. *New England Journal of Medicine*, 1973, **288**, 560–562. (a)

BLEECKER, E. R., & ENGEL, B. T. Learned control of ventricular rate in patients with atrial fibrillation. *Psychosomatic Medicine*, 1973, **35**, 161–175. (b)

BRADY, J. P. Metronome-conditioned relaxation: a new behavioral procedure. *British Journal of Psychiatry*, 1973, **122**, 729–730.

BRADY, J. P., LUBORSKY, L., & KRON, R. E. Blood pressure reduction in patients with essential hypertension through metronome-conditioned relaxation: a preliminary report. *Behavior Therapy*, 1974, **5**, 203–209.

BRADY, J. V. Ulcers in "executive" monkeys. *Scientific American*, 1958, **199**, 95–103.

BRENER, J. A general model of voluntary control applied to the phenomena of learned cardiovascular change. In P. A. Obrist, A. H. Black,

J. Brener, & L. V. DiCara (Eds.), *Cardiovascular psychophysiology*. Chicago: Aldine, 1974.

BRENER, J., EISSENBERG, E., & MIDDAUGH, S. Respiratory and somatomotor factors associated with operant conditioning of cardiovascular responses in curarized rats. In P. A. Obrist, A. H. Black, J. Brener, & L. V. DiCara (Eds.), *Cardiovascular psychophysiology*. Chicago: Aldine, 1974.

BRENER, J., & KLEINMAN, R. A. Learned control of decreases in systolic blood pressure. *Nature*, 1970, **226**, 1063–1064.

BRENER, J., KLEINMAN, R. A., & GOESLING, W. J. The effects of different exposures to augmented sensory feedback on the self-control of heart rate. *Psychophysiology*, 1969, **5**, 510–516.

BROWN, B. B. Recognition of aspects of consciousness through association with EEG alpha activity represented by a light signal. *Psychophysiology*, 1970, **6**, 442–452.

BRUDNY, J., GRYNBAUM, B. B., & KOREIN, J. Spasmodic torticollis: treatment by feedback display of the EMG. *Archives of Physical Medicine and Rehabilitation*, 1974, **55**, 403–408.

BUDZYNSKI, T. H. Biofeedback procedures in the clinic. *Seminars in Psychiatry*, 1973, **5**, 537–547.

BUDZYNSKI, T. A systems approach to some clinical applications of biofeedback. *Proceedings of the Biofeedback Research Society*, 1974, p. 105. (Abstract)

BUDZYNSKI, T., STOYVA, J., & ALDER, C. Feedback-induced muscle relaxation: application to tension headache. *Journal of Behavior Therapy and Experimental Psychiatry*, 1970, **1**, 205–211.

BUDZYNSKI, T. H., STOYVA, J. M., ADLER, C. S., & MULLANEY, D. J. EMG biofeedback and tension headache: a controlled outcome study. *Psychosomatic Medicine*, 1973, **35**, 484–496.

BUNCH, M. E. The effect of electric shock as punishment in human maze learning. *Journal of Comparative Psychology*, 1928, **8**, 343–359.

BYKOV, K. M. *The cerebral cortex and the internal organs*. W. H. Gantt (Trans. and Ed.) New York: Chemical Publishing Co., 1957.

CARMONA, A., MILLER, N. E., & DEMIERRE, T. Instrumental learning of gastric tonicity responses. *Psychosomatic Medicine*, 1974, **36**, 156–163.

CHIANG, B. N., PERLMAN, L. V., OSTANDER, L. D., Jr., & EPSTEIN, F. H. Relationship of premature systoles to coronary heart disease and sudden death in the Tecumseh epidemiologic study. *Annals of Internal Medicine,* 1969, **70,** 1159–1166.

CORDAY, E., GOLD, H., DEVERA, L. B., WILLIAMS, J. H., & FIELDS, J. Effect of the cardiac arrhythmias on the coronary circulation. *Annals of Internal Medicine,* 1959, **50,** 535–553.

CORDAY, E., & IRVING, D. W. Effect of cardiac arrhythmias on the cerebral circulation. *American Journal of Cardiology,* 1960, **6,** 803–807.

CRIDER, A., SCHWARTZ, G. E., & SHAPIRO, D. Operant suppression of electrodermal response rate as a function of punishment schedule. *Journal of Experimental Psychology,* 1970, **83,** 333–334.

CRIDER, A., SHAPIRO, D., & TURSKY, B. Reinforcement of spontaneous electrodermal activity. *Journal of Comparative and Physiological Psychology,* 1966, **61,** 20–27.

DATEY, K. K., DESHMUKH, S. N., DALVI, C. P., & VINEKAR, S. L. "Shavasan": a yogic exercise in the management of hypertension. *Angiology,* 1969, **20,** 325–333.

DICARA, L. V., & MILLER, N. E. Changes in heart rate instrumentally learned by curarized rats as avoidance responses. *Journal of Comparative and Physiological Psychology,* 1968, **65,** 8–12. (a)

DICARA, L. V., & MILLER, N. E. Instrumental learning of systolic blood pressure responses by curarized rats: dissociation of cardiac and vascular changes. *Psychosomatic Medicine,* 1968, **30,** 489–494. (b)

DICARA, L. V., & MILLER, N. E. Instrumental learning of vasomotor responses by rats: learning to respond differentially in the two ears. *Science,* 1968, **159,** 1485–1486. (c)

DICARA, L. V., & WEISS, J. M. Effect of heart-rate learning under curare on subsequent non-curarized avoidance learning. *Journal of Comparative and Physiological Psychology,* 1969, **69,** 368–374.

DUNBAR, F. *Psychosomatic diagnosis.* New York: Paul B. Hoeber, 1943.

EDDLEMAN, E. E., Jr., RESNIK, W. H., & HARRISON, T. R. Disorders of rate, rhythm, and conduction. In J. V. Harrison, R. D. Adams, I. L. Bennett, W. H. Resnik, G. W. Thorn, & M. M. Wintrobe (Eds.), *Principles of internal medicine.* New York: McGraw-Hill, 1966.

EDELBERG, R. Electrical activity of the skin: its measurement and uses in psychophysiology. In

N. S. Greenfield & R. A. Sternbach (Eds.), *Handbook of psychophysiology.* New York: Holt, Rinehart & Winston, 1972.

ENGEL, B. T. Operant conditioning of cardiac function: a status report. *Psychophysiology,* 1972, **9,** 161–177.

ENGEL, B. T. Clinical applications of operant conditioning techniques in the control of the cardiac arrhythmias. *Seminars in Psychiatry,* 1973, **5,** 433–438.

ENGEL, B. T., & BLEECKER, E. R. Application of operant conditioning techniques to the control of the cardiac arrhythmias. In P. A. Obrist, A. H. Black, J. Brener, & L. V. DiCara (Eds.), *Cardiovascular psychophysiology.* Chicago: Aldine, 1974.

ENGEL, B. T., & CHISM, R. A. Operant conditioning of heart rate speeding. *Psychophysiology,* 1967, **3,** 418–426.

ENGEL, B. T., & GOTTLIEB, S. H. Differential operant conditioning of heart rate in the restrained monkey. *Journal of Comparative and Physiological Psychology,* 1970, **73,** 217–225.

ENGEL, B. T., & HANSEN, S. P. Operant conditioning of heart rate slowing. *Psychophysiology,* 1966, **3,** 176–187.

FAIRBAIRN, J. F., JUERGENS, J. L., & SPITTELL, J. A., Jr. (Eds.) *Allen-Barker-Hines, peripheral vascular diseases.* (4th ed.) Philadelphia: W. B. Saunders, 1972.

FOWLER, R. L., & KIMMEL, H. D. Operant conditioning of the GSR. *Journal of Experimental Psychology,* 1962, **63,** 563–567.

FRENCH, D., LEEB, C., & FAHRION, S. Self-induced scrotal hyperthermia: an extension. *Proceedings of the Biofeedback Research Society,* 1974, p. 62. (Abstract)

GANNON, L., & STERNBACH, R. A. Alpha enhancement as a treatment for pain: a case study. *Behavior Therapy and Experimental Psychiatry,* 1971, **2,** 209–213.

GREEN, E. E., GREEN, A. M., & WALTERS, E. D. Voluntary control of internal states: psychological and physiological. In T. X. Barber, L. V. DiCara, J. Kamiya, N. E. Miller, D. Shapiro, & J. Stoyva (Eds.), *Biofeedback and self-control 1970: an Aldine Annual on the regulation of bodily processes and consciousness.* Chicago: Aldine-Atherton, 1971.

GREENE, W. A. Operant conditioning of the

GSR using partial reinforcement. *Psychological Reports,* 1966, **19,** 571–578.

GUTMANN, M. C., & BENSON, H. Interaction of environmental factors and systemic arterial blood pressure: a review. *Medicine,* 1971, **50,** 543–553.

HAHN, W. W. A look at the recent history and current developments in laboratory studies of autonomic conditioning. *Proceedings of the Biofeedback Research Society,* 1974, p. 94. (Abstract)

HARRIS, A. H., FINDLEY, J. D., & BRADY, J. V. Instrumental conditioning of blood pressure elevations in the baboon. *Conditional Reflex,* 1971, **6,** 215–226.

HARRIS, A. H., GILLIAM, W. J., FINDLEY, J. D., & BRADY, J. V. Instrumental conditioning of large magnitude, daily, 12-hour blood pressure elevations in the baboon. *Science,* 1973, **182,** 175–177.

HEFFERLINE, R. F. Learning theory and clinical psychology—an eventual symbiosis. In A. J. Bachrach (Ed.), *Experimental foundations of clinical psychology.* New York: Basic Books, 1962.

HEFFERLINE, R. F., & BRUNO, L. J. J. The psychophysiology of private events. In A. Jacobs & L. B. Sachs (Eds.), *The psychology of private events.* New York: Academic Press, 1971.

HEFFERLINE, R. F., & KEENAN, B. Amplitude-induction gradient of a small human operant in an escape-avoidance situation. *Journal of the Experimental Analysis of Behavior,* 1961, **4,** 41–43.

HENSON, D. E., & RUBIN, H. B. Voluntary control of eroticism. *Journal of Applied Behavior Analysis,* 1971, 4, 37–44.

HERBURG, L. J. The hypothalamus and the aetiology of migraine. In R. Smith (Ed.), *Background to migraine.* London: Heinemann, 1967.

HULL, C. L. *Essentials of behavior.* New Haven: Yale University Press, 1951.

JACOBS, A., & FELTON, G. S. Visual feedback of myoelectric output to facilitate muscle relaxation in normal persons and patients with neck injuries. *Archives of Physical Medicine and Rehabilitation,* 1969, **50,** 34–39.

JACOBSON, A. M., HACKETT, T. P., SURMAN, O. S., & SILVERBERG, E. L. Raynaud phenomenon. Treatment with hypnotic and operant technique. *Journal of the American Medical Association,* 1973, **225,** 739–740.

JACOBSON, E. *Progressive relaxation.* (2nd ed.) Chicago: University of Chicago Press, 1938.

JACOBSON, E. *Anxiety and tension control. A physiological approach.* Philadelphia: Lippincott, 1964.

JAMES, W. *The principles of psychology.* New York: Holt, Rinehart & Winston, 1890.

JOHNSON, H. J., & SCHWARTZ, G. E. Suppression of GSR activity through operant reinforcement. *Journal of Experimental Psychology,* 1967, **75,** 307–312.

JOHNSON, R. J. Operant reinforcement of an autonomic response. *Dissertation Abstracts,* 1963, 24, 1255–1256. (Abstract)

KAMIYA, J. Operant control of the EEG alpha rhythm and some of its reported effects on consciousness. In C. Tart (Ed.), *Altered states of consciousness.* New York: John Wiley, 1969.

KAMIYA, J., BARBER, T. X., DiCARA, L. V., MILLER, N. E., SHAPIRO, D., & STOYVA, J. (Eds.) *Biofeedback and self-control: an Aldine Reader on the regulation of bodily processes and consciousness.* Chicago: Aldine-Atherton, 1971.

KANNEL, W. B., GORDON, T., & SCHWARTZ, M. J. Systolic versus diastolic blood pressure and risk of coronary heart disease. *American Journal of Cardiology,* 1971, **27,** 335–343.

KAPLAN, B., EEG biofeedback and epilepsy. Paper presented at the meeting of the American Psychological Association, Montreal, August 1973.

KHACHATURIAN, Z., KERR, J., KRUGER, R., & SCHACHTER, J. A methodological note: comparison between period and rate data in studies of cardiac function. *Psychophysiology,* 1972, **9,** 539–545.

KIMBLE, G. A., & PERLMUTER, L. C. The problem of volition. *Psychological Review,* 1970, **77,** 361–384.

KIMMEL, H. D., PENDERGRASS, V. E., & KIMMEL, E. B. Modifying children's orienting reactions instrumentally. *Conditional Reflex,* 1967, **2,** 227–235.

KLEINMAN, K. M., & GOLDMAN, H. Effects of biofeedback on the physiological and cognitive consequences of essential hypertension. *Proceedings of the Biofeedback Research Society,* 1974, p. 37. (Abstract)

KRAFT, T. The use of behavior therapy in a psychotherapeutic context. In A. A. Lazarus

(Ed.), *Clinical behavior therapy.* New York: Brunner/Mazel, 1972.

LACHMAN, S. J. *Psychosomatic disorders: a behavioristic interpretation.* New York: John Wiley, 1972.

LANCE, J. W., & ANTHONY, M. Thermographic studies in vascular headache. *The Medical Journal of Australia,* 1971, **1**, 240–243.

LANG, P. J. Learned control of human heart rate in a computer directed environment. In P. A. Obrist, A. H. Black, J. Brener, & L. V. DiCara (Eds.), *Cardiovascular psychophysiology.* Chicago: Aldine, 1974.

LANG, P. J., RICE, D. G., & STERNBACH, R. A. The psychophysiology of emotion. In N. S. Greenfield & R. A. Sternbach (Eds.), *Handbook of psychophysiology.* New York: Holt, Rinehart & Winston, 1972.

LANG, P. J., & TWENTYMAN, C. T. Learning to control heart rate: binary versus analogue feedback. *Psychophysiology,* 1974, **11**, 616–629.

LANGER, P., & CROCCEL, L. *Le phénomène de Raynaud: aspects cliniques, étiopathogeniques et thérapeutiques.* L'Expansion Scientifique Française, Paris, 1960.

LAWS, D. R., & RUBIN, H. B. Instructional control of an autonomic sexual response. *Journal of Applied Behavior Analysis,* 1969, **2**, 93–99.

LAZARUS, A. *Behavior therapy and beyond.* New York: McGraw-Hill, 1971.

LEVENE, H. T., ENGEL, B. T., & PEARSON, J. A. Differential operant conditioning of heart rate. *Psychosomatic Medicine,* 1968, **30**, 837–845.

LEVENSON, R. W., MANUCK, S. B., STRUPP, H. H., BLACKWOOD, G. L., & SNELL, J. D. A biofeedback technique for bronchial asthma. *Proceedings of the Biofeedback Research Society,* 1974, p. 11. (Abstract)

LEWIS, T. *Vascular disorders of the limbs: described for practitioners and students.* London: Macmillan, 1949.

LISINA, M. I. The role of orientation in the transformation of involuntary into voluntary reactions. In L. G. Voronin, A. N. Leontiev, A. R. Luria, E. N. Sokolov, & O. S. Vinogradova (Eds.), *Orienting reflex and exploratory behavior.* Moscow: Akad. Pedag. Nauk RSFSR, 1958 (in Russian); Washington, D.C.: American Psychological Association, 1965 (in English).

LOWN, B., & WOLF, M. Approaches to sudden death. *Circulation,* 1971, **44**, 130–142.

LUTHE, W., & SCHULTZ, J. H. *Autogenic therapy, medical applications.* Vol. 2. New York: Grune & Stratton, 1969.

LYNCH, J. J., & PASKEWITZ, D. A. On the mechanisms of the feedback control of human brain wave activity. *Journal of Nervous and Mental Disease,* 1971, **153**, 205–217.

LYNCH, W. C., HAMA, H., KOHN, S., & MILLER, N. E. Instrumental learning of vasomotor responses: a progress report. *Proceedings of the Biofeedback Research Society,* 1974, p. 68. (Abstract)

MARINACCI, A. A. *Clinical electromyography.* Los Angeles: San Lucas Press, 1955.

MARINACCI, A. A. The basic principles underlying neuromuscular re-education. In D. Shapiro, T. X. Barber, L. V. DiCara, J. Kamiya, N. E. Miller, & J. Stoyva (Eds.), *Biofeedback and self-control 1972: an Aldine Annual on the regulation of bodily processes and consciousness.* Chicago: Aldine, 1973.

MARINACCI, A. A., & HORANDE, M. Electromyogram in neuromuscular re-education. *Bulletin of the Los Angeles Neurological Society,* 1960, **25**, 57–71.

MELZACK, R. *The puzzle of pain.* New York: Basic Books, 1973.

MERRILL, J. P. Hypertensive vascular disease. In J. V. Harrison, R. D. Adams, I. L. Bennett, W. H. Resnik, G. W. Thorn, & M. M. Wintrobe (Eds.), *Principles of internal medicine.* New York: McGraw-Hill, 1966.

MILLER, N. E. Learning of visceral and glandular responses. *Science,* 1969, **163**, 434–445.

MILLER, N. E. Applications of learning and biofeedback to psychiatry and medicine. In A. M. Freedman, H. I. Kaplan, & B. J. Sadock (Eds.), *Comprehensive textbook of psychiatry—II.* Baltimore: Williams & Wilkins, 1975.

MILLER, N. E., & BANUAZIZI, A. Instrumental learning by curarized rats of a specific visceral response, intestinal or cardiac. *Journal of Comparative and Physiological Psychology,* 1968, **65**, 1–7.

MILLER, N. E., BARBER, T. X., DiCARA, L. V., KAMIYA, J., SHAPIRO, D., & STOYVA, J. (Eds.) *Biofeedback and self-control 1973: an Aldine Annual on the regulation of bodily processes and consciousness.* Chicago: Aldine, 1974.

MILLER, N. E., & CARMONA, A. Modification of a visceral response, salivation in thirsty dogs, by instrumental training with water reward. *Journal of Comparative and Physiological Psychology*, 1967, **63**, 1–6.

MILLER, N. E., & DiCARA, L. V. Instrumental learning of urine formation by rats; changes in renal blood flow. *American Journal of Physiology*, 1968, **215**, 677–683.

MILLER, N. E., & DWORKIN, B. R. Visceral learning: recent difficulties with curarized rats and significant problems for human research. In P. A. Obrist, A. H. Black, J. Brener, & L. V. DiCara (Eds.), *Cardiovascular psychophysiology*. Chicago: Aldine, 1974.

MITTLEMANN, B. & WOLFF, H. G. Affective states and skin temperature experimental study of subjects with "cold hands" and Raynaud's syndrome. *Psychosomatic Medicine*, 1939, **1**, 271–292.

MOORE, N. Behavior therapy in bronchial asthma: a controlled study. *Journal of Psychosomatic Research*, 1965, **9**, 257–276.

MULHOLLAND, T. Feedback electroencephalography. *Activitas Nervosa Superior*, 1968, **10**, 410–438.

NOWLIS, D. P., & KAMIYA, J. The control of electroencephalographic alpha rhythms through auditory feedback and the associated mental activity. *Psychophysiology*, 1970, **6**, 476–484.

OBRIST, P. A., HOWARD, J. L., LAWLER, J. E., GALOSY, R. A., MEYERS, K. A., & GAEBELEIN, C. J. The cardiac-somatic interaction. In P. A. Obrist, A. H. Black, J. Brener, & L. V. DiCara (Eds.), *Cardiovascular psychophysiology*. Chicago: Aldine, 1974.

OGDEN, E., & SHOCK, N. W. Voluntary hypercirculation. *American Journal of Medical Sciences*, 1939, **198**, 329–342.

OSTFELD, A. M. *The common headache syndromes: biochemistry, pathophysiology, therapy*. Springfield, Ill.: Charles C. Thomas, 1962.

OTTENBERG, P., STEIN, M., LEWIS, J., & HAMILTON, C. Learned asthma in the guinea pig. *Psychosomatic Medicine*, 1958, **20**, 395–400.

PAPPAS, B. A., DiCARA, L. V., & MILLER, N. E. Learning of blood pressure responses in the non-curarized rat: transfer to the curarized state. *Physiological Behavior*, 1970, **5**, 1029–1032.

PARRY, P. Effect of reward on performance of hyperactive children. Unpublished doctoral dissertation, McGill University, 1973.

PASKEWITZ, D. A., & ORNE, M. T. Visual effects on alpha feedback training. *Science*, 1973, **181**, 360–363.

PATTERSON, G. R. *Families: applications of social learning to family life*. Champaign, Ill.: Research Press Co., 1971.

PINKERTON, P. The enigma of asthma. *Psychosomatic Medicine*, 1973, **35**, 461–462.

PLUMLEE, L. A. Operant conditioning of increases in blood pressure. *Psychophysiology*, 1969, **6**, 283–290.

QUINN, J. T., HARBISON, J. J. M., & McALLISTER, H. An attempt to shape human penile responses. *Behaviour Research and Therapy*, 1970, **8**, 213–216.

RACHMAN, S., & TEASDALE, J. *Aversion therapy and behavior disorders: an analysis*. Coral Gables, Fla.: University of Miami Press, 1969.

RASKIN, M., JOHNSON, G., & RONDESTVEDT, J. W. Chronic anxiety treated by feedback-induced muscle relaxation. *Archives of General Psychiatry*, 1973, **28**, 263–267.

RAZRAN, G. The observable unconscious and the inferable conscious in current Soviet psychophysiology: interoceptive conditioning, semantic conditioning, and the orienting reflex. *Psychological Review*, 1961, **68**, 81–147.

RICE, D. G. Operant GSR conditioning and associated electromyogram responses. *Journal of Experimental Psychology*, 1966, **71**, 908–912.

ROBERTS, A., KEWMAN, D. G., & MACDONALD, H. Voluntary control of skin temperature: unilateral changes using hypnosis and feedback. *Journal of Abnormal Psychology*, 1973, **82**, 163–168.

ROBERTS, A. H., SCHULER, J., BACON, J., & ZIMMERMAN, R. L. Individual differences and autonomic control: absorption, hypnotic susceptibility and the unilateral control of skin temperature. *Proceedings of the Biofeedback Research Society*, 1974, p. 67. (Abstract)

ROBERTS, L. E. Operant autonomic conditioning in paralyzed rats. *Proceedings of the Biofeedback Research Society*, 1974, p. 94. (Abstract)

ROSEN, R. C. Suppression of penile tumescence by instrumental conditioning. *Psychosomatic Medicine*, 1973, **35**, 509–514.

ROSEN, R. C. Implications of biofeedback for sexual dysfunction. *Proceedings of the Biofeedback Research Society*, 1974, p. 12. (Abstract)

ROSEN, R. C., SHAPIRO, D., & SCHWARTZ, G. E.

Voluntary control of penile tumescence. *Psychophysiology,* 1974, **11**, 230–231. (Abstract)

ROSENFELD, J. P., RUDELL, A. P., & FOX, S. S. Operant control of neural events in humans. *Science,* 1969, **165**, 821–823.

RUCH, T. C., PATTON, H. D., WOODBURY, J. W. & TOWE, A. H. (Eds.) *Neurophysiology.* (2nd ed.) Philadelphia: W. B. Saunders, 1965.

RUGH, C. D., & SOLBERG, W. K. The identification of stressful stimuli in natural environments using a portable biofeedback unit. *Proceedings of the Biofeedback Research Society,* 1974, p. 54. (Abstract)

SAINSBURY, P., & GIBSON, J. F. Symptoms of anxiety and tension and accompanying physiological changes in the muscular system. *Journal of Neurology, Neurosurgery, and Psychiatry,* 1954, **17**, 216–224.

SARGEANT, H. G. S., & YORKSTON, N. J. Verbal desensitisation in the treatment of bronchial asthma. *Lancet,* 1969, **7634**, 1321–1323.

SARGENT, J. D., WALTERS, E. D., & GREEN, E. E. Psychosomatic self-regulation of migraine headache. *Seminars in Psychiatry,* 1973, **5**, 415–428.

SCHERF, D., & SCHOTT, A. *Extra systoles and allied arrhythmias.* New York: Grune & Stratton, 1953.

SCHULTZ, J. H., & LUTHE, W. *Autogenic therapy.* Vol. 1. New York: Grune & Stratton, 1969.

SCHUMACHER, G. A., & WOLFF, H. G. Experimental studies of headache. *Archives of Neurological Psychiatry,* 1941, **45**, 199–214.

SCHWARTZ, G. E. Voluntary control of human cardiovascular integration and differentiation through feedback and reward. *Science,* 1972, **175**, 90–93.

SCHWARTZ, G. E. Biofeedback as therapy: some theoretical and practical issues. *American Psychologist,* 1973, **28**, 666–673.

SCHWARTZ, G. E., & SHAPIRO, D. Biofeedback and essential hypertension: current findings and theoretical concerns. *Seminars in Psychiatry,* 1973, **5**, 493–503.

SCHWARTZ, G. E., SHAPIRO, D., & TURSKY, B. Learned control of cardiovascular integration in man through operant conditioning. *Psychosomatic Medicine,* 1971, **33**, 57–62.

SCHWARTZ, G. E., SHAPIRO, D., & TURSKY, B. Self-control of patterns of human diastolic blood pressure and heart rate through feedback and reward. *Psychophysiology,* 1972, **9**, 270. (Abstract)

SHAPIRO, D. Role of feedback and instructions in the voluntary control of human blood pressure. *Japanese Journal of Biofeedback Research,* 1973, **1**, 2–9. (in Japanese)

SHAPIRO, D. Operant-feedback control of human blood pressure: some clinical issues. In P. A. Obrist, A. H. Black, J. Brener, & L. V. DiCara (Eds.), *Cardiovascular psychophysiology.* Chicago: Aldine, 1974.

SHAPIRO, D., BARBER, T. X., DiCARA, L. V., KAMIYA, J., MILLER, N. E., & STOYVA, J. (Eds.) *Biofeedback and self-control 1972: an Aldine Annual on the regulation of bodily processes and consciousness.* Chicago: Aldine 1973.

SHAPIRO, D., & CRIDER, A. Operant electrodermal conditioning under multiple schedules of reinforcement. *Psychophysiology,* 1967, **4**, 168–175.

SHAPIRO, D., CRIDER, A. B., & TURSKY, B. Differentiation of an autonomic response through operant reinforcement. *Psychonomic Science,* 1964, **1**, 147–148.

SHAPIRO, D., & SCHWARTZ, G. E., Biofeedback and visceral learning: clinical applications. *Seminars in Psychiatry,* 1972, **4**, 171–184.

SHAPIRO, D., SCHWARTZ, G. E., NELSON, S., SHNIDMAN, S., & SILVERMAN, S. Operant control of fear-related electrodermal responses in snake-phobic subjects. *Psychophysiology,* 1972, **9**, 271. (Abstract) (a)

SHAPIRO, D., SCHWARTZ, G. E., & TURSKY, B. Control of diastolic blood pressure in man by feedback and reinforcement. *Psychophysiology,* 1972, **9**, 296–304. (b)

SHAPIRO, D., TURSKY, B., GERSHON, E., & STERN, M. Effects of feedback and reinforcement on the control of human systolic blood pressure. *Science,* 1969, **163**, 588–590.

SHAPIRO, D., TURSKY, B., & SCHWARTZ, G. E. Control of blood pressure in man by operant conditioning. *Circulation Research* (Supplement I) , 1970, **26–27**, 27–32. (a)

SHAPIRO, D., TURSKY, B., & SCHWARTZ, G. E. Differentiation of heart rate and systolic blood pressure in man by operant conditioning. *Psychosomatic Medicine,* 1970, **32**, 417–423. (b)

SHAPIRO, D., & WATANABE, T. Timing characteristics of operant electrodermal modification: fixed interval effects. *Japanese Psychological Research,* 1971, **13**, 123–130.

SHNIDMAN, S. R. Avoidance conditioning of skin potential responses. *Psychophysiology*, 1969, **6**, 38–44.

SHNIDMAN, S. R. Instrumental conditioning of orienting responses using positive reinforcement. *Journal of Experimental Psychology*, 1970, **83**, 491–494.

SHNIDMAN, S., & SHAPIRO, D. Instrumental modification of elicited autonomic responses. *Psychophysiology*, 1971, **7**, 395–401.

SIROTA, A. D., & MAHONEY, M. J. Relaxing on cue: the self-regulation of asthma. *Journal of Behaviour Therapy and Experimental Psychiatry*, 1974, **5**, 65–66.

SIROTA, A. D., SCHWARTZ, G. E., & SHAPIRO, D. Voluntary control of human heart rate: effect on reaction to aversive stimulation. *Journal of Abnormal Psychology*, 1974, **83**, 261–267.

SLUCKI, H., ÁDÁM, G., & PORTER, R. W. Operant discrimination of an interoceptive stimulus in rhesus monkey. *Journal of the Experimental Analysis of Behavior*, 1965, **8**, 405–414.

SNYDER, C., & NOBLE, M. E. Operant conditioning of vasoconstriction. *Journal of Experimental Psychology*, 1968, **77**, 263–268.

SOLBERG, W. K., & RUGH, J. D. The use of biofeedback devices in the treatment of bruxism. *Journal of the Southern California Dental Association*, 1972, **40**, 852–853.

STERMAN, M. B. Neurophysiologic and clinical studies of sensorimotor EEG biofeedback training: some effects on epilepsy. *Seminars in Psychiatry*, 1973, **5**, 507–525.

STERMAN, M. B., HOWE, R. C., & MACDONALD, L. R. Facilitation of spindle-burst sleep by conditioning of electroencephalographic activity while awake. *Science*, 1970, **167**, 1146–1148.

STEVENS, S. S. Matching functions between loudness and ten other continua. *Perception and Psychophysics*, 1966, **1**, 5–8.

STEVENSON, I. P., DUNCAN, C. H., WOLF, S., RIPLEY, H. S., & WOLFF, H. G. Life situations, emotions, and extra systoles. *Psychosomatic Medicine*, 1949, **11**, 257–272.

STOYVA, J., BARBER, T. X., DiCARA, L. V., KAMIYA, J., MILLER, N. E., & SHAPIRO, D. (Eds.) *Biofeedback and self-control 1971: an Aldine Annual on the regulation of bodily processes and consciousness*. Chicago: Aldine-Atherton, 1972.

STOYVA, J., & BUDZYNSKI, T. Cultivated low-arousal—an anti-stress response? In L. V. DiCara

(Ed.), *Recent advances in limbic and autonomic nervous system research*. New York: Plenum, 1974.

STROEBEL, C. F., & GLUECK, B. C. Biofeedback treatment in medicine and psychiatry: an ultimate placebo? *Seminars in Psychiatry*, 1973, **5**, 379–393.

STUART, R. B., & DAVIS, B. *Slim chance in a fat world: behavioral control of obesity*. Champaign, Ill.: Research Press, 1972.

SURWIT, R. S. Biofeedback: a possible treatment for Raynaud's disease. *Seminars in Psychiatry*, 1973, **5**, 483–490.

SURWIT, R. S., & SHAPIRO, D. Skin temperature feedback and concomitant cardiovascular changes. *Proceedings of the Biofeedback Research Society*, 1974, p. 69. (Abstract)

TAUB, E., & EMURIAN, C. Autoregulation of skin temperature using a variable intensity feedback light. Paper presented at the second annual meeting of the Biofeedback Research Society, 1972.

TAUB, E., EMURIAN, C., & HOWELL, P. Further progress in training self-regulation of skin temperature. *Proceedings of the Biofeedback Research Society*, 1974, p. 70. (Abstract)

TEPLITZ, T. A. Operant conditioning of blood pressure: a critical review and some psychosomatic considerations. *Communications in Behavioral Biology*, 1971, **6**, 197–202.

THOMAS, L. J., TIBER, N., & SCHIRESON, S. The effects of anxiety and frustration on muscular tension related to the temporomandibular joint syndrome. *Dental Research*, 1973, **36**, 763–768.

THORNDIKE, E. L. *An experimental study of rewards*. New York: Columbia University Teacher's College, 1933, publication no. 580.

TROWILL, J. A. Instrumental conditioning of the heart rate in the curarized rat. *Journal of Comparative and Physiological Psychology*, 1967, **63**, 7–11.

TURSKY, B., SHAPIRO, D., & SCHWARTZ, G. E. Automated constant cuff-pressure system to measure average systolic and diastolic blood pressure in man. *IEEE Transactions on Biomedical Engineering*, 1972, **19**, 271–276.

VAN TWYVER, H. B., & KIMMEL, H. D. Operant conditioning of the GSR with concomitant measurement of two somatic variables. *Journal of Experimental Psychology*, 1966, **72**, 841–846.

VOLOW, M. R., & HEIN, P. L. Bi-directional

operant conditioning of peripheral vasomotor responses with augmented feedback and prolonged training. *Psychophysiology,* 1972, **9,** 271. (Abstract)

WALTON, D. The application of learning theory to the treatment of a case of bronchial asthma. In H. J. Eysenck (Ed.), *Behavior therapy and the neuroses.* New York: Pergamon Press, 1960.

WEISS, H. D. The physiology of human penile erection. *Annals of Internal Medicine,* 1972, **76,** 793–799.

WEISS, T., & ENGEL, B. T. Operant conditioning of heart rate in patients with premature ventricular contractions. *Psychosomatic Medicine,* 1971, **33,** 301–321.

WICKRAMASEKERA, I. Electromyographic feedback training and tension headache: preliminary observations. *American Journal of Clinical Hypnosis,* 1972, **15,** 83–85.

WILLERSON, J. T., THOMPSON, R. H., HOOKMAN, P., HERDT, J., & DECKER, J. L. Reserpine in Raynaud's disease and phenomenon: short-term response to intra-arterial injection. *Annals of Internal Medicine,* 1970, **72,** 17–27.

WOLFF, H. G. *Headache and other head pain.* (2nd ed.) New York: Oxford University Press, 1963.

WOLPE, J. *Psychotherapy by reciprocal inhibition.* Stanford, Calif.: Stanford University Press, 1958.

WOLPE, J., & LAZARUS, A. A. *Behavior therapy techniques.* Oxford: Pergamon Press, 1966.

WYRWICKA, W., & STERMAN, M. B. Instrumental conditioning of sensorimotor cortex EEG spindles in the waking cat. *Physiology and Behavior,* 1968, **3,** 703–707.

YEMM, R. Masseter muscle activity in stress. *Archives of Oral Biology,* 1969, 14, 1437–1439. (a)

YEMM, R. Variations in the electrical activity of the human masseter muscle occurring in association with emotional stress. *Archives of Oral Biology,* 1969, 14, 873–878. (b)

Behavioral Approaches to Treatment of Neuroses

4

HAROLD LEITENBERG

This chapter reviews behavioral approaches to treatment of two neurotic disorders—phobia and obsessive-compulsive neurosis. These neuroses were chosen because (1) depression is covered in some detail in chapter 5 of this book; (2) it is difficult to distinguish between anxiety neurosis and either severe agoraphobia or neurotic depression, and it is still unclear whether or not entirely different treatment approaches are really indicated; therefore, anxiety neurosis has been omitted; (3) relatively little evaluation of behavioral treatment of other classic neurotic disorders (e.g., hysterical neurosis, "existential" neurosis) has taken place; (4) considerable research time and effort *has* been expended in the development and analysis of behavioral therapies for phobia and obsessive-compulsive neurosis, and as will be seen from the review of this research literature, treatment approaches for these two disorders have been developed along strikingly similar lines.

Before elaborating on the treatment issues, it may be helpful to briefly discuss (1) what is meant by neuroses, and (2) how often neurotic disorders are encountered in the general population and in clinical settings. Unfortunately these are complex issues without satisfactory answers. Let us deal with the definitional question first. Almost every textbook in psychology and psychiatry defines five major types of neurosis. They are:

1. *Anxiety neurosis:* chronic anxiety of variable intensity supposedly unreferrable to specific situations.
2. *Phobia:* extreme fear and avoidance of specific objects or situations which the individual objectively recognizes should not be fear-provoking.
3. *Obsessive-compulsive reaction:* intense repetition of compulsive checking and washing rituals; undesired thoughts of illness, contamination, doing injury to others; and avoidance of situations that might provoke these.
4. *Hysterical neurosis:* includes conversion reactions such as functional limb paralysis, blindness, deafness, and dissociative reactions such as fugue states, amnesia, multiple personality.
5. *Depressive neurosis:* intense feelings of dejection, helplessness, and hopelessness accompanied by sleeping and eating problems.

These diagnostic categories provide an appearance of clarity and order that may be misleading. Differential diagnosis is notoriously unreliable (e.g., Derogatis, Lipman, Covi, & Rickels, 1972; Schmidt & Fonda, 1956; Zigler & Phillips, 1961). Actually, the distinctions between different neurotic syndromes are not clear-cut, neither providing accurate descriptions nor signifying discrete etiologies or prescriptions for separate treatment plans. Furthermore the distinctions between specific neurotic disorders and psychotic disorders are often blurred. We have seen instances, for example, of arguments among clinicians as to whether a patient is suffering from a personality disorder with phobic reactions or from a phobia with secondary personality deficits. Treatment plans seem to be guided much more by the specific excess and deficit behaviors an individual patient exhibits than by a diagnostic label. And in some instances diagnosis may actually inhibit consideration of alternative treatment approaches. The extreme social phobic who believes people think he looks, talks, and walks "funny" may be classified as a schizophrenic with paranoid delusions. As a result many clinicians would consider it quite inappropriate to treat the social phobia with behavioral means.

Derogatis, Lipman, Covi, and Rickels (1971) recently tried to clear the waters somewhat by doing a factor analysis study of the common complaints associated with neurotic disorders. Five clusters of symptoms or problem behaviors were defined.

1. *Somatization:* muscle soreness, numbness or tingling in parts of body, heavy feelings in arms or legs, weakness in parts of body, pains in heart or chest, hot or cold spells, pains in lower part of back, sweating, trouble getting breath, feeling low in energy or slowed down, difficult in speaking when excited, faintness or dizziness, lump in throat, headaches.

2. *Anxiety:* feeling fearful, nervousness or shakiness inside, suddenly scared for no reason, feeling tense or keyed up, heart pounding or racing, having to avoid certain things, places, etc.

because of fear, trembling, worrying or stewing about things, difficulty falling or staying asleep.

3. *Depression:* thoughts of ending life, feeling blue, loss of sexual interest or pleasure, feeling hopeless about future, poor appetite, feeling lonely, constipation, crying easily, feeling no interest in things, worrying or stewing about things, feeling people are unfriendly, feeling inferior to others, feeling others don't understand you, feelings of being trapped or caught, feeling easily annoyed or irritated, uncontrollable temper outbursts, blaming yourself for things.

4. *Interpersonal sensitivity:* feeling easily annoyed or irritated, feeling critical of others, feeling others do not understand you, uncontrollable temper outbursts, easily hurt feelings, feeling inferior to others, feeling of being trapped or caught, feeling people are unfriendly.

5. *Obsessive-compulsive:* having to check and double-check, having to do things very slowly to insure correctness, mind going blank, trouble remembering things, difficulty making decisions, trouble concentrating, worried about sloppiness/carelessness, feeling confused, having to ask others what you should do, feeling blocked/stymied in getting things done, blaming yourself for things, feeling no interest in things, difficulty speaking when excited.

It is clear that there may be considerable overlap in the complaints of a patient said to be suffering from phobia and the complaints of a patient said to be suffering from anxiety neurosis or neurotic depression. It is also clear that although the above list of problems seems long, it is still incomplete. If a problem-oriented list were derived for each neurotic patient, many more items would undoubtedly be included. For example, it would be unusual to find clients suffering from central neurotic behavior problems who did not, at the same time, have interpersonal problems at home and on the job, and who did not devaluate themselves and have poor self-concepts.

The idea of compiling lists of problem behaviors for individual neurotic patients raises another issue. We are not in a good position to say whether or not neuroses should be defined by the presence of some critical "symptom" or by some arbitrary total number of symptoms (although it is clear that neurotic patients exhibit a greater number of neurotic behaviors than "normal controls," cf. Kellner & Sheffield, 1973). Undoubtedly questions of intensity, chronicity, and scope of the problem enter into conclusions about the presence or absence of a full-fledged, conspicuous neurotic disorder as distinguished from the simple presence of specific neurotic behaviors. However, this sort of distinction tends to be unreliable and of little utility. The more pertinent concern is not pinning a particular label on an individual but rather having an accurate list of problems and effective solutions.

This brings us to the second question. How large a problem is neurosis, how debilitating are its symptoms, and how many people have neurotic disorders? Unfortunately determinations of incidence or prevalence of psychoneuroses are bedevilled by the definitional and diagnostic quandaries just discussed. Furthermore, because neurotic behaviors will not typically result in consultation with a physician or mental health professional (Ryle, 1967), statistics derived from these sources will be vastly disparate from those derived from surveys of the general population. For example, neuroses are said to account for only 4% of all first hospital admissions (Kutash, 1965). Yet, in Great Britain it has been estimated that from 7% to 21% of the patients that consult a physician in *general practice* do so because of neurotic behavior problems (Kellner, 1966; Rycroft, 1968); questionnaires administered to random samples of the general population further raise these estimates. When Ryle (1967) administered the Cornell Medical Index to 110 working class families, "minimal neurosis" was defined as a score of 16 or more and "definitely neurotic" as a score of 31 or more. Eighty-two of the 110 people obtained a score above 31. Similarly, the Midtown Manhattan Study (Srole, Langner, Michael, Opler, & Rennie, 1962) indicated that only

18% of the general population were *not* at least mildly impaired by psychological problems, and that approximately 25% were considered to have a marked degree of disturbance. Specific breakdowns into conventional diagnostic entities were not made. Nonetheless, this works out to a staggering figure of over 50 million people. The rough estimate that at least 10 million people in the United States suffer from neurotic behavior problems (Kutash, 1965) may actually be quite conservative. It is certainly clear that this is a matter for serious concern, and that effective preventative and therapeutic programs must be developed.

This chapter is organized around the usual diagnostic system for neurotic disorders rather than around lists of a wide variety of excess and deficit behaviors. This is the path that treatment-oriented research has so far taken and we will follow it here. Treatment of phobia will be discussed first, followed by a review of the research literature on behavioral treatment of obsessive-compulsive neurosis. One of the major purposes of this chapter is to review in detail those studies that illustrate how and why emphasis in the treatment of both disorders has shifted from an initial focus on first modifying subjective experiences of anxiety to the current focus on first modifying overt avoidance behavior.

Phobia

Although minor fears are common in children and adults, real phobia is estimated to be present in only about 77 out of 1000 persons (Agras, Sylvester, & Oliveau, 1969). Phobias so disabling as to cause inability to work or manage common household tasks have a still lower estimated proportion, only 2 out of 1,000 persons (Agras et al., 1969). Phobic states are reported to be the major complaint in only 2% to 3% of outpatients (Marks, 1970).

By far the most common clinical phobia

is *agoraphobia:* a fear of going out into open spaces and public areas (such as streets and stores), of travel, and sometimes of just leaving home, or conversely, remaining home alone. Anxiety with somatic and autonomic components is a major feature of this disorder. In addition, agoraphobia patients often have a fear of fainting, and losing control in public due to anticipated recurrence of panic attacks—approximately 50% to 60% of patients suffering from phobia have this syndrome (Marks, 1970). Agoraphobia usually has an onset between ages 18 and 25 and two-thirds of patients seen for this problem are women. Aside from agoraphobia, the major clinical phobias are illness and injury phobia, social phobia, animal phobia, and other miscellaneous specific phobias, e.g., heights, storms, etc. (Agras et al., 1969; Marks, 1969).

There are few studies of the long-term course of untreated phobia. After initial identification in an epidemiological survey, a follow-up of 30 phobics who had not sought or obtained any treatment during a five-year interval was accomplished (Agras, Chapin, & Oliveau, 1972). The results indicated that 100% of children's phobias improved substantially or completely recovered by the end of five years, whereas only 43% of adults' phobias improved during this time, 20% of the adults remained unchanged and 33% were rated worse. The authors point out "that these findings do not confirm Eysenck's (1966) impression that 72% of adult neurotic patients will recover without treatment by the end of two years, and that 90% will have improved in five years time. Either phobia has a worse prognosis than other neuroses, or the studies examined by Eysenck are inadequate. In either case, the base rate of improvement that behavior therapy must now beat no longer appears so formidable.

It is also important to note that long-term follow-up studies of phobic patients who received forms of treatment other than behavior therapy have not reported results much different from the above 43% figure for untreated phobias. In a 23-year follow-up of 19 phobic patients who had received brief out-patient psychotherapy (average of 12 sessions), Errara and Coleman (1963) found that only 1 of the 19 was completely recovered and 12 of the 19 had not shown improvement. Roberts (1964) interviewed 38 agoraphobics 18 months to 16 years following in-patient treatment consisting of psychotherapeutic support, medication, and "firm encouragement to go out." He found that only 23% were completely recovered. Miles, Barabee, and Finesinger (1951) performed a long-term evaluation of 62 cases of anxiety neurosis following in-patient psychotherapy. Only 8% were considered recovered and 14% much improved.

The question that needs to be considered here is whether or not recent developments in behavior therapy give cause for greater optimism, and more specifically to examine what the findings have been in regard to treatment of phobia. Four behavioral approaches to treatment will be reviewed: systematic desensitization, reinforced practice, participant modeling, and flooding in reality. As will be seen, the latter three approaches are relatively new and have an important feature in common—they all try to reduce phobic anxiety and avoidance behavior by arranging rapid and direct exposure to actual rather than, as in the case of systematic desensitization, imagined phobic stimuli.

SYSTEMATIC DESENSITIZATION

The first and by now most thoroughly studied behavior therapy technique used to treat phobia is systematic desensitization (Wolpe, 1958). The three major components of systematic desensitization are: (1) construction of a graduated hierarchy of anxiety-provoking scenes, and arrangement of these in an order such that the first scene elicits minimal anxiety and the last scene evokes considerable anxiety: (2) training the patient in deep muscle relaxation usually via the Jacobsen (1938) technique, although hypnotic induction techniques, drugs, and biofeedback have also been employed for this purpose; (3) having the patient visualize each of the scenes while in the relaxed state. Examples of typical hierarchies, detailed descriptions of the muscle relaxation training procedure, and demonstrations of actual desensitization therapy sessions can be found in Wolpe and Lazarus (1966) and Wolpe (1969).

Provoked anxiety is minimal in systematic desensitization because the scenes are imagined rather than real, because the scenes are arranged in a very gradual manner, because progression is delayed until each preceding item can be visualized without anxiety, and most importantly, because the patient is completely relaxed while imagining each scene. Wolpe (1958) believed that muscle relaxation was an anxiety antagonist which would inhibit autonomic arousal. Wolpe suggested that relaxation would suppress or inhibit the anxiety producing properties of phobic stimuli, and thus the bond between these stimuli and the former anxiety response would be weakened.

Since Wolpe's original publication (1958), various alternative theoretical explanations as well as various procedural components of systematic desensitization have been exhaustively researched. Work in this area has taken several directions. At first numerous case studies were presented simply to illustrate the wide range of anxiety disorders that could be treated by systematic desensitization. A second series of studies evaluated outcome. A third effort tried to elucidate the process underlying the apparent success of systematic desensitization. A fourth approach involved experimental manipulations of the systematic desensitization procedure to determine what elements were most essential, and what elements might be added for effectiveness. Areas explored included the presence or absence of relaxation, the extent of anxiety reduction prior to movement up the hierarchy, the necessity of the hierarchy

itself, the use of imagined versus real phobic stimuli, standardized versus individualized hierarchies, automated versus therapist presentation of relaxation instructions and hierarchy series, and the role of therapeutic expectancies.

Because comparable phobic patients are not in large supply or readily available for research purposes, many studies have made use of "phobia analogues." Severe fear of snakes, rats, spiders, examinations, and public speaking in college students has been substituted for clinical phobia with resultant confusion about the similarity of clinical and nonclinical phobias and the overall usefulness of analogue studies (Bernstein & Paul, 1971). Without question, however, the availability of these phobia analogues has led to a tremendous outpouring of publications and dissertations dealing with systematic desensitization. Because a number of excellent reviews and theoretical discussions of this topic already exist (Bandura, 1969; Davison & Wilson, 1973; Lang, 1969; Paul, 1969; Rachman, 1967; Wilkins, 1971; Wilson & Davison, 1971), no attempt will be made to cover this vast literature here. Another major reason for bypassing the bulk of this research is that it all seems to be leading away from systematic desensitization and into other behavioral techniques that may be more efficient and effective. Procedural studies as well as studies directed at explaining the process that makes systematic desensitization work seem to be converging. The underlying mechanism of systematic desensitization is not what it was originally thought to be, and in fact can be better implemented via other behavioral approaches. Before pursuing this point further, however, it might be helpful to provide a brief overview of the major clinical outcome studies with systematic desensitization. This will provide some perspective in evaluating the material that follows. Although recent evidence suggests that other behavioral strategies might be more effective than systematic desensitization in treatment of phobia, the evidence does not in any way imply that systematic desensitization alone is not effective.

OUTCOME STUDIES. All large-scale outcome studies in psychotherapy suffer similar difficulties. It is seldom a simple matter to isolate the specific therapeutic procedure under study from other nonspecific factors. Pre- and posttest measures that are objective, reliable, clinically relevant, and unbiased are always hard to achieve. Long-term follow-up is essential but difficult. Comparable patients to be assigned to alternative treatment groups or to no-treatment control groups are not easily available. In the case of systematic desensitization, large-scale outcome studies have been done not only with volunteer subjects in analogue studies, but also with phobic patients. These latter studies are, of course, of greater interest. Instead of mentioning all of these clinical studies, the "landmark" studies are sufficient to show the relative effectiveness of systematic desensitization.

An uncontrolled clinical trial was the first outcome report provided (Wolpe, 1958). The results of a sample of 210 mixed neurotic patients seen in private practice were quite impressive. Wolpe claimed that 90% of these patients were either improved or cured upon completion of treatment. This sample, however, excluded dropouts, i.e., those receiving less than 15 treatment sessions. If dropouts were included and considered failures, then only 75% of those who started treatment would have showed marked improvement. No follow-up data were provided.

Lazarus (1961) reported similar results but in the context of a much more sophisticated study. Eighteen phobic patients received systematic desensitization (in groups), and 17 control patients received "interpretive" group therapy. Of the 18 systematic desensitization patients, 13 recovered in an average of 20 sessions (72% improvement rate). A nine-month follow-up indicated no relapse or symptom substitution. Only two

of the group therapy patients were symptom free after a mean of 22 sessions. The remaining 15 patients from the control group were subsequently desensitized. Ten recovered in a mean of 10 sessions. This was a rather impressive demonstration of the superiority of systematic desensitization.

Lazarus (1963) also reported a large uncontrolled outcome study of 126 neurotic cases. Systematic desensitization was not used exclusively (assertive training and behavior rehearsal were incorporated as necessary). Lazarus determined that 62% of the patients were markedly improved or fully recovered. It should be noted that circumscribed or specific monosymptomatic phobias were intentionally excluded from this sample since Lazarus felt that systematic desensitization was already proven for those cases and now needed to be evaluated in patients suffering from more diffuse and pervasive neurotic disorders.

Analogue studies by Lang and his associates (Lang & Lazovik, 1963; Lang, Lazovik, & Reynolds, 1965) and Paul and his associates (Paul, 1966, 1967, 1968; Paul & Shannon, 1966) should also be mentioned here. They represent breakthroughs for pure experimental analysis of systematic desensitization with precise measures of outcome and adequate controls. Lang and Lazovik (1963) conducted a well designed snake phobia experiment which opened the floodgates for this sort of research. The ability to touch a harmless snake upon completion of treatment was used as a criterion measure of success. Seven out of 13 subjects receiving systematic desensitization were able to do this as compared to only 2 out of 11 for a no-treatment control group. Treatment was limited to only 11 sessions, and it was noted that subjects who progressed through 15 or more of the 20 hierarchy items improved significantly more than subjects who did not get this far. Presumably the 54% cure rate, which is much lower than in preceding studies, might have been increased if more sessions were held or if a less stringent criterion of improvement (touching snake) had been employed. In a subsequent study, Lang et al. (1965) added a pseudotherapy group that went through the initial steps of relaxation training and hierarchy construction but did not receive the actual desensitization procedure. Instead therapy sessions were devoted to discussion of nonphobic material. There was a significant difference between the systematic desensitization group and the two control groups (pseudotherapy and no treatment) with the latter two groups showing little gain and no difference between them.

Paul (1966) presented a detailed and rather extensive study of volunteer college students suffering from speech anxiety. Five groups were established: systematic desensitization in imagination, insight-oriented psychotherapy, social attention placebo, untreated control, and noncontact control. Numerous measures were taken in the form of questionnaires, psychometric tests, independent behavioral ratings of speech performance, anxiety ratings while speaking, and physiological measures. The systematic desensitization group did significantly better than all others on subjective, behavioral, and physiological measures. Follow-up questionnaires at two years showed that the percentage improved was 85% for desensitization, 50% for insight psychotherapy and placebo, and 22% for untreated controls. A similar study by Paul and Shannon (1966) was done using the group desensitization procedures employed by Lazarus (1961). Five groups of 10 subjects each were compared. The treatment conditions were similar to the previous study, namely, group systematic desensitization, individual systematic desensitization, individual insight-oriented psychotherapy, attention placebo, and untreated controls. There were no significant differences in effects of group and individual systematic desensitization, and both of these groups had outcomes superior to the three comparison control groups. These differences were sustained on a two-year follow-up (Paul, 1968).

Unfortunately, such neat experimental designs with multiple outcome measures are seldom possible with neurotic patients (as distinguished from volunteers). Nevertheless, a valiant attempt along these lines has been made at the Maudsley Hospital in London. The Maudsley studies are important since phobic patients, unlike phobic volunteers, usually have more crippling phobias as well as other behavior problems. A series of retrospective studies was first completed (Cooper, 1963; Cooper, Gelder, & Marks, 1965; Marks & Gelder, 1965). The Cooper et al. (1965) paper presents the cumulative findings from all three studies. Seventy-seven patients (29 agoraphobics, 12 other phobics, 13 writer's cramp, 10 obsessive rituals, 13 miscellaneous) received some combination of behavior therapy techniques. Unfortunately, this was seldom systematic desensitization alone. Fifty-five control cases who did not receive any form of behavior therapy were found in the hospital records. Retrospective studies such as these are, of course, easily criticized (Paul, 1969). Nevertheless the results with phobic patients suggest that behavior therapy did better than other treatment procedures. At one-year follow-up, 70% of the phobic patients treated with systematic desensitization (plus in vivo practice, assertive training, drugs in some unspecified mix) were considered improved, whereas only 52% of phobic patients that had other forms of therapy (drugs, individual psychotherapy, leucotomy, but no behavior therapy) were considered improved.

The Maudsley group next conducted a series of controlled prospective studies where patients were initially matched and then assigned to different treatment groups. In the first study (Gelder & Marks, 1966), 20 severe agoraphobics (three-fourths were unable to leave house unaccompanied) were matched in terms of age at treatment, age at symptom onset, symptom duration, type of symptom, initial severity of phobia, degree of general anxiety, scores on symptom checklist of phobia, ratings of family, and social adjustment. All patients were treated in the hospital and, unfortunately, treatment was again a complex mix of behavior therapy techniques (systematic desensitization, graded retraining, assertive training) although systematic desensitization predominated. In addition, 6 of the 10 patients received medication. The control group received individual psychotherapy and 7 of 10 control patients were also on medication. Ratings by patients, therapists, and an independent assessor yielded disappointing results in that no significant difference between groups was found. Seven out of 10 patients in each group showed improvement on their main phobia; 4 out of 10 were rated much improved with behavior therapy; 2 out of 10 were rated much improved with the control treatment.

Gelder, Marks, Wolff, and Clarke (1967) compared the effects of individual psychotherapy, group psychotherapy, and systematic desensitization (usual confounding with in vivo practice assignments and assertive training). Sixteen patients were assigned each to group therapy and systematic desensitization conditions, and 10 were assigned to individual psychotherapy. Agoraphobia, social phobia, and specific phobias of thunder, heights, darkness, and birds were included in the sample. The agoraphobics were less severely disabled than in the prior study. At 18-month follow-up, multiple ratings indicated that 9 of 16 systematic desensitization patients were much improved, while only 2 of 16 for group therapy and only 3 of 10 for individual psychotherapy, were improved. In a subsequent study (Gelder & Marks, 1968), 7 of the group psychotherapy patients who had failed to respond during either 18 months of group therapy or during a 6-month follow-up period were treated with systematic desensitization. Mean improvement in phobic symptoms was three times as great following 4 months of desensitization as compared to the degree of improvement observed in the preceding 2-year period.

In another experiment (Marks, Gelder, & Edward, 1968), hypnosis was compared to systematic desensitization. Six agoraphobics, 4 social phobics and 4 specific phobics (animals, storms, heights) were assigned to systematic desensitization and the same distribution was assigned to hypnosis. Forty-six percent of desensitization patients and 39% of hypnosis patients also received medication at some stage during treatment. At the end of three months treatment, 7 systematic desensitization patients were rated much improved, whereas only 3 of 14 hypnosis patients were so rated.

McConaghy (1970), in reviewing these series of experiments conducted at the Maudsley, points out that although individual studies often failed to yield statistically significant differences between systematic desensitization and other treatments, this was largely due to small sample size. The trend was clearly and consistently in favor of systematic desensitization. Approximately half the patients treated with desensitization showed marked improvement whereas only a quarter of control subjects treated with other therapies did so.

Finally, when we consider the controlled studies of Lazarus (1961), Lang and Lazovik (1963), Paul (1966), and Paul and Shannon (1966) it seems safe to conclude that systematic desensitization is demonstrably more effective than both no treatment and every psychotherapy variant with which it has so far been compared.

INTERPRETATION OF OUTCOME.   Why does systematic desensitization work? Almost every aspect of the systematic desensitization procedure has at some time been experimentally demonstrated to be unessential. For example, deep muscle relaxation or pairing of relaxation with phobic scenes may not always be critical (Agras, Leitenberg, Barlow, Curtis, Edwards, & Wright, 1971; Aponte & Aponte, 1971; Marshall, Strawbridge, & Kettner, 1972; Nawas, Welsh, & Fishman, 1970; Rachman, 1968b; Rachman & Hodgson, 1967; Waters, McDonald, & Koresko, 1972); and graduated hierarchies and gradual progression through the hierarchy may not be necessary (Cohen, 1969; Krapfl & Nawas, 1970; Miller & Nawas, 1970; Nawas, Fishman, & Pucel, 1970; Wolpin & Pearsall, 1965). Many of these studies, however, can be dismissed because of methodological faults and small samples. Also it is important to note that occasional failure to find a significant difference between, let us say, a progressive hierarchy and a nonprogressive hierarchy does not mean that one can logically conclude there is no difference. Conventional statistical designs only permit us to say that the null hypothesis (no difference) could not be rejected. Even more importantly, aside from Agras et al. (1971), all these experiments used volunteer subjects with circumscribed fears rather than clinical phobias. Obviously, certain procedural elements may be more essential in treatment of severe phobias in patients than they are in treatment of animal fears or test anxiety. Nevertheless, there is reason to look elsewhere to try to determine the essential components of systematic desensitization. These reasons include: the influence of various social and cognitive factors on systematic desensitization (Wilkins, 1971); the disrepute of counterconditioning theories (although subjects may no longer show anxiety to phobic stimuli following systematic desensitization, they hardly ever show signs of conditioned relaxation); the similar disrepute of reciprocal inhibition theories of systematic desensitization (anxiety is not equivalent to muscle tension and muscle relaxation hardly precludes experience of subjective anxiety).

A predominant feature of systematic desensitization is that it gradually induces subjects to expose themselves to actual feared stimuli and situations they have been avoiding. Phobic scenes are imagined and the function of relaxation may simply be to facilitate such exposure; subjects are less likely to try to escape the phobic scenes described by the therapists when they are relaxed. Also mental relaxation may promote concentration and thus more vivid phobic imagery. In addition, during the course of systematic desensitization it is customary to instruct patients to confront in *reality* those phobic situations which they have already been able to *imagine* without concomitant anxiety. Given that patients believe the rationale of systematic desensitization, and given their prior success in imagination, it is now more likely than ever before that they will take this all important next step.

Wolpe (1963) stated that "there is almost invariably a one-to-one relationship between what the patient can imagine without anxiety and what he can experience in reality without anxiety [p. 1063]." Empirical evidence, however, indicates otherwise. Lang et al. (1965) and Davison (1968) in snake phobic studies reported that the amount of progress made in a behavioral test with the real feared object after desensitization was far less than the amount of progress made in imagination. Also when subjects did reach the same point in reality they often reported anxiety in doing so. Agras (1967) reported similar findings with five agoraphobic patients. Improved performance in the actual feared situation lagged well behind progress in desensitization in all but one patient. Barlow, Leitenberg, Agras, and Wincze (1969) demonstrated this transfer gap in a direct experimental fashion. They compared the effect of systematic desensitization on volunteer college subjects afraid of snakes in two conditions. In the first, relaxation was paired with imagined scenes of the snake; in the second, relaxation was paired with a real snake. Otherwise the conditions were identical; the same relaxation exercises and the same progressive hierarchy were employed. The subjects who were exposed to the real object could maintain their relaxed state because the snake was gradually moved closer to them; they did not actively move closer to the snake. There were 10 subjects in each group matched on the basis of pretest scores of ability to approach a harmless boa contained in a glass cage. All subjects were seen until they completed the hierarchy or for a maximum of 10 sessions, whichever came first. Pretest and posttest behavioral and physiological measures were obtained by an experimenter who did not know which group subjects were assigned to.

In group 1 (imagined object), only 3 of the 9 subjects who completed the hierarchy reached the corresponding point in the behavioral approach test. In group 2 (real object) all 10 subjects completed the hierarchy and 9 out of 10 reached the corresponding point in the behavioral approach test. Although both groups improved, there was a significantly greater amount of change in group 2. The mean posttest score for group 1 (step 12) represented placing one's bare hand on the snake, while the mean posttest score for group 2 (step 17) indicated an ability to pick up the snake in one hand and hold it for 30 seconds. GSR response to five imagined scenes and to the actual presence of the snake placed in three different locations also indicated greater anxiety reduction as a result of prior exposure to the real feared object rather than the imagined object. In group 1 the reduction in GSR to imagined scenes approached the .05 level of significance, while there was little difference in GSR to the real situations. In group 2, however, GSR to both imagined and real situations was significantly reduced. These data indicate that systematic desensitization in imagination reduced physiological response to scenes in imagination; however, in the real situation anxiety was still quite high. Subjective reports of anxiety corresponded in this case to the GSR data. Similar reports of the benefit of adding real life exposure to systematic desensitization can be found in Garfield, Darwin, Singer, and McBrearty (1967) and Sherman (1972).

Systematic desensitization seems to work because it indirectly encourages patients to expose themselves to actual feared objects. Such a conclusion fits well with what is known from basic research on fear reduction and extinction of avoidance behavior in animals (Wilson & Davison, 1971). In reviewing the work of Nelson, these authors remark, ". . . that the provision of a stimulus that supposedly elicits an anxiety competing response (food, chlorpromazine) facilitates extinction of fear through the increased exposure to the CS which it can bring about. When these additional stimulus conditions are arranged so as *not* to provide such increased exposure . . . they result in *poorer* reduction in fear [p. 5]."

The idea that exposure to feared stimuli is the crucial and necessary ingredient in treatment of phobia is not a new one. In his paper "Turnings in the Ways of Psychoanalytic Therapy," Freud (1924) wrote: "One can hardly ever master a phobia if one waits till the patient lets the analysis influence him to give it up . . . one succeeds only when one can induce them through the influence of analysis to go about alone and to struggle with their anxiety while they make the attempt [p. 400]." Andrews (1966) in his review of psychotherapy approaches to phobia similarly concludes that the therapist must use his directive role as leverage to urge the patient to venture out of safety and confront fear arousing situations. Obviously one must take care to insure that such confrontation is within the manageable capacity of the patient. The patient should be in a position where he or she is likely to succeed in such approach behavior and thus gain confidence to go further next time.

If systematic desensitization then, is no more than a method of promoting exposure to actual phobic stimuli, we must ask whether other behavioral approaches can achieve this same goal more rapidly and effectively. The answer from several fronts seems to be yes. Three separate areas of research need to be reviewed: the work at the University of Vermont on reinforced practice, the work at Stanford University on participant modeling and contact desensitization, and the work at the Maudsley Hospital in London on prolonged exposure or flooding. Each of these projects and techniques will be evaluated in considerable detail since they represent the major new developments in this area.

"Reinforced practice," "shaping," "successive approximation," and "in vivo desensitization" are all therapeutic formats aimed at achieving essentially the same goal: to reduce phobic avoidance behavior and anxiety by gradually increasing the subject's contact with real life rather than imagined phobic stimuli. Graded exposure to real fear-provoking stimuli has long been used in overcoming avoidance behavior. Sporadic and for the most part uncontrolled case reports have appeared in the literature beginning with Jones (1924). (See also Bernstein & Beaty, 1971; Freeman & Kendrick, 1960; Herzberg, 1941; Jersild & Holmes, 1935; Lazarus, Davison, & Polefka, 1965; Meyer, 1957).

The research project at the University of Vermont, however, represents the first systematic and experimental exploration of factors that might facilitate such graduated training of approach behavior.

The strategy of the Vermont project was first to isolate significant therapeutic variables using single-case experimental methodology in phobic patients (Leitenberg, 1973). For the most part, the series of studies made use of the withdrawal design in which the effects on a direct measure of a central symptomatic behavior were continuously monitored as a function of introducing, withdrawing, and reintroducing a particular therapeutic variable in sequence. Subsequently, the therapeutic effectiveness of some of these same variables were evaluated in isolation and in combination in conventional between-group experimental designs with both clinical patients and volunteers exhibiting a variety of severe common fears (animals, heights, and darkness).

The initial therapeutic variable studied was social reinforcement—praise delivered contingent upon observed changes in desired behavior (Agras, Leitenberg, & Barlow, 1968). This variable was experimentally analyzed in three agoraphobic patients (two women, 23 and 39 years old, and one 36-year old man who had been severely phobic for 1, 15, and 16 years respectively, all having numerous fears including fears of walking alone, traveling alone, crowds, illness, and death. The two women had been unable to leave their homes alone, and the man had been able to manage only a five-minute drive to work with difficulty. All three patients were admitted to the University of Vermont clinical research center, a six-bed hospital-attached research ward in which patients can be treated without charge.

The detailed procedure and results for subject 1 (the 23-year-old woman) will be summarized here. It should be noted that previous in-patient psychiatric treatment had not altered her condition.

One of the central symptomatic behaviors in agoraphobia is difficulty in leaving a dependent situation. Thus, both time spent away and distance walked alone from the Clinical Research Center were used as indicators of phobic behavior. These were measured by mapping out a "course" from the Center to downtown, with landmarks identified at 25-yard intervals for over a mile. The subject was asked to stay on the course, to note the point at which she turned back, and was told, "We would like to see how far you can walk by yourself without experiencing undue tension. We find that repeated practice in a structured situation often leads to progress." Two sessions were held each day. Each session lasted half an hour, unless the patient stayed out longer than 20 minutes on the first trial, in which case the session was ended on return. At the end of each trial the patient reported the point reached in her walk. Since much of the course was easily observable, frequent checks of the patient's behavior were made throughout each phase of the study, con-

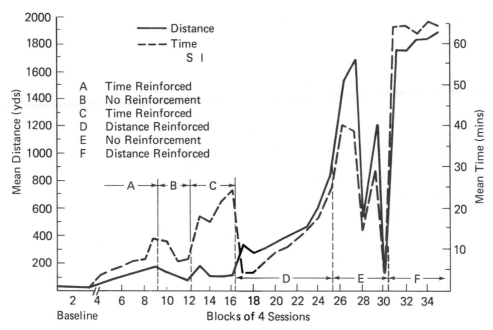

FIGURE 4–1   The effect of social reinforcement **and** nonreinforcement upon the time spent away and distance walked from the hospital by an agoraphobic patient (Agras, Leitenberg, & Barlow, 1968). Reprinted from Archives of General Psychiatry **19:425**, 1968. Copyright, American Medical Association.

firming the accuracy of her verbal report. The duration of each walk was timed by the therapist with a stop watch. The patient was not told how long she had been away from the Center.

During the baseline period the therapist maintained a pleasant relationship with the patient, but made no comment on the distance walked or time spent away. Reports of improvement made by the patient were also ignored.

Following the baseline, six experimental phases were held in sequence, as shown in Figure 4–1. These consisted of reinforcement of time spent away from the unit, nonreinforcement, reinforcement of time away again, reinforcement of distance walked.

Reinforcement consisted of praise such as, "Good . . . you're doing well . . . excellent" given with appropriate enthusiasm. During the reinforcement phase, remarks about progress made by the patient to the nursing staff were also praised. Nonreinforcement consisted of returning to baseline conditions and stopping selective

praise, but taking special care to maintain a generally pleasant, supportive attitude toward the patient. In this way a distinction between general support and differential reinforcement could be made.

In the reinforcement phase, the first trial of each day and all trials meeting the criterion were reinforced. The criterion was usually established as the mean between the previous criterion and the next highest trial, allowing behavior to be steadily shaped. Thus, if the patient has been reinforced at a criterion of 5 minutes, and spent 10 minutes away on the next trial, the criterion became 7.5 minutes. The patient now had to be away for at least 7.5 minutes to be reinforced, but the patient was not told of changes in criterion.

The results for this patient are summarized in Figure 4-1. During the baseline period, the patient showed no change in behavior. Following the introduction of reinforcement, both time away and distance walked alone showed a sustained increase. When reinforcement was withdrawn in the second phase, there was a clear reversal in performance. During this phase, the patient complained of feeling depressed and blamed herself for "doing so poorly." The addition of reinforcement in the next phase led to a steady rise in time spent away from the unit, but distance walked did not increase. This occurred because the patient was walking in circles by a turnabout outside of the hospital. This illustrates the selective effect of social praise since only the behavior reinforced, namely time spent away from the unit, increased.

The specific effect of reinforcement was demonstrated in another way in the next experimental condition when (without telling the patient) the criterion for reinforcement was changed from time away to distance walked. As seen in Figure 4–1, there was an immediate decrease in the amount of time spent away, and a sharp increase in distance walked, to the highest point since the beginning of the experiment. On the day of the change the patient complained that she "was doing very badly and was not able to stay out as long as before." This suggests that she was not aware of the change in reinforcement criterion, even though her behavior responded appropriately. For the remainder of this phase, distance walked alone increased steadily. Then reinforcement was removed for the second time. A marked spurt in performance occurred, during which the patient doubled her distance walked. This phenomenon parallels the initial extinction burst found in the animal laboratory (Keller & Schoenfield, 1950). The short-lived spurt was followed by a drop in performance which almost replicated the initial symptomatic behavior of the patient. Reinstatement of reinforcement for distance walked in the last experimental phase led to rapid reacquisition of the lost behavior and to further improvement.

By the end of the study, the patient was able to walk alone downtown. This behavior transferred to other situations so that she could walk where she pleased. In addition, her associated fears of crowds, choking, and dying also disappeared. Follow-up one year after treatment showed her to be symptom free.

The results for the other two patients were similar although less dramatic since only distance walked was reinforced and since baseline phases were less stable. Nevertheless it was clear in each case that the addition of contingent social praise facilitated approach behavior (declines in phobic avoidance behavior) and that withdrawal of such praise hampered progress.

The ability of praise contingent upon small gains in performance to increase approach behavior (exposure to phobic stimuli) and consequently decrease phobic avoidance behavior was also experimentally demonstrated with other types of phobia, including claustrophobia (Agras, Leitenberg, Barlow, & Thomson, 1969) and injury phobia (Leitenberg, Wincze, Butz, Callahan, & Agras, 1970). In these studies, reinforcement was manipulated in the context of a structured situation where patients gradually and repeatedly practiced doing what they were initially unable to do. For example, a claustrophobic had to stay in enclosed spaces for progressively longer periods of time; an agoraphobic had to walk and stay alone in open and crowded places. The effects of such repeated practice, whether or not accompanied by explicit social reinforcement, was next explored in five phobic patients (Leitenberg, Agras, Edwards, Thomson, & Wincze, 1970). The opportunity to practice was introduced, withdrawn, and reintroduced in sequence to determine whether phobic behavior would be reduced only during practice phases.

The procedure and data from only one of these patients will be summarized here. (It should be noted that the results of the other four patients were essentially the same.) The patient was a 25-year-old married male, with an admitting diagnosis of phobic reaction. He expressed a strong fear of strangers and crowds and indicated that he had not been able to go to work for the past four months (he got as far as the door of the factory once, and as far as the parking lot twice during this period); he had only been shopping once in eight months when he "purchased several items and left as quickly as possible." He reported feeling tense and anxious in the store with sensations of "fiery warmth" in his chest and back, tingling in his feet radiating up to his chest, dizziness, and near blackout.

The training situation consisted of entering a large discount department store and staying there "until he felt any undue anxiety." The therapist remained outside and timed with a stop watch how long he stayed in the store. Two sessions were held per day, one at 11 A.M. and one at 4 P.M. with one trial per session. A sample of three large stores was available from which two were randomly selected every day. A crowd of moderate size was usually present in each of the stores at these times. During the practice phase, whenever the patient stayed in the store for a longer time than his previous high time he was enthusiastically praised. (It should be noted that contingent praise was provided in only two of these five cases.) If the time declined or stayed the same, he was not praised. There were three phases to the experiment, each lasting five days. The opportunity to practice in the situation he formerly avoided was available in the first and third phases, while verbal "psychotherapy" was conducted for five consecutive days in the second phase. Themes discussed during this second phase were his anger and resentment over his wife's poor housekeeping (this may have played a part in his phobia since he stated, "If she won't do her share, I'll just quit too"); his use of hospitalization as a way of forcing his wife to shape up; his excessive demands and lack of cooperation at home; his necessary recognition that his own behavior, not the behavior of others, was the basis of his problem. Psychotherapy was conducted by an enthusiastic intern who was not involved in the rest of the experiment. Obviously this was not designed as a test of long-term psychotherapy, but was rather a control for attention and non-specific therapeutic expectancies.

The results are depicted in Figure 4–2.

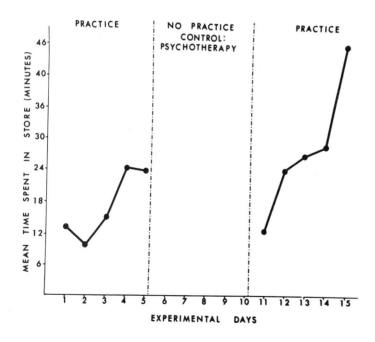

FIGURE 4–2   Time spent in crowded stores as a function of practice and no-practice conditions (Leitenberg, Agras, Edwards, Thomson, & Wincze, 1970).

The mean time stayed in the stores rapidly increased over the five days in which practice was possible.

Even the first point of 12 minutes may reflect the effect of practice since the day before the experiment began, the patient was pretested in a number of different stores and averaged only 5 minutes per entry. (The purpose of the pretest was to provide an empirical basis for selecting which stores to use in the acual experiment.) When practice was interrupted in phase 2 and verbal psychotherapy substituted in its place as a control procedure, the effect was a clear drop in the time subject stayed in the store. When practice was reinstated, there was a substantial increase in performance.

In each of the cases then, the opportunity to practice nonphobic behavior in a gradual structured manner was introduced, withdrawn, and reintroduced in sequence, while the amount of therapist attention, the therapeutic milieu, and instructions designed to increase expectancies for change were kept constant. Patients only showed positive change in a specific behavior measure during practice phases; when practice was removed, performance either regressed or stayed the same. When practice was reinstated, phobic avoidance behavior began to decline again.

Partly as a consequence of the specific behavioral focus and the graduated learning (practice) procedure, and partly because of the emphasis on continuous assessment and objective measurement, the target behavior in these studies was made overt and observable to both therapist and patient alike. Throughout therapy the patient usually saw that his behavior was gradually changing in the desired direction. In another study an attempt was made to experimentally manipulate such knowledge of performance (Leitenberg, Agras, Thomson, & Wright, 1968). This was most easily done in the case of patients suffering from phobias that involved some measure of time. For example, for a crowd phobia, increased time spent in a store might be a target; for an illness phobia, the target might be increased time in a hospital lobby; a claustrophobic would strive for increased time in an enclosed space.

In a discrete practice trial situation, information concerning performance could be given to the patient either during or at the end of a trial. In the first case reported below, feedback was provided throughout the trial; in others it was provided at the end of each practice trial with little apparent difference.

This subject was a 51-year-old claustrophobic woman. She reported that although her fears started in childhood, they had become more intense and incapacitating since the death of her husband seven years earlier. She said she could not stay in a house by herself, in a room with a closed door, in a cinema, in a church, or in a car alone for more than three or four miles. Her son indicated that for years he had had to stand outside ladies' rooms holding the door ajar because she was afraid to have it closed. She also expressed fears of choking and indicated that she had occasional "throat spasms."

A room four feet wide and six feet long illuminated by a 100 watt shaded bulb provided a situation in which the patient's claustrophobia could be measured. While in the room, the patient sat in a chair and was not allowed to read or engage in any other activity such as knitting, doing crossword puzzles, etc.

At the start of the first feedback phase, the patient received the following instructions: "You have been improving nicely. In order to further reduce your fears we will continue this repeated practice with a slight change. Larry will no longer remain just outside the room. Instead, he will be in the recording room at the other end of the corridor. Remember you are to come out of the room as soon as you feel the slightest discomfort or anxiety, and you are to go back only after you rest a while" (typically one minute). It was then pointed out: "In order to increase the accuracy of our recording we have installed an automatic timer that will operate when the door is closed. In order to check on the timer we want you to use a stopwatch to keep track in each trial of the time you spend in the room." She was shown how to work the stopwatch and told to record the exact time for each trial on a slip of paper. She was also told not to wear a wristwatch "as it might distract you from paying attention to the stopwatch." At the end of each session this paper was collected by the therapist. He did not mention if the times she recorded corresponded with times recorded by the automatic timer; nor did he praise her for any increase in time spent in the room.

In the no-feedback phase, the patient was told that the stopwatch had broken and had been sent out for repairs. This explanation was accepted without question (she made no attempt to wear a wristwatch during this phase). When the last trial of a session ended, the therapist told the patient that the session was over. He did not comment on her performance and gave neither

information about the time spent in the room nor praise such as "that was fine," "you did well," etc.

When feedback was resumed, the patient was told that the stopwatch had been repaired and that the earlier procedure of having a double-check on accuracy of measurement would be reinstated. As in the first feedback phase, no praise was provided for improved performance.

An attempt was made to provide an equally supportive, encouraging, and friendly social environment during all three phases. The nurses were not aware of shifts in experimental procedure and the psychiatrist and experimenters were repeatedly reminded to try to talk to the patients in the same amount and manner throughout the experiment. No effort was made, however, to confirm objectively that this was indeed done.

The major findings are summarized in Figure 4–3. Mean time per trial spent in the

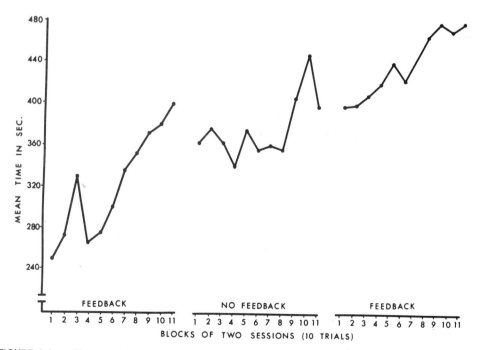

FIGURE 4–3   Time spent in a closed room by a claustrophobic as a function of feedback and no-feedback conditions (Leitenberg, Agras, Thomson, & Wright, 1968).

closed room increased progressively during the first feedback phase. When the stopwatch was removed in the no-feedback phase, there was a drop in time which leveled before any rise began to reappear. Although this late rise was not sustained (performance in the last two sessions of the no-feedback phase returned to the level exhibited at the end of the preceding feedback phase), it was rather marked, and was presumably due to repeated practice trials. As the results of the next phase suggest, however, feedback appeared to hasten and sustain this practice effect. When feedback was reinstated, time in the room immediately increased and continued to move steadily upwards throughout the remainder of the experiment.

The next experiments explored whether or not praise plus feedback had additive therapeutic effects. (It should be noted that in each of these experimental cases the target behavior involved an increase in time spent in contact with feared stimuli. When time is the target behavior, accurate knowledge of slight gains in performance usually depends upon external validation. Unlike an agoraphobic who can tell if he or she has walked further or not on any given trial, a claustrophobic cannot easily tell without a watch whether or not he or she stayed in the closed room 40 seconds rather than 30 seconds on any given trial.) In the first case, feedback alone was initially provided and praise was added to see if the rate of progress would be more rapid. Praise was then withdrawn while feedback was maintained, etc. The results indicated a steady rate of progress during feedback with no further benefit resulting from the addition of contingent praise. In five other phobic patients the order was reversed. Praise was initially provided without any accompanying feedback. Subsequently feedback was added to praise and then once again feedback was withdrawn and praise maintained. When the sequence of phases was switched in order to study the effects of adding feedback to praise (rather than the effect of adding

praise to feedback) the results were more interesting. The procedure and data from one representative case will be described.

This was a 56-year-old woman who was seen as an in-patient on the research unit. Four years before admission, she was treated for depression with ECT in another hospital. She reported that on the first day of release, while drying dishes at her brother's house, she picked up a knife and was overcome by the fear that she would use it to hurt someone. Since that time she reported avoiding contact with any pointed object that could be used to hurt someone. Although there were some clear obsessive features to this patient, the absence of any compulsive ritual and the extensive phobic avoidance behavior led us first to concentrate on the phobic component.

Since this patient had been avoiding situations (e.g., kitchens, gift shops) where she might come into contact with sharp implements, it was thought that a first therapeutic step would be to provide repeated practice in just looking at a sharp knife. Once this was achieved, handling knives alone and in the presence of others would be gradually reestablished.

In order to quantify the patient's knife fear and at the same time provide a structural situation for training, a box with a sliding door was constructed so that opening the door exposed a knife and activated an elapsed time meter located in an adjoining room. There were three practice sessions per day with 10 trials per session and 45-second intertrial intervals. A trial consisted of opening and closing the door to expose and conceal the knife. She was told that "during these sessions we want you to practice opening the door and looking at the knife for as long as you can without feeling the slightest anxiety. You are to close the door as soon as you feel any discomfort or upset. Through repeated practice we expect that you will gradually be able to increase your times." The therapist was not in the room during these training sessions. Closed circuit TV was used for monitoring purposes throughout the experiment with the patient's knowledge, and an intercom system enabled easy communication between patient and the therapist.

As indicated in Figure 4–4, there were six sequential phases to this experiment: praise alone, praise plus feedback, praise alone, no praise or feedback, praise alone, praise plus feedback. Praise involved remarks such as "excellent," "good," "that was great," etc., whenever the patient's trial time exceeded a progressively increasing criterion. For example, if the criterion for delivering praise on trial 9 had been 20 seconds, and she looked at the knife on this trial for 40 seconds, she was praised, and the criterion for trial 10 was set at 30 seconds. The new criterion, then, was an increment of one-half the difference between

the old criterion and the next exhibited increase. The patient was not informed about shifts in criterion.

When feedback was added, the therapist would report over the intercom at the conclusion of each trial, "That was X seconds," and then deliver praise if the prescribed criterion had been met. In addition, at the end of each session in the feedback phases, he would report the cumulative time spent in observing the knife.

Figure 4–4 shows that there was no discernible progress in the first phase when praise alone was provided. When feedback was added, however, performance steadily improved. When feedback was subsequently removed, the rate of progress continued without any regression. In the next phase, when both praise and feedback were

FIGURE 4–4   Time in which a knife was kept exposed by a phobic patient as a function of praise, feedback plus praise, and no feedback or praise conditions (Leitenberg, Agras, Allen, Butz, and Edwards, 1975).

omitted, patient's performance stopped improving after an initial brief gain. When praise alone was reinstated there was no further improvement. When feedback was added again, however, a steady rate of improvement was observed. Essentially this same pattern was obtained in four other phobic cases (social phobia, crowd phobia, storm phobia, illness-injury phobia) in which this particular experiment was attempted. Apparently, knowledge of actual performance was more important than therapist praise in getting progress started. Once precise feedback had been received, however, and performance had started to improve in a regular fashion, then more general praise alone could sustain this rate of improvement.

The importance of precise feedback (knowledge of performance) in treatment of phobia has since been experimentally confirmed in two other laboratories. Rutner (1973) conducted an analogue study with female undergraduate students who initially would not get closer than two feet to a rat enclosed in a cage, and who in baseline would not look at a rat for longer than 30 seconds; Rutner found that feedback was the factor most responsible for increased observation times. Of perhaps greater relevance because of the patient population studied, Emmelkamp and Ultee (1974), in studying 20 agoraphobics, found no significant difference in amount of progress between feedback alone and feedback plus praise conditions. In a crossover design, the amount of time clients were able to spend outside increased equally and significantly in both treatment conditions, no matter which came first.

It might be noted parenthetically that feedback is also an integral element of the systematic desensitization procedure. Progress is made known each time a step in the imaginary hierarchy is successfully passed. The possible benefit of such feedback in conventional systematic desensitization has yet to be experimentally analyzed.

Although no systematic attempt has been made to experimentally determine the importance of therapeutic set in the series of single-case experiments performed at Vermont with phobic patients, there is little doubt that expectancies of improvement, the typical authoritative context in which therapy is conducted, and the rationale of the therapeutic procedure as it is explained to the patient all contribute to success of treatment. Such expectancies and demand characteristics have been demonstrated to contribute to systematic desensitization (Leitenberg, Agras, Barlow, & Oliveau, 1969; Oliveau, Agras, Leitenberg, Moore, & Wright, 1969) and to behavioral scores obtained in avoidance tests (Miller & Bernstein, 1972) as well as to other forms of psychotherapy and social influence procedures (Frank, 1961; Goldstein, 1962; Orne & Evans, 1965). Thus, it is likely they are crucial ingredients here as well.

In summary, then, these single-case experiments point to four major therapeutic elements: (1) repeated graduated practice in aproaching actual phobic stimuli and situations; (2) social reinforcement for small gains in performance; (3) trial-by-trial feedback of precise measures of performance; (4) instructions designed to arouse expectations of gradual success. How, then, does this combined package compare with no-treatment controls and alternative behavior therapy procedures?

Leitenberg and Callahan (1973) reported a series of four experiments in which the combined reinforced practice procedure was compared to no-treatment controls in conventional between-group experimental designs. These experiments were also designed to determine whether or not common fears (including adults' fear of heights, harmless snakes, and painful electric shock, and young children's fear of darkness) could be overcome by a common training procedure, even though these fears have different origins, courses, and chronicity (Marks, 1969). In each of the four experiments, subjects who experienced the reinforced practice procedure improved their performance by a significant and substantial margin as compared to untreated control subjects. These results suggest that regardless of different etiologies, regardless of whether or not fears are "rational" or "irrational," and regardless of whether or not fears are transitory or long-lasting, the same reinforced practice treatment procedure can be equally effective in reducing escape-avoidance behavior.

Barlow, Agras, Leitenberg, and Wincze (1970) compared the effectiveness of systematic desensitization in imagination with the reinforced practice procedure. Subjects were undergraduate women afraid of snakes. They were matched on a behavioral pretest of approach to a harmless two- to three-foot boa and then assigned to either reinforced practice or conventional systematic desensitization. The experimenter who conducted pre- and posttests was not aware of subject groupings. A hierarchy containing 19 items describing approach to the snake was used for both groups but no relaxation training was provided for the reinforced practice group. Subjects in the reinforced practice group were instructed as follows: "We find that repeated practice in a structured situation is useful in reducing fears such as yours." The location of the snake (a glass cage in a room across the hall), was shown to the subject. She was then given the list of hierarchy items and told to go into the room and practice approaching the snake. The instructions continued, "When you have gone as far as you wish, come back and tell me at what point in the hierarchy you stopped, which I will record, then we will have another trial. On any particular trial you may do as many steps as you like, or none at all. . . ." At the end of the trial the subject returned to the original room and reported the point that had been reached on the hierarchy. She then received praise such as, "Good . . . congratulations!" or "You're doing much better . . . that's fine!" for reports of improvement. If the subject did not improve after three or more trials, her report would be met by a blank

stare followed by a change of conversation. An average of 4 (range 3 to 5) such trials was held per session. Intertrial intervals lasted 1 to 2 minutes, and sessions lasted approximately 20 minutes. For both groups, treatment was terminated when subjects completed either the hierarchy or 10 sessions.

Although both groups improved, there was a greater degree of progress for the reinforced practice group than for the desensitization group. The mean pretest score for both groups was step 7 which represented reaching into the cage with a glove on but not touching the snake. The mean posttest score for the desensitization group (step 12) represented placing one's bare hand on the snake, while the mean posttest score for the reinforced practice group (step 16) indicated an ability to pick up the snake in one hand and hold it for 20 seconds. These differences were statistically significant. GSR in the actual presence of the snake was also found to be more reduced following reinforced practice than following systematic desensitization in imagination.

Two between-group comparisons of reinforced practice with other forms of behavioral treatment of phobia have also been made with clinical subjects. Crowe, Marks, Agras, and Leitenberg (1972) contrasted systematic desensitization in imagination, implosion in imagination, and reinforced practice. Fourteen patients with various types of phobia took part in this experiment (five cases of agoraphobia, and the rest social, crowd, animal, height, and miscellaneous phobias). All patients were seen on an out-patient basis.

In a crossover design, each patient received each form of treatment. Following preparatory interviews and behavioral and rating scale assessments, the first treatment procedure was introduced and carried out in four 50-minute sessions, which were held twice a week. After another assessment, the second treatment was introduced and carried out in the same way. After a third assessment, the third treatment was introduced. Following the third treatment, there was a final assessment.

Desensitization was administered as described by Wolpe (1958), the only major difference being the small number of sessions given. Relaxation training and hierarchy construction had been carried out in the preparatory sessions. Each of the four treatment sessions began with 10 minutes of relaxation, followed by presentation of the anxiety-provoking scenes for 40 minutes. The patient signalled clear visualization of the described scene and 10 seconds later was asked to stop imagining it, to relax, and to signal whether visualization had caused "anxiety" or no anxiety, by raising the left or right index finger. Thirty seconds later the next presentation took place. Progress to the next step in the hierarchy took place after two presentations of a scene without signalled anxiety.

Implosion was carried out according to the description of Hogan and Kirchner (1967) using mainly environmental cues as the material for the imagined scenes. Hypothetical psychodynamic cues (Stampfl & Levis, 1967) have been recommended for inclusion in implosive sessions, but here they were used sparingly and were closely linked with what the patient had described in the preparatory interviews. Material that seemed to be causing a strong emotional reaction was repeated and elaborated. In height phobias, for example, the patient might be asked to imagine himself entering a 40-story building. His apprehension and anxiety during the ascent in the elevator to the roof garden would be described. The patient would then be taken by a friend to the edge of the garden and would unwittingly lean on a brick wall which, as it collapsed, turned out to be right on the edge of the building. The patient's feelings would be described as he fell over the remains of the wall, gradually lost his balance, hung by his hands from the bricks, and swung out over the street 40 stories below. Those parts of the narrative which

had caused obvious emotional reactions would be repeated again and again until they became ineffective and other situations involving heights would be added until they failed to produce a reaction. Each of these sessions lasted 40 minutes with an additional 5 minutes or so before and after the session for discussion of subjective reactions or new sources of anxiety arising in the patient during presentation.

Reinforced practice involved a graded approach to the feared object or situation with instructions to the patient not to make himself unduly anxious, but to try and complete as many steps in the approach course as possible. Praise was given when the patient exceeded a criterion, and the criterion itself was raised in accordance with improvement in performance. For example, if a height phobic had completed 15 steps of the fire escape on the last behavioral test, this became the starting criterion. If the next performance was 17 steps, praise would be given, and the criterion would be raised to 16 steps, the mean of the "best" performance and the previous criterion. A subsequent performance less than 16 steps would meet with no comment, but one of 16 steps or more would be praised. Patients were always given feedback regarding the level of their performance in cases where this was not obvious to them. Occasionally, participant modeling was introduced (Bandura, Blanchard, & Ritter, 1969) as in the case of two animal phobics in whom the initial approach to the animal was very difficult to shape. Here the therapist handled the animal while the patient approached. The therapist quickly withdrew while praising the patient for continued contact with the animal, thus retaining the reinforced practice paradigm. The treatment was administered for four 40-minute sessions to match the time of exposure to stimuli in the other two therapies. Crowe et al. (1972) point out that 4 sessions of each form of treatment is not typical. If given alone, they would each normally be administered for approximately 15 sessions. Nevertheless this short-term, time limited comparison did yield some interesting results.

On the behavioral avoidance measures, an analysis of variance showed a significant treatment effect. A multiple range test indicated that reinforced practice was significantly superior to desensitization; implosion was in an intermediate position. There was no significant difference between the three therapies on the various symptom rating scales.

At the conclusion of the study, patients were asked which treatment they preferred and which they thought most effective. Ten patients thought reinforced practice was most effective, whereas only 4 thought desensitization was most effective. Preferences, however, were a complete turnaround. Only 1 patient preferred reinforced practice, whereas 11 preferred systematic desensitization. This discrepancy might be accounted for in part by the shortened versions of each therapy. Reinforced practice is the only one of the three that involves exposure to the actual feared stimuli, and, especially in the beginning, this must be a more arduous and demanding therapy than the two imagination-based therapies. In any case, effectiveness is presumably of greater importance than preference. For example, I may prefer not to have surgery, but when this alternative works better than others available, I would choose the more effective procedure.

A final study in which reinforced practice was compared to another behavior therapy was conducted by Everaerd, Rijken, and Emmelkamp (1973) in the Netherlands. They used 14 agoraphobic subjects with a crossover design. Six 90-minute sessions of reinforced practice were compared with six sessions of "flooding." (The flooding procedure is described in detail in a later section of this chapter.) Half the subjects received reinforced practice first, and half received flooding first. The target for reinforced practice was increased time (not distance per se) spent away from the starting point, the patient's house. Each flooding session consisted of two parts: 45 minutes of

imagined exposure plus 45 minutes of exposure in reality to the agoraphobic situation. Both treatments led to significant and essentially equivalent improvement on measures of avoidance behavior, phobic anxiety scale, phobic avoidance scale, and the fear survey schedule. The authors point out that a significant change from external to internal control on Rotter's I-E test took place only following the reinforced practice procedure, suggesting that this treatment, more than flooding, gave the clients the idea they could influence their own behavior. This could be an important factor in sustaining gains during follow-up, but as yet there is no hard evidence to support this supposition.

Although the major behavioral therapy used in the treatment of neurotic disorders has to date been systematic desensitization, the studies so far reviewed suggest that reinforced practice is a viable alternative. It is important to note that these two therapies are based on different assumptions. Systematic desensitization assumes that anxiety must be inhibited before avoidance behavior can be expected to decline. Although it seems reasonable to suppose that anxiety reduction must precede behavioral change, there is no direct evidence to support this hypothesis, and on a priori basis the converse appears equally reasonable. The results of the Vermont studies (discussed above) indirectly suggested that patients could gradually learn to act differently in spite of anxiety, and that as a result of such changed behavior, anxiety would subsequently subside. In such an instance, anxiety reduction would be a consequence rather than a cause of behavior change. Leitenberg, Agras, Butz, and Wincze (1971) directly tested these two alternatives. Simultaneous trial by trial measures of heart rate and approach behavior in the actual feared situation were obtained during treatment of nine phobic cases. It was reasoned that Wolpe's hypothesis would be supported if heart rate tended to decrease before phobic avoidance behavior was observed to do the same. On the other hand, the behavioral hypothesis would be supported if phobic behavior declined before any decline in heart rate was noted.

As it turned out, a number of different relationships were observed. In some cases heart rate increased as phobic avoidance behavior decreased; in other cases there was a parallel decline; in still others there was a decline in phobic behavior without any accompanying change in heart rate; and finally in several cases heart rate decreased only after phobic behavior had declined. These data clearly suggest that physiologically defined anxiety need not always be inhibited first in order to obtain desired behavior changes during treatment of phobia. In fact, anxiety reduction may often be a consequence rather than a cause of behavioral change.

Subjective reports of anxiety as well as physiological indices of anxiety may also change after, rather than before, behavioral change. For example, an experimental evaluation of systematic desensitization (Lang et al., 1965) found that decreased reports of anxiety followed rather than preceded reductions in overt avoidance behavior. The general social psychological literature on attitude change also suggests that the direct behavioral strategy is most efficient and effective. Persuasive communications may affect beliefs and attitudes, but seldom have much effect upon overt actions (Festinger, 1964). Instead, enduring attitude change is made more likely by first getting a person to engage in new behavior.

There is general agreement that the treatment of phobia should be concerned with at least three components: extreme avoidance behavior, excess physiological arousal provoked by phobic stimuli, and subjective reports of fear and anxiety. In essence the reinforced practice approach represents a direct behavioral strategy for treatment. Focus on reducing overt avoidance behavior, however, does not neglect cognitive and physiological components

since these are expected to change as a result of prior changes in overt avoidance behavior. This strategy directly contrasts with systematic desensitization's assumption that it is best to first attack subjective and physiological aspects of anxiety. The empirical evidence, so far, seems to favor the behavioral strategy.

PARTICIPANT MODELING (THE STANFORD PROJECT)

Observing other people's behavior and the consequences of such behavior can often affect the observer's own verbal, motor, and social behavior (Bandura & Walters, 1963). Recently the potential applicability of modeling procedures in psychotherapy has been considered (for reviews of this literature see Bandura, 1969, 1971; Rachman, 1972). In particular, Bandura and his associates at Stanford University have begun to experimentally explore the use of symbolic and live modeling in reducing fear motivated behavior in children and adults (Bandura & Barab, 1973; Bandura et al., 1969; Bandura, Grusec, & Menlove, 1967; Bandura & Menlove, 1968; Blanchard, 1970; Ritter, 1968, 1969a, 1969b).

A major outgrowth of this research has been the development of a technique called participant modeling or contact desensitization which closely resembles the reinforced practice therapy described above. Participant modeling, like reinforced practice, involves gradual exposure to and practice in approaching phobic situations. Social reinforcement and feedback, however, are not stressed. Instead graded demonstrations of nonphobic behavior by a therapist-model in the presence of the subject is the main therapeutic component.

The first study in this series was conducted with 48 nursery school children (Bandura et al., 1967). Following a 14-step pretest of approach behavior to a cocker spaniel, subjects with equivalent fear were assigned to four treatment groups. (It is important to note that although only one-third of the children exhibited extreme signs of avoidance behavior, all children were used in the study. A separate analysis for the most fearful population was *not* reported.) The first group observed a fearless peer model exhibit progressively more difficult interactions with a dog in the context of a jovial party. There were eight 10-minute treatment sessions conducted on four consecutive days. Each session involved groups of four children. After the party was well underway (hats, cookies, prizes, etc.), the experimenter entered the room carrying the dog. He was followed by a four-year-old male model who was unknown to most of the children. The dog was initially placed in a playpen located across the room from a large table at which the children were seated. The model then performed prearranged sequences of interactions with the dog for three minutes. In successive sessions, physical restraints on the dog were gradually removed and closer and more active interactions with the dog (e.g., scratching stomach, feeding dog by hand) were modeled. A second group of children observed the same sequence of modeled approach responses but not in a party atmosphere. A third group was exposed to the dog during the eight sessions but did not observe a model interact with the dog. Instead the dog was confined in the playpen during the first four sessions and placed on a leash outside the playpen in the remaining four sessions. A fourth group was not exposed to either the dog or the model. Instead they just participated in the parties.

Posttests and a one-month follow-up were conducted with the same dog and an unfamiliar dog to determine generalization. There was no significant difference between the two types of modeling experience (party and non-party context) but both modeling groups improved significantly more than the control groups. The terminal behavior on the approach test involved standing alone in the room and in the playpen with the dog. Sixty-seven percent of the children in the modeling groups were able to do this compared to 33% of controls.

In a subsequent study of young children afraid of dogs, Bandura and Menlove (1968) examined the effectiveness of filmed models as distinguished from the live models of the prior experiment. One group observed a film in which multiple models interacted in a graded manner with a dog. Another group saw a film in which only a single peer model interacted with a dog, and a control group saw a movie which contained no animals. Both groups who saw the film of model(s) interacting with the dog did significantly better on the posttest than the control group; and there was a slightly greater improvement for the multiple model condition than for the single model condition. But the most important finding was that the degree of improvement was much less in this study than in the previous one, indicating that symbolic modeling is much less powerful than live modeling.

Ritter (1968) introduced the procedure of contact desensitization (subsequently called participant modeling) which has turned out to be much more effective than pure modeling (observation alone). In contact desensitization the subject not only observes the experimenter and peer model interact with the feared stimulus; he also has opportunities to make physical contact with the model and the phobic object. For example, while the experimenter was holding a snake, the subject would come up and touch it. A comparison of pure modeling and contact desensitization was made with children aged 5 to 11 who exhibited moderate fear of snakes. In addition to the observation-alone group (vicarious extinction) and contact desensitization group, there was a no-treatment control group (Ritter, 1968). Following only two 35-minute treatment sessions, 80% of the contact desensitization children, 53.5% of the observation-alone children, and none of the controls completed the terminal task (sitting in a chair with arms at sides while snake remains in lap for 30 seconds).

Ritter (1969b) points out that contact desensitization or participant modeling has three main components: (1) the model (therapist) demonstrates the desired behavior to the subject; (2) the therapist uses physical prompts to assist in response replication, e.g., the subject is encouraged to hold on to the therapist's hand while they make joint approach responses; (3) the therapist's assistance is gradually faded out with continuing independent practice by the subject.

In contact desensitization the function of the therapist-model is complex. In addition to being instructive and reassuring, the therapist-model is also a motivating force. Demand characteristics of the graded practice sessions are probably heightened and provide a further spur to behavioral progress and subsequent feelings of accomplishment and confidence.

Ritter (1969a, 1969b) experimentally analyzed the importance of joint participation (actual physical contact with therapist-model) in two studies with height phobics. Contact desensitization was more effective than modeling without actual physical contact. Participant modeling, in turn, was superior to observation without graded practice of actual approach behavior. Blanchard (1970) also found that participant modeling in which subjects gradually made actual contact with a snake after observing a model's demonstrations was more effective than just observing a model engage in non-fearful approach behavior.

The most conclusive and comprehensive experiment in this series was reported by Bandura et al. (1969). They compared the relative effectiveness of four procedures in reducing snake phobia: (1) graduated live modeling with guided participation; (2) symbolic modeling (film showing young children, adolescents, and adults engage in graduated interactions with snakes); (3) systematic desensitization in imagination; (4) no treatment (control).

By far the most effective procedure in reducing specific and generalized avoidance behavior, fear arousal, and attitude change was live modeling plus guided participation. Systematic desensitization and symbolic modeling fell midway between the no-treatment control group's performance and the participant modeling group's performance. Ninety-two percent of the participant modeling group was able to engage in the final terminal behavior on the post-treatment test, whereas only 33% of the symbolic modeling group achieved this level.

Once again it is clear that a procedure which trains fearful subjects to approach gradually real phobic stimuli is more effective than systematic desensitization (or for that matter symbolic modeling or observation alone).

A major limitation of the research done to date on participant modeling is the non-clinical nature of the populations studied. Because no research has been conducted with phobic patients, the true usefulness of participant modeling treatment of severe phobia remains in question. A useful topic for future research would be a direct comparison of reinforced practice with participant modeling in *clinical phobia;* the similarity of the two procedures indicates that a combination of the two would probably work better than either alone.

FLOODING (THE MAUDSLEY PROJECT)

Flooding is a behavioral treatment of phobia which, like reinforced practice and participant modeling, stresses exposure to real phobic stimuli. Unlike the other two, however, flooding is not a graduated procedure. No attempt is made to keep anxiety to a minimum. The whole technique is based on getting the patient into the feared situation as soon as possible and maintaining the exposure for prolonged periods of time. (Some sessions have lasted as long as eight hours and minimum time is typically one hour.)

The flooding procedure employed at the Maudsley Hospital for treatment of clinical phobia in many respects resembles the response prevention procedure explored in the animal laboratory to promote rapid extinction of avoidance behavior. Extinction of avoidance behavior has long been a popular topic of basic research in animal conditioning laboratories. Solomon, Kamin, and Wynne (1953) demonstrated that a well established avoidance response is highly resistant to the typical extinction procedure of simply removing shock from the situation. In the laboratory, a dog or rat is first trained to jump over a hurdle in response to a light signalling the imminent onset of shock. The light will typically precede shock by about 10 seconds. If the animal jumps before this period is concluded the shock does not go on and the signal light is terminated. Soon the animal is avoiding shock regularly; he jumps immediately following light onset. Since shock was initially needed to motivate the animal to learn the avoidance response, one would think that the removal of shock would cause the animal to stop engaging in avoidance behavior. Unfortunately, extinction of well established avoidance behavior is not so simple. Removing shock does not lead to rapid extinction of the avoidance response because the animal cannot detect that shock has been removed if he continues to emit the avoidance response. Since jumping over the hurdle previously led to the termination of the signal light and omission of shock, the experimenter's disconnection of shock has changed nothing as far as the animal's experience is concerned. Furthermore, escape from the signal light alone by now has probably assumed reinforcing properties. Only if the animal *fails to jump* within the prior time limits set between onset of signal and onset of shock can he discover that shock is no longer forthcoming. Like the phobic patient, however, the well trained animal will not voluntarily "reality test."

One supplementary procedure which will facilitate extinction is the repeated prevention of the avoidance response. This forces the animal to remain in the presence of the fear provoking signal until the signal terminates without receipt of the primary aversive shock stimulus. Following such "response prevention" the animal, when subsequently given the opportunity to engage in avoidance behavior, does so less often than the animal who undergoes a conventional extinction procedure. Considerable evidence has been amassed to convincingly indicate that temporary response prevention will hasten the overall course of extinction of avoidance responding in animals (Baum, 1970; Wilson & Davison, 1971).

Although physical constraints and mechanical prodding are not used to expose human subjects as fully as possible to phobic stimuli, social constraints are unhesitatingly employed. The therapist's recommendations and reassurances, statements about more rapid and effective treatment procedure, forewarning of possible experiences of anxiety, warnings that if patients drop out early from treatment they might be made worse rather than better, and the presence of the therapist during actual exposure sessions all serve as motivating forces to discourage phobic avoidance behavior.

Flooding, as currently used by the Maudsley group, must be distinguished from the implosion technique developed by Stampfl (Stampfl & Levis, 1967). Implosion relies solely on description of high-anxiety scenes in imagination rather than prolonged exposure to phobic situations in reality. Also, implosion deliberately provokes anxiety by exaggerating phobic stimuli (e.g., height phobia scenes would intentionally describe the subject being hung over a cliff's edge). Implosion also tries to heighten anxiety by involving psychodynamic content (interpretation of repressed sexuality, hostility to parents, etc. are incorporated into imaginal scenes.) Implosion in imagination does not appear to succeed as well as systematic desensitization in imagination and need not concern us further here. (For recent reviews of the implosion literature see Ayer, 1972; and Morganstern, 1973.)

In most of the Maudsley studies, flooding in imagination was combined with flooding in reality. Gradually, the flooding procedure developed from imagined scenes alone to imagined scenes plus practice to prolonged practice without any imagined scenes. Experiments which have relied only upon imagined scenes belong more appropriately in the category of implosion and will not be discussed.

An initial pilot study with four patients was reported by Boulougouris and Marks (1969). In this study the early influence of the implosion technique was apparent in two ways. First, phobic scenes in imagination were exaggerated in order to provoke anxiety. For example, a spider phobic was asked to imagine she was alone in a room with black hairy spiders that surrounded her, crawled up her legs and arms, bit her, and entered her mouth and nose while she screamed uncontrollably and helplessly. As soon as anxiety appeared to habituate, the therapist would switch to a new variant on the theme. This sort of continuing escalation was maintained for one hour. Second, patients were asked to encounter the phobic situation in reality only *after* fantasy sessions had first eradicated most signs of anxiety (presumably via a habituation process). Later studies in this series typically incorporated practice sessions into treatment more rapidly and more often than in this pilot study, and attempts to deliberately provoke anxiety above and beyond what was already elicited by the real phobic stimulus were abandoned. In this initial study there were a total of 2 to 3 sessions per week and a mean of 10 flooding sessions in fantasy and 4 in reality. Three of four patients were reported to be free of their main phobia at a one-year follow-up. One patient failed to improve.

A subsequent experiment compared the short-term effects of flooding with systematic desensitization (Marks, Boulougouris, & Marset, 1971). Sixteen phobic patients

(nine agoraphobics, seven miscellaneous specific phobics) served as subjects. For half the sample, six sessions of systematic desensitization were given first and six sessions of flooding were given second. For the other eight subjects the order was reversed: flooding came first and was followed by systematic desensitization. The fifth and sixth sessions of both treatments were followed immediately by 70 minutes of in vivo desensitization, or of flooding in the real situation rather than in imagination.

A number of rating scales filled out by therapist, patient, and an independent assessor served as the major outcome measures. Although physiological measures were also obtained, objective behavioral measures of phobic avoidance behavior were not taken. When first and second treatments were combined, analyses of variance showed flooding to be superior to desensitization as measured by: combined therapist's and independent assessor's ratings of main phobia and total phobia; declines in heart rate increase during main phobic fantasy; spontaneous fluctuations of skin conductance and maximum deflection of skin conductance during phobic talk. Compared to flooding, systematic desensitization did not show significantly greater improvement on any measure.

The next study showed the shift from flooding in imagination to flooding in reality more clearly (Watson, Gaind, & Marks, 1971). Ten patients with specific phobias who had shown only little improvement in a prior trial of flooding in fantasy alone (Watson & Marks, 1971) served as subjects. Some patients were told that fantasy sessions were preliminary to practice sessions, and two patients had treatment in practice only. (Furthermore, for the last few patients, both contingent praise and, where appropriate, modeling were incorporated into these two-hour practice sessions.) On the average, patients received approximately five hours of treatment spread over two to three sessions. The results, in general, indicated a greater and more rapid diminution of the phobia following treatment in reality than following treatment in fantasy. No residual fear or avoidance reappeared during follow-up.

An important variable to consider in flooding in reality is the duration of each practice trial. Siegeltuch and Baum (1971), in a study of response prevention with rats, found that longer exposure times were more effective in reducing avoidance behavior. Similar findings have also been reported in an analogue experiment with high school girls exhibiting fear of snakes (Miller & Levis, 1971). Marks (1972) summarized an unpublished clinical study that yielded similar results. Sixteen chronic agoraphobic patients received practice sessions either 120 or 30 minutes in length. Total practice time was equated over treatment. Thus one group received fewer but longer sessions, whereas another group received a greater number of shorter sessions. Marks (1972) reports that long flooding in reality was significantly superior to short flooding in reducing phobia. (Flooding in fantasy where scenes were described over a tape recorder were completely ineffective regardless of length of session.)

As Baum and Poser (1971) point out, behavior of patients during flooding must be watched. If practice sessions are maintained for a long enough time, the initial increase in anxiety provoked by sudden contact with the feared situation will have a chance to dissipate. Sessions should be maintained until patients begin to exhibit signs of nonfearful behavior. This, of course, may require considerable time. Corroborative evidence for this view is derived from Stern and Marks' experiment with agoraphobics whose "reduction of subjective anxiety and of tachycardia was greater in the second hour than in the first hour of long flooding." Watson, Gaind, and Marks (1972) also found that tachycardia tended to be greatest at the beginning of sessions.

Unlike reinforced practice and participant modeling, flooding does not permit patients to progress at a self-determined gradual pace. They are moved into the most phobic situation as soon as possible and then provided continuous exposure, usually for two hours. Thus the amount of distress that patients can expect to experience, especially in the first few flooding sessions, is quite great. Marks et al. (1971) report they were initially reluctant to employ this technique because of its likely unpleasantness to patients. To their surprise, however, they found that patients readily accepted the procedure and that dropouts were no greater than during systematic desensitization in imagination. Nevertheless, they argue, it would be desirable to make the treatment less anxiety provoking.

A subsequent experiment attempted to achieve this goal by combining a sedative (Diazepam) with prolonged exposure (Marks, Viswanathan, Lipsedge, & Gardner, 1972). Three conditions were compared: (1) Two-hour sessions of flooding in practice given four hours after drug ingestion when pharmacologic effects should be waning; this timing was designed to avoid the dissociation often noted between behavior in drug and undrugged states; (2) flooding one hour after drug ingestion when drug should be at peak effect; (3) flooding after placebo. Eighteen patients with specific phobias served as subjects. The flooding treatment was explained and the patients told that the therapists were testing whether treatment could be further improved by addition of medication. As in all the other later studies at the Maudsley, flooding involved continuous exposure to the actual phobic situation. The authors indicated that sessions were conducted in as pleasant a fashion as possible (although exposure always resulted in initial anxiety), with the therapist modeling contact with the phobic object when necessary and praising the patient each time he made progress. The authors point out that "emphasis was on continued contact with all aspects of the phobic situation until no further anxiety could be detected physiologically or clinically."

Flooding in reality produced significant

improvement under all three treatment conditions with a slight suggestion of greater change under the "waning" Diazepam condition. Mean rating of unpleasantness of sessions, however, were equivalent (and surprisingly in light of some of the anectdotal reports, not all that high). Thus, the major purpose of the drug was not achieved. On the other hand, unpleasantness might have received similar ratings because the Diazepam permitted faster (more intense) exposure to the stimulus. The mean time it took the peak Diazepam group to touch the phobic object in the first session was 13 minutes, while it took 32 minutes for the waning condition, and 39 minutes for placebo. Since Marks et al., (1972) mention several instances of fainting and screaming, it is obvious, however, that acute distress was still often present in initial sessions.

A recent flooding study is interesting because of the unusual problem treated (Lamontagne & Marks, 1973). Two patients had been unable to urinate in public bathroom facilities (at work, at gas stations, etc.) for 33 and 20 years, respectively. Both patients were told not to urinate in the morning and to drink five cups of coffee prior to the start of the 3 P.M. treatment session. Treatment consisted of sending patients to the lavatory and waiting for them to succeed no matter how long it took. They were told not to come out until they had passed urine in the beaker, that after a while their anxiety in the situation would decline and they would be able to urinate. Praise for success was employed and there was no deliberate attempt to provoke anxiety. Of course, simply insisting that patients engage in an activity which they have avoided in the past was likely to cause considerable anxiety. During the first three sessions, the therapist waited a certain distance outside the lavatory door; he gradually progressed closer until by the fifteenth session the therapist was able to wait inside with the patient.

In the first session one patient took two hours to urinate and the other took one-half hour. By session 10 there was less than a one-minute delay for both patients. They also voided steadily increasing amounts of urine during successive sessions. These gains had generalized to other lavatories and been maintained at nine-month follow-up.

BEHAVIOR THERAPY OF PHOBIA: CONCLUSIONS

Reinforced practice, participant modeling (contact desensitization), and flooding in practice (prolonged exposure) have all been demonstrated to be more effective behavioral treatments of phobia than systematic desensitization in imagination. Their common element is the direct exposure of the patient to actual phobic stimuli. This is not a new or unusual therapeutic element but the evidence is quite striking that it works, and works better than any other therapeutic approach and better than no therapy at all. At this time there are not many other behavior disorders or treatments for which a similar categorical conclusion can be stated. It is also noteworthy that these treatment procedures correspond closely to what works best in overcoming fear and avoidance behavior in basic animal laboratory research. Thus, no matter how simply these procedures seem, there is a firm empirical and theoretical foundation for their success (most other therapeutic approaches to behavior disorders lack such support).

It is still unclear how important the different emphases of reinforced practice, participant modeling, and prolonged exposure procedures may turn out to be. Both reinforced practice and participant modeling promote gradual and progressive approaches to actual phobic stimuli, whereas flooding promotes more sudden and continuous exposure. Only one tentative comparison between reinforced practice and flooding with phobic patients has been reported (Everaerd et al., 1973), and both treatments showed approximately equal effectiveness in eliminating agoraphobia. There is more patient distress, however, in flooding, and if both procedures are equally effective in other respects, then reinforced practice would be preferable simply because it is less anxiety-provoking and unpleasant for the patient. Everaerd et al., (1973) also suggests that the reinforced practice procedure gives the patient a greater feeling of control over his own behavior. More comparisons with similar populations and measures are needed, however, before any firm choice can be made between gradual reinforced practice and sudden prolonged exposure.

No direct comparisons of modeling with either reinforced practice or flooding in phobic patients have yet been made. In fact, one of the major limitations of the development of modeling to date is the absence of any controlled research with phobic patients (as distinguished from research with circumscribed common fears of volunteer populations). Future research should compare, in a clinical population, reinforced practice (repeated gradual practice, feedback of ongoing objective measures of behavior, contingent praise) with participant modeling (modeling of nonphobic behavior, joint participation). The more significant question, of course, is whether or not the two procedures together work significantly better than either one alone in reducing various clinical phobias. It is noteworthy that the Maudsley group seems to have incorporated in some unsystematic manner features of both of these techniques in their prolonged exposure treatment paradigm.

One other issue of some practical and theoretical significance is the often observed dissociation between the three major components of phobia: avoidance behavior, physiological arousal, and subjective reports of anxiety. The evidence, so far, indicates considerable individual variation. Some patients show simultaneous change in all three modalities. Others show common change in behavior and physiological arousal with subjective reports of anxiety lagging behind. And still others show concomitant change in behavior and subjective report with little

alteration in physiological response. Since reinforced practice, modeling, and in vivo flooding most directly attack overt behavior, however, it is not surprising to find that avoidance behavior generally declines first. It would be facile to argue that what a patient is able to do is more important than what he says he feels or what his heart does. Luckily this issue appears to be beside the point. Typically, behavioral change is simply a forerunner of delayed improvement in physiological response and subjective reports of anxiety. In fact, reductions in phobic avoidance behavior may be not only a precursor of improvement in other modalities but also the most important cause of such change. Customary thinking in this area (especially theorizing associated with systematic desensitization in imagination) may have followed the wrong track. It does not seem necessary to first reduce anxiety (as defined subjectively or physiologically) in order to reduce phobic avoidance behavior. The reverse corollary seems at least as accurate. In many instances avoidance behavior must be reduced before anxiety can be subsequently expected to decline. Reinforced practice, participant modeling, and flooding in reality are three behavioral procedures which strive to achieve this goal in a direct and efficient manner. The procedures have been clearly delineated, they have been systematically researched, and their effectiveness has been generally well proven. Considering the traditional muddle of psychotherapy, one can ask for little more.

Obsessive-Compulsive Neurosis

Obsessional thinking and compulsive rituals are the defining features of obsessive-compulsive neurosis. Obsessional thoughts have been described as repetitive, intrusive, and frightening ideas, images, impulses, and beliefs. Obsessional fears of doing injury to others and of illness and contamination are probably the most common. Unlike the delusions of grandeur and persecution of paranoid psychotics, the obsessive thoughts are rejected by the neurotic patient. He does not want to have these thoughts and struggles against them. Also unlike the psychotic, the obsessive-compulsive patient is ambivalent about the veracity of his disturbing thoughts. He simultaneously believes them and doesn't believe them.

Compulsive rituals are repetitive and stereotyped acts such as excessive handwashing and checking. These behaviors reach extreme dimensions; for example, handwashing is often so frequent that the skin becomes sore and red. The rituals are often bizarre and completely disruptive of normal activities. One patient I worked with used to sit on the toilet for more than eight hours a day. Another had a fear of doing injury to others when driving and constantly had to retrace her route to make sure that she had not run anybody over when she felt the slightest bump in the road. Soon she could not drive at all. A third patient thought that if her infants were not immediately given a head-to-toe bath after they soiled their diapers, the whole house would be contaminated. Once, while at grandmother's house, the child was only sponged down and not bathed thoroughly before she had played with some toys and wandered through several rooms at home the next day. Although the mother had seen the child's diapers changed the night before and felt the grandmother did a good job, and although she could not see or smell any remnants of the child's soiling, the mother still felt compelled to thoroughly wash and disinfect every piece of floor and furniture the child had come into contact with during this period. The doorhandles on the car and the door of the house were included. Marks (1973) describes a woman with a 20-year history of compulsive handwashing centering around a fear of tuberculosis infection. She was unable to feed her child for fear of infecting him and hours had to be spent boiling bottles and utensils. The child was

seldom allowed outside the playroom and the home was not swept because dust was thought to contain TB germs. Thus a thick layer of dust accumulated on the floor. When the husband returned from work and appeared at all dirty, he had to strip completely naked outside the home before he was allowed to enter and put new clothes on. It is difficult to convey on paper the distraught qualities of a severe obsessive-compulsive patient, but the above descriptions may hint at the terrible suffering and interference with daily functioning so often encountered in these patients.

It was once believed that a reliable distinction could be made between anxiety-reducing rituals and anxiety-evelating rituals (Wolpe, 1958; Eysenck & Rachman, 1965). Recent experimentation, however, indicates that most rituals reduce the patients distress. Hodgson and Rachman (1972) studied in detail the effects of touching "contaminated" objects and subsequent washing in obsessive-compulsive neurotics. All 12 patients reported a marked increase in subjective anxiety when brought in contact with contaminating material. This anxiety was subsequently reduced when patients engaged in their washing ritual. Surprisingly, interrupting the ritual did not increase subjective distress. Pulse rate measures showed a similar but statistically insignificant trend.

An identical study was carried out with another 12 patients in which repetitive checking rather than handwashing was the major element in the ritual (Roper, Rachman & Hodgson, 1973). Walker and Beech (1969) had previously reported that prolonged haircombing, washing, and clothes-changing rituals in a single patient had increased rather than decreased anxiety. In the sample of patients studied by Roper et al., however, results were different. It was found that, like the handwashers, checkers reduced their anxiety by engaging in checking compulsions, but unlike the handwashers, the checker's level of anxiety or discomfort after carrying out what they considered to be harmful acts was lower than that evoked in handwashers after touching "contaminating" material. Apparently the uncertainty that normally evoked the checking ritual was considerably reduced by the presence of a therapist. Also 5 of the 12 checking patients did indicate occasional increases in anxiety after checking. Whether checking reduced anxiety or not seemed to depend in part on prior "mood state" and how long the checking ritual was prolonged. If a few checks did not suffice, then increasing difficulty in determining when to stop and increasing subjective experiences of anxiety were more likely. As in the study of obsessional handwashers, no significant effects on pulse rate were noted, and therapist interruptions of the checking ritual did not cause further increases in anxiety.

There are a number of theoretical articles dealing with the possible etiology of obsessive-compulsive behaviors (Metzner, 1963; Rachman, 1971; Taylor, 1963; Walton, 1960; Walton & Mather, 1963). Although these papers offer various conditioning phenomena to explain the origins of obsessive-compulsive neurosis, they have not proved particularly useful in the development and evaluation of behavioral approaches to treatment, and thus will not be considered further here.

Obsessive-compulsive neurosis accounts for only 1% of the psychiatric in-patient and out-patient population. Although it is not a common disorder, it is particularly disabling and resistant to conventional treatment (insight-oriented psychotherapy, extensive psychoanalysis, chemotherapy, ECT, and even as a last extreme, leucotomy, have all been of little avail). Goodwin, Guze, and Robins (1969) reviewed the findings of 13 published outcome studies containing adequate sized samples and long-term follow-up periods. Five of these studies were conducted in England, two in the United States, three in Scandinavian countries, and one each in Germany, Switzerland, and Hong Kong. The number of patients in each study ranged from 13 to 130. Cutting across all these studies, the mean percent of patients who were rated as "improved" at follow-up was only 38%. Improved does not mean completely free of symptomatic behavior. If the latter criterion had been employed, the outcome of these studies would undoubtedly have been even poorer. It is clear that more effective treatment procedures need to be developed for obsessive-compulsive disorders.

BEHAVIORAL TREATMENT

An interesting parallel exists between the development of behavioral strategies of treatment for obsessive-compulsive neurosis and for phobia. Both have shifted away from systematic desensitization in imagination toward direct attacks on overt behavior. In treatment of obsessive-compulsive neurosis, however, the shift was not controversial because systematic desensitization was not effective in treating this disorder in the first place. Rather than having to determine whether a proven behavioral or learning approach could be improved by developing more direct methods (e.g., training patients to approach actual phobic stimuli), clinicians were confronted with a series of studies which indicated that systematic desensitization did not provide much benefit for obsessive-compulsive patients. Cooper et al. (1965), in their retrospective analysis of the results of behavior therapy, noted that only 3 of 10 obsessive-compulsive patients treated by systematic desensitization showed any improvement. Four out of 9 patients treated in more "traditional" manners also showed improvement. Further instances of failures in smaller samples were reported by Furst and Cooper (1970), Marks, Crowe, Drewe, Young, and Dewhurst (1969), and Walton and Mather (1963). Considering traditional difficulties in getting negative findings published in professional journals, these dismal results are not easily countered by an occasional uncontrolled report of a single case treated successfully with systematic desensitization (e.g., Rackensberger & Feinberg, 1972).

The breakthrough paper in this area is attributed to Meyer (1966); his two subjects were suffering from severe and chronic obsessive-compulsive neuroses. Subject 1 was a 37-year-old married woman who for the past three years had engaged in extensive washing and cleaning rituals. She considered a wide range of objects and situations "contaminated," and she feared that if she made contact with these materials she would pass on some disease to her baby. Although she had been hospitalized three times before and had received ECT, drugs, psychotherapy, and systematic desensitization, she did not improve. Subject 2 was a 47-year-old married woman with a 36-year history of having blasphemous thoughts which she alleviated by repeating any activity on hand a certain number of times. Meyer reported that she underwent a leucotomy at age 32 and then had psychoanalysis for 11 years. Neither of these major therapeutic interventions proved helpful.

The essence of the behavioral therapy employed with these two patients was (1) preventing rituals from taking place, while at the same time (2) exposing the patient to thoughts and situations that normally evoked such rituals. As we will see, the combination of these two procedures is critical if treatment is to prove successful. Either component alone is relatively ineffective.

In order to control performance of the first subject's washing behavior, the taps in her room were turned off and the authors note that persuasion, reassurance, and encouragement were used to prevent the patient from unnecessary and excessive washing and cleaning behavior. At the same time the patient was instructed to touch door knobs, handle dust bins, and touch her child's toys and bottles. It was also arranged for her to take trips on the bus and subway and to go shopping. Intensive 24-hour nursing supervision was used initially to insure against performance of compulsive washing

behavior. After several weeks, supervision was gradually withdrawn.

The second patient was required to imagine having intercourse with the Holy Ghost, to swear aloud, to eat sausage, to walk straight without looking down and stopping. After each session, special care was taken to prevent her from performing rituals. Again, intensive supervision was gradually reduced after several weeks. Also, her husband was brought into several treatment sessions in order to teach him how to prevent his wife from engaging in ritualistic behavior.

A 14-month follow-up for subject 1 indicated that she was considerably improved. Although some avoidance behavior and compulsive washing were still present, it was substantially reduced. The patient was able to engage in most normal daily behaviors— go to the movies, take walks, go shopping, etc. She had joined a tennis club, had resumed her teaching career, and had resumed having sexual relations with her husband.

The results for subject 2 were equally impressive. She had kept daily records of obsessive thoughts and rituals throughout the 22-month follow up period and these had been reduced to negligible levels. Activities at home and outside home were no longer being interfered with. She had obtained a teaching job and was doing so well that she had recently received a promotion.

These two basic therapeutic ingredients —rigorous prevention of compulsive rituals and exposure to actual stimuli and situations that in the past triggered compulsive acts—were examined next by Levy and Meyer (1971) in a sample of eight obsessive-compulsive patients. The patients were continuously supervised during waking hours, and nurses were instructed to prevent patients from carrying out rituals. The patients were engaged in other activities, distracted, cajoled, and very occasionally, with patient's consent, mildly restrained in order to prevent the compulsive behavior. When total prevention had been achieved. the patients were gradually exposed to situations which previously evoked rituals. During this one- to four-week period, continuous supervision was maintained and patients were prevented from engaging in compulsive behavior. Supervision was then gradually withdrawn.

Follow-ups of one to six years were obtained. In every case, there was a marked decline in compulsive behavior with concurrent declines in self-ratings and therapist ratings of anxiety and depression. Six of the eight patients were considered "much improved" (a 75% or greater decrease in compulsive rituals), and two were considered "improved" (50% to 74% decreases in compulsive behavior). Although the authors point out the absence of control groups and the limitations of subjective ratings obtained from only subject and therapist, these outcomes are still impressive. All but one of these patients had previously received extensive treatment via other methods including antidepressants, tranquilizers, ECT, leucotomy, psychotherapy, and psychoanalysis and had shown little improvement.

A more controlled analysis of Meyer's treatment strategy was performed at the Maudsley Hospital with 15 chronic obsessive-compulsive patients (Hodgson, Rachman, & Marks, 1972; Rachman, Hodgson, & Marks, 1971). All patients had to agree to a minimum in-patient stay of seven weeks. The first week was devoted to interviews and testing and was followed by three weeks of a relaxation control treatment. During this three-week period, one session per day was scheduled in which patients went through tape recorded relaxation exercises. In the last 10 minutes of each session, general inquiries about health and mood were made and patients were requested to think about one of their obsessive problems.

At the end of the relaxation control phase, patients were assigned to three different treatment groups: participant modeling, flooding in practice, and modeling plus flooding. Modeling group subjects first constructed a graded hierarchy of situations

which caused anxiety and compulsive behavior. For example, for a patient afraid of contamination from hospitals the items in the hierarchy were: (1) touching bandage; (2) touching dirty lint; (3) touching medicine; (4) touching a kidney bowl; (5) touching hypodermic syringe; (6) touching a faked TB sample; (7) approaching hospital; (8) touching ambulances; (9) entering a hospital casualty waiting room; (10) walking around hospital touching walls, doorknobs, etc. The patients were encouraged to engage in each of these behaviors starting with the one that produced the *least* anxiety. In each session the therapist first demonstrated (modeled) the behavior, and the patient was asked to follow suit. The second group underwent a flooding (prolonged exposure in reality) procedure. A hierarchy was constructed, but patients were encouraged and persuaded—not forced—to enter the *most* disturbing situation first. The therapist did not model desired approach behavior but he did provide a "calming and reassuring" presence throughout the 40- to 60-minute sessions. The third group received a combination of modeling plus flooding. Patients were urged to carry out activities at the top of a hierarchy after closely observing these activities being performed by the therapist.

It is important to note that patients in all three types of exposure conditions were encouraged to refrain from carrying out compulsive rituals following therapy sessions. Continuous nursing supervision as in the Meyer studies, however, was not provided.

A variety of rating, behavioral, and psychometric measures were taken before treatment, after three weeks of the relaxation control treatment, after three weeks of either participant modeling, flooding in practice, or the two combined, and after a six-month follow up. All three treatment procedures caused significantly greater improvement than the relaxation control procedure on all measures of obsessive-compulsive behavior. There was also some slight evidence on some of the rating scales that the combined flooding and modeling procedure might have been more effective than either flooding or modeling alone. At the end of the six-month follow-up, however, there were no significant differences between the three treatment procedures, although the trend favored modeling alone and modeling plus flooding rather than flooding alone. At follow-up, two of the five patients in the flooding alone group were rated as much improved, whereas four out of five patients in each of the other groups were considered much improved.

Five of the patients failed to show any improvement following treatment. It is striking that four of these five patients did not comply with instructions to stop engaging in rituals between sessions. It is not surprising to find poor outcomes when patients continue to wash after making contact with "contaminating" substances. Contact is meaningless if the escape valve of the ritual is still available. As Meyer (1966) points out, expectations of dire consequences can be countered only if *both* response prevention and exposure to feared stimuli are provided. Only when both ingredients are present is true extinction made possible by allowing the patient to discover that the terrible consequences he anticipated are not forthcoming.

The importance of preventing rituals in behavioral treatment of obsessive-compulsive neurosis was even more clearly demonstrated in a series of five single-case experimental studies (Mills, Agras, Barlow & Mills, 1973). They found that exposure alone and controls for expectations had no effect, but that response prevention (water taps turned off, supervision, etc.) dramatically reduced performance rituals. An encouraging aspect of this study was that relatively short periods of response prevention (just one week) produced substantial and lasting reductions in compulsive behavior.

A recent paper by Boulougouris and Bassiakos (1973) provided one additional piece of information about the response prevention plus exposure method of treatment of obsessive-compulsive neuroses. Two patients with contamination fears and washing rituals and one patient with repetitive checking rituals served as subjects in this study. A combination of flooding in imagination, flooding in reality, and response prevention was used to treat these patients. At nine-month follow-up the typical positive outcome was obtained on patient's, therapist's, and independent assessor's rating of total obsessions, anxiety, and depression. In addition, physiological measures of subject's skin conductance and heart rate when they were thinking about and touching "contaminated" objects were also substantially reduced.

As Marks (1973) points out, treatment by exposure with response prevention requires considerable patient cooperation and motivation. Patients must be told before they enter the hospital what will transpire and what will be expected of them. A caution first voiced by Levy and Meyer is that "the line between firm but sympathetic control and unpleasant and inhumane bullying is a thin one indeed and all too easy to cross when one has devoted a lot of time and energy to a patient who relentlessly and monotonously pursues an unchanging course [1971, p. 1118]." There is no question that considerable therapist skill and patient trust is needed to successfully restrict performance of rituals since such restriction is likely to elicit some anguished responses in patients.

In many ways compulsive rituals are attempts to escape or avoid aversive stimuli. And as indicated in the prior section on treatment of phobia, there is now considerable experimental data emanating from animal conditioning laboratories that lend support to clinical research findings. The key to rapid extinction of avoidance behavior in animals is to prevent physically such behavior from occurring in order to expose subjects to formerly conditioned fear arousing stimuli. Avoidance behavior is found to be substantially reduced following such exposure.

With severe and chronic obsessive-compulsive behavior, continuous daily supervision and elimination of free access to normal washing facilities closely approximates physical restraint and anxiety is often experienced in the initial treatment phase. Nevertheless, response prevention is surely preferable to years and years of intolerable suffering. In some cases of obsessive-compulsive neurosis, instructions, reinforcements, feedback, graduated practice, and modeling may bring subjects into contact with feared stimuli but not suffice to control performance of rituals. When this happens, response prevention via continuous supervision (e.g. removing free access to washroom facilities) is clearly appropriate as long as the procedure is first explained and agreed to by the patient.

It is apparent that prevention of rituals is most easily accomplished in in-patient settings where continuous surveillance and objective recording of behavior are easily arranged. Treatment in the hospital, however, is probably not sufficient. Each of the above studies points to the advisability of teaching spouses how to encourage ritual prevention and how to encourage patients to maintain exposure to formerly feared stimuli. If this is not done, gains made in the hospital may be quickly lost when the patient returns home. One question that has not been addressed in any large scale or by any controlled study, however, is whether or not response prevention plus exposure can be successfully administered solely on an out-patient basis. A strategy employed at Vermont to try to bring rituals under control in the home combined features of symptom scheduling and paradoxical intention (Frankl, 1960; Gertz, 1966). Patients were instructed to engage in their rituals only at prescribed periods of the day regardless of whether they had an urge to do so during those times or not. Once this was achieved, the number of "ritual periods" during the day was gradually reduced. At the same time, sessions were arranged in which the subjects practiced coming into contact

with stimuli they had been avoiding. Practice at home was also prescribed via carefully constructed tasks. For severe cases, however, it seems that more efficient and effective treatment can be provided in a situation where closer supervision is initially possible.

At long last we can express cautious optimism about therapy for obsessive-compulsive behaviors. Because controlled research is still somewhat sparse, assurance must be much more guarded than in the case of phobia. Nevertheless, although much more work needs to be done, the past few years have seen some remarkably consistent findings. The formula for successful treatment seems to be prevention of compulsive rituals while teaching patients to approach rather than avoid anxiety arousing situations, objects, and thoughts which formerly led to the performance of such rituals.

One subject not yet covered in this section is treatment of obsessions where compulsive rituals are not present. The published literature on this topic is most unsatisfactory. Occasional uncontrolled case reports of "thought stopping" techniques and "shock aversion" techniques have appeared (e.g., Kenny, Solyom, & Solyom, 1973; Stern, 1970). But until more systematic controlled research with larger samples of patients is reported, a review of this area would be premature.

Summary and Conclusions

Behavioral treatments of two specific neuroses, phobia and obsessive-compulsive disorders, have been reviewed. Reinforced practice, participant modeling, and flooding in practice all seem to be demonstrably more effective than systematic desensitization in imagination in treatment of phobia, and it therefore seems logical to choose among these three in practice. Although these techniques have many elements in common, there are certain differences in emphasis and procedure. More controlled outcome studies with clinical populations will be needed before any final determination can be made as to which of the three is preferable or whether some combination is indicated.

There is one further caution. Although evaluative research has favored reinforced practice, participant modeling, and flooding in practice over systematic desensitization in imagination, this does not necessarily imply ready usage of these techniques in standard clinical practice. All too often prosaic practical matters, publicity, and what a therapist "feels comfortable with" seem to be as important as data in determining therapeutic choice. Time and consistent findings are the only counter to such human roadblocks.

The literature on behavioral treatment of obsessive-compulsive neurosis is more problematic than the literature on phobia. Early work with systematic desensitization was unsuccessful, and the first inkling of a breakthrough was Meyer's (1966) study. Although controlled follow-up research on Meyer's work has been conducted, the optimism of consistent positive findings must be tempered by the small number of patients involved in these subsequent studies. Even with this qualification, however, there is now at least some solid reason to be hopeful. The approach that seems to work consists of two components: (1) compulsive rituals are prevented via extensive supervision and persuasion (response prevention): (2) simultaneously, subjects are exposed to the situations, thoughts, and stimuli that customarily would have provoked compulsive rituals. The second component can make use of reinforced practice, participant modeling, and flooding in practice procedures developed for reducing avoidance behavior in treatment of phobia. It is not as easy, however, to implement the first component. In severe and chronic cases of obsessive-compulsive neurosis, around-the-clock supervision may be necessary. Although this is never easy to arrange, the studies in the Maudsley Hospital indicate it can be done. The remarkable results reported to date certainly warrant the extra therapeutic effort.

Neurotic patients usually have many problems that go beyond the specific anxieties, avoidance behaviors, obsessional thoughts, and compulsive rituals associated with phobia and obsessive-compulsive neurosis. Although these latter specific "symptoms" are of central concern, the other difficulties also are often quite pressing. Marital conflict, job and financial difficulties, sexual inadequacies, existential uncertainties, family concerns about children and in-laws, for example, are common. Although we have not dealt with these topics in this chapter, it is clear that they cannot be ignored in providing a full clinical service.

More general neurotic styles of interpersonal functioning have also been omitted from this review and again not because they are unimportant concerns for effective clinical practice. Lazarus (1971) in particular has argued that behavior therapists cannot safely afford to ignore these broader concerns, and in many ways he is right. A catalogue of creative clinical techniques to deal with neurotic life styles, however, would divert attention from that which is so attractive about the behavioral treatment approach to specific phobias and obsessive-compulsive neurosis. Detailed description of treatment procedures, objective evaluation of the effective components of treatment, and direct evaluation of changes in specific patient behaviors has been the *sine qua non* of progress in this area, and any neglect of this empirical approach would be disastrous.

This empirical approach need not be abandoned, but instead can be extended to reach some of the other problem behaviors of neurotic patients. For example, a characteristic problem of many neurotic clients is lack of appropriate assertive behavior. The inability to find the happy medium between submissive behavior and aggressive behavior, the ability to stand up for one's rights in interpersonal confrontations, the inability to express either positive or negative feelings in a forthright and direct fashion are common complaints. Although this has been known for a long time and although clinicians oriented toward application of "principles of learning theory" have long espoused the usefulness of assertive training (e.g., Salter, 1949; Wolpe and Lazarus, 1966), it is only recently that systematic research in this area has begun. As a result of the experimental studies of McFall and his associates (McFall & Lillesand, 1971; McFall & Marston, 1970; McFall & Twentyman, 1973) and Rathus (1972; 1973a; 1973b), there is now a better understanding on the training techniques most likely to lead to desired changes in assertive behavior. Although this line of research has been mainly conducted with the "normal" college population and in a few instances with the more "captive" clinical population of psychotic in-patients (Eisler, Hersen, & Miller, 1973), there is little doubt that more directly relevant studies with neurotic patients will be forthcoming shortly.

Although most behavioral research on treatment of neurotic disorders has been limited to the central symptoms of either phobic avoidance behavior and anxiety or obsessive-compulsive rituals, it would be a mistake to conclude that these other areas of concern are being neglected by behaviorally oriented clinicians. Unfortunately, however, research is only beginning to catch up to routine clinical practices. Thus it would be premature for a chapter such as this to deal with these more diffuse topics.

In pointing out gaps, one must be wary not to lose sight of what has been achieved. Tremendous strides have been made in developing and evaluating behavioral treatment plans for phobia and obsessive-compulsive neurosis. As earlier literature on the more disappointing results of traditional psychotherapeutic techniques would indicate, attaining a larger degree of success with these two specific disorders is no minor accomplishment.

References

AGRAS, W. S. Transfer during systematic desensitization therapy. *Behaviour Research and Therapy*, 1967, **5**, 193–200.

AGRAS, W. S., CHAPIN, H. N., & OLIVEAU, D. C. The natural history of phobia. *Archives of General Psychiatry*, 1972, **26**, 315–317.

AGRAS, W. S., LEITENBERG, H., & BARLOW, D. H. Social reinforcement in the modification of agoraphobia. *Archives of General Psychiatry*, 1968, **19**, 423–427.

AGRAS, W. S., LEITENBERG, H., BARLOW, D. H., CURTIS, N. A., EDWARDS, J., & WRIGHT, D. Relaxation in systematic desensitization. *Archives of General Psychiatry*, 1971, **25**, 511–514.

AGRAS, W. S., LEITENBERG, H., BARLOW, D. H., & THOMSON, L. E. Instructions and reinforcement in the modification of neurotic behavior. *American Journal of Psychiatry*, 1969, **125**, 1435–1439.

AGRAS, W. S., SYLVESTER, D., & OLIVEAU, D. The epidemiology of common fears and phobia. *Comprehensive Psychiatry*, 1969, **10**, 151–156.

ANDREWS, J. D. W. Psychotherapy of phobias. *Psychological Bulletin*, 1966, **66**, 455–480.

APONTE, J. F., & APONTE, C. E. Group preprogrammed systematic desensitization without the simultaneous presentation of aversive scenes with relaxation training. *Behavior Research and Therapy*, 1971, **9**, 337–346.

AYER, W. A. Implosive therapy: a review. *Psychotherapy: Theory, Research, and Practice*, 1972, **9**, 242–250.

BANDURA, A. *Principles of behavior modification.* New York: Holt, Rinehart & Winston, 1969.

BANDURA, A. Psychotherapy based upon modeling principles. In A. E. Bergin & S. L. Garfield (Eds.), *Handbook of psychotherapy and behavior change.* New York: John Wiley, 1971.

BANDURA, A., & BARAB, P. G. Processes governing disinhibitory effects through symbolic modeling. *Journal of Abnormal Psychology*, 1973, **82**, 1–9.

BANDURA, A., BLANCHARD, E. B., & RITTER, B. The relative efficacy of desensitization and modeling approaches for inducing behavioral, affective, and attitudinal changes. *Journal of Personality and Social Psychology*, 1969, **13**, 173–179.

BANDURA, A., GRUSEC, J. E., & MENLOVE, F. L. Vicarious extinction of avoidance behavior.

Journal of Personality and Social Psychology, 1967, **5**, 16–23.

BANDURA, A., & MENLOVE, F. L. Factors determining vicarious extinction of avoidance behavior through symbolic modeling. *Journal of Personality and Social Psychology,* 1968, **8**, 99–108.

BANDURA, A., & WALTERS, R. H. *Social learning and personality development.* New York: Holt, Rinehart & Winston, 1963.

BARLOW, D. H., AGRAS, W. S., LEITENBERG, H., & WINCZE, J. F. An experimental analysis of the effectiveness of "shaping" in reducing maladaptive avoidance behavior: an analogue study. *Behaviour Research and Therapy,* 1970, **8**, 165–173.

BARLOW, D. H., LEITENBERG, H., AGRAS, W. S., & WINCZE, J. P. The transfer gap in systematic desensitization: an analogue study. *Behaviour Research and Therapy,* 1969, **7**, 191–196.

BAUM, M. Extinction of avoidance responding through response prevention (flooding). *Psychological Bulletin,* 1970, **74**, 276–284.

BAUM, M., & POSER, E. G. Comparison of flooding procedures in animals and man. *Behaviour Research and Therapy,* 1971, **9**, 249–325.

BERNSTEIN, D. A., & BEATY, W. E. The use of *in vivo* desensitization as part of a total therapeutic intervention. *Journal of Behavior Therapy and Experimental Psychiatry,* 1971, **2**, 259–265.

BERNSTEIN, D. A., & PAUL, G. L. Some comments on therapy analogue research with small animal "phobias." *Journal of Behavior Therapy and Experimental Psychiatry,* 1971, **2**, 225–237.

BLANCHARD, E. B. The generalization of vicarious extinction effects. *Behaviour Research and Therapy,* 1970, **8**, 323–330.

BOULOUGOURIS, J. C., & BASSIAKOS, L. Prolonged flooding in cases with obsessive compulsive neurosis. *Behaviour Research and Therapy,* 1973, **11**, 227–231.

BOULOUGOURIS, J. C., & MARKS, I. M. Implosion (flooding)—a new treatment for phobias. *British Medical Journal,* 1969, **2**, 721–723.

COHEN, R. The effects of group interaction and progressive hierarchy presentation on desensitization of test anxiety. *Behaviour Research and Therapy,* 1969, **7**, 15–26.

COOKE, G. The efficacy of two desensitization procedures in an analogue study. *Behavior Research and Therapy,* 1966, **4**, 17–24.

COOPER, J. E. A study of behavior therapy in thirty psychiatric patients. *Lancet,* 1963, **1**, 411–415.

COOPER, J. E., GELDER, M. G., & MARKS, I. M. Results of behavior therapy in 77 psychiatric patients. *British Medical Journal,* 1965, **1**, 1222–1225.

CROWE, M. J., MARKS, I. M., AGRAS, W. S., & LEITENBERG, H. Time-limited desensitization, implosion and shaping for phobic patients: a crossover study. *Behaviour Research and Therapy,* 1972, **10**, 319–328.

DAVISON, G. C. Systematic desensitization as a counter conditioning process. *Journal of Abnormal Psychology,* 1968, **73**, 91–99.

DAVISON, G. C., & WILSON, G. T. Processes of fear reduction in systematic desensitization: cognitive and social reinforcement factors in humans. *Behavior Therapy,* 1973, **4**, 1–21.

DEROGATIS, L. R., LIPMAN, R. S., COVI, L., & RICKELS, K. Neurotic symptom dimensions. *Archives of General Psychiatry,* 1971, **24**, 454–464.

DEROGATIS, L. R., LIPMAN, R. S., COVI, L., & RICKELS, K. Factorial invariance of symptom dimensions in anxious and depressive neuroses. *Archives of General Psychiatry,* 1972, **27**, 659–665.

EISLER, R. M., HERSEN, M., & MILLER, P. M. Effects of modeling on components of assertive behavior. *Journal of Behavior Therapy and Experimental Psychiatry,* 1973, **4**, 1–6.

EMMELKAMP, P. M. G., & ULTEE, K. A. A comparison of "successive approximations" and "self-observation" in the treatment of agoraphobia. *Behavior Therapy,* 1974, **5**, 606–613.

ERRARA, P., & COLEMAN, J. V. A long term follow-up study of neurotic phobic patients in a psychiatric clinic. *Journal of Nervous and Mental Disease,* 1963, **136**, 276–271.

EVERAERD, W. T., RIJKEN, H. M., & EMMELKAMP, P. M. A comparison of "flooding" and "successive approximation" in the treatment of agoraphobia. *Behaviour Research and Therapy,* 1973, **11**, 105–117.

EYSENCK, H. J. The effects of psychotherapy: an evaluation. *Journal of Consulting and Clinical Psychology,* 1952, **16**, 319–324.

EYSENCK, H. J. *The effects of psychotherapy.* New York: International Science Press, 1966.

EYSENCK, H. J., & RACHMAN, S. *The causes and cures of neurosis.* San Diego: Knapp, 1965.

FESTINGER, L. Behavioral support of opinion change. *Public Opinion Quarterly,* 1964, **28,** 404–417.

FRANK, J. D. *Persuasion and healing.* Baltimore: Johns Hopkins Press, 1961.

FRANKL, V. E. Paradoxical intentions: a logotherapeutic technique. *American Journal of Psychotherapy,* 1960, **14,** 520–535.

FREEMAN, H. L., & KENDRICK, D. C. A case of cat phobia. *British Medical Journal,* 1960, **2,** 497–502.

FREUD, S. *Collected papers.* Vol. 2. London: Hogarth Press, 1924.

FURST, J. B., & COOPER, A. Failure of systematic desensitization in 2 cases of obsessive-compulsive neurosis marked by fears of insecticides. *Behaviour Research and Therapy,* 1970, **8,** 203–206.

GARFIELD, Z. H., DARWIN, P. L., SINGER, B. A., & McBREARTY, J. F. Effect of *in vivo* training on experimental desensitization of a phobia. *Psychological Reports,* 1967, **20,** 515–519.

GELDER, M. G., & MARKS, I. M. Severe agoraphobia: a controlled prospective trial of behavior therapy. *British Journal of Psychiatry,* 1966, **112,** 309–319.

GELDER, M. G., & MARKS, I. M. Desensitization and phobias: a crossover study. *British Journal of Psychiatry,* 1968, **114,** 323–328.

GELDER, M. G., MARKS, I. M., WOLFF, H. E., & CLARKE, M. Desensitization and psychotherapy in the treatment of phobic states: a controlled inquiry. *British Journal of Psychiatry,* 1967, **113,** 53–73.

GERTZ, H. O. Paradoxical intention in obsessives. *American Journal of Psychiatry,* 1966, **23,** 548–553.

GOLDSTEIN, A. P. *Therapist-patient expectancies in psychotherapy.* New York: Pergamon Press, 1962.

GOODWIN, D. W., GUZE, S. B., & ROBINS, E. Follow-up studies in obsessional neurosis. *Archives of General Psychiatry,* 1969, **20,** 182–187.

HERZBERG, A. Short treatment of neuroses by graduated tasks. *British Journal of Medical Psychology,* 1941, **19,** 19–36.

HODGSON, R. J., & RACHMAN, S. The effects of contamination and washing in obsessional patients. *Behaviour Research and Therapy,* 1972, **10,** 111–117.

HODGSON, R., RACHMAN, S., & MARKS, I. M. The treatment of chronic obsessive-compulsive neurosis: follow-up and further findings. *Behaviour Research and Therapy,* 1972, **10,** 181–189.

HOGAN, R. A., & KIRCHNER, J. A. Preliminary report of the extinction of learned fears via implosive therapy. *Journal of Abnormal Psychology,* 1967, **72,** 106–109.

JACOBSON, E. *Progressive relaxation.* Chicago: University of Chicago Press, 1938.

JERSILD, A. T., & HOLMEN, F. B. Children's fears. *Child Development Monographs,* 1935, **20.**

JONES, M. C. The elimination of children's fears. *Journal of Experimental Psychology,* 1924, **7,** 382–390.

KELLER, F.. S., & SCHOENFELD, W. W. *Principles of psychology.* New York: Appleton-Century-Crofts, 1950.

KELLNER, R. The seasonal prevalence of neurosis. *British Journal of Psychiatry,* 1966, **112,** 69–70.

KELLNER, R., & SHEFFIELD, B. F. The one week prevalence of symptoms in neurotic patients and normals. *American Journal of Psychiatry,* 1973, **130,** 102–105.

KENNY, F. T., SOLYOM, L., & SOLYOM, C. Faradic disruption of obsessive ideation in the treatment of obsessive neurosis. *Behavior Therapy,* 1973, **4,** 443–457.

KRAPFL, J., & NAWAS, M. Differential ordering of stimulus presentation in systematic desensitization. *Journal of Abnormal Psychology,* 1970, **75,** 333–337.

KUTASH, S. B. Psychoneuroses. In B. B. Wolman (Ed.), *Handbook of clinical psychology.* New York: McGraw-Hill, 1965.

LAMONTAGNE, Y., & MARKS, I. M. Psychogenic urinary retention: treatment by prolonged exposure. *Behavior Therapy,* 1973, **4,** 581–585.

LANG, P. J. The mechanics of desensitization and the laboratory study of human fear. In C. M. Franks (Ed.), *Behavior therapy: appraisal and status.* New York: McGraw-Hill, 1969.

LANG, P. J., & LAZOVIK, A. D. Experimental desensitization of a phobia. *Journal of Abnormal and Social Psychology,* 1963, **66,** 519–525.

LANG, P. J., LAZOVIK, A. D., & REYNOLDS, J. J. Desensitization, suggestibility and pseudo-therapy. *Journal of Abnormal Psychology,* 1965, **70,** 395–402.

LAZARUS, A. A. Group therapy of phobic disorders by systematic desensitization. *Journal of Abnormal and Social Psychology*, 1961, **63**, 504–510.

LAZARUS, A. A. The results of behavior therapy in 126 cases of severe neurosis. *Behaviour Research and Therapy*, 1963, **1**, 69–79.

LAZARUS, A. A. *Behavior therapy and beyond.* New York: McGraw-Hill, 1971.

LAZARUS, A. A., DAVISON, G. C., & POLEFKA, D. A. Classical and operant factors in the treatment of a school phobia. *Journal of Abnormal Psychology*, 1965, **70**, 225–229.

LEITENBERG, H. The use of single-case methodology in psychotherapy research. *Journal of Abnormal Psychology*, 1973, **82**, 87–101.

LEITENBERG, H., AGRAS, W. S., ALLEN, R., BUTZ, R., & EDWARDS, J. Feedback and therapist praise during treatment of phobia. *Journal of Consulting and Clinical Psychology*, 1975, **43**, 396–404.

LEITENBERG, H., AGRAS, W. S., BARLOW, D. H., & OLIVEAU, D. C. Contribution of selective positive reinforcement and therapeutic instructions to systematic desensitization therapy. *Journal of Abnormal Psychology*, 1969, **74**, 113–118.

LEITENBERG, H., AGRAS, W. S., BUTZ, R., & WINCZE, J. P. Relationship between heart rate and behavioral change during the treatment of phobias. *Journal of Abnormal Psychology*, 1971, **78**, 59–68.

LEITENBERG, H., AGRAS, W. S., EDWARDS, J. THOMSON, L. E., & WINCZE, J. P. Practice as a psychotherapeutic variable. An experimental analysis within single cases. *Journal of Psychiatric Research*, 1970, **7**, 215–225.

LEITENBERG, H., AGRAS, W. S., THOMSON, L. E., & WRIGHT, D. E. Feedback in behavior modification: an experimental analysis in two phobic cases. *Journal of Applied Behavior Analysis*, 1968, **1**, 131–137.

LEITENBERG, H., & CALLAHAN, E. J. Reinforced practice and reduction of different kinds of fears in adults and children. *Behaviour Research and Therapy*, 1973, **11**, 19–30.

LEITENBERG, H., WINCZE, J. P., BUTZ, R. A. CALLAHAN, E. J., & AGRAS, W. S. Comparison of the effects of instructions and reinforcement in the treatment of a neurotic avoidance response: a single case experiment. *Journal of Behavior Therapy and Experimental Psychiatry*, 1970, **1**, 53–58.

LEVY, R., & MEYER, V. Ritual prevention in obsessional patients. *Proceedings Royal Society of Medicine*, 1971, **64**, 1115–1118.

MARKS, I. M. *Fears and phobias.* New York: Academic Press, 1969.

MARKS, I. M. Agoraphobic syndrome (phobic anxiety state). *Archives of General Psychiatry*, 1970, **23**, 539–553.

MARKS, I. M. Perspectives on flooding. *Seminars in Psychiatry*, 1972, **4**, 129–138.

MARKS, I. M. New approaches to the treatment of obsessive-compulsive disorders. *Journal of Nervous and Mental Disease*, 1973, **156**, 420–426.

MARKS, I., BOULOUGOURIS, J., & MARSET, P. Flooding versus desensitization in the treatment of phobic patients: a crossover study. *British Journal of Psychiatry*, 1971, **119**, 353–375.

MARKS, I. M., CROWE, M., DREWE, E., YOUNG, J., & DEWHURST, W. G. Obsessive compulsive neurosis in children. *British Journal of Psychiatry*, 1969, **115**, 991–998.

MARKS, I. M., & GELDER, M. G. A controlled retrospective study of behavior therapy in phobic patients. *British Journal of Psychiatry*, 1965, **111**, 561–573.

MARKS, I. M., GELDER, M. G., & EDWARDS, G. Hypnosis and desensitization for phobias: a controlled prospective trial. *British Journal of Psychiatry*, 1968, **114**, 1263–1274.

MARKS, I. M., VISWANATHAN, R., LIPSEDGE, M. S., & GARDNER, R. Enhanced relief of phobias by flooding during waning Diazepam effect. *British Journal of Psychiatry*, 1972, **121**, 493–505.

MARSHALL, W. L., STRAWBRIDGE, H., & KELTNER, A. The role of mental relaxation in experimental desensitization. *Behaviour Research and Therapy*, 1972, **10**, 355–366.

McCONAGHY, N. Results of systematic desensitization with phobias re-examined. *British Journal of Psychiatry*, 1970, **117**, 89–92.

McFALL, R. M., & LILLESAND, D. B. Behavior rehearsal with modeling and coaching in assertion training. *Journal of Abnormal Psychology*, 1971, **37**, 313–323.

McFALL, R. M., & MARSTON, A. R. An experimental investigation of behavior rehearsal in assertion training. *Journal of Abnormal Psychology*, 1970, **76**, 295–303.

McFALL, R. M., & TWENTYMAN, C. T. Four experiments on the relative contribution of rehearsal, modeling, and coaching to assertion training. *Journal of Abnormal Psychology,* 1973, **81**, 199–219.

METZNER, R. Some experimental analogues of obsession. *Behaviour Research and Therapy,* 1963, **1**, 231–236.

MEYER, V. The treatment of two phobic patients on the basis of learning principles. *Journal of Abnormal and Social Psychology,* 1957, **55**, 261–266.

MEYER, V. Modification of expectations in cases with obsessional rituals. *Behaviour Research and Therapy,* 1966, 4, 273–280.

MILES, H. H. W., BARRABEE, M. S., & FINESINGER, J. E. Evaluation of psychotherapy with a follow-up study of 62 cases of anxiety neurosis. *Psychosomatic Medicine,* 1951, **13**, 83–105.

MILLER, B. V., & BERNSTEIN, D. A. Instructional demand in a behavioral avoidance test for claustrophobic fears. *Journal of Abnormal Psychology,* 1972, **80**, 206–210.

MILLER, B. V., & LEVIS, D. J. The effects of varying short visual exposure times to a phobic test stimulus on subsequent avoidance behavior. *Behaviour Research and Therapy,* 1971, **9**, 17–21.

MILLER, H., & NAWAS, M. Control of aversive stimulus termination in systematic desentitization. *Behaviour Research and Therapy,* 1970, **8**, 57–63.

MILLS, H. L., AGRAS, S., BARLOW, D. H., & MILLS, J. R. Compulsive rituals treated by response prevention. *Archives of General Psychiatry,* 1973, **28**, 524–529.

MORGANSTERN, K. P. Implosive therapy and flooding procedures: a critical review. *Psychological Bulletin,* 1973, **79**, 318-334.

NAWAS, M., FISHMAN, S., & PUCEL, J. A standardized systematic desensitization program applicable to group and individual treatment. *Behaviour Research and Therapy,* 1970, **8**, 49–56.

NAWAS, M., WELSH, W., & FISHMAN, T. The comparative effectiveness of pairing aversive imagery with relaxation, neutral tasks, and muscular tension in reducing snake phobia. *Behavior Research and Therapy,* 1970, **8**, 63–68.

OLIVEAU, D. C., AGRAS, W. S., LEITENBERG, H., MOORE, R. C., & WRIGHT, D. E. Systematic desensitization, therapeutically oriented instructions, and selective positive reinforcement. *Behaviour Research and Therapy,* 1969, 7, 27–33.

ORNE, M. T., & EVANS, E. J. Social control in the psychological experiment: antisocial behavior

and hypnosis. *Journal of Personality and Social Psychology,* 1965, **1**, 189–200.

PAUL, G. L. *Insight versus desensitization in psychotherapy.* Stanford, Calif.: Stanford University Press, 1966.

PAUL, G. L. Insight versus desensitization two years after termination. *Journal of Consulting Psychology,* 1967, **31**, 333–348.

PAUL, G. L. Two-year follow up of systematic desensitization in therapy groups. *Journal of Abnormal Psychology,* 1968, **73**, 119–130.

PAUL, G. L. Outcome of systematic desensitization. In C. M. Franks (Ed.), *Behavior therapy: appraisal and status.* New York: McGraw-Hill, 1969.

PAUL, G. L., & SHANNON, D. T. Treatment of anxiety through systematic desensitization in therapy groups. *Journal of Abnormal Psychology,* 1966, **71**, 124–135.

RACHMAN, S. Systematic desensitization. *Psychological Bulletin,* 1967, **67**, 93–103.

RACHMAN, S. *Phobias: their nature and control.* Springfield, Ill.: Charles C. Thomas, 1968. (a)

RACHMAN, S. The role of muscular relaxation in desensitization therapy. *Behavior Research and Therapy,* 1968, **6**, 159–166. (b)

RACHMAN, S. Obsessional ruminations. *Behaviour Research and Therapy,* 1971, **9**, 229–237.

RACHMAN, S. Clinical applications of observational learning, imitation, and modeling. *Behavior Therapy,* 1972, **3**, 379–397.

RACHMAN, S., & HODGSON, R. J. Studies in desensitization. IV. Optimum degree of anxiety reduction. *Behavior Research and Therapy,* 1967, **5**, 251–252.

RACHMAN, S., HODGSON, R., & MARKS, I. The treatment of chronic obsessive-compulsive neurosis. *Behaviour Research and Therapy,* 1971, **9**, 237–247.

RACKENSBERGER, W., & FEINBERG, A. N. The treatment of severe handwashing compulsion by systematic desensitization: a case report. *Journal of Behavior Therapy and Experimental Psychiatry,* 1972, **3**, 123–127.

RATHUS, S. A. An experimental investigation of assertive training in a group setting. *Journal of Behavior Therapy and Experimental Psychiatry,* 1972, **3**, 81–86.

RATHUS, S. A. Investigation of assertive behavior through videotape-mediated assertive models and direct practice. *Behaviour Research and Therapy*, 1973, **11**, 57–65 (a)

RATHUS, S. A. A 30-item schedule for assessing assertive behavior. *Behavior Therapy*, 1973, **21**, 398–405. (b)

RIMM, D. C., & MAHONEY, M. J. The application of reinforcement and participant modeling procedures in the treatment of snake phobic behavior. *Behaviour Research and Therapy*, 1967, **7**, 369–376.

RITTER, B. The group desensitization of children's snake phobias using vicarious and contact desensitization procedures. *Behaviour Research and Therapy*, 1968, **6**, 1–6.

RITTER, B. Treatment of acrophobia with contact desensitization. *Behaviour Research and Therapy*, 1969, **7**, 41–45. (a)

RITTER, B. The use of contact desensitization, demonstration plus participation and demonstration alone in the treatment of acrophobia. *Behavior Research and Therapy*, 1969, **7**, 157–164. (b)

ROBERTS, A. H. Housebound housewives: a follow-up study of a phobic anxiety state. *British Journal of Psychiatry*, 1964, **110**, 191–197.

ROPER, C., RACHMAN, S., & HODGSON, R. An experiment on obsessional checking. *Behaviour Research and Therapy*, 1973, **11**, 271–277.

RUTNER, I. T. The effects of feedback and instructions on phobic behavior. *Behavior Therapy*, 1973, **4**, 338–348.

RYCROFT, C. *Anxiety and Neurosis.* London: Penguin Press, 1968.

RYLE, A. *Neurosis in the ordinary family.* Philadelphia: Lippincott, 1967.

SALTER, A. *Conditional reflex therapy.* New York: Capricorn, 1949.

SCHMIDT, H. O., & FONDA, C. P. The reliability of psychiatric diagnosis: a new look. *Journal of Abnormal and Social Psychology*, 1956, **52**, 262–267.

SHERMAN, A. R. Real life exposure as a primary therapeutic factor in the desensitization treatment of fear. *Journal of Abnormal Psychology*, 1972, **79**, 19–28.

SIEGELTUCH, M. B., & BAUM, M. Extinction of well-established avoidance responses through response prevention (flooding). *Behaviour Research and Therapy*, 1971, **9**, 103–109.

SOLOMON, R. L., KAMIN, L. J., & WYNNE, L. C. Traumatic avoidance learning: the outcomes of several extinction procedures with dogs. *Journal of Abnormal and Social Psychology*, 1953, **48**, 291–302.

SROLE, L., LANGNER, T. S., MICHAEL, S. T., OPLER, M. K., & RENNIE, T. A. C. *Mental health in the metropolis, midtown Manhattan study*, Vol. 1. New York: McGraw-Hill, 1962.

STAMPFL, T. G., & LEVIS, D. J. Essentials of implosive therapy. *Journal of Abnormal Psychology*, 1967, **72**, 496–503.

STERN, R. Treatment of a case of obsessional neurosis using thought-stopping techniques. *British Journal of Psychiatry*, 1970, **117**, 441–442.

TAYLOR, J. G. A behavioral interpretation of obsessive compulsive neurosis. *Behaviour Research and Therapy*, 1963, **1**, 237–244.

WALKER, V. J., & BEECH, H. R. Mood state and ritualistic behavior of obsessional patients. *British Journal of Psychiatry*, 1969, **115**, 1261–1263.

WALTON, D. The relevance of learning theory to the treatment of an obsessive compulsive state. In H. J. Eysenck (Ed.), *Behavior therapy and the neuroses.* New York: Pergamon Press, 1960.

WALTON, D., & MATHER, M. D. The application of learning principles to the treatment of obsessive compulsive states in the acute and chronic phases of illness. *Behaviour Research and Therapy*, 1963, **1**, 163–174.

WATERS, W. F., McDONALD, D. G., & KORESKO, R. L. Psychophysiological responses during analogue SD and non-relaxation control procedures. *Behaviour Research and Therapy*, 1972, **10**, 381–393.

WATSON, J. P., GAIND, R., & MARKS, I. M. Prolonged exposure: a rapid treatment for phobias. *British Medical Journal*, 1971, **1**, 13–15.

WATSON, J. P., GAIND, R., & MARKS, I. M. Physiological habituation to continuous phobic stimulation. *Behaviour Research and Therapy*, 1972, **10**, 269–279.

WATSON, J. P., & MARKS, I. M. Relevant and irrelevant fear in flooding: a crossover study of phobic patients. *Behavior Therapy*, 1971, **2**, 275–293.

WILKINS, W. Desensitization: social and cognitive factors underlying the effectiveness of Wolpe's procedure. *Psychological Bulletin*, 1971, **76**, 311–317.

WILSON, G. T., & DAVISON, G. C. Processes of fear reduction in systematic desensitization:

animal studies. *Psychological Bulletin*, 1971, **76**, 1–14.

WOLPE, J. *Psychotherapy by reciprocal inhibition*. Stanford, Calif.: Stanford University Press, 1958.

WOLPE, J. Quantitative relationships in the systematic desensitization of phobias. *American Journal of Psychiatry*, 1963, **119**, 1062–1068.

WOLPE, J. *The practice of behavior therapy*. New York: Pergamon Press, 1969.

WOLPE, J., & LAZARUS, A. A. *Behavior therapy techniques: a guide to the treatment of neuroses*. London: Pergamon Press, 1966.

WOLPIN, M., & PEARSALL, L. Rapid deconditioning of a fear of snakes. *Behaviour Research and Therapy*, 1965, **3**, 107–111.

ZIGLER, E., & PHILLIPS, L. Psychiatric diagnosis and symptomology. *Journal of Abnormal and Social Psychology*, 1961, **63**, 69–75.

Depression

MARTIN E. P. SELIGMAN
DAVID C. KLEIN
WILLIAM R. MILLER

5

Depression may be the most common major form of psychopathology. Yet it is likely the least adequately investigated and most dimly understood. We hope to shed some light on this disorder first by reviewing the theoretical and therapeutic literature and then by proposing a theory of our own which integrates much of this literature.

Our chapter has four sections:[1]

1. examination of the symptoms and classification of depression;

2. review of the major theories;

3. review of the therapies for depression, with an emphasis on behavior therapy;

Preparation of this chapter was supported by National Institute of Mental Health grants MH19604 to Martin E. P. Seligman and MH1998903 to Aaron T. Beck.

[1] We have largely omitted physiological and genetic consideration from our review. Although we believe these to be important, they fall beyond the scope of this chapter. For reviews of this literature, the interested reader should consult Glassman (1969), Rubin and Mandell (1966), Schildkraut (1965), and Whybrow and Mendels (1969). In addition, we are omitting a discussion of mania which is generally considered to have a physiological basis (cf. Kraines, 1965).

4. presentation of the learned helplessness model of depression.

Symptoms of Depression

We are all familiar, at least casually, with what depression looks like. Sadness, passivity, crying spells, thoughts of suicide, feelings of hopelessness, helplessness, and worthlessness, indecisiveness, loss of interest in the world, loss of appetite, and susceptibility to fatigue and boredom are all common symptoms of the disorder.

The prevalence of depression is staggering. The National Institute of Mental Health (Williams, Friedman, & Secunda, 1970) estimates that "4 to 8 million Americans may be in need of professional care for the depressive illnesses." In addition, this disorder, unlike most other forms of psychopathology, can be lethal. "One out of every 100 persons afflicted by a depressive illness will die a suicidal death." The economic cost is also enormous. Loss of productivity and cost of treatment amount to "between 1.3 and 4.0 billion dollars per annum."

Beck (1967) obtained the distributions of

symptoms considered relevant to depression in 966 psychiatric patients, assigned to four groups on the basis of psychiatric ratings of depth of depression (none, mild, moderate, and severe), regardless of primary diagnosis. Four classes of symptoms were identified—affective, cognitive, motivational, and physical. Table 5–1 presents the percentages of patients showing each of the various symptoms. It can be seen from the table that there is no one symptom that all depressed patients have. Like other words from ordinary parlance, "depression" denotes a family or cluster of symptoms with no single defining feature.[2]

Types of Depression

The considerable confusion concerning the classification of depression can be attributed to its varying definitions as well as to its large number of subtypes. Depression has been variously defined as a mood, a symptom, a syndrome, and a nosological entity. In discussing problems in classification,

[2] See Wittgenstein (1953; paragraphs 66-77) for a brilliant exposition of the general argument against necessary conditions as defining features of words in natural languages.

Mendels (1968) listed some of the subtypes of depression that have been described:

A short list would include psychotic, neurotic, reactive, psychotic reactive, involutional, agitated, endogenous, psychogenic, symptomatic, presenile, senile, acute, chronic, and, of course, manic-depressive psychosis and melancholia (minor and major); as well as depression in sexual perversion, alcoholic depressive symptoms resulting from organic disorder (p. 1549).

The two most widely used classifications for depression are the scheme of the American Psychiatric Association (1968) and the endogenous versus reactive classification. The APA classification consists of two major divisions of "affective disorders"—the psychotic and neurotic. The psychotic affective disorders include involutional melancholia, manic-depressive illness, and psychotic depressive reaction; depressive neurosis is the only neurotic affective disorder. In addition, other disorders with an affective component are included within the APA system: cyclothymic personality is listed as a personality disorder and schizoaffective disorder is listed as a subtype of the schizophrenic reaction.

The endogenous-reactive concept of depression has caused a great deal of contro-

TABLE 5–1   Distribution of symptoms among depressed and nondepressed psychiatric patients

	Depressed (n = 751)	Non-depressed (n = 224)		Depressed (n = 751)	Non-depressed (n = 224)
Affective symptoms			*Cognitive symptoms*		
Dejected mood	50–88%[a]	23%	Low self-evaluation	60–81%	38%
Self-dislike	64–86	37	Negative expectation	55–87	22
Loss of gratification	65–92	35	Self-blame and criticism	67–80	43
Loss of attachments	37–64	16	Indecisiveness	48–76	23
Crying spells	44–83	29	Distorted self-image	33–66	12
Loss of mirth response	29–52	8	*Physical symptoms*		
Motivational symptoms			Loss of appetite	40–72	21
Loss of motivation	65–86	33	Sleep disturbance	60–87	40
Suicidal wishes	31–74	12	Loss of libido	38–61	27
			Fatigability	62–78	40

[a] Range of symptom frequency for patients with degree of depression ranging from mild to severe.
Adapted from Beck, 1967.

versy in psychiatry and psychology (Partridge, 1949). This classification is based primarily upon etiology—endogenous depressions are presumably caused by internal factors (biochemical, hormonal, or genetic) whereas reactive depressions are presumably caused by external factors (e.g., stress, psychological trauma, and conflict).

A number of factor analytic studies attempted to determine whether depression is a unitary or a binary phenomenon. The results of these studies were highly consistent. Mendels (1970) compared the results of seven of the studies (Carney, Roth, & Garside, 1965; Hamilton & White, 1959; Hordern, 1965; Kiloh & Garside, 1963; Mendels & Cochrane, 1968; Rosenthal & Gudeman, 1967; Rosenthal & Klerman, 1966) to see if they agreed on the direction (positive or negative) and significance of a given item's factor loading. He found that the results of the seven studies were in perfect agreement for eight items and in 75% agreement for nine additional items. Several investigators (cf. Carney et al., 1965; Kiloh & Garside, 1963) have argued that the results of these studies demonstrate that there are two distinct types of depression which differ in symptomatology and prognosis, while others (cf. Kendell, 1968) have concluded that depression is a unitary phenomenon. Eysenck (1970) has persuasively argued that this disagreement in interpretation is due to a misunderstanding of the statistical methods used and has asserted that the results of the factor analytic studies conclusively favor the binary view.

So, a number of factor analytic studies have confirmed the binary view of depression. Typically, the two factors identified have been labelled endogenous and reactive depressions. Comparison of the results of these studies (Mendels, 1970) shows that endogenous depression is characterized by retardation, severe depression, lack of reactivity to the environment, loss of interest in life, somatic symptoms, no precipitating stress, middle of the night insomnia, lack of self-pity, history of previous episodes, weight loss, early-morning awakening, guilt, absence of features of hysterical or inadequate personality, and suicide. On the other hand, reactive depression shows less retardation, less severe depression, more reactivity to the environment, less loss of interest in life, fewer somatic symptoms, precipitating stressors, less middle of the night insomnia, more self-pity, fewer prior episodes, less weight loss, less early-morning awakening, less guilt, more hysterical or inadequate personality features, and fewer suicides.

The fact that two independent symptom clusters have been identified does not necessarily support the endogenous-reactive dichotomy. The endogenous-reactive distinction is theoretically an *etiological* distinction and we cannot conclude that the etiologies are different merely because two symptom clusters exist.

Winokur (1973) developed a comprehensive classification scheme based on studies of family constellations of affective disorder. There are three major categories: (1) normal grief, which may be equivalent to reactive depression; (2) secondary depression, which is a depressive episode in the presence of preexisting, nonaffective psychopathology; and (3) primary affective disorder, which is mania or depression without any other psychiatric disorder. Primary affective disorder is further divided into unipolar (depressive) and bipolar (manic-depressive) types. The unipolar is subdivided into (1) pure depressive disease, typified by the late onset male; and (2) depression spectrum disease, typified by the early onset female.

Ultimately, diagnostic systems are of value only if they predict, especially if they predict which treatment is most likely to be successful. There is some evidence to indicate that patients' scores on the endogenous and reactive factors (of the factor analytic studies) predict response to electroconvulsive shock with endogenous depressives improving more (Carney et al., 1965). However, the relationship of the APA classification and Winokur's classification to response to various types of treatment has not yet been determined. In addition, no studies have demonstrated that either psychological therapy in general, or any particular form of psychotherapy—behavioral, cognitive, or psychodynamic—is more effective with one type of depression than another. Finally, even if two etiologically distinct types of depression were identified, one endogenous and one reactive, it does not follow that two corresponding therapies, one somatic and one psychological, would be needed.

Psychological Theories of Depression

EARLY THEORIES

Description of depression are found in the most ancient medical records. Around 400 B.C., Hippocrates gave the first written account of "melancholia," the early term for depression. He recognized it as a mental disease along with epilepsy, mania, and paranoia. A physiological cause for the illness was stressed: melancholia literally means "black bile" and an abundance of black bile moving upward toward the brain was the accepted etiology. Aristotle (approximately 350 B.C.) recognized a melancholic temperament in all great thinkers, poets, artists, and statesmen. Aretaeus of Cappadocia (approximately 80 A.D.) provided what is generally considered to be the best early clinical description of the disease. He considered mania and melancholia to be two expressions of a recurrent, but potentially curable illness. Melancholic patients were described as "restless, sad, dismayed, sleepless," "seized with terror if the affection makes progress," and "thin by their agitation and loss of refreshing sleep." Also, "at a more advanced age, they complain of a thousand futilities and they desire death" [Zilboorg & Henry, 1941, p. 76].

After the domination by spiritual healers during the Middle Ages, Felix Platter emerged in the late 1500s as the first great systematist. He described melancholia as "a kind of mental alienation in which imagination and judgment are so perverted that without any cause the victims become very sad and fearful [Diethelm & Hefferman, 1965, p. 15]." Platter felt that terror from an unforeseen accident was the most common cause and he recommended drugs, dietary advice, bleeding, and/or cauterization as treatment.

Kraepelin (1921) was the first to isolate manic-depressive insanity as a disease entity. He distinguished many forms of the disorder (e.g., mania, melancholia) and gave excellent clinical descriptions of each type. He separated manic-depressive insanity from the other major category of mental disorders, dementia praecox, on the following basis: dementia praecox was a progressive, deteriorating disorder, whereas manic-depressive insanity was episodic and nondeteriorating. Kraepelin viewed this disorder as hereditary. Although he paired mania with depression, the melancholic form of this disorder is the focus of this chapter. There is no longer reason to believe that mania and depression invariably or even predominantly occur together. Depression without mania is commonplace.

PSYCHODYNAMIC THEORIES[3]

The ideas of Karl Abraham (1927a; 1927b) led to a psychoanalytical theory of depression. In 1911, Abraham claimed that hatred is the dominant feeling in the premorbid depressive but this hatred is unacceptable to the person and is therefore repressed and

[3] Many contributions to the psychodynamic theories of depression have been made (cf. Gero, 1936; Jacobson, 1946, 1953, 1954; Klein, 1948; Rado, 1928). Rather than radically changing the fundamental psychodynamic theory, these authors have suggested minor modifications in its structure. The discussion presented here should give a basic understanding of the theory, but the reader interested in a more complete review of the literature is referred to Garma (1947), Rosenfeld (1959), and especially Mendelson (1960).

projected. The person feels hated by others and comes to believe that he is hated because of his inborn defects. Hence, he becomes depressed. Abraham found evidence of repressed hostility in depressives' dreams of criminality and attempts to get revenge on others. The patients, however, do not attribute their violent impulses to sadism but rather to their own defects. They are strongly masochistic and the guilt they feel because of their impulses adds to the pleasure they receive from suffering and from constantly thinking about themselves. Because they cannot make a lasting libidinal attachment, the patients become autoerotic, their behavior becomes inhibited, and they thus satisfy the unconscious tendency toward a "negation of life."

Freud (1955) actually formulated the fundamental psychoanalytic explanation of depression. He compared melancholia with the normal process of mourning, hoping that the comparison would help explain melancholia as a pathology. When a loved object is lost, reality testing shows the mourner that he must withdraw his libidinal attachments to the object. Because the attachments are normally very strong, the ego can only slowly accept reality but eventually it is freed from the object.

Melancholia, according to Freud, sometimes occurs when there is *no* apparent object loss and therefore appears related to an unconscious loss. Freud found it strange that the mourner believes that an object external to himself has been lost, but the melancholic locates the loss within himself. The resolution of this problem introduced the crucial mechanism in the etiology of melancholia. Freud noted that in all cases, the melancholic's self-accusations better described the love-object or potential love-object rather than the melancholic himself. Upon the loss of the love-object, the freed libido is withdrawn into the ego rather than being directed to another object. The freed libido is used to establish an identification of the ego with the lost object by introjection and the ego is thus enabled to criticize

itself as an object. By substituting identification for object love, the patient regresses to the oral phase of the libido, where the infant was unable to distinguish himself from his environment and many object-relations were ambivalent. Because of this ambivalence, some of the freed libido from the abandoned object-cathexis fuels a sadism directed toward the self.

We should also note Bibring's (1953) psychodynamic theory of depression which, like the theory we shall propose, sees helplessness as the central theme of depression.

> To summarize: What has been described as the basic mechanism of depression, the ego's shocking awareness of its helplessness in regard to its aspirations, is assumed to represent the core of normal, neurotic, and probably also psychotic depression. It is further assumed on the basis of clinical material that such traumatic experiences usually occur in early childhood and establish a fixation of the ego to the state of helplessness. This state is later on regressively reactivated whenever situations arise which resemble the primary shock condition [p. 39].

It seems a worthless endeavor to criticize specific aspects of the psychoanalytic theory of depression. Whether the lost object is actually introjected into the ego, whether the object is "split" (see Rado, 1928), and whether the depressive is orally fixated are all questions which are posed on a theoretical level. Discussion of these topics cannot lead to a definitive evaluation. Grinker, Miller, Sabshin, Nunn, and Nunnally (1961) stress the lack of clinical data in analytic writings. When data are supplied, they are used only as catalysts for discussions of various intrapsychic phenomena. Psychoanalytic theory is ambiguous and remote from observables and therefore makes few directly testable predictions. Depression is probably predisposed and some types of events seem more likely than others to precipitate a depressive episode, but couching these statements in dynamic terms may even *retard* understanding. As Salzman (1962) writes: "Is there any justification for proposing complicated theories to explain phenomena that can be comprehended in simpler terms [p. 28]?" The cognitive and behavioral theories that follow are less complex explanations that are more closely tied to the observable phenomena of depression.

COGNITIVE THEORIES

Beck (1963, 1964, 1967, 1970b, 1971) has challenged the generally accepted view of depression as an affective disorder. He does not consider the cognitive manifestations of depression (e.g., low self-esteem, hopelessness, and helplessness) to be secondary to the affective disturbance. Beck asserts that the sequence that perception leads to cognition and emotion in normals (in which cognitions determine affect), exists also in depressives. Unlike normal cognitions, depressive cognitions are dominated by idiosyncratic processes and content. These cognitions determine the affective response in depression.

Beck examined the idiosyncratic thought content of depressives and discovered distorted and unrealistic conceptions. Patients' verbalizations and free associations revealed recurring themes of low self-regard, deprivation, self-criticism and self-blame, overwhelming problems and duties, self-commands and injunctions, and escapist and suicidal wishes. These cognitions are distorted and unrealistic because patients tend to exaggerate their faults and the obstacles in their path.

Beck divides the erroneous conceptualizations of the depressed patient into the "cognitive triad." The patient views his world, himself, and his future in a negative way. As this triad becomes increasingly dominant, the patient becomes progressively more depressed and shows other noncognitive symptoms of depression. Because the person has been rejected or believes he has been rejected, he feels sad. Because all tasks seem insurmountable and boring, he

shows paralysis of the will and wants to escape. When these feelings are intensified and coupled with feelings of helplessness and worthlessness, he becomes extremely dependent and may attempt suicide.

Melges and Bowlby (1969) stress the importance of hopelessness in depression. Hope and hopelessness refer to a person's estimate of his ability to achieve certain goals; this estimate depends on prior success with specific goals as well as on effectiveness in achieving goals generally. A depressive is hopeless about his future when he (1) believes his skills will no longer be effective in reaching his goals; (2) believes he has failed because of his own incompetence and must rely upon others; and (3) feels his previous efforts at long-term goals have failed. Although the depressive feels he is incapable of attaining his goals, they remain important and he is preoccupied with them.

Lichtenberg (1957) also believes that the depressive is hopeless about attaining his goals, and stresses that the depressive blames himself for his failures. Lichtenberg describes three types of depression which progress in severity as belief in hopelessness moves from a specific situation (least severe) to a whole behavior style to total satisfaction from the environment (most severe). The more severe cases show intense feelings of worthlessness, more passivity, and less trust. Lichtenberg traces the genesis of depression to the development of expectancies of attaining goals during the helpless stage of infancy and during childhood, when behavior styles are begun.

Schmale (1958) and Engel (1968) have indicated that hopelessness and helplessness make a person more susceptible to depression as well as to illness and death. Schmale claimed that loss or threat of loss is related to anger, fear, and especially hopelessness and helplessness. He studied hospitalized patients and found that disease onset frequently immediately followed some significant change in a relationship. Engel also studied hospitalized patients and found that a profound feeling of psychological impotence precedes illness and death. Patients feel both hopeless and helpless; they have a depreciated image of themselves; they have lost gratification in their lives, their futures seem bleak. In our words, they seem depressed. The cognitive aspects of depression, therefore, seem powerful enough not only to be related to psychomotor retardation, weight loss, sleeplessness, etc., but also to medical illness and possibly death.

Mowrer (1969) presented a rather novel view of depression. He observed the program at Daytop Village, a drug rehabilitation center, and claimed that the program actually worked on depression without mentioning it. Part of the therapy consisted of examining one's cognitions of anger, controlling the anger, and expressing it verbally. Mowrer referred to the theories and practices of Daniel H. Casriel, a New York psychiatrist, who believes that American children are infused with the Protestant Work Ethic which stresses that work is the supreme virtue and that one's acceptance as a person is dependent upon his productivity. Furthermore, children are taught to show emotional control to avoid possibly exposing themselves to ridicule or dislike. Depression results from discouragement and defiance of orders to work. In other words, depression does not cause work inhibition; depression is caused by work inhibition. Therapy is a matter of repudiating the Work Ethic and openly asking others for love. Although the theory and therapy of depression presented by Mowrer are unique, they are related to a framework like Beck's where the cognitions leading to depression are illogical and must be repudiated. Mowrer suggests, however, that cognitive distortions are considerably more widespread than Beck would have us believe and that it may be necessary to change the attitudes of a whole country to get rid of depression.

The cognitive theories presented above possess a distinct advantage over the dynamic theories in that they speak in language that is closely related to observable phenomena. Rather than stressing some infantile experience that is not likely to be convincingly discovered, cognitive theorists usually deal with the present cognitive structure of the depressive. Although their systems are necessarily based on hypothetical constructs and their primary data are almost wholly subjective, the theories seem sufficiently close to reality to be testable. In addition, cognitive theorists have shown a refreshing disinclination to engage in etiological speculation and have contributed a great deal to descriptions of thinking in depression, an area that has been neglected by both psychoanalysts and behaviorists for too long. Their work must play an integral role in any comprehensive theory of depression.

BEHAVIORAL THEORIES

A recent advance in theories of depression has been made by behaviorists. Formulations have been presented and corresponding therapies have been devised. To date, no breakthroughs have occurred but the field seems promising if it can attain a scientific rigor that other theories have lacked.

Ferster (1965) described behavior pathology as a direct result of an individual's interaction with his environment and an outcome of his reinforcement history. He demanded both a topographic and a functional analysis of behavior. A topographic analysis simply describes what has occurred without reference to antecedents or consequences. A functional analysis, which Ferster considered to be more important, describes the relation of the behavior to the environment and specifies controlling environmental events which are potentially manipulable. Ferster considered depression to be the lowered frequency of emission of positively reinforced behavior. So, a functional analysis of variables that control the emission of such behavior is directly applicable to both the etiology and the therapy of depression.

Ferster (1966) presented an animal analogue of such an analysis, with depression being characterized by retardation of psychomotor and thought processes with a notable reduction or absence of previously successful behaviors. He did not deny the existence of thought and mood disorders but he considered them to be secondary. Animal experiments suggest a number of ways to sharply reduce the occurrence of a behavior: (1) require large amounts of a behavior to produce reinforcement; (2) present aversive stimuli; (3) produce a sudden change in the environment by removing an important object which is either a reinforcer or a discriminative stimulus. If the lost object controlled a large amount of a person's behavior, this behavior may drop out. Ferster described depression as a reduction of the total repertoire rather than just a reduction of one or two responses. As such, no one of the above processes alone is likely in itself to produce depression.

Moss and Boren (1972) extended Ferster's analysis and presented clinical examples of effects of various reinforcement contingencies. In their view, the two major environmental conditions associated with depressive behavior are insufficient positive reinforcement and aversive control. Insufficient compliments to a housewife and an increase in the amount of work required to achieve the same rewards are examples of a high behavior/reinforcement ratio. Withdrawal of a positive reinforcer is illustrated by a salesman who is suddenly no longer obtaining sales with behaviors which previously brought success. Interruption of a behavior chain is exemplified by an executive who loses his job while working toward a long-range goal. Aversive control includes punishment, avoidance, and escape. Moss and Boren's analysis of depression provides "a preliminary model for the behavioral analysis of clinical problems" and it deserves further attention.

Lazarus (1968) also views depression as a function of inadequate or insufficient reinforcers. Agreeing with Ferster, Lazarus con-siders the depressive to be virtually on an extinction schedule with lack of reinforcement resulting in a weakened repertoire. Lazarus then goes one step further by proposing and demonstrating therapeutic methods consistent with his theoretical ideas. These methods are reviewed in our section on therapy.

Lewinsohn, Weinstein, and Shaw (1968) have explored depression through a social-learning theory framework. They claim that not only environmental events, but also organismic traits and states (such as a lack of social skill) can bring about a low positive reinforcement rate. This low reinforcement rate reduces activity and verbalization. In addition, social reinforcers (such as sympathy, interest, and concern) maintain the depressive behavior. Liberman and Raskin (1971) have also stressed the role of secondary gain in depression.

Costello (1972) disagreed with the loss of reinforcement view of depression. He claimed that these behavioral theories explain loss of interest only in those parts of the environment related to the reinforcer and do not explain the *general* loss of interest characteristic of depression. Costello stated that a *loss in reinforcer effectiveness* causes depression and that such a loss can be due to either endogenous biochemical and neurophysiological changes or to the disruption of a chain of behavior. This theory is parsimonious in that it postulates only one mechanism for depression but it has little empirical support as yet.

A number of investigators have attempted to reproduce phenomena of human depression in animals and thus provide an animal model of depression. McKinney and Bunney (1969) have outlined the advantages of animal models and have presented certain requirements for any such model. They feel that an animal model is necessary because biological variables can be directly studied and because social and interactional variables important in depression can be systematically manipulated.

Ivanov-Smolensky (1928) described a dog

that showed depressive-like behaviors after being unable to discriminate between two compound stimuli in a classical conditioning experiment. His explanation was based on the Pavlovian concept of cortical irradiation and depression was seen as resulting from massive cortical inhibition. We know of no further work on this model.

Much of the evidence for an animal model of depression comes from separation studies. Senay (1966) described some of the depressive-like states observed in animals that had been separated from some important object. He attempted to replicate these observations in the laboratory by making himself the only human figure involved in the early rearing of German Shepherd pups. When he left the dogs alone for two months, the dogs with "approach" temperaments began to approach an observer even more than they had before separation; dogs with "avoidance" temperaments showed increased avoidance and/or aggression. Reunion with Senay first resulted in an intensification of their response to separation followed by a return to preseparation levels. Although Senay's data point to the potential behavioral changes that can be produced in animals by separation, they may not relate directly to depression.

McKinney, Suomi, and Harlow (1971), Suomi and Harlow (1972), and Suomi (1973) presented striking evidence for depressive-like phenomena in rhesus monkeys. By using a range of traumatic procedures, these investigators have produced behaviors that look very much like the anaclitic depression reported by Spitz (1946) in human infants. Spitz reported maturational retardation, protest, and despair in children who were separated from their mothers between the ages of 6 and 18 months. Suomi and his coworkers went beyond Spitz's model and produced profound maturational arrest along with protest (locomotion and vocalization) and despair (self-clasping and huddling). Kaufman and Rosenblum (1967) reported that infant monkeys who were separated from their mothers showed pro-

test and despair. McKinney et al. (1971) reported that repetitive, short-term peer separations resulted in protest and despair with each separation. Recovery occurred upon reunion. Furthermore, when these monkeys were nine months old, they were behaving at three-month levels on measures of clinging, self-orality, locomotion, exploration, and play. Suomi and Harlow (1972) reported the behaviors of young monkeys confined to pits. These pits were intuitively designed to create a "well of despair." An animal could eat, drink, and move a little in the pit but after a few days, it typically huddled in the bottom. After six weeks of confinement, the monkeys were put in regular home cages and were tested in playroom sessions with other monkeys. The confinement "produced severe and persistent psychopathological behavior of a depressive nature [p. 14]." The monkeys showed virtually no social behavior, and spent much of their time self-clasping and huddling, and little or no time locomoting or exploring the environment. Their behavior was even more impoverished than that of animals who had been allowed to see and hear other monkeys but who were reared in isolated cages. Furthermore, there was no significant improvement in the behavior of the pitted monkeys over the eight months of testing despite the fact that there was no more pitting. Suomi (1973) reported that pitting during repetitive peer separations increases the deficits attributable to the separations alone.

These reactions in monkeys closely parallel Spitz's (1946) anaclitic depression but the pit data show that an attachment bond does not necessarily have to be formed before the effects can be produced. Suomi, Harlow, and McKinney (1972) have reported that some monkeys who showed typical deficits after isolation were "cured" by contact with younger, clinging monkeys. The temptation to generalize these findings to humans is enormous and it should be indulged to some extent in future experimentation. Although this appears to be a

promising model, we must keep in mind that adult depression is our topic of interest. Nothing is known about the relation of adult depression to anaclitic depression.

Behavioral theories and animal models of depression may well provide an explanation for the disorder. The laboratory tools available to the behaviorist are impressive. Isolating variables that can be experimentally manipulated, especially with animals, can lead to important etiological and therapeutic findings. If there has been a weakness in this area, it is overly simplistic application of operant principles to the complexities of depressive behavior. At the end of this chapter, we shall propose a theory of depression based on an animal model which attempts to wrestle with more of the complexities of the disorder.

Therapy

We now turn to a critical discussion of the modalities of therapy for depression. The more clinically oriented reader may find this section particularly useful since it provides a "pharmacopeia" of available techniques.[4] We begin with a brief consideration of general psychotherapeutic and psychodynamic approaches to treatment, and then detail the cognitive and behavioral therapies that have been employed. We will also point out methodological inadequacies and make suggestions for more definitive research on the effectiveness of the various therapies.

PSYCHOTHERAPY

Because of the lack of controlled studies of psychotherapy with depressed patients, we cannot compare it to other forms of therapy. Therefore, we will merely outline the various treatment techniques and approaches that have been suggested in the literature.

[4] We will omit discussion of pharmacological and other somatic therapies for depression since they are beyond the scope of this chapter.

A more extensive review of this subject can be found in Beck (1967).

The therapeutic techniques suggested by Ayd (1961) are typical of those suggested by other nonanalytic therapists and will be discussed here in some detail. Ayd considers it most useful during the initial sessions for the patient to learn "that he has a known illness for which treatment is available and from which he can expect to recover [p. 117]." Ayd also tells the patient that depression has a physical basis, and he provides repeated reassurance and feedback about improvement.

Ayd considers it best for the therapist not to mention "underlying dynamics." However, he stresses the importance of analyzing the precipitating events, determining the degree to which ongoing stressors can be eliminated, and preparing the patient to cope with similar future events. Explanations for the depression and discussion of the possibility of relapses are postponed until the depression has subsequently cleared.

In addition, Ayd urges the therapist to consult with and advise the patient's family in order to obtain new information about the patient, to relieve some of the stress on the family caused by the illness, to reduce any hostility that the family expresses toward the patient as a result of the illness, and to obtain the family's cooperation in the treatment. Finally, Ayd suggests rest and relaxation, involving a temporary reduction in work or even a leave of absence. Presumably, such measures are needed to isolate the depressive from additional environmental stress.

Campbell (1953) and Kraines (1957) agree with Ayd in urging the therapist to explain to the patient that the depression has a physical basis and can be cured. They also urge the therapist to be reassuring while allowing the patient to ventilate his problems. Campbell suggests occupational therapy and reading to provide relaxation and a sense of satisfaction, while Kraines disagrees and encourages social activity.

These therapeutic techniques can best be considered supportive. For a discussion of insight-oriented psychotherapy with depressives we must turn to the psychoanalytic literature. The psychoanalytic process contains certain features that are constant, regardless of the particular disorder that is being treated. The psychoanalytic treatment of depression and other disorders is designed to bring intrapsychic conflict into conscious awareness through interpretation of resistances, free association, and the working through of the transference. Examples of detailed case study reports of the psychoanalytic treatment of depressed patients may be found in Gero (1936) and Jacobson (1946, 1971).

No studies comparing the effectiveness of psychotherapy and psychoanalysis with other psychological therapies (e.g., behavioral and cognitive) or with no treatment have been reported. The comparison with no-treatment controls is especially important, since psychotherapy and psychoanalysis are generally long-term treatment procedures and depression itself is usually short-term (Kraines, 1957; Lundquist, 1945; Paskind, 1929, 1930).

COGNITIVE THERAPY

Cognitive therapy has been defined as "a set of operations focused on a patient's cognitions (verbal or pictorial) and on the premises, assumptions, and attitudes underlying these cognitions [Beck, 1970a, p. 187]." Beck (1967, 1970a) has been the leading proponent of cognitive therapy for depression, and the discussion here will be restricted to his treatment techniques. He believes that cognitive therapy interrupts the "downward spiral" of depression in which a specific loss leads to sadness about the loss which leads to feelings of giving up which lead to further sadness and loss.

Beck's (1967) cognitive therapy proceeds through four stages. During the first stage, the therapist surveys the patient's life history data to identify major maladaptive

patterns, such as a tendency to see himself as a loser. Instead of calling depression a physical disease (as advocated by Ayd, Campell, and Kraines), Beck tells the patient that the disorder results from the development of maladaptive attitudes, overreaction to specific stresses, and the unfortunate occurrence of traumatic events.

The second stage of treatment might be called an educational phase: the patient is taught to focus upon and identify depression-generating cognitions which Beck labels "automatic thoughts." (For example, the patient may automatically think, "I'm repulsive," whenever he is introduced to someone.) The next stage involves "distancing" or increasing the patient's objectivity toward these depressive cognitions. Distancing is accomplished by pointing out to the patient that his depressive cognitions distort reality, by having the patient and therapist apply rules of logic to the cognitions, and by having the patient review and check the observations on which the cognitions were based.

When the patient is able to identify his depressive cognitions and recognizes that these cognitions are invalid, the fourth stage of therapy "neutralizes" the depressive cognitions. Whenever the patient recognizes a cognition as invalid, he recites the reasons that it is invalid. This leads to reductions in the intensity and frequency of the cognition and the accompanying affect.

Beck considers cognitive therapy to be useful after the low point of depression. He suggests that cognitive therapy should be used in conjunction with supportive therapy during the depressive episode. However, Beck notes that cognitive therapy is effective even during the depressive episode with reactive depressives.

In summary, a treatment procedure involving the identification and modification of depressives' inappropriate and inaccurate cognitions has been proposed. Case studies of cognitive therapy with depressives may be found in Beck (1967). Unfortunately, no controlled studies with depressed patients have yet compared the effectiveness of cognitive therapy with other therapies or with no treatment.

BEHAVIOR THERAPY

MODIFICATION OF VERBAL BEHAVIOR. Lewinsohn and his associates (cf. Robinson & Lewinsohn, 1973b) have utilized the Premack principle in attempts to modify "depressed talk" (e.g., complaining about misfortunes, guilt, and sadness). According to Premack (1959), high frequency responses can reinforce low frequency responses. Since "depressed talk" is a high frequency behavior in depressives, it should be capable of reinforcing lower frequency "nondepressed" or "healthy talk." Robinson and Lewinsohn (1973a) suggested that damping down depressed talk may be therapeutically useful because depressed talk is likely to result in avoidance of the depressives by others.

Robinson and Lewinsohn assigned 20 depressed female college students to one of four groups: (1) the Premack group which had light onset contingent upon nondepressed talk—during the light, depressed talk was permitted; (2) the contingent control group which also had light onset contingent upon nondepressed talk but for whom the light permitted some other *low frequency* behavior; (3) a deprivation control group which was restricted from depressed talk during no light periods and allowed depressed talk during the light; light onset, however, was not contingent upon nondepressed talk (light onset was yoked to light onset in the Premack group); (4) the free talk control group which had no light onset and no restrictions on verbal behavior. Baseline rates of verbal behavior were obtained, and subjects' spontaneous conversation was coded according to topic, using categories described by Lewinsohn (unpublished). The treatment lasted one hour.

After treatment, the Premack group had significantly increased nondepressed talk over its baseline rate and also showed significantly more nondepressed talk than both the free talk and contingent control groups. However, the Premack group did not differ significantly from the deprivation control group. These results suggest that increases in nondepressed talk were due to the restrictions imposed upon depressed talk rather than to reinforcement of nondepressed talk by depressed talk.

Robinson and Lewinsohn (1973a) also reported a case study designed to increase a depressive's rate of speech. The patient was a chronically depressed male. The amount of therapy time available to the patient was made contingent upon the patient's rate of speech, regardless of the topic. After a change in rate had been obtained, the contingency was altered so that a buzzer sounded each time the patient's rate of speech fell below a certain rate. The patient showed a considerable increase in his rate of speech during treatment. During a subsequent extinction phase, the rate of speech decreased to baseline level. Finally, speech rate again increased following reinstatement of the treatment.

These studies demonstrate the effectiveness of operant procedures in altering the frequency of depressed talk and in increasing the speech rate of depressives. However, they are deficient in a number of ways. No report has been made on generalization of the treatment effects to extratherapeutic situations. No adequate follow-up data have been reported. Only vague references have been made as to why reducing depressed talk or increasing speech rate should affect other depressive symptomatology.

The remaining studies of behavior therapy of depression are concerned with treatment of the depression itself rather than with verbal behavior. We will discuss individual, group, and family behavior therapies separately.

INDIVIDUAL BEHAVIOR THERAPY. Lewinsohn et al. (1968) reported a method of treatment similar to the methods discussed above for modifying verbal behavior. The patient was a 22-year-old male who had become depressed and had threatened suicide following his divorce. The patient was also troubled by financial problems and an inability to make decisions concerning career goals. The therapist began each treatment session by asking the patient whether or not he had made any concrete attempts to improve his financial status and career difficulties. If definite action had been taken, the therapist would then listen to the patient's depressed talk. If, however, little or no concrete action had been taken, the therapist would terminate the session, suggesting that the patient return in a few days. Within a few weeks the patient had made and acted upon a number of decisions. The patient also reported that he felt "much better."

One obvious deficiency in this case study is the lack of any objective measure of depression. In addition, it is not at all clear that improvement was the result of reinforcement of more adaptive, low frequency behaviors by the high frequency depressed talk. Termination of the treatment sessions might have acted as a powerful punishment for not making career decisions; increased therapeutic contact may have acted as a positive reinforcer of adaptive behavior independent of the patient's increased opportunity to engage in depressed talk.

Lewinsohn (unpublished) recently used individualized activity schedules in the treatment of 10 depressed patients. The patients noted their frequency of participation in the events and completed the Depression Adjective Checklist (DACL) at the end of each day of the 10-week study, which included an initial 30-day base level period. The 10 activities which were most highly correlated with a patient's mood during the base level period were selected, and the treatment time available to the patient was made contingent upon his participation in the 10 activities. The actual treatment sessions were termed "nondirective." Lewinsohn reported that the frequency of partici-

pation in the 10 selected events increased significantly over treatment and that mean MMPI Depression score decreased. Unfortunately, Lewinsohn did not report the effect of treatment on DACL scores and did not include a control group. In addition, activity level was obtained solely by self-report and the patients had been informed of the contingency between treatment time and activity level prior to treatment.

Seitz (1971) reported on a treatment procedure with a severely depressed female patient. This treatment was based upon the Premack principle and upon Homme's (1965) hypothesis that thoughts follow the same laws as behavior. The basic procedure was to insure that high frequency behavior followed immediately upon the occurrence of positive thoughts. Seitz did not report how such a sequence of events was "insured." The only outcome information was that, "At the end of nine sessions, she reported that she had not felt so well in years [p. 426]."

Lazarus (1968) proposed three treatment procedures for reactive depression. He viewed depression as a result of inadequate or insufficient reinforcers. The reduced reinforcement then leads to decrements in response frequency and quality. The first treatment procedure, called time "projection with positive reinforcement," is illustrated by a student who had become depressed following a break-up with her boyfriend and who had eventually attempted suicide. Using hypnosis, Lazarus had the patient imagine herself engaging in rewarding experiences at progressively more distant times in the future. The rewarding experiences described to the patient were all behaviors which she had enjoyed prior to the depression. Before the patient was brought out of the trance, she was told to remember the time projection sequence and to "return to the present" feeling as she did during the trance. Lazarus reported that the patient felt immediate improvement. Except for a few episodes of "gloom," she was reported to have been free of depressive symptoms at one-week and one-year follow-ups without any further treatment. Lazarus reported the use of future time projection with a total of 11 patients. After one session of treatment, 6 were judged to have responded excellently, 2 to have improved moderately, and 3 to be unimproved. Neither the criteria for degree of improvement nor the identity of the judge(s) was reported.

The second technique proposed by Lazarus was called "affective expression." He suggested that the expression of anger, amusement, affection, sexual excitement, and anxiety acted to break up depression. No supporting data were presented.

Finally, Lazarus proposed "behavioral deprivation and retraining" for the treatment of depression. He suggested that an enforced period of sensory deprivation might make the depressive more susceptible to environmental stimuli. Lazarus' suggestions are intriguing and they merit controlled experimentation. It should be noted, however, that the procedures seem only loosely derived from the theory of insufficient positive reinforcement.

Morita therapy (Kora, 1965), a Japanese treatment for neurosis, is similar to Lazarus' third suggestion. It involves: (1) absolute bed rest for four days to one week; (2) a week of light work; (3) a week of heavy work; and (4) a life training period. Bed rest presumably creates a "state of hunger for stimuli" and leads the patient to realize that "...abulia runs counter to his true nature and that activity alone is something natural to him [p. 626]." Kora termed depressives "weak-willed" personalities who did not respond to Morita therapy. Such patients either failed to endure the period of bed rest or remained in bed without feeling any boredom. No studies using Morita therapy to explicitly treat depression have been reported.

Burgess' (1968) view of depression differs from that of Lazarus. Burgess identified two behavior classes: (1) a performing behavior class consisting of task-oriented behaviors, and (2) a depressive behavior class consisting of the various symptoms of depression.

She proposed that depression results from the simultaneous extinction of performing behaviors and reinforcement of depressive behaviors ("secondary gain") rather than from extinction alone. Her method of treating depression involves, therefore, the reacquisition of performing behaviors and extinction of depressive behaviors.

Burgess provided case reports for six patients treated for depression. In all cases, extinction of depressive behaviors consisted of the therapist's ignoring such behaviors. Two methods were used to reinstitute performing behaviors. First, environmental manipulations were used to reinstate lost reinforcers. For example, a depressed student with a history of accomplishment in money-making ventures recovered after obtaining a part-time job. When reinforcers could not be reinstated by environmental manipulation, patients were presented with a series of tasks of progressively increasing difficulty. Social reinforcement in the form of therapist approval and attention was made contingent upon successful completion of each task. Burgess reported that four of the six patients remained symptom free six to nine months after treatment, while one patient had suffered a relapse at two-month follow-up and one patient was still in treatment. Interestingly, although no assertive training was used, Burgess noted the appearance of more assertive behaviors as the patients improved. Burgess reported at least some improvement in all cases after three weeks of treatment.

As in the studies reviewed above, Burgess' outcome measures unfortunately consisted mainly of patients' self-reports of how they felt and the therapist's subjective estimate of improvement. Furthermore, as Burgess noted, "Case reports . . . are not adequate to establish the efficacy of any treatment method. The need for controlled research is obvious [p. 199]." This problem is particularly acute with depression, which usually dissipates in time.

Beck, Seligman, Binik, Schuyler, and Brill (unpublished data) used a graded task assignment like Burgess' on 24 hospitalized depressives. These patients were given a graded task assignment in a one-hour test session and were socially reinforced upon successful completion of each step. First, they were asked to read a paragraph aloud. Then they read a new paragraph aloud and with expression. Then, they were asked to read another with expression and to interpret it in their own words. Then they read aloud with expression plus interpretation and argued for the author's point of view. Finally, the patients were asked to choose one of three topics and give an extemporaneous speech. Nineteen of the 24 showed substantial immediate elevation in mood as measured by a self-rating scale. Unfortunately, no follow-up was done so the mood swing may be only transitory. In addition, no control group was run.

Wolpe (1971) suggested that reactive depression conforms to the definition of neurosis as a "... *persistent, unadaptive habit acquired by learning in an anxiety-generating situation* [p. 367]." Wolpe described three situations in which reactive depression is seen and suggested a method of treatment for each. The first involves an exaggerated and prolonged reaction to loss. He suggested that anxiety should be treated by systematic desensitization and that a schedule for systematically rewarding the patient's efforts should be devised in the manner described by Burgess (1968). The second situation involves severe anxiety. Here, Wolpe suggested treatment of anxiety with desensitization or assertive training. He noted that, in his experience, depression ceases to appear once anxiety has been overcome. The final situation involves a failure to control interpersonal situations. The suggested treatment is assertive training to overcome interpersonal anxiety and systematic reinforcement of selected motor behavior. Wolpe did not report any data on the use of these treatments.

Stampfl and Levis (1967) claimed that implosion therapy has been successfully used in the treatment of neurotic and psychotic disorders, including depressive reac-

tions and affective psychoses. Hogan (1968) reported the case history of a patient in whom depression was a major feature. The depression seemed related to a fear of rejection. In addition, the patient had sexual and marital problems, as well as multiple phobias. The patient had been diagnosed as an acute schizophrenic. Among the scenes the patient imagined in implosion therapy were several related to rejection themes: "... the patient pictured herself abandoned on an ice island without love or companionship and a scene where the client was buried alive while friends and family stood by the grave rejecting and criticizing her [p. 425]." The patient's MMPI Depression score decreased markedly. A number of informants (family physician, social worker, husband) reported a marked improvement both at the termination of treatment and at a four-month follow-up. The presence of multiple psychological problems in the patient makes it especially difficult to assess the specific effect of the implosion therapy upon this patient's depression.

In summary, a number of behavioral techniques have been used or suggested for the individual treatment of depression: (1) positive reinforcement of nondepressed behaviors and thoughts; (2) time projection; (3) affective expression; (4) Morita therapy; (5) graded task assignment; (6) systematic desensitization and assertive therapy; and (7) implosion. Most of these studies are in the form of case histories involving only a few subjects and not employing control groups. At this time, it is not possible to evaluate the effectiveness of individual behavior therapy in the treatment of depression.

GROUP BEHAVIOR THERAPY.   Lewinsohn et al. (1968) and Lewinsohn, Weinstein, and Alper (1970) described a group treatment for depression that emphasized analysis of the form of group interactions rather than analysis of feelings and attitudes or content of interactions. The procedure was designed to inform patients about the social consequences of their behaviors, to establish behavioral goals, to use the social reinforcement of the group to reinforce behaviors consistent with these goals, and to extinguish inconsistent behavior. Ongoing interactions in the group were coded and plotted individually for each patient, and these data were presented to the group at regular intervals. Lewinsohn et al. (1970) hypothesized that such feedback enhances social skills and facilitates behavior change.

They selected nine depressed undergraduates for treatment. The group met with two therapists over a period of three months. The coding and plotting of interactions identified particular problems. For example, two very passive subjects emitted very few responses and, as a result, few responses were directed toward these subjects. After this was pointed out to the group, the group reinforced increases in rate of responding for these two patients. At the conclusion of therapy, the patients were retested on the MMPI Depression scale, the Feelings and Concerns Checklist, and the Interpersonal Behavior Scale (Dyer, 1967). Mean scores on the three scales showed improvement. However, no statistical analysis of these data was reported.

FAMILY THERAPY. Lewinsohn and his associates (cf. Lewinsohn et al, 1968) have included home observations, coding of family interactions, and consultations with the patient's family as an integral part of the diagnostic process and treatment of depression. Using this procedure, the therapist can identify specific behavioral goals and involve the patient's family in the process of achieving these goals.

Lewinsohn and Atwood (1969) reported the case study of a 38-year-old female. Coding of family interactions indicated that the patient initiated many interactions with the family members but that the family initiated very few interactions with her. The patient was seen individually and with her husband over a period of three months. Treatment was aimed at altering the pattern of family interactions, as well as at encouraging the patient to engage in new activities outside the family. A follow-up visit revealed a change in the pattern of family interactions. The patient initiated fewer interactions toward her husband, while the husband initiated more interactions toward the patient. Self-rating scales indicated considerable elevation in mood.

Lewinsohn and Shaffer (1971) reported three additional case studies in which treatment was accompanied by home observations and coding of family interactions. In two of the case studies, the patient was seen individually following the initial home observation. In the remaining case, the patient was seen individually, as well as jointly with her husband. As in the case discussed above, therapy was directed at the modification of family interactions. For two of the cases, post-therapy home observations indicated that family interactions had changed in a manner consistent with the treatment goals. No outcome was reported for the third case.

Liberman's (1970) family therapy approach is similar to that of Lewinsohn and his associates in that it emphasizes identification of those family interactions that act as reinforcers of maladaptive behavior. Liberman (1970) and Liberman and Raskin (1971) illustrated this approach with case studies of depressives. In one case, for example, the husband of a depressed patient was told to spend more time at home with his wife and was shown, through a modeling procedure, how to reinforce his wife's nondepressed behaviors. In another case, Liberman and Raskin first obtained base rates of nondepressed and depressed behaviors by home observation of the patient and her family. The therapist instructed the family members about ways to reinforce the patient's nondepressed behaviors and told the family to ignore the depressive behaviors. During the first two weeks of therapy, the rate of nondepressed behavior increased and the rate of depressed behavior decreased. Next, the family was told to revert to its former mode of interacting. During this reversal phase, the patient's nondepressed behaviors decreased, while her depressed behaviors increased. Finally, treatment contingencies were restored, and the patient began to improve again. The authors reported that the patient was symptom free at a one-year follow-up.

In summary, a number of studies have focused upon the identification of maladaptive modes of family interaction and have modified reinforcement contingencies within the family. These case studies have succeeded in decreasing depressed behavior and in increasing coping behavior. Again, it is unfortunate that all of the studies to date have been case studies. As with the studies of individual behavior therapy, the lack of sufficient numbers of subjects, the lack of control groups, the use of therapists and patients as raters of improvement, and the lack of adequate follow-up preclude evaluation of the effectiveness of these treatment procedures. However, the occasional use of pre- and posttherapy administration of standard assessment devices by Lewinsohn and his group and of a reversal design by Liberman and Raskin is encouraging. A major contribution by Lewinsohn and his associates is the development of a highly reliable system for coding family interactions.

ANTIDEPRESSION MILIEU THERAPY. Taulbee and Wright (1971) discussed a number of "attitude therapy programs" initiated at the Tuscaloosa, Alabama Veterans Administration Hospital in which every staff member who comes in contact with a given patient responds to the patient with a single prescribed attitude.

The Anti-Depressive (AD) program involves the attitude of "Kind-Firmness" (KF): patients are dealt with in a kind but firm manner, and patients are required to complete menial and monotonous tasks assigned to them without receiving any positive social reinforcement. Aggressive responses are encouraged and reinforced. When the patient emits depressed behavior,

he is placed in the "sanding room" where he engages in such tasks as sanding a small block of wood, counting tiny seashells, and mopping floors. These activities are supervised by nursing assistants who forbid the patient to talk and continually point out all imperfections in the patient's work. Within a few hours, the patient typically becomes overtly hostile and "blows up." The patient is then allowed out of the room, and the staff responds to his aggressiveness with acceptance.

Taulbee and Wright reported two pilot studies of the effectiveness of the AD program. In the first study, six patients were randomly assigned to each of two groups—the AD group and a control group receiving "ego-building" tasks and antidepressant medication. Posttreatment evaluation indicated that the AD group had improved significantly more than controls in positive self-concept, level of depression and anxiety, and ability to admit to psychological problems. In a second study, 22 subjects were placed in the AD program, while 9 control subjects were given an unspecified, control treatment. Pre- and posttherapy administration of the MMPI indicated that there was no significant change in control subjects. The AD group, on the other hand, showed significant decreases on the depression and other scales of the MMPI.

Taulbee and Wright (1971) also reported on a more extensive study of the effectiveness of the AD program. Depressed patients were randomly assigned to one of six treatment groups: (1) KF only; (2) KF with placebo; (3) KF with antidepressant drugs; (4) AF[5] only; (5) AF with placebo; and (6) AF with antidepressant drugs. The MMPI and Leary's Interpersonal Chicklist (Leary, 1956) were administered on four occasions. Six weeks after the beginning of treatment, subjects in all AF and KF groups showed significant decreases in depressive, anxious,

[5] Active friendliness (AF) is an attitude in which attention, reassurance, and support are provided for the patient.

and obsessive symptoms and in somatic preoccupation. KF, but not AF, subjects showed less passivity and dependency. However, at a six-month follow-up, the KF subjects had maintained their improvement, while the AF subjects had regressed somewhat.

So, the AD program appears to be an effective method for the treatment of depression in hospitalized patients. Unfortunately, this treatment cannot be easily used with out-patients since a main feature of the program is the *highly consistent* reinforcement contingencies of the patient's environment.

TOKEN ECONOMY SYSTEMS.   Recent studies have used token economies in the treatment of depression. Reisinger (1972) examined the effects of positive reinforcement and response cost on the excessive crying and lack of smiling responses in an institutionalized patient diagnosed as an "anxiety-depressive." During the baseline phase of the experiment, frequencies of crying and smiling under typical hospital conditions were measured. Next, token reinforcement for smiling and token costs for crying were instituted. Marked increases in the frequency of smiling responses and decreases in the frequency of crying responses were observed. Removal of the experimental contingencies (extinction) was followed by relatively small decreases in smiling and increases in crying responses. Reversal of the experimental contingencies (i.e., token reinforcement for crying and token costs for smiling) resulted in further decreases in smiling and increases in crying responses. The final treatment phase consisted of token and social reinforcement for smiling and ignoring of crying, followed by a fading out of the token reinforcement. In this phase, marked increases in smiling responses and decreases in crying responses were again observed. These changes were maintained following the fading out of token reinforcement. The patient, a 20-year-old female who had been hospitalized for 6 years, was discharged 20 weeks after the start of treatment. A follow-up 14 months after discharge indicated that the patient had not been rehospitalized and had not been referred for additional treatment. Unfortunately, Reisinger did not report what, if any, other treatment the patient had received during the 20 weeks of his study.

Hersen, Eisler, Alford, and Agras (1973) used a single case design to study the effects of a token economy on the depressive behaviors of three institutionalized neurotic depressives. The target behaviors—talking, smiling, and motor activity—were rated by ward nurses on the Behavioral Rating Scale (Williams, Barlow, & Agras, 1972). The patients were given tokens upon the completion of behaviors classified as work, occupational therapy, responsibility, and personal hygiene. This study differs from Reisinger's in that the target behaviors were not directly subject to token reinforcement or token costs.

In the baseline phases of the baseline-contingency-baseline design, tokens were contingent upon the performance of the work behaviors, but since privileges were not contingent upon tokens, the tokens were worthless. During the contingency management phase, privileges were issued in exchange for tokens. For the first baseline period, the rate of depressive behaviors was high and the number of tokens earned was low. Introduction of token reinforcement was followed by large increases in the frequency of target behaviors and the number of tokens earned. The rate of depressive behaviors and number of tokens earned in the two baseline periods were similar. Unfortunately, a reintroduction of the experimental contingencies was prevented by the early discharge of one patient and changes in medication in the other two patients.

Hersen et al. suggested that the increase in work behaviors caused by tokens resulted in more social contact and interaction. Presumably, this increased social contact then resulted in elicitation and more natural reinforcement of the talking, smiling and motor target behaviors.

The Reisinger and Hersen et al. studies suggest that token economy systems may be effective in the treatment of depression. Additional studies are certainly needed since these two studies examined only four patients who may have been quite atypical. Reisinger's patient was an "anxiety-depressive" who had apparently been hospitalized continuously for six years from the age of 14, while Hersen et al's three patients were *hospitalized,* neurotic depressives.

SUMMARY OF BEHAVIOR THERAPY. A number of investigators have reported successful treatment of depression with behavioral techniques in individual, group, family, antidepression milieu, and token economy therapy. An adequate assessment of the effectiveness of these behavior therapies cannot be made at this time, however. With only a few exceptions, the existing studies have been case histories or preliminary reports. Adequate assessments of improvement and of control groups have been virtually nonexistent. Given such preliminary success, the time has come for investigators in this area to carry out systematic and well designed studies. Fortunately, there now exists a substantial literature on psychotherapy research designs (cf. Kiesler, 1971; Meltzoff & Kornreich, 1970). There is no reason that appropriate studies cannot be carried out on the effectiveness of different therapies for depression. Only then will we be entitled to conclude that behavior therapy actually works in depression.

Learned Helplessness: A Model of Depression[6]

We now present our theory of depression. The learned helplessness model is, we believe, compatible with more facts of depression than alternate theories we have reviewed. Although it is a model of reactive

[6] Much of this material also appears in Seligman (1974).

depression, we shall discuss its relationship to endogenous depression as well. This section presents the common characteristics of learned helplessness (a laboratory phenomenon first observed in animals) and depression. The argument will be fairly structured since too often investigators have discovered and analyzed dramatic bits of maladaptive behavior in their animals and unconvincingly suggested that they had illuminated some form of psychopathology in man. Pavlov (1927) found that conditioned reflexes of dogs disintegrated when the experimenter made discrimination problems increasingly difficult. Liddell (1953) found that restrained sheep given many conditioning trials stopped making conditioned flexion responses to signals paired with shock. Both Pavlov and Liddell claimed they had demonstrated "experimental neuroses." Masserman (1943) and Wolpe (1958) found that hungry cats would not eat in compartments in which they had been shocked, and claimed that they had brought "phobias" into the laboratory. Maier (1949) found that rats formed response fixations when confronted with insoluble discrimination problems and explained the findings as "frustration." The experimental analysis of these phenomena was reasonably thorough, but to argue that they represented human psychopathology was inappropriate. Worse, the arguments were usually plausibility arguments that did not lend themselves readily to disconfirmation. How would one *test* whether Masserman's cats had phobias, anyway? Let us try to state some rules of argument for claiming that an animal phenomenon provides a model of a form of psychopathology in man.

GROUND RULES

Four lines of evidence can be used to compare similarities between behavioral phenomena: (1) symptoms—behavioral and physiological; (2) etiology; (3) cure; and (4) prevention. We cannot expect any actual experimental phenomenon to meet all these criteria for any actual form of psycho-pathology, but making the argument explicit has two advantages: it makes similarity claims more testable and it helps to narrow the definition of the clinical phenomenon. As two phenomena converge on one or two of the lines of evidence, investigators can test the model by looking for similarities predicted along the other lines. For example, say that learned helplessness in animals presents behavior similar to reactive depression in man and that the etiologies of the two are similar. If we discover that the only way to cure learned helplessness is to forcibly expose subjects to responding that produces relief, we can predict that the central theme for therapy of depression in man should be the recognition that responding is effective in producing reinforcement. If this is tested and confirmed, the model is strengthened. Strengthening such a model empirically works two ways: if a therapy helps reactive depression in man, does its animal analogue relieve learned helplessness?

In addition to enhancing testability, a model sharpens the definition of the clinical phenomenon. The laboratory phenomenon of learned helplessness is well defined. Depression, as we saw in our first section, does not have a necessary condition which defines it. Rather, it is a convenient diagnostic label which denotes a constellation of symptoms, no one of which is necessary. Clinical labels denote a family of phenomena, "a complicated network of similarities overlapping and crisscrossing" (Wittgenstein, 1973, paragraph 66). A well defined laboratory model does not mirror the open-endedness of the clinical label, rather it clips it off at the edges by imposing necessary conditions on it. Thus, if a particular model of depression is valid, some phenomena, formerly classified as depression, may be excluded. We are engaged in an attempt to refine the nosology: we do not believe that learned helplessness models all phenomena now called "depression." Rather, we propose that there are "helplessness depres-sions," characterized by passive individuals with negative cognitive sets about the effects of their own actions, who become depressed upon the loss of an important source of gratification, have a given prognosis, a preferred set of therapies, and perhaps a given physiology. Some phenomena not now called depression will be included, e.g., the catastrophe syndrome (Wallace, 1957), while others now called depression will be excluded, e.g., manic-depression. Learned helplessness concentrates on those depressions which begin as a reaction to loss of control over gratification and relief of suffering, and in which the individual is slow to initiate responses, believes himself to be powerless and hopeless, and has a negative outlook on the future.

SYMPTOMS OF LEARNED HELPLESSNESS

When an experimentally naive dog receives escape-avoidance training in a shuttle box, the following behavior typically occurs: at the onset of the first traumatic electric shock, the dog runs frantically about until it accidentally scrambles over the barrier and so escapes the shock. On the next trial, the dog crosses the barrier more quickly than on the preceding trial. This pattern continues until the dog learns to avoid shock altogether. Overmier and Seligman (1967) and Seligman and Maier (1967) found a striking difference between this pattern of behavior and that exhibited by dogs given inescapable electric shocks in a Pavlovian hammock. The inescapably shocked dog's first reactions to shock in the shuttle box are much the same as those of a naive dog. However, in dramatic contrast to a naive dog, it soon stops running and sits or lies, quietly whining, until shock terminates. The dog does not cross the barrier and escape from shock. Rather, it seems to give up and passively accept the shock. On succeeding trials, the dog continues to fail to make escape movements and takes as much shock as the experimenter chooses to give.

There is another peculiar characteristic

of the behavior of dogs that have first experienced inescapable shock. They will occasionally jump the barrier early in training and escape, but then revert to taking the shock; they fail to profit from exposure to the barrier jumping–shock termination contingency. In naive dogs, a successful escape response is a reliable predictor of future, short-latency escape responses.

The escape-avoidance behavior of over 150 dogs that had received prior inescapable shock has been studied. Two-thirds of these dogs did not escape; the other third escaped and avoided in normal fashion. It is obvious that failure to escape is highly maladaptive since it means that the dog takes 50 seconds of severe, pulsating shock on each trial. In contrast, only 6% of experimentally naive dogs failed to escape in the shuttle box. So any given dog either fails to escape on almost every trial or learns normally. An intermediate outcome is rare.

A typical experimental procedure that produces failures to escape shock is as follows. On the first day, the subject is strapped into a hammock and given 64 unsignalled, inescapable electric shocks, each 5.0 seconds long and 6.0 ma intensity. The shocks occur randomly in time. Twenty-four hours later, the dog is given 10 trials of signalized escape-avoidance training in the shuttle box. The onset of the conditioned stimulus (dimmed illumination) begins each trial, and the CS remains on until the trial ends. The CS-US interval is 10 seconds. If the dog jumps the barrier (set at shoulder height) during this interval, the CS terminates, no shock occurs, and the trial ends. Failure to jump during the CS-US interval leads to a 4.5 ma shock which remains until the subject jumps the barrier. If the subject fails to jump the barrier within 60 seconds after the CS onset, the trial automatically terminates. The shuttle box performance that typically results is that the group pretreated with inescapable shocks responds much more slowly than does the group not so pretreated.

We use the term "learned helplessness" to describe the interference with adaptive responding produced by inescapable shock and also as a shorthand to describe the process which we believe underlies the behavior (see the section on etiology below). So, learned helplessness in the dog is defined by two behaviors: (1) dogs pretreated with uncontrollable shock *fail to initiate responses* to escape shock or are slower to make responses than naive dogs, and (2) if the dog does make a response which turns off shock it has *more trouble learning that responding is effective* than does a naive dog.

Learned helplessness is not an isolated phenomenon. In addition to the studies of Overmier and Seligman (1967) and Seligman and Maier (1967), such interference was reported in dogs by Carlson and Black (1957), Leaf (1964), Maier (1970), Overmier (1968), Seligman and Groves (1970), and Seligman, Maier and Geer (1968). Deficits in escaping or avoiding shock after experience with uncontrollable shock have been observed in rats. A large number of early studies using rats have shown interference as a consequence of inescapable shock (Brookshire, Littman, & Stewart, 1961; Brown & Jacobs, 1949; Denenberg, 1964; Denenberg & Bell, 1960; Dinsmoor, 1958; Dinsmoor & Campbell, 1956a, 1956b; Levine, Chevalier, & Korchin, 1956; Mowrer, 1940; Mullin & Mogenson, 1963; Weiss, Krieckhaus & Conte, 1968). Unlike the dog, these rats did not sit and take shock; they were merely slower to escape. In addition, it also is possible that these effects resulted from freezing rather than learned helplessness (Miller & Weiss, 1969; Weiss, et al., 1968). Recently Looney and Cohen (1972), Maier, Albin, and Testa (1973), Seligman and Beagley (1975), and Seligman, Rosellini, and Kozak (1975) have found techniques which produce profound doglike interference in the rat. The crucial variable is the *voluntariness* of the response tested. To the extent that the escape response is reflexively elicited by shock, it is not interfered with: fixed ratio 1 (FR1) bar press or shuttling proceeds smoothly even after prior inescapable shock. When the response requirement is increased, however, learned helplessness results. Rats given prior inescapable shock sit and take shock when the escape response requires FR2 or FR3 performances. Rats given equivalent prior escapable shock perform FR2 and FR3 efficiently. Inescapable shock given to weanling rats also produces escape learning deficits when the rats are adults (Hannum, Rosellini, & Seligman, 1975). Cats (Seward & Humphrey, 1967; Thomas & Balter, 1975) and goldfish (Behrand & Bitterman, 1963; Padilla, Padilla, Ketterer, & Giacalone, 1970) also show escape-avoidance deficits following inescapable shock. In addition, a number of studies give substantial confirmation to the existence of learned helplessness in man, across a variety of uncontrollable training tasks, on a variety of test tasks (Hiroto, 1974; Hiroto & Seligman, 1975; Klein, Fencil-Morse, & Seligman, 1975; Klein & Seligman, 1975; Miller & Seligman, 1975a; Racinskas, 1971; Roth & Kubal, 1975; Williams & Moffat, 1974). Helpless subjects fail to escape noise and shock and fail to solve cognitive problems, providing evidence for both the response initiation deficit and the cognitive deficit found in helpless animals.

Inabilty to control trauma not only disrupts shock escape, but also debilitates adaptive behaviors across a range of situations not involving shock. McCulloch and Bruner (1939) reported that rats given inescapable shocks were slower than controls to learn to swim out of a water maze; Braud, Wepman, and Russo (1969) reported similar findings in mice. Brookshire et al. (1961, experiment 6) reported that inescapable shocks given to weanling rats disrupted food-getting behavior in adulthood when the rats were very hungry, and Rosellini and Seligman (1975) found that inescapable shock produced deficits in hurdle-jump escape from frustration in the rat. Also, tonic immobility can be produced by inescapable shock in chickens (Maser & Gallup, 1975).

Situations involving uncontrollable events other than shock can produce effects similar to failure to escape shock. Escape deficits are produced by inescapable tumbling (Anderson & Paden, 1966) as well as by unsolvable problems and loud noise (Hiroto & Seligman, 1975; Klein & Seligman, 1975), and passivity is produced by defeat in fighting (Khan, 1951). Harlow, Harlow, and Suomi (1971) reported that 45-day-old monkeys made helpless by 45 days of confinement to a narrow pit showed deficits later in locomotion, exploration, and social behavior. Seligman (1975) has reviewed and discussed the generality of the effects of inescapable USs across species and situations at greater length.

In addition to passivity and retarded response-relief learning, four other characteristics of learned helplessness are relevant to depressive symptoms in man. First, helplessness has a time course. In dogs, inescapable shock produces transient as well as nontransient interference with escape (Overmier & Seligman, 1967) and avoidance (Overmier, 1968). Twenty-four hours after *one* session of inescapable shock, dogs are helpless, but if intervals longer than 48 hours elapse, responding is normal. This is also true of goldfish (Padilla et al., 1970) With multiple sessions of inescapable shock, helplessness is not transient (Seligman & Groves, 1970; Seligman, Maier, & Geer, 1968). Weiss (1968) found a parallel time course for weight loss in rats given uncontrollable shock, but other than this no such time course has been found in the rat or other species (e.g., Anderson, Cole, & McVaugh, 1968; Seligman et al., 1975). In spite of the fact that nontransient learned helplessness occurs, one session of inescapable shocks may produce a physiological depletion which is restored with time. Weiss, Stone, and Harrell (1970) speculated that depletion of some substance such as norepinephrine may be partially responsible for the transient form of helplessness.

Second, helpless animals show reduced aggression. Maier, Anderson, and Lieberman (1972) and Powell and Creer (1969) reported that rats given inescapable shock showed reduced shock-elicited aggression toward other rats. Rats given equivalent prior escapable shock showed enhanced aggression.

Third, Seligman, Marques, and Radford (unpublished data) found that dogs given inescapable shock as puppies showed lower dominance in food getting situations than dogs given escapable shock or no shock. Uncontrollable shock also suppresses food oriented and perhaps sexual and social behavior. Weiss (1968) reported that uncontrollable shock retarded weight gain more than did controllable shock in rats. Mowrer and Viek (1948) and Lindner (1968) reported more anorexia in rats given inescapable shock than in rats given escapable shock. Harlow et al. (1971) and Suomi and Harlow (1972) have reported severe and lasting deficits in play and social behavior in monkeys that had been pitted. Recently in our laboratory, we have found that rats given prior inescapable shock do not copulate with oestrous females.

Fourth, a few facts are beginning to come to light about the physiology of helplessness. Weiss at al. (1970) and Weiss, Glazer, and Pohorecky (1975) found reductions in norepinephrine when shock was inescapable. Thomas and Balter (1975) found that blocking cholinergic activity with atropine, thus releasing inhibited nor-adrenergic activity, broke up learned helplessness effects. We do not know at the present time whether NE depletion is merely a correlate, or if it plays a causal role in learned helplessness. (See Maier & Seligman, 1975, for a discussion of the role of norepinephrine in helplessness).

In summary, experience with prior uncontrollable trauma produces six effects related to depression. The two basic effects are: (1) animals and men become passive in the face of later trauma, i.e., they are slower to initiate responses to alleviate trauma and may not respond at all, and (2) animals and men are retarded at learning that their responses control trauma, i.e., if they make a response which produces relief, they may

have trouble "catching on" to the response-relief contingency. In addition, learned helplessness (3) dissipates in time, and is associated with (4) lowered aggression, (5) loss of food, social, and sexual behaviors, and (6) whole brain norepinephrine depletion and septal activation.

RELATIONSHIP OF THE SYMPTOMS OF LEARNED HELPLESSNESS TO DEPRESSION

The six symptoms of learned helplessness discussed above all have parallels in depression.

1. *Lowered response initiation*. Passivity is perhaps the major behavioral symptom of depression. All clinical descriptions include it. Psychomotor retardation differentiates depressives from normals and is a direct instance of reduced voluntary response initiation (Franz, 1906; Friedman, 1964; Hall & Stride, 1954; Huston & Senf, 1952; Lundholm, 1922; Martin & Rees, 1966; Payne & Hewlett, 1960; Shapiro & Nelson, 1955; Wells & Kelley, 1920). It should be noted that schizophrenics also show severe psychomotor retardation (Hall & Stride, 1954; Huston & Senf, 1952; Miller, 1975; Payne & Hewlett, 1960; Shapiro & Nelson, 1955); learned helplessness claims that depressive retardation is caused by a belief in response-reinforcement independence (see the section on etiology below) while schizophrenic retardation has some other cause. Intellectual slowness, and learning, memory, and IQ deficits are all symptoms of depression (Callagan, 1952; Davidson, 1939; Fisher, 1949; Kendrick, Parboosingh, & Post, 1965; Martin & Rees, 1966; Mason, 1956; Miller, 1975; Payne, 1961; Payne & Hewlett, 1960; Post, 1966; Teasdale & Beaumont, 1971; Walton, White, Black, & Young, 1959). These can be interpreted as resulting from reduced motivation to initiate such voluntary responses as memory scanning and test taking. Depressives engage in fewer activities and show reduced interpersonal responding and reduced voluntary nonverbal communication (Ekman & Friesen, 1974; Hinchliffe, Lancashire, & Roberts, 1971; Lewinsohn & Graf, 1973; Lewinsohn & Libet, 1972; Lewinsohn & Shaffer, 1971; Libet & Lewinsohn, 1973). These deficits all reflect the lowered response initiation in learned helplessness.

Recent experiments in our laboratory demonstrate a striking similarity between the lowered response initiation of learned helplessness and depression. In each of these studies, nondepressed students exposed to uncontrollable events, in the form of inescapable noise (Klein & Seligman, 1975; Miller & Seligman, 1975a) or unsolvable concept formation problems (Klein et al., 1975), showed subsequent performance deficits when compared to nondepressed subjects exposed to controllable events or no events. Moreover, depressed subjects who had received no prior experience showed performance deficits relative to comparable nondepressed subjects. Deficits were found for anagram performance (Klein et al., 1975; Miller & Seligman, 1975a). and shuttlebox noise escape (Klein & Seligman, 1975). So, naturally-ocurring depression was associated with performance deficits wholly parallel to those induced by a helplessness pretreatment in nondepressed subjects.

2. *Negative cognitive set.* Depressives show a "negative cognitive set," which directly mirrors the difficulty that helpless subjects have in learning that responding succeeds in producing relief. Depressives believe that their actions are doomed to failure; even when they perform successfully, they perceive failure. Beck (1967) sees this as the single most prominent feature of depression. Friedman (1964) found that depressed patients performed more poorly than normals in reaction to a light signal and recognition time for common objects, but even more striking was their subjective estimate of how poorly they thought they would do: "When the examiner would bring the patient into the testing room, the patient would immediately protest that he or she could not possibly take the tests, was unable to do anything, or felt too bad or too tired, was incapable, hopeless, etc. . . . While performing adequately the patient would occasionally and less frequently reiterate the original protest, saying 'I can't do it,' 'I don't know how,' etc. [p. 243]."

Miller and Seligman (1973) assessed negative cognitive set by looking at depressed and nondepressed college students' perceptions of reinforcement contingencies in chance and skill tasks. The tendency to perceive reinforcement as response-independent or as response-dependent was determined by examining changes in the subjects' verbalized expectancies for success following success and failure. In a skill task, depressed subjects perceived reinforcement as more response-independent than nondepressed subjects. This response-independent perception increased with increasing depth of depression. In a chance task where reinforcement actually was response-independent, the perception of reinforcement was not correlated with depression. Miller, Seligman, and Kurlander (1975) found the response-independent perception to be specific to depression; controls matched for anxiety level showed no deficit.

Klein and Seligman (1975) and Miller and Seligman (1975b) directly demonstrated the parallel between the negative cognitive set in learned helplessness and depression. In both studies, nondepressed subjects exposed to inescapable noise perceived skill task reinforcement as more response-independent than nondepressed subjects exposed to escapable noise or no noise. In addition, depressed subjects receiving no noise showed skill task perceptions of response-reinforcement independence (replicating Miller & Seligman, 1973, and Miller et al., 1975). Noise pretreatment and depression level had no effect on chance task perceptions. So, the effects of learned helplessness and depression on perception of reinforcement were parallel. Furthermore, cognitive performance deficits were associated with both learned helplessness and depression in a number of studies (Klein et al., 1975; Klein & Seligman, 1975; Miller & Seligman, 1975a). In each of these studies, measures were obtained that assessed the degree to which subjects were able to benefit from successful test task responding (either anagram solution or noise escape). In all studies, depressed controls were impaired on the cognitive measure relative to nondepressed controls, and nondepressed subjects receiving uncontrollable events exhibited deficits relative to nondepressed subjects receiving controllable events or no events. Learned helplessness and depression produced similar effects on measures that more directly assess cognitive, rather than response initiation deficits.

So, the perceptual set in depression consists of the belief that success and failure are independent of skilled responding. Negative cognitive set may also explain the poor discrimination learning of depressives (Martin & Rees, 1966) and be partly responsible for the lowered cognitive abilities (cf. Payne, 1961).

3. *Dissipation in time.* Depression, like learned helplessness, seems to have a time course. Wallace (1957) reported that following sudden

catastrophes, depression occurs for about a day or so and then functioning returns to normal. It seems possible that multiple traumatic events intervening between the initial disaster and recovery might potentiate depression considerably, as we have found with dogs. We should also note that endogenous or process depression is characterized by cyclic fluctuations of weeks or months between depression and mania. Moreover, it is commonly thought that almost all depressions dissipate in time, although whether the period lasts days, weeks, months, or years is a matter of some dispute (cf., Kraines, 1957; Lundquist, 1945; Paskind, 1929, 1930).

4. *Lack of aggression.* The lowered aggression of depressives is such a salient symptom that psychoanalysts view introjected hostility as the central explanatory principle of depression. We do not believe that the increased self-blame in depression results from hostility turned inward but it seems undeniable that hostility, even in dreams (Beck & Hurvich, 1959; Beck & Ward, 1961), is reduced in depression. This symptom corresponds to the lack of aggression in learned helplessness.

5. *Loss of libido and appetite.* Depressives commonly show reduced interest in food, sex, and interpersonal relations. This symptom corresponds to the anorexia, weight loss, and sexual and social deficits characteristic of learned helplessness.

6. *Norepinephrine depletion and cholinergic activity.* The catecholamine hypothesis of affective disorders proposed by Schildkraut (1965) claims that depression in man is associated with the deficiency of NE at receptor sites in the brain, and that elation may be associated with its excess. This is based on evidence that imipramine, a drug that increases the amount of NE in the central nervous system possibly by blocking its reuptake, breaks up depression. Klerman and Cole (1965) and Cole (1964) reported positive results of imipramine over placebos. Monoamineoxidase (MAO) inhibitors, which prevent the breakdown of NE, may be useful in relieving depression (Cole, 1964; Davis, 1965). Reserpine, a drug which depletes NE, produces depression in man. There is also some suggestion of cholinergic mediation of depression. Janowsky, El-Yousef, Davis, and Sekerkehj (1973) reported that physostigmine, a cholinergic stimulator, produced depressive affect in normals. Atropine, a cholinergic blocker, reversed

these symptoms. So, there are suggestions of NE depletion and cholinergic involvement in both depression and learned helplessness. However, Mendels and Frazer (1974) reviewed the behavioral effects of drugs that deplete brain catecholamines and argued that the behavioral changes associated with reserpine are better interpreted as a psychomotor retardation-sedation syndrome than as depression. Moreover, selective depletion of brain catecholamines by alpha-methyl-para-tyrosine (AMPT) and parachloro-phenylalanine fails to produce some of the key features of depression, despite the fact that these drugs produce a consistently greater reduction in amine metabolite concentration than occurs in depression. So, depletion of catecholamines, in itself, seems insufficient to account for depression.

Finally, we should mention that Grinker et al. (1961) reported the "factor describing characteristics of hopelessness, helplessness, failure, sadness, unworthiness, guilt and internal suffering" to be the essence of depression," when subjectively reported [pp. 228–229].

Even though the symptoms of learned helplessness and depression have a great deal in common there are substantial gaps. First, two symptoms of uncontrollable shock may or may not be found in depression. Stomach ulcers occur more frequently and more severely in rats receiving uncontrollable shock that in those receiving controllable shock (Weiss, 1968, 1971a, 1971b, 1971c). We know of no study examining the relationship of depression to stomach ulcers. Secondly, uncontrollable shock produces more anxiety, measured subjectively, behaviorally, and physiologically, than controllable shock. Whether depressed people are more anxious than others is not clear. Beck (1967) reported that although both depression and anxiety can be observed in some individuals, only a small positive correlation exists over a population of 606 in-patients. Miller et al. (1975) found very few depressed college students who were not anxious. We can speculate that anxiety and depression are related in the following way:

when a man or animal is confronted with a threat or a loss, he responds initially with fear or anxiety. If he learns that the threat is wholly controllable, anxiety, having served its function, disappears. If he remains uncertain about controllability, anxiety remains. If he learns or is convinced that the threat is utterly uncontrollable, depression replaces anxiety.

There are also a number of facts about depression which have been insufficiently investigated in learned helplessness. For example, certain depressive symptoms—dejected mood, feelings of self-blame and self-dislike, loss of mirth, suicidal thoughts and crying—cannot be investigated in animals. Now that learned helplessness has been reliably produced in man, we can determine whether any or all of these states occur. In addition there are a number of features of depression that could be but have not been investigated in both helpless animals and helpless men. Among these are the distraction effect (Foulds, 1952); visual, spatial, and temporal perceptual distortions (Cameron, 1936; Dilling & Rabin, 1967; Dixon & Lear, 1962; Fisher, 1964; Friedman, 1964; Mezey & Cohen, 1961; Miller, 1975; Payne & Hewlett, 1960; Wapner, Werner, & Krus, 1957; Wohlford, 1966); sleep disturbance; and fatigability. We know of no evidence that *disconfirms* the correspondence of symptoms in learned helplessness and depression.

ETIOLOGY OF LEARNED HELPLESSNESS

The causes of learned helplessness are reasonably well understood. It is not trauma per se that produces interference with later adaptive responding, but *not having control over trauma.* This distinction between controllable and uncontrollable reinforcement is central to the phenomenon and theory of helplessness.

Learning theorists have viewed the relations between instrumental responding and outcomes that organisms could learn as a line depicting the conditional probability

of a reinforcement following a response $p(RFT/R)$. This line varies from zero to 1. At 1, every response produces a reinforcement (continuous reinforcement). At zero, a response never produces reinforcement (extinction). Intermediate points on the line represent various degrees of partial reinforcement. A simple line, however, does not exhaust relations between response and outcomes to which organisms are sensitive. Rewards or punishments sometimes occur when no specific response has been made. It would be a woefully maladaptive subject that could not learn such a contingency. We can better describe instrumental learning by using the two-dimensional space shown in Figure 5-1. The x-axis ($p(RF/R)$) represents the traditional dimension, conditional-probability of reinforcement, following a response.

Orthogonal to the conditional probability of reinforcement, given a response, is the conditional probability of reinforcement, given the absence of *that* response. This dimension is represented along the y-axis. We believe that Ss learn about variations along *both* dimensions conjointly. Thus, S may learn the extent to which relief occurs when it does not make a specific response at the same time as it learns the extent to which relief occurs when it does make a specific response. Systematic changes in behavior occur with systematic changes along both dimensions.

Most learning theorists agree that organisms can learn about the contingencies within this instrumental training space, including the crucial 45° line (e.g., Catania, 1971; Church, 1969; Gibbon, 1970; Maier et al., 1969; Poresky, 1970; Premack, 1965; Rescorla, 1967, 1968; Seligman, Maier, & Solomon, 1971; Wagner, 1969; Watson, 1967; Weiss, 1968).

The traditional training line has been thoroughly explored (e.g., Ferster & Skinner, 1957; Honig, 1966). The points in the training space which are of special concern for helplessness are those that lie along the 45° line (x, y, where x = y). Whether or not the

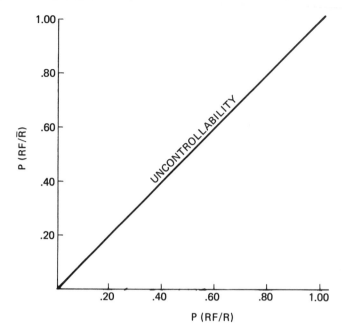

FIGURE 5–1   The instrumental training space. The x- and y-axes represent the relationships between
S's response and a reinforcer outcome. They are conditional probabilities, or contingencies, arranged by
E. The 45° line represents a special condition that exists when the reinforcer is uncontrollable because
P(RF/R) = P(RF/R) (Seligman, Maier, & Solomon, 1971).

organism responds, it still gets the same density of reinforcement. The conditional probability of reinforcement, given a specific response, *does not differ* from the conditional probability of reinforcement in the absence of that response. Responding and reinforcement are independent.

The concept of control is defined within this instrumental training space. Any time the organism can do or can refrain from doing something that changes what it gets, it has control. Specifically, a response stands in control of a reinforcer *if and only if:*

$$p(RFT/R) \neq p(RFT/R)$$

That is, the probability of reinforcement given a response is different from the probability of reinforcement in the absence of that response. Furthermore, when a response will not change what S gets, the response and reinforcement are independent.

Specifically, when a response is independent of a reinforcer:

$$p(RFT/R) = p(RFT/R)$$

When this is true of all responses, S *cannot control* the reinforcer, the outcome is uncontrollable, and nothing the organism does matters.

The passivity of dogs in the face of trauma and their difficulty in benefiting from response-relief contingencies result, we believe, from their having learned that responding and trauma are independent—that trauma is uncontrollable. This is the heart of the learned helplessness hypothesis. The hypothesis states that when shock is inescapable, the organism learns that responding and shock termination are independent (the probability of shock termination given any response doesn't differ from its probability in the absence of that response). Learning that trauma is uncontrollable has three effects:

1. *Motivational:* The probability that the subject will initiate responses to escape is reduced because part of the incentive for making such responses is the expectation that they will bring relief. If the subject has previously learned that its responses have no effect on trauma, this contravenes the expectation. Thus the organism's motivation to respond is undermined by experience with reinforcers it cannot control. It should be obvious to the reader that this motivational effect is what we believe underlies passivity in learned helplessness and, if the model is valid, in depression.

2. *Cognitive:* Learning that responding and shock are independent makes it more difficult to learn that responding *does* produce relief when the organism makes a response which actually terminates shock. In general, if one has acquired a cognitive set in which A is irrelevant to B it will be harder to learn that A can produce B. By the helplessness hypothesis, this mechanism is responsible for the difficulty that helpless dogs have in learning that responding produces relief, even after they respond and successfully turn off shock. Further, if the model is valid, it is this mechanism which produces the "negative cognitive set" of depression.

3. *Affective or emotional:* When a traumatic stimulus is introduced into a situation, it produces fear and anxiety. Three kinds of learning can now occur and each modulates affect differently: (a) if an organism learns that it can control the stimulus, anxiety disappears; (b) if an organism is uncertain about control (neither a nor c has asymptoted), anxiety remains; (c) if an organism learns that it cannot control the stimulus, anxiety is displaced by the affective components of depression.

Taken together, a and b account for the fact that uncontrollable trauma produces more stress than controllable trauma. C, we believe, is the affective concomitant with learning that responding is useless. This affect accompanies the motivational passivity and negative cognitive set we have described (see Maier et al., 1969; Seligman et al., 1971; and Seligman, 1975, for a more rigorous statement of the helplessness hypothesis and the relevant evidence.)

We have tested and confirmed this hypothesis in several ways. We began by ruling out alternative hypotheses: it is unlikely that our dogs have either become adapted (and therefore not motivated enough to escape shock) or sensitized (and therefore too disorganized to escape shock) by pretreatment with shock; making the shock very intense or very mild in the shuttle box does not attenuate the phenomenon. Further, it is unlikely that the dogs have learned during inescapable shock (by explicit or superstitious reinforcement or punishment) some motor response pattern which competes with barrier jumping in the shuttle box; interference occurs even if the dogs are paralyzed by curare and can make no overt motor responses during shock. Seligman and Maier (1967) performed a direct test of the hypothesis that it is learning that shock is uncontrollable, and not shock per se, that causes helplessness. An escape group was trained in the hammock to press a panel with the nose or head in order to turn off shock. A yoked group received shocks identical to the shocks delivered to the escape group. The yoked group differed from the escape group only with respect to the degree of instrumental control which it had over shock; for pressing the panel in the yoked group did not affect the programmed shocks. A naive control group received no shock in the hammock.

The yoked group was significantly poorer at shuttlebox escape than the escape or naive control groups. Six of the eight subjects in the yoked group failed to escape shock. Thus the helplessness hypothesis was supported.

Maier (1970) provided more dramatic confirmation of the hypothesis. In response to the criticism that it is not a cognitive set that is learned during uncontrollable trauma, but rather a motor response (reinforced by shock termination) that antagonizes barrier jumping, Maier reinforced the most antagonistic response he could find. One group of 10 dogs (passive-escape) was tied down in the harness and had panels pushed to within a quarter of an inch of the sides and top of their heads. Only by *not* moving their heads, by remaining passive and still, could these dogs terminate shock. Another group of 10 (yoked) received the same shock in the hammock, but it was independent of responding. A third group received no shock. A response-learning source of helplessness predicts that when the dogs are later tested in the shuttle box, the passive-escape group should be the most helpless since it has been explicitly reinforced for not moving during shock. The cognitive-set view makes a different prediction: These dogs could control shock, even though it took a passive response to do it; some response, even one which competes with barrier jumping, produced relief, and the dogs should not learn response-reinforcement independence. As predicted, the dogs in the yoked group were predominantly helpless in the shuttle box escape, and the naive controls escaped normally. The passive-escape group at first looked for "still" ways of minimizing shock in the shuttle box. Failing to find these, they all began to escape and avoid. Thus it was not trauma per se nor interfering motor habits that produced failure to escape, but having learned that no response at all can control trauma.

So, learning that responding and reinforcement are independent causes retarded response initiation, but does it also cause a negative cognitive set which interferes with forming later associations? Evidence from four different areas in the recent animal learning literature supports the prediction that independence between events retards later learning that events are correlated. (1) Seligman (1968) reported that when stimulus and shock were presented independently, rats later were retarded at learning that a second stimulus predicted shock. (2) Bresnahan (1969), and Thomas, Freeman, Svinicki, Burr, and Lyons (1970) reported that experience with the value of one stimulus

dimension presented independently of food retarded a rat's ability to discriminate along other dimensions. (3) McKintosh (1965) reviewed a substantial discrimination learning literature which points to the conclusion that when values along a stimulus dimension are independent of reinforcement, animals are retarded at discrimination learning when values along this dimension are later correlated with reinforcement. Bainbridge (1973), Kemler and Shepp (1971), Maier (1949), and Mellgren and Ost (1971) have found that rats and children acquire discriminations based on previously irrelevant stimuli very slowly. (4) Engberg, Hansen, Welker, and Thomas (1973) and Gamzu and Williams (1971) reported that pigeons exposed to independence between a lighted key and grain are retarded at acquiring "autoshaping" when the lighted key later signals grain. Engleberg et al. dubbed this retardation learned laziness, an appetitive analogue and learned helplessness.

In summary, one cause of laboratory produced helplessness seems to be learning that one cannot control important events. Learning that responding and reinforcement are independent results in a cognitive set which has three basic effects: fewer responses to control reinforcement are initiated, associating successful responding with reinforcement becomes more difficult, and the affect of depression, preceded by anxiety, occurs.

RELATIONSHIP OF THE ETIOLOGY OF LEARNED HELPLESSNESS TO DEPRESSION

Some of the events which typically precipitate depression are: failure in work or school; death, loss, rejection or separation from loved ones; physical disease; and growing old. We believe that the depressed patient has learned or believes that he cannot control those elements of his life which relieve suffering or bring him gratification. In short, he believes that he is helpless. Consider a few of the common precipitating events: What is the meaning of job failure or incompetence at school? Frequently it means that a person's efforts have been in vain; his responses have failed to bring about the gratification he desires. When an individual is rejected by someone he loves, he can no longer control this significant source of gratification and support. When a parent or lover dies, the bereaved is powerless to produce love from the dead person. Physical disease and growing old are helplessness situations in which the person finds his own responses ineffective and must often be cared for by others. So, we would predict that it is not life events that produce depression (cf. Alarcon & Cori, 1972) but uncontrollable life events. As mentioned above, Bibring (1953), Lichtenberg (1957), Beck (1967), and Melges and Bowlby (1969) have all theorized that helplessness is central to the etiology of depression.

The previously mentioned studies by Klein et al. (1975), Klein and Seligman (1975), and Miller and Seligman (1975a; 1975b) are relevant here. In each of these studies, strikingly similar test task performance was found for depressed subjects who received no pretreatment and nondepressed subjects pretreated with uncontrollable events. Clearly, the fact that noncontingent reinforcement results in behavioral deficits in nondepressed subjects paralleling those found in naturally-occurring depression does not *prove* that the depression was produced by uncontrollable events. However, if experiments continue to demonstrate a variety of similarities between depression and helplessness induced by uncontrollability, then the hypothesis that learned helplessness and depression are parallel phenomena with the same etiology will be strengthened.

Our etiological theory dictates that it is *reactive* depression that is analogous to learned helplessness. Is there any theoretical relation between endogenous and reactive depression? We would speculate that there is a fundamental common element: both endogenous and reactive depressives believe that they are helpless. Reactive depression results from severe trauma over which a person learns he has no control, while the most mild circumstances will trigger the endogenous depressive's belief in uncontrollability.

It has been suggested that depression is caused by extinction procedures or the *loss* of reinforcers (Ferster, 1966; Kaufman & Rosenblum, 1967; Lewinsohn et al., 1968; Liberman & Ruskin, 1971; McKinney & Bunney, 1969). There is no contradiction between the learned helplessness and extinction views of depression; helplessness, however, is more general. This is a subtle point and needs some elucidation. Extinction commonly refers to a set of contingencies in which reinforcement is withdrawn from the situation so that the subject's responses (as well as lack of responses) no longer produce reinforcement. Loss of reinforcers, as in the case of the death of a loved one, can be viewed as an extinction procedure. In conventional extinction procedures, the probability of the reinforcer occurring is zero whether or not the subject responds. It is important to realize that such extinction is a special case of independence between responding and reinforcement (the origin of the graph in Figure 5-1). Reinforcement, however, may also have a probability greater than zero, and still be presented independent of responding. This is the typical helplessness paradigm, and such procedures cause responding to decrease in probability (e.g., Rescorla & Skucy, 1969). A view, therefore, which talks about independence between responding and reinforcement subsumes the extinction view and in addition suggests that situations in which reinforcers still occur, but independent of responding, also will cause depression.

Is a net loss of reinforcers necessary for depression, or can depression occur when there is only loss of control without loss of reinforcers? Would a Casanova who slept with seven new girls every week become depressed if he found out that it was not his amatory prowess, but rather his wealth or his fairy godmother that made him popular? This is a theoretically crucial case, but we can only speculate about what would happen. It is appropriate to mention "success" depression in this context. When a person, after years of striving, finally reaches a goal such as becoming APA president or getting a Ph.D., depression often ensues. This puzzling phenomenon is clearly a problem for any loss view of depression. From a helplessness view, success depression may occur because reinforcers are no longer contingent on present responding. After years of goal directed instrumental activity, one now gets his reinforcers because of who he is rather than for what he is doing. The common clinical impression that beautiful women get depressed and attempt suicide frequently also seems relevant: positive reinforcers abound but not because of what she *does* but because of how she looks. Would children raised with abundant positive reinforcers which they got independently of what they did become clinically depressed?

Finally, we do not wish to maintain that helplessness is the only route to reactive depression. The absolute quality of life also affects mood; certain events are inherently cheering or depressing regardless of whether they are controllable. Holding the quality of life constant, whether events are controllable or uncontrollable will push mood in the direction of euphoria or dysphoria. Controllable events will be less depressing or more cheering than uncontrollable ones (Klinger, 1975). But Handel's "Messiah" played uncontrollably will still be more cheering than cancer induced by one's own smoking.

THERAPY FOR LEARNED HELPLESSNESS

One treatment invariably cures helplessness in dogs and rats. According to the helpless-ness hypothesis, the helpless dog does not try to escape because he expects that no instrumental response will produce shock termination. By forcibly exposing the dog to the fact that responding produces reinforcement, this expectation should be changed. Seligman et al. (1968) found that forcibly dragging the dog from side to side in the shuttle box, so that getting to the other side terminated shock, cured helplessness. The experimenters pulled three chronically helpless dogs back and forth across the shuttle box with long leashes. This was done during CS and shock, with the barrier removed. After being pulled across the center of the shuttle box (thus terminating shock and CS) 20, 35, and 50 times, respectively, each dog began to respond on his own. Then the barrier was replaced and the subject continued to escape and avoid. The recovery from helplessness was complete and lasting, and this finding has been replicated with over two dozen helpless dogs.

The behavior of animals during "leash pulling" was noteworthy. At the beginning of the procedure, a good deal of force had to be exerted to pull the dog across the center of the shuttle box. Less and less force was needed as training progressed. A stage was typically reached in which a slight nudge of the leash would drive the dog into action. Finally, each dog initiated its own response, and thereafter failure to escape was very rare. The initial problem seemed to be one of "getting going."

Other procedures had little success. Removing the barrier, calling to the dog from the safe side, dropping food into the safe side, and kicking the dangerous side of the box all failed. Until the correct response occurred repeatedly, the dog was not effectively exposed to the response relief contingency. It is significant that so many forced exposures were required before the dogs responded on their own. This observation supports the interpretation that motivation to initiate responses during shock was low, and that the ability to associate successful responses with relief was impaired (see Seligman, et al., 1975, for a description of a similar therapeutic procedure for helpless rats).

It should also be mentioned that time (Overmier & Seligman, 1967), electroconvulsive shock (Dorworth, 1971), atropine (Thomas & Balter, 1975), and the antidepressant drug pargyline (Weiss et al., 1975) have all been reported to be successful in alleviating learned helplessness.

RELATIONSHIP OF CURE OF LEARNED HELPLESSNESS TO DEPRESSION

According to the helplessness view, successful therapy for depression should have the patient discover and believe that his responses produce the gratification he desires—that he is, in short, an effective human being. Consonant with their helplessness centered views of the etiology of depression, Bibring (1953), Beck (1967), and Melges and Bowlby (1969) all stressed that reversing helplessness alleviates depression.

Central to most of the therapies we have reviewed is inducing the patient to discover that responding produces the reinforcement he desires. In antidepression milieu therapy, the patient is *forced* to emit anger—one of the most powerful responses people have for controlling others. When this response is dragged out of his depleted repertoire, he is powerfully reinforced. (Beck's (1970) cognitive therapy is aimed at similar goals. He sees success manipulations as changing the negative cognitive set ("I'm an ineffective person") of the depressed person to a more positive set, and argues that the primary task of the therapist is to change the negative expectional schema of the depressed patient to a more optimistic one. In both Burgess' therapy and the graded task assignment, the patient makes instrumental responses of gradually increasing difficulty and each is reinforced. Similar-

ly, all instrumental behavior therapy, by definition, arranges the contingencies so that responding controls reinforcement, and the patient's recognition of this relationship should alleviate depression. Lewinsohn's therapies call for participation in activity and other nondepressed behavior to control therapy time. In assertive training, the patient emits social responses which bring about a desired change in his environment.

As in learned helplessness, time has been found to alleviate depression. ECT, which alleviates helplessness, probably alleviates endogenous depression (Carney et al., 1965), but its effects on reactive depression are unclear. The role of atropine is largely unknown (but see Janowsky et al., 1973).

In a recent series of human helplessness studies, Klein and Seligman (1975) demonstrated that deficits associated with both depression and learned helplessness are reversed if subjects are exposed to success experiences. Three groups were used—nondepressed inescapable-noise, nondepressed no-noise, and depressed no-noise groups. Following pretreatment, nondepressed inescapable-noise and depressed no-noise subjects were allowed to solve 0, 4, or 12 concept formation problems. Then, subjects performed on either the noise escape task of Hiroto (1974) or the skill and chance tasks of Miller and Seligman (1973). As noted earlier, nondepressed inescapable-noise and depressed no-noise subjects showed similar deficits on noise escape and skill expectancy changes relative to nondepressed no-noise subjects when not allowed to solve the concept formation problems. However when these subjects successfully solved 4 or 12 problems following pretreatment, their deficits disappeared. Nondepressed inescapable-noise subjects and depressed no-noise subjects no longer showed noise escape deficits, nor did they show skill perceptions of response-reinforcement independence. So, experience in controlling reinforcement reversed the performance and perceptual deficits of both learned helplessness and depression.

We believe that this study provides a useful method for testing the effectiveness of any therapy for depression in the laboratory. Since we can bring depression into the laboratory in both its naturally-occurring state and in the form of learned helplessness, we can see what reverses it. Will assertive training, emotive expression, or atropine given to helpless and depressed subjects in the laboratory reverse the symptoms of depression and helplessness enumerated above?

The outcome of therapy is a poor test of theory, indeed. However, most of the therapies for depression reviewed above have features consistent with the learned helplessness model. In addition, the Klein and Seligman (1975) study directly confirms a number of the model's therapeutic predictions.

PREVENTION OF LEARNED HELPLESSNESS

Dramatic successes in medicine have come more frequently from prevention than from treatment, and we would hazard a guess that inoculation and immunization have saved many more lives than cure. Surprisingly, psychotherapy is almost exclusively limited to curative procedures, and preventative procedures rarely play an explicit role. In the studies of dogs, behavioral immunization provided an easy and effective means of preventing learned helplessness.

The helplessness viewpoint suggested a way to immunize dogs against inescapable shocks. Initial experience with escapable shocks should interfere with learning that responding and shock termination are independent. The relevant experiment was done by Seligman and Maier (1967). One group of dogs was given 10 escape-avoidance trials in the shuttle box before inescapable shocks in the hammock. Interference with subsequent escape-avoidance behavior was eliminated. That is, immunized dogs continued to respond normally when placed in

the shuttle box 24 hours after inescapable shock treatment in the hammock. Another interesting finding was that dogs that learned to escape shock in the shuttle box pressed the panels four times as often in the hammock during the inescapable shocks as did naive dogs, even though pressing panels had no effect on shock. Such panel pressing probably indicates the dog's attempts to control shock. Seligman, Marques, and Radford (unpublished data) extended these findings by first letting the dogs escape shock by panel pressing in the hammock. This was followed by inescapable shock in the same place. The experience with control over shock termination prevented the dogs from becoming helpless when they were later tested in a new apparatus, the shuttle box.

As in the dog, we have been able to immunize rats against the delibitating effects of inescapable shock. Rats first exposed to a session of escapable shock did not subsequently become helpless when exposed to inescapable shock (Seligman et al., 1975). More recently, we have found lifelong immunization against helplessness: rats given escapable shock at weaning did not become helpless when given inescapable shock as adults (Hannum et al., 1975).

Other findings from our laboratory support the idea that experience in controlling trauma may protect organisms from the helplessness caused by inescapable trauma. Recall that among dogs of unknown history, helplessness is a statistical effect: approximately two-thirds of dogs given inescapable shock become helpless, while one-third respond normally. About 5% of naive dogs are helpless in the shuttle box without any prior experience with inescapable shock. Why do some dogs become helpless and others not? Could it be possible that those dogs who do not become helpless even after inescapable shock have had a prelaboratory history of controllable trauma? Seligman and Groves (1970) tested this hypothesis by raising dogs singly in cages in the laboratory. Relative to dogs of variegated history, these dogs had very limited experience controlling anything. Cage-reared dogs proved to be more susceptible to helplessness: it took four sessions of inescapable shock to produce helplessness one week later in dogs of unknown history, but only two sessions of inescapable shock in the hammock to cause helplessness in the cage-reared dogs. Lessac and Solomon (1969) also reported that dogs reared in isolation seem prone to interference with escape. Thus, dogs who are deprived of natural opportunities to master reinforcers in their developmental history may be more vulnerable to helplessness than naturally immunized dogs.

RELATIONSHIP OF PREVENTION OF LEARNED
HELPLESSNESS TO PREVENTION OF
DEPRESSION

Almost everyone sometimes loses control over the reinforcements that are significant to him: parents die, failure occurs. Everyone also becomes at least mildly and transiently depressed in the wake of such events. But why are some people hospitalized for long periods and others resilient? We can only speculate about this, but the data on immunization against helplessness guide our speculations. The life histories of individuals who are particularly resilient to depression may have been filled with mastery. These people may have had extensive experience controlling and manipulating the sources of reinforcement in their lives, and may therefore perceive the future optimistically. People who are particularly susceptible to depression may have had lives full of situations in which they were helpless to influence their sources of suffering and gratification.

Although it seems reasonable that extensive experience controlling reinforcement might make one more resilient from depression, how about the person who has met only with success, the person who has rarely had to cope with anxiety? Is an individual whose responses have always succeeded more susceptible to depression when con-

fronted with situations beyond his control? Too much experience controlling reinforcers might not allow the development and use of coping against failure, just as too little control might prevent the development of coping.

One can also look at successful therapy as preventative. After all, therapy is usually not focused just on undoing past problems. It also should arm the patient against future depressions. Would therapy for depression be more successful if it were explicitly aimed at providing the patient with a wide repertoire of coping responses that he could use in future situations when he finds he cannot control reinforcement by his usual responses?

Finally, we can speculate about child rearing. What kind of experiences can best protect our children against the debilitating effects of helplessness and depression? A tentative answer from the learned helplessness view is that childhood should be full of experiences in which the child's own actions are instrumental in bringing about gratification and removing annoyances.

SUMMARY OF LEARNED
HELPLESSNESS AND DEPRESSION

We have reviewed the symptoms, etiology, cure, and prevention of learned helplessness. In many respects, the major symptoms of helplessness parallel those of depression. We have suggested that the cause of both reactive depression and learned helplessness is the belief that responding does not control important reinforcers. Finally, we have speculated that the methods which succeeded in curing and preventing learned helplessness have their parallels in the cure and prevention of depression. Table 5-2 summarizes the similarities between learned helplessness and depression. Much remains to be tested, but we believe that a common theme has emerged: both depression and learned helplessness have at their core the belief in the futility of active responding.

TABLE 5–2

Symptoms

Learned Helplessness	*Depression*
1. Passivity.	1. Passivity.
2. Difficulty learning that responses produce relief.	2. Negative cognitive set.
3. Dissipates in time.	3. Time course.
4. Lack of aggression.	4. Introjected hostility.
5. Weight loss, anorexia, social and sexual deficits.	5. Weight loss, anorexia, social and sexual deficits.
6. Norepinephrine depletion and cholinergic activity.	6. Norepinephrine depletion.
7. Ulcers and stress.	7. Ulcers(?),[a] cholinergic activity and stress (?).
	8. Feelings of helplessness.

Cause

Learning that responding and reinforcement are independent.	Belief that responding is useless.

Cure

1. Directive therapy: forced exposure to responding producing reinforcement.	1. Recovery of belief that responding produces reinforcement.
2. Electroconvulsive shock.	2. Electroconvulsive shock.
3. Time.	3. Time.
4. Anticholinergics and norepinephrine stimulants (?).	4. Norepinephrine stimulants and anticholinergics (?).

Prevention

Inoculation with mastery over reinforcement.	(?)[a]

[a] "?" means "unknown."

References

ABRAHAM, K. The first pregenital stage of the libido (1916). In *Selected papers of Karl Abraham, M.D.* Ed. by E. Jones, trans. by D. Bryan & A. Strachey. London: Hogarth Press, 1927. (a)

ABRAHAM, K. Notes on the psycho-analytical investigation and treatment of manic-depressive insanity and allied conditions (1911). In *Selected papers of Karl Abraham, M.D.* Ed. by E. Jones, trans. by D. Bryan & N. Strachey. London: Hogarth Press, 1927. (b)

AKISKAL, H. S., & McKINNEY, W. T. Jr. Depressive disorders: toward a unified hypothesis. *Science*, 1973, **182**, 20–29.

ALARCON, R. D., & CORI, L. The precipitating event in depression. *Journal of Nervous and Mental Disease*, 1972, **155**, 379–391.

AMERICAN PSYCHIATRIC ASSOCIATION. *Diagnostic and statistical manual of mental disorders.* (2nd ed.) Washington, D.C.: APA, 1968.

ANDERSON, D. C., COLE, J., & McVAUGH, W. Variations in unsignaled inescapable preshock as determinants of responses to punishment. *Journal of Comparative and Physiological Psychology*, 1968, **65**, (Monogr. Suppl. 1–17).

ANDERSON, D. C., & PADEN, P. Passive avoidance response learning as a function of prior tumbling trauma. *Psychonomic Science*, 1966, **4**, 129–130.

AYD, F. J. Jr. *Recognizing the depressed patient.* New York: Grune & Stratton, 1961.

BAINBRIDGE, P. L. Learning in the rat: Effect of

early experience with an unsolvable problem. *Journal of Comparative and Physiological Psychology*, 1973, **82**, 301–307.

BECK, A. T. Thinking and depression. I. Idiosyncratic content and cognitive distortions. *Archives of General Psychiatry*, 1963, **9**, 324–333.

BECK, A. T. Thinking and depression. II. Theory and therapy. *Archives of General Psychiatry*, 1964, **10**, 561–571.

BECK, A. T. *Depression: clinical, experimental, and theoretical aspects*. New York: Hoeber, 1967.

BECK, A. T. Cognitive therapy: nature and relation to behavior therapy. *Behavior Therapy*, 1970, **1**, 184–200. (a)

BECK, A. T. The core problem in depression: the cognitive triad. *Science and Psychoanalysis*, 1970, **17**, 47–55. (b)

BECK, A. T. Cognition, affect, and psychopathology. *Archives of General Psychiatry*, 1971, **24**, 495–500.

BECK, A. T., & HURVICH, M. S., Psychological correlates of depression. I. Frequency of "masochistic" dream content in a private practice sample. *Psychosomatic Medicine*, 1959, **21**, 50–55.

BECK, A. T., & WARD, C. H. Dreams of depressed patients: characteristic themes in manifest content. *Archives of General Psychiatry*, 1961, **5**, 462–467.

BEHRAND, E. R., & BITTERMAN, M. E. Sidman avoidance in the fish. *Journal of the Experimental Analysis of Behavior*, 1963, **13**, 229–242.

BIBRING, E. The mechanism of depression. In P. Greenacre (Ed.), *Affective disorders*. New York: International Universities Press, 1953.

BRAUD, W., WEPMANN, B., & RUSSO, D. Task and species generality of the "helplessness" phenomenon. *Psychonomic Science*, 1969, **16**, 154–155.

BRESNAHAN, E. L. Effects of intradimensional and extradimensional equivalence training, and extradimensional discrimination training upon stimulus control. Paper presented at the meeting of the American Psychological Association, Washington, D.C., September 1969.

BROOKSHIRE, K. H., LITTMAN, R. A., & STEWART, C. N. Residue of shock trauma in the white rat: a three factor theory. *Psychological Monographs*, 1961, **75**, (10, Whole No. 514).

BROWN, J., & JACOBS, A. The role of fear in the motivation and acquisition of responses. *Journal of Experimental Psychology*, 1949, **39**, 747–759.

BURGESS, E. P. The modification of depressive behaviors. In R. D. Rubin & C. M. Franks (Eds.), *Advances in behavior therapy*. New York: Academic Press, 1968.

CALLAGAN, J. E. The effect of electro-convulsive therapy on the test performances of hospitalized depressed patients. Unpublished doctoral dissertation, University of London, 1952.

CAMERON, D. E. Studies in depression. *Journal of Mental Science*, 1936, **82**, 148–161.

CAMPBELL, J. D. *Manic-depressive disease*. Philadelphia: Lippincott, 1953.

CARLSON, N. J., & BLACK, A. H. Traumatic avoidance learning: the effects of preventing escape responses. *Canadian Journal of Psychology*, 1957, **14**, 21–28.

CARNEY, M. W. P., ROTH, M., & GARSIDE, R. F. The diagnosis of depressive syndromes and the prediction of E.C.T. response. *British Journal of Psychiatry*, 1965, **111**, 659–674.

CATANIA, A. C. Elicitation, reinforcement, and stimulus control. In R. Glaser (Ed.), *The nature of reinforcement*. New York: Academic Press, 1971.

CHURCH, R. M. Response suppression. In B. A. Campbell & R. M. Church (Eds.), *Punishment and aversive behavior*. New York: Appleton-Century-Crofts, 1969.

COLE, J. O. Therapeutic efficacy of antidepressant drugs. *Journal of the American Medical Association*, 1964, **190**, 448–455.

COSTELLO, C. G. Depression: loss of reinforcers or loss of reinforcer effectiveness? *Behavior Therapy*, 1972, **3**, 240-247.

DAVIDSON, M. Studies in the application of mental tests to psychotic patients. *British Journal of Medical Psychology*, 1939, **18**, 44–52.

DAVIS, J. Efficacy of tranquilizing and antidepressant drugs. *Archives of General Psychiatry*, 1965, **13**, 552–572.

DENENBERG, V. H. Effects of avoidable and unavoidable shock upon mortality in the rat. *Psychological Reports*, 1964, **14**, 43–46.

DENENBERG, V. H., & BELL, R. Critical periods for the effects of infantile experience on adult learning. *Science*, 1960, **131**, 227–228.

DIETHELM, A., & HEFFERMAN, T. Felix Platter and psychiatry. *Journal of the History of Behavioral Science*, 1965, **1**, 10–23.

DILLING, C. A., & RABIN, A. I. Temporal experience in depressive states and schizophrenia. *Journal of Consulting Psychology*, 1967, **31**, 604–608.

DINSMOOR, J. Pulse duration and food deprivation in escape from shock training. *Psychological Reports*, 1958, 4, 531–534.

DINSMOOR, J., & CAMPBELL, S. L. Escape-from-shock training following exposure to inescapable shock. *Psychological Reports*, 1956, **2**, 34–49. (a)

DINSMOOR, J., & CAMPBELL, S. L. Level of current and time between sessions as factors in adaptation to shock. *Psychological Reports*, 1956, **2**, 441–444. (b)

DIXON, N. F., & LEAR, T. E. Perceptual regulation and mental disorder. *Journal of Mental Science*, 1962, **108**, 356–361.

DORWORTH, T. R. The effect of electroconvulsive shock on "helplessness" in dogs. Unpublished doctoral dissertation, University of Minnesota, 1971.

DYER, R. The effects of human relations training on the interpersonal behavior of college students. Unpublished doctoral dissertation, University of Oregon, 1967.

EKMAN, P., & FRIESEN, W. V. Non-verbal behavior in psychopathology. In R. J. Friedman and M. M. Katz (Eds.), *The psychology of depression: contemporary theory and research*. Washington, D.C.: Winston-Wiley, 1974.

ENGBERG, L. A., HANSEN, G., WELKER, R. L., & THOMAS, D. R. Acquisition of key-pecking via autoshaping as a function of prior experience: "learned laziness" *Science*, 1973, **178**, 1002–1004.

ENGEL, G. A life setting conducive to illness. The giving-up—given-up complex. *Bulletin of the Menninger Clinic*, 1968, **32**, 355–365.

EYSENCK, H. J. The classification of depressive illnesses. *British Journal of Psychiatry*, 1970, **117**, 241–250.

FERSTER, C. B. Classification of behavioral pathology. In L. Krasner & L. P. Ullman (Eds.), *Research in behavior modification*. New York: Holt, Rinehart & Winston, 1965.

FERSTER, C. B. Animal behavior and mental illness. *Psychological Record*, 1966, **16**, 345–356.

FERSTER, C. B., & SKINNER, B. F. *Schedules of reinforcement*. New York: Appleton-Century-Crofts, 1957.

FISHER, K. A. Changes in test performance of ambulatory depressed patients undergoing electro-shock therapy. *Journal of General Psychology*, 1949, **41**, 195–232.

FISHER, S. Depressive affect and perception of up-down. *Journal of Psychiatric Research*, 1964, **2**, 25–30.

FOULDS, G. A. Tempermental differences in maze performance. II. The effect of distraction and of electroconvulsive therapy on psychomotor retardation. *British Journal of Psychology*, 1952, **43**, 33–41.

FRANZ, S. I. The times of some mental processes in the retardation and excitement of insanity. *American Journal of Psychology*, 1906, **17**, 38–68.

FREUD, S. Mourning and melancholia (1917). In *The standard edition of the complete psychological works of Sigmund Freud*. Trans. and ed. by J. Strachey. London: Hogarth Press, 1955.

FRIEDMAN, A. S. Minimal effects of severe depression on cognitive functioning. *Journal of Abnormal and Social Psychology*, 1964, **69**, 237–243.

GAMZU, E., & WILLIAMS, D. A. Classical conditioning of a complex skeletal response. *Science*, 1971, **171**, 923–925.

GARMA, A. Psychoanalytic investigations in melancholias and other types of depressions. *Yearbook of Psychoanalysis*, 1947, **3**, 75–108.

GERO, G. The construction of depression. *International Journal of Psychoanalysis*, 1936, **17**, 423–461.

GIBBON, J. Contingency spaces and random controls in classical and instrumental conditioning. Paper presented at the meeting of the Eastern Psychological Association, Atlantic City, April 1970.

GLASSMAN, A. H. Indoleamines and affective disorders. *Psychosomatic Medicine*, 1969, **2**, 107–114.

GRINKER, R., MILLER, J., SABSHIN, M., NUNN, R., & NUNNALLY, J. *The phenomena of depressions*. New York: Hoeber, 1961.

HALL, K. R. L., & STRIDE, E. Some factors affecting reaction times to auditory stimuli in mental patients. *Journal of Mental Science*, 1954, **100**, 462–477.

HAMILTON, M., & WHITE, J. M. Clinical syndromes in depressive states. *Journal of Mental Science*, 1959, **105**, 985–998.

HANNUM, R. D. ROSELLINI, R. A., & SELIGMAN, M. E. P. Retention of learned helplessness and immunization in the rat from weaning to adulthood. Submitted for publication, 1975.

HARLOW, H. F., HARLOW, M. K., & SUOMI, S. J. From thought to therapy: lessons from a primate laboratory. *American Scientist,* 1971, **59,** 538–549.

HERSON, M., EISLER, R. M., ALFORD, G. S., & AGRAS, W. S. Effects of token economy on neurotic depression: an experimental analyss. *Behavior Therapy,* 1973, **4,** 392–397.

HINCHLIFFE, M. K., LANCASHIRE, M., & ROBERTS, F. J. Depression: defense mechanisms in speech. *British Journal of Psychiatry,* 1971, **118,** 471–472.

HIROTO, D. S. Locus of control and learned helplessness. *Journal of Experimental Psychology,* 1974, **102,** 187–193.

HIROTO, D. S., & SELIGMAN, M. E. P. Generality of learned helplessness in man. *Journal of Personality and Social Psychology,* 1975, **31,** 311–327.

HOGAN, R. A. The implosive technique. *Behaviour Research and Therapy,* 1968, **6,** 423–431.

HOMME, L. E. Perspectives in psychology: control of coverants, the operants of the mind. *Psychological Record,* 1965, **15,** 501–511.

HONIG, W. H. (Ed.) *Operant behavior: theory and research.* New York: Appleton-Century-Crofts, 1966.

HORDERN, A. *Depressive states, a pharmacotherapeutic study.* Springfield, Ill.: Charles C. Thomas, 1965.

HUSTON, P. E., & SENF, R. Psychopathology of schizophrenia and depression. I. Effect of amytal and amphetamine sulfate on level and maintenance of attention. *Amercan Journal of Psychiatry,* 1952, **109,** 131–138.

IVANOV-SMOLENSKY, A. G. The pathology of conditioned reflexes and the so-called psychogenic depression. *Journal of Nervous and Mental Disease,* 1928, **67,** 346–350.

JACOBSON, E. The effect of disappointment on ego and superego formation in normal and depressive development. *Psychoanalytic Review,* 1946, **33,** 129–147.

JACOBSON, E. Contribution to the metapsychology of cyclothymic depression. In P. Greenacre (Ed.), *Affective disorders.* New York: International Universities Press, 1953.

JACOBSON, E. Transference problems in the psychoanalytic treatment of severely depressive patients. *Journal of the American Psychoanalytic Association,* 1954, **2,** 594–606.

JACOBSON, E. *Depression: comparative studies of normal, neurotic, and psychotic conditions.* New York: International Universities Press, 1971.

JANOWSKY, D. S., EL-YOUSEF, M. K., DAVIS, J. M., & SEKEREHJ, H. J. Parasympathetic suppression of manic symptoms by physostigmine. *Archives of General Psychiatry,* 1973, **28,** 542–547.

KAHN, M. W. The effect of severe defeat at various age levels on the aggressive behavior of mice. *Journal of Genetic Psychology,* 1951, **79,** 117–130.

KAUFMAN, J. C., & ROSENBLUM, L. A. The reaction to separation in infant monkeys; anaclitic depression and conservation-withdrawal. *Psychosomatic Medicine* 1967, **29,** 648–675.

KEMLER, D., & SHEPP, B. The learning and transfer of dimensional relevance and irrelevance in children. *Journal of Experimental Psychology,* 1971, **90,** 120–127.

KENDALL, R. E. *The classification of depressive illness.* Institute of Psychiatry Mandsley Monographs, Number 18. London: Oxford University Press, 1968.

KENDRICK, D. C., PARBOOSINGH, R., & POST, F. A Synonym Learning Test for use with elderly psychiatric subjects: a validation study. *British Journal of Social and Clinical Psychology,* 1965, **4,** 63–71.

KIESLER, D. J. Experimental designs in psychotherapy research. In A. E. Bergin & S. L. Garfield (Eds.), *Handbook of psychotherapy and behavior change: an empirical analysis.* New York: John Wiley, 1971.

KILOH, L. G., & GARSIDE, R. F. The independence of neurotic depression and endogenous depression. *British Journal of Psychiatry,* 1963, **109,** 451–463.

KLEIN, D. C., FENCIL-MORSE, E., & SELIGMAN, M. E. P. Learned helplessness, depression, and the attribution of failure. Submitted for publication, 1975.

KLEIN, D. C., & SELIGMAN, M. E. P. Reversal of performance deficits and perceptual deficits in learned helplessness and depression. Submitted for publication, 1975.

KLEIN, M. A contribution to the psychogenesis of manic-depressive states. In *Contribution to psychoanalysis 1921–1945.* London: Hogarth Press, 1948.

KLERMAN, G. L., & COLE, J. O. Clinical and pharmacology of imipramine and related antidepressant compounds. *Pharmacological Review,* 1965, **17**, 101–141.

KLINGER, E. Consequences of commitment to and disengagement from incentives. *Psychological Review,* 1975, **82**, 1–25.

KORA, T. Morita therapy. *International Journal of Psychiatry,* 1965, **1**, 611–640.

KRAEPELIN, E. *Manic-depressive insanity and paranoia.* Translated by R. M. Barclay. Edinburgh: E. and S. Livingstone, 1921.

KRAINES, S. H. *Mental depressions and their treatment.* New York: Macmillan, 1957.

KRAINES, S. H. Manic-depressive syndrome: a diencephalic disease. Paper presented at Annual Meeting of the American Psychiatric Association, New York, 1965.

LAZARUS, A. A. Learning theory and the treatment of depression. *Behaviour Research and Therapy,* 1968, **6**, 83–89.

LEAF, R. C. Avoidance response evocation as a function of prior discriminative fear conditioning under curare. *Journal of Comparative and Physiological Psychology,* 1964, **58**, 446–449.

LEARY, T. Multilevel measurement of interpersonal behavior: a manual for the use of the interpersonal system of personality. Berkeley: Psychological Consultation Service, 1956.

LESSAC, M., & SOLOMON, R. L. Effects of early isolation on the later adaptive behavior of beagles: a methodological demonstration. *Development Psychology,* 1969, **1**, 14–25.

LEVINE, S., CHEVALIER, J., & KORCHIN, S. The effects of early shock and handling on later avoidance learning. *Journal of Personality,* 1956, **24**, 475–493.

LEWINSOHN, P. M. Manual of instructions for the behavior ratings used for the observation of interpersonal behavior. Unpublished manuscript, University of Oregon, 1968.

LEWINSOHN, P. M., & ATWOOD, G. E. Depression: a clinical-research approach. *Psychotherapy: Research and Practice,* 1969, **6**, 166–171.

LEWINSOHN, P. M., & GRAF, M. Pleasant activities and depression. *Journal of Consulting and Clinical Psychology,* 1973, **41**, 261–268.

LEWINSOHN, P. M., & LIBET, J. Pleasant events, activity schedules, and depressions. *Journal of Abnormal Psychology,* 1972, **79**, 291–295.

LEWINSOHN, P. M., & SHAFFER, M. Use of home observations as an integral part of the treatment of depression: preliminary report and case studies. *Journal of Consulting and Clinical Psychology,* 1971, **37**, 87–94.

LEWINSOHN, P. M., WEINSTEIN, M. S., & ALPER, T. A behavioral approach to the group treatment of depressed persons: a methodological contribution. *Journal of Clinical Psychology,* 1970, **26**, 525–532.

LEWINSOHN, P. M., WEINSTEIN, M. S., & SHAW, D. Depression: a clinical-research approach. In R. D. Rubin & C. M. Frank (Eds.), *Advances in behavior therapy.* New York: Academic Press, 1968.

LIBERMAN, R. Behavioral approaches to family and couple therapy. *American Journal of Orthopsychiatry,* 1970, **40**, 106–118.

LIBERMAN, R. P., & RASKIN, D. E. Depression: a behavioral formulation. *Archives of General Psychiatry,* 1971, **24**, 515–523.

LIBET, J., & LEWINSOHN, P. M. The concept of social skill with special reference to the behavior of depressed persons. *Journal of Consulting and Clinical Psychology,* 1973, **40**, 304–312.

LICHTENBERG, P. A definition and analysis of depression. *Archives of Neurology and Psychiatry,* 1957, **77**, 519–527.

LIDDELL, H. *Emotional hazards in animals and man.* Springfield, Ill.: Free Press, 1953.

LINDNER, M. Hereditary and environmental influences upon resistance to stress. Unpublished doctoral dissertation, University of Pennsylvania, 1968.

LOONEY, T. A., & COHEN, P. S. Retardation of jump-up escape responding in rats pretreated with different frequencies of noncontingent electric shock. *Journal of Comparative and Physiological Psychology,* 1972, **78**, 317–322.

LUNDHOLM, H. Reaction time as an indicator of emotional disturbances in manic-depressive psychoses. *Journal of Abnormal Psychology,* 1922, **17**, 292–318.

LUNDQUIST, G. Prognosis and course in manic-depressive psychoses. *Acta Psychiatrica Neurologica Supplement,* 1945, Supplement No. 35.

MACKINTOSH, N. J. Selective attention in animal learning. *Psychological Bulletin,* 1965, **64**, 124–150.

MAIER, N. R. F. *Frustration.* Ann Arbor: University of Michigan Press, 1949.

MAIER, S. F. Failure to escape traumatic shock: incompatible skeletal motor responses or learned helplessness? *Learning and Motivation,* 1970, **1,** 157–170.

MAIER, S. F., ALBIN, R. W., & TESTA, T. J. Failure to learn to escape in rats previously exposed to inescapable shock depends on nature of escape response. *Journal of Comparative and Physiological Psychology,* 1973, **85,** 581–592.

MAIER, S. F., ANDERSON, C., & LIEBERMAN, D. A. Influence of control of shock on subsequent shock-elicited aggression. *Journal of Comparative and Physiological Psychology,* 1972, **81,** 94–100.

MAIER, S. F., & SELIGMAN, M. E. P. Learned helplessness: theory and evidence. *Journal of Experimental Psychology: General,* 1975, in press.

MAIER, S. F., SELIGMAN, M. E. P., & SOLOMON, R. L. Pavlovian fear conditioning and learned helplessness. In B. A. Campbell & R. M. Church (Eds.), *Punishment.* New York: Appleton-Century-Crofts, 1969.

MARTIN, I., & REES, L. Reaction times and somatic reactivity in depressed patients. *Journal of Psychosomatic Research,* 1966, **9,** 375–382.

MASER, J. P., & GALLUP, G. G. Jr. Tonic immobility in chickens: catalepsy potentiation by uncontrollable shock and alleviation by imipramine. *Psychosomatic Medicine,* 1974, **36,** 199–205.

MASON, C. F. Pre-illness intelligence of mental hospital patients. *Journal of Consulting Psychology,* 1956, **20,** 297–300.

MASSERMAN, J. H. *Behavior and neurosis.* Chicago: University of Chicago Press, 1943.

McCULLOCH, T. L., & BRUNER, J. S. The effect of electric shock upon subsequent learning in the rat. *Journal of Psychology,* 1939, **7,** 333–336.

McKINNEY, W. T. Jr., & BUNNEY, W. E. Jr. Animal model of depression. *Archives of General Psychiatry,* 1969, **21,** 240–248.

McKINNEY, W. T. Jr., SOUMI, S. J., & HARLOW, H. F. Depression in primates. *American Journal of Psychiatry,* 1971, **127,** 1313–1320.

MELGES, F. T., & BOWLBY, J. Types of hopelessness in psychopathological process. *Archives of General Psychiatry,* 1969, **20,** 690–699.

MELLGREN, R. L., & OST, J. W. P. Discriminative stimulus preexposure and learning of an operant discrimination in the rat. *Journal of Comparative and Physiological Psychology,* 1971, **77,** 179–187.

MELTZOFF, J., & KORNREICH, M. *Research in psychotherapy.* New York: Atheron Press, 1970.

MENDELS, J. Depression: the distinction between syndrome and syndrome. *British Journal of Psychiatry,* 1968, **114,** 1549–1554.

MENDELS, J. *Concepts of depression.* New York: John Wiley, 1970.

MENDELS, J., & COCHRANE, C. The nosology of depression: the endogenous-reactive concept. *American Journal of Psychiatry,* 1968, **124,** 1–11 (May Supplement).

MENDELS, J., & FRAZER, A. Brain biogenic amine depletion and mood. *Archives of General Psychiatry,* 1974, **30,** 447–451.

MENDELSON, M. *Psychoanalytic concepts of depression.* Springfield, Ill.: Charles C. Thomas, 1960.

MEZEY, A. G., & COHEN, S. I. The effect of depressive illness on time judgment and time experience. *Journal of Neurology, Neurosurgery, and Psychiatry,* 1961, **24,** 269–270.

MILLER, W. R. Psychological deficit in depression: a review. *Psychological Bulletin,* 1975, **82,** 238–260.

MILLER, W. R., & SELIGMAN, M. E. P. Depression and the perception of reinforcement. *Journal of Abnormal Psychology,* 1973, **82,** 62–73.

MILLER, W. R., & SELIGMAN, M. E. P. Depression and learned helplessness in man. *Journal of Abnormal Psychology,* 1975, **84,** 228–238. (a)

MILLER, W. R., & SELIGMAN, M. E. P. Learned helplessness, depression, and the perception of reinforcement. *Behavior Research and Therapy,* 1975, in press. (b)

MILLER, W. R., SELIGMAN, M. E. P., & KURLANDER, H. Learned helplessness, depression, and anxiety. *Journal of Nervous and Mental Disease,* 1975, in press.

MOSS, G. R., & BOREN, J. J. Depression as a model for behavioral analysis. *Comprehensive Psychiatry,* 1972, **13,** 581–590.

MOWRER, O. H. An experimental analysis of "regression" with incidental observations on "reaction formation." *Journal of Abnormal and Social Psychology,* 1940, **35,** 56–87.

MOWRER, O. H. New directions in the understanding and management of depression. *International Psychiatry Clinics,* 1969, **6,** 317–360.

MOWRER, O. H., & VIEK, P. An experimental analogue of fear from a sense of helplessness.

Journal of Abnormal and Social Psychology, 1948, **43**, 193–200.

MULLIN, A. D., & MOGENSON, G. J. Effects of fear conditioning on avoidance learning. *Psychological Reports,* 1963, **13**, 707–710.

OVERMIER, J. B. Interference with avoidance behavior: failure to avoid traumatic shock. *Journal of Experimental Psychology,* 1968, **78**, 340–343.

OVERMIER, J. B., & SELIGMAN, M. E. P. Effects of inescapable shock upon subsequent escape and avoidance learning. *Journal of Comparative and Physiological Psychology,* 1967, **63**, 23–33.

PADILLA, A. M., PADILLA, C., KETTERER, T., & GIACALONE, D. Inescapable shocks and subsequent avoidance conditioning in goldfish, Carrasius Avratus. *Psychonomic Science,* 1970, **20**, 295–296.

PARTRIDGE, M. Some reflections on the nature of affective disorders arising from the results of prefrontal leucotomy. *Journal of Mental Science,* 1949, **95**, 795–825.

PASKIND, H. A. Brief attacks of manic-depressive depression. *Archives of Neurology and Psychiatry,* 1929, **22**, 123–134.

PASKIND, H. A. Manic-depressive psychosis in private practice: length of attack and length of interval. *Archives of Neurology and Psychiatry,* 1930, **23**, 789–794.

PAVLOV, I. P. *Conditioned reflexes.* Translated by G. V. Anrep. New York: Dover, 1927.

PAYNE, R. W. Cognitive abnormalities. In H. J. Eysenck (Ed.), *Handbook of abnormal psychology.* New York: Basic Books, 1961.

PAYNE, R. W., & HEWLETT, J. H. G. Thought disorder in psychotic patients. In H. J. Eysenck (Ed.), *Experiments in personality.* Vol. 2. London: Routledge & Kegan Paul, 1960.

PINCKNEY, G. Avoidance learning in fish as a function of prior fear conditioning. *Psychological Reports,* 1967, **20**, 71–74.

PORESKY, R. Noncontingency detection and its effects. Paper presented at the meeting of the Eastern Psychological Association, Atlantic City, April 1970.

POST, F. Somatic and psychic factors in the treatment of elderly psychiatric patients. *Journal of Psychosomatic Research,* 1966, **10**, 13–19.

POWELL, D. A., & CREER, T. L. Interaction of developmental and environmental variables in shock-elicited aggression. *Journal of Compar-*

ative and Physiological Psychology, 1969, **69**, 219–225.

PREMACK, D. Toward empirical laws. I. Positive reinforcement. *Psychological Review,* 1959, **66**, 219–233.

PREMACK, D. Reinforcement theory. In M. Jones (Ed.), *Nebraska Symposium on Motivation.* Lincoln: University of Nebraska Press, 1965.

RACINSKAS, J. R. Maladaptive consequences of loss or lack of control over aversive events. Unpublished doctoral dissertation, Waterloo University, Ontario, Canada, 1971.

RADO, S. The problem of melancholia. *International Journal of Psychoanalysis,* 1928, **9**, 420–438.

REISINGER, J. J. The treatment of "anxiety-depression" via positive reinforcement and response cost. *Journal of Applied Behavior Analysis,* 1972, **5**, 125–130.

RESCORLA, R. A. Pavlovian conditioning and its proper control procedures. *Psychological Review,* 1967, **74**, 71–80.

RESCORLA, R. A. Probability of shock in the presence and absence of the CS in fear conditioning. *Journal of Comparative and Physiological Psychology,* 1968, **66**, 1–5.

RESCORLA, R. A., & SKUCY, J. Effect of response independent reinforcers during extinction. *Journal of Comparative and Physiological Psychology,* 1969, **67**, 381–389.

ROBINSON, J. C., & LEWINSOHN, P. M. Behavior modification of speech characteristics in a chronically depressed man. *Behavior Therapy,* 1973, **4**, 150–152. (a)

ROBINSON, J. C., & LEWINSOHN, P. M. Experimental analysis of a technique based on the Premack Principle changing verbal behavior of depressed individuals. *Psychological Reports,* 1973, **32**, 199–210. (b)

ROSELLINI, R. A., & SELIGMAN, M. E. P. Failure to escape shock after repeated exposure to inescapable shock. Submitted for publication, 1975.

ROSENBLATT, B. P. The influence of affective states upon body image and upon the perceptual organization of space. Unpublished doctoral dissertation, Clark University, Worcester, Mass., 1956.

ROSENFELD, H. An investigation into the psycho-analytic theory of depression. *International Journal of Psychoanalysis,* 1959, **40**, 105–129.

ROSENTHAL, S. H., & GUDEMAN, J. E. The endogenous depressive pattern: an empirical investigation. *Archives of General Psychiatry*, 1967, **16**, 241–249.

ROSENTHAL, S. H., & KLERMAN, G. L. Content and consistency in the endogenous depressive pattern. *British Journal of Psychiatry*, 1966, **112**, 471–484.

ROTH, S., & KUBAL, L. The effects of noncontingent reinforcement on tasks of differing importance: facilitation and learned helplessness effects. *Journal of Personality and Social Psychology*, 1975, in press.

RUBIN, R. T., & MANDELL, A. J. Adrenal cortical activity in pathological emotional states: a review. *American Journal of Psychiatry*, 1966, **123**, 387–400.

SALZMAN, L. *Developments in psychoanalysis.* New York: Grune & Stratton, 1962.

SCHILDKRAUT, J. J. The catecholamine hypothesis of affective disorders: a review of supporting evidence. *American Journal of Psychiatry*, 1965, **122**, 509–522.

SCHMALE, A. H. Jr. Relationship of separation and depression to disease. I. A report on a hospitalized medical population. *Psychosomatic Medicine*, 1958, **20**, 259–277.

SEITZ, F. C. Behavior modification of depression. Proceedings of the 79th Annual Convention of the American Psychological Association, 1971.

SELIGMAN, M. E. P. Chronic fear produced by unpredictable shock. *Journal of Comparative and Physiological Psychology*, 1968, **65**, 402–411.

SELIGMAN, M. E. P. Depression and learned helplessness. In R. J. Friedman & M. M. Katz (Eds.), *The psychology of depression: contemporary theory and research.* Washington, D.C.: Winston-Wiley, 1974.

SELIGMAN, M. E. P. *Helplessness.* San Francisco: W. H. Freeman, 1975.

SELIGMAN, M. E. P., & BEAGLEY, G. Learned helplessness in the rat. *Journal of Comparative and Physiological Psychology*, 1975, **88**, 534–541.

SELIGMAN, M. E. P., & GROVES, D. Non-transient learned helplessness. *Psychonomic Science*, 1970, **19**, 191–192.

SELIGMAN, M. E. P., & MAIER, S. F. Failure to escape traumatic shock. *Journal of Experimental Psychology*, 1967, **74**, 1–9.

SELIGMAN, M. E. P., MAIER, S. F., & GEER, J. The alleviation of learned helplessness in the dog. *Journal of Abnormal and Social Psychology*, 1968, **73**, 256–262.

SELIGMAN, M. E. P., MAIER, S. F., & SOLOMON, R. L. Unpredictable and uncontrollable aversive events. In F. R. Brush (Ed.), *Aversive conditioning and learning.* New York: Academic Press, 1971.

SELIGMAN, M. E. P., ROSELLINI, R., & KOZAK, M. Learned helplessness in the rat: reversability, time course, and immunization. *Journal of Comparative and Physiological Psychology*, 1975, **88**, 542–547.

SENAY, E. C. Toward an animal model of depression: a study of separation behavior in dogs. *Journal of Psychiatric Research*, 1966, 4, 65–71.

SEWARD, J., & HUMPHREY, G. L. Avoidance learning as a function of pretraining in the cat. *Journal of Comparative and Physiological Psychology*, 1967, **63**, 338–341.

SHAPIRO, M. B., & NELSON, E. H. An investigation of the nature of cognitive impairment in co-operative psychiatric patients. *British Journal of Medical Psychology*, 1955, **28**, 239–256.

SPITZ, R. A. Anaclitic depression. In A. Freud, W. Hoffer, & E. Glover (Eds.), *The psychoanalytic study of the child.* Vol. 2. New York: International Universities Press, 1946.

STAMPFL, T. G., & LEVIS, D. J. Essentials of impulsive therapy: a learning-theory based psychodynamic behavioral therapy. *Journal of Abnormal Psychology*, 1967, **6**, 496–503.

SUOMI, S. J. Repetitive peer separation of young monkeys: effects of vertical chamber confinement during separations. *Journal of Abnormal Psychology*, 1973, **81**, 1–10.

SUOMI, S. J., & HARLOW, H. F. Depressive behavior in young monkeys subjected to vertical chamber confinement. *Journal of Comparative and Physiological Psychology*, 1972, **80**, 11–18.

SUOMI, S. J., HARLOW, H. F., & McKINNEY, W. T. Jr. Monkey psychiatrists. *American Journal of Psychiatry*, 1972, **128**, 927–932.

TAULBEE, E. S., & WRIGHT, H. W. A psychosocial-behavioral model for therapeutic intervention. In C. D. Spielberger (Ed.), *Current topics in clinical and community psychology.* Vol. 3. New York: Academic Press, 1971.

TEASDALE, J. D., & BEAUMONT, J. G. The effect of mood on performance on the Modified New Word Learning Test (Walton-Black). *British*

Journal of Social and Clinical Psychology, 1971, **10,** 342–345.

THOMAS, D. R., FREEMAN, F., SVINICKI, J. G., BURR, D. E., & LYONS, J. Effects of extradimensional training on stimulus generalization. *Journal of Experimental Psychology,* 1970, **83,** (Pt. 2), 1–22.

THOMAS, E., & BALTER, A. Learned helplessness: amelioration of symptoms by cholinergic blockade of the septum. Submitted for publication, 1975.

WAGNER, A. R. Stimulus selection and a "modified continuity theory." In G. H. Bower & J. T. Spence (Eds.), *The psychology of learning and motivation.* Vol. 3. New York: Academic Press, 1969.

WALLACE, A. F. C. Mazeway disintegration: the individual's perception of socio-cultural disorganization. *Human Organization,* 1957, **16,** 23–27.

WALTON, D., WHITE, J. G., BLACK, D. A., & YOUNG, A. J. The modified word-learning test: a cross-validation study. *British Journal of Medical Psychology,* 1959, **32,** 213–220.

WAPNER, S., WERNER, H., & KRUS, D. M. The effect of success and failure on space localization. *Journal of Personality,* 1957, **25,** 752–756.

WATSON, J. S. Memory and "contingency analysis" in infant learning. *Merrill-Palmer Quarterly of Behavior Development,* 1967, **13,** 55–76.

WEISS, J. M. Effects of coping response on stress. *Journal of Comparative and Physiological Psychology,* 1968, **65,** 251–260.

WEISS, J. M. Effects of coping behavior in different warning signal conditions on stress pathology in rats. *Journal of Comparative and Physiological Psychology,* 1971, **77,** 1–13. (a)

WEISS, J. M. Effects of coping behavior with and without a feedback signal on stress pathology in rats. *Journal of Comparative and Physiological Psychology,* 1971, **77,** 22–30. (b)

WEISS, J. M. Effects of punishing the coping response (conflict) on stress pathology in rats. *Journal of Comparative and Physiological Psychology,* 1971, **77,** 14–21. (c)

WEISS, J. M., GLAZER, H. L., & POHORECKY, L. A. Coping behavior and neurochemical changes: an alternative explanation for the original "Learned Helplessness" experiments. In G.

Serban & A. Kling (Eds.), *Animal models in human psychobiology.* New York: Plenum Press, 1975, in press.

WEISS, J. M., KRIECKHAUS, E. E., & CONTE, R. Effects of fear conditioning on subsequent avoidance behavior. *Journal of Comparative and Physiological Psychology,* 1968, **65,** 413–421.

WEISS, J. M., STONE, E. A., & HARRELL, N. Coping behavior and brain norepinephrine in rats. *Journal of Comparative and Physiological Psychology,* 1970, **72,** 153–160.

WELLS, E. L., & KELLEY, C. M. Intelligence and psychosis. *American Journal of Insanity,* 1920, **77,** 17–45.

WHYBROW, P. C., & MENDELS, J. Toward a biology of depression: some suggestions from neurophysiology. *American Journal of Psychiatry,* 1969, **125,** 1491–1500.

WILLIAMS, J. G. BARLOW, D. H., & AGRAS, W. S. Behavioral measurement of severe depression. *Archives of General Psychiatry,* 1972, **27,** 330–333.

WILLIAMS, R. L., & MOFFAT, G. H. Escapable/inescapable pretraining and subsequent avoidance in human subjects. *Bulletin of the Psychonomic Society,* 1974, 4, 144–146.

WILLIAMS, T. A., FRIEDMAN, R. J., & SECUNDA, S. K. Special report: the depressive illnesses. Washington, D.C.: National Institute of Mental Health, November 1970.

WINOKUR, G. The types of affective disorders. *Journal of Nervous and Mental Disease,* 1973, **156,** 82–96.

WITTGENSTEIN, L. *Philosophical investigations.* New York: Macmillan, 1953.

WOHLFORD, P. Extension of personal time, affective states, and expectation of personal death. *Journal of Personality and Social Psychology,* 1966, **3,** 559–566.

WOLPE, J. *Psychotherapy by reciprocal inhibition.* Stanford, Calif.: Stanford University Press, 1958.

WOLPE, J. Neurotic depression: experimental analog, clinical syndromes, and treatment. *American Journal of Psychotherapy,* 1971, **25,** 362–368.

ZILBOORG, G., & HENRY, G. W. *A history of medical psychology.* New York: W. W. Norton, 1941.

Behavioral Treatment of the Chronic Mental Hospital Patient

6

J. R. STAHL
HAROLD LEITENBERG

The total number of patients residing in state and county mental hospitals has consistently declined since 1955. In that year there were 560,000 psychiatric patients in public mental hospitals. By 1970 the number had decreased to 350,000, despite an increase in the United States population from 166 to 205 million during the same period (United States Public Health Service, 1969, 1970; Yolles, 1967).

The reduction in the population of psychiatric in-patients has been attributed to a number of factors, among them the introduction of phenothiazines, the development of community mental health facilities and other out-patient clinics, the establishment of after-care facilities for released patients, and the development of alternate resources for the aged (Bartholow & Tunahan, 1967; Bellak & Loeb, 1969; Greenblatt, Solomon, Evans, & Brooks, 1965; Klein & Davis, 1969; Lamb, 1968; Pasamanick, Scarpitti, & Dinitz, 1967).

Epidemiological surveys have indicated, however, that only a certain proportion of the psychiatric population is affected by current forms of intervention and that the response of this subgroup alone accounts for the decline in the resident population.

Jones and Sidebothem (1962) suggest that each public hospital consists, in effect, of two separate facilities: one, a rapid turnover hospital for acute, short-term patients, and the other a custodial facility for a long-term, chronic population. Research has indicated that approximately two-thirds of all public mental hospital residents fall into this second, chronic group (Glass, 1965).

For patients who do not respond quickly to traditional hospital treatment, the probability of successful readaptation to community living is low, since length of hospitalization has been found to be inversely correlated with probability of release (Dunham & Weinberg, 1960; Odegard, 1961). After two years of hospitalization the probability of discharge is only about 6% (Gurel, 1966; Hassall, Spencer, & Cross, 1965; Ullman, 1967); after five years of continuous hospitalization, the chance of release is still less (Greenblatt et al., 1965).

In addition, many chronic patients who *are* released are rehospitalized within six months (Brown, Carstairs, & Topping, 1958; Fairweather, Sanders, Cressler, & Maynard, 1969; Vitale, 1964; Vitale & Steinbach, 1965; Wohl, 1964). Miller (1965) followed up a sample of patients who had been hospitalized two or more years prior to discharge and found that 93% had been rehospitalized within five years. Lamb (1968) has estimated that half the public mental hospital population is made up of "hard core" chronic patients who are unacceptable even for shelter care placement; for this group the probability of discharge is essentially zero.

The failure of traditional psychiatric techniques to effect significant improvement in chronic mental hospital patients stimulated the growth of two behavioral approaches to treatment: the ward-wide token economy system and the individualized reinforcement program.

The major focus of this chapter will be on the token economy system with primary consideration given to an evaluation of therapeutic effectiveness rather than to a detailed description of how to institute a token economy. After a review of the effects of token economies on chronic psychiatric patients has been completed, a brief survey will be made of the broad range of specific "psychotic" behaviors that have been treated with individualized behavioral programs.

Token Economy:
Definition, Aims, and Rationale

The first report of a ward-wide token economy system for chronic psychiatric patients was published in 1965 by Ayllon and Azrin. Essentially, a token economy is a program which provides patients with tokens (money) following occurrences of therapeutically desirable behaviors. These tokens are exchangeable for a wide variety of on-ward and off-ward activities, privileges, and commodities.

The overall rationale underlying a token economy system for chronic hospitalized patients is deceptively simple: in order to increase relevant everyday adaptive behavior (walking, talking, participating in group activities, engaging in self-care and work behaviors, etc.) it may be necessary to break these behaviors into small components and

to regularly reinforce (reward) instances of such behavior when they do occur. The token economy provides new sources of motivation and incentive in order to promote clinically relevant changes in patient behavior. It is designed to reduce the apathy and dependence so often seen in the long-term patient. The token economy is a means of teaching people in a salient and direct fashion that their own behavior immediately influences what happens to them. If a withdrawn patient earns a token every time he talks to peers or to staff, an initially artificial but presumably rewarding consequence is now attached to a behavior that had been lacking and that otherwise no longer has any intrinsic reinforcing properties. A large vein of optimism underlies the token economy system. The assumption is being made that meaningful changes in chronic patients' behavior can be generated by systematic manipulation of the immediate social environment consequences of such behavior.

The actual implementation of a token economy system requires: (1) specification of therapeutically desirable behaviors that can be reliably observed and recorded; (2) delivery of tokens contingent upon the occurrence of these behaviors; (3) discovery of effective back-up reinforcers (items of exchange for tokens); and (4) a balance between "wages" and "prices," between the number of tokens that can be earned and the number that can be spent.

There are many practical problems related to implementation, but space does not allow us to go into them here. (See Ayllon & Azrin, 1968 and Schaefer & Martin, 1969, for details of implementation.) Some minimal discussion of typical target behaviors and typical reinforcers, however, is necessary. Paul (1969) delineated three broad areas of functioning where appropriate responses must be developed if the chronic patient is to succeed outside the hospital. These are (1) resocialization, consisting of self-care behaviors, interpersonal interaction skills, and social interests; (2) instrumental role performance, consisting of occupational skills and housekeeping behaviors; and (3) reduction in the frequency, intensity, or timing of bizarre or "symptomatic" behaviors.

A majority of the token economies reported to date (for example, Ayllon & Azrin, 1965; Lloyd & Garlington, 1968; Steffy, Hart, Craw, Torney, & Marlett, 1969; Winkler, 1970) have focused primarily on self-care behaviors, job performance, and the control of grossly disruptive or violent behaviors. Concentration upon these, as opposed to more complex social responses, was necessitated in many instances by the limited range of behaviors initially emitted by chronic patients.

Schaefer and Martin (1966) and Atthowe and Krasner (1968) were among the first to focus token economy programs on the set of behaviors termed the "institutionalization syndrome" (Paul, 1969). A number of researchers (Bockoven, 1963; Goffman, 1961; Kantor & Gelineau, 1965; Zusman, 1967) have observed that long-term patients tend to develop a typical set of behaviors characterized by withdrawal, dependency, and general apathy toward their environment. Hunter, Schooler, and Spohn (1962) time-sampled the behavior of 100 chronic patients and observed total immobility during 44% of the waking day. Only 2.7% of the patients' time was spent in social interaction. Greenblatt, York, and Brown (1955) reported that only 7% of chronic patients become involved in any way in on-ward activities.

The token reinforcement programs of Schaefer and Martin (1966) and Atthowe and Krasner (1968) attempted to foster activity by reinforcing social interaction, decision making, planning, and various forms of assertive behavior. Other programs (Ellsworth, 1969; Lawson, Greene, Richardson, McClure, & Pandina, 1971; O'Brien, Azrin, & Henson, 1969) have been designed to increase the frequency of social interactions among patients and participation in group activities.

Few programs have included specific procedures for dealing with "symptomatic"

behaviors, e.g., hallucinations, word salad, etc. Ayllon and Azrin (1968) have defended this policy by pointing out that the elimination of symptoms alone would not restore the patient's social functioning. Furthermore, they assert, society is willing to tolerate symptoms so long as the individual is a self-sustaining functional member. The modification of such behaviors, however, does remain a significant problem, and the issue will be addressed again later in the chapter.

The most critical aspect of a token economy system is the choice of items and activities for which tokens can be exchanged. Reinforcers that have been employed include meals, choice of special foods, the opportunity for privacy, access to recreational and entertainment activities, music, reading materials, writing materials, leave from the ward, social interactions with professional staff, devotional opportunities, commissary items (such as candy, cigarettes, and clothing), musical instruments, the use of a locked cabinet, the choice of a particular chair, television, selection of one's social company at mealtimes, items from store catalogs, and the use of a mattress with springs rather than cots. In short, it has been assumed that if the token system is to be maximally effective, it should mediate as many possible sources of reinforcement as can be arranged. Does this mean that patients may be deprived of essential rights? Where should the line be drawn between what is given freely and what must be earned? There are two typical responses to these questions. First, minimal behavior is initially required for receipt of tokens so that in effect patients never really lack the essentials (meals, beds with springs, etc.). Second, it is indeed advisable *not* to deprive patients of what they are already accustomed to having without charge. Instead, wherever possible new sources of reinforcement that are not typically available should be added to the hospital environment (e.g., bicycles, pets, fishing trips, etc.) and these new items and activities should be the major items of exchange for tokens. This is not an easy issue to resolve, however, because some chronic hospitalized patients may only be motivated by relatively basic and primitive reinforcers, and many public hospitals operate with very limited budgets (and imagination). The greatest concern is that powerful reinforcers not be used to coerce behaviors that cannot be demonstrated to be therapeutic. It would be a travesty if token economy systems were used to promote compliant behaviors for the benefit of staff rather than for the benefit of patients, and although unlikely, this possibility is real enough and must be guarded against diligently. For a more extended discussion of this ethical issue, see chapter 18 in this book and Wexler (1973) on the legal ramifications of the token economy system.

The most obvious and controversial distinctions between a token economy system and the monetary system that we are all used to involve the type of behaviors that are being compensated and the fact that patients should have to purchase desired items and activities in a hospital setting. Of course, one could take general issue with the possible "evils" of a materialistic system that we all operate under and the possible harm that can result from further propagating such a system in a treatment environment for mentally ill patients. Instead of exploring abstract arguments, however, it would seem preferable to examine in detail the evidence indicating whether or not token economies, in fact, do work for the benefit of chronic hospitalized patients.

THERAPEUTIC EFFECTS
AND EXPERIMENTAL ANALYSES

Ayllon and Azrin (1965) sought to demonstrate that the behavior of minimally functioning chronic psychiatric patients could be brought under the control of comprehensive ward contingencies. Subjects were obtained by accepting the patients whom the supervisors of the hospital's other wards wished to have transferred. The subjects were 45 females, ranging in age from 24 to 74. They had been hospitalized an average of 16 years.

Ayllon and Azrin performed a series of experiments investigating the extent to which token reinforcement controlled work performance. Aspects of their methodology weakened this demonstration. For example, they experimentally analyzed whether onward work performance would be maintained if token payment was discontinued. At the onset of the no-token phase, however, patients were instructed that they were being given a "vacation without pay," thus confusing a changed instructional set with actual withdrawal of token reinforcement.

Despite such shortcomings, Ayllon and Azrin did demonstrate the effectiveness of token reinforcement in maintaining job performance, increasing the performance of on-ward assignments, altering voluntary job preferences, and increasing the frequency of self-care behavior. It was clearly shown that the frequency of emission of target responses decreased when the response-reinforcement relationship was disrupted either by delivering tokens noncontingently, allowing free access to reinforcers, or reinforcing alternative responses.

One of the achievements of the program was that it increased the level of performance of nearly all subjects, irrespective of age, education, or years of hospitalization. Of 65 subjects, only 7 failed to perform at least one hour's work per day for a minimum of 40 days (Ayllon & Azrin, 1968).

The focus of the Ayllon and Azrin study was in-hospital behaviors. They have maintained (1968) that once functional behaviors were established, many symptomatic behaviors were no longer present. Little information, though, is provided regarding discharge and rehospitalization, and so there is little evidence that patients who were able to work consistently in the hospital could function outside of that setting. Since no direct measures of "symptomatic" responses were given, it is difficult to conclude that significant reductions in these behaviors did commonly occur.

While Ayllon and Azrin (1965) were concerned primarily with work performance, the focus of a study by Lloyd and Garlington (1968) was personal care. The subjects were 13 females, diagnosed as chronic schizophrenic, who had been hospitalized at least five years. Seven types of self-care behaviors, including hair combing, make-up, neatness and cleanliness of clothing, bed making, and eating were rated.

During phases 1 and 3 of the experiment, tokens were provided noncontingently at a morning pay station. During phases 2 and 4, tokens were contingent on behavior ratings. The results indicated that contingent tokens could control personal care behaviors. The behavior rating means were lower during phases 1 and 3, and analysis of the responding of each subject individually showed that whenever experimental conditions were changed the ratings of all patients did change in the direction of the mean.

The Lloyd and Garlington study complemented the work of Ayllon and Azrin by investigating personal care behaviors and by providing pretreatment baseline data. Schaefer and Martin (1966) also looked at some different behaviors and applied additional techniques. The focus of their study was the apathetic behaviors often evidenced by chronic psychiatric patients. The authors characterized apathy as an extremely limited and undifferentiated behavioral repertoire with respect to environmental stimuli. Forty female patients living on an experimental ward were studied. The time-sampling technique of Ayllon (1963) was employed to obtain 30 behavioral samples for each subject, spaced evenly in half-hour intervals for five-day periods. The checklist used allowed for the recording of mutually exclusive behaviors (walking, sitting, lying, etc.), concomitant behaviors (talking, reading, listening, etc.) and idiosyncratic behaviors. Apathy was operationally defined as a subject's engaging in one mutually exclusive behavior without the simultaneous performance of a concomitant behavior.

Subjects were assigned randomly to the experimental and control groups. All subjects continued to live on the token economy ward, but the control subjects received tokens noncontingently. The target behaviors were personal hygiene, work performance, and social interaction. The social interaction contingencies involved reinforcement for asking questions, emitting social amenities, speaking in group sessions, etc. Specialized procedures were instituted for individual patients. An effort was made to treat the control group in the manner in which patients are routinely dealt with on psychiatric wards.

The subjects who received tokens contingent upon desirable behaviors showed an impressive decrease in apathetic behaviors. A comparison of their apathy scores at the beginning and end of treatment revealed a very significant (.005 level) decline. The control subjects, by comparison, declined only slightly.

The study is one of a very small number in the token economy literature to employ a randomly assigned control group. Although the overall differences between the two groups were clearly significant, some representation of the variability within groups would have permitted a clearer understanding of the effects of the different procedures. The results also would have been more persuasive had more pains been taken to standardize the treatment that the controls received. The staff on the token economy ward was instructed to "treat the controls in the way in which you would treat patients before you ever heard of the analysis of behavior." This treatment was to entail verbal admonitions and praise, but only to the extent and in the manner in which these would be administered in a conventional ward program. Because the ward staff had been employing behavioral techniques for two years, however, it is doubtful that this plan could have been effectively carried out. A comparison with a control group from a different ward would have been preferable.

The effects produced in the experimental group, however, were significant in themselves. Furthermore, the success which graduates of the program achieved outside the hospital was compared with other treatment programs. The return rate of patients discharged from the token economy was 14%, while the rate from the hospital overall was 28.7%, and the rate in the state (overall) was 35%.

Atthowe and Krasner (1968) also made modification of apathetic behaviors the focus of a study. Their program was designed to foster activity, responsibility, planning for the future, and responsible decision making. Of the 86 subjects, patients in a V.A. hospital, one-third were over 65. Prior to the token economy, 60% had required constant supervision. Only 25% had grounds privileges, and only 15% were considered able to function in a boarding home. The design of the study involved a six-month baseline, a three-month shaping period, and an eleven-month experimental period. During shaping, many patients had to be escorted to the canteen, shown how to use the tokens, and cajoled into purchasing items which seemed to interest them.

The program specifically reinforced personal care, attendance at scheduled activities, helping on the ward, and interacting with patients or staff. Contingencies, though, were extended to all routine activities. In order to facilitate the transfer of training to other stations, token reinforcement was associated with social approval. Whenever a token was delivered, the administrator was to smile and express approval.

The results indicated increased responsibility and self-sufficiency. There was a dramatic increase in the number of patients who were arising on time, making the bed, and leaving the sleep area by the specified time. Improvements in the number of patients shaving, showering, and dressing appropriately were as significant.

A reduction in apathy and an increase in activity was suggested by increased attendance at group activities, gains in social interaction and communication at weekly group meetings, and a three-fold increase in the number of patients going out on passes and drawing weekly cash. A greater interest in the outside world was indicated by the numbers of persons requesting leave from the hospital. Prior to the token economy, 80% of the patients had not been off the hospital grounds in at least eight months. Eleven months after the establishment of the reinforcement program, 19% had had overnight or longer passes, 17% had had day passes, and 13% had gone on one or more 30-day trial visits.

Atthowe and Krasner reported marked increases in a number of behaviors not before investigated in the token economy setting. More information, though, could have been gleaned from their data had they presented them differently. Changes in behaviors were represented in terms of means and percentages, obscuring the changes that were occurring in individual subjects. The amount of variability among patients in response to different therapeutic techniques was not provided. It was not always possible to determine whether the improvement in behavior resulted from the performance of a few high responders or many low responders (Allen & Magaro, 1971).

The increase reported in the number of patients leaving the hospital after the establishment of the token economy was impressive. The term of the experiment, however, was approximately two years, and there has been a progressive trend in hospital administration favoring discharge, especially since the development of community treatment facilities. A comparison with the discharge rates on other wards would have controlled for this variable. The readmission rate for discharged patients which Atthowe and Krasner reported was not greatly improved by the token economy. No systematic techniques, however, were employed to foster generalization.

Ellsworth (1969) described the establishment of a token economy on a chronic ward where a milieu or "total push" program had not succeeded in effecting improvement. Thirty patients from a locked ward of the V.A. hospital were selected. They were characterized as dirty, carelessly dressed, passive, uninterested in hospital activities, and socially isolated.

The token economy was established in two phases. Token reinforcement contingencies were first applied at occupational therapy, where patients were reinforced for appropriate performance and fined for non-participation or disruptive behavior. The tokens were exchangeable for canteen items. Next, reinforcement contingencies were extended to the whole program. Self-care, performance of on-ward jobs, activity, and social behavior were rewarded.

The effects of the token reinforcement program were assessed through staff ratings which were made prior to the inception of the program and at three one-month intervals after its start. Comprehensive data are not reported, but significant improvement was observed in meal behaviors and in participation in scheduled activities (occupational therapy, recreational programs, etc.). The effects of the program as reflected by discharge data were impressive. Twenty of 28 patients were discharged, and only two rehospitalized, during the first year of the program. After two years, 32 of 44 had been released and had adapted to the community.

Steffy et al. (1969) described the application of a token economy program to a special ward which housed severely regressed and aggressive patients. The average length of stay among the patients on the ward was 20 years; the ages ranged from 18 to 74. The behavioral problems ranged from extreme withdrawal to homicidal aggression. Only 19% of the subjects could respond correctly to a set of six general orientation questions. The immediate goals of the project were to improve mealtime behaviors and self-care behaviors at bed-

time. Reinforcement was administered for reporting to the dining room, refraining from outbursts at meals, changing one's own garments, retiring at the designated time, and refraining from behaviors that would interfere with the sleep of other patients.

The token program was effective in each of these areas of study. The number of patients missing meals and the number of persons evicted from the dining room for violent behavior were both dramatically reduced. The only measure of bedtime behaviors was number of tokens earned. Although an indication of how these behaviors actually changed after the introduction of tokens would have been preferred, the data that are presented do show that the number of individuals receiving tokens for meeting the bedtime criteria did steadily increase.

Although only very short baselines were obtained and other demonstrations of experimental control were lacking, the improvements effected seemed quite substantial. After one year of treatment, 16 of the original 36 subjects were able to be placed in community boarding homes, and three more were transferred to wards that housed more typical patients. Of the patients who were placed in the community, only four have been returned to the hospital after two years. Considering the limited nature of the specific procedures employed, the authors concluded that response generalization must have occurred.

The token economy established by Winkler (1970) also dealt with violent behaviors. Activity, self-care, work performance, and planning for the future were programmed. The subjects were 66 females hospitalized an average of 12 years. Fines were made contingent upon violence and loud noise. To insure payment of fines, the costs of all items were doubled for three days following a subject's refusal to pay a fine.

Staff received no formal training, and despite their initial misgivings about the efficacy of the program, every type of behavior that was reinforced improved. Experimental control was demonstrated with several behaviors. The fines levied for noise and violent behavior were discontinued during 14 occupational therapy sessions, while being maintained on the ward. Noise and violence increased at occupational therapy, but not on the ward. The reinstitution of fines at occupational therapy resulted in a decrease in the undesirable responses. Similar control was demonstrated with regard to performance on assembly work assignments. The number of tokens paid had been contingent upon work output. When a specified number of tokens were delivered each day irrespective of output, an immediate reduction in performance occurred.

Another token economy dealing with severely regressed patients was reported by McReynolds and Coleman (1972). Forty-eight patients from the "back ward" of a state hospital were studied. They ranged in age from 18 to 83 years and averaged more than 13 years of hospitalization. The patients lacked the most basic skills and interpersonal processes: only 10% were capable of dressing themselves; 70% could not bathe themselves; 40% would not feed themselves; none had off-ward assignments; none would even carry their own food trays. Prior to the institution of the token economy, there had been no discharges or transfers from the ward in two years.

Reinforcement for desirable behavior was introduced gradually. Tokens were first delivered for carrying a food tray, next for the appropriate use of eating utensils, then for the performance of grooming behaviors, participation in recreational activities, and so on. One year after the establishment of the token economy, substantial gains had been made in eating, grooming, dressing, and involvement in activities on and off the ward. All patients carried their trays and engaged in appropriate eating behaviors. Thirty of 47 bathed and dressed themselves. Twelve had off-ward work assignments, and 11 attended occupational therapy. Thirteen had been transferred to and were able to function on an open ward. Five had made one or more home visits, and seven had been successfully placed in the community. Two others awaited discharge.

Changes in staff attitude were nearly as dramatic. Prior to the establishment of the token economy, the staff estimated that only 20% of the ward's patient's were responsive to either hospital staff or to other patients, and that none was suitable for eventual discharge. After one year, the staff reported feeling that 100% of the patients were responsive and that 30% were capable of adjustment outside. These changes were further dramatized by comparing the attitudes of the token economy staff with the attitudes of the staff on other wards. Token economy staff felt that 80% of the patients would benefit from treatment, while others felt that 50% would benefit, even though the token economy ward was a "back ward" and the others were not. Token economy staff felt that 75% of the patients were fully aware of themselves and responsible for their behaviors, while the staff of other wards felt that only 20% of their patients were so. The token economy staff felt that 90% of their patients experienced "normal human emotions," while staff on other wards felt that way about only 50% of their patients.

Although changes in patients' behavior are obviously the most important concern, such reported changes in staff attitude and behavior are also significant. Two difficulties are often encountered with respect to staff in the establishment of a token economy (McReynolds & Coleman, 1972). One concerns the general resistance which personnel often manifest upon the introduction of a new approach that requires alterations in their former routines. The other has to do with pessimistic expectations concerning the likelihood of improvement in most patients. Such expectations can effect the consistency with which reinforcement contingencies are applied. McReynolds and Coleman attribute the positive change in staff expectancies to the nature of the treatment program.

Because behaviors are specifically defined and monitored in a token economy, effects of therapy are much more readily observable. Furthermore, since the token economy forces the staff to attend to appropriate rather than disruptive behaviors, patients are automatically viewed from a more positive perspective. Finally, McReynolds and Coleman point out that "praise and attention given to the token ward from both inside and outside the hospital served to ... engender a feeling of pride in their role as *treatment* personnel and their patients as legitimate, worthwhile therapy candidates" [p. 33, italics in original]. Katz, Johnson, and Gelfand (1972) likewise observed that objective data on patients' performance may have reinforcing value for staff. More consistent performance by staff following the establishment of a token economy suggests that they find their jobs more rewarding. Winkler (1970) reports that staff absenteeism decreased by 24% four months after the institution of a token economy. Absenteeism in a control ward decreased by 3% during the same period. Ayllon and Azrin (1968) report that requests for days off or time off were reduced dramatically in their token economy.

Herson, Eisler, Smith, and Agras (1972) reported on a token economy for patients who were younger and more acute than those described in most studies. The mean age of the subjects was 26; 49% had never been hospitalized previously for psychiatric problems. The token economy program accommodated only six patients at a time, but data on 27 subjects were reported. Target behaviors were defined under the categories of work assignments, occupation therapy, responsibility (e.g., being on time for appointments), and personal hygiene. Reinforcers consisted of off-ward privileges and weekend passes. Off-ward privileges, however, were available noncontingently after working hours and on weekends. Fines were levied for disruptive behaviors.

Results were reported in terms of number of points earned. The initiation of reinforcement contingencies produced a substantial increase in point earnings over baseline. A bonus clause was later added to the system which allowed patients to earn $5 if they worked at least two hours on five consecutive days. The technique produced no change in point earnings. A $10 bonus, however, produced a significant increase. The effectiveness of the system was also demonstrated experimentally. When the reinforcement contingencies were suspended and privileges provided noncontingently, point earnings decreased. When the reinforcement contingencies were reinstituted, point earnings increased substantially. Anecdotally, the authors reported that under baseline conditions these young patients assumed a passive, inactive attitude characteristic of chronically hospitalized patients. Herson et al. also observed that the reinforcement program effected improvements in the ability of patients to make decisions and to plan ahead with respect to both in-hospital activities and extrahospital adjustments. Subjects reported that the high level of activity fostered by the program kept them from ruminating and countered depressed feelings.

Lloyd and Abel (1970) have described long-term changes in patient behavior. The changes in the behavior of 39 males and 13 female patients were assessed during the first 21 months of a token economy. After the first month of the program's operation, the patients were divided into groups. Group C patients were restricted to the ward except for scheduled activities. A member of this group could progress to group B by earning 200 tokens in a 3-week period. Members of group B had grounds privileges and could make home visits. Membership in this group was maintained by meeting a token-earning quota of 700 tokens per week. If a patient earned 10,000 tokens in any 11-week period, he advanced to group A. Patients in this group were housed in a different building and were officially out of the token program.

Patients living on the token economy

ward received tokens at pay stations three times per day. Personal care and work behaviors were reinforced at these times. Target responses were subdivided so that all patients were capable of earning tokens. During the evening, patients could earn tokens for engaging in social interaction. Individual shaping programs were instituted when necessary.

Lloyd and Abel reported that two-thirds of all changes in ward position represented improvements in socially acceptable behavior. There were 60 movements from C to B, 43 from B to C, 21 from B to A, 18 from A to discharge. Terminal status included 13 patients discharged from the hospital, 6 in group A, 12 in B, 12 in C, and 9 removed to different wards. Terminal position was not related to type of medication nor to psychiatric diagnosis (which included different types of schizophrenia, chronic brain syndrome, and mental deficiency). The authors note that the proportion of patients discharged increased on the ward after the token economy was established even though the criteria for release were more stringent after establishment of the token system.

One of the earliest token economies for psychiatric patients also employed a "leveled" system. The program, at Patton State Hospital, has been described by Bruce (1966) and by Gericke (1965). Patients were divided into three groups. Poorly functioning patients and new patients made up the "orientation group," which comprised 60% of the ward's population. They were housed in a dormitory that was furnished with bare essentials (i.e., no drapes, no bedspreads). Members of this group earned tokens by engaging in self-care behaviors, on-ward jobs, and social interactions. Target behaviors were also defined individually for specific patients. Tokens were exchangeable for meals, sleeping facilities, and television privileges. Fines were levied for grossly inappropriate behaviors such as urinating on the floor. Response costs also were applied to other maladaptive behaviors. For example, if a patient habitually wandered off,

he was required to pay a more responsible patient to "baby-sit." Fees were charged for unusual services requested of the staff such as help in bathing.

Patients who progressed to the "middle group" were housed under more desirable conditions. Each patient was assigned a private, well furnished room. Dining facilities also were more attractive. The costs of all items was higher on this level than on the lower level. Each patient transferred to this group was expected to be ready for discharge within five months; if he was not, he was returned to the orientation group.

Prior to discharge, patients were placed in a "ready-to-leave group." Though located within the hospital, the living conditions on this "ward" approximated those of the outside. Many members of this group commuted to jobs outside the hospital. The purpose of this level was to firmly establish socially desirable behaviors under conditions that simulated the extra-hospital environment. Very stiff fines were levied for any behaviors that would be inappropriate in the community.

Neither Gericke nor Bruce provide actual data on patient change within the program, but anecdotal evidence suggested the efficacy of the procedures. Patients were reported to take more responsibility for arising from bed and for being on time for activities. Patients were generally more active and engaged more frequently in social behavior. The impressions of both ward staff and hospital administration were very positive.

Allen and Magaro (1971), in evaluating change in token economies, noted that most studies have emphasized overall changes in the ward rather than changes that occur in individual patients. Such an emphasis makes it difficult to assess the extent to which different patients respond to the procedures and the extent to which behavior changes as a function of the token reinforcement program. In most reports there are indications that some withdrawn patients undergo no change whatsoever and that some patients undergo dramatic change as a result of minimal intervention. The conditions that precede behavioral change should be isolated by demonstrating the progress of individual patients.

Allen and Magaro set out to examine more closely the effects of reinforcement contingencies at the individual level. The subjects were 39 schizophrenics who had been hospitalized an average of 17 years. Attendance at 90-minute occupational therapy (OT) periods were studied. Thirty occupational therapy sessions were divided into five conditions: six free sessions, six where subjects were paid three tokens before OT, six more free sessions, six sessions where it was announced that those attending would receive three tokens after OT, and six more free sessions.

The results showed that subjects could be divided into groups on the basis of when they started attending OT. Group 1 started attending by the third free session, Group 2 started during the second condition, and Group 3 during the fourth condition. A final group never attended OT. Age and length of hospitalization were not significant variables. Subjects who could be characterized as belonging in Group 1 attended OT whether they were reinforced or not, but they made the most responses in the reward condition (4). The effect of the token economy on these subjects was to stimulate responses already being emitted at a relatively high frequency. There were nine subjects in Group 1 and 9 in Group 2. The attendance of Group 1 subjects seemed to prime the attendance of Group 2 subjects. The responses of these two groups accounted for the high-low-high attendance pattern over the first three conditions. The effect of the reinforcement procedure on the five subjects in Group 3 was to initiate responding, indicating that the program had its greatest effect here. The 16 subjects in Group 4 never responded. Four of these seemed to be functioning generally at the level of Group 1 subjects, but they had no interest in occupational therapy. This suggests the efficacy of offering reinforcement

for alternative (and equally desirable) target behaviors.

Due to the nature of the study, the generality of the conclusions must be limited. Only one response was studied, and the duration of the experiment was not long. Additional investigations focusing on patterns of responding among individual patients are indicated. Allen and Magaro suggest, however, that the results obtained do have implications for other programs. They emphasize the importance of identifying patients by their responses and categorizing them according to the method described. Group 4 type patients should be immediately transferred to an intensive treatment ward. Group 1 and 2 type patients may be placed in any ward and encouraged to plan for discharge. Group 3 patients should form the hospital's token economy ward.

Lawson et al. (1971) reported on a token economy program in which patient groups were constructed according to baseline data on activity level. The subjects were psychotic residents of a maximum security correctional hospital. During a 15-day baseline, behaviors of the hospital population were time-sampled, and 41 subjects were selected who were dependent, apathetic, and generally "institutionalized." On the basis of baseline data, subjects were divided into five groups. The most behaviorally active were assigned to Group 1 and the least active to Group 5. Target behaviors included personal care, attendance at scheduled activities, and participation in various work assignments. All contingencies were ward-wide, and no individualized reinforcement programs were carried out. Tokens were exchangeable for commissary items such as cigarettes, fruit, soda, candy, soap, records, clothing, and jewelry.

Token earnings increased during the three-month duration of the study. Group differences with respect to token earnings were statistically significant. Patients in Group 1 (those most active during baseline) consistently earned the greatest amount of tokens, while those in Group 5 earned the least. When interviewed, the more active patients were more likely to express feelings of increased control over their own behavior. The results suggested to the authors that a global program is likely to have its greatest impact on patients who are initially more active.

All patients, though, did earn tokens and did engage regularly in the reinforcing activities available. The frequency of patients leaving the unit to participate in off-ward activities increased. On weekends, when fewer reinforcing activities were available, patients tended to become apathetic. During the course of the program, however, 14 patients were transferred to higher functioning wards. Two subjects were able to return to prison and were not rehospitalized during a one-year follow-up.

The studies so far reviewed have demonstrated that token economy systems can produce beneficial changes in chronic mental hospital patients. Personal care, social interaction, job performance, and participation in occupational therapy, recreation, and social activities have all been shown to improve as a function of ward-wide reinforcement programs. At the same time, aggressive behavior and apathy have declined. In addition several of these studies have attributed increased hospital discharge and decreased recidivism rates to token economy programs. An interesting side effect on staff behavior and attitude has also been observed. For example, a few articles mentioned declines in absenteeism, and Mc-Reynolds and Coleman (1972) found that staff expectations regarding patients became much more positive.

Once it has been demonstrated that a therapeutic procedure works, the next question that needs to be objectively evaluated is whether or not it works better than available alternatives.

COMPARATIVE OUTCOME STUDIES

A number of studies have sought to evaluate token economy procedures by com-

paring their effects with those achieved by other programs. The Schaefer and Martin (1966) study described above compared the performance of patients subject to reinforcement contingencies to the performance of patients exposed to "traditional" hospital procedures. The patients in the token economy program evidenced a significant decrease in apathetic behaviors, while the behavior of the control patients changed only slightly. Patients discharged from the token economy were more successful than control patients in readjusting to community life.

Marks, Sonoda, and Schalock (1968) compared token reinforcement to "relationship therapy" with respect to their effects on social behavior, work performance, and communication skills. Twenty-two males who had been hospitalized an average of 15 years served as subjects. The relationship therapy was conducted on an individual basis by two attendants, two psychology graduate students, one physician, and four research assistants. The treatment sought to deepen self-understanding and increase self-acceptance and autonomy. It was administered one hour per day, five days per week, for 10 to 13 weeks. The reinforcement therapy involved administering tokens for desirable behaviors. Target behaviors were altered weekly according to what behaviors seemed to need improvement. Each subject received both therapies, the order balanced. Change within each subject on each of 18 ratings was assessed. Measures included behavioral ratings, the Hospital Adjustment Scale, tests of mental efficiency, associative looseness, speed of work set, social skills, and self-concept.

The subjects showed improvements on 12 of 18 ratings, but there were few consistent differences between the effects of the two methods. Both therapies produced more improvement than was made in a former study wherein subjects received drug therapy. Since the effects of reinforcement and relationship therapy were similar, the authors conclude that reinforcement was preferable because the costs of employing it are much less. They also state, however, that relationship therapy may enhance the patients' sensitivity to reinforcement contingencies.

The authors suggest that the failure to obtain greater differences between treatments may have resulted from difficulties in keeping the two treatments distinct; however, other contaminating factors were also present. All the standard hospital programs were continued during the course of the experiment. Further, the delivery of tokens was not standardized. Rather, payment was "left to the discretion of the staff," and was meant to reflect staff judgment of the patient's compliance with efforts to keep him progressing toward "higher levels of achievement." Marks et al. felt that this schedule was preferable to a more standardized one. Such a hypothesis might have been profitably pursued in a different study, but for the purposes of a comparison of reinforcement therapy with relationship therapy a more defined method of administering tokens would have been preferable.

Hartlage (1970) compared reinforcement with traditional psychotherapy techniques. Twenty-two student nurses each received five hours of training in applying reinforcement and five hours in applying psychotherapy (interpreting statements, encouraging insight, etc.). Each therapist worked with two subjects, applying one type of therapy to each. The subjects were 44 females, hospitalized an average of 17 years. Therapy was administered one hour each day for seven weeks.

The Hospital Adjustment Scale indicated that the contingent reinforcement group was superior after treatment with respect to the overall score and with respect to the communication and interpersonal relations subscales. The therapists' global ratings favored the subjects who had received contingent reinforcement. As in the Marks et al. study, difficulties were reported in keeping the two techniques separate. Here, too, results were contaminated by the fact that other hospital procedures were continued

during the experiment. In addition, it could be argued that therapists could hardly be trained in psychotherapy in five hours. The conclusion that Hartlage draws, however, does seem warranted. For untrained therapists, the employment of reinforcement therapy is preferred.

Gripp and Magaro (1971) compared patients on a token economy ward with control patients on other wards. The reinforcement program was similar to that of Atthowe and Krasner (1968), except that the staff here was larger and more specially trained. The staff was especially selected for their willingness to apply new techniques and to approach patients optimistically. The regular staff was supplemented by 10 psychology graduate students for the first half of the study. Subjects on the token economy ward received tokens for performance of on-ward and off-ward jobs and for engaging in certain desirable behaviors. A number of rating scales (Psychotic Reaction Profile, Nurses' Observation Scale for In-Patient Evaluation, etc.) were administered at the start of the program and after six months.

Results indicated that the token economy patients improved on seven of 10 scales, while control subjects improved on only two. Subjects in the token economy group became more social, more purposeful, less agitated, and less confused. Data for individual patients, however, were not presented. Furthermore, the scales used did not always produce comparable results. Scales which purported to measure the same traits or abilities (e.g., "social relations" and "social competence") varied in their results. Other problems, also, made interpretation of the data difficult. Patients were not assigned to the different wards randomly. The staff on the token economy ward was specially selected. Treatment on the control ward was not described in detail and may have been custodial. Most importantly, a comparison between the token economy group and the control group was never really made—all comparisons were made over time within each group rather than between groups.

A study conducted by Shean and Zeidberg (1971) did compare the patients in a token economy with a control group matched for age, diagnosis, and length of hospitalization. The control group lived on a different ward, but the staff-to-patient ratio was the same on both wards. Fifty-five subjects from each group were studied. The token economy program reinforced self-care, social responses incompatible with bizarre behavior. The control ward offered traditional custodial treatment. The two wards were compared on rating scales, instrumental role activity, and self-care at 6- and 12-month intervals.

The results were presented primarily in terms of means and statistical transformations. Changes in individual patients were obscured, and differences between the experimental and control groups were sometimes difficult to assess. However, the effects of one year of hospitalization were clearly different in the two groups. In the token economy group, where reinforcement was contingent upon socially approved behavior, significant increases in self-care and interpersonal behaviors were observed. Control subjects, by contrast, showed significant decreases on several indices of behavioral adjustment. On the Motility-Affect-Cooperation-Communication (MACC) Behavior Adjustment Scale, the token economy subjects increased on cooperation, communication, and social contact, while control subjects deteriorated on these same subscales. No direct measure of the frequency of "bizarre" behavior was made, but the experimental subjects required significantly lower levels of medication.

Heap, Boblitt, Moore, and Hord (1970) compared token reinforcement with traditional treatment in preparing patients for readaptation to the community, evaluating the programs both in terms of within-hospital performance and extra-hospital adjustment. The 20 most unmanageable and/or bizarre patients on a neuropsychi-atric unit were selected for the token economy. The remaining patients on the unit were assigned randomly to the token economy and to either one or two control wards. The experimental and control groups consisted of 45 patients each, comparable in age, length of hospitalization, education, and diagnosis.

Target behaviors within the token economy were determined individually for each patient and emphasized desirable social behaviors (self-care, work performance, interpersonal skills, etc.). All patients earned tokens for their participation in an elaborate ward government program. Patients were also assigned to small groups which met biweekly, with an attendant eliciting and modifying social responses. Reinforcers included meals, canteen items, and recreational activities. Fines were administered for ward rule violations and for bizarre behaviors. The control wards were basically custodial.

Within-hospital measures consisted of grooming and self-care (care of room, possessions, physical needs, and recreational behavior). During a 14-day baseline, self-care performance varied randomly. During a 14-day phase when performance was monitored and feedback administered, self-care behavior increased slightly. When social reinforcement was added to the "checking" procedure, performance improved substantially; and when tokens were added, the largest increment was obtained. Similar results were reported for grooming behavior.

After 6 months, only 11 of the 45 patients initially assigned to the token economy remained, including just four of the 20 "severe" cases. After 35 months, 478 patients had passed through the token economy program. Sixty-eight percent had been discharged or furloughed, and 14% of these had been rehospitalized. For the whole hospital, the rate of return from furlough during the same time period was 50%.

The results clearly demonstrated the superiority of the experimental procedure over custodial treatment. It was not possible, unfortunately, to determine from the data the relative contribution to the overall effect made by the various techniques (token reinforcement for specific responses, group discussions, ward government, increased staff attention) that comprised the experimental procedure.

Birky, Chambliss, and Wasden (1971) compared a token economy program with a traditional psychiatric approach that provided more active therapy than most custodial programs. As in the Heap et al. (1970) study, the focus of evaluation was patient readaptation to the community. The token economy provided ward-wide contingencies for self-care behaviors and on-ward jobs. The patients also attended classes designed to develop skills that are important outside the hospital, such as food preparation, housekeeping, and shopping. Frequent trips to the community and participation in community activities were programmed. In addition, individualized reinforcement contingencies were instituted for each patient. The control group was comprised of two open wards. Chemotherapy and weekly ward meetings were provided for all patients, while selected patients also received individual psychotherapy. Subjects in the control and experimental groups did not differ in education, diagnosis, marital status, or length of hospitalization.

Release and recidivism data after 14 months of treatment revealed no significant differences between the token economy ward and the traditional programs with respect to the total number of patients discharged or to the number of patients remaining outside the hospital for at least six months. The data indicated, however, that the token economy was more successful than the other programs in discharging patients who were chronic. The patients discharged from the token economy had been hospitalized a significantly greater number of years than those discharged from the traditional programs.

The failure of Birky et al. to find many differences between the effects of reinforce-

ment therapy and traditional treatment may have been at least in part a function of the measures employed. As the authors note, successful adaptation in the community is not determined totally by treatment variables, but rather is influenced by outside factors, such as the amount of support available to the patient from his family and from after-care agencies. Many patients may improve greatly in treatment yet fail in the community or fail to be discharged because of outside factors.

Maley, Feldman, and Ruskin (1973) avoided discharge measures in comparing different treatment programs by developing objective, standardized tests of behavioral functioning. The subjects were 40 female schizophrenics who had been hospitalized more than six years. Half were randomly assigned to a token economy, while half remained on their original wards and received the treatment available. The token economy was similar to that of Ayllon and Azrin, focusing on self-care, social interaction, and appropriate work performance.

Behavioral functioning was measured in a standardized interview and by videotape ratings. The interview procedure was comprised of four parts: (1) 17 questions relating to orientation for time, place, and person; (2) a spending task that required the patient to purchase items and make change; (3) a task requiring discrimination of colors and various geometric figures; and (4) a command task that required the subject to perform specific behaviors. A videotape made of the interview was rated by three naive graduate students according to items of the MACC Behavioral Adjustment Scale.

The results clearly demonstrated the effectiveness of the token reinforcement procedures. The token economy subjects, in comparison to the controls, were significantly better oriented, more adept in making monetary transactions, and superior in following commands. They exhibited significantly more cooperation and more appropriate mood and did not display as much anxiety, unusual motor activity, or bizarre behavior.

The behaviors assessed by Maley et al. were clearly behaviors of importance for treatment, and the results unequivocally supported the effectiveness of reinforcement procedures in developing behaviors necessary for release and community adjustment. Aspects of the testing procedure, however, made controlled comparisons with the other wards difficult. Although the token economy subjects had not been specifically trained on any of the responses tested, similarity between the token economy ward and the test setting might have biased test outcome. The token economy subjects might have been less anxious in the test situation and more motivated to perform for the experimenter. The consistent use of tokens by the experimental subjects would influence the performance on the monetary tasks. Motor performance and general responsiveness could have been affected by the level of medication, which likely varied between the wards.

Many important treatment and assessment variables are controlled in a long-term comparative study still being conducted in Illinois by Gordon Paul and associates (Paul, 1971). The effectiveness of token reinforcement and milieu therapy are being compared with respect to the development of social, work, and personal care behaviors.

Subjects are chronic schizophrenics matched in age, socioeconomic level, length of hospitalization, and other descriptive variables. The milieu treatment program focuses on problem solving, group pressure, and the communication of expectations and needs. A trained paraprofessional staff rotates between the two treatment wards. Measures include a time-sample behavioral checklist and three assessment instruments shown to be reliable and valid with chronic populations: the Social Breakdown Syndrome Gradient Index, the Nurses' Observational Scale for Inpatient Evaluation, and the Minimal Social Behavior Scale (Lentz, Paul, & Calhoun, 1971).

The longterm effectiveness of the two procedures has not yet been determined, but Paul, Tobias, and Holly (1972) have reported on the contribution of psychotropic medication to both treatment procedures. Low dosage phenothiazine therapy is commonly believed to be effective in controlling psychotic behavior (Bellak & Loeb, 1969; Klein & Davis, 1969), and more than 85% of chronic psychiatric patients are maintained on medication. On both the milieu and token economy wards two patient subgroups were formed. Maintenance medication was continued in one group, while drugs were abruptly withdrawn and replaced with placebo medication in the other group. Neither patients, staff administering the medication, nor observers were aware of the manipulation.

Treatment continued for 17 weeks. The results indicated that medication did not contribute to the effectiveness of either reinforcement or milieu therapy. Degree of improvement was similar among the drug-maintained and placebo subjects, although medication appeared to temporarily impair the response of patients to the treatment programs. Not a single incident of "acute psychotic episode" was observed when medication was withdrawn. The authors conclude that where an active treatment program exists, medication should be discontinued.

In the studies reviewed above, token economy programs were compared with traditional custodial treatment and with other active therapy programs. Relative to other treatments, token economy procedures were found to be effective in modifying self-care behavior, in developing social and interpersonal skills, in fostering cooperation and activity, and in modifying emotional behavior in a positive direction. Data on discharge and recidivism have supported the effectiveness of the token economy procedures with chronically hospitalized patients.

Few studies, however, were totally adequate with respect to experimental controls. Large between-group discrepencies in staff competency and incomplete specification of conditions in control programs are recurrent problems. At least one study (Birky et al., 1971) failed to find decided differences between the effects of reinforcement therapy and an active traditional program. Additional evaluative research appears warranted.

Carlson, Herson, and Eisler (1972) have asserted that the experimental evaluation of token reinforcement procedures requires comparison of the token economy with two different control groups. One of the control conditions should be an attention placebo. All procedures employed in the token economy would be employed in this group, but would be administered noncontingently. The other control group should be exposed to a standard hospital program that actively employs traditional treatments, including chemotherapy, individual and group psychotherapy, occupational therapy, and milieu techniques.

Controlled comparisons of this sort could have wide implications for the determination of public hospital policy. Foster (1969) analyzed all the costs involved in operating a token economy for 32 patients and a custodial ward for the same number of patients. For a full year of operation, the cost of the token economy was only $424 more than the custodial program. If token economy programs are indeed effective in making possible the discharge of long-term chronic patients who make up two-thirds of the population of public facilities, the employment of token economies as standard treatment could produce enormous financial savings.

PROBLEMS IN THE APPLICATION OF TOKEN ECONOMY PROCEDURES

Ayllon and Azrin (1965) reported that 18% of their subjects were relatively unaffected by the reinforcement procedures. Steffy et al. (1969) reported that the behavior of six of their eight socially withdrawn patients was not much altered. Atthowe and Krasner (1968) reported no marked behavior change for 10% of their subjects. There is, in fact, a small percentage of patients in almost all token economy programs (Kazdin & Bootzin, 1972) who remain unaffected by the procedures. This failure seems due, in individual instances, to either practical problems of implementation or to the institution of an inadequate or inappropriate operant paradigm.

The major problems in implementation include consistent reinforcement of target responses, the minimization of peer or other reinforcement for undesirable behaviors, monitoring the application of contingencies, and the escaping of contingencies. Most of these problems are technical ones, however, and space limitations do not permit a full discussion here.

A general means of providing for the successful implementation of a program, though, is to enlist the patients' cooperation in it. Planning programs in conjunction with the subjects, assigning them duties of administration, entering into contractual agreements, and emphasizing their responsibility all encourage the subjects' involvement. Dominguez, Acosta, and Carmona (1972) demonstrated that patients can be reliably employed within a token economy to observe behavior, distribute tokens, tabulate earnings, and graph data.

With regard to the application of inadequate paradigms, at least four types of shortcomings are obvious. The first problem concerns the behaviors that are reinforced. In attempting to reinforce only adaptive behaviors, the early token economy programs (Ayllon & Azrin, 1965; Atthowe & Krasner, 1968) focused primarily on behaviors that were somewhat complex (e.g., work performance). Many subjects in these programs had been hospitalized a number of years, however, and had become very inactive. Failure of some patients to respond, therefore, was due to their not emitting any of the behaviors that the system reinforced.

This problem has been recognized, and most recent token economies have subdivided each target response into components that are simple enough for all patients to emit. Programs have reinforced any behavior that is at all in a positive direction for a particular patient. A subject may be initially reinforced, for instance, for sitting in the middle of a floor rather than lying there.

The second problem concerns the absence of effective reinforcers for particular subjects. Ayllon and Azrin (1968) have indicated that this was a crucial factor with respect to the patients who did not respond to their program. One possible solution to this problem is to utilize as reinforcers the only high-frequency behaviors that these subjects demonstrate—in many cases, eating and sleeping. Food, of course, should not be withheld, but the type of food available may be manipulated. A nutritionally complete, but uninteresting, diet could be provided free, while any other food would require tokens. Sleep behavior can be similarly manipulated. The privilege of sleeping on a mattress with a spring, as opposed to a cot, can be a very effective reinforcer.

Mitchell and Stoffelmayr (1973) employed sitting as a reinforcer with extremely inactive schizophrenics who did not respond to tangible reinforcement. Sitting was made contingent upon the completion of a specified amount of work. The effectiveness of the procedure in increasing work performance was demonstrated experimentally. There is a danger, however, in using such primitive sources of reinforcement. Although many medical interventions are in and of themselves unpleasant (e.g., surgery), one must always be on the lookout to promote the most humane means of achieving desired therapeutic ends. Use of the above reinforcers can probably be depended upon in extreme cases, but they should only be used as a last resort with proper safeguards against abuses. Such procedures may be effective in initiating minimal activity, but

in order to develop and maintain a level of behavior that would be adaptive on the outside, additional and more imaginative reinforcers must be added and employed at maximum efficiency.

Periodic reviews of the items that were being purchased were made in the first token economies (Ayllon & Azrin, 1968) to insure the use of all reinforcers. More sophisticated procedures have since evolved. Kagel and Winkler (1972) support the use of economic principles. Economic theory provides a frame of reference for conceptualizing relationships between income and expenditures and phenomena such as inflation. It also provides rational bases for decisions concerning the management of wages and prices. Winkler (1972) has put forward a number of techniques for disrupting the output equilibrium which tends to develop when savings reach certain levels. In different situations, it may be necessary to manipulate the prices of certain items, extend the range of items available, or require that tokens be spent within a specified number of days after delivery (force spending).

With respect to the manipulation of prices, research by Winkler (1971) has indicated that a rise in the price of certain items (e.g., tea) will produce an increase in token spending, but a rise in the cost of other items (e.g., cigarettes) will have an opposite effect. It was also shown that as income increases, the proportion of tokens spent on needs decreases while that which is spent on luxuries increases. This suggests that if a disruption in equilibrium is desired, and one wishes to accomplish this by extending the range of goods available, the best sort of goods to introduce are luxury items.

Fethke (1972) has criticized Winkler's failure to consider the real income implications of some of the experimental manipulations that he performed. When the price of cigarettes is decreased, for example, consumers may anticipate that the reduction is temporary and may therefore buy and store cigarettes. This will, of course, alter the demand both during and after the price reduction phase. In general, Fethke has suggested that any accumulation of tokens is to be discouraged, as wealth permits a degree of independence from current contingencies.

A third major problem with which token economies contend is that little feedback is received from patients regarding the ways in which the program is affecting them. Chronic patients have learned in many cases not to communicate their needs, problems, or the possible solutions to these. O'Brien et al. (1969) instituted a program to reinforce suggestions from patients. The procedure involved priming suggestions and then acting upon them immediately. Thirteen patients in a token economy ward were the subjects. The age range was 29 to 69; the average length of hospitalization, 18 years. A suggestion was defined as a direct request for a change in or an addition to the ward treatment program. Questions were systematically asked concerning how the patient was doing, what he would like to have, and what changes he would like to see. The purpose of these questions was to prime responses. They were asked in a situation where it was possible for the therapist to take immediate action (e.g., by writing an order) upon a patient's request.

The results showed that the number of suggestions by patients increased as a direct function of the percent granted. The number of patients making requests in a group meeting increased as a function of the probability that the staff member would follow the suggestion. The increased responsiveness resulted in the staff's discovery of previously unrevealed medical problems and the discovery of new reinforcers. Greater initiative and assurance was noted among patients.

The last major problem regarding effectiveness concerns individualized contingencies. The first reports in the token economy

literature implied or stated that ward contingencies were sufficient to modify all relevant behaviors. Ayllon and Azrin (1965; 1968) expressed the belief that once functional behaviors are established, "symptomatic" behaviors will disappear. Lloyd and Abel (1970) suggested that their individual shaping procedures could be eliminated if the overall ward rules were more appropriate.

Upper (1973) designed a program to deal with individual problem behaviors on a ward-wide basis. All nursing personnel administered fines in the form of violation tickets. The fines applied to behaviors not usually covered by ward-wide contingencies —for example, shouting, destroying property, obscenity, nudity, and possessing contraband. Patients who engaged in no violations on a particular day received bonus tokens. During an eight-week experimental period, a statistically significant reduction in the frequency of target behaviors was obtained.

If fines are relied upon heavily, however, the program incentives may be destroyed. The accumulation of fine debts by a particular patient may result in his exclusion from back-up reinforcers. In a program described by Doty, McInnis, and Paul (1974), 75% of the patients possessed standing fines and were making inadequate progress toward reducing the debts.

To cope with the problem, two new rules were created: (1) eligibility to spend tokens for back-up reinforcers could be purchased by making a payment on a standing fine; (2) a proportional pay-off schedule reduced a patient's debt as a function of the amount of time that passed without his incurring a new fine—for example, after two days the fine could be paid off at a ratio of 1:3, after eight days 1:10, after 14 days 1:20. These procedures were effective in increasing payments on fines and in reducing the frequency of some types of undesirable behavior.

There is another potential problem to wide-scale use of fines. Some undesirable behaviors occur at very low frequencies, e.g., once a week, or once a month, or even once every three months. Contingencies cannot be readily employed in these instances. For example, angrily breaking the dishes on the average of once a month is sufficient to cause placement in the more disturbed wards, but the low frequency makes a fine system relatively useless.

It was always hoped that all forms of undesirable behavior might be supplanted merely by strengthening more desirable behavior. In the chronic mental hospital population, however, there is only minimal evidence to either support or contradict this notion. On the positive side, O'Brien and Azrin (1972) reinforced self-care and social skills in a female schizophrenic and observed a decrease in her formerly high rate of screaming. It may be more difficult, however, to functionally displace covert maladaptive thinking processes in this manner.

It has never been demonstrated, for instance, that delusions may not exist concurrently with adequate work responses. This is an important issue with regard to the maintenance of patients outside the hospital. Symptomatic behaviors may well be tolerated on a hospital job, but the expression of delusions or bizarre ideas is the behavior most frequently resulting in the rehospitalization of released patients (Hoenig & Hamilton, 1966; Lorei, 1967; Sanders, Smith, & Weinman, 1967).

The need to attack certain behavioral problems directly and individually has been acknowledged in a number of recent reports (Herson et al., 1972; Pomerleau, Bobrove, & Harris, 1972; Shean & Zeidberg, 1971). Whether it will be necessary to institute individual programs in *every* token economy, or whether ward-wide contingencies can effectively modify *all* symptomatic behaviors, is still an open question. Up to the present, however, the failure of ward-wide programs to deal adequately with the extreme problems of individual subjects has been one factor in the token economy's lack of success with some patients. The following

section will consider individualized approaches to specific problem behaviors.

Individualized Procedures

As noted in the introduction to this chapter, a detailed review will not be made of individual treatment approaches distinct from token economy programs.[1] However, a survey of the behaviors targeted and the therapeutic techniques employed will reflect the scope of this literature.

A number of studies have attempted to modify or establish various self-care behaviors. Mertins and Fuller (1963) employed food, praise, and shaping techniques (instructions and aid) to increase the frequency of shaving among regressed psychotic patients. Milby, Stenmark, and Horner (1967) applied social reinforcement to increase self-wheeling behavior in a psychotic patient who was confined to a wheelchair. Wagner and Paul (1970) applied several different procedures to reduce incontinence on a ward of chronic mental patients.

Considerable attention has been devoted to the development of appropriate self-care behaviors at meals. Ayllon and Haughton (1962) shaped promptness for meals by gradually reducing the time limit for entering the dining area. An increase in self-feeding behavior was observed when coaxing and feeding by aides was eliminated. Ayllon and Azrin (1964) decreased objectionable cafeteria behavior by delaying the delivery of food. They also investigated instruction, reinforcement, and instruction plus reinforcement in teaching patients to select proper eating utensils. Ayllon (1965) utilized withdrawal of social reinforcement to diminish the tendency of a psychotic patient to linger in the dining area following meals.

Several programs have dealt with excesses or deficits in eating. Agras (1967) reported

[1] Individualized procedures have been reviewed by James A. Mulick in an unpublished manuscript, "Behavior Therapy with Chronic Psychiatric Patients," University of Vermont, 1973.

on a hospitalized male schizophrenic who had ceased to eat regularly three years prior to treatment. Staff were instructed to ignore his refusals to eat, and food was made available only at regular specified times. Moore and Crum (1969) treated a chronic schizophrenic female for obesity using response contingent withdrawal of social reinforcement. The patient was weighed daily. If she had lost weight the therapist praised her; if she had gained, the therapist expressed disapproval and asked her to return to the ward.

The overuse of drugs is a significant problem in public mental hospitals. Typically, medication is prescribed freely, and patients who have become chronic and adapted to the "sick" role often request medication more frequently than is needed. Parrino, George, and Daniels (1971) sought to decrease this latter behavior via reinforcement techniques. The subjects were 19 males and 19 females on a token economy ward where tokens were earned for personal care and through individual programs. An effort was made to reduce the freqency of requests for PRN (*pro re nata,* "as needed") medication by charging tokens. The requests involved primarily minor tranquilizers, sleeping pills, and aspirin. During a baseline period females requested 170 pills per week and males 60 per week.

During phase 1, PRNs could be received free at a certain time, but cost two tokens each at other times (in a 16-token per day economy). During this phase the number of requests were reduced to 71 per week for females and 19 for males. During phase 2 scheduled PRNs cost two tokens; at unscheduled times they cost four tokens each. Requests by females were reduced to 54, while requests by males did not decrease. During phase 3 all PRNs cost four tokens. Requests were reduced to 20 and two, for females and males respectively.

A variety of behaviors disruptive to ward life have been dealt with effectively. The hoarding of towels and clothes has been treated by stimulus satiation (Ayllon, 1963).

The annoying behavior of a psychotic patient who continually entered the nurses' station was extinguished by ignoring her (Ayllon & Michael, 1959). Compulsive handwashing in a hospitalized psychotic patient was eliminated by extinction and social reinforcement (Baily & Atchinson, 1969). Abusive speech, assaultive behavior, and other disruptive responses have been modified by withdrawing attention and reinforcing incompatible responses, and by using fines (Ayllon & Michael, 1959; Sushinsky, 1970).

A number of studies have been directed toward verbal behavior. Procedures used to reinstate speech in mute or near-mute psychotics have included modeling, response shaping, and social and tangible reinforcement (Baker, 1971; Sabatasso & Jacobson, 1970; Sherman, 1965; Wilson & Walters, 1966). Programs have focused on the expression of affect (Weiss, Krasner, & Ullman, 1963), the occurrence of self-referred affect statements in interviews (Salzinger & Pisoni, 1958; Salzinger & Portnoy, 1964), and the modification of affect responses on the ward (Reisinger, 1972).

Complex verbal responses have been studied, including the conditioning of common associations (Sommer, Witney, & Osmond, 1962; Ullman, Krasner, & Edinger, 1964) and the occurrence of "sick talk" and "healthy talk" in interview situations (Ullman, Forsman, Kenny, McInnis, Unikel, & Zeisset, 1965). Meichenbaum (1969) decreased the percentage of "sick talk" and increased the abstractness of responses in a comprehensive study of verbal behavior. Little (1966) investigated the effects of social interaction on abstract thinking.

Several procedures have been used to develop social responses in chronic patients. King, Armitage, and Tilton (1960) employed a problem-solving apparatus that required complex motor responses and socially cooperative behavior. Ayllon and Haughton (1962) made entrance to the dining hall contingent upon the operation of an apparatus that required the cooperation of two patients. Leitenberg, Wincze, Butz, Callahan, and Agras (1970) applied token reinforcement to modify the social behavior of a chronic patient, and Ullman, Krasner, and Collins (1961) investigated a group approach.

INDIVIDUALIZED PROCEDURES APPLIED TO DELUSIONAL BEHAVIOR

Delusional behavior in chronic schizophrenics has been more thoroughly investigated in the context of individualized behavior programs. Delusions, or beliefs maintained despite evidence to the contrary, are common in psychoses (Rettersöl, 1966). Hallucinations (perceptions in the absence of corresponding external stimuli) may also be associated with delusional thought (DSM–II, 1968). Delusional behavior has been researched in the behavior modification literature more completely than any other form of psychotic behavior. Two factors which may have stimulated these efforts are (1) the important role played by delusional behavior in the re-hospitalization of furloughed patients (Paul, 1969), and (2) the ineffectiveness of traditional psychotherapeutic techniques in modifying paranoid ideation (Grinspoon, Ewalt, & Shader, 1967; May, 1968).

The majority of behavior modification approaches to delusional behavior have employed positive reinforcement. Typically, "normal" verbalizations are rewarded with tangible and/or social reinforcers, while delusional speech is ignored. A small number of studies have employed desensitization or self-control techniques.

Rickard, Dignam and Horner (1960) and Rickard and Dinoff (1962) were among the first to apply operant techniques to the treatment of delusional behavior. A 60-year-old male psychotic was interviewed in 45-minute sessions. During one phase of treatment, the therapist turned away from the patient whenever speech was delusional. Interest and approval were expressed whenever verbalizations were appropriate. Rational speech increased by 100% during reinforcement.

A number of other studies employed similar procedures without experimental controls. When Kennedy (1964) expressed disapproval of delusional speech and socially reinforced rational speech, "sick talk" decreased substantially. Drugs, however, had been introduced simultaneously with the initiation of the reinforcement procedure, making it impossible to attribute the effects to one agent. Rashkis (1966) treated four chronic delusional patients as a group. Positive social reinforcement was administered for rational talk and negative comments for inappropriate speech. No actual data on delusional speech were presented, but all patients were discharged after 23 sessions. Other studies have employed token reinforcement (Hertz, Migler, & Feingold, 1968) and the contingent attention of the nursing staff (Ayllon & Michael, 1959; Lindsley, 1960).

Ayllon and Haughton (1964) reported the first experimental demonstration of operant control of delusional speech. The verbal behavior of three hospitalized patients was systematically monitored during a baseline of 15 to 20 days. Nurses interacted with the patients during three-minute intervals and rated all responses as "psychotic" or "neutral." During one phase of the study, the nurses' attention (and occasionally cigarettes and candy) were contingent upon delusional speech, while attention was withheld for neutral speech. These contingencies produced an increase in delusional speech and a decrease in neutral speech. When the contingencies were reversed, delusional speech decreased and neutral speech increased.

In another controlled study, Wincze, Leitenberg, and Agras (1972) examined the effects of feedback and token reinforcement on delusional behavior. The subjects were 10 paranoid schizophrenics who had been hospitalized an average of 12 years. A list of 105 delusional statements was compiled for each patient. For each treatment session,

15 statements were randomly drawn and a question was asked regarding each statement. During feedback phases, the patient was informed whether or not his response to a question was correct (i.e., rational). During reinforcement phases, the patient was reinforced with tokens for correct responses. Generalization of effects were tested by: (1) time-sampling ward behavior, and (2) administering an independent psychiatric interview following each phase of the study. Reinforcement produced a substantial decrease in the delusional behavior of six of the nine patients who completed the study. Instruction without reinforcement was found to be ineffective. No change in percentage of delusional speech was observed, however, on the ward or in the psychiatric interviews.

Generalization of treatment effects was assessed in a study conducted by Liberman, Teigen, Patterson, and Baker (1973). The subjects were four chronic paranoid schizophrenics who had been hospitalized an average of 17 years. The nursing staff held 10-minute interviews with each patient four times per day. In addition, each patient met with a particular therapist every evening for a 30-minute "chat" over snacks. This session served as a reinforcer and as a means of measuring generalization.

During baseline, the evening chats and snacks were provided noncontingently. During the first phase of treatment, the 10-minute interviews with the nurses were terminated as soon as the patients' speech became delusional, and the length of the evening chat was proportional to the amount of time spent in interview with the nursing staff. This procedure produced a statistically significant reduction in delusional speech in all four subjects.

During a second treatment phase, reinforcers were faded. When the evening chat was available only two nights per week, three of the subjects maintained their former level of rational speech. In a third phase of treatment, two of the subjects were exposed to questioning designed to provoke delusional speech. Under these conditions the percentage of rational talk decreased, but still remained greater than the baseline level.

Throughout the study, the patients were free to express delusional material during the evening chats. However, three of four showed a decrease in delusional speech during these sessions, and two of the four showed an increase in rational speech. The amount of generalization observed in this study was greater that that reported by Wincze et al. (1972). The authors suggest that increased generalization may have resulted from their use of social rather than token reinforcement. The methodology employed in the two studies, however, differed in many respects.

Liberman (1972) employed time out (TO) from positive reinforcement in treating a delusional patient who had been hospitalized 13 years. The patient was interviewed in 30-minute sessions. Whenever the patient spoke delusionally, the interview was interrupted for five minutes. The procedure produced a decrease in the average rate of delusions during interviews and during observation periods. When the contingencies were suspended, the rate of delusions increased in both settings. Reinstitution of the contingencies again produced a decrease in delusions. During the course of the study, the patient's medication was gradually reduced from 600 mg. chlorpromazine per day to zero medication.

Relaxation and desensitization procedures have also been employed in treating chronic delusional patients. Cowden and Ford (1962) applied systematic desensitization (SD) with two chronic paranoid schizophrenics. Treatment with one subject focused on a phobic inability to socialize. By the end of therapy, hallucinations, ideas of reference, and other unusual thoughts had ceased. A second subject treated was not able to achieve relaxation.

Zeisset (1968) studied 48 patients who

were hospitalized an average of 64 months and who demonstrated hallucinatory or delusional speech. Patients were divided into four groups. Group 1 received SD; Group 2 received progressive relaxation training; Group 3 received attention plus the suggestion that the therapy was effective; Group 4 was a no-treatment control. On a behavioral checklist both experimental groups (1 and 2) improved significantly more than either control group, but did not differ from each other. On a self-report measure of anxiety, the pooled data from groups 1 and 2 was significantly lower than the pooled data from the two control groups. There were no significant differences on ward measures.

Two studies reported SD with delusional patients who were not chronic. Wickramasekera (1967) treated a hospitalized female, diagnosed as paranoid schizophrenic. SD and instruction were employed in dealing with the patient's anxious feelings about sexual relations with her husband. The procedure was effective in eliminating delusional thoughts. Slade (1972) utilized SD in training an 18-year-old psychotic male who reported auditory hallucinations. A hierarchy of situations concerning the subject's home and family was employed. Auditory hallucinations decreased from 15.8% of times sampled during baseline to 1.9% during follow-up.

Self-control techniques have been employed with psychotic patients who were not chronic. Rutner and Bugle (1969) employed a self-monitoring technique to treat hallucinatory behavior in a hospitalized patient. During the first phase of the study the patient privately recorded the occurrence of hallucinatory behavior. During the second phase a public chart was maintained and social reinforcement was administered. Self-reports of hallucinatory behavior decreased to a low level during phase 1. During phase 2, the frequency decreased to 0 and remained at that level. Bucher and Fabricatore (1970) employed a self-shock technique to treat hallucinations in a hospitalized male. The procedure temporarily eliminated the hallucinations, but the problem returned after the patient was released from the hospital.

Liberman (1972) described an unpublished study by Patterson who recorded psychotic patients' reports of auditory hallucinations and employed the recordings in a satiation paradigm. The patients were exposed to the content of their hallucinations for one and a half hours per day over 40 to 80 days A decrease in hallucinatory behavior was observed in each patient.

In summary, a considerable amount of research has been devoted to the control of delusional behavior. Although only four studies (Ayllon & Haughton, 1964; Liberman, 1972; Liberman et al., 1973; Wincze et al., 1972) employed adequate experimental controls, it has been clearly demonstrated that delusional speech can be controlled through operant techniques. An important unresolved question is whether delusional "thought" is modified by the same methods. The issue is especially important in the case of paranoid patients who have acted violently on the basis of delusional beliefs and who are incarcerated under criminal law. The modification of delusional speech under these circumstances involves weighty legal and moral responsibilities to society. In attempting to assess, or to modify, delusional thought, it is possible only to deal with overt delusional behavior. If the patient's verbal behavior is rational under a variety of stimulus conditions, it might be justifiably inferred that his beliefs are rational. Risks are necessarily involved, however, and where possible other correlates of verbal behavior should be measured.

Summary and Conclusions

There seems to be clear evidence that token economies and individualized behavioral interventions can cause clinically relevant changes in chronic mental hospital patients' behavior. There is also some data to support the tentative conclusion that reinforcement programs are more effective than other conventional treatment programs provided in state and VA hospital settings. Nevertheless, reinforcement programs in and of themselves cannot be considered panaceas.

Patients who have been hospitalized for 10 to 30 years pose a major problem for society. Family ties have often been lost; job opportunities are almost nil. Even though a token economy may have brought the patient to a surprisingly satisfactory level of functioning in the hospital, the opportunity for leading a productive life on the outside is still severely impaired. Statistics on increased release from hospital or reduced return to hospital following release are encouraging but not sufficient. Former state hospital patients can be vegetating in boarding houses and be leading no happier a life out of hospital than they led in hospital.

The implicit assumption underlying any treatment is that the program will help the patient to function in the natural environment. The extent to which the effects of token reinforcement procedures transfer to settings outside the hospital has not been sufficiently addressed. Several techniques have been suggested to help promote such transfer. Although we will review these, it should be noted that large-scale experiments to assess maintenance of reinforcement effects of specific behaviors in the outside environment have not yet been conducted. After-care or continuity of care following participation in reinforcement programs in mental hospitals has been a relatively neglected research area.

Most forms of behavior are maintained in the natural environment by social approval and peer pressure. Several token economies (Atthowe & Krasner, 1968; Cohen, Florin, Grusche, Meyer-Osterkamp, & Sell, 1972; McReynolds, 1972) and a number of studies of verbal operant conditioning in psychiatric patients (Baker, 1971; Drennen, Gallman, & Sausser, 1969; Kale, Kay, Whelan, & Hopkins, 1968) have paired praise with tokens or other tangible reinforcement in order to enhance the reinforcing value of praise. Stahl, Thomson, Leiten-berg and Hasazi (1974) experimentally demonstrated that this could indeed be accomplished. Three socially unresponsive psychiatric patients were studied in a within-subject multiple baseline design. Praise was administered contingent upon the occurrence of target responses. Prior to its being paired with tokens, praise was ineffective as a reinforcer. However, praise acquired reinforcing properties through being consistently associated with token reinforcement.

Pomerleau et al. (1972) designed a program to extend the token economy procedures to include a greater use of social reinforcers. Patients were organized into pairs and polydyads in order to promote mutual responsibility in the performance of work assignments and to facilitate the development of the socially cooperative behaviors that are crucial outside of the hospital. The system was designed to supplement ward contingencies by bringing group pressure to bear on irresponsible patients. The program designated groups of patients and made the group responsible for the behavior of each of its members in the completion of assigned tasks. Over three years, more than 55% of the patients entering the program left the hospital and were able to remain outside.

Transfer of treatment effects to the extra-hospital environment should also be enhanced if characteristics of the treatment program simulate conditions outside the hospital. Toward this end it is possible to manipulate the delay in time between the occurrence of a response and the delivery of reinforcement and the delay between the delivery of tokens and the opportunity to exchange them for other reinforcers (Kazdin, in press). Atthowe and Krasner (1968) delayed payment for job performance until the end of the week with better functioning patients.

The establishment within a token economy of institutions that the patients will encounter outside has been suggested by Kagel and Winkler (1972). Banks, stores, and small factories should become a part of the hospitals. To date this has never been accomplished to the extent necessary.

A related approach to the facilitation of transfer effects involves directly shifting the discriminitive stimuli for reinforcement to the extra-hospital environment. Exposure to the outside environment and reinforcement under those conditions may be programmed by providing frequent trips outside the hospital (Kelley & Henderson, 1971). Liberman (1971) has reported on the adaptation of token economy procedures to an open day-treatment setting, and Henderson and Scoles (1970) established a residential treatment facility in the community. The aim of this program was to develop vocational behaviors, social adjustment, and counter-symptom behavior. Patients were referred to as "residents" and were regarded as responsible for their behavior. In order to develop social skills, there were regularly scheduled dances, discussion groups, and other recreational activities. Patients were rewarded for performance in these events at four different levels of social participation. As a subject improved, the program provided for progressively longer stays outside of the treatment setting. A comparison with matched subjects from the state hospital and general hospital revealed that this facility tended to keep the patients longer per admission, but that the average length of hospitalization and rehospitalization was shorter. It showed as well that the token economy subjects spent more time in the community and more time employed.

Training family members or other persons from the patients' natural environment in the application of behavioral principles is a procedure of considerable promise (Henderson & Scoles, 1970). Cheek, Laucius, Mahncke and Beck (1971) have investigated procedures for training relatives of discharged patients to observe behavior, analyze interactions, and administer rewards and punishments systematically. Many learned to apply the procedures effectively, and most thought the training valuable.

The issue of generalization and maintenance of reinforcement effects outside of hospital is not the only area where considerably more work is needed. For example, it is still unclear whether or not the bulk of psychotic behaviors exhibited by mental hospital patients can in fact be modified by reinforcement programs. Agitated depression, manic behaviors, disordered thinking processes, hallucinations—the bulk of psychotic behavior has been virtually ignored. Although it is probably true that in very regressed patients these "exotic" behaviors may not occur very frequently, they are seen often enough to be considered a continuing problem for token economies. As yet, there is little direct evidence that such low-frequency psychotic behaviors can be directly and permanently affected by reinforcement procedures. Although reinforcement techniques should not be expected to answer all the problems exhibited by chronic psychotic patients, the boundaries of effectiveness have yet to be empirically drawn.

There has been a fantastic worldwide growth of reinforcement programs in mental hospitals during the past 10 years. Although there is reason to believe that the potential of these programs has yet to be fully realized, unbridled enthusiasm would be misplaced. Such reinforcement programs have undoubtedly made a major contribution to treatment of the chronic mental hospital patient; it is equally apparent, however, that they represent only a partial answer.

References

AGRAS, W. S. Behavior therapy in the management of chronic schizophrenia. *American Journal of Psychiatry*, 1967, **124**, 240–243.

ALLEN, D., & MAGARO, P. A. Measures of change in token economy programs. *Behavior Research and Therapy*, 1971, **9**, 311–318.

ATTHOWE, J. M., & KRASNER, L. Preliminary report on the application of contingency reinforcement procedures (token economy) on a "chronic" psychiatric ward. *Journal of Abnormal Psychology,* 1968, **73**, 37–43.

AYLLON, T. Intensive treatment of psychotic behavior by stimulus satiation and food reinforcement. *Behavior Therapy and Research,* 1963, **1**, 53–61.

AYLLON, T. Some behavioral problems associated with eating in chronic schizophrenics. In L. P. Ullman & L. Krasner (Eds.), *Case studies in behavior modification.* New York: Holt, Rinehart & Winston, 1965.

AYLLON, T., & AZRIN, N. H. Reinforcement and instructions with mental patients. *Journal of the Experimental Analysis of Behavior,* 1964, **7**, 327–331.

AYLLON, T., & AZRIN, N. H. The measurement and reinforcement of behavior of psychotics. *Journal of the Experimental Analysis of Behavior,* 1965, **8**, 357–383.

AYLLON, T., & AZRIN, N. H. *The token economy: a motivational system for therapy and rehabilitation.* New York: Appleton-Century-Crofts, 1968.

AYLLON, T. & HAUGHTON, E. Control of the behavior of schizophrenic patients by food. *Journal of the Experimental Analysis of Behavior,* 1962, **5**, 343–352.

AYLLON, T., & HAUGHTON, E. Modification of symptomatic verbal behavior of mental patients. *Behaviour Research and Therapy,* 1964, **2**, 87–97.

AYLLON, T., & MICHAEL, J. The psychiatric nurse as a behavioral engineer. *Journal of the Experimental Analysis of Behavior,* 1959, **2**, 323–334.

BAILEY, J., & ATCHISON, T. The treatment of compulsive hand-washing using reinforcement principles. *Behaviour Research and Therapy,* 1969, **7**, 327–329.

BAKER, R. The use of operant conditioning to reinstate speech in mute schizophrenics. *Behaviour Research and Therapy,* 1971, **9**, 329–336.

BARTHOLOW, G. W., & TUNAHAN, B. Role of the community mental health center in the rehabilitation of the long-hospitalized patient. In J. H. Masserman (Ed.) *Current psychiatric therapies.* New York: Grune & Stratton, 1967.

BELLAK, L., & LOEB, L. *The schizophrenic syndrome.* New York: Grune & Stratton, 1969.

BIRKY, H. J., CHAMBLISS, J. E., & WASDEN, R. A comparison of residents discharged from a token economy and two traditional psychiatric programs. *Behavior Therapy,* 1971, **2**, 46–51.

BOCKHOVEN, J. S. *Moral treatment in American psychiatry.* New York: Spring, 1963.

BROWN, G. W., CARSTAIRS, G. M., & TOPPING, G. Post-hospital adjustment of chronic mental patients. *Lancet,* 1958, **2**, (7048), 685–688.

BRUCE, M. Tokens for recovery. *American Journal of Nursing,* 1966, **66**, 1799–1802.

BUCHER, B., & FABRICATORE, J. Use of patient-administered shock to suppress hallucinations. *Behavior Therapy,* 1970, **1**, 382–385.

CARLSON, C. G., HERSON, M., & EISLER, R. M. Token economy programs in the treatment of hospitalized adult psychiatric patients: current status and recent trends. *Journal of Nervous and Mental Disease,* 1972, **155**, 192–204.

CHEEK, F. E., LAUCIUS, J., MAHNCKE, M., & BECK, R. A behavior modification program for parents of convalescent schizophrenics. In R. D. Rubin, A. A. Lazarus, H. Fensterheim, & C. M. Franks (Eds.), *Advances in behavior therapy.* New York: Academic Press, 1971.

COHEN, R., FLORIN, I., GRUSCHE, A., MEYER-OSTERKAMP, S., & SELL, J. The introduction of a token economy in a psychiatric ward with extremely withdrawn chronic schizophrenics. *Behaviour Research and Therapy,* 1972, **10**, 69–74.

COWDEN, R. C., & FORD, L. I. Systematic desensitization with phobic schizophrenics. *American Journal of Psychiatry,* 1962, **119**, 241–245.

DOMINGUEZ, B., ACOSTA, T. F., & CARMONA, D. Discussion: a new perspective: chronic patients as assistants in a behavior rehabilitation program in a psychiatric institution. In S. W. Bijou & E. Ribes-Inesta (Eds.), *Behavior modification: issues and extensions.* New York: Academic Press, 1972.

DOTY, D. W., MCINNIS, T., & PAUL, G. L. Remediation of negative side-effects of an on-going response-cost system with chronic mental patients. *Journal of Applied Behavior Analysis,* 1974, **7**, 191–198.

DRENNEN, W., GALLMAN, W., & SAUSSER, G. Verbal operant conditioning of hospitalized psychiatric patients. *Journal of Abnormal Psychology,* 1968, **74**, 454–458.

DSM-II Diagnostic and Statistical Manual of Mental Disorders. Washington, D.C.: American Psychiatric Association, 1968.

DUNHAM, H. W., & WEINBERG, S. U. *The culture*

of the state mental hospital. Detroit: Wayne State University Press, 1960.

ELLSWORTH, J. R. Reinforcement therapy with chronic patients. *Hospital and Community Psychiatry,* 1969, **20**, 238–240.

FAIRWEATHER, G. W., SANDERS, D. H., CRESSLER, D. L., & MAYNARD, H. *Community life for the mentally ill: an alternative to institutional care.* New York: Aldine, 1969.

FETHKE, G. C. The relevance of economic theory and technology to token reinforcement systems: a comment. *Behaviour Research and Therapy,* 1972, **10**, 191–192.

FOSTER, J. The economies of behavior modification programs. Paper presented at the annual meeting of the American Psychological Association, 1969.

GERICKE, O. L. Practical use of operant conditioning procedures in a mental hospital. *Psychiatric Studies and Projects,* 1965, **3**, 2–10.

GLASS, A. J. The future of large public mental hospitals. *Mental Hospitals,* 1965, **16**, 9–22.

GOFFMAN, E. *Asylums.* Garden City, N.Y.: Doubleday, 1961.

GREENBLATT, M., SOLOMON, M., EVANS, A., & BROOKS, G. *Drugs and social therapy in chronic schizophrenia.* Springfield, Ill.: Charles C Thomas, 1965.

GREENBLATT, M., YORK, R. H., & BROWN, E. L. *From custodial to therapeutic patient care in mental hospitals.* New York: Russell Sage Foundation, 1955.

GRINSPOON, L., EWALT, J., & SHADER, R. Long term treatment of chronic schizophrenia: a preliminary report. *International Journal of Psychiatry,* 1967, 4, 116–128.

GRIPP, R. F., & MAGARO, P. A. A token economy program evaluation with untreated control group comparisons. *Behaviour Research and Therapy,* 1971, **9**, 137–149.

GUREL, L. Release and community stay in chronic schizophrenia. *American Journal of Psychiatry,* 1966, **122**, 892–899.

HARTLAGE, L. C. Subprofessional therapists' use of reinforcement versus traditional psychotherapeutic techniques with schizophrenics. *Journal of Consulting and Clinical Psychology,* 1970, **34**, 181–183.

HASSALL, C., SPENCER, A. M., & CROSS, K. W. Some changes in the composition of a mental hospital population. *British Journal of Psychiatry,* 1965, **111**, 420–428.

HEAP, R. F., BOBLITT, W. E., MOORE, C. H., & HORD, J. E. Behavior-milieu therapy with chronic neuropsychiatric patients. *Journal of Abnormal Psychology,* 1970, **76**, 349, 354.

HENDERSON, J. D., & SCOLES, P. E. A community-based behavioral operant environment for psychotic men. *Behavior Therapy,* 1970, **1**, 245–251.

HERSON, M., EISLER, R. M., SMITH, B. S., & AGRAS, W. S. A token reinforcement ward for young psychiatric patients. *American Journal of Psychiatry,* 1972, **129**, 233–242.

HERTZ, S., MIGLER, B., & FEINGOLD, L. Rapid modification of psychotic verbal behavior. Unpublished manuscript, 1968.

HOENIG, J., & HAMILTON, M. W. The schizophrenic patient in the community and his effect on the household. *International Journal of Social Psychiatry,* 1966, **12**, 165–176.

HUNTER, M., SCHOOLER, C., & SPOHN, H. E. The measurement of characteristic patterns of ward behavior in chronic schizophrenics. *Journal of Consulting Psychology,* 1962, **26**, 69–73.

JONES, K., & SIDEBOTHAM, A. *Mental hospitals at work.* London: Routledge & Kegan Paul, 1962.

KAGEL, J. H., & WINKLER, R. C. Behavioral economics: areas of cooperative research between economics and applied behavioral analysis. *Journal of Applied Behavior Analysis,* 1972, **5**, 335–343.

KALE, R. J., KAYE, J. H., WHELAN, P. A., & HOPKINS, B. L. The effects of reinforcement on the modification, and maintenance, and generalization of social responses of mental patients. *Journal of Applied Behavior Analysis,* 1968, **1**, 307–314.

KANTOR, D., & GELINEAU, V. Social processes in support of chronic deviance. *International Journal of Social Psychiatry,* 1965, **11**, 280–289.

KATZ, R. C., JOHNSON, C. A., & GELFAND, S. Modifying the dispensing of reinforcers: some implications for behavior modification with hospitalized patients. *Behavior Therapy,* 1972, **3**, 579–588.

KAZDIN, A. E. Recent advances in token economy research. In M. Hersen, R. M. Eisler, & P. M. Miller (Eds.), *Progress in behavior modification.* New York: Academic Press, in press.

KAZDIN, A. E., & BOOTZIN, R. R. The token

economy: an evaluative review. *Journal of Applied Behavior Analysis,* 1972, **5**, 343–372.

KELLEY, K. M., & HENDERSON, J. D. A community-based operant learning environment. II. Systems and procedures. In R. D. Rubin, H. Fensterheim, A. A. Lazarus, & C. M. Franks (Eds.), *Advances in behavior therapy.* New York: Academic Press, 1971.

KENNEDY, T. Treatment of chronic schizophrenia by behavior therapy. *Behaviour Research and Therapy,* 1964, **2**, 1–6.

KING, G. F., ARMITAGE, S. G., & TILTON, J. R. A therapeutic approach to schizophrenics of extreme pathology: an operant-interpersonal method. *Journal of Abnormal Psychology,* 1960, **61**, 276–286.

KLEIN, D. F., & DAVIS, J. M. *Diagnosis and drug treatment of psychiatric disorders.* Baltimore: Williams & Wilkins, 1969.

LAMB, H. R. Release of chronic psychiatric patients into the community. *Archives of General Psychiatry,* 1968, **19**, 39–44.

LAWSON, R. B., GREENE, R. T., RICHARDSON, J. S., McCLURE, G., & PANDINA, R. J. Token economy program in a maximum security correctional hospital. *Journal of Nervous and Mental Disease,* 1971, **152**, 199–205.

LEITENBERG, H., WINCZE, J. P., BUTZ, R. A., CALLAHAN, E. J., & AGRAS, W. S. Comparison of the effects of instructions and reinforcement in the treatment of a neurotic avoidance response. *Journal of Behavior Therapy and Experimental Psychiatry,* 1970, **1**, 53–58.

LENTZ, R. J., PAUL, G. L., & CALHOUN, J. F. Reliability and validity of three measures of functioning with "hard-core" chronic mental patients. *Journal of Abnormal Psychology,* 1971, **78**, 69–76.

LIBERMAN, R. P. Behavior modification and community mental health. *California Mental Health Research Digest,* 1971, **9**, 88–90.

LIBERMAN, R. P. Behavior modification of schizophrenia: a review. *National Institute of Mental Health Schizophrenia Bulletin,* 1972, **6**, 37–48:

LIBERMAN, R. P., TEIGEN, J., PATTERSON, R., & BAKER, V. Reducing delusional speech in chronic paranoid schizophrenics. *Journal of Applied Analysis,* 1973, **6**, 57–64.

LINDSLEY, O. R. Characteristics of the behavior of chronic psychotics as revealed by free-operant conditioning methods. *Diseases of the Nervous System,* 1960, **21**, 66–78.

LITTLE, L. K. Effects of interpersonal interaction on abstract thinking performance in schizophrenics. *Journal of Consulting Psychology,* 1966, **30**, 158–164.

LLOYD, K. E., & ABEL, L. Performance on a token economy psychiatric ward: a two year summary. *Behaviour Research and Therapy,* 1970, **8**, 1–9.

LLOYD, L. E., & GARLINGTON, W. K. Weekly variations in performance on a token economy psychiatric ward. *Behaviour Research and Therapy,* 1968, **6**, 407–410.

LOREI, T. W. Prediction of community stay and employment for released psychiatric patients. *Journal of Consulting Psychology,* 1967, **31**, 349–357.

MALEY, R. F., FELDMAN, G. L., & RUSKIN, R. S. Evaluation of patient improvement in a token economy treatment program. *Journal of Abnormal Psychology,* 1973, **82**, 141–144.

MARKS, J., SONODA, B., & SCHALOCK, B. Reinforcement versus relationship therapy for schizophrenics. *Journal of Abnormal Psychology,* 1968, **73**, 397–402.

MAY, P. *Treatment of schizophrenia.* New York: Science House, 1968.

McREYNOLDS, W. T., & COLEMAN, J. Token economy: patient and staff changes. *Behaviour Research and Therapy,* 1972, **10**, 29–34.

MEICHENBAUM, D. H. The effects of instruction and reinforcement on thinking and language behavior in schizophrenics. *Behaviour Research and Therapy,* 1969, **7**, 101–114.

MERTINS, G. C., & FULLER, G. B. Conditioning of molar behavior in regressed psychotics. I. An objective measure of personal habit training with "regressed" psychotics. *Journal of Clinical Psychology,* 1963, **19**, 333–337.

MILBY, J. B., STENMARK, D. E., & HORNER, R. F. Modification of locomotive behavior in a severely disturbed psychotic. *Perceptual and Motor Skills,* 1967, **25**, 359–360.

MILLER, D. Worlds that fail. I. Retrospective analysis of mental patients' careers. *California Mental Health Research Monograph,* 1965, No. 6.

MITCHELL, W. S., & STOFFELMAYR, B. E. Application of the Premack principle to the behavioral control of extremely inactive schizophrenics.

Journal of Applied Behavior Analysis, 1973, **6**, 419–423.

MOORE, C. H., & CRUM, B. C. Weight reduction in a chronic schizophrenic by means of operant conditioning procedures: a case report. *Behaviour Research and Therapy,* 1969, **7**, 129–131.

O'BRIEN, F., & AZRIN, N. H. Symptom reduction by functional displacement in a token economy: a case study. *Journal of Behavior Therapy and Experimental Psychiatry,* 1972, **3**, 205–207.

O'BRIEN, F., AZRIN, N. H., & HENSON, K. Increased communications of chronic mental patients by reinforcement and by response priming. *Journal of Applied Behavior Analysis,* 1969, **2**, 23–29.

ODEGARD, O. Pattern of discharge and readmission in psychiatric hospitals in Norway, 1926 to 1955. *Mental Hygiene,* 1961, **45**, 185–193.

PARRINO, J. J., GEORGE, L., & DANIELS, A. C. Token control of pill-taking behavior in a psychiatric ward. *Journal of Behavior Therapy and Experimental Psychiatry,* 1971, **2**, 181–185.

PASAMANICK, B., SCARPITTI, F. R., & DINITZ, S. *Schizophrenics in the community.* New York: Appleton-Century-Crofts, 1967.

PAUL, G. L. Chronic mental patient: current status—future directions. *Psychological Bulletin,* 1969, **71**, 81–94.

PAUL, G. L. Chronically institutionalized mental patients: research and treatment. Paper presented to the Third Annual Conference on Behavior Modification, Los Angeles, California, 1971.

PAUL, G. L., TOBIAS, L. L., & HOLLY, B. L. Maintenance psychotropic drugs in the presence of active treatment programs. *Archives of General Psychiatry,* 1972, **27**, 106–115.

POMERLEAU, O. F., BOBROVE, P. H., & HARRIS, L. C. Some observations on a controlled social environment for psychiatric patients. *Journal of Behavior Therapy and Experimental Psychiatry,* 1972, **3**, 15–21.

RASHKIS, H. A. How behavior therapy affects schizophrenics. *Diseases of the Nervous System,* 1966, **27**, 505–510.

REISINGER, J. J. The treatment of "anxiety-depression" via positive reinforcement and response cost. *Journal of Applied Behavior Analysis,* 1972, **5**, 125–130.

RETTERSÖL, N. *Paranoid and paranoic psychoses.* Springfield, Ill.: Charles C Thomas, 1966.

RICKARD, H. C., DIGNAM, P. J., & HORNER, R. F. Verbal manipulation in a psychotherapeutic relationship. *Journal of Clinical Psychology,* 1960, **16**, 364–367.

RICKARD, H. C., & DINOFF, M. A follow-up note on "Verbal manipulation in a psychotherapeutic relationship." *Psychological Reports,* 1962, **11**, 506.

RUTNER, I. T., & BUGLE, G. An experimental procedure for the modification of psychotic behavior. *Journal of Consulting and Clinical Psychology,* 1969, **33**, 651–653.

SABATASSO, A. P., & JACOBSON, L. J. Use of behavioral therapy in the reinstatement of verbal behavior in a mute psychotic with chronic brain syndrome: a case study. *Journal of Abnormal Psychology,* 1970, **76**, 322–324.

SALZINGER, K., & PISONI, S. Reinforcement of affect responses of schizophrenics during the clinical interview. *Journal of Abnormal and Social Psychology,* 1958, **57**, 89–90.

SALZINGER, K., & PORTNOY, S. Verbal conditioning in interviews: application to chronic schizophrenics and relationship to prognosis for acute schizophrenics. *Journal of Psychiatric Research,* 1964, **2**, 1–9.

SANDERS, R., SMITH, R. S., & WEINMAN, B. S. *Chronic psychosis and recovery.* San Francisco: Jossey-Bass, 1967.

SCHAEFER, H. H., & MARTIN, P. L. Behavioral therapy for "apathy" of hospitalized schizophrenics. *Psychological Reports,* 1966, **19**, 1147–1158.

SCHAEFER, H. H., & MARTIN, P. L. *Behavioral therapy.* New York: McGraw-Hill, 1969.

SHEAN, G. D., & ZEIDBERG, Z. Token reinforcement therapy: a comparison of matched groups. *Journal of Behavior Therapy and Experimental Psychiatry,* 1971, **2**, 95–105.

SHERMAN, J. A. Use of reinforcement and imitation to reinstate verbal behavior in mute psychotics. *Journal of Abnormal and Social Psychology,* 1965, **70**, 155–164.

SLADE, P. D. The effects of systematic desensitization on auditory hallucinations. *Behaviour Research and Therapy,* 1972, **10**, 85–91.

SOMMER, R., WITNEY, G., & OSMOND, H. Teaching common associations to schizophrenics. *Journal of Abnormal and Social Psychology,* 1962, **65**, 58–61.

STAHL, J. R., THOMSON, L. E., LEITENBERG, H.,

& HASAZI, J. E. The establishment of praise as a conditioned reinforcer in socially unresponsive psychiatric patients. *Journal of Abnormal Psychology,* 1974, **83**, 488–496.

STEFFY, R. A., HART, J., CRAW, M., TORNEY, D., & MARLETT, N. Operant behavior modification techniques applied to severely regressed and aggressive patients. *Canadian Psychiatric Association Journal,* 1968, **14**, 59–67.

SUSHINSKY, L. W. An illustration of a behavioral therapy intervention with nursing staff in a therapeutic role. *Journal of Psychiatric Nursing and Mental Health Services,* 1970, **8**, 24–26.

ULLMANN, L. P. *Institution and outcome: a comparative study of psychiatry hospitals.* New York: Pergamon, 1967.

ULLMANN, L. P., KRASNER, L., & COLLINS, B. J. Modification of behavior through verbal conditioning: effects in group therapy. *Journal of Abnormal and Social Psychology,* 1961, **62**, 128–132.

ULLMANN, L. P., KRASNER, L., & EDINGER, R. L. Verbal conditioning of common associations in long-term schizophrenics. *Behaviour Research and Therapy,* 1964, **2**, 15–18.

ULLMANN, L. P., FORSMAN, R. G., KENNY, J. W., McINNIS, T. L., UNIKEL, I. P., & ZEISSET, R. M. Selective reinforcement of schizophrenics' interview responses. *Behaviour Research and Therapy,* 1965, **2**, 205–212.

UNITED STATES PUBLIC HEALTH SERVICE. NIMH reports continued drop in patient population. *Psychiatric News,* 1969, 4 (10), 16.

UNITED STATES PUBLIC HEALTH SERVICE. Population dip in institutions cited in report. *Psychiatric News,* 1970, 5 (5), 28.

UPPER, D. A "ticket" system for reducing ward rules violations on a token economy program. *Journal of Behavior Therapy and Experimental Psychiatry,* 1973, 4, 137–140.

VITALE, J. H. The emergence of mental hospital field research. In G. W. Fairweather (Ed.), *Social psychology in treating mental illness.* New York: John Wiley, 1964.

VITALE, J. H., & STEINBACH, M. The prevention of relapse of chronic mental patients. *International Journal of Social Psychiatry,* 1965, **11**, 85–95.

WAGNER, B. R., & PAUL, G. L. Reduction of incontinence in chronic mental patients: a pilot project. *Journal of Behavior Therapy and Experimental Psychiatry,* 1970, **1**, 29–38.

WEISS, R. L., KRASNER, L., & ULLMANN, L. Responsibility of psychiatric patients to verbal conditioning: "success" and "failure" conditions and the pattern of reinforced trials. *Psychological Reports,* 1963, **12**, 423–426.

WEXLER, D. B. Token and taboo: behavior modification, token economies and the law. *California Law Review,* 1973, **61**, 81–109.

WICKRAMASEKERA, I. The use of some learning theory derived techniques in the treatment of a case of paranoid schizophrenia. *Psychotherapy: Theory, Research and Practice,* 1967, 4, 22–26.

WILSON, F. S., & WALTERS, R. H. Modification of speech output of near-mute schizophrenics through social-learning procedures. *Behaviour Research and Therapy,* 1966, 4, 59–67.

WINCZE, J. P., LEITENBERG, H., & AGRAS, W. S. The effects of token reinforcement and feedback on delusional verbal behavior of chronic paranoid schizophrenics. *Journal of Applied Behavior Analysis,* 1972, **5**, 247–262.

WINKLER, R. C. Management of chronic psychiatric patients by a token reinforcement system. *Journal of Applied Behavior Analysis,* 1970, **3**, 47–55.

WINKLER, R. C. The relevance of economic theory and technology to token reinforcement systems. *Behaviour Research and Therapy,* 1971, **9**, 81–88.

WINKLER, R. C. A theory of equilibrium in token economies. *Journal of Abnormal Psychology,* 1972, **79**, 169–173.

WOHL, S. A. Follow-up community adjustment. In G. W. Fairweather (Ed.), *Social psychology in treating mental illness.* New York: John Wiley, 1964.

YOLLES, S. Patient release hits peak. *Science News,* 1967, **92**, 107.

ZEISSET, R. M. Desensitization and relaxation in the modification of psychiatric patients' interview behavior. *Journal of Abnormal Psychology,* 1968, **73**, 18–24.

ZUSMAN, J. Some explanations of the changing appearance of psychotic patients: antecedents of the social breakdown syndrome concept. *International Journal of Psychiatry,* 1967, **3**, 216–237.

Training of Marital Skills:
Some Problems and Concepts

7

G. R. PATTERSON
R. L. WEISS
HYMAN HOPS

The research designed to investigate marital interactions is limited in both quality and quantity. In the Kuhnian sense (Kuhn, 1970), the area seems destined to occupy a permanent niche as "*pre*scientific." We assume that the reason for this lag in development is due to the complexity which characterizes this area of research. Complexity, in this context, refers to the number of innovations required of an investigator who wishes to measure and/or change marital interactions.

Several of the most creative behavior modifiers had initiated research into this area by the mid-1960s (Goldiamond, 1965; Lazarus, 1968; Stuart, 1968; Tharp, 1963). However, at the time of this writing there are few, if any, studies which provide even minimally acceptable data demonstrating change following intervention. It is fair to say that most of the published work to date is characterized by inappropriate assessment and lack of specification of either the antecedents or general parameters for marital conflict (Olson, 1972).

The aims of this chapter are to: (1) evaluate the relevance of altering marital interaction; (2) delineate the sense in which marital interaction poses complex problems for investigation; (3) outline a behavioral formulation of the antecedents and concomitants of marital interaction; (4) discuss assets and liabilities of devices currently available for assessing changes in marital interaction; and (5) review the empirical studies.

The Social Relevance of Marital Conflict Research

Although the family is presented on TV as being a viable social unit, survey data consistently suggest the "happy family" concept to be a myth. Studies in England (Rutter, Tizard, & Whitmore, 1970; Wolff, 1967) and America (Griffith, 1952; MacFarlene, Allen, & Honzik, 1962) have showed that at least 1 parent in 10 had a child with one or more major problems. For example, 5.7% (Rutter et al., 1970) and 4% (MacFarlene et al., 1962, respectively, complained of their children's "stealing;" 16.1% and 15% of "lying;" and in the English study, 15% complained of "fighting."

Survey research for middle and upper middle class couples has shown steady declines in general marital satisfaction during the first 10 years of marriage (Feldman, 1971). Several studies showed about one couple in seven to be unhappy (Bradburn & Caplovitz, 1965; Rollins & Feldman, 1970). Since 1890, the proportion of couples seeking divorce has approximately doubled every 30 years, to the point where currently one marriage in three ends in divorce (Christensen, 1964).

If such data indict the system as inefficient in socializing children and keeping adults contented, additional data give it a countenance yet more grim. Twenty-eight percent of all murders occur among family members (Federal Bureau of Investigation, 1968). Twenty percent of police deaths and 40% of their staff injuries occur during attempts to intervene in family quarrels (Bard, 1969). Forty percent of the women from lower socioeconomic classes and 23% from the middle class complain of physical abuse as a major reason for their decision to obtain a divorce (Steinmetz & Strauss, 1971).

There are also data that show that even "normal" couples are confronted by conflict about once a week and distressed couples at least once a day (Birchler, Weiss, & Wampler, 1972). In the present context, it is assumed that the failure of many couples to acquire conflict resolution skills leads to a dissolution of the family as a social system. When this occurs, adaptive behaviors are no longer maintained but are replaced by coercive control and/or escape-avoidance behaviors. Certainly, finding a means for ameliorating such a process would constitute socially relevant research.

Some Complex Issues

Several problems confront the marital conflict researcher. First, interventions aimed at changing the behavior of children in the home (Wahler, Winkle, Petersen, & Morrison, 1965) or classroom (Walker & Buckley, 1973) are relatively uncomplicated. Adults in these settings hold most of the key contingencies which control the behavior of the child. The child, in turn, holds relatively few of the contingencies which maintain the adult. Such inequities make for ease in intervention. However, such inequities do not characterize marital interactions. Here, both members hold relatively equal shares of the reinforcing contingencies (Azrin, Master, & Jones, 1973; Stuart, 1969, 1972). Intervention with couples in severe conflict requires simultaneous changes in contingencies for both members of the dyad. Presumably, each will change the reinforcers which he or she provides for the other. The clinician must be prepared to design and monitor two programs simultaneously, usually in an atmosphere of tension and mistrust.

Second, many behaviors central to marital conflict are low base rate occurrences which do not lend themselves to the use of observation data. Within behavior modification, the use of direct observation (e.g., token culture classrooms, institutional management, parent training, and the Kansas Achievement Place) has led to rapid gains. It is simply not practical, however, to send observers into homes to wait for the occurrence of the "one conflict per day."

Third, the complaints of the couple are often vaguely defined and seem to vary from one couple to another. If one takes the complaints at face value, then it would seem necessary to innovate programs to handle the spectrum of clinical phenomena—anxiety, physical abuse, money problems, relations with relatives, child management, sexual difficulties of all kinds, depression, and lack of affection. The range, difficulty, and ambiguity of such complaints are sufficient to give pause to the most obdurate social engineer.

Fourth, great advances in behavior modification research have been made using the ABAB reversal and multiple response designs as described by Sidman (1960) and others. The intervention effects obtained with this design offer compelling support for the efficacy of contingency manipulations as witnessed by most of the papers appearing in the *Journal of Applied Behavior Analysis*. To date, none of these more powerful designs has been employed within the field of marital conflict. Most experienced clinicians suspect that even if the couple could return to baseline in an ABA, they would strongly reject any such proposal. Whatever the reason, the omission of this model may have contributed to the slow development in the marital conflict area.

Fifth, as noted by several reviewers (Christensen, 1964; Olson, 1970, 1972), much of the traditional literature concerned with specifying antecedents for marital conflict behavior is highly speculative in nature and poorly researched.

The sections that follow address themselves to each of these issues.

Speculations About Antecedents and Concomitants of Marital Conflict

As shown in the Birchler et al. (1972) study, distressed couples report approximately three times as many conflicts as do nondistressed couples. Conflict is defined here as an interchange in which one or both members of a dyad demand immediate change in the behavior of the other person and the other person does not comply. Initially, such a demand for behavior change is probably expressed as a "request" and is likely followed by a discussion of some sort. If this produces the desired result, then conflict does not ensue. However, two or three nonreinforced discussions are likely to be followed by a request which is accompanied by an aversive stimulus of some kind, e.g., "Damn it, you're just like your mother . . ."

It is assumed that when one member introduces an aversive stimulus, the interchange shifts into a "coercion process" (Patterson & Cobb, 1971, 1973; Patterson & Reid, 1970). An aversive stimulus is presented in either of two ways. It can be delivered contingently following a certain response which is to be suppressed, or it can be presented prior to the behavior which is to be manipulated and then withdrawn only when the other person complies. "Punishment" and "negative reinforcement" describe the processes involved in coercion. In either case, over repeated trials both members of the dyad are changed. The person presenting the aversive stimulus is reinforced for behaving unpleasantly by the rapid changes brought about in the behavior of the victim. The victim's compliant behavior is strengthened by negative reinforcement. As the behavior changes, the aversive stimulus is withdrawn and/or the punishment is terminated.

It is assumed, however, that as one person begins using aversive stimuli, the "victim" will reciprocate and will also use aversive stimuli. Data for interactions of adolescents showed a p of .75 that an unfriendly act would be followed by an unfriendly act (Raush, 1965). In general, both members of a dyad quickly become involved in the use of aversive stimuli.

Data reported by Birchler et al. (1972) showed that distressed couples reported significantly higher mean rates of aversive consequences received at home than did a sample of nondistressed couples. Vincent (1972) analyzed data from the same samples which showed that in the laboratory, distressed couples were also significantly more aversive in their interchanges.

In keeping with this hypothesis, Reid (1967) found that the family member who "gave" the highest rate of aversive stimuli also "received" the highest rate as reflected in an average correlation of +.65. The studies of nondistressed couples by Birchler et al. (1972) and Wills (1971) showed correlations of .26 ($df = 11$; $p > .05$) and .61 ($df = 7$; $p > .05$) respectively for ordinal rankings of spouses on rates with which they exchanged "displeasures" during the day. A comparable analysis of exchanges for distressed couples by Birchler et al. (1972) produced correlations of .54 ($df = 11$; $p < .05$).

Evidently, there is a low level equity holding for the exchange of aversive stimuli.

The third aspect of the coercion process (Patterson & Cobb, 1973, p. 162) concerns a hypothesized increment over trials in the intensity of aversive stimuli used by both members. In addition, as their skill level increases there may be an increase in the length of any given aversive interaction. Both persons are being hurt in these interchanges. Given that one person suddenly intensifies the stimuli being presented, the other person is likely to withdraw from the interaction. Over a series of trials, each member is reinforced in this manner and each gradually escalates the intensity of pain being inflicted on the other. Prior training, or a general "trait of aggressiveness," are not thought to be prerequisites for physical assault in cases such as these. The escalation proceeds until one person consistently exhibits escape/avoidance behavior and thus becomes the "victim."

It is predicted that for married couples the increasing level of aversive stimuli is accompanied or followed by a decrease in the level of positive consequences exchanged. Birchler et al. (1972) found a significantly higher mean level of "pleasures" from the daily reports of nondistressed compared to distressed couples for interactions at home. Using data from the same samples, Birchler (1972) and Vincent (1972) also found significantly higher rates of coded positive consequences in laboratory interactions for nondistressed couples when they worked in a problem-solving situation. Presumably, reciprocity also holds when one examines the exchanges of positive consequences. Reid (1967) found a mean correlation of $+.55$ among families when investigating observed exchanges of positive behaviors. Similarly, for a sample of seven nondistressed couples (Wills, 1971), the correlations between spouses' mean daily reports of positive consequences received at home were 1.00 ($df = 7; p < .01$). In another study, for a sample of 12 nondistressed and 12 distressed couples (Birchler et al., 1972), the correlations were .97 ($df = 11; p < .01$) and .74 ($p < .01$) respectively.

Given that a member's demand for immediate behavior change is accompanied by an aversive stimulus, it is likely (Raush, 1965) that the other member will immediately respond with a similar stimulus. This in turn elicits a counterresponse. At this juncture, the problem-solving aspect of the interchange has been effectively sidetracked. A couple can repeatedly attempt to solve the problem, sidetrack each other, and thus fight endlessly without altering the behavior which initiated the first discussion.

Presumably, distressed couples have the usual problem-solving skills in their repertoire, but no longer apply them to their own interactions. Vincent (1972) has showed that members of distressed couples display at least the "normal problem-solving skills" when interacting with opposite sex strangers. However, these skills were not in evidence when the distressed spouses themselves worked together on solving interpersonal problems.

As the conflicts escalate in intensity, one would expect the members to begin spending less time together. Stuart (1969) noted that his distressed couples had reduced rates of sexual activity and spent less time talking together. Data provided by Weiss, Hops, and Patterson (1973) showed that distressed couples shared fewer recreational activities; global ratings of marital satisfaction as measured on the Locke-Wallace (1959) also showed less satisfaction for the distressed couples.

SUMMARY

The coercion process begins when one member of the dyad demands immediate behavior changes and accompanies the demand with an aversive stimulus. This, in turn, elicits an aversive reaction from the other member and produces a general increase in the overall rate of aversive behavior. As the aversive interchanges lengthen, they are likely to be accompanied by intensified aversive stimuli, and are likely to lead to a general reduction in use of positive consequences, reduced frequency of social interchanges (talking, sex, recreation), and general marital dissatisfaction.

Assessment:
Some Problems and Procedures

Most couples' training occurs in the office or seminar room (Goldstein & Francis, 1969; Knox, 1972; Lazarus, 1968; Liberman, 1970; Stuart, 1969; Turner, 1972). Measures of behavior change within that setting should be obtained. Indeed, several devices exist for coding such dyadic interactions (Carter & Thomas, 1973; Hops, Wills, Weiss, & Patterson, 1972; Olson & Ryder, 1970). Presumably, such data would sample several different aspects of the couples' behavior such as their use of aversive and supporting consequences, problem-solving skills, etc. It should be noted that only a few investigators have provided data demonstrating *any* changes in the behavior of the couple in the training setting.

Given measures of change in the training setting, it would also seem necessary to demonstrate generalization of effects to interactions within the home. Here the current investigators make a better showing in that several have employed self-report measures for this purpose. However, the data collected have been of variable quality. The assessment procedures used to measure both kinds of changes will be covered in the sections that follow.

ASSESSMENT WITHIN THE TREATMENT SETTING

A number of indirect measures have been developed to assess couples' problem-solving or negotiating skills (Deutsch & Kraus, 1964; Goodrich & Boomer, 1963; Strodbeck, 1961).

More recently, procedures have begun to develop which propose to directly measure such interchanges. Carter and Thomas (1973) presented 27 different categories describing disruptions in marital interchanges. Although it has not yet been used to collect systematic data, the outline of the code system looks promising.

The Inventory of Marital Conflicts (IMC) was developed by Olson and Ryder (1970). It utilizes a variant of the Strodbeck (1961) revealed differences method. The spouses are given vignettes which put them into a potential conflict setting since each has an explanation of behaviors slightly at variance with the other. The set of conflict-inducing vignettes constitutes a relatively standardized task in which the couples are required to resolve the differences. In negotiating these disagreements, they display behaviors which are coded into 29 categories having to do with information, opinions, suggestions, positive and negative support, and structural categories (Olson & Ryder, 1970, p. 446).

The Marital Interaction Coding System (MICS) was developed by Hops et al. (1972). During baseline, couples are asked to resolve four of their own conflicts. These conflicts are identified from the intake interview. The MICS contains 30 code categories, some of which were developed for use as an observation coding system appropriate for aggressive children (Patterson, Ray, Shaw, & Cobb, 1969). The verbal and nonverbal categories sampled by the MICS index constructive or problem-solving behaviors, supportive and aversive behaviors, instances of affection and disdain, and sidetracking. The data are recorded sequentially from videotapes of the couple's interactions. Behaviors of both individuals are categorized for each 30-second interval.

Coders require extensive training in order to use the system effectively. The research by Reid (1970) showed a dramatic drop in observer agreement when, following training, they were placed in presumably unmonitored field situations. Later studies by Reid and DeMaster (1972) showed that observer pairs participating in regular retraining sessions maintained satisfactory levels of observer agreement. For this reason, observers received continuous training.

In an attempt to validate the MICS code systems, Birchler (1972) and Vincent (1972) analyzed different aspects of interactions obtained in a laboratory setting. The studies were based upon data from the same 12 distressed and 12 nondistressed couples reacting to the Olson-Ryder vignettes. Distressed couples displayed significantly lower rates of "positive consequences" and significantly higher rates of "aversive behaviors" (Birchler, 1972). Patterson, Hops, and Weiss (1975) compared pre- and post-intervention means for each code category, separately for a clinical sample of 10 husbands and wives. After treatment, there were five significant changes obtained for husbands and four for wives. The changes suggested a more direct and nonaversive approach to problem solving for couples. These two sets of findings suggest that the MICS code was moderately sensitive to differences between distressed and nondistressed couples and to changes brought about by intervention.

The more recent validation of the MICS was provided by Lerner (1973). Behavioral ratings in one setting were used to define "dominant" and "submissive" subjects. Subsequently, *ad hoc* dyads were formed in which subjects worked together to resolve several mild conflict situations. Their interactions were coded with the MICS, and were grouped into categories of positive reactions (agreement, attentiveness, compromise, humor, etc.) and aversive reactions (criticism, put-down, ignoring, no response, etc.). The results indicated that compatible dyads comprised of a dominant and a submissive subject were significantly higher on positive behavior codes and significantly lower on negative behavior codes than were incompatible dyads (dominant-dominant). There was also significant agreement between rated attraction to the partner and MICS categories denoting positive reactions.

The intervention study by Patterson, Hops, and Weiss (1975) provided an additional bit of validation data. Baseline data showed that wives who were identified in their husbands' daily reports as giving higher rates of "pleasures" at home also showed higher rates of "facilitating behavior" (MICS) in the problem-solving situation in the laboratory. The rank order correlation of .85 ($df = 8$; $p < .01$) between baseline measures of these variables was highly significant. The comparable correlation for husbands was .61 ($df = 8$; $p > .05$). There were no significant correlations with the laboratory measure of "disruption" (MICS).

These preliminary findings suggest that coding changes in couples' behavior prior to, during, and following training may be feasible. At this point, however, only one of the three available code systems has been explored in even a preliminary fashion.

EVALUATING CHANGES IN MARITAL INTERACTION

Some investigators have used observation data collected within the home to assess the generalizability of training effects. By and large, however, this would not seem to be a feasible technique because many of the phenomena one wishes to alter (e.g., conflicts, clearly positive or aversive consequences) seem to be low base rate events. For example, in a sample of 27 normal families, each observed for 6 to 10 hours in their homes, the mothers showed only .096 "approvals" per minute; .001 "yells;" and .166 "laughs." Bernal, Gibson, Williams, and Pesses (1971) devised an ingenious procedure which overcomes some of the difficulties. A tape recorder was equipped with a timer to sample family interaction. A comparison with data obtained by direct observation in the home showed a correlation (over days) of .89 ($p < .02$) for mothers' "commands" as sampled by the two procedures. There are also commercial devices available which activate a tape recorder when the interactions reach certain decibel levels. A third possibility, currently being explored, is to have the parents turn on the tape recorder when embroiled in heated interactions with their children.

Most investigators currently use some variant of self-report as a means of evaluating outcome (Azrin et al., 1973; Goldstein & Francis, 1969; Stuart, 1972; Turner, 1972). The general feeling is that systematic self-report data constitute a necessary, but not sufficient, criterion measuring change in interaction. The problem revolves around the size of the units involved. We believe that the more global the judgment and the larger the time interval being sampled, the more likely the couple's self-report data will tend not to covary with other criterion measures.

Perhaps the least effective evaluation procedure is to require the couple to synthesize the outcome of multiple problems over the entire training program in a single rating along with an improved–not improved dimension. One of the few consistent findings from evaluation of traditional psychotherapy was the lack of covariation between the judgments of the client and those of the therapist (Board, 1959; Cartwright & Roth, 1957; Storrow, 1960). Similarly, Olson's (1969) review showed little or no correlation between direct observation and family members' global judgments of family role, authority patterns within family, or dominance. We would view such judgments as being too global.

Even when restricting the judgments to a single and presumably more specific variable such as "fear of X," the correlations between self-report and observed behavior accounted for only 9% to 25% of the variance in studies reviewed by Fazio (1969). Similarly, Birchler and Weiss (1970) found no correlation between observed and reported rates of social reinforcement when both sampled the same 20 minutes of interaction! Even restricting the judgments to a simple motor act (e.g.,

smoking), in a specific setting produced a correlation of only .61 between self-report and observed behavior (McFall, 1970).

Knox (1972), Locke and Wallace (1959), and Stuart (1972) have constructed scales which constitute global samples for areas of marital discord. In the same vein, the MAITAI (cf. Weiss et al., 1973) presents a listing of 84 recreational events (watching TV, going out for dinner, playing catch). In the Birchler (1972) and Vincent (1972) samples, distressed couples were significantly different from the nondistressed sample in percentage of events shared with spouse. The "Areas of Change" questionnaire (cf., Weiss et al., 1973) was designed to provide a sample of specific behaviors spouses wanted changed in each other, as well as to indicate whether the same behaviors should be changed in the self. Its product moment correlation with the more traditional Locke-Wallace (1959) was found to be in the .70s for each of two samples, and its measure of internal consistency (alpha) was .89. Each of these self-report measures is insufficient evidence for change. Few of them have any validation data; none of them is supported by adequate studies. The units of behavior remain large and therefore liable to the distortions noted earlier. Although each investigator may wish to include self-report data as necessary evidence for change in interaction, additional criterion measures should also be used.

Traditionally, it has been assumed that requiring the couple to tabulate daily the occurrence of specific behaviors provided both reliable and valid data (Goldstein & Francis, 1969; Rappaport & Harrel, 1972; Stuart, 1969). It is important to note that this assumption has seldom, if ever, been tested. In addition to questioning the unexplored psychometric characteristics of such data, Olson (1972) also pointed out that most marital interaction studies sample changes in only one or two behaviors. He went on to stress the need for multilevel assessment of changes in marital interaction, a position with which we heartily concur. The early papers by Stuart (1969) and Weiss et al. (1973) are examples of such beginnings.

As part of the multicriteria assessment approach of the Oregon group (Hops et al., 1972), the pleasure (P) and displeasure (D) measures seemed most promising. The behaviors being tabulated were reasonably well defined and of narrow bandwidth. The time intervals were also rather small, i.e., recall for the past 24 hours. During the intake interview, each spouse was given the "Checklist of Ps and Ds." The list had evolved gradually from extended interviews with problem and nonproblem couples. Each member identified the particular behaviors of the spouse which were pleasing or displeasing. The frequency of the Ps and Ds and the amount of time the couple spent together were obtained by daily phone contact. Efforts to have the family members collect such data over an interval of a few days or a week have simply not worked consistently. The daily call seemed necessary.

The existing data suggest some modest validity for this approach. Weiss et al. (1973) obtained a P/D ratio of 4 to 3 for the distressed couples in contrast to 29 to 7 for nondistressed couples. The "t" tests for these differences showed them to be significant at $p < .005$ levels. There was a significant correlation of .54 between the couples' P/D ratios and their Locke-Wallace scores (marital satisfaction). There was also a correlation of .56 between the intake interviewer's ratings of distress and the couples' P/D ratio for data obtained during the baseline study which followed.

Wills et al. (1974) showed that for normal couples, the daily reports of Ps and Ds correlated significantly with their more global daily ratings of marital satisfaction. The across-subjects analysis identified displeasures as accounting for a large portion of variance in spouses' ratings of marital satisfaction.

In summary, there has been only the barest of beginning in the development of multiple criteria for use in evaluating changes in marital interaction. Only two coding systems have actually been used to collect data measuring pre- and postinteractions in the laboratory setting. A limited amount of reliability and validity data were available for only one of these code systems. The limitations of broad spectrum self-report were also discussed. Some relevant attempts to obtain more precise self-report data were described, together with a limited amount of validation evidence for the latter.

Intervention Strategies

Intervention in marital conflicts has taken two forms. One approach trains both members of the dyad simultaneously and the other trains only a single member. Lazarus (1968) applied systematic desensitization and assertion training to one member of a dyad for a variety of sexual and marital problems, ranging from frigidity to communication difficulties. Goldstein and Francis (1969) successfully taught a group of wives to use social reinforcers to shape their husbands' desirable behaviors and extinguish their undesirable behaviors. We believe that for most marital problems the single member approach will have limited utility. However, there are no studies comparing the dyadic to the single member approach. The dyadic approach generally emphasizes training in communication skills, contingency management, and negotiation. The training is always carried out jointly (Carter & Thomas, 1973; Rappaport & Harrel, 1972; Stuart, 1969, 1972; Turner, 1972; Weiss et al., 1973).

Although only a limited number of studies are available, it is apparent that there is a surprisingly high degree of overlap in the procedures used by the different investigators. This probably reflects extensive communication between marital investigators. Generally, the training sessions described by investigators were highly structured, and the clients were encouraged specifically to practice at home.

Several investigators stressed the use of reinforcement language in training couples (Liberman, 1970; Rappaport & Harrel, 1972). However, only a few took a systematic approach to the problem. Turner (1972), for example, required the couples to read *Marriage Happiness* (Knox, 1972) or *Families* (Patterson, 1971). The latter was also required reading in the training procedures described by Weiss et al. (1973).

Great emphasis is placed on teaching couples how to pinpoint or use simple operational terms when describing behaviors which may be subject to change in themselves and their partners (Stuart, 1969; Welch & Goldstein, 1972). As a concomitant, many (Azrin et al., 1973; Stuart, 1972) stress the importance of using nonaversive labels when stating such requests for change. For example, Patterson and Hops (1972) replayed videotapes of couples who then tracked their own use of ambiguous or aversive language in negotiating sessions. They were trained to substitute, for example, "wash the dishes an hour after suppertime" for "she's no good as a housekeeper."

Many behaviorally oriented therapists recognize that communication training alone is probably insufficient to change behavior in marital conflict. But couples are taught the important concept that changes in each other's behavior are negotiable. They are given specific training in negotiating simultaneous desirable changes in each other's behavior. For example, a husband might agree to reduce his drinking behavior in exchange for less nagging from his wife.

These skills emphasize the use of contingency contracts, a procedure introduced by Homme, Csanzi, Gonzales, and Rechs (1970) and adapted by Stuart (1969, 1972) for use with marital conflict. Many of the negotiated contracts corresponded to the *quid pro quo* interchanges described so lucidly by Lederer and Jackson (1968). In the contingency contract model, the wife contracts to change one or more of her behaviors for a change in the husband's behavior(s) and vice versa. For example, Stuart's (1969) husbands could earn sex or physical affection from their wives by increasing their conversational interactions with them, a behavior change often requested by the wives. If the husbands failed to talk, the wives would withhold sex; the husbands therefore had to make their move first. In such models, both spouses' behavioral changes were similarly yoked and any partner could decide to sabotage the agreement. To avoid this problem, Patterson and Hops (1972) had their couples draw up contracts in which behavior changes in the spouses were controlled by independent consequences, i.e., consequences independent of whether the other changes. When one of the partners violated the agreement, that person earned a prestipulated consequence. For example, one could provide positive consequences for compliance rather than aversive consequences for noncompliance. This emphasis upon accelerating positive behaviors was in accord with the position taken by Stuart (1969). More extensive experience with such contracts led Weiss et al. (1973) to stress the use of positive rather than aversive consequences. Typically, the positive and aversive consequences were separate for each member and negotiated in advance. For example, if the husband returns from work at a reasonable hour, he gets his favorite dessert that evening. If he fails, his wife may earn a nickel for each minute that he is late. If the wife has kept the house well ordered for a week, she may then get an extra evening's bowling with her league team. On the other hand, each evening for which dinner is late or the house is in a mess earns a dollar for her husband to spend any way he wishes. Telephone calls each day ascertain whether the couple is following their contract and also makes it possible to remedy problems which may have developed with its application.

Length of treatment, although variable, was short by traditional standards. Turner (1972) held six two-hour group sessions; Azrin et al. (1973) met twice weekly for a total of eight sessions; and Stuart alternated contacts weekly after the fourth week for a total of 10 sessions. Depending on the problems involved, Patterson et al. (1975) varied treatment from 2 to 13 weeks, with an average of six sessions per couple. There were, however, several additional hours of telephone contact between sessions.

Most investigators have studied simple cases of marital conflict. Few of the couples had applied for divorce or were actually separated; many of the couples were well educated, upper middle class. For example, in the Azrin et al. (1973) study, 10 of the 12 husbands were students. Welch and Goldstein (1972) used a similar sample, as did Patterson et al. (1975). At this early juncture, it is probably wise to select such cases in that it enables the investigators to learn without being overwhelmed. It should also be noted, however, that the early samples of Stuart (1969) and Liberman (1970) involved couples with more severe long-standing problems.

Follow-up data have been collected by three studies (Azrin et al., 1973; Stuart, 1969; Patterson et al. (1975) at intervals of 1 month, 6 to 7 months, and 12 to 24 months, respectively. Although all provided data which supported the maintenance of treatment effects, the data consisted entirely of global self-reports obtained by telephone or mail. A more adequate evaluation of the persistence of treatment effects must await the collection of more rigorous follow-up data.

Certainly, these techniques seem reasonable as opening gambits for this type of research. What is needed, however, are (1) replication of treatment effects for con-

secutive cases by the same investigator; (2) replications by investigators from other laboratories; (3) comparison of these treatment effects to untreated control groups; and (4) multiple criteria assessments at baseline, during and following intervention. Given that a "treatment package" survived such a series of studies, then it should be necessary to carry out analyses of the contributions of the individual components, e.g., teaching concepts and language, pinpointing, negotiating, construction of contracts, skills in use of positive reinforcers. The four steps would constitute the minimal requirements for placing intervention procedures on a reasonable scientific footing.

Summary

The last decade's work in the area of marital conflict consists entirely of exploratory investigations by a small number of investigators. With the rare exception of R. B. Stuart, most researchers publish a few case studies, unsupported by data, and move on to more accessible problems. There has been difficulty in obtaining high quality data showing changes in behavior in the training setting and in generalization to other settings. Because of the problems involved, most investigators have employed gross measures of self-report. The research literature reviewed suggested that these measures were inadequate. Some alternative procedures were described.

A general formulation was given for describing the process by which "normal" individuals may get caught up in the process of using aversive stimuli to control each other's behavior. The process presumably escalates to the point where both members begin to avoid each other as defined by reduced rates of social interaction, sex, and recreation. Presumably, the formulation specified not only process and outcome variables for marital interaction, but also implied means by which they might be measured.

Finally, the reviewed material suggested a surprising degree of homogeneity in treatment approaches. However, in view of the paucity of evaluated data, there is no basis for deciding whether this implies a good or bad state of affairs.

References:

AZRIN, N. H., MASTER, B. M., & JONES, R. Reciprocity counseling: a rapid learning-based procedure for marital counseling. *Behaviour Research and Therapy*, 1973, **11**, 1–18.

BARD, M. Extending psychology's impact through existing community institutions. *American Psychologist*, 1969, **24**, 610–612.

BERNAL, M. E., GIBSON, D. M., WILLIAMS, D. E., & PESSES, E. I. A device for recording automatic audiotape recording. *Journal of Applied Behavior Analysis*, 1971, 4, 151–156.

BIRCHLER, G. R. Differential patterns of instrumental affiliative behavior as a function of degree of marital distress and level of intimacy. Unpublished doctoral dissertation, University of Oregon, 1972.

BIRCHLER, G. R., & WEISS, R. L. Instrumental affiliative behavior and self-awareness. Paper presented at the meeting of the Western Psychological Association, Los Angeles, April 1970.

BIRCHLER, G. R., WEISS, R. L., & WAMPLER, L. D. Differential patterns of social reinforcement as a function of degree of marital distress and level of intimacy. Paper presented at the meeting of the Western Psychological Association, Portland, Oregon, April 1972.

BOARD, F. A. Patients' and physicians' judgments of outcome of psychotherapy in an outpatient clinic: a questionnaire investigation. *Archives of General Psychiatry*, 1959, **1**, 185–196.

BRADBURN, N. M., & CAPLOVITZ, D. *Reports on happiness*. Chicago: Aldine-Atherton, 1965.

CARTER, R. D., & THOMAS, E. J. Modification of problematic marital communication using corrective feedback and instruction. *Behavior Therapy*, 1973, 4, 100–109.

CARTWRIGHT, D. S., & ROTH, I. Success and satisfaction in psychotherapy. *Journal of Clinical Psychology*, 1957, **13**, 20–26.

CHRISTENSEN, H. T. *Handbook of marriage and the family*. Chicago: Rand McNally, 1964.

DEUTSCH, M., & KRAUS, R. M. Studies of interpersonal bargaining. In M. Shubik (Ed.), *Game theory and related approaches to social behavior*. New York: John Wiley, 1964.

FAZIO, A. F. Verbal and overt behavioral assessment of a specific fear. *Journal of Consulting and Clinical Psychology*, 1969, **33**, 705–709.

FEDERAL BUREAU OF INVESTIGATION. *Crime in the United States: uniform crime reports*. Washington, D.C.: U.S. Government Printing Office, 1968.

FELDMAN, H. The effects of children on the family. In A. Michel (Ed.), *Family issues of employed women in Europe and America*. The Netherlands: Lieden Press, 1971.

GOLDIAMOND, I. Self control procedures in personal behavior problems. *Psychological Report*, 1965, **17**, 851–868.

GOLDSTEIN, M. K., & FRANCIS, B. Behavior modification of husbands by wives. Paper presented at the meeting of the National Councils on Family Relations, Washington, D.C., 1969.

GOODRICH, D. W., & BOOMER, S. Experimental assessment of marital modes of conflict resolution. *Family Process*, 1963, **2**, 15–24.

GRIFFITH, W. B. Behavior differences of children as perceived and judged by parents, teachers, and children themselves. *Institute of Child Welfare Monograph*, Minneapolis: University of Minnesota Press, 1952, No. 25.

HOMME, L., CSANZI, A., GONZALES, M., & RECHS, J. *How to use contingency contracting in the classroom*. Champaign, Ill.: Research Press, 1970.

HOPS, H., WILLS, T., WEISS, R., & PATTERSON, G. R. Marital interaction coding system (MICS). Unpublished manuscript, University of Oregon and Oregon Research Institute, 1972. (See NAPS Document #02077 for 29 pages of supplementary material. Order from ASIS/NAPS, c/o Microfiche Publications, 440 Park Ave. So., New York, New York 10017. Remit in advance for each NAPS accession number $1.50 for microfiche or $5.00 for photocopies. Make checks payable to Microfiche Publications.)

KNOX, D. *Marital happiness: a behavioral approach to counseling*. Champaign, Ill.: Research Press, 1972.

KUHN, T. S. *The structure of scientific revolutions.* Vol. 2, No. 2. Chicago: University of Chicago Press, 1970.

LAZARUS, A. A. Behavior therapy and marriage counseling. *Journal of the American Society of Psychosomatic Dentistry and Medicine,* 1968, **15,** 49–56.

LEDERER, W. J., & JACKSON, D. D. *The mirages of marriage.* New York: Norton, 1968.

LERNER, L. F. Actual versus expected compatibility in the problem-solving dyad. Unpublished doctoral dissertation, University of Oregon, 1973.

LIBERMAN, R. Behavioral approaches to family and couple therapy. *American Journal of Orthopsychiatry,* 1970, **40,** 106–118.

LOCKE, H. J., & WALLACE, K. M. Short marital adjustment and prediction tests: their reliability and validity. *Marriage and Family Living,* 1959, **21,** 251–255.

MacFARLENE, J., ALLEN, L., & HONZIK, M. *A developmental study of the behavior problems of normal children between 21 months and 14 years.* Berkeley and Los Angeles: University of California Press, 1962.

McFALL, R. M. Effects of self-monitoring on normal smoking behavior. *Journal of Consulting and Clinical Psychology,* 1970, **35,** 135–142.

OLSON, D. H. The measurement of family power by self report and behavioral methods. *Journal of Marriage and the Family,* 1969, **31,** 545–550.

OLSON, D. H. Marital and family therapy: integrative review and critique. *Journal of Marriage and the Family,* 1970, **32,** 501–538.

OLSON, D. H. Behavior modification research with couples and families: a system analysis, review, and critique. Paper presented at the meeting of the Association for the Advancement of Behavior Therapy, New York, October 1972.

OLSON, D. H., & RYDER, R. G. Inventory of marital conflicts (IMC): an experimental interaction procedure. *Journal of Marriage and the Family,* 1970, **32,** 443–448.

PATTERSON, G. R. *Families: applications of social learning to family life.* Champaign, Ill.: Research Press, 1971.

PATTERSON, G. R., & COBB, J. A. A dyadic analysis of "aggressive" behaviors. In J. P. Hill (Ed.), *Minnesota symposia on child psychology.* Vol. 5. Minneapolis: University of Minnesota Press, 1971, 72–129.

PATTERSON, G. R., & COBB, J. A. Stimulus control for classes of noxious behaviors. In J. F. Knutson (Ed.), *The control of aggression: implications from basic research.* Chicago: Aldine-Atherton, 1973, 144–199.

PATTERSON, G. R., & HOPS, H. Coercion, a game for two: intervention techniques for marital conflict. In R. E. Ulrich & P. Mountjoy (Eds.), *The experimental analysis of social behavior.* New York: Appleton-Century-Crofts, 1972, 424–440.

PATTERSON, G. R., HOPS, H., & WEISS, R. L. Interpersonal skills training for couples in the early stages of conflict. *Journal of Marriage and the Family,* 1975, May 1975, 295–303.

PATTERSON, G. R., RAY, R. S., SHAW, D. A., & COBB, J. A. Manual for coding of family interaction, 1969. See Document #01234 for 33 pages of material. Order from ASIS/NAPS, c/o Microfiche Publications, 440 Park Ave. So., New York, New York 10017. Remit in advance $5.45 for photocopies or $1.50 for microfiche. Make checks payable to Microfiche Publications.

PATTERSON, G. R., & REID, J. B. Reciprocity and coercion: two facets of social systems. In C. Neuringer & J. L. Michael (Eds.), *Behavior modification in clinical psychology.* New York: Appleton-Century-Crofts, 1970, 133–177.

RAPPAPORT, A. F., & HARREL, J. A behavioral-exchange model for marital counseling. The *Family Coordinator,* 1972, **21,** 203–212.

RAUSH, H. L. Interaction sequences. *Journal of Personality and Social Psychology,* 1965, **2,** 487–499.

REID, J. B. Reciprocity and family interaction. Unpublished doctoral dissertation, University of Oregon, 1967.

REID, J. B. Reliability assessment of observation data: a possible methodological problem. *Child Development,* 1970, **41,** 1143–1150.

REID, J. B., & DeMASTER, B. The efficacy of the spot-check procedure in maintaining the reliability of data collected by observers in quasi-natural settings: two pilot studies. *Oregon Research Institute Research Bulletin,* 1972, **12,** No. 8.

ROLLINS, B. C., & FELDMAN, H. Marital satisfaction over the family life cycle. *Journal of Marriage and the Family,* 1970, **2,** 20–28.

RUTTER, M., TIZARD, J., & WHITMORE, W. *Education health and behavior.* New York: John Wiley, 1970.

SIDMAN, M. *Tactics of scientific research.* New York: Basic Books, 1960.

STEINMETZ, S. K., & STRAUSS, M. A. Some myths about violence in the family. Paper presented at the meeting of the American Sociologist Convention, Houston, Texas, 1971.

STORROW, H. A. The measurement of outcome in therapy. *Archives of General Psychology,* 1960, **2**, 142–146.

STRODBECK, F. L. Husband and wife interaction over revealed differences. *American Sociological Review,* 1961, **16**, 468–473.

STUART, R. B. Token reinforcement in marital treatment. Paper presented at the meeting of the Association for the Advancement of Behavior Therapy, San Francisco, 1968.

STUART, R. B. Operant interpersonal treatment for marital discord. *Journal of Consulting and Clinical Psychology,* 1969, **33**, 675–682.

STUART, R. B. Behavioral remedies for marital ills: a guide to the use of operant-interpersonal techniques. Paper presented at the International Symposium on Behavior Modification, Minneapolis, Minnesota, October 1972.

THARP, R. G. Psychological patterning in marriage. *Psychological Bulletin,* 1963, **60**, 90–117.

TURNER, A. J. Couple and group treatment of marital discord: an experiment. Unpublished manuscript, 1972.

VINCENT, J. P. Problem-solving behavior in distressed and non-distressed married and stranger dyads. Unpublished doctoral dissertation, University of Oregon, 1972.

WAHLER, R. G., WINKLE, G. H., PETERSEN, R. F., & MORRISON, D. C. Mothers as behavior therapists for their own children. *Behaviour Research and Therapy,* 1965, **3**, 113–124.

WALKER, H., & BUCKLEY, N. R. Teacher attention to appropriate and inappropriate classroom behavior: an individual case study. *Focus on Exceptional Children,* 1973, **5**, 5–11.

WEISS, R. L., HOPS, H., & PATTERSON, G. R. A framework for conceptualizing marital conflict, a technology for altering it, some data for evaluating it. In L. A. Hamerlynck, L. C. Handy, & E. J. Mash (Eds.), *Behavior change: methodology concepts and practice.* Champaign, Ill.: Research Press, 1973.

WELCH, J. C., & GOLDSTEIN, M. K. The differential effects of operant-interpersonal intervention. Paper presented at the meeting of the Association for the Advancement of Behavior Therapy, New York, 1972.

WILLS, T. A. The measurement of pleasurable and displeasurable events in marital relationships. Unpublished master's thesis. University of Oregon, 1971.

WILLS, T. A., WEISS, R. L., & PATTERSON, G. R. A behavioral analysis of the determinants of marital satisfaction. *Journal of Consulting and Clinical Psychology,* 1974, **42**, 802–811.

WOLFF, S. Behavioral characteristics of primary school children referred to psychiatric departments. *British Journal of Psychiatry,* 1967, **113**, 885–893.

Management of Sexual Disorders

8

ISAAC M. MARKS

This review will deal with that majority of sexual disorders in which there is no physical pathology. Nonorganic sexual problems can be divided into three broad classes which are not mutually exclusive. The first involves *failure of function,* which is sometimes termed sexual dysfunction. This includes three forms of male impotence and several varieties of female frigidity. When these disorders have always been present they are called "primary;" if they develop after an initial period of normal function they are labelled "secondary." Failures of sexual function are often associated with sexual anxiety, fear or disgust, and other complications like social deficits.

Impotence is a generic term which includes premature ejaculation and failure of erection (erectile impotence), which often occur together, and the rarer condition of ejaculatory failure despite adequate and prolonged erection. Frigidity ranges from extreme sexual phobias (where the woman cannot bear to be touched anywhere on her body, even by a child) to more localized vaginismus where anxiety and spasm occur only on attempted penetration. Either of these might be sufficiently severe to result in nonconsummation of marriage. Severe vaginismus and nonconsummation can co-exist with normal orgasm through mutual masturbation. The least severe form of "frigidity" is anorgasmia, where coitus might actually be pleasurable but orgasm unattainable. Some have argued that this is a normal biological variant (Cooper, 1969).

The second main class of sexual problem concerns *attraction to an unusual object or activity for sexual gratification.* These are the sexual deviations, which include homosexuality, transvestism, fetishism, exhibitionism, voyeurism, sadomasochism, and anal intercourse. Sexual deviations may be associated with fear of heterosexuality, social deficits, and other difficulties. However, they are also perfectly compatible with normal heterosexual functioning.

Transsexualism is the third class of sexual disorder. It is a disturbance of gender role or identity in which the subject feels he or she belongs to the sex opposite to that of his or her physical features. It is usually associated with cross-dressing, though not necessarily to reach orgasm.

Frequency

The commonest problems for which help is sought in medical and psychological clinics are failures of function such as impotence and frigidity. Less frequently seeking help are the sexual deviants. The commonest deviation in the clinic is homosexuality; the next most frequent is exhibitionism, which is the commonest adult sexual offense in Britain (Rooth, 1971) and many other countries. Transsexualism is rare in the clinic and very rare in the community, the overall incidence being perhaps one in a million of the normal population. Homosexuality apart, the great majority of sexual deviants are males, and very few reports of females are to be found in the literature (Kinsey, Pomeroy, & Martin, 1953).

The frequency with which sexual problems present for treatment is not a reliable guide to their prevalence in the community. Current figures for the community prevalence of most sexual problems are unavailable and it is hard to visualize practicable epidemiological studies which could be done at present to produce hard knowledge of this kind.

The incidence given by Kinsey (1948) for erectile impotence was 0.1% of males under 20, 0.8% under 30, 1.9% under 40, 6.7% under 50, 18.4% under 60, 27% under 70, and 75% under 80, although numbers in old age were small. Out of 4,108 adult males, 66 (1.6%) had lasting erectile impotence; however, only 6 (0.1%) had failure of ejaculation, although this is the normal situation in preadolescent males and sometimes in old age. Kinsey et al. (1953) found that female anorgasmia after marriage fell from 25% at 1 year to 17% at 5 years and 11% by 20 years of marriage while nonconsummation occurred in less than 1% of marriages. Anorgasmia was less common in the younger generation, perhaps reflecting changes in social attitudes.

Persistent homosexuality is the commonest sexual deviation in the community, occurring in about 4% of adult males, and in rather fewer women (Kinsey et al., 1948; 1953). It is fortunate for therapists that most homosexuals do not seek to change their orientation because clinics would otherwise be overwhelmed. Exhibitionists seek treatment only when difficulties, usually legal, arise from their activities. The characteristics of clients who seek treatment for sexual problems at clinics are not necessarily the same as those of untreated people with similar sexual behavior. Siegelman (1972a; 1972b) found that nonclinical male and female homosexuals who answered a questionnaire were as well adjusted as comparable heterosexuals. Masculine homosexuals were better adjusted than feminine homosexuals. Homosexuals who seek help in changing their orientation tend to have other neurotic problems and in that respect resemble other neurotics more than do nonclinical homosexuals (Feldman, 1973). These differences between clinical and nonclinical populations need to be kept in mind.

Causation

In a chapter on management of sexual disorders, detailed discussion of etiology is out of place. Only a few points deserve comment. Little systematic knowledge about the origins of sexual disorder is available and there are few experiments to help us interpret the data, although some failures of sexual function can apparently be traced to traumatic or anxiety-laden experiences in earlier years. For deviations, there is much evidence showing that absence of a stable relationship with the father in Western cultures is associated with homosexuality, transvestism, exhibitionism, and transsexualism. It is still a mystery why, given similar paternal deficits, some become homosexual while others become transsexual, transvestite, or exhibitionist.

Cerebral function appears normal in most persons with sexual problems. However, early brain damage can render an individual vulnerable to abnormal sexual behavior. In epileptic out-patients, Kolarsky, Freund, Machek, & Polak (1967) found that sexual *deviations* were associated with temporal lobe damage prior to age two. The lesions of sexually deviant subjects began earlier than did those of nondeviant patients. Kolarsky et al. suggested that "an early brain lesion destroys primordial programs controlling the selection of stimuli and activities, the learning of which are necessary for further specification and elaboration of these primordial programs. Aberrant sexual programs may develop as a compensation, provided that the brain lesion is present during a critical period of life . . ." which in man is unlikely to be beyond age two.

Not only deviation but also sexual *hypoactivity* is associated with temporal lobe damage (Kolrasky et al, 1967). Temporal lobe epilepsy is associated with lack of sexual drive (Blumer & Walker, 1967); after a temporal lobectomy, absence of seizures is accompanied by return of sexual responsiveness. Medial temporal structures thus appear important for normal sexual activity.

An ingenious experiment by Rachman (1966) and Rachman and Hodgson (1968) showed that young males can develop deviant erections in a classical conditioning situation where pictures of high-heeled boots are followed repeatedly by those of nude women. In contrast, young men conditioned only weak erections to several patterns (Langevin & Martin, 1975). Some stimuli may be more prepotent than others in their ability to become associated with sexual behavior (Marks, 1972). The narrow range of fetish objects appears nonrandom when the character and the objects of pornography are considered, given the wide range of stimuli to which the average male is exposed during formative years. Seligman's notion of preparedness (Seligman & Hager, 1972) is potentially useful here and could be tested experimentally (Marks, 1972).

Assessment for Treatment

Although it would be facile to regard all sexual problems as "learned maladaptive reactions"—a term which merely masks our ignorance—effective treatment luckily does not depend upon precise knowledge of causation.

The chief considerations in the treatment of patients with sexual problems appear in Table 8–1. An essential aspect of

TABLE 8–1   Considerations in assessment of sexual problems

Contributing Problems

Depression
Drugs
Physical illness (endocrinal, metabolic, neurological, other)
Impotence/Frigidity ⟷ sexual deviance
Marital and/or other interpersonal disharmony
Social anxiety and/or deficits

Sexual History Since Puberty

Puberty
Masturbation (frequency and accompanying fantasies)
Coitus (frequency and accompanying fantasies and difficulties)
Hetero- and/or homosexual relationships (stability and quality)
Deviant practices and fantasies (frequency and content)

Implications for Management

Does dysfunction need to improve?
Does deviance need to decrease?

management is clear definition of the problem by adequate history taking and precise delineation of sexual behavior. The subject may seek aid ostensibly for a sexual problem at a time when he is undergoing severe depression, a grief reaction at loss of a lover, or marital disharmony. A patient may be referred for an apparently sexual disorder when in fact other pathology is responsible. An extreme example encountered by the author is a man who was referred for exhibitionism but whose exposing in fact resulted from gross posttraumatic brain damage. A less obvious instance is a manic-depressive woman who sought to change her lesbianism repeatedly each time she had a depressive swing; between depressive episodes she remained contented as a homosexual.

Two couples illustrate the difficulty of separating marital disharmony from sexual problems (Marks, Gelder, & Bancroft, 1970). The partner in one had been unhappy and distant for 20 years. His wife insisted that he be treated for his rubber fetishism. This disappeared after three weeks' aversion therapy, upon which he felt much more attracted to his wife and sought her affections. She, however, not only turned from him with indifference but told him that she had formed an attachment to another man. He required support and antidepressant medication for his ensuing depression, from which he recovered without relapse of his fetishism. He continued normal coitus with his wife despite her liaison. The second couple had argued frequently before treatment, and the wife had insisted on therapy. The husband's deviant sexual behavior ceased after aversion therapy, but the wife then complained that her husband's depression and "sulks" were more difficult to bear than his cross-dressing and she forced him to leave the home.

Having excluded serious depression, marital disorder, schizophrenia, and cerebral or other organic pathology, overall appraisal may indicate that the sexual complaint is the main problem. Once this problem has been defined, one can proceed to treatment according to the particular features of the case. A detailed clear sexual history is required to decide subsequent management. It must include the subject's physical and sexual development, the age of puberty, outlets since then (including *masturbation,* its frequency, and its accompanying fantasies over the years), *coital frequency* (and accompanying fantasies and difficulties), duration of heterosexual and homosexual relationships (and their stability and quality), and *deviant practices* and *fantasies.* The subject's personality style and activities, and the presence or absence of other psychological problems also require assessment.

Treatment Research

Tables 8–2 and 8–4 (see p. 259 and p. 267) summarize the options for management of the two main problem areas—failure of heterosexuality and deviant activity. Interpersonal anxieties and deficits can complicate both these areas and may require social skills training procedures in their own right. It is still unknown how much improvement in heterosexuality can generalize to reducing deviance and interpersonal deficits and vice versa. Common sense suggests that each area requires its own approach, but only research will tell whether a homosexual, for example, will benefit most from aversion therapy alone, or from aversion to his deviance combined with desensitization to heterophobia (if this is present) and training in heterosexual skills.

Unfortunately, few firm guidelines have emerged to date. Although research is improving, the bulk of the existing literature consists of uncontrolled reports, usually of single cases and rarely of series. There are few adequately controlled investigations of single subjects or of series of patients, so current conclusions are very tentative. It would be pointless in this review to cat-

TABLE 8–2   Management of sexual dysfunction: impotence and frigidity

I Treat any contributory problems.

II Obtain a detailed history (behavior analysis).

III Treat client and partner, client alone, or client and surrogate.

IV One or two therapist(s) can be same sex as patient; opposite sex of patient; or a male-female team.

V Counseling and providing sexual and interpersonal information

    A. with or without marital or other interpersonal therapy (contract/interpretative).
    B. with or without social skills training (modeling, role rehearsal, role reversal, repeated practice with feedback correction).

VI Exposure of patient to sexual behavior; exposure can be:

    A. slow (desensitization) or fast (flooding)
    B. in fantasy or in vivo, and can include:

        1. repeated practice with feedback to and from therapist (verbal, videotape, direct observation)
        2. general relaxation (muscular or with drugs such as methohexitone)
        3. hierarchy items given by therapist, patient, or spouse, with or without emotional reexperiencing of hierarchy events
        4. sensate focus with or without initial ban on coitus and initial nudity
        5. pelvic exercises (relaxation and contraction)
        6. digital genital exploration (done by self and spouse)
        7. dilators passed by therapist, patient, spouse
        8. self-masturbation with or without spouse, orgasmic conditioning
        9. coital position
      10. squeeze technique
      11. superstimulation
      12. shaping or fading
      13. modeling (film, video, or live)

alogue all uncontrolled case reports except where these are of special interest. More attention will be devoted to these rare studies which are reasonably well controlled. Until recently, experimental treatment of sexual disorders has been hampered by cultural taboos which lately have eased, enabling more systematic work to be done.

From controlled studies there is slight evidence that imaginal desensitization plus social skills training is useful in treating sexual dysfunction (see p. 264) and that aversion and self-regulation can reduce deviance (see Table 8–6, p. 279). All other methods are based on uncontrolled work; these of course cannot be ignored and clinical progress has been made from unsystematic experiments, but clearer definition of techniques and their indications will greatly increase the ability of therapists to help their clients. Table 8–2 and 8–4 are as much a list of research problems which remain to be explored as they are of techniques at the disposal of the therapist. These techniques will be discussed presently.

MEASURES OF CHANGE

With improving methodology more measures of sexual function have become available. The best measure—direct observation of sexual behavior—is as yet rarely possible, although Serber (1974) used videotape recordings, and Masters and Johnson (1970) and other laboratories have observed sexual behavior directly. Indirect information is obtained by interviews which detail sexual behavior (Bancroft, 1970a, 1970b; Birk, Huddleston, Miller, & Cohler, 1971; Chabot, personal communication). Attitude scales to measure sexual anxiety were used by Obler (1973); Bentler (1968) described questionnaires regarding sexual activity in males and females. Self-report measures of sexual orientation were described by Feldman and MacCulloch (1971), while Marks and Sartorius (1968) devised attitude scales to measure any sexual attraction in a semantic differential format. Questionnaire measures of effeminate behavior were described by Schatzberg, Westfall, Blumetti, & Birk (1975).

Direct measures of sexual arousal are provided by mechanical measures of penile erection or of vaginal warmth or color. Numerous devices have been used (Bancroft, Gwynne Jones, & Pullan, 1966; Barlow, Becker, Leitenberg, & Agras, 1970; Freund, 1960; Johnson & Kitching, 1969; McConaghy, 1967). Although these autonomic measures might seem the best indicators of sexual function, the result in a laboratory does not necessarily reflect performance in the natural situation (Bancroft, 1971). They need to be used in conjunction with other evidence of sexual attitude and behavior.

Indirect measures of sexual interest are described by Hess, Seltzer, & Shlien (1965) and Solyom and Miller (1965) who measured pupillary and finger plethysmograph responses respectively to pictures of men and women. These are remote indices compared to other methods of sex research. Measures of genital arousal were reviewed by Jovanovic (1971), while Zuckerman (1971) gave a detailed critique of these and many other physiological correlates of sexual arousal.

The value of using movies rather than photos in measuring sexual responses was noted by McConaghy (1974) in a controlled experiment. Twelve medical students saw two series of neutral and sexually stimulating films and slides; each stimulus was preceded a few seconds earlier by geometric figures. Subjects showed greater erections to films than to slides of females. Furthermore, their conditioned erections were greater to geometric figures seen before films than before slides of nude girls. Conditioned erections to circles correlated significantly with unconditioned erections to nudes.

It is obvious that the best measures for a given investigation depend on the purpose of that study, and no rigid prescriptions can be offered. In general, the broader the sets of observations available the better. Ideally one requires interview data from both client and partner, direct observation, physiological measures and attitudes, and long-term follow-up. This ideal is likely to remain unattainable for some years to come.

Treatment of Sexual Dysfunction: Impotence and Frigidity

The first step in management of failed sexual function is adequate delineation of the difficulty. Psychological causes include severe depression and marital disharmony. Organic causes of impotence occur in fewer than 5% of patients in psychiatric practice (Johnson, 1968) but should be suspected when erections never occur at any time. Organic factors and drugs can be readily excluded as causes of impotence by a history of normal erections in the early morning or at other times. Excessive alcohol is a well known cause as Shakespeare recognized: "Lechery, Sir, it provokes and unprovokes, it provokes desire but it takes away performance [*Macbeth*, Act 2, scene 3]." Impotence may correlate with the start of medication such as phenothiazines, monoamine oxidase inhibitors, and hypotensive agents such as guanethidine, or with use of drugs like heroin or morphine. In some men there is a history of normal sexual activity until sudden failure due to "brewer's droop," fatigue, or his partner's behavior. This failure can lead to anticipatory fear of impotence at the next attempt which produces the very result which is dreaded, and secondary impotence then becomes established. A few men may have constitutionally and persistently low sex interest, although they are physically normal in other respects. At the other extreme, abnormally high expectations can lead to a complaint of impotence as with one 20-year-old man who reported himself abnormal when he could "only" complete sexual relations six times a night. Rarely, ignorance of normal sexual processes can contribute to impotence.

In the treatment of impotence and frigidity the largest series so far is the uncontrolled one of Masters and Johnson (1970). Variants of their methods have been described by Bancroft (1972) and Brown (1972). Their chief principles are: (1) the couple is treated together rather than as an individual; (2) relevant sexual attitudes are modified as appropriate; and (3) the sexual partners learn to caress one another in the nude ("sensate focus") while there is a ban on intercourse. When the partners are comfortable with this, sensate focus is continued along with specific techniques for particular problems—graduated stimulation is used for erectile impotence and anorgasmia; the squeeze technique for premature ejaculation; graded dilators for vaginismus; and superstimulation for ejaculatory failure. Throughout treatment a hierarchical approach is adopted in which the couple progresses from less to more difficult tasks and good communication is always fostered. The couple must learn to give pleasure to one another in order to receive it ("give to get").

The work of Masters and Johnson (1970) is now so well known as to be part of the general culture. A popular exposition of their technique is given in a paperback by Belliveau and Richter (1970). Books like these and diagrams and films about normal sex can be valuable instructional media for patients. Masters and Johnson's overall results are encouraging. Excellent results were obtained in the treatment of premature ejaculation where 98% of patients obtained adequate control. In erectile impotence, success rate was 74% of secondary and 60% of primary impotence patients. In failure of ejaculation, emission was obtained in 82% of subjects. All cases of nonconsummation engaged in coitus after treatment and a five-year follow-up showed satisfactory outcome in 80% of patients with primary and 75% with secondary frigidity. However, the Masters and Johnson work is uncontrolled, and many factors in the complicated package of treatment could have contributed toward their results. Their couples pay fees and are treated in a special clinic far from home in a honeymoon setting. Problems are sometimes encountered in the transfer of treatment gains from the clinic to the home. An expensive male and female therapist team is used for each couple.

Bancroft (1972) has adapted the approach to the prevailing environment under the National Health Service in Britain. He uses only one therapist and does not find this a disadvantage. In a controlled study Mathews (1975, unpublished) found that one therapist produced results similar to those of a male-female therapist team. During the initial session he sees each partner first separately and then together; during this time he explains the principles of sensate focus and bans them from having intercourse. This reduces the anxiety which arises when patients feel they have to perform well. From the third session on, he sees the couple jointly during "briefing sessions" in which attitudinal and behavioral problems are worked through. At these sessions, he discusses behavior between sessions, explores attitudes, and modifies new behavioral goals. Brown (1972) uses a male-female therapist team in a similar setting.

Couples in treatment have to have a *commitment to change*. The Masters and Johnson approach involves *education* by day and *performance* by the couple at night; performance is reported to the therapist in detail the next day, and the therapist provides corrective *feedback* to improve subsequent performance.

Certain techniques are methods of graduated exposure or desensitization. *Sensate focus* is a form of desensitization in vivo whereby partners become used to fondling one another's bodies without anxiety or embarrassment. Methods of vaginal dilation use the same principle.

The *squeeze* technique for premature ejaculation teaches response control. A variant of the squeeze technique was originally described by Semans (1956). In this, masturbation without emission was practised repeatedly with the aim of prolonging the time of erection before ejaculation was reached. Masters and Johnson ask the women to masturbate the penis until the man indicates ejaculation is imminent, upon which she inhibits ejaculation by squeezing the glans penis with her fingers.

The emphasis on *good communication* and round table discussions reduces friction between partners which might have led to poor performance. The effects of simple counseling should not be overlooked (Faulk, 1971). Brown (1967) reported that patients were successful in obtaining orgasm after but few sessions of counseling from several therapists. The Masters and Johnson approach can thus be seen as exercising its effect partly through the easing of interpersonal tensions, enhancement of communication, education with repeated practice and corrective feedback, graduated exposure, and response control.

A major research effort is now testing the various components of the Masters and Johnson package. The most obvious question is whether two therapists are required, as this adds greatly to the cost. Mathews' work implies that two therapists are generally unnecessary. Another question is whether couples need to be treated together, or whether similar results would be obtained if only one member of a couple were treated or if both were seen separately. The last would help indicate the contribution made simply by improving communication between the partners. Other issues that should be tested are whether the initial ban on intercourse removes fear of failure; how clients who have no partner can be helped by treatment alone; and whether or not surrogates should be employed.

Masters and Johnson noted that couples who were unwilling to apply lubricants during sexual exercises did less well. Brown (1972) found that a prognostic feature was the readiness of the couple to allow time for treatment and for sexual encounter in a relaxed atmosphere. In addition, patients with secondary impotence or frigidity who once functioned reasonably well have a better prognosis than those who have never achieved normal sexual relations.

Chabot (personal communication, 1973) has summarized the treatment components used by many different workers in sexual dysfunction. These and their outcomes are given in Table 8–3. They include the factors just mentioned, plus items like simple advice and explanation, insight into other aspects of personality function, desensitization in fantasy, relaxation through muscular exercises or drugs (methohexitone), and effects of vaginal examination with dilators or digitally.

The contribution of *feedback* to performance is described by Serber (1974). His couples engage in sexual relations in a room with a videotape recorder which switches on automatically when they enter. The couple subsequently view the videotape with the therapist, who discusses problems and their solution with the couple. They then keep the tape. This feedback procedure is said to increase the accuracy of treatment monitoring and self-report.

Graded exposure to different aspects of sexual behavior has been used in various ways by many workers:

Self-masturbation by women has been incorporated deliberately in a Masters and Johnson program for the treatment of orgasmic dysfunction (Lopiccolo & Lobitz, 1972). They describe a nine-step program of masturbation designed to lead a woman to heterosexual coital orgasm as an adjunct to a 15-session treatment program involving husband and wife. The husband is aware of the wife's program and is involved from the seventh step onward. The authors describe the treatment of eight women who had never previously had orgasm but attained it during the program.

The use of **orgasmic reconditioning** during graded exposure in vivo was described by Wilson (1973). His female patient could experience orgasm during mutual masturbation, but could not tolerate intercourse due to vaginismus. She worsened during seven sessions of desensitization in fantasy and in vivo (in vivo desensitization consisted of insertion of her own and her fiance's finger intravaginally). She was then required to engage in foreplay and *just before orgasm* to imagine the tip of her own finger intravaginally. When this was tolerated she had to imagine her own finger progressively further in and longer before orgasm. Eventually real was substituted for imagined finger insertion, first by herself and then by her fiance. Within two months normal intercourse was occurring regularly.

Faulk (1973) cited several authors who treated frigidity by graded exposure in one form or another. Hastings (1967) found that some women benefited from practicing masturbation to orgasm and then progressing by stages to full coital orgasm. Kegal (1953) and Davis (1957) recommended **exercise of the pubococcygeus muscle** to increase sexual appreciation. Dawkins and Taylor (1961) and Freidman (1962) taught women **digital exploration** of their own genitals plus insight therapy with about 70% success in previously unconsummated marriages Ellison (1968) reported 87% success using insight therapy and **dilators** in 100 cases. Haslam (1965) described treatment of two women by passing graduated dilators which were left in situ for 10 minutes at a time after which the patient would pass them. Treatment time was only 2½ hours for one patient and 8 hours for the other. Cooper

(1969) noted a similar method with the husband being present at later stages of the wife's dilation.

Cooper's patient eventually engaged in coitus, but did not obtain orgasm. Most other authors did not report results about orgasm. Faulk (1971) noted that in frigidity not associated with nonconsummation, although almost half of 40 patients received substantial benefit in terms of pleasure and adjustment in treatment with dilators and insight therapy, only 5 achieved regular orgasm. Patients with the best prognosis in his study had a good relationship with their husbands and higher anxiety in sexual matters. Whether the frigidity was primary or secondary was less important.

Desensitization in imagination has been used for frigidity by Lazarus (1963) with full sexual adjustment being obtained in 9 of 16 patients after a mean of 29 sessions. Madsen and Ullman (1967) modified the method by getting the husband to present the hierarchies, and Brady (1966) used methohexitone sodium successfully to induce relaxation. O'Gorman (1972) described the use of **group desensitization** in fantasy of frigid women while counseling the spouses in other groups. None of these studies was controlled.

The use of modeling has been limited. Some workers encourage couples to watch films of sexual activity, while others have actually had normal couples copulate in front of clients to demonstrate technique. As they become freely available, films of normal sexual activities may assume an increasingly important role in the education of couples with sexual dysfunction.

A large controlled investigation of sexual dysfunction (Obler, 1973) selected 64 volunteer students (60% male) out of 235 referred from university clinics on the basis of Manifest Anxiety Scale scores and interviews. These students were all well motivated and intelligent. They were divided into three matched groups: (1) desensitization for 45 minutes weekly over 15 weeks; (2) traditional group therapy 1½ hours weekly over 10 weeks; and (3) no treatment. The researcher carried out all treatment. Desensitization included not only hierarchy images facilitated by seeing sexual films and slides, but also four sessions of assertive training and role play of sex-related social situations.

Results showed significant increases in the success/experience ratio for the desensitized group, and for females over the no-treatment control and for males over both other groups. The GSR and heart rate decreased more in the desensitized group. Desensitized subjects also showed significantly more gains than both other groups on scales measuring specific sexual stress, and more gains than the no-treatment control on the Manifest Anxiety Scale. Eighty percent[1] of the desensitized subjects became "sexually functional" and at 18-month follow-up no regression was found. Some improvement was also found in the other two groups. The author commented on the value of graphic aids for the presentation of hierarchy images.

A problem in interpreting results of this study is that Obler's desensitization included role rehearsal methods which might have contributed even more to the effect than the desensitization in fantasy. Another difficulty is that sexual dysfunction includes a wide range of disorders. No data are given which can separate premature ejaculation from erectile impotence, nonconsummation of marriage, vaginismus, or anorgasmia (or whether these were primary or secondary). Furthermore, volunteer student populations are not necessarily comparable to more broad spectrum clinic populations. Phobic patients are usually more disturbed and difficult to treat than phobic volunteers, especially students (Marks, 1969; Olley & McAllister, 1974), and the same might apply to persons with sexual problems. The report

is too compressed to allow assessment of the seriousness of the sexual problems treated and the follow-up data are inadequate. There is also a lingering possibility that the volunteer population had a subcultural disbelief in traditional group treatment, or a strong belief in desensitization, since two volunteers refused to have group treatment instead of desensitization.

Couples with sexual dysfunction formed part of a series of marital problems treated in a controlled trial of several forms of marital therapy by Crowe (1976, in preparation). He contrasted a directive behavioral approach which included contracts with a more interpretative form of psychotherapy and with a supportive approach. All 3 approaches used a single therapist with patients treated conjointly with their spouses. Although the 3 approaches were equally effective in producing a significant reduction in marital pathology, the directive behavioral approach produced significantly more improvement in sexual and general adjustment than did the supportive treatment. Interpretative treatment was intermediate in effect. The superiority of directive treatment derived from results in couples whose main problem was sexual dysfunction.

Most of the literature on male *impotence* is uncontrolled. Friedman (1968) reported the use of **desensitization in imagination** with intravenous methohexitone in 19 cases. Sixteen patients with "erective disorders" were treated over 6 to 15 sessions. A 12-month follow-up indicated that 8 out of 10 patients who had suffered from impotence and 3 out of 6 patients who had suffered from premature ejaculation were improved. Three patients who had suffered from failure of ejaculation were only slightly improved after 29 treatments.

Secondary impotence has been treated by **shaping** (Wanderer, personal communication). The patient was fitted with a penis transducer and a female therapist on the other side of a one-way screen was able to see on a dial how much erection the patient was producing to heterosexual slides. Initi-

---

[1] The 80% figure contrasts with Chabot's 39% figure in Table 8–3. This 39% was computed from Obler's tables, which suggests that only 9 out of 22 subjects were successful on more than 50% of occasions, which is not an impressive result.

TABLE 8–3　Treatment components in studies of sexual dysfunction

	Group session	Conjoint session	Simple advice and explanation	Insight oriented	Desensitization in fantasy	Muscular/drug relaxation	Modelling and role playing	Advice to "stop" sexual intercourse	Vaginal examination plus dilators, or digital self-examination	Medication	Squeeze (Semans) technique	(Auto)hypnosis	Advice to masturbate to erotic stimuli	Number of cases	Success rate (%)	Average number of sessions
VAGINISMUS																
Dawkins & Taylor (1961)		(x)	x	x					x					63	70	4
Ellison (1968)		(x)	x	x				x	x					100	87	6
Freidman (1962)			x	x					x					100	71	6
Fuchs et al. (1973)			x		(x)	x		x	x				(x)	34	91	10
Haslam (1965)			x			x			x					2	100	10
Masters & Johnson (1970)	x	x	x					x	x					29	100	14
Michel-Wolfromm (1954)			x	x					x					22	73	12
ORGASMIC DYSFUNCTION																
Brady (1966)					x	x		x						5	80	12
Courtenay (1968)				x										7	43	10
Faulk (1971)			x	x						(x)				28	50	?
Lazarus (1963)					x	x		x						16	56	29
Lobitz & Lopiccolo (1972)	x	x					x	x					x	23	70	15
Madsen & Ullman (1967)	x				x	x		x						7	?	?
Masters & Johnson (1970)	x	x	x					x						342	80	14
IMPOTENCE																
Cooper (1969)		(x)	x	(x)	x									31	42	20
Friedman (1968)					x	x								10	80	9
Johnson (1968)		(x)	x	(x)						(x)				28	39	?
Lobitz (1972)	x	x					x	x						6	66	15
Masters & Johnson (1970)	x	x	x					x						245	72	14
PREMATURE EJACULATION																
Cooper (1969)	x	x					x				x			10	10	20
Friedman (1968)					x	x								6	50	11
Johnson (1968)			x	(x)						(x)				7	29	?
Lobitz & Lopiccolo (1972)	x	x						x			x			6	100	15
Masters & Johnson (1970)	x	x	x					x			x			182	98	14
Semans (1956)	x	x									x			8	100	?
FAILURE OF EJACULATION																
Cooper (1969)	x	x				x								13	46	20
Friedman (1968)					x	x								3	0	29
Johnson (1968)			x											3	33	?
Masters & Johnson (1970)	x	x	x					x						17	82	14
MISCELLANEOUS SEXUAL DYSFUNCTIONS																
Obler (1973)			x		x	x		x						22	39	15
Obler (1973)	x					x								20	5	10

(x) = not all patients received the particular treatment component.　　Adapted from Chabot (personal communication, 1973).

ally, the therapist praised small erections and gradually increased her criterion for praise to full erections. The patient did well. His impotence had dated back to an incident when he failed with a girlfriend who had then teased him about it.

Graded manual stimulation was reported to be useful in the treatment of a patient who had penile pain during thrusting and ejaculation in coitus (Sharpe & Meyer, 1973). The patient's wife touched his penis to find which areas of the glans and which forms of stimulation were painful. Starting with the easiest areas, the wife rubbed first the shaft and then the glans of the penis repeatedly while the patient was distracted by reading pornography. Distraction was then gradually withdrawn. The patient felt no pain during 14 sessions of treatment over three months, and at a three-week follow-up was symptom free.

Sometimes **brief contact with a therapist** can enhance performance. An impotent patient seen by the author found that he was able to perform normally for short periods after contact with the therapist by phone, letter, or in a brief interview. When failure of sexual function is associated also with sexual deviance, treatment may need to be directed to the deviance as well. Simpler methods can be quite valuable. An example comes from a couple treated by the author who had an unconsummated marriage of three years' duration. The husband was pedophiliac until the time of consultation, and impotent during the only four attempts he ever made at sexual intercourse during the honeymoon. Treatment consisted of instruction to sleep in the nude and fondle one another with an initial ban on coitus followed by graduated steps toward intercourse. Normal regular sexual relations were established within a month after only two treatment sessions. These miracle cures, however, are unusual.

The only controlled study of fantasy desensitization in impotence is that of Kockott, Dittmar, & Nusselt (1975). They treated 24 males (mean age 31) with co-operative partners for erectile impotence. Patients were assigned at random into three groups matched for age, intelligence, neuroticism, and whether impotence was primary or secondary. Subjects were either (1) given 14 sessions of desensitization in fantasy with an initial ban on coitus; (2) given 4 sessions of routine treatment over 16 weeks plus medication and advice; or (3) placed on the waiting list for 16 weeks. The two treated groups showed greater (but not significantly more) overall improvement and increase in erections. The desensitized patients could imagine intercourse with a woman they had just met with significantly decreased anxiety compared to the other two groups. The overall results of desensitization in fantasy with a ban on coitus were thus unimpressive. The authors commented on the many factors which maintained impotence including social anxiety, anxiety about level of performance, unrealistic sexual standards, a very limited range of sexual behavior, and an attitude that sex is dirty. The treated patients who had not improved in this study then received a modified Masters and Johnson approach combined with sex education. Of the 12 patients, 8 were improved. This method thus seemed superior to systematic desensitization alone.

Another controlled study is in progress (Chabot, personal communication) which looks at a Masters and Johnson program directed at sexual dysfunction alone compared with that plus attention to interpersonal relationships on a wider basis. Other controlled studies are in progress (Ascher, Phillip, & Wolpe; Bancroft, personal communication; Everaerd; Lopiccolo, unpublished).

In summary, therapy research into failure of sexual function is still in its infancy. Many workers with varying uncontrolled methods have reported good results. Controlled research is under way into overall outcome and into treatment components. It seems likely that different combinations of techniques will be required for different problems and indications for these will need to be delineated.

Treatment of Sexual Deviation

When there is an attraction for an unusual sexual object or mode of sexual stimulation, this attraction has to be reduced before the client can be considered improved. Sexual deviations do not necessarily correlate with the presence of heterophobia and although improvement in fears of heterosexuality can sometimes lead to resolution of sexual deviance as well, this is by no means the rule. The problems in treatment are of decreasing the deviant attraction and, where necessary, of treating the heterophobia and increasing heterosexual skills.

Psychological treatments of sexual deviations have a memorable history, and in the 1890s Schrenck-Notzing in Germany devised a program of desensitization in vivo for homosexuals (see Bancroft, 1970b). In 1935, Max wrote his pioneering account of electric aversion in homosexuals, but such treatment was not taken up again systematically until a generation later. Many other methods have developed and are evolving further. Unfortunately, controlled investigations are the exception rather than the rule so that few firm conclusions can be drawn at the present time. We need more systematic work using refined techniques in well selected homogenous populations of deviants with adequate follow-up of a year or more.

ETHICAL ISSUES

Unpleasant treatments, such as aversion, are adopted with understandable reluctance by therapists Any treatment foisted on a patient against his will is generally undesirable, but it is especially so with aversion therapy. The therapeutic unpleasantness has to be balanced against the continuation of the patient's problem, and he has to fully understand what is required in therapy before he gives consent. (We should remember that the unpleasantness of aversion therapy can be exaggerated.) In a study by Hallam, Rachman, and Falkowski (1972), most deviants and alcoholics rated aversion therapy as less unpleasant that a visit to the dentist.

Another ethical issue is that homosexuality is regarded by many as a normal variant of behavior rather than as a disorder and that society's attitude needs to be changed rather than the client's. Although

TABLE 8–4   Management: decreasing deviance

 I Treat any contributory problems.

 II Obtain a detailed history (behavior analysis).

 III Use any measures necessary to improve sexual dysfunction (see Table 8–2).

 IV Use aversion (electric, chemical, shame, or covert or smell sensitization) administered by therapist or patient to:
    A. deviant cues (fantasy, slides, films, narrative, in vivo–erections to any of these)
    B. classical/instrumental conditioning backward, aversion relief
    C. aversion immediately on contact or delayed
    D. partial or complete reinforcement

 V Pairing deviant and heterosexual stimuli (fading, shaping).

 VI Instruct in masturbation exercises and orgasmic conditioning.

 VII Teach patient self-regulation of deviant impulses

---

there is much cogency to this view, a homosexual who wants to change his orientation because he feels life would be easier as a heterosexual has the right to obtain help. It is unrealistic to ask him to wait the century or more that it may take for society to become geared to varying sexual orientations. Similarly, although exhibitionism may be a harmless activity, it is only humane to help an exposer lose the urges that bring him into conflict with the law.

The ethics of aversion therapy are in principle no different from those of any other treatment provided it is given with discretion and compassion, and with the patient's overall needs always in mind. It may be easier to help a pedophile to become homosexual rather than a heterosexual, for example. The target of treatment needs to be worked out by consensus with the patient, his partner, and the therapist. Full heterosexuality need not be the aim in all cases.

DECREASE DEVIANT BEHAVIOR

AVERSION. Research in aversion through 1969 has been ably summarized by Rachman and Teasdale (1969). Useful reviews of work in homosexuality are those of Feldman (1973) and Feldman and MacCulloch (1971). A second review of work in deviants is by Bancroft (1974).

Aversion therapy can take many forms. The aversive stimulus can be paired with any type of deviant cue, including fantasies, photographs, slides, narratives, or real life situations. The timing of the aversive stimulus can vary from the moment of contact with the deviant cue (either immediate or delayed) to only after erections or other signs of arousal appear to the deviant cues. The aversive stimulus can be given once or many times, regardless of the patient's behavior, or terminating only when the deviant behavior or erection ceases. Reinforcement can be partial or complete. Aversion can be paired with relief stimuli (usually

heterosexual) at the moment the aversive stimulus ceases.

Many aversive stimuli have been used. *Chemical* aversion was used widely until a few years ago (e.g., Barker, 1965; Cooper, 1963; Freund, 1960; Lavin, Thorpe, Barker, Blakemore, & Conway, 1961; Morgenstern, Pearce, & Rees, 1965; Oswald, 1961; Raymond, 1956). There is only one controlled study of this method (McConaghy, 1969, 1970). *Electric* aversion has been studied (including several controlled investigations) more than any other form. It has been given by classical conditioning, avoidance conditioning, backward conditioning, and aversion relief. Recently *covert sensitization* has often been used, though only one report was controlled (Barlow, Agras, Leitenberg, Callahan, & Moore, 1972). Other pilot aversive methods used in sexual deviations include *smell sensitization* (Colson, 1972; Maletzky, 1973) and *shame aversion* (Serber, 1972). *Aversive tickling* (Greene & Hoats, 1971) has not been reported in sexual deviations, nor has *scoline apnoea*. An *elastic band worn around the wrist* can be held taut and snapped back suddenly to sting the skin as effectively as any shock apparatus. It is simple, and the patient can use it as a "self-regulator" or "thought-stopper" as well as an aversive stimulus.

Chemical aversion. This has fallen into disfavor because, compared with electric aversion, it is more cumbersome, less precise, and potentially dangerous. In addition, fewer trials are possible, it cannot be self-administered, and it must be given in a medical setting. McConaghy and his co-workers performed a controlled study of chemical aversion (McConaghy, 1969, 1970; McConaghy, Proctor, & Barr, 1972). They assigned 40 homosexual patients at random to apomorphine or electric aversion. Treatment lasted for five days in the hospital. Apomorphine patients were shown slides on 28 occasions of males they found attractive, each occasion being associated with nausea produced by apomorphine injection. Electric aversion patients read aloud a series of phrases descriptive of homosexual activity and immediately received a painful electric shock to the fingertips. After 14 trials a heterosexual slide was seen 5 times without shock. This procedure was termed "aversion relief" though usually this label is used when shock regularly precedes a relief stimulus (not just once per session as in this design). Each patient experienced over one thousand pairings of phrases and shocks during the course of treatment, given over 15 sessions. Little difference was found between the effectiveness of apomorphine and electric aversion. At two-week follow-up, patients had significantly decreased erections to nude male pictures but had not increased erections to female pictures. At six months follow-up, half the patients had decreased in homosexual and increased in heterosexual feelings. Among these patients, the decrease in homosexual feelings correlated with the decrease in erections to male slides.

At a year's follow-up (McConaghy, 1970), little difference was apparent between the efficacy of apomorphine and aversion therapy. Of the 35 subjective reports received at follow-up, 10 patients showed marked, 15 some, and 10 no improvement. Only 7 had changed to a predominantly heterosexual adjustment. Others felt more able to control their feelings. Of 9 married men who attended at follow-up, 6 thought their marital sexual relationships had markedly improved. No consistent relationship was found between response to treatment and conditionability of erections as measured at initial assessment.

In a further report, McConaghy and Barr (1973) noted that another group of homosexuals who had had electric aversion ("avoidance conditioning") showed no significant differences from those described above who received apomorphine aversion or aversion relief. During avoidance conditioning, the patient was presented with 20 slides of males which could be rejected to avoid a painful electric shock on two-thirds of presentations; on remaining occasions the patient could not avoid shock.

Electric aversion. Three forms of electric aversion were compared by McConaghy and Barr (1973). They assigned 46 homosexuals at random (mean age 25) to classical, avoidance, or backward electric aversion conditioning. Each subject was treated in 14 sessions as an in-patient for 5 days. During treatment, 60 slides of male children, adolescents, and adults were shown for 10 seconds at a time. On some occasions following the removal of the male slide and cessation of shock, subjects assigned to avoidance or backward conditioning were also shown 30 slides of nude or partially clothed young adult women. Follow-up, usually with booster shock, was at monthly intervals for six months and again at one year.

Results showed no significant differences between these three forms of electric aversion. Subjects who attended for six or more booster treatments at follow-up did best. At one-year follow-up, half the subjects reported decreased homosexual feelings and half reported increased heterosexual feelings. A quarter showed increase in coital frequency and a quarter showed decrease in homosexual relations, the correlation between these being significant.

There was no significant relationship between outcome and a measure of "appetitive conditionability"—erections to red circles preceding female movies and to green triangles preceding male movies. However, there was a significant correlation between outcome and a measure of aversive conditioning—the GSR to tones preceding shocks. The fact that backward conditioning equalled the other two forms of aversion in efficacy suggested that aversion therapy does not act by setting up conditioned reflexes. Patients treated with aversion did not show arm withdrawal to the shocks or report anxiety if they viewed homosexual pictures after treatment. Instead they reported less sexual interest and showed fewer erections to these pictures. Patients under the age of 30 were more likely to commence heterosexual intercourse after treatment.

In another study (1975, in press) McConaghy compared the effect of backward and forward classical "conditioning" in homosexuals. Shocks were given either before or after 15 men saw slides of male nudes. In a contrasting condition, 16 homosexual men had "positive conditioning" in which male nudes were followed by female nudes or vice versa, in a balanced design. All patients had 14 sessions over 5 days, with 4 trials per session, and 3 minute intervals between trials. Neither treatment had a significant effect on erections. Aversion produced significantly greater change in orientation according to the therapist's assessment of homosexual and heterosexual interest at 1 and 12 month follow-up, but the therapist knew which treatments the patients had had. There was no correlation between change in erections and in behavior. Back and forward "conditioning" had equal effects for aversive and for positive "conditioning."

The reduction in homosexuality obtained by McConaghy and coworkers was less than that obtained by Feldman and MacCulloch (1971). These investigators treated 43 homosexual patients (including 7 pedophiles) by electric shock given in an anticipatory avoidance paradigm; follow-up lasted a year or more. Shocks were given while the subject viewed slides of males on a screen. Slides of males could sometimes be turned off prior to receipt of a shock. Immediately after the slides of males left the screen, a slide of a female was introduced as a relief stimulus, on a variable-ratio basis. Patients could request the return of a female slide at times, this request being met occasionally. About 24 stimulus presentations were given per 30-minute session (average number of sessions being 18 to 20) on an in-patient basis. Thirty-six of the 43 patients who began treatment completed it. Of these, 25 were significantly improved at the end of the year. Success was defined as cessation of homosexual behavior, the use of no more than occasional and mild homosexual fantasy and/or mild homosexual interest in directly observed

males, together with strong heterosexual fantasy or behavior. Posttreatment measures were a structured clinical interview and a sexual orientation questionnaire. Within-treatment measures were of avoidance response latencies and changes in pulse rate to the male slides that were used as conditional stimuli. Measures cohered in indicating change or not. Prognosis was best in patients with a prior history of pleasurable heterosexual behavior and without a "weak-willed" or "attention-seeking" personality. This relationship held even when controlled for age.

Feldman and MacCulloch (1971) also carried out a controlled trial in 30 more homosexuals who were randomly assigned to treatment by anticipatory avoidance learning, classical conditioning, or psychotherapy. Aversion treatment was given over 24 half-hour sessions, and psychotherapy over 12 one-hour sessions. After 24 sessions, 6 aversion patients were crossed over to the alternative form of aversion in a further 24 sessions, while 7 psychotherapy patients whose orientation failed to change then received aversion. Bias against psychotherapy was not excluded from the design. Follow-up was an average of 44 weeks. Both aversive techniques were equally successful with most patients who had a prior heterosexual history. Of the 27 patients who finally had aversion therapy, 17 showed successful change in sexual orientation at a mean of 46 weeks follow-up. Of the 2 patients who received psychotherapy only, one failed to improve and one defaulted at follow-up. All three treatments were almost totally unsuccessful in patients without a history of prior heterosexuality.

An elegant controlled comparison of electric aversion and imaginal desensitization was made by Bancroft (1970b). He randomly assigned 30 patients to treatment by desensitization in fantasy to fears of heterosexuality or to electric aversion. There were 30 treatment sessions, each lasting one hour. In half the aversion sessions, patients were shocked when they developed

TABLE 8–5   Results of aversion and desensitization in homosexuality.[a] (Significance of pre-post changes seen in figures 8–1, 2, and 3)

		Sexual Behavior		Sexual Attitudes		Erections	
		Hetero	*Homo*	*Hetero*	*Homo*	*Hetero*	*Homo*
Pretreatment—end of treatment	Aversion	ns[b]	<.01	<.01	<.001	<.05	<.05
	Desensitization	ns	<.001	<.02	ns	<.05	ns
Pretreatment—6-month follow-up	Aversion[c]	ns	<.01	ns	<.01	not tested	
	Desensitization[c]	ns	<.001	<.005	ns		

[a] Aversion and desensitization never differed significantly from each other.
[b] ns = not significant.
[c] Excluding dropouts.
SOURCE: Adopted from Bancroft (1970b).

erections to slides of males and in half the sessions patients were shocked on reporting the production of homosexual fantasies. Measures of change consisted of ratings of sexual behavior and attitude, and actual erections to slides.

Table 8-5 and Figures 8-1, 8-2, and 8-3 show Bancroft's results. Immediately after treatment only aversion significantly reduced erections and attitudes to males; erections and attitudes to females increased significantly both with aversion and with desensitization. On no measure at the end of treatment did aversion differ significantly from desensitization. At six to nine months follow-up only 5 of the averted and 5 of the

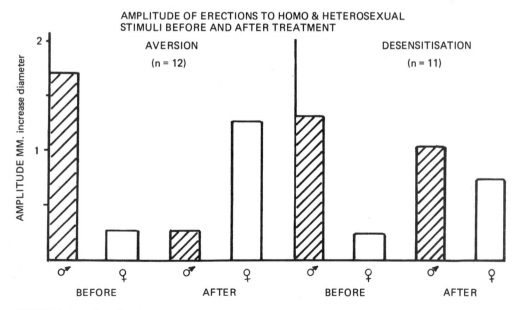

FIGURE 8–1   Erectile change: these histograms show the mean increase in erections to homosexual (shaded) and heterosexual (unshaded) pictures before and after treatment in the two treatment groups. Increases in erection are measured as millimeter increase in diameter of the penis (Bancroft, 1970b).

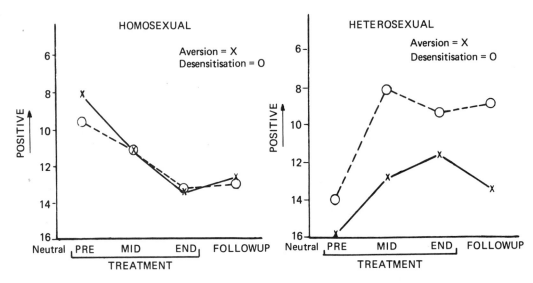

FIGURE 8–2   Attitude change: these graphs show the mean scores for the sexual scales on the semantic differential for the four occasions of testing (start of treatment, midtreatment, end of treatment, and follow-up). A neutral score is 16; anything less than this reflects a more positive attitude (Bancroft, 1970b).

desensitized patients were improved— change in orientation was less obvious than with Feldman and MacCulloch. Erections were not measured, but there was a slight suggestion that desensitized patients showed more heterosexual behavior; both aversion and desensitization significantly reduced homosexual behavior; aversion significantly improved homosexual attitudes and desensitization heterosexual attitudes. Only 1 case showed persistent signs of conditioned anxiety. Desensitization worked better in patients who had shown previous anxiety about heterosexuality. Aversion improved heterosexual erections more in younger and less in anxious patients.

The value of heterosexual arousal for outcome was suggested by one finding. At the end of treatment, although homosexual erections decreased in many patients, more of those with heterosexual interest (attitudes and erections) subsequently did well at six months follow-up.

Bancroft made the important observation

that changes often began in patients two months *before* treatment (see Figure 8-3). This reviewer has also observed this at times. It suggests that motivation is an important factor.

Another careful comparison of electric aversion with a nonaversive (placebo) control was reported by Birk et al. (1971). Of 60 homosexual referrals, 18 were selected for treatment and 16 remained after two years treatment. During these two years, they all received group psychotherapy with a male and female cotherapist team. At the end of the first year's group therapy the sample was assigned at random to shock or placebo conditioning. This was followed immediately by 12 hours of individual treatment and another year's group psychotherapy. A total of 20 to 25 half-hour conditioning sessions were given over six weeks. Each patient selected his own male and female pictures for use in sessions. There were 25 pictures per session given at intervals of 20 seconds. Within each session several forms of electric aversion were given: avoidance trials with escape by a female slide, classical conditioning with inevitable shock, delayed escape, delayed avoidance, and intertrial approach learning. Placebo conditioning controls received no shock but instead saw an amber light and were told that this was "associative conditioning."

After 12 sessions of conditioning none of the 8 placebo patients and 5 of the 8 aversion patients showed changed sexual feelings. One year after the end of conditioning 2 of the 5 improved aversion patients remained free of homosexuality and were active heterosexually. On the Kinsey ratings, aversion was significantly better than placebo at the end of conditioning but not at the end of follow-up. However, homosexual cruising, petting, and orgasm was significantly decreased at the end of follow-up in aversion patients compared to placebo conditioning subjects (Figures 8-4a & b). Really good results were obtained in only 2

out of 8 patients with aversion and in none of those who received placebo conditioning.

Total treatment time was 79 to 140 hours, most of which was spent in group psychotherapy. The design of the experiment precludes accurate assessment of the contribution made by group psychotherapy to the changes, as it was balanced across aversive and placebo conditioning. However, the poor results in the psychotherapy and placebo group suggests that group psychotherapy was not very useful unless one posits a specific interaction between it and aversion. Overall change was less than that obtained by Feldman and MacCulloch, but the evidence did favor contingent shock over contingent light where both were given in the context of group psychotherapy.

Tanner (1974a) compared male homosexuals on a waiting list control with those receiving electric aversion therapy. The latter showed significantly more erection and

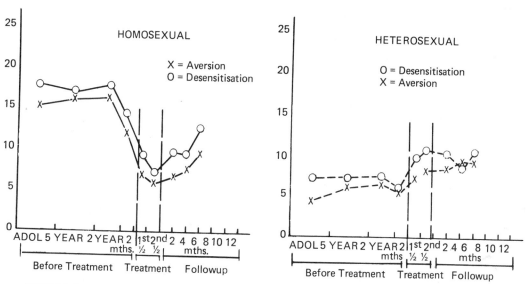

SEXUAL BEHAVIOUR RATING

FIGURE 8–3   Behavior change: these graphs show the mean ratings for the two treatment groups for homosexual and heterosexual behavior. The first four points represent the pretreatment periods (adolescence, five-year period, two-year period, and two months period). Between the two vertical lines are the two scores for the first and second half of treatment. Following this are the follow-up scores for two monthly periods (Bancroft, 1970b).

subjective arousal to female slides, and more sexual thoughts, socializing, and sex with females.

The controlled studies to date all concern homosexuality. One controlled comparison has also been made of aversion in exhibitionism (Rooth & Marks, 1974). Twelve persistent chronic exposers were treated as in-patients; 10 of these had been convicted for exhibitionism. A parallel study with

long-term follow-up was not practicable, so instead a design was adopted which examined changes in feelings and behavior three days after the end of each form of treatment. Three treatments were given, one form of treatment per week over three consecutive weeks, in a balanced incomplete Latin square design. The treatments were aversion, self-regulation, and muscular relaxation chosen as a placebo control method,

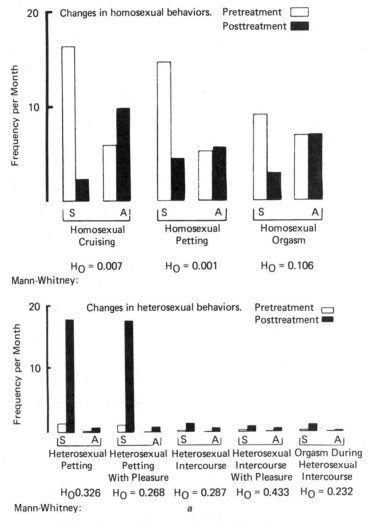

FIGURE 8–4 a & b   Change in homosexuals one year after aversive or placebo conditioning. Patients in both conditions also had two years group psychotherapy. S = aversion (shock); A = placebo (associative conditioning). (Birk et al., 1971). Reprinted from the Archives of General Psychiatry, October 1971, Vol. 25. Copyright 1971, American Medical Association.

unlikely to have a specific effect on the target problem. There were eight therapist sessions a week, each session lasting an hour. During aversion, patients were shocked either on reporting that they had produced an image of exposing, or during their rehearsal and description of an exposure act in front of a mirror. Shocks were given on all trials, followed by the aversion relief of conversation with the therapist. There were about 15 trials per session. Shocks were given from a portable shock box to the subject's forearm. In the second half of the trial patients were also required to shock their own exposure fantasies in their own rooms, and to administer self-aversion to their forearm with a portable shock-box in potential exposure situations.

In self-regulation sessions, discussions elucidated internal and external triggers of the exposure impulse-response chain, and a repertoire of alternative behaviors (e.g., smoking, mental arithmetic, reading) was selected for use in interrupting the early stage of sequences that might lead to exposure. To enhance awareness of deviant behavior patterns, prerecorded accounts of typical acts were repeatedly played back while the subject exposed to himself in the mirror and tried to express his feelings about the situation. In the second half of the trial, patients spent an additional daily session on self-administered covert sensitization in their rooms, and were also required to rehearse self-regulation techniques in provocative situations. The aversive and self-regulation procedures overlapped to the extent that the self-administered aversion that patients carried out between sessions could be construed as a form of self-regulation while the covert sensitization that patients practiced during self-regulation could be regarded as a form of aversion.

Relaxation treatment consisted of Jacobson's method of progressive muscular relaxation. In the second half of the trial the patients carried out daily relaxation sessions in their room. They also went into tempting situations each day, with the instruction that they should counteract incipient tension by attempting to generate feelings of mental and physical relaxation.

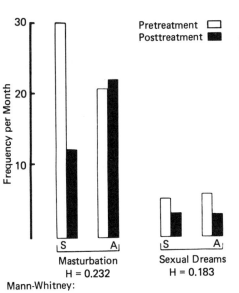

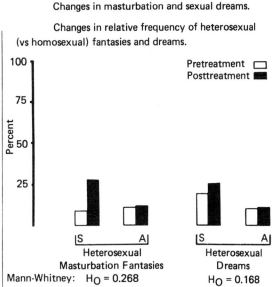

Changes in masturbation and sexual dreams.

Changes in relative frequency of heterosexual (vs homosexual) fantasies and dreams.

b

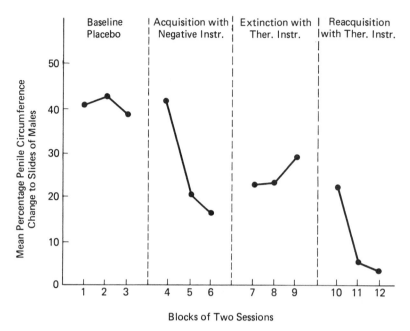

FIGURE 8–5   Change in homosexuals using covert sensitization versus repeated imagery (Barlow et al., 1972).

Aversion had the best results and self-regulation the next best, whereas relaxation was ineffective. Measures of change were necessarily based mainly on self-reports. Aversion produced significant improvement on four measures, self-regulation on two, and relaxation on none. Aversion was significantly superior to self-regulation and relaxation on two measures. Self-regulation was significantly superior to relaxation on only one measure. Aversion was most effective when given as the first treatment; on one measure self-regulation was potentiated when preceded by aversion. Follow-up results could be attributed to any or all of the three treatments because of the crossover design. At 12 to 14 months follow-up, significant improvement continued despite the chronicity and severity of the disorder before treatment. However, of the 12 patients, 7 had reexposed at some stage and, of the 10 with convictions, 4 had been reconvicted.

Covert sensitization. This form of aversion utilizes as noxious stimuli the patient's fantasies rather than an external agent such as injection or shock (Barlow, Leitenberg, & Agras, 1969; Callahan & Leitenberg, 1973; Cautela & Wisocki, 1971; Davison, 1968; Harbert, Barlow, Hersen, & Austin, 1973). During covert sensitization, a patient is asked to imagine himself engaging in the undesired behavior. When this is achieved he is asked to imagine at the same time a noxious scene. For example, a pedophile might be asked to imagine himself masturbating a little boy who then proceeds to vomit all over both of them. The noxious scene need not be disgusting, but could instead be anxiety-provoking. Kolvin (1967) described the treatment of a 14-year-old boy who put his hand up women's skirts in the street. This image was paired with sensations of falling out of bed while dreaming of falling from a great height. This patient received only seven half-hour sessions over three weeks and remained much improved at 13 months follow-up. (He also received advice about how to approach girls.) Curtis and Presley (1972) treated a homosexual by pairing homosexual images with anxiety-provoking ones such as a man brandishing a knife while threatening to castrate the subject unless he complied with homosexual demands, or the subject's wife looking in through a car window at the subject about to begin a homosexual encounter.

A small controlled study of covert sensitization (Barlow et al., 1972) examined the contribution of therapeutic instructions to the procedure. Four homosexuals were told that covert sensitization would increase their sexual deviation and that simply visualizing deviant images repeatedly was therapeutic. They then received treatment in a repeated measures design which consisted of (1) repeated visualization of deviant images (no pairing); then (2) covert sensitization with negative instructions; then (3) no pairing; then (4) covert sensitization with more positive instructions. The number of sessions and pairings was matched across covert sensitization and the preceding condition except on one occasion. Subjects were treated three to five times weekly, three as out-patients and one as an in-patient, to a total of 28 to 42 sessions.

Results shortly after sessions (Figure 8-5) showed that, regardless of instructions, erections to male slides were reduced significantly more after covert sensitization than after visualizing deviant images without the nauseating image. One patient did improve during a no-pairing condition but there was a suggestion that he might have used covert sensitization himself at this stage. Only four subjects were used in this study, but results suggested that overall instructions and patient expectations played but a minor role in covert sensitization in the short term.

An attempted comparison of covert sensitization with electric aversion was reported by Callahan and Leitenberg (1973) in six sexual deviants (three homosexuals, two exhibitionists, and one transvestite trans-sexual). The two forms of aversion produced similar improvement in erections to deviant stimuli and frequency of deviant sexual behavior. Covert sensitization produced greater suppression of deviant urges than did shock. Unfortunately, the balance of design which the authors planned could not be attained, making adequate comparison of the two treatments impossible, and significance figures of differences was not reported.

The long-term effects of covert sensitization remain to be demonstrated in a controlled fashion. Since subjects learn to summon up their own noxious fantasies when they have deviant temptations, the method can be regarded as a form of self-regulation.

Smell sensitization. This method pairs deviant stimuli with unpleasant smells. Colson (1972) treated a homosexual by pairing narrations of homosexuality with inhalations of ammonia and ammonium sulphide. The patient was said to be improved after three sessions and six weeks follow-up. Maletzky (1973) paired deviant stimuli with inhalations from a bottle containing valeric acid. The patient had homosexual fellatio urges and was treated by 15 sessions of smell sensitization to deviant images and to tape recorded descriptions of his deviant behavior. He was much improved at a one-year follow-up. Coitus with his wife continued normally after as before treatment. The report briefly mentions eight other homosexuals who improved, and another who achieved only partial remission. Smell sensitization could be regarded as a form of chemical aversion but noxious inhalations are obviously more practicable than injections.

Shame aversion. In this form of therapy, the patient performs his deviant sexual act in front of several people for up to half an hour. For treatment to be aversive, the patient must be ashamed or embarrassed at being observed while performing his deviant act. Staff are enlisted to act as "partners" in the presence of other mental health workers (Serber, 1970, 1972). In sessions, a frotteur would rub against a girl, or a pedophile might touch a young person's hair, back, and arms. Serber (1972) reported five male deviants who received shame aversion as the sole treatment; all showed some repetition of their deviance by six months follow-up. Ten other patients received shame aversion over two weeks, plus graduated retraining which included assertive training (the "stand up for yourself" type) and heterosexual social retraining with a female therapist. Further retraining was assisted by a full length mirror and audio tape recorder for immediate feedback. The retraining included modeling, behavior rehearsal, and role playing, and was carried out once or twice a week over a three-month period.

Of the 10 patients who received shame aversion plus social retraining, 8 did not repeat their deviant behavior during a one-year follow-up. Two improved but continued some deviant behavior. Serber suggested that patients with marked heterosexual deficit might begin heterosexual retraining *before* applying aversion.

Shame aversion was also used successfully by Reitz and Keil (1971) with an exhibitionist. Patterson (personal communication) employed it with an exhibitionist pedophile who described a detailed fantasy about his most attractive deviant stimulus on a tape recorder. This tape recorded fantasy was then played back to the patient in the presence of seven nurses who meanwhile looked at the stimulus picture—a charming 8-year-old girl. After two sessions the patient remained well to six weeks follow-up. No controlled studies of shame aversion are yet available though it has obvious potential applicability to exhibitionism, where the response of the victim can be important.

One prim and naive patient of the author's showed the effect of shame in another context. He was asked to buy sadomasochistic pictures in the red-light district of London for use in his aversion. On return to hospital he expressed such shock at the atmosphere in which his perversion was practiced that he lost his deviant urges and required no further treatment.

General issues of aversion therapy. Table 8-6 summarizes the results of controlled studies of aversion in sexual deviance. Little difference was found between the efficacy of chemical or electrical methods (McConaghy, 1969), or between different forms of electric aversion (Bancroft, 1970a, 1970b; Feldman & MacCulloch, 1971; McConaghy & Barr, 1973). Electric aversion was not found superior to desensitization (Bancroft, 1970a, 1970b), but was to placebo conditioning (Birk et al., 1971), brief psychotherapy (Feldman & MacCulloch, 1971), self-regulation, and muscular relaxation (Rooth & Marks, 1973). Barlow et al. (1972) found that covert sensitization was significantly superior to repeated deviant imagery alone. Significant differences in all these studies referred to decreases in deviance, not to increases in heterosexuality. All concerned homosexuality, except the study by Rooth and Marks which involved exhibitionism. All used parallel designs with follow-up except Barlow et al. who used a repeated measures design, and Rooth and Marks who used an incomplete Latin square. The design of the two latter studies allowed interpretation only of short-term effects of procedures. None except Bancroft paid much attention to decreasing heterosexual anxiety and increasing heterosexual skills.

The unpleasantness of aversion therapy varies greatly depending upon its mode of administration. Perceived aversiveness increases with strength of shock and greater delay before its receipt (Franzini, 1970). There is no evidence that extreme unpleasantness is important. Tanner (1973b) compared a 5mA strength of shock with self-selected strength (average 3 to 4.5mA) in 26 male homosexuals having aversion treatment. The 5mA group improved slightly more, but had a higher dropout rate. Marks and Gelder (1967) used just

TABLE 8–6   Controlled group studies of aversion in sexual deviance

Author	Subjects (n)	Comparison (n per condition in brackets)	Number of sessions: out-patient (OP) or in-patient (IP)	Outcome for deviance
Bancroft (1970a, 1970b)	homosexuals (30)	1. desensitization in fantasy (30) 2. electric aversion (30)	30 OP & IP 30 } sessions	equally effective
Barlow et al. (1972)	homosexuals (4)	1. covert sensitization 2. repeated deviant imagery (repeated measures design)	28 to 42 OP and IP sessions	covert sensitization significantly superior
Birk et al. (1971)	homosexuals (16)	Group psychotherapy plus 1. electric aversion (8) 2. placebo conditioning (8)	OP 2 years 25 in month 25 in month	electric aversion significantly superior
Feldman & MacCulloch (1971)	homosexuals (30)	Electric aversion 1. Classical conditioning (10) 2. anticipatory avoidance (10) 3. psychotherapy (10)	24 ½-hour 24 ½-hour } IP 12 1-hour } sessions	aversions 1 and 2 equally effective; psychotherapy ineffective
McConaghy (1969, 1970) McConaghy et al. (1972)	homosexuals (40)	1. apomorphine (20 subjects) 2. electric aversion (20 subjects)	28 injections 15 sessions 5 days IP	equally effective
McConaghy (1975)	homosexuals (31)	1. electric conversion (15) 2. positive conditioning (16)	14 IP over 5 days	aversion better on therapist's ratings, not on erections forward = backward conditioning
McConaghy & Barr (1973)	homosexuals (46)	Electric aversion 1. classical conditioning (15) 2. anticipatory avoidance (16) 3. backward conditioning (15)	14 IP 6 } sessions	all equally effective
Rooth & Marks (1974)	exhibitionists (12)	1. electric aversion 2. self-regulation 3. muscular relaxation (8 per condition, incomplete Latin square)	8 8 } IP sessions 8	electric aversion significantly best; self-regulation second best; relaxation ineffective

enough shock to overcome the pleasure which patients experienced from deviant stimuli; the aim was not to produce suffering but to abolish pleasure. The patients of Hallam et al. (1972) rated electric aversion as less unpleasant than a dental visit. Aversion can thus be given humanely in a manner which is acceptable to most patients. Obviously, however, if more pleasant and equally effective treatments can be found, these should replace aversive methods.

Emotional reactions during aversion (Marks & Gelder, 1967)—including short-lived anxiety, depression, irritability, hostility, and embarrassment—require skilled clinical management at times. In patients with multiple problems it can be difficult to sort out which responses are directly due to aversion, which to loss of deviance, and which to other problems. In general, masochistic patients avoid shocks and do not seek these painful stimuli as a fresh source of gratification (Marks & Gelder, 1967; Marks et al., 1970; Marks, Rachman, & Gelder, 1965). Their masochism involves a few specialized cues only, and most stimuli which are painful for others are painful for them as well. Despite these findings, therapists need to be alert to the remote possibility of masochists becoming shock fetishists.

Although the evidence suggests that aversion decreases deviance more than other methods, it is not absolutely conclusive, and the overall effects are not startlingly large even when significant. There is also evidence that aversion to deviant stimuli can increase heterosexual erections and desires in the short term (Bancroft, 1970a, 1970b) but the mechanism and durability of this effect is obscure. An agreed prognostic factor is the favorable effect of some prior heterosexual interest. This has been used as a determinant of subsequent heterosexual behavior (Bancroft, 1970a, 1970b; Feldman & MacCulloch, 1971; Marks et al., 1970; Rooth & Marks, 1973).

Some patients change before treatment begins. In their cases aversion seems simply to enhance a process which has already begun (e.g., Bancroft, 1970a, 1970b; see Figure 8-3). Although aversion is unlikely to act solely by straightforward conditioning in most patients, labeling this process as "cognitive" is not particularly helpful except to indicate directions for further possible research.

Aversion is commonly described as a "conditioning" treatment, but evidence that it works mainly by setting up conditioned anxiety responses is unimpressive (Bancroft, 1970a, 1970b; Hallam & Rachman, 1972; Marks et al., 1970; McConaghy & Barr, 1973). Lasting conditioned anxiety is exceptional during aversion. Hallam et al. (1972) demonstrated increases in heart rate to deviant fantasies after successful aversion, but another study (Hallam & Rachman, 1972) reported that such increases were also found in alcoholics (reacting to alcoholic stimuli) who improved with both aversive and nonaversive procedures. The usual response of patients who improve after aversion is to report indifference to rather than anxiety about their formerly attractive stimuli (Marks et al., 1970; Hallam et al., 1972). On semantic differential scales, attitudes toward deviant objects changed from attractive to simply neutral rather than aversive (Bancroft, 1970b). This is seen clearly in Figure 8-6. The paradox is that, though aversion therapy works, it produces changes which are neutralizing rather than aversive.

Far from anxiety being associated with improvement, to aversion the opposite was found by Marks et al. (1970) and Bancroft (1970a, 1970b). Outcome at follow-up of transvestites and fetishists after aversion was significantly *negatively* correlated with anxiety scores for "myself" after three days aversion and with "electric shocks" on admission, and with devalued scores on admission for "other people with the same trouble as me." Morgenstern et al. (1965) found that of transvestites treated by apomorphine aversion, those who were less anxious and less introverted on admission did best.

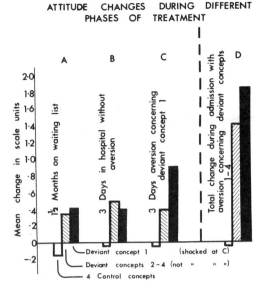

FIGURE 8–6   Change in attitudes in 17 transvestites and fetishists after periods on a waiting list, and in the hospital with and without aversion. Devaluation of deviant attitudes of the groups as a whole began only with aversion therapy and reached significance (>1.0 scale units) after two to three weeks of in-patient aversion. Control concepts concerning unshocked nonsexual ideas did not change (Marks et al., 1970). Reprinted with permission of *British Journal of Psychiatry.*

Similarly, Feldman and MacCulloch (1971) found the best prognosis in homosexuals with stable personalities who were least neurotic. In general, therefore, aversion seems to work best in patients with higher self-esteem and less anxiety before and during treatment.

The importance of an *aversive* stimulus is suggested by the results of Birk et al. (1971) in which a placebo conditioning procedure produced inferior results. However, this does not argue for *conditioning* processes; only a noncontingent shock control could prove this, and such has not yet been reported in sexual deviants. The fact that backward conditioning has produced as good results as forward conditioning (McConaghy & Barr, 1973) argues against conventional conditioning mechanisms. That the precise form of aversion is not important (Table 8-6) indicates that the mechanisms of change are still poorly understood. Morgenstern et al. (1965) found that outcome to apomorphine aversion did not correlate with classical eyeblink conditioning; they

thought that outcome did correlate with instrumental verbal conditioning; though Rachman and Teasdale (1969, p. 162) questioned this conclusion. McConaghy and Barr (1973) found that outcome to electric aversion did not correlate with classical appetitive conditioning (erection to green triangles seen before male slides) although it did correlate with classical aversive conditioning (GSR to tone before male slides). In the absence of a general factor of conditionability across stimulus-response systems, it is less useful to think in terms of general conditionability than to attend to the precise S-R systems involved. The concepts of stimulus prepotency (Marks, 1969, 1972) and species preparedness for some S-R connections rather than others (Seligman & Hager, 1972) suggest ideas for developing more powerful therapeutic tools. For example, electric shock is an unnatural stimulus to connect with sexual responses. Smell might be more potent, and a trial of smell sensitization versus electric aversion in sexual deviations is overdue. Other stimuli such as apnoea to scoline injections are less acceptable ethically.

During aversion treatment attitudes, changes in erections and behavior tend to be parallel, although the usual sequence is not clear and may depend upon the way in which aversion is applied (e.g., aversion to erections may produce decrement in those before change in attitude and vice versa). Marks and Gelder (1967) found that changes in attitudes and erections closely followed systematic application of aversion to different cues. Figures 8-7 and 8-8 show how attitudes and erections changed to particular items as those items were shocked, while unshocked items remained unaffected. Both patients relapsed during follow-up. That the attitude changes hold true for groups as well as individuals is seen in Figure 8-9. Ratings are evaluative and sex scales on a semantic differential format devised by Marks and Sartorius (1968). Changes of less than one scale unit can be regarded as random. Significant devaluation

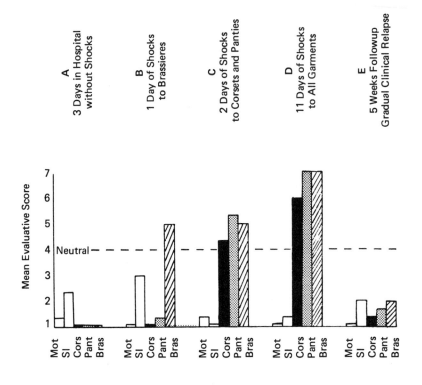

Mean Evaluative Score

A — 3 Days in Hospital without Shocks
B — 1 Day of Shocks to Brassieres
C — 2 Days of Shocks to Corsets and Panties
D — 11 Days of Shocks to All Garments
E — 5 Weeks Followup Gradual Clinical Relapse

Evaluative Change with Selective Aversion

1 = good, friendly, approachable   7 = bad, unfriendly, distant

Mot = Mother   Bras = Brassieres   Cors = Corsets

SI = Sexual Intercourse   Pant = Panties

FIGURE 8–7   Specificity of attitude change with electric aversion in a transvestite. The patient relapsed at five-week follow-up. Scores are mean of three 7-point evaluative scales—good-bad, friendly-unfriendly, approachable-distant (Marks & Gelder, 1967). Reprinted with permission of *British Journal of Psychiatry*.

to deviant concepts began only with introduction of aversion, first involving concept one and then concerning concepts one to four. Control nonsexual concepts did not change throughout treatment.

Aversion treatment is not a cure-all and has to be used with other methods of treatment as part of an overall plan of clinical management. Though many effects of aversion cannot be accommodated readily into a conditioning framework, certain phenomena undoubtedly suggest conditioning type processes. Perhaps surprisingly, the clearest evidence for conditioning comes from shocked fantasies. Clear conditioned aversion of fantasies was found with generalization gradients in a minority of cases, and suggests that aversion can produce cognitive changes akin to conditioning. This phenomenon will be termed "experimental repression" (suppression).

Experimental repression. Hallam and Rachman (1972) found that the time it took four successfully treated deviants to imagine deviant fantasies (latencies) more than doubled after treatment, while the latencies remained unchanged in three unsuccessfully treated patients. A similar phenomenon was found by Marks and Gelder (1967), Marks (1968), and Gelder and Marks (1970). It occurred only in about a third of patients and did not necessarily correlate with improvement. No obvious difference separated "repressors" from "nonrepressors." Nonrepressors continued to imagine their deviant fantasies easily although with diminished pleasure as their deviance receded. Repressors tended to lose their deviance as repression developed, but could relapse later. The loss of fantasy repression did not necessarily herald relapse of deviant behavior.

Repressors' images that were repeatedly shocked gradually became more difficult to visualize: "It's like when you see something out of the corner of your eye and look in that direction and it's not there. It's like trying to push through a tangle of cobwebs to hold a picture for a moment." Some reported that as they tried to concentrate on the required scene another would take its place: "I can't seem to get a picture. I keep getting something else instead." Patients' language described an involuntary event outside their control: "Whenever I tried to put the stocking on my leg, in my mind's eye I managed to get it to the knee, and then it snapped back as though pulled by elastic." Patients seemed anxious when they could not obtain the image, and relieved if they finally succeeded. In the early stages of repression the image might produce sexual arousal and erection but these diminished as the image became unattainable. Once repression was established it

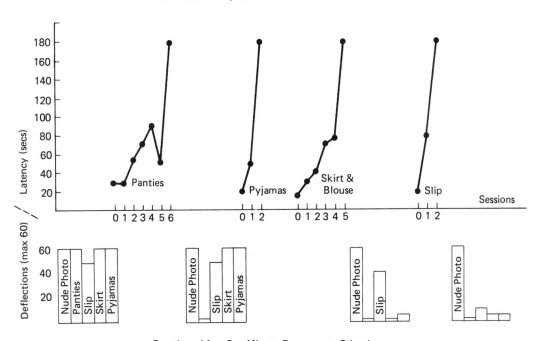

FIGURE 8–8   Specificity of erectile change with electric aversion in a transvestite. The patient relapsed one year after treatment. Top half depicts sequence of objects averted in treatment (Marks & Gelder, 1967). Reprinted with permission of *British Journal of Psychiatry.*

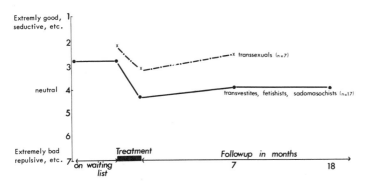

COURSE OF DEVIANT ATTITUDES BEFORE AND AFTER
ELECTRIC AVERSION

FIGURE 8–9   Course of deviant attitudes over a two-year follow-up. Attitudes to deviant activities changed significantly from pleasurable and did not become actually disagreeable for the group as a whole. Scores are mean change on three 7-point evaluative scales—good-bad, friendly-unfriendly, approachable-distant—and three sex scales—seductive-repulsive, sexy-sexless, erotic-frigid—taken from Marks and Sartorius (1968) Marks et al., (1970).

continued for variable lengths of time in the absence of shock. It might last for several hours early in treatment, or for many months later on. Generalization gradients became apparent in the repressed material, examples of which are detailed by Gelder and Marks (1970).

A homosexual patient treated by the author illustrates the features of repression with generalization gradients and accompanying changes in attitude and erections. Figure 8-10 shows an increase in fantasy latencies without shock threat during aversion in a married homosexual (whose favorite activities were with a friend, "John," and male hitchhikers). The latencies to these fantasies increased with shocks, and

an erotic generalization gradient can be seen on the right. Seeing John or a hitchhiker, rather than embracing them, was not repressed. The erotic generalization gradient is seen even more clearly in Figure 8-11; the fact that immediate shock threat did not affect the gradient is seen in Figure 8-12. Attitude changes and loss of erections coincided with the increase in latency of repressed fantasies (Figure 8-13).

Several observations suggest that this phenomenon is not due to the patient's desire to please the therapist or to avoid shock. First, the gradual increase in latency during repression is not the most rapid strategy to avoid shock; in laboratory experiments subjects prefer immediate to delayed shock

SELECTIVE   REPRESSION   OF   SHOCKED   FANTASIES

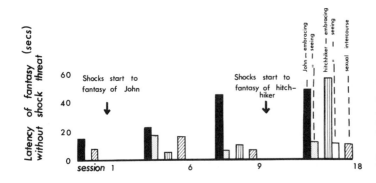

FIGURE 8–10   Experimental repression of deviant fantasies in a homosexual during aversion. Favorite fantasies of embracing John and a male hitchhiker increased only in latency after aversion, while less erotic fantasies of simply seeing them were not repressed. Heterosexual intercourse was visualized normally.

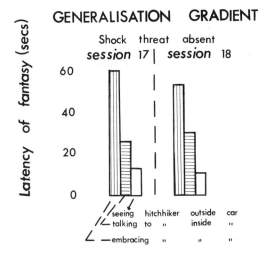

FIGURE 8–11   Erotic generalization gradient of the patient in Figure 8–10. The most erotic fantasy—embracing a male hitchhiker inside a car—had the longest latency. The least erotic fantasy—seeing a male hitchhiker outside the car—was visualized easily with a short latency.

(Cook & Barnes, 1964). Second, it is very difficult for a patient to fake curves of increasing latency, for this requires psychological sophistication as well as an unusually accurate ability to estimate the passage of time. Third, early in treatment, erections often start shortly before the patient signals that he has a clear image, so that therapists are able to predict when the patient will signal the presence of a fantasy. Fourth, continuous recordings of palmar skin conductance show that spontaneous fluctuations of skin conductance change specifically during fantasies. Fifth, the generalization gradients in the repressed material argue that the process is a learned avoidance response rather than a voluntary act.

The results were also in line with experiments with students who were instructed to produce associations to 15 words (Eriksen & Kuethe, 1956). Their associations to 5 of these words were followed by shocks. Associations that were accompanied by the aversive experience declined rapidly, while the frequency of nonpunished associations

remained unchanged over 16 trials. The decrement in associations occurred whether or not subjects were aware of the punishment contingency.

FADING.   Fading gradually changes deviant stimuli in a heterosexual direction during periods of sexual arousal. The technique has been used by Bancroft (1971) with a 28-year-old masochist. The patient produced repeated full erections to fantasies of being beaten by a man dressed only in a loin cloth. The fantasy of dressing the man fully or exposing his genitalia resulted in less erection; the fantasy of being beaten by a woman resulted in even less. The therapist informed the patient that his fantasies indicated some homosexuality. This thought distressed the patient, who opted to become more heterosexual. After this decision he began to get full erections to the fantasy of being beaten by a naked woman. This fantasy was then systematically modified. The fantasy whip used to beat the patient was gradually made shorter until it gave way to a simple slap of the woman's hand. The imagined slap gave way to direct sensual stimulation while tied up at the woman's mercy. The patient in his fantasy was then progressively released from bondage, free-

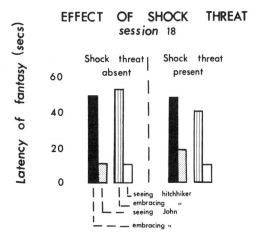

FIGURE 8–12   Once established, shock threat did not affect repression (patient in Figure 8–10).

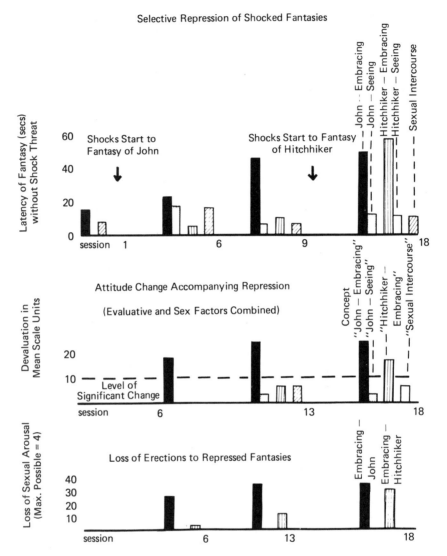

FIGURE 8–13   Evaluation of and erections to deviant fantasies changed as the fantasies became repressed (patient in Figure 8–10).

ing at first one leg and then all four limbs. Then in imagery he became gradually more active until he was taking the dominant role in sexual intercourse. Changes in fantasy depended upon continuing erection to the preceding fantasy. When the erection diminished the patient was asked to return to an earlier fantasy and subsequent changes

were made more gradually. After 18 sessions the patient responded consistently to normal heterosexual fantasies.

Beech, Watts, and Poole (1971) increased heterosexual arousal to women in a pedophile by pairing sexual arousal to pictures of young girls with slides of increasingly older females. Pictures of increasingly older women were substituted as erections developed. Interest in young girls declined without aversion. Jarman and Marks (unpublished) produced similar results with fading in a masochistic patient who, however, relapsed three months later.

A slightly different fading approach was used by Gold and Neufeld (1965). A homosexual patient was asked to imagine himself standing in a toilet beside a most unprepossessing old man whom he would not normally solicit. This image was modified so that the man became slightly more attractive but was associated with a prohibition like a policeman standing by. If the patient signalled that he had no desire to approach the man in such circumstances he was asked to further modify the image so that the man became progressively more sexually attractive and the prohibition became less and less. Eventually the patient was able to imagine rejecting an attractive young man with no prohibitions operating, and to prefer a woman. The patient improved in 10 sessions over three weeks and remained entirely heterosexual at one year follow-up.

Barlow and Agras (1973) described a similar procedure in three homosexuals. They superimposed slides of nude females on slides of nude males. The female slides were faded in as the subject maintained 75% of a full erection to the male slide. Erections decreased when fading was reversed, and increased again when fading was resumed. Unfortunately, because the control and experimental procedures were given over different lengths of time, conclusions about their relative efficacy are not possible. Homosexual arousal diminished in two subjects at follow-up and one Kinsey subject actually became heterosexual. Further experiments with fading procedures would be desirable.

SHAPING.   There are pilot reports of the use of operant methods with sexual problems. Quinn, Harbison, and McAllister (1970) described a homosexual man who relapsed after electric aversion and desensi-

tization. He was then deprived of fluid and shown a selection of male and female slides. When he requested female slides or showed progressively greater erections to them he received a drink of lime-juice. Erections increased over 20 sessions, as did heterosexual attitude.

SELF-REGULATION.   This method defines the precise conditions under which self-control is deficient and trains the client to control his impulses by interrupting the response chain (e.g., by switching thoughts). Bergin (1969a) described the treatment of a male and a female homosexual with this method. Both patients did well until 10 to 12 months follow-up.

The only controlled trial of self-regulation to date (Rooth & Marks, 1973) was discussed in the section on aversion. Self-regulation had a significant short-term effect but less so than aversion. The method required the patient and therapist to discuss the most recent exhibitionistic urges; data were obtained from a time sheet and daily self-regulation form. Choice points were identified and, when faced with alternative moves, the patient was instructed to take the action less likely to lead to exposure. Possible future situations were rehearsed and responded to. For example, one patient became resentful when he felt unfairly treated at work or at home and would then plan to expose over the next few days. He was instructed to challenge such resentful moods and to articulate the covert decision to expose which was made at this point. Many patients disguised their decision to expose by pretending they wanted to go out for a walk. During self-regulation they become more aware of their exposure plans.

As the patient moved toward a potential exposure situation, e.g., a park or train, he had to become aware of the situation and its danger. Then he had to execute an *alternative* behavior which would decrease the likelihood of exposure—e.g., walk away from young girls, look at a shop window, read a newspaper, memorize verse, solve crossword puzzles, think of his family, look at a photograph of his children, or think of a policeman coming. The latter is a form of covert sensitization.

On the measure that improved most with self-regulation, the effect was significantly greater when it was preceded by electric aversion. The possibility of a treatment combining both methods thus arises. One patient said that he felt unable to apply self-regulation when exhibitionistic urges were very strong, but was able to do so when their strength had been reduced by aversion.

Canton-Dutari (1973), working in Panama, trained several young males to control their homosexual arousal with a combination of desensitization, aversion, and self-regulation by a breathing-contraction technique; thereafter they were asked to masturbate to heterosexual stimuli. The patient was first taught to relax all his muscles; he was then shown how to diminish sexual arousal by alternately contracting and relaxing his thighs while breathing with his abdominal muscles. Having mastered this technique, the patient was instructed to masturbate as his sole sexual outlet for three weeks and to try to prolong the erection as long as possible. During this time if he became homosexually aroused he was to practice the control breathing-contraction technique. Then for three weeks he was given electric aversion while imagining homosexual fantasies and looking at homosexual slides and films. The patient was then instructed to masturbate in the presence of heterosexual stimuli, the aim being to prolong erections rather than to achieve orgasm. After 12 weeks in treatment the patient's relationship with his male therapist was analyzed and compared with other male relationships in actual situations. Canton-Dutari treated 54 homosexuals who had a mean age of only 17 and found that 90% achieved worthwhile results in terms of changed sexual orientations up to four years follow-up. Comparable results were obtained in 12 other patients even when aversion was omitted from the treatment approach (Canton-Dutari, 1976). The homosexual samples were younger than most reported in the literature and therefore had a higher probability of achieving heterosexuality.

INCREASING HETEROSEXUAL BEHAVIOR

The major therapeutic endeavor in sexual deviations has been to reduce the strength of deviant impulses rather than to increase heterosexual behavior. (This topic has been well reviewed by Barlow, 1973.) It is still an open question what proportion of sexual deviants also have heterosexual anxiety and deficits. A sample of homosexual students showed that many disliked or feared heterosexuality, rather than feeling neutral toward it (Ramsay & van Velzen, 1968). However, there are undoubtedly sexual deviants who have normal heterosexual skills without heterophobia, and in such patients it seems more useful to simply reduce the deviant urges.

In those deviants with heterosexual anxiety and deficits, it is hard to say how much decrease in deviance would result from production of a heterosexual repertoire. Several case reports (Bond and Hutchinson, 1960; Huff, 1970; Kraft, 1967; Stevenson & Wolpe, 1960) have adopted this approach, all reporting on homosexuality except Bond and Hutchinson, who reported on exhibitionism. Figure 8–14 shows how one homosexual lost his deviant urges as heterosexual desires developed during desensitization in fantasy. Such reports give no reliable guide to practitioners as to when to opt for reducing heterophobia and increasing heterosexual skills, and when to reduce deviance. An optimal strategy might be a combination of both techniques. A patient's history might serve as a guide. For example, an exhibitionist often exposes when depressed or tense after an argument with a wife or a boss, and the deviant behavior is tension-reducing as well as sexual. In such a

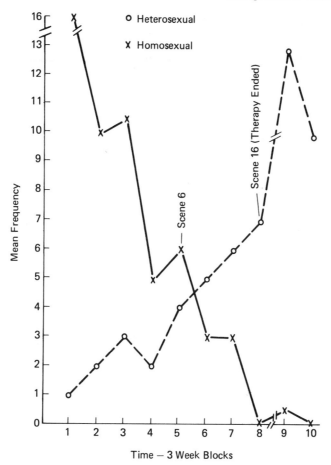

FIGURE 8–14   Decrease in homosexual urges as heterosexual interest increased during desensitization in fantasy, n = 1. Follow-up was to six months (Huff, 1970).

patient, reducing the depression or interpersonal tension by itself, without attention to heterosexuality or the deviance, can diminish the deviant impulse. Another case in point is a sadistic patient of the author's who lost his deviance after aversion treatment. He had a history of depression in earlier years and in the two years after aversion developed further transient depressive episodes. During these episodes the sadistic fantasies would return, only to disappear after the depression remitted with tricyclic antidepressive drugs.

There is no clear-cut relationship be-tween the presence of deviance and heterosexuality; in some cases, one seems reciprocal to the other, and in others they are independent. The author has known transvestites and exhibitionists to engage in repeated heterosexual intercourse in a vain attempt to keep their deviant urges at bay. There are many causes of deviant behavior, only one of which is heterosexual anxiety or deficit. In subjects where this is clearly a contributing factor, it would seem logical to try to increase heterosexual behavior. Several methods have been used in this endeavor.

DESENSITIZATION. Case reports of desensitization in homosexuality come from Huff (1970), Kraft (1967), and Lopiccolo (1971). The most systematic study to date is Bancroft's (described earlier). Only 1 of his 15 patients who were desensitized in fantasy lacked heterosexual anxiety and he dropped out of treatment. The result of imaginal desensitization was modest: only 5 of the 15 showed marked improvement at follow-up of nine months.

A technique to improve desensitization by warmth, empathy, and emotional experiencing of hierarchy events was described by Bergin (1969b). The patient also received eight sessions of self-regulation to control lesbian impulses. During desensitization, progress in construction of a heterophobic hierarchy was slow. The patient was then relaxed and asked to associate her feelings to hierarchy items. Although relaxed, she spoke of topics laden with anxiety and anger, the affect decreasing with discussion. Desensitization seemed accelerated with this guided fantasy approach. Bergin suggested that if a relaxed client were encouraged to discuss feelings, memories, and ideas in relation to each hierarchy item, the relaxation would be paired with many affective and symbolic aspects of the traumatic events being discussed. He cited Weitzman's observation that when a psychoanalytic patient loses or represses significant dream material, many new associations can be invoked by relaxing the patient and presenting the last remembered dream image repeatedly until there is no anxiety associated with it.

Barlow's conclusion seems valid that no experimental evidence indicates that desensitization in fantasy increases heterosexual responsiveness. Research is needed using *in vivo* methods with clearly heterophobic patients.

SOCIAL RETRAINING. Assertive training, modeling, and behavior rehearsal might be used to increase heterosexual skills. Pilot reports of their use come from Blitch and Haynes (1972), Hanson and Adesso (1972), Serber (1972), and Stevenson and Wolpe (1960). Cautela and Wisocki (1969) used male therapists to administer covert sensitization and thought stopping for homosexual deviance, and female therapists to desensitize heterophobia and offer information about dating and feminine behavior. No technique in this crucial field is definitely of value as controlled investigations still have to appear.

PAIRING. Pairing of sexual arousal with heterosexual stimuli is another theoretically feasible manner of evoking heterosexual behavior. Fading and shaping, described earlier, are variations of pairing. Moan and Heath (1972) paired heterosexual stimuli and behavior with septal stimulation from an electrode implant. Herman, Barlow, and Agras (1974) reported single case studies in which homosexuals were shown female slides as conditioned stimuli and male slides as unconditional stimuli. Unfortunately, the number of sessions differed greatly across the various experimental conditions, thus precluding firm conclusions from the data.

Barlow (1973) cites several workers who paired sexual arousal in masturbation with heterosexual stimuli in the treatment of homosexuality (Annon, 1971; Canton-Dutari, 1973; Marquis, 1970; Thorpe, Schmidt, Brown, & Castell, 1964), sadomasochism (Davison, 1968; Marquis, 1970; Mees, 1967), voyeurism (Jackson, 1969), and heterosexual pedophilia (Annon, 1971). This method is also called orgasmic conditioning. Subjects usually masturbate to pictures or fantasies which progressively resemble the heterosexual target.

Evans (1968) noted that of 10 exhibitionists treated by aversion, those who had deviant masturbatory fantasies did significantly worse than those with normal masturbatory fantasies. However, such conclusions are not warranted because masturbatory fantasies themselves are as much a sign of deviance as its cause; hard experimental data are needed that modifying such fantasies leads to permanent change in fantasies and behavior.

Aversion relief pairs a heterosexual stimulus with cessation of a noxious stimulus. This might be classified as a form of aversion since the effect of electric aversion given as backward conditioning is similar to that given as forward conditioning (McConaghy & Barr, 1973). Aversion relief has been used on its own or with other methods to treat homosexuality, transvestism, fetishism, and voyeurism (Abel, Levis, & Clancy, 1970; Feldman & MacCulloch, 1971; Gaupp, Stern, & Ratliffe, 1971; Mandel, 1970; McConaghy, 1970; Solyom & Miller, 1965; Thorpe et al., 1964). Barlow (1973) concludes that evidence still fails to support the value of aversion relief in increasing heterosexual behavior.

Transsexuals are much more difficult to treat than other deviants and there are no successful reports of improving adult transsexuals in the long term. Marks et al. (1970) failed to improve any of seven transsexuals with electric aversion over two years follow-up, in contrast to transvestites, fetishists, and sadomasochists (see Figures 8–9 and 8–15). Barlow, Reynolds, & Agras (1973) reported

successful change of gender identity in a 17-year-old male transsexual after one year of intensive in-patient treatment; this included 8 unsuccessful sessions of fading, 48 unsuccessful sessions of aversion, 30 sessions of modeling plus video feedback, and 24 sessions of heterosexual fantasy training. Green, Newman, & Stoller (1972) reported successful treatment of five very effeminate boys and their parents. The boys were aged two to seven when treatment started. Treatment consisted of developing a close relationship between the male therapist and the boys, stopping parental encouragement of feminine behavior, interrupting the excessively close relationship between mother and son, enhancing the role of father and son, and generally promoting the father's role within the family. Results indicated that effeminate young boys could develop more masculine gender roles after years of treatment.

GENERAL CONSIDERATIONS

We have dealt with sexual deviations as though they were all equivalent. In fact, there may be important differences in treat-

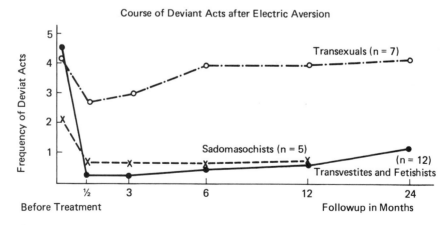

FIGURE 8–15   Course of deviant acts of transsexuals and other deviants over two years following electric aversion. Transvestites and sadomasochists did quite well, but transsexuals did uniformly badly (Marks et al., 1970). Reproduced with permission of *British Journal of Psychiatry*.

ment approaches to particular forms of deviation (e.g., homosexuals as opposed to exhibitionists or masochists). Treatment of homogeneous groups of deviants is necessary to delineate particular problems. All controlled studies have been of homosexuals except for one study of exhibitionists. A summary of these appeared in Table 8–6. The different conditions treated and described in a series of single case reports are listed in Table 8–7. Nearly half concern homosexuality. Uncontrolled homogeneous studies of exhibitionists were described by Evans (1968); studies of transvestites and fetishists were reported by Morgenstern et al. (1965) and Marks et al. (1970).

An obvious factor complicating the treatment of homosexuals is the subculture to which they often belong. A homosexual wishing to make the transition to heterosexuality may also need to break with his previous social environment. Some transvestites and transsexuals also belong to special subcultures with a vested interest in their continuing deviant behavior.

In conclusion, research into the behavioral treatment of sexual disorders is still in its infancy, and few questions have been satisfactorily answered by systematic study. Various forms of impotence and frigidity can be treated successfully by complex treatment packages which include commitment to change, fostering of good communication, education, repeated sexual practice under guidance, and graduated exposure to sexual behavior and specific techniques when in-

TABLE 8–7   Behavioral treatment reports classified by sexual deviation

EXHIBITIONISM	Bond & Hutchinson, 1960; Callahan & Leitenberg, 1973; Evans, 1968; Feldman et al., 1968; Fookes, 1968; Kushner & Sandler, 1966; Reitz & Keil, 1971; Rooth & Marks, 1974; Serber, 1970, 1972; Wickramasera, 1968.
HOMOSEXUALITY	Bancroft, 1969, 1970a, 1970b; Barlow et al., 1969, 1970; Bergin, 1969a, 1969b; Birk et al., 1971; Blitch & Haynes, 1972; Callahan & Leitenberg, 1973; Canton-Dutari, 1973; Cautela & Wisocki, 1969, 1971; Colson, 1972; Curtis and Presley, 1972; Discipio, 1968; Feldman & MacCulloch, 1971; Fookes, 1968; Freund, 1960; Gold & Neufeld, 1965; Gray, 1970; Hallam & Rachman, 1972; Hanson & Adesso, 1972; Herman et al., 1973; Huff, 1970; Kraft, 1967; Larson, 1970; Levin et al., 1968; Maletzky, 1973; Mandel, 1970; Marquis, 1970; Max, 1935; McConaghy & coworkers, 1969, 1970, 1972, 1973; Moan & Heath, 1972; Oswald, 1962; Quinn et al., 1970; Solyom & Miller, 1965; Stevenson & Wolpe, 1960; Tanner, 1973; Thorpe et al., 1964.
PEDOPHILIA	Barlow et al., 1969; Beech et al., 1971; Callahan & Leitenberg, 1973; Feldman & MacCulloch, 1971; Hallam & Rachman, 1972; Rooth & Marks, 1974; Serber, 1970, 1972.
SADOMASOCHISM	Davison, 1968; Feldman et al., 1968; Hallam et al., 1972; Marks & coworkers, 1965, 1967, 1968, 1970; Marquis, 1970; Mees, 1966.
TRANSVESTISM AND FETISHISM	Barker, 1965; Bond & Evans, 1967; Callahan & Leitenberg, 1973; Clark, 1963; Cooper, 1963; Feldman et al., 1968; Fookes, 1968; Hallam & Rachman, 1972; Hallam et al., 1972; Kushner, 1965; Lavin et al., 1961; Marks & coworkers, 1967, 1968, 1970; McGuire & Vallance, 1964; Oswald, 1962; Raymond, 1956; Serber, 1972; Stevenson & Wolpe, 1960; Thorpe et al., 1964.
VOYEURISM	Beech et al., 1971; Gaupp et al., 1971; Hallam & Rachman, 1972; Jackson, 1969.
OTHER	Harbert et al., 1973 (incest); Kolvin, 1967 (putting hand up women's skirts); Serber, 1972 (frotteurism).

dicated like the squeeze method and super-stimulation. The value of various components is currently under investigation. Deviant behavior can often be reduced by several aversive methods, though the effects are not dramatic. Aversive stimuli seem to play an important role, though conditioning mechanisms account for only a small proportion of all the features found in aversion treatment. Many methods have been tried to foster heterosexuality, but systematic research in this direction has only just started. The development of social skills in patients with sexual problems is an important area which might yield large dividends.

Summary

Sexual problems without physical pathology fall into three broad classes which are not mutually exclusive: (1) failure of function, or sexual dysfunction (including impotence —failure of erection, premature ejaculation, failure of ejaculation; and frigidity—sexual phobias, vaginismus, anorgasmia); (2) sexual deviations, where there is an attraction to an unusual object or activity for gratification; and (3) transsexualism, where the subject feels he belongs to the opposite sex to that denoted by his anatomy.

Impotence and frigidity are the commonest sexual problems in clinics and the community. Homosexuality is the commonest deviation in the community, while exhibitionism is the most frequent sexual offense in Britain. Homosexuality apart, most sexual deviants are men. Transsexualism is rare.

Little is known about causation. Temporal lobe pathology is sometimes associated with sexual hypoactivity and deviations. Experimental fetishes have been produced by conditioning. A stable relationship with the father is absent in many deviants.

Treatment requires clear formulation of the problem by adequate case history and behavioral analysis. Conditions to be excluded include depression, grief reaction, marital disharmony, and organic pathology. Literature reports of treatment are mainly of uncontrolled cases or series. Systematic controlled studies are rare, and usually concern aversion in homosexuality. Sex therapy research is still in its infancy, and all conclusions must thus be tentative.

The largest series concerning sexual dysfunction is the uncontrolled one of Masters and Johnson (1970). Possible therapeutic components include commitment to change, facilitation of good communication, education by day and performance by night with subsequent corrective feedback from therapists. The principle of graduated exposure is implicit in procedures such as sensate focus, masturbation programs, finger or instrumental dilation of the vagina, and desensitization in fantasy with or without drugs. More specific components are the squeeze technique for premature ejaculation, and superstimulation for failure of ejaculation and anorgasmia. None of these components has been unequivocally demonstrated to be of value, though results of the total approach are encouraging. One therapist may be as good as a male–female therapist team. Other questions that need to be answered by controlled research are: do two therapists do better than one? Do couples treated together do better than when partners are treated separately? What are the values of initial ban on coitus, orgasmic conditioning, and modeling? One controlled study of volunteers with sexual dysfunction suggests the value of a broad "desensitization" package which would include exposure to sexual films and slides, assertive training, and role play of sex-related social situations. A controlled study of desensitization in fantasy alone for impotence found it had little therapeutic effect; when the failures were treated by a broader Masters & Johnson approach, they did much better.

Sexual deviants can be treated by methods to decrease deviance, to increase heterosexuality, or both. Common sense suggests the latter only when heterosexual anxiety or deficits are present, but research is lacking. Techniques to diminish deviant behavior are usually aversive; the unpleasantness of such treatments varies and can be overestimated, and needs to be balanced against the inimical results of the subject continuing his deviant behavior. Full cooperation in treatment is essential.

Aversive stimuli include injected chemicals, electric shocks, unpleasant covert fantasies, unpleasant smells, and social shaming situations. One controlled study found chemical and electric aversion equally helpful, and three others found differing forms of electric aversion to have similar effects, including backward conditioning. One worker found electric aversion superior to a placebo procedure and another found it superior to psychotherapy. The only comparison between desensitization in fantasy and electric aversion found them equally but only modestly helpful. In a short-term study covert sensitization was superior to repeated deviant imagery. All these reports concerned homosexuality. In exhibitionism a short-term study found electric aversion to be superior to self-regulation which in turn was better than relaxation. Controlled research is required in sexual deviants of noncontingent versus contingent shock, and of shock versus smell sensitization.

The foregoing results all concern decrease in deviance. Aversive methods are useful but certainly not a cure-all. Extreme unpleasantness is unnecessary. Emotional reactions during treatment require skilled clinical management. Masochistic patients can respond well to aversion and lasting shock; shock fetishism has fortunately not yet been reported. Evidence is unimpressive that aversion works mainly by conditioning mechanisms, though conditioning effects are undoubtedly found, especially in experimental repression of fantasies. Self administered forms of aversion like self-shocking or covert sensitization can be construed as methods of self-regulation rather than aversion. Shocked fantasies can resemble covert avoidance responses, with increased latencies along generalization gradients, and accompanying changed attitudes and loss of erections. In general, aversion therapy is not aversive in that shocked material changes from being attractive to neutral rather than attractive to disagreeable. Anxiety is associated with a poorer outcome to aversion. During aversion, improvement tends to occur in attitudes, behavior, and erections at parallel, but varying, speeds.

Other methods of reducing deviance include fading, operant shaping, and self-regulation. Only the latter has had controlled study. Techniques to increase heterosexual behavior reported modest results in one controlled study of desensitization; in addition, social retraining, pairing of deviant sexual arousal with heterosexual stimuli (as in orgasmic conditioning), fading, shaping, and aversion relief have all been tried. None except the first has yet been tested in adequately controlled designs.

Adult transsexuals have not been treated with lasting success. Several transsexual boys and a teenage male developed normal gender identity after intensive and prolonged treatment by social retraining methods (modeling, shaping, and extensive role rehearsal).

References

ABEL, G., LEVIS, D., & CLANCY, J. Aversion therapy applied to taped sequences of deviant behavior in exhibitionism and other sexual deviations: a preliminary report. *Journal of Behavior Therapy and Experimental Psychiatry,* 1970, **1**, 59–66.

ANNON, J. S. The extension of learning principles to the analysis and treatment of sexual problems. *Dissertation Abstracts International,* 1971, **32** (6–B), 3627.

BANCROFT, J. H. J. Aversion therapy of homosexuality. *British Journal of Psychiatry,* 1969, **115**, 1417–1431.

BANCROFT, J. H. J. A comparative study of two

forms of behavior therapy in the modification of homosexual interest. M.D. thesis, University of Cambridge, 1970. (a)

BANCROFT, J. H. J. A comparative study of aversion and desensitization in the treatment of homosexuality. In L. E. Burns, & J. H. Worsley (Eds.), *Behavior Therapy in the 1970's.* Bristol, England: Wright, 1970. (b)

BANCROFT, J. H. J. The application of psychophysiological measures to the assessment and modification of sexual behavior. *Behaviour Research and Therapy,* 1971, 9, 119–130.

BANCROFT, J. H. J. Paper presented at the Second Annual Meeting of European Association of Behavior Therapy, Wexford, September 1972.

BANCROFT, J. H. J. *Deviant sexual behavior.* Oxford: Oxford University Press, 1974.

BANCROFT, J. H. J., GWYNNE JONES, H. G., & PULLAN, B. R. A simple transducer for measuring penile erection, with comments on its use in the treatment of sexual disorders. *Behaviour Research and Therapy,* 1966, 4, 239–241.

BARKER, J. A. Behavior therapy for transvestism: a comparison of pharmacological and electrical aversion techniques. *British Journal of Psychiatry,* 1965, 111, 268–276.

BARLOW, D. H. Increasing heterosexual responsiveness in the treatment of sexual deviation. A review of the clinical and experimental evidence. *Behavior Therapy,* 1973, 4, 655–671.

BARLOW, D. H., & AGRAS, W. S. Fading to increase heterosexual responsiveness in homosexuals, 1973.

BARLOW, D. H., AGRAS, W. S., LEITENBERG, H., CALLAHAN, E. J., & MOORE, R. C. The contribution of therapeutic instruction to covert sensitization. *Behaviour Research and Therapy,* 1972, 10, 411–415.

BARLOW, D. H., BECKER, R., LEITENBERG, H., & AGRAS, W. S. A mechanical strain gauge for recording penile circumference change. *Journal of Applied Behavior Analysis,* 1970, 3, 73–76.

BARLOW, D. H., LEITENBERG, H., & AGRAS, W. S. The experimental control of sexual deviation through manipulation of the noxious scene in covert sensitization. *Journal of Abnormal Psychology,* 1969, 74, 596–601.

BARLOW, D. H., REYNOLDS, E. J., & AGRAS, W. S. Gender identity change in a transsexual. *Archives of General Psychiatry,* 1973, 28, 569–576.

BEECH, H. R., WATTS, F., & POOLE, A. D. Classical conditioning of sexual deviation: a preliminary role. *Behavior Therapy,* 1971, 2, 400–402.

BELLIVEAU, K., & RICHTER, L. *Understanding human sexual inadequacy.* New York: Hodder Paperbacks, 1970.

BENTLER, P. M. Heterosexual behavior assessment. *Behaviour Research and Therapy,* 1968, 6, 21–30.

BERGIN, A. E. A self-regulation technique for impulse control disorders. *Psychotherapy: Theory, Research and Practice,* 1969, 6, 113–118. (a)

BERGIN, A. E. A technique for improving desensitization via warmth, empathy and emotional reexperiencing of hierarchy events. In R. D. Rubin, C. M. Franks, & A. A. Lazarus (Eds.), *Proceedings of the association for advancement of the behavioral therapies.* New York: Academic Press, 1969. (b)

BIRK, L., HUDDLESTON, W., MILLER, E., & COHLER, B. Avoidance conditioning for homosexuality. *Archives of General Psychiatry,* 1971, 25, 314–323.

BLITCH, J. W., & HAYNES, S. N. Multiple behavioral techniques in a case of female homosexuality. *Journal of Behavior Therapy and Experimental Psychiatry,* 1972, 3, 319–322.

BLUMER, D., & WALKER, A. E. Sexual behavior in temporal lobe epilepsy. *Archives of Neurology,* 1967, 16, 37–43.

BOND, I. K., & EVANS, D. R. Avoidance therapy: its use in 2 cases of underwear fetishism. *Canadian Medical Asociation Journal,* 1967, 96, 1160–1162.

BOND, I. K., & HUTCHINSON, H. C. Application of reciprocal inhibition therapy to exhibitionism. *Canadian Medical Association Journal,* 1960, 83, 23–25.

BRADY, J. P. Brevital relaxation treatment of frigidity. *Behaviour Research and Therapy,* 1966, 4, 71–77.

BROWN, D. G. Female orgasm and sexual inadequacy. In R. Brecher & E. Brecher (Eds.), *Analysis of human sexual response.* Deutsch, 1967.

BROWN, P. Paper presented at the Second Annual Conference of Behavior Therapy, Wexford, September 1972.

CALLAHAN, E. J., & LEITENBERG, H. Aversion therapy for sexual deviation: contingent shock and covert sensitization. *Journal of Abnormal Psychology*, 1973, **81**, 60–73.

CANTON-DUTARI, A. The treatment of homosexuality: a model for controlling active homosexual behavior. *Archives of Sexual Behavior*, 1974, **3**, 367–372.

CANTON-DUTARI, A. Combined intervention for controlling unwanted homosexual behavior: Part II. *Archives of Sexual Behavior*, 1976, in press.

CAUTELA, J. R., & WISOCKI, P. A. The use of male and female therapists in the treatment of homosexual behavior. In R. Rubin & C. Franks (Eds.), *Advances in behavior therapy*. New York: Academic Press, 1969.

CAUTELA, J. R., & WISOCKI, P. A. Covert sensitization for the treatment of sexual deviations. *Psychological Record*, 1971, **21**, 37–48.

CLARK, D. F. Fetishism treated by negative conditioning. *British Journal of Psychiatry*, 1963, **109**, 695–696.

COLSON, C. E. Olfactory aversion therapy for homosexual behavior. *Journal of Behavior Therapy and Experimental Psychiatry*, 1972, **3**, 1–3.

COOK, J. O., & BARNES, L. W. Choice of delay of inevitable shock. *Journal of Abnormal Social Psychology*, 1964, **68**, 669–672.

COOPER, A. J. A case of fetishism and impotence treated by behavior therapy. *British Journal of Psychiatry*, 1963, **109**, 649–652.

COOPER, A. J. An innovation in the "behavioral" treatment of a case of non-consummation due to vaginismus. *British Journal of Psychiatry*, 1969, **115**, 721–722.

COURTENAY, M. *Sexual discord in marriage*. London: Tavistock Publications, 1968.

CURTIS, R. H., & PRESLEY, A. S. The extinction of homosexual behavior by covert sensitization: a case study. *Behaviour Research and Therapy*, 1972, **10**, 81–84.

DAVIS, M. *The sexual responsibility of women*. William Heinemann, 1957. (Cited by M. Faulk, Factors in the treatment of frigidity. *British Journal of Psychiatry*, 1971, **119**, 53–56.

DAVISON, G. C. Elimination of a sadistic fantasy by a client-centered counter-conditioning technique. *Journal of Abnormal Psychology*, 1968, **73**, 84–89.

DAWKINS, S., & TAYLOR, R. Non-consummation of marriage: a survey of 70 cases. *Lancet*, 1961, **2**, 1029–1033.

DISCIPIO, W. Modified progressive desensitization and homosexuality. *British Journal of Medical Psychology*, 1968, **41**, 267–272.

ELLISON, C. Psychosomatic factors in unconsumated marriage. *Journal of Psychosomatic Research*, 1968, **12**, 61–65.

ERIKSEN, C. W., & KUETHE, J. L. Avoidance conditioning of verbal behavior without awareness: a paradigm of repression. *Journal of Abnormal Social Psychology*, 1956, **53**, 203–209.

EVANS, D. R. Masturbatory fantasy and sexual deviation. *Behaviour Research and Therapy*, 1968, **6**, 17–20.

FAULK, M. Factors in the treatment of frigidity. *British Journal of Psychiatry*, 1971, **119**, 53–56.

FAULK, M. Frigidity—a critical review. *Archives of Sexual Behavior*, 1973, **2**, 257–266.

FELDMAN, M. P. Aversion therapy for sexual deviations: a critical review. *Psychological Bulletin*, 1966, **65**, 65–79.

FELDMAN, M. P. Abnormal sexual behavior in males. In H. J. Eysenck (Ed.), *Handbook of abnormal psychology*. (2nd ed.). London: Pitman, 1973.

FELDMAN, M. P., & MacCULLOCH, M. J. *Homosexual behavior: therapy and assessment*. Oxford: Pergamon, 1972.

FELDMAN, M. P., MacCULLOCH, M. J., MacCULLOCH, M. L. The aversion treatment of a heterogeneous group of 5 cases of sexual deviation. *Acta Psychiatrica Scandinavia*, 1968, **44**, 113–123.

FOOKES, B. H. Some experiences in the use of aversion therapy in male homosexuality, exhibitionism and fetishism. *British Journal of Psychiatry*, 1968, **115**, 339–341.

FRANZINI, L. R. Magnitude estimations of the aversiveness of the interval preceding shock. *Journal of Experimental Psychology*, 1970, **84**, 526–528.

FREIDMAN, L. J. *Virgin wives: a study of unconsummated marriages*. Philadelphia: Lippincott, 1962.

FREUND, K. Some problems in the treatment of homosexuality. In H. J. Eysenck (Ed.), *Behavior therapy and the neuroses*. Oxford: Pergamon, 1960.

FRIEDMAN, D. The treatment of impotence by brietal relaxation therapy. *Behaviour Research and Therapy*, 1968, **6**, 257–261.

FUCHS, K., HOCH, Z., et al. Desensitization therapy of vaginismus. *International Journal of Clinical and Experimental Hypnosis*, 1973, **21**, 144–156.

GAUPP, L. A., STERN, R. M., & RATLIFF, R. G. The use of aversion relief procedure in the treatment of a case of aversion. *Behavior Therapy*, 1971, **2**, 585–588.

GELDER, M. G., & MARKS, I. M. Transsexualism and faradic aversion. In R. Green & and J. Money (Eds.), *Transsexualism and sex reassignment*. Baltimore: Johns Hopkins, 1970.

GOLD, S., & NEUFELD, I. L. A learning approach to the treatment of homosexuality. *Behaviour Research and Therapy*, 1965, **2**, 201–204.

GRAY, J. J. Case conference: behavior therapy in a patient with homosexual fantasies and heterosexual anxiety. *Journal of Behavior Therapy and Experimental Psychiatry*, 1970, **1**, 225–232.

GREEN, R., NEWMAN, L. E., & STOLLER, R. J. Treatment of boyhood "transsexualism." *Archives of General Psychiatry*, 1972, **26**, 213–217.

GREENE, R. J., & HOATS, D. L. Aversive tickling: a simple conditioning technique. *Behavior Therapy*, 1971, **2**, 389–393.

HALLAM, R. S., & RACHMAN, S. Some effects of aversion therapy on patients with sexual disorders. *Behaviour Research and Therapy*, 1972, **10**, 171–180.

HALLAM, R., RACHMAN, S., & FALKOWSKI, W. Subjective, attitudinal and physiological effects of electrical aversion therapy. *Behaviour Research and Therapy*, 1972, **10**, 1–13.

HANSON, R. W., & ADESSO, V. J. A multiple behavioral approach to male homosexual behavior: a case study. *Journal of Behavior Therapy and Experimental Psychiatry*, 1972, 323–325.

HARBERT, T. L., BARLOW, D. H., HERSEN, M., & AUSTIN, J. B. Measurement and modification of incestuous behavior: a case study. *Psychological Reports*, 1973, **34**, 79–86.

HASLAM, M. T. The treatment of psychogenic dyspareunia by reciprocal inhibition. *British Journal of Psychiatry*, 1965, **111**, 280–282.

HASTINGS, D. W. *Impotence and frigidity*. Boston: Little, Brown, 1963. Also chapter in R. & E. Brecher (Eds.), *Analysis of Human Sexual Response*. Deutsch, 1967.

HERMAN, S. H., BARLOW, D. H., & AGRAS, W. S. An experimental analysis of classical conditioning as a method of increasing heterosexual arousal in homosexuals. *Behavior Therapy*, 1974, **5**, 33–42.

HESS, E. H., SELTZER, A. L., & SHLIEN, J. M. Pupil response of hetero- and homosexual males to pictures of men and women: a pilot study. *Journal of Abnormal Psychology*, 1965, **70**, 165–168.

HUFF, F. W. The desensitization of a homosexual. *Behaviour Research and Therapy*, 1970, **8**, 99–102.

JACKSON, B. A case of voyeurism treated by counterconditioning. *Behaviour Research and Therapy*, 1969, **7**, 133–134.

JOHNSON, J. *Disorders of sexual potency in the male*. Oxford: Pergamon, 1968.

JOHNSON, J., & KITCHING, R. A mechanical transducer for phallography. *Biomedical Engineering*, September 1969, 416–418.

JOVANOVIC, U. J. The recording of physiological evidence of genital arousal in human males and females. *Archives of Sexual Behavior*, 1971, **1**, 309–320.

KEGAL, A. H. Letter to the editor. *Journal of American Medical Association*, 1953, **153**, 1303–1304.

KINSEY, A. C., POMEROY, W. B., & MARTIN, C. E. *Sexual behavior in the male*. Philadelphia: Saunders, 1948.

KINSEY, A. C., POMEROY, W. B., & MARTIN, C. E. *Sexual behavior in the female*. Philadelphia: Saunders, 1953.

KOCKOTT, G., DITTMAR, F., & NUSSELT, L. Systematic desensitization of erectile impotence: a controlled study. *Archives of Sexual Behavior*, 1975, in press.

KOLARSKY, A., FREUND, J., MACHEK, J., & POLAK, O. Male sexual deviation. *Archives of General Psychiatry*, 1967, **17**, 735–743.

KOLVIN, I. "Aversive imagery" treatment in adolescents. *Behaviour Research and Therapy*, 1967, **5**, 245–249.

KRAFT, T. A case of homosexuality treated by systematic desensitization. *American Journal of Psychotherapy*, 1967, **21**, 815–821.

KUSHNER, M. The reduction of a longstanding fetish by means of aversive conditioning. In L. P. Ullman & L. Krasner (Eds.), *Case studies in behavior modification*. New York: Holt, Rinehart & Winston, 1965.

KUSHNER, M., & SANDLER, J. Aversion therapy

and the concept of punishment. *Behaviour Research and Therapy,* 1966, **4,** 179–186.

LANGEVIN, R., & MARTIN, M. Can erotic responses be classically conditioned? *Behavior Therapy,* 1975, **6,** 350–355.

LARSON, D. E. An adaptation of the Feldman and MacCulloch approach to treatment of homosexuality by the application of anticipatory avoidance learning. *Behaviour Research and Therapy,* 1970, **8,** 209–210.

LAVIN, N., THORPE, J., BARKER, J., BLAKEMORE, C., & CONWAY, C. Behavior therapy in a case of transvestism. *Journal of Nervous and Mental Disorders,* 1961, **133,** 346–353.

LAZARUS, A. A. Treatment of frigidity by systematic desensitization. *Journal of Nervous and Mental Disorders,* 1963, **136,** 272–278.

LEVIN, S., HIRSCH, I., SHUGAR, G., & KAPCHE, R. Treatment of homosexuality and heterosexual anxiety with avoidance conditioning and systematic desensitization: Data and case report. *Psychotherapy: Theory, Research and Practice,* 1968, **5,** 160–168.

LOBITZ, W. C., LOPICCOLO, J. New methods of the behavioral treatment of sexual dysfunction. *Journal of Behavior Therapy and Experimental Psychiatry,* 1972, **3,** 265–271.

LOPICCOLO, J. Systematic desensitization of homosexuality. *Behavior Therapy,* 1971, **2,** 394–399.

LOPICCOLO, J., & LOBITZ, W. C. The role of masturbation in the treatment of orgasmic dysfunction. *Archives of Sexual Behavior,* 1972, **2,** 163–171.

MADSEN, C. H., & ULLMAN, L. P. Innovations in the desensitization of frigidity. *Behaviour Research and Therapy,* 1967, **5,** 67–68.

MALETSKY, M. M. "Assisted" covert sensitization: a preliminary report. *Behavior Therapy,* 1973, **4,** 117–119.

MANDEL, K. H. Preliminary report on a new aversion therapy for male homosexuals. *Behaviour Research and Therapy,* 1970, **8,** 93–95.

MARKS, I. M. Aversion therapy. *British Journal of Medical Psychology,* 1968, **41,** 47.

MARKS, I. M. *Fears and phobias.* New York: Academic Press, 1969.

MARKS, I. M. Phylogenesis and learning in the acquisition of fetishism. *Danish Medical Bulletin,* 1972, **19,** 307–309.

MARKS, I. M., & GELDER, M. G. Transvestism and fetishism: clinical and psychological changes during faradic aversion. *British Journal of Psychiatry,* 1967, **113,** 711–739.

MARKS, I. M., GELDER, M. G., & BANCROFT, J. H. J. Sexual deviants two years after aversion. *British Journal of Psychiatry,* 1970, **117,** 173–185.

MARKS, I. M., RACHMAN, S., & GELDER, M. G. Methods for assessment of aversion treatment in fetishism with masochism. *Behaviour Research and Therapy,* 1965, **3,** 253–258.

MARKS, I. M., & SARTORIUS, N. A contribution to the measurement of sexual attitude. *Journal of Nervous and Mental Diseases,* 1968, **114,** 323–328.

MARQUIS, J. N. Orgasmic reconditioning: changing sexual object choice through controlling masturbation fantasies. *Journal of Behavior Therapy and Experimental Psychiatry,* 1970, **1,** 263–271.

MASTERS, W., & JOHNSON, V. *Human sexual inadequacy.* Boston: Little, Brown, 1970.

MATHEWS, A. M. Paper to Annual Meeting of British Association of Behavioural Pyschotherapy, York, 1975.

MAX, L. W. Breaking up a homosexual fixation by the conditioned reaction technique. *Psychological Bulletin,* 1935, **32,** 734.

McCONAGHY, N. Penile volume change to moving pictures of male and female nudes in heterosexual and homosexual males. *Behaviour Research and Therapy,* 1967, **5,** 43–48.

McCONAGHY, N. Subjective and penile plethysmograph responses following aversion-relief and apomorphine aversion therapy for homosexual impulses. *British Journal of Psychiatry,* 1969, **115,** 723–730.

McCONAGHY, N. Subjective and penile plethysmograph responses to aversion therapy for homosexuality: a follow-up study. *British Journal of Psychiatry,* 1970, **117,** 555–560.

McCONAGHY, N. Penile volume responses to moving and still pictures of male and female nudes. *Archives of Sexual Behavior,* 1974, **3,** 565–570.

McCONAGHY, N. *Behavior research therapy,* in press.

McCONAGHY, N., & BARR, R. F. Classical, avoidance and backward conditioning treatments of homosexuality. *British Journal of Psychiatry,* 1973, **122,** 151–162.

McCONAGHY, N., PROCTOR, D., & BARR, R. Subjective and penile plethysmography responses to aversion therapy for homosexuality: a partial replication. *Archives of Sexual Behavior*, 1972, **2**, 65–78.

McGUIRE, R. J., & VALLANCE, M. Aversion therapy by electric shock: a simple technique. *British Medical Journal*, 1964, **1**, 151–153.

MEES, H. L. Sadistic fantasies modified by aversive conditioning and substitution. *Behaviour Research and Therapy*, 1966, **4**, 317–320.

MICHEL-WOLFRUMM, H. Causes et traitement du vaginisme. *Fr. Gyn. Obst.*, 1954, **49**, 30.

MOAN, C. E., & HEATH, R. G. Septal stimulation for the initiation of heterosexual behavior in a homosexual male. *Journal of Behavior Therapy and Experimental Psychiatry*, 1972, **3**, 23–30.

MORGENSTERN, F. S., PEARCE, J. F., & REES, W. L. Predicting the outcome of behavior therapy by psychological tests. *Behaviour Research and Therapy*, 1965, **2**, 191–200.

OBLER, M. Systematic desensitization in sexual disorders. *Journal of Behavioral Therapy and Experimental Psychiatry*, 1973, **4**, 93–101.

O'GORMAN, et al. Paper presented at the Second Annual Meeting of European Association of Behavior Therapy, Wexford, September 1972.

OLLEY, M., & McALLISTER, H. A comment on treatment analogues for phobic anxiety states. *Psychological Medicine*, 1974, **4**, 463–469.

OSWALD, I. Induction of illusory and hallucinatory voices with consideration of behavior therapy. *Journal of Mental Science*, 1962, **108**, 196–212.

QUINN, J., HARBISON, J., & McALLISTER, H. An attempt to shape human penile responses. *Behaviour Research and Therapy*, 1970, **8**, 213–216.

RACHMAN, S. Sexual fetishism: an experimental analogue. *Psychological Record*, 1966, **16**, 293–296.

RACHMAN, S., & HODGSON, R. J. Experimentally induced "sexual fetishism:" a replication and development. *Psychological Record*, 1968, **18**, 25–27.

RACHMAN, S., & TEASDALE, J. *Aversion therapy*. Oxford: Pergamon, 1969.

RAMSAY, R. W., & VAN VELZEN, V. Behavior therapy for sexual perversions. *Behaviour Research and Therapy*, 1968, **6**, 233.

RAYMOND, M. J. Case of fetishism treated by aversion therapy. *British Medical Journal*, 1956, **2**, 854–857.

REITZ, W. E., & KEIL, W. E. Behavioral treatment of an exhibitionist. *Journal of Behavior Therapy and Experimental Psychiatry*, 1971, **2**, 67–69.

ROOTH, F. G. Indecent exposure and exhibitionism. *British Journal of Hospital Medicine*, 1971, **9**, 521–534.

ROOTH, F. G., & MARKS, I. M. Persistent exhibitionism: short-term response to self-regulation and relaxation treatment. *Archives of Sexual Behavior*, 1974, **3**, 227–248.

SCHATZBERG, A., WESTFALL, M., BLUMETTI, A., & BIRK, L. Effeminacy: a quantitative rating scale, and variation with social content. *Archives of Sexual Behavior*, 1974, **4**, 43–52.

SELIGMAN, M., & HAGER, J. *Biological Boundaries of Learning*. New York: Appleton-Century-Crofts, 1972.

SEMANS, J. H. Premature ejaculation. *Southern Medical Journal*, 1956, **49**, 353–357.

SERBER, M. Shame aversion therapy. *Behavior Therapy and Experimental Psychiatry*, 1970, **1**, 219–221.

SERBER, M. Shame aversion therapy with and without heterosexual training. In *Advances in behavior therapy*. New York: Academic Press, 1972.

SERBER, M. The employment of videotape recording as an adjunct to the treatment of sexual dysfunction. *Archives of Sexual Behavior*, 1974, **3**, 377–380.

SHARPE, R., & MEYER, V. Modification of "cognitive sexual pain" by the spouse under supervision. *Behavior Therapy*, 1973, **4**, 285–287.

SIEGELMAN, M. Adjustment of homosexual and heterosexual women. *British Journal of Psychiatry*, 1972, **120**, 477–481. (a)

SIEGELMAN, M. Adjustment of male homosexuals and heterosexuals. *Archives of Sexual Behavior*, 1972, **2**, 9–25. (b)

SOLYOM, L., & MILLER, S. A. A differential conditioning procedure as the initial phase of the behavior therapy of homosexuality. *Behaviour Research and Therapy*, 1965, **3**, 147–160.

STEVENSON, I., & WOLPE, J. Recovery from sexual deviations through overcoming non-sexual neurotic responses. *American Journal of Psychiatry*, 1960, **116**, 737–742.

TANNER, B. A. A comparison of automated aversive conditioning in a waiting list control in the modification of homosexual behavior in males. *Behavior Therapy*, 1974, 5, 29–32 (a).

TANNER, B. A. Shock intensity and fear of shock in the modification of homosexual behavior in males by avoidance learning. *Behaviour Research and Therapy*, 1973, 11, 213–218. (b)

THORPE, J., SCHMIDT, E., BROWN, P. T., & CASTELL, D. Aversion-relief therapy: a new method for general application. *Behaviour Research and Therapy*, 1964, 2, 71–82.

WICKRAMASERA, I. The application of learning theory to the treatment of a case of sexual exhibitionism. *Psychotherapy: Theory, Research and Practice*, 1968, 5, 108–112.

WILSON, G. T. Innovations in the modification of phobic behaviors in two clinical cases. *Behavior Therapy*, 1973, 4, 426–430.

ZUCKERMAN, M. Physiological measures of sexual arousal in the human. *Psychological Bulletin*, 1971, 75, 297–329.

Children
and
Youth

Behavior Modification with Psychotic Children

9

O. IVAR LOVAAS
CRIGHTON D. NEWSOM

This chapter will report on certain recent findings pertaining to the behavioral treatment of severely psychotic children. Childhood psychosis is a broad diagnostic category which refers to children who have failed to a rather extreme extent in their social, emotional, and intellectual development. "Childhood schizophrenia" and "early infantile autism" are among the terms that are used, often quite arbitrarily, to classify severely psychotic children. However, the implications of different diagnoses for the treatment of these children has yet to be established, and we will therefore use the terms "psychotic," "schizophrenic," and "autistic" interchangeably. Let us clarify our reasons for doing so in somewhat more detail, since there exists in some quarters a great deal of controversy over the use of these terms.

It is well known that if a behaviorally deficient child has been seen in more than one clinic, he is very likely to have been given more than one diagnosis. He could, in fact, have a record containing several theoretically incompatible diagnoses (schizophrenia, autism, brain-damaged, and retardation, for example). The published guidelines for diagnosing children into

these various categories are not uniform, and the difficulty stems partly from the fact that there is considerable behavioral overlap between these various kinds of children. The reason for using a diagnosis in the first place is that it tells us the reasons behind a child's present problem and it indicates how far a child will proceed with a particular kind of treatment. It has, of course, been demonstrated that there exist distinct etiologies and treatment outcomes for certain kinds of mentally retarded children, such as those with Down's Syndrome and those with phenylketonuria. Such differential etiologies and treatment outcomes justify the use of distinctive diagnostic terms. But such a degree of physiological or behavioral specificity has not yet been shown to exist between children labeled schizophrenic, autistic, and psychotic. In practice, these categories are of no more use than the terms "familial" and "undifferentiated," which are applied to the majority of retarded children and fail to convey any precise information about etiology or prognosis. Nor are the boundaries between psychotic and retarded children very clear. In the future we may find that many children who are now considered psychotic will be considered retarded and vice versa. Until we know more about the merits of entertaining different diagnoses for these children, that is, until we have gained enough knowledge to specify in some detail the etiology and prognosis of these psychological difficulties, it is safe to pay scant attention to these diagnostic labels, and instead to focus our treatment efforts at helping the child with his *behavioral* deviations. The behavior therapist's strategy, then, is to treat behavioral excesses and deficiencies rather than to attempt the remediation of some hypothetical underlying disease process such as "autism." When we can successfully treat various behaviors, then any child may benefit, regardless of his diagnosis.

Before we describe the rationale for the behavioral treatment of psychotic children in more detail, it would probably be helpful to contrast this approach to the more traditional approaches to the problem. This may help to make our position on the diagnostic situation seem less arbitrary because the history of the treatment of psychotic children very clearly illustrates the futility of premature attempts to resolve questions of etiology and prognosis.

Historical Considerations

Kanner (1943) was the first person to suggest that there may exist a distinct type of psychotic child known as autistic. Kanner pointed to emotional aloofness and insistence on the maintenance of sameness as particularly diagnostic of autism. He refrained from postulating a specific etiology, although he did suggest that the typical parents of autistic children were cold, detached, unaffectionate, and emotionally insulated. Other psychodynamically oriented writers, like Bettelheim (1967), were quick to seize on this apparent correlation between child deviance and parental rejection. The etiology of autism, from this point of view, centered on the child's being raised in an environment that was singularly cold and destructive. The child's subsequent withdrawal to his inner "autistic world" was a defense against parents who rejected him, frightened him, and perhaps threatened his very existence. It was postulated that the parents' angry rejection of the child was the cause behind the child's failure to form a meaningful, warm, affectionate relationship toward people; consequently, he never moved on developmentally to relate himself to ("cathect") the external world. His behaviors were seen as symptoms of this combined effect of fear of his parents' anger toward him and the correlated failure of "reality testing" (or "ego" development). For example, an analytically oriented person may point to the excessive body rocking of autistic children as symptomatic of primitive attempts to reaffirm, through ritualism and monotony, their limited hold on an otherwise fluctuating and frightening world. A child's self-destructive behaviors may be seen as symptomatic of his attempts to injure his mother because his mother hurt him, and when he hits himself he is, in his own reality, hitting her back.

Given this particular etiology, it followed that the treatment of the child from a psychodynamic point of view would consist of attempts by therapists, parents, and teachers to create a loving, accepting, understanding, and warm adult-child relationship—which the parents had supposedly failed to provide—in the hope that the child would accept the adult in a therapeutic relationship. He would then move out toward the world, relate himself to that world, and concurrently lose the various "symptoms" of autism. Because of this new emotional relationship to the adults around him, the child would acquire appropriate behaviors quite automatically without anyone specifically teaching them to him.

It is interesting to note that the particular treatment that psychodynamically oriented theorists have prescribed for autistic children appears not to differ substantially from the prescribed treatment for schizophrenic children or for psychotic children in general. The multiplication of different kinds of psychotic children on paper, according to various assumptions about etiology and prognosis, has had little, if any, practical impact on treatment considerations. In practice the various kinds of psychotic children have been treated very much alike, that is, as children who need a great deal of noncontingent love and affection, which would presumably effect certain internal changes in the child and thereby produce a behavioral reorganization.

Large, comprehensive formulations such as the psychodynamic attempts to understand autism have not been adequately evaluated and perhaps they never will be. But it is important to note that on the empirical level the outcome studies on psychoanalytic attempts to treat psychotic children have failed to yield significant results. Kanner and Eisenberg (1955), Brown (1960), and Rutter (1966) have all reported data indicating that autistic children treated in accordance with psychoanalytic principles did not do significantly better than children who received no treatment at all. Merely providing a loving, understanding milieu (to replace the hostile, cold environment supposedly provided by the parents) does not seem to help these children. Similarly, more laboratory-like experimental studies which were designed to test the major psychodynamic formulations regarding autism have failed to support the necessary assumptions. For example, research has failed to identify the parents as cold and detached, or any other emotionally deficient type (Pitfield & Oppenheim, 1964; Rimland, 1964; Schopler & Reichler, 1972; Wolff & Morris, 1971).

What we saw, then, during the 1940s and 1950s was the appearance of Dr. Kanner's suggestion that a distinct group of psychotic children be singled out and labeled "autistic," followed by a great deal of vigorous

support for the creation of a new diagnostic category to recognize this condition, for which people like Bettelheim postulated a distinct etiology and prescribed a supposedly distinct treatment. By the early 1960s, as data failed to support these theoretical formulations, an attitude of reservation and pessimism characterized the treatment of autistic children; therapists felt they were giving a lot but not getting much back. It was in this kind of atmosphere, of a pessimistic prognosis and confusion about etiology, that the first behavioral approach to the treatment of autistic children was begun.

Reinforcement Theory and Autism

The first attempt to understand the behavior of autistic children within a behavioristic framework was made by Ferster (1961). He argued that in the absence of acquired reinforcing aspects of social stimuli (as well as a lack of acquired reinforcers in general), the very impoverished behavioral repertoires of autistic children would naturally follow. The primary contribution of Ferster's theoretical argument lies not in its etiological speculations, which have never received experimental confirmation, but in the explicit and concrete way in which it relates learning theory to the psychotic child's current patterns of behavior. There have been some general efforts to relate learning theory to psychopathology in the past, but perhaps no one presented the argument as directly and clearly as did Ferster. We shall come back to a more detailed presentation of his view later.

Shortly after this theoretical analysis appeared, Ferster and DeMyer (1961) reported a set of experiments in which autistic children were exposed to very simple but highly controlled environments where they could learn relatively simple behaviors (such as pulling levers or matching to sample) for reinforcers which were functional in maintaining these behaviors over time. These studies were the first to show that the behavior of autistic children could be related lawfully to certain explicit environmental contingencies; these children could, in fact, be taught to comply with certain aspects of reality.

Let us briefly summarize a behavioral analysis of autism in terms of that part of learning theory which we have relied upon to help us in our treatment projects with psychotic children. Using the concepts of learning theory one can view a child's development as consisting of (1) the development of behavioral repertoires, and (2) the acquisition of stimulus functions. If we look at autistic children from a behavioral perspective, their most deviant feature is their behavioral deficiency. They have little, if any, behavior which would help them function in society. Therefore, a therapeutic program for autistic children may focus on how to strengthen certain behaviors, such as appropriate play and speech. One may strengthen such behaviors by *reinforcing* their occurrence. When they are initially absent, such behaviors may be prompted or gradually shaped by rewarding successive approximations to their final form. We shall give numerous examples of such programs designed to increase the behavioral repertoires of autistic children. Conversely, it is also true that some behaviors are too strong in autistic children. This is particularly true of tantrums and self-destructive behavior, and we attempt to decrease their strength either by withholding those reinforcers which may be maintaining them (*extinction*), or by systematically applying aversive stimuli contingent upon their occurrence (*punishment*). In short, it is quite possible to develop treatment programs where one works directly with the child's behaviors, increasing some and decreasing others by the use of whatever reinforcers and punishers are functional for that child. In the programs which we will discuss in this chapter, the emphasis lies in the development of appropriate behaviors with the use of primary reinforcers (such as food) in conjunction with prompting and prompt-fading techniques.

As new behaviors are learned, the child's environment simultaneously begins to acquire "meaning," or what might technically be referred to as "stimulus functions," for him. Internal and external events to which the child attends when he responds acquire the capacity to evoke those responses in the future. A stimulus which sets the occasion upon which a certain behavior will be reinforced and others will not is called a *discriminative stimulus* or S^D. We say that *stimulus control* exists to the extent that a given behavior reliably occurs when a given stimulus is present and does not occur when it is absent. Another aspect of the acquisition of stimulus functions has to do with symbolic rewards and punishers, which are known technically as secondary, acquired, or *conditioned* reinforcers and punishers. In normal development, certain parts of the child's environment which were neutral when he was born come to acquire reinforcing or punitive functions for him. One can think of many good examples to illustrate this point, and it is particularly obvious that within the area of social functioning much of this kind of learning takes place. The presence or absence of an approving smile, although neutral to the newborn infant, gradually assumes reinforcing functions as the child interacts with people around him. The primary reason that the acquisition of these conditioned reinforcers is so important lies in their contribution to the acquisition of complex social and intellectual behaviors. Normal children appear to acquire normal behaviors to the extent that there exists a variety of conditioned reinforcers to support such behavioral development. Since autistic children generally do not respond to praise, smiles, hugs, interpersonal closeness, being correct, and other events which reinforce so much behavior in normal children, it is reasonable to expect their behavioral development to be correspondingly deficient. Thus, much of an autistic child's failure to acquire appropriate behavior can be viewed as the result of a more basic failure of his environment to acquire motivational meaning for him; that is, his environment occasions little "normal" behavior because it contains few "normal"—conditioned—reinforcers. This was the essence of Ferster's (1961) theoretical analysis of autism. One can conceive of conditioned reinforcers as being "causes" of behavior. To address one's therapeutic work to the development and rearrangement of reinforcing stimuli would seem to strike at the base of the autistic child's problem. Yet there has been surprisingly little work done in this area. We will consider this point again in more detail when we discuss motivation.

Shortly after Ferster's first papers appeared, several studies were published describing the treatment of autistic children with behavior modification procedures. These studies were characterized by relatively powerful research designs, and most of the thrust of behavior modification research continues to derive from its adherence to such sound designs. Usually, the behavioral studies have employed within-subject replication designs so that one can be reasonably certain that the treatment which is given does in fact help a child. But since the early studies were limited to a single child or just a few children, or limited themselves to interventions with just a few behaviors, it was difficult to assess the overall effectiveness of behavior modification. Within a short time, however, the early findings were independently replicated and extended by investigators in other laboratories and clinics. Let us briefly review some of the first studies which employed behavioral techniques in the treatment of autistic children.

In one of the best known early studies, Wolf, Risley, and Mees (1964) used shaping, extinction, and time out to treat a three-year-old autistic boy who would not eat properly, lacked normal social and verbal repertoires, was self-destructive, and refused to wear glasses necessary to preserve his vision. The child's behavior improved markedly during treatment, and a subsequent follow-up study (Wolf, Risley, Johnston, Harris, & Allen, 1967) showed that he continued to improve after discharge from the program, to the point where he was able to take advantage of a public school education program. In another early study, Hewett (1965) described a procedure for building speech in children who were speech deficient or mute. He used a shaping procedure to increase the child's attending behavior, then systematically rewarded the child for vocalizations that eventually matched those modeled by the therapist. Under this procedure the child acquired the beginnings of meaningful language.

Around the time that this work was being conducted, there appeared conceptually important studies demonstrating errorless discrimination learning (Terrace, 1963) and generalized imitation (Baer & Sherman, 1964). These studies led to the development of techniques which enormously increased the therapeutic power of behavior modification procedures with behaviorally deficient children. Consider imitative behavior as an example. As Bandura (1969) has argued, it may be literally impossible to shape highly complex behaviors a step at a time. Complex behaviors seem often to be acquired through imitation, but until the Baer and Sherman (1964) study appeared, we did not have a technology for establishing imitation where none existed. These investigators showed that if a child were reinforced for imitating some of a model's behaviors, the child would also begin to imitate the model's other behaviors, even though these had not been explicitly reinforced. They viewed imitation as a discrimination: the child discriminates the similarity between his and the model's behavior as the occasion for reinforcement. Although the Baer and Sherman study dealt with normal children who already imitated, its results provided a conceptual and methodological basis for building imitative behavior in nonimitating children. Thus, Metz (1965) first showed how one could use reinforcement to build nonverbal imitative behaviors in autistic children. Lovaas, Berberich, Perloff, and Schaeffer (1966) showed that it was possible, through the use of a discrimination-learning paradigm, to build imitative verbal behavior in previously mute autistic children. These early behavioral studies showed that it was quite possible to take learning principles discovered in animal laboratories and apply them to socially and clinically relevant behaviors in humans (such as atavisms, self-help skills, and language). From these studies have come the beginnings of a comprehensive technology of treatment for psychotic children (Kozloff, 1974; Lovaas, 1976). We have moved very quickly in work with a difficult clinical population in the short span of 15 years, which takes us from Ferster's (1961) theoretical behavioral analysis of autism to the present day. Obviously, this is a very new field that has experienced a promising start.

Behavioral Description of Psychotic Children

Let us briefly describe in more detail how severely autistic children actually behave when first seen and what their parents say about them. An autistic child often appears different from normal children during his first year of life; and certainly by the time he is two years old he is dramatically different from normal children. He can be described in terms of the following characteristics.

APPARENT SENSORY DEFICIT. We may move directly in front of the child, smile and talk to him, yet he will act as if no one is there. We may not feel that the child is avoiding or ignoring us, but rather that he simply does not seem to see or hear. The mother also reports that she did, in fact, incorrectly suspect the child to be blind or deaf. At one time or another she has taken him for a medical examination, but he was not diagnosed as blind or deaf insofar as his behavioral limitations permitted testing. As we get to know the child better, we become aware of the great variability in this obliviousness to stimulation. For example, although the child may give no visible reaction to a loud noise, such as a clapping of hands directly behind his ears, he may orient to the crinkle of a candy wrapper or respond fearfully to a distant and barely audible siren. Similarly, though he does not notice the comings or goings of people around him, or other major changes in his visual field (turning off the lights may have no effect on his behavior), he will sometimes spot a small piece of candy on a table some 20 feet away from him. An operant vision test recently developed in our laboratory indicates that most severely psychotic children have normal distance acuity thresholds (Newsom & Simon, Note 1). Obviously, he is not blind or deaf in the way we usually use these terms.

SEVERE AFFECT ISOLATION. Another characteristic that we frequently notice is that attempts to love and cuddle and show affection to the child encounter a profound lack of interest on the child's part. Again, the parents relate that the child seems not to know or care whether he is alone or in the company of others. The child is indifferent to being liked by the family. As a small baby he does not cup or mold when he is held, and does not respond with anticipation to being picked up. He does not laugh or smile appropriately, if at all. And he does not seem sad or depressed; he does not cry or seem hopeless or bewildered.

SELF-STIMULATION. A most striking kind of behavior in these children centers on very repetitive stereotyped acts, such as rocking their bodies when in a sitting position, twirling around, flapping their hands at the wrists, or humming a set of three or four notes over and over again. The parents often report that their child has spent entire days gazing at his cupped hands, staring at lights, spinning objects, etc.

TANTRUMS AND SELF-MUTILATORY BEHAVIOR. Although the child may not engage in self-mutilation when we first meet him, often the parents report that the child sometimes bites himself so severely that he bleeds; or that he beats his head against walls or sharp pieces of furniture so forcefully that large lumps rise and his skin turns black and blue. He may beat his face with his fists. Some of the children bear scars from their self-mutilation—for example, skin discolorations that remain from bite wounds on the inside of their wrists. We are likely to trigger self-mutilatory behavior in such a child if we impose some restriction on his movement (e.g., holding him still) or if we attempt to impose even minimal standards for appropriate behavior (e.g., by requesting the child to sit at a desk or table). Sometimes the child's aggression will be directed outward against his parents or teachers in the most primitive form of biting, scratching, and kicking. Some of these children absolutely tyrannize their parents by staying awake and making noises all night, tearing curtains off the window, spilling flour in the kitchen, etc., and the parents are often at a complete loss as to how to cope with these behaviors.

ECHOLALIC AND PSYCHOTIC SPEECH. Most of these children are mute; they do not speak, but they may hum or occasionally utter simple sounds. The speech of those who do talk may be echoes of other people's attempts to talk to them. For example, if we address a child with the question, "What is your name?" the child is likely to answer, "What is your name?" (preserving, perhaps, the exact intonation of the one who spoke to him). At other times the echolalia is not immediate but delayed; the child may repeat statements he has heard that morn-ing or on the preceding day, or he may repeat TV commercials or other such announcements. He may have almost the same deficiency in receptive speech as he has in expressive speech.

BEHAVIORAL DEFICIENCIES. Although the presence of the behaviors sketched above is rather striking, it is equally striking to take note of many behaviors that the autistic child does *not* have. At the age of 5 or 10, he may, in many ways, show the behavioral repertoire of a 1-year-old child. He has few if any self-help skills but needs to be fed and dressed by others. He may not play with toys, but put them in his mouth, or tap them repetitively with his fingers. He shows no understanding of common dangers. One has to be careful not to let the child walk in the street unassisted, because he may walk directly in front of an oncoming car.

OTHER CONSIDERATIONS. Many diagnosticians now consider it important that the child's motor development fall within the normal range in order to diagnose autism as distinct from retardation. Thus, in order for the child to be diagnosed autistic it is necessary to many that he sat up, crawled, and walked at a normal age. Similarly, many diagnosticians look for isolated signs of average or perhaps above average intellectual functioning in the way that the child manipulates certain people or objects in his environment or in behavior suggesting superior memory. For example, some autistic children appear to be particularly clever at manipulating their parents by throwing tantrums; others are particularly skillful in assembling and disassembling mechanical objects such as clocks or watches. Some autistic children give evidence of unusual memory, in that they detect minor changes in the furniture arrangement of their living room (even though they were not there when the changes were made) and become extremely upset. Others may be able to recite songs, series of numbers, or other kinds of material, which indicates an extensive rote memory. This last diagnostic task, of inferring intact intellectual functioning, is admittedly the most difficult one, which no doubt contributes significantly to the problem of discriminating autistic children from other types of children with severe behavioral retardation.

In any case, what one usually sees when first meeting an autistic child who is 2, 3, or even 10 years of age is a child who has all the external physical characteristics of a normal child—that is, he has hair, and he has eyes and he has a nose, and he may be dressed in a shirt and trousers—but who really has no behaviors that one can single out as distinctively "human." The major job then, for a therapist—whether he's behaviorally oriented or not—would seem to be a very intriguing and significant one, namely, the creation or construction of a truly human behavioral repertoire where none exists. Shortly we will see how behavioral psychologists tried to accomplish this task. First, however, we will discuss self-destructive behavior—surely one of the most bizarre and awesome phenomena that one will ever encounter—and self-stimulatory behavior, a kind of "pathological play" which can consume the greater part of the child's waking hours. We consider these topics first because the effective management of these behaviors is an essential prerequisite to any serious attempt to help psychotic children.

Managing Self-destructive Behavior

A significant number of children diagnosed as psychotic or severely retarded manifest, at one time or another in their lives, self-destructive behavior. This behavior consists primarily of head banging (against walls and furniture); arm banging (against sharp corners); beating themselves on their heads or in their faces with their fists or knees;

and biting themselves on wrists, arms, and shoulders. In some children, the self-destructive behavior can be severe enough to pose a major problem for the child's safety. Thus, one can frequently see that such children have removed large quantities of flesh from their bodies, torn out their nails, opened wounds in their heads, broken their noses, etc. Such severe forms of self-destruction often require restraints, either in the form of camisoles ("straitjackets") or by tying the child's feet and arms to his bed. Sometimes the self-destructive behavior is sporadic; at other times it is long-lasting, necessitating such prolonged use of restraints that one can observe structural changes, such as demineralization, shortening of tendons, or arrested motor development, secondary to disuse of limbs.

The self-destructive child poses major psychological problems for those who take care of him, in the form of anxiety, demoralization, and hopelessness. Parents and institutional personnel must be constantly aware of the immediate threat to the child, either directly through tissue damage or indirectly through infections. There are secondary problems associated with self-destructive behavior which center on the curtailment of growth (psychological and otherwise) in the child who has to be restrained. The authors know of no treatment that invariably alleviates self-destructive behavior. The most common form of treatment consists of some combination of drugs, supportive verbal therapy, and occasional electroconvulsive therapy. There is no evidence to demonstrate that any of these forms of treatment is effective; they could make the child worse.

Prior to the behavioral work on self-destruction there existed a number of hypotheses as to the causes of such behavior. Freud (1954), for example, thought that self-destructive behavior, particularly in young children, provided cues to establish "body reality." Similarly, Greenacre (1954) proposed that self-destruction promoted "solidification" of the body image. Other psychodynamically oriented people, like Hartman, Kris, and Loewenstein (1949) considered a child's self-destructive behavior to be attempts of the child to punish his mother. It was supposed that the mother rejected the child, and, further, that the child differentiated poorly between himself and his mother. Others thought of head banging as being auto-erotic, hence as providing its own reinforcement, while still others considered it to be an attempt by the child to stimulate himself in an otherwise nonstimulating environment.

These highly speculative theories were undoubtedly well intentioned, and that is about the most that can be said for them. In a moment, we will see the destructive effects of the type of treatment they led to. The behavioral work, on the other hand, presents data which clearly shows self-destructive behavior to be social operant behavior. Whatever its origins may be, the eventual strength of this particular behavior is determined by the kind of social consequences which it produces. It is therefore possible to treat self-destructive behavior effectively by withholding its usual social consequence, the attention it receives from other people in the child's environment.

Very early we had some indications from a study reported by Wolf et al., (1964) that the withdrawal of attention can eliminate self-destructive behavior. They used it effectively with a five-year-old boy whom they placed in isolation contingent on his throwing tantrums or injuring himself. Later, Hamilton, Stephens, and Allen (1967) also used social isolation to eliminate head and back banging in a severely retarded institutionalized girl. Their subject was physically confined in a chair located away from ward activities (and hence social reinforcement) for a 30-minute period contingent upon each occurrence of self-destructive behavior. The self-destructive behavior was eliminated very rapidly

and apparently did not recur over a nine-month follow-up period.

In these studies involving contingent social isolation, or time out, it could be argued that the experience of being placed in isolation reduces self-destructive behavior because it involves an interruption of ongoing behavior and a possibly aversive social interaction, and not necessarily because it involves the removal of social attention. The hypothesis that self-destruction is maintained by its social consequences is, however, directly supported by evidence that the complete removal of all social consequences results in the elimination of self-destructive behavior. Let us first present data on one self-destructive child who underwent social extinction (Bucher & Lovaas, 1968). Figure 9-1 shows a record of the self-destructive behavior of an eight-year-old boy whose self-destruction is plotted as cumulative curves. The first eight extinction sessions are presented. In each session the child was left alone unrestrained for a 90-minute period of time. Observe that at first his rate was very high; he hit himself more than 2,700 times during the first extinction period. Note, however, that only half an hour into the first session his rate began falling slightly, which was our first inkling that the treatment might work. Gradually over these first eight sessions the rate of his self-destructive behavior decreased until it reached zero in the eighth session. Similar support for the effect of extinction on self-destruction was provided in a paper by Lovaas, Freitag, Gold, and Kassorla (1965) and later by Lovaas and Simmons (1969).

If self-destructive behavior is operant behavior, then it should show the opposite effect (an increase in strength) if social reinforcement is presented contingent on its occurrence. In an early study (Lovaas, et al., 1965) we had quite accidentally observed that on certain days, when we attended to a child's self-destructive behaviors by verbalizing our concern about

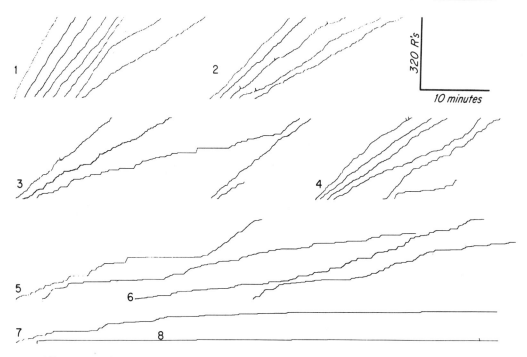

FIGURE 9–1   Cumulative self-destructive responses of an autistic boy during eight successive extinction sessions (Bucher & Lovaas, 1968). Reprinted with permission of University of Miami Press.

the child, the self-destruction increased, only to decrease on the days when we did not similarly attend to the self-destruction.

A singularly good example of how detrimental such attention can be is presented in Figure 9-2, which gives data on an 11-year-old self-destructive boy (Lovaas & Simmons, 1969). Again these data are presented as cumulative curves. Numbers 1 and 2 refer to the first and second 10-minute sessions that formed a base rate of self-destruction; he was left free to hit himself and no one did anything about it. Self-destructive behavior was at a very low level because this child, Gregg, had just completed a prolonged series of extinction sessions. Number 3 refers to the third 10-minute session where the approach was changed as follows: on the average of every fifth time Gregg hit himself, we would attend to him for 30 to 60 seconds, comforting him and allowing him to play with

some drawers, closet doors, and wooden blocks, which we knew that he liked to play with. This kind of intervention is shown by the diagonal hatchmarks. It is apparent that when we administered such "treatment" his rate of self-destruction increased. In session 4, we withdrew comments and his self-destructive behavior again extinguished. Then we reintroduced the comments and attention contingent on self-destruction in session 5; note how detrimental this "therapeutic" intervention was: self-destructive responses increased and were maintained at a very steady rate. But the effect was reversible, as we can see in sessions 6 and 7, when we refrained from reinforcing his self-destruction, and his rate again decreased to manageable levels.

It seems that we have isolated an intervention (attention contingent on self-destruction) which is extremely dangerous to administer. In session 5 (Figure 9-2), when we reintroduced the treatment, Gregg hit himself some 300 times in the short period of 10 minutes. It would have been quite possible to extend this intervention in certain ways so as to force Gregg to kill himself. For example, we could have thinned the reinforcement schedule to increase his rate of hitting himself and, through selective reinforcement, gradually moved the locus of his self-inflicted injury so as to make him more vulnerable to permanent, perhaps fatal, damage. Specifically, we could have shaped him to hit his eyes or throat. Neither a laboratory nor an explicit shaping program is necessary to bring about such results; unintentional shaping of this

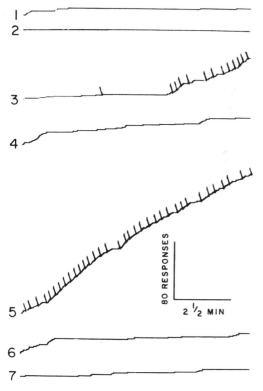

FIGURE 9–2   Cumulative self-destructive responses of Gregg during seven successive sessions. Diagonal hatchmarks in sessions 3 and 5 indicate occurrences of adults' attention contingent on self-destruction. Extinction was in force during the other sessions. (Lovaas & Simmons, 1969). Copyright 1969 by the Society for the Experimental Analysis of Behavior, Inc.

sort can occur in natural settings and produce the same effects. It is significant to note that this dangerous form of treatment—expressing concern, affection, and understanding to a child when he injures himself—was the treatment of choice for self-destructive children only some 10 years ago, and it is probably more prevalent even today than are other forms of intervention.

The most compelling evidence to support the social operant nature of self-destruction can be found in the high degree of stimulus control which the environment exercises over such behavior. Since self-destructive behavior is maintained by reinforcement we can expect it to come under the stimulus control of those aspects of the environment which signal the availability of social reinforcement. Since it is the social environment that shapes and maintains such behavior, and since people cannot attend to and reinforce the behavior in all situations, some situations will be discriminative for self-destruction while others will not.

One of the best examples of such high degree of stimulus control can be illustrated by discussing some data obtained with Beth, a nine-year-old, self-destructive, psychotic girl. We had initially taught Beth, through prompting and the use of social attention and food reinforcement, to sing and to dance and, in general, to behave appropriately when we sang particular kinds of nursery school songs to her. After about two months of this kind of training she improved markedly in her singing and dancing and she looked very good. Throughout this training she gave no signs of self-destruction. We then discontinued giving her attention and food contingent on appropriate singing and dancing. We were still nice and friendly to her; we just did not reinforce her singing and dancing. We wanted to see if her singing and dancing would maintain itself without our experimental reinforcement. This is what happened: (1) for the first couple of days she increased her singing and dancing, as often happens with any behavior when it is first put on extinction; (2) over the next two weeks her singing and dancing gradually fell off in strength; and (3) about two weeks into the extinction condition, when the singing and dancing were quite low, there began a surprising rise in self-destructive behavior which peaked at 22 days into extinction. At this particular time, her self-destruction was extremely vicious and she was bleeding profusely from her head. We did not discontinue the study, however, but allowed her to hit herself. Gradually her self-destruction decreased in strength so that some 50 days into extinction she had essentially ceased her self-destructive behavior as well as her singing and dancing. We will discuss a possible explanation of the increase in self-destruction momentarily, after considering some additional data on Beth. It took some time before Beth's self-destruction fell to zero, and during that time we performed some operations which are of interest. Consider Figure 9-3, where frequency of self-destruction is given on the ordinate and sessions, with various procedural manipulations, are given on the abscissa. Two of these manipulations are relevant to the present discussion. In sessions 30-32 and 34-37 we withdrew our attention from her altogether. In the other sessions we were smiling, being friendly, and happily interacting with her, but in these particular sessions we just ceased to smile and look happy; instead, we took on very sober and uninterested demeanors. Note that this operation had no effect on her self-destruction. Finally, in sessions 44, 46 and 48, we changed from the song we had taught her and sang a completely new song to her. Notice that in these sessions her self-destruction fell to zero.

Now let us raise the following questions, and they may be somewhat difficult to answer. First, why is it that we observed a rise in self-destructive behavior when Beth underwent extinction for appropriate social behavior (singing and dancing)? Second, why is it that we could completely withdraw all forms of attention and affection and interest in her and leave her self-destructive behavior unaffected? Third, why did her self-destructive behavior drop to zero when we introduced the new songs?

Remember that we are looking for instances of S^D control over self-destruction. Let us deal with the third question first, since the argument about stimulus control over self-destruction is illustrated most clearly during sessions 44, 46, and 48. When the new songs were introduced in these sessions, her self-destruction dropped to zero and she seemed essentially "cured." Why did she stop hitting herself? We will argue that the new songs were *not* S^Ds for self-destruction because they had never been associated with extinction. That the old song was indeed discriminative for self-destructive behavior is shown by the return of self-destructive behavior to its former level when the old song was reintroduced in sessions 45 and 47.

Now let us consider the question of why the complete removal of all attention to Beth in sessions 30-32 and 34-37 failed to affect Beth's self-destructive behavior. Clinically, one might expect that such a gross and "drastic" operation would provoke self-destruction (by her feeling rejected, for example). We conclude that the removal of *noncontingent* attention is *not* an S^D for self-destruction. If an environmental event fails to predict a given consequence for some behavior, it never acquires stimulus control over that behavior. In the present case, facial expressions which were unrelated to Beth's behavior were very unreliable predictors of the consequences of self-destructive behavior.

Finally, with regard to the rise and subsequent decline of Beth's self-destructive responding during extinction, let us advance the following considerations. Beth's singing and dancing behaviors had been under the stimulus control of the song we were playing, which had been a reliable predictor that such behaviors as singing and dancing would be reinforced by our atten-

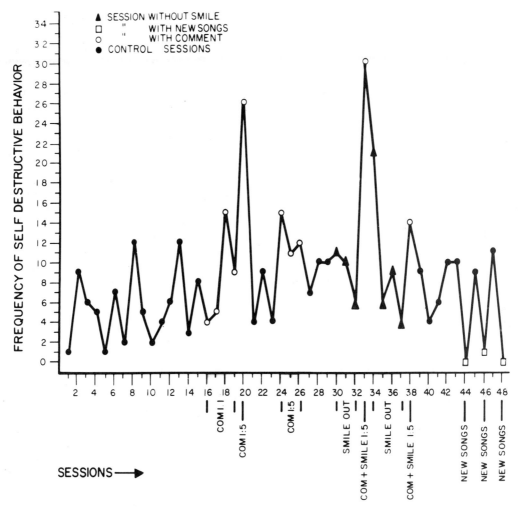

FIGURE 9–3   Frequency of self-destructive responses during sessions when adults withdrew attention from entire sessions (30–32, 34–37), when new songs were introduced (44, 46, 48), and when adults commented on self destruction (16–20, 24–26, 33, 38) (Lovaas, et al., 1965). Reprinted with permission of *Journal of Experimental Child Psychology*.

tion and praise. However, when our smiles and praise were no longer strictly contingent on her singing and dancing, Beth soon discriminated the extinction condition, as shown by the fact that she began responding very much in accordance with what we know about the effects of extinction. There was an initial increase in the magnitude of singing and dancing, which was accompanied by an increase in appropriate verbal behavior (this was not recorded, but she was overheard to say clearly, "Take me out of here."). These appropriate behaviors were not reinforced, so they declined in strength and were replaced by self-destructive behavior. The extinction of appropriate behaviors, then, appears to have been discriminative for self-destruction. We suspect that the two-week delay in the appearance of self-destructive behavior was due to the fact that Beth exhausted her repertoire of social behavior in a hierarchical manner during the course of the extinction sessions. The first behaviors to appear and then decline were those most recently acquired in the laboratory. Beth had been self-destructive since she was three years old; from her case history we knew that she had a long history of responding self-destructively in the presence of adults who reliably gave her attention whenever she did so. In our laboratory, adults were failing to attend to her appropriate social behaviors, thus reproducing a stimulus situation which ordinarily signalled to Beth that self-destructive behavior would gain attention. Therefore, Beth initiated self-destructive behavior in the laboratory. As it continued to go unreinforced, it eventually declined. These observations, along with others like them, led us to abstract the general rule that the withholding of reinforcement from a previously reinforced alternative response can function as a discriminative stimulus for self-destructive behavior (Lovaas et al., 1965).

We have discussed stimulus control over self-destruction in some detail to illustrate how powerful such control can be, producing quite rapid and major changes. Other examples are provided by children whose self-destructive behavior serves as an escape response: they "use" self-destruction like normal children "use" tantrums, to get out of situations where demands are placed on them. For example, Carr, Newsom, and Binkoff are now completing a study of an autistic boy whose rate of self-hitting is very high when simple requests known to be in the child's repertoire are made (e.g., "Point to the door."), but whose rate drops immediately to negligible levels when requests are withdrawn. Clinically speaking, stimulus control is an example of what is meant when it is argued that psychopathology is situational. That is, people we label as abnormal do not act abnormally all the time, but rather one can observe an "abnormal" person to act completely normally in certain situations. We have not as

yet systematically capitalized on such stimulus control; most behavior modification work, like our own, has been largely limited to investigations of reinforcement control.

Let us now turn to studies on the punishment of self-destructive behavior. At the present time, this operation constitutes the most significant intervention, in terms of probable success, for self-destructive behavior.

What we have observed, essentially, is that when a physically aversive stimulus is given contingent on a self-destructive behavior, then that behavior decreases sharply or is terminated altogether. The first study to report such an effect was published by Lovaas, Schaeffer, and Simmons (1965), in which a painful electric shock was given contingent on "psychotic" behavior (self-stimulation and tantrums, including self-destruction) in two five-year-old old boys. Their psychotic behavior decreased almost immediately to zero. This finding has been replicated both by us and by investigators in a number of other laboratories (Corte, Wolf, & Locke, 1971; Lovaas & Simmons, 1969; Merbaum, 1973; Risley, 1968; Tate & Baroff, 1966).

The use of a physical punishment like electric shock with children who have psychological handicaps introduces a whole range of ethical and moral questions which have to be answered. Many of these questions fall beyond the scope of this chapter, which is primarily concerned with the evaluation of empirical data. Suffice it to say that there are times when a child is so self-destructive that extinction operations cannot be undertaken, for the simple reason that the child may kill himself during the extinction run. We have also reasoned that the primary moral justification for the use of punishment centers on the use of a relatively small pain in the present to prevent a relatively large pain in the future. Many forms of therapeutic intervention in medicine and dentistry are based on specifically the same kind of rationale. What we can most usefully examine at this point, in some detail, are certain empirical data which lend strong support to such an argument on the ethics of punishment.

Let us examine the effect of shock on self-destruction in the case of John, an eight-year old boy with a history of self-destruction going back to the time he was two. This study is reported in detail in another publication (Lovaas & Simmons, 1969), but we will present enough detail here to illustrate some of its more important points. We observed John's self-destruction in two situations, "John during lap" and "John during room." In the first situation John's restraints were removed, and the

attending nurse sat him sideways on her lap. During the "in room" sessions he was left free to move about in his bedroom, in the company of two adults. These observations took place in the same ward and were made on a daily basis, each observation lasting five minutes. In addition to recording the frequency of his self-destructive behavior, a record was kept of the amount of time that he attempted to avoid the nurse (defined as struggling to get off her lap) and the amount of time he whined.

The data on John during the lap sessions are presented in the upper half of Figure 9-4. The abscissa gives the days, the experi-

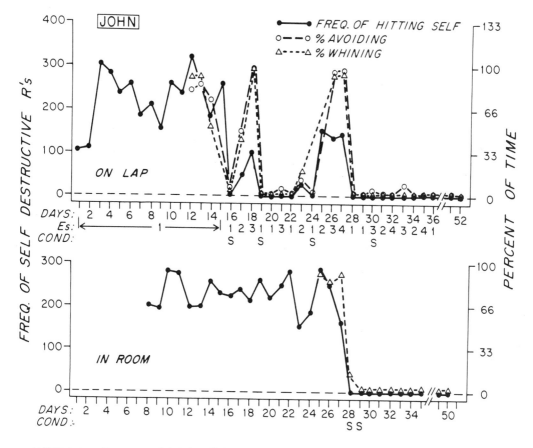

FIGURE 9–4   Frequency of John's self-destructive responses and percentage of time spent avoiding adults and whining during sessions with and without shock punishment. (Top: 5-minute sessions when John was on nurse's lap. Bottom: 10-minute sessions in a separate room.) The abscissa gives the daily sessions, the attending experimenter, and shock sessions (S) (Lovaas & Simmons, 1969). Copyright 1969 by the Society for the Experimental Analysis of Behavior, Inc.

menter (one of four adults) present during each session, and condition (S = shock punishment session). The ordinates give frequency of self-destructive behavior and percent of time that John was avoiding and whining during the session. (Because of mechanical failures in the recording apparatus, some data are missing for some sessions.) The first 15 days were used to obtain his base rates. As can be observed, his rates stayed about the same over these 15 days, neither improving nor getting worse. Punishment, in the form of one-second electric shock on the leg, was delivered by a hand-held inductorium. The punishment was introduced in session 16 with dramatic results. John received a total of 12 shocks distributed over sessions 16, 19, 24, and 30. There was a two-week span between sessions 36 and 51, and it can be observed that his rate was low, even without shock, after that time period.

Two additional observations are of interest. The first pertains to the generalization of the suppression effect across experimenters. Up to session 29 he was punished only by experimenter 1. The suppression effected by experimenter 1 generalized only partly to the other experimenters. By sessions 25, 26, and 27, his rate of self-destructive behavior with the nonpunishing adults was climbing alarmingly. In other words, he started to form a discrimination between the adult who punished him for self-destruction and those who did not. In session 30, experimenter 3 also punished John for self-destruction, with the effect of producing generalization across other experimenters.

The second observation of interest pertains to the generalization of shock effects to behaviors that were not punished. As self-destructive behavior was decreased by shock, John avoided the attending adult less and also whined less. Apparently, avoiding, whining, and self-destructive behavior fell within the same response class. These data indicate that the side effects of punishment were desirable. Informal clini-

cal observations further confirmed these findings (John was observed by some 20 staff members), and the nurse's notes reported less distance and less fussing.

There are a number of important questions left to be answered:

1. How much shock is necessary to suppress the self-destruction and how should that shock be distributed over time? We bring this up because an occasional child has been brought to our attention who has received a series of shocks without concomitant suppression of his self-destruction. It is our clinical guess that unless the child shows marked suppression, at least within one situation or with one person, within 5 to 10 shocks, he will not suppress with shock, and it is pointless to continue. We have no hard data on that. To be maximally effective, the shock should follow every self-destructive response as closely in time as possible.

2. When one has a choice, which procedure—shock or extinction—produces the most durable results with the least undesirable side effects? The answer is simply not known at present.

3. How can the high degree of situationality (discriminability) of the shock effects be reduced? Such situationality probably varies across children, so that those with long, varied, and complex reinforcement histories for self-destruction show the most discriminated effects. What this implies is that if punishment to suppress self-destruction is to be maximally therapeutic, it has to be administered by more than one person in more than one environment. Obviously, it would be particularly harmful if the child were simultaneously positively reinforced for self-destruction by other persons or in other situations. Apart from using shock in several different settings, exactly how we might maximize generalization (in order to minimize shocks) is not known. In any case, there is ample evidence indicating that, with sufficient effort on the therapist's part, shock can have general and beneficial effects (Corte et al., 1971; Kushner, 1970; Lovaas, Schaeffer, & Simmons, 1965; Lovaas & Simmons, 1969; Merbaum, 1973; Risley, 1968; Tate, 1972; Tate & Baroff, 1966; and others, as reviewed in Bachman, 1972, and Bucher & Lovaas, 1968).

4. Is it really worth subjecting the child to the pain of punishment, even though it reduces his self-mutilation, if he develops other, more serious

problems as the result of being shocked? Surprisingly, the data show the side effects of shock to be desirable. There appears to be an immediate *increase* in socially directed behavior, such as eye contact and physical contact, as well as a simultaneous *decrease* of a large number of inappropriate behaviors, such as whining, fussing, and self-isolation. Such desirable side effects have been reported by others besides ourselves. Risley (1968) specifically recorded some of the desirable side effects of shock treatment. He found that eye contact with the experimenter and desirable imitative responses increased after electric shock and vigorous shaking were used as punishers for different responses. Hamilton, Stephens, and Allen (1967) described their children ". . . to be more socially outgoing, happier, and better adjusted in the ward setting . . . [p. 856]." White and Taylor (1967) reported that their patients, after shock treatment. ". . . appeared to be more aware of and to interact more with the examiner . . . [p. 32]." We reported similar findings in an earlier study (Lovaas, Schaeffer, & Simmons, 1965). We have a filmed record that quite dramatically portrays the beneficial changes in John.

One observation would seem to contraindicate the use of aversive stimuli, at least when one is working to facilitate language. We observed a decrease in a child's babbling and an increase in echolalic speech when the child was placed in an aversive situation (Bucher & Lovaas, 1968, p. 129, Figure 12). We are not sure why this occurred, although we have observed similar effects with other children. A possible alternative to punishment in speech therapy is time out. McReynolds (1969) has shown that time out can be used to decelerate inappropriate behavior and to increase the probability of correct verbalizations in speech training.

5. Why have the side effects of punishment usually been desirable changes rather than undesirable ones, as might be predicted by theories of "symptom substitution?" Some of these behavioral changes obviously occur for rather "mechanical" reasons: elimination of whining makes it possible for smiling to occur, for example. Perhaps more important, it is easier for a child released from his "compulsive" self-destruction to come into contact with more rewarding aspects of his environment. Some of the beneficial changes will be specific to individual children. For example, the suppression of self-destruction in one child permitted surgery for her cataracts

and thereby contributed to the alleviation of her restricted vision. Some of the behavioral changes accompanying shock probably occur because reinforcements have been given to the child for behaving appropriately when faced with aversive stimuli in the past. Finally, certain behaviors may be elicited by shock as an unconditioned stimulus; certain kinds of stress, fears, or pain may call forth socially oriented behavior at a purely biological level.

6. Although the immediate side effects of punishment point in a desirable direction, can we be optimistic about long-term behavioral change? We can supply few data which exceed a couple of months follow-up, and in the case of only two children have we had the opportunity to conduct follow-ups for as much as one year, while the suppression of self-destruction was being maintained. It seems reasonable that if social reinforcement controlled the self-destructive behavior in the first place, then that reinforcement, being unaltered in strength through punishment operations, should retain the power to build other equally undesirable behaviors. If the child had to resort to self-destruction to gain some attention from his attending adults, then it seems reasonable that these adults, unless taught to respond to more appropriate behavior, would repeat themselves and begin shaping some similarly alarming behavior (such as feces smearing or eating, aggression toward other children, etc.). Within reinforcement theory terms, the suppression of one behavior may be discriminative for a large number of other behaviors, some more and some less desirable than the suppressed one. We recommend that no one undertake to punish self-destructive behavior unless he is prepared to invest considerable time and effort in explicitly building and maintaining adaptive behaviors which will have a chance of displacing self-destructive behavior as a means of obtaining social reinforcers. The extent to which reinforcement for behavior incompatible with self-destructive behavior enhances the durability of the shock--suppression effects is not known, although the animal literature suggests it to greatly extend the effects. It would also seem virtually to guarantee that the side effects of shock are desirable. Needless to say, in order for us to achieve an adequate technology for the use of punishment, which would make all of us more certain about exactly what it is that we are getting, a lot more work has to be done.

7. Other, somewhat more theoretical, questions have not yet been explored. For example, why does the very brief pain over a small area which is associated with shock delivery terminate responding which in itself entails the much more prolonged and widespread pain associated with self-destructive behaviors of all types? Two considerations seem relevant. First, the child has never had the opportunity to adapt to the pain of the shock, as he has to the pain of his self-mutilation. Shock punishment is introduced suddenly and at full strength. Self-destructive blows, on the other hand, usually build up gradually to full intensity over a period of months or years. It is well established that an organism will continue responding despite a high-intensity punishing stimulus whose final intensity is approached gradually, but will stop responding if a less intense punisher is presented at full strength from the start (Masserman, 1946; Miller, 1960). Second, stimuli which would serve as punishers under ordinary conditions can become discriminative for reinforcement if they are differentially associated with reinforcement (e.g., Azrin & Holz, 1966, pp. 419–424, 428). If the child receives sympathy and attention more reliably when he is self-destructive than when he is not, the presence of pain will become associated with reinforcement, whereas the absence of pain will become associated with nonreinforcement.

Analysis of Self-stimulatory Behavior

One of the most salient characteristics of the autistic child, or any child with a severely limited behavioral repertoire, is his large amount of stereotyped, repetitive behavior, such as rocking, hand flapping, head rolling, etc. We have referred to such behavior as *self-stimulatory*, because the child seems to "use" the behavior to stimulate himself. Although slightly fewer than half of all psychotic children engage in self-destructive behavior, and even fewer require psychological or medical treatment for such behavior, all the psychotic children we have seen engage in self-stimulation.

In a previous study (Lovaas, Litrownik, & Mann, 1971) we described self-stimulatory behavior in the following way:

Usually such behavior is stereotyped and repetitive and appears to have no observable effects upon the child's social environment, instead providing the child with sensory input from the movements of his own body. Sometimes these behaviors are rather gross, as when the child rocks his body, either in a sitting or standing position, jumps up and down on both feet, paces the room, or flaps his arms. Sometimes the behavior is more subtle, such as when the child "regards" his cupped hand, moves his eyes by rolling or crossing them, stares out of the corners of the eye, presses his finger into the same spot on the body, walks in a peculiar gait, either on toes or with a "rolling gait" on the soles of his feet. Sometimes it involves the interaction of two or more body parts, as when the child flips his hands rhythmically with fingers extended in front of his eyes. It may involve the use of objects which the child often will spin, such as coins, or ash trays, at which point they will be drawn to a flickering visual input, approaching it to within a couple of inches, maintaining a rigid and glazed facial appearance, flapping arms vividly at the wrists, perhaps also jumping up and down. Seemingly, they will generate similar stimulation by running back and forth in front of a picket fence, or twirling a string by their fingers in front of their eyes. Sometimes the behavior seems primarily supported by tactual input, as in rocking, poking at the body, or mouthing. Sometimes the behavior has primarily olfactory support, as in children who smell objects handed to them. At other times there seems to be a preponderance of visual feedback involved, as in spinning, gazing, or rolling of the eyes. At other times auditory feedback seems predominant, as when the child emits the same pattern of three tones, repeatedly, for hours and days at a time [p. 40].

In our early studies (discussed in Lovaas, 1967), we paid scant attention to this behavior since the self-stimulation gradually decreased in strength without any direct intervention when appropriate behavior was shaped up. Typically, the self-stimulatory behaviors would return when the appropriate behaviors were extinguished. We observed a similar inverse relationship between appropriate (social, intellectual) behavior and self-stimulation in normal children. When such children were placed in a situation that prevented social or intellectual behaviors, such as a barren room, they engaged in various forms of self-stimulation, some of which were virtually identical to those exhibited by the psychotic children. One can observe a similarly high proportion of self-stimulation in infants before their acquisition of social behaviors.

It was this inverse relationship between the two behaviors (self-stimulatory motor behavior and appropriate social or intellectual behavior) which led us to hypothesize that the proprioceptive-kinesthetic sensory feedback from such behaviors (e.g., rocking) is reinforcing. Sometimes external sensory reinforcers appear to be involved, as in the case of certain self-stimulatory behaviors like object-spinning, string-twirling, and gazing. Most psychotic and severely retarded children have impoverished social and intellectual repertoires, so it seems hardly surprising that they develop strong and elaborate behaviors for sensory consequences. We raised a more theoretical question when we considered that the central nervous system required a certain level of sensory input to function adequately (cf. Leuba, 1955; Zubek, 1969) and that behavior (including self-stimulatory behavior) generated the sensory input which maintained some optimal level of activity in the central nervous system. The latter hypothesis would seem to render self-stimulation biologically meaningful, but psychologically meaningless. Thus, we view psychoanalytic attempts to "interpret" self-stimulatory behavior, on the assumption that it has symbolic, communicative functions, as indicating a total misunderstanding of the significance of self-stimulation and definitely nontherapeutic. Additionally, we wondered about the range of behaviors which may be considered self-stimulatory and we suggested that self-stimulatory behavior may be representative of other forms of psychotic behavior. It is possible, for example, that hallucinatory behavior is a form of covert self-stimulatory behavior.

As we gained more experience in the treatment of these children, it became more and more apparent that their self-stimulatory behavior would sometimes actively interfere with the acquisition of new behaviors. An observation from one of our first studies (Lovaas, et al., 1971) will help to illustrate this point.

> The children could either obtain food, or avoid shock, by walking across a room within 5 seconds of a signal. This is an extremely simple task, and the children were very hungry and the shock very painful. It was therefore quite incredible to observe that when the child was halfway across the room, and literally inches and seconds away from safety, that he would visually fixate on a shiny door handle ("gets hooked" was the expression used), cock his head and start flapping his arms. He would repeatedly, this way, miss the opportunity to eat, despite his extensive food deprivation, or he would receive shock. In fact we made no substantial progress in the two cases we saw until we first had suppressed the large amount of self-stimulatory behavior with shock [p. 40].

This observation led to more systematic investigations of the blocking effect of self-stimulation on responsivity to external stimuli in autistic children. Lovaas et al. (1971) studied the auditory responsivity of three groups of children (mute autistics, autistics with echolalic speech, and normals) under two conditions: when the children were engaged in self-stimulation and when they were free from self-stimulatory behavior. The children were trained to approach a dispenser for candy reinforcement at the sound of a tone. The time interval between the onset of the tone and subject's approach was labelled his response latency. We found that (1) the presence of self-stimulatory behavior was associated with increased response latencies for the mute autistics; (2) the response latencies of the latter group decreased as subjects received increased training in responding to the auditory stimulus; (3) the amount of self-stimulatory behavior varied inversely with the magnitude of reinforcement for other behavior; (4) in a preliminary way, we obtained some control over the response latencies by experimentally manipulating the amount of self-stimulatory behavior.

A subsequent study by Koegel and Covert (1972) gives particularly clear data that self-stimulatory behavior interferes with the acquisition of new behaviors. They attempted to teach three autistic children, characterized by high levels of self-stimulatory behaviors, a simple discrimination (to respond on a bar in the presence of a light and a tone, and *not* to respond in the absence of these stimuli). They used food reinforcers for correct responding, but the autistic children made no progress on this discrimination until the experimenters suppressed the self-stimulation (by yelling "no" and, if necessary, slapping the subject on the hands contingent on self-stimulatory behavior). When they suppressed the self-stimulation the children acquired the correct discrimination.

There are several related studies which may help to understand these findings at a physiological level. For example, Stone (1964) reported sleep-like EEG activity following self-stimulatory behavior in blind children. This finding led Stone to speculate that the stimulation involved in some self-stimulatory behaviors is sleep-inducing. Brackbill, Adams, Crowell, and Gray (1966), working with normal children, found decreased arousal levels (and more rapid onset of sleep) under conditions of continuous auditory stimulation. They suggested that almost any continuous, monotonous stimulation, including tactile and kinesthetic, would produce a similarly decreased arousal level. Other forms of self-stimulation may result in a blockage of environmental input by increasing, rather than decreasing, arousal level. Sroufe, Stuecher, and Stutzer (1973) found that finger-flicking in an autistic boy was associated with heart rate acceleration. They related their findings to Lacey's (1967) conclusion that heart rate acceleration correlates with the withdrawal of attention from the external environment.

In our attempts to understand the relationship between self-stimulatory behavior and decreased responsivity to external stimulation at the level of overt behavior, we have considered the implications of viewing the stimulation arising from self-stimulatory behavior as strongly reinforcing. Our data (Lovaas, et al., 1971; Koegel & Covert, 1972) suggest that the child is confronted with a choice between two kinds of reinforcers: self-stimulatory (sensory) reinforcers as opposed to food and social reinforcers. The extent to which he either self-stimulates or behaves appropriately in a situation in which he has already learned some appropriate behavior reflects the relative strengths of the two kinds of reinforcers. Insofar as he is satiated or completely unable to respond correctly, he will attend to stimuli associated with self-stimulatory reinforcement, i.e., certain internal kinesthetic and proprioceptive stimuli or external stimuli such as spinning objects, flickering lights, his own hand and finger movements, etc. If he is hungry and the response is already learned or very easy to learn, he will attend to stimuli associated with food reinforcement. A similar interpretation has been advanced by Azrin, Kaplan, and Foxx (1973). They emphasize the low probability of success by psychotic and retarded children in performing "outward-directed" (social and intellectual) behaviors, with the result that "inward-directed" (self-stimulatory) behaviors become dominant. Thus it often becomes necessary to punish self-stimulatory behavior, at least within the therapy situation, in order to increase the probability that the child will attend to those environmental events which will teach him to function more adaptively than he already does.

The aspects of self-stimulatory behavior that are most relevant to the treatment of psychotic children can be summarized as follows:

1. Self-stimulatory behaviors in psychotic children appear to be incompatible with the acquisition of socially appropriate behaviors, and the child's therapist may have to actively suppress self-stimulation in order to facilitate the child's learning. Baumeister and Forehand (1973) have reviewed a number of studies indicating that self-stimulatory behaviors may be reduced or eliminated by the use of punishment and by shaping incompatible responses. A recently reported technique which merits further investigation is "positive practice overcorrection" (Azrin, Kaplan, & Foxx, 1973; Epstein, Doke, Sajwaj. Sorrell, & Rimmer, 1974; Foxx & Azrin, 1973). Under this procedure, the child is required to practice correct behaviors for several minutes each time he engages in self-stimulatory behavior.

2. The large degree of attention which psychotic children pay to self-stimulatory stimuli is apparently a function of the limited power of socially controlled reinforcers to maintain more appropriate attending behaviors.

3. It may be convenient to view self-stimulatory behavior as operant behavior maintained by the sensory reinforcers (Kish, 1966) that such behavior generates. We might conceive, then, of two broad categories of operants—*self-stimulatory* and *extrinsic* or *social*—distinguished in terms of who controls the reinforcer. The child himself controls the reinforcers of self-stimulatory operants. Others control the reinforcers of extrinsic or social operants, and others, therefore, control the acquisition and maintenance of appropriate behavior. This distinction raises a number of interesting problems for further research. In particular it invites a more detailed analysis of the importance of self-stimulatory reinforcers. This is properly a question of motivation, and we shall return to discuss this problem in a later section of this chapter.

Self-destructive and self-stimulatory behaviors fairly well exhaust the larger part of the repertoires of severely psychotic children. There are several other interesting behaviors considered to be characteristic of autistic children which have not been investigated empirically, or which have been investigated without yielding a satisfactory understanding of their controlling variables. Behaviors such as those assumed to indicate a preference for order (e.g., lining up toys or other objects in neat rows, resisting changes in furniture arrangement), a strong liking for music, and an unusually well-developed rote memory remain to be analyzed experimentally. Echolalic speech is one of those behaviors about which we know very little despite years of effort. However, some very recent work is beginning to clarify the picture somewhat. Carr, Schreibman, and Lovaas (Note 2) have shown that one of the factors governing immediate echolalia is the incomprehensibility of speech stimuli. Echolalic autistic children selectively echoed questions and commands to which no appropriate responses were possible, and did not echo questions and commands to which they could make appropriate responses. When taught responses to previously meaningless verbalizations, the children stopped echoing them. Regarding delayed echolalia, our current working hypothesis is that some forms of it constitute complex verbal self-stimulation. Lovaas, Varni, Koegel, and Lorsch (Note 3) have found that delayed echolalia does not extinguish over a large number of sessions in controlled situations where no nutritive or social reinforcement is obtainable. In this respect, delayed echolalia resembles the "verbal play" exhibited by young normal children when they are alone.

Let us now turn to an examination of programs which have been devised to help these children acquire normal, socially adaptive behaviors. We will limit ourselves to a review of some programs designed to build spoken language in psychotic children. Language is the most complex of the behaviors which have been taught to these children, and language training programs subsume many of the procedures for establishing more "elementary" behaviors.

Building Language

Most children acquire language without anyone knowing quite how it happens and we are ignorant of the process which underlies this acquisition. Unfortunately, some children do not learn to speak under normal conditions, and others speak very strangely, perhaps constantly echoing what they hear. Such children need help to develop language, but in order to help them, we need to find ways to improve existing methods for teaching language. Several courses of action are possible. We could conceive of the child's language problems as symptomatic of an underlying psychodynamic aberration, and perhaps attempt to alleviate this aberration. Or, if any speech is present, we could study the utterances in terms of the formal (topographical) properties of his speech, perhaps analyzing the relationships between different words and noting changes in vocabulary and grammar over time. Then it might be possible to speculate on the child's cognitive dysfunctions and to provide him with a number of relatively nonspecific remedial experiences.

On the other hand, rather than focus exclusively on the emotional or cognitive aspects of language, we might view it functionally and attempt to remediate it by manipulating current environmental events as precisely as possible in order to produce known behavioral effects. Although this approach may not tell us very much about the origin of the child's language problem, it may bring about important changes now. Further, what the behavior therapist learns through the programming of events necessary for the shaping and elaboration of language in the autistic child can prove useful to many: to parents and professionals engaged in remedial language training with any child or adult, to experimental psychologists concerned with the generality and limitations of principles of learning, and to theoretical psychologists and psycholinguists interested in relating such findings to speculative accounts of language acquisition.

The rationale underlying the behavioral treatment of language disorders is that a child who acquires language must acquire two things. First, he must acquire a large number of *vocal response topographies* of differing levels of complexity. One of these levels includes phonemic behavior (basic speech sounds); another level concerns morphemic behavior (words and parts of words); and a third concerns grammatical behavior (arrangement of words in sentences). Of course, a large repertoire of vocal behavior does not in itself constitute language; vocal behavior can easily exist without "meaning." One can observe such behavior in the form of vocal imitation, or a parroting back of words. Infants are said to pass through a stage of imitating the utterances of others. Some psychotic and brain-damaged children come close to this in instances of echolalic speech (as when the child says, "How are you?" in response to the adult's question, "How are you?"). In order for a child's vocal output to acquire meaning it must be appropriate to its stimulus context, that is, certain aspects of the child's environment must acquire certain *stimulus functions* which serve to regulate the occurrence of his verbal behavior. To accomplish this a child must learn (1) which stimulus conditions, be they external or internal, give rise to which verbal utterances; and (2) what stimulus functions the utterance itself should possess (that is, what further verbal or nonverbal behavior, in himself or others, may be evoked by that utterance). In linguistics, the term semantics most closely resembles our use of the term stimulus functions. This definition of language (in terms of functional relationships between verbal behavior and the child's internal and external environments) is most closely associated with Bloomfield (1933) within the field of American linguistics; Skinner (1957) is its best known contemporary spokesman.

Whether this view of language is correct or not, it is useful in attempts at teaching language, since it relates to some rather well known principles of behavior change. Perhaps it does not attribute enough "novelty" or "uniqueness" to language, since any response can be described in similar terms. A smile, for example, shares the same properties—it is a behavioral topography which acquires meaning to the extent that it acquires stimulus control over other behaviors, and comes to be controlled by stimulus events which surround it. Skinner has argued repeatedly that verbal behavior is operant behavior, shaped and maintained by the individual's verbal community, and it is this argument which is considered to be unique and radical in his analysis of language.

The goal of our work on language is to teach verbal behavior approximating normal adult language as closely as possible to developmentally retarded (autistic) children who appear to have little or no understanding or use of language. In working with nonlinguistic children, we soon realize how handicapped they are without language. Instead of our being able to tell them what to do, we have to move them physically through the desired behaviors. When we have to delay meeting their needs, there is no effective way to tell them to delay gratifications. When they become emotionally attached to us, there is no way to tell them, when we leave for the day, that we will return tomorrow. If they want something, they have no easy way to tell us what they want. Our goal is for language to become a means for facilitating social interaction, to help the child to deal better with his feelings. We are also interested in learning how his language might regulate his own behavior. Once, early in our work, we had in the back of our minds some notion that if the child learned to talk, somehow a "conception of himself" would emerge, that he might become "more defined as a person," that he might show more self-control. One of the most important things we have learned since then is that "self-concept" and "self-awareness" do not emerge automatically, but have to be taught. Thus we place considerable emphasis on teaching the child to describe his own behaviors, experiences, and inner states.

BUILDING A VERBAL TOPOGRAPHY

Before we start working on language per se, we prepare the child for the teaching situation. Obviously, if the child is self-mutilative, we attempt to suppress that behavior. Also, we now make a special effort to suppress self-stimulatory behavior so as to prevent inattentiveness. We typically punish such behavior, using whatever stimuli are functional. (Usually a loud "no" or a slap is sufficient.) Exactly how low a level of self-stimulation is required for learning to take place has not been determined, but we assume the lower the better.

Concurrently, the teacher attempts to establish some early forms of stimulus control. That is, the teacher may request the child to perform some simple behavior such as sitting quietly in a chair. Since even such a minimal request often evokes tantrums or self-destructive behavior, the establishment of this basic stimulus control and the reduction of aggression and self-destructive behaviors proceed together. It is generally impossible to work on the acquisition of appropriate behaviors until one has achieved some reduction of the pathological behaviors.

We start language training by attempting to build verbal behavioral topographies through imitation. The basic program involves building various discriminations. One can teach a discrimination by reinforcing a response that occurs when a stimulus is presented and attended to, and withholding reinforcement if the response occurs to another stimulus. When this is done consistently, a particular stimulus acquires stimulus control over the response; it "triggers" or "cues" the response. An imitative response is one which has the same topography as its controlling behavioral stimulus. The verbal imitation training consists of the following steps. In Step 1, the therapist increases the child's vocalizations by rewarding him (usually with food) contingent upon such behavior. We do this with mute children in order to get some vocal behavior with which to work. In Step 2, the child is trained to make a temporal discrimination: his vocalizations are reinforced only if they occur within about five seconds of the therapist's vocalizations. In Step 3, finer discriminations of the therapist's vocal topography are reinforced. The child is rewarded for making successively closer approximations to the therapist's speech sound until he matches the particular sound given by the therapist (e.g., emits "a" when the therapist says "a"). In Step 4, the therapist repeats Step 3 with another sound very dissimilar to the first one (e.g., "m"), intersperses this sound with the previous one, and reinforces the child for correct productions only. Increasingly finer discriminations are required as new sounds are added, then syllables, words, and sentences are taught as the child becomes able to master them.

The course of acquisition of verbal imitation is presented in Figure 9-5, which shows the data for Billy and Chuck, the first two children we taught to imitate. The phonemes or words are presented in lower case letters on the days they were introduced and practiced, and in capital letters on the

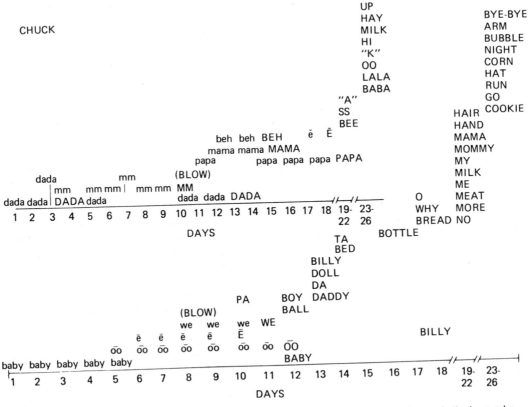

FIGURE 9–5   The first 26 days of verbal imitation training for Billy and Chuck, psychotic boys who were mute before training. The sounds and words are printed in lower case letters on the days they were introduced and in capitals on the days they were mastered (Lovaas, O. I., *Behavioral treatment of autistic children*, published by General Learning Press. © 1973 General Learning Corporation. Reprinted by permission.

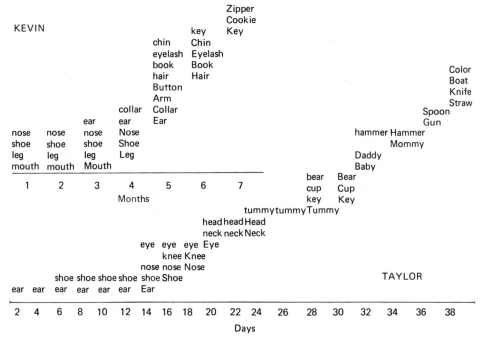

FIGURE 9–6   Acquisition of a label by two previously mute psychotic boys. Introduction and mastery of labels are differentially indicated by lower-case and capital letters as in Figure 9–5. The different scales of the abscissae indicate the range of acquisition rates for psychotic children (Lovaas, *Behavioral treatment of autistic children*). Published by General Learning Press. © 1973 General Learning Corporation. Reprinted by permission.

days they were mastered. The curves are positively accelerated: each child learned at an increasing rate (more and more behavior per unit time) the longer he was in the program. As training progressed, each learned new verbal discriminations more and more easily. They were "learning to learn."

TEACHING STIMULUS FUNCTIONS (MEANINGS)

Although a child may learn to imitate the speech of others, he does not simultaneously know the meanings of the words he utters. A program for the establishment of meaningful speech involves establishing a *context* for speech, which we view as two basic discriminations. The first is "expressive" discrimination in which the stimulus is nonverbal and the response is verbal (e.g., labeling and describing). The second is "receptive" discrimination in which the stimulus is verbal but the response is nonverbal (as in language "comprehension," when the child comes under the verbal control of others). Most language situations involve components of both discriminations. The speech program based on these two discriminations begins with simple labeling of common objects and events and is made functional as soon as possible. For example, as soon as a child knows the label for a food, he is fed contingent on asking for that food. The program gradually moves on to making the child increasingly proficient in language, including training in more abstract terms (such as pronouns, adjectives, etc.), some grammar (such as the tenses), and the use of language to please others (as in recall or storytelling).

Figure 9-6 gives an example of how one of these "meaning acquisitions" occurs. It shows the acquisition of verbal labels of common everyday events (objects and behaviors) in two previously mute psychotic children. Note the high degree of similarity between Figures 9-5 and 9-6. The similarity of the data is probably attributable to the lawfulness of the underlying process, discrimination learning.

It might be useful to present our program for a more complex language behavior, the acquisition of correct receptive and expressive speech pertaining to *time*, because this program helps illustrate the degree of behavioral complexity we have achieved with some of these children. The object of the time program is to introduce the child to terms which denote common ways in which we order events in time. This is the first step in helping the child to relate his behavior to events in the past, present, and future, to begin to reconstruct what has happened to him, and to plan for events to come.

We usually begin with the term "first," although, in retrospect, one may be better off beginning with "last," since the spatial and temporal cues are more recent. We collect a large pool of some 30 common, everyday objects that the child has previously learned to label and randomly pick any five objects from that pool for Set 1. These objects are then returned, and a set of five new objects is picked to become Set 2, etc. To begin training, the therapist places Set 1 (e.g., key, cup, pencil, watch, ring) in front of the child and tells him to touch three of them in a certain order (e.g., touch watch, then cup, then ring). The therapist asks the child, "What was the *first*?" The desired response (e.g., "The watch was first") is prompted. After the child has learned the correct response, Set 1 remains but it is rearranged and a new selection of three objects is touched, the question is repeated, the response is prompted, etc. After the child reaches criterion (e.g., five successive correct trials), Set 1 is replaced by Set 2. Once the child has reached criterion on several sets, training on the concept

"first" is terminated and the next concept, "last," is introduced. "What was last?" is taught in the same manner as was "What was first?" After it is mastered, the two concepts are alternated in a mixed order, with the same set of objects being used for both. That is, after the child has touched three objects in a certain order, he is asked which was touched first, and, after responding, is asked which was touched last. "After" and "before" are taught next. Using the same materials and the same method of stimulus presentations as were used previously, the therapist asks, for example, "What did you touch after (before) the watch?"

Some data on the acquisition of the concepts of "first" and "last" are presented in Figure 9-7. Scott was five years old and echolalic; his data show that he required 120 trials on Set 1 to correctly identify the object that he touched first. He arrived at mastery within 20 trials on Set 2, and was errorless from the beginning on both Sets 3 and 4. It is apparent that he learned to discriminate the temporal relationship between sequential events. Since Scott had not previously been exposed to any temporal ordering of the particular objects in Sets 3 and 4, and could not use any nontemporal cues to respond correctly, we may conclude that it was the temporal order in which he touched the objects that he was attending to. Furthermore, since he had never been confronted with these particular stimuli before (the ordering of the objects in Sets 3 and 4) and had not been taught these particular verbal sequences before (e.g., "boat was first"), we can argue that his behavior was truly novel and creative. It is correct to say that he was taught to "generate" (produce his own) correct phrases to stimulus situations he had previously not encountered.

Notice again the "learning to learn" phenomena, both over sets and over concepts. In the mixed condition, we see that these autistic children acquired a relatively complex "intellectual" behavior. On each trial they had to remember the order in

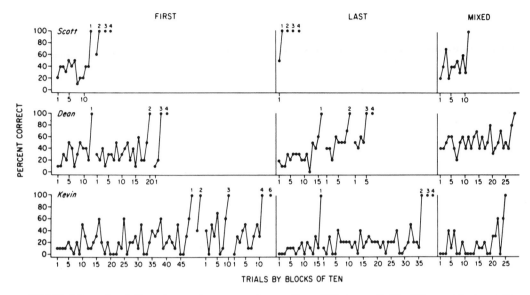

FIGURE 9-7   Acquisition of correct responses to questions, "What was first/last?" over blocks of 10 trials. The numbers 1 through 6 above the acquisition curves refer to the various sets of objects used in training.

which they touched three objects, and then, in accordance with a subsequent instruction, verbalize the name and temporal location of one of the objects. Notice also the heterogeneity among the children, in particular, how slow Kevin (six-year-old mute) was in comparison with the others. Between blocks 10 and 45 on the concept "first," which corresponds to trials 100 through 450, Kevin was apparently not learning anything. The data show that we have to learn more about teaching complex discriminations in order to better help children like Kevin. Presumably, a training program that starts with only two objects and gradually introduces additional objects would be easier for such a child.

We have produced a film (Lovaas, 1969) that shows the use of the language training procedures described above, as well as others, with severely psychotic children. The program is presented in detail in a book (Lovaas, 1976). Additional language training procedures appear in the very useful books by Kent (1974) and Kozloff (1974).

There is a host of problems one invites when attempting to build a complex behavior like language, and space allows for only a cursory mention of some of the more important ones. Some of these problems, such as discrimination learning, can be related to the work with lower animals that underlies our efforts in language teaching. We are particularly in need of more knowledge on ways to bring about efficient shifts in stimulus control, especially in connection with the use of prompt stimuli. Let us relate some other gaps in our knowledge of language acquisition to the more usual ways in which people talk about language, i.e., its phonetic, semantic, and syntactic aspects. It might be helpful to relate our data, as well as data from others, to these three divisions, beginning with semantics.

SEMANTICS

A major question in language development concerns the acquisition of meaning, which is studied in the field of semantics. How do verbal utterances become associated to the appropriate context? There are at least two dimensions to this "context:" the environmental stimulus input that triggers the verbal behavior and the verbal behavior as input, triggering further behaviors in either the speaker or the listener.

In our own efforts to build language in autistic children, we have repeatedly found that, through differential reinforcement, verbal behavior may come under the control of a large range of environmental stimuli, external and internal (Lovaas, 1976). We have taught discriminations between purely internal events such as "known" and "unknown" material, and among minute differences between statements like "Ricky is a bad boy," "Is Ricky a bad boy?" and "Ricky is a big boy." We have described a procedure which brings verbal behavior under the control of stimuli which are very subtle and dynamic, such as the temporal and spatial relations between objects and behaviors. Skinner (1957) has speculated extensively on the power of reinforcement in bringing verbal behavior under appropriate stimulus control; our data support his speculations. Our data on semantics are perhaps our strongest point and relate to a small body of similar investigations that have been published over the last few years.

One of the more detailed accounts of operant procedures for language acquisition, including semantics, is contained in the work of the Kansas group. These studies describe prompting, fading, timing of reinforcement, stimulus rotation, and a number of special procedures similar to those employed in our studies. In their first study, Wolf et al. (1964) were able to establish a 10-word labeling vocabulary in a three-and-a-half-year-old psychotic echolalic boy. Detailed procedures and results were not given in the 1964 report for the labeling program, but were extensively reviewed in a later article (Risley & Wolf, 1967). The 1967 study is particularly interesting since it involved four psychotic children with echolalic speech and attempted to establish broader classes of functional speech.

The procedures they employed are strikingly similar to those we have outlined, even though the two programs were developed independently. Their data also reflect the positive acceleration (savings over tasks) that characterizes our results. The authors also comment on many of the same learning difficulties we have encountered, such as the loss of previously mastered material as new stimuli are introduced and the difficulty of shifting behavior from the prompt to the training stimuli.

Hewett's (1965) study is one of the earliest reports of a behavioral approach to the acquisition of a beginning language repertoire. He worked with a four-and-a-half-year-old mute autistic boy, building both a basic labeling vocabulary as well as some basic components of conversational speech. His procedures overlap those that we have described. Thus prompting, fading, and stimulus rotation are all mentioned by Hewett as part of his training procedures. He employed a comprehensive reinforcement environment, underscoring the importance of an "artificial' motivational system in working with psychotic children. Within a six-month period Hewett's child was reported to have acquired a 32-word vocabulary, which was increased to 105 words one year later. Several other accounts of programs designed to establish labeling behavior are reported by Cook and Adams (1966), Risley and Wolf (1966); Salzinger, Feldman, Cowan, and Salzinger (1965); and Sloane, Johnston, and Harris (1968).

Another group of related studies is concerned with teaching verbal comprehension, i.e., appropriate nonverbal responses to verbal instructions, questions, and commands (Davison, 1964; Hartung, 1970; Schell, Stark, & Giddan, 1967; Stark, Giddan, & Meisel, 1968). For example, Stark et al. (1968) describe procedures for teaching a five-year-old autistic boy to choose a pictured object or letter named by the therapist and to execute certain motor responses upon request. Their data show the acceleration of the child's acquisition in the decreasing number of trials required for mastery over successive responses.

Relevant literature on the acquisition of abstractions (pronouns, prepositions, etc.) is more scarce than that for simple labeling (Risley & Wolf, 1967; Sailor & Taman, 1972). Sailor and Taman evaluated the effects of using the same stimulus objects to train both "on" and "in" as opposed to using a different pair of objects with each word. They found that acquisition of correct usage of the prepositions was much more likely to occur when each word was trained with a separate set of objects.

Historically, most writers in the field of language have not debated the importance of learning or experience in the establishment of meaning. Perhaps this is why there are so few investigators researching this area. Yet there are obviously many issues related to the acquisition of semantics that have not been resolved (Segal, 1975). Particularly, it seems there will be surprising findings on what constitutes a stimulus, which apparently is the critical issue in teaching semantics. We need to see much more work concerned with what the child is learning about his environment when he is reinforced, how subtle a difference between stimuli he can be taught to respond to, how broad a range of events may constitute a stimulus, and so on. If we turn our attention to the acquisition of grammatical skills, on the other hand, we can see the beginning of a significant amount of relevant literature.

SYNTAX

Although many investigators envision some role for differential reinforcement and modeling in the acquisition of semantics, they often feel syntactical (grammatical) behavior is too complex to be acquired through learning processes as we now know them. This problem probably derives in

part from early attempts to define responses solely in topographical, rather than functional, terms and to consider response generalization in terms of physical structure rather than functional relatedness. Such definitional attempts placed severe limitations on the flexibility of learning theory formulations and virtually excluded grammatical behavior as being learned. The expression of grammatically correct word sequences (sentences) requires a large repertoire of verbal chains of responses with different and interchangeable topographical features. The problem is complicated by the fact that people will speak grammatically correct sentences even though those particular sequences of words may never have been reinforced (or practiced) in the past. Brown and Bellugi (1964) put it this way: "Children are able to understand and construct sentences (and grammatical forms) they have never heard but which are nonetheless well formed, i.e., well formed in terms of the general rules that are implicit in the sentences the child has heard [p. 151]." This observation led many linguists to postulate certain theoretical concepts such as the concept of "generative" grammar, or "rule-generated" language, and to endow these concepts with many neurologically based (innate) determinants.

The argument that language has strong innate determinants is, of course, not new. For centuries, psychologists and philosophers who have given thought to the origins of human behavior, and who have wondered how complex behaviors such as language come about, have emphasized one or the other of two viewpoints: the characterization of language as determined by innate organic structures, in contrast to the view that language is learned or determined by environmental or experiential variables. The first position, the nativistic one, is currently most closely associated with Chomsky (1965) and Lenneberg (1964). The environmentalist position has been most closely associated with Skinner (1957), Mowrer

(1960), and to some extent with Berko (1958), Brown and Fraser (1964), and Ervin (1964). Hopefully our data will lend more credence to one of these positions than the other.

In other publications (Lovaas, 1976) we have presented data to show that, by certain reinforcement operations, the children we worked with came to understand and correctly express novel and grammatically correct sentences. How can we conceptualize such flexibility within learning theory? It is in this regard that we find the concept of *response class* directly useful. This concept allows for the occurrence of behavior which has not been specifically reinforced in the past, provided other responses within the same class have been reinforced. Most critics of learning approaches to language appear not to be fully cognizant of the response class concept. The notion of response classes, however, is not new. Skinner (1935) considered responses which had different topographies but satisfied a common contingency of reinforcement as constituting a functional response class. The members of a response class are related, in that an operation that changes the strength of one response indirectly alters the strength of the other responses (Bijou & Baer, 1967, p. 78; Segal, 1972). A "simple" illustration of this concept can be found in shaping the barpress of a rat: if a rat has been rewarded for a barpress with its left foot, then it is more probable that in the future the rat will also press the bar with its right foot or its head and "express" a similar wide range of new appropriate behaviors which have not been previously reinforced. All these different responses, whose probabilities have been altered because of the change in the strength of one response, are said to constitute a response class. To illustrate the notion of response classes in language development, let us suppose that an infant is rewarded for emitting the phoneme "ah." One may well observe an increase in a large range of other phonemes (such as "oh" and "ee"), and in facial movements, even though these ad-

ditional responses were never directly reinforced. We would say that we had isolated a response class. Perhaps the most interesting implication of this concept is that the members of a response class cannot be known a priori; what does or does not constitute a class is an empirical question. We know we have isolated a class when the members of that class react in a lawful manner to reinforcement (or some other environmental intervention).

How does this notion of response classes help us understand the acquisition of grammatical forms? One of the earliest reports relating the concept of a response class to grammatical forms comes from the study by Salzinger et al. (1965). They observed the language development in one child who was reinforced for the response "gimme candy." Subsequently they observed an increase in the use of the "gimme ———" response with a whole series of new words and even strings of words without the additional "specific reinforcement of these combinations." Examples include, "gimme tape," "gimme office," "gimme wait," "gimme no more cloudy again," and several others, including a perfectly logical, although ungrammatical, request for assistance, "gimme pick it up." The concurrent appearance of these (functionally similar) responses illustrates the concept of the response class.

Several other investigators have presented data relating verbal response classes to the acquisition of grammatical forms. Guess, Sailor, Rutherford, and Baer (1968) presented data on the acquisition of plurals by a 10-year-old retarded girl (*c.f.* their Figure 1, p. 301). The child was taught the plural forms of three object labels she had previously mastered in singular forms. After this training, she correctly generalized the plural form to other objects. That is, after she had learned the plural label for some objects she would now use the correct plural label with *new* objects even though she had not been specifically trained to pluralize these labels. It was this observation that led the authors to argue that the plural morpheme may be conceptualized as a (generalized) response class, thus explaining the appearance of behavior that has not been directly taught. Schumaker and Sherman (1970) used similar imitation and reinforcement procedures to teach three retarded children to use verbs in past and present progressive tense. Their results showed that the children correctly produced past and present tense forms of *untrained* verbs within each inflectional class used in training.

Our own data replicate and extend the studies we have just reviewed. For example, our work on the inflectional affix "ed" (Lovaas, 1976) directly supports Schumaker and Sherman's (1970) work as well as the work of Guess et al. (1968) and Sailor (1971) on the plural affix. The children were indeed acquiring very broad classes defined in terms of the endings of words. Consider again our data on the acquisition of pronouns and prepositions, or our data on temporal terms (Lovaas, 1976). It is apparent that the children learned to respond with correct terminology (sentences) even though a particular sentence, in its physical topography, had never been taught to the child or previously expressed by him. For example, the child might say "I touched (object-noun) *before* (object-noun)." The object-nouns originally used in the training of this particular sentence form were replaced only by other object-nouns, previously trained in isolation (i.e., as labels).

The evidence that word classes (which are defined, for example, by certain morphemes) function as response classes provides the basis for an argument that children can also learn what positions different word classes may occupy in a given kind of sentence. This is a complex matter, since it is true that a particular word class may occupy a number of positions depending upon a number of environmental and motivational variables. It is this complexity which has led some investigators to propose that a speaker must know the rules of sentence structure in order to properly combine word classes.

Our question here is whether such rules can be considered to be the definitions of higher order verbal response classes, i.e., whether the reinforcement of the permissible orders of word classes (and the nonreinforcement of nonpermissible orders) can create response classes of sentence length. As Salzinger (1968) expresses this idea, "A second kind of complexity is introduced by response classes of a somewhat larger size than, say, word classes. To the outside observer these response classes appear to be quite obviously based on rules. Thus . . . the 'rule' for sentence type is a grammatical one or a series of these having to do with the arrangement of words and phrases [p. 123]". We may speak of words as forming the response unit of interest when we discuss the acquisition of word classes, and sentences as forming the responses when we speak of the acquisition of sentence structures.

Our work (Lovaas, 1976) demonstrates that one can prompt and differentially reinforce a child for arranging words into sentences and that as a function of this training, he will then combine new words into grammatically correct sentences. All our echolalic children, and most of the mutes, acquired such verbal behavior. Data presented by Salzinger (1968) and by Garcia, Guess, and Byrnes (1973) support this possibility as well. A study by Wheeler and Sulzer (1970) provides us with a very direct illustration. They worked with an eight-year-old boy, variously diagnosed brain-damaged, retarded, and autistic, who spoke in what is sometimes referred to as "telegraphic" English, leaving out most of the articles and auxillary verbs. Through a combination of chaining, imitative prompting, and differential reinforcement techniques, the child was trained to use a particular kind of sentence structure to describe a standardized set of pictures. The sentences were of the form, "The (noun) is (present participle of the verb) the (noun)," e.g., "The man is smoking the pipe." Since the use of this form generalized to sets of untrained and novel stimuli, the authors argued that a functional response class had been established.

Risley, Reynolds, and Hart (1970) have also presented procedures and data which support the feasibility of using prompts and differential reinforcement to build and extend sentence structure. Working with culturally disadvantaged, linguistically impoverished children in a program they refer to as "Narration Training" (which is very similar to our "Spontaneity Training"), they give the following account of their method:

> If the child had responded to the question, "What did you see on the way to school?" with, "A doggie," the teacher nodded and said, "What kind of doggie?" The child answered, "A German Shepherd." The teacher praised, gave him an M & M and then asked again, "What did you see on the way to school?" He answered, "A doggie;" the teacher looked expectantly, raised her eyebrows and waited. The child then said, "A German Shepherd doggie," and was praised and given an M & M. The next time that the child responded to the question with, "A German Shepherd doggie," the teacher nodded, smiled, and asked what the doggie was doing; to which the child responded "Fighting." this was reinforced and the child again was asked, "What did you see on the way to school?" The child responded, "A German Shepherd doggie;" the teacher raised her eyebrows and waited and the child said, "A German Shepherd doggie was fighting."

They present data on how the effects of this training generalized to new situations that had not been specifically trained.

Similar success at building sentences has been reported by Stevens-Long and Rasmussen (1974). They worked with an autistic boy, and by using imitative prompts and reinforcement, built both simple and compound sentences. They also present data that this behavior was under reinforcement control and generalized to new stimulus situations in which the child had received no direct training.

Finally, working with animals (chim-panzees), Gardner and Gardner (1971) and Premack (1970, 1971) provide very strong support for the concept of response classes and the power of discrimination training in building sentence structure. One is struck by the large amount of initial apparent similarity between their procedures and the ones we have reported with autistic and retarded children. Consider, for example, Premack's (1970) report on training Sarah in the acquisition of prepositions. Here he speaks of choosing and rotating stimuli in such a fashion as to allow Sarah to discriminate the correct dimensions of the training stimulus (". . . to assure that our subject uses syntactic definitions from the beginning . . . [p. 114]"), using prompts to facilitate the desired response (". . . to bring about the desired behavior by limiting the probability of other kinds of behavior . . . [p. 114]"), and testing for generalization to new (untrained) stimuli. Both Premack and the Gardners observed positive acceleration as a characteristic feature of the acquisition, and both studies note a substantial amount of stimulus generalization and interchangeability of responses within a given class.

It is apparent from our data and similar research on semantics and syntax that the concepts of response class and stimulus generalization can account, at least in part, for linguistic performances that far exceed any simple-minded notion of what one should consider as learned behavior. It is also true, of course, that we would have been unable to remediate as well as we did had our procedures merely taught specific response topographies. Most objections to behavior change interventions based on learning models fail to recognize the response class concept, and base their objections on unduly narrow conceptions of the terms *stimulus* and *response*. To the extent that these key terms are misunderstood, critics of learning interventions do not come to grips with the issues of "what is learned" or "what can be learned." The reader who wants to familiarize himself more extensively with the conceptual basis of the response-class model and its relationship to the acquisition of complex behavior may want to read excellent discussions on this topic by Baer, Guess, and Sherman (1972), MacCorquodale (1969, 1970), Segal (1972), Sherman (1971), and Wiest (1967). Exactly how far this notion of response classes can be usefully extended is not known at present. Research such as we have reported here does help to define classes of stimuli and classes of responses that can become functional through operant language-training programs.

PHONETICS

It would seem a simple matter to engineer programs for phonological development once we already had some knowledge of how to teach a child semantics and grammar. But this is not necessarily so. Let us introduce the problems involved.

We began our efforts to accelerate phonological development in mute autistics through a straightforward shaping procedure. We attempted to reinforce their spontaneous vocalizations through successive approximations toward recognizable words. Rheingold, Gewirtz, and Ross (1959) had already shown such reinforcement control over the vocalizations of three-month-old infants, and suggested the feasibility of a reinforcement model to account for phonological development.

After several months of shaping vocalizations through successive approximations we succeeded in increasing the rate of the reinforced sound (e.g., "ma"). However, the shaping contingency restricted the output of other sounds and the first target word ("ma") disappeared as soon as we began to reinforce approximations to the second target word ("dee"). Obviously, we weren't getting anywhere and we made no particular progress on phonological development until we developed procedures for the acquisition of verbal imitative behavior (Lovaas et al., 1966). In this study we built verbal imitative behavior through a set of discriminations

where the child's vocal response had to resemble its stimulus (the adult's vocalization). Several developments preceded our study, and the Baer and Sherman (1964) model of "generalized imitation" formed the most important base.

The use of discrimination training procedures to build verbal imitative behavior obviously assures some progress in phonological development for the mute child. Our data, as well as the results of other workers cited earlier, confirm that. But casual observations also show large differences between the "imitation trained" previously mute child and the echolalic child, who already imitates the adult's speech. It is striking to observe how clearly and effortlessly the echolalic child imitates the adult's speech. Generally, they speak frequently and "play" with speech. The imitative behavior of the previously mute children, on the other hand, often stays closely dependent on the experimental reinforcers, frequently deteriorates ("drifts" away from criterion), sounds stilted, etc. In general, our language program has not been as successful for the mutes as for the echolalics. If the child is already echolalic, even though he does not know the meaning of his verbalizations, nor how to arrange them in appropriate sentences, then speech remediation is relatively easy. In other words, we usually succeed when we have to rearrange verbal behavior (syntax) and bring it under appropriate stimulus control (semantics). But we are less successful in creating and maintaining new verbal topographies. In work with a child who remains essentially mute after intensive, repeated attempts to teach words, it may be useful to try to teach manual signs like those used with deaf children (Creedon, Note 4; Webster, McPherson, Sloman, Evans, & Kuchar, 1973).

There are some interesting exceptions to our failure at phonological training. A few mute children became echolalic, that is, their word production suddenly became extensive and took on the qualities of the echolalic child's imitations. Hewett (1965) and Hartung (1970) have described what is probably the same phenomenon in their subjects. We will discuss this problem again in the section on motivation.

Generalization and Follow-Up Results

We now have some data that provide an estimate of the changes one might expect in autistic children undergoing behavior therapy (Lovaas, Koegel, Simmons, & Long, 1973). We examined three measures of the generality of treatment effects: (1) stimulus generalization, the extent to which behavior changes that occurred in the treatment environment transferred to other situations; (2) response generalization, the extent to which changes in a limited set of behaviors effected changes in a larger range of behaviors; and (3) maintenance over time (or durability), how long therapeutic effects lasted.

Let us illustrate the kinds of treatment changes and follow-up data we have collected by presenting certain data on the first children we treated. We recorded five behaviors in a free-play situation (which was different from the treatment environment), and in the presence of people who had not treated the child. This would give us an estimate of the extent to which our treatment produced stimulus generalization. Two of the behaviors—*self-stimulation* and *echolalia*—were inappropriate. Three were appropriate: *appropriate verbal*, which was speech related to an appropriate context, understandable, and grammatically correct; *social nonverbal*, which referred to appropriate nonverbal behavior that depended on cues given by another person for its initiation or completion; and *appropriate play*, which referred to the use of toys and objects in an appropriate, age-related manner. The recordings were made before treatment started, at the end of 12–14 months of treatment, and in a follow-up evaluation conducted some 1 to 4 years after treatment was terminated. The children were divided into two groups—those who were discharged to a state hospital and those who remained with their parents.

The data are presented in Figure 9-8. If one examines the changes in the children's behavior between B and A, it is apparent that they improved with treatment. After 12 months of treatment there was a substantial reduction in inappropriate behaviors and a corresponding increase in appropriate ones. The follow-up data (F) pose a warning: the children who were discharged to a state hospital lost what they had gained in treatment. They increased their psychotic behavior (self-stimulation and echolalia) and lost what they had gained of social nonverbal behavior, as well as appropriate verbal and appropriate play behaviors. On the other hand, the children who stayed with their parents maintained their gains or improved further. For the children who went to the state hospital and regressed, a brief reinstatement of behavior therapy could temporarily reestablish the original therapeutic gains.

These findings clearly emphasize certain important points underlying the use of behavior modification with psychotic children. It is not enough to help the child acquire appropriate behaviors and to overcome the inappropriate ones; it is also necessary to provide maintaining conditions that ensure that the improvements will last. To promote generalization and maintenance of the treatment effects, we now teach the child's parents to become the child's primary therapists. The parents have to pass a small "test" before we accept them as clients: they have to learn how to record behavior reliably, and they have to demonstrate that (with our help) they can gain control over one of their child's behaviors. We will discuss a few of the skills we teach the parents in a later section of this chapter.

Current Research on Perception

Even under the best of treatment conditions, behavior modification with severely psychotic children is usually a long, slow

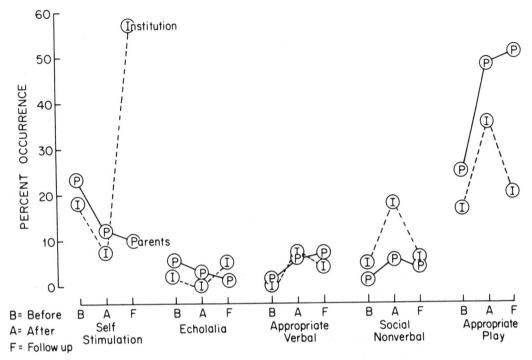

FIGURE 9–8   Percentage of time psychotic children engaged in five classes of behaviors during sessions conducted before treatment (B), after treatment (A), and at follow-up (F). "I" refers to the average results for four children who were institutionalized after treatment; "P" refers to the average results for the nine children who lived with parents after treatment (From Lovaas, Koegal, Simmons, & Long, 1973). Copyright 1973, Society for the Experimental Analysis of Behavior, Inc.

process. Further, behavioral gains achieved at considerable cost in therapeutic time and effort may prove to be easily reversible. The techniques in use today are preliminary steps toward the more powerful treatment programs that can be developed as additional knowledge about the characteristics of psychotic children becomes available. In this section we will first present our current research on perception, particularly the results and implications of our work on stimulus overselectivity. We will relate certain problems and possible solutions in the use of prompting and prompt-fading techniques, which are particularly relevant to the education of psychotic children. We will then review some recent work on generalization and memory. We will then move on to a discussion of some new studies that attempt to expand our understanding of motivation and the reinforcers available to

help autistic children learn. Finally, we will discuss some recent research on how to train teachers and parents to work with autistic children.

Perceptual abnormalities of one kind or another figure prominently in all comprehensive descriptions of autistic children (e g., Creak, 1964; Hermelin & O'Connor, 1970; Hingtgen & Bryson, 1972; Lovaas, 1967; Ornitz, 1973; Ornitz & Ritvo, 1968; Rimland, 1964; Rutter, 1968). The large variety of unusual perceptual behaviors attributed to autistic children suggests that there is probably not a "key" deficit that, once isolated, would "explain" autism. It seems more likely that many aspects of perceptual functioning will be found to be abnormal.

The investigation of attention seems especially timely in view of accumulating evidence that autistic children perform poorly in some visual and auditory discrimination tasks (Hermelin & O'Connor, 1965, 1967; Hingtgen & Coulter, 1967; Ottinger, Eweeney, & Loew, 1965; Wasserman, 1969). Assuming adequate motivation and absence of sensory impairment, subnormal discrimination performance suggests attentional deficits. Hermelin and O'Connor (1965), for example, remarked that the autistic children in their study who failed to learn simple visual discriminations "did not seem to 'see' the figures on the stimulus card, though they did 'look' at them [p. 459]." Other studies indicate that autistic children have particular difficulties when they are expected to learn about stimuli presented in more than one modality. Cowan, Hoddinott, and Wright (1965) found that only 2 of 12 autistic children were able to associate simple shape or color words with corresponding visual stimuli. Bryson (1970) noted that autistic children performing matching-to-sample tasks disregarded additional auditory stimuli during visual and small motor tasks and disregarded extra visual stimuli when making vocal responses. She suggested that the tasks were either so easy or so difficult that the provision of additional stimuli in another modality had no effect.

STIMULUS OVERSELECTIVITY

A number of recent studies in our laboratories have explored attentional deficits in autistic children. The results of these studies provide substantial evidence for the conclusion that many autistic children attend to environmental stimuli highly selectively, much more selectively than do normal children of the same age. Operationally, the data show that their behavior comes under the control of a very limited number of the stimuli which, in terms of normal functioning, should control responding. Conversely, many stimuli which an observer would consider highly salient and which reliably signal the consequences for given behaviors remain nonfunctional in the

regulation of the autistic child's behavior. We have referred to this finding as "stimulus overselectivity" (Lovaas, Schreibman, Koegel, & Rehm, 1971) because the only other suitable term, "selective attention," has acquired many diverse meanings (see Mostofsky, 1970), none of which adequately conveys the extreme degree to which many autistic children do in fact selectively attend.

In the initial study (Lovaas, et al., 1971) we trained normal, retarded, and autistic children to respond to a complex stimulus consisting of simultaneously presented visual, auditory, and tactile components. After each child had learned to respond reliably in the presence of this complex and to inhibit responding in its absence, the components were presented separately to see which were controlling correct responding. We found that the normals responded uniformly to all three of the cues, the retardates usually responded to two of them, but the autistics responded primarily only to one. After this testing was completed, the children were trained to respond to whatever component had remained the least functional by presenting that component by itself. All the children quickly learned to respond reliably to whatever component had been previously nonfunctional, and continued to respond to it and to the other components when the test condition was reinstated. Thus, no one sensory modality seems impaired in autistic children. Rather, these findings indicate that when autistic children encounter multiple stimuli, only a restricted range of those stimuli gain control of their behavior.

Subsequent research has supported and extended the findings of the first study. We have found that autistic children show stimulus overselectivity when presented with stimuli in only two sensory modalities, such as vision and audition (Lovaas & Schreibman, 1971). Initially we thought that the children had difficulty only in attending to stimuli in more than one modality at a time, that, in a sense, they had difficulty "shifting" across modalities, or difficulties in "turning on" more than one modality at a time. However, we subsequently found that the children had difficulty with any complex or multiple-cue input, even if it fell within one modality. Koegel and Wilhelm (1973) reported overselectivity when the children were confronted with a multiplicity of cues within the visual modality, and Reynolds, Newsom, and Lovaas (1974) showed autistic children to be overselective within the auditory modality. Auditory overselectivity may be part of the explanation of the autistic child's severe language handicap.

One of the studies we carried out on overselectivity has rather obvious implications for understanding the autistic child's failure to show appropriate social behavior. Schreibman and Lovaas (1973) taught normal and autistic children to discriminate between lifelike male and female figures. Subsequent tests showed that normal children distinguished between the figures on the basis of a large number of cues, particularly the figures' heads, but autistic children used some minor and irrelevant feature, such as the figures' shoes. For example, if we removed the shoes from the figures after the child had learned to tell the figures apart, he would suddenly lose the discrimination only to regain it in additional training by using an equally minute and irrelevant feature. We suggested that this finding may relate to the autistic child's recognition of people. If an autistic child habitually distinguishes between people on the basis of a socially irrelevant and changeable feature such as a piece of clothing, it seems hardly surprising that many individuals fail to acquire stable meaning for him.

Our concern with treatment has led us to look for evidence of overselectivity in more applied settings, where the most important stimuli are the complex, multidimensional cues provided by human beings. For example, in verbal imitation training (Lovaas et al., 1966) the child is taught to imitate his therapist's vocalizations, which typically consist of simultaneously occurring visual and auditory stimuli. The situation is further complicated if the therapist uses manual prompts and thus provides tactile input. The initial report on overselectivity (Lovaas et al., 1971), includes some data illustrating the possibility that the child's imitative vocalizations may initially come under the control of only the therapist's lip movements, as though he never hears the sound of the vocalizations. Perhaps stimulus overselectivity partly explains the very slow progress of some autistic children in speech training. In any case it seems advisable to make periodic checks for the presence of auditory stimulus control and to minimize as much as possible the use of additional (potentially interfering) cues.

In a study recently completed in our lab, Rincover and Koegel (in press) were concerned with the possible contribution of stimulus overselectivity in the failure of many autistic children to transfer treatment gains across settings (Birnbrauer, 1968; Lovaas, et al., 1973; Risley, 1968). In this experiment, one teacher individually taught 10 autistic children to perform a simple behavior upon request, e.g., "Touch your nose." Immediately after each child had learned the new behavior, a second teacher took him outside the building and made the same request to determine whether the behavior would transfer to another adult in a new setting. Four of the 10 children were unable to perform the behavior outside, which suggested that their behavior in the classroom had not come under the control of the appropriate stimuli. In order to determine whether their failure to generalize was due to overselective attention during training, cues which were present in the classroom were systematically introduced outside. These tests showed that three of the children had failed to learn the verbal request because they had selectively attended to cues provided by incidental behaviors of the first teacher during training. In the case of one child, for example, the child's responding was controlled by incidental movements of the first teacher's hand. Subsequently, when the second teacher simply raised his hand in a similar way in the outside setting, the child did generalize appropriately. These results clearly emphasize the importance of not assuming that generalization will take place simply because of a vaguely defined "similarity" between treatment and extratreatment settings. The therapist or teacher must ensure that the stimuli that are expected to control a behavior *after* treatment do in fact control behavior *during* treatment.

Our follow-up data suggest an apparent failure of autistic children to learn by observing others and imitating their behaviors. This type of learning is usually referred to as "observational learning" or "S-S learning" (Bandura, 1969). Varni, Lovaas, and Koegel (Note 5) obtained data suggesting that stimulus overselectivity may prevent the vicarious acquisition of new behaviors in an observational learning situation. In this experiment, the child sat at a table across from two adults (a model and a teacher). On the table in front of the model rested two objects, each of which was used in the execution of an associated response. The child was required to watch the model while the teacher commanded, e.g., "phone," and the model then picked up the handset of a toy telephone and was rewarded by the teacher. We wanted to know the extent to which the child could learn what to do with the objects by merely observing the model handle the objects in accordance with the teacher's instructions. After observing 20 repetitions of the model doing what the teacher requested, the child took the model's seat and was given the same command by the teacher. If the child failed to produce the correct response, he returned to his original position to watch the teacher-model interaction another 20 times before being tested again. This succession of 20 observation trials followed by one test trial continued until the child responded correctly on a test trial, or until he had performed

1,000 trials without success. Correct performance on a test trial was taken to indicate that observational learning had occurred, since the child was never rewarded until he had responded correctly on a test trial. After a second response involving a second object was learned, and tests showed that the child remembered both responses, the child was given 10 additional test trials with the two verbal commands presented in random order. Ten of 14 children learned at least two responses, but only 3 of the 10 responded correctly when the two commands were presented randomly. The other 7 children had attended primarily to the visual stimuli of the model's actions, with the teacher's commands serving only as undifferentiated "go" signals. In a second study involving the same observational learning paradigm, Varni and Everett (Note 6) found that the majority of autistic children at each of three age levels (5–7, 8–10, and 11–16 years) performed no better than 1-year-old normal children and much worse than 3- or 5-year-old normal children.

The difficulty which some autistic children show in learning about all the cues in a situation involving "vicarious" reinforcement seems to help our understanding of their severely impoverished behavioral repertoires. Undoubtedly, many of the complex and subtle behaviors which are shown by normal children are learned by watching social interactions of various kinds; a child who does not naturally learn in this way can be expected to function at a relatively simple level without special training.

The existence of stimulus overselectivity may be of considerable value in explaining certain deficiencies in the behavior of autistic children in other learning situations, as we have suggested elsewhere (Lovaas et al., 1971). The acquisition of several kinds of behavior requires a shift in stimulus control, such that new stimuli substitute for previous ones in the regulation of behavior. The inability of the autistic child to come under the control of appropriate stimuli has important implications for understanding his problems in the following important areas:

1. The acquisition of stimulus control by an elaborate environmental context underlies meaningful speech. Most autistic speech (e.g., echolalia) is meaningless in the sense that it is contextually impoverished. For example, a word like "happy" may occur only in response to another person vocalizing "happy," and not to a larger context such as the child's own feelings of happiness, signs of happiness in others, and so on. This contextual impoverishment may be the result of the difficulty autistic children have in making the shift from imitative, echoic control of vocalizations to control by more appropriate stimuli.

2. Many emotional behaviors are considered to be acquired through classical conditioning. For this kind of learning to take place, it is essential that the child attend to two stimuli simultaneously or in close temporal contiguity. The difficulty with which the autistic child receives simultaneously presented sensory inputs could account for his failure to acquire appropriate affective responses. A similar analysis can be applied to conditioned, or symbolic, reinforcers: the failure of smiles and praise to influence his behavior may be related to his inability to associate them with other reinforcers.

3. In most teaching situations, the autistic child is not left to himself to discover the correct answer. Instead, the teacher provides him with extra cues to facilitate correct responding and to minimize errors. She may point to an object to be identified, say a word to be mastered, or manually guide a motor response to be learned. Several investigators have argued that the provision of such extra stimuli, or *prompts*, helps the child to acquire new behaviors and new discriminations (Lovaas et al., 1966; Metz, 1965; Risley, 1968). However, it may be very difficult to remove the prompt without simultaneously losing the child's performance. In our clinical work we have often observed a child to lose an apparently well-learned response, immediately when we drop a prompt abruptly. Sometimes it is possible to remove the prompt gradually (fade it) in small steps. Such a procedure may increase the probability that the child will shift attention from the prompt to the training stimuli, but autistic chil-

dren sometimes do not make this shift. The stimulus overselectivity hypothesis, in fact, suggests that the provision of additional stimuli in a prompt procedure may *prevent* the child from learning a discrimination. Since most prompt procedures require the child to attend to multiple cues simultaneously (because the prompt and training stimuli occur contiguously), they create a situation where stimulus overselectivity is very likely to occur. Let us examine some relevant research in more detail.

PROMPT AND PROMPT-FADING TECHNIQUES

Koegel (1971) reported findings consistent with the overselectivity hypothesis in showing the deleterious effects on learning when extra cues are used as prompts. He pretrained autistic and normal subjects to respond differentially to two colors. Then the colors were presented simultaneously with training stimuli (black forms) in four tasks (e.g., red with superimposed X and green with O). In the criterion discriminations, the training stimuli appeared alone after the colors were eliminated either abruptly or gradually. It was found that autistic children usually failed to transfer from the prompt to the training stimulus whether the prompt was removed abruptly or was gradually faded out. Interestingly, the autistic children did acquire these same discriminations when prompts were *not* used in training. Koegel's data suggested that the use of extra cues in teaching autistic children may be exactly what makes it so difficult for them to learn. They may respond selectively to the prompt as long as it is available, reverting to chance performance when it disappears because they have learned nothing about the training stimuli. This may be especially likely to happen when the discrimination involves difficult stimuli. A recent study by Russo (Note 7) clarifies this finding further; he reports that autistic children shift from an ordinary finger-pointing prompt to the training stimulus more readily when the task is easy (e.g., black versus white) than when it is difficult (e.g., vertical line versus line tilted four degrees from vertical).

In some of the studies on overselectivity reviewed above, occasional autistic subjects showed little or no evidence of overselective attention, while some normal subjects did show such evidence. A study by Wilhelm and Lovaas (in press) indicates that overselectivity is more closely related to the child's mental age (and becomes more and more acute the lower that age is) than to the child's diagnosis. In the Wilhelm and Lovaas study, mentally retarded children (not diagnosed as autistic) showed stimulus overselectivity to a degree inversely proportional to mental age. Therefore, one would expect overselectivity most often among lower functioning autistic children and very young normal children than among higher functioning autistics and older normal children. Evidence supporting this expectation has recently been obtained (Kovattana & Kraemer, 1974; Schover & Newsom, Note 8).

Those who design teaching programs for autistic children would do well to focus their efforts according to a conception of "attention as something taught rather than something immutable to be measured [Ray, 1972, p. 293]". The discovery and elaboration of techniques designed to teach autistic children how to attend to all the relevant stimuli in learning situations would contribute significantly to our ability to educate them. At present we can suggest two procedures that may be helpful in certain cases. First, it is probably better to train the child on the components of the complex separately prior to combining them. If the child's responding is initially brought under the control of each component in isolation, the probability that responding will subsequently be controlled by only one of the components when they occur simultaneously should be reduced. This suggestion is prompted by the finding that children trained to respond to a previously nonfunctional component when that component was trained in isolation continued to respond

to that component, as well as to the other components of the complex, in additional test sessions (Lovaas et al., 1971). Second, overtraining the discrimination may result in control by more than one component. Recall that the tests for stimulus control in the above studies were carried out immediately after some discrimination criterion was reached. It is possible that prolonged training would in some cases have resulted in the development of control by more than one aspect of the stimulus compounds used. For example, four of the seven children who initially attended only to visual cues in the observational learning experiment subsequently came under appropriate auditory control during additional observation trials in which the two command-response sequences were presented randomly.

In many practical situations one is less interested in teaching autistic children to attend to multiple cues than in teaching them to attend to a distinctive feature that will enable them to discriminate between stimuli. Here, the problem is to redirect overselective attention rather than to overcome it. Recently, Schreibman (1975) found that fading programs can be designed to take advantage of overselectivity in teaching difficult visual and auditory discriminations. She noted that in Koegel's (1971) study the autistic children had become very good at discriminating minute differences in the color prompt even though they failed to transfer from the color prompt to the training stimulus. Apparently, stimulus overselectivity had functioned to decrease attention to nonprompt dimensions but to *enhance* attention to the prompt dimension. The significant contribution in Schreibman's study was the incorporation of the prompt *within* the training stimulus.

Schreibman wanted to teach the child to tell the difference between various geometric forms which were difficult to discriminate. In everyday life the developing child is asked to make a great number of such discriminations between stimuli which differ only slightly in form, such as a smile and a frown, the letters b and d, and so on. In one of Schreibman's visual discriminations the children were required to touch one of two stick figures printed on cards. These figures were identical except that one had his arm raised. The teacher initially tried to help the child by pointing to the correct figure. The autistic children failed to learn, even though the teacher went through extensive and elaborate prompt-fading procedures. The children discriminated between increasingly fine pointing cues, but did not transfer their responses from the teacher's finger to the correct figure. It was as if they saw only the teacher's finger and not the figure she was pointing to. Schreibman then changed her approach by exaggerating the critical feature of the positive figure. She made up a "correct" card which had a large black diagonal stripe across its surface. She left the "incorrect" card blank. The autistic children learned this initial simple discrimination relatively rapidly. Then the incorrect stimulus, an inverted V, was gradually faded in on the blank card. Then the sizes of the stripe and the V were gradually reduced. Finally, when the child could discriminate between the lines that were to represent the figures' arms (a raised versus a lowered arm), the other, irrelevant parts of the figures (head, legs, etc.) were

slowly faded in. Figure 9-9 illustrates the steps in Schreibman's study. She suggested that the use of the finger-pointing prompt prevented discrimination learning because it constituted an additional, "extra-stimulus" cue to which the autistic children responded overselectively, preventing the acquisition of control of responding by the S^D complex. The use of a within-stimulus prompt, however, resulted in learning because the critical part of the S^D complex itself constituted the prompt.

The point of Schreibman's study is, of course, that the environment which helps the normal child does not necessarily help, and may in fact retard, the deviant child. Instead of putting the blame entirely on the child and considering him unteachable, we do better to analyze and redesign our educational materials and procedures. Schreibman's study is a promising beginning, and emphasizes the critical importance of further research on prompting and fading ("attention-shaping") procedures for the development of effective teaching programs for autistic children.

STIMULUS GENERALIZATION

Rimland (1964) and Goldstein (1959) have suggested that the critical disability shared by autistic children is their impaired con-

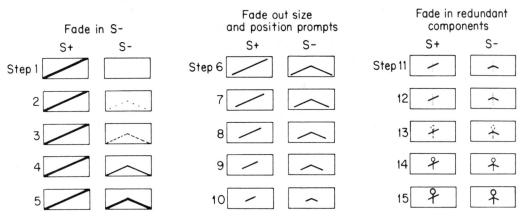

FIGURE 9–9   The within-stimulus prompt and fading steps used to teach discrimination between two stick figures. The criterion discriminanda appear in Step 15 (Schreibman, 1975). Copyright 1975, Society for the Experimental Analysis of Behavior, Inc.

ceptual ability, based on defective stimulus generalization. In applied settings, potential problems in generalization can often be neutralized by the provision of reinforcement for appropriately generalized responses (Craighead, O'Leary, & Allen, 1973; Lovaas et al., 1973). In basic research, problems of under- and over-generalization have been traced to unintended sources of stimulus control. The Rincover and Koegel (in press) study discussed earlier indicated that the psychotic child's failure to generalize a response from one stimulus complex to another can be traced to the acquisition of stimulus control by irrelevant stimuli which are not present in the test situation. An unpublished study by Newsom and Collins complements this finding by showing that data apparently indicative of "excessive generalization" is produced when the irrelevant stimuli *are* present in the test situation. Mute autistic children 8 to 14 years old and normal children 8 to 10 years old were taught to label a triangle with the phoneme "ah;" they were then tested with geometric shapes of varying numbers of sides (3-, 4-, 5-, 6-, 7-, and 10-sided figures) and a blank card. Unreinforced test trials were interspersed among intermittently reinforced trials with the triangle until each figure and the blank card had been presented 12 times. The generalization gradients of the six normal children showed strong control by the shapes of the forms: the "ah" response always occurred to the triangle, occasionally to the square, but never to the more complex forms. In contrast, four of the five autistic children showed no control by shape—they produced the phoneme to every form and to the blank card each time they were presented. Each of these children produced high, flat generalization gradients, suggesting that their responses were controlled by the experimenter's card presentations and not by the figures on the cards. Similarly, in speech training the child's first label may often be evoked by one or more of the irrelevant events accompanying the presentation of

the object, such as the therapist's orienting toward the child, lifting a hand, etc., in addition to or instead of the object itself (Lovaas, 1976). In the second phase of the study, the children were taught to say "ee" to the 10-sided figure, required to respond discriminatively during random presentations of the 3- and 10-sided figures, and given a second generalization test identical to the first. Now the shape dimension exerted stimulus control over every child's vocalizations during testing; the "ah" phoneme occurred almost exclusively to the triangle, while the "ee" response occurred primarily to the decagon. Thus it was relatively easy to remediate the "conceptual" behavior of the psychotic children so that it resembled that of the normal children in this study. Although much work in this area remains to be done, these preliminary investigations indicate that problems attributed to generalization deficits can be understood and approached therapeutically with the use of stimulus control methodology (Ray & Sidman, 1970).

MEMORY

Although we have thus far emphasized the role of overselective attention in the perceptual anomalies of autistic children, we should point out that memory deficiencies also appear to be important. Hingtgen and Bryson (1972) have specifically suggested that impaired memory may contribute to the psychotic child's generally poor performance on discrimination tasks. Although this proposal has yet to be tested directly, experimental studies have indicated that psychotic children, particularly those without functional speech, may perform very poorly on tasks involving short-term memory skills (Hagen, Winsberg, & Wolff, 1968; O'Connor & Hermelin, 1965). We suspect that the systematic investigation of memory would add much to our understanding of the autistic child's learning difficulties. Clearly, a child must be able to associate events separated in time and to remember instructions if any significant learning is to take place.

Experiments concerned with the short-term visual memory of autistic children in a conditional discrimination have been initiated by Newsom in collaboration with Marlyn Perkins and Dennis Russo. In a preliminary phase of this work, three severely retarded nonverbal psychotic children were trained to a strict criterion of accuracy on a simultaneous match-to-sample task, then shifted to a zero-delay matching task. On each trial a red or a green light transilluminated the center key of a three-key panel. A press on the center key turned off its light and simultaneously turned on a red light behind one of the side (choice) keys and a green light behind the other. Then a press on the side key whose color matched that of the center key was reinforced with an edible and the sound of a chime. When 90% or more of the 48 trials in a session were correct for three consecutive sessions, a titrating delay procedure (Cumming & Berryman, 1965) was instituted. In the titrating-delay procedure, the first trial of each session included a delay of zero seconds between the offset of the center key light and the onset of the choice lights. When the subject made two consecutive correct responses, the delay advanced to 0.5 second, then to 1.0 second after another two correct responses, and so on. Thus, every second correct response in a row resulted in a 0.5-second increment in the delay, and every error resulted in a decrement of 0.5 second. We used the titration procedure to measure memory for colors because it remains sensitive to the subject's ongoing performance, and thus avoids the disruptive emotional behavior likely to be induced by a testing procedure including numerous delay values currently impossible for the subject. Additionally, we were interested in determining whether this particular titration procedure would act to "shape" memory, since its gradual introduction of longer delays constituted a temporal fading program.

The three subjects tested under these conditions showed profound memory deficits. In the first test session, mean delays ranged from 0.5 to 2.0 seconds, with 3.5 seconds being the maximum delay at which any child achieved two consecutive correct responses. Two of these children were exposed to this procedure for 30 additional sessions, but the mean delay values never rose above 6 seconds. It remains to be investigated whether a titration procedure that includes many more than two steps at each delay value before advancing to a longer delay would improve performance to a greater extent. On the other hand, it may be more efficient and useful to teach explicit rehearsal responses that would enable the child to bridge the delay.

Current Research on Motivation

Motivational variables affect both the acquisition of new learning as well as maintenance of that which is learned. In the kind of behavioristic system we have followed, the question of motivation becomes a question concerning the effectiveness of reinforcers. Can we understand the autistic child's problems by analyzing how certain events become reinforcers? Let us try.

It seems safe to assume that at birth most of what happens around the child is essentially neutral to him; most of the stimuli he encounters neither reward nor punish him. But as he interacts with his environment, various stimuli acquire rewarding and punishing functions for him. For example, his mother's smile, though initially not affecting him, becomes a reward as he has certain experiences with it; we say it acquires reinforcing functions. The child learns new behaviors to obtain that smile. Stimuli that have acquired reinforcing power are called conditioned (secondary) reinforcers.

Let us be more explicit about the interaction between conditioned reinforcers and behavioral development. Although the child's behavior during the first few months of life seems regulated by primary (biological) reinforcers and punishers, such as food and pain, conditioned reinforcers and punishers soon take over an essential controlling function. To illustrate, the mother may respond to the baby's various behaviors by stroking him, cuddling him, or feeding him. We say that she administers primary reinforcing stimuli that shape and maintain his various behaviors. Later in the child's life, however, she is less likely to give primary reinforcers but rather to respond with conditioned reinforcing stimuli (e.g., smiles, praise, and hugs).

Many stimuli generated by other people —including closeness, affection, support of peers, approval, etc.—can serve as conditioned reinforcers. We speculate that when a child emerges as a human being, he does so essentially because his behaviors are reinforced by stimuli from his social environment. For example, a child may visually fixate on his mother's face to the extent that her face has reinforcing properties for him. If her face possessed no reinforcing function for him (he did not "care" one way or the other about her face) he probably would not look at her. It is usually appropriate to consider looking an operant behavior; that is, behavior that exists insofar as there exist reinforcing stimuli to maintain it. To illustrate further, the child may seek others if closeness to other people is reinforcing for him. And he may repeat his first syllables and words because he hears himself sound like his parents; that is, the matching of stimulus inputs has acquired reinforcing properties for him. Apparently an enormous variety of emotional and intellectual behaviors are regulated by conditioned reinforcers, that is, environmental consequences which have *acquired* their rewarding properties.

Given these assumptions, it can be speculated that an autistic child has failed to develop behaviorally because his natural environment is not sufficiently reinforcing for him. If his developmental failure was based on a deficiency in social and other acquired reinforcers, as Ferster (1961) claimed it was, then an intervention at this level would seem to strike at the very heart of the problem. A treatment program centered on the establishment of conditioned reinforcers would give the child's everyday social environment (his parents, teachers, peers, etc.) the tools with which to build and modify the myriad behaviors necessary for the child to function effectively. In a sense, the child's behavioral changes would "take care of themselves," assuming he returned from treatment to a normal environment that provided sufficient reinforcers for him.

When we first began to treat autistic children we explored this alternative of enriching and normalizing reinforcing stimuli for these children. We did succeed in establishing certain social stimuli as reinforcing for the autistic child, using either pain reduction (Lovaas, Schaeffer, & Simmons, 1965) or food presentations (Lovaas et al., 1966). For example, we delivered social stimuli (smiles, verbal approval) at the same time as the child was fed, hoping that he would associate the social stimuli with the pleasurable biological ones. Further, we reasoned that parents normally acquire reinforcing properties not only because they are associated with the delivery of pleasurable events, but also because they help their children escape frightening situations. Therefore we constructed a dangerous environment for the child and proceeded to rescue him from that danger. In brief, we delivered a painful but physically harmless electric shock through the floor, which was turned off as soon as the child sought us out. Ideally we would have liked to help him overcome fear of a more "natural" aversive stimulus than shock, but autistic children seem quite void of natural fears. Although we produced some very durable reinforcers in these ways, their effectiveness was ultimately limited to the treatment room and the procedures were too cumbersome to be of much practical significance. For example, the child showed great affection for us when in the "dangerous" room, but more and more returned to his previous autistic behaviors outside it, since strong consequences were not present to ensure the maintenance of social behavior.

When we finally designed our treatment environment, we sidestepped the child's motivational deficiency by selecting powerful, largely primary reinforcers such as food and pain. For example, the children were fed only if they behaved appropriately. But there are certain serious problems inherent in the use of primary reinforcers. Primary reinforcers are "artificial" for the older children since such reinforcers exist only in specially constructed environments, such as our treatment environment. One observes limited maintenance with artificial reinforcers—the behaviors one builds with those reinforcers are limited largely to those environments where such reinforcers are available. Our use of primary reinforcers is part of the reason why the children showed behavior losses when they were institutionalized on discharge from us. The institutional environment, like most environments, did not prescribe contingent primary reinforcers for the children, hence the behaviors we had built were extinguished. The child's parents, on the other hand, had been specifically taught by us how to use powerful reinforcers, and because the parents used reinforcers their children did not lose the progress they had made. But this is only a partial solution. The ideal treatment would normalize the child's motivational structure so that his everyday environment could help him.

What can we do at this point? We can try harder to find efficient and practical ways of building conditioned social reinforcers, that is, we can pursue the motivation problem as a problem in the acquisition of conditioned reinforcers. Or, we can take another view: perhaps our analysis has placed too much emphasis on the social consequences of behavior. Maybe most of

normal human behavior is *not* maintained by social or extrinsic reinforcement.

We now know from research with animals and normal children that organisms respond to obtain reinforcing stimuli unrelated to social or primary reinforcers. Normal children will respond just to obtain sensory input, such as changes in light intensity, sound productions, and so on. It seems as if organisms have a "need" for sensory stimulation, as has been indicated by studies on the effects of prolonged sensory restriction (Zubek, 1969). Similarly, psychotic children give evidence of the same "craving" for stimulation in their rocking, spinning, twirling, jumping and other repetitive, stereotyped behaviors. We have labeled this behavior self-stimulatory because it seems to have no other function than providing the child with sensory input from his own behavior; the sensory feedback he gives himself seems very "important" to him. For example, Newsom and Ferris (Note 9) have found that if one of a child's predominant forms of self-stimulation is temporarily eliminated, another self-stimulatory response immediately increases in strength to replace it. Various kinds of self-stimulatory behavior can be observed in normal infants, children, and adults when they have nothing else to do.

We have therefore proposed (Lovaas, 1976) that there exist *two kinds of operants* depending on the kind of reinforcers that maintain the operant. We may talk about *extrinsic* or *social operants* when other people control the reinforcer, and hence shape and maintain the behavior. And we may talk of *self-stimulatory operants* when the reinforcer for a class of responses is completely controlled by the person himself, as in the case of sensory reinforcement. Presumably, a response may be shaped by social stimuli, but maintained by self-stimulatory ones. The next question that faces us, then, is to what extent is common, everyday, normal human behavior self-stimulatory? Obviously, certain behaviors qualify—many forms of play, listening to music, and watching movies. But let us also speculate that many instances of language or thought—such as daydreaming, mulling on the present, ruminating over the past, exhorting and soothing oneself with words, conversing with others in "mental dialogues" —have the same self-stimulating function. It is virtually impossible to "pull a blank;" one is always thinking. Since there is often scant evidence that one is actually solving any problems or achieving any social effects by these thoughts, it seems unlikely that the reinforcers which maintain them are extrinsic or social. Rather, many instances of language and thought may be prime examples of self-stimulatory behavior. We recently found some excellent examples of such high rate responding which seems maintained independently of extrinsic reinforcement (Lovaas et al., Note 3). We attached microphones to echolalic autistic and young normal children, and obtained recordings of their vocalizations while they were alone. In this way we obtained up to 40 one-hour recording sessions on some children, and we observed, interestingly enough, that the children kept up a constant chatter throughout, with no signs of falling or rising rates. Had the high rate of this verbal behavior been a function of extrinsic (social) reinforcement, then one might have expected some decrease in rate as the child began to discriminate that speech during the recording sessions (which remained unaltered throughout) never resulted in reinforcement. We concluded, therefore, that such speech was self-stimulatory. The lack of such ("vocal play") behavior may be the major stumbling block in our attempts to build spontaneous speech in mute psychotic children. We are able to teach both syntax and semantics, but we have often failed to establish and maintain adequately high rates of verbal behavior in initially mute children. Although there may be an abundance of external reinforcement for vocalizing, vocalizing itself may never act as a reinforcer. Such mute children are reminiscent of deaf children, who generally stop babbling after infancy.

The above considerations lead to the suggestion that an essential problem in motivational research with psychotic children concerns the discovery of those conditions that replace inappropriate self-stimulatory behavior with socially appropriate forms of self-stimulation (such as play, language, and thought). One effort in this direction has been made by Koegel, Firestone, Kramme, and Dunlap (1974). They first trained autistic children to play appropriately with toys, using food and social reinforcers, and found that self-stimulatory behavior invariably replaced toy play when extrinsic reinforcers were withdrawn. However, when self-stimulation was temporarily eliminated, appropriate play rose to a high level and continued in the absence of extrinsic reinforcement. The children were apparently becoming responsive to the sensory reinforcement inherent in a "normal" type of self-stimulation (appropriate play), rather than being limited to more primitive, or "pathological," varieties of self-stimulation.

The importance of learning more about motivational variables has also led to a systematic inquiry into the reinforcing effects of certain sensory stimuli for psychotic children (Rincover, Newsom, & Carr, Note 10). We asked teachers of three autistic children what kind of sensory stimulation was preferred by each child. When brief presentations of these stimuli (low frequency strobelight, popular music, etc.) were contingent on correct responses, it was possible to use such stimuli to teach certain basic discriminations and language skills. This finding replicates earlier results reported by Fineman (1968) and Kerr, Meyerson, and Michael (1965). We then set out to investigate how powerful these sensory stimuli were in supporting behavior by delivering such stimuli contingent on barpress responses according to an FR 5 schedule. It was found that the reinforcement effects were highly idiosyncratic—the child who worked for music did not work for the strobelight, and vice versa. Second, the sensory stimuli maintained responding over a long period of time; for example, one child started responding at a rate of 38 responses per minute, which fell below 5 responses per minute only after 52 weeks during which he experienced four 15-minute sessions per week. Third, after the child had eventually been brought to apparent satiation, a minor change in the sensory stimulation (such as changing the music) yielded another 30 sessions with approximately 15,000 barpresses.

This study shows that sensory stimuli can be very powerful, long-lasting reinforcers that compare favorably to the appetitive reinforcers usually employed in behavior therapy with psychotic children. However, it is important to note that the ability of a particular sensory event to function as a reinforcer for a particular child can only be determined empirically. One can observe the child in his natural environment or talk to someone who has already done so, such as a parent or teacher, to narrow down the range of alternatives to be tried in therapeutic work. If the child spends a considerable amount of time self-stimulating with a particular object, an attempt could be made to exploit the reinforcement potential of that object by making access to it for brief periods contingent on appropriate behavior. Although we have not studied this possibility in sufficient detail as yet, its investigation may contribute much to a solution of the motivational problems that exist in work with psychotic children.

Research on Treatment Skills and Classroom Development

Until very recently, behavior therapy with psychotic children was something of an art and was strictly limited to the interaction between one professional therapist and one child. Under such conditions, effective techniques benefit only a fraction of the many children who need help. Thus it is extremely important to identify specific skills and procedures that parents and teachers must have to work effectively with individual children in tutorial situations and with groups of children in classrooms.

TRAINING TEACHERS AND PARENTS

Some very useful information on the skills essential in behavior therapy is provided in a study by Koegel, Russo, Rincover, Everett and Dimalanta (Note 11). Experienced observers evaluated the performances of teachers according to the extent to which they used five skills in teaching new behaviors to autistic children. The skills were: (1) presentation of instructions concisely and clearly, (2) use of effective prompts, (3) responsive, efficient shaping, (4) application of immediate and appropriate consequences, and (5) maintenance of distinctive intertrial intervals. During baseline sessions, none of the 11 teachers used these techniques more than half the time they worked with the children. Consequently, none of the children showed any improvement on any of the behaviors being taught. The teachers then participated in a one-week training program in which they read operational definitions of each of the five behavior modification techniques and watched video-taped demonstrations of the correct and incorrect use of each of the techniques. After this training, all 11 teachers used the techniques correctly more than 90% of each session; every child showed measureable improvement on each behavior being taught. It is of considerable interest to note that prior to the training carried out in this study, all the teachers had described themselves as familiar with behavior modification principles and had assumed that they were using them consistently in their work.

The importance of training that focuses on fundamental behavioral techniques was also demonstrated by Glahn (1975). The parents of a group of psychotic children were evaluated for their ability to teach new behaviors to their children. They were unable to produce measureable improvements until after they were given training which consisted of watching an experienced therapist teach a given behavior to a child. Although the parents were subsequently able to teach the behavior they had observed during training, they were unable to teach other behaviors that they had not observed being taught by the demonstrator. Therefore, a second training program was conducted in which the parents were trained to identify correct and incorrect use of each of the five techniques listed above. Following this training, the parents were able to teach their children a variety of new and different behaviors. In other words, modeling was insufficient; only added training and instruction in basic learning principles assured an effective parent-teacher.

These studies clearly indicate that teachers and parents who are naive with respect to both clinical psychology and learning theory can be trained in the use of effective treatment techniques within a very short period of time *if* the training explicitly deals with fundamental skills. To be sure, there undoubtedly are limits on how far these teachers and parents can take their children without further training and supervision. However, there are a great many relatively simple things that every psychotic child needs to learn and that can be taught by teachers and parents if they are proficient in the essentials of behavior therapy (Schreibman & Koegel, 1975). Detailed accounts of the successful implementation of parent training programs in the home have been presented by Kozloff (1973) and by Nordquist and Wahler (1973).

CLASSROOM TREATMENT

Several investigators have reported varying degrees of success in implementing methods for teaching groups of autistic children in classroom settings (Elgar, 1966; Halpern,

1970; Hamblin, Buckholdt, Ferritor, Kozloff, & Blackwell, 1971; Martin, England, Kaprowy, Kilgour, & Pilek, 1968; Rabb & Hewett, 1967). Koegel and Rincover (1974) illustrated some of the difficulties encountered in establishing an orderly, productive class and provided a systematic procedure for introducing group instruction. In the first part of this study, eight autistic children were individually taught to attend to the teacher, to imitate nonverbal responses, and to label objects. After a given child achieved a criterion of at least 80% appropriate responses in the one child–one teacher situation, his performance of those behaviors was measured in test sessions with one to one, two to one, and eight to one child-teacher ratios. Although correct responding on previously mastered tasks was maintained in the one to one test sessions, the performance of each child deteriorated when he was tested with only one other child present and deteriorated even further when seven other children were present. Additional observations of the children in a group of eight during weekly sessions in which the teacher attempted to train new behaviors indicated that no new learning occurred.

The second phase of the Koegel and Rincover (1974) study assessed the effects of gradual, rather than abrupt, increases in group size. First, two children sat side by side, facing the teacher, while two teaching assistants sat directly behind the children. Training was conducted just as it was in one to one treatment, except that now only the assistants provided the necessary prompts and reinforcers. For example, the teacher might say, "Touch your ear," to one child and the assistant would prompt the child to touch his ear (by moving the child's hand) and reinforce the response with an edible. The procedure was then repeated with the second child. Over trials the prompts were faded out. When both children reached a criterion of 80% or more correct responses without prompts, the reinforcement schedule was reduced to an

FR 2 schedule so that a given child was rewarded after performing two correct responses. At this point, these two children were grouped with two other children who had achieved the same criterion to form a class of four children, one teacher, and two assistants. Since each child was now responding twice for one reward, each assistant could provide prompts and rewards for two children. All four children were again brought to an 80% correct response criterion, and the reinforcement schedule was gradually thinned to FR 4. These children were then grouped with four others who had reached the same criterion to form the final class size of eight. When all the children again reached a high level of correct responding, the reinforcement schedule was further thinned to a FR 8, so that each child was rewarded for every eighth correct response on the average. Both assistants were then removed from the classroom. As a result of this gradual introduction of additional children and progressive leaning of the reinforcement schedule, a classroom situation was achieved in which the children would reliably and accurately respond to instructions and questions for very infrequent rewards. Significantly, the children's responses were not merely repetitions of previously acquired behaviors—the teacher was able to introduce a standard preschool curriculum and teach new behaviors. In a very short time the children were engaging in various activities such as telling time, reading first grade books, printing the letters of the alphabet, and solving simple arithmetic problems.

As the children became proficient in these complex behaviors, their individual differences in ability became increasingly important and it was obvious that group instruction would have to be supplemented with individualized programs. But to work individually, the children would have to be taught to engage in a long sequence of behavior without constant supervision by the teacher. Rincover and Koegel (Note 12) conceptualized the problem as one requiring the shaping of increasingly longer chains of responses to each instructional S^D. Initially, for example, the teacher would hand the child a sheet of paper with a single arithmetic problem and tell him to do his arithmetic. As soon as the child wrote the correct answer to the problem, he was rewarded. Later, worksheets with a gradually increasing number of problems were provided, and the teacher left the child alone to work on them for longer and longer periods of time. Eventually, each child was able to work alone for as long as 15 or 20 minutes. Thus the teacher could circulate among the children, provide each with a task appropriate to his current level of ability, and return a little later to check the child's work and reward him. Several benefits resulted from this personalized system of instruction. Each child worked on the academic task which was most appropriate for him and was allowed to work at his own rate. Each child worked and learned throughout much of the school day, instead of remaining idle or behaving inappropriately while the teacher attended to other children. Finally, and very importantly from an economic standpoint, only one teacher and one teacher's aide were required to conduct this class of 8 to 10 autistic children.

These studies show that classroom programs can be designed and implemented to provide significant educational experiences for autistic children. Further, because the effects of alternative programs were measured and evaluated, the authors were able to demonstrate that certain once plausible assumptions had to be rejected. For example, the combined effect of one to one treatment and repeated exposure to the eight to one classroom situation during a six month period failed to result in a classroom environment where autistic children could learn new behaviors. The transition from one to one treatment to classroom education had to be systematically programmed. Similarly, it proved impossible to assume that children who were able to behave very appropriately in the immediate presence of a teacher were also able to continue behaving appropriately in the teacher's absence. Instead, the ability to persist in carrying out a series of appropriate responses had to be constructed gradually, step by step. Clearly, the establishment of successful classrooms for psychotic children requires an imaginative approach to problems that usually do not even exist in classrooms for normal and less severely handicapped children. The studies just described indicate that some of these problems are being detected and solved.

SELECTING CHILDREN

The primary weaknesses in behavior modification with psychotic children, as we outlined in the follow-up paper (Lovaas et al., 1973), concerned the slow rate of change and the reversibility of the therapeutic gains. We have tried to tackle these problems in three ways. (1) We are attempting to acquire a better understanding of the autistic child per se, for example, by investigating his perceptual and motivational deviations. (2) We are attempting to generalize and otherwise extend the treatment environment, by means of, for example, the teacher- and parent-training programs we have just reviewed. Consistent with these efforts, attempts are also now being made (Russo, Miners, & Lovaas, Note 13) to seek treatment models which avoid reliance on large, impersonal, and nontherapeutic institutional environments, and instead emphasize the concept of professional foster or "teaching" homes. This involves an effort to extend the Kansas Achievement Place model for delinquents (Phillips, 1968) to psychotic children. (3) Finally, we are attempting to optimize the treatment effects by the *selection* of patients. It is clear that psychotic children have shown great variability in their response to our efforts, with an occasional child becoming normal. The child's age at onset of treatment seemed most closely correlated with rapid, irreversible changes—the youn-

ger the child the better his prognosis. This led to our young-autism (before 30 months) treatment project (Lovaas, Koegel, & Schreibman, 1973), where the results are most encouraging—the changes occur quite rapidly, large behavior classes seem involved, and the therapeutic effects appear to be permanent. We have focused the treatment effort on teaching the child's parents how to teach the child in order to extend the treatment program to all the child's waking hours.

One can offer several hypotheses as to why the young autistic child should do better than the older one. Apparently they have acquired fewer behaviors (such as tantrums and inattention to external stimuli) which interfere with treatment. Also, they may be easier to bring under the control of generalized conditioned reinforcers, which we see as essential to support the necessary social and intellectual behaviors. That is, the older and more experienced the child, the less likely it will be that social stimuli such as smiles and attention will achieve control over his behavior. The kind of exclusive control such stimuli must possess for normal development to take place is, in all probability, not easily acquired after infancy, because such stimuli are thereafter rarely associated with more basic reinforcers (food, warmth, pain reduction, etc.). It would seem that normal people work hard to obtain social reinforcers because they get "hooked" on these events early in life, prior to a history of discrimination training which might render these reinforcers effective in certain situations only. In this chapter we have reviewed several studies, involving primarily older autistic children, which showed that they can discriminate between situations in which social stimuli are reliably backed up by food or shock and situations in which they are not. Perhaps young children can be considered somewhat like pigeons that are shifted from a multiple schedule in which food is available for pecking when the key is either red or green to one in which food is available only in red and never in green (cf. Reynolds, 1961). Inexperienced pigeons are relatively slow to learn that green is no longer correlated with reinforcement, and may never show complete extinction in green. Young children are like inexperienced pigeons in that they are organisms with limited practice in forming discriminations who can be expected to generalize appropriate behaviors readily and extensively across people and situations. In any case, our work with young autistic children looks very encouraging at the present time.

Conclusion

Let us conclude by briefly mentioning what we see as some of the significant contributions of the behavioral approach to the understanding and treatment of severely psychotic children.

1. The primary contribution, from which everything else derives, is the *methodology* used by behavior therapists when they work with psychotic children or persons from any other population (Baer, Wolf, & Risley, 1968; Leitenberg, 1973). The key components of this methodology are (a) *measurement*, the precise specification of the therapeutic interventions used and the behavioral changes observed; and (b) *experimentation*, the manipulation of treatment variables to assess their causal status and to determine the replicability of their effects. The use of such a methodology gives us an enormous advantage over traditional psychotherapists, because it forces us to center our inquiry on proposals that are capable of being disproved relatively quickly. Thus, we are able to distinguish effective interventions from merely plausible ones. To do so, we have to maintain a deep respect for the individuality and complexity of each child we treat. This fact apparently still escapes those who assume that an insistence on methodological rigor in the evaluation of treatment entails the "dehumanization" of the children. The major value of behavioral methodology is that it is atheoretical (Risley, 1972); it therefore allows the clinician (or parent or teacher or nurse or speech therapist) sufficient freedom to test effectively whatever treatment intervention he or she desires.

2. The elimination of the most grossly patho-logical behaviors of the psychotic child has been accomplished through the use of punishment and extinction operations, especially when incompatible responses are trained simultaneously. Thus, the management of self-destruction, tantrums, and the more obvious forms of self-stimulation is within the capacity of anyone who avails himself of the existing technology.

3. The establishment of many appropriate behaviors, including eye contact, affectionate responses, academic skills, and receptive and expressive language is feasible for many psychotic children through the use of imitation, prompting, shaping, and differential reinforcement operations. The successes which have been achieved with procedures incorporating these techniques constitute an important basis for optimism in treatment endeavors. The technology, for the elaborate construction of complex behaviors, such as propositional language, may be possible only to highly trained behavior modification specialists at the present time. Acquisition of beginning social, intellectual, and self-help skills, on the other hand, can probably be accomplished by anyone with minimal training in behavior therapy.

4. The identification of specific perceptual dysfunctions has been advanced through the use of nonverbal procedures borrowed from experimental psychology. Such methods have made possible the isolation of a severe attention deficit—stimulus overselectivity—which appears to underlie many of the psychotic child's learning difficulties. Knowledge of the existence of this problem has so far led to at least one general principle for the design of teaching programs for behaviorally deficient children: emphasize the distinctive feature of the positive stimulus in prompting the acquisition of a discrimination. As we learn more about how stimulus control can be established and transferred we should become increasingly able to overcome the perceptual handicaps of psychotic children.

5. The education of psychotic children in classroom environments approximating those of less-severely disturbed and normal children has become eminently feasible. It is now possible to teach meaningful academic skills to psychotic children relatively efficiently and economically. Further knowledge of exactly what parents and teachers must be able to do and improved methods for training parents and teachers will undoubtedly lead to radical changes in society's approach to the treatment of psychotic children.

6. Our ignorance of motivational variables may be a major deterrent to the development of more optimal treatment programs at present. The reliance on experimental (treatment-specific) reinforcers, rather than the building of more normal, everyday ones, probably accounts for much of the response- and stimulus-specificity associated with our therapeutic accomplishments to date. Such specificity requires that considerable attention be given to the redesign of the child's posttreatment environment in order to prevent reversals of treatment gains.

Although we have touched on a variety of topics relating to psychotic children in this chapter, we have failed to mention much interesting and important work that could profitably have been discussed. Recent reviews which examine other aspects of theory, treatment, and research are those by Churchill, Alpern, and DeMyer (1971), Hermelin and O'Connor (1970), Hingtgen and Bryson (1972), Jennings (1970), Leff (1968), Ornitz (1973), Ross (1974), Rutter (1971), and Yates (1970).

Reference Notes

1. NEWSOM, C. D., & SIMON, K. M. *A simultaneous discrimination procedure for measuring subjective visual acuity in nonverbal children.* Manuscript submitted for publication, 1975.

2. CARR, E. G., SCHREIBMAN, L., & LOVAAS, O. I. *Control of echolalic speech in psychotic children.* Manuscript submitted for publication, 1975.

3. LOVAAS, O. I., VARNI, J. W., KOEGEL, R. L., & LORSCH, N. *Some observations on the nonextinguishability of children's speech.* Manuscript submitted for publication, 1975.

4. CREEDON, M. P. *A simultaneous communication learning program: rationale and results.* Paper presented at the meeting of the American Psychological Association, Montreal, August 1973.

5. VARNI, J. W., LOVAAS, O. I., & KOEGEL, R. L. *An experimental analysis of the components of observational learning: autistic children as subjects.* Paper presented at the meeting of the Western Psychological Association, San Francisco, April 1974.

6. VARNI, J. W., & EVERETT, N. *Observational learning in normal and autistic children.* Manuscript submitted for publication, 1975.

7. RUSSO, D. C. *Variables influencing transfer from prompt to training stimuli in autistic children: difficulty of the discrimination.* Manuscript submitted for publication, 1975.

8. SCHOVER, L. R., & NEWSOM, C. D. *Overselectivity, developmental level, and overtraining in autistic and normal children.* Manuscript submitted for publication, 1975.

9. NEWSOM, C. D., & FERRIS, C. D. *Interactions among self-stimulatory responses in psychotic children.* Manuscript submitted for publication, 1975.

10. RINCOVER, A., NEWSOM, C. D., & CARR, E. G. *Identifying and using sensory reinforcers.* Paper presented at the meeting of the Western Psychological Association, San Francisco, April 1974.

11. KOEGEL, R. L., RUSSO, D. C., RINCOVER, A., EVERETT, N., & DIMALANTA, P. *A method for assessing and training teachers in behavior modification with autistic children.* Manuscript submitted for publication, 1975.

12. RINCOVER, A., & KOEGEL, R. L. *Treatment of psychotic children in a classroom environment. II. Unsupervised learning.* Manuscript submitted for publication, 1975.

13. RUSSO, D. C., MINERS, W. S., & LOVAAS, O. I. *Use of teaching homes for the treatment of psychotic children.* Paper presented at the meeting of the American Psychological Association, New Orleans, September 1974.

References

AZRIN, N. H., & HOLZ, W. C. Punishment. In W. K. HONIG (Ed.), *Operant behavior: areas of research and application.* New York: Appleton-Century-Crofts, 1966.

AZRIN, N. H., KAPLAN, S. J., & FOXX, R. M. Autism reversal: eliminating stereotyped self-stimulation of retarded individuals. *American Journal of Mental Deficiency*, 1973, **78**, 241–248.

BACHMAN, J. A. Self-injurious behavior: a behavioral analysis. *Journal of Abnormal Psychology*, 1972, **80**, 211–224.

BAER, D. M., GUESS, D., & SHERMAN, J. Adventures in simplistic grammar. In R. L. Schiefelbusch (Ed.), *Language of the mentally retarded.* Baltimore: University Park Press, 1972.

BAER, D. M., & SHERMAN, J. Reinforcement control of generalized imitation in young children. *Journal of Experimental Child Psychology*, 1964, **1**, 37–49.

BAER, D. M., WOLF, M. M., & RISLEY, T. R. Some current dimensions of applied behavior analysis. *Journal of Applied Behavior Analysis*, 1968, **1**, 91–97.

BANDURA, A. *Principles of behavior modification.* New York: Holt, Rinehart & Winston, 1969.

BAUMEISTER, A. A., & FOREHAND, R. Stereotyped acts. In N. R. Ellis (Ed.), *International review of research in mental retardation* (Vol 6). New York: Academic Press, 1973.

BERKO, J. The child's learning of English morphology. *Word,* 1958, **14**, 150–177.

BETTELHEIM, B. *The empty fortress.* New York: Free Press, 1967.

BIJOU, S. W., & BAER, D. M. *Child development: readings in experimental analysis.* New York: Appleton-Century-Crofts, 1967.

BIRNBRAUER, J. S. Generalization of punishment effects—a case study. *Journal of Applied Behavior Analysis*, 1968, **1**, 201–211.

BLOOMFIELD, L. *Language.* New York: Holt, 1933.

BRACKBILL, Y., ADAMS, G., CROWELL, D. H., & GRAY, M. L. Arousal level in neonates and preschool children under continuous auditory stimulation. *Journal of Experimental Child Psychology,* 1966, **4**, 178–188.

BROWN, J. L. Prognosis from presenting symptoms of preschool children with atypical behavior. *American Journal of Orthopsychiatry,* 1960, **30**, 382–390.

BROWN, R., & BELLUGI, U. (Eds.). *The acquisition of language.* Yellow Springs, Ohio: Antioch Press, 1964.

BROWN, R., & FRASER, C. The acquisition of syntax. *Child Development Monographs,* 1964, **29**, 43–79.

BRYSON, C. Q. Systematic identification of perceptual disabilities in autistic children. *Perceptual and Motor Skills,* 1970, **31**, 239–246.

BUCHER, B., & LOVAAS, O. I. Use of aversive stimulation in behavior modification. In M. R. Jones (Ed.), *Miami symposium on the prediction of behavior, 1967: aversive stimulation.* Coral Gables, Fla.: University of Miami Press, 1968.

CHOMSKY, N. *Aspects of the theory of syntax.* Cambridge, Mass.: MIT Press, 1965.

CHURCHILL, D. W., ALPERN, G. D., & DeMYER, M. K. (Eds.). *Infantile autism: proceedings of the Indiana University colloquium.* Springfield, Ill.: Charles C Thomas, 1971.

COOK, C., & ADAMS, H. E. Modification of verbal behavior in speech deficient children. *Behaviour Research and Therapy,* 1966, **4**, 265–271.

CORTE, H. E., WOLF, M. M., & LOCKE, B. J. A comparison of procedures for eliminating self-injurious behavior of retarded adolescents. *Journal of Applied Behavior Analysis,* 1971, **4**, 201–213.

COWAN, P. A., HODDINOTT, B. T., & WRIGHT, B. A. Compliance and resistance in the conditioning of autistic children: an exploratory study. *Child Development,* 1965, **36**, 913–923.

CRAIGHEAD, W. E., O'LEARY, K. D., & ALLEN, J. S. Teaching and generalization of instruction-following in an "autistic" child. *Journal of Behavior Therapy and Experimental Psychiatry,* 1973, **4**, 171–176.

CREAK, M. The schizophrenic syndrome in childhood: progress report of a working party. *British Medical Journal,* 1964, **2**, 889–890.

CUMMING, W. W., & BERRYMAN, R. The complex discriminated operant: studies of matching-to-sample and related problems. In D. I. Mostofsky (Ed.), *Stimulus generalization.* Stanford, Calif.: Stanford University Press, 1965.

DAVISON, G. C. A social learning therapy programme with an autistic child. *Behaviour Research and Therapy,* 1964, **2**, 149–159.

ELGAR, S. Teaching autistic children. In J. K. Wing (Ed.), *Early childhood autism: clinical, educational, and social aspects.* London: Pergamon Press, 1966.

EPSTEIN, L. H., DOKE, L. A., SAJWAJ, T. E., SORRELL, S., & RIMMER, B. Generality and side effects of overcorrection. *Journal of Applied Behavior Analysis,* 1974, **7**, 385–390.

ERVIN, S. M. Imitation and structural change in children's language. In E. H. Lenneberg (Ed.), *New directions in the study of language.* Cambridge, Mass.: MIT Press, 1964.

FERSTER, C. B. Positive reinforcement and behavioral deficits of autistic children. *Child Development,* 1961, **32**, 437–456.

FERSTER, C. B., & DEMYER, M. K. The development of performances in autistic children in an automatically controlled environment. *Journal of Chronic Diseases,* 1961, **13**, 312–345.

FINEMAN, K. R. Visual-color reinforcement in establishment of speech by an autistic child. *Perceptual and Motor Skills,* 1968, **26**, 761–762.

FOXX, R. M., & AZRIN, N. H. The elimination of autistic self-stimulatory behavior by overcorrection. *Journal of Applied Behavior Analysis,* 1973, **6**, 1–14.

FREUD, A. Problems of infantile neurosis: a discussion. *The Psychoanalytic Study of the Child,* 1954, **9**, 9–71.

GARCIA, E., GUESS, D., & BYRNES, J. Development of syntax in a retarded girl using imitation, reinforcement, and modelling. *Journal of Applied Behavior Analysis,* 1973, **6**, 299–310.

GARDNER, B. T., & GARDNER, R. A. Two-way communication with an infant chimpanzee. In A. Schrier & F. Stollnitz (Eds.), *Behavior of nonhuman primates* (Vol. 4). New York: Academic Press, 1971.

GLAHN, T. J. *Effects of modelling techniques versus instruction in operant principles for teaching behavior modification procedures to parents.* Unpublished master's thesis, University of California, Santa Barbara, 1975.

GOLDSTEIN, K. Abnormal mental conditions in infancy. *Journal of Nervous and Mental Diseases,* 1959, **128**, 538–557.

GREENACRE, P. Problems of infantile neurosis: a discussion. *The Psychoanalytic Study of the Child,* 1954, **9**, 18–24.

GUESS, D., SAILOR, W., RUTHERFORD, G., & BAER, D. An experimental analysis of linguistic development: the productive use of the plural morpheme. *Journal of Applied Behavior Analysis,* 1968, **1**, 292–307.

HAGEN, J. W., WINSBERG, B., & WOLFF, P. Cognitive and linguistic deficit in psychotic children. *Child Development,* 1968, **39**, 1103–1117.

HALPERN, W. I. Schooling of autistic children. *American Journal of Orthopsychiatry,* 1970, **40**, 665–671.

HAMBLIN, R. L., BUCKHOLDT, D., FERRITOR, D., KOZLOFF, M., & BLACKWELL, L. *The humanization processes: a social, behavioral analysis of children's problems.* New York: John Wiley, 1971.

HAMILTON, J., STEPHENS, L., & ALLEN, P. Controlling aggressive and destructive behavior in severely retarded institutionalized residents. *American Journal of Mental Deficiency,* 1967, **71**, 852–856.

HARTMAN, J., KRIS, E., & LOEWENSTEIN, R. M. Notes on the theory of aggression. *The Psychoanalytic Study of the Child,* 149, **3**, 1–36.

HARTUNG, J. R. A review of procedures to increase verbal imitation skills and functional speech in autistic children. *Journal of Speech and Hearing Disorders,* 1970, **35**, 203–217.

HERMELIN, B., & O'CONNOR, N. Visual imperception in psychotic children. *British Journal of Psychology,* 1965, **56**, 455–460.

HERMELIN, B., & O'CONNOR, N. Perceptual and motor discrimination in psychotic and normal children. *Journal of Genetic Psychology,* 1967, **110**, 117–125.

HERMELIN, B., & O'CONNOR, N. *Psychological experiments with autistic children.* London: Pergamon Press, 1970.

HEWETT, F. M. Teaching speech to an autistic child through operant conditioning. *American Journal of Orthopsychiatry,* 1965, **35**, 927–936.

HINGTGEN, J. N., & BRYSON, C. Q. Recent developments in the study of early childhood psychoses: infantile autism, childhood schizophrenia, and related disorders. *Schizophrenia Bulletin,* 1972, **5**, 8–54.

HINGTGEN, J. N., & COULTER, S. K. Auditory control of operant behavior in mute autistic children. *Perceptual and Motor Skills,* 1967, **25**, 561–565.

JENNINGS, W. B. *Early infantile autism: a review.* Memphis: Memphis Board of Education, 1970.

KANNER, L. Autistic disturbances of affective contact. *Nervous Child,* 1943, **2**, 181–197.

KANNER, L., & EISENBERG, L. Notes on the follow-up studies of autistic children. In P. H. Hoch & J. Zubin (Eds.), *Psychopathology of childhood.* New York: Grune & Stratton, 1955.

KENT, L. R. *Language acquisition program for the severely retarded.* Champaign, Ill.: Research Press, 1974.

KERR, N., MEYERSON, L., & MICHAEL, J. A procedure for shaping vocalizations in a mute child. In L. P. Ullman & L. Krasner (Eds.), *Case studies in behavior modification.* New York: Rinehart & Winston, 1965.

KISH, G. B. Studies of sensory reinforcement. In W. K. Honig (Ed.), *Operant behavior: areas of research and application.* New York: Appleton-Century-Crofts, 1966.

KOEGEL, R. L. *Selective attention to prompt stimuli by autistic and normal children.* Unpublished doctoral dissertation, University of California, Los Angeles, 1971.

KOEGEL, R. L., & COVERT, A. The relationship of self-stimulation to learning in autistic children. *Journal of Applied Behavior Analysis,* 1972, **5,** 381–387.

KOEGEL, R. L., FIRESTONE, P. B., KRAMME, K. W., & DUNLAP, G. Increasing spontaneous play by suppressing self-stimulation in autistic children. *Journal of Applied Behavior Analysis,* 1974, **7,** 521–528.

KOEGEL, R. L., & RINCOVER, A. Treatment of psychotic children in a classroom environment. I. Learning in a large group. *Journal of Applied Behavior Analysis,* 1974, **7,** 45–59.

KOEGEL, R. L., & WILHELM, H. Selective responding to the components of multiple visual cues by autistic children. *Journal of Experimental Child Psychology,* 1973, **15,** 442–453.

KOVATTANA, P. M., & KRAEMER, H. C. Response to multiple visual cues of color, size, and form by autistic children. *Journal of Abnormal Child Psychology,* 1974, 4, 251–261.

KOZLOFF, M. A. *Reaching the autistic child: a parent training program.* Champaign, Ill.: Research Press, 1973.

KOSLOFF, M. A. *Educating children with learning and behavior problems.* New York: John Wiley, 1974.

KUSHNER, M. Faradic aversive controls in clinical practice. In C. Neuringer & J. L. Michael (Eds.), *Behavior modification in clinical psychology.* New York: Appleton-Century-Crofts, 1970.

LACEY, J. I. Somatic response patterning and stress: some revisions of activation theory. In M. H. Apley & R. Trumbull (Eds.), *Psychological stress: issues in research.* New York: Appleton-Century-Crofts, 1967.

LEFF, R. Behavior modification and the psychoses of childhood: a review. *Psychological Bulletin,* 1968, **69,** 396–409.

LEITENBERG, H. The use of single-case method-ology in psychotherapy research. *Journal of Abnormal Psychology,* 1973, **82,** 87–101.

LENNEBERG, E. H. Language disorders in childhood. *Harvard Educational Review,* 1964, **34,** 152–177.

LEUBA, C. Toward some integration of learning theories: the concept of optimal stimulation. *Psychological Reports,* 1955, **1,** 27–33.

LOVAAS, O. I. A behavior therapy approach to the treatment of childhood schizophrenia. In J. P. Hill (Ed.), *Minnesota symposia on child psychology* (Vol. 1). Minneapolis: University of Minnesota Press, 1967.

LOVAAS, O. I. *Behavior modification: teaching language to psychotic children.* New York: Appleton-Century-Crofts, 1969. (Film)

LOVAAS, O. I. *Language acquisition programs for nonlinguistic children.* New York: Irvington Publishers, 1976.

LOVAAS, O. I., BERBERICH, J. P., PERLOFF, B. F., & SCHAEFFER, B. Acquisition of imitative speech by schizophrenic children. *Science,* 1966, **151,** 705–707.

LOVAAS, O. I., FREITAG, G., GOLD, V. J., & KASSORLA, I. C. Experimental studies in childhood schizophrenia: analysis of self-destructive behavior. *Journal of Experimental Child Psychology,* 1965, **2,** 67–84.

LOVAAS, O. I., KOEGEL, R. L., & SCHREIBMAN, L. *Experimental studies in childhood schizophrenia.* Research Project MH 11440-07, National Institute of Mental Health, 1973.

LOVAAS, O. I., KOEGEL, R. L., SIMMONS, J. Q., & LONG, J. S. Some generalization and follow-up measures on autistic children in behavior therapy. *Journal of Applied Behavior Analysis,* 1973, **6,** 131–165.

LOVAAS, O. I., LITROWNIK, A., & MANN, R. Response latencies to auditory stimuli in autistic children engaged in self-stimulatory behavior. *Behaviour Research and Therapy,* 1971, **9,** 39–49.

LOVAAS, O. I., SCHAEFFER, B., & SIMMONS, J. Q. Experimental studies in childhood schizophrenia: building social behavior in autistic children by use of electric shock. *Journal of Experimental Research in Personality,* 1965, **1,** 99–109.

LOVAAS, O. I., & SCHREIBMAN, L. Stimulus over-selectivity of autistic children in a two-stimulus situation. *Behaviour Research and Therapy,* 1971, **9,** 305–310.

LOVAAS, O. I., SCHREIBMAN, L., KOEGEL, R. L., & REHM, R. Selective responding by autistic children to multiple sensory input. *Journal of Abnormal Psychology,* 1971, **77**, 211–222.

LOVAAS, O. I., & SIMMONS, J. Q. Manipulation of self-destruction in three retarded children. *Journal of Applied Behavior Analysis,* 1969, **2**, 143–157.

MACCORQUODALE, K. B. F. Skinner's "Verbal behavior:" a retrospective appreciation. *Journal of the Experimental Analysis of Behavior,* 1969, **12**, 831–841.

MACCORQUODALE, K. On Chomsky's review of Skinner's "Verbal behavior." *Journal of the Experimental Analysis of Behavior,* 1970, **13**, 83–99.

MARTIN, G. L., ENGLAND, G., KAPROWY, E., KILGOUR, K., & PILEK, V. Operant conditioning of kindergarten classroom behavior in autistic children. *Behaviour Research and Therapy,* 1968, **6**, 281–294.

MASSERMAN, J. H. *Principles of dynamic psychiatry.* Philadelphia: Saunders, 1946.

MCREYNOLDS, L. V. Application of timeout from positive reinforcement for increasing the efficiency of speech training. *Journal of Applied Behavior Analysis,* 1969, **2**, 199–205.

MERBAUM, M. The modification of self-destructive behavior by a mother-therapist using aversive stimulation. *Behavior Therapy,* 1973, **4**, 442–447.

METZ, J. R. Conditioning generalized imitation in autistic children. *Journal of Experimental Child Psychology,* 1965, **2**, 389–399.

MILLER, N. E. Learning resistance to pain and fear: effects of overlearning, exposure, and rewarded exposure in context. *Journal of Experimental Psychology,* 1960, **60**, 137–145.

MOSTOFSKY, D. I. (Ed.). *Attention: contemporary theory and analysis.* New York: Appleton-Century-Crofts, 1970.

MOWRER, O. H. *Learning theory and the symbolic processes.* New York: John Wiley, 1960.

NORDQUIST, V. M., & WAHLER, R. G. Naturalistic treatment of an autistic child. *Journal of Applied Behavior Analysis,* 1973, **6**, 79–87.

O'CONNOR, N., & HERMELIN, B. Visual analogies of verbal operations. *Language and Speech,* 1965, **8**, 197–207.

ORNITZ, E. M. Childhood autism: a review of the clinical and experimental literature. *California Medicine,* 1973, **118**, 21–47.

ORNITZ, E. M., & RITVO, E. R. Perceptual inconstancy in early infantile autism. *Archives of General Psychiatry,* 1968, **18**, 76–98.

OTTINGER, D. R., SWEENEY, N., & LOEW, L. H. Visual discrimination learning in schizophrenic and normal children. *Journal of Clinical Psychology,* 1965, **21**, 251–253.

PHILLIPS, E. L. Achievement place: token reinforcement procedures in a home-style rehabilitation setting for "pre-delinquent" boys. *Journal of Applied Behavior Analysis,* 1968, **1**, 213–223.

PITFIELD, M., & OPPENHEIM, A. N. Child rearing attitudes of mothers of psychotic children. *Journal of Child Psychiatry,* 1964, **5**, 51–57.

PREMACK, D. A functional analysis of language. *Journal of the Experimental Analysis of Behavior,* 1970, **14**, 1–19.

PREMACK, D. Language in chimpanzee? *Science,* 1971, **172**, 808–822.

RABB, E., & HEWETT, F. M. Development of appropriate classroom behaviors in a severely disturbed group of institutionalized children with a behavior modification model. *American Journal of Orthopsychiatry,* 1967, **37**, 313–314.

RAY, B. A. Strategy in studies of attention: a commentary on D. I. Mostofsky's "Attention: contemporary theory and analysis." *Journal of the Experimental Analysis of Behavior,* 1972, **17**, 293–297.

RAY, B. A., & SIDMAN, M. Reinforcement schedules and stimulus control. In W. N. Schoenfeld (Ed.), *The theory of reinforcement schedules.* New York: Appleton-Century-Crofts, 1970.

REYNOLDS, B. S., NEWSOM, C. D., & LOVAAS, O. I. Auditory overselectivity in autistic children. *Journal of Abnormal Child Psychology,* 1974, **2**, 253–263.

REYNOLDS, G. S. An analysis of interactions in a multiple schedule. *Journal of the Experimental Analysis of Behavior.* 1961, 4, 107–117.

RHEINGOLD, H. L., GEWIRTZ, J. L., & ROSS, H. W. Social conditioning of vocalizations. *Journal of Comparative and Physiological Psychology,* 1959, **25**, 68–73.

RIMLAND, B. *Infantile autism: the syndrome and its implications for a neural theory of behavior.* New York: Appleton-Century-Crofts, 1964.

RINCOVER, A., & KOEGEL, R. L. Setting generality and stimulus control in autistic children. *Journal of Applied Behavior Analysis,* in press.

RISLEY, T. The effects and side effects of the use of punishment with an autistic child. *Journal of Applied Behavior Analysis,* 1968, **1**, 21–34.

RISLEY, T. Behavior modification: an experimental-therapeutic endeavor. In R. Rubin, H. Fensterheim, J. Henderson, & L. Ullmann (Eds.), *Advances in behavior therapy.* New York: Academic Press, 1972.

RISLEY, T., REYNOLDS, N., & HART, B. Behavior modification with disadvantaged preschool children. In R. H. Bradfield (Ed.), *Behavior modification: the human effort.* San Rafael, Calif.: Dimensions Publishing Co., 1970.

RISLEY, T., & WOLF, M. M. Experimental manipulation of autistic behaviors and generalization into the home. In R. Ulrich, T. Stachnik, & J. Mabry (Eds.), *Control of human behavior.* Glenview, Ill.: Scott, Foresman & Co., 1966.

RISLEY, T., & WOLF, M. M. Establishing functional speech in echolalic children. *Behaviour Research and Therapy,* 1967, **5**, 73–88.

ROSS, A. O. *Psychological disorders of children: a behavioral approach to theory, research, and therapy.* New York: McGraw-Hill, 1974.

RUTTER, M. Prognosis: psychotic children in adolescence and early adult life. In J. K. Wing (Ed.), *Early childhood autism: clinical, educational, and social aspects.* London: Pergamon Press, 1966.

RUTTER, M. Concepts of autism: a review of research. *Journal of Child Psychology and Psychiatry,* 1968, **9**, 1–25.

RUTTER, M. (Ed.). *Infantile autism: concepts, characteristics, and treatment.* London: Churchill Livingstone, 1971.

SAILOR, W. Reinforcement and generalization of productive plural allomorphs in two retarded children. *Journal of Applied Behavior Analysis,* 1971, **4**, 305–310.

SAILOR, W., & TAMAN, T. Stimulus factors in the training of prepositional usage in three autistic children. *Journal of Applied Behavior Analysis,* 1972, **5**, 183–190.

SALZINGER, K. On the operant conditioning of complex behavior. In J. M. Shlien (Ed), *Research in psychotherapy* (Vol. 3). Washington, D.C.: American Psychological Association, 1968.

SALZINGER, K., FELDMAN, R., COWAN, J., & SALZINGER, S. Operant conditioning of verbal behavior of two young speech-deficient boys. In L. Krasner & L. Ullmann (Eds.), *Research in*

behavior modification. New York: Holt, Rinehart & Winston, 1965.

SCHELL, R. E., STARK, J., & GIDDAN, J. G. Development of language behavior in an autistic child. *Journal of Speech and Hearing Disorders,* 1967, **32**, 51–64.

SCHOPLER, E., & REICHLER, R. J. How well do parents understand their own psychotic children? *Journal of Autism and Childhood Schizophrenia,* 1972, **2**, 387–400.

SCHREIBMAN, L. Effects of within-stimulus and extra-stimulus prompting on discrimination learning in autistic children. *Journal of Applied Behavior Analysis,* 1975, **8**, 91–112.

SCHREIBMAN, L., & KOEGEL, R. L. Autism: a defeatable horror. *Psychology Today,* 1975, **8**, 61–67.

SCHREIBMAN, L., & LOVAAS, O. I. Overselective response to social stimuli by autistic children. *Journal of Abnormal Child Psychology,* 1973, **1**, 152–168.

SCHUMAKER, J., & SHERMAN, J. A. Training generative verb usage by imitation and reinforcement procedures. *Journal of Applied Behavior Analysis,* 1970, **3**, 273–287.

SEGAL, E. F. Induction and the provenance of operants. In R. M. Gilbert & J. R. Millenson (Eds.), *Reinforcement: behavioral analyses.* New York: Academic Press, 1972.

SEGAL, E. F. Psycholinguistics discovers the operant: a review of Roger Brown's "A first language: the early stages." *Journal of the Experimental Analysis of Behavior,* 1975, **2**, 149–158.

SHERMAN, J. A. Imitation and language development. In H. W. Reese (Ed.), *Advances in child development and behavior* (Vol. 6). New York: Academic Press, 1971.

SKINNER, B. F. The generic nature of the concepts of stimulus and response. *Journal of General Psychology,* 1935, **12**, 40–65.

SKINNER, B. F. *Verbal behavior.* New York: Appleton-Century-Crofts, 1957.

SLOANE, H. N., JOHNSTON, M. K., & HARRIS, F. R. Remedial procedures for teaching verbal behavior to speech deficient or defective young children. In H. N. Sloane and B. MacAuley (Eds.), *Operant procedures in remedial speech and language training.* Boston: Houghton Mifflin, 1968.

SROUFE, L. A., STUECHER, H. U., & STUTZER, W. The functional significance of autistic behavior for the psychotic child. *Journal of Abnormal Child Psychology,* 1973, **1**, 225–240.

STARK, J., GIDDAN, J. J., & MEISEL, J. Increasing verbal behavior in an autistic child. *Journal of Speech and Hearing Disorders,* 1968, **3**, 42–48.

STEVENS-LONG, J., & RASMUSSEN, M. The acquisition of simple and compound sentence structure in an autistic child. *Journal of Applied Behavior Analysis,* 1974, **7**, 473–479.

STONE, A. A. Consciousness: altered levels in blind retarded children. *Psychosomatic Medicine,* 1964, **26**, 14–19.

TATE, B. G. Case study: control of chronic self-injurious behavior by conditioning procedures. *Behavior Therapy,* 1972, **3**, 72–83.

TATE, B. G., & BAROFF, G. S. Aversive control of self-injurious behavior in a psychotic boy. *Behaviour Research and Therapy,* 1966, 4, 281–287.

TERRACE, H. S. Discrimination learning with and without "errors." *Journal of the Experimental Analysis of Behavior,* 1963, **6**, 1–27.

WASSERMAN, L. M. *Discrimination learning in autistic children.* Unpublished doctoral dissertation, University of California, Los Angeles, 1969.

WEBSTER, C. D., McPHERSON, H., SLOMAN, L., EVANS, M. A., & KUCHAR, E. Communicating with an autistic boy by gestures. *Journal of Autism and Childhood Schizophrenia,* 1973, **3**, 337–346.

WHEELER, A. J., & SULZER, B. Operant training

and generalization of a verbal response form in a speech deficient child. *Journal of Applied Behavior Analysis,* 1970, **3**, 139–147.

WHITE, J. C., & TAYLOR, D. Noxious conditioning as a treatment for rumination. *Mental Retardation,* 1967, **6**, 30–33.

WIEST, W. Some recent criticisms of behaviorism and learning theory. *Psychological Bulletin,* 1967, **7**, 214–225.

WILHELM, H., & LOVAAS, O. I. Stimulus overselectivity: a common feature in autism and mental retardation. *American Journal of Mental Deficiency,* in press.

WOLF, M. M., RISLEY, T., JOHNSTON, M., HARRIS, F., & ALLEN, E. Application of operant conditioning procedures to the behavior problems of an autistic child: a follow-up and extension. *Behaviour Research and Therapy,* 1967, **5**, 103–112.

WOLF, M. M., RISLEY, T., & MEES, H. Application of operant conditioning procedures to the behavior problems of an autistic child. *Behaviour Research and Therapy,* 1964, **1**, 305–312.

WOLFF, W. M., & MORRIS, L. A. Intellectual and personality characteristics of parents of autistic children. *Journal of Abnormal Psychology,* 1971, **77**, 155–161.

YATES, A. J. *Behavior therapy.* New York: John Wiley, 1970.

ZUBEK, J. P. (Ed.) *Sensory deprivation: fifteen years of research.* New York: Appleton-Century-Crofts, 1969.

Mental Retardation

10

JAY S. BIRNBRAUER

The mentally retarded are a diverse group ranging from the kid in the neighborhood who is "slow" and attends a special school to children and adults who are so handicapped as to be unable to sit up or ambulate and who thus receive total nursing care. "Officially," mental retardation refers to significantly subaverage general intellectual functioning and significant deficits in adaptive behavior which are manifest during the development period (Grossman, 1973). Subaverage general intellectual functioning means two or more standard deviations below the mean on a test of general intelligence such as the Stanford-

Binet and Wechsler Intelligence Scale for Children. The stipulation that it originates during the development period (up to 18 years of age) is intended to exclude persons whose functioning deteriorates as a result of psychoses, strokes, and so on. Defining and measuring "adaptive behavior" has been a problem, but the term is meant to convey that the label, "mental retardation," should not be applied solely on the basis of an intelligence test, but rather only if the person also lags significantly behind the norms in the development of motor and self-help skills, academic learning, and social behavior. Adaptive behavior is measured most commonly by such rating scales as the Vineland Social Maturity Scale (Doll, 1947) and the Cain-Levine Social Competency Scale (Cain, Levine, & Elzey, 1963). Estimates of the incidence of mental retardation range from 3–5% of the population.

This large and heterogeneous group has been divided into four levels: mild, moderate, severe, and profound. Those in the mildly retarded group may not be noticeably different until school age, and they are likely then to be assigned to "ed-

A preliminary summary of this chapter, written in collaboration with Mr. Francisco Barrera, was presented at the 6th Annual Gatlinburg Conference on Research and Theory in Mental Retardation, Gatlinburg, Tenn. March 1973. I am very much indebted to Mr. Barrera and regret that distance made it impractical to continue collaboration through completion of this chapter.

I also wish to thank Mr. Jack E. James and Dr. Ronald G. Hicks of the University of Western Australia for their thoughtful comments about earlier drafts of this chapter, and Miss Kerry Evans, who so patiently and carefully typed the manuscript.

ucable" classes, classes emphasizing vocational skills in adolescence, and absorbed into the general population. Increasingly, the mildly retarded, who comprise 90% of the retarded population, are admitted to institutions only if the family or community is unable to provide appropriate training opportunities. The trend is, however, to care for and educate all retardates in their homes, day care centers, special classes, sheltered workshops, and hostels rather than commit them to large, depersonalizing institutions.

Moderately retarded children, depending on their cooperativeness and their having obtained such skills as bladder and bowel control, attend classes for the "trainable." In these classes, the emphasis, generally speaking, is upon motor coordination, social and verbal skills, self-help, appearance, good work habits, and navigation. The severely and profoundly retarded most often have been assigned to custodial wards, institution nurseries, and infirmaries. Typically, the condition of these wards is appalling and the ratio of residents to staff so high that the staff are hardpressed to provide clean and safe surroundings (Blatt & Kaplan, 1966).

The causes of mental retardation are numerous and include rare metabolic anomalies, CNS damage caused in a variety of ways, chromosomal anomalies (the most common being Down's Syndrome, or mongolism), and severely deprived rearing conditions. Quite frequently in particular cases, etiology is not known, which probably accounts for the absence of diagnostic category in many of the studies to be reviewed. (See Baroff, 1974, Heber, 1959, 1961, Grossman, 1973, and Robinson & Robinson, 1965, for information about definition, classification, and causes of mental retardation.)

Reports of research in behavior modification with the retarded began to appear in 1964. Prior to that, Ellis (1963) wrote a theoretical account of how toilet training might be accomplished through systematic application of learning principles. The only

experimental paper was Fuller's (1949) demonstration of conditioning of arm movements of a profoundly retarded, completely dependent adolescent. Basic research in learning began in earnest in the latter part of the fifties in laboratories established by Bijou (Orlando, Bijou, Tyler, & Marshall, 1961), Zeaman and House (Zeaman & House, 1963), Ellis and others associated with Peabody College at the time (Ellis, Barnett, & Pryer, 1960), Barrett and Lindsley (1962), Spradlin and colleagues (Spradlin & Girardeau, 1966), and Zigler (1962). According to Gardner and Selinger's (1971) summary of their survey of research in learning (Gardner, Selinger, Watson, Saposnek, & Gardner, 1970), prior to 1956 less than 10 articles per year had been published. In 1960, 50 articles pertaining to learning appeared. None was applied in nature. In the years 1965–1968, the total had increased to 110 articles per year, of which, in 1968, 22% were categorized as "applied behavior change."

The aims, procedures, and designs of the applied research have been as varied as the population itself, and the research has been conducted with persons at all levels of retardation and in all of the settings in which retardates reside, study, and work. In preparing this review, I have concentrated upon published studies in which data were presented and control groups or within-subject control data were part of the design. A second criterion was that the work be conducted in nonlaboratory settings except when a laboratory happened to be used as a clinic or classroom. (See Weisberg, 1971, for a review of operant laboratory research.) A final criterion for inclusion was that the subjects, or some of the subjects, be retarded as defined above.

The chapter is divided into five sections as follows: Research Strategies; Research in Educational Settings; Research in Wards; Research in Vocational Settings; and Appraisal and Recommendations. In the first four sections, I try to convey the questions that have been asked and the experimental designs and procedures employed with a minimum of critical commentary.

Research Strategies

The investigator interested in applied research has three options available: (1) The investigator may begin with an experimental question and find a suitable setting in which to conduct the study. (2) The investigator may build an applied laboratory to study a problem of interest to an agency and the investigator, i.e., establish a demonstration classroom, ward, or program. (3) The investigator cooperates with agents—teachers, parents, and nursing staff—to solve particular problems as they arise.

The first option, the more familiar one to school and institution personnel, consists of assigning subjects to a group or groups who receive instruction in a particular "subject" outside their regular classrooms or domiciles. The earliest studies of this type evaluated programmed instruction (e.g., Malpass, Hardy, Gilmore, & Williams, 1964), and methods of toilet training and other self-help skills (e.g., Bensberg, Colwell, & Cassel, 1965). Recently, this strategy has been employed by D. Ross (1970), S. Ross (1969a, 1969b), and Ross and Ross (1972) in a very interesting series of experiments that will serve as a model for research of this kind. The advantages of this tack are greater control of conditions, minimal amount of intrusion in the institutional program, and limited responsibility for the subjects. That is, one need only assume responsibility for limited periods of time each day for so many weeks. The major disadvantage is that the work may have no impact upon institutional programs, because it is conducted without regard for the practical problems that staff with multiple responsibilities for many children face.

The second approach is to take advantage of opportunities to develop demonstration projects. The Rainier School Programed Learning Classroom (Bijou,

Birnbrauer, Kidder, & Tague, 1966; Birnbrauer, Bijou, Wolf, & Kidder, 1965), the sheltered workshop at Murdoch Center (Baroff & Tate, 1966), and the ward-wide program of Girardeau and Spradlin (1964) were among the first of these projects to be publicized. This approach continues to be followed (Baker, Stanish, & Fraser, 1972; Colwell, Richards, McCarver, & Ellis, 1973). The strategy, however, is fraught with practical administrative problems and may yield slight returns of a research nature in comparison with the investment of time and resources. The main advantage is that such work is more likely to be noticed by staff and administrators and pave the way for further research and implementation.

The third strategy, which accounts for the bulk of the reported experiments, is to assist teachers, attendants, and parents with particular problems in behavioral management. The well-known study of controlling hyperactivity, by Patterson, Jones, Whittier, and Wright (1965), was the first of this type to appear. Since the work is conducted *in situ* by regular staff, it is less liable to the criticism of impracticality and entails much less cost than demonstration projects. Further, each study trains staff in behavior modification principles. In order to gain control of circumstances and ensure consistent application of procedures, however, the investigator must spend a fair amount of time in instruction and overseeing. At one extreme, an investigator may have spent no greater time than that required to train a laboratory assistant, but at the other extreme, no doubt investigators have had to give up after considerable investment of time.

Except in studies of the last type, which demanded single-subject experimental designs, investigators have employed both single-subject and group-statistical designs. The measures of change run the gamut from standardized tests of intelligence and rating scales of social maturity to frequency of "hits and misses" of toilets, errors in academic programs and self-feeding, and turns of screw drivers. Generally speaking, the results with *in situ* behavioral measures are far more dramatic than those with standardized measures.

Research in Educational Settings

The experimental questions that have been asked and the representative studies to be reviewed are as follows:

1. How effective is programmed instruction with the mentally retarded? (Blackman & Capobianco, 1965; Malpass et al., 1964)

2. How does performance of pupils in token economy classes compare with the gains of pupils taught in conventional ways (Ayllon & Kelly, 1972; Baker, Stanish, & Fraser, 1972) and pupils taught in identical ways with token reinforcement omitted? (Birnbrauer, Wolf, Kidder, & Tague, 1965; Dalton, Rubino, & Hislop, 1973; Hewett, Taylor, & Artuso, 1969; Zimmerman, Zimmerman, & Russell, 1969)

3. What are the relative effects of token reinforcement for appropriate behavior and token loss for inappropriate behavior? (Kaufman & O'Leary, 1972)

4. How effective are instructional programs that emphasize teacher modeling, social reinforcement, and tokens? (D. Ross, 1970; S. Ross, 1969a, 1969b; Ross & Ross, 1972, 1973)

5. Will delayed access to "free time" and other privileges serve to improve in-class behavior? (Edlund, 1971; Greene & Platt, 1972; Osborne, 1969; Sulzbacher & Houser, 1968; Wasik, 1970)

6. What are the effects of "time out from positive reinforcement" (TO) in the form of brief periods of restraint or removal from the classroom? (Lahey, McNess, & McNess, 1973; Perline & Levinsky, 1968; Pendergrass, 1972)

7. Does reinforcement of behavior in one setting influence the same behavior at another time? (Hislop, Moore, & Stanish, 1973; Patterson, 1965; Patterson et al, 1965; Whitman, Caponigri, & Mercurio, 1971; Whitman, Burish, & Collins, 1972) How may improved behavior be maintained? (Kaufman & O'Leary, 1972)

8. How is the behavior of other children in the class affected by differential reinforcement of "target" subjects? (Broden, Bruce, Mitchell, Carter, & Hall, 1970; Kazdin, 1973)

9. What are the effects of reinforcement, instructions, class of behavior, and setting conditions upon the maintenance of "generalized antecedent stimulus control" of behavior? (See Table 10-1.)

PROGRAMMED INSTRUCTION

Blackman and Capobianco (1965) constructed primary reading and arithmetic programs suitable for machine presentation to adolescents, and assigned subjects whose reading and arithmetic achievement was at the first-grade level to two groups. The "machine" group spent approximately 2 hours per week working on the programs for an academic year. The control group received "conventional" instruction. In addition to before-and-after administration of standardized achievement tests, and a test based on the programs, the children were rated monthly on general classroom behavior by the teachers and trained observers. The results were that both groups made small (about 2 months), but statistically significant, gains in achievement but did not differ from each other. The "machine" group's general behavior, however, improved significantly, whereas the control subjects did not.

In accounting for the negative academic result, the authors probably were not being unduly modest in explaining that the programs, which the authors had not evaluated beforehand, were not optimal. From an experimental point of view, the important message in this study is the need for a control group that receives special attention of a different sort.

Another study vividly illustrates this need. Malpass et al. (1964) obtained significantly different gains in word recognition and spelling when their programmed groups were compared with groups receiving conventional teaching of the same words, but automated instruction was *not* superior to tutorial instruction. While the

TABLE 10–1   Studies of generalized stimulus control

A. AS A FUNCTION OF REINFORCEMENT CONTINGENCIES

1. average preschool-age children:	Baer & Sherman (1964)
2. autistic children:	Metz (1965)
	Lovaas et al. (1966)
	Risley & Wolf (1967)
3. retarded children:	Baer, Peterson, & Sherman (1967)
	Barton (1970)
	Peine, Gregersen, & Sloane (1970)
	Martin (1971)
	Whitman, Zakaras, & Chardos (1971)
	Bry & Nawas (1972)

B. AS A FUNCTION OF CLASS OF BEHAVIOR TRAINED

1. imitative/nonimitative:	Peterson (1968)
2. topography of motor responses:	Garcia, Baer, & Firestone (1971)
	Acker, Acker, & Pearson (1973)
3. English/foreign words; nonsense syllables:	Brigham & Sherman (1968)
	Burgess et al. (1970)
	Whitehurst (1971)
4. grammatical (syntactical) class:	Guess et al. (1968)
	Guess (1969)
	Schumacher & Sherman (1970)
	Wheeler & Sulzer (1970)
	Baer & Guess (1971)
	Sailor (1971)
	Bennett & Ling (1972)
	Garcia, Guess, & Byrnes (1973)

C. AS A FUNCTION OF SETTING AND ANTECEDENT STIMULI

1. instructions:	Steinman (1970a, 1970b)
	Bufford (1971)
	Steinman & Boyce (1971)
	Martin (1972)
2. experimenter presence/absence:	Peterson et al. (1971)
	Peterson & Whitehurst (1971)
3. antecedent/consequent stimulus control:	Epstein et al. (1973)

Note.—Several studies in B and C also show effects of response consequences.

authors could point to the economic advantage of automated instruction, they could not attribute the results to use of programming techniques.

Studies comparing programmed instruction with other approaches did not appear after 1965. The principal reasons were the realizations that the content of programs was of utmost importance, that programming was exceedingly tedious, that the costs of conducting truly convincing studies, as the above-mentioned studies illustrate, were very high indeed given the gains reported

until then, and that the best of programs did not obviate the need for motivating pupils and teaching other prerequisites as well (Birnbrauer, Kidder, & Tague, 1964). Since then, of course, programs have been published commercially, and descriptions of programs (e.g., Wunderlich, 1972) and analyses of the performance of individual children on programmed materials have been reported (Bijou, 1968; Sidman & Stoddard, 1966, 1967). It must be said that the promises made about programmed instruction have not materialized. (For other reviews of programmed instruction with the retarded, see Greene, 1966, and Malpass, 1968.)

The tokens in common use have been check marks and poker chips. When check marks are used, each child has a sheet of paper divided into squares in which the teacher inserts a check (tick) as behavior meeting the criteria occurs. Poker chips, naturally, tend to be used with younger and more severely retarded children. At the end of the lesson or period, the marks or chips are exchanged for items from a variety of objects ("back-up reinforcers") such as candy, gum, toys, and school supplies or are applied to a large prize, an outing perhaps. Of course, at the onset of the program, the children may have to be taught the value of the tokens by providing opportunities to exchange more frequently (Zimmerman, Zimmerman, & Russell, 1969). Once in operation, a token system can become quite complicated and may in itself be useful in teaching numerical skills, budgeting, and the like. Indeed, Hewett et al. (1969) speculated that daily experience in counting tokens may have played a part in producing the gains in arithmetic achievement that their token groups showed.

Birnbrauer, Wolf, Kidder, and Tague (1965) assessed the role that token reinforcement and tangible backup played in their two programmed classes by discontinuing the token system *in toto* for 21 or 35 days. Although the children had been receiving instruction with the system for at least 3 months, performance data were provided for only the 21 days before termination of tokens. After the period with no tokens, the system was reinstated, with data being provided for 30 days of the second token period. Three patterns of result were described. On the measures recorded, items completed, correct responses, and frequency of TO, 5 of the 15 children worked as well without tokens as they had with them. The produc-

tivity of six other children declined, but their general level of cooperativeness as indicated by frequency of being sent to the TO room did not change. Four children's performances changed for the worse in productivity and disruptiveness. With all children but one, former high levels were recorded after the system was reinstated. The results indicated that the token system was valuable for most of the children.

Zimmerman, Zimmerman, and Russell (1969) reported very similar results with a group of severely retarded boys during lessons in instruction following. In all control and token sessions, the teacher praised the boys for responding correctly to an instruction. (Other aspects of the control procedures were described in detail and maintained during token sessions.) Four of the seven boys' performances varied with reinforcement condition, i.e., the boys followed more instructions when tokens were dispensed; one boy followed instructions throughout, one boy did not throughout, and one improved gradually in such a way as to permit no conclusion. The investigators also used TO, i.e., placed a boy in an adjoining room for a very brief count to 15 by the teacher. Their *impression* was that the procedure was effective and that most TOs were applied during control sessions.

Hewett, Taylor, and Artuso (1969), in an ambitious undertaking, were interested in testing the effects of tokens in their "engineered" classroom for the educationally handicapped. While not retarded, their pupils would seem to have similar behavioral characteristics, for they were described as "educationally retarded" and "adjustment problems." The design of the study is a nice one and the procedures, in several ways, elegant. The pupils were matched on IQ, CA, and achievement scores and assigned randomly to six classes, which they attended for an academic year. The teachers were assigned to classes at random as well. Achievement tests were administered outside of the class by the same examiners at the beginning of term, at midyear, and at the end of the study. Attention to task was recorded daily by two observers in each class for the entire year! The basic curricular structure and physical design of the classes were the same.

The classes differed in that one never received tokens, one received tokens throughout the year, two received tokens until midyear at which time tokens were discontinued, and two received tokens after the midyear testing. Token reinforcement, checkmarks administered at 15-minute intervals for work completed correctly, was associated with significantly greater gains in arithmetic achievement and in significantly higher task attention scores. It is noteworthy that, in contrast to the results of Birnbrauer et al. (1965), task attention increased further in the groups after tokens were discontinued.

In considering reasons for gains in arithmetic and not other areas of achievement, I would argue, as Hewett et al. imply, that token reinforcement can be expected to facilitate learning, but that instructional programs will determine the *nature* of academic gains. Dalton, Rubino, and Hislop (1973), however, have reported results that in part contradict this view. They used the same arithmetic and language lessons with two matched groups of retarded children in an eight-week summer school program. One class received praise and tokens while the other group received social reinforcement alone. The children did *not* differ on measures of in-class behavior. My prediction would be that since the lessons were the same and the children appeared to be equally attentive to them, academic gains would be similar. Gains were similar in language skills, but only the token group improved significantly in arithmetic. Therefore, tokens, possibly because of the counting, ordering, and so on involved (Hewett et al., 1969), apparently do contribute to acquisition of numerical skills.

A study by Baker, Stanish, and Fraser (1972) deserves comment because of its blending of group and individual research strategies and the use of a control group, which has both practical and informational advantages over the "conventional methods" group frequently employed. Baker et al. established a classroom for 4- to 7-year-old severely and moderately retarded "problem" children with the aim of preparing them for regular special-education classes. The procedures in the experimental class included dispensing poker chips, which were exchangeable for toys, sweets, and snacks, and time out (TO)—placing a child in a separate small room for 5 minutes when tantrums and other misbehavior occurred. Ten children of similar age and IQ who were *not* regarded as problems were selected as controls. They remained in their regular classes, which were located in five different schools. The daily schedules were the same in control and experimental classes, and all classes used volunteers, permitting 1:1 ratios of "adults" to pupils. Trained raters not connected with the program scored TV playbacks of the classes.

Within the experimental class, conditions were as follows: 5 weeks of baseline, 7 weeks of treatment with tokens and TO, 1 week of baseline, and 1 week of treatment. Thus, within the token class an ABAB experiment was conducted. The authors reported negative behavior in class over these conditions in the experimental class and over the corresponding period of time in the control classes. Negative behavior declined in the control classes to a large, but statistically nonsignificant, degree. The token group's negative behavior, in contrast, declined significantly after tokens were instated, and group members were significantly better behaved than the control subjects throughout the token period.

Baker et al.'s design permits, first, within-subject comparison of the effects of procedures with a baseline, which includes the effects of being removed from regular classes and placed in a special group. Second, between-subject comparisons control for the effects of time in conventional classes. Baker et al. have not compared their procedures with the "best" alternative classes, of course. It also would have been interesting to observe the effects of informing those responsible for the regular classes that the children being observed were behaving as poorly as the "problem" children. On the other hand, one cannot criticize Baker et al. for having picked a poor class or having designed a "straw man" to serve as a control. Without even considering the savings involved in having to establish only one classroom, I think their strategy has much to commend it.

Miller and Schneider (1970) also varied conditions within a token class while comparing before-and-after performance with a control group. Miller and Schneider's between-group comparison, unlike Baker et al.'s design is immediately subject to the criticism that the program was compared with the teaching of one teacher whose methods were not described.

These several replications give strong support to the value of token reinforcement to classroom management of pupils varying widely in functioning level. The results, when standardized measures of academic achievement are considered, are far less dramatic.

Performance during tests has also been shown to be influenced significantly by reinforcement (Ayllon & Kelly, 1972; Edlund, 1972). Ayllon and Kelly (1972) evaluated performance on the Metropolitan Readiness Test before and after 6 weeks of a token class and a "conventional" class. The interesting feature of their study is that the children were assembled in one group for testing, and at posttesting, half of the test was administered with token reinforcement and half without. The division was accomplished simply by presenting odd items in one condition and even items in the other. Although the pupils from the token class performed better than the control class at both sittings, the control subjects performed significantly better during token administration than they had without tokens. Unfortunately, token administration and order

were confounded. Nevertheless, the sensitivity of standardized tests to manipulations such as reinforcement should not pass unnoticed. The practical implications are especially striking in the study by Edlund (1972). He administered the Stanford-Binet twice to children whose mean IQ was 82 on the first testing. During the second test, 7 weeks later, one-half of the subjects were given M&Ms for correct responses. The control group, tested in the standard way, gained a median of 1 IQ point. Those earning M&Ms gained a median of 12 points; the mean IQ for the group became 94.

TOKEN REWARD VS. TOKEN COST

It has been a fairly standard, although controversial, practice to give tokens for appropriate behavior and also to take them away following instances of inappropriate behavior. Aside from data showing that one of Birnbrauer et al.'s boys studied more when token loss was in effect, empirical data have not been reported until recently (Burchard & Barrera, 1972; Kaufman & O'Leary, 1972). The study by Burchard and Barrera is described in a later section on control of aggressive behavior in wards.

Kaufman and O'Leary (1972) conducted an exemplary study—nicely done and completely reported. They organized two reading classes for adolescents in a psychiatric hospital. Throughout the study, the classroom rules were the same and the teacher attempted to shape and maintain appropriate behavior with differential social reinforcement. To check on this, her behavior was observed for 30 minutes of *each* 45-minute class meeting. The categories of teacher behavior recorded included praise, touches, reprimands, and attention to a student's work or question. The records show that she behaved in a remarkably consistent manner across phases in both classes. In one class the students could earn as many as 10 tokens per interval (reward class); in the other, they were given 10 tokens at the beginning of each interval and could lose as many (cost class). For the between-class comparison, the pupils had been assigned so that the groups were matched on CA, sex, diagnostic, WISC IQ, Wide Range Achievement Test grade levels, level of disruptive behavior in class, and the teacher's subjective ratings of the pupils.

The cost and reward procedures did not differ in effectiveness; both classes were significantly better behaved during token phases. The difference between the two systems was, it should be noted, entirely verbal. In the cost class, the teacher recited a pupil's offenses and took a token from the pupil's token container (located in the front of the room) for each offense. In the reward class, she recited positive behaviors and added tokens to the containers. The results, therefore, may not apply to situations in which pupils are given the tokens and then asked to return them. Nevertheless, Kaufman and O'Leary were technically correct in labeling this condition "cost." It is valuable to learn that one can emphasize verbally either positive or negative behavior and accomplish the desired ends so long as the payoff is the same to the pupils. Although Kaufman and O'Leary's students were not mentally retarded, I should think the results would be much the same for mentally retarded students.

MODELING, SOCIAL REINFORCEMENT, AND TOKENS

Studies which come close to the ideal design for comparing methods of instruction have been reported by Sheila and Dorothea Ross, who are systematically developing curricula for teaching cognitive and motor skills to young, mildly retarded children. The studies differ essentially from one to another in the objectives of training—social problem solving (S. Ross, 1969a), motor skills (S. Ross, 1969b), game skills and number concepts (D. Ross, 1970), listening skills (Ross & Ross, 1972), and problem solving and planning (Ross & Ross, 1973). In each study, the experimental method of instruc-

tion was a combination of modeling correct behavior, requiring that the children respond, and reinforcing correct behavior with stars backed up by prizes. Instruction was conducted for short sessions (30 minutes or less) to individuals or small groups outside of class for a period of 2 to 9 months. The control groups received identical periods of time outside of class and were given symbolic and tangible reinforcers while, for example, playing the same games (Ross, 1970) or hearing a "creative multimedia program" depicting the same social incidents (Ross, 1969a). In other words, the investigators attempted to match the children's experiences out of class in as many ways as possible except the systematic use of modeling and reinforcement. Replication with independent observation of the teachers' behavior during these sessions will be necessary to say how successful they were in accomplishing their aims, but one cannot help but be impressed by the care the authors displayed. Another feature of their studies was the administration of their tests to average subjects, thus permitting assessment of the social and academic significance of gain scores. Each study reported highly significant findings favoring the experimental group, and in the two instances in which data on average subjects were available, the mean performance of the retardates equalled and exceeded that of their peers of average intelligence.

In sum, Ross and Ross asked, "How effective will instruction based on modeling and reinforcement be with educable (mildly) retarded children?" and controlled for: (1) the effects of individual or small-group attention outside of class; (2) the effects of the regular teachers knowing who were and who were not experimental subjects; and (3) the effects of receiving tokens and tangibles. Ross and Ross did not control for effects of experimental bias, of course, since that would have required other investigators, and for possible effects of the examiners being familiar with the children's group assignment. On balance, the studies are exemplary, and it may be especially encouraging to know that such studies can be conducted in schools.

FREE TIME AND OTHER PRIVILEGES

Free time appealed to investigators as an alternative to tokens and edibles because it was much less costly and more acceptable to teachers, parents, and administrators. Also, since free time entailed a delay in reinforcement, it became a challenge to devise ways of providing immediate feedback to bridge the delay between behavior and back-up reinforcement. Wasik (1970) used check marks (tokens) to accomplish these ends. Sulzbacher and Houser (1968) provided the teacher with a display like a desk calendar that all of the children could see. Whenever a child offended by giving the "third finger salute" or making verbal reference to it, she flipped over a card which signaled loss of 1 minute. On the other hand, Osborne (1969) merely instructed the teacher to say, "You forgot, no break" when a child left her seat at an inappropriate time. Apparently, a number of procedures will be effective, as all of the studies report significant decreases in inappropriate behavior when the programs were in effect. Apparently, also, in keeping with the results of Kaufman and O'Leary (1972), the programs that have structured the rules in terms of loss for misbehavior have been as successful as those emphasizing gain for appropriate behavior.

Since the studies of this topic were straightforward ABAB or replicated AB designs, I will not discuss them further except to call attention to the variety of procedures investigators have used. Procedures ranged from careful administration of check marks signifying time earned in a specially planned classroom (Wasik, 1970) to teachers' ratings that were passed on from period to period, culminating in free time at the end of the school day (Greene & Platt, 1972), and teachers' ratings that parents exchanged for privileges after school (Edlund, 1971).

TIME OUT FROM POSITIVE REINFORCEMENT (TO)

In addition to loss of tokens and loss of special privileges in the future, response-contingent periods of social isolation (Birnbrauer et al., 1965; Lahey et al., 1973; Pendergrass, 1972), interruption and separation from the group (Zimmerman et al., 1969), and restraint (Perline & Levinsky, 1968) have been employed in experimental and regular classes for the retarded to suppress resistive and aggressive behavior. Birnbrauer et al. (1965) reported that use of the TO area was greater during the no-token phase of their study, a finding that is consistent with the rationale of seclusion, i.e., that seclusion be associated with a marked reduction in positive reinforcement. The study, however, had a major flaw: applications of TO, not the frequency of pupil behavior meeting the criteria for TO, were recorded by the teachers. Assuming reliable counting of TO, it is not trivial that the teachers used TO more frequently during the no-token phase; it may be, however, that a different interpretation is in order.

The contribution of TO to the success of token classes has been assessed in only one study (Perline & Levinsky, 1968). The "maladaptive" behavior (aggressive behavior, stealing, throwing, and out-of-seat behavior) of four disruptive, severely retarded children was observed in two classes per day for 20 days. The 20 days were allotted to three phases as follows: baseline consisting of "usual" procedures (5 days); tokens for two subjects, tokens *plus* restraint for two subjects (10 days); tokens for both groups (5 days). Maladaptive behavior declined dramatically in both groups with instatement of tokens, but no detectable differences was obtained between the restraint and no-restraint conditions. The authors, however, do not report how often, if at all, restraint was used, nor reliabilities of data.

Studies that have shown TO to be effective in decreasing inappropriate behavior in classes for the retarded have been conducted by Pendergrass (1972) and Lahey,

McNess, and McNess (1973). Pendergrass applied 2 minutes in a specially constructed booth to reduce the following behaviors: repeatedly banging toys on objects and people, and lip biting (S1); tearing string and autistic arm movements (S2). Using a multiple-response baseline, only one of the two behaviors was followed by TO, and the phases were arranged so that while one child was in the TO condition, the other was not. Since with S1, both behaviors decreased with TO, the multiple design was aborted, but the effect was replicated later. Lahey et al. (1973) found, in an ABAB design, suppression of an "obscene verbal tic," with 5 minutes of seclusion per offense or until the child had been quiet for 1 minute. Enforced practice of the tic previously had not been effective, and the procedure was highly aversive to teacher and others.

Pendergrass queried why TO affected the behavior of nonsocial children—time out from what? It is tempting to suggest that the effect was due to interruption of the activity and lack of opportunity to continue (assuming the toys and strings were taken away), but this explanation does not account for lip biting. TO is discussed more fully later in the section on aggressive behavior in wards. For a good discussion of methodological and theoretical problems, see Drabman and Spitalnik (1973).

TRANSFER AND MAINTENANCE

The lack of generalization or transfer of effects has plagued workers with the retarded of all persuasions, including behavior analysts. In the first within-subject experiment conducted, it was observed that behavior acquired during intervention extinguished when the procedures were discontinued; trainers found that quite good pupils were no longer good when the cup of M&Ms was not present. So every study that has reported recovery of baseline or that the effects were achieved with only the reinforced response in a multiple-response design was reporting that the effects were specific—did not generalize. From the perspective that behavior is a function of contingencies, such findings are to be expected.

One suggestion for effecting generalization, made by Patterson et al. (1965) and many others since then, is to strengthen behavior that the group will reinforce. In their study of a hyperactive 10-year-old, after observing the amount of time the boy did not attend, wiggled, and walked about the room, Patterson et al. taught him to attend to work by sounding a buzzer that signified he had earned a candy. This training was conducted outside of the classroom, but his behavior in class was observed prior to each session. Since no improvement in class was observed after 9 days, the apparatus was brought to class, and the child earned, by attending, candies and pennies for the entire class. His classmates were asked to assist. His behavior in the period preceding these sessions improved and remained at the new acceptable level during seven follow-up observations.

Patterson et al.'s interpretation of the results was that a hyperactive child is aversive to other children. By teaching him to be quieter and simultaneously involving the other children, his classmates began to interact with the subject and to reinforce appropriate behavior; the previous cycle of hyperactive-aggressive behavior leading to reduced reinforcement from peers was reversed. Buell, Stoddard, Harris, and Baer (1968), applying a similar rationale, taught a young child who was socially withdrawn to play on the nursery school's outdoor equipment. In addition to recording play, they also observed several types of social behavior. The result was an increase in outdoor play *and* social behavior, with the latter presumably being a product of the child's being brought closer to other children engaged in similar enjoyable activities. This principle, the "Relevance of Behavior Rule," is discussed by Ayllon and Azrin (1968, p. 49).

In another study of hyperactivity, Patterson (1965) was also successful in attenuating hyperactivity during pre-conditioning-session observations and suggested that the improved behavior was due to the presence of the observer/experimenter in the classroom. This explanation too, is plausible. Whitman, Caponigri, & Mercurio (1971) reduced hyperactivity first out of class and then within. At follow-up, 3 weeks later, the child's behavior was greatly improved.

I have wondered if the results of Patterson et al. were attributable in part to the fact that the observation periods immediately preceded conditioning. The authors did take precautions to avoid the child's discriminating that a session was due by having the observers view from behind a one-way screen and apparently scheduling sessions at different times of the day. It is nonetheless usually very difficult to eliminate all cues in nonlaboratory situations. (Observers make noise. Teachers show signs of anticipation, etc.) The hypothesis has been put to rest for me by Whitman, Burish, and Collins (1972), who scheduled test sessions after conditioning sessions. These investigators were interested in teaching two moderately retarded males to converse. They measured the effects of training in play sessions with two girls of similar age with an ABAB design. During A, the boys and girls were instructed to play while observers counted social and nonsocial verbalizations and social behavior. During B, the play sessions continued. In addition, an experimenter met with just the boys beforehand and reinforced conversation with tokens and approval. Conversational speech during test sessions varied with experimental condition. Of course, there are many variables to which these results might be attributed, but it is clear that order of training and test sessions did not seem to matter. In addition, the presence of the same observers in test and training sessions did not influence the results. (How much more informative this study would have been if instead of no sessions during A, the investigators had spent comparable amounts of time with the boys in other activities.) See

also Paloutzian, Hasazi, Striefel, and Edgar (1971).

Hislop, Moore, and Stanish (1973) describe briefly their strategy for ensuring improved behavior in regular classes. Disruptive, uncontrollable children were assigned to a token classroom in the morning while remaining in regular afternoon classes. Behavior was rated in both classes. In addition to shaping appropriate behavior in the token class, the investigators consulted with regular teachers and families. At followup, 3–6 months later, the children's behavior was very much improved. The report is too brief to be evaluated as an experiment but may be useful as a guide to establishing similar programs.

At the moment, the most certain way of effecting transfer and maintenance of gains is to modify the procedures employed in regular classes and fade out the degree of control in the special class. (Although it might appear more practical to not have special classes and modify the classes in the first instance, it is generally true that teachers and administrators have to be convinced that the results will be worth the effort. Also, it is usually too much to ask of teachers. They are quite apt to have referred a child after much trial, error, and grief, and thus have "had it." Gaining improved behavior in one situation does make the task much easier in a second, and in the future the teacher involved might employ more systematic procedures or ask for assistance sooner.)

Two other approaches to maintaining gains have been studied: self-evaluation and teaching pupils to differentially reinforce others. Self-evaluation, an aspect of self-control, has been suggested by many as a possible means of phasing out tokens or other externally controlled programs while maintaining improved behavior. In the final phase of Kaufman and O'Leary's (1972) investigation of token reward and token cost systems, the pupils decided how many tokens they had earned or lost. Self-evaluation was successful for the seven days in which it was used. Although it is unfortunate that the self-evaluation phase was so short, earlier in the study in like periods of time with no token reinforcement, the pupils' behavior had shown marked changes for the worse. Thus, the results were encouraging, but a recent replication has found quite the opposite (Santogrossi, O'Leary, Romanczyk, & Kaufman, 1973). These papers, together with Walker and Buckley (1972), warrant careful study and followup.

Rather than teach retardates to conform or place them in token classes and the like, Graubard, Rosenberg, and Miller (1971) set out to teach children in special classes to modify the behavior of peers and teachers. For example, if a student was regarded as a problem and the student felt that the teacher did not like him, the student was taught to reinforce positive teacher response by establishing eye-to-eye contact, nodding, thanking the teacher for help, and so on. Graubard et al. reported several successful cases. The beauty of the approach is that the pupils' behavior is changed for the better through instructions and role-playing, and maintenance is, as it were, built in through the modified teaching behavior. It would be naive to suppose that one experience would suffice for the pupils to apply the skills to other social problems, but a program to accomplish that would be well worth the effort.

Very little is known about effecting maintenance and transfer. In contrast to work with other populations and work with retardates in self-help skills, these problems do not seem to be receiving the attention they deserve in educational settings.

EFFECTS ON OTHER CHILDREN

Behavior modifiers frequently are asked about the effects of intervention on other children in the class, usually with concern that other children will be affected adversely. It has already been seen in Patterson's work that peers can be quite helpful in programs, at least when they share the rewards, but until recently no study has assessed the effects of reinforcing one retarded child on others in a position to observe. Two studies (Broden, Bruce, Mitchel, Canter, & Hall, 1970; Kazdin, 1973) using only praise found that both the praised and observing child improved. The studies were conducted in quite different ways, and their designs are worth detailed consideration.

Broden et al.'s subjects were two disruptive, mildly retarded boys in a second-grade class. Pupil attention to task and teacher attention to pupils were recorded. During baseline, the teacher followed usual procedures and was reported to have attended to the boys when their behavior was appropriate, about twice per 30 minutes. The boys were attending about 33% of the period. The teacher was then instructed to differentially attend to $S1$ but continue as usual with $S2$. The third phase consisted of the reverse, i.e., $S2$ was attended to differentially. In the fourth and fifth phases, the teacher was asked to resume baseline procedures for both boys and attend to both boys respectively. The results clearly support that the boy being reinforced attended considerably more often, and his peer increased also. It is noteworthy that overall attention to task levels became quite high with what appears to have been very little change in the teacher's behavior. Since she was also instructed to not attend when the boys were misbehaving, it is rather a pity that attention to misbehavior could not have been recorded also.

Broden et al. suggested the following reasons for the effect on the observer: (1) when the teacher praised she often approached the children, and proximity of teacher may well evoke "getting down to work"; (2) as one student became more industrious, he reinforced peer inattentiveness less often; and (3) modeling.

Kazdin (1973) conducted his study in such a way as to rule out each of the above explanations. He employed two pairs of children with one child of each pair as the target subject and the second as the observer. An experimenter sat with them throughout the study, thus controlling for hypothesis (1). In experimental phases, the experimenter delivered praise to the target subject without specifying the behavior being praised, i.e., "Good Mary." After a baseline phase, praise was dispensed to the target child contingent upon task attention. After reinstating baseline, praise was given to the same child contingent upon *inattention*, thus testing hypotheses (2) and (3). In the final phase, attention was again praised. The observing children were more attentive to task in each of the reinforcement phases than they were in baseline, despite the fact that the target subject's behavior remained at essentially baseline level when inattention evoked the experimenter's praise. The reader should find these papers by Broden et al. (1970) and Kazdin (1973), particularly the latter's discussion of the discriminative properties of reinforcement, provocative.

"GENERALIZED" ANTECEDENT STIMULUS CONTROL

The final dimension along which the effects of reinforcement training may generalize is to other behavior of the individual. As mentioned earlier, very often such generalization does not occur; the pupil seemingly learns only precisely what he is taught. For example, once a student has been taught through modeling, physical guidance, and reinforcement to emit a response such as raising his hand when hand raising is demonstrated by the teacher who simultaneously says "Do this," that experience could cause the pupil to scratch his left ear when the teacher scratches her left ear and says "Do this." Typically, however, the pupil *who requires training in handraising in response to the demonstration and instruction* will not scratch his left ear. He does nothing, fidgets, moves to get out of his chair, or raises his hand.

If the teacher continues and demonstrates left ear scratching, guides the child's hand to his own left ear, and reinforces differentially, the pupil will come to scratch his left ear to the verbal and physical demonstration. Then, if the teacher *raises her hand*, the pupil may do nothing or scratch his ear. The pupil has been taught again to make a specific response. If the teacher persists and teaches the child to scratch when she scratches and raise his hand when she raises her hand, the pupil learns this discrimination. With training in additional responses, the number of trials to learn a new response diminishes until the point is reached at which the child copies novel demonstrations on the first presentation. Furthermore, the pupil does so, and continues to do so, even though some responses do not earn reinforcement. This phenomenon was called "generalized imitation" by Baer and Sherman (1964); "generalized" because some responses were emitted correctly without ever having been taught or reinforced and "imitation" because the particular response the pupil made was controlled by the response that the teacher demonstrated. This discovery has generated a number of studies, for it has significant theoretical and practical implications. Much of this reasearch is summarized in Table 10-1.

From the point of view of theory, the phenomenon is puzzling because behavior that is consistently not reinforced should extinguish and because it is difficult to specify the dimension of generalization. That is, the child has learned "to do what the model does," a variety of topographically different acts. Several hypotheses have been suggested (Baer & Sherman, 1964; Bandura & Barab, 1971; Gewirtz & Stingle, 1968; Steinman, 1970a, 1970b) and have prompted some of the research. The finding is significant also because it demonstrated that imitation can be developed by operant principles as Skinner (1953, 1957) theorized. There need be, and actually is, no basis for dispute between advocates of modeling (Bandura, 1969) and operant theorists. The former have studied the conditions affecting imitation in those who have acquired the prerequisites. Generalized imitation procedures can be seen as a method for establishing the requisite skills.

I shall not discuss this research for two reasons. First, space does not permit doing justice to the topic. Second, in discussing the theoretical arguments I could obscure the main points, as often happens when findings are the subject of theoretical debate. The main points for applied investigators are: (1) The phenomenon occurs, and it has been replicated several times with subjects including average 2-year-olds (Whitehurst, 1971), severely retarded children, and a deaf 3-year-old (Bennet & Ling, 1972); (2) The procedures have been extended to situations in which verbal commands were used (e.g., Martin, 1971) and in which nonimitative behavior was reinforced (e.g., Peterson, 1968). Thus, the phenomenon is now more correctly called "generalized antecedent stimulus control" of which generalized imitation is just one form; (3) For the first time, we can describe a set of procedures for teaching severely retarded and seriously disturbed persons to imitate and follow instructions on first presentation. The training is tedious; it is not always successful and the effects are difficult to maintain (Browning, 1971; Lovaas, Koegel, Simmons, & Long, 1973); it requires 1:1 instruction, but fortunately nonprofessional persons have been found quite suitable (Guess, Rutherford, Smith, & Ensminger, 1970). My recommendation is that we exploit the considerable beginnings that have been made.

CONCLUSION

One can indeed effect dramatic changes in the classroom behavior of retardates with manipulation of response consequences. At this time, it seems absurd to even question the possibility of effecting such changes. One problem, maintenance of gains, has been discussed. Another problem is that

whereas class behavior has been affected in impressive ways, academic learning has not been. Grim, Bijou, and Parsons (1973) offer an answer. Ironically, the work takes us full circle to programmed instruction, analysis of task requirements, and reinforcement for the steps involved in problem solution. Grimm et al. had two children in their token class who were apparently diligent enough but made 40% or more errors in arithmetic. The teacher's practice was to intermittently check the pupils' work, giving praise and tokens for correct problems and offering help, e.g., modeling the steps to solution, as needed. To test the hypothesis that reinforcement was too delayed, the children were provided with tutors who gave tokens and praise as problems were completed correctly and who ignored incorrect solutions. Error rate did not change. In the next stage, the children were required to emit overtly each link in the chain of responses leading to correct solution. Verbal feedback such as "That's good counting," was given by the tutor when the component response was correct. When errors occurred, the tutor interrupted, modeled the correct response, and required the child to repeat the step until it was correct. The final response, the solution, earned praise and tokens as before. Solution responses, of course, immediately approached 100% correct. Then, the tutors gradually eliminated feedback for the presolution responses until the boys were making fewer than 10% errors with no feedback prior to the solution. After about eight sessions at this level, the tutors gave instructions to complete the problems and withdrew until completion or the study session was over, at which time problems were checked. Performance declined to approximately 80% correct. Additional experimental phases were conducted and the effects replicated.

My reasons for mentioning the study are to second Grimm et al.'s suggestion that task analysis receive renewed attention and to point out that their procedures were very similar to those used successfully by O'Brien and colleagues (O'Brien & Azrin, 1972; O'Brien, Bugle, & Azrin, 1972) to teach profoundly retarded children to feed themselves. This work is described in the next section.

Research in Wards

When psychologists began to explore the potential of behavior modification in training self-help and social skills on wards for the severely and profoundly retarded in 1963–64, they had entered unknown and unfriendly territory indeed. "Custodial" areas of institutions were visited rarely by professionals other than nurses and physicians, who usually visited as infrequently and quickly as possible. These wards were repositories for persons who could not be trained, and the function of attending staff was to maintain safe and clean surroundings. The absolute minimum of staff, furnishings, toys, and activities was provided, staff training was nil, staff turnover, very high, and morale, very low. (Although not as generally true now as then, these attitudes and conditions still predominate.) Such circumstances, obviously, do not lend themselves to research.

The first goal had to be to prove to oneself and local staff that training could be effective, and the first behaviors chosen were those most aversive to staff—eating habits and attending to toilet needs. The rationale was that a tidy child will be reacted to more positively and will have more opportunities to learn. Important contributing factors were Ellis' (1963) theoretical model, which provided guidelines for toilet training, and the fact that food, a potent reinforcer, gave a starting point for training in self-feeding. In other words, the need for such training was clear, and there were some ideas as to how to go about conducting the training.

At first, positive reinforcement, extinction, and careful instruction in small steps were emphasized. Punishment was con-

demned (Bensberg, 1965). But ward attendants continually confronted urgent problems that they could not avoid. Whereas educational programs were selective and teachers could send children back to their wards because of misconduct, ward attendants did not have these options. Consequently, and rather quickly, investigators were challenged to assist with the "truly difficult" cases—children who were self-injurious (Tate & Baroff, 1966) and assaultive and destructive (Hamilton, Stephens, & Allen, 1967). The urgency of the problems brought punishment into use. We find a large number of studies of punishment—seclusion, restraint, removal from the dining table, electric shock, and most recently "overcorrection" (Foxx & Azrin, 1972, 1973). The use of punishment is the major difference between research on wards and the research discussed in the previous section.

The research will be discussed by target behavior, e.g., self-initiated use of toilet and reduction of self-injurious behavior. This arrangement will permit one to see the variety of ways in which similar goals have been approached and measured. It does mean, though, that the reader interested in a particular set of procedures will find pertinent studies under each subheading.

STUDIES WITH MULTIPLE OBJECTIVES
(TABLE 10–2)

In these studies, groups of profoundly retarded boys and girls were selected to receive instruction in following simple commands, dressing, using utensils at meals, communication, and using the toilet. The trainers were selected attendants, with an interesting exception being the employment of "foster grandparents" (Gray & Kasteler, 1969). The method of teaching, usually 1:1, included instructions and modeling, tangible and social reinforcement for small bits of behavior, and extinction of inappropriate behavior. Improvement was mea-

TABLE 10–2   Selected studies of behavioral techniques to strengthen self-help and social behavior

Study	Subjects	Measure and Design	Duration	Comments
Bensberg, Colwell, & Cassell (1965)	7 profound ("lowest" on ward)	Mod. VSMS[a] monthly; 4 subjects in special unit; 3 transferred to special unit later	7 mos.; all day or 2 sessions/day	Large gains mostly in first month
Minge & Ball (1967)	6 profound (IQ 10–24)	Instruction following (11 behaviors) pre-mid-post; matched untreated controls	2 mos.; 2 sessions/day	Significant gains in E[b] group only; gains fast at first
Kimbrell, Luckey, Barbuto & Love (1967)	40 profound	VSMS pre-post; E groups and matched controls divided by age: Young—CA[e] 8 yrs.–8 mos.; Old—CA 14 yrs.–4 mos.	7 mos.; all day	SA[d] gain of 7 mos. (young) and 3.4 mos. (old). Significantly different from controls
Leath & Flournoy (1970)	33 profound	Follow-up assessment of Kimbrell et al.'s subjects	—	Non-significant changes
Gray & Kasteler (1969)	140 profound	VSMS pre-post; controls on same ward received increased attention only	1 year 4 hrs./day	Employed "foster grandparents"; both groups increased significantly; E & C[e] groups significantly different at posttest
Lawrence & Kartye (1971)	21 profound and severe	Cain-Levine Soc. Comp. Scale; training (B); no training (A); training (B) design	B—12 mos. A— 4 mos. B—10 mos.	Results varied among skills
Colwell, Richards, McCarver, & Ellis (1973)	47 profound and severe	Dressing, feeding, toileting scales, and Stanford-Binet pre-post	7 mos. (mean) 15 hrs./day	Short-stay residential facility; significant gains in all areas

a Modified Vineland Social Maturity Scale.
b Experimental.
c Mean chronological age.
d Average social age.
e Control.

sured by rating scales of dubious reliability. Of the studies in Table 10-2, only Colwell et al. (1973) reported reliability of the ratings.

The studies do not include adequate control groups. In one exception (Gray & Kasteler, 1969), control subjects resided on the same ward and thus received increased attention and opportunities. They were not, however, assigned "foster grandparents" to train them. The results were that the control subjects improved significantly over the year of the program, but the groups receiving special training improved significantly more. Other studies had no control groups (Bensberg et al., 1965; Colwell et al., 1973) or no treatment controls (Kimbrell et al., 1967; Minge & Ball, 1967), while Lawrence and Kartye (1971) conducted a within-group (ABA) study.

Thus, it does not require a very experienced eye to criticize these studies as experiments. It should be remembered, however, that their purpose was to demonstrate that children of the level of functioning sampled could be taught. That purpose was served, although the gains were modest and, as Leath and Flournoy (1970) found in their assessment of children three years after training, continued improvement could not be expected.

The study by Colwell et al. (1973) is noteworthy on several counts. First, the data were obtained in a short-stay facility housing 32 children, which was designed to permit observation for the collection of data and training. The building seems to be a model that all states would do well to adopt (see also Fingado, Kini, Stewart, & Redd, 1970). Second, impressive gains were realized. The average gain in MA, for example, was 3.36 mos over an average stay of 7.1 mos. Third, the reliability of the scales used was analyzed in two ways: (1) the standard method in which two raters score the same sequence and (2) comparisons of scores obtained by judges who observed different samples of behavior, i.e., on two different days. The latter, in that it gives

a measure of stability and reflects the way in which the scales would be used most often, strikes me as a very valuable additional piece of information. Since the authors make no mention of the fate of these youngsters after graduation, we must hope that provisions have been made for continued training and await further reports.

TOILET TRAINING (TABLE 10-3)

Standard practice on custodial wards, believe it or not, was (still is in many institutions) to "potty" the residents *en masse* on a schedule such as on awakening, before and/or after meals, and before retiring. The doors to the toilet area were locked at other times. Residents who wet or soiled their beds were awakened periodically and sent to the toilet. Accidents were quite frequent. For example, Levine and Elliott (1970) counted an average of 22.8 accidents per week on wards housing 103 profoundly retarded children and adults.

Essentially two methods of obtaining daytime bladder and bowel control have been studied. The first is a method similar to that used by parents to toilet train: the child is placed on the toilet at times when the child is most likely to go, praised and perhaps rewarded with tangibles for going, and reprimanded, punished physically, or ignored when accidents occur. It is not, however, possible to totally ignore accidents, for the child does need changing and washing. In wards, where children generally receive very little attention, how to react to accidents was considered of crucial importance. The procedures used included a minimum of 15 minutes between accident and changing (Baumeister & Klosowski, 1965), reprimands (Hundziak et al., 1965), restraint (Giles & Wolf, 1966), and shaking, reprimand, "overcorrection," and 1 hour TO (Azrin & Foxx, 1971).

Studies using this method (Dayan, 1964; Baumeister & Klosowski, 1965; Hundziak et al., 1965; Giles and Wolf, 1966; Levine

TABLE 10-3   Representative studies of toilet training

Study	Subjects	Measure and Design	Duration	Comments
Baumeister & Klosowski (1965)	11 profound	"Hits & misses"; AB; training—scheduling; hits: tangible reinforcement; misses: 15 min. in wet/soiled clothes[a]	A—30 days B—70 days	Demonstration program
Hundziak, Maurer, & Watson (1965)	29 severe & profound. Random assignment to 3 groups	C[b] group—no treatment; E[c] groups-scheduling; "hits": tangible or social reinforcement only; "misses"; scolding (?)	14 days of adaptation; 27 days of training	"Hits" increased in tangible-reinforcement group. "Misses" did not decline. Successful transfer to ward
Giles & Wolf (1966)	5 profound	"Hits"—self-initiated and when scheduled. AB case studies	A—30 days B—60 days	Procedures tailored to subject
Van Wagenen, Meyerson, Kerr, & Mahoney (1969)	8 profound	Wet-alarm pants; "forward" training	≤15 days (45 hours)	Demonstration
Mahoney, Van Wagenen, & Meyerson (1971)	3 average CA—20 mos. 5 profound to moderately retarded; parent referred	Modifications of above; baseline, training, followup	A—5 days B—≤48 hours	Clear description of procedures
Levine & Elliott (1970)	103 profound	Misses; scheduling & behavior shaping	10 weeks	Demonstration on ward with limited staff
Azrin & Foxx (1971)	9 profound	Wet-alarm pants; automatic "toilet-chair," etc.; maintenance procedures	A—3 days, B—≤ 14 days; maintenance—140 days	Incontinence eliminated
Sloop & Kennedy (1973)	42 profound; matched & randomly assigned to 2 groups	Wet nights; C group—scheduled potting; E group—buzzer pad apparatus	A—7 nights B—to criterion	50% of E group, 5% of C group met criterion; 33% dry at follow-up

a The design was Baseline-Training (AB) with hits and misses recorded. Training consisted of potting child at times when elimination was probable (scheduling). Elimination was followed by tangible reinforcer, and accidents were ignored with changing taking place 15 min. later.

b Control.

c Experimental.

& Elliott, 1970; Azrin & Foxx, 1971) reported success in at least increased "hits" (urination or defecation in toilet) and/or decreased "misses." As an indication of what may be accomplished under "normal" ward conditions, the weekly rate of accidents in the Levine and Elliott study declined from 22.8 to 9.4 in 10 weeks. At the other extreme, Azrin and Foxx (1971) obtained 80% reduction after 1–14 days of very intensive (8 hours per day) training in which (1) moisture-sensitive pants signalled accidents; (2) toilet chairs signalled urination/defecation; (3) edible and social reinforcers were dispensed at 5-minute intervals if person was dry and after elimination in toilet; (4) pottying was scheduled every 30 minutes for 20 minutes or until voiding occurred, whichever came first; (5) dressing/undressing was shaped; and (6) fluids were offered every 30 minutes.

Prior to the work of Azrin and Foxx (1971) and Azrin, Bugle, and O'Brien (1971), a number of difficulties with the scheduling method had been noted. Aside from the time required and the fact that it often failed, teaching urination/defecation by placing a person on the potty does not teach self-initiated use of the toilet. According to parents, this step "just happens" as it did with one of Giles and Wolf's (1966) five subjects. (These authors recorded both "hits" and self-initiated toilet behavior; achieving self-initiated behavior required additional procedures in four of the five cases.) A second major difficulty, particularly with persons whose pattern of elimination is unpredictable, is arranging schedules so as to maximize the likelihood of elimination in the toilet. Frequent placement on the toilet supplemented by suppositories and control of liquid and food consumption appears necessary. In the Azrin and Foxx plan, a child could have spent as much as 5 hours of the 8-hour training period seated on the toilet. Finally, although Hundziak et al. (1965) reported transfer of training after their subjects returned to

their ward, other studies could not substantiate that transfer had been obtained.

What Azrin and Foxx have done is take all of these factors into consideration and constructed a "total push" package for training *and* maintenance that worked. The procedures are no doubt tedious for the attendants, but this short-term investment should be more than repaid in long-term gains. The procedures also involve more aversive consequences than those described, at least for some residents, because "over-correction" pursuant to accidents includes having the child undress, bathe, clean the soiled area, and wash the soiled pants. Many retardates, particularly at the profound level, do not comply when merely asked to perform such duties.

The second method has been developed by Van Wagenen and his associates (Van Wagenen, Meyerson, Kerr & Mahoney, 1969; Van Wagenen & Murdock, 1966; Mahoney, Van Wagenen, & Meyerson, 1971). Van Wagenen et al. (1969) argued that the scheduling method is backward and proposed instead that the chain of responses (from urge-to-eliminate through elimination in the right place) be trained as one pattern of behavior beginning with the cues to eliminate. They also used moisture-sensitive pants, but when the tone sounded, the trainer shouted "No," thereby, it was hoped, momentarily stopping urination, and quickly took the child to the toilet where urination continued or resumed. The child was then reinforced. After a number of these trials, the next step was to fade out the trainer's participation until the tone was sufficient to evoke the chain. The final step was to teach anticipation of urination and eliminate the tone. In their 1969 paper, Van Wagenen et al. demonstrated that the method had promise. Eight profoundly retarded youngsters were assigned three at a time to a room adjacent to the toilets for 3–4 hours a day. High liquid consumption was induced. All were trained within about 45 hours (15 days) to respond to the tone by going to the toilet and urinating. The authors described several problems that they encountered. The major ones to me were eliminating dependence upon the tone and maintaining the behavior.

Mahoney et al. (1971) demonstrated a variation that seems more efficient. As in the earlier study, the pants alarm was used, and the children were trained in small groups near the toilets. In the first phase, however, the tone was controlled remotely by the trainer, and going to the toilet, lowering pants, and assuming the appropriate stance in response to the tone were taught. That is, the experimenter sounded the tone and with verbal and physical prompts taught the child to move to the toilet, where he was reinforced and the trial ended. When that behavior was reliable, reinforcement was withheld until pants were lowered. After the child learned to assume the correct position with pants lowered to the sound of the tone without prompting, liquids were offered frequently and urinating in the toilet was added as a requirement for reinforcement. When this sequence was achieved, the auditory signal was eliminated. Success was measured in a 3-day posttest during which time the parents received instruction in the procedure. Terminal performance defined as "Walk to commode, lower pants, urinate in commode, pull pants. *No* prompts or auditory signal." (p. 178) was obtained by seven of their eight subjects in 17–48 hours. These seven made a total of four errors in the 3-day posttests. (The eighth subject urinated frequently but only a few drops at a time. "Dribbling" might be an insufficient stimulus for both the moisture detector and the child.) Followup was inadequate for any conclusion about long-term gains. So, on that count we shall have to wait, although there is every reason to believe that a maintenance program will be necessary.

As yet, neither method has been replicated by independent investigators and, of course, the two methods have not been

compared experimentally. Given the available information and guessing that Azrin and Foxx' subjects were not as "bright" or as cooperative as Mahoney et al.'s, Azrin and Foxx' approach has the advantages of being faster and effective in all cases. In addition, the package included an explicit long-term maintenance program and was effective in reducing soiling by over 90%. Another factor to be considered is that Mahoney et al. gave no assurance that their records of responding were reliable. Nevertheless, I hope that the "forward" method is followed up and refined, for the amount of time required was not appreciably greater and the procedures apparently were much less aversive to trainers and trainees alike.

Nocturnal bladder and bowel control, although a serious problem, has received little attention in the literature. I would suggest that the reasons are simply that investigators do not like working at night, and the night shifts in institutions are drastically understaffed. As I mentioned earlier, a common procedure is to awaken enuretic residents periodically and send them to the toilet with the expectation that wet and soiled linen will be reduced and possibly residents will become continent. In unpublished work, my colleagues and I kept reasonably reliable records of bedwetting for about a year on one ward and found that the method was not even effective in minimizing bed changes.

Two approaches have been studied experimentally—Mowrer and Mowrer's (1938) pad and buzzer conditioning apparatus, and teaching retention during the day.

The pad and buzzer technique has been evaluated by Sloop and Kennedy (1973). They obtained what they considered disappointing results with two groups (11 males and 10 females). In comparison with 21 untreated control subjects matched for frequency of wet nights, age, and IQ, the number of residents meeting their criterion of 13 dry nights was statistically significant (1 Control vs. 11 Experimental subjects) but

4 of the 11 successful subjects relapsed within 36 to 72 days. Thus, in the long term, 33% of the treated group remained dry. These results need not be taken as reason to give up. A 50% return in 11 weeks, in the absence of alternatives, is excellent, and relapses might have been prevented had the apparatus been left in place. As Sloop and Kennedy say, the method is economical, but the indications are that additional methods are needed. The second method has been developed by Kimmel and colleagues (Kimmel & Kimmel, 1970; Paschalis, Kimmel, & Kimmel, 1972) and consists simply of prompting the child to report when he needs to urinate during the day and instructing him to wait—briefly at first and then for longer periods. In the controlled study by Paschalis et al., impressive results were obtained. It seems reasonable that this training supplemented by the buzzer and pad apparatus would be more efficient than either used alone.

It seems to me that we now have techniques for toilet training even the most profoundly retarded persons and have entered a stage of refinement, implementation, and maintenance.

SELF FEEDING (TABLE 10–4)

Mealtimes in custodial wards can be unbelievably chaotic. The residents feed themselves by hand or more directly by face to plate, steal food from each other, throw and spill food and utensils, and make quite a mess of themselves and the dining room in the process. The resident-to-staff ratio, usually higher than 10:1, is often worse than it sounds because staff are occupied in feeding those who are physically disabled, who refuse to eat, and who are in physical restraints. Crisis intervention and cleaning up occupy the remainder of staff's time.

No one questioned that backward chaining and manual guidance, i.e., guiding the child's hand in filling the utensil (spoon) and in bringing the spoon to the mouth, releasing just prior to spoon in mouth, and in gradual steps relaxing the guidance further and further from the mouth (Bensberg, 1965), was the method of training to use. The major problems were: (1) arranging the 1:1 instruction that certainly would be necessary at first; (2) choosing methods for reacting to errors, thievery, and the like; (3) providing for maintenance of training; and (4) designing practical and sensitive recording systems. Positive reinforcement, food, was built in and supplemented by praise and touch. But it must be noted, the residents' methods of eating were swifter and surer ways of procuring the food. Thus, it should not be surprising that the emphasis in the studies in Table 10–4 was upon reactions to inappropriate behavior.

Although one can question the reliability of the data in all of the studies except those by Azrin's group (Azrin & Armstrong, 1973; O'Brien, Bugle, & Azrin, 1972) and Barton, Guess, Garcia, and Baer (1970), the studies taken together demonstrate the following: (1) Short-term interruption of eating will effectively suppress errors and inappropriate behavior. Several variations of procedures have been employed. Barton et al. (1970) removed the plate for 15 seconds for offenses other than stealing, which was followed by removal from the dining room. Stealing was so treated because removing the offender's plate would in no way interfere with the act of stealing. Other studies suggest less drastic remedies, however. Martin, McDonald, and Omichinski (1971) withdrew the child's chair from the table for 15 seconds and Henrikson and Doughty (1967) said "bad" and quickly held the child's hands. It appears that the least punitive and intrusive procedure, namely, interruption of the act alone, is sufficient. Implementation obviously does require 1:1 training, however. (2) Maintenance programs must be included (Groves & Carroccio, 1971; O'Brien, Bugle & Azrin, 1972). O'Brien and Azrin (1972) have provided one model with data supporting its effectiveness. (3) Punishment for errors, regardless of

TABLE 10-4 Selected studies of training in self-feeding

Study	Subjects	Measure and Design	Duration	Comments
Hamilton & Allen (1967)	59 profound & severe	Inapprop. meal behavior, AB; removal from dining room (DR)	A—7 days B—50 days 1 yr. later	60/day reduced to 10/day in 7 days; typical ward conditions
Henrikson & Doughty (1967)	4 profound	E's "interruptions"; social reinforcement and holding hand down 1:1	11 wks. + 2 wks. transfer to DR	Demonstration
Zeiler & Jervey (1968)	1 profound (previously tied while fed)	Self-feeds & aided spoonful; 1:1 shaping	46 meals 14 mos. followup	Demonstration
Barton, Guess, Garcia, & Baer (1970)	16 profound & severe	Several behaviors; multi-R design; removal from DR; 15-sec. plate removal	120 meals	Reliable data; clear results
Groves & Carroccio (1971)	24 severe & profound	Utensil used & hands in food; removal from DR; 10-sec. plate removal; usual DR conditions	14 weeks	Demonstration with limited staff
Martin, McDonald, & Omichinski (1971)	4 profound	4 deceleration targets; ABAB; social reinforcement; 15-sec. chair removal	100 meals	Employed student trainers
O'Brien, Bugle, & Azrin (1972)	1 profound outpatient	Precisely defined self-feeds with spoon; interruption & manual guidance	Five 4-min. meals/day; 66 meals	Demonstrates need for maintenance program
O'Brien & Azrin (1972) Exp. 1	6 E[a], 5 C[b] profound-to-mild adults	Errors; manual guidance; interruptions & "no"; 30-sec. plate removal; pre- and posttests & followup	Exp. 1: 2 meals of training	All experimental subjects improved; maintenance program
O'Brien & Azrin (1972) Exp. 2	6 E, 6 C profound-to-moderate adults		Exp. 2: Ca. 9 meals	
Azrin & Armstrong (1973)	11 E, 11 C profound; average comparison group	Same as above & overcorrection for errors	Nine 15-min. meals/day for E ≤ 12 days	Level attained equivalent to average groups

[a] Experimental
[b] Control

the form it takes, will not suffice in all cases. O'Brien, Bugle, and Azrin (1972) in a very nice experiment repeatedly measured effects by following training trials with unguided test trials. After baseline, "interruption-extinction" was used to prevent handfeeding. The child, rather than turning to using the spoon, simply stopped. In a subsequent phase, interruption-extinction and manual guidance were combined with success.

As with toilet training, Azrin's group has organized a very efficient "total effort" package that incorporates the best features of earlier work and thinking about the problems of training in self-feeding. A unique aspect is their conducting the training in several short sessions per day. One can imagine a cadre of specially trained teachers to bring eating habits to the level desired or to assist parents in doing so. Ward staff and parents could then implement the simpler maintenance programs. Frequent short sessions reduce the likelihood of teacher and child fatigue (the training is strenuous!) while ensuring that the trainees are not deprived of food, allowed to feed themselves in their preferred ways, or fed by staff at other times.

OTHER SELF-HELP SKILLS AND SOCIAL BEHAVIOR

Ward training programs in a wide variety of other skills have been described and studied experimentally. With the exception of language training, which for the most part has been studied in the context of "generalized antecedent stimulus control," other areas have received only sporadic attention and therefore will not be discussed.

AGGRESSIVE BEHAVIOR, SELF-INJURIOUS BEHAVIOR, AND RUMINATION

Like other people, retardates throw tantrums, assault others, and hit themselves, when they are deprived of desired objects, attention, and activities, when they are con-

fronted by situations in which previously they have suffered failure, deprivation, and punishment, and when they are attacked or taunted. Much of this behavior is normal in the sense that the contingencies are understandable and the behavior can be managed once an analysis of the behavior has been conducted. Thus, the literature on management of behavior with other groups is applicable to the majority of retardates, and one usually need not resort to the special techniques to be discussed in this section. Treatment, consisting of relatively simple, consistently applied procedures, has been successful even though the behavior had been occurring for some time and was very unpleasant. Three examples of what I mean follow:

1. Wolf, Birnbrauer, Williams, and Lawler (1965) suspected from its pattern of occurrence that a child's vomiting was escape from, or avoidance of, school and other situations. Thus, the program called for the child to be sent to school despite vomiting and to remain in school no matter what the rate of vomiting was. In time, vomiting ceased and the student took part in class activities. (The classroom was one in which the teacher reinforced appropriate behavior liberally with attention and edibles.) There probably were more efficient tactics that could have been, and probably would have to be, used, because not many teachers would be willing or able to tolerate the program. Nevertheless, the behavior was lawful and responded as it should have, if the analysis of its causes was correct.

2. Wiesen and Watson (1967) provide another instructive illustration. Paul, a severely retarded institutionalized boy, continually "hung around" adults, untied their shoe laces, and grabbed, pulled, and hit them. During baseline, approximately 120 such incidents were reported per day. The authors judged this behavior to be "attention-seeking," and it no doubt was "attention-getting." Their plan consisted of steps to ensure minimal adult response and to increase interaction with peers. Intervention consisted of "No" and nothing more if Paul stopped. On the other hand, if he repeated, he was placed outside the cottage door for 5 minutes. In addition,

the staff arranged for another child to give Paul M&Ms when Paul approached him. (The accomplice received M&Ms as well.) In 21 days, the rate declined to fewer than 5 incidents per day.

3. Webster and Azrin (1973) described successful use of 2 hours of bedrest to significantly reduce long-standing aggressive, self-injurious, and other aversive behaviors of severely and profoundly retarded adults. During baseline, extended periods of bedrest were administered on a response-independent schedule to test the effects of rest as a general calming influence. An average rate of seven incidents per day was recorded for the eight subjects. Within 5 days of requiring 2 hours rest contingent upon incidents, the mean rate declined to 0.2 per day. It remained at that level for 75 days, and the authors reported that since the patients' behavior had improved greatly, they were visited more often, and some were released from the institution. Very wisely, Webster and Azrin rigged the beds so that if the residents moved off the bed an alarm sounded. Without that, the procedure obviously would be impractical in most wards.

Clearly, as Webster and Azrin comment, the method could not be used with persons who would not stay in bed when instructed. In that case, what does one do? In the cases of Paul and Laura, suppose they had run away or endangered themseves or others? (Paul had ample opportunity to do so. Fortunately he did not, although he did strip and soil himself, for which Wiesen and Watson added 3 minutes to his time outside.) Once aversive behavior becomes strong, parents and institutional staff often find themselves one or more steps behind, and, inevitably, in every institution, there are some residents who are physically restrained all of the time and/or are drugged to the gills because of uncontrollable behavior, whose teeth have been pulled because the residents bit others or themselves, and whom staff are both afraid to be near and afraid to leave alone with other residents. Such persons were the subjects of the studies in Table 10–5.

As can be seen from the table, the aversive consequences used have been shock, isola-tion, physical restraint, slaps, and "overcorrection." In most cases, differential reinforcement of other behavior (DRO) was also reportedly used, but I have included that only when the authors described what was dispensed and the schedule.

PARAMETERS OF TO.   Restraint or seclusion (TO) has been applied upon occurrence of the target behavior for 1 minute to 2 hours, with provision in some cases for extension of the time if the subject was not quiet or was in other ways being uncooperative at the end of the elapsed time. (I wonder if experimenters actually have released subjects who were misbehaving when the time was up. That is, have they simply omitted mention of extending the time?)

Two studies of the relationship between length of TO and effectiveness have been reported. White, Nielsen, and Johnson (1972) compared 1, 15, and 30 minutes of TO with 20 severely and moderately retarded children whose average age was 11 years, 6 months. The behaviors included the full range—aggressive behavior, self-injurious behavior, tantrums, and running away. The children were divided randomly into three groups, the treatment of each group differing in the order of exposure to the three TO intervals. After baseline (no TO), one group, for example, received 1 minute TO, baseline, 30 minutes TO, baseline, 15 minutes TO, and finally baseline. The individual results included all possible combinations of effects. For the group as a whole, the two longer TO intervals were significantly more effective than the 1 minute TO, but there was an order effect. The 1 minute TO was as effective with the group who was exposed to it first; in the other two groups, 1 minute TO increased the number of deviant behaviors.

Subject characteristics, e.g., social age, did not correlate with success, nor was response related to baseline levels. The authors make no mention of relationship between type of behavior subjected to TO and effectiveness, possibly because of small

TABLE 10–5   Selected studies of suppression of aggressive, self-stimulatory, and self-injurious behavior and rumination

Behavior/Study	Contingencies
ASSAULTIVE/DESTRUCTIVE BEHAVIOR	
Hamilton, Stephens, & Allen (1967)	30–120 min. in restraint chair
Birnbrauer (1968)	shock
Bostow & Bailey (1969)	2 min. in seclusion room; DRO[a]
Vukelich & Hake (1971)	up to 120 min. in restraint chair; DRO
White, Nielsen, & Johnson (1972)	1, 15, or 30 min. in seclusion room
Foxx & Azrin (1972)	30 min. "restitution training" (overcorrection)
SELF-INJURIOUS (SIB)/SELF-STIMULATORY BEHAVIOR	
Tate & Baroff (1966)	shock and 3 sec. TO from contact
Hamilton, Stephens, & Allen (1967)	30—120 min. in restraint chair
Peterson & Peterson (1968)	positive reinforcement (DRO)
Risley (1968)	shock
Lovaas & Simmons (1969)	extinction; shock
Whaley & Tough (1970)	shock punishment and shock avoidance
Corte, Wolf, & Locke (1971)	shock; DRO; extinction
Thomas & Howard (1971)	whirlpool baths and perceptual motor training; disapproval and TO from physical contact
White, Nielsen, & Johnson (1972)	1, 15, or 30 min. in seclusion room
Foxx & Azrin (1973)	DRO; slaps; overcorrection
RUMINATION	
White & Taylor (1967)	shock
Luckey, Watson, & Musick (1968)	shock
Kohlenberg (1970)	shock of anticipatory stomach contractions

a Differential reinforcement of other behavior.

numbers and/or low reliability of the categories. (The dependent variable analyzed was total deviant behavior; only reliability of total scores was reported.) Although the study is of theoretical interest and practically valuable in that it demonstrated that 15 minutes was as effective as 30 minutes for all three groups, the individual results, it should not be overlooked, clearly say that placing children in seclusion contingent upon offenses will not only be ineffective in suppressing some behavior but will also worsen behavior in some cases.

Burchard and Barrera (1972) compared 5 minutes TO, 30 minutes TO, and response costs of 5 and 30 tokens. Their subjects were mildly retarded "delinquent" adolescents who resided in a token economy cottage. It was a complex study with results that I have difficulty interpreting. (The number of differences in design, especially the baseline conditions, which included both 5 minutes TO and 5 token response cost, make comparisons with White et al. 1972, impossible.) The authors concluded that the longer interval and higher response cost were equally effective and significantly more effective than the lower values of TO and response cost with five subjects. The opposite relationships held for their sixth subject. Since they replicated each condition with each subject, Burchard and Barrera were able to observe that the higher values of each increased in effectiveness across exposures, whereas the lower values remained at essentially the level obtained initially. Anyone interested in analyzing TO should first study these papers by Burchard and Barrera (1972) and White et al. (1972) carefully. Both have very nice features.

At this time, how long TO intervals should be to be effective and under what circumstances is an entirely open question. Although Burchard and Barrera and White et al. both found that the shorter intervals were, in general, least effective, there are reasons for believing that the duration of TO, beyond some minimum to allow the offender and staff to "cool off," is not as important a variable as others. Indeed, it may eventuate that duration is completely unimportant. In studies of self-feeding, the important feature seemed to be consistent interruption of the behavior. It should be noticed also that in the dining room, the trainers had clearly defined alternative behaviors to teach and immediately after the brief interruption resumed instruction *in those alternative behaviors*. My hunch is that the most effective plan involving TO is to quickly interrupt offensive behavior, return the offender to the scene as soon as he "calms down," and model and reinforce-alternative behaviors as is done in be-

havioral rehearsal, role-playing, and some forms of overcorrection. This recommendation is admittedly difficult to implement and, with assaultive persons, not without risks to staff and others. It may be necessary to conduct rehearsal of alternative behavior at a somewhat later time, perhaps involving other persons and settings at first.

Other parameters of TO have not been studied with retardates. Hamilton, Stephens, and Allen (1967) state that TO seemed most effective in cases presenting a single problem behavior, less effective with behavior that varied in frequency and intensity, and least effective when a variety of aversive behaviors was emitted. The relationship has not been reported by others, but it makes sense. Insofar as a single class of behavior can be better defined and its occurrence predicted, treatment ought to be applied more consistently and immediately, thus enabling faster learning. Hamilton et al. also raised a question, which applies no matter which punishing consequence is in use, with a subject presenting multiple aversive responses: Does one apply the consequence to one class at a time or to all responses from the outset?

TO vs. SHOCK. The effectiveness of TO has been contrasted with that of shock in two studies. Risley (1968) reported that seclusion administered by the parent at home had no effects upon his subject's climbing, despite reasons for supposing that parental attention was maintaining the dangerous behavior. Shock used subsequently resulted in nearly complete suppression in the situation in which it was applied. In an extended study of the self-injurious behavior of a blind autistic boy, Sam, Tate and Baroff (1966) first tested the efficacy of 3 seconds of TO in the form of silence and discontinuation of physical contact in an ABAB design. The data were gathered while Sam was walking with two assistants. During A, face slapping was ignored. During TO phases (B), the assistants immediately and abruptly released their hands and remained out of contact until 3 seconds of no SIB had elapsed. During the first phase of five TO sessions, the SIB rate was substantially lower (0.1 responses per minute in contrast to 6.6 during baseline), and there seemed to be some carryover of effect when ignoring was reinstated. The second exposure to TO was not as effective. In view of the seriousness of the behavior, total suppression was the aim. Hence, shock was employed with quite dramatic success. The report was written after 167 days of the shock program, and the last 20 days had been SIB free. Although neither of these studies was a convincing demonstration, others have reported similar experiences.

TO vs. Overcorrection. TO and overcorrection have not been compared systematically, although Foxx and Azrin (1972) included TO among the treatments that had failed prior to their successful use of overcorrection. A careful analysis of TO and overcorrection would be valuable. TO, if administered according to the rationale proposed originally, consists of removing an individual from opportunities for positive reinforcement. After the time has been served, positive reinforcement in conjunction with training and other activities is resumed until the next offense occurs. Overcorrection involves a period of very close contact with a trainer during which the patient engages in work, such as cleaning, in "restitution overcorrection," or exercises in the case of "positive practice overcorrection" (Foxx & Azrin, 1972, 1973). During overcorrection, the patient is forcibly prevented from emitting offensive behavior and physically guided through the appropriate behavior as necessary.

The two methods are alike in interrupting and temporarily preventing offensive behavior (except, of course, if the behavior is self-stimulatory and can continue in TO). They are different in that overcorrection often uses the period of time to train alternative appropriate behavior. The two methods are obviously different in the demands upon trainers. It is conceivable that the outcome of analysis would include, first, that overcorrection is indicated if the behavior functions to prevent demands, contact, and attention, i.e., is avoidance behavior. TO, under those circumstances, would constitute positive reinforcement. Second, the two procedures in immediate succession might be more effective than either one alone. Indeed, since shock immediately stops the target behavior and often results in patients being quite attentive (Lovaas & Simmons, 1969; Risley, 1968; Tate & Baroff, 1966), the combination of shock and overcorrection might be most efficient.

Shock Punishment. The results with electric shock administered upon each occurrence of unwanted behavior have been quite consistent across the behaviors to which it has been applied—aggressive behavior, SIB, and rumination—and may be summarized by reference to Corte, Wolf, and Locke (1971). (1) The behavior, often, is suppressed almost completely in the first session. (2) The results usually are limited to the situation or situations in which shock was administered and to the presence of the person who administered it or the presence of the shock device. (3) Situational and person generality can be increased by administering the shock in a number of different circumstances. (4) The negative side-effects of punishment that were anticipated have not materialized, although if the patient is free to fight and flee, he may well do so, as has been my experience, and that can be a problem. Several authors have reported positive "side-effects" instead (Lovaas & Simmons, 1969; Risley, 1968; Tate & Baroff, 1966; Whaley & Tough, 1970). (5) Long-term maintenance programs are necessary. Kohlenberg (1970), who has conducted the most careful study of the application of shock to eliminate rumination, followed the case for about a year. During the 10-month ward program, the child was gaining weight, and shock had not been used for five months. Nevertheless, the report ends with the statement, "vomiting appears to have become a problem again" (Kohlenberg, 1970, p. 245). It should be noted that although investigators using shock have emphasized the specificity of efforts, and rightly so, it is doubtful that the effects are *more* specific than those obtained with other approaches. That is, it has become an accepted fact of life among behavior modifiers that generality and maintenance must be programmed—somehow.

An alternative method of using shock was described in a brief case report by Whaley and Tough (1970). Their subject pounded his head and ears and was consequently in continual restraints when they entered the case. After reducing the rate significantly with response-contingent shocks, they used shock to train clutching toys, a response incompatible with SIB. That is, shock was administered independently of SIB, and the child's hand was guided to a toy, at which time shock ceased. The child rapidly learned to hold the toy and avoid shock; other toys were substituted without difficulty. "Several months" after the program was terminated, the boy was still completely free of restraint. active, and making progress in social and self-help skills. The belief that answers to the problems under discussion will be found in successfully training incompatible behaviors is widely held. Whaley and Tough's method is unusual in that a specific alternative behavior was trained on the basis of shock avoidance when shock was it its peak of effectiveness.

DIFFERENTIAL REINFORCEMENT OF OTHER BEHAVIOR (DRO). Although DRO has not stood up in comparison with shock (Corte, Wolfe, & Locke, 1971) and overcorrection (Foxx & Azrin, 1973), that it can be effective has been demonstrated by Peterson and Peterson (1968) with self-injurious behavior and Vukelich and Hake (1971) with extremely dangerous choking behavior. Although one can question whether other in-

vestigators really tried to make DRO work, the truth is that DRO with people of the type under consideration requires considerable expertise and time. It is quite likely also that without a maintenance program, the effects are no more enduring than those obtained with shock and overcorrection.

Many readers will be appalled by the techniques under discussion. The procedures are distasteful and painful. We seem, however, to have so few alternatives. We could wish, as I do, that these problems were prevented by early training relying principally on differential positive reinforcement. We could pretend that such problems do not exist and leave parents and staff to do the best they can. We can pursue the beginnings that have been made with the intent of refining procedures so as to maximize success and minimize pain and indignity. That option is the one that will and should be taken.

Research in Vocational Settings

Since I cannot improve upon Marc Gold's comprehensive and provocative review of research in vocational habilitation of the retarded (Gold, 1973), I will just touch the main points.

Opportunities to engage in work under supervision have been made available to the retarded in three ways: (1) apprenticeships to institutional employees; (2) extended care or permanent sheltered workshops; and (3) transitional workshops. In addition, classes in "manual arts" or vocational training are included in institutional and community school programs. The typical program of habilitation combines academic instruction, vocational classes, and on-the-job training in graduated steps of independence and duration. For example, an institutional resident might spend the morning in an academic class, the afternoon in vocational training class and/or sheltered workshop, and also work part-time in the kitchen, laundry, warehouse, etc. When the resident is judged ready, off-campus employment is found, and the trainee works part-time in such positions as domestic, "bag boy" in a local market, service station attendant, laborer, and nursing aide. The next step is full-time employment and living off campus in hostels, with family or employer, or on one's own. On paper, the plan is quite a reasonable one in that on-the-job expectations are graduated, the amount of responsibility and freedom increases gradually, and the experiences are concrete. The discrepancy between plan and implementation, however, is often great.

The most noticeable discrepancy, as Gold emphasizes, is that although opportunities exist, *"training . . . almost without exception refers to exposure rather than treatment, or, it refers to placing clients on a job station where it is hoped training occurs."* (Gold, 1973, p. 100). Crosson (1969) notes that the usual pattern is to find work that retardates can do instead of training. Even supervisors with the best of intentions about training have been handicapped by lack of training themselves, low expectations, the necessity to meet production deadlines, and, in institutions at least, the fact that typically everything is provided free. Thus, the plan tends to select already good workers (and too often to hold on to them) rather than provide training. One need then was to develop facilities suitable for training, tasks that were both useful and measurable, and programs of instruction. Much of the literature consists of descriptions of facilities and programs (cf. Baroff & Tate, 1966; Crosson, 1969; Gold, 1968; Tate & Baroff, 1967).

A second presumed problem was that there were no incentives for production or quality other than those used personally by supervisors. The most obvious one, money, usually was dispensed noncontingently in pitifully small amounts, e.g., 50 cents and a pack of cigarettes per week, and thus the relationship between work and pay was obscure, to say the least. Secondly, since every-thing was free, there was scant opportunity to acquire skills in money management. (The pay scale for workers in institutions and sheltered workshops has been the subject of heated debate recently. In general, it has risen sharply; in some cases, to union rates.)

The situation was a natural for testing the effects of token and monetary rewards for units of work. That is, changes in incentive systems would seem an obvious solution to increasing productivity and improving other work habits, and workshops would appear to be good research settings as they have the following positive features for research: (1) The work is highly repetitive and culminates in tangible products that lend themselves to reliable measurement. (2) Other measures, such as arriving on time, can be recorded easily. (3) Workshops, like classes, may refuse highly disruptive workers. (4) In those workshops catering to permanent workers, the work force is reasonably stable. On the other hand, in addition to the disadvantages shared with other applied settings such as limited staff who may be disinterested in research, workshops often have the significant disadvantage of being dependent upon contracts. This dependency means that sometimes there may be no work to be completed, and at others, there is a rush to meet a deadline. While this feature adds realism to the setting, investigators must at least control for fluctuations in work available and the atmosphere that prevails when production lags behind schedule and be prepared for research aims being pre-empted by the need to meet a deadline.

For this reason, among others, the studies of various monetary and token systems such as Huddle (1969), Hunt & Zimmerman (1969), and Logan, Kinsinger, Shelton, & Brown (1971) and other approaches to increase productivity by manipulating motivation, e.g., goal setting by the workers and the presence of a model worker (Kliebhan, 1967) and video-taped playback of on-the-job performance (De Roo and Haralson,

1971), are of disappointing quality. Klieb-han (1967) is noteworthy, however, in that both the goal-setting and model-present conditions did significantly (statistically) increase productivity; the study also illustrates the point made earlier that simple procedures are worth trying. In addition, the work deserves followup because of the implications that worker goal setting has for maintenance of effects. De Roo and Haralson's (1971) preliminary report of the possible advantage of TV playback also deserves attention. Although the methodology of this research may be criticized on one or more grounds, together the authors have more than demonstrated that rate, quality, and complexity of work can be improved greatly. I agree with Gold's conclusion that important groundwork has been completed and that we should turn now to developmental research in which we exploit principles of programming and devise systems that can and will be used, i.e., that are practical.

That high-quality research can be conducted in vocational training settings has been demonstrated by Schroeder (1972b). Actually, the series of experiments is an excellent illustration of applied behavior analysis independent of setting and is one of the few instances in which applied research has produced new findings. The studies were conducted in the workshop described by Baroff and Tate (1966) and used automatically recorded tool movements as one of the dependent variables (Schroeder, 1972a; Schroeder & Yarbrough, 1971). Three experiments were reported: (1) comparison of rates of tool usage and product completion under fixed-internal (FI), fixed-ratio (FR), and response-independent, i.e., time-dependent, schedules of reinforcement; (2) measurement of the interaction between work required per movement and value of FR reinforcement; and (3) measurement of the effects of varying amounts of reinforcement with differing schedules of reinforcement. The 10 men and women who served as subjects were 23–43 years of age with IQs 31–73 (mean 47). Immediate reinforcement of tool movements, e.g., stripping insulation from wire tips with pliers, consisted of an automatically dispensed light flash and counter point. Points were exchanged at the end of each hour session for poker chips of four different values, which permitted holding pay per session constant across the different schedules of reinforcement. The subjects, all "old hands," were quite familiar with the various ways in which the tokens could be spent. To allow adaptation to the new working conditions, points were dispensed on a time-dependent schedule for 6 weeks. Then the subjects were exposed to FR and FI schedules of different values for 10 one-hour sessions per schedule. As FI values were increased from 1 minute to 60 minutes, both movements and work completed declined in accordance with expectations from laboratory data. As FR values increased from 5 to 300 (600) movements to points earned, productivity increased with two workers as expected, but decreased with the third.

In the second study, Schroeder asked if the discrepant results with FR were due to the fact that the amount of work per movement was greater for the third subject. With a subject who previously had shown the expected increase in productivity with increases in FR, Schroeder varied precisely the amount of work per movement. The results confirmed that while the work was easy, rates increased with FR, but when the work was difficult, increasing the FR was accompanied by a decline in movements. Products completed was virtually nil at all values.

Although it seems intuitively obvious that more frequent reinforcement would be necessary to maintain hard work, this interaction has not been demonstrated previously, and pay schedules in society, in terms of physical labor and dullness, are quite the opposite. (Perhaps we should not complain when those who perform the hardest work for the least pay work slowly, aperiodically, and not at all.) Schroeder's third study indicates that the solution may not be found in increasing amount of pay per response. When amount per movement increased, rates declined on each of the schedules tested (FR 50, VR 75, FI 10, VI 10). In other words, work output varied so that essentially the same income was maintained across schedules. The research has shown some constraints on what can be accomplished with adjustments in schedules and amounts of reinforcement.

Gold (1973) argues that giving retardates more interesting and challenging work will be more effective than extrinsic reinforcement systems and that the rates of productivity of retardates are low because of the dull, repetitive work provided. Insofar as dull work and hard work may be equated, Schroeder's results confirm the latter point. Whether or not interesting and varied work experiences will provide more than a partial alternative remains to be seen.

Finally, some contend that the behaviorist's emphasis upon on-the-job productivity misses the mark, for retardates often are seen as good workers but unacceptable because of appearance, behavioral peculiarities, and the like. Often, too, the retarded worker is dissatisfied because of isolation and loneliness on and off the job. While not for a moment contending that these other factors are not extremely important, I call attention to the findings of Chaffin (1969), which suggest a relationship between productivity and employers' judgments of success. The work was clever in conception, but since the reliability of the data is highly questionable, it requires replication. Nonetheless, it seems to me that employers are much more tolerant of "peculiarities" in good workers. Thus, production rate should not be dismissed too quickly.

Appraisal and Recommendations

In the preceding sections, I have described the questions investigators have asked, the designs and procedures used in educational, ward, and vocational settings, and the opportunities and constraints that each setting presents. In this section, I will summarize (1) flaws in research design and methodology that I have noted, and (2) findings that have some generality and recommendations.

RECURRING METHODOLOGICAL AND DESIGN ERRORS

GROUP STATISTICAL STUDIES. I suggest the studies of Azrin and Armstrong (1973). Baker, Stanish, and Fraser (1972), Hewett, Taylor, and Artuso (1969), Kaufman and O'Leary (1972), S. Ross (1969a, 1969b), D. Ross (1970), and Ross and Ross (1972, 1973) as models of good experimental designs.

The most common deficiencies of the group research reviewed are:

1. Control group and description of control conditions. Since increased attention of an undefined nature has been found to improve the behavior of retardates (e.g., Gray & Kasteler, 1969) and considerable gains have been noted in the beginning of special training (e.g., Bensberg, Colwell, & Cassel, 1965), studies that do not increase attention, provide opportunities, and provide a changed environment for control subjects, i.e., include an "active" control, simply are not informative. Baker et al. did not have an active control group but used an equivalent. They measured effects of the new environment and then introduced their experimental procedures. The other studies listed above included active control groups.

2. Control for agent: subject ratios and for attention to, and selection of, agents. Hewett et al. (1969), after training the teachers as a group, assigned them to classes at random. They also consulted with each class equally often. Kaufman and O'Leary used the same teacher, observed the teacher's behavior daily, and included the teacher's ranking of the students as one of the matching variables. Azrin and Armstrong used volunteers for the training of control subjects, which is fair enough, but we are left to wonder if the volunteers received the same amount of

encouragement and attention as the experimental trainers. It is, of course, easy for investigators to convey their expectations and affect the outcomes thereby.

3. Assignment to groups. Since schools and institutions cannot (indeed should not) move persons around to suit the needs of a research project, I cannot be critical of experimenters on this point as long as they describe how assignment was accomplished or happened. I think we will need to be patient and rely on replications.

4. Failure to report who observed or examined the subjects, reliability of measurement, and definitions of recorded behavior. Although improvement is marked with regard to defining behavior and reliability estimates, the omission of comments about the examiners or raters continues to be very common, and a number of very difficult problems with the use of observers remain unsolved. See Johnson & Bolstad (1973) and Romanczyk, Kent, Diament, & O'Leary (1973).

5. Failure to give assurance that procedures were carried out as designed. Like the observation of subject behavior, observing agent behavior is a difficult problem. Most experimenters do not appear to agree with the need for recording agent behavior, and it has only recently been discussed at all (Birnbrauer, 1971).

6. Practical significance of results. The majority of behavior modification studies have used specially designed scales from which it is difficult to judge the practical or educational significance of the changes obtained. Two methods for overcoming this problem occur to me. The first is to gather comparative or criterion data on the scales used. For example, Azrin and Armstrong observed staff table manners, the Rosses administered some of their tests to peers of average ability, Huddle (1967) obtained estimates of the number of rectifiers nonretarded workers assembled, and Baker, Stanish, and Fraser observed children who were not regarded as problems by their regular teachers. The second method is to take other measurements, concurrently and at posttesting, using other devices and independent evaluators. Colwell et al. (1973), for example, administered standardized tests of intelligence as well as rated performance of self-help skills. Investigators have to be careful here, though, to choose criterion measures that are valid themselves and that tap the skills that the program was designed to teach. This decision, in part, will be based on the intended audience. Parents and institutional staff may be encouraged to continue training in other areas by a child's dressing itself. School authorities, on the other hand, have been more impressed by standardized test results.

Investigators often try to convey the importance of changes by describing what happened to the subjects after the program —"The clients were accepted into programs for which they previously had been judged unsuitable." Such statements are not sufficient unless the decisions were based on independent assessment.

A third method, indeed *the* method in the eyes of many, is performance during follow up. Except in those rare instances in which a specifically prescribed follow-up program is involved, I categorically dismiss this criterion. It is confounded by conditions during follow up and based on the unfounded notion that people can be psychologically prepared at time A to be happy, productive, and cooperative in any and all circumstances at time B. We can expect programs to produce skills necessary to gain entry as measured by independently administered scales, but we should not expect clients to remain at that level and improve further, if prescriptions for aftercare are not given and followed.

A final general point about the design of group studies pertains to the selection of subjects. We are taught to select subjects randomly from some population and assign them to experimental conditions randomly with or without matching on appropriate variables. That's fine. The point I wish to make, however, is simply that populations most often are defined in terms of demographic variables, age, sex, standardized test results, clinical diagnosis, and the like, and these variables may not be relevant to the effectiveness of behavioral treatments. It is curious that the standard way of defining populations is perpetuated in view of widespread acceptance that clinical diagnoses are unreliable and that generalizations made about women, particular age groups, the poor, etc., crumble with the slightest touch.

STUDIES OF INDIVIDUAL SUBJECTS. Most of the criticisms levelled at group studies above apply also to studies of individual subjects.

1. Choice and description of control conditions. Baseline conditions often are described as "conventional," and changes in procedure from baselines to treatments are, we may infer, several. Consequently, we do not know with what the treatment is being compared and, equally important, the conditions during baseline that were important to the success of the treatment. Our failure to emphasize baseline conditions and the role they play in choosing a treatment procedure no doubt accounts for the oft-reported inability of others to replicate success in their situations. We have reached the stage of development in which the most valuable studies will be those that include the equivalent of "active" control groups, i.e., "active" baseline conditions.

2. Agent: subject ratios and agent selection. Since the same agents participate across conditions, generally agent:subject ratios remain constant, but investigator expectations certainly can be operative and have not been controlled. A common procedure is to collect original baseline data at the same time as agents are being trained and other changes are made. The dangers are (1) that unstable baseline conditions may cloud or overdramatize the magnitude of treatment effects, and (2) the treatment may not be applicable where agent-subject patterns of interaction have had a longer history. Santogrossi et al. (1973) may illustrate the opposite possibility. One explanation of their failure to replicate the earlier study by Kaufman and O'Leary (1972) is that they introduced the change more rapidly.

3. Assignment to groups. Assignment of subjects to groups usually is not relevant, but comparable problems exist. For example, in the Perline and Levinsky (1968) study mentioned earlier, subjects were divided into two groups during the phase in which restraint was tested. The basis for such divisions should be random assignment. Another design in which subject assignment is relevant is application of procedures at different times to different subjects, i.e.,

multiple designs across subjects (Baer, Rowbury, Baer, Herbert, Clark, & Nelson, 1971). It is important to control the order in which subjects are treated. I am not suggesting that order be decided by lot beforehand, but rather to state a priori the criteria that will be used to shift from baseline to treatment.

4–6. Individual analyses share all of the problems mentioned above with respect to reliability and meaningfulness of data.

7. Variability within phases. Single-subject designs, if properly conducted and reported, make inferential statistics unnecessary. Reports traditionally presented all data from each phase or the final portion of each phase. Thus, variance was discernible and readers could assess for themselves whether or not differences between phases were reliable. Recently, however, investigators have presented just average data per phase with no mention of variability and no statistical analysis. This practice asks readers to accept too much on faith. Proper reporting requires either complete pictorial presentation of the data or descriptive statistics of within-phase variablility and, when there is doubt, statistical analysis of the results as well.

Three other points unique to studies of individual subjects need to be added. First, interpretation of single-subject designs requires both replication of procedures *and* replication of results. That is, when baseline is reinstated in an ABAB design, behavior must return to near baseline levels; in multiple designs, changes in behavior must correlate with introduction of the experimental procedures in the other situations or to the other behaviors, and not before. Investigators sometimes interpret changes that do not conform to these patterns to mean that the procedure was not only effective but also generalized. That interpretation may be correct, but proper demonstrations still require replication; when generalization appears to have occurred, the entire study needs replication.

Second, investigators will need to be wary of cumulative effects and be careful in their interpretations of "multi-treatment designs" (Birnbrauer, Peterson, & Solnick,

1974). Multi-treatment designs consist of applying different procedures in succession. For example, Foxx and Azrin (1973) Study I—"Barbara"—tested the effects of (A) non-contingent (free) reinforcement, (B) DRO, (C) slapping, and (D) overcorrection upon a child's mouthing of objects. Free reinforcement was the baseline procedure and was reinstated *only* when a procedure effected changes in mouthing. Thus each procedure was instated against a common base *rate* of behavior, but not a common set of baseline *conditions*. Foxx and Azrin assumed that because the behavior being recorded did not change, the procedure was neutral or functionally equivalent to free reinforcement. This assumption could well be untenable. The order of procedures in Foxx and Azrin, following the rule they specified, was ABCAD. DRO (B) had no observable effects and thus the slapping phase (C) followed immediately. C reduced mouthing considerably. Hence, baseline (A) was reinstated before overcorrection (D) was tested. A question that we should ask is: Would the effects have been the same if the design had been ABACAD? In addition, would the procedures have aligned themselves in degree of effectiveness in the same way if the order had been ADABAC? Although more time-consuming, the clearest design is one in which baseline procedures are reinstated regardless of effects of preceding procedure.

Third, many query how subjects are selected for single-subject investigations. The answer should be that subjects are selected on the basis of probability of success with the experimental techniques. Rather than select subjects randomly, in clinical research, procedures *should* be fitted to subjects and subjects selected for the procedure of interest. The principles of behavior analysis, not to mention professional ethics, are actually seriously violated by selecting subjects and procedures randomly. The mistake behavior modifiers have made is to fail to report how subjects

were selected or, as usually is the case, how procedures were selected.

CURRENT STATUS OF KNOWLEDGE AND RECOMMENDATIONS

Despite the criticisms and generally negative stance expressed above, a number of conclusions can be stated without hesitation.

1. Combined use of modeling and reinforcement principles has been shown to be more effective than less systematic approaches in increasing a number of skills. Persons who contend that they can do as well now bear the burden of proof. Specifically, I cite Azrin and colleagues' packages for suppressing aversive behaviors and teaching self-initiated toilet behavior and self-feeding, and remedial classes employing programmed materials, token reinforcement systems, and modeling, of which there are a number of variants.

By and large, the results in academic settings have been more impressive when the behavior measured was classroom behavior, e.g., attention to work. Thus, while we can be confident in our knowledge of how to increase the amount of time spent working arithmetic problems, for example, we cannot with existing programs be optimistic about the amount of improvement in arithmetic that will be realized. It is clear to me that we need turn our attention once again to the contents and objectives of training. The time has come to combine what we have learned about controlling attention and work habits with different curricula leading to different objectives. For example, it should be profitable to analyze the components of "strategies," "hypothesis testing," "problem solving," and "abstracting relevant information" and developing programs to teach these complex repertoires.

2. Combinations of instructions, demonstrations, physical guidance, and reinforcement have effected changes in an impressive *variety* of responses with many retardates in many contexts. The response consequences that may serve as reinforcers or aversive stimuli seem to be limitless. Whereas Fuller (1949) used food to shape arm movements in a crib-bound profound retardate, Bailey and Meyerson (1969) demonstrated the same effect with vibration. Webster and Azrin (1973) reported that 2 hours of en-

forced bed rest contingent on misbehavior suppressed misbehavior quite rapidly. There are numerous examples of positive effects being obtained by merely making attention/praise contingent on appropriate behavior, but Herbert et al. (1973) have demonstrated that differential attention can have the opposite effect. While, on the one hand, response consequences obviously do not achieve all goals, on the other hand, workers with the retarded should certainly be alerted by now to the necessity of controlling response consequences.

Indications are, however, that we would be wise to investigate further the traditional stance of operant conditioners that the combination of positive reinforcement and extinction, i.e., ignoring incorrect behavior, is most effective. It has been known for some time that the combination " 'Right'—no response" is less effective than "no response—'wrong' " in teaching (cf. Cairns, 1970). There is no question that ignoring behavior in some training situations results in a chain of correct *and* incorrect behavior (Bijou & Orlando, 1961; Talkington, 1971).

3. Several studies support that response-reinforcer contingency is an essential aspect of some *improvements* in behavior (Hart, Reynolds, Baer, Brawley, & Harris, 1968; Redd & Birnbrauer, 1969, with noncontingent reinforcement; Baer et al., 1967, with delayed reinforcement; Burchard, 1967, with prepayment). That behavior may be *maintained* with less precise response-reinforcer relationships is another matter that has received virtually no attention. Studies in which changes from contingent to noncontingent reinforcement are not announced are rare indeed.

4. Generally speaking, studies have effected changes in rates of behavior that existed prior to intervention. Intervention programs have increased an infrequently occurring response or brought certain behaviors under stimulus, situational, or agent control. The major and significant exceptions are the procedures developed for establishing "generalized stimulus control." These procedures are both theoretically exciting and extremely useful.

5. Retardates are very sensitive to reinforcement contingencies, i.e., they acquire discriminations very rapidly. With positive reinforcement and punishment alike, *as each has been used in experiments*, retarded persons have proved to be more resilient than rigid. Another way of stating this conclusion is that generalization and transfer of training infrequently occur spontaneously.

With no intention of belittling the magnitude of the problems of maintaining and generalizing gains, we may have exaggerated discriminations and induced rapid recovery of baseline behaviors by the designs of our experiments and the severe limitations imposed upon agent behavior. Birnbrauer et al. (1965), for example, might have discontinued tokens successfully in those classes, if the teachers had been allowed to use their own resources, e.g., occasionally set goals before going on an outing and employ special incentive systems for selected students. As another example, rarely in practice would an agent ignore other positive behavior as is required in multiple baselines; one would expect that teachers, parents, and staff would reinforce desirable behavior wherever it occurred and whatever its nature. But generalization and maintenance are problems, and they have only begun to be explored, e.g., training in self-evaluation (e.g., Kaufman & O'Leary, 1972) and in modifying the behavior of others (Graubard, Rosenberg, & Miller, 1971), and prescribing programs for maintenance and generalization. Another approach not yet used with retardates is that of role playing or behavioral rehearsal in varying circumstances.

6. Punishment effects dramatic decreases in behavior temporarily. In the early sixties punishment was frowned upon because its effects were presumed to be temporary, and it elicited undesirable side effects. The undesirable side effects have not materialized, but the view that its effects would be temporary has been substantiated. Although I can still think of no alternative but to apply severe punishment in some cases, I have seen nothing that has led me to change my opinion that suppression is at best only the beginning of a program of habilitation (Birnbrauer, 1968).

7. The variables controlling such repetitive acts as self-injurious behavior remain a puzzle.

In conclusion, in that retarded persons treated with behavior modification techniques are still retarded, the results are disappointing. In that strides have been made in developing ways of working with the retarded and an unprecedented amount of information has been accumulated, the results are encouraging indeed. The literature is a solid foundation to build upon. Changes in methodology and climate have occurred so that it is now much easier to gain support from families, institutions, and schools, and we are methodologically more sophisticated.

Although we can be severely critical of observational systems presently in use, 10 years ago few investigators had any experience in, or interest in, obtaining data in naturalistic situations. Such experience is now widely accepted as part of the training of students in psychology. Hardware to make the task of observation simpler and more accurate has been developed; the literature includes some ingenious techniques and certainly a wide variety to choose from.

We have also learned that it is feasible to work with clients so as to measure patient progress for the sake of both the client and the advancement of knowledge. The number of persons prepared to experimentally analyze behavior in natural settings has increased dramatically. Whereas once they were interlopers, they are now sought. Measurement, once considered a luxury that could not be afforded, now is recognized as an integral part of therapy and education. Finally, we now have much more realistic ideas of the magnitude of the problems. We appreciate the amount of sheer work involved in implementing behavioral programs. We know that intervention affects the community of the client and vice versa and that effective programs require attention to the total social system within which the client moves.

References

ACKER, L. E., ACKER, M. A., & PEARSON, D. Generalized imitative affection: Relationship to prior kinds of imitation training. *Journal of Experimental Child Psychology,* 1973, **16**, 111–125.

AYLLON, T., & AZRIN, N. H. *The token economy: A motivational system for therapy and rehabilitation.* New York: Appleton-Century-Crofts, 1968.

AYLLON, T., & KELLY, K. Effects of reinforcement on standardized test performance. *Journal of Applied Behavior Analysis,* 1972, **5**, 477–484.

AZRIN, N. H., & ARMSTRONG, P. M. The "mini-meal"—A method of teaching eating skills to the profoundly retarded. *Mental Retardation,* February 1973, **11**, 9–13.

AZRIN, N. H., BUGLE, C., & O'BRIEN, F. Behavioral engineering: Two apparatuses for toilet training retarded children. *Journal of Applied Behavior Analysis,* 1971, 4, 249–253.

AZRIN, N. H., & FOXX, R. M. A rapid method of toilet training the institutionalized retarded. *Journal of Applied Behavior Analysis,* 1971, 4, 89–99.

BAER, D. M., & GUESS, D. Receptive training of adjectival inflections in mental retardates. *Journal of Applied Behavior Analysis,* 1971, 4, 129–139.

BAER, D. M., PETERSON, R. F., & SHERMAN, J. A. The development of imitation by reinforcing behavioral similarity to a model. *Journal of the Experimental Analysis of Behavior,* 1967, **10**, 405–416.

BAER, D. M., ROWBURY, T., BAER, A. M., HERBERT, E., CLARK, H. B., & NELSON, A. A programmatic test of behavioral technology: Can it recover deviant children for normal public schooling? In M. E. Meyer (Ed.), *Early learning, the Second Western Washington Symposium on Learning.* Bellingham: Western Washington State College, 1971, pp. 112–133.

BAER, D. M., & SHERMAN, J. A. Reinforcement control of generalized imitation in young children. *Journal of Experimental Child Psychology,* 1964, **1**, 37–49.

BAILEY, J., & MEYERSON, L. Vibration as a reinforcer with a profoundly retarded child. *Journal of Applied Behavior Analysis,* 1969, **2**, 135–137.

BAKER, J. G., STANISH, B., & FRASER, B. Comparative effects of a token economy in nursery school. *Mental Retardation,* August 1972, **10**, 16–19.

BANDURA, A. *Principles of behavior modification.* New York: Holt, Rinehart & Winston, 1969.

BANDURA, A., & BARAB, P. G. Conditions governing nonreinforced imitation. *Developmental Psychology,* 1971, **5**, 244–255.

BAROFF, G. S. *Mental retardation: nature, cause, and management.* New York: Wiley, 1974.

BAROFF, G., & TATE, B. A demonstration sheltered workshop in a state institution for the retarded. *Mental Retardation,* June 1966, **4,** 30–34.

BARRETT, B., & LINDSLEY, O. R. Deficits in acquisition of operant discrimination and differentiation shown by institutionalized retarded children. *American Journal of Mental Deficiency,* 1962, **67,** 424–436.

BARTON, E. S. Inappropriate speech in a severely retarded child: A case study in language conditioning and generalization. *Journal of Applied Behavior Analysis,* 1970, **3,** 299–307.

BARTON, E. S., GUESS, D., GARCIA, E., & BAER, D. M. Improvement of retardates' mealtime behaviors by timeout procedures using multiple baseline techniques. *Journal of Applied Behavior Analysis,* 1970, **3,** 77–84.

BAUMEISTER, A., & KLOSOWSKI, R. An attempt to group toilet train severely retarded patients. *Mental Retardation,* December, 1965, **3,** 24–26.

BENNETT, C. W., & LING, D. Teaching a complex verbal response to a hearing-impaired girl. *Journal of Applied Behavior Analysis,* 1972, **5,** 321–327.

BENSBERG, G. J. (Ed.) *Teaching the mentally retarded.* Atlanta: Southern Regional Education Board, 1965.

BENSBERG, G. J., COLWELL, C. N., & CASSEL, R. H. Teaching the profoundly retarded self-help activities by behavior shaping techniques. *American Journal of Mental Deficiency,* 1965, **69,** 674–679.

BIJOU, S. W. Studies in the experimental development of left-right concepts in retarded children using fading techniques. In N. R. Ellis (Ed.), *International review of research in mental retardation.* Vol. 3. New York: Academic Press, 1968, pp. 65–96.

BIJOU, S. W., BIRNBRAUER, J. S., KIDDER, J. D., & TAGUE, C. Programmed instruction as an approach to teaching of reading, writing, and arithmetic to retarded children. *The Psychological Record,* 1966, **16,** 505–522.

BIJOU, S. W., & ORLANDO, R. Rapid development of multiple schedule performances with retarded children. *Journal of the Experimental Analysis of Behavior,* 1961, **4,** 7–16.

BIRNBRAUER, J. S. Generalization of punishment effects—A case study. *Journal of Applied Behavior Analysis,* 1968, **1,** 201–211.

BIRNBRAUER, J. S. Contingency management research. *Educational Technology,* 1971, **11,** 71–77.

BIRNBRAUER, J. S., BIJOU, S. W., WOLF, M. M., & KIDDER, J. D. Programed instruction in the classroom. In L. P. Ullman & L. Krasner (Eds.), *Case studies in behavior modification.* New York: Holt, Rinehart & Winston, 1965, pp. 358–363.

BIRNBRAUER, J. S., KIDDER, J. D., & TAGUE, C. Programing reading from the teacher's point of view. *Programed Instruction,* 1964, **3,** (7), 1–2.

BIRNBRAUER, J. S., PETERSON, C. R., & SOLNICK, J. V. The design and interpretation of studies of single subjects. *American Journal of Mental Deficiency,* 1974, **79,** 191–203.

BIRNBRAUER, J. S., WOLF, M. M., KIDDER, J. D., & TAGUE, C. Classroom behavior of retarded pupils with token reinforcement. *Journal of Experimental Child Psychology,* 1965, **2,** 219–235.

BLACKMAN, L. S., & CAPOBIANCO, R. J. An evaluation of programmed instruction with the mentally retarded utilizing teaching machines. *American Journal of Mental Deficiency,* 1965, **70,** 262–269.

BLATT, B., & KAPLAN, F. *Christmas in purgatory.* Boston: Allyn & Bacon, 1966.

BOSTOW, D. E., & BAILEY, J. B. Modifications of severe disruptive and aggressive behavior using brief timeout and reinforcement procedures. *Journal of Applied Behavior Analysis,* 1969, **2,** 31–37.

BRIGHAM, T. A., & SHERMAN, J. A. An experimental analysis of verbal imitation in preschool children. *Journal of Applied Behavior Analysis,* 1968, **1,** 151–158.

BRODEN, M., BRUCE, C., MITCHELL, M. A., CARTER, V., & HALL, R. V. Effects of teacher attention on attending behavior of two boys at adjacent desks. *Journal of Applied Behavior Analysis,* 1970, **3,** 199–203.

BROWNING, R. M. Treatment effects of a total behavior modification program with five autistic children. *Behaviour Research and Therapy,* 1971, **9,** 319–327.

BRY, P. M., & NAWAS, M. M. Is reinforcement necessary for the development of a generalized imitation operant in severely and profoundly retarded children? *American Journal of Mental Deficiency,* 1972, **76,** 658–667.

BUELL, J., STODDARD, P., HARRIS, F., & BAER, D. M. Collateral social development accompanying reinforcement of outdoor play in a preschool child. *Journal of Applied Behavior Analysis,* 1968, **1**, 167–173.

BUFFORD, R. K. Discrimination and instructions as factors in the control of nonreinforced imitation. *Journal of Experimental Child Psychology,* 1971, **12**, 35–50.

BURCHARD, J. D. Systematic socialization: A programmed environment for the habilitation of antisocial retardates. *Psychological Record,* 1967, **17**, 461–476.

BURCHARD, J. D., & BARRERA, F. An analysis of timeout and response cost in a programmed environment. *Journal of Applied Behavior Analysis,* 1972, **5**, 271–282.

BURGESS, R. L., BURGESS, J. A., & ESVALDT, K. C. An analysis of generalized imitation. *Journal of Applied Behavior Analysis,* 1970, **3**, 39–46.

CAIN, L. F., LEVINE, S., & ELZEY, F. F. *Manual for the Cain-Levine Social Competency Scale.* Palo Alto: Consulting Psychologist Press, 1963.

CAIRNS, R. B. Meaning and attention as determinants of social reinforcer effectiveness. *Child Development,* 1970, **41**, 1067–1082.

CHAFFIN, J. D. Production rate as a variable in the job success or failure of educable mentally retarded adolescents. *Exceptional Children,* 1969, **35**, 533–538.

COLWELL, C. N., RICHARDS, E., McCARVER, R. B., & ELLIS, N. R. Evaluation of self-help habit training. *Mental Retardation,* June 1973, **11**, 14–18.

CORTE, H. E., WOLF, M. M., & LOCKE, B. J. A comparison of procedures for eliminating self-injurious behavior of retarded adolescents. *Journal of Applied Behavior Analysis,* 1971, **4**, 201–213.

CROSSON, J. E. A technique for programming sheltered workshop environments for training severely retarded workers. *American Journal of Mental Deficiency,* 1969, **73**, 814–818.

DALTON, A. J., RUBINO, C. A., & HISLOP, M. W. Some effects of token rewards on school achievement of children with Down's syndrome. *Journal of Applied Behavior Analysis,* 1973, **6**, 251–259.

DAYAN, M. Toilet training retarded children in a state residential institution. *Mental Retardation,* 1964, **2**, 116–117.

DE ROO, W. M., & HARALSON, H. L. Increasing workshop production through self-visualization on videotape. *Mental Retardation,* August 1971, **9**, 22–25.

DOLL, E. A. *Vineland Social Maturity Scale: Manual of directions.* Minneapolis: American Guidance Service, 1947.

DRABMAN, R., & SPITALNIK, R. Social isolation as a punishment procedure: A controlled study. *Journal of Experimental Child Psychology,* 1973, **16**, 236–249.

EDLUND, C. V. Changing classroom behavior of retarded children: Using reinforcers in the home environment and parents and teachers as trainers. *Mental Retardation,* 1971, **9**, 33–36.

EDLUND, C. V. The effect on the test behavior of children, as reflected in the I.Q. scores, when reinforced after each correct response. *Journal of Applied Behavior Analysis,* 1972, **5**, 317–319.

ELLIS, N. R. Toilet training the severely defective patient: An S-R reinforcement analysis. *American Journal of Mental Deficiency,* 1963, **68**, 98–103.

ELLIS, N. R., BARNETT, C. D., & PRYER, M. W. Operant behavior in mental defectives: Exploratory studies. *Journal of the Experimental Analysis of Behavior,* 1960, **3**, 63–69.

EPSTEIN, L. H., PETERSON, G. L., WEBSTER, J., GUANIERI, C., & LIBBY, B. Comparison of stimulus control and reinforcement control effects on imitative behavior. *Journal of Experimental Child Psychology,* 1973, **16**, 98–110.

FINGADO, M. L., KINI, J. F., STEWART, K., & REDD, W. H. A thirty-day residential training program for retarded children. *Mental Retardation,* December 1970, **8**, 42–45.

FOXX, R. M., & AZRIN, N. H. Restitution: A method of eliminating aggressive-disruptive behavior of mentally retarded and brain damaged patients. *Behaviour Research and Therapy,* 1972, **10**, 15–27.

FOXX, R. M., & AZRIN, N. H. The elimination of autistic self-stimulatory behavior by over-correction. *Journal of Applied Behavior Analysis,* 1973, **6**, 1–14.

FULLER, P. R. Operant conditioning of a vegetative human organism. *American Journal of Psychology,* 1949, **62**, 587–590.

GARCIA, E., BAER, D. M., & FIRESTONE, I. The development of generalized imitation within topographically determined boundaries. *Journal of Applied Behavior Analysis,* 1971, 4, 101–112.

GARCIA, E., GUESS, D., & BYRNES, J. Development of syntax in a retarded girl using procedures of imitation, reinforcement, and modelling. *Jour-*

nal of Applied Behavior Analysis, 1973, **6,** 299–310.

GARDNER, J. M., & SELINGER, S. Trends in learning research with the mentally retarded. *American Journal of Mental Deficiency,* 1971, **75,** 733–738.

GARDNER, J. M., SELINGER, S., WATSON, L. S., SAPOSNEK, D. T., & GARDNER, G. M. Research on learning with the mentally retarded: A comprehensive bibliography. *Mental Retardation Abstracts,* 1970, 7, 417–453.

GEWIRTZ, J. A., & STINGLE, K. G. Learning of generalized imitation as the basis for identification. *Psychological Review,* 1968, **75,** 374–397.

GILES, D. K., & WOLF, M. M. Toilet training institutionalized, severe retardates: An application of operant behavior modification techniques. *American Journal of Mental Deficiency,* 1966, **70,** 766–780.

GIRARDEAU, F. L., & SPRADLIN, J. E. Token rewards in a cottage program. *Mental Retardation,* 1964, 2, 345–351.

GOLD, M. W. Preworkshop skills for the trainable: A sequential technique. *Education and Training of the Mentally Retarded,* 1968, **3,** 31–37.

GOLD, M. W. Research on the vocational habilitation of the retarded: The present, the future. In N. R. Ellis (Ed.), *International review of research in mental retardation.* Vol. 6. New York: McGraw-Hill, 1973, pp. 97–147.

GRAUBARD, P. S., ROSENBERG, H., & MILLER, M. B. Student applications of behavior modification to teachers and environments or ecological approaches to social deviancy. In E. A. Ramp & B. L. Hopkins (Eds.), *A new direction for education: Behavior analysis.* Vol. 1. Lawrence, Kans.: The University of Kansas Support and Development Center for Follow Through, 1971, pp. 80–101.

GRAY, R. M., & KASTELER, J. M. The effects of social reinforcement and training on institutionalized mentally retarded children. *American Journal of Mental Deficiency,* 1969, **74,** 50–56.

GREENE, F. M. Programmed instruction techniques for the mentally retarded. In N. R. Ellis (Ed.), *International review of research in mental retardation.* Vol. 2. New York: Academic Press, 1966, pp. 209–239.

GREENE, R. J., & PRATT, J. J. A group contingency for individual misbehaviors in the classroom. *Mental Retardation,* June 1972, **10,** 33–34.

GRIMM, J. A., BIJOU, S. W., & PARSONS, J. A problem-solving model for teaching remedial arithmetic to handicapped young children. *Journal of Abnormal Child Psychology,* in press.

GROSSMAN, H. J. (Ed.) *Manual on terminology and classification in mental retardation.* (Rev. ed.) Washington, D.C.: American Association on Mental Deficiency, 1973.

GROVES, I. D., & CARROCCIO, D. F. A self-feeding program for the severely and profoundly retarded. *Mental Retardation,* June 1971, **9,** 10–12.

GUESS, D. A. A functional analysis of receptive language and productive speech: Acquisition of the plural morpheme. *Journal of Applied Behavior Analysis,* 1969, **2,** 55–64.

GUESS, D. A., RUTHERFORD, G., SMITH, J. O., & ENSMINGER, E. Utilization of sub-professional personnel in teaching language skills to mentally retarded children: An interim report. *Mental Retardation,* April 1970, **8,** 17–23.

GUESS, D. A., SAILOR, W., RUTHERFORD, G., & BAER, D. M. An experimental analysis of linguistic development: The productive use of the plural morpheme. *Journal of Applied Behavior Analysis,* 1968, **1,** 297–306.

HAMILTON, J., & ALLEN, P. Ward programming for severely retarded institutionalized residents. *Mental Retardation,* 1967, **5,** 22–24.

HAMILTON, J., STEPHENS, L., & ALLEN, P. Controlling aggressive and destructive behavior in severely retarded institutionalized residents. *American Journal of Mental Deficiency,* 1967, **71,** 852–856.

HART, B. M., REYNOLDS, N. J., BAER, D. M., BRAWLEY, E. R., & HARRIS, F. R. Effect of contingent and non-contingent social reinforcement on the cooperative play of a preschool child. *Journal of Applied Behavior Analysis,* 1968, **1,** 73–76.

HEBER, R. F. A manual on terminology and classification in mental retardation. *American Journal of Mental Deficiency Monograph Supplement,* 1959, 64 (Rev. ed. 1961).

HENRIKSEN, K., & DOUGHTY, R. Decelerating undesirable mealtime behavior in a group of profoundly retarded boys. *American Journal of Mental Deficiency,* 1967, **72,** 40–44.

HERBERT, E. W., PINKSTON, E. N., HAYDEN, M. L.,

Sajwaj, T. E., Pinkston, S., Cordua, G., & Jackson, C. Adverse effects of differential parental attention. *Journal of Applied Behavior Analysis,* 1973, **6,** 15–30.

Hewett, F. M., Taylor, F. D., & Artuso, A. A. The Santa Monica Project: Evaluation of an engineered classroom design with emotionally disturbed children. *Exceptional Children,* 1969, **35,** 523–529.

Hislop, M. W., Moore, C., & Stanish, B. Remedial classroom programming: Long-term transfer effects from a token economy system. *Mental Retardation,* April 1973, **11,** 18–20.

Huddle, D. D. Work performance of trainable adults as influenced by competition, cooperation, and monetary reward. *American Journal of Mental Deficiency,* 1967, **72,** 198–211.

Hundziak, M., Maurer, R. A., & Watson, L. S. Jr. Operant conditioning in toilet training of severely mentally retarded boys. *American Journal of Mental Deficiency,* 1965, **70,** 120–124.

Hunt, J. G., & Zimmerman, J. Stimulating productivity in a simulated sheltered workshop setting. *American Journal of Mental Deficiency,* 1969, **74,** 43–49.

Johnson, S. M., & Bolstad, O. D. Methodological issues in naturalistic observation: Some problems and solutions for field research. In F. R. Clark & L. A. Hamerlynck (Eds.), *Critical issues in research and practice: Proceedings of the Fourth Banff International Conference on Behavior Modification.* Champaign, Ill.: Research Press, 1973, in press.

Kaufman, K. F., & O'Leary, K. D. Reward, cost, and self-evaluation procedures for disruptive adolescents in a psychiatric hospital school. *Journal of Applied Behavior Analysis,* 1972, **5,** 293–310.

Kazdin, A. E. The effect of vicarious reinforcement on attentive behavior in the classroom. *Journal of Applied Behavior Analysis,* 1973, **6,** 71–78.

Kimbrell, D. L., Luckey, R. E., Barbuto, P. F. P., & Love, J. G. Operation dry pants: An intensive habit-training program for severely and profoundly retarded. *Mental Retardation,* February 1967, **5,** 32–36.

Kimmel, H. D., & Kimmel, E. An instrumental conditioning method for the treatment of enuresis. *Journal of Behavior Therapy and Experimental Psychiatry,* 1970, **1,** 121–123.

Kliebhan, J. Effects of goal-setting and modelling on job performance of mentally retarded adolescents. *American Journal of Mental Deficiency,* 1967, **72,** 220–226.

Kohlenberg, R. J. The punishment of persistent vomiting: A case study. *Journal of Applied Behavior Analysis,* 1970, **3,** 241–245.

Lahey, B. B., McNess, M. P., & McNess, M. C. Control of an obscene "verbal tic" through time-out in an elementary classroom. *Journal of Applied Behavior Analysis,* 1973, **6,** 101–104.

Lawrence, W., & Kartye, J. Extinction of social competency skills in severely and profoundly retarded females. *American Journal of Mental Deficiency,* 1971, **75,** 630–634.

Leath, J. R., & Flournoy, R. L. Three year follow-up of intensive habit-training program. *Mental Retardation,* June 1970, **8,** 32–34.

Levine, M. N., & Elliott, C. B. Toilet training for profoundly retarded with a limited staff. *Mental Retardation,* June 1970, **8,** 48–50.

Logan, D. L., Kinsinger, J., Shelton, G., & Brown, J. M. The use of multiple reinforcers in a rehabilitation setting. *Mental Retardation,* June 1971, **9,** 3–6.

Lovaas, O. I., Berberich, J. P., Perloff, B. F., & Schaeffer, B. Acquisition of imitative speech by schizophrenic children. *Science,* 1966, **151,** 705–707.

Lovaas, O. I., Koegel, R., Simmons, J. Q., & Long, J. S. Some generalization and follow-up measures on autistic children in behavior therapy. *Journal of Applied Behavior Analysis,* 1973, **6,** 131–165.

Lovaas, O. I., & Simmons, J. Q. Manipulation of self-destruction in three retarded children. *Journal of Applied Behavior Analysis,* 1969, **2,** 143–157.

Luckey, R. E., Watson, C. M., & Musick, J. K. Aversive conditioning as a means of inhibiting vomiting and rumination. *American Journal of Mental Deficiency,* 1968, **73,** 139–142.

Mahoney, K., Van Wagenen, R. K., & Meyerson, L. Toilet training of normal and retarded children. *Journal of Applied Behavior Analysis,* 1971, **4,** 173–182.

Malpass, L. P. Programmed instruction for retarded children. In A. A. Baumeister (Ed), *Mental retardation.* London: University of London Press, 1968, pp. 212–231.

MALPASS, L. F., HARDY, M. W., GILMORE, A. S., & WILLIAMS, C. F. Automated instruction for retarded children. *American Journal of Mental Deficiency,* 1964, **69**, 405–412.

MARTIN, G. L., McDONALD, S., & OMICHINSKI, M. An operant analysis of response interactions during meals with severely retarded girls. *American Journal of Mental Deficiency,* 1971, **76**, 68–75.

MARTIN, J. A. The control of imitative and non-imitative behaviors in severely retarded children through "generalized instruction following." *Journal of Experimental Child Psychology,* 1971, **11**, 390–400.

MARTIN, J. A. The effect of incongruent instructions and consequences on imitation in retarded children. *Journal of Applied Behavior Analysis,* 1972, **5**, 467–475.

METZ, J. R. Conditioning generalized imitation in autistic children. *Journal of Experimental Child Psychology,* 1965, **2**, 389–399.

MILLER, L. K., & SCHNEIDER, R. The use of a token system in project Head Start. *Journal of Applied Behavior Analysis,* 1970, **3**, 213–220.

MINGE, M. R., & BALL, T. S. Teaching of self-help skills to profoundly retarded patients. *American Journal of Mental Deficiency,* 1967, **71**, 864–868.

MOWRER, O. H., & MOWRER, W. M. Enuresis: A method for its study and treatment. *American Journal of Orthopsychiatry,* 1938, **8**, 436–459.

O'BRIEN, F., & AZRIN, N. H. Developing proper mealtime behaviors of the institutionalized retarded. *Journal of Applied Behavior Analysis,* 1972, **5**, 389–399.

O'BRIEN, F., BUGLE, C., & AZRIN, N. H. Training and maintaining a retarded child's proper eating. *Journal of Applied Behavior Analysis,* 1972, **5**, 67–72.

ORLANDO, R., BIJOU, S. W., TYLER, R. M., & MARSHALL, D. A. A laboratory for the experimental analysis of developmentally retarded children. *Psychological Reports,* 1961, **7**, 261–267.

OSBORNE, J. G. Free-time as a reinforcer in the management of classroom behavior. *Journal of Applied Behavior Analysis,* 1969, **2**, 113–118.

PALOUTZIAN, R. F., HASAZI, J., STREIFEL, J., & EDGAR, C. L. Promotion of positive social interaction in severely retarded young children. *American Journal of Mental Deficiency,* 1971, **75**, 519-524.

PASCHALIS, A., KIMMEL, H. D., & KIMMEL, E.

Further study of diurnal instrumental conditioning in the treatment of enuresis nocturna. *Journal of Behavior Therapy and Experimental Psychiatry,* 1972, **3**, 253–256.

PATTERSON, G. R. An application of conditioning techniques to the control of a hyperactive child. In L. P. Ullmann and L. Krasner (Eds.), *Case studies in behavior modification.* New York: Holt, Rinehart & Winston, 1965, pp. 370–375.

PATTERSON, G. R., JONES, R., WHITTIER, J., & WRIGHT, M. A. A behavior modification technique for the hyperactive child. *Behaviour Research and Therapy,* 1965, **2**, 217–226.

PEINE, H. A., GREGERSEN, G. F., & SLOANE, H. N. A program to increase vocabulary and spontaneous verbal behavior. *Mental Retardation,* April 1970, **8**, 38–44.

PENDERGRASS, V. E. Timeout from positive reinforcement following persistent, high-rate behavior in retardates. *Journal of Applied Behavior Analysis,* 1972, **5**, 85–92.

PERLINE, I. H., & LEVINSKY, D. Controlling maladaptive classroom behavior in the severely retarded. *American Journal of Mental Deficiency,* 1968, **73**, 74–78.

PETERSON, R. F. Some experiments on the organization of a class of imitative behaviors. *Journal of Applied Behavior Analysis,* 1968, **1**, 225–235.

PETERSON, R. F., MERWIN, M. R., MOYER, T. J., & WHITEHURST, G. J. Generalized imitation: The effects of experimenter absence, differential reinforcement and stimulus complexity. *Journal of Experimental Child Psychology,* 1971, **12**, 114–128.

PETERSON, R. F., & PETERSON, L. R. The use of positive reinforcement in the control of self-destructive behavior in a retarded boy. *Journal of Experimental Child Psychology,* 1968, **6**, 351–360.

PETERSON, R. F., & WHITEHURST, G. J. A variable influencing the performance of nonreinforced imitative behavior. *Journal of Applied Behavior Analysis,* 1971, **4**, 1–10.

REDD, W. H., & BIRNBRAUER, J. S. Adults as discriminative stimuli for different reinforcement contingencies with retarded children. *Journal of Experimental Child Psychology,* 1969, **7**, 440–447.

RISLEY, T. R. The effects and side effects of punishing the autistic behaviors of a deviant child. *Journal of Applied Behavior Analysis,* 1968, **1**, 21–34.

RISLEY, T. R., & WOLF, M. M. Establishing functional speech in echolalic children. *Behaviour Research and Therapy,* 1967, **5**, 73–88.

ROBINSON, H. B., & ROBINSON, N. M. *The mentally retarded child: A psychological approach.* New York: McGraw-Hill, 1965.

ROMANCZYK, R. G., KENT, R. N., DIAMENT, C., & O'LEARY, K. D. Measuring the reliability of observational data: A reactive process. *Journal of Applied Behavior Analysis,* 1973, **6**, 175–186.

ROSS, D. M. Incidental learning of number concepts in small group games. *American Journal of Mental Deficiency,* 1970, **74**, 718–725.

ROSS, D. M., & ROSS, S. A. The efficacy of listening training for educable mentally retarded children. *American Journal of Mental Deficiency,* 1972, **77**, 137–142.

ROSS, D. M., & ROSS, S. A. Cognitive training for the EMR child: Situational problem solving and planning. *American Journal of Mental Deficiency,* 1973, **78**, 20–26.

ROSS, S. A. Effects of intentional training in social behavior on retarded children. *American Journal of Mental Deficiency,* 1969, **73**, 912–919. (a)

ROSS, S. A. Effects of an intensive motor skills training program on young educable mentally retarded children. *American Journal of Mental Deficiency,* 1969, **73**, 920–926. (b)

SAILOR, W. Reinforcement and generalization of productive plural allomorphs in two retarded children. *Journal of Applied Behavior Analysis,* 1971, 4, 305–310.

SANTOGROSSI, D. A., O'LEARY, K. D., ROMANCZYK, R. G., & KAUFMAN, K. F. Self-evaluation by adolescents, in a psychiatric hospital school token program. *Journal of Applied Behavior Analysis,* 1973, **6**, 277–287.

SCHROEDER, S. R. Automated transduction of sheltered workshop behaviors. *Journal of Applied Behavior Analysis,* 1972, 4, 106–109. (a)

SCHROEDER, S. R. Parametric effects of reinforcement frequency, amount of reinforcement, and required response force on sheltered workshop behavior. *Journal of Applied Behavior Analysis,* 1972, 5, 431–442. (b)

SCHROEDER, S. R., & YARBROUGH, C. C. Programming and automated recording in a sheltered workshop. *Mental Retardation,* December 1972, **10**, 9–11.

SCHUMAKER, J., & SHERMAN, J. A. Training generative verb usage by imitation and reinforcement procedures. *Journal of Applied Behavior Analysis,* 1970, **3**, 273–287.

SIDMAN, M., & STODDARD, L. T. Programming perception and learning for retarded children. In N. R. Ellis (Ed.), *International review of research in mental retardation.* Vol. 2. New York: Academic Press, 1966, pp. 151–208.

SIDMAN, M., & STODDARD, L. T. The effectiveness of fading in programming a simultaneous form discrimination for retarded children. *Journal of the Experimental Analysis of Behavior,* 1967, **10**, 3–15.

SKINNER, B. F. *Science and human behavior.* New York: Macmillan, 1953.

SKINNER, B. F. *Verbal behavior.* New York: Appleton-Century-Crofts, 1957.

SLOOP, E. W., & KENNEDY, W. A. Institutionalized retarded nocturnal enuretics treated by a conditioning technique. *American Journal of Mental Deficiency,* 1973, **77**, 717–721.

SPRADLIN, J. E., & GIRARDEAU, F. L. The behavior of moderately and severely retarded persons. In N. Ellis (Ed.), *International review of research in mental retardation.* Vol. 1. New York: Academic Press, 1966, pp. 257–298.

STEINMAN, W. M. Generalized imitation and the discrimination hypothesis. *Journal of Experimental Child Psychology,* 1970, **10**, 79–99. (a)

STEINMAN, W. M. The social control of generalized imitation. *Journal of Applied Behavior Analysis,* 1970, **3**, 159–167. (b)

STEINMAN, W. M., & BOYCE, K. D. Generalized imitation as a function of discrimination difficulty and choice. *Journal of Experimental Child Psychology,* 1971, **11**, 251–265.

SULZBACHER, S. I., & HOUSER, J. E. A tactic to eliminate disruptive behaviors in the classroom: Group contingent consequences. *American Journal of Mental Deficiency,* 1968, **73**, 88–90.

TALKINGTON, L. W. Response-chain learning of mentally retarded adolescents under four conditions of reinforcement. *American Journal of Mental Deficiency,* 1971, **76**, 337–340.

TATE, B. G., & BAROFF, G. S. Aversive control of self-injurious behavior in a psychotic boy. *Behaviour Research and Therapy,* 1966, 4, 281–287.

TATE, B. G., & BAROFF, G. S. Training the mentally retarded in the production of a complex product: A demonstration of work potential. *Exceptional Children,* 1967, **33**, 405–408.

THOMAS, R. L., & HOWARD, G. A. A treatment program for a self-destructive child. *Mental Retardation,* December 1971, **9,** 16–18.

VAN WAGENEN, R. K., MEYERSON, L., KERR, N. J., & MAHONEY, K. Field trials of a new procedure for toilet training. *Journal of Experimental Child Psychology,* 1969, **8,** 147–159.

VAN WAGENEN, R. K., & MURDOCK, E. E. A transistorized signal-package for toilet training of infants. *Journal of Experimental Child Psychology,* 1966, **3,** 312–314.

VUKELICH, R., & HAKE, D. F. Reduction of dangerously aggressive behavior in a severely retarded resident through a combination of positive reinforcement procedures. *Journal of Applied Behavior Analysis,* 1971, **4,** 215–225.

WALKER, H. M., & BUCKLEY, N. K. Programming generalization and maintenance of treatment effects across time and across settings. *Journal of Applied Behavior Analysis,* 1972, **5,** 209–224.

WASIK, B. H. The application of Premack's generalization on reinforcement to the management of classroom behavior. *Journal of Experimental Child Psychology,* 1970, **10,** 33–43.

WEBSTER, D. R., & AZRIN, N. H. Required relaxation: A method of inhibiting agitative-disruptive behavior of retardates. *Behaviour and Research Therapy,* 1973, **11,** 67–78.

WEISBERG, P. Operant procedures with the retardate: An overview of laboratory research. In N. R. Ellis (Ed.), *International review of research in mental retardation.* Vol. 5. New York: Academic Press, 1971, pp. 113–145.

WHALEY, D. L., & TOUGH, J. Treatment of a self-injuring mongoloid with shock-induced suppression and avoidance. In R. Ulrich, T. Stachnik, & J. Mabry (Eds.), *Control of human behavior.* Vol. 2. Glenview, Ill.: Scott, Foresman & Co., 1970, pp. 154–155.

WHEELER, A. J., & SULZER, B. Operant training and generalization of a verbal response form in a speech-deficient child. *Journal of Applied Behavior Analysis,* 1970, **3,** 139–147.

WHITE, G. D., NIELSEN, G., & JOHNSON, S. M. Timeout duration and the suppression of deviant behavior in children. *Journal of Applied Behavior Analysis,* 1972, **5,** 111–120.

WHITE, J. C., & TAYLOR, D. J. Noxious conditioning as a treatment for rumination. *Mental Retardation,* February 1967, **5,** 30–33.

WHITEHURST, G. J. Generalized labeling on the basis of structural response classes by two young children. *Journal of Experimental Child Psychology,* 1971, **12,** 59–71.

WHITMAN, T. L., BURISH, T., & COLLINS, C. Development of interpersonal language responses in two moderately retarded children. *Mental Retardation,* October 1972, **10,** 40–45.

WHITMAN, T. L., CAPONIGRI, V., & MERCURIO, J. Reducing hyperactive behavior in a severely retarded child. *Mental Retardation,* June 1971, **9,** 17–19.

WHITMAN, T. L., ZAKARAS, M., & CHARDOS, S. Effects of reinforcement and guidance procedures on instruction-following behavior of severely retarded children. *Journal of Applied Behavior Analysis,* 1971, **4,** 283–291.

WIESEN, A. E., & WATSON, E. Elimination of attention-seeking behavior in a retarded child. *American Journal of Mental Deficiency,* 1967, **72,** 50–52.

WOLF, M. M., BIRNBRAUER, J. S., WILLIAMS, T., & LAWLER, J. A note on apparent extinction of the vomiting behavior of a retarded child. In L. Ullmann & L. Krasner (Eds.), *Case studies in behavior modification.* New York: Holt, Rinehart & Winston, 1965, pp. 364–366.

WUNDERLICH, R. A. Programmed instruction: Teaching coinage to retarded children. *Mental Retardation,* October 1972, **10,** 21–23.

ZEAMAN, D., & HOUSE, B. J. The role of attention in retardate discrimination learning. In N. R. Ellis (Ed.), *Handbook of mental deficiency.* New York: McGraw-Hill, 1963, pp. 159–223.

ZEILER, M. D., & JERVEY, S. S. Development of behavior: Self-feeding. *Journal of Consulting and Clinical Psychology,* 1968, **32,** 164–168.

ZIGLER, E. Rigidity in the feebleminded. In E. P. Trapp and P. Himelstein (Eds.), *Research readings on the exceptional child.* New York: Appleton-Century-Crofts, 1962, pp. 141–162.

ZIMMERMAN, E. H., ZIMMERMAN, J., & RUSSELL, D. Differential effects of token reinforcement on instruction-following behavior in retarded students instructed as a group. *Journal of Applied Behavior Analysis,* 1969, **2,** 101–118.

Behavior Modification and Juvenile Delinquency

11

JOHN D. BURCHARD
PAUL T. HARIG

This chapter reviews the literature on the use of behavior modification techniques in the prevention and modification of delinquent behavior. Three general questions will be considered: what are some of the different ways that behavior modification has been used to prevent or modify delinquent behavior; how effective has it been; and what implications does it have for the future? Before we begin to deal with these questions, a number of related issues should be clarified.

First, this review will not consider many so-called behavior modification programs that have little resemblance to applied learning theory or a systematic, empirical approach to treatment. Unfortunately, there have been in recent years a number of questionable, highly coercive procedures implemented within penal institutions, in which "behavior modification" is often a euphemism for drug control, psychosurgery, and confinement. The objectives of these programs are often narrow, repressive control of behavior without a view toward the amelioration of life problems or therapy in the positive sense.

Second, the focus of this chapter is on youths who have a high probability of becoming adjudicated delinquent. In that sense we are talking about a class of people whose credentials involve the commission of certain behaviors (which are often poorly defined), being apprehended (which is usually infrequent), and being declared delinquent or unmanageable by a judge (who is often inconsistent). Given this rather loosely defined class of people, it is the modification of specific behaviors rather than a class of people that we wish to evaluate. The fact that we are reviewing research that relates to a heterogeneous population whose selection is rather capricious and arbitrary poses some obvious problems with respect to the generalization of the findings. Although we believe the results would apply to those individuals who display similar behavior but are not apprehended or prosecuted, we cannot be sure because we have no way of studying these persons. That may not be so important, however, since the task at hand seems to be to develop ways to take those youths who are already labeled delinquent or pre-delinquent and divert them from a juvenile justice system that appears to do more harm than good (Arbuckle & Litwack, 1960; Menninger, 1968). Also, it should be noted that by evaluating those programs that attempt to modify delinquent behavior, we may be addressing only a part of the problem. Of equal if not more importance may be the modification of those aspects of society that develop and maintain delinquent behavior and then arbitrarily select out a few as its scapegoats.

Third, by prevention programs we are referring to those secondary preventive efforts that focus on youths who are displaying a high frequency of antisocial behavior but as yet have not been adjudicated delinquent. This is distinguished from the primary preventive programs such as day care programs or educational efforts that attempt to instill in everyone a proper degree of socialization.

Fourth, we will not attempt to cover every program that lays claim to the successful modification of delinquent behavior. While this may have been possible a few years ago, the recent proliferation of such programs has been too extensive to permit such a task. Rather, we will try to analyze in some depth a few programs in three different areas: institutional programs, community-based residential programs, and community-based prevention programs. For a broader coverage of these areas, the reader is referred to two excellent reviews (Braukmann & Fixsen, 1974; Costello, 1972) and a comprehensive book entitled *Behavior Therapy with Delinquents* (Stumphauzer, 1973).

Institutional Programs

In this section we will discuss three institutional programs that utilized a behavioral technology to rehabilitate the juvenile offender: the CASE Project at the National Training School for Boys in Washington, D.C., the Intensive Training Program at Murdoch Center in North Carolina, and the Youth Center Research Project in California. These three programs were chosen because they represent comprehensive behavioral programs that differ significantly in terms of how the behavioral technology was applied and evaluated.

Before discussing particular characteristics of each program, however, it is important to identify some of the more common aspects of most behavior modification programs that operate within an institutional setting. It is hoped that this will provide a meaningful background for discussing the three programs in question.

In most institutional behavior modification programs, there is a similar overall strategy. The first step is to develop a special environment with prescribed contingencies in which predetermined behaviors are reinforced, not reinforced, or punished in accordance with specific reinforcement schedules. The purpose of such an environment is to obtain rapid and extensive behavioral change wherein behaviors that are regarded as adaptive are strengthened while maladaptive behaviors are weakened. Within this special environment, the reinforcement or punishment usually involves the delivery or removal of an event, consumable, or privilege, which is most often mediated through some form of "token." Also, the specific nature of the contingencies is typically adjusted until the desired behavioral change is obtained. Once this has occurred, the final step is to replace the artificial contingencies that produced the behavioral change with more natural contingencies. This might be done abruptly through the placement of the resident into his natural environment or through some form of gradual transition such as a halfway house program.

While the token economy is used to regulate the reinforcement and punishment contingencies in most institutional programs, another method of contingency control involves the behavioral contract, which usually specifies, in writing, the relationship between a particular behavior and its consequence. Because of the multitude of behavioral targets that are the subject of most residential programs, the contracting system appears most suitable for community-based outpatient programs where the focus is on the modification of a few specific behaviors. However, a combination of the two is obviously possible, and possibly desirable, depending upon the nature and goals of a particular program. The reader is referred elsewhere for further discussion of the theoretical and practical issues related to token economies (Kazdin & Bootzin, 1972) and behavioral contracting (Stuart, 1971; Tharp & Wetzel, 1969).

Related to this general strategy are some rather important assumptions. First, that the tokens that control access to a wide variety of objects and events are initially more reinforcing than intermittent praise and approval, consequences that are more natural and possibly easier and less costly to administer. Second, that by pairing praise and approval with the administration of tokens, praise and approval themselves will become more powerful and effective reinforcers. Third, that the behaviors being reinforced or strengthened are those behaviors that would enable the youth to adjust to his or her noninstitutional community environment. Fourth, that through the use of artificial contingencies involving token reinforcers a behavioral repertoire can be developed that will be maintained in the natural environment. Fifth, that the staff that is taught the behavioral techniques that are utilized in the program do in fact administer reinforcement and punishment in accordance with the predetermined reinforcement schedule. Sixth, that the behavioral change that does occur in a function of the procedures that program advocates claim were administered.

Although the three programs we will discuss appear to have adapted the general strategy and assumptions mentioned above, they also differ in some important ways. For example, with respect to research strategy, one of the three focused mostly on an evaluation of the total program in terms of pre- and posttest measures (CASE), another dealt more with the development and evaluation of specific intervention procedures (Intensive Training Program), while the third involved a comparison of a behavioral program to one based on the theory of transactional analysis (Youth Center Research Project). Further discussion of these similarities and differences and some of the general issues related to institutional behavior modification programs will follow a brief discussion of each of the three projects.

CASE II

One of the first residential behavior modification programs within an institutional setting was established by Harold Cohen and his colleagues at the National Training School for Boys (NTSB) in Washington, D.C. (Cohen, 1968; Cohen & Filipczak, 1971). Cohen, a professional architect, became involved through a special interest in the design of motivationally oriented environments (Cohen, 1967a, 1967b). In 1965, he conducted an 8-month demonstration project with 16 volunteer student inmates. Assigned the acronym CASE I (Contingencies Applicable to Special Education—phase I), the project's goals were to affect the residents' attitudes (motivation) towards school and to raise their specific academic skills to expected grade-age norms for typical public school youngsters.

Cohen based his project on the observation that the typical reinforcers for academic achievement (grades, promotions, diplomas) were not effective for the National Training School inmates. Case I created and used special facilities at the school as response contingencies to motivate study behavior and learning. Cohen provided a lounge with a juke box, television, vending machines, etc., in the project's amusement area; a store; and private study offices in addition to general study areas within the facilities.

All of the participants were high school dropouts who had encountered some degree of academic failure before Case I. By their own admission, they had little or no interest in school work, and they were clearly not motivated by learning for its own sake. The intervention was designed around points earned for academic performances as immediate, extrinsic rewards. These points functioned as the only means by which the student inmates could acquire access to the back-up reinforcers provided in these special areas. Cohen (1967a) reported a typical illustration of the power of his system:

> When he (a student) was assigned to a program he stated, "Man, what's in it for me? If I go and learn all this (junk), I'm going to go on being considered a "nigger" anyway and they're going to s--- all over me." After a moment I said, "You're probably right— but do you like Coca Cola?" And he said, "Yeah." And I said "Well, if you give out the right answers until you get ten points, you can take these ten points and you can buy yourself a Coke." He started working.

In this pilot project, Cohen was able to demonstrate significant increases in the volunteer participants' educational level, as measured by objective achievement tests, and a marked change in their attitudes towards school, as reported by the National Training School staff. Encouraged by these results and the desire to extend the project to a 24-hour basis, the Case staff sought additional funds for the project and, as a result, were able to relocate in their own four-story building on the grounds of the school in 1966. The Case II model (Cohen, Filipczak, Bis, & Cohen, 1966), which followed the 6-month demonstration project (Case I), involved 25 fourteen- to eighteen-year-old inmates (students) from the institution's population who were representative of the entire inmate population in terms of race, type of commitment (federal vs. District of Columbia), and type of offense (primarily breaking and entering, theft, and assault). The primary objective of Case II was to strengthen academic behaviors to enable the student to reenter the public school system (Cohen, 1968). To accomplish

this a comprehensive point (token) system was established whereby points were contingent upon a criterion performance of 90% on individualized program material. However, in the early part of the program, a student could earn some points for simply "studying," and towards the end each student had an opportunity to earn extra points by participating in group academic settings that were more analogous to the traditional classroom environment. With such points students could purchase a variety of items and events including a private room, various commissary items, better cafeteria food, time in a recreational lounge that provided opportunities for pool, watching TV, and socializing with friends, etc. Students remained in the program until their release was approved by their parole board. The average length of stay was approximately 8 months.

For the most part the project was evaluated in terms of a nonexperimental, sequential analysis. The primary data consisted of achievement and intelligence test results obtained before, during, and after a student was in the program, and a multitude of data collected on each student's performance on the point system and on the programmed instructional material. The evaluation was sequential because the procedures changed from time to time, either as a function of a student's progress or in an attempt to make the program more effective and/or more responsive to the needs of students or staff. Such changes are often unavoidable, if not desirable, in such programs that involve the development of new techniques with multiple staff and students. The Case II program was nonexperimental in that there was no systematic effort to compare any specific procedures, nor was there any systematic comparison with a control group of inmates who were similar to the Case II students but did not participate in the Case II program.

Due to the lack of tight experimental control, it is not possible to make any firm conclusions regarding the immediate or long-range behavioral effects of the CASE program. However, it can be said that a rather complex token economy program was established and maintained operative for approximately 2 years, that most of the points were contingent upon academic behavior, and that the students spent close to 90% of their available study time engaging in academic-related behavior (Cohen & Filipczak, 1971). In addition, a number of tentative conclusions can be made. First, it appears likely that the Case II students made significantly greater progress in certain basic academic skills than non-Case inmates (and possibly even noninstitutionalized peers) during the time they were in the program. According to the data, the entire group of Case II students improved an average of one to two grade levels during their 8-month length of stay. While this change may be partially a function of increased familiarity with the tests, the examiners, or "testing" per se, it seems likely that some significant improvement did occur. In addition, Cohen reports an average increase of 12.5 IQ points over the duration of the project. However, this finding is less significant since the students earned points during the second test administration but not the first.

A second tentative conclusion is that the increase in academic skills is a function of both programmed instructional material *and* the reinforcement or token economy program that was established to shape and maintain the student's performance through the individually programmed academic assignments. Since non-CASE inmates did not seem to have access to programmed materials, it could be argued that by merely making such material available a similar outcome could have been obtained. While this may be true for a noninstitutionalized population of peers, there are many descriptive accounts of institutional programs involving youthful offenders that discuss in detail the difficulty in getting most inmates to work seriously on any "academic" task without the use of external incentives.

In addition to the tentative conclusions mentioned above, Cohen makes an additional conclusion that relates to the basic assumption involved in Case II. The assumption is that through the improvement of basic academic skills an inmate is better able to adjust to his noninstitutional environment. Cohen's support for this assumption is based upon follow-up data collected on 27 of the original 37 students who had spent at least 90 days in the Case II program (10 students could not be located). Of the 27, eleven were released directly from the project (CASE-Only students), and 16 were transferred from CASE II to another institutional program before their final release (CASE-Plus students). Considering the two groups separately, the recidivism rate for a 3-year period was 36.4% for the CASE-Only group and 68.8% for the CASE-Plus group.

Many complex issues are raised in trying to interpret such data. While the overall recidivism rate on the national level seems to be about 50–60% (Arbuckle & Litwack, 1960; Kennedy, 1964), there are many well-known problems related to the reliability and validity of recidivism data. The CASE program is compared with the National Training School (NTS) recidivism rate of 76% during the first year (Cohen & Filipczak, 1971). According to Cohen's data, 27% of the CASE-Only students recidivated during the first year, while the recidivism rate for the CASE-Plus students was 62.5%. However, there is little assurance that the CASE II students were, in fact, representative of the overall NTS population (the placement of students with CASE II was not random) or that the data collection procedures were the same for both groups (for example, the recidivism data for NTS appear to have been obtained before CASE II even started).

There is also the problem that approximately 25% of the CASE population was not included in the CASE II follow-up data. Although these "lost" students probably did not return to NTS, it is possible that they did end up in some other correctional facility. Finally, it is not clear how to interpret the comparison of the "CASE-Only" with the "CASE-Plus" students. Were the "CASE-Plus" students the more difficult cases with whom the CASE program was not successful, or was the decision to divert to another penal program a function of pre–Case II decisions or institutional policy?

Nevertheless, there are some data to suggest that those students who participated in the CASE program were better able to avoid further institutional commitment than students who did not participate in that program. Why they might have been able to avoid further institutionalization is a separate question. Was it because of their experience in a structured program where they were held accountable for some of their behavior? Had they learned something about regulating their own behavior in order to obtain greater reinforcement? Did their increased academic skills result in greater self-confidence and achievement in community-based settings? Was their increased academic skill even related to their ability to adjust outside of an institution? Although these are important questions, they are obviously impossible to answer on any empirical basis. Nevertheless, Cohen has provided us with a very promising beginning in terms of the application of a behavioral technology for the rehabilitation of the delinquent offender within an institutional setting.

INTENSIVE TRAINING PROGRAM

At about the same time that Cohen started the CASE Project, the senior author and his associates were developing the Intensive Training Program (ITP) at Murdoch Center, a state institution for the mentally retarded. The ITP, which was in existence for approximately 6 years (1965–1971), was designed to habilitate the adolescent retardate who displayed high frequencies of antisocial behavior. Approximately 70 boys

between the ages of 12 and 20 were involved in this program.

Essentially, the ITP involved first placing the resident in a controlled environment (Intensive Training Unit—ITU) where the consequences of his behavior could be regulated as systematically as possible. Within the ITU, the reinforcement system involved a token economy similar to that of CASE II in that tokens, administered for specific, predetermined behaviors, were exchangeable for a wide variety of backup reinforcers (commissary items, privileges, money, etc.). However, the ITU token economy differed from that of the CASE program in two major ways. First, the token consisted of small, multiple-sized aluminum discs instead of marks on a card (points). Although the ITU first began with a point system, it was readily apparent that the more tangible coins were more appropriate for youths functioning within the mildly retarded and borderline ranges of intelligence. Second, the program involved the total residential environment, and therefore tokens were administered for personal, social, recreational, and vocational behaviors as well as academic behaviors.

The primary contingencies in the ITU involved the immediate administration of tokens (paired with praise and approval) for appropriate behavior, the withholding of attention for mildly inappropriate behavior, and the removal of tokens and brief isolation (time out and seclusion) for those behaviors that the staff felt they could not ignore (e.g., certain forms of profanity and aggression and property destruction). The nature of these contingencies was periodically adjusted on an individual basis wherever specific behavioral objectives were not obtained.

As the resident progressed and displayed increasing degrees of adaptive behavior, the reinforcement and punishment contingencies were gradually modified in the direction of those that exist in the community (e.g., an increasing percentage of tokens were administered for vocational behaviors, with the "payments" being more intermittent but involving a larger number of tokens). Once the behavior was being maintained on more natural contingencies, the resident was gradually phased out of the ITU at Murdoch Center and into a half-way house in the community where he was confronted with even more realistic responsibilities and contingencies. In the event that there was a relapse during the transition from the more structured and artificial ITU environment to the community, some of the more powerful token contingencies were temporarily reestablished in order to regain control.

Although the ITP appears to have been a logical application of the behavioral model to the habilitation of the antisocial retardate within an institutional setting, questions pertaining to its overall effectiveness are difficult if not impossible to answer on an empirical basis. The primary research strategy in the ITP involved the development and evaluation of procedures for modifying specific behaviors. Unfortunately, there was no systematic attempt to track particular variables on all the residents before, during, and after their placement in the program (e.g., the CASE program), nor was there any systematic comparison with a similar group of residents who either did not go through the ITP or who went through some other type of program (e.g., the California Youth Center Research Project). The primary reason for not having a control group was mostly political. In order to obtain what was thought to be the full support of the administration, all those residents who were displaying the most serious behavioral problems were included in the program. Frustrations with the failure of the administration's previous strategy for coping with these residents, which was to separate (put one or two boys into each living unit) and medicate, seemed to preclude a "no treatment" control group, and there were not sufficient funds or staff to

develop an alternative program. Instead of tracking some uniform variables across all residents, the primary emphasis was on the formulation and modification of individual targets, which varied from one resident to another. Through hindsight it would appear that considerable standardized pre-post data (in all five of the target category areas) should have been collected.

Two types of research were conducted in the ITP. The first, the individualized case study, involved four steps: (1) the definition of a specific behavior to be developed, strengthened, or weakened; (2) the objective measurement of that behavior; (3) the administration of an intervention program to modify the behavior; and (4) adjusting the intervention program when necessary in order to obtain the desired change in behavior (for a more detailed discussion of this type of research see Birnbrauer, Burchard, & Burchard, 1970). While this type of approach appeared very therapeutic with many of the residents, it did not generate the kind of empirical data that is essential for a comprehensive program evaluation.

The second type of research dealt with the evaluation of specific procedures. There are two examples of this. One study assessed the effects of token reinforcement on classroom and workshop attendance (Burchard, 1967). Utilizing a conventional ABA design, it was demonstrated that the primary variable responsible for high rates of attendance at both of these activities was the token reinforcement. During condition B, when token reinforcement was made noncontingent on attendance, the residents almost completely discontinued going to the classroom and the workshop. To counteract the set of a "paid vacation," the boys were told at the beginning of the noncontingent phase that it was very important that they continue going to class (workshop) but that they were making good progress and that their tokens would just be given to them in advance. While the boys' verbal behavior reflected their enthusiasm for the classroom (workshop) and their intention to keep up their good attendance, their nonverbal behavior spoke otherwise. Although these data demonstrate how to increase and maintain the attendance of the ITP resident in school or on a job, they also demonstrate the problem of generalization; as soon as more natural contingencies are introduced, the behavior deteriorates.

The second example involves a study that was conducted to analyze the effects of two different magnitudes of time out and response cost (Burchard & Barrera, 1972). Different magnitudes of response cost (5 and 30 tokens) and time in time out (5 minutes and 30 minutes) were analyzed. For the experimental analysis, a multiple-schedules design was utilized in which six residents were exposed to each of the four different punishment conditions at different times. The results indicated that for five of the boys, the larger magnitudes of response cost and isolation were the most suppressive, but for the sixth boy the opposite was true. There were two important implications of this study. First, it points out the importance of defining punishment in terms of the effect on behavior. For whatever reason, the frequency of the target behavior of the sixth boy increased when the consequences involved the greater magnitude of response cost and isolation. To categorically refer to these techniques as punishment is confusing and can interfere with the discovery of ways to bring the behavior of the atypical individuals under optimal control. The second implication relates to possible advantages of the response cost procedure. Although the response cost did not appear to be any more effective in suppressing the undesirable behavior, it required less time and training to administer, the resident did not waste time sitting in an empty room or behind a partition, and he was confronted with the challenge of quickly returning to the scene that prompted the disruption to see if he could bring his own behavior under control.

Obviously this is only one study, but it points up the need for more comparison studies that analyze different procedures for modifying a particular type of behavior.

Because of the controversy surrounding the use of punishment, some additional comment is necessary. There are those behavior modifiers who argue that aversive control should not be a part of any behavior modification program. This would seem to be a little idealistic, particularly with respect to programs for the acting-out adolescent. Groups of such individuals within a residential context create a very volatile, competitive atmosphere much like that that exists in most athletic contests. And in order to maintain order and complete most athletic contests, it is important that there be such things as rules and regulations that are backed up by some form of penalty whenever any violations occur. The important point would seem to be that the rules and penalties are minimal and that one has a positive experience from playing the game. The rationale was similar in the ITP. Mild punishment procedures were instituted to "keep the lid on the situation" so that positive reinforcement could be used to shape and maintain a multitude of adaptive behaviors that were incompatible with the behaviors that seemed responsible for the youths' institutionalization.

In an effort to minimize aversive control, extinction was used for minor forms of undesirable behavior that seemed to be at least partially maintained by the attention of the staff. It is quite possible that additional aversive control could have been avoided through the development and utilization of techniques to control peer attention (see Patterson, 1965) and to strengthen behaviors that were incompatible with the undesirable behavior. Unfortunately, this was not done.

While the ITP offered a more comprehensive residential program than the CASE II program, there is even less empirical evidence with which to determine its overall success. After one year the recidivism rate was approximately 25–35%. However, in dealing with a population of youths for whom there is no standardized policy of incarceration (e.g., the delinquent retardate), it is difficult to know what a recidivism rate means. It would certainly not be appropriate to compare these subjects with inmates at the National Training School, because quite different youths were placed in their respective institutions for quite different reasons. Further, the ITP did not have the kind of support staff that could have made a comprehensive survey of the participants' adjustment in their home environments. Rather, the contribution of this project is more in its evaluative data, which compare specific procedures within the institutional program, and in the description of a comprehensive and complicated system of habilitation. Like CASE, the program contains elaborate procedures for developing a special environment to produce optimal behavioral change together with a host of subjective data concerning problems and issues that related to those procedures. It would be desirable if future programs such as these could be committed to more rigorous empirical analysis than has been conducted thus far.

YOUTH CENTER RESEARCH PROJECT

While there have been numerous replications of token economy programs within institutions, comparative studies to determine possible differences in treatment effects between institutional programs are quite rare. One of the major methodological handicaps to this type of research is the noncomparability of the various settings (Chassan, 1967). The range of possibilities for confounding differences in therapists, subjects, or setting variables seems staggering. Besides possible differences in the composition of resident populations, there could be numerous administrative nuances, potential differences among experience levels of staff, and treatment biases that may confound the results and make it a priori impossible to conduct a valid comparison. A possible solution to this problem was demonstrated by Carl Jesness and his associates (Jesness,

DeRisi, McCormick, & Wedge, 1972; Jesness & DeRisi, 1973).

The Youth Center Research Project was conducted at two institutions of the California Youth Authority. A unique feature of the setting was that both institutions were situated adjacently in the same geographical area (near Stockton, California) and were very similar in their organizational structure, staffing patterns, and physical layout. Each of the facilities, the O. H. Close School and the Karl Holton School, was designed to house approximately 400 youngsters in eight 50-bed living halls. When the project began, boys in the age range of 15 to 21 were being assigned to both institutions. The similarities enabled Jesness to randomly assign residents to one of the two units.

The two treatment models used in this comparative study were expected to differ on their basic assumptions about human behavior, etiology of delinquency, and the manner by which delinquent behavior is changed. At the O. H. Close School, a program of transactional analysis was implemented. Transactional analysis is essentially a psychodynamic personality theory that focuses attention on the individual's self-concept and his subjective perceptions that influence his response to the external world. Transactional analysis deals with much broader patterns of behavior than are ordinarily targeted by the behavior modifier (Jesness et al., 1972). The therapist attempts to help his client sort out his perceptions and expectations and find the alternatives to his present course. Counseling sessions serve as an important vehicle of treatment, in which both client and therapist seek to structure treatment goals and make bilateral commitments (or contracts) to a plan of action. A more comprehensive discussion of transactional analysis is available in Berne (1963).

The behavior modification program conducted at the Karl Holton School employed a variety of techniques including systematic desensitization, extinction, assertive training, and avoidance conditioning. However, the most basic strategy was the use of a token economy coupled to a form of behavior contracting. Three kinds of behavioral targets were managed in the Karl Holton program (Jesness & DeRisi, 1973). The first was "convenience behavior," management and administrative targets that were interpreted as important to the "efficient, orderly function of the institution." These encompassed the everyday routines of institutional living such as getting up on time, dressing properly, keeping the living area neat and clean, being courteous and cooperative with peers and staff, following rules, and completing assignments. Academic behavior was also reinforced in the facility's school. The final target area concerned "critical behavior deficiencies" identified by a behavior checklist and assumed to be most likely to increase the probability of a youth's failing his parole. These critical deficiencies were usually phrased in very general terms (e.g., friendliness, responsibility, considerateness), which were then subdivided into typical examples of the target category.

The incentive system at the Karl Holton School had both long-term and immediate reinforcement systems. On a long-term basis, the opportunity for a parole hearing was made contingent upon a specified level of behavior change as determined through success on the token economy. In order to be referred for a Board hearing, a youngster needed to earn a specified percentage of points in each of the three target areas. It was required that 45% of the youth's points be earned by convenience behavior, 28% by academic behavior, and 27% by the correction of critical behavior deficiencies (Jesness had not offered a rationale for the particular distribution used there). As an additional contingency, a boy needed to accumulate earnings of a minimum number of points for actual release from the institution. This critical number was 7,875 and reflected the average accumulative point earning that would allow a resident to earn his way out in approximately 30 weeks.

In addition to the long-term reinforcers, there was a microeconomy of intermediate reinforcers used to purchase privileges, goods, and services from the institution. Typical reinforcement menus included the opportunities for furlough and day pass, bringing in personal clothing, renting a private room, and using various recreational facilities. The point system had a certain degree of flexibility because the critical deficiencies were handled through behavioral contracts. Thus the youngster and staff worked out contingencies for additional targets as these were necessary.

In addition to the overall behavioral management system, the Karl Holton program evolved an independent token economy to handle the academic area. This became necessary because of several flaws in the overall system. Among them was inflation, which resulted from the staff's failure to charge for all reinforcers. Further, as a result of poor bookkeeping practices in some of the residence halls (Jesness & DeRisi, 1973), many students often found themselves bankrupt from accidental overspending and were inadvertently deprived of the tangible backup reinforcers. Students too deep in debt because of overspending or fines for misbehavior quickly lost interest and motivation to perform on schoolwork. Several boys found themselves confronted with the prospect of having to work their way out of debt before they could even get referred for a parole hearing. Because of these inadequacies, an independent token economy was established strictly for the classroom program. The reinforcement menu included various school supplies, the opportunity to take class smoking breaks or purchase refreshments, and the opportunity to work on independent-study projects. Jesness and DeRisi reported that the introduction of school points increased the rate of class participation and reduced the occurrence of inappropriate in-class behaviors. As a result of this success, the school point system was expanded to an auto mechanics program in which the students filed behavioral contracts on which they earned school points for the completion of behavioral objectives relating to class assignments.

The O. H. Close transactional analysis program was conducted around small group sessions that met twice weekly. An average of eight boys met with a caseworker, who negotiated treatment contracts with each youngster. These contracts specified what goals a boy had set for himself and were of three kinds, academic, small group, and overall social behavior. Most small-group contracts were aimed at broad changes in the youth's way of responding in social situations. Likewise, at school he was encouraged to set individual goals for himself and to negotiate ways by which the staff could help the youngster to achieve his objectives. No explicit reinforcement consequences, however, were arranged for adherence to the contracts.

Outcome data based on the comparison of these two types of institutional programs revealed a number of differences. The average length of stay in the Holton behavior modification program was significantly longer than in the Close transactional analysis program. Residents at Close gave their staff higher ratings in competence and likeability than did residents at Holton. In both schools, youth workers received higher ratings from boys on their case load than from those not on their case load, yet no relationship was found between ratings of caseworker competence made by supervisors and those made by residents. Finally, the differences in likeability between Close and Holton were also reflected in the way that the residents rated living units, almost all halls at Close receiving higher ratings than the highest rated hall at Holton.

Jesness noted that there were serious administrative problems in developing both programs. He feels that both staff and residents were able to read the messages conveyed by the behavior of certain administrators, who asked more questions about the cleanliness of the facilities or security procedures than about the quality of the groups, the number of behavior contracts

written, or improvement on target behaviors. Thus, the institution still reflected what Jesness called "age-old conflicts between treatment and custody, and between residents' needs and staff convenience."

Analysis of the occurrence of rule infractions at both institutions suggested that there was an eventual drop in the rate of incidents of reported misconduct and a continuing reduction in the number of boys sent to detention, which dropped more than 60% at both schools. Staff members also agreed that when detention was used, it was used for a different reason and for briefer periods.

Overall it seems to Jesness that the transactional analysis program appeared to provide a more satisfactory treatment model in terms of consumer satisfaction. However, this may have been due to the fact that staff in the behavior modification program were often required to behave in a different role, being firm and unyielding in their expectations of performance from boys who were not used to such structure. Jesness adds the qualification that among the subjects who complained most about the Holton program were those characterized as "social manipulators," those youths especially prone to trying to obtain reinforcers on demand, according to their own wishes.

Another view of the differential effects of the programs was given in an analysis by personality subtypes. In Jesness's interpretation, youngsters who were more capable of insight and responsibility benefited the most from the transactional analysis. On the other hand, the same subgroup participated more vigorously in behavior modification projects, completing more contracts, earning points at a higher rate, and receiving fewer behavior checks.

Because both treatment programs substantially reduced the amount of major rule violations and promoted a more relaxed, noncustodial social climate, Jesness concluded that both techniques offer desirable features and that the optimal program should have a blend of the obvious strengths of each system. Since both paradigms operate within a contracting system, the prospects for such a synthesis may be considerable.

A 12-month followup of subjects paroled from both institutions indicated that both groups were about the same with respect to the percentage of parole violators (31.4% for the transactional analysis program; 31.9% for the behavior modification program). These rates were significantly lower than the parole violation rates of subjects released from those institutions in the two previous years. The parole violation rates were also significantly different than those of comparable populations of inmates released from two similar California Youth Authority institutions. During the followup year, two of these facilities had an average parole violation rate of over 46%, and there were no significant differences in these rates over previous years at those institutions. Thus, it was clear that both treatment programs significantly affected the probability of successful readjustment upon release from the treatment programs, especially when compared to similar institutions within the system. Because this followup was only for a 12-month period, one must, of course, be cautious when interpreting these statistics as evidence of long-term adjustment. Yet, the data appear to confirm that changes in the institutional climate of a reformatory, at least with respect to two different theoretical approaches, can be moderately beneficial to the inmates. Unfortunately, the nature of the research that was conducted does not disclose which aspects within each "treatment package" were the most beneficial.

DISCUSSION

Prior to our discussion of the above programs, we outlined a general strategy together with several assumptions related to the use of behavior modification techniques in institutional settings. Although we have mentioned several differences with respect to those programs, the general strategy is similar. Before considering behavior modification programs in other settings, we would like to further discuss some of those assumptions.

With respect to the first assumption, the three programs mentioned above provide some objective evidence to suggest that the more material, "token" reinforcers are more powerful than social consequences such as praise, approval, recognition, etc. However, additional data may not be essential since there seems to be a general consensus that social consequences are relatively weak reinforcers for modifying and strengthening the behavior of youth who engage in high frequencies of antisocial behavior. Not only is this relationship almost inherent in the definition of the delinquent (antisocial), but there are considerable data similar to the study cited above (Burchard, 1967) that demonstrate that once token reinforcement is removed, the target behavior tends to deteriorate.

It would appear that the second assumption, which relates to increasing the power of social reinforcers through repeated association with the more material reinforcers, is less obvious. Where generalization to more natural contingencies does occur, it may be that the individual has acquired a greater tolerance of delays in material reinforcement rather than a greater attraction for intermittent praise and approval. If so, this may mean that in order for generalization to occur, greater emphasis should be placed on rearranging stimulus conditions in the natural environment rather than relying so much on the behavior being maintained by those contingencies that already exist (this is the approach adopted by Patterson and his colleagues, which will be discussed in a later part of this chapter).

The third assumption, which deals with the relevance of the target behaviors for community survival, is generally dealt with on an a priori basis. This may eventually turn out to be unfortunate. With respect to the CASE programs, the emphasis was almost exclusively on academic behaviors, while the other two programs seemed to decide arbitrarily what was best for the resident with respect to all aspects of community adaptation. While there is some logic (and benefit) to this procedure, we know of no instance where there was a systematic effort to determine what behaviors are the most critical (either positive or negative) with respect to an individual's ability to adapt to his or her own natural environment. Obviously, what is adaptive in one family or community setting may not be adaptive in another, a characteristic that social service agencies who make adolescent foster placements have been aware of for some time. It would seem desirable for institutional personnel to conduct an analysis of family and community characteristics of their residents similar to that suggested by Kanfer and Saslow (1965, 1969), before they establish their treatment objectives. Since many of their residents come from low-income and minority families, it may be that a disproportionate emphasis on decreasing profanity and increasing academics and cleanliness, may not be all that adaptive (Kimbles, 1973).

The fourth assumption, which states that the behavior, once modified in the special environment, will be maintained in the natural environment, appears to be a very tenuous assumption that has been discussed to some extent in conjunction with the previous two assumptions. The evidence suggests that this is probably true to the extent that the behavior is relevant to the natural environment but, even then, there probably needs to be some modification of the contingencies that exist in that particular setting (Wahler, 1969). Actually, none of the three programs discussed above dealt very extensively with the problem of generalization because of their physical remoteness from the community and the practical problems involved in moving residents in and out of an institution.

The fifth and sixth assumptions pertain to the extent to which procedures are actually administered in accordance with the manner in which they are described by the program advocates. It would seem that this involves a very important assumption that receives very little attention in the literature. We mention this not because we believe that program administrators deliberately deceive their readers and listeners when they write or talk about their programs. Rather, we believe that there are many critical variables related to institutional administration and policies and staff selection and training that can interfere with, and even sabotage, a behavior modification program and that often what is not discussed in a typical research paper can have significant programmatic implications. For example, it is generally assumed that an institutional environment offers almost unlimited potential for establishing an "educational" environment with optimal conditions for behavioral change. Because the institutional environment is relatively small, self-contained, and administered by people whose primary interest should be one of rehabilitating the resident and returning him or her to the most natural environment as soon as possible, the institution should be a good location for programs involving behavior modification.

There are several problems, however, that can seriously mitigate the potential advantages of this situation. One is that the staff of a behavior modification program may not be able to obtain sufficient control of the institutional environment. Even though administrators may verbalize a desire for having their own behavior modification program, they may not be willing to allow the program director to select and train his own staff, eliminate or change irrelevant, irrational, or even maladaptive institutional policies (e.g., regimentation, marching, mail censure, bedtime hours, segregation of sexes, restricted times for taking showers, changing clothes, and smoking, and profanity and physical abuse restrictions that only apply to the residents). In defense of institutions, such policy changes should not be regarded as simple accommodations that can be granted overnight. Although many existing policies are difficult to defend (except to say, "We've always done it that way"), it should be recognized that the behavior of the administration may be as stable and resistant to change as the antisocial behavior of the resident. Additional time might be well spent developing techniques to modify the behavior of those who control the destiny of behavior modification programs as well as with those who are generally regarded as its clients.

A similar problem may exist with the staff of a behavior modification program. It is relatively easy to modify the verbal behavior of the staff in terms of the jargon of behavioral technology. Corresponding changes in nonverbal behavior may be a different matter. For example, at one point, the staff of the ITP at Murdoch Center was well versed in the technique of extinction. However, some systematic observational data indicated a significant discrepancy between their description of their behavior and how they actually behaved. Therefore, a game was devised whereby residents were reinforced in the process of teaching staff how to use extinction (Burchard & Harig, 1974). It would seem that such techniques, which offer on-the-job training and the shaping and reinforcement of actual staff behavior, probably are much more productive than the more conventional, didactic form of instruction. (For further discussion of problems related to the accountability of staff behavior see Burchard, 1969, and Lachenmeyer, 1969.)

A final note on program evaluation. The three programs we have discussed illustrate different methods of program evaluation ranging from the individual case study to the more complex experimental comparison of two different treatment programs. Obviously, not all program directors are interested in conducting research at all of these levels, and, even if they were, it is doubtful that very many could obtain the necessary administrative and financial support to do so. However, it would seem that at a min-

imum each and every behavior modification program should include a tight data collection system that would document empirically whether or not specific behavioral targets are in fact being modified. Without such a system, the perpetuation or change of any particular treatment procedure is determined on the subjective, arbitrary basis that has been so unproductive in the development of most therapeutic procedures. While the more elaborate experimental comparisons of different procedures and programs are important, we believe they should be secondary to a system that determines what behavioral change is taking place with each individual program resident.

Community-based Residential Programs

One of the most significant developments in juvenile rehabilitation and prevention programs during the second half of this century is the advocacy of community-based halfway houses and group foster homes for youngsters who have been committed for delinquent or unmanageable behavior. These youngsters who, like their mentally ill counterparts, were formerly contained in large state institutions a great distance from home are now more likely to receive help in their own cities and towns, with a view toward their readjustment in their home environment.

On a national level, this trend has been even more impressive as whole states convert their juvenile correction programs from the old institutional model. The growth of community-based alternatives has been so rapid that it is virtually impossible to list them all. Keller and Alper (1970) reviewed several sources of interest in these community-based facilities, the most important being public concern over spiraling crime rates combined with a general dissatisfaction with the demonstrated ineffectivess of the institutional treatment either as a resource for rehabilitation or as a deterrent to future delinquent behavior. Moreover, there is a growing awareness that as delinquency originates in the community, the most effective programs for preventing and modifying delinquent behavior are probably located there as well.

When behavior modifiers undertake residential programs in the community, they find several conspicuous advantages over the large institutional settings. On the surface, these differences alleviate many problems pertaining to the transition between treatment environment and home environment, including the perilous step of transferring a resident from the artificial contingencies maintained within the institution to more natural contingencies likely to maintain behavior at home. It is apparent that the typical state institution has many characteristics and policies that could not be found in the natural environment and, therefore, interfere with the rehabilitation process. For example, the large resident-to-staff ratio forces many management problems that can only be met through regimentation; everyone gets up, dresses, eats, showers, does his job, goes to bed, etc., at the same time and under clearly specified conditions that primarily involve aversive control. While this may be necessary in order to prevent chaos and confusion, it does not necessarily build behavioral repertoires that are relevant for making an appropriate adjustment in the community. Because the youth has not learned to regulate his own behavior, the modified behavior usually undergoes rapid deterioration as soon as the structure and aversive control are removed. But this is only to scratch the surface with respect to the inherent differences between institutional and community-based environments. Given the concentrated emphasis in most institutions on custody and security, it is becoming all too apparent that the institutional experience renders one less, rather than more, capable of community survival.

Ordinarily built around a family unit, with fewer residents and more similarity to an average home, community-based programs have many more stimulus features of a youth's natural environment, which should facilitate generalization. And because these programs attempt to fit the youth into the real world, the youth is less apt to label himself as bad and the "treatment" as punishment. Instead, the focus can be shifted to his learning to live a productive life in the community. A related advantage of community-based strategies is that the therapist and youth can work more effectively with *real* problems (school success; job; peer group; parents) that are significant in terms of the youth's community adjustment, not simply problems of the institution itself. Our review of behavioral programs within institutions demonstrates that many intervention tactics are oriented toward the preservation of the order of the system. This pitfall is illustrated by Karachi and Levinson's (1970) discussion of the token economy at the Robert F. Kennedy Youth Center (KYC) in Morgantown, West Virginia, which replaced the National Training School for Boys. The token system at KYC provides a method by which students earn points for "good behavior." Essentially, points are earned for the completion of chores, cooperative behaviors within the cottage area, and effort and accuracy in academic and vocational instruction. Karachi and Levinson described the KYC staff as "form bound" with respect to the type of behavior that gets rewarded. That is, the staff frequently rely upon the various rating forms devised to suggest general ways students could be rewarded, rather than developing their own individualized goals. Points tend to be earned for such activities as getting up on time, remaining silent in the classroom, being seated during class, and so forth—those behaviors that go into maintaining a "smooth institution." Similarly, in his analysis of the Karl Holton School, Jesness reported that 45% of the resident's daily earnings were expected to be made on "convenience points," which were for behaviors "important to the efficient, orderly function of the institution" (Jesness, DeRisi, McCormick, & Wedge, 1972). These behaviors included maintenance chores, promptness, peer and staff interactions, and rule keeping.

In view of the rather clear focus on dealing with problems that occur in the community, through interventions designed to minimize the contrast between a youngster's natural home and the treatment environment, the critical questions to ask about these community-based residential programs are whether in fact they are more effective in dealing with the real problems in the natural environment and, thus, whether they lead to more generalization of treatment effects than has previously been realized through institutional approaches.

ACHIEVEMENT PLACE

By far, the most outstanding example of a behavioral intervention based upon a community setting is Achievement Place in Lawrence, Kansas. Both in terms of public exposure and the volume of experimental research that has been conducted in the treatment program there, Achievement Place stands as a model for intervention programs in the natural environment. We shall review the available literature on this project in some detail in order to arrive at some conclusions about the advantages of community-based programs over institutional models.

The Achievement Place model is a family-style program of group foster care for 6 to 8 adolescents who have been adjudicated delinquent or dependent-neglect and placed in state custody. Its residents have characteristically been caught in the spiral of academic failure, theft, vandalism, truancy, drug abuse, defiance, or physical and verbal aggression. These problems are seen as expressions of the failure of the youths' past environments to provide the instructions, examples, and feedback necessary to develop appropriate behaviors

(Phillips, Phillips, Fixsen, & Wolf, 1972). The program seeks to correct those deficits through modeling, practice and instruction, and feedback mediated by a motivational system based upon a token economy and administered by teaching-parents, professionally trained mediators who are the program's primary staff members.

Achievement Place is "community based" in that it calls upon a board of community representatives to set standards and identify behaviors that tend to be rewarded or sanctioned in the community. One of the principal goals of the program is to teach a youngster how to recognize the predictable consequences of various behaviors. Presumably, the youth will abandon behaviors that ordinarily get punished in the community in favor of those actions that earn praise, status, and a good reputation from the community.

In order to convey this feedback, the program is organized around rules and consequences, fines, and rewards. The goal behaviors include academic conduct, personal care and home-maintenance responsibilities, and a variety of social skills. Achievement Place is intended to be a microcosm of the values of the local community, so that the youth can learn what kind of behavior gets reinforced there: expressions of appropriate behavior, i.e., academic achievement, cooperation, taking responsibility, are rewarded, and occurrences of inappropriate behavior, i.e., lying, stealing, academic failure, and fighting, are punished.

Residents at Achievement Place are taught to recognize these consequences through a multilevel motivational system. When a youngster first enters the program, he receives the maximum amount of structured feedback through the point system. Appropriate behaviors are immediately followed by point earning and praise, whereas inappropriate responses are followed by fines and practice of desirable alternative behaviors (which can, in turn, earn back some of these lost points). The points can be used to purchase various privileges in the token economy, according to a series of schedules that instructs the youth about the system. The Achievement Place token economy is thus both a positive and a negative system (earnings and fines), flexible enough to permit the reinforcement and punishment of specific, individualized target behaviors.

The designers of Achievement Place make a direct translation between the concept of "self-control" and successful performance on the point system. Residents who obtain the necessary level of performance can purchase the right to go on a merit system, avoiding the token economy by demonstrating satisfactory conduct in the absence of points or fines. The developers feel that this is a means of fading a youth into a normal source of reinforcement and feedback—social praise, satisfaction, and status. Nevertheless, the possibility of returning to the point system is still present as a backup, and the resident must periodically prove his eligibility to remain on the point-free status. When a youngster has demonstrated that he can fare well on a merit system, he is subsequently transferred

to his or her natural home, where the teaching-parents devise a prototype token economy to help the natural parents or guardians maintain the behaviors learned at Achievement Place.

The experimental foundations of Achievement Place are documented in six years of published research. Its proponents are clearly among the most prolific writers within the behavior modification literature, and a number of very interesting studies still await publication. However, this review will focus mainly on those studies that are currently available and that pertain to the experimental analysis of various program attributes.

Table 11-1 lists nine such investigations on various aspects of the Achievement Place program. We shall attempt a systematic analysis of the research based on these reports. These nine articles review 30 different experiments, involving a total of 127 subjects in different experimental manipulations. (Experiment No. 9 in reference number 9 only provides data on the validation of a dependent variable and, therefore, was not included in this analysis.) The extent to which the same subject was

TABLE 11–1   The nine studies involved in the analysis of the achievement place research program

Reference	No. of Separate Experiments	No. of Subjects In All Experiments
1. Phillips, E. L. (1968)	5	13
2. Bailey, J. S., Wolf, M. M., & Phillips, E. L. (1970)	3	7
3. Bailey, J. S., Timbers, G. D., Phillips, E. L., & Wolf, M. M. (1971)	2	2
4. Phillips. E. L., Phillips, E. A., Fixsen, D. L., & Wolf, M. M. (1971)	4	19
5. Braukmann, C. J., Maloney, D. M., Fixsen, D. L., Phillips, E. L., & Wolf, M. M. (1972)	3	6
6. Fixsen, D. L., Phillips, E. L., & Wolf, M. M. (1972)	2	12
7. Kirigin, K. A., Phillips, E. L., Fixsen, D. L., & Wolf, M. M. (1972)	1	6
8. Fixsen, D. L., Phillips, E. L., & Wolf, M. M. (1973)	2	13
9. Phillips, E. L., Wolf, M. M., & Fixsen, D. L. (1973)	8	49
	Total = 30	Total = 127

involved in different experimental manipulations is not always known. In some instances, however, it is clear that the same subject did participate in different experiments. In analyzing these nine studies, we will use the 30 experiments as our data base. The purpose of this is to try to provide a comprehensive and objective assessment of the Achievement Place research program. This does not mean that there are not differences between the research program and the treatment program. Obviously there are many behavioral targets, intervention programs, etc., that are a basic part of the Achievement Place program but are not included in these nine studies, and in some instances, what is included may create a distorted picture of what takes place. Nevertheless, our purpose is to review research findings, not program descriptions, and the manner in which we have analyzed them seems the most efficient way to accomplish that goal.

TARGET BEHAVIORS. Table 11-2 summarizes seven different categories of target behaviors that were examined in the 30 different experiments. From this table it can be seen that the most frequent interventions reported in the research literature have focused upon bedroom and bathroom cleaning and similar maintenance tasks. However, these were not necessarily interventions in their own right. It appears that some of the justification for the utilization of housekeeping measures was that they afforded quantifiable and highly reliable outcome measures sensitive to various types of supervision, strategies for shaping reliable reporting of behavior, and so forth.

Academic and social behaviors received the next greatest degree of attention in the developmental research of Achievement Place. On the academic side, daily report cards, which the youth carried between his classes and the group home, were utilized to provide feedback on disruptive class conduct and overall class participation. Similarly, completion of homework assignments was mediated through feedback with the youth's regular teachers and through direct observation in the group home. The general focus of those studies related to social skills was to change various aspects of a youngster's behavior that promoted his negative image or reputation in the community. In this regard, the various targets dealt with the suppression or elimination of noxious mannerisms and the development of appropriate interview skills.

TABLE 11–2   Target behaviors of the nine different studies

Target Behaviors	No. of Experiments	(References— See Table 11–1)
Maintenance behaviors (bedroom and bathroom cleaning)	10	(1, 4, 9)
Social behaviors (interview skills and inappropriate speech)	7	(1, 3, 5)
Academic behaviors (homework, classroom participation, disruptions, etc.)	5	(1, 2, 7)
Program administration (self- and peer-report of maintenance behaviors and participation in family conference)	4	(6, 8)
Other (punctuality, saving points, watching evening news)	4	(1, 4)
Total = 40		

The next largest set of experimental manipulations focused upon aspects of program administration, whereby a youngster was taught to administer the system or to participate in various activities thought to reflect self-government. One of these studies (Fixsen, Phillips, & Wolf, 1972) focused on how to get boys to be more accurate in evaluating their own and their peers' performance with respect to keeping their rooms neat and clean. Another study (Fixsen, Phillips, & Wolf, 1973) examined the variables that influenced the youngster's participation in family conference; a time was set aside for group meetings, discussion of house rules, and deliberation on the consequences for various infractions. The final category includes all other targets, such as punctuality, saving points, and watching evening news.

METHODOLOGY. All of the nine studies referred to in Table 11–2 utilized a single-subject experimental analysis with each subject serving as his own control. In most cases the findings have been replicated both across and within subjects. There was considerable variation in the specific type of experimental design, including AB interventions (e.g., Phillips, 1968), reversal or withdrawal designs (e.g., Phillips et al., 1971), multielement factorial design of an ABCDC nature (e.g., Phillips, Wolf, & Fixsen, 1973), multiple-baseline designs (e.g., Bailey et al., 1972), and time-lagged intersubject replications or multiple-base-line-across-person designs (e.g., Braukmann et al., 1972). For further discussion of these various designs see Glass, Wilson, & Gottman, 1974.

One of the outstanding features of these studies has been the manner in which operational response definitions have been established and reliable data collection systems have been maintained. Often, by focusing on certain nonreactive measures that were highly quantifiable (e.g., level of bathroom cleaning as an index of a peer manager supervisory skill), the investigators were able to obtain high interrater reliability for the behavior under investigation.

In our survey, the most widely employed designs were multielement and multiple-base-line studies in which the experimental effect was contrasted for its own sake. In the case of the multielement study, various techniques were analyzed sequentially on an intersubject basis. In the multiple-baseline designs, techniques were systematically replicated to demonstrate their general effect across several behaviors. Although such designs are a useful strategy to parcel out the various factors that make an intervention work, it overlooks the fact that the purpose of Achievement Place is purportedly to make a youth independent of its various systems. With this fact in mind, the priority of studies that examine response generalization becomes obvious. Certainly it is useful to demonstrate that an intervention procedure in the artificial or structured environment produces a reliable effect (e.g., the acceleration or deceleration of target behavior from baseline level). Yet, this information is of dubious utility unless one can also determine the residual effects of that intervention, or its generalization, to the natural environment. More will be said about the problem of generalization later.

The only other point to be made is to reemphasize the need for more evaluative research that, in this case, would compare the Achievement Place model with other strategies of intervention. As will be seen below, the research related to Achievement Place demonstrates a successful modification of almost all of the target behaviors that were specified. This does not necessarily mean, however, that the program is any more effective than other programs or no program at all in obtaining long-range community adjustment. Phillips et al. (1972) suggested that Achievement Place was superior to both reform school or probation on a youth's chance for improvement and continued avoidance of the juvenile justice system. However, these data do not represent unbiased samples, and some controlled comparison studies involving randomized placement of residents are needed. Fortunately, a number of group homes built upon the Achievement Place model have recently opened, and a few such studies are now under way.

TYPES OF INTERVENTION. Achievement Place operates on a token economy in which points are both earned and lost for various behaviors. As Phillips et al. (1972) noted, this flexible kind of a system provides certain advantages to the behavior modifier. Various appropriate behaviors that have low baseline levels can be strengthened using only positive points. Conversely, high-rate noxious behaviors can be eliminated using only fines. In other situations, the system provides differential reinforcement of certain behaviors, depending upon their operant level. For these responses, either a positive or negative consequence can be applied.

Table 11-3 summarizes the mode of contingency control that was utilized in the 30 experiments that were surveyed.

As seen in the summaries of the targets of these experiments, the utilization of various contingencies did tend to correspond to the general Achievement Place token economy description. Prosocial targets at initially low base rates tended to result in positive reinforcement only, while mild punishment was the consequence for those behaviors that were targeted exclusively as inappropriate. Other behaviors, such as housekeeping tasks, received differential reinforcement and punishment based on their relative occurrence or qualitative level. In most instances this category seemed to include behaviors that were within the youth's repertoire but were not expected to occur without administering points for their occurrence and removing points for their absence.

It should be noted that the medium of control (positive versus negative) reflected in this research survey does differ somewhat from the procedures suggested in the Teaching-Family Handbook (Phillips et al., 1972, pp. 36–42). Table 11-4 presents a summary of the point earnings and fines that are suggested in the handbook for two behavioral categories, social behaviors and indoor maintenance tasks (cleaning, polishing, dusting, sweeping, etc.). With respect to social behaviors, 39 inappropriate behaviors are specified that might result in a response cost, whereas there are 41 maintenance behaviors that can result in earning points. This would indicate that there is no guarantee that a youth will earn back his points engaging in the prosocial or appropriate counterparts of the activity that may have lost him points. Since the token economy is arranged between social, maintenance, and academic behaviors, it might be more likely to find a youth who lost a significant

TABLE 11–3   Medium of contingency control utilized in the 30 experiments

Positive Reinforcement (Earn Points Only)		Negative Reinforcement (Lose Points Only)		Both Positive and Negative Reinforcement	
Interview skills	(2)	Articulation errors	(2)	Classroom behavior	(4)
Family conference	(2)	Aggressive speech	(1)	Reliable peer and self report	(2)
Homework	(1)	Punctuality	(2)	News quizzes	(1)
Savings	(1)	Inappropriate Speech	(1)	Room cleaning	(10)
Totals	7		6		17

TABLE 11–4   Approximate point consequences suggested by teaching-family handbook

Behavioral Categories	No. of Behaviors Defined	% Behaviors That Lost Points	% Behaviors That Earned Points	Total Possible Earnings	Total Possible Losses
Social behaviors	44	89%	14%	6,600	109,900
Maintenance behaviors (indoor)	41	—	100%	23,800	—

amount of points on a social or academic category earning these back through an unrelated maintenance task.

RESULTS

In terms of demonstrating functional relationships between the target behaviors and the intervention procedures, the results are very impressive. In over 90% of the experiments there was a significant change in the target behavior, and in each case that change was demonstrated to be a function of a particular intervention. The only instances where a significant behavioral change did not occur involved an attempt to improve room cleaning performance through self and peer reports (Fixsen, Phillips, & Wolf, 1972) and two experiments (Exp. 2 & 6) comparing the effectiveness of different ways to administer the point system to produce clean bathrooms (Phillips, Phillips, Wolf, & Fixsen, 1973). In both cases, however, additional experiments were conducted in which some form of experimental control was established.

The positive results include many specific relationships that cannot be mentioned in a review such as this. However, it is important to note the wide variety of behaviors that can be readily modified given the environmental control and a token economy program like that that exists at Achievement Place. No matter whether the targets involve doing homework, behaving appropriately in school, making appropriate eye contact in an interview, cleaning one's room, expressing oneself at family conference,

monitoring one's own performance, or depositing points in the bank, new behaviors can be developed and the frequency of old behaviors can be modified given the appropriate manipulation of contingencies that control powerful reinforcers.

While the power with which a token economy program can produce rapid behavioral change has been demonstrated in numerous other studies involving both delinquent and nondelinquent subjects, there are aspects of the above nine studies that lead to new and important areas of investigation. First, there is an increasing emphasis on the modification of social behaviors. While there has been no reluctance in the literature to identify the importance of modifying social behaviors, especially with delinquent and predelinquent youths, there is a dearth of data on this subject in the area of behavior modification. Much of the reason for this seems to relate to the methodological problems encountered in dealing with a behavior that is difficult to define, involves other people, and takes place in a multitude of different settings (Burchard, 1969). Nevertheless, the fact that seven of the above experiments involved the successful modification of social behavior is encouraging. In addition, we have seen at least one prepublication manuscript that pertains to the modification of a youth's negative reaction to the loss of points. It would seem that any intervention that enables predelinquent youth to control their tempers and relate more effectively would adults and authority figures would be desirable.

The second positive development involves the utilization of youths in the administration and analysis of the Achievement Place system (Fixsen, Phillips, & Wolf, 1972; Fixsen, Phillips, & Wolf, 1973; and to some extent, Phillips, Wolf, & Fixsen, 1973). In general, the results demonstrate that the youths can be taught how to reliably monitor their behavior; that youths participate more in family conference when *they* can set the consequences of rule violations; and that the youths not only prefer a democratically elected peer manager of maintenance tasks but that they perform best under that particular system.

One of the major criticisms of behavior modification programs is that the programs involve a perpetuation of the lopsided power relationship between youths and the adult authority figure, and that, at best, they only teach the youths to conform to "established" ways of doing things. According to some of these critics, a more meaningful and effective strategy would be to teach youths how to take a more active role in obtaining what they want. In other words, instead of being taught that "if they do X they'll get Y," they should be taught to become more actively involved in defining their objectives and formulating and experimenting with different ways that they and their peers can obtain those objectives. It would seem that the three studies mentioned above reflect a desire at Achievement Place to move in that direction. What remains to be seen is whether or not such a strategy does in fact help youths to adjust more effectively to the community.

DISCUSSION

The Achievement Place program represents a comprehensive and impressive example of how behavior modification techniques can be used in a community-based residential program for delinquent youths. Anyone attempting such an effort could certainly benefit from a detailed review of all the research that has been done there. However, in developing new programs, we think the emphasis should not be on how can one do what Achievement Place did, but rather, how can one utilize what Achievement Place has done to develop an even more effective program. In this regard, there are three issues related to the Achievement Place program that we feel warrant further attention: the relevance of the target behaviors, the use of aversive control, and the problem of generalization.

First, the relevance of some of the target behaviors is questionable. In selecting behavior modification targets, we feel there are two important criteria that must be considered; first, is the behavior relevant in terms of the youth's ultimate adaptation to his natural environment, and second, can the behavior be objectively defined so that its occurrence can be monitored reliably (Birnbrauer, Burchard, & Burchard, 1970). Because these two criteria are not always compatible, it is often necessary to make compromises in one or the other or both. In the case of Achievement Place, there may be an overemphasis on meeting the latter criterion at the expense of the former. We are referring primarily to the multitude of behavioral targets that relate to the maintenance of a clear and orderly household. While it may be possible to obtain reliable data by defining a task in terms of the absence of dust greater than one-quarter inch in diameter, the absence of dirt on a white glove that is wiped over a window still, or the absence of a crease longer than 4 inches in a bedspread, the relationship of such targets to a successful community adjustment is debatable.

In addition to the more obvious scientific arguments related to the need for reliable data (e.g., many intervention procedures can be evaluated in terms of their effect on such behavior, an increased certainty that the frequency of the target behavior is in fact changing, etc.), the staff of Achievement Place also claim that these behaviors do generalize to the natural environment where they are maintained by natural reinforcement. According to one staff member, it gives the youth an effective way to reinforce the behavior of his or her parents that wasn't there before. If these things are true, we hope that they can be validated empirically in the near future. On the surface it would appear that this part of the program only models and reinforces compliance to tasks that relate more to a career as a butler or maid than to return to a low-income family (77% of the residents) that is probably receiving welfare assistance (Phillips, Phillips, Fixsen, & Wolf, 1972). It should be noted that the issue is not whether youths should be taught to pick up after themselves, make their beds, and wash their hands before they eat. The issue is one of emphasis. A daily room inspection procedure that includes 21 criteria measured with rulers and white gloves seems to constitute a certain degree of overkill, especially given the relatively limited amount of time to deal with many of the more social (and antisocial) behaviors that are more directly responsible for the youths' being there.

A second and related issue that should be considered in developing a program such as Achievement Place involves the question of aversive control. With respect to the maintenance targets, it may be that Achievement Place pays a considerable price for its clean household. It would appear from the data that moderate aversive control must be exerted over the residents to maintain these standards. This is suggested in the data presented in one of the experiments involving room-cleaning behavior (Phillips, Phillips, Fixsen, & Wolf, 1971). During baseline, four boys performed at near 100% criteria under conditions where a performance below 80% criteria resulted in a loss of 500 points and a performance above 80% resulted in a gain of 500 points. When the point contingencies were removed, a number of threats, demands, and social contin-

gencies were demonstrated to be ineffective in maintaining a high level of room cleaning behavior. The authors describe this condition in the following manner:

> During this condition there was no point consequences for room cleaning. However, several probes were made during the No-Points condition: the feedback was discontinued and reinstated; the boys were threatened that "If you boys don't start cleaning your rooms it will be necessary to start points on rooms again"; they were given instructions that "Boys, your rooms are a mess. Clean them up as soon as possible"; and it was demanded that "Boys, your rooms are a mess. I want you to go up and clean your rooms *now*!"

An important question is why were the boys less willing to clean their room in the absence of the point contingency (even when demanded to do do)? While one explanation is that they could no longer *earn* points for room cleaning, other data would suggest that it was the point loss that was really controlling their behavior. For example, in that same study, data are presented that indicate that boys are much more inclined to watch television news if the contingency involves a point loss as compared to a large point earning (1,000 points). Also, data are presented that imply that the best way to enhance punctuality is through a point fine (although it was not contrasted with a point gain for not being tardy). Another study demonstrates that the way to obtain more accurate and reliable self- and peer-reports of room cleaning is to increase the point *loss* for those items marked incorrectly (Fixsen, Phillips, & 1972).

As with the issue related to the relevance of the behavioral targets, the question is not whether aversive control should be utilized but rather under what conditions and how often. Its rather extensive use in the Achievement Place program is best illustrated in the experiments in self-government

(Fixsen, Phillips, & Wolf, 1973). The purpose of the experiments was to evaluate ways to enhance participation in a semi-self-government system. The important point here is that youth participation dealt almost exclusively with rule violations and the determination of guilt and punishment. The study lasted 4 months and involved 7 boys. During that time there were 80 "trials" involving rule violations, which resulted in 58 fines totaling 1,020,750 points. The mean fine was 17,600 points, and the median was 5,000 points. This would suggest that in the Achievement Place token economy one of the more significant ways in which points are spent is for rule violations.

While it may be necessary and desirable to utilize aversive control to modify certain types of antisocial and disruptive behavior, it is also necessary to consider overuse of aversive control. At Achievement Place there are 99 rules that a resident can violate. While they all may reflect undesirable behavior, it is not clear that the best way to modify those behaviors is through aversive control. There are known adverse side effects of aversive control, and for this reason it would seem beneficial to explore other strategies to suppress certain types of inappropriate behavior. For example, one area of research on the Achievement Place motivational system that remains to be explored is the application of DRO (differential reinforcement for other behavior) contingencies for the *nonoccurrence* of certain target behaviors. If this reinforcement schedule was employed, a youth might receive points for short intervals during which aggressive speech was not recorded. On intuitive grounds, this approach should have some major advantages over the response-cost strategy now employed, because the youth could get reinforced for engaging in various incompatible alternative behaviors. Yet, the experimental comparison still awaits a rigorous test.

One of the most critical questions related to the use of aversive control pertains to the third issue we would like to discuss: the generalization of behavioral change to the natural environment. There is considerable evidence in the Achievement Place research that indicates that a fine or response cost is an effective way to modify high-frequency inappropriate behavior. Aversive control also seems to be the primary workhorse for accelerating the frequency of many behaviors (primarily academic and maintenance) that, in and of themselves, are relatively unreinforcing. But an important question is what are the effects of these procedures on the behavior after the youth leaves Achievement Place?

Formulating questions about generalization is somewhat like a game that might go something like this: At the start, there are two things to worry about. Will the behavioral change be maintained in the natural environment or won't it? If it will, then there is nothing to worry about. If it won't, then there are two more things to worry about. Does the lack of generalization reflect the type or level of the reinforcement schedule that produced the behavioral change in the first place, or did the behavior fail to generalize because of a lack of supporting contingencies in the community? If the problem pertained to the schedule you have little to worry about. You go back to the treatment setting and strengthen the desirable behavior, preferably through a positive reinforcement schedule. However, if the problem is with the supporting contingencies in the natural environment, then you have two more things to worry about. Should you reprogram the natural environment to provide supporting contingencies, or should you build in a resistance to the lack of supporting contingencies through intermittent reinforcement, fading, or overlearning? And so on . . .

Obviously the game is one in which these questions can be formulated ad infinitum. With generalization, the unfortunate part is that there will probably always be something to worry about; this is the nature of the beast! It's hard enough to try to determine whether or not behavior has changed, and if so why, let alone trying to determine whether or not the change also occurred in a completely different setting.

With respect to Achievement Place, most of the focus is still on the first question: will the behavioral change be maintained in the natural environment or won't it? There are no data on the generalization of behavior to other environmental settings except in terms of the very gross, subjective nature of anecdotal parental reports. In several studies, follow-up data are provided on a few behaviors (inappropriate speech and room cleaning) in the same setting, which demonstrates the suppression of undesirable responses but only insofar as the subjects still lived at the group home where nonspecific contingencies may have actually confounded this effect (Bailey, Timbers, Phillips, & Wolf, 1971; Phillips, 1968; Phillips, Phillips, Fixsen, & Wolf, 1971). Also, there were two studies in which systematic changes were made on contingencies in an attempt to maintain behavior under more "natural" conditions (Bailey, Wolf, & Phillips, 1970; Phillips, Phillips, Fixsen, & Wolf, 1971). In both of these instances, daily point consequences that were demonstrated to have produced a change in behavior were administered less frequently (but for a correspondently larger point loss or gain depending on one's performance). The procedure, referred to as fading, was very successful as far as it went. Yet there is still a considerable gap between the performance of room cleaning behavior in Achievement Place, where one can stand to gain or lose a large number of points (depending upon whether or not the contingency is being applied that day), and the performance of such behavior 3 months or even 2 weeks after the youth has returned home. A next step in the fading procedure might be to gradually introduce noncontingent conditions in which the behavior is only maintained by social reinforcement and there is no risk of a point loss. If this were done, it would be important that the youth understand the no-risk clause.

It should also be noted that although the Achievement Place data contain innumerable examples of precise behavioral control through the withdrawal of the (artificial) point contingencies, each one of these demonstrations also illustrates the problem of generalization. At some point it is desirable to have the behavior occur merely for the asking (or shouting or demanding). It would appear that part of the answer to this dilemma lies in the programming of the transition from the artificial to the natural environment, much as has been done in the two fading experiments.

A final point on the issue of generalization pertains to what may be a problem of too much stimulus control. There is some indication that those behaviors that respond best to reinforcement control are the least apt to generalize across time and settings once the contingency is withdrawn (Hartman & Atkinson, 1973). In the Achievement Place program, it would appear that each youth is involved in many experiments in which he learns the nature of differential reinforcement. During the "no point" condition, he learns that he doesn't have to exhibit those behaviors that he can readily perform when points are forthcoming. The behavior quickly becomes under the precise control of the point contingency. However, when he returns home there may be few stimuli associated with the reinforcement condition that existed at Achievement Place (e.g., different people, different reinforcers, no daily report cards, etc.). To what extent, then, does a youth who returns home tell himself he is in a "no points" condition?

Another example of this problem of stimulus control is illustrated in a recent Achievement Place manuscript that deals with vocational training (Ayala, Minkin, Phillips, Fixsen, & Wolf, 1973). In this study, several boys were given jobs cleaning gas station rest rooms in preparation for reentry into the community. What is interesting is that after spending many months cleaning the Achievement Place bathroom, their performance in the gas stations was only at criteria when they were provided with immediate feedback, instruction, and supervision (it should be noted that the authors place a slightly different interpretation on these data). In other words, the behaviors were within the boys' response repertoire, but without specific stimulus conditions the behaviors did not occur. Perhaps this illustration gives us a clue to the generalization problem. In order to solve the dilemma of generalization, more attention should be paid to certain characteristics of the natural environment: what behaviors are apt to be reinforced in that environment; how does one modify the behavior of relevant people in that environment; and how can we teach those people how to maintain the control that has been established. Until this happens, we will have a lot to worry about with respect to the problem of generalization.

Community-based Prevention Programs

In spite of the numerous advantages of Achievement Place and related forms of residential, community-oriented programs, economic and practical constraints limit their utility as a general strategy of treatment.

It must be recalled that the Achievement Place staff typically work with youngsters who have been placed in their custody by the juvenile court. This process requires formal adjudication and the legal separation of the youths from their natural families. Thus the staff controls a very powerful contingency, namely, the opportunity for a youth to return home on a permanent basis, given adequate performance in Achievement Place. This fact may be a significant determinant in the youth's willingness to accept the partial aversive control exerted by the Achievement Place system. It is certainly questionable whether any youngster would accept such a structure as a free

agent. One pertinent question to ask is what kind of programs can one devise in situations where adjudication is unlikely?

Even if it were possible to obtain formal commitment on every "predelinquent" youth, it would certainly not be economical to conduct all intervention within a residential framework. According to the estimates of Phillips and Wolf (1972), the total costs for the first year for group homes for 100 youths (including construction and operating costs) would be $1,250,000, which is only 25% of the initial cost of state training schools but still exceeds $12,000 per youth. A problem with this approach at the local level is that residential intervention limits the number of youngsters served to six or eight at a time, for an average duration of 12–15 months. Thus the issue is not only that all youths may not require residential treatment, but also that relatively few could be served even if all did.

The second major point is that although community-based residential programs can often approximate the natural environment much more effectively than institutions can, the problem of generalization of newly acquired behaviors is still present, and supplementary intervention to transfer these behaviors to the natural environment is still required. The staff of Achievement Place have devised an elaborate "homeward bound" system to accommodate the transition (Phillips, Phillips, Fixsen, & Wolf, 1972). This approach involves a limited transfer of Achievement contingencies to the youth's own home, under supervision of the teaching-parents. Parents are involved in the treatment programs after the fact, in order to get the youths to maintain behaviors that the parents may not necessarily be able to shape. Unfortunately, this model has not produced extremely durable results, and the Achievement Place staff typically functions in a "doctor-patient" relationship with parents even after the youngster has been released from the program (Phillips, 1973).

These issues highlight the need for a third type of intervention program, focused upon the direct modification of deviant behaviors within a youngster's natural environment. Not only can this model function on a preventive basis with youth for whom residential treatment programs are not feasible or practical, but it also serves as a necessary step in the transition of youths from these residential, structured programs to their natural homes. In this section we will examine four different programs—the Social Learning Project (parent training) developed by Gerald Patterson and his associates at the Oregon Research Institute; the Family and School Consultation Project (behavior contracting) developed by Richard Stuart and his associates in Michigan; the PICA/PREP program (community intervention) developed by Cohen and his associates in Silver Springs, Maryland; and the Hunt School Project (youth center) developed by Burchard and his associates in Burlington, Vermont.

SOCIAL LEARNING PROJECT

The work of Patterson and his associates on the Social Learning Project differs from the intervention programs we have previously discussed on several fundamental points. In the first place, Patterson's focus is on prevention rather than on rehabilitation. The target population he has worked with consists of younger children (6–13 years old) who have not been formally adjudicated. In fact, the majority of youngsters the project has served have not even come to the attention of outside authorities and, typically, referrals have been directly from parents, on a child guidance clinic basis. Despite these differences, the resemblance of the referral problems of these youngsters to those of their older counterparts and the similarity of Patterson's treatment approach to other community-based interventions make it quite relevant to discuss his research here.

The Social Learning Project was begun by Patterson in order to make a systematic investigation of interrelationships between family members and their reciprocal influence on rates of various target behaviors such as coercion, aggression, and conflict. Much of the impetus for Patterson's work came from preliminary case studies with preschool children with mild conduct problems. In an early investigation with a 5-year-old in kindergarten (Patterson & Brodsky, 1966), for example, Patterson attempted to broaden the focus of behavior modification beyond the single-target intervention. The child's problem behaviors included tantrums, physical aggression, hyperactive behavior, and peer conflict, which were apparently precipitated by the youngster's separation from his mother each morning at school. Patterson conceptualized the situation in terms of the *antecedents* of the deviant behavior. The youngster's oppositional or negative responses were interpreted as a link in a response chain elicited by anxiety. Patterson and Brodsky treated the symptoms with an anxiety-reducing paradigm including flooding and modeling. In addition, they modified the reaction of the youngster's parents to these tantrums, so as to limit the availability of social reinforcers for the noxious responses. In their discussion of this case, Patterson and Brodsky make a comment that is very informative about their approach to behavioral procedures used to shape or extinguish behaviors. The intervention only served to rearrange social behaviors within already existing hierarchies. In their view, the therapist's function is to initiate the first link in a chain reaction of dyadic social responses, yet such a chain clearly would not exist unless the child had been conditioned previously to social behaviors. Another key point in their discussion is the realization that major changes in behavior occur within social environments that support or sabotage change produced in treatment. Patterson was among the first to maintain that the demonstration of behavior change within the laboratory and other special environments is irrelevant unless those responses can be shown to generalize on a long-term basis within the natural environment.

Despite these perceptions, Patterson's early interventions all suffered from the same problems of a limited persistence of the treatment effect, leading him to conclude that it is probably more reasonable to design interventions that act directly on the relevant social agents of the child rather than to alter the child's deviant behavior and then determine the effect of that change upon the reinforcement schedules of relevant social agents (Patterson, McNeil, Hawkins, & Phelps, 1967). Subsequently, he produced a series of investigations focused on "reprogramming" of the social environments of the various subjects.

In the first general study (Patterson et al., 1967), Patterson worked with a 5-year-old youngster who was withdrawn, isolated, and emitted several bizarre behaviors. The goal was to reprogram the parents and the child to be more mutually reinforcing. Patterson instituted a series of behavioral interventions. He first trained the mother to use positive reinforcers, then trained her to initiate more social contacts with her son. In turn, he trained the child to function as a more effective social reinforcer for the parents and trained the child to initiate more social contacts with them. The major tool in this intervention was a programmed text that Patterson developed to teach reinforcement principles to parents. After the parents had read the text, Patterson shaped attending responses in the youth to the experimenter's reinforcement. Then, he faded this response to the mother, teaching her to elicit and bring smiles under her control. In order to provide sources for generalization, he encouraged the parents to practice this procedure outside of the experimental trials. With a novel twist, Patterson shaped the parents by using a fee reduction for reports of their effectiveness. Finally, Patterson taught the mother

to attend to the child's presence, shaping him to be around her, and then reinforcing the youngster for compliance to the mother's instructions and requests.

Data were collected for a 2-month follow-up period, in addition to pretreatment and treatment phases. The results indicated a progressive increase in the proportion of "warm" responses between parent and child and a marked reduction in the youngster's social isolation. Similarly, a check of the child's social behavior in a nursery school classroom at 5 weeks posttermination revealed no differences from a normal control in social skills or rates of interaction.

Because the intervention presumably dealt with the general patterns of social interaction, it is probable that these results do reflect generalization across situations. However, pre-post analyses are usually vulnerable to a number of threats to invalidity arising from the historical influence of uncontrolled variables, and it is at least plausible that changes in the child's behavior could have been the artifact of influences not directly related to treatment. These issues are not paramount to Patterson's strategy, however, because he describes the therapist's effort as the first step in a chain (Patterson & Brodsky, 1966), and it can be argued that it is not really relevant to attempt to analyze what changes are due to direct manipulations and what are due to uncontrolled improvements in the client's social situation. In another sense, however, it would be beneficial to know the extent to which specific procedures contribute to the subsequent behavioral change, or if, in fact, they are even necessary.

Again, in his discussion of this study, Patterson asserted that he did not *teach* adaptive behaviors. In his interpretation, the speed of the intervention (which took only 4 weeks) suggested that the behaviors were not being shaped, but rather that the program produced a small increment in certain kinds of social behaviors that already existed. Patterson concluded that a previous history of socialization is apparently a necessary antecedent for short-term interventions. Thus the typical outpatient treatment program should presuppose that the individual has been almost completely socialized. Obviously, this restriction imposes a limitation on the general usefulness of Patterson's approach with delinquent youngsters. However, it is difficult to fully assess the implication of Patterson's proviso, because there are no objective data with which to discriminate between real deficits and poor stimulus control for various behaviors. Such data, which would obviously be difficult to obtain, were not the focus of Patterson's study. However, if Patterson's assumption is correct, further research is necessary in order to be able to reliably assess which youth are most likely to benefit from his particular parent training program.

Patterson extended his social engineering technology in a study with six boys (aged 4–12) with multiple behavior targets (Patterson, Ray, & Shaw, 1968). Since Patterson made the assumption that generalization and persistence of effect are less a matter of stimulus generalization than a function of reinforcement control, the focus of his treatment was to teach the parents to function as social engineers. Each of the interventions applied conventional behavior modification strategies. The difference was mainly that the treatment process took place in the home, administered by family members, instead of at the clinic or laboratory. In the case of one 4-year-old boy, the parents were trained to conduct a DRO reinforcement schedule for nonaggressive interactions with the youth's siblings, and the whole family was encouraged to reward compliance to directions from the mother. In the case of a 6-year-old, who frequently fought with his older brothers, the intervention also included the use of a time-out strategy. Another illustration of Patterson's comprehensive approach is seen in the case of an 11-year-old boy referred for hyperactive and bizarre behaviors. Patterson initially provided the parents with his programmed

text. Then the father was taught to dispense positive reinforcers to control his son's behavior. The remaining family members were taught to observe the father and reward him for effective behavior. In turn, the father was encouraged to practice withholding criticism and demands on other family members.

It should be noted that studying the programmed text alone does not appear to appreciably reduce rates of deviant interaction (Patterson, et al., 1967, 1968, 1973), which is not surprising in view of the limited impact that instructions alone have on therapeutic outcome. Nevertheless, many therapists agree that it is often useful to start clients with preparatory reading in order to induce a cooperative set and familiarize clients with the technical jargon of behavioral intervention.

Patterson conducted a followup between baseline periods, intervention, and at 12 months post termination for these six families. Comparison of baseline and termination data in the home showed a range of 62–75% reduction in the base rates of total deviant behaviors. Follow-up data demonstrated persistence in three-quarters of the families for whom data were available. Further, the average amount of professional time involved in the intervention was only 22.8 hours. These data indicated that his intervention strategy was both effective and efficient.

Patterson's interest in the social environment has also been influenced by his studies of aggressive behavior in children. In his definition of aggression (Patterson, Littman, & Bricker, 1967), aggressive responses are operants—high-rate, high-intensity demands for a reaction from the environment. They are extremes in the class of assertive behaviors. Stimuli associated to various motivational states (hunger, fear, frustration, anger, social deprivation) become eliciting stimuli for aggressive behavior; the termination of these aversive motivational states further strengthens the aggressive response. The authors obtained experimental verification of this hypothesis through observations at two nursery schools. Making observations on 2,583 aggressive acts of 9 aggressive children, they found that the sequence of aggressive responses could be predicted on the basis of the aggressor-victim contingencies of reinforcement. The consequences provided by the victim were a basis for strengthening or suppressing assertive-aggressive behaviors. Moreover, a study of the protocols for 20 passive subjects suggests that aggressive behavior could be developed by successful counterattacks upon the aggressors. The result of the brief series of counterattacks was to increase the strength of the set of assertive behaviors in passive subjects.

The observation that aggressive behavior depended upon the social environment precipitated a series of interventions in families of social aggressors. Generalizing the observations from nursery school children, Patterson replicated the "social engineering" approach with a number of families of aggressive boys who were referred because of high rates of coercive behavior (Patterson, Cobb, & Ray, 1973). These parents were trained to modify the occurrence of these noxious patterns within their families. Patterson employed a coding system of 29 behavior categories divided into responses and consequences. *Response events* included commands, cries, occasions of humiliation or negativism, laughs, whines, yells, and touches. *Consequence events* included ignoring, approving, compliance, disapproval, noncompliance, attention, or no response. The study employed a comprehensive observation schedule in which, on 6–10 occasions, two 5-minute segments of continuous data were collected by professional observers on all family members. Following the initial baseline data collection, the families were introduced into a sequential series of parent training procedures. First, parents were taught the basic social learning theoretical framework through the programmed textbook (Patterson & Guillion, 1968). When parents could

make accurate responses to questions based on the text, they were taught how to pinpoint targets and collect data on behaviors they wanted to modify in their children. Following this step, the parents were invited to a group whose goal was to teach specific management techniques, plan behavior change programs, and support role-playing exercises and group reinforcement for each of the families' data-keeping assignments. In a final step, after 10–12 weeks in the group, staff members from the project conducted home visits and consultations on specific intervention programs, if necessary.

The parent groups consisted of 3 or 4 sets of parents who met weekly; each family received 30 minutes of the group time, during which they discussed the various interventions and assignments they had conducted the previous week. Parents were trained in two sets of behavior management techniques: first, token point systems—early in the program, parents were taught how to negotiate behavioral contracts with their children, mediated through various point systems or similar contingencies. These programs introduced positive, noncoercive reciprocal control within the families. The second procedure was a *time-out* strategy, for responding to occurrences of specified noxious behavior. Regardless of whether time out was the optimal response on the parents' part, Patterson et al. felt the procedure was useful in that it reduced amounts of physical abuse, which often occurred within families when parents attempted coercive countercontrol of their children.

The experimental design used to test the effect of treatment was based upon pre- and post measures of the various behaviors. Because of the wealth of data collected by the observational technique, Patterson et al. were able to obtain descriptive (correlational) data on a series of dependent variables: (1) targeted coercive behaviors of the aggressive child, which were the specific behaviors targeted during the parent training program; (2) nontargeted coercive behaviors of the aggressive child, which were other elements in the response class of coercive behaviors that were not picked as targets by the parents; (3) rates of coercive behavior of the siblings, which were occurrences of coercive responses by brothers or sisters of the targeted child.

Patterson et al. obtained follow-up data on 9 of the 13 cases. In terms of the targeted, coercive behaviors, these showed a slight overall decrease in proportion to the total behaviors observed. The rate per minute of coercive behavior declined from .32 at baseline to .12 by the twelfth-month followup. Despite this overall decrease, Patterson did not find response generalization with reference to nontargeted, coercive behaviors of the various subjects' repertoire. For these behaviors, there were relatively few changes over baseline rates at the twelfth-month follow-up. Examining the effects of generalization on the coercive behaviors in siblings, Patterson et al. found that a reduction of 50% from baseline levels had occurred by termination. However, this was a brief effect, the data showing a gradual drift in post termination rate towards the initial baseline frequency. Their general impression from these findings was that parents need specific training for specific problems, and generalization is unlikely to occur and be maintained unless carefully programmed. One of the problems may have been that parents changed their function as behavioral engineers as the initial referral problems became less frequent. At least the parents' daily report of the occurrence of specific referral problems declined markedly from baseline to termination, dropping from 59% of the target problem reported daily in the baseline period to 28% observed at least once per day at the termination of treatment.

Patterson's intervention program with aggressive boys was further replicated with 11 consecutive referrals to the Social Learning Project (Patterson & Reid, 1971, 1973). As before, the four outcome criteria for treatment included: (1) systematic observations of targeted deviant child behavior during baseline and termination; (2) parents' reports of the frequency of selected problems; (3) parents' global ratings of improvement; and (4) amount of professional time involved in the intervention.

Fourteen of the 29 codes for family interactions were listed a priori as deviant or noxious (Patterson, 1972). These included noncompliance, destructive behaviors, teasing or hitting, yells or cries, humiliations or disapprovals, or any high-rate behavior.

Follow-up data proved quite similar to the previous study. Targeted, coercive behaviors of the aggressive child declined from an average rate of .41 per minute to .15 at termination, a 64% reduction in targeted behavior for the families. Again, nontarget behaviors of a deviant child showed only a weak change that was not substantially different from baseline levels. Behaviors declined from an average rate of .21 to a mean of .16 responses per minute. Parental reports declined in a similar fashion from 61.2% of referral problems reported each day during baseline periods down to 34% reported at termination. The average professional time involved in the intervention was 31.4 hours, which is comparable to the 25.7 hour average that occurred in the original study.

Interventions on conflict and oppositional responding deal perhaps more indirectly with aspects of delinquent or predelinquent behavior, concentrating on many elements of the parent-child relationships that are of major relevance to delinquency prevention. However, Reid and Patterson (1973) and Reid and Hendricks (1973) have conducted parent training projects that change the focus of intervention from social aggression to more specific delinquent "behavior" patterns, particularly stealing behavior. The instigating factor for this change appears to be that direct home intervention does not work as well in families of youngsters who also steal. Reid and Hendricks analyzed all the treatment cases seen by the Oregon Project between 1967 and 1971, for which good observation data were available. Of a total sample of 25 families, Reid and Hendricks's analysis revealed that although the intervention was quite effective on the average, those boys who were reported to steal (i.e., boys in treatment for social aggression who also stole) were helped much less by the project. Using a success criterion of 33% reduction in rate of target behaviors, 9 of 11 nonstealers obtained successful treatments, whereas only 6 of 14 stealers improved to the same degree. These results suggest that treatment was twice as effective for families of nonstealers. Similarly, as a result of treatment, the average change from baseline to termination in rate per minute of deviant behavior declined .46 for nonstealers, while stealers showed a mean reduction of only .17. The difference between these rates was highly significant.

While these differences are apparent, it is still true that Patterson's success rates for these families were still at par with, or above in some cases, outcome rates for traditional therapies (Bergin & Garfield, 1971). Moreover, Patterson used strict improvement criteria based on highly objective and reliable measurement, eschewing rating scales or symptom checklists, making his data a very conservative estimate. Thus, it would be erroneous to characterize his social engineering approach as a failure with families of stealers or to assume that there is anything generic to stealers that precludes successful behavioral treatment. As will be discussed below, it is probable that the families of stealers had a number of additional handicaps, perhaps socioeconomically determined, that confounded the intervention. The essence of this lesson is simply that behavioral interventions should look to all aspects of the social environment for clues to a client's pattern of responding.

Reid and Hendricks (1973) reanalyzed the family observation data in terms of the general social characteristics of the youngsters and their families. Both stealers and nonstealers were compared to a sample of normal controls. It appears that stealers

were less in conflict with their family in terms of observable, negative coercive behaviors than the nonstealers in the social aggression project. However, stealers ranked the lowest on rates of positive behaviors in these family interactions. Data on mothers parallel the findings for the mothers' sons. On the basis of these analyses, it appears that stealers and their families have more distant, loose social ties than nonstealers or controls. The authors suggest that these parents may not have powerful enough social reinforcers at their command to be systematically or effectively employed within the social-learning treatment paradigm. Reid and Hendricks interpret this low rate of positive and negative social exchange as a picture of a rather boring family climate, which may serve to motivate the youth to seek developmental experiences and positive reinforcers in unsupervised, extra-family settings.

Another significant finding of the analysis of these observation data was that stealers did not display high rates of out-of-control behaviors. The apparent discrepancy between the referral information and the observational data may be based upon the fact that the youngster displays his deviant behavior outside of the home. If true, as Reid and Hendricks suggest, the reason the parent training program produced minimal results might be that there is little deviant behavior occurring within the actual home setting upon which the procedure can work.

Having switched the focus of the Social Learning Project to the exclusive study and treatment of families of children who steal, Reid and Hendricks (1973) summarized their initial impressions of 5 referral families. Twenty-seven referrals had been made to the project since the transition, yet only 5 of the referrals actually began treatment. The authors characterized the typical lack of poor parental motivation on these problems:

The parents phone to request treatment immediately following the child's being apprehended for stealing; they either miss the intake appointment or cancel it with one of the following explanations—the problem has ceased to exist, one of the parents (usually said to be the father) refuses to cooperate, or the parents have reconsidered the incident and now feel that the child was unjustly accused. The message behind these cancellations appears quite clear: the parents were upset at the time the child was apprehended, but after the incident had blown over there is little motivation to enter treatment. [p. 216]

Further information about this project is provided through a summary of the first 10 referrals who had begun treatment (Reid & Patterson, 1973). It appeared that these families had a higher level of disorganization than those referred for the social aggression interventions and presented problems different from families of social aggressors. Some of these characteristics included: (1) the families developed a pattern of missed appointments and failure to carry out assignments; (2) the parents seemed disinclined to monitor or track their children's behavior; (3) the parents spent much more time involved in activities away from the home, and children in the family were typically unsupervised for long periods each day; (4) the factor most common was the parents' failure to identify stealing as theft. They either ignored such occurrences or relabeled the behavior when they detected it in their child. That is, they were more willing to accept the youngster's explanation that he had either "borrowed," been "given," or "found" a particular item. Reid and Patterson observe that stealing is, unlike social aggression, a rather invisible, low-rate set of responses, which is seldom aversive to parents unless authorities coerce them to get help. In this respect, there appear to be different sources of motivation for families of social aggressors and families of stealers. In the case of the former, the noxious behaviors occur at high rates at home in such a way as to be aversive to the parents. In the case of the latter, the youngsters are involved in extra-family deviant

behaviors that only indirectly affect the parents. While the deviant behavior in families of social aggressors motivates the parents to participate in treatment, the deviant responses of families of stealers (in the few cases where these are detected) motivate the parents only to seek treatment as a way of calming the authorities.

Based upon the dynamics of the families involved in treatment, Reid and Patterson suggested several strategies for intervention that deviated slightly from the original approach. First, before parents of stealers could use the behavior management training, they needed to learn to label each event of stealing as such. It was hoped that this awareness would motivate them to actually engage in the program. If the parents' acceptance of this knowledge failed to motivate them, an attempt would be made to use extrinsic reinforcers to increase their participation. Reid and Patterson have employed techniques such as daily phone calls, intervention with the authorities, and the use of a $60 per month parenting salary contingent upon parental cooperation in treatment. Second, it was assumed that once the parents learned to track and identify all stealing, and when they had sufficient motivation to do something about it, then the same techniques found to be successful with families of social aggressors could be employed. In general, the three phases might be referred to as learning how to track one's children, learning how to label the occurrences of the specific deviant behavior, and learning effective interventions. With these exceptions, the Reid and Patterson intervention was identical to that for the previously studied nonstealers.

In their preliminary evaluation of 7 families, Reid and Patterson reported intervention effects in terms of cumulative rate of parents' reports of stealing events over 2-week periods. In most cases, low occurrence of stealing was effectively suppressed by such interventions as time out, if the parent-reported data can be believed. The monetary value of the stolen articles was also reduced for the children actually treated by the project. These preliminary observations suggest that a relatively minor change in the intervention strategy makes it possible to modify one other form of delinquent behavior (stealing). This research is continuing at the present time.

On its face value, the Social Intervention Project is an attractive intervention strategy for delinquency treatment programs. Nevertheless, it is unlikely that these techniques are a panacea to cure all social ills.

One of the areas in which additional research is necessary concerns work with families who come for treatment through third-party referrals, namely, the courts or youth-serving agencies. To date, the Social Learning Project has worked exclusively with self-referred families. Despite the low motivation that is seen in families of youngsters who behave antisocially outside of the home, these families differ from a still more apathetic population in that they have taken the initiative to secure some form of treatment. It is more often the case that parents react in helpless or ineffective ways in response to a crisis precipitated by their child's misbehavior in the community. There may be unforeseen problems when the project's staff makes the initial contact with parents rather than parents with the clinic, as in Patterson's case. One could speculate that the expectation of these families might differ significantly. Parents who bring their children for treatment may at least expect some degree of success, whereas parents who do not contact the clinic for help may have little expectation of meaningful improvement in their children and, hence, operate on the "Rosenthal Effect" to preclude any change.

A similar problem can be encountered with parents who are unwilling to cooperate in their child's treatment. Even in the worst situations, Patterson's intervention dealt with families who responded to the coercion of authorities to find treatment for their children. This may not always be the case with parents who also have problems with the law, civil authority, and so forth. One of the premises of community treatment is that there will be someone in the community to mediate the therapy, in addition to professional staff. The absence of a cooperative parent, either by virtue of separation or neglect, is a significant handicap for this strategy. On the other hand, the generality of the social engineering approach requires only that significant others in the environment, not necessarily the parents, act as behavioral engineers. It should be possible then to train older brothers, court-appointed guardians or foster parents, or other significant persons in the youth's environment to function as behavioral mediators.

A point to be made in favor of the Social Learning Project is that the research methodology employed is among the most sophisticate in behavioral research. The 29-category behavior coding system was ordinarily managed by professional observers who periodically retrain and calibrate their performance with a supervisor. Moreover, the data are collected according to the stream of behavioral interactions, such that sequential analysis is possible for the various behaviors. This latter feature has been extensively employed in theoretical research on stimulus control of noxious behavior, which has been conducted concurrently with the social engineering project. The major problem is that the extent to which the behavior is influenced by the observers is not well understood. However, until we can resolve the ethical issues involved in the collection of data unbeknownst to the family, this procedure seems to be the most productive.

Another outstanding feature of Patterson's work is the care taken to amass systematic follow-up data on the effects of treatment. This illustrates his contention that the effectiveness of training cannot be assessed by simply comparing baseline to treatment changes in the behavioral measures (Patterson et al., 1973). Thus, his analyses have included a series of baseline observations, several during the intervention phase, and at a number of months posttermination. For example, in the 1973 study, home observations were made on a regular schedule throughout baseline intervention and followup. Six or 10 baseline observations were obtained prior to intervention. During intervention, two observation sessions occurred after the parents had read the programmed text, following 4 and 8 weeks of parent training, and at the termination of the intervention program. During the follow-up period, two observations were done each month after termination through the sixth month and then bimonthly through the twelfth month following termination (Patterson et al., 1973). Within these periods of observation, the two nonconsecutive 5-minute periods of data collected for each family member were subdivided into 30-second intervals, each 30 seconds containing an average of 5 behavioral sequences. On the surface, it might appear that many more data were collected than was necessary to demonstrate the effectiveness of the program. However, the rigor in Patterson's research is mandated by the unreliability of parents as observers, even when using precise definitions of a single class of problem behaviors (Peine, 1970). Previous research on the accuracy of parental estimates and treatment outcomes had made Patterson very cautious about depending on this type of report as the main source of data. Within his past research, 10–20% of the families reported dramatic "cures" very early in intervention that were not supported by the findings from the observers (Patterson et al., 1973). Such rigorous experimental practice, therefore, may be even more necessary when dealing with families referred for treatment under jurisdiction of the courts or probation. It is easy to imagine how a parent eager to escape the coercion to participate in a family therapy program, or pressured by relatives, neighbors, or friends to let their child "off the hook," might underestimate the frequency of noxious behaviors and hence inflate the number of false positive treatment effects. This issue is a thorny problem for behavior analysts dealing in delinquency treatment programs. Obviously, it is in the client's best interest to report improvement since improvement is directly linked to one's freedom from sentence or further legal entanglement. On the other hand, it is seldom possible to have a staff of highly trained, professional observers who are able to conduct systematic observations on a regular basis. Yet, it does seem necessary to provide independent sources of confirmation for therapeutic change when dealing in a family situation, and equally important to maintain a suitable follow-up evaluation in order to determine the durability of the treatment effect as time after termination increases.

Finally, it should be noted that although the research of Patterson and his colleagues has dealt primarily with a *process* evaluation of the social intervention procedure, some impressive *outcome* data comparing essentially the same procedure with other forms of family intervention are presently available. In a very extensive, well-controlled study, Alexander and Parsons (1973) compared short-term behavioral intervention that incorporated much of the Patterson procedure (as well as the behavioral contracting procedure described by Stuart below) with a client-centered procedure, a psychodynamic-oriented procedure, and a no-treatment control. The study involved 99 families who were referred by the Salt Lake County Juvenile Court to the Family Clinic at the University of Utah over a 13-month period of time. On the basis of tightly defined behavioral measures, it was demonstrated that the families who received the behavioral intervention ended up displaying better negotiation-communication skills (e.g., more equal verbal interaction, less silence, and more constructive interruptions) than the other groups and that the youths in those families displayed significantly less recidivism during a 6–18-month follow-up period. Although the data are not conclusive, the magnitude of the study and the quality of its control suggest that a behaviorally oriented parent or family training program is one of the more effective types of intervention that has been developed to date.

FAMILY AND SCHOOL COUNSELING PROJECT

One of the practical shortcomings of Patterson's social engineering technique, when applied to families of delinquent adolescents, is that the parents may not have the social repertoire to effectively apply contingencies, or the parent-child relationship may have deteriorated to such a degree that the conventional strategies are ineffectual. Roland Tharp and Ralph Wetzel (1969) were among the first to deal with these problems in a community-based intervention program. Their Behavior Research Project worked with a number of families of delinquent and predelinquent youngsters. Tharp and Wetzel often found parents who could not talk productively with their children and children who could only react in a negative or oppositional manner to a parental overture. In such cases, they felt the most effective approach was to depersonalize the interactions and minimize the need for parent-child verbalization, since they were largely aversive. The authors described several instances where the behavior analyst, or consultant, functioned in the role of arbitrator to develop negotiation skills in the family. Their most formal arrangement was the *behavioral contract*, which the consultant helped arrange. These contracts stated the expectations and contingencies as they concerned all parties, and the contracts became the principal form of treatment. Tharp and Wetzel reported the case of one youth who had a hostile and aggressive relationship with his stepfather. The behavior analyst was successful in negotiating a contract under which the youth could obtain a car for his personal use in return for weekly repayment through specified chores and responsiveness to house curfew.

It was noted that the interpersonal interactions never became friendly, but the contact was successful in improving the youth's behavior at home.

Similar observations have been made by Richard Stuart (1971) in his work with the Family and School Consultation Project. Stuart compared delinquent and non-delinquent families for their rate of aversive stimulation and found that parent-child interactions in the delinquent families were significantly less positive and were oriented to a greater extent on negative feedback. Because these families were not sources of positive reinforcement for the youngsters, it might not be surprising that the children's behavior was controlled by peer groups and contingencies outside of the home. Stuart has advocated behavioral contracting for these families on the rationale that the etiology of delinquency is the paucity of opportunities for positive reinforcement in the home (1971). Stuart sees behavioral contracts as a structured means of scheduling the exchange of positive reinforcements between parent and child, when reciprocal patterns of reinforcement have broken down within families. He has stipulated four assumptions behind behavioral contracting. First, he assumes that the receipt of positive reinforcement in an interpersonal situation is a privilege rather than a right. In families, parents and their children should have access to positive reinforcers on a reciprocal basis. For example, an adolescent might wish free time, and in the reciprocal exchange the parent might wish to know where his child goes when he leaves home.

The second assumption underlying behavioral contracts is that the most effective interpersonal agreements provide for an equity or quid pro quo in the value of the interchange of reinforcers. Inherent in the use of behavioral contracts is the notion of fairness between the payoff or reinforcers between parties.

The third assumption made in using behavioral contracts is that they increase the value of the interpersonal exchange in direct proportion to the range, rate, and magnitude of the positive reinforcers mediated by the exchange. Thus, it is assumed that the behavioral contract can lead to an improvement in the parent-child relationship as more of these negotiations are conducted.

Stuart's fourth and final assumption about the concept of contracting is that rules create freedom. That is, rules prevent arbitrary sanctions or unspecified consequences and give an individual the freedom to engage or not engage in a particular activity at his own choice. This is particularly useful in families where there is great uncertainty or inconsistency with respect to rule enforcement. The behavioral contract provides a structured basis upon which the youth may choose a certain course of action that will have predictable consequences, that is, either the opportunity to choose to take advantage of a privilege or the predictable denial of that privilege or some other prespecified sanction.

Stuart (1971) has further specified the essential elements in a good behavioral contract. The first three deal with the need to detail the privileges or consequences that each party expects to gain after fulfilling his exact responsibilities. Stuart also recommends a bonus clause in a behavioral contract simply for complying with the terms of the contract. These extra privileges are designed to reward periods of near-flawless compliance with responsibilities. Finally, Stuart suggests the use of some monitoring or feedback technique to provide sources of verbal reinforcement, setting the occasion for positive comments, which themselves strengthen the desirable behaviors. In a case study provided with this discussion (Stuart, 1971), two examples of a contract between a teenager and her parents over the girl's response to curfew are used as an illustration. The first contract was a more unilateral agreement, stipulating the parent's desired terms. This was much less successful than one that called for a degree of negotiation on the youngster's part. Unlike Thorp and Wetzel's use of behavioral contracts to depersonalize the intervention, Stuart's work suggests that contracts function best as a catalyst to a more effective parent-child interaction.

The importance of this point appears to be borne out in a series of studies conducted with the Family and School Consultation Project between 1970 and 1973 (Stuart & Tripodi, 1973; Stuart & Lott, 1972; Jayaratne, Stuart, & Tripodi, 1974). These studies involved large, factorial designs in which therapist, client, and treatment variables were analyzed in order to determine the relative effect of these factors. On the basis of their research, there appear to be three major influences in the success of behavior contracting (Stuart & Lott, 1972). First, it appears that families with strong histories of constructive negotiation are more amenable to this approach, although Stuart and Lott could not identify any outward characteristics that appeared to be highly correlated with success. Second, it seems that the immediacy of conflict is an important factor. That is, a family's willingness to negotiate appears to depend upon the need for successfully resolving some pressing family conflict. In Stuart's research, these factors were less critical than the third influence, which is the therapist's skill in structuring a climate of compromise in which no one loses face. This finding seems to parallel the role of labor mediator, whose skill rests in his ability to "bob and weave," bringing both parties together without unnecessary confrontation. Thus it appears that while behavioral contracts are indeed useful, their implementation should not be oversimplified. The tactics of inducing a compromise using a contract rivals, in Stuart's opinion, the intervention mechanisms themselves.

The work of Tharp and Wetzel and Stuart et al. builds from the social engineering technology promulgated by the Patterson group and yet points out the definite need for additional procedural strategies.

The best behavioral interventions are worthless when they are not implemented correctly or when they are unwittingly sabotaged by the client (Davison, 1973). Stuart's research on contracting highlights the need not only to teach families the mechanics of behavioral engineering but also to ensure that they are predisposed to implement these.

PICA-PREP

Most of the programs thus far discussed have focused on the modification of deviant behavior patterns in youngsters whose problems were severe enough to warrant some form of intensive therapy. An equally important area concerns programs whose aim is to strengthen appropriate behavior in the hope of forestalling a serious problem at some later time. Programs of this type take one step backward in the behavioral chain to focus on certain antecedent events that are presumed to be of some importance in the development of a well-adjusted personality. The notion of early prevention follows from the assumption that some persons may be more vulnerable to certain factors that are related, at least conceptually, to the etiology of juvenile delinquency. For example, deficiencies in basic academic skills, not in themselves a reason for adjudication, may predispose a youngster to certain alternative responses in a classroom (such as being disruptive, not paying attention, cutting classes, or, ultimately, truancy) that may lead to adjudication. Because the link between vulnerability and actual incidence of a disorder is seldom clear cut (Rolf & Harig, 1974), one must be extremely cautious in characterizing the clients of these prevention programs as "predelinquents," because their school-related referral problems may never result in their becoming delinquent.

One example of a prevention project is PICA, or Programming Interpersonal Curricula for Adolescents, a research and demonstration project that was conducted by Harold Cohen and his associates at the Institute for Behavioral Research in the Washington, D.C. area (Cohen, Filipczak, Slavin, & Boren, 1971). PICA was designed to help underachieving youngsters whose academic and behavioral problems often got them in trouble with school officials and could be part of a larger pattern of disruptive behavior in their homes and the community. The model used to implement the PICA project was a part-time educational program, similar to work-study activities widely used by schools as a way to deal with potential dropouts. The PICA program differed from other work-study programs in that the contract pertained to actual academic learning. In many respects, the PICA program was an extension of Cohen's CASE project at the National Training School for Boys. In the first 3 years, PICA's physical location was a special facility in Silver Springs, Maryland. Participating junior high school students were transported from schools in the District of Columbia and adjoining towns. This special facility served as an educational laboratory whose objectives were to permit both observation and shaping of individual study behavior and maintenance of appropriate in-class behaviors approximating those required in the student's schools. These students participated in a token economy in which they earned or lost depending on how well they improved their behavioral and academic skills. Achievement was rewarded by monetary reinforcements that could be used to purchase privileges in a student lounge. The monetary rewards were based on a "work unit" concept devised to take into account the difficulty or effort required in an academic achievement as well as the simple time to completion. Students worked on numerous self-instructional materials designed to improve English and mathematics skills.

A typical PICA day began when the student punched in at a time clock in the educational laboratory. On arrival, the student was permitted to go to a lounge area furnished with a soda machine, a candy dispenser, and a radio. He could relax there for a few minutes until being called to report for his morning assignments. The self-instruction materials were worked on in private study carrels equipped with electrical outlets to power teaching machines available for the student's use.

Following Cohen's penchant for environmental design, the PICA self-instructional process was designed so that the youngster would have numerous opportunities to succeed. Following a pretest to determine those elements that he needed to learn, a student would be assigned a specific unit or part of an instructional program and would be expected to complete the assigned program at a predetermined criterion level (100% for all mathematics programs; 90% for most English programs) in order to receive payment. This academic work could take any of several different forms, including tape recordings or teaching machines. If a student experienced difficulty with the material, teacher help was available upon request. When the assigned work had been completed, it was checked by the staff to determine whether the criterion level for payment and advancement had been met. If the student had demonstrated his proficiency, he was paid a portion of the money he had earned, and his work units were recorded. The remainder would be paid at the end of the sessions. If he did not meet criterion, the system provided a series of back-up tutorial assistance and alternate forms of the instructional programs. In addition to this remedial English and math instruction, the PICA project provided an interpersonal skills program on subject matter considered to be important for teenagers, such as law and order, drugs, and sex. The educational goal of each of these issues was to help the youths define their options and consider the probable consequences associated with each of the options. As the program developed, the interpersonal skills curricula were expanded to include such topics as design science, operant behavior,

and behavioral issues. In addition there was a "how to" curriculum that dealt with the general skills useful in surviving in school. The subject matter for the various classes included how to follow written instructions, how to follow oral instructions, and how to take tests. Each of these was followed by a laboratory session in which the youngster practiced the various skills. The PICA project also included a curriculum on teenagers' rights and responsibilities (TARR), which was designed to provide teenagers with effective strategies for solving or avoiding problems. The subject matter in these sessions included familiarization with the juvenile justice system. Other problem-solving curriculum included units on sex education, behavior modification, drug abuse, and a unit on life in the parents' times, which was a 12-lesson course designed to give the students information and insights about the kinds of experiences that their parents had had when they were in their adolescent period.

Of their total day in PICA (2½ hours), students spent nearly 60% of their time on the self-instruction materials and 30% of the daily session working directly with teachers, including test checks, assistance, and various classes. The outcome data were described in terms of actual grade changes for the pre-PICA and PICA-year final scores for 11 students who completed the program. The mean grade increase for English and mathematics was 3.04 as compared with a grade increase of 1.14 for all other non-tutored classes. Group results on standardized reading surveys indicated significant increases in language abilities, with almost double the expected increase in reading comprehension skills during the treatment year. Similarly, students' mathematics abilities (as determined by standardized tests) doubled over the previous year's levels.

In 1971, at the invitation of the principal of one of the junior high schools, the PICA staff moved their program to the school facility. They trained volunteer teachers from the math and English departments in the use of the behavior management techniques and learning materials that had been developed in the PICA laboratory. After relocating to the junior high school, the project was renamed PREP, or Preparation Through Responsive Educational Programs. Approximately 80 PREP students were divided into 5 groups of 16 each. Each participant spent approximately three hours of his school day at the PREP "Skills Center." In addition, parents of these students were selected for parent training sessions for the establishment of contingency management programs in the home.

As in the PICA contingency program, PREP students received points for completed work units and for productive, cooperative behavior. They lost points for inappropriate behavior such as sleeping on the job, damaging equipment, or missing other classes. Students could use their points for the purchase of various back-up reinforcers such as use of a student lounge or taking the opportunity to become a teacher's aide. The interpersonal skills classes were included with the basic remedial skills components.

Although the complete data for the PREP program have not been reported, the preliminary results are similar to PICA's. Behavior and academic school writings by the teachers of regular classes indicated near or above 90% appropriate performance, and the PREP participants bettered the average attendance for all students in the school for the previous year. The parent training classes, which were held once a week for the first semester and only once a month during the second, resulted in nearly 70% attendance in voluntary classes, and a number of behavior management programs were developed by families at home. The PREP staff was also able to initiate a parents newsletter and establish a new level of home-school coordination through individual parent consultation projects.

The PREP program represents a careful extension of laboratory research to an applied setting. The contingency management techniques and instructional programs had been piloted through PICA for 3 years prior to the program's introduction into the school. A strong point of the program was that it employed a carefully structured system that clearly defined staff and student roles and behavioral consequences. In addition, it had a comprehensive set of strategies to determine accountability, and the procedures it employed had already produced impressive results in the laboratory.

However, in the process of moving from the laboratory to the school, the program ran into substantial resistance (Filipczak, 1973). In the community, politicians, reporters, and other citizens were expressing concerns about modern mathematics, the morality of behavior modification, conditioning children like rats in a cage, etc., while school administrators and staff were locked in internal struggles in an effort to side with what was beneficial to them and disown what wasn't. Thus, the problems that plague efforts to adopt behavioral programs within institutions also exist in the community. This is not all that surprising since the essence of behavior modification is to change what other people do in relationship to the subject and his or her behavior. In most instances, people resist change and things that are new. What seems more surprising is that more attention has not been spent on these administrative aspects of behavior modification. The following observations reflect the importance of these practical issues with respect to one behavior modification program in the public schools (Filipczak, 1973).

Observation 1. *Somebody out there doesn't like you.* In other words, no matter what kind of a program one operates, there will inevitably be someone in the community who takes issue with the program's philosophy, goals, or practices. Many laymen of the community have reservations about scientists and fear that they might be making guinea pigs of children. Filipczak felt that it was most important to define the participating group the project served and foster their support as a way of enlisting community support in the face of harsh criticism.

Observation 2. *Homework doesn't stop after graduate school.* Simply put, every community-based program had better thoroughly cover all of the procedural details for working with schools or other public agencies. In some situations, departures from established protocol, even when done out of ignorance, can be very costly in terms of the institutional resistance created.

Observation 3. *The public press is going to find you out.* Implicit in this corollary is the warning to expect public criticism from misinterpretations, erroneous reporting, and emotional editorials against behavior modification techniques.

Observation 4. *Traditional results both do and do not mean something.* The ways that scientists communicate among themselves are often meaningless methods of public communications. PREP's graphic and statistical representations were often useless and unsatisfying means of presenting concerned individuals with information. More informative information was conveyed though personal discussions with students, testimonials from parents, live and recorded video observations, and informal meetings with staff members.

Observation 5. *Unplanned activities may be more important than your most sophisticated efforts.* In other words, the spontaneous efforts of supporters of a program may be more important to a program's success than planned public relations strategies or formal tactics to counter adverse public opinion. In the case of PREP, a massive letter-writing campaign to school board members by interested parents and an avalanche of personal telephone calls were more useful that staff meetings or special reports.

Observation 6. *Everything takes more time than you think it will.* In other words, many unforeseen contingencies in any community-based project make it very unlikely that all the research objectives will be met. Each controversy or crisis inevitably influences the overall results of the project itself.

Observation 7. *If you and the community have done your jobs, things will get better.* In other words, the careful development of support from participants and consumers of the project's services and the establishment of community liaisons are investments that are very well made and

can mean the difference between project failure and success.

The clear message of Filipczak's comments is that the behavior modifier planning to go into the community faces a great deal of work beyond the simple application of learning principles. Above and beyond the consideration of the problems of various clients, there is a separate but equally important need to consider the environment in which the program itself will function and the individuals who manipulate the contingencies by which the project managers themselves are reinforced.

HUNT SCHOOL PROGRAM

Like the PICA/PREP program, the Hunt School Program focuses on early prevention, or the identification and modification of school behaviors that are at least correlated with the adjudication of delinquency. Such behaviors include high frequencies of absenteeism, classroom disruptions and fighting, stealing, and prolonged academic failure. The Hunt School Program is located at Lyman C. Hunt Junior High School in Burlington, Vermont, and is one of several delinquency prevention programs operated by the Burlington Youth Service Bureau.

In 1972 the Youth Service Bureau was conducting a behavioral counseling program similar to that described by Tharp and Wetzel (1969). Utilizing the contracting procedure described by Stuart (1971), trained staff of the bureau worked with mediators in the youth's environment to establish incentives for the modification of specific target behaviors. While the program appeared to be very successful for most youths in the lower age range (9–13), some difficulties were encountered in trying to reach many of older youths. The primary problem appeared to be that for many of these youths the mediators (parents, relatives, and other adults who were intimately involved with the youths) did not control the most powerful reinforcers. While an allowance, special privileges, additional time with the mediators, etc., were reinforcing to a younger youth, the primary interest of the older adolescents seemed to be access to, and participation in, their peer groups. Unfortunately for many parents, the youths' only time at home was between 3 A.M. and 2 P.M., asleep. And all too often, any effort to modify this pattern resulted in the youths sleeping elsewhere. Therefore, the primary purpose of the Hunt School Program was to create an environment comprised of many youths that would permit specific individuals to be dealt with in the context of their peers.

The Hunt School Project was developed over a period of 2 years and consisted of three phases. In Phase 1, a youth center was established at the school and operated two nights a week (Burchard, Harig, Miller, & Amour, 1974). The purpose of this phase was to determine (1) would youths who were having difficulty adjusting to school and the community attend the center on a regular basis, and (2) could a token economy program be established to modify behavior within the center. To accomplish the first objective, the center was limited to about 90 youths who were selected or "invited" by a small group of youths who had had multiple police contacts and had been involved in numerous negative incidents within the school. Also, a variety of activities and events was created at the center (gymnastics, street hockey, basketball, a coffee house, arts and crafts, and library) in order to attract the youths' attention and participation. In general, the token economy involved points being earned for time spent in the different activity areas (with a greater number of points being earned for participation in the less preferred activities, such as doing academic work in the library) and points being spent for refreshments in the coffee house and for gift certificates at a local discount store.

In general, the results of Phase 1 indicated that most of the youths who were invited to the center did attend on a regular basis and that those with multiple police contacts attended as much, if not more, than youth with no previous police contacts. Also, through the use of a multiple-schedule design, which alternated between contingent sessions (points administered for time spent in specific activity areas) and noncontingent sessions (points administered merely for the asking), two major effects were demonstrated. On contingent nights, youths spent significantly more time in that area that paid the most points (e.g., the library) and less time in those areas that paid no points (the bathroom, hallways, front steps, etc.). The subjective data indicated that on contingent nights the center was not only more orderly but also contained a more reinforcing atmosphere.

Phase 2 continued the recreational opportunities of the youth center but focused on providing services to the school and to particular youths having social or academic problems. A number of intervention techniques were examined to determine their relative effectiveness in resolving these school adjustment problems.

The first study (Miller & Burchard, 1974) examined the utility of behavioral contracting procedures, with access to youth center activities as reinforcers to develop and maintain either daily school attendance or appropriate classroom behavior. Fifty-five students carried rating cards to two classes each day. The rating cards were of two types: attendance cards and daily behavior cards. Attendance cards provided the teacher with a space where information on the youth's attendance was indicated. The daily behavior cards listed a number of common appropriate or inappropriate classroom behaviors. The students earned points according to the number of behavior cards turned in. These contingencies were affected only by the teacher's signature, not by ratings. Initially, youths contracted to carry only the attendance cards. Results showed that the token economy system could easily be used to maintain high rates of card-carrying behavior. This step was necessary in order to maintain a consistent level of participation by the youths. Previous experience indicated that unless there was an explicit contingency, these youngsters were very unreliable at carrying the cards to and from their classes. When the card-carrying behavior was established at sufficient strength, a number of case studies were conducted to assess the effect of the feedback properties of the various ratings. This study yielded an interesting interaction: as seen in independent observation of their classroom behaviors, students did much better in class on days in which they carried the behavior cards and received specific feedback than on days when they carried attendance cards only. Youngsters who earned a series of positive ratings (which were relatively infrequent events in school) continued to do well, whereas low ratings and a series of negative feedback made certain students less inclined to carry the cards at all. Miller and Burchard (1974) suggested that the students who received low ratings may have decreased their card carrying as a result of the social punishment they received each day from teachers. Certainly, feedback techniques of this sort impose a thorny problem, as they risk sensitizing an already-failing youngster to his shortcomings and may make him less inclined to want to change them.

In an extension of research on the behavior cards, Stahl, Lefebvre, Fuller, and Burchard (1974) compared the effectiveness of traditional behavioral contracting, behavioral rehearsal of appropriate classroom behaviors, and a self-evaluation procedure that involved matching student self-assessments to teachers' ratings. Teachers' ratings of attitudes and class participation and an observational measure of on-task and disruptive behavior were used as dependent variables. The results after 6 weeks of intervention indicated that only the traditional contracting group made significant improvement on attitude and participation

measures and the school conduct indices. The self-evaluation group improved only on participation ratings and on-task behavior. Unexpectedly, the behavior rehearsal group showed no consistent improvement on any of the measures. The authors suggested that since the youths were not reinforced for performing the rehearsed behavior in school, they may never have attempted these more appropriate ways of responding.

Having demonstrated that the Youth Center could (1) be conducted on a token economy and (2) be used as an effective reinforcer in groups and single-case intervention programs, Phase 3 of the project attempted to develop procedures for conducting a community-operated program. This change in orientation was necessary to make the model more adaptable to communities that would not have the manpower resources of college students or the financial backing of research grants. The objectives of Phase 3 were to phase the college students and staff out of the Youth Center's administration and to enlist and train three levels of staff from the community: junior high school students, adult volunteers, and high school student assistants. In order to provide income for the project, mainly to provide incentives for the junior high and high school students, each of the youths who attended the center was charged an admission fee of 25¢ per evening. The format of the Youth Center continued to be based upon the token economy, and student staff members earned their points for helping out on the project. Since the main objective was to evaluate the performance of the new staff members, three operational measures of performance were made: attendance, job ratings by supervisors, and performance on cleanup. The peer staff received feedback in the form of correction or praise for their activities. The outcome data indicated that the training program was successful in making the students proficient in their jobs. It was also clear that while staff attendance averaged only 78% and turnover was about 50% for the 15 weeks of the program, the center continued to operate efficiently, due to the large pool of replacement staff available from among the youngsters.

During the final 4 weeks of the center, adult volunteers were employed as supervisors. In general, the findings indicated that adults with little prior experience could be trained in a short time to assume many of the administrative tasks required in the operation of the program.

One of the elements that was clearly lacking from Phase 3 was the application of the program's contingencies to academic or school-related problems. Originally, it was expected that the school guidance counselors would assume the role that staff members had taken under Phase 2 with respect to behavioral contracting. Apparently this is not apt to happen unless such a procedure is specifically programmed in advance.

One noteworthy point about the Youth Center Project is that it represents a voluntary token economy. With most token economies there has usually been some implied form of coercion, in that the subjects were a captive audience being offered the opportunity to participate in the token economy in contrast to some existing program that maintained their presence through aversive control. In a school setting, for example, a youth has little ultimate choice but to attend or be found truant, and even in a program like PICA or PREP, the alternative is a much more aversive classroom setting. In an institution, a resident has little ultimate choice but to respond to the contingencies or go without significant privileges. The Youth Center Project, on the other hand, was maintained without coercion; the numbers were invited but not required to attend; they were not brought by staff members or forced to remain within the building; the burden of maintaining their participation within the program was, therefore, put upon the staff, who strove to make the evening as enjoyable and as reinforcing as possible. The

youths attended not for fear of losing something significant, but because they liked to attend.

Conclusions

Clearly, the programs and projects that have been reviewed in this chapter point to some rather impressive and encouraging advances in the treatment or rehabilitation of youths who engage in high frequencies of anti-social behavior. The behavioral approach has been most impressive in producing a rapid change in behavior, especially in those programs where there is maximum environmental control (e.g., institutions and group homes). On the other hand, those some programs are most plagued by the problem of generalization. For example, with respect to institutional programs, it appears that successful behavior modification is of limited benefit unless some effort is spent modifying the behavior of parents, teachers, peers, etc., in the youth's natural environment. However, if a youth must be removed from home, it would appear that placement in a community-based home such as Achievement Place would be more beneficial than placement in an institution many miles from home. Although there are many pressures from irate parents, teachers, law enforcement officials, etc., to remove a delinquent youth from the community, the youth's relationship with those same individuals usually constitutes much of the problem, and it does not appear that a prolonged "time out" from the community leads to an effective solution to those problems.

We do not intend to imply, however, that behavior modifiers should not continue to conduct programs in institutions. As long as society continues to utilize such facilities, something needs to be done for the youths who are placed there, and there are no data that point to a more effective strategy of intervention.

With respect to the nonresidential, community-based procedures (family and parent training programs, behavioral contracting, youth centers, etc.), there is considerable evidence of promising effects on an individual basis. With the exception of the study by Alexander and Parsons (1973), however, there are few data that compare the behavioral approach with other forms of intervention.

There appear to be two important trends in this area, both of which are yet to be supported by much empirical data. One is a change in focus from a rather narrow perspective on the youth to a greater emphasis on the people and conditions in the youth's environment that are either maintaining the problem behavior or might be instrumental in alleviating it. This would include programs that attempt to change irrational policies in institutions, programs that attempt to develop effective community action in low-income families, programs like PREP, which direct an all-out effort on school personnel, and programs like the Hunt Youth Center, which attempt to work with the youths' peer groups and train com-

munity volunteers to function as paraprofessionals and implement programs of their own. The second trend involves an effort to teach youths the technology of behavior modification in order to enable them to obtain their objectives in ways more effective and socially acceptable (Gray, Grawbard, & Rosenberg, 1974).

Both trends seem to suggest that, in the long run, it may be more effective with some youths to help them change their environment rather than to focus directly on a change in their own behavior. It is conceivable that such an approach would not only stimulate greater involvement and a greater degree of self-esteem, but that it might also lead to greater generalization. The evidence seems to suggest that when a youth perceives himself as having produced a change in the behavior of others, he is more apt to continue to engage in the behavior that produced that change than if he perceives that someone else did it for him. However, much more research is needed before such a claim can be made with any degree of certainty.

References

ALEXANDER, J. F., & PARSONS, B. V. Short-term behavioral intervention with delinquent families. Impact on family process and recidivism. *Journal of Abnormal Psychology,* 1973, **81,** 219–225.

ARBUCKLE, D., & LITWACK, L. A. A study of recidivism among juvenile delinquents. *Federal Probation,* 1960, **2,** 44–46.

AYALA, H. E., MINKIN, N., PHILLIPS, E. L., FIXSEN, D. L., & WOLF, M. M. Achievement Place: The training and analysis of vocational behaviors. Paper presented at the meeting of the American Psychological Association, Montreal, Canada, 1973.

BAILEY, J. S., TIMBERS, G. D., PHILLIPS, E. L., & WOLF, M. M. Modification of articulation errors of predelinquents by their peers. *Journals of Applied Behavior Analysis,* 1971, **4,** 265–281.

BAILEY, J. S., WOLF, M. M., & PHILLIPS, E. L. Home-base reinforcement and the modification of predelinquents' classroom behavior. *Journal of Applied Behavior Analysis,* 1970, **3,** 223–233.

BERGIN, A. E., & GARFIELD, S. L. (Eds.) *Handbook of psychotherapy and behavioral change: An empirical analysis.* New York: Wiley, 1971.

BERNE, Eric. *Games people play: The psychology of human relationships.* New York: Grove Press, 1964.

BIRNBRAUER, J. S., BURCHARD, J. D., & BURCHARD, S. N. Wanted: Behavior analysts. In R. H. Bradfield (Ed.), *Behavior modification: The human effort.* San Rafael: Dimensions, pp. 19–76.

BRAUKMANN, C. J., & FIXSEN, D. L. Behavior modification with delinquents. In M. Hersen, R. M. Eisler, & P. M. Miller (Eds.), *Progress in behavior modification.* New York: Academic Press, in press.

BRAUKMANN, C. J., MALONEY, D. M., FIXSEN, D. L., PHILLIPS, E. L., & WOLF, M. M. An analysis of a selection interview training package. Paper presented at the meeting of the American Psychological Association, Honolulu, Hawaii, 1972.

BURCHARD, J. D. Systematic socialization: A programmed environment for the habilitation of anti-social retardates. *The Psychological Record,* 1967, **17,** 461–476.

BURCHARD, J. D. Residential behavior modification programs and the problem of uncontrolled contingencies: A reply to Lackenmeyer. *Psychological Record,* 1969, **19,** 259–261.

BURCHARD, J. D., & BARRERA, F. An analysis of timeout and response cost in a programmed environment. *Journal of Applied Behavior Analysis,* 1972, **5,** 271–282.

BURCHARD, J. D., HARIG, P. T., MILLER, R. B., & AMOUR, J. New strategies in community-based intervention. In E. L. Ribes-Inesta (Ed.), *The experimental analysis of delinquency and social aggression.* New York: Academic Press, in press.

CHASSAN, J. B. *Research design in clinical psychology and psychiatry.* New York: Appleton-Century-Crofts, 1967.

COHEN, H. Educational therapy. *Arean,* 1967, **82,** 220–225. (a)

COHEN, H. MODEL: Motivationally oriented designs for an ecology of learning. Paper presented at the meeting of the American Educational Research Association, New York, February 1967. (b)

COHEN, H., & FILIPCZAK, J. *A new learning environment.* San. Francisco: Josey-Bass, 1971.

COHEN, H. L., FILIPCZAK, J. A., SLAVIN, J., & BOREN, J. *Programming interpersonal curricula for adolescents (PICA)—Project year three: A laboratory model.* Silver Springs, Md.: Institute for Behavioral Research, October 1971.

COSTELLO, J. Behavior modification and corrections. The Law Enforcement Assistance Administration. (National Technical Information Service #PB-223-629/AS), 1972.

DAVISON, G. C. Counter-control in behavior modification. In L. A. Hamerlynck, L. C. Handy, & E. J. Mash (Eds.), *Behavioral change: Methodology, concepts and practice.* Champaign, Ill.: Research Press, 1973, pp. 153–168.

FIXSEN, D. L., PHILLIPS, E. L., & WOLF, M. M. Achievement Place: The reliability of self-reporting and peer-reporting and their effect on behavior. *Journal of Applied Behavior Analysis,* 1972, **5,** 19–33.

FIXSEN, D. L., PHILLIPS, E. L., & WOLF, M. M. Achievement Place: Experiments in self-government with predelinquents. *Journal of Applied Behavior Analysis,* 1973, **6,** 31–49.

GLASS, G. V., WILLSON, V. L., & GOTTMAN, J. M. Design and analysis of time-series experiments. Unpublished manuscript, University of Colorado, 1974.

GRAY, F., GRAUBARD, P. S., & ROSENBERG, H. Little brother is changing you. *Psychology Today,* 1974, **8,** 42–45.

HARTMAN, D. P., & ATKINSON, C. Having your cake and eating it too: A note on some apparent contradictions between therapeutic achievements and design requirements in $N = 1$ studies. *Behavior Therapy,* 1973, **4,** 589–591.

JAYARATNE, S., STUART, R. B., & TRIPODI, T. Methodological issues and problems in evaluating treatment outcomes in the family and school consultation project, 1970–1973. In P. D. Davidson, F. W. Clark, & L. A. Hamerlynck (Eds.), *Evaluation of behavioral programs.* Champaign, Ill.: Research Press, 1974, pp. 141–174.

JESNESS, C. F., & DERISI, W. J. Some variations in techniques of contingency management in a school for delinquents. In J. S. Stumphauzer (Ed.), *Behavior therapy with delinquents.* Springfield, Ill.: Charles C. Thomas, 1973, pp. 196–235.

JESNESS, C. F., DERISI, W. J., MCCORMICK, P. M., & QEDGE, R. F. *The Youth Center research project.* Sacramento: American Justice Institute, 1972.

KANFER, F. H., & SASLOW, G. Behavior analysis: An alternative to diagnostic classification. *Archives of General Psychiatry,* 1965, **12,** 529–538.

KANFER, F. H., & SASLOW, G. Behavioral diagnosis. In C. M. Franks (Ed.), *Behavior therapy: Appraisal and status.* New York: McGraw-Hill, 1969, 417–444.

KARACHI, L., & LEVINSON, R. B. A token economy in a correctional institution for youthful offenders. *The Howard Journal of Penology and Crime Pevention,* 1970, **13,** 20–30.

KAZDIN, A. E., & BOOTZIN, R. R. The token economy: An evaluative review. *Journal of Applied Behavior Analysis,* 1972, **5,** 343–372.

KELLER, O. J., & ALPER, B. S. *Halfway houses.* Lexington, Mass.: Heath, 1970.

KENNEDY, R. F. Halfway houses pay off. *Crime and delinquency,* 1964, **10,** 4–7.

KIMBLES, S. L. Behavior therapy and the black

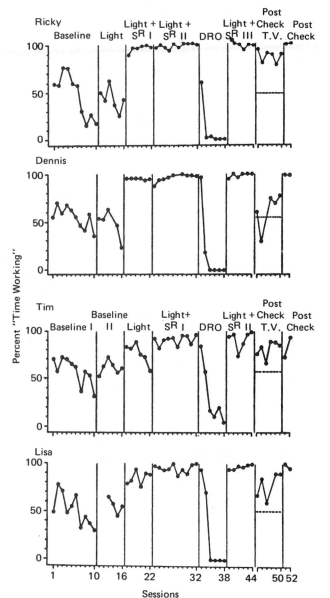

FIGURE 13–2   Graph showing percentage "time working" for all students. (From Surratt, Ulrich, & Hawkins, 1969.) Copyright 1969 by the Society of Experimental Analysis of Behavior, Inc.

(1975), Evans and Oswalt (1968), Coleman (1970), and Brooks and Snow (1972). For example, Evans and Oswalt asked two fourth-grade and two sixth-grade teachers to select one or two students in their classes whom they thought were capable of doing better work. After baseline data, consisting of weekly spelling, math, social studies, or science test scores, were obtained for the target children and the rest of the class, the teachers implemented the following procedure. Five minutes before recess or dismissal time once each day, the teachers asked the target children one question related to material covered that day. The entire class was dismissed early or was read a story if the target child answered the question correctly. Continued observations of weekly test scores clearly showed (in five of the six target children) that the target children's test scores improved when the rewards for the class were contingent on the target children's responses.

Several studies have also been conducted utilizing the Type-II procedure (Barrish, Saunders, & Wolf, 1969; Long & Williams, 1973; Medland & Stachnik, 1972; Ascare & Axelrod, 1973, Sulzbacher & Houser, 1970; Axelrod, 1973; Harris & Sherman, 1973; Packard, 1970; Graubard, 1969; and Grandy, Madsen, & DeMersseman, 1973). Three of these demonstrated the effectiveness of a procedure dubbed the "Good Behavior Game" by its originators, Barrish et al. (1969). Although the procedures varied somewhat, the basic elements included dividing the class into two teams, discussing appropriate and inappropriate behaviors with the class, giving the team a mark if anyone on the team broke a rule, and rewarding the team with the fewest marks (or both teams if no more than a criterion number of marks were received) with extra recess, first in line for lunch, special projects, etc. Medland and Stachnik (1972) added a procedure for dealing with children who continually precluded a team from winning—the individuals could be voted out of the game for a day and had to study in isolation. Harris and Sherman (1973) analyzed separately the effects of no reward, varying the criterion, recording the marks publicly (on the blackboard) or privately (at the teacher's desk), and dividing the class into teams versus treating the class as a whole. Measures of academic performance were also obtained. The results were as follows. Playing the game

with no consequence reduced disruptive behavior to some extent but not as dramatically as when early dismissal could be won. When the criterion was eight marks, disruptive behavior occurred with greater frequency than when the criterion was four marks. Public and private marking did not differentially affect the rates of disruptive behavior. Dividing the class into teams was somewhat more effective than treating the class as a whole. Only small improvements in academic behavior were related to playing the game.

In many ways, the Type-III procedure, in which the individual child is only indirectly involved, is most deserving of the label "group contingency." However, this procedure is much more limited in its applicability than the others, primarily because there are only a limited number of behaviors that are group behaviors. In fact, the only behavior that has been studied with a Type-III paradigm is the level of noise in the classroom. Schmidt and Ulrich (1969) recorded class noise with a sound-level meter. A timer was set for ten minutes. If the decibel (dB) level exceeded 42 dB, the experimenter signaled the class, and the timer was reset. Each time the timer ran the full 10 minutes, the class earned 2 extra minutes of recess and a 2-minute break. Wilson and Hopkins (1973) successfully reduced the noise level in junior high school home economics classes using radio music as a reinforcer. Whenever the noise level exceeded criterion, the radio was turned off for a minimum of 20 seconds and until the noise level was below criterion for 20 seconds.

While group procedures may be easier for the teacher to implement than individualized token programs, the relative effectiveness of group and individual procedures is a necessary consideration. Four of the studies mentioned above made this comparison. While the types of contingencies employed varied across the studies, the findings consistently revealed either no difference between group and individual contingencies (Axelrod, 1973) or small differences in favor of group contingencies (Long & Williams, 1973; Grandy, Madsen, & DeMersseman, 1973; and Rosenbaum et al., 1974). In addition to ease of implementation, the factor of peer influence has been suggested as a contributor to the success of group contingencies. Data on overt indications of peer influence have not usually been collected. However, Graubard (1969) noted that spontaneous reminders of the effect on the group of an individual's transgressions did occur and usually came from those scoring highest on a class sociometric device. Axelrod (1973) recorded students' threats of punishment for deviant behavior in one of his classes and found that more threats occurred during the group contingency phase than when individual contingencies were in effect. The specific role of peer influence in group contingencies needs further study, perhaps within the context of whether the program is based on reward or response cost.

The research on reward programs in recent years shows that there has been a trend toward more frequent use of natural reinforcers (extra recess, special activities, and privileges) and less frequent use of tangible rewards (candy, trinkets, and money). Of the approximately 21 articles reported in this section on reward programs published since 1970, twice as many programs employed natural reinforcers rather than tangibles (14/7). Whether the focus was on social or academic behaviors did not alter this ratio appreciably (8/3 and 6/4, respectively).

There are two other general types of reward programs that merit discussion: home-based programs and contingency contracting. Home-based programs vary on most of the same dimensions that other reward programs do, e.g., behaviors focused on and types of reinforcers. They differ in that while the tokens are dispensed at school, the back-up reinforcers are administered at home. The tokens are in the form of a note from the teacher, which may be as simple as a smile or as detailed as ratings on several behaviors. Although it is the authors' impression that daily or weekly reports home are used frequently by practicing behavior modifiers and appear as parts of general treatment packages (Hawkins, 1971; O'Leary & Kent, 1974), there has been little systematic evaluation of the effectiveness of sending notes home. Using simple AB designs, two studies have been shown that home-based incentive programs can effectively improve the behavior of children in a learning disabilities class (McKenzie, Clark, Wolf, Kothera, & Benson, 1968) and of children diagnosed as hyperactive (Jacob, O'Leary, & Price, 1973). Bailey, Wolf, and Phillips (1970) demonstrated in a series of experiments with boys in a special foster home facility that reports sent home every day effectively improved study behavior and decreased class rule violations. The daily reports were not effective when the predelinquent boys received good reports regardless of their behavior or when they received backups at home regardless of the quality of the daily reports. In one experiment, daily reports were shifted to reports twice a week with little deleterious effect on the students' study behavior. Hawkins, Sluyter, and Smith (1972) also showed the importance of the back-up reinforcers at home. Daily reports without backups to the child alone or to the child and parent were not effective. Home-based programs have clear advantages for the teacher, and they seem to work in spite of the relatively long delay between the occurrence of the desired behavior and the reinforcer. However, such programs depend heavily on the consistent and contingent application of the rewards by the parents, who may not always be cooperative.

The discussion of contingency contracting has been placed at the end of this section for two reasons: (1) contracting can involve any or a combination of the techniques described above; (2) it has not been well researched or well defined. Credit is usually given to Lloyd Homme (e.g., Homme, Csanji, Gonzales, & Rechs, 1969) for first describing contingency contracting. The unique aspect of contracting appears to be that there is a written statement of contingencies that is formulated and agreed upon both by the child and by the teacher and/or parent. However, the "contract" is not always written (MacDonald, Gallimore, & MacDonald, 1970), and the child does not necessarily participate in or agree to the writing of the contract (Cantrell, Cantrell, Huddleston, & Wooldridge, 1969). In fact, in the published literature, it is often unclear that there is any difference between what is labeled "contingency contracting" and what would be recognized as a well-designed reward program (Homme et al., 1969). Finally, to the authors' knowledge, there is no research focusing on either of the two aspects of contracting that could distinguish the procedure from other reward programs, viz., the written nature of the contract and the negotiation of the agreement. Judging from research with delinquents (Stuart, 1971), however, the authors feel that written contracts with significant input on the part of the adolescent may be a fruitful approach for dealing with older children who have school problems.

Punishment

In 1970 and 1971, the present authors searched for experimental articles evaluating the effects of punishment in the classroom for inclusion in a book on classroom management (O'Leary & O'Leary, 1972). There were only a few articles that reported experimental evaluations occurring in the classroom. The scene is not appreciably different today. In addition to the theoretical bias of many behavior modifiers against punishment, there are various practical problems involved in conducting classroom research on punishment. Local school boards and granting agencies are often strongly against it. The choice of effective punishers is difficult. While there are certain punishers that might be effective, they may be impractical from the school's point of view, e.g., time-out rooms, spending time in a principal's office, and staying after school. Nonetheless, teachers are confronted with daily problems where some form of punishment seems desirable. Hitting, kicking, poking a neighbor with a sharp pencil, and running around the room are behaviors that do not easily extinguish. As O'Leary et al. (1971) and MacMillan, Forness, and Trumball (1973) noted, praising appropriate behavior and ignoring all inappropriate behavior may well give some children the message that "it's OK to hit and run around." In brief, it would appear that only under contrived situations is some form of punishment, at least in the form of negative feedback or verbal reprimands, *unnecessary*. The present authors are convinced that punishment research must be done not only because it is occasionally necessary to use aversive controls but also because teachers do use some forms of punishment and at a rate that may be unduly high. Recall, for example, the data reported by Madsen et al. (1970) showing that 77% of teacher-student interactions were negative. Fortunately, in the past 5 years, some applied research on classroom punishment has appeared. These studies will be categorized under three basic headings: (1) response cost, (2) time out, and (3) reprimands. Before considering these studies, various definitions will be given. The terms "negative reinforcement" (an *increase* in response frequency that occurs when the response either terminates or avoids an aversive stimulus) and "punishment" are so frequently confused by those with a smattering of information about behavior modification that we suggest that the term "negative reinforcement" be avoided wherever possible. Even restricting oneself to the term "punishment" creates definitional problems, since it is defined differently even by people within the general behavior modification framework.

> Punishment has been defined as a consequence of behavior which reduces the future probability of that behavior or as an operation in which an aversive stimulus is made contingent upon a response. The aversive stimulus is defined as one whose avoidance or termination is reinforcing. For example, children generally will do things to avoid being spanked and they will do things to terminate loud noises. The spanking and the loud noises are thus called aversive stimuli. In practice, however, few investigators have actually determined whether their subjects will work to escape or avoid a presumably aversive stimulus such as a loud tone or a mild shock before the investigators make the shock or tone contingent upon some response that they wish to suppress. They simply pick some stimulus such as shock or a tone which they *presume* a child would escape or avoid (and thus by definition would be aversive) and then make the shock or tone contingent upon some behavior they wish to weaken. Consequently, most research on punishment deals with testing various stimuli, which are assumed to be aversive, to see if they will weaken a response. In addition, the withdrawal of a positive reinforcer is considered a form of punishment. That is, if one removes a child from a pleasant classroom or an activity which the child obviously likes when the child displays inappropriate behavior, the operation is called time-out from positive reinforcement. In summary, punishment here refers to the presentation of a stimulus assumed to be aversive or to the removal of a presumed positive reinforcer when the subject performs some response one wishes to weaken (Reprinted with permission from K. Daniel O'Leary and Susan G. O'Leary, *Classroom Management*, 1972, Pergamon Press, Inc.).

RESPONSE COST

Kaufman and O'Leary (1972) compared a reward and a cost program for hospitalized adolescent psychiatric patients, in two hour-long, after-school remedial reading classes. In one class, the subjects earned poker chips that were placed in a jar every 15 minutes and were exchangeable for prizes in a special store on the ward after dinner (reward). In the other class, the subjects had all possible tokens (also exchangeable for prizes in the store) placed in a jar at the beginning of the class, and every 15 minutes the student could lose tokens (cost). As can be seen in Figure 13–3, the reward and cost programs were dramatically effective in reducing disruptive behavior, but they were not different from each other. In the last phase of the study, when students were asked to evaluate their own behavior, the disruptive behavior remained very low in both classes. The reward and cost programs did not differentially affect attendance or academic output. Bucher and Hawkins (1973) also found reward and cost programs to be equally effective for four academic underachievers. Like Kaufman and O'Leary, Bucher and Hawkins did not even detect reward versus cost differences in the intervals just after the addition or subtraction of points was announced. The authors of both studies, however, sounded notes of caution. While neither cost contingency had negative side effects, a cost procedure may prompt a teacher to look for the bad rather than the good behaviors and to increase her criticism, threats, and reprimands. In addition, timing of the subtraction of tokens may be critical. If a ward attendant or teacher took tokens away from adolescents *immediately* upon completion of the undesired behavior, more disruption might ensue than if the administration of point consequences occurred at fixed time intervals. For example, if tokens were taken from an angry adolescent just after he was in a verbal battle with a classmate, the adolescent might be more likely to curse the teacher than if the token removal occurred 10 minutes after the altercation.

In ongoing token systems, reward and cost may be effectively utilized together, as illustrated by McLaughlin and Malaby (1972)

COMPARISON OF DAILY MEAN DISRUPTIVE BEHAVIOR IN REWARD AND COST CLASSES

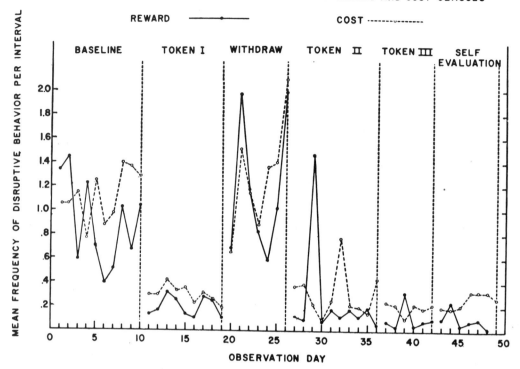

FIGURE 13–3   Comparison of daily mean disruptive behavior in reward and cost classes. (Kaufman and O'Leary, 1972). Copyright 1972 by the Society for the Experimental Analysis of Behavior, Inc.

in a "normal" combined fifth- and sixth-grade classroom. The behaviors and their positive and negative consequences are listed below in Table 13–1. While the fines or loss of points may seem high, 20 of the 25 class members evaluated the program very favorably. Most important, this system illustrates the combined use of reward and cost, which, on the basis of the authors' observations, seems to be the manner in which most ongoing token programs should operate.

TIME OUT FROM REINFORCEMENT

The procedure most commonly labeled "time out" or "time out for reinforcement" is social isolation. On occasions, "time out" may refer to loss of adult attention or loss

of the opportunity to earn tokens. The use of the term "time out from reinforcement" presupposes that a person is being removed from a reinforcing environment, but procedurally such an assessment is seldom ·if ever made. As Drabman and Spitalnik (1973) emphasized, the simple placement of a child in a socially restricted environment contingent upon deviant behavior should be properly defined as social isolation, not time out from reinforcement.

The few investigations using time out, which assessed whether the environment or portions thereof were indeed reinforcing to the child, used a combination of time out and a token reinforcement program. Because of this, the effects of time out from reinforcement per se cannot usually be evaluated. For example, Wasik, Senn, Welch, and Cooper (1969) reported on a

TABLE 13–1   Behaviors and the number of points that they earned or lost. Copyright 1972 by the Society for the Experimental Analysis of Behavior, Inc.

Behaviors That Earned Points	Points
1. Items correct	6 to 12
2. Study behavior, 8:50–9:15	5 per day
3. Bring food for animals	1 to 10
4. Bring sawdust for animals	1 to 10
5. Art	1 to 4
6. Listening points	1 to 2 per lesson
7. Extra credit	Assigned value
8. Neatness	1 to 2
9. Taking home assignments	5
10. Taking notes	1 to 3
11. Quiet in lunch time	2
12. Quiet in cafeteria	2
13. Appropriate noon hour behavior	3
Behaviors That Lost Points	**Points**
1. Assignments incomplete	Amount squared
2. Gum and candy	100
3. Inappropriate verbal behavior	15
4. Inappropriate motor behavior	15
5. Fighting	100
6. Cheating	100

successful modification procedure that simultaneously involved praise, withholding of praise, and social isolation. Similarly, Walker, Mattson, and Buckley (1971) utilized praise, tokens, and time out in an experimental classroom for children with behavior problems; and Sibley, Abbott, and Cooper (1969) used praise and time out to decrease the assaultive behaviors of a kindergarten boy.

One of the most interesting recent applications of a social isolation procedure was that of Lahey, McNees, and McNees (1973). A 10-year-old student with an IQ of 76 was enrolled in an elementary class of educable mentally retarded children because of his disruptive behavior, namely, uttering obscene words. His obscene utterances (usually a four-letter expression for sexual intercourse) were accompanied by a facial twitch. Following the use of massed practice (frequent repetition of the behavior under instruction), which had only a partially suppressive effect, time out in a well-lighted 4-by-10-foot room adjoining the classroom was clearly effective in reducing the obscenities.

One of the best designed evaluations of social isolation was conducted by Drabman and Spitalnik (1973) in a classroom for emotionally disturbed children. Social isolation was the single manipulated variable. Social isolation was clearly effective in reducing the two manipulated disruptive behaviors, out-of-seat behavior and aggression. Vocalization was not manipulated but was observed as a control behavior. No changes were observed in the frequency of vocalization. Of interest was the absence of any effect on nontarget children. Finally, the frequency of the two punished behaviors did not significantly increase when the social isolation procedure was terminated.

Time out and social isolation have been utilized and evaluated in special rather than regular or normal classrooms. Even in special classrooms, time out is not a very popular procedure with principals and teachers. Its use was viewed so negatively in Eugene, Oregon, several years ago that it resulted in cries of torture chamber treatment and clamors in several newspapers. Even where pressure from the news media does not result in the cessation of time-out utilization, teachers often do not continue its use if it does not result in an immediate reduction in the undesired behavior. One major reason for teachers' dislike of time out is that it may be difficult to get the child or adolescent into the isolation area. In short, a bouncer is often required; consequently, the authors here recommend that time out be used very, very discriminately and usually only after other methods have been tried.

REPRIMANDS

There are two studies that showed the effectiveness of soft reprimands or reprimands that were made audible only to the child being reprimanded (O'Leary & Becker, 1968; O'Leary, Kaufman, Kass, & Drabman, 1970). After it was observed that the usual form of reprimands was audible to most of the class, teachers were asked to change the reprimands so that only the child being reprimanded could hear the reprimands. Using an individual subject design, it was clearly shown that for very disruptive children, a soft reprimand was more effective in reducing disruptive behavior than a loud reprimand. While the teachers admitted that the utilization of soft reprimands took more effort initially than giving a loud reprimand, they felt that in the long run the use of loud reprimands was a vicious cycle—the more the child was reprimanded loudly, the more he misbehaved.

Thomas, Becker, and Armstrong (1968) demonstrated that a high disapproval rate was related to an increase in disruptive behavior in "a good class with above-average distribution of ability and no 'bad' kids." While the category of disapproval behavior included behaviors other than reprimands

such as spanking, shaking, threats, and frowning, one may infer that reprimands constituted a high percentage of the negative behavior observed. In a related study mentioned earlier, Madsen, Becker, Thomas, Koser, and Plager (1968) found that "sit down" reprimands increased the frequency of out-of-seat behavior. Conversely, when the children were praised for in-seat behavior, they tended to remain in their seats. In both the above studies, the reprimands were largely audible to many class members, and the loud reprimand may have functioned in a manner similar to that in the O'Leary et al. (1970) and O'Leary and Becker (1968) studies.

MacMillan et al. (1973) have an excellent review of punishment in the classroom, and some of their points deserve repeating here. There is a continuum of teacher behaviors ranging from spanking and withdrawal of love to verbal reprimands and mild social disapproval that will decrease undesirable student behaviors. The alternatives chosen must take the maturity of the child and the social mileu into account. On the basis of the Aronfreed (1968) and Parke (1969) research, which indicated that giving a child a reason or a verbal explanation for the prohibition not to play with an attractive toy (e.g., "that toy is for another boy"; "that toy breaks very easily") decreased playing with the forbidden toy, MacMillan argued that a reason should accompany punishment.

Modeling

Much of the original work on modeling was directed at assessing the effects of viewing films depicting aggression on children's behavior in a laboratory setting. More recently, such research has been conducted in the classroom proper by Friedrich and Stein (1973). Nursery school children were shown aggressive cartoons (*Batman* and *Superman*), prosocial programs (*Mister Rogers Neighborhood*) and neutral films.

The children viewed these films daily for 9 weeks, and their behavior was observed in the classroom. Children who viewed the aggressive cartoons showed a decrease in obeying rules and tolerance of frustration. In addition, those children who watched the aggressive cartoons and who were initially most aggressive (above the group mean) showed more interpersonal aggression than those who viewed the neutral programs. In contrast, children who watched the prosocial programs showed higher levels of persistence than those children who watched the neutral films. This work is commendable for it is one of the few modeling studies that evaluated the effects of repeated viewing of certain programs and that included repeated observations in the natural environment.

O'Connor (1969, 1972) and Evers and Schwarz (1973) effectively modified the behavior of socially isolated *preschool* children by having them view a 23-minute film depicting a graduated sequence of children interacting socially. O'Connor (1972) found that the children in the modeling conditions maintained their improved social behavior better than those children receiving shaping with praise, although this result was not found by Evers and Schwarz (1973). In sum, it is now clear that social interactions of nursery school children can be increased after the single viewing of a relatively brief modeling film.

To our knowledge, there is no research investigating the effect of modeling on the classroom behavior of elementary or secondary school children. There are, however, two sources of information that indirectly indicate the potential usefulness of modeling. Zimmerman and Pike (1972) observed the frequency with which second graders asked questions in a small-group prototype of a classroom story period. Modeling by the experimenter-teacher plus praise increased question-asking considerably, while praise alone did so only slightly. Prototypes of classrooms provide better information regarding the application of modeling procedures in the classroom than laboratory situations, but research is sorely needed with dependent measures in the classroom.

Research demonstrating changes in untreated children when target children are either participants in token programs (Bolstad & Johnson, 1972) or the recipients of systematic teacher attention (Broden et al., 1970) points to the possible importance of children modeling the behavior of their peers. It should be noted that there are extensive problems in interpreting this "generalization" literature. The vicarious reinforcing effect of teacher proximity, the cueing properties of the teacher, the influence of decreasing disruption, perhaps the "threat" value of the teacher's nearness, and modeling may all be aspects of the effects represented in the above studies. If there is any approach to changing children's classroom behavior that deserves more attention, it is modeling. Modeling studies are relatively easy to execute in laboratory settings and such studies abound in the literature. Unfortunately, with the exception of work with nursery school children, intervention research regarding the effects of modeling in a classroom is practically nonexistent.

Instructional Techniques

Behavioral researchers interested in classroom management problems have recognized and discussed the need to deal with the students' academic behaviors as well as their social behaviors (Ayllon & Roberts, 1974; O'Leary & Drabman, 1971; Winett & Winkler, 1972; O'Leary & O'Leary, 1972). Initially, investigators first looked for changes in academic behavior as a result of establishing contingencies for social behavior or for a combination of social and academic behavior. Then the effects of establishing contingencies directly on academic responses were studied. At this point, the emphasis is still largely on the consequences of academic behavior (e.g., Grimm, Bijou,

& Parson, 1973). Even though it has always been apparent to classroom researchers that many problem children have serious academic difficulties that are not solely due to or remediable by consequences to social or academic behavior, the antecedents to academic responses, i.e., the instructional stimuli, have been generally ignored by those involved in applied classroom research (Berman, 1973). This is not to say that such research is entirely lacking. For example, there is evidence that consistently supports the effectiveness of programmed instruction as a supplementary teaching tool.

Atkinson[2] (1968) reported the first year's results of teaching first graders reading via computer-assisted instruction (CAI). Half the children in one school received CAI reading and half were taught by the classroom teacher. At the end of the year, the CAI children scored significantly higher on the California Achievement Test (except for the comprehension subtest) and the Hartley Reading Test. Similarly, Williams, Gilmore, and Malpass (1968) found that when culturally deprived, slow-learning first graders received extra reading instruction in programmed formats, they improved significantly more (Gates Primary Reading Test) than students receiving only regular classroom instruction. Half of the students who were exposed to programmed material used workbooks and half were given the same material via teaching machines. No differences were observed between modes of presentation. In another analysis of instructional format (Reese & Parnes, 1970), a programmed creativity course for high school seniors was found to be more effective when taught in class by an instructor than when the students worked independently in workbooks. Unfortunately, demonstrating that programmed instruction adds signifi-

cantly to the effects of "usual classroom instruction" is not equivalent to demonstrating its superiority.

A recent comprehensive review (Jamison, Suppes, & Wells, 1974) of instructional media (i.e., traditional classroom instruction, instructional radio, instructional television, programmed instruction, and computer-assisted instruction) reached the following conclusions. There is no consistent pattern linking input variables of traditional instruction to student achievement, with the possible exceptions that smaller class sizes may improve the performance of elementary school students and that teachers' verbal ability contributes to learning. On the whole, no differences were found in the effectiveness of programmed instruction, instructional radio (plus printed material), instructional television, and computer-assisted instruction as compared to the effectiveness of traditional instruction. Programmed materials may save the student time, and slower students may improve more with supplementary computer-assisted instruction.

In addition to program evaluation, applied behavioral analysis of more subtle aspects of instructional techniques is needed. Two examples of this type of research are found in Lovitt and Curtiss (1968) and Lovitt and Smith (1972). Lovitt and Curtiss examined the effects of having an 11-year-old boy verbalize an arithmetic problem prior to making a written response. Correct answer rate increased and error rate decreased as a result of this manipulation. An equally simple procedure, the use of clearly stated instructions, was shown to affect the variety and length of sentences that a 9-year-old boy used in describing pictures (Lovitt & Smith, 1972). These procedures, verbalization of the problem and explicit instructions, may seem obvious, but the reader should note that the same has been said regarding praise. To suppose that fine-grained analyses of instructional procedures are either someone else's business (i.e., the educator's) or are unimportant for

---

2 The researchers mentioned in this paragraph do not necessarily align themselves with a behavioral approach, but their instructional work is readily integrated into such an approach.

understanding and modifying complex classroom behavior would be shortsighted. Thus, like modeling, analyses of instructional variables seem long overdue by behavior modifiers.

Self-Management

During the past three or four years, research on and teaching of self-control have been strongly emphasized and advocated (Bandura, 1969; Goldfried & Merbaum, 1973; Kanfer, 1970). Initially, a number of studies appeared that demonstrated the efficacy of self-control procedures in laboratory analogue experiments, but now several studies have been conducted that evaluated the role of self-management in applied clinical or educational settings. Both types of studies will be reviewed here in detail. They will be subsumed under the following headings: (1) self-determination of goals and reinforcement standards, (2) self-recording, (3) self-evaluation, and (4) self-reinforcement.

SELF-DETERMINATION OF GOALS AND REINFORCEMENT STANDARDS

There are no classroom studies known to these authors in which goals clearly determined by subjects were compared with identical goals superimposed upon subjects. Drabman (1973) varied goal selection versus goal imposition simultaneously with peer versus teacher administration of a token program. The programs in which goals were selected by the students and in which the students themselves distributed tokens were more successful than the programs in which teachers determined the goals and administered the reinforcers. Unfortunately, the extent to which the students actually felt that they were instrumental in setting the goals (desired behaviors) of the classroom may have been minimal and, as mentioned previously, goal determination was confounded with type of administration of program. While the children were told that

they were to be involved in the design of the program, in fact they could only suggest the rules that had already been posted, e.g., come to class on time, sit in seat, do not leave seat without permission, and keep quiet.

It is, of course, difficult to give children and adolescents—particularly very disruptive ones—complete freedom in selecting classroom goals. However, with some teacher supervision, such students would probably select reasonable goals. One program where adolescents have been taught rule development is Achievement Place, a family-style treatment program for adolescents (Phillips, Phillips, Fixen, & Wolf, 1972). Basically, the adolescents had rules imposed upon them initially; and they were gradually taught to (1) establish new rules and modify old rules; (2) give reasons for each rule; and (3) establish consequences for rule violations. While the emphasis in Achievement Place was on consequences for actions, special attention was paid to rule development, and the development of rules in many instances was tantamount to developing goals. Teachers clearly involve children in some classroom decisions, but the effects of such student involvement in the decision-making process have not been evaluated. It is no accident that current work on student involvement with goal determination and rule making occurred with adolescents. One simply cannot thrust rules upon older children and expect to obtain compliance. Young children, too, would probably respond positively to involvement in rule making and learn important lessons in the process.

Bandura and Perloff (1967) investigated self- versus external-imposition of standards of reinforcement in a laboratory situation. Children in one condition selected their own reinforcement criteria for work on a motor task (wheel cranking), and they administered their own rewards upon reaching those standards. A yoked control group had rewards imposed upon them and were given rewards by the experimenter.

Noncontingent reinforcement and no-incentive controls were also employed. There was no significant difference in performance between the self- and externally-imposed contingent reinforcement conditions, but both of these groups showed greater productivity than the control subjects. Following this study, Lovitt and Curtiss (1969), Glynn (1970), Felixbrod and O'Leary (1973), Felixbrod and O'Leary (1974), and Felixbrod (1974) all investigated aspects of self-determination of standards. These studies have been reviewed in detail by Felixbrod (1974). With few exceptions, one can conclude from present evidence that a self-determined reinforcement standard results in productivity equivalent to an externally determined reinforcement standard. For those interested in research applications, however, the warning by Felixbrod and O'Leary (1973) must be heeded. As long as children realize that there are no aversive consequences for imposing very lenient standards of reinforcement, they will often do so. In brief, if relatively high standards of reinforcement are to maintained, some surveillance and social reinforcement for high standard setting generally must be used.

In a recent study by Price and O'Leary (1974), four first-grade children were selected from a special class of children with behavioral problems. The teacher referred the four children because she thought they had low performance standards. During the initial 5-day period, the children were given math and reading problems consecutively and were asked to select the number of problems they wanted to complete. No feedback was given to the children by the experimenter during this initial standard selection period. Treatment sessions then followed in which children received praise plus a hug or a pat on the back for a 10% increase in standard setting in math only. Additionally, for one child who was not responsive to praise from the experimenter, a visit to the head of the school was utilized as a reinforcer. No reading problems were given to the children during the treatment phase. All children increased their standard setting and, more important, during a second 5-day baseline phase in which no praise for high standards was given, the high standards were maintained and generalized to the reading task.

SELF-RECORDING

Self-recording and self-evaluation might be considered by some to be identical. Here we wish to refer to self-evaluation as a procedure requiring the child to evaluate his behavior on a subjective basis (e.g., evaluate your behavior on a 1–10 scale) and to self-recording as a checking or monitoring of behaviors that requires minimal amounts of judgment (counting the number of problems complete). Actually, there is a continuum of judgment involved, and categorization is sometimes difficult, e.g., recording whether one is studying or not. For our purposes here, however, we will classify the recording of study time as self-recording. Broden, Hall, and Mitts (1971) has a junior high school girl record studying time and a junior high school boy record the times he talked out of turn. In the first instance, self-recording consisted of making a "+" or "−" mark on a specially prepared sheet ("when she thought of it") to indicate whether she was studying or not. The boy simply was asked to make a hatch mark on a 2-by-5 card ("every time he talked without permission"). An important aspect of the plan was that the students deposited their daily records with a counselor who praised the students for improvement. Thus, in essence, the intervention was counselor praise plus self-recording. The intervention was effective for the girl but had only a transitory positive effect for the boy. Salzberg (1972) also reported a failure of self-recording of progress in influencing the number of quizzes passed in two classes. Self-recording has been utilized within the context of token reinforcement programs and is often an integral part of such programs. Santogrossi

(1974) evaluated the effects of self-recording on the number of academic units correctly completed per class session in an after-school reading token program. He found peer and teacher recording of units completed more influential than self-recording on the actual number of correctly completed units; the self-recording group was better than a control group whose progress was not recorded (except by the experimenters).

Cheating is a potential problem with any self-recording procedure, and it is a special problem where the self-recording is related to immediate payoff as in a token reinforcement program. Using only small candies as reinforcers, Dietz (1973) found that third- to fifth-grade students deliberately misscored 15% of their answers. To reduce cheating, two types of teacher checking were then introduced: an intermittent checking system and a checking system that was gradually faded out. His results suggested that when all checking was terminated, the students who experienced the intermittent checking cheated less. Finally, Glynn, Thomas, and Shee (1973) employed a self-recording procedure with second-grade children in a "typical" class with "no special problems." A tape recorder was introduced into the classroom that produced intermittent beeps randomly during a 1- to 5-minute period. Each child was provided with a card on which he placed a check each time a beep occurred and he or she was "on task." The actual self-recording phase of this study followed several group contingency phases, and it appeared that the self-recording procedure was as effective as the group contingencies. While the percentage of on-task behavior declined markedly when the children stopped evaluating and no longer received rewards for their efforts, their on-task behavior was higher than it had been at the beginning of the token program. The present authors seriously question whether a procedure involving intermittent audible beeps in a classroom would be accepted by many teachers. In fact, such a procedure could be distracting in a normal classroom.

SELF-EVALUATION

Self-evaluation per se has been evaluated in two studies with disruptive students. Santogrossi, O'Leary, Romanczyk, and Kaufman (1973) found that while adolescent boys' self-evaluations of their classroom behavior on a 10-point scale correlated highly with teachers' ratings and with evaluations made by independent observers, the self-evaluations did not lead to a reduction in disruptive behavior. Similarly, Turkewitz, O'Leary, and Ironsmith (1975) found that self-evaluation per se did not influence disruptive classroom behavior of very disruptive children. In brief, self-evaluation by itself seems to have little influence on disruptive classroom behavior.

Many classroom studies focusing on self-management have included self-evaluation as a critical component of a more extensive behavioral intervention program. For example, Bolstad and Johnson (1972) had children evaluate their own behavior. The children's evaluations were redeemable for reinforcers dispensed by the experimenter in the token program. A comparison external-regulation group experienced a standard teacher-administered token reinforcement program. The children who were taught to self-evaluate were slightly less disruptive during the reinforcement as well as during the extinction periods.

Drabman, Spitalnik, and O'Leary (1973) taught children drawn from classes for "emotional disturbance" to evaluate their own behavior in a token program on a 1–10 rating scale. The children were told that they could award themselves as many as 5 points for appropriate social behavior (being quiet, not disturbing others) and 5 points for academic behavior (completing assignments, getting items correct). Following a baseline period, three of four 15-minute periods were designated as token periods. One of the four 15-minute periods was randomly chosen at the beginning of each day as the nontoken, or control, period. The children were told at the beginning of each day which three 15-minute periods were designated as token periods and which period was designated as the control period. In order to teach honest self-evaluation, the children's self-evaluations were checked with those of the teacher, and points were awarded or subtracted depending upon how closely the children's ratings matched the teacher's ratings. Not only was the token program associated with a sharp reduction in disruptive behavior, but, more important, during the nontoken or generalization period disruptive behavior was also markedly reduced.

Turkewitz, O'Leary, and Ironsmith (1975) replicated the Drabman et al. (1973) results and, in addition, showed that during a final extinction phase the rates of disruptive behavior remained quite low. Turkewitz et al. (1975) faded both teacher checking of the self-evaluation as well as the back-up reinforcers.

In summary, based on the efforts of Bolstad and Johnson (1972), Drabman, Spitalnik, and O'Leary (1973), and Turkewitz, O'Leary, and Ironsmith (1975), it appears that self-evaluation procedures in the context of token reinforcement programs offer promise for producing long-range treatment effects. The rates of disruptive behavior following removal of the programs remained low, and in two studies generalization of effects was seen to segments of the hour when the token program was not operative (Drabman et al., 1973; Turkewitz et al., 1975). However, until more comparative studies similar to that of Bolstad and Johnson are executed, it cannot be stated unequivocally that self-evaluation procedures per se are key factors in producing generalization. Very gradual fading of reinforcers and the random nature of the control periods in the Drabman et al. (1973) and Turkewitz et al. (in press) studies may have been critical elements in producing generalization. From a clinical and educational standpoint, it would clearly

seem wise to incorporate self-evaluation procedures into a token program. The children like them, and self-evaluation appears to have a salutary effect. Self-evaluation, however, is something that requires external monitoring at least on occasion, and it is a skill that, like many other skills, must be carefully taught.

SELF-REINFORCEMENT

Generally, self-reinforcement refers to the changing of behavior through self-produced consequences. Such consequences may be overt or covert, as exemplified by statements to oneself or the purchase of an item as a reward for one's efforts. As such, the self-reinforcement process here refers to one aspect of the more general self-management paradigm.

The Bolstad and Johnson (1972) experiment described earlier involved a component of self-regulation in that "subjects were given complete control over dispensing reinforcers to themselves [p. 444]." In brief, subjects could take items like pens, pencils, and children's readers from specially labeled boxes. However, in a phase prior to the purported transfer of control of reinforcers to the subjects, the children's evaluations were matched against those of observers in the classroom. In addition, the child was watched as he availed himself of goods from the reward boxes. Thus the condition in which a child was to pick from the reward boxes based on self-evaluations of his behavior was not a condition without some surveillance since the observers were in the classroom. In short, although the term self-reinforcement was used sporadically throughout the article, its use was somewhat strained in that the child was not completely free to avail himself (at least in a perceived sense) of rewards, since the experimenter dispensed the back-up reinforcers.

In a comparison of self-determined, experimenter-determined, and chance-determined token reinforcement treatments. Glynn (1970) recorded the test scores of girls in four ninth-grade history-geography

classes. He reported that the self-determined and externally determined reinforcement programs were equally efficacious and that both were superior to the chance-determined and no-reinforcement groups. However, the term self-reinforcement may well have been a misnomer. The girls could earn prizes by turning in credits (tokens); they were told to award themselves from zero to five tokens, but no rules or suggestions were made for making such a decision. Envelopes for tokens were used to minimize social influence, but there were checks by the experimenter on the amount of reward taken.

If the term self-reinforcement refers to complete freedom to avail oneself of some goods such as candy or money without surveillance, it seems that such a procedure is unlikely to succeed in reducing disruptive behavior or increasing academic response rates of "problem" students. Even the most moral or ethical adults would be sorely tempted and most likely enticed by complete freedom to avail themselves of extra cash from a box as payment for a week's work if there were no aversive consequences. Self-reinforcement procedures would seem most reasonably applied where individuals are taught to make positive comments to themselves. For example, a child or teenager who is depressed could be taught to recognize small accomplishments in himself, to praise himself for them, and to dwell on such thoughts occasionally. A child could be taught to praise and encourage himself for improving drawing skills or athletic prowess; in both instances talking to oneself while engaging in the task might prove helpful. While self-praise or self-reinforcement is ultimately linked to some external monitoring such as teacher or parental feedback, its use is potentially quite valuable in shaping and maintaining behavior.

Generalization and Maintenance

Any chapter on classroom management would be incomplete without an updated report on how behavior modifiers are faring in the battle to remove the albatross of generalization from around their necks. The term generalization in the behavioral literature has been used rather loosely, but briefly the issue is as follows. The large majority of school children learn and behave reasonably well without token programs, group contingencies, and often without much teacher attention. It is therefore assumed that an ideal intervention would culminate in the maintenance of adequate academic and social behavior in the absence of special procedures and in the presence of only those reinforcers available to "normal" children, e.g., report cards, occasional praise, and personal satisfaction. More specifically, the effects of classroom intervention should maintain themselves when the procedures are not in effect (e.g., the following year); they should generalize to other situations (e.g., to the regular class if the intervention occurs in a special class) and to behaviors other than those directly being changed (e.g., swearing if the target behavior has been aggression). These three types of effects have been referred to as maintenance of effects across time (following the removal of a program) and generalization across situations and responses. Evidence for maintenance and generalization is obtained in any of several ways: follow-up observations after the program has been officially terminated, simultaneous observations on nontargeted behavior or during times of the day when the program is not in effect, anecdotal information, and questionnaires and tests administered before and after the treatment is implemented.

Research reporting *no* evidence for generalization has been very plentiful in the past. Several explanations have been proffered for these failures to find generalization. Generalization will not occur spontaneously; it must be programmed (Baer, Wolf, & Risley, 1968). Usually, researchers do not include procedures designed to enhance generalization in their intervention programs. Another major source of the difficulty involves factors that encourage discrimination rather than generalization. For example, the use of the typical ABA design may operate against producing generalization. Sudden and complete shifts in contingencies are designed to teach discrimination rather than lead to maintenance. In addition to the multitude of very successful reversals that have been reported and which would inhibit generalization primarily across time, Wahler (1969) has shown that children appear to discriminate between situations (i.e., home versus school) when the intervention occurs in one situation and not the other. Similar findings have been reported when the token and nontoken situations are at different times of the day (Meichenbaum, Bowers, & Ross, 1968; O'Leary, Becker, Evans, & Saudargas, 1969; Wolf, Giles, & Hall, 1968). The results relevant to generalization across responses are more complicated but suggest that generalization is not likely to occur when the responses are very dissimilar (Ferritor et al., 1972). In effect, it appears that any factor that facilitates the discrimination between intervention and nonintervention times, situations, or responses decreases the likelihood that generalization will be observed.

The remainder of this discussion will focus on research that has systematically attempted to understand and produce generalization. There are a number of studies, e.g., Blanchard and Johnson, 1973; O'Leary, Drabman, and Kass, 1973, that have reported generalization but that did not assess the parameters critical in its production. Since these results did not provide clear indications of how to produce generalization, they will not be reviewed.

One approach to producing generalization emphasizes programming the environment, and the other emphasizes programming the individual. Clearly, the two approaches are not mutually exclusive but rather reflect a strategic emphasis. Environmental reprogramming has included factors such as fading reinforcers, reducing the differences between token and nontoken

settings, and redirecting peer attention from disruptive to appropriate behavior. Several examples of the environmental reprogramming effort follow. O'Leary and Becker (1967) were able to gradually fade the exchange of backups from every day to every 5 days without an increase in disruptive behavior. Bailey, Wolf, and Phillips (1970) successfully faded from daily reports home to the parents to reports twice per week. However, neither of these studies withdrew the programs entirely. Turkewitz, O'Leary, and Ironsmith (1975) did withdraw the program entirely. These authors combined a token program and edible backups with a self-evaluation program. The first component to be faded was teacher monitoring of the accuracy of the self-evaluations. When teacher monitoring was no longer occurring, back-up reinforcers were faded. During the final 5 days of the study, the children received no backups, teacher monitoring did not occur, the children continued to evaluate their own behavior, and the level of disruptive behavior remained low.

Another environmental reprogramming approach is exemplified by the work of Walker and Buckley (1972) and entails programming certain aspects of the treatment procedures into the child's posttreatment environment. Walker and Buckley admitted 44 children for 2 months of treatment in an experimental classroom. The children were then assigned to one of the following four groups for the purpose of studying generalization effects when the children were returned to their regular classes: (1) peer reprogramming (essentially a group contingency procedure); (2) equating stimulus conditions (a continuation of almost all of the procedures employed in the experimental class); (3) teacher training in behavior modification; and (4) a control group. The data analysis reported by Walker and Buckley has been criticized by Cone (1973). Cone's reanalysis took into account differential baseline levels and the amount of change during treatment. This reanalysis indicated that the percentages of baseline to treatment change that persisted during the 2-month followup for the four groups were 44.8% (peer reprogramming), 52.2% (equating stimulus conditions), 49.0% (teacher training), and 33.0% (control). Cone's discussion should be thoroughly considered by anyone involved in assessing change and generalization over time and situations. Walker and Buckley demonstrated three procedures for producing partial maintenance of their treatment effects across time and situations, but no clear differences in the relative effectiveness of peer reprogramming, equating stimulus conditions, and teacher training were found.

Drabman (1973) also successfully reprogrammed the posttreatment environment by employing feedback as a maintenance strategy in a state hospital classroom. The students' levels of disruptive behavior remained low when ratings by either the teacher or peer captain were continued following withdrawal of back-up reinforcers.

The second basic approach to the study of generalization recognizes the difficulties involved in reprogramming the child's posttreatment environment and suggests that the children themselves can be reprogrammed by teaching them self-control procedures. Presumably, self-control skills could be used on a continuing basis by the children after the formal aspects of the treatment were terminated. Several studies have demonstrated that children can be taught to veridically evaluate their behavior (see previous self-management section). Kaufman and O'Leary (1972) and Santogrossi, O'Leary, Romanczyk, and Kaufman (1973) found that the frequency of disruptive behavior remained low when teacher evaluations were discontinued and back-up reinforcers were dispensed contingent on self-evaluations. Drabman, Spitalnik, and O'Leary (1973) and Turkewitz, O'Leary, and Ironsmith (1975) obtained generalization to a 15-minute control period of a 1-hour reading class that combined self-evaluation and a token pro-

gram. The only study that compared the relative effects on generalization of self-regulation and external (experimenter) regulation was that of Bolstad and Johnson (1972). Their design is illustrated in Figure 13-4. It is important to note that the four most disruptive children from each of several classes were randomly assigned to one of the conditions—NR_1 (untreated control), ER, SR_1, and SR_2. The NR_1 students were not involved in the token program at all but were in classes where three other disruptive children were involved in a token program. The NR_2 (also untreated) children were all in one class containing no treated children. Using raw-score analyses, self-regulation and external-regulation procedures were found to be equally effective.[3] Therefore, the argument that self-control procedures should enhance generalization was not clearly supported. The data on the NR_1 group are particularly interesting. Although these children did not show as much improvement during the treatment phases, their behavior did improve and was indistinguishable from the treated children during the final generalization phase. This result suggests that a teacher who has several problem children in the class may be able to effect changes in all the children's behavior by utilizing behavioral procedures with only a portion of the children.

In spite of the widely recognized need for research in the area of generalization and maintenance of behavior, surprisingly little progress has been made, and some difficult issues have become apparent. For instance, should the effect of treatment on other nontreated children in the class observed by Bolstad and Johnson (1972) and by Broden et al. (1970) be considered generalization, or should the effect be more appropriately discussed in terms of modeling, cueing, or

[3] An analysis of difference scores showed that the self-regulation groups decreased their disruptive behavior more from baseline than did the external-regulation group.

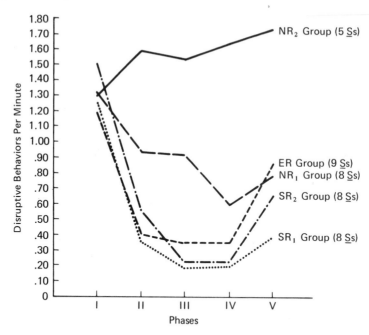

FIGURE 13-4   Average disruptive behavior per minute of groups. During phase I (baseline), disruptive behaviors were observed in class. During phase II (external regulation), children in all experimental groups (ER, SR₁, and SR₂) were awarded points after class for fewer disruptions. During phase III, ER group remained on external regulation, while the self-regulation groups (SR₁ and SR₂) were trained to record and report their own behavior and were given points for accurate reports of fewer disruptions. Phase IV was the same as phase III except that points were given for children reporting few disruptions regardless of the accuracy of their reports. In phase V (extinction), no points were given, and only the SR₁ group was still required to record and report on disruptive behavior (Bolstad & Johnson, 1972). Copyright 1972 by the Society for the Experimental Analysis for Behavior, Inc.

vicarious reinforcement? Is it reasonable to consider disruptive behaviors on the same generalization continuum with correct answers (Ferritor et al., 1972), or is the incompatibility of the behaviors or their position in the child's response hierarchy more relevant? Can we use follow-up data from the teacher-attention studies (e.g., Hall, Lund, & Jackson, 1968) as evidence for maintenance when in all probability the teacher is continuing the treatment during followup? How much programming of the child's new environment (e.g., Walker & Buckley, 1972) are we willing to allow and still describe the persistence of his appropriate behavior as maintenance?

It is clear that many factors can operate to produce what is sometimes mislabeled generalization or maintenance. These factors (e.g., relationships between behaviors, modeling) need to be studied in their own right. The assessment of generalization and maintenance when the treatment involves high rates of teacher attention must include data during times of reduced rates of praise (e.g., in art class or during the following year). Finally, it is the authors' opinion that treatment effects must be maintained in the absence of any procedures that are not normally used by classroom teachers before it can be said that generalization has been demonstrated. There are three possible exceptions to this: continued alteration of the relative amounts of the teacher's positive and negative interactions with the child; maintenance of slightly higher levels of praise, especially where particularly disruptive children are involved; and the continuation of any procedures that the child himself might use, for example, self-evaluation and systematically attending to the behavior of fellow students and teachers (as in Graubard et al., 1971). We agree with Baer et al. (1968) that generalization will not occur spontaneously and must be programmed, but because of the presently unsolved difficulties involved in training teachers to use behavioral procedures independent of supervision (see below), most of this programming will have to occur as part of the intervention. In the long run, we will have to depend largely on our abilities to teach children with problems to function in the world without a great deal of ever-continuing aid—not on society's ability to provide a constant therapeutic environment.

Teacher Training

Anyone who tries to implement behavioral procedures in the classroom quickly realizes that teacher training is a central concern. Several procedures for training teachers have been studied, and the results are fairly clear. Instructions to the teacher regarding the definition of target behaviors and the systematic use of attention do not effectively increase the frequency or appropriateness of teacher praise (Cossairt, Hall, & Hopkins, 1973). Giving the teacher graphical and/or verbal feedback at the end of the day regarding her behavior, either alone or in combination with instructions, is also ineffective (Cossairt et al., 1973; Rule, 1972; Saudargas, 1972). However, Cooper, Thomson, and Baer (1970) gave teachers feedback (frequencies of praise and failure to praise appropriate child response) every 10 minutes and successfully increased the percentage of time the teachers spent attending to their students' appropriate behaviors.

Another type of feedback has also been found to be an effective means of teacher training: self-recording of videotapes. Thomas (1971) described the results of a procedure whereby teachers viewed segments of their teaching behavior after being shown tapes illustrating the definition of target behaviors, how to record and graph behavior, and how to praise. Saudargas (1972) expanded on Thomas' (1971) findings and showed that the teachers' praise rate changed not only when the teachers were being taped but also at times of the day when only observers were present. Self-recording of videotapes has been compared to daily instructions and feedback (Rule, 1972) and was found to be slightly more effective.

Rule (1972) also observed the effect of having the experimenter praise the teacher for every 5 minutes of appropriate teaching behavior. When the teacher's behavior fell below the criterion level, the experimenter took over the teacher role and modeled appropriate behavior for approximately 5 minutes. This combination of direct interventions led to more appropriate teacher behavior than did either instructions and feedback or video recording. Rule stated that being replaced by the experimenter was highly aversive to the teachers and that the teachers changed their behavior to avoid that consequence. Unless the consultant has very good rapport with the teacher or control over important reinforcers, direct intervention contingent on poor teacher behavior would clearly be a hazardous training procedure.

Praise is one of the most powerful teacher training procedures. Cossairt et al. (1973) demonstrated the superiority of graphical feedback combined with praise from the experimenter at the end of the day over either instructions or feedback alone. The experimenter was able to fade feedback and praise without the teachers' rates of praise decreasing substantially. In addition, the students' attending behavior did not improve until the experimenter began praising the teacher. It should also be remembered that Graubard et al. (1971) taught students to attend systematically to their teachers with the result that positive interactions with the teacher increased while negative interactions decreased. Students as well as experimenters, principals, and parents may be effective teacher trainers.

In summary, praise or frequent feedback appears to be the most useful teacher-training procedure, especially since video equipment is not widely available. Instructions, the procedure most commonly used by practicing clinicians, simply do not produce the desired results. While these findings are encouraging, there are several problems associated with the teacher-training research published to date that seriously limit its applicability.

First of all, the number of subjects (teachers) represented in the research is small: Cossairt et al. (1973)—3 teachers; Rule (1972)—9 teachers; Cooper et al. (1970)—2 teachers; Thomas (1971)—4 teachers; Saudargas (1972)—2 teachers; and Graubard (1971)—14 teachers. It would be particularly interesting to see an evaluation of training procedures not only with larger numbers of teachers but also with teachers who are "resistant" to behavioral approaches or to having their behavior modified. Second, the discriminative function of observers has been documented (e.g., Surratt & Ulrich, 1969), and the existing data do not tell us how the teachers behave when they are not being observed. Using children as observers without a teacher's consent raises serious ethical questions. Visits from the principal would prompt good behavior —but perhaps only during his visit. Product measures (result on weekly quizzes) are one viable solution. Alternatively, with teacher permission, random videotaped sequences of teacher-child interactions across a semester or academic year would provide some critical evidence regarding behavior maintenance in a research setting, although it would not be practical for school districts

to use video procedures routinely. Finally, the question of how to produce maintenance is as yet unanswered.

Methodological Issues[4]

One of the hallmarks of behavior modification has been its emphasis on direct measurement of behavior *in situ*. Unlike most of the preceding therapeutic endeavors, behavior modification experimenters usually eschewed rating scales and instead focused on placing an observer in the home, school, or ward. It was held by many that direct observation of a behavior was superior to standardized personality tests and factorially derived rating systems, even though the latter assessment tools often had well-defined statistical properties (Bijou, Peterson, & Ault, 1968; O'Leary, 1972). In the past 2 years, behavior modifiers have begun to question the above assumption because researchers are finding that direct measurement has its own set of methodological problems that raises doubts about data obtained under certain conditions. This soul searching was best exemplified by the 1972 Banff Conference in Alberta, Canada. As Mash (1973) noted, the most recurrent theme of the presenters, who were selected from three university centers noted for behavior modification, was "a general concern for quality of data—and more specifically with issues of *experimental design, data collection, and data analysis* [p. 3]." It was long felt that when an observer was sent to a school, home, or ward, what the observer reported was what was there. It has now become apparent that what is reported is not necessarily what is there. Despite the general constancy of the classroom environment, researchers have found that numerous problems plague observa-

[4] This final section on methodological issues will be of interest to readers working in applied settings only from the standpoint of research evaluation. However, readers actively involved in research should seriously consider the problems discussed.

tional methodology in the classroom. Let us consider some of these problems.

EXPECTATION

In 1967, Scott, Burton, and Yarrow published a study that purported to demonstrate that the observers' knowledge of the experimental hypothesis leads to biased classroom data. That study has been amply criticized for methodological problems (Kent, O'Leary, Diament, & Dietz, 1974), but nonetheless it has served as a seminal influence in the field. Kent et al. (1974) found that knowledge of experimental hypotheses per se did not influence objective recordings of classroom behavior. On the other hand, knowledge of experimental hypotheses did alter global ratings of classroom behavior. O'Leary, Kent, and Kanowitz (1975) found that knowledge of experimental hypotheses *plus* contingent feedback from an experimenter did influence observer data. That is, if an experimenter gave a subject (observer) praise or reproof contingent upon receiving data consistent with experimental hypotheses, the subject produced data consistent with the hypotheses. One major implication of the above findings is that investigators may not have to be overly concerned that knowledge of an experimental hypothesis alone will be sufficient to distort data. Such results should be of consolation to investigators who have experimentally evaluated token reinforcement programs in classrooms, for it is impossible to prevent observers from knowing when a token program begins and from knowing that the token program is designed to reduce disruptive behavior and increase appropriate behavior. However, evaluative feedback to observers on a daily basis could seriously influence data collection. For example, assume that an investigator went to a very unruly class and initiated a token program that seemed quite successful on the basis of anecdotal teacher reports and casual observation. If observers then handed data sheets to the investigator that indicated

a decreasing rate of disruptive behavior and the investigator reacted with great enthusiasm, it is quite likely that some distortion of data could occur. Thus, at the least, evaluative feedback to observers should be eliminated. While information feedback (e.g., "things seem to be going well") to observers may be necessary in order to maintain motivation, investigators should be particularly careful not to react differentially to data that confirm their experimental hypothesis.

DRIFT

When a large number of observers are trained simultaneously to some criterion of reliability and then assigned randomly to separate groups to conduct observations of *identical* videotapes, observers from the different groups often record different rates of behavior. The different rates of recorded behavior that are obtained are felt to result from what Patterson (1969) and O'Leary and Kent (1973) refer to as drift. This drift apparently results from idiosyncratic group definitions of a behavioral observation code that emerge in the process of comparing reliability and discussing the definitions of the behavior code. Drift has been unequivocally documented by Kent (1972) and Kent, O'Leary, Diament, and Dietz (1974), and it has very serious implications for researchers from any area employing observational methodology.

If an investigator wishes to repeatedly observe a large number of classrooms in the evaluation of some treatment, he cannot simply assign one team of observers to one classroom wing and another team to the other, since in the absence of any real treatment differences, drift can artificially produce differences attributable to treatment. With large treatment differences and a large number of observers, drift is probably a minor problem. On the other hand, it is possible that drift will produce large error variance, which can prevent small treatment differences from being detected. In order to minimize drift, it is necessary to have some method of recalibrating or retraining observers after their initial training sessions. In addition, it is wise to employ a number of independent observer groups across all experimental conditions so that drift of any particular group does not prejudice one's data. Probably the best method to avoid the drift problem is to videotape the experiment and, following the completion of the experiment, have observers watch tapes from the various experimental conditions in a random sequence.

REACTIVITY OF OBSERVATION

Johnson and Bolstad (1973) reveiwed the effect of an observer's presence on the subjects being observed. As Johnson and Bolstad noted, Webb, Campbell, Schwartz, and Sechrest (1966) have defined reactivity in terms of any measurement procedure that influences the behavior of a subject. The Johnson and Bolstad review was extensive and covered reactivity in both home and school settings. The researchers reasonably concluded that the studies that have purported to show evidence for minimal reactivity have been "based on data of questionable meaning and/or restricted to highly specific circumstances" (Barker & Wright, 1955; Purcell & Brady, 1965; Martin, Gelfand, & Hartmann, 1971). Johnson and Bolstad (1973) reviewed other studies from which one would conclude that reactivity is a significant problem. For example, Polansky, Freeman, Horowitz, Kirwin, Papanis, Rappaport, and Whaley (1949) found that delinquent children began to aggress against the observers during the second week of observations in a summer camp. White (1972) found that the activity level of a family was markedly reduced when the family thought that an observer was present. Studies investigating reactivity in a classroom are rare. A recent study (Kent, Fisher, & O'Leary, 1974) compared the rates of disruptive behavior of a class of emotionally disturbed children in a university laboratory classroom both when the observer was in the room and when the observer was behind a one-way mirror. Data were collected during baseline and treatment conditions. Significant reactivity effects were obtained on only 1 of 10 categories, but for that category, not attending, reactivity interacted with baseline and treatment. During baseline, rates of disruptive behavior were highest when observers were present in the classroom; but during treatment, rates of disruptive behavior were lowest when observers were present. Finally, Hursh, Baer, and Rowbury (1974) found that teachers in an experimental classroom exhibited more of the behaviors deemed appropriate when the observers were in the room than when they were behind a one-way mirror.

Despite some teachers' opinions that children's behavior is not influenced by the observers' presence, it seems fair to say that reactivity is operative at times. In many instances, an observer simply cannot "fade into the woodwork." Some very unruly elementary school children have harassed observers repeatedly despite myriad attempts to reduce reactions of observers to the children. Reactivity may vary as a function of the type of classroom, with more reactivity occurring in classrooms for groups of disruptive children than in classrooms where only one "problem child" is being observed (O'Leary & Kent, 1974). Age of the children, proximity of observer to the child being observed, the reasons given to the children for the observer's presence, and reactions of the observer to the child are but a few of the factors that might influence reactivity and that deserve experimental evaluation.

REACTIVE NATURE OF RELIABILITY ASSESSMENT

It is generally assumed that if one uses an observer to collect data, there should be periodic checking of the reliability of the observer. Presumably, such periodic checks help prevent the drift discussed earlier. It is assumed that if high reliability is found during the periodic checks, the data obtained on days when reliability is not checked are very similar to the data obtained when the reliability is checked. Finally, there is a tacit assumption that reliability is the same whether or not the reliability checker informs the observer that he is being checked. A study by Reid (1970) drew this latter assumption into serious question. He found that observers obtained median reliabilities of .75 when they were aware that reliability was being assessed. However, reliabilities dropped to a median of .51 when the observers were told that their reliability would not be assessed further.

Romanczyk, Kent, Diament, and O'Leary (1973) and Kent, O'Leary, Diament, and Dietz (1974) replicated the Reid (1970) finding and in addition found that knowledge of the *particular* assessor with whom recordings were to be checked was a factor that influenced reliability. Romanczyk et al. (1973) had different reliability checkers adopt different criteria, and he found that observers would match the idiosyncracies of different reliability checkers. Reliability assessment was also found to affect the rates of behavior reported. Only 80% as much behavior was recorded when reliability was not assessed as when reliability was assessed.

The findings of Reid (1970), Romanczyk et al. (1973), and Kent et al. (1974) argue for covert or surreptitious checking of reliability. Since the recorded rates of target behaviors may be higher under conditions of frequent overt reliability checks, it would seem wise to have reliability checks equally distributed throughout experimental conditions. In many studies, frequent reliability checks are obtained during training and baseline phases, while fewer are obtained during treatment. It is possible that spuriously high differences between baseline and treatment may be obtained under such conditions.

SUBJECTIVITY: THE BANE OF OBSERVATIONAL METHODOLOGY

Througout the behavior modification literature there has been an attempt to clearly define target behaviors. Nonetheless, definitions of most social behaviors, such as aggression, cooperation, compliance, and attending, involve considerable subjectivity. While high reliabilities are often reported in the behavioral literature, these reliabilities are usually between one observer and a single reliability checker. Many people do not realize, however, that reliability becomes much more difficult to obtain when all possible reliabilities among 10 people are checked. In fact, any rule that reliability has to be .85 or higher is ridiculous. One has to know under what conditions the reliability was obtained, e.g., between 2 people, among 10 people, and whether the observer knew that the reliability was being checked. Even under conditions where observers know reliability is being checked, it will sometimes be difficult to obtain average reliabilities among 20 individuals that exceed .70 or .75, for example, when observing aggression or attending. Consequently, it is of primary importance to improve the definitions of target behaviors currently used and to search for simply recorded behaviors that correlate highly with more complex behaviors. For example, instead of recording attending, one might observe a product measure such as items completed correctly (Ferritor et al., 1972). As O'Leary and Kent (1973) have argued, however, even when recording a dependent product measure such as items complete, judgmental factors are not eliminated because it is also important to record independent variables such as teacher praise, prompts, and affection. Observations of the latter variables, of course, are highly influenced by judgmental factors. If investigators are interested in detecting small-treatment effects, such as responsiveness to small amounts of praise or affection, it is of utmost importance to reduce as much of the subjectivity in the behavioral definitions as possible. The most obvious trend that should emerge from the methodological problems associated with observation is a shift toward multimeasurement evaluation. Clearly, there is not a single index of truth. While some behavior modifiers have decried the use of standardized tests and rating scales, we hope that they will become increasingly aware that their present evaluation tools have a host of their own problems.

EXPERIMENTAL DESIGNS

Design problems in classroom and behavioral research have been discussed at length by Baer, Wolf, and Risley (1968), Baer (1971), O'Leary and Drabman (1971), Kazdin (1973), O'Leary and Kent (1973), and Stuart (1973). Advantages and disadvantages of individual and group designs are discussed in these articles, and, most important, it is increasingly recognized that both designs have their merits. Particularly as was argued by Baer (1971) and O'Leary and Kent (1973), control group designs are of special current significance. Critics of behavior modification no longer repeatedly question whether certain procedures work; they now ask how the procedures' effects compare with other treatment programs. In an age of accountability, such a question is legitimate and even more likely to be asked than in the past.

Certain behavioral programs like Head Start-Follow Through classroom programs are under national evaluation, and many groups are being compared in terms of their effects on academic and social development. Because of the effort involved in implementing token programs, it is probable and desirable that cost effectiveness analyses be made of such programs and compared to other classroom interventions. Because of recent skepticism about using certain drugs

with hyperactive children (Sroufe & Stewart, 1973), comparative studies of drugs and behavior modification will certainly appear more frequently in the future (Christensen & Sprague, 1973). Finally, because of maturational changes in behavior such as short attention span, fighting, and demanding adult attention (Schectman, 1971), extended individual subject designs will not be convincing to some.

An interesting appraisal of the pros and cons of control group designs was presented by Stuart (1973) in his analysis of ethical choice points in research design. With the recent emphasis on protection of human subjects, Stuart's chapter is highly recommended. As alternatives to no-treatment or placebo control groups, Stuart suggests the possible use of contrast groups (groups who get an alternative treatment) and control group monitoring procedures. Control group monitoring is used during the experiment to detect any particularly deleterious changes that might occur in the untreated subjects. Any subjects who show such changes are assigned to treatment. The first procedure, use of contrast groups, suffers from the inability to answer the question of whether the subjects would have improved without treatment or if treatment made them worse. The second procedure, control group monitoring, suffers from a possibility of eliminating detection of treatment effects because the worst cases are removed from the control group and assigned to treatment. However, if one is dealing with very serious problems, such as classroom aggression, which might become worse over time, these two alternatives to standard control groups offer protection to subjects and allow research to be executed in a most humane manner.

Suggested Directions

As a result of reviewing the recent literature on behavior modification in the classroom, we feel that certain areas deserve critical attention. There is almost no evidence for the effectiveness of behavioral procedures in the high school and only minimal evidence in the junior high school. A similar lack of research focusing on the problems of withdrawn children persists.

The observational systems used in most behavior modification research tend to be idiosyncratic to the particular research team, making comparisons across studies difficult. One solution would be to encourage wider use of the more frequently used observational codes. Since this has not occurred even though many researchers have been aware of the problem, we would suggest that investigators include a standardized assessment procedure (e.g., rating scales) along with observations.

With certain notable recent exceptions, the major dependent variables used in classroom research have been variations of disruptive behavior, for example, summary measures of disruption, talking out, and being out of seat. A visitor* to our laboratory school which has a decided behavior modification focus recently remarked that our measurement devices used to assess change failed to capture the positive atmosphere of the class. That is, they failed to assess variables such as positive peer interaction, empathic responses of the children to one another, and behaviors indicating independence and self-responsibility. The avowed attempts to integrate behavior modification and open-classroom approaches should prompt some change in dependent variables, but the most successful efforts will probably come from professionals trained in educational measurement or behavior modification, since a nonresearch atmosphere often surrounds open-education environments.

Contingency management has so dominated the behavioral literature that environmental factors in public school classrooms have received almost no systematic research

* Dr. Ernst Beier, Dept. of Psychology, Univ. of Utah.

attention. The effects of seating arrangements and pupil location in the classroom (Delefes & Jackson, 1972) have been evaluated for some time; size of class or group, the role of televised teaching, curriculum elements, the role of family or age-vertical grouping, cluster versus contained classroom structure, and the presence of a child with special disabilities are but a few environmental factors that would seem worthy of study.

Research on self-control is proliferating and, as noted earlier in this chapter, results are exciting. The roles of choice, self-evaluation, self-determination of standards, self-reinforcement, and general cognitive strategies for self-control (Robin, Schneider, & Dolnick, 1974) are being systematically evaluated. Children will work for the opportunity to choose among a variety of math tasks (Taffel, 1974), and there is some evidence that children will work harder when given such a choice. Teaching self-evaluation and self-reinforcement skills appears a very promising arena, but results that should have an impact on the daily role of the classroom teacher are just beginning to emerge. As mentioned above, modeling is also a procedure that deserves considerably more attention.

Although Baer, Wolf, & Risley (1968) convincingly argued that generalization must be programmed rather than lamented, little systematic work has been done to evaluate such programmatic efforts. Generalization has been reported in a number of studies (Ferritor et al., 1972), and maintenance of effects across time has occurred (Bolstad & Johnson, 1972; Walker & Buckley, 1972; Turkewitz et al., 1975; Patterson, 1974). Nonetheless, the critical parameters necessary for producing generalization or maintenance are simply not known.

Rationales, explanations, and reasoning have been largely ignored in the behavior modification literature with children despite the fact that two of the influential proponents of social learning, Bandura and

Walters (1963), argued more than a decade ago that such cognitive factors deserve serious attention. Given the findings of Taffel, O'Leary, and Armel (1974), which showed that reasoning was slightly superior to praise in maintaining interest in the task in a tutorial mathematics setting, reasoning clearly warrants further investigation. As parents, to deny the importance of reasoning seems to contradict our best common sense.

Comparative evaluations of various approaches to disadvantaged children in elementary schools have been undertaken on a massive scale by the federal government (Follow-Through programs). The full results of those evaluations will be made public in the next few years,[5] but initial results regarding academic achievement of thousands of children indicate that 2 behavioral approaches (Engelmann-Becker and Bushell) have fared better than approximately 20 other approaches, including Piagetian and open-education approaches (*Behavior Today*, 1972). To give you some notion of the dramatic nature of the instructional affects in behaviorally oriented classrooms, let us cite just one example. Becker (1973) has shown that children gain an aver-

age of 1.5 reading grade levels and 1.0 math grade levels per year in the Engelmann-Becker Follow-Through Program, whereas the expected gains for such groups without this program are approximately .6 grade levels per year. More efforts of this sort are sorely needed. For example, few comparative evaluations of behavioral and non-behavioral methods have been made regarding special classes or "mainstreaming" (i.e., keeping the child with emotional or learning disabilities in the regular class while providing a support system with remedial work and counseling).

Finally, with the exception of work regarding daily reports home and the aforementioned Follow-Through programs, almost no research exists regarding a total family treatment program. Given the rather specific effects of most treatment interventions, the difficulty in producing long-term effects, and the frequent association between child problems and marital discord, it seems fruitful to expand our treatment efforts to include both child and family problems. While teachers can often exacerbate or diminish a child's problems, they certainly are not responsible for the presence of the problem in many—if not most—instances. Classroom problems stem from a complex of organic, family, environment, and classroom factors, and it seems myopic to concentrate our treatment efforts on only one front, namely, the classroom.

---

[5] A full report of the evaluations of Follow-Through programs is being prepared by ABT Associates, Cambridge, Massachusetts.

References

ARONFREED, J. Aversive control of socialization. In W. J. Arnold (Ed.), *Nebraska symposium on motivation*. Lincoln: University of Nebraska Press, 1968.

ASCARE, D., & AXELROD, S. Use of a behavior modification procedure in four "open" classrooms. *Psychology in the Schools*, 1973, **10**, 243–248.

ATKINSON, R. C. Computerized instruction and the learning process. *American Psychologist*, 1968, **23**, 225–239.

AXELROD, S. Comparison of individual and group contingencies in two special classes. *Behavior Therapy*, 1973, **4**, 83–90.

AYLLON, T., & ROBERTS, M. D. Eliminating discipline problems by strengthening academic performance. *Journal of Applied Behavior Analysis*, 1974, **7**, 71–76.

BAER, D. M. Behavior modification: You shouldn't. In E. A. Ramp & B. L. Hopkins (Eds.), *A new direction for education: Behavior analysis*. Vol. 1. Lawrence, Kans.: University of Kansas, Support and Development Center for Follow Through, 1971.

BAER, D. M., WOLF, M. M., & RISLEY, T. R. Some current dimensions of applied behavior analysis. *Journal of Applied Behavior Analysis,* 1968, **1**, 91–97.

BAILEY, J. S., WOLF, M. M., & PHILLIPS, E. L. Home-based reinforcement and modification of predelinquents' classroom behavior. *Journal of Applied Behavior Analysis,* 1970, **3**, 223–233.

BANDURA, A. *Principles of behavior modification.* New York: Holt, Rinehart & Winston, 1969.

BANDURA, A., & PERLOFF, B. Relative efficacy of self-monitored and externally imposed reinforcement systems. *Journal of Personality and Social Psychology,* 1967, **7**, 111–116.

BANDURA, A., & WALTERS, R. H. *Social learning and personality development.* New York: Rinehart & Winston, 1963.

BARKER, R. G., & WRIGHT, H. F. *Midwest and its children: The psychological ecology of an American town.* New York: Row, Peterson, 1955.

BARRISH, H. H., SAUNDERS, M., & WOLF, M. M. Good behavior game: Effects of individual contingencies for group consequences on disruptive behavior in a classroom. *Journal of Applied Behavior Analysis,* 1969, **2**, 119–124.

BECKER, W. C. Some necessary conditions for the controlled study of achievement and aptitude. Paper presented to the CTB/McGraw-Hill Invitational Conference on the Aptitude-Achievement Distinction. Carmel, California, February 1973.

BECKER, W. C., MADSEN, C. H. Jr., ARNOLD, C. R., & THOMAS, D. R., The contingent use of teacher attention and praise in reducing classroom behavior problems. *The Journal of Special Education,* 197, **1**, 287–307.

Behavior Today. 3 (46). Del Mar, Calif.: Ziff-Davis, 1972, p. 1.

BERMAN, M. L. Instructions and behavior change: A taxonomy. *Exceptional Children,* 1973, **39**, 644–650.

BIJOU, S. W. Experimental studies of child behavior, normal and deviant. In L. Krasner & L. P. Ullmann (Eds.), *Research in behavior modification.* New York: Holt, Rinehart & Winston, 1965.

BIJOU, S. W., PETERSON, R. F., & AULT, M. H. A method to integrate descriptive and experimental field studies at the level of data and empirical concepts. *Journal of Applied Behavior Analysis,* 1968, **1**, 175–191.

BLANCHARD, E. B., & JOHNSON, R. A. Generalization of operant classroom control procedures. *Behavior Therapy,* 1973, **4**, 219–229.

BOLSTAD, O. D., & JOHNSON, S. M. Self-regulation in the modification of disruptive classroom behavior. *Journal of Applied Behavior Modification,* 1972, **5**, 443–454.

BRIGHAM, T. A., GRAUBARD, P. S., & STANS, A. Analysis of the effects of sequential reinforcement contingencies on aspects of composition. *Journal of Applied Behavior Analysis,* 1972, **5**, 421–429.

BRODEN, M., BRUCE, C., MITCHELL, M. A. CARTER, V., & HALL, R. V. Effects of teacher attention on attending behavior of two boys at adjacent desks. *Journal of Applied Behavior Analysis,* 1970, **3**, 199–203.

BRODEN, M., HALL, R. V., & MITTS, B. The effect of self-recording on the classroom behavior of two eighth grade students. *Journal of Applied Behavior Analysis,* 1971, **4**, 191–200.

BROOKS, R. B., & SNOW, D. L. Two case illustrations of the use of behavior modification techniques in the school setting. *Behavior Therapy,* 1972, **3**, 100–103.

BROWN, P., & ELLIOT, R. Control of aggression in a nursery school class. *Journal of Experimental Child Psychology,* 1965, **2**, 103–107.

BUCHER, B., & HAWKINS, J. Comparison of response cost and token reinforcement systems in a class for academic underachievers. In R. D. Rubin & J. P. Brady (Eds.), *Advances in behavior therapy.* Vol. 4. New York: Academic Press, 1973.

BUCKLEY, N. K., & WALKER, H. M. Free operant teacher attention to deviant child behavior after treatment in a special class. *Psychology in the Schools,* 1971, **8**, 275–284.

CANTRELL, R. P., CANTRELL, M. L., HUDDLESTON, C. M., & WOOLDRIDGE, R. L. Contingency contracting with school problems. *Journal of Applied Behavior Analysis,* 1969, **2**, 215–220.

CARLSON, C. S., ARNOLD, C. R., BECKER, W. C., & MADSEN, C. H. The elimination of tantrum behavior of a child in an elementary classroom. *Behaviour Research and Therapy,* 1968, **6**, 117–119.

CHRISTENSEN, D. E., & SPRAGUE, R. Reduction of hyperactive behavior by conditioning procedures alone and combined with methylphenidate (Ritalin). *Behaviour Research and Therapy,* 1973, **11**, 331–334.

COLEMAN, R. A conditioning technique applicable to elementary school classrooms. *Journal of Applied Behavior Analysis,* 1970, **3**, 293–297.

CONE, J. D. Assessing the effectiveness of programmed generalization. *Journal of Applied Behavior Analysis,* 1973, **6**, 713–718.

COOPER, M. L., THOMSON, C. L., & BAER, D. M. The experimental modification of teacher attending behavior. *Journal of Applied Behavior Analysis,* 1970, **3**, 153–157.

COSSAIRT, A., HALL, R. V., & HOPKINS, B. L. The effects of experimenter's instructions, feedback, and praise on teacher praise and student attending behavior. *Journal of Applied Behavior Analysis,* 1973, **6**, 89–100.

DELEFES, P., & JACKSON, B. Teacher-pupil interaction as a function of location in the classroom. *Psychology in the Schools,* 1972, **9**, 119–123.

DIETZ, A. The effects of teacher feedback on veridicality of self-evaluation on an individualized reading task. Unpublished undergraduate honors study, SUNY, Stony Brook, N.Y., 1973.

DRABMAN, R. S. Child- versus teacher-administered token programs in a psychiatric hospital school. *Journal of Abnormal Child Psychology,* 1973, **1**, 68–87.

DRABMAN, R. S., & SPITALNIK, R. Social isolation as a punishment procedure: A controlled study. *Journal of Experimental Child Psychology,* 1973, **16**, 236–249.

DRABMAN, R. S., SPITALNIK, R., & O'LEARY, K. D. Teaching self-control to disruptive children. *Journal of Abnormal Psychology,* 1973, **82**, 10–16.

EVANS, G. W., & OSWALT, G. L. Acceleration of academic progress through manipulation of peer influence. *Behaviour Research and Therapy,* 1968, **6**, 189–195.

EVERS, W. L., & SCHWARZ, J. C. Maintaining social withdrawal in preschoolers: The effect of filmed modeling and teacher praise. *Journal of Abnormal Child Psychology,* 1973, **1**, 248–256.

FELIXBROD, J. J. Effects of prior locus of control over reinforcement on current performance and resistance to extinction. Unpublished doctoral dissertation, SUNY, Stony Brook, N.Y., 1974.

FELIXBROD, J. J., & O'LEARY, K. D. Effects of reinforcement on children's academic behavior as a function of self-determined and externally imposed contingencies. *Journal of Applied Behavior Analysis,* 1973, **6**, 241–250.

FELIXBROD, J. J., & O'LEARY, K. D. Self-determination of academic standards by children: Toward freedom from external control. *Journal of Educational Psychology,* 1974, **66**, 845–850.

FERRITOR, D. E., BUCKHOLDT, D., HAMBLIN, R. L., & SMITH, L. The noneffects of contingent reinforcement for attending behavior on work accomplished. *Journal of Applied Behavior Analysis,* 1972, **5**, 7–17.

FRIEDRICH, L. K., & STEIN, A. H. Aggressive and prosocial television programs and the natural behavior of preschool children. *Monographs of the Society for Research in Child Development,* 1973, **38**, No. 4.

GLYNN, E. L. Classroom applications of self-determined reinforcement. *Journal of Applied Behavior Analysis,* 1970, **3**, 123–132.

GLYNN, E. L., THOMAS, J. D., & SHEE, S. M. Behavioral self-control of on-task behavior in an elementary classroom. *Journal of Applied Behavior Analysis,* 1973, **6**, 115–124.

GOETZ, E. M., & BAER, D. M. Social control of form diversity and the emergence of new forms in children's blockbuilding. *Journal of Applied Behavior Analysis,* 1973, **6**, 209–217.

GOLDFRIED, M., & MERBAUM, M. *Behavior change through self-control.* New York: Holt, Rinehart & Winston, 1973.

GRANDY, G. S., MADSEN, C. H. Jr., & DEMERSSEMAN, L. M. The effects of individual and interdependent contingencies on inappropriate classroom behavior. *Psychology in the Schools,* 1973, **10**, 488–493.

GRAUBARD, P. S. Utilizing the group in teaching disturbed delinquents to learn. *Exceptional Children,* 1969, **36**, 267–272.

GRAUBARD, P. S., ROSENBERG, H., & MILLER, M. B. Student applications of behavior modification to teachers and environments or ecological approaches to social deviancy. In E. A. Ramp & B. L. Hopkins (Eds.), *A new direction for education: Behavior analysis 1971.* Vol. 1. Lawrence, Kans.: University of Kansas, Support and Development Center for Follow Through, 1971.

GRIMM, J. A., BIJOU, S. W., & PARSONS, J. A. A problem-solving model for teaching remedial arithmetic to handicapped young children. *Journal of Abnormal Child Psychology,* 1973, **1**, 26–39.

HALL, R. V., FOX, R., WILLARD, D., GOLDSMITH, L., EMERSON, M., OWEN, M., DAVIS, F., & PORCIA,

E. The teacher as observer and experimenter in the modification of disputing and talking-out behaviors. *Journal of Applied Behavior Analysis,* 1971, 4, 141–149.

HALL, R. V., LUND, D., & JACKSON, D. Effects of teacher attention on study behavior. *Journal of Applied Behavior Analysis,* 1968, **1**, 1–12.

HARRIS, V. W., & SHERMAN, J. A. Use and analysis of the "Good Behavior Game" to reduce disruptive classroom behavior. *Journal of Applied Behavior Analysis,* 1973, **6**, 405–417.

HAWKINS, R. P. The School Adjustment Program: Individualized intervention for children with behavior disorders. In E. A. Ramp & B. L. Hopkins (Eds.), *A new direction for education: Behavior analysis 1971.* Vol. 1. Lawrence, Kans.: University of Kansas, Support and Development Center for Follow Through, 1971.

HAWKINS, R. P., SLUYTER, D. J., & SMITH, C. D. Modification of achievement by a simple technique involving parents and teacher. In M. Harris (Ed.), *Classroom uses of behavior modification.* Columbus, Ohio: Charles Merrill, 1972.

HOMME, L., CSANJI, A. P., GONZALES, M. A., & RECHS, J. R. *How to use contingency contracting in the classroom.* Champaign, Ill.: Research Press, 1969.

HOPKINS, B. L., SCHUTTE, R. C., & GARTON, K. L. The effects of access to a playroom on the rate and quality of printing and writing of first and second grade students. *Journal of Applied Behavior Analysis,* 1971, 4, 77–87.

HURSH, H. B., BAER, D. M., & ROWBURY, T. A pilot project to examine whether teachers "turn on" only when observers are present. Unpublished manuscript, Western Carolina Center, Morgantown, N.C., 1974.

JAMISON, D., SUPPES, P., & WELLS, S. The effectiveness of alternative instructional media: A survey. *Review of Educational Research,* 1974, 44, 1–67.

JACOB, R. G., O'LEARY, K. D., & PRICE, G. H. Behavioral treatment of hyperactive children: An alternative to medication. Unpublished manuscript, SUNY, Stony Brook, N.Y., 1973.

JOHNSON, S. M., & BOLSTAD, O. D. Methodological issues in naturalistic observation: Some problems and solutions for field research. In L. A. Hamerlynck, L. C. Handy, & E. J. Mash (Eds.), *Behavior change: Methodology, concepts, and practice.* Champaign, Ill.: Research Press, 1973.

KANFER, F. Self-regulation: Research, issues, and speculations. In C. Neuringer & J. L. Michael (Eds.), *Behavior modification in clinical psychology.* New York: Appleton-Century-Crofts, 1970.

KAUFMAN, K. F., & O'LEARY, K. D. Reward, cost, and self-evaluation procedures for disruptive adolescents in a psychiatric hospital school. *Journal of Applied Behavior Analysis,* 1972, 5, 293–310.

KAZDIN, A. Methodological assessment considerations in evaluating reinforcement programs in applied settings. *Journal of Applied Behavior Analysis,* 1973, 517–531.

KENT, R. N. Expectancy bias in behavioral observation. Unpublished doctoral dissertation, SUNY, Stony Brook, N.Y., 1972.

KENT, R. N., FISHER, J. E., & O'LEARY, K. D. Observer presence as an influence on child behavior in a classroom setting. Unpublished manuscript, SUNY, Stony Brook, N.Y., 1974.

KENT, R. N., O'LEARY, K. D., DIAMENT, C., & DIETZ, A. Expectation biases in observational evaluation of therapeutic change. *Journal of Consulting and Clinical Psychology,* 1974, **42**, 774–780.

KIRBY, F. D., & SHIELDS, F. Modification of arithmetic response rate and attending behavior in a seventh grade student. *Journal of Applied Behavior Analysis,* 1972, 5, 79–84.

KRASNER, L., & KRASNER, M. Token economies and other planned environments. In *Yearbook of the National Society for the Study of Education,* 1973, pp. 351–384.

KUYPERS, D. S., BECKER, W. C., & O'LEARY, K. D. How to make a token system fail. *Exceptional Children,* 1968, **35**, 101–109.

LAHEY, B. B., McNEES, M. P., & McNEES, M. C. Control of an obscene "verbal tic" through time-out in an elementary school classroom. *Journal of Applied Behavior Analysis,* 1973, **6**, 101–104.

LONG, J. D., & WILLIAMS, R. L. The comparative effectiveness of group and individually contingent free time with innercity junior high school students. *Journal of Applied Behavior Analysis,* 1973, **6**, 465–474.

LOVITT, T. C., & CURTISS, K. A. Effects of manipulating an antecedent on mathematics response rate. *Journal of Applied Behavior Analysis,* 1968, **1**, 329–333.

LOVITT, T. C., & CURTISS, K. A. Academic response rate as a function of teacher and self-imposed contingencies. *Journal of Applied Behavior Analysis,* 1969, **2**, 49–53.

LOVITT, T. C., & SMITH, J. O. Effects of instructions on an individual's verbal behavior. *Exceptional Children,* 1972, **38,** 685–694.

MacDONALD, W. S., GALLIMORE, R., & MacDONALD, G. Contingency counseling by school personnel: An economical model of intervention. *Journal of Applied Behavior Analysis,* 1970, **3,** 175–182.

MacMILLAN, D., FORNESS, S. R., & TRUMBALL, B. M. The role of punishment in the classroom. *Exceptional Children,* 1973, **40,** 85–96.

MADSEN, C. H., BECKER, W. C., & THOMAS, D. R., Rules, praise, and ignoring: Elements of elementary classroom control. *Journal of Applied Behavior Analysis,* 1968, **1,** 139–150.

MADSEN, C. H., BECKER, W. C., THOMAS, D. R., KOSER, L., & PLAGER, E. An analysis of the reinforcing function of "sit down" commands. In R. K. Parker (Ed.), *Readings in educational psychology.* Boston: Allyn & Bacon, 1968.

MADSEN, C. H., MADSEN, C. K., SAUDARGAS, R. A., HAMMOND, W. R., & EGAR, D. E. Classroom RAID (Rules, Approval, Ignore, Disapproval): A cooperative approach for professionals and volunteers. Unpublished manuscript, University of Florida, Tallahassee, Fla., 1970.

MALONEY, K. B., & HOPKINS, B. L. The modification of sentence structure and its relationship to subjective judgments of creativity in writing. *Journal of Applied Behavior Analysis,* 1973, **6,** 425–434.

MARTIN, M. F., GELFAND, D. M., & HARTMANN, D. P. Effect of adult and peer observers on boys' and girls' responses to an aggressive model. *Child Development,* 1971, **42,** 1271–1275.

MASH, E. J. Methodological problems and developments. In L. A. Hamerlynck, L. C. Handy, & E. J. Mash (Eds.), *Behavior change: Methodology, concepts and practice.* Champaign, Ill.: Research Press, 1973.

McALLISTER, L. W., STACHOWIAK, J. G., BAER, D. M., & CONDERMAN, L. The application of operant conditioning techniques in a secondary school classroom. *Journal of Applied Behavior Analysis,* 1969, **2,** 277–285.

McKENZIE, H. S., CLARK, M., WOLF, M. M., COTHERA, R., & BENSON, C. Behavior modification of children with learning disabilities using grades as tokens and allowances as back-up reinforcers. *Exceptional Children,* 1968, **4,** 745–752.

McLAUGHLIN, T. F., & MALABY, J. Intrinsic reinforcers in a classroom token economy. *Journal of Applied Behavior Analysis,* 1972, **5,** 263–270.

MEDLAND, M. B., & STACHNIK, T. J. Good behavior game: A replication and systematic analysis. *Journal of Applied Behavior Analysis,* 1972, **5,** 45–51.

MEICHENBAUM, D. H., BOWERS, K. S., & ROSS, R. R. Modification of classroom behavior of institutionalized female adolescent offenders. *Behaviour Research and Therapy,* 1968, **6,** 343–353.

O'CONNOR, R. D. Modification of social withdrawal through symbolic modeling. *Journal of Applied Behavior Analysis,* 1969, **2,** 15–22.

O'CONNOR, R. D. Relative efficacy of modeling, shaping, and the combined procedures for modification of social withdrawal. *Journal of Abnormal Psychology,* 1972, **79,** 327–334.

O'LEARY, K. D. Diagnosis of children's behavior problems. In H. C. Quay & J. Werry (Eds.), *Psychopathological disorders of childhood.* New York: Wiley, 1972.

O'LEARY, K. D., & BECKER, W. C. Behavior modification of an adjustment class: A token reinforcement program. *Exceptional Children,* 1967, **33,** 637–642.

O'LEARY, K. D., & BECKER, W. C. The effects of the intensity of a teacher's reprimands on children's behavior. *Journal of School Psychology,* 1968, **7,** 8–11.

O'LEARY, K. D., BECKER, W. C., EVANS, M. B., & SAUDARGAS, R. A. A token reinforcement program in a public school: A replication and systematic analysis. *Journal of Applied Behavior Analysis,* 1969, **2,** 3–13.

O'LEARY, K. D., & DRABMAN, R. S. Token reinforcement programs in the classroom: A review. *Psychological Bulletin,* 1971, **75,** 379–398.

O'LEARY, K. D., DRABMAN, R. S., & KASS, R. E. Maintenance of appropriate behavior in a token program. *Journal of Abnormal Child Psychology,* 1973, **1,** 127–138.

O'LEARY, K. D., KAUFFMAN, K. F., KASS, R. E., & DRABMAN, R. S. The effects of loud and soft reprimands on the behavior of disruptive students. *Exceptional Children,* 1970, **37,** 145–155.

O'LEARY, K. D., & KENT, R. N. Behavior modification for social action: Research tactics and problems. In L. A. Hamerlynck, L. C. Handy, & E. J. Mash (Eds.), *Behavior change: Method-*

ology, concepts, and practice. Champaign, Ill.: Research Press, 1973.

O'LEARY, K. D., & KENT, R. N. A behavioral consultation program for parents and teachers of children with conduct problems. Paper presented at the meeting of the American Psychopathological Association, March 7, 1974, Boston, Mass. Proceedings of Conference to be published by APPA, Fall, 1975 (Editor, Robert L. Spitzer).

O'LEARY, K. D., KENT, R. N., & KANOWITZ, J. Shaping data collection congruent with experimental hypotheses. *Journal of Applied Behavior Analysis,* 1975, **8**, 43–51.

O'LEARY, K. D., & O'LEARY, S. G. *Classroom management: The successful use of behavior modification.* New York: Pergamon, 1972.

PACKARD, R. G. The control of "classroom attention": A group contingency for complex behavior. *Journal of Applied Behavior Analysis,* 1970, **3**, 13–28.

PARKE, R. D. Effectiveness of punishment as an interaction of intensity, timing, agent nurturance, and cognitive structuring. *Child Development,* 1969, **40**, 213–235.

PATTERSON, G. R. An application of conditioning techniques to the control of a hyperactive child. In L. P. Ullmann & L. Krasner (Eds.), *Case studies in behavior modification.* New York: Holt, Rinehart & Winston, 1965.

PATTERSON, G. R. A community mental health program for children. In L. A. Hamerlynck, P. O. Davidson, & L. E. Acker (Eds.), *Behavior modification and mental health services.* Calgary, Canada: University of Calgary Press, 1969.

PATTERSON, G. R. Interventions for boys with conduct problems: Multiple settings, treatments, and criteria. *Journal of Consulting and Clinical Psychology,* 1974, **42**, 471–481.

PATTERSON, G. R., JONES, R., WHITTIER, J., & WRIGHT, M. A. A behavior modification technique for the hyperactive child. *Behaviour Research and Therapy,* 1965, **2**, 217–226.

PHILLIPS, E. L., PHILLIPS, E. A., FIXSEN, D. L., & WOLF, M. M. *The teaching-family handbook.* Lawrence, Kans.: University of Kansas Printing Service, 1972.

POLANSKY, N., FREEMAN, W., HOROWITZ, M., IRWIN, L., PAPANIS, N., RAPPAPORT, D., & WHALEY, F. Problems of interpersonal relations in research on groups. *Human Relations,* 1949, **2**, 281–291.

PRICE, G., & O'LEARY, K. D. Teaching children to develop high performance standards. Unpublished manuscript, SUNY, Stony Brook, N.Y., 1974.

PURCELL, K., & BRADY, K. Adaptation to the invasion of privacy: Monitoring behavior with a miniature radio transmitter. *Merrill-Palmer Quarterly,* 1965, **12**, 242–254.

REESE, H. W., & PARNES, S. J. Programming creative behavior. *Child Development,* 1970, **41**, 413–423.

REID, J. B. Reliability assessment of observation data: A possible methodological problem. *Child Development,* 1970, **41**, 1143–1150.

RICKARD, H. C., MELVIN, K. B., CREEL, J., & CREEL, L. The effects of bonus tokens upon productivity in a remedial classroom for behaviorally disturbed children. *Behavior Therapy,* 1973, **4**, 378–385.

ROBIN, A. Behavior modification and open education: Strange bedfellows. Unpublished manuscript, SUNY, Stony Brook, N.Y., 1974.

ROBIN, A. SCHNEIDER, M., & DOLNICK, M. The turtle technique: A systematic evaluation. Unpublished manuscript, SUNY, Stony Brook, N.Y., 1974.

ROMANCZYK, R. G., KENT, R. N., DIAMENT, C., & O'LEARY, K. D. Measuring the reliability of observational data: A reactive process. *Journal of Applied Behavior Analysis,* 1973, **6**, 175–186.

ROSENBAUM, A., O'LEARY, K. D., & JACOB, R. G. Behavioral interventions with hyperactive children: Group consequences as a supplement to individual contingencies. *Behavior Therapy,* 1975, **6**, 315–323.

RULE, S. A comparison of three different types of feedback on teachers' performance. In G. Semb (Ed.), *Behavior analysis and education—1972.* Lawrence, Kans.: University of Kansas, Support and Development Center for Follow Through, 1972.

SALZBERG, B. H., WHEELER, A. A., DEVAR, L. T., & HOPKINS, B. L. The effect of intermittent feedback and intermittent contingent access to play on printing of kindergarten children. *Journal of Applied Behavior Analysis,* 1971, 4, 163–171.

SALZBERG, C. L. Freedom and responsibility in an elementary school. In G. Semb (Ed.), *Behavior analysis and education—1972.* Lawrence, Kans.: University of Kansas, Support and Development Center for Follow Through, 1972.

SANTOGROSSI, D. A. Self-reinforcement of achievement in an academic (reading) task. Unpublished doctoral dissertation, SUNY, Stony Brook, N.Y., 1974.

SANTOGROSSI, D. A., O'LEARY, K. D., ROMANCZYK, R. G., & KAUFMAN, K. F. Self-evaluation by adolescents in a psychiatric hospital school token program. *Journal of Applied Behavior Analysis*, 1973, **6**, 277–288.

SAUDARGAS, R. A. Setting criterion rates of teacher praise: The effects of video tape feedback in a behavior analysis Follow Through classroom. In G. Semb (Ed.), *Behavior analysis and education—1972*. Lawrence, Kans.: University of Kansas, Support and Development Center for Follow Through, 1972.

SCHECHTMAN, A. Age patterns in children's psychiatric symptoms. *Child Development,* 1971, **41**, 683–693.

SCHMIDT, G. W., & ULRICH, R. E. Effects of group contingent events upon classroom noise. *Journal of Applied Behavior Analysis*, 1969, **2**, 171–179.

SCHNEIDER, M. Turtle technique in the classroom. *Teaching Exceptional Children,* 1974, **7**, 22–24.

SCHUTTE, R. C., & HOPKINS, B. L. The effects of teacher attention on following instructions in a kindergarten class. *Journal of Applied Behavior Analysis*, 1970, **3**, 117–122.

SCOTT, P., BURTON, R. V., & YARROW, M. Social reinforcement under natural conditions. *Child Development*, 1967, **38**, 53–63.

SIBLEY, S., ABBOTT, M., & COOPER, B. Modification of the classroom behavior of a "disadvantaged" kindergarten boy by social reinforcement and isolation. *Journal of Experimental Child Psychology*, 1969, 4, 281–287.

SOLOMON, R. W., & WAHLER, R. G. Peer reinforcement control of classroom problem behavior. *Journal of Applied Behavior Analysis*, 1973, **6**, 49–56.

SROUFE, L. A., & STEWART, M. A. Treating behavioral problem children with stimulant drugs. *New England Journal of Medicine*, 1973, **239**, 407–413.

STAATS, A. Development, use, and social extensions of reinforcer systems in the solution of human problems. Paper presented at a conference on behavior modification, Honolulu, Hawaii, January 1969.

STUART, R. B. Behavioral contracting within the families of delinquents. *Journal of Behavior Therapy and Experimental Psychiatry*, 1971, **2**, 1–11.

STUART, R. B. Notes on the ethics of behavior research and intervention. In L. A. Hamerlynck, L. C. Handy, & E. J. Mash (Eds.), *Behavior change: Methodology, concepts, and practice*. Champaign, Ill.: Research Press, 1973.

SULZBACHER, S. I., & HOUSER, J. E. A tactic to eliminate disruptive behaviors in the classroom: Group contingent consequences. In R. Ulrich, T. Stachnik, & J. Mabry (Eds.), *Control of human behavior*. Vol. 2. Glenview, Ill.: Scott, Foresman & Co., 1970.

SURRATT, P. R., ULRICH, R. E., & HAWKINS, R. P. An elementary student as a behavioral engineer. *Journal of Applied Behavior Analysis*, 1969, **2**, 85–92.

TAFFEL, S. J. The influence of choice and interest level of academic tasks on children's academic activity. Unpublished doctoral dissertation, SUNY, Stony Brook, N.Y., 1974.

TAFFEL, S. J., O'LEARY, K. D., & ARMEL, S. The effects of reasoning and praise on academic behavior. *Journal of Educational Psychology,* 1974, **66**, 291–295.

THOMAS, D. A., BECKER, W. C., & ARMSTRONG, M. Production and elimination of disruptive classroom behavior by systematically varying teacher's behavior. *Journal of Applied Behavior Analysis,* 1968, **1**, 35–45.

THOMAS, D. R. Preliminary findings on self-monitoring for modifying teaching behaviors. In E. A. Ramp & B. L. Hopkins (Eds.), *A new direction for education: Behavior analysis*. Vol. 1. Lawrence, Kans.: University of Kansas, Support and Development Center for Follow Through, 1971.

TURKEWITZ, H., O'LEARY, K. D., & IRONSMITH, M. Producing generalization of appropriate behavior through self-control. *Journal of Consulting and Clinical Psychology*, 1975, **43**, 577–583.

WAHLER, R. G. Setting generality: Some specific and general effects of child behavior therapy. *Journal of Applied Behavior Analysis*, 1969, **2**, 239–246.

WALKER, H. M., & BUCKLEY, N. K. Programming generalization and maintenance of treatment effects across time and setting. *Journal of Applied Behavior Analysis*, 1972, **5**, 209–224.

WALKER, H. M. MATTSON, R., & BUCKLEY, N. K.

The functional analysis of behavior within an experimental class setting. In W. C. Becker (Ed.), *An empirical basis for change in education.* Chicago: Science Research Associates, 1971.

WARD, M. H., & BAKER, B. L. Reinforcement therapy in the classroom. *Journal of Applied Behavior Analysis,* 1968, **1,** 323–328.

WASIK, B., SENN, K., WELCH, R., & COOPER, B. Behavior modification with culturally deprived school children. *Journal of Experimental Child Psychology,* 1969, **2,** 181–194.

WEBB, E. J., CAMPBELL, D. T., SCHWARTZ, R. D., & SECHREST, L. *Unobtrusive measures: A survey of non-reactive research in the social sciences.* Chicago: Rand McNally, 1966.

WHITE, G. D. Effects of observer presence on mother and child behavior. Unpublished doctoral dissertation, University of Oregon, 1972.

WILLIAMS, C. F., GILMORE, A. S., & MALPASS, L. F. Programmed instruction for culturally deprived slow-learning children. *The Journal of Special Education,* 1968, **2,** 421–427.

WILLIS, J. W., MORRIS, B., & CROWDER, J. A remedial reading technique for disabled readers that employs students as behavioral engineers. *Psychology in the School,* 1972, **9,** 67–70.

WILSON, C. W., & HOPKINS, B. L. The effects of contingent music on the intensity of noise in junior high home economics classes. *Journal of Applied Behavior Analysis,* 1973, **6,** 269–275.

WINETT, R. A., KRASNER, L., & KRASNER, M. Child-monitored token reading program. *Psychology in the Schools,* 1971, **8,** 259–262.

WINETT, R. A., & WINKLER, R. C. Current behavior modification in the classroom: Be still, be quiet, be docile. *Journal of Applied Behavior Analysis,* 1972, **5,** 499–504.

WOLF, M. M., GILES, D. K., & HALL, V. R. Experiments with token reinforcement in a remedial classroom. *Behaviour Research and Therapy,* 1968, **6,** 51–64.

ZIMMERMAN, B. J., & PIKE, E. O. Effects of modeling and reinforcement on the acquisition and generalization of question-asking behavior. *Child Development,* 1972, **43,** 892–907.

ZIMMERMAN, E. H., & ZIMMERMAN, J. The alteration of behavior in a special classroom situation. *Journal of the Experimental Analysis of Behavior,* 1962, **5,** 59–60.

Deviant Child Behavior Within the Family: Developmental Speculations and Behavior Change Strategies

14

ROBERT G. WAHLER

Therapeutic work with families almost always begins with a concern about one member of the family. That person is considered deviant by the family or by the community in which the family lives. Thus, the beginning focus of therapy centers around one individual within this group of people. However, after the initial labeling process takes place, a more complex state of affairs ensues—this is true of all approaches to family therapy as well as the behavior modification orientation. The present chapter is an attempt to explore this latter strategy as it is applied to families in which a child is the initial therapeutic target.

A Behavioristic Conception of the Family

Treatment strategies evolve, in part, from the conceptual model of deviance employed by the person responsible for directing the treatment. Family treatment is based on a model arguing that the individual cannot be considered as an entity apart from the social system in which he behaves. This general conception was initiated by early,

nonbehavioristic, family therapists such as Bateson, Jackson, Haley, and Weakland (1956). From their view, the family is a structured system of interbehaving people. The structure is such that the behavior of any member of the system depends on the interbehaviors of other members in that grouping. Thus, if a child in the system is considered deviant, one explanation of his deviance lies in the interbehavior of other family members. Their behaviors contribute to his deviance, and his deviant behaviors in turn feed back support to their behaviors. According to this kind of "feedback loop" notion, deviant behavior is not viewed as dysfunctional; rather, it is seen as an appropriate response to contingencies presented by the system.

While we have yet to see a formal statement of behavioristic conceptions of the family, such a position would undoubtedly be much like that proposed by Bateson and his colleagues. Since most behavioristic family therapists are guided by social learning theory (see Tharp & Wetzel, 1969), the argument that family members behave in an interdependent fashion is bound to strike a responsive behavioristic chord. These interdependencies are presently conceptualized in terms of reinforcing and discriminative stimuli provided by the various behaviors of family members. Thus, the child's problem behavior is seen as controlled by reinforcers and discriminative stimuli dispensed by the child's caretakers and siblings. However, the question of who is controlling whom is not this simple. One could also attempt an analysis of factors that determine the behaviors of the latter stimulus dispensers. From this perspective the child's problem behaviors could be conceptualized as stimulus events that partially control the actions of his caretakers and siblings. Here, the "loop" is completed, and the assignment of responsibility or blame to any one family member requires an arbitrary decision.

Figure 14–1 provides a simple schematic illustration of the theoretical process by which families operate. According to the process, the child's behavior (normal and deviant) is a function of dyadic interchanges with father and mother. The parents' approaches and reactions to the child operate as patterns of cues and reinforcers, determining those behaviors he will display in the home setting. In addition, since the child's behaviors also function as cues and reinforcers for the parents, the parents' contingency patterns are at least partially maintained by the child.

It will also be seen in Figure 14–1 that each parent's contingency pattern for the child is partially determined by father-mother interchanges. For example, mother's dispensing of cues and reinforcers for the child could be a result of father's particular set of cues and reinforcers dispensed to mother. In the same manner, father's contingency pattern for the child ought to depend partly on his wife's interactions with him. Thus, the child's behavior may be viewed as directly maintained by each parent, and the parents' maintenance behaviors are also multiply determined. One should note that the simple addition of one more family member to the triad shown in Figure 14–1 would complicate this maintenance question considerably.

Before moving further into this behavioristic conception of the family, it should be noted that the model does not explain *why* caretaker and child have reinforcement value for each other, nor does it explain *why* family members reinforce some behaviors and not others. In other words, the model is primarily a *descriptive* speculation on the interbehaviors of family members. Like most strategies that underlie behavior modification, this one attempts to minimize the construction of hypothetical events to explain phenomena.

DEVIANT CHILD BEHAVIOR WITHIN THE FAMILY

At some point in a child's life, his parents, or members of the larger community, may

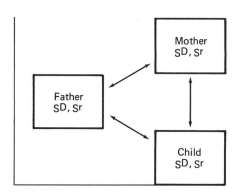

FIGURE 14–1   A social learning theory conception of the family. Each person is viewed as a source of discriminative stimuli (S^D) and reinforcing stimuli (S^r) for other family members.

decide that some aspects of his behavior are deviant. That is, he may do things (e.g., stealing) or fail to do things (e.g., schoolwork) that become distressful to his parents. However, according to social learning theory, this distress cannot be taken to mean that the child's deviance does not serve some function within the family. As outlined in Figure 14–1, the child's deviant behavior is maintained by reinforcers provided by other family members—and his deviant actions serve to reinforce these family members for their supporting behaviors. In a very real sense, the child's deviance is "locked" into the family system.

These arguments are made complete by further speculations on the development of such deviance supporting systems. The notion that a child's deviant behavior is "reinforcing" to other family members attributes both positive and aversive properties to the child's behavior. That is, he can reinforce others by presenting them with certain behaviors (e.g., clinging), and he can reinforce by terminating certain behaviors (e.g., screaming). In both cases, the outcome could involve a mutual strengthening of the child's deviant behavior and those family member behaviors that are reinforcing to the child. In essence there are two kinds of such "trap" situations that can develop within a family.

1. THE POSITIVE REINFORCER TRAP.

In this situation, a family member or members find some aspect of the child's behavior reinforcing (e.g., clinging); they in turn provide reinforcers for the child when he emits such behavior. An impending trap is evident if further production of this behavior would create problems (e.g., refusing to leave mother's side). Thus, a child behavior can be reinforcing to family members at one time yet aversive to them at a later time. The classic example of such a trap is seen in the development of extreme dependency behavior. Here, a caretaker finds the child's requests for help quite reinforcing and therefore consistently provides reinforcers for this behavior. The ensuing high fre-

quency of "help asking" and absence of self-help skills may continue to be reinforcing to the caretaker until new situations are imposed on the family, such as the child's entry into school. Since the child does not possess the kinds of behaviors that allow his successful entry into this new system, problems are created for the family. The dependent behaviors that were formerly reinforcing to the caretaker now become a source of punishment.

2. THE NEGATIVE REINFORCER TRAP.

In the author's experience, this kind of trap situation is the most common process in the development of deviant child behavior. The process assumes that some child behaviors are aversive to other family members (e.g., screaming). When the child dispenses such negative reinforcers, a caretaker may discover that there are quick and efficient ways of terminating these aversive stimuli. Often, the most effortless of these escape methods involves dispensing positive reinforcers to the child. This done, the child ceases his aversive behavior (temporarily), and the caretaker has thus been reinforced for using that particular method. Unfortunately, the child has also been reinforced for the very behavior that the caretaker wishes to suppress. As seen from the child's perspective (Patterson & Reid, 1970), the child is on the road to developing "coercive" means of relating to other members of his family. If these aversive behaviors become characteristic features of the child, other family members may experience enough distress to consider the child deviant. Yet, like the caretaker in the positive reinforcer trap situation, these people are now "locked" into a set of contingencies that continue to support the child's deviant behavior.

Aggressive behavior is perhaps the most obvious example of child behaviors that can be developed through negative reinforcer traps. Such behaviors are often aversive to adults, and it is thus likely that the behaviors may sometimes function to coerce reinforcers from a harried caretaker. For example, imagine a child in a supermarket, kicking and screaming following his mother's refusal to place a carton of popsicles in the shopping basket. It would not be unusual to see the parent respond by "giving in" and placing the popsicles in the basket. By providing this reinforcer, the parent will most likely escape the aversive tantrum situation; but, at the same time, the child has also been reinforced for using this particular coercive technique. Given that this kind of interaction between parent and child occurs often enough, the child is likely to become increasingly assertive, finally to the point where his parents seek psychological help.

We have purposefully neglected discussion of parent-parent interactions in the development of these trap situations. This aspect of the simple triad outlined in Figure 14–1 undoubtedly contributes to the likelihood that such traps will emerge within the family. However, since parent-parent interactions are discussed in considerable detail by Patterson, Weiss, and Hops (chapter 7), we need not present this material here.

CARETAKER MOTIVATION TO CHANGE DEVIANT CHILD BEHAVIOR

If the family does in fact operate as a system of mutually reinforcing members, it would seem unlikely that any member would seek change within that system. In this sense, the above family model appears inconsistent, arguing on the one hand that the child's deviant behavior and the behavior of other family members are mutually supporting, yet on the other hand supposing that the child's deviance can lead to a caretaker's decision to find ways of discontinuing this support.

However, this inconsistency is more apparent than real. First, it must be realized that the family is a system within a larger community system. While child and caretaker might be mutually supportive, the child may at the same time be punishing to another system in the community (e.g., school). Members of this latter system are then likely to set contingencies for the caretakers, motivating them to seek ways of modifying the child's behavior. In the author's experience, caretaker motivation to change deviant child behavior usually stems from this kind of between-system interaction. Public school systems, family relatives and friends, juvenile courts, and other community agencies are commonly instrumental in caretaker decisions to produce change within the family.

Caretaker motivation for family change can also come from within the family. The argument that caretaker and child are "locked into" a pattern of interbehaviors does not preclude the possibility of new caretaker behaviors, motivated by the child but not directed to the child. This possibility is most clearly illustrated in negative reinforcer trap situations. Here, while caretaker response to the child's aversive behaviors is to produce reinforcers for the child, these aversive behaviors may also set the occasion for other caretaker behaviors not directed to the child. That is, while the caretaker may continue to escape the aversive behaviors by providing reinforcers for the child, at the same time the caretaker may also look outside the family for other methods. The seriousness of such a search would probably depend on how aversive the child's behavior becomes to the caretaker.

Child behavior can also motivate caretaker change efforts through the caretaker's personal set of child development norms. Parents expect to see certain child behaviors (e.g., speech) at certain age periods; other behaviors, such as feminine actions in a boy, they do not expect to see. Once discriminated by the caretaker as a normative deviation, the behavior (or lack of it) may become aversive to the caretaker, thus motivating the caretaker's efforts to seek change.

Parental Categories of Deviant Child Behavior

There are some common factors in the kinds of child behaviors judged to be deviant by family caretakers. The author has found it useful to categorize these behaviors into four classes. These deviance categories differ in descriptive features of the behaviors they summarize and, to some extent, they differ in terms of which intervention techniques are appropriate to the modification of the behaviors. The utility of such a taxonomy will be presented in this section and in a later section dealing with treatment strategies.

OPPOSITIONAL BEHAVIOR

Probably the most common behaviors classified as deviant by parents are those that involve rule breaking or noncompliance with parental instructions (Patterson, 1964; Roach, 1958). Sometimes these actions involve assertive activities, such as fighting, and sometimes the actions are more passive, such as ignoring parental instructions. However, both cases share a common function, namely, an opposition to rules and instructions established by the parents.

The specific ways in which children can oppose parental rules and instructions are numerous, but some appear rather regularly in those children who are referred for treatment. For example, refusals to do work, frequent demands, fighting with peers or siblings, property destruction, stealing, and lying are often mentioned by parents seeking help for their children's "oppositional" behavior.

Social learning theory speculations on the development of oppositional behaviors have been offered by Patterson and his colleagues (Patterson & Reid, 1970; Patterson, Cobb, & Ray, 1970). In essence, these investigators conceptualize the developmental process as similar to the previously discussed "negative reinforcer trap." According to their "coercion hypothesis" (Patterson & Reid, 1970), extremely oppositional children are adept at coercing reinforcers from their parents. The children collect the lion's share of reinforcers in the family and give very few in return. It is assumed that much

of the children's coercive behaviors can be classified as "mands" (i.e., behaviors aimed at specific environmental consequences). Mands such as hitting, nagging, and whining appear functionally geared to obtain one class of reinforcers—compliance with the instructional content of the mand. Parents who typically provide such compliance reinforcers are in turn reinforced by the child's temporary termination of his aversive manding behavior, thus completing the "trap."

Data supporting the coercion hypothesis have been collected by the Patterson group. The researchers' naturalistic observations of families containing assertive oppositional children showed that these children obtained more positive consequences than did any other single family member (Patterson & Reid, 1970). While these data cannot be taken to support a *developmental* view of the coercion hypothesis, they do lend credence to the question of how oppositional behaviors might be *maintained* within the family.

Parents of oppositional children also commonly report that they frequently shout at, hit, or otherwise punish the oppositional child (Becker & Krug, 1965). The previously cited observational work by Patterson and Reid (1970) lends empirical support to these parental reports. The investigators' findings showed that the oppositional child not only obtained most of the positive attention within the family, but he also received most of the negative feedback. At first glance, this finding would appear incompatible with the notion that oppositional behaviors are maintained by positive (i.e., parental compliance) reinforcers. However, it may well be that these aversive events occur only after a series of successful coercion attempts by the child. There are no clear data yet available to evaluate this contention, but clinical accounts suggest that parental punishment of oppositional children usually occurs after a number of parent-compliant responses to the children's rule-breaking actions. If this is indeed the case, it would not be surprising to find that the parents' use of punitive methods is ineffective.

Another question raised by the Patterson and Reid findings concerns the actual reinforcement and punishment functions of parental attention for oppositional children. It is possible that the so-called "negative" parental attention is in fact "positive" for the child, and parental behaviors judged by observers as "positive" do not serve such a function. One consistent finding has emerged from investigations dealing with this issue. Oppositional children are relatively unresponsive to approval dispensed by their parents (Patterson, 1969; Wahler, 1969a). While parental compliance might serve as a reinforcer for these children, it seems clear that the usual sorts of parental affection are not very reinforcing to them. Thus, the typical picture presented by oppositional children and their parents appears to be "aversion oriented." There is little positive value inherent in either party's behaviors; both frequently dispense negative reactions to the other person, but only the child seems successful in obtaining anything positive from such interchanges. Parental compliance with the child's mands is probably a powerful maintenance factor for the child's behavior patterns.

One might guess that continued development of the above family interactions could only result in the child's acquisition of a rather narrow social repertoire. He might be expected to approach other social systems (school, peer group) in much the same way that he has learned to respond to his parents —coercively. Eventually his rule-breaking behavior might expand to the point where he violates legal statutes; at the very least he could be expected to alienate others.

Several follow-up studies of oppositional children who attracted the attention of outpatient psychological agencies support these predictions (e.g., Morris, 1956; Robins, 1966). In these studies, children referred for treatment because of stealing, fighting, school truancies, refusal to obey parental instructions, and other oppositional actions were quite likely to be considered deviant as adolescents and adults. The Robins study, for example, showed that when these children and a matched control group were compared, the former contributed disproportionally as adults to major crimes, psychosis, and marginal employment records. It is clear that extremely oppositional children are unlikely to "outgrow" their problems.

BEHAVIOR DEFICITS

This parental deviance category is probably noted earlier in the child's life than is true of the oppositional category. The term "behavior deficit" has reference to an absence of sizeable segments of the child's expected behavior repertoire. As noted by many pediatricians, parents expect to observe behavior segments such as walking, talking, and social approaches at fairly specific and early points in the child's life. Although the age ranges during which such segments actually do appear are broad (Gesell & Amatruda, 1941), many parents seem to use the early end of the range as their normative criteria.

Some children, labeled variously by clinicians as retarded, brain damaged, autistic, or schizophrenic, do not produce important behavior classes within or beyond the normative age ranges. In these cases, the behavior deficit category does become a deviance category.

Language problems appear to constitute a principal aspect of behavior-deficient children. Language, in this case, refers to the child's verbal and nonverbal communication skills, as well as his comprehension of such information when presented to him by his environment. When a child is considered within the behavior deficit category (often with labels such as retarded, autistic, or brain damaged), it is likely that some important features of his expressive and/or receptive language skills will be missing. The deficiencies may range from an across-the-board depression in all linguistic skills to specific deficiencies in the communication process.

Another commonly reported feature of behavior-deficient children has to do with what might be termed "self-help" skills. These usually include grooming, bowel and bladder control, dressing, walking, and eating. Again, as in the case of language deficiencies, the children may fail to acquire the entire range of such behaviors or may lack specific skills.

Given the absence of important language and self-help skills, it is not surprising to also find that behavior-deficient children are restricted in terms of social skills. Some show no interest in adult or peer interactions; others, while they may frequently initiate social contact, fail to do so in ways that might ensure positive responses from others. By and large, these children are isolated in terms of the usual forms of social contact.

The above deficiencies constitute frequently noted gaps in behavior repertoires. However, a complete picture of behavior-deficient children must include some of the typical things that the children *do* as well as the things they don't do. Many of the solitary activities of behavior-deficient children are simple and repetitive. It is not unusual to observe these children engaged in ritualistic manipulations of objects and their own bodies. At times, the self-stimulatory actions may include self-injurious behaviors such as face slapping and head banging. These simplistic and sometimes bizarre behaviors are commonly cited by parents and other onlookers as evidence of the child's extreme deviance.

As mentioned previously, the social repertoires of behavior-deficient children are restricted. Those children who are socially responsive often approach others in ways considered inappropriate. The term "inappropriate" has reference to the child's failure to observe implicit rules of social interaction (e.g., hugging a total stranger). Parents of socially responsive, behavior-deficient children typically pinpoint such actions as undesirable and inhibitory to the child's social contact with others.

Social learning theory speculations on these developmental failures have been offered by Bijou (1966) and by Ferster (1961). Both investigators have pointed out that while physical defects might underlie many behavior deficits, there is yet good reason to pursue environmental causes. In the first place, the most recent survey of evidence relating to physical bases for behavior deficits revealed confirmation in only 15% of the cases studied (*American Psychologist*, 1970, pp. 267–268). Secondly, physical defects are bound to interact with environmental factors in the sense that the former are likely to restrict the child's exposure to environmental events that might prove necessary to normal development. It is the latter possibility that Bijou considers in presenting his developmental speculations.

Bijou's analysis of behavior deficits grants the possibility that physical defects (hereditary and/or congenital) might be responsible for initial deficiencies in a child's behavior repertoire. However, it is then possible that these deficiencies might be progressively accentuated through social contingencies within the family. In essence, the expected contingency pattern is one in which parents and siblings fail to provide reinforcers for developmental changes in the child's language, self-help, and social skills. Instead, the caretakers are likely to further impede the acquisition of these skills by reinforcing incompatible behaviors such as passivity, primitive skills (for example, pointing and grunting), or temper tantrums.

It is probable that negative reinforcer trap situations adequately describe these family contingency patterns. Many parents of behavior-deficient children report that it was simply "easier" to reinforce the child's passivity through feeding and clothing him than to withhold reinforcers contingent upon small advances in self-help skills. In addition, it is "easier" to respond and comply with a child's primitive communications (e.g., pointing) than to demand more complex linguistic skills. Withholding reinforcers is also likely to lead to an acceleration of such primitive mands, to the point that the child becomes quite aversive through screaming, self-injury, and property destruction. Obviously, providing reinforcers for "status quo" behaviors avoids many negative consequences for parents and siblings alike.

Presently, there are no data available to evaluate the above speculations. However, recent data taken within institutional settings show that such contingency patterns appear to operate in settings with behavior-deficient children (Braginsky & Braginsky, 1971). These investigators supported earlier observational findings pointing to minimal staff attention to developmental changes in child behavior (Dennis & Najarian, 1957). In addition, their findings showed that behavior-deficient children are by no means unresponsive to their social environments. Rather, their primitive behaviors appeared functionally geared to obtaining reinforcers available within the institution, thus probably contributing to the inhibition of developmental skills. If this sort of trap situation occurs within institutional settings, it is possible that the same kind of situation operates within families.

As we argued in the case of oppositional children, it seems likely that behavior-deficient children will become progressively more restricted in their behavior repertoires if they continue to operate within the kind of trap situation described by Bijou (1966) and Braginsky and Braginsky (1971). Follow-up data presented by a number of investigators confirm this expectation. For example, Skeels (1966), in a 30-year follow-up study of behavior-deficient children who remained in the kind of institution studied by Braginsky and Braginsky, showed progressive deterioration in the children's behavioral skills. Even those behavior-deficient children whose deficiencies are thought by some to be largely due to environmental conditions show such deterioration over

time (Eisenberg, 1956). In the latter study, most of a sample of children classified as autistic were found to be profoundly retarded in intellectual and social skills by late adolescence. Thus, as is the case for oppositional children, prognosis for change in behavior-deficient children is unfavorable.

AGE-INAPPROPRIATE BEHAVIORS

While parents are often quick to notice the absence of expected behaviors in their children, they also become concerned to a lesser extent about behaviors that persist beyond an age when most children no longer produce them.

Most children form close attachments to one or more caretakers during the first 2 years of life (see Schaffer & Emerson, 1964). During this time it is not unusual to note the child's distress (fear and/or depression) upon separation from the caretaker or similar distress upon exposure to novel situations or people. Gradually, however, these specific dependencies tend to diminish, and the child spends progressively more time exploring his social and physical environment. On the other hand, with some children these specific caretaker dependencies persist well beyond the first few years of life, leading to shyness and isolation from the larger social and physical environment. Such dependencies, including the accompanying fears and depressions, are now age-inappropriate behaviors.

In addition to (and possibly related to) the above dependencies are other commonly mentioned age-inappropriate behaviors. Bed wetting, soiling, thumb sucking, and "baby talk" are often mentioned by parents seeking for help for this class of behavior problems. These behaviors cluster together in the sense that all are expected from very young children.

Often the age-inappropriate category is not applied to a child until he reaches school age. Prior to that time, many parents appear only mildly concerned about the child's immaturity. They may readily admit that they are "spoiling" the child through frequent reinforcement of his caretaker dependent actions, but they also note his quite adequate development in general. Most of these children are bright, verbally adept, and socially reinforcing to others. However, the child's required entry into the new and unfamiliar school environment may quickly alter parental impressions of his age-inappropriate behaviors. The child's reluctance or refusal to leave the caretaker and his fears and loneliness in the new environment often lead a parent to view the formerly reinforcing behaviors as deviant.

Gewirtz (1972) has offered a social learning theory view concerning the development of normal dependencies in children, a view that lends itself nicely to speculations on how such dependencies might persist into age-inappropriate behaviors.

Gewirtz makes an important distinction between dependence and attachment, the latter term referring to a singular attachment between child and caretaker and the former describing a child's attachment to multiple caretakers. Data showing that children vary considerably in the number of their caretaker attachments during the first 2 years of life have been presented in support of Gewirtz's distinction (Schaffer & Emerson 1964). Schaffer and Emerson's study discovered a positive correlation between the number of attachments formed by a child within the family and the number of family members who routinely interact with that child. In cases where a single family member was the principal interaction agent, a single, usually intense, attachment was developed between the child and that caretaker. In contrast, children formed multiple, less intense attachments in families where caretaking responsibilities were shared by several family members.

The clinical importance of these findings with normal children is suggested by differences in the degree and duration of separation distress elicited in young children with multiple versus singular attachments. Several investigators (Spitz & Wolf, 1946; Mead, 1962) have presented data showing that separation distress is more severe and prolonged for children with close attachments to a single caretaker. These findings suggest that trap situations leading to age-inappropriate behaviors are most likely to occur in families where singular-caretaker–child attachments are formed.

The nature of such trap situations is alluded to by Gewirtz (1961) in an analysis of potential problems connected with social attachments. Gewirtz views the normal attachment process in terms of positive stimulus control; in essence, we might assume that both child and caretaker behaviors are developed and maintained by mutually dispensed, positive social reinforcers. The child's clinging, smiling, and cooing are positive reinforcers for the caretaker, and that adult's tactual, auditory, and visual stimulation functions in the same capacity for the child. In fact, Etzel and Gewirtz (1967) presented an interesting experimental demonstration of this process with two 6- to 20-week-old infants in a boarding nursery. Thus, an extended development of singular, intense attachments might well occur through positive reinforcer traps. Both child and caretaker might maintain the dependency relationship through appropriately contingent dispensing of their positive social reinforcers. By the time the caretaker categorizes the child's dependent behavior as deviant, both members of the pair are likely to be "locked into" their dependency relationship. Not only is the child's age-inappropriate behavior positively reinforcing to the caretaker; the child's distress upon separation is likely to be quite punishing to that caretaker (one 8-year-old known to the author threatened his mother with suicide when she attempted to leave him with a baby sitter on several occasions).

Despite the dramatic and sometimes frightening separation features of age-inappropriate behavior problems, these children show a favorable prognosis for change over time. The previously quoted follow-up study by Robins (1966) showed that dependent, shy, anxious, and otherwise age-inappropriate behavior problems in childhood were not likely to persist into adulthood. Probably the requirement in this country that all children enter a social system other than home is a factor here. The child's forced entry into public school makes it probable that he will form new attachments. If an intense, prolonged attachment within the family is in fact the basis of age-inappropriate behaviors, such a required shift in the child's social interactions might be expected to be therapeutic.

CROSS-GENDER BEHAVIOR

By the time children reach preschool age, most have acquired aspects of behavior patterns that are predictable on the basis of the child's sex and societal pressures. Boys tend to produce more assertive and gross-motor actions than do girls; the latter generally prefer less competitive games, such as "house," and both sexes interact most frequently with same-sex members (Walters, Pearce, & Dahms, 1957; Koch, 1944).

Some children of this age have not acquired the above gender-appropriate behavior patterns and instead display behaviors characteristic of their opposite sex. Girls, commonly referred to as "tomboys," may come to resemble boys, both in terms of behaviors and clothing preferences; likewise, some boys ("sissies") may develop characteristically feminine behaviors. While such cross-gender behavior patterns are not uncommon in children (particularly for girls), the phenomenon can constitute a deviance category in terms of the social consequences of such patterns.

Cross-gender behavior patterns in young children have been the subject of several clinical and developmental investigations. By and large, the outcomes of these studies point to some clearly different social consequences for tomboys and sissies. Tomboyish behavior is usually regarded positively

by parents and peers alike (Kagen & Moss, 1962). These girls appear at ease with both male and female peers and often assume leadership roles. On the other hand, sissified behavior usually results in negative consequences for the boy who consistently produces such behavior (Kagen & Moss, 1962; Stoller, 1970). He is usually scorned by his peer group and often leads a lonely life of isolation. The fact that adults are also likely to consider sissies as deviant is seen in the differential proportion of boys versus girls referred for psychological help because of cross-gender behavior. A survey by Green (1969) revealed that virtually all such referrals were boys.

Compared to the previously discussed deviance categories, cross-gender problems include a broader range of specific behaviors. For cross-gendered boys (where the case for a deviance label seems justified), the behaviors considered could involve a complete matching of the typical things that females do. The imitative behavior covered by such a matching has been discussed within a social learning framework by Bandura and Walters (1963) and Mischel (1970). These investigators assume that imitative learning is a basic process in the development of all social behavior and gender behaviors in particular. While their speculations are geared to the acquisition of gender-appropriate behaviors, they consider the same process to operate in the development of cross-gender behaviors.

The likelihood that a child will imitate a model is influenced by reinforcement of the child's imitative actions and by the reinforcement value of the model. The latter factor appears to be determined both by the model's history of providing reinforcers for the child-observer and the degree of control that the model has over reward dispensing in general. That is, laboratory studies have shown that models who provide frequent social reinforcers for children will be readily imitated by these children (see Bandura & Huston, 1961). In addition, an even more powerful imitative influence appears tied to the model's degree of control over dispensing such reinforcers, regardless of whether or not the child-observer receives them. Further laboratory work by Bandura, Ross, and Ross (1963) showed this phenomenon clearly and presented suggestive evidence on the acquisition of cross-gender behaviors. In this study, boys and girls were most likely to imitate the reinforcer-controlling model, regardless of the model's sex.

More naturalistic studies, in which parents were the models, provided support for the Bandura group's contention that control over reward dispensing is a significant factor in children's imitation of gender behaviors (Hetherington, 1965; Hetherington & Frankie, 1967). These studies investigated relationships between parental "dominance" (degree of reinforcer control within the family) and children's performance of gender behaviors as well as the children's direct imitation of parental behaviors. Results were clearer for boys than girls. In mother-dominant families, boys tended to be behaviorally less similar to the father and more likely to imitate the mother. Thus, as suggested by the laboratory studies, cross-gender behaviors in boys might be acquired in families where the mother has primary control of reinforcers.

Several clinical case studies of cross-gendered boys provide speculative information on the kind of mother-son trap situation that can lead to the child's consistent imitation of feminine behaviors. As in the case of age-inappropriate behaviors, positive reinforcer trap situations appear to be involved. These mothers apparently find their sons' dependency actions reinforcing *and* their more effeminate behaviors as well (Giffin, Johnson, & Litin, 1954; Litin, Giffin, & Johnson, 1956). In turn, the mothers may reinforce these behaviors with approval and often physically seductive actions. For example, in one case reported by the above investigators, the mother slept with her son and had shown him her vagina a number of times. Thus, as Bandura and Walters (1963) argue, female characteristics are not only

associated with reinforcement for the boy (therefore increasing the likelihood that he will imitate such actions) but the mother may also actively reinforce these imitations.

As with age-inappropriate behaviors, cross-gender behaviors are not usually considered deviant by parents until another social system affects the family. In this case, it is usually the cross-gendered boy's peer group that is instrumental in parental decisions to seek treatment for the boy. Other boys' tendencies to punish effeminate behaviors of their group members make it likely that sissified boys will lead unhappy lives outside their homes. It is often this sort of punishment that leads parents to look for psychological help.

The classification of cross-gender behaviors by boys as deviant is supported by several longitudinal studies as well as previously mentioned peer group consequences during childhood. First, it is clear that cross-gendered boys are likely to continue their feminine activities into adulthood (Kagen & Moss, 1962). More important, however, is the consistent finding that these adults are apt to suffer adjustment problems that are even more severe than those in childhood (see Green & Money, 1969). Adult transsexuals are subject to frequent ostracism and arrest and, not surprisingly, suffer severe depressions (Pauly, 1969). Cross-gendered girls, on the other hand, are not likely to continue their masculine activities past adolescence (Kagen & Moss, 1962). Thus, while a deviance label for tomboys is unwarranted, it is clearly supported for the sissified boy.

Situational Aspects of Deviant Child Behavior

The preceding classes of deviant child behavior are intended to describe the principal complaints of parents who seek psychological help for their children. It would be erroneous, however, to presume that these behaviors, or any class of behaviors for that matter, are *characteristic* features of a child.

For example, an "oppositional" child is unlikely to produce his noncomplaint behaviors consistently across all settings within the home. He may be extremely coercive "when company comes" or "when mother is fixing dinner" yet show none of this behavior "at breakfast" or "when father comes home."

Perhaps a hallmark feature of social learning theory is the assumption that children's social behaviors are maintained by specific events within the child's environment (see Bijou & Baer, 1961). That is, regardless of what the child's parents and other relatives did to *develop* his social behaviors, the *maintenance* of these behaviors ought to depend on the actions of those people who make up the child's current environment. In other words, the positive and negative reinforcer trap situations referred to earlier must continue to operate if the child's deviant behavior is to continue to occur.

It is probable that maintenance factors (i.e., reinforcer traps) in deviant child behavior are situational. A host of naturalistic-observational studies of both normal and deviant child social behaviors point clearly to the fact that these behaviors are not produced consistently by a child in all of his environmental settings (see Mischel, 1968, for a review of situational factors in child social behavior). Thus, a reinforcer trap may be reliably operative "when mother is fixing dinner," but just as reliably non-operative "when father comes home" or when the child is in the school classroom.

Observational data showing the situational nature of deviant child behavior have been presented for all four of the previously discussed classes of deviant child behavior. Rekers and Lovaas (1973) in a most thorough family study of a cross-gendered boy discovered that the boy's effeminate behaviors were specific to certain environmental settings. Likewise, Gewirtz (1954) showed that dependency behaviors do not occur uniformly within an environment but depend on specific situations within that setting. As for oppositional behavior, Wahler (1969b) demonstrated a similar phenomenon with an extremely coercive kindergarten-age boy. In this case, the boy's refusals to obey instructions were shown to depend functionally on the settings in which he was observed. Finally, Sajwaj, Twardosz, and Burke's (1972) observational descriptions of several behavior-deficient children revealed wide variation in each child's behaviors over several environmental situations. No doubt the children's major behavior deficits (e.g., language) were consistently evident across situations. However, when one looks at what these children *do*, situational determinants appear to be as strikingly operative for them as for all other children.

The situational nature of deviant child behavior has at least two important implications as far as treatment strategies are concerned:

1. The effective clinician, in line with the views of Barker (1965), must consider ecological as well as psychological factors in working with problem children. Clearly, the child's behavior must be viewed within the various environmental contexts in which it occurs. Developmental information acquired via interview or present-day information based on observing the child in a single environmental setting (e.g., clinic) may not be sufficient to initiate a successful treatment program.

2. If deviant child behavior is indeed tied to specific situations, maintenance factors are likely to operate within these situations. As we argued previously, reinforcer traps may become well established in some environmental situations but not in others. If these situations can be specified and the trap operations within them described, behavior modification along the lines of Tharp and Wetzel (1969) becomes the logical course of intervention. Here the clinician becomes a consultant whose goals are to utilize this information to train caretaker and child to eliminate the day-to-day trap situations. If the child's deviance is indeed maintained by ongoing, day-to-day social interactions within the family, such a treatment strategy makes perfect sense. Regardless of the child's history, ther-

apeutic changes ought to occur if certain critical situational factors are modified. The following sections describe some strategic approaches to this sort of modification within the family.

Assessment Strategies Within the Family

Assuming that situational reinforcer traps are responsible for the maintenance of deviant child behavior, the initial task of intervention must entail specification and description of these traps. Characteristic of all behavior modification strategies, direct observation of family interactions is emphasized in producing assessment information. Once the consultant has a picture of the specific family interbehaviors that make up these traps, he is in a position to take remedial action. Thus, before turning to an examination of remediation, it would be wise to describe the assessment process.

ASSESSMENT PROCEDURES: I. THE INTERVIEW

Obviously, all assessment efforts in outpatient work begin by talking with the principals involved. Unfortunately, few family investigators have bothered to describe in any systematic fashion these initial procedures. The author and a colleague (Wahler & Cormier, 1970) have attempted to specify some of the usual steps that occur in such an "ecological interview."

Most behavioristic family consultants view the interview as serving two broad functions:

1. An educational experience for the parents and perhaps the child as well. In order to comprehend and implement the consultant's suggestions, parents ought to have a workable grasp of social learning theory principles. In the author's experience, most parents do not view their children's actions from this perspective. They tend to attribute continued occurrences of the child's deviant behavior to developmental factors (e.g., "We spoiled him when he was a baby") or to hypothetically present internal events (e.g., "There's something wrong with his mind"). As

Goldiamond (1969) pointed out, the interview can serve to focus parental attention on the immediate environmental situations that maintain behavior as well as teaching parents some basic notions about reinforcement operations.[1]

2. Secondly, the interview ought to permit an initial specification of probable reinforcer traps and the situations in which they occur. Here, the consultant needs to get specific information on what the child does and/or does not do, as well as how the parents and other relatives respond to the behavioral occurrences. While this information could be inaccurate, at least the consultant has some idea where to begin in his formulations of behavior categories for later direct observation.

A focus on situations that typically occur in the family's day-to-day living is profitable for several reasons. First, the direct observations necessary to complete an assessment must be initially geared to some specific time period. That is, observers, whether they be professionals or family members, need to know where to begin their task. The author has been impressed by parents' abilities to accurately specify those situations that most reliably set the occasion for their children's deviant behaviors. With sufficiently detailed situational questions, most parents can provide a range of home situations that differ in the likelihood that their child will produce his or her problem actions. For the author, common examples have been "when I am trying to fix dinner," "when all the kids are in the house together," and "bedtime."

Given a specification of multiple problem situations, the consultant has the option to begin an assessment in any one or all of the situations. Having such an option is desirable because some situations may present difficulties in implementing an intervention program. For example, "when I am trying to fix dinner" might be a

[1] Several inexpensive parent training manuals are available to assist the clinician in this process. See Patterson (1971), Patterson & Gullion (1968), and Becker (1971) in the reference section of this chapter.

highly likely problem situation, but it could be a poor selection in which to initiate the intervention program. The mother might be so completely involved in competing activities that she could not attend in sufficient detail to the unfamiliar procedures of intervention. One mother known to the author was primarily concerned about her behavior-deficient son's tantrums in the family car. While it was discovered that this problem occurred in three other home situations as well, her pressing interest was in handling the car situation. It soon became obvious to her, however, that her mastery of the author's suggested assessment and behavior-change techniques would be quite difficult if she was also expected to drive the car. In this case, intervention training was initiated in one of the home situations, with the understanding that the car situation would be next in priority once the mother had received adequate training as a behavior modifier.

In addition to focusing on multiple situations within the family, the interview should also yield information on a range of behaviors produced by the child within these situations. By and large, most parents tend to summarize their children's problem behaviors under a single label (e.g., "he's stubborn"), or they tend to concentrate on those singular problem behaviors that arouse most concern within the family (e.g., stealing). As in the previously discussed case of situations, providing a range of specific problem behaviors allows a selection of targets for the initial intervention training. Again, some problem behaviors are more difficult to deal with than others, and it would be wise to begin intervention with the behaviors that are least difficult to modify. A rule of thumb in selecting such behaviors is that those behaviors that the parents describe as occurring in their presence are more readily dealt with than behavior occurring elsewhere. For example, stealing is a very difficult behavior to mod-

ify, probably because it occurs in situations where adults are not present.

Sometimes the child himself can provide useful information in the interview setting. Keeping in mind that trap situations are maintained by *all* people involved in the trap, the child's view of situations and behaviors ought to be considered as well as the views of his caretakers. Verbally adept children can often provide information on how parents generally respond in trap situations, which leads to the possibility that the child could take part in the observational procedures that follow.

ASSESSMENT PROCEDURES: II OBSERVATION

A successful interview ought to allow a preliminary specification of situations to be examined and the behaviors to be observed in these situations. At this point it becomes important to be exceedingly specific about *what* is to be observed. That is, the consultant must formulate behavior categories permitting reliable coding of family inter-behaviors.

Most family consultants believe that category construction should begin by obtaining narrative running records of the child's family interactions (see Bijou, Peterson, & Ault, 1968, for a detailed discussion of this process). Such a sample of concrete actions not only permits a validity check on interview information, it also helps to ensure agreement among all principals concerning category definitions. Rules for the grouping of narrative record behaviors into categories are somewhat arbitrary; as long as observer use of the category system is reliable and the resultant category counts reflect family problem interactions, the consultant has done his job adequately.

The author has found it helpful to utilize four guidelines in the grouping process:

1. Behaviors that appear to cluster together in time may constitute a single category. For ex-

ample, a child's whining, nagging, and complaints may be found to co-occur in time, leading to their grouping as a single category; a parent's shouting and screaming, if they co-occur, might be considered together (e.g., "negative attention"). Of course, one could consider each of these specific behaviors as a single category, and some family consultants prefer to deal with such simplistic units. Certainly, observer agreement is bound to be higher if molecular categories are used. However, one needs to strike a balance between observer reliability and category breadth. Utilizing observer agreement as the only criterion for category construction could lead to an inordinate number of these units and communication between parents and consultant might be hampered.

2. A second guideline in category construction utilizes parental behaviors as "anchor points." Some child behaviors may cluster together in their relationship to a particular behavior produced by another family member. For example, parental instructions may often lead to a child's refusal to obey, and these noncompliances could constitute a single category. In the author's experience, many aspects of child problem behavior are geared to implicit family rules set by parents. Requiring parents to make this rule system explicit may produce some useful anchor points for category construction.

3. Parent and consultant attitudes and values should also be considered as determinants of those behaviors summarized by a category. A number of behaviors might be grouped together following the "cluster" guidelines, yet, a parent may be very worried about some of these behaviors and little concerned about the others. Therefore, the category ought to reflect this differential concern through limiting its scope or through the construction of multiple categories instead of one. For example, a "rule-breaking" category might be formulated by use of the second guideline discussed in this section. However, parent and consultant might be most concerned about the child's assertive rule-breaking actions (such as fighting with siblings), or the greatest concern may be aroused by stealing. In this case, multiple categories rather than a single broad one would be called for.

4. Finally, it should be remembered that observers must be able to agree on the occurrence and nonoccurrence of a category, and the parents (who may also be the observers) must be able to track these occurrences in order to serve as behavior modifiers. People vary in their abilities to perform these tasks, and the number of behavioral instances summarized by a category will be limited by this consideration.

As an end product, a set of categories should be available to observers. These units should permit the observers to obtain a quantitative picture of the child's problem and desirable behavior and of family-member reactions to this behavior. The latter categories would be conceptualized as possible reinforcing and punishing events.

Observer selection will probably be dictated by resources available to the consultant. To avoid bias, professional observers are a good choice (the author has for some time employed and trained unskilled housewives in this capacity). However, if such personnel are not available, the parents themselves can serve this function (see Patterson, Ray, & Shaw, 1969), and some consultants have even utilized the problem child as an observer (see Lovitt & Curtis, 1969).

The actual counting of the categories is typically done in two ways. For categories that occur at moderate to high rates (e.g., self-stimulation), the observer watches the child for a set time interval and at the end of that interval records on paper a single occurrence or nonoccurrence of a category. That is, regardless of whether the category occurs once, several times, or continues for the duration of the interval, its maximum score is one. Multiple categories can be scored for the interval, but each is limited to a single occurrence. Such a rule facilitates observer agreement on the number of category occurrences. Time interval length is arbitrary, but very short intervals (e.g., 10 seconds) will facilitate observer agreement.

The total number of time intervals that constitutes an observation period is also arbitrary. Most family investigators employing time interval recording have sampled at least 100 intervals within a period, but all such studies have utilized professional observers. Needless to say, it would be difficult for a family member to operate as a family member and also conduct such intensive observational work. However, some recent data by Kubany and Sloggett (1973), taken within a school classroom setting, indicate that far fewer intervals may provide an adequate sample of moderate- to high-rate behaviors. In this study, the teacher was required to serve as an observer of a problem child in her classroom. In addition, she was expected to conduct her teaching duties as usual, probably a more difficult task than caretaking within a family.

The teacher's observational equipment included an ordinary kitchen bell timer and a sheet of paper with a list of variable time intervals spaced, on the average, 4 minutes apart. She was told to set the timer for the first interval on the list; when the bell sounded she was to quickly observe the target child and classify his behavior *at that moment* into a prearranged category system. She then reset the timer for the next interval, and so on for a 20-minute observation period. Her daily sample of the child's behavior thus amounted to only four or five time intervals.

During the same 20-minute observation periods, a professional observer using the teacher's category system sampled the target child's behavior every 15 seconds. This procedure therefore resulted in a sample of 80 time intervals per day. Percentages of category occurrences over the 50 days of the study were then compared for the teacher observer and the professional observer. The two sets of percentages were virtually identical, indicating that the teacher's brief time samples produced a representative picture of the child. Thus, it is probably not unrealistic to expect a family member to serve as an observer of his or her interactions with the problem child.

A second kind of counting procedure is used for categories that occur at low rates (e.g., stealing). Here the observer must be a

family member because the tracking procedure must occur continuously. That is, the caretaker is required to record every episode occurrence of the category. This is a difficult procedure to maintain in spite of the fact that recording is usually only required a few times per day. The author has experimented with an "episode" form in which a parent is told to record category episodes immediately on a daily log sheet. The log sheets are then picked up when a professional observer visits the family. However, we have been disappointed in parental performance on this continuous recording procedure. Most parents simply do not do the recording on a regular, everyday basis. Presently, we are resorting to daily telephone calls to the parent, asking that person to recall category episodes that occurred during the day. This procedure ensures regular recording but of course suffers in requiring parental recall over the day. In addition, no procedure has yet been devised to determine the reliability of this sort of category counting procedure. Despite these problems, efforts must be made to record low-rate events. Often these category occurrences are central features of the child's problem behavior.

The amount of time devoted to all of the preceding pretreatment "baseline" observations will obviously vary across families. In the author's experience, one to two weeks of daily observations usually result in a fairly stable picture of the child's behavior and family-member response to that behavior.

A professional observer should provide at least some input in the baseline to evaluate the reliability of parental recording. A professional's presence will undoubtedly influence family interbehavior and may extend baseline length because of the time required to habituate the family to the newcomer. There are no set rules to determine when a stable baseline has been obtained. The author's preferred method is to split the obtained observation periods into early and late halves to compare average category occurrences. If the average category occurrences have the same relative rank ordering in the two halves, one might conclude that stability has been obtained, and thus intervention should proceed.

Intervention Strategies Within the Family

A successful baseline assessment ought to provide some fairly clear guidelines for intervention. A quantitative picture of those child behaviors to be accelerated and those to be weakened should be available to evaluate intervention success. In addition, some index of how other family members have maintained the problem behaviors may become available. It then becomes a matter of rearranging stimulus contingencies within the family. It is hoped that such a rearrangement would be designed to ensure that the child's major source of family based reinforcers would be obtainable only through behaviors deemed desirable by the combined judgment of caretakers and consultant.

REINFORCER SELECTION

The consultant should not be too disappointed to discover minimal baseline information on the child's major reinforcers. With professional observers, these trap-supporting events are often detected within baseline category counts. However, if family members serve as observers, their self-observations of reward dispensing may not prove informative (in the author's experience). Despite this problem, discussions with the child and other family members will ordinarily provide a range of these events.[2] Following Premack (1963), the discussions

[2] The reader may be surprised at the heavy reliance on self-report data in an approach that places strong emphasis on direct observation. Unfortunately, observational technology has not progressed to the point where behavior modifiers can realistically operate with it alone.

should be geared to those activities that the child engages in most frequently, since the events involved in these activities are likely to be powerful reinforcers (e.g., TV set). Given a listing of probable reinforcers or reinforcing activities and their relative values, this job is complete.

PUNISHMENT

Ideally, the task of intervention should utilize positive reinforcers only. For ethical reasons, punishment is an undesirable feature of any therapeutic intervention. However, to exclude this procedure from the consultant's collection of techniques is to seriously hamper intervention efforts in some cases. That is, discontinuing family reinforcers for a child's problem behaviors often leads initially to an increased output of these behaviors. In line with this differential reinforcement procedure, family members would be required to ignore these accelerated behaviors. Unfortunately, there are cases in which this tactic is simply not feasible, from an ethical as well as practical view. For example, it might prove possible to weaken self-injurious behaviors through ignoring their occurrences. However, the possible damage to the child in the process must be considered. An extended weakening of self-injurious behavior might prove to be far more harmful to the child than the use of punishment to more quickly suppress these actions. To take another example, a parent would be hard pressed to ignore extremely assertive behaviors by a child. To do so would probably result in painful outcomes for other family members.

From the author's perspective, punishment has to be considered as an intervention technique. Various kinds of punishment have been reported in the research literature, but the most commonly used procedure for families is "time out" (see Leitenberg's 1965 review for a detailed discussion of the procedure). In essence, time out refers to a means of ensuring that the child be denied access to positive reinforcers for a short time interval. Typically this means that the child is isolated in a bedroom or bathroom for 5 or 10 minutes. The time-out area should be relatively barren in terms of available reinforcers (e.g., toys), and a means of keeping the child in this area may be necessary (e.g., locked door).

It is possible that more extreme forms of punishment may be required to suppress certain problem behaviors. Several investigators have used electric shock or slapping for the self-injurious actions of behavior-deficient children (Risley, 1968; Lovaas, Koegel, Simmons, & Long, 1973). However, neither of these studies attempted to compare the effectiveness of these procedures with the more moderate time-out procedure. It may well be that time out is not an effective punisher for these extreme behavior deviations, although two investigations showed otherwise (Wolf, Risley, & Mees, 1964; Nordquist & Wahler, 1973). The question is an empirical one; if the consultant has to recommend a punishment procedure, the initial selection should be based on some sort of "aversiveness criterion." The procedure least aversive to the family probably ought to be employed first. In the author's experience, time out fits this standard as the mildest of those punitive techniques commonly employed in behavior modification work.

SETTING THE CONTINGENCIES

Once a decision has been made as to likely reinforcers for the child and whether or not a punishment procedure is to be employed, the stage is set to implement the intervention program. The author's preference is to meet with all family members to discuss the setting of stimulus contingencies. Here the program is made clear to everybody, including the child if he can comprehend the information. A principal purpose of such a discussion is to clarify the actual management of reinforcing and punishing contingencies. Most family consultants prefer to use token or point systems to manage the

dispensing of reinforcers. Such a system requires the parents to award a set number of points or tokens whenever the child produces a desirable target behavior. In addition, parental approval—in whatever form the parent feels comfortable providing—is to follow these desirable behaviors. As the child accumulates points, he may "spend them" by obtaining reinforcers from the previously discussed listing. Of course, the more valuable the reinforcer (e.g., fishing trip), the higher the point cost. If siblings are within the family, it is ethically desirable to include them in the management program.

In the case of behavior-deficient children, more immediate access to reinforcers may be necessary. If the child is unable to comprehend relationships between accumulated points and reinforcers, the parent will be required to dispense reinforcers immediately upon the child's production of desirable behaviors.

The previously discussed observation system must be continued for several reasons. First, it allows an evaluation of change in the problem child. Secondly, the training of parents is facilitated by this sort of monitoring. Here, the importance of an outside observer again comes into play. Parents may require short-term feedback as to their accuracy in implementing the new contingencies. This feedback has been provided by postobservation discussions (see Wahler, 1969b), direct radio transmission to the parent (Wahler, Winkel, Petersen, & Morrison, 1965), videotape replay (Bernal, 1969), and graphic presentations of observational category counts (Friedman, 1971).

While the contingency management program must be followed closely in the beginning of intervention, less structured family interactions may be possible later. That is, once desirable changes occur in the child's behavior, it might prove feasible to maintain the changes with a more informal means of tracking and reinforcing the child's behavior. It must be noted that contingency management procedures require effort from parents and are quite unlike natural family interactions. Because of these factors, it is probably unreasonable to expect an indefinite employment of the procedures. The consultant must eventually move the family members toward their more usual means of interacting yet, ensure that the child's desirable behaviors continue to be his principal means of gaining family attention and other reinforcers. This process will be discussed in more detail in a later section dealing with follow-up aspects of intervention.

We now turn to an examination of the above procedures as they have been applied to various sorts of child behavior problems. In these sections, it is instructive to note those differences in intervention techniques that appear to be a function of the type of behavior problem.

INTERVENTION STRATEGIES FOR OPPOSITIONAL BEHAVIOR

Most investigations of contingency management procedures for this sort of problem have found it necessary to employ a time-out contingency as part of the program. In large part this decision has been governed by parental difficulty in ignoring extremely coercive actions by some of these children (see Patterson, Cobb, & Ray, 1970). Although Wagner and Ora (1970) demonstrated successful parent use of contingency management without time out, their program was aimed at very young (ages 2–3 years) oppositional children. By the time these children reach school age (when they are most likely to be referred for treatment), it would be difficult for most parents to successfully ignore the children's coercive actions. For example, the clinical impressions of Patterson, Cobb, and Ray (1970) pointed to some predictable sequences in the interbehaviors of school-age oppositional children and their parents. The Patterson group discovered that these parents typically ignored the children's initial manding behaviors. However, the

children would then usually accelerate these rule-breaking activities, and the parents found these later, high-rate, high-amplitude behaviors too aversive to ignore.

In addition to the Patterson group, a number of other investigators have shown that a combination of positive reinforcement and time out will lead to desirable changes in oppositional behavior (Hawkins, Peterson, Schweid, & Bijou, 1966; Zeilberger, Sampen & Sloane, 1968; Johnson, 1971). The author (Wahler, 1969a) found similar outcomes and also demonstrated a positive "side effect" of such a dual-contingency program. In this study, parental reinforcement values for the children were found to increase as a function of parental use of time out and differential attention. Not only did the children become more cooperative, but both parent and child appeared to obtain more enjoyment out of each other's company.

Little systematic inquiry has been directed to the success of these programs in modifying low-rate problem behaviors produced by oppositional children (e.g., stealing, truancy). Since these behaviors are not likely to occur in the presence of a parent, indirect means of dealing with the behaviors must be employed. These either take the form of a long-range reinforcement contingency (e.g., points for a weekly reduction in episode reports) or, more commonly, a generalization strategy. The latter approach assumes that increments in the child's prosocial behaviors in parental presence will affect problem episodes elsewhere. Unfortunately, an extensive intervention study of stealing by Reid and Hendriks (1972) showed little success in altering this problem behavior.

At this point, little can be said about the effectiveness of family contingency programs for low-rate deviant behaviors. No doubt part of the problem is due to difficulties in monitoring these behaviors. Until observational technologies provide a reliable means of detecting low-rate occurrences, prognosis for changing these behaviors must remain guarded.

INTERVENTION STRATEGIES FOR BEHAVIOR DEFICITS

Of all behavior disorders, behavior deficits call for the most intensive of intervention efforts. Because of the precision required in contingency management of the deficits, most attempts to work with these children have occurred in institutional settings (see Birnbrauer, Wolf, Kidder, and Tague, 1965; Lovaas, Schaeffer, & Simmons, 1965). Recently, however, efforts to train parents to conduct this sort of precision teaching have been initiated (Lindsey, 1966; Lovaas, Koegel, Simmons, & Long, 1973; Nordquist & Wahler, 1973).

The above contingency management programs have typically focused on two aspects of the child's problem behavior. First, efforts are made to weaken behaviors that would interfere with the teaching process (e.g., self-stimulation, temper tantrums). Punishment appears necessary to accomplish this goal. In fact, Herbert, Pinkston, Sajwaj, Pinkston, Cordua, and Jackson (1972) found that differential parent attention alone actually *increased* the rates of these disruptive behaviors in behavior-deficient children. The increases proved quite stable and thus could not be attributed to the usual initial acceleration of problem behaviors following an ignoring tactic. Adding a time-out contingency, however, resulted in quick reductions in the deviant actions.

Granted that the child becomes attentive to the parent through weakening of his disruptive behaviors, the precision teaching process can begin. Most of these programs have been geared to the child's language deficiencies, which are probably the most crippling of the children's deficits. Following the pioneering work of Lovaas and his associates (see Lovaas, Koegel, Simmons, & Long, 1973), initial efforts have been designed to strengthen the child's imitation of parental nonverbal and verbal behavior. These investigators have argued that high probabilities of imitation are critical prerequisites to language development. Once the child reliably imitates a parent, it be-

comes possible for the parent to model and shape approximations to normal speech (see Guess, Sailor, Rutherford, & Baer, 1968, for a detailed discussion of this procedure).

In addition to disruptive behavior, another major obstacle to the above teaching process has to do with the usually restricted range of reinforcers for behavior-deficient children. In some cases the children appear to be responsive only to biological stimuli (e.g., food); some of those who are responsive to nonbiological stimuli (e.g., social approval) appear to satiate rather quickly in terms of the reinforcement value of these events (Nordquist & Wahler, 1973). Thus, it is not surprising to find that most family investigations of the teaching process have employed biological reinforcers (Risley & Wolf, 1966). Of course, because of satiation problems, the teaching program can only be implemented a few times daily.

Recently Nordquist (1973) developed a teaching technique that may overcome the above reinforcer problem. The Nordquist procedure first requires the parent to conduct a Premack (1963) analysis of reinforcing activities naturally available in the child's home. This is accomplished by having the parent record those child activities that occur most frequently during the day (e.g., object manipulations). Assuming that these activities are reinforcing to the child, the parent now attempts to track them during the day. Whenever the parent notices one of these episode occurrences (e.g., beginning to swing on a swing), she interrupts it, preferably at its beginning. A modeling cue is then presented (e.g., clap hands) and, if the child imitates, he is allowed to continue the interrupted activity.

The parent is also required to record episode occurrences, the nature of the required imitative act, and whether or not a successful imitative act occurred. Nordquist reports that parents can carry out all procedures in addition to regular caretaking duties with little difficulty. The advantages of this type of program over the more traditional structured-session approach are as follows: First, since many different reinforcers are utilized over a lengthy time period, satiation is less likely to occur. Secondly, the teaching process is not restricted to a few limited time periods. The parents' periodic use of the procedure over the entire day should not only permit a relatively large number of teaching experiences; the carry-over problem from teaching session to the rest of the child's day is avoided as well.

Teaching of self-help and social skills as well as language would presumably follow the child's acquisition of imitative behavior. While only language teaching has been extensively studied within the family, other skills would probably be taught in a similar fashion.

The success of parent-operated contingency management programs for behavior-deficient children has been limited. It seems clear that family interactions with these children can become much more enjoyable through such procedures (see Lovaas, Koegel, Simmons, & Long, 1973). Self-injurious behaviors and other aggressive behaviors have been significantly reduced in several family-based investigations (Risley, 1968). In addition, improvements have been obtained in self-help skills (Foxx & Azrin, 1973), social skills (Wetzel, Baker, Roney, & Martin, 1966), and language skills (Nordquist & Wahler, 1973). However, it has yet to be shown that these deficiencies (particularly language) can be completely remedied. By and large, the behavior repertoires of these children following family treatment have lagged well behind those of other children of comparable ages.

INTERVENTION STRATEGIES FOR AGE-INAPPROPRIATE BEHAVIORS

Contingency management consultants have reported clearest success in dealing with these age-inappropriate behaviors. In most cases, differential reinforcement procedures alone have shown to be extraordinarily effective in modifying the broad class of

dependency behaviors that constitute the problem. In part, the success of positive reinforcent procedures may be due to the high responsivity of dependent children to social reinforcers (Ferguson, 1961). Unlike many oppositional and behavior-deficient children, most dependent children seem to find a broad range of events reinforcing, particularly social events.

In line with the above impressions of high parent reinforcement value for dependent children, most parent programs have been aimed at teaching the parents to ignore age-inappropriate behaviors and to provide approval as well as other potential reinforcers for more mature behaviors. For example, parents have been trained to use such a technique in alleviating their children's fears of parent separation (Patterson, 1966; Ayllon, Smith, & Rogers, 1970). In this type of problem, it has also proven important to establish a similar contingency management program in the outside home setting avoided by the child (usually school). In these studies, the children were rewarded by parental praise and material reinforcers for independent home behaviors *and* approximations to school attendance. School personnel did likewise for the children's appropriate classroom behavior. While it is clear that differential reinforcement alone may successfully alter the home-based dependency actions (also see Wahler, Winkel, Paterson, & Morrison, 1965), some sort of physical force may prove necessary to ensure the child's reliable entry into the school setting (Ayllon, Smith, & Rogers, 1970).

Other forms of age-inappropriate actions such as bedwetting, soiling, and constipation have likewise shown improvement through differential parent reinforcement. While bedwetting has traditionally been treated by behaviorists through classical conditioning procedures (e.g., Mowrer & Mowrer, 1938), more recent family investigations have shown the effectiveness of parent reinforcement procedures as well (Nordquist, 1971; Kimmel & Kimmel, 1970). Likewise, soiling (Conger, 1970) and constipation (Lal & Lindsley, 1968) have been modified through similar home-based procedures. In this connection it should be noted that Foxx and Azrin (1973) have packaged an effective toilet training technique that is suitable for use by parents.

It is often true that age-inappropriate behavior problems include physical distress in addition to anxiety and depression. In those cases where separation distress is the principal presenting problem, it is not unusual to also note the child's somatic complaints such as stomach and head pains, vomiting, and even asthmatic attacks (see Marks, 1969). Usually, these complaints have no physical basis. Anecdotal accounts suggest that the somatic problems are alleviated when the separation problem is modified (Ayllon, Smith, & Rogers, 1970). Some family consultants have considered the more serious somatic problems as direct targets for contingency management and have presented data to show successful parent differential reinforcement control of asthmatic attacks (Neisworth & Moore, 1972) and psychogenic convulsions (Gardner, 1967).

Thus, most family treatment programs for age-inappropriate behaviors have achieved relatively rapid success in producing change within the family. In view of the favorable prognosis for these behavior problems in general (Robins, 1966), this success is probably not surprising.

INTERVENTION STRATEGIES FOR CROSS-GENDER BEHAVIOR

This section must be brief because of the very limited attention given to cross-gender behavior by behavioristic family consultants. Until a larger number of such investigations are reported, little can be said about effective intervention approaches within the family.

The pioneering work of Money and his associates (Money, Hampson, & Hampson, 1955; Money, 1963) points to the probability that intervention must begin early in

the child's life if success is to be obtained. These nonbehavioristic investigators discovered that their therapeutic efforts were unlikely to succeed if the cross-gendered boy had been reared in the feminine role for the first few years of life. Thus, whatever the intervention strategy, it seems evident that an effort must be initiated while the child is quite young.

Only recently have social learning theory consultants attempted to explore the use of contingency management procedures in family-based intervention for cross-gendered boys. Rekers and Lovaas (1971; 1972; 1973) have developed a set of procedures that appear potentially effective for preschool-aged boys. In a report of an exceptionally thorough intervention program for a 5-year-old boy, Rekers and Lovaas (1973) concentrated their consultative efforts on the boy's mother. Consistent with the previously reviewed developmental speculations, she appeared to be a central maintenance factor in the boy's feminine behaviors. The intervention tactics were similar to those employed for oppositional behaviors. While the initial procedures involved differential reinforcement only, the boy became increasingly coercive when the mother ignored his feminine behaviors. Therefore, the consultants deemed it necessary to employ a punishment contingency (variable use of point loss, time out, or spankings by father).

As expected in view of the broad-scale behavior changes required for cross-gendered children, the Rekers and Lovaas program continued far longer than most contingency management programs. These consultants found it necessary to keep the formal contingencies in operation for a 10-month period. At the end of that time, the boy's behavior was indistinguishable from that of most 6-year-old boys—certainly a dramatic therapeutic success.

To date, the Rekers and Lovaas work is the only behavioristic effort at family intervention for cross-gendered boys. Thus, it is premature to make any sort of generalizations about necessary intervention techniques.

The Maintenance of Behavior Change Within the Family

The preceding investigations have demonstrated the utility of behavioristic strategies in establishing behavior change conditions within the family. Most of these studies included experimental manipulations of the treatment conditions, thus permitting conclusions as to the role of these conditions in producing the therapeutic benefits. In the 15 years since Williams (1959) first showed the potential value of social learning principles as guidelines for family consultation, much progress has been evident. It is clear that a technology of family intervention is now available to the public under the supervision of a knowledgeable consultant. However, the field has yet to provide much evidence that the family can operate therapeutically without the consultant. Only a handful of follow-up studies are available to evaluate the stability of therapeutic changes over time, and most of these were rather casually conducted through telephone, letter, or brief visits by the consultant. The few studies that did obtain direct observational assessments of posttreatment outcomes yielded some interesting results. Two of these (Hawkins, Peterson, Schweid, & Bijou, 1966; Herbert & Baer, 1972) reported maintenance of the therapeutic gains but were limited to 24 days and 2 months, respectively. The most thorough follow-up assessment yet reported showed similar results but indicated that the parents were rather narrowly competent as behavior managers (Patterson, Cobb, & Ray, 1970). That is, although targeted behavior problems remained below baseline rates over 12 months following treatment, the parents showed little evidence of competence in dealing with other, less serious, problem behaviors produced by their children.

The Patterson group's work remains as the single piece of evidence that relatively brief periods of family consultation (average of 31.5 hours) can produce lasting therapeutic benefits. However, it must be noted that many of the parents required retraining experiences during followup, and 7 of the 27 families dropped out of the treatment program prior to followup. One implication of these findings is that the consultant's successful departure from the family may be difficult to arrange. In fact, several parent training programs that provided less intensive consultative coverage than did Patterson's program reported very discouraging results. For example, only 46% of the parents in Mira's (1970) training program successfully completed training. Worse yet, Rickert and Morrey (1970) were able to keep only 6 of 20 parents involved in their program. All in all, these findings indicate that the consultant must plan some sort of maintenance strategy to ensure long-term therapeutic success.

As mentioned earlier, contingency management procedures require a good deal of work for parents and are quite unlike most natural family interactions. However, with the exception of the teaching procedures for behavior-deficient children, most consultants think of the formal management as a temporary phase, designed to alter child behavior and to train the parents to more informally maintain the improved family interactions. Ideally, the parents should acquire a general competency in principles of contingency management, allowing them to analyze and solve any further child behavior problems within the family. At the very least they should become capable of dealing with those presenting problems for which they received their training. While there is little evidence pointing to success in attaining the former goal, the latter goal, as stated earlier, has been attained with the aid of periodic consultative contacts during followup (Patterson, Cobb, & Ray, 1970). Presently, the fading of consultative contact has been the sole means of supporting therapeutic changes after termination of the formal contingency program. We have yet to see other systematic ways of fading the program to more natural family interactions.

Another facet of the maintenance issue concerns parental motivation to support therapeutic changes in their children's behavior. The high attrition rates shown by Mira (1970) and Rickert and Morrey (1970) must seriously question the often-voiced assumption that improvements in child problem behavior will serve to maintain those parent reinforcement contingencies that produced the improvements. In line with Arnold's (1973) conclusions, desirable changes in child problem behavior do not appear sufficient to motivate continued parent use of the appropriate reinforcement contingencies. It may well be that many families slip back into the trap situations that were likely precursors to the child's deviant behavior.

In all likelihood, the maintenance problem will be approached in future work through two strategies: First, since it seems evident that some families need the support of other social systems to maintain therapeutic gains, a broader approach to intervention may be necessary. As Patterson, Cobb, and Ray (1970) have noted, some families may require consultative contact indefinitely. Of course, such contact could conceivably be arranged through systems that are part of the usual family community (e.g., school system, church). In any case, if this course of action is pursued, the consultant will need to think in terms of social systems much larger than the family. Subsystems of a community, such as the church, already influence the behavior of family members. It might prove possible to recruit volunteers from these groups who could then be trained in principles of contingency management. In fact, such a volunteer program was established in a small Appalachian community by the author and a colleague (Wahler & Erickson, 1969).

A second support strategy would focus on a more thorough examination of the family than we have yet seen in the research literature. As noted in the introductory section of this chapter, a social learning theory conception of the family entails more than simple dyadic interchanges between parent and child. Triadic and even quadradic interchanges involving the problem child are possible, given the presence of at least two parents and a sibling. It may well be that the maintenance of therapeutic interactions between parent and child will entail establishing supporting contingencies between parents and between parents and siblings. However, as Haley (1971) has pointed out, behavioristic work with families to date has been limited to dyadic interactions. Perhaps the parent-parent interchange studies presented by Patterson, Weiss, and Hops in this book will mark a beginning in this direction.

In all probability, future behavioristic work with families will employ both of the preceding strategies. A stable shift in family interactions with a problem child may require far-reaching changes within and beyond the family.

References

ARNOLD, J. E. A technology of parent training. Unpublished manuscript, University of California, Santa Barbara, June 1973.

AYLLON, T., SMITH, D., & ROGERS, M. Behavioral management of school phobia. *Journal of Behavior Therapy and Experimental Psychiatry,* 1970, **1**, 125–138.

BANDURA, A., & HUSTON, ALETHA C. Identification as a process of incidental learning. *Journal of Abnormal Social Psychology,* 1961, **6**, 311–318.

BANDURA, A., ROSS, D., & ROSS, S. A. Imitation of film-mediated aggressive models. *Journal of Abnormal Social Psychology,* 1963, **66**, 3–11. (a)

BANDURA, A., & WALTERS, R. H. *Social learning and personality development.* New York: Holt, Rinehart & Winston, 1963.

BARKER, R. G. Explorations in ecological psychology. *American Psychologist,* 1965, **20,** 1–14.

BATESON, G., JACKSON, D. D., HALEY, J., & WEAKLAND, J. Toward a theory of schizophrenia. *Behavioral Science,* 1956, **1,** 251–264.

BECKER, W. *Parents are teachers: A child management program.* Champaign, Ill.: Research Press, 1970.

BECKER, W. C., & KRUG, R. S. The parent attitude research instrument—A research review. *Child Development,* 1965, **36,** 329–365.

BERNAL, M. Behavioral feedback in the modification of brat behaviors. *Journal of Nervous and Mental Disease,* 196, **148,** 375–385.

BIJOU, S. W. Theory and research in mental (developmental) retardation. *Psychological Record,* 1963, **13,** 95–110.

BIJOU, S. W., & BAER, D. M. *Child Development. Vol. 1. A systematic and empirical theory.* New York: Appleton-Century-Crofts, 1961.

BIJOU, S. W., PETERSON, R. F., & AULT, M. H. A method to integrate descriptive and experimental field studies at the level of data and empirical concepts. *Journal of Applied Behavior Analysis,* 1968, **1,** 175–191.

BIRNBRAUER, J. S., WOLF, M. M., KIDDER, J. O., & TAGUE, C. E. Classroom behavior of retarded pupils with token reinforcement. *Journal of Experimental Child Psychology,* 1965, **2,** 210–235.

BRAGINSKY, D. D., & BRAGINSKY, B. M. *Hansels and Gretels: studies of children in institutions for the mentally retarded.* New York: Holt, Rinehart, & Winston, 1971.

CONGER, J. The treatment of encopresis by the management of social consequences. *Behavior Therapy,* 1970, **1,** 386–390.

DENNIS, W., & NAJARIAN, P. Infant development under environmental handicap. *Psychological Monographs,* 1957, **71** (7).

EISENBERG, L. The autistic child in adolescence. *American Journal of Psychiatry,* 1956, **112,** 607–612.

ETZEL, B. D., & GEWIRTZ, J. L. Experimental modification of caretaker maintained highrate operant crying in a 6- and a 20-week-old infant (Infans tyrannotearus): Extinction of crying with reinforcement of eye contact and smiling. *Journal of Experimental Child Psychology,* 1967, **5,** 303–317.

FERGUSON, P. E. The influence of isolation, anxiety, and dependency on reinforcer effectiveness. Unpublished master's thesis, University of Toronto, 1961.

FERSTER, C. B. Positive reinforcement and behavioral developments of autistic children. *Child Development,* 1961, **32,** 437–456.

FOXX, R. M., & AZRIN, N. H. *Toilet training the retarded: A rapid program for day and nighttime independent toileting.* Champaign, Ill.: Research Press, 1973.

FRIEDMAN, P. H. Personalistic family and marital therapy. In A. Lazarus (Ed.), *Clinical behavior therapy.* New York: Science House, 1971, in press.

GARDNER, J. Behavior therapy treatment approach to a psychogenic seizure case. *Journal of Consulting Psychology,* 1967, **31,** 209–212.

GESELL, A., & AMATRUDA, C. *Developmental diagnosis.* New York: Holber, 1941.

GEWIRTZ, J. L. Attachment, dependence, and a distinction in terms of stimulus control. In J. L. Gewirtz (Ed.), *Attachment and dependency.* Washington, D.C.: V-H Winston and Sons, 1972.

GEWIRTZ, J. L. Three determinants of attention-seeking in young children. *Monographs of the Society for Research in Child Development,* 1954, **19** (2, Whole No. 59).

GEWIRTZ, J. L. A learning analysis of the effects of normal stimulation, privation and deprivation on the acquisition of social motivation and attachment. In B. M. Foss (Ed.), *Determinants of infant behavior.* New York: Wiley, 1961, pp. 213–303.

GIFFIN, M. E., JOHNSON, A. M., & LITIN, E. M. Antisocial acting out: 2. Specific factors determining antisocial acting out. *American Journal of Orthopsychiatry,* 1954, **24,** 668–684.

GOLDIAMOND, I. Justified and unjustified alarm over behavioral control. In O. H. Milton & R. G. Wahler (Eds.), *Behavior disorders: Perspectives and trends.* Philadelphia: Lippincott, 1969, pp. 235–240.

GREEN, R. Childhood cross-gender identification. In R. Green and J. Money (Eds.), *Transsexualism and sex reassignment.* Baltimore: Johns Hopkins Press, 1969, pp. 23–36.

GREEN, R., & MONEY, J. *Transsexualism and sex reassignment.* Baltimore: John Hopkins Press, 1969.

GUESS, D., SAILOR, W., RUTHERFORD, G., & BAER, D. M. An experimental analysis of linguistic development: The productive use of the plural morpheme. *Journal of Applied Behavior Analysis*, 1968, **1**, 225–235.

HALEY, J. *Changing families: A family therapy reader.* New York: Grune & Stratton, 1971, pp. 272–284.

HERBERT, E., & BAER, D. Training parents as behavior modifiers: Self recording of contingent attention. *Journal of Applied Behavior Analysis*, 1972, **5**, 139–149.

HERBERT, E., PINKSTON, E., HAYDEN, M., SAJWAJ, T., PINKSTON, S., CORDUA, G., & JACKSON, C. Adverse effects of differential parental attention. *Journal of Applied Behavior Analysis*, 1973, **6**, 15–30.

HETHERINGTON, E. M. A developmental study of the effects of sex of the dominant parent on sex-role preference, identification, and imitation in children. *Journal of Personality and Social Psychology*, 1965, **2**, 188–194.

HETHERINGTON, E. M., & FRANKIE, G. Effect of parental dominance, warmth, and conflict on imitation in children. *Journal of Personality and Social Psychology*, 1967, **6**, 119–125.

JOHNSON, J. Using parents as contingency managers. *Psychological Reports*, 1971, **29**, 703–710.

KAGEN, J., & MOSS, H. *Birth to maturity.* New York: Wiley, 1962.

KOCH, H. L. A study of some factors conditioning the social distance between sexes. *Journal of Social Psychology*, 1944, **20**, 79–107.

KUBANY, E. S., & SLOGGETT, B. B. A coddling procedure for teachers. *Journal of Applied Behavior Analysis*, 1973, **6**, 339–344.

KUMMEL, H. D., & KUMMEL, E. An instrumental conditioning method for the treatment of enuresis. *Journal of Behavior Therapy and Experimental Psychiatry*, 1970, **1**, 121–123.

LAL, H., & LINDSLEY, O. Therapy of chronic constipation in a young child by rearranging social contingencies. *Behaviour Research and Therapy*, 1968, **6**, 484–485.

LEITENBERG, H. Is time-out from positive reinforcement an aversive event? A review of the experimental evidence. *Psychological Bulletin*, 1965, **64**, 428–441.

LINDSLEY, O. R. An experiment with parents handling behavior at home. *Johnstone Bulletin*, 1966, **9**, 27–36.

LITIN, E. M., GIFFIN, M. E., & JOHNSON, A. M. Parental influences in unusual sexual behavior in children. *Psychoanalysis Quarterly*, 1956, **25**, 37–55.

LOVAAS, O. I., KOEGEL, R., SIMMONS, J. Q., & LONG, J. S. Some generalization and follow-up measures on autistic children in behavior therapy. *Journal of Applied Behavior Analysis*, 1973, **6**, 131–164.

LOVAAS, O. I., SCHAEFFER, B., & SIMMONS, J. Building social behavior in autistic children by use of electric shock. *Journal of Experimental Research in Personality*, 1965, **1**, 99–109.

LOVITT, T. C., & CURTIS, K. A. Academic response rate as a function of teacher and self-imposed contingencies. *Journal of Applied Behavior Analysis*, 1969, **2**, 49–53.

MARKS, I. M. *Fears and phobias.* New York: Academic Press, 1969.

MEAD, M. A cultural anthropologist's approach to maternal deprivation. In *Deprivation of maternal care.* Public Health Paper No. 14. Geneva: World Health Organization, 1962, pp. 45–62.

MIRA, M. Results of a behavior modification training program for parents and teachers. *Behaviour Research and Therapy*, 1970, **8**, 309–311.

MISCHEL, W. *Personality and assessment.* New York: Wiley, 1968.

MISCHEL, W. Sex-typing and socialization. In Paul H. Mussen (Ed.), *Carmichael's manual of child psychology.* Vol. 2. (3rd ed.) New York: Wiley, 1970.

MONEY, J. Cytogenic and psychosexual incongruities with a note on space-form blindness. *American Journal of Psychiatry*, 1963, **119**, 820–827.

MONEY, J., HAMPSON, J. G., & HAMPSON, J. L. An examination of some basic sexual concepts: Evidence of human hermaphroditism. *Bulletin of the Johns Hopkins Hospital*, 1955, **97**, 301–319.

MORRIS, H. H. Aggressive behavior disorders in children: A follow-up study. *American Journal of Psychiatry*, 1956, **112**, 991–997.

MOWRER, O., & MOWRER, W. Enuresis: A method for its study and treatment. *American Journal of Orthopsychiatry*, 1938, **8**, 436–459.

NEISWORTH, J. T., & MOORE, F. Operant treatment of asthmatic responding with the parent as therapist. *Behavior Therapy*, 1972, **3**, 95–99.

NORDQUIST, V. M. The modification of a child's

enuresis: Some response-response relationships. *Journal of Applied Behavior Analysis*, 1971, **4**, 231–247.

NORDQUIST, V. M. Naturalistic treatment of childhood autism. Final report, NIMH research grant MH 21100–01, 1973.

NORDQUIST, V. M., & WAHLER, R. G. Naturalistic treatment of an autistic child. *Journal of Applied Behavior Analysis*, 1973, **6**, 79–88.

PATTERSON, G. R. An empirical approach to the classification of disturbed children. *Journal of Clinical Psychology*, 1964, **20**, 326–337.

PATTERSON, G. A learning theory approach to the treatment of the school phobic child. In L. P. Ullmann and L. Krasner (Eds.), *Case studies in behavior modifications*. New York: Holt, Rinehart & Winston, 1966, pp. 278–285.

PATTERSON, G. R. Behavioral intervention procedures in the classroom and in the home. In A. E. Bergin & S. L. Garfield (Eds.), *Handbook of psychotherapy and behavior change*. New York: Wiley, 1969, pp. 751–775.

PATTERSON, G. *Families: Applications of social learning to family life*. Champaign, Ill.: Research Press, 1971.

PATTERSON, G. R., COBB, J. A., & RAY, R. S. A social engineering technology for retraining aggressive boys. In H. Adams & L. Unikel (Eds.), *Georgia symposium in experimental clinical psychology*. Vol. 11. Oxford: Pergamon, 1970.

PATTERSON, G. R., & GULLION, M. E. *Living with children*. Champaign, Ill.: Research Press, 1968.

PATTERSON, G., & GULLION, N. *Living with children: New models for parents and teachers*. Champaign, Ill.: Research Press, 1968.

PATTERSON, G., RAY, R., & SHAW, D. Direct intervention in families of deviant children. *Oregon Research Institute Bulletin* (Rev.), 1969. (a)

PATTERSON, G. R., & REID, J. B. Reciprocity and coercion: Two facets of social systems. In C. Neuringer and J. Michael (Eds.), *Behavior modification in clinical psychology*. New York: Appleton-Century-Crofts, 1970.

PAULY, I. Adult manifestations of male transsexualism. In R. Green and J. Money (Eds.) *Transsexualism and sex reassignment*. Baltimore: Johns Hopkins Press, 1969, pp. 37–58.

PREMACK, D. Prediction of the comparative reinforcement values of running and drinking. *Science*, 1963, **139**, 1062–1063.

REID, J. B., & HENDRICKS, A. F. C. J. A preliminary analysis of the effectiveness of direct home intervention for treatment of pre-delinquent boys who steal. *ORI Research Monograph*, 12 (8).

REKERS, G. A. *Pathological sex-role development in boys: Behavioral treatment and assessment*. Ann Arbor: University Microfilms, 1972.

REKERS, G. A., & LOVAAS, O. I. Experimental analysis of cross-sex behavior in male children. *Research relating to children: ERIC Clearinghouse on early childhood education* (Bulletin 28), 1971, 68. (abstract)

REKERS, G. A., & LOVAAS, O. I. Behavioral treatment and assessment of childhood cross-gender problems. Paper presented at the 53rd annual meeting of the Western Psychological Association, Anaheim, Calif., April 13, 1973.

RICKERT, D. C., & MORREY, R. S. Parent training in precise behavior management with mentally retarded children. Final report, U.S. Office of Education, Project No. 9-8-016, January 1972.

RISLEY, T. R. The effects and side effects of punishing the autistic behaviors of a deviant child. *Journal of Applied Behavior Analysis*, 1968, **1**, 21–34.

RISLEY, T., & WOLF, M. M. Experimental manipulation of autistic behaviors and generalization into the home. In R. Ulrich, T. Stachnik, & J. Mabry (Eds.), *Control of human behavior*. Glenview, Ill.: Scott, Foresman & Co., 1966, pp. 193–198.

ROACH, J. L. Some social-psychological characteristics of child guidance clinic caseloads. *Journal of Consulting Psychology*, 1958, **22**, 183–186.

ROBINS, L. N. *Deviant children grown up: A sociological and psychiatric study of sociopathic personality*. Baltimore: Williams & Wilkins, 1966.

SAJWAJ, T., TWARDOSZ, S., & BURKE, M. Side effects of extinction procedures in a remedial preschool. *Journal of Applied Behavior Analysis*, 1972, **5**, 163–175.

SCHAFFER, J. R, & EMERSON, P E. The development of social attachments in infancy. *Monographs of the Society for Research in Child Development*, 1964, 29 (2).

SKEELS, H. M. Adult status of children with contrasting early life experience. *Monographs of the Society for Research in Child Development*, 1966, 31 (3).

SPITZ, R. A., & WOLF, K. Anaclitic depression. *Psychoanalytic study of the Child,* 1946, **2,** 313–342.

STOLLER, R. J. Psychotherapy of extremely feminine boys. *International Journal of Psychiatry,* 1970, **9,** 278–282.

THARP, R. G., & WETZEL, R. J. *Behavior modification in the natural environment.* New York: Academic Press, 1969.

WAGNER, L., & ORA, J. Parental control of the very young severely oppositional child. Paper presented at the meeting of the Southeastern Psychological Association, Louisville, Kentucky, 1970.

WAHLER, R. G. Oppositional children: A quest for parental reinforcement control. *Journal of Applied Behavior Analysis,* 1969, **2,** 159–170. (a)

WAHLER, R. G. Setting generality: Some specific and general effects of child behavior therapy. *Journal of Applied Behavior Analysis,* 1969, **2,** 239–246. (b)

WAHLER, R. G., & CORMIER, W. H. The ecological interview: A first step in outpatient child behavior therapy. *Journal of Behavior Therapy and Experimental Psychiatry,* 1970, **1,** 293–303.

WAHLER, R. G., & ERICKSON, M. Child behavior therapy: A community program in Appalachia. *Behaviour Research and Therapy,* 1969, **7,** 71–78.

WAHLER, R. G., WINKEL, G. H., PETERSON, R. F., & MORRISON, D. C. Mothers as behavior therapists for their own children. *Behaviour Research and Therapy,* 1965, **3,** 113–124.

WALTERS, J., PEARCE, D., & DAHMS, L. Affectional and aggressive behavior of preschool children. *Child Development,* 1957, **28,** 15–26.

WETZEL, R., BAKER, J., RONEY, M., & MARTIN, M. Outpatient treatment of autistic behavior. *Behavior Research Therapy,* 1966, 4, 169–177.

WILLIAMS, C. The elimination of tantrum behavior by extinction procedures. *Journal of Abnormal Social Psychology,* 1959, **59,** 269.

WOLF, M., RISLEY, T., & MEES, H. Application of operant conditioning procedures to the behavior problems of an autistic child. *Behavioral Research Therapy,* 1964, **1,** 305–312.

ZEILBERGER, J., SAMPEN, S. E., & SLOANE, H. N. Jr. Modification of a child's problem behaviors in the home with the mother as therapist. *Journal of Applied Behavior Analysis,* 1968, **1,** 47–58.

General

Behavior Modification in the General - Hospital Psychiatric Unit

W. STEWART AGRAS

15

The general hospital has not been a favored site for the application of behavior modification techniques, although one ward-wide program (Hersen, Eisler, Smith, & Agras, 1972) and a number of applications in individual cases (Smith & Carlin, 1972; Alford, Blanchard, & Buckley, 1972) have been described. Why this lack compared with the explosive application in schools, halfway houses, mental hospitals, prisons, and even the U.S. Army (Ayllon & Roberts, 1972)? To answer this question, we need to examine the administrative structure of the general-hospital unit and determine how it differs from other settings.

The Unit—Structure and Function

The general-hospital psychiatric unit is a recent development; only 5% of units open in 1965 existed before 1923, and only 20% had been in operation before the end of World War II (Glasscoate & Kanno, 1965). Now these facilities admit more patients each year than mental hospitals.

ADMINISTRATION

The psychiatric ward is administered in the same way as other parts of the general hospital. A board, often composed of prominent citizens, is responsible for the hospital's functioning, and day-to-day management is delegated to a hospital administrator, who is responsible for the physical plant and all patient-support services except medical care. The physician who attends patients belongs to the hospital medical staff by which he is governed. Large hospitals are departmentalized, with psychiatry being one such department; rules, regulations, and procedures regarding therapy are drawn up by the psychiatrists. The average psychiatric attending staff numbers 10 (Glasscoate & Kanno, 1965), and each physician is responsible for the care of his own patients within the general limits described above. In a few general hospitals (usually teaching units), there is a full-time psychiatric staff and a full-time psychiatrist administratively in charge of the unit. The implication of this structure is that patient care is usually programmed by individual physicians, although occasional programs are organized by a full-time psychiatric administrator.

MILIEU

The unit is most frequently a floor or part of a floor of the general hospital, with rooms arranged like those of other medical floors, with private or semiprivate rooms, long corridors, and a nurses' station. The median size is 27 beds, usually about 8% of the hospital's total (Glasscoate & Kanno, 1965). Most units go beyond the medical floors; almost all (97%) have a day room, and just over half have occupational therapy facilities; but only a third have an exercise area, and, as in many mental hospitals, there isn't much to do (Rosenhan, 1973). Thus the opportunity for patients to emit adaptive behavior, particularly work skills, is limited.

TREATMENT

Patients demonstrating the entire range of psychopathological conditions are admitted to the general hospital (see Table 15-1). Of

TABLE 15-1   Diagnoses for 161 consecutive admissions to a general-hospital psychiatric unit

Diagnosis	Number	%
Organic brain syndrome	20	12
Schizophrenia	13	
Psychotic depression	8 > Psychosis 14	
Mania	3	
Anxiety reaction	9	
Phobic reaction	3	
Conversion reaction	3 > Neurosis 24	
Obsessive-compulsive reaction	5	
Depressive reaction	20	
Personality disorder	45	27
Situational disorder	32	23

SOURCE: University of Mississippi Medical Center, 1973.

161 consecutive admissions to a teaching hospital, 12% had an organic cause for their disturbed behavior and were diagnosed as organic brain syndrome, 14% were diagnosed as psychotic, while the remainder fell into fairly equal proportions of neurosis, personality disorder, and situational reactions. The average patient stay is 20 days, with a range nationally from 3 to 117 days. In the usual general-hospital unit, some 10% of patients are committed to state hospitals for further treatment (Glasscoate & Kanno, 1965).

A variety of treatment methods are commonly used. Most units (92%) employ both electroshock and psychopharmacologic agents and, in addition, use both individual and group psychotherapy, and often milieu therapy. Thus there is a brisk flow of patients through the average general-hospital unit, and a variety of treatments are applied to the patients.

STAFF

As noted above, 10 psychiatrists attend patients on the average psychiatric unit. In addition, about 30% of all units have psychiatric residents, 40% have social workers, but only 7% have a psychologist. Since there is one nurse for each two to seven beds and, in addition, a full complement of nursing assistants, it is clear that the general-hospital unit is well staffed (Glasscoate & Kanno, 1965).

Behavior Modification: Why the Slow Application?

Several features of the general-hospital unit appear responsible for the sparse application of behavior modification techniques. First, unlike, in a state hospital or similar institution, no one person is in a position to direct a program for all patients in a given unit. In the general hospital, the patient is treated by one of the many psychiatrists on the staff, and even a psychiatric administrator has relatively little control over treatment. It is even less likely that a psychologist—and psychologists have been the main innovators in institutions—can direct a program, since the general hospital operates on traditional medical lines, and there are relatively few psychologists in general hospitals.

Second, patients are not usually committed to the general hospital; only 1% of general hospitals accept patients solely by commitment, and only 38% accept committed patients under any circumstances (Glasscoate & Kanno, 1965). Thus patients may leave at any time and usually have access to the facilities of the general hospital and even the community. Again, this is the opposite of the institution. There, patients live full-time within the institution, and control over reinforcers, an essential element of most programs, is almost total.

Third, the excellent staffing patterns and provision of care on a private basis within the general hospital are in sharp contrast to the situation in mental hospitals or other institutions. The great need for more effective treatment in the state hospital has led to the adoption of techniques such as the token economy because care can be improved without adding large numbers of highly paid professionals to the staff. Thus the demand for change within a general-hospital psychiatric unit is less. Moreover, there are not large numbers of long-stay patients, who have so far been the main target population for behavior modification.

Finally, the general hospital provides a more restricted milieu than does a state hospital. No work is available for patients, and even the social situations are relatively restricted. Thus there is less opportunity to shape adaptive skills, than in an institution with its many work areas. And yet the general-hospital psychiatric unit has traditionally been considered a place where persons can learn something helpful about problem interpersonal behavior, usually conceptualized under the rather vague term "milieu therapy." Thus we will first review

ward-wide applications of behavior modification and then consider applications to the individual.

Ward-wide Application of Behavior Modification

MILIEU THERAPY

One of the most popular traditional approaches to behavior change in the general hospital has been milieu therapy. This technique is often vaguely described, and there have even been suggestions that it lacks a technology (Edelson, 1964). However, the aims and methods of a leading exponent of the technique are of interest since they fit in well with the stated aims of behavior modification.

Abroms (1969) describes two main aims of milieu therapy: setting limits and teaching social skills. By setting limits he means reducing the frequency of, or eliminating, behaviors such as destructiveness, delusional and other bizarre behaviors, rule-breaking behavior, and social withdrawal (including depression). Reduction of such behavior is also a goal of behavior modification (Agras, 1972). Among social skills Abroms (1969) singles out teaching spatial and temporal orientation to the disoriented patient, teaching assertive behavior, occupational skills such as searching for a job, interviewing skills, being on time, and recreational skills. These aims fit in well with the most frequently listed problem behaviors of patients admitted to a general-hospital psychiatric unit, as noted in Table 15-2 (see section on presenting problems).

To achieve these aims, milieu therapy relies on a decision-making process involving both patients and staff and upon feedback of information to patients and staff through frequent meetings. While this procedure would seem insufficient to produce behavior change in the light of findings concerning reinforcement and extinction of deviant behavior, it is a step in the right

TABLE 15–2   The 20 most frequent problem behaviors identified
in 40 consecutive admissions to a general-hospital unit

Rank	Problem	% of total number
1	Depression	10
2	Somatic complaints	10
3	Marital problems	6
4	Family problems	6
5	Work problems	5
6	Suicide attempt	5
7	Alcoholism	4
8	Socially inappropriate behavior	4
9	Social withdrawal	4
10	Hallucination	3
11	Sleep disturbance	3
12	Delusional statements	2
13	Memory disturbance	2
14	Obesity	2
15	Rapid speech	1
16	Overactivity	1
17	Mutism	1
18	Agitation	1
19	Impotence	1
20	Combative behavior	1

direction and is founded on the notion that deviant behavior is learned and can be modified within a structured social context.

TOKEN ECONOMY

Only one token economy on an open ward in a general hospital has been reported (Hersen, Eisler, Smith, & Agras, 1972). The unit was part of a Veterans Administration hospital where the relationship between patient and staff differs from that of the usual private hospital, thus facilitating establishment of the program, which involved young patients, many of whom were hospitalized for the first time, with a relatively short stay ($x = 29.7$ days).

The basic aim of the program was to increase the patients' general activity level and to simulate normal working and, to a lesser extent, social behavior. The four main target behaviors selected were: work, occupational therapy, responsibility, and personal hygiene. Within each category, behaviors were precisely defined and points

assigned to each behavior. For example, being on time to take medication was part of the responsibility item, and one point was given each time that behavior occurred. Work behavior took place within actual hospital departments, giving patients the opportunity to be supervised by the kinds of employers they would have to face when discharged.

A unique aspect of the program was the banking hour each morning, when points earned or lost the previous day were tabulated and patients were given cards for recording that day's points, which would be tabulated the next day and signed by a staff member (signatures were randomly checked for authenticity).

Points earned were exchangeable for a variety of privileges, such as weekend passes, phone calls, and access to television or the day room during working hours. The relative cost of each privilege was determined by a prestudy questionnaire wherein patients ranked all possible privileges. An orange card signed by a supervisor indicated privileges and their time limit. Fines were imposed for certain behaviors and were entered by the staff on a card that was sent to the banking office.

EFFICACY

The effects of the program were studied systematically over a 6-month period in four experimental phases. During baseline condition, patients were given points contingent upon performance, but the points were not exchangeable; in the next phase, points were exchangeable for privileges at various rates of exchange; after this there was a return to baseline conditions; the last phase was a return to reinforcement conditions.

The results of these maneuvers are shown in Figure 15-1. During the baseline period, when the entire token system was in effect except that points were not exchangeable for anything, a low rate of the target behaviors (as measured by number of points earned) occurred. Introduction of the token exchange for privileges led to doubled output, while removal of this arrangement caused a return to low output; and reintroduction produced high output again. It is interesting that composition of the patient group changed throughout the experiment as patients were admitted and discharged.

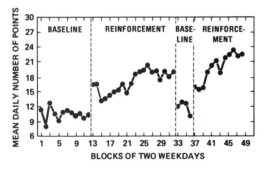

FIGURE 15-1   Performance (as measured by number of points earned) of patients within a token economy on a general-hospital ward. During baseline conditions, nonexchangeable tokens were given contingent upon performance (Hersen, Eisler, Smith, & Agras, 1972).

Immediately upon admission, new patients adapted to the work output of the group as a whole: low under baseline conditions, high under reinforcement conditions. These data clearly indicate that the activity levels of acutely hospitalized patients can be controlled by applying environmental contingencies to target behaviors.

Moreover, the program had a number of beneficial side effects. Requiring patients to plan each day's activity increased their ability to foresee and forestall difficulties that would occur after discharge. This skill is of obvious importance in patient management.

Problems in the Token Economy

In the program just described, each staff member was carefully trained in applying reinforcement, extinction, and punishment procedures, and also in data collection and management. This training, completed before the economy went into operation, took one month and helped to avoid the kind of problems reported by Smith and Carlin (1972), whose nursing staff and aides "vociferously complained that the patient was really psychotic and should not be punished for her crazy behavior." The "punishment" referred to was a combination of ignoring tantrums, followed by time out in the patient's room for persistent tantrums. Moreover, other staff members vented their "negative feelings toward the program" by substituting their own techniques, such as tying the patient down for several hours at a time or giving extra medication—most undesirable outcomes demonstrating a lack of understanding of the principles of behavior modification.

Hersen et al. (1972) forestalled another potential problem, patient dissatisfaction with the program, by giving each patient a handbook that detailed the rules of the program. In addition, regular patient-staff meetings dealt with problem areas and patient grievances.

Toward a Behavioral Milieu

The motivational system just described and milieu therapy programs have certain similarities. These include giving precise feedback about behavior by means of tokens and fines or by comments in group meetings, carefully defining and explaining the rules of the unit, holding patient-staff meetings to deal with mutual problems, and assigning patients responsibility for some aspects of the program (e.g., banking and individual scheduling).

Milieu programs have been widely accepted in the general hospital, perhaps because the values of such programs coincide with those of both patients and staff. Just as the token economy in a general hospital takes on certain features of milieu programs, so an extension of milieu therapy using the principles and procedures of behavior modification seems logical.

One example of such an extension has appeared in the literature (Kass, Silvers, & Abroms, 1972). The target population was five young women between 17 and 25 years old, diagnosed as hysterical personalities, who were treated as a subgroup within an ongoing general-hospital milieu therapy program. Four of the five patients had been admitted by way of the emergency room following attempted suicide. The psychiatric unit was fairly typical of such wards, admitting all types of patients, with an average stay of 20 days.

Hysteria was defined as a set of maladaptive behaviors. These included difficulty in meeting responsibilities, more accurately defined as inadequate rule following; inappropriate displays of anger and tantrums; suicidal threats; somatic complaints; and unassertive behavior (e.g., opportunities to speak or act are not taken or not effectively carried out). Different patients displayed different combinations of these behaviors, and problems unique to each patient were also defined as concretely and precisely as possible.

The basic program revolved around a required schedule of activities from 7:00 A.M. to 11:00 P.M.: for example, 4:00 P.M.—socializing with community in day room, 4:30 P.M.—group schedule meeting (make up schedule for next day), 5:30 P.M.—dinner, and so on. Not adhering to the schedule resulted in loss of certain privileges that were individually defined. Thus smokers could not smoke, hearty eaters were denied second helpings or snacks, and the fastidious groomer, which included all the hysterical patients, would be deprived of makeup and other toiletries.

Behaviors such as physical complaints or tantrums were dealt with by negative social feedback from the patient group, while adaptive behavior resulted in positive feedback. Assertive training, which included role-playing, was also used to develop and practice more adequate interpersonal behavior. While the authors present no data to demonstrate the efficacy of the particular contingencies used, they do note that four out of the five patients had a reasonably good outcome.

Demonstrations such as this and the motivational system described earlier suggest that the environment of the general-hospital psychiatric unit can be arranged to optimize social learning. Moreover, individual programs to deal with specific problems can be developed within such environments.

Individual Applications of Behavior Modification

A necessary precursor to the modification of behavior is precise definition and measurement of the problem to be changed. Unfortunately, the psychiatric approach in the general hospital is based upon the traditional approach to physical problems, in which patients' complaints are sorted into symptoms that, combined with findings from physical examination and the laboratory, are refined into disease patterns and diagnoses. Broad psychiatric diagnoses such as schizophrenia are not measurable, nor are constructs such as intrapsychic conflict or defenses; therefore, the patient's progress is usually documented in descriptive notes in the medical chart without precise quantification. As long as psychiatric charts are kept in this way, behavior modification will be difficult to introduce.

Within the last few years, however, a new development has occurred in medical record keeping relevant to behavior modification. This approach (Weed, 1968; Hurst & Walker, 1972) dissects medical illness into concrete objective problems and organizes the record such that the fate of each problem is tracked until it is resolved.

The Problem-oriented Record

The essence of the problem-oriented approach is that following collection of an identified data base (which includes history, physical examination, and pertinent laboratory tests), the patient's complaints, symptoms, and signs are translated into concrete, measurable problems. The course of each problem is then tracked, and changes due to interventions or complications are documented. One of the best ways to track behavior change, of course, is by a graph.

As an example of problem definition we may consider the case of a black girl, aged 15 years, who was referred to a psychiatric unit by her physician. For 2 months she had been "having hallucinations" in which she reported seeing "people killing each other." One scene was of someone killing a baby with a knife. She also awakened early at night, screaming and saying that she had seen violent happenings. Two days before admission she thought she "heard voices talking" telling her "to kill someone." Just before hospitalization she grabbed a large knife, started to shout and scream, and had to be held down by her mother.

Briefly, it was found that the girl was living at home under crowded conditions with her mother and several younger siblings, including a baby. Her mother worked at night, and the patient was then responsible for managing the house, a job she was "tired of." Her older sister, who had left home a few months earlier, had "seen things at night," which had been cured when she began to sleep with the patient. Two months before admission, the patient's boyfriend threatened to kill her, and just before the "hallucinations" began she learned that a good friend had been killed by her husband.

On examination, apart from being somewhat uncooperative, the patient showed no objective evidence of psychopathology. However, she wakened screaming the first night on the unit.

A usual diagnostic workup would probably note the various complaints and diagnose adolescent situational reaction or, perhaps, hysterical neurosis, dissociative type, with night terrors. But for the problem-oriented record, this is not enough. In this case the problem list read:

1. Nightmares—waking up early in the evening screaming
2. Bizarre verbal statements—seeing scenes of violence, hearing voices
3. Home problems, too heavy responsibilities when mother is working

The first problem was measured by charting the frequency of nightmares as defined, the second by recording every such bizarre statement made to the nursing staff. The third, of course, is not measurable within the confines of the hospital. However, it appeared that the third problem might be the most critical and that the first two problems effectively allowed the patient to avoid looking after the children, particularly the baby, since she implied to the family that she might kill it.

The course of the first two problems can be seen in Figure 15-2. The morning of the third hospital day the patient was told that she would be able to leave the floor to visit

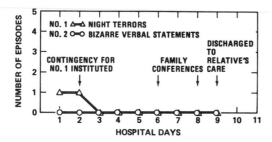

FIGURE 15-2   Excerpt from patient's chart documenting the course of two problem behaviors during hospitalization.

the hospital gift shop, providing that she made no complaints of bad dreams the evening before. Thereupon nightmares dropped to zero, i.e., the patient no longer woke up screaming and did not complain of frightening dreams. No more bizarre statements were made to the nursing staff. A family conference was held concerning the third problem, and it was decided that the patient should go to live with an aunt in a nearby town. A baby-sitter was found to look after the younger children while their mother was working. Note that very little charting of the patient's progress beyond the graph was required.

It has been found that the presenting situation of most psychiatric patients can be dissected into discrete problems (Hayes-Roth, Longabaugh, & Ryback, 1972), although there will be some disagreement among different observers. In this way, a more precise description of behavior emerges than when only global diagnoses are considered.

Presenting Problems

Table 15-2 presents a detailed analysis of the problems of 40 consecutive admissions to the same general-hospital unit from which the diagnoses listed in Table 15-1 were obtained. Each patient was considered in detail by a multidisciplinary group; the final list of problems in each case represents the consensus achieved by the time the patient was discharged.

While a diversity of problem behaviors exists (35 categories in all), there are some interesting commonalities. The most frequent problems were (1) depression, defined as verbal complaints of sadness, depression, or despair, accompanied by certain behavioral manifestations (e.g., absence of laughter), and (2) somatic complaints, defined as any repeated complaint about body function. Although these behaviors are much in evidence in the hospital, the next set of problem behaviors, marital, family, and work problems, are not exhibited in the psychiatric unit. Moreover, the next two behaviors (suicide attempts and alcohol consumption) are also rarely seen in the hospital because of the precautions taken to stop them. The last three, social inappropriateness, social withdrawal, and complaints or behavior suggesting hallucinations, are, of course, all demonstrated on the ward.

Thus patients on the psychiatric unit exhibit some, but not all, of these behavior problems, which were severe enough to cause admission to a hospital. This suggests that behavior modification in the general hospital must often focus on problems outside: much of what is done must be directed toward relieving the distressing family or interpersonal situation that precipitated admission.

The two most common problems encountered on a general-hospital unit are depression and somatic complaints. Has behavior modification anything to contribute in handling such problems? The answer must be a qualified *yes*.

DEPRESSION

Williams, Barlow, and Agras (1972) recently studied behavioral measurement of depression in a general-hospital psychiatric unit. To simplify their study, they chose only patients with a diagnosis of psychotic depression, in whom depressive behavior was marked, and who presented serious clinical problems. The investigators measured the following behaviors: talking, smiling, motor activity, and time out of room. Each of these behaviors was precisely defined and its presence or absence recorded by nursing aides at 16 randomly selected times each day. With brief training the psychiatric aides reached an agreement rate of at least 96% for each category of behavior. The investigators then compared behavioral measurement with two standard measures of depression, the Beck Depressive Inventory, essentially a self-report, and the Hamilton Rating Scale, based upon a psychiatric interview. The behavioral measure correlated well with the other two scales and nicely demonstrated patient progress during hospitalization; moreover, the task and cost of administration was small compared with other scales.

Following on this work, Hersen, Eisler, Alford, and Agras (1973) studied the effects of the token economy described earlier on three patients with a diagnosis of neurotic depression. The thesis examined was that by motivating the patient to work, the essentially incompatible behavior of being depressed would be eliminated. To avoid bias, depression was measured during non-working hours, using behavioral measures. The experiment consisted of a baseline period in which tokens with no extrinsic value were given contingently, a reinforcement period when the tokens were exchangeable for privileges, and a return to baseline. In each case the patients worked more when the reinforcement condition was in effect than during either baseline period. Moreover, the patients' depressive behavior improved markedly only during the reinforcement phase. This finding adds further impetus for developing motivational systems to increase the activity of general-hospital psychiatric patients, since such a system tends to improve the most common behavior problem faced on such units, namely, depression.

A number of other studies tackle depressive behavior more directly (Lewisohn, Weinstein, & Shaw, 1969; Reisinger, 1972). Reisinger, albeit working with an institutionalized patient, directly modified crying and smiling in a patient with "anxiety-depression." When observed to be smiling, the patient was given tokens that were later backed up by social reinforcement, and the patient was fined when observed to be crying. In this way smiling was reinstated and crying eliminated. That this change was due to the reinforcement and punishment procedures was demonstrated by reversing the contingencies, causing smiling to decrease and crying to increase. The patient was discharged and 14 months later appeared well. This procedure could, of course, be incorporated into an activity-motivating token economy.

SOMATIC COMPLAINTS

The second most frequent behavior problem observed in the sample of general-hospital psychiatric patients is their tendency to complain about bodily ailments that have no physiological basis. Such complaints sometimes accompany depressive behavior, but not infrequently the complaints alone lead to hospitalization, having been reinforced by social attention within the patient's environment. Measurement presents no problem: either all complaints heard can be recorded or time samples can be taken, during which a member of the staff converses with the patient for a defined time and records the number of complaints. Since such behavior appears to be maintained by social reinforcement (Leitenberg, Agras, & Thomson, 1968), an extinction procedure in which complaints are ignored is appropriate. However, this is difficult to achieve in practice unless all patients and staff cooperate in the program. Moreover, it is important that staff do not decrease the overall amount of time they spend with the patient, i.e., that appropriate behavior continues to be reinforced.

AN ILLUSTRATIVE CASE. Mrs. M. B., an 87-year-old woman, was admitted to the psychiatric unit at the request of her physician. For several weeks she had been complaining frequently of "backache," "headache," and "stomach trouble," taking medication such as aspirin and tranquilizers too frequently, and calling her physician many times a day. He was concerned that she might endanger her life with a drug overdose or perhaps injure herself accidentally while intoxicated from taking drugs.

The patient's husband had died 2 months before, following a prolonged illness. The patient now lived alone and was frequently observed crying about her husband's death. Interestingly, some 10 years previously, the patient's husband had been severely injured, following which Mrs. M. B. was hospitalized with "complaints about her ear, dizziness, and hysterical crying."

Otherwise the patient's behavior had been reasonably stable. She graduated from nursing school and worked steadily as a nurse until she was over 80. She married relatively late, at the age of 50, having led an active social life. Her marriage was described as happy and stable.

Problem list. Following initial data collection, a number of specific behavior problems were outlined: (1) somatic complaints; (2) frequent crying spells associated with grief; (3) excessive self-medication.

Behavioral measurement. Staff were asked to record every instance of somatic complaint and crying spells during their contacts with the patient. As an index of medication, she was allowed to take as many aspirin as she wished up to 15 each day, and the number was recorded. No other medications were prescribed.

Treatment program. Thorough physical examination revealed osteoporosis of the spine with partial collapse of a vertebra, which doubtless caused some back pain. No specific treatment was indicated for this condition.

During initial interview the patient avoided talking about her husband and the events surrounding his death; at the same time she cried frequently, behavior that had been noted at home. It was postulated that her grief over her husband's death would be lessened if she could stop avoiding stimuli

associated with his death. She was therefore encouraged to talk about her husband and to look at his picture in daily sessions lasting 1 hour. As can be seen, frequency of crying (see Figure 15-3) declined quickly, and the patient became able to discuss freely her husband, his death, and her loneliness.

Somatic complaints (see Figure 15-3) were fairly frequent and quite bothersome to the staff. On the second hospital day, staff were instructed to ignore all the patient's complaints by walking away from her. However, they were also asked to spend at least as much time with her as previously. As shown in Figure 15-3, complaints at first increased in number and then steadily decreased. Aspirin taking followed the trend for complaints. By the eighth day, complaints and aspirin taking were at acceptable levels.

At this point, discussions with the patient and her few remaining relatives were begun to work out future plans. Relatives and the treatment staff both favored having the patient enter a nursing home where she would be less lonely. This she absolutely refused to do. We then suggested a trial visit home. Note that complaints and aspirin taking increased before going home. While at home, the patient reported marked loneliness, and upon her return to hospital complaints again reached a high level. Despite feelings of loneliness, the patient still insisted upon returning home, believing that she could pick up old friendships and

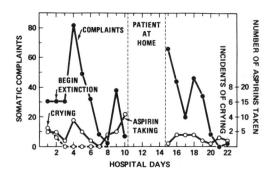

FIGURE 15–3   Graph demonstrating the course of three problem behaviors during hospitalization.

thus gain the necessary social support. Her complaints steadily lessened, and by discharge they were at an acceptable level, as was aspirin taking. Followup indicated maintenance of this pattern of behavior.

These kinds of data, of course, do not demonstrate the efficacy of the treatment procedures used but rather indicate how a behavioral viewpoint may contribute to treatment.

FURTHER APPLICATIONS

The above examples of the treatment of depression and of somatic complaints illustrate the application of behavior modification procedures to the two most common problems in the general hospital psychiatric unit. How have they been applied to other clinical problems?

Taking the traditional diagnostic categories listed in Table 15-1 together with the more common problem behaviors (see Table 15-2), we find much work in some categories and little in others. Thus there are no reported applications of behavioral techniques to the management of the organic psychoses or of manic depressive psychosis, but such techniques have been applied to numerous patients diagnosed as schizophrenic (see chapter 5 for examples), although most studies have been confined to chronic schizophrenia, which is not common in the general-hospital unit. Nevertheless, behavioral techniques have modified delusional behavior (Liberman, Teigen, Patterson, & Baker, 1973; Patterson & Teigen, 1973), in particular, which is ranked twelfth (see Table 15-2), and other bizarre and antisocial behaviors, for example, mutism, ranked seventeenth (Isaacs, Thomas, & Goldiamond, 1960). The procedures most frequently applied have been differential social attention (ignoring maladaptive and attending to adaptive behavior). the token economy, including individually arranged reinforcement programs (Wincze, Leitenberg, & Agras, 1972), and occasionally punishment (Tate & Baroff, 1966). These

studies suggest that some inappropriate behaviors of the schizophrenic can be modified, although the amount of benefit obtained in patients with acute schizophrenia and the interaction between behavioral and pharmacologic approaches in such patients are at present not known.

For the neuroses, which account for about one-quarter of admissions to the general hospital, more work has been done (see chap. 4), resulting in many procedures useful in general-hospital psychiatry. Patients with anxiety states often demonstrate clear conditions under which anxiety and avoidance behavior occur. Such cases may be treated similarly to phobic states in which the environmental stimuli controlling avoidance behavior are more obvious. Research over the last 10 years (Agras, 1972, pp. 150–153; Marks, 1973) suggests that exposure to avoided situations is the critical procedure common to most therapeutic approaches to phobia or phobic like conditions. The effectiveness of any particular therapy may well depend on the efficiency with which the patient is exposed to the full range of feared and avoided environmental stimuli. In any event, systematic desensitization (Wolpe, 1958), implosion (Stampfl & Levis, 1967; Marks, 1972), and reinforced practice (Agras, Leitenberg, & Barlow, 1968) can all be used to treat both anxiety states and phobias, although some evidence suggests that flooding and reinforced practice are the most effective techniques (Marks, 1972; Crowe, Marks, Agras, & Leitenberg, 1972; Everaerd, Rijken, & Emmelkamp, 1973).

In the case of obsessive-compulsive neurosis, the combination of treating the phobic components with reinforced practice, flooding, or modeling, all of which facilitate exposure to avoided environmental events, and response prevention, in which compulsive behavior is prevented from occurring, has been demonstrated to be effective (Mills, Agras, Barlow, Baugh, & Mills, 1973). In addition, some of the less common conditions such as anorexia nervosa (see chap. 2) have been successfully treated with reinforcement and feedback procedures.

While the treatment of neurotic conditions still forms the core of a behavioral approach to the problems of individuals, a beginning has been made in treating personality disorders. Personality disorders may be viewed as distortions of interpersonal behavior in which either inappropriate behavior is exhibited toward others or a deficit occurs in one or more aspects of interpersonal behavior. Assertive training (Sherman, 1973) is one example of a treatment approach to a common interpersonal deficit, although work in this area has not progressed much beyond the level of case report. Nevertheless, the technique, which consists of a combination of instructions, modeling, and reinforcement of verbal and nonverbal behaviors concerned with more effective communication, is a model for training other classes of interpersonal behavior. Similarly, a couples or family approach, in which the responses of each partner to the other are systematically modified, often using a contract (Liberman, 1972) that outlines the contingencies for both desired and undesired behavior, is likely to develop into a well-researched therapeutic endeavor. Since marital and family problems rank third and fourth in the problem behaviors encountered within the general hospital (see Table 15-2), this approach is most relevant.

Specific behavior disorders such as the sexual deviations, including homosexuality, can be treated with aversive therapy, which has proved more effective than psychotherapy, and recently several innovative approaches to fostering heterosexual behavior have been reported (see chap. 8). Finally, a number of alternative approaches have been developed for treating alcoholism, a problem ranked seventh in frequency on the general-hospital psychiatric unit. These approaches include aversive conditioning using emetine or apmorphine (Miller & Barlow, 1973), perhaps most profitably carried out in groups, and an analysis of family or social interaction, eliminating factors that reinforce drinking. The most comprehensive program of this type has been described by Hunt and Azrin (1973), whose data confirm its effectiveness compared with a group receiving no treatment.

Behavior Analysis and Somatotherapy

Many different kinds of treatment are used in the general-hospital psychiatric unit, including somatic therapies such as electroconvulsive shock or administration of pharmacologic agents. An important contribution of behavioral analysis to the management of patients in the general hospital may be in assessing the effects of somatic treatment.

MEASUREMENT

Continuous objective measurement of target behaviors can lend precision to the global clinical judgments of nurses and physicians and can lead to more adequate decisions about changes in treatment.

AN ILLUSTRATIVE CASE. Mrs. R. L., a 50-year-old woman, was admitted to hospital with a history and behavior typical of the diagnosis of psychotic depression. She reported that for several months she had found housework increasingly difficult, had lost interest in outside activities, could no longer enjoy her sexual relationship with her husband, was waking at three or four every morning, had a poor appetite, and had lost 25 pounds by the time of admission. She felt that life was not worth living and that her family might be better off without her. She spent much time in her hospital room with the shades drawn.

On examination she answered questions slowly, was preoccupied with past failings, and had a very depressed facies. Behavioral measurement (Williams et al., 1972) for depression was started to provide a running record of her course in hospital.

After the initial workup was completed, she was started on Imipramine 200 mg. daily. After 8 days (see Figure 15–4), it was clear that she was not responding to medication, and so electroshock therapy (EST) was administered on alternate days. As shown in Figure 15-4, her response to this treatment was immediate and steady, and she was discharged some 20 days later. The objective behavioral record (of talking, smiling, motor activity, and time out of room) facilitated decisions about changes in the therapeutic regimen (e.g., starting and stopping EST) and nicely documented the course of hospitalization.

In this case, measurement of a target behavior demonstrated that an antidepressant drug had no effect and that electroshock therapy was apparently effective in treating a woman with deep depression. However, since electroshock therapy was not discontinued at any time, we cannot be absolutely sure that improvement was due to that therapy. In the next case, the effect of a drug was evaluated by briefly discontinuing it while behavioral measures were taken.

AN ILLUSTRATIVE CASE. D. M., a 16-year-

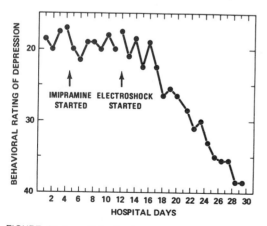

FIGURE 15–4   Behavioral measurement of depression, illustrating response to treatment during a 30-day hospital course.

old black youth, was referred to the psychiatric unit from a local training school where he had proved unmanageable due to repeated temper tantrums, "hallucinations," and persistent attention seeking. He had been diagnosed by psychologic testing as mildly mentally retarded.

His history revealed that he was brought up in an environment marred by severe social and economic deprivation. Three years before admission his parents had divorced, leaving him in the care of his mother, who was unable to discipline him. Eventually he was referred by the local youth court to a training school for the delinquent.

A careful workup, including chromosomal analysis, revealed no major physical abnormalities. However, psychologic testing (Reitan) indicated brain damage weakly lateralized to the right hemisphere. Direct behavioral observation showed temper tantrums, statements such as "I am seeing (or hearing) things," with sometimes elaborate descriptions of such events, stealing food from other patients' plates, eating with his fingers, begging for money, food, or cigarettes, and exposing himself. The nursing staff regarded him as a time-consuming, difficult-to-manage patient.

A structured management program was devised in which appropriate behavior such as getting up on time, cleaning his room, dressing and grooming neatly, completing school assignments, and helping the nursing staff earned tokens; inappropriate behavior as described earlier resulted in loss of tokens. Tokens could be spent on extra snacks, watching television, cigarettes, telephone calls, and time off the ward. In this system, the daily total of tokens earned and fined provided an index of appropriate and inappropriate behavior. The results are presented in Figure 15-5. During the first 6 days of the program, while appropriate behavior reached desirable levels, inappropriate behavior also steadily increased, despite the addition of a time-out procedure (brief

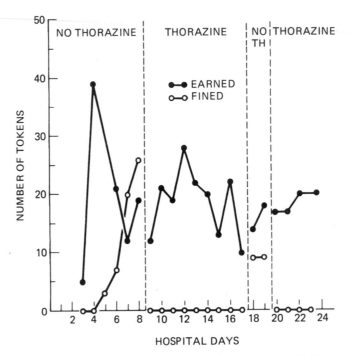

FIGURE 15–5   Behavior of an adolescent in response to chlorpromazine added to a token economy, as indicated by tokens earned or fined.

confinement in an isolation room) contingent upon tantrums and begging behavior.

Chlorpromazine (300 mg. daily in divided doses) was therefore introduced in an attempt to reduce this patient's impulsivity. A rather dramatic effect occurred, in which desirable behavior was maintained and undesirable behavior (tantrums, begging, food stealing) was completely eliminated. The amount of chlorpromazine was reduced to 200 mg. daily, to eliminate drowsiness.

Next, a short clinical test of the drug's efficacy was made by stopping the chlorpromazine. Inappropriate behavior immediately increased, and the nursing staff demanded that the medication be continued. Financial considerations prevented further clinical analysis; however, it would have been desirable to drop the behavioral management program to determine its contribution to therapy, if any.

This case nicely illustrates the use of experimental analysis of behavior in the clinic, to determine whether a treatment technique is useful for a particular patient. While this study demonstrated the effect of adding a drug to a behavioral program, the opposite sequence was recently studied experimentally (Liberman, Davis, Moon, & Moore, 1973). Their patient had been repeatedly hospitalized with a diagnosis of paranoid schizophrenia, and she made frequent delusional statements. The authors measured the frequency of such statements during several interviews each day in a 14-day baseline condition, while the patient was given 600 mg. of chlorpromazine daily. Then, while drug therapy continued, a time-out procedure was begun: the patient was taken to, and remained in, her room for 5 minutes whenever she made a delusional statement during an interview; such statements were almost completely eliminated during the 24 days of this condition. When time out ceased during the final phase of this study (and chlorpromazine was continued), delusional behavior steadily increased.

Neither of these studies considered the interaction between drug and behavioral therapies, nor has this question been studied systematically. Combined treatment may quite possibly be the most effective approach to many behavioral disorders, and since individuals with the same problem behaviors may differ in their response to either approach, a clinical experimental analysis in which the problem behavior is measured, and the effect of various combinations of therapies observed, should be used more frequently in the clinic. Contingency management may turn out to be particularly useful in dealing with specific behaviors not affected by drug therapy and in reinforcing the gains in adaptive behavior promoted by drugs.

Summary and Future Application

The influence of behavior modification on general-hospital psychiatry has been less than and different from its influence on other institutions. Since control of the general-hospital ward and of patient care lies in many hands, the first applications have been piecemeal individual therapeutic endeavors rather than ward-wide programs. Thus the general hospital is more likely to utilize a technique-oriented behavior therapy than scientifically oriented behavior modification, which is an experimental therapeutic endeavor (Risley, 1970).

Beyond the individual application of behavior therapy, we have seen three methods that move toward an experimental approach to therapy: (1) behavioral extensions of existing milieu therapy; (2) behavior measurement; (3) clinical use of the experimental analysis of behavior.

BEHAVIORAL MILIEU

In the first application, the principles and procedures of behavior modification provide a much needed technology (Edelson, 1964) for existing milieu therapy programs. It probably makes little difference whether the application takes the form of a token economy (Hersen et al., 1972) with modifications derived from ward management or milieu principles, or of a milieu therapy program with the addition of procedures based on behavior modification (Kass, Silvers, & Abroms, 1972). The major principles in either case are precise definition of problem behavior, objective measurement, contingency management, and clear expectancies and open communication among all participants, whether patients or staff.

MEASUREMENT

The second application extends, and to some extent replaces, present methods of psychiatric and psychological evaluation. Direct behavioral observations replace the impressionistic and anecdotal accounts of patient interaction with which charts are now liberally sprinkled. Many of the key pathologic behaviors exhibited on a psychiatric unit can be measured objectively using the technique of time sampling, in which the presence or absence of a well-defined unit of behavior is recorded 10, 20, or more times each day, at randomly chosen intervals. This method, which allows behavior to be recorded graphically, can be combined, as we have seen, with the problem-oriented record to give a running account of each precisely defined problem. This graphic account can be supplemented by briefly described subjective aspects of behavior, although many subjective descriptions can also be quantified by self-report scales, either for general use as in depression (Beck, Ward, & Mendelson, 1961), or individually tailored for each patient (Shapiro & Nelson, 1955). Quantification is preferable to description where possible, since changes and trends can be more quickly identified from a graph than from a paragraph.

BEHAVIOR ANALYSIS

The final application examined was the clinical use of an experimental method, the single-case experiment. Given an objective record of behavior, the effect of any treatment can be determined by instituting it, stopping it, and then reinstituting it. While this may not always be necessary or even desirable, in many circumstances such an analysis benefits both patient and therapist.

THE FUTURE UNIT

These methods will probably be applied with increasing frequency to the management of the general-hospital patient without unduly disturbing present organizational and staffing patterns. But extensive use of behavior modification will require changes in the environment of the general hospital.

If the environment governs much behavior, then changes in the physical environment, staffing patterns, and the social structure of the psychiatric ward will be necessary to optimize therapeutic behavior change. Some such changes follow from the applications already discussed; others are needed for more extensive applications. Thus, if behavioral measures are to be widely used, special technicians must be trained whose full-time job will be to observe, record, and estimate the reliability of behavioral measures. In addition, they will chart their observations, maintaining a clear flow sheet that represents each problem graphically and shows when each therapeutic or major environmental change occurred. Without such technicians neither behavioral measurement nor the behavioral problem-oriented record is possible.

The remaining staff require intensive training in behavior change techniques. All staff should be expert behavior modifiers,

and some should be able to teach the principles and procedures to patients, for there is no doubt that patients themselves must become therapeutic agents, since they form a major part of each other's social environment.

To accomplish this latter goal, the structure of the milieu therapy meeting might be used. Frequent meetings of small patient groups with the staff involved in their care would permit problem behavior to be publicly defined and systematic programming of social interaction by both patients and staff to be developed (Abroms, 1969). Ways of measuring and recording behavioral problems and alternative strategies could be discussed at these meetings, and a final program worked out. Moreover, in this way both patients and staff would be continually learning how to apply the principles of behavior change to concrete situations. One effect on the patient may be to enhance the generalization of therapeutic effects to the natural environment as the patient learns the principles behind new ways of changing his own and others' behavior.

Such a program would be enhanced by an overall token or point economy concentrating on certain basic adaptive behaviors. The exact behaviors chosen should depend on the type of population: while manual work and daily planning were suitable for the group of veterans described earlier, they would not be relevant for a group on the upper socioeconomic level. Instead, communication skills and social interaction might be the target behaviors selected. Facilitating such adaptive behaviors will require both alteration in the physical structure of most psychiatric units and the development of work situations. Ideally, such changes in environment or program would be analyzed experimentally, to determine that the desired effects were being obtained.

Finally, some form of patient government, in which patients and staff can revise the overall rules of operating the unit, seems desirable. Again, the effects of changes should be measured, to determine if the goal is being attained. Indeed, continual monitoring of the goals of an inpatient program—increased social interaction or lessened ward disturbance—should give a clearer picture of how a unit functions than is presently obtainable. Such accurate informational feedback should, in turn, lead to changes in ward management.

GENERALIZATION OF BEHAVIOR CHANGE

As we noted in Table 15-2, many problems of general-hospital psychiatric patients occur at home or at work. In addition, adaptive behavior changes that occur in the hospital must be transferred to, and maintained in, the outside world. One way to accomplish these aims is to work with significant persons such as family members to change their behavior so as to enhance or maintain the patient's behavior change. Such changes can be brought about by direct instructions to relatives, by modeling, or by supervised practice. Moreover, home-based reinforcement systems (Bailey, Wolf, & Phillips, 1970; Nordquist & Wahler, 1973) or contingency management by means of a behavioral contract (Cantrell et al., 1969) can be developed.

A second way to ensure generalization of behavior change is to form a network of collaborative community programs that take advantage of existing natural reinforcement contingencies and turn them to therapeutic advantage. For example, youth courts exert control through legal contingencies, which can be made part of an overall therapeutic program; judges and counselors can learn to use legal constraints in a positive way. A behavioral contract be-

tween parents and a predelinquent adolescent can, for example, be given legal status, with brief detention in a youth center as one of the contingencies. Similarly, the general-hospital unit should stimulate formation of therapeutic environments in the community; these would of course be designed along behavior modification lines.

Finally, if behavior analysis and modification are taken seriously, the general-hospital psychiatric unit will concern itself not only with changing deviant behavior but with promoting positive behavior change. It will develop programs leading toward fulfillment of human potential and toward more healthful living. Such programs might include shaping behavior to improve physical health, for example, eating less and enjoying exercise more, as well as to achieve what is called mental health, for example, enhancing interpersonal skills such as the ability to enjoy more satisfying social and sexual relationships. The effect of such programs on prevention of behavioral deviance would need to be studied experimentally.

Programs to ensure adequate generalization of behavior change, and aimed at preventing disability, require a very different physical environment from the usual general-hospital psychiatric unit. The hospital bed would be deemphasized and reduced considerably in number; self-care facilities, along motel lines, would suffice for most patients and would promote adaptive behavior change, while the most space would be allotted to programs that emphasized work, socializing, and outpatient health maintenance. Such developments are quite congruent with the aims of a community-oriented psychiatry or psychology and should therefore fit easily within plans for future mental health programs.

References

Abroms, G. M. "Defining milieu therapy." *Archives of General Psychiatry,* 1969, **21**, 553–560.

Agras, W. S. (Ed.) *Behavior modification: Principles and clinical applications.* Boston: Little, Brown, 1972, pp. 1–27.

Agras, W. S., Leitenberg, H., & Barlow, D. H. "Social reinforcement in the modification of agoraphobia." *Archives of General Psychiatry,* 1968, **19**, 423–427.

ALFORD, G. C., BLANCHARD, E. B., & BUCKLEY, T. M. "Treatment of hysterical vomiting by modification of social contingencies: A case study." *Journal of Behavior Therapy and Experimental Psychiatry,* 1972, **3**, 209–212.

AYLLON, T., & AZRIN, N. H. *The token economy: A motivational system for therapy and rehabilitation.* New York: Appleton-Century-Crofts, 1968.

AYLLON, T., & ROBERTS, M. D. "The token economy: Now." In W. S. Agras (Ed.), *Behavior modification: Principles and clinical applications.* Boston: Little, Brown, 1972.

BAILEY, J. S., WOLF, M. M., & PHILLIPS, E. L. "Home-based reinforcement and the modification of predelinquents' classroom behavior." *Journal of Applied Behavior Analysis,* 1970, **3**, 223–233.

BECK, A. T., WARD, C. H., & MENDELSON, M. "An inventory for measuring depression." *Archives of General Psychiatry,* 1961, **4**, 561–571.

CANTRELL, R. P., CANTRELL, M. L., HUDDLESTON, C. M., & WOOLRIDGE, R. L. "Contingency contracting with school problems." *Journal of Applied Behavior Analysis,* 1969, **2**, 215–220.

CROWE, M. J., MARKS, I. M., AGRAS, W. S., & LEITENBERG, H. "Time-limited desensitization, implosion, and shaping for phobic patients: A crossover study." *Behaviour Research and Therapy,* 1972, **10**, 319–328.

EDELSON, M. *Ego psychology, group dynamics and the therapeutic community.* New York: Grune & Stratton, 1964.

EVERAERD, W., RIJKEN, H. M., & EMMELKAMP, P. "A comparison of flooding and successive approximation in the treatment of agoraphobia." *Behaviour Research and Therapy,* 1973, **11**, 105–118.

GLASSCOATE, R. M., & KANNO, C. K. *General hospital psychiatric units: A national survey.* Baltimore: Garamond/Pridemark Press, 1965.

HAYES-ROTH, F., LONGABAUGH, R., & RYBECK, R. "The problem-oriented record and psychiatry." *British Journal of Psychiatry,* 1972, **121**, 27–34.

HERSEN, M., EISLER, R. M., ALFORD, G. S., & AGRAS, W. S. "Effects of token economy on neurotic depressions: An experimental analysis." *Behavior Therapy,* 1973, **4**, 420–425.

HERSEN, M., EISLER, R. M., SMITH, B. S., & AGRAS, W. S. "A token reinforcement ward for young psychiatric patients." *American Journal of Psychiatry,* 1972, **129**, 228–233.

HUNT, G. M., & AZRIN, N. H. "A community-reinforcement approach to alcoholism." *Behaviour Research and Therapy,* 1973, **11**, 91–104.

HURST, J. W., & WALKER, H. K. *The problem oriented system.* New York: Medcom Press, 1972.

ISAACS, W., THOMAS, J., & GOLDIAMOND, I. "Application of operant conditioning to reinstate verbal behavior in psychotics." *Journal of Speech and Hearing Disorders,* 1960, **25**, 8–12.

KASS, D. J., SILVERS, F. M., & ABROMS, G. M. "Behavioral group treatment of hysteria." *Archives of General Psychiatry,* 1972, **26**, 42–50.

LEITENBERG, H., AGRAS, W. S., & THOMSON, L. E. "A sequential analysis of the effect of selective positive reinforcement in modifying anorexia nervosa." *Behaviour Research and Therapy,* 1968, **6**, 211–214.

LEWINSOHN, P. M., WEINSTEIN, M. S., & SHAW, D. A. "Depression: A clinical research approach." In R. Rubin & C. M. Franks (Eds.), *Advances in Behavior Therapy.* New York: Academic Press, 1969.

LIBERMAN, R. P. *A guide to behavioral analysis and therapy.* New York: Pergamon, 1972, pp. 303–317.

LIBERMAN, R. P., DAVIS, J., MOON, W., & MOORE, J. "Research design for analyzing drug-environment-behavior interactions." *Journal of Nervous and Mental Disorders,* 1973, **156**, 432–439.

LIBERMAN, R. P., TEIGEN, J. R., PATTERSON, R., & BAKER, J. "Reducing delusional speech in chronic, paranoid schizophrenics." *Journal of Applied Behavior Analysis,* 1973, **6**, 57–64.

MARKS, I. M. "Flooding (implosion) and allied treatments." In W. S. Agras (Ed.), *Behavior modification: Principles and clinical applications.* New York: Little, Brown, 1972.

MARKS, I. M. "Reduction of fear: Toward a unifying theory." *Canadian Psychiatric Association Journal,* 1973, **18**, 9–12.

MILLER, P., & BARLOW, D. H. "Behavioral approaches to the treatment of alcoholism." *Journal of Nervous and Mental Disease,* 1973, **157**, 10–20.

MILLS, H. L., AGRAS, W. S., BARLOW, D. H., BAUGH, J. R., & MILLS, J. R. "The treatment of compulsive rituals by response prevention: A sequential analysis of treatment variables." *Archives of General Psychiatry,* 1973, **28**, 524–529.

NORDQUIST, V. M., & WAHLER, R. G. "Naturalistic treatment of an autistic child." *Journal of Applied Behavior Analysis,* 1973, **6,** 79–98.

PATTERSON, R. L., & TEIGEN, J. R. "Conditioning and post-hospital generalization of nondelusional responses in a chronic psychotic patient." *Journal of Applied Behavior Analysis,* 1973, **6,** 65–70.

REISINGER, J. O. "The treatment of 'anxiety-depression' via positive reinforcement and response cost." *Journal of Applied Behavior Analysis,* 1972, **5,** 125–130.

RISLEY, T. R. "Behavior modification: An experimental-therapeutic endeavor." In L. A. Hamerlynck, P. O. Davidson & L. E. Acker (Eds.), *Behavior modification and ideal mental health service.* Calgary, Canada: University of Calgary Press, 1970.

ROSENHAN, D. L. "On being sane in insane places." *Science,* 1973, **179,** 250–257.

SHAPIRO, M. B., & NELSON, E. H. "An investigation of an abnormality of cognitive function in a cooperative young psychotic: An example of the application of experimental method in a single case." *Journal of Clinical Psychology,* 155, **28,** 239–256.

SHERMAN, R. A. *Behavior modification: Theory and practice.* Monterey, Calif.: Brooks-Cole, 1973, pp. 104–118.

SMITH, R. C., & CARLIN, J. "Behavior modification using interlocking reinforcement on a short-term psychiatric ward." *Archives of General Psychiatry,* 1972, **27,** 386–389.

STAMPFL, T. G., & LEVIS, D. J. "Essentials of implosive therapy: A learning-theory-based psychodynamic behavioral therapy." *Journal of Abnormal Psychology,* 1967, **72,** 496–511.

TATE, B. G., & BAROFF, G. S. "Aversive control of self-injurious behavior in a psychotic boy." *Behaviour Research and Therapy,* 1966, 4, 281–287.

WEED, L. L. "Medical records that guide and teach." *New England Journal of Medicine,* 1968, **278,** 593–599, 652–657.

WILLIAMS, J. G., BARLOW, D. H., & AGRAS, W. S. "Behavioral measurement of severe depression." *Archives of General Psychiatry,* 1972, **27,** 330–333.

WINCZE, J. P., LEITENBERG, H., & AGRAS, W. S. "The effects of token reinforcement and feedback on the delusional verbal behavior of chronic paranoid schizophrenics." *Journal of Applied Behavior Analysis,* 1972, **5,** 247–262.

WOLPE, J. *Psychotherapy by reciprocal inhibition.* Stanford, Calif.: Stanford University Press, 1958.

Behavior Analysis and Therapy in Community Mental Health

16

ROBERT PAUL LIBERMAN
LARRY W. KING
WILLIAM J. DE RISI

In the Community Mental Health Centers Act of 1963, a "bold new approach to mental health" in the United States was unveiled. Cooperation of federal, state, and local governments was to bring about intensive treatment and early intervention for those labeled "mentally ill" at sites close to their homes. A concurrent reduction in the resident populations of large, custodial, state hospitals was anticipated as an indirect benefit of community-based services. Locally developed and operated programs were to be easily and readily available to those who needed them. The services were to be comprehensive: inpatient, outpatient, partial hospitalization, aftercare, and emergency care were to be provided for psychotics, retardates, neurotics, drug and alcohol abusers, children and adults, those in crisis, and those trying to cope with

The work described in this chapter was supported by NIMH Grant No. 1R01MH19880-01A1 from the Mental Health Service Research & Development Branch, Division of Mental Health Services; and by a 314(d) grant from the California Department of Health. The authors are grateful for the support and encouragement provided by Mr. James Cumiskey, Dr. Marie MacNabola, and Dr. Howard Davis of the NIMH Mental Health Services Development Branch.

adjustment problems of everyday life. Finally, programs developed under the Community Mental Health Centers Act were to be oriented toward prevention through consultation and education as well as treatment (Beigel & Levenson, 1972). The community mental health movement has been termed the third "revolution" in the history of psychiatry, with the first two being the humanization of treatment by Pinel, Tuke and Dix, and the influence of psychoanalysis.

This chapter outlines the philosophy and goals of the community mental health and behavior modification movements, reviews behavioral research in community settings, and describes the application of behavioral techniques to the various services of a typical, comprehensive community mental health center. The strengths and weaknesses of the behavioral model in this applied setting are described, and suggestions are made for its more effective use.

In the 10 years since the Mental Health Act was passed, over 200 centers have become operational with an additional 200 having been funded. Each center is intended to serve a "catchment" area, defined as a geographic area containing no less than 75,000 and no more than 200,000 people. Given the average catchment area size of 100,000 people, 2,000 community mental health centers are needed to serve the current population of the United States.

Community mental health centers currently provide a wide range of services, including inpatient care designed to support the patient's functional capabilities and, at the same time, to strengthen the social setting to which he will return. Inpatient care at community mental health centers is brief, almost always less than 14 days' duration. Partial hospitalization, generally referred to as "day treatment," provides rehabilitation for 6 to 8 hours per day, 5 days a week. Patients come to "day treatment" after a period of inpatient care or as an alternative to hospitalization and begin by spending all day at the center. Later, attendance is reduced to half-days or less. Evening treatment is provided for patients who hold jobs but who require continued support and treatment. Outpatient services in the community mental health center include both individual and group psychotherapy, most often offered once per week. Emergency or crisis services are provided on a 24-hour basis. Trained staff members, who range from psychiatric technicians to psychologists and psychiatrists, respond to clients who walk in or telephone for assistance. Resolution of the crisis is the primary goal, with referral for continuing care being an integral part of the intervention.

Indirect services are provided to other community agencies, such as schools, aftercare facilities, social welfare, the courts, and law enforcement. These services typically include consultation for diagnosis and disposition, training, and program development and evaluation. Mental health education to the public and to community "gatekeepers" is disseminated via lectures, seminars, workshops, and the mass media.

By design, the community mental health center should be a magnet for drawing together those who have unmet needs and the community resources necessary to meet these needs. Since the centers serve well-defined geographic areas, community mental health center staffs are charged with the responsibility of gathering information necessary for planning client-oriented services and acting as a change agent for the community. The activities of the community mental health center are guided by citizens' advisory councils and are geared toward reducing disability and chronicity. The services provided are supposed to be equivalent in comfort and quality to those found in the private-care sector.

Although the national goal of 2,000 centers is only 10% attained, the "bold new approach to mental health" has been criticized on a number of important issues (Cowen, 1973; Chu & Trotter, 1973; Schwartz, 1972). Admissions to state hospitals have increased despite declines in the resident populations. Another mental health bureaucracy has been created, critics say, one that is as unresponsive and impotent as the one it was to replace. More damaging, the charge is made that mental health professionals do not have the expertise to solve the nation's mental health problems.

Few take issue with the philosophical points of departure for the community mental health movement—continuity of care, rapid restoration of vocational and social adjustment, reduction of time spent away from family and job in hospitals, treatment close to the home setting, training of indigenous nonprofessionals and community gatekeepers, and involvement of the total community in program planning and evaluation; the challenge for community mental health workers lies in the implementation of these lofty goals.

Behavioral Approaches to Community Mental Health Services

Another "revolution" in psychology has been the advent of behavioral approaches to problems in education and mental health. Behavior analysis and therapy can be viewed as potentially contributing the "working muscles" to the "philosophical skeleton" of community mental health ideology. In principle, behavioral methods:

are brief and economical to apply.

can be used by paraprofessionals without graduate education.

are more effective when conducted close to the patient's natural environment, which promotes generalization.

can be evaluated because their objectives are specified and operationalized.

are effective with a wide variety of behavioral problems across patients from varying social classes.

offer a tangible means of carrying out primary, secondary, and tertiary prevention through consultation and education, early intervention, and rehabilitation.

The emphasis in an ideal mental health service should be on outcome. Mental health services are improved by demonstrating what does *not* work or what interventions lead to improvements in the client's behavior. Building evaluation of outcome into the mental health delivery system begins to answer recent criticism of the community mental health center measurement. Therapeutic efforts ideally should contribute to advances in our basic knowledge and technology by being experimental in execution or by yielding pre-experimental, pilot data (Risley, 1972).

MacDonald, Hedberg, and Campbell (1971) argue that a behavioral model would improve the effectiveness of the community mental health system. The special advantages of the behavioral approach are rooted in its basic empiricism. Its understandable language, tools, and techniques can be applied to a much larger sample of community residents. MacDonald and his colleagues (1971) redefine the consultant model of Nagler and Cooper (1969) from a behavioral standpoint. The community mental health model can be more responsive to the

problems of the entire community if goals are specified and interventions carried out on the reinforcement contingencies operating on the broader social level. Behaviorists should move out of the therapist role and into the consultant-educator role. Training "gatekeepers" and other mediators in the community in behavioral analysis and therapy will multiply the consultant-educator's effect on the population at risk. Deprofessionalizing the role of change agent reduces the cost of the therapeutic process. In describing a parent workshop in a community mental health center, Liberman (1973) maintains that training community citizens in behavioral techniques returns "power to the people" in a meaningful way.

The behaviorist also can act as a consultant–systems engineer. By focusing interventions on community decision makers, changes can be made in the positive and negative aspects of the community system. By conducting functional, behavioral analyses of problems that affect the entire community and offering solutions to decision makers, the consultant–systems engineer fulfills his role.

In order to provide some perspective on the direction of behavioral research in the community, four behavioral journals were surveyed. The contents of *Journal of Applied Behavior Analysis, Behaviour Research and Therapy, Behavior Therapy,* and *Journal of Behavior Therapy and Experimental Psychiatry* were examined from January 1968 through August 1973. Of the total articles published in these sources, 113, or 13%, were found to have been performed in the community. To be considered a community-based study, the research or treatment must have been carried out outside a laboratory, large hospital, or academic institution with subjects from clinical populations. Analogue studies were omitted, as were studies done in schools. Studies or reports that included both school and some other community setting were included for analysis. Each study or report was analyzed to determine (1) the research or treatment setting, (2) the source of data, (3) the presence or absence of multiple types of measures, (4) the recruitment of subjects, (5) the generalization measures employed, and (6) the role of the author-consultant. These data are summarized in Table 16–1.

By far the most frequently used treat-ment setting in behavioral community studies is the client's own home. Very few studies specifically mentioned that they were performed in a community mental health center. Unusual settings included stores, weight-reduction clubs, a motel conference room, casinos, theaters, and summer camps.

TABLE 16–1   Characteristics of behavioral studies carried out in community settings and published during 1968–73

TREATMENT OR RESEARCH SETTING	Number	%
Home	73	40.1
Day treatment	3	1.6
Outpatient setting	23	12.6
Special treatment facility	20	11.1
School	11	6.0
Day care preschool	28	15.4
Unusual setting	24	13.2
	182	100.0
SOURCES OF SUBJECTS		
Selected	108	95.6
Unselected	5	4.4
	113	100.0
SOURCES OF DATA		
Direct observation	56	46.3
Permanent products	17	14.1
Ratings, tests	13	10.7
Official records	6	4.9
Hearsay, anecdotal	10	8.3
Self-report	19	15.7
	121	100.0
MULTIPLE OUTCOME MEASURES TAKEN		
Yes	63	55.8
No	50	44.2
	113	100.0
FOLLOW-UP OR GENERALIZATION MEASURES TAKEN		
Time	39	33.1
Response	18	15.3
Setting	5	4.2
None	56	47.4
	118	100.0
INTERVENTION ROLE		
Therapist	64	38.3
Educator	83	49.7
Systems engineer	20	12.0
	167	100.0

Note.—Total number of cases/studies included in this analysis=113.

There was more than one setting for 17.7% of the studies.

Important for the consideration of these data is the *source of subjects*. Most studies —95.6%—made use of *selected* subjects; that is, subjects were chosen to fit the particular treatment paradigm being tested. The remainder of the studies indicated that subjects were included in the study because they presented themselves at the treatment facility. The use of *unselected* subjects provides a most stringent test of any treatment procedure and closely approximates the conditions found in community treatment settings. Subjects were selected for the severity of their symptoms or for extremely low rates of some behavior of interest.

Data presented in these studies were gathered from a variety of sources. The most frequently reported source was direct observation, accounting for almost half the instances of data collection reported. Many studies reported data arising from several sources; for example, direct observation of behavior plus self-reports by subjects. The sources of data were coded into two categories, "hard" and "soft." Direct observation and permanent products of behavior were considered to yield "hard" data. Hard data were reported in 60% of the studies reviewed. Measurement in applied settings can give rise to such methodological problems as experimenter bias, reactivity, and obtrusiveness. The applied researcher can take steps to reduce error that might be introduced by the use of these "hard" measures. (King, 1973a; Kazdin, 1973; Johnson & Bolstand, 1973). Almost 25% of the total sources were "soft," deriving from anecdotal reports (hearsay), or self-reports of subjects. The remaining 15% depended on measurement techniques that were once obligatory in clinical psychological studies —ratings, standardized tests, and official records.

Over half the studies reported data from more than one behavioral dimension or source. Measures taken on more than one response modality or multilevel measures made on the same aspect of behavior are important to a thorough analysis of experimental or treatment outcome. Collecting follow-up data after the termination of the formal study is completed is the most common method of assessing generalization. One-third of the studies surveyed included some measure of generalization over time. Only a few authors attempted to measure generalization across responses. The measurement of several responses to test for broad effects of treatment can serve to answer the criticism that behavioral treatment has a narrow focus.

As opposed to the traditional role of the mental health practitioner as therapist behavioral research has emphasized the role of consultant-educator from its inception. Ayllon and Michael's (1959) work in training hospital nurses in operant techniques is a classic case. Zeilberger, Sampen, and Sloane (1968), Wahler (1969a, 1969b; Wahler & Erickson, 1969), and Cantrell (1969) all taught behavioral treatment techniques to parents, who thereby served as primary therapists in their own homes. This emphasis on the training of nonprofessionals to be primary therapists has continued in the behavioral literature.

Authors were classified according to their reported behavior as primary therapist, educator of those who carried out treatment, or systems engineer who was acting to change an organization or its policies. It was found that authors seldom wear only one hat during research and demonstration projects. Half of the roles that could be discriminated in these studies were judged to be educator roles. Relatively few roles were judged to fall into the systems-engineer category. Considering the increased response cost in doing research in the community and the even greater effort of attempting to change an organization or agency, the 12% of the studies that attempted a systems intervention seem a respectable amount at the present time.

Attempts to alter human service systems have been reported. Target systems range from a half-way house for chronic psychotics (Henderson, 1970) to day care for preschool children (Miller & Schneider, 1970; Herman, 1971; LeLaurien & Risley, 1972). Other authors have attempted to gain experimental control in settings unusual for psychological research. Burgess and his colleagues (1971) studied the littering behavior of children in a public theater. Miller (1970) initiated a self-help, group program for welfare clients. Herbert and her associates (1972) used mothers to develop and evaluate a technique for the measurement of the behavior of autistic and hyperactive children. These studies can be classified under the heading of community development.

Two studies currently under way in Alabama and California are introducing behavior technology into the operation of comprehensive mental health services being offered to geographically defined populations. In Huntsville, Alabama, A. Jack Turner and his colleagues are completing a 3-year program supported by the National Institutes of Mental Health (NIMH) to test the feasibility of employing an operant learning approach to all activities associated with a comprehensive community mental health center. In this program, which serves all of Madison County, "empiricism has been adopted totally and behavior modification where feasible" (Turner, 1972). Measurement of outcome and isolation of the effective elements of treatment are goals that receive the highest priority. Turner has altered the personnel system as it applies to the employees of the center. Wages and prerequisites are now dispensed in a manner that more closely approximates a ratio, instead of the usual interval, schedule of reinforcement. All employees and all other agencies that enter into cooperative agreements with the center negotiate performance contracts on a yearly basis. A cost-accounting system for all aspects of the care-giving program has been developed. Since the evaluation of programs is based exclusively on quantifiable behaviors, and since all activities of the center are further quantified within a time frame, direct and indirect cost accounting is a reality.

In the Huntsville program, accountability is stressed not only as a necessary evil but as an ethical necessity and a prerequisite to empiricism. Services that do not meet goals are either redesigned for further evaluation or dropped. All services are evaluated in terms of outcome measures; for example, readmission rates in state hospitals, length of periods between hospitalizations, percentage of goal attainment, and frequency and duration of jailings of mentally disturbed persons. In addition, Turner and his colleagues are accepting responsibility for reducing undesirable community statistics, such as various types of vehicular accidents.

In assisting other community agencies, such as courts, welfare, and police, Turner employs the consultant first as a *model,* then as a *trainer* to shape appropriate behavior, and finally as a *generalization agent,* with a gradually decreasing frequency of contacts with the agency. This approach fits closely the MacDonald-Hedberg-Campbell model of consultant as therapist, educator, and systems engineer. Efforts at altering a social service delivery system first require demonstration by the consultant that he or she is competent as a therapist, and later as an educator or shaper of trainee behavior. If either of these steps is lacking, the consultant cannot easily establish himself as a credible agent of change and faces an uphill struggle in altering the social systems.

The other large-scale program designed to demonstrate the effectiveness of behavioral therapies in a comprehensive community mental health center is located in Oxnard, California, and is being developed by Liberman and his colleagues. Supported by an applied research grant from the Mental Health Services Research and Development Branch of the NIMH, this 3-year project is titled "Behavioral Analysis and Modification in a Community Mental Health Center."

The BAM Project

The Behavior Analysis and Modification (BAM) Project[1] aims to introduce and evaluate behavioral approaches for the wide variety of clinical problems that are encountered in a typical, comprehensive community mental health center. Most innovations reported here have occurred in the Day Treatment Center and with indirect services for parents and schools. The BAM Project has also developed and assessed behavioral methods in outpatient, emergency, inpatient, and aftercare settings.

Oxnard, the largest city in the county of Ventura, is located 50 miles north of Los Angeles and has a population of 80,000. Mexican-Americans, many of whom speak only Spanish, account for 30% of the population. The mental health center has a total catchment area that includes three cities and a population of 140,000. The community is supported largely by agriculture, but there are many light industries, a large state hospital, and two large naval bases in the area.

The Oxnard Community Mental Health Center is located in the commercial center of the city of Oxnard and thus it is easily accessible by car and bus. It is housed in an oblong, two-story building, adjoining a Knights of Columbus hall, and has no iden-

tification as a *medical* center. The center was renamed the Oxnard Center for Problems in Living to avoid stigma associated with mental illness, especially among the Mexican-American population. Out of 25 staff members, 5 are bilingual, and outreach services are provided in the barrio of Oxnard. The outpatient clinic has a staff of three psychiatric social workers and two clinical psychologists. A mobile emergency team consisting of two mental health technicians and a mental health nurse is on call 24 hours a day.

The Day Treatment Center of the mental health center has a staff of 11.[2] There are two occupational therapists, three psychiatric nurses, four psychiatric technicians, and two nonprofessional mental health assistants. The staff members also perform activities in the outpatient, emergency, aftercare, and consultation sectors of the mental health center. The Day Treatment Center consists of homey and comfortably furnished living rooms, a dining room and kitchen, an occupational-therapy crafts room, and three offices for staff and for staff-patient consultation.

Prior to the onset of the BAM Project funding the NIMH, the senior author spent 18 months working at the Oxnard Mental

[1] Drs. Rafael Canton, Sarah Miller, and Stephen Coray of the Ventura Health Services Agency have made the efforts described in this chapter a true collaboration between a community mental health program and a research and evaluation project. Their warm support and interest in new and innovative approaches to mental health care have aided and nurtured the BAM Project from its inception to the present. The authors also acknowledge the assistance of Dr. Louis Jolyon Wert, Chairman and Professor, Department of Psychiatry, UCLA School of Medicine.

[2] The commitment to trying and evaluating new methods of clinical treatment by the clinical staff of the Oxnard Mental Health Center has made the BAM Project possible. The authors are honored to be colleagues of Edith Asbury, Jim Bedwell, Dick Blaesing, Ed Bryan, Richard Gonzalez, Lalo Perez, Karen Halter, Ann Hansen, Charlotte Hoffer, Griselda Lopez, Gayle McDowell, Monica Myron, Al Rivera, Johnie Roberts, Ray Rocha, Nancy Sanders, S. Stansfeld Sargent, Leona Smith, Vikki Smith, and Genie Wheeler. The diligent and stimulating efforts of a large research team have kept the BAM Project going through thick and thin. The authors recognize the important contributions made to this chapter by Nancy Austin, Jan Levine, Robert Aitchison, Robert Drury, Mary Hernandez, Aurora de la Selva, Janet Merrill, Janet Brown, Paul Gabrinetti, Susan Heyl, and David Wood. In particular, Nancy Austin's tireless efforts in preparing the manuscript and writing the summary are greatly appreciated.

Health Center part-time as a psychiatrist. Essential groundwork and preparation of the staff for the intensive training program of 1972–75 were conducted in gradual steps, responsive to the progress and needs of the staff. Negative stereotypes toward behavior modification were dispelled as the senior author developed friendly, supportive, and collaborative relationships with the clinical staff and with the administrative hierarchy at the county's mental health department headquarters in Ventura. Difficult cases were taken on by the senior author on referral from the clinical staff, and training was begun on a case supervision basis. A token economy was initiated with monitoring of the transactions being shared by staff and patients (Liberman, 1971a; Liberman, 1973).

In June 1972, NIMH funding permitted the establishment of a six-person BAM Project team, including two behavioral psychologists (the second and third authors), a psychiatrist (the first author), and three research assistants. The BAM Project offices were deliberately set up in space adjoining the clinical area of the mental health center. The BAM Project team quickly became an intrinsic part of the clinical operations, with emphasis on catalyzing program development and evaluation in a consultative fashion.

The goals of the BAM Project are:

1. To train the clinical staff in behavior analysis and modification

2. To have the staff adopt behavioral assessment and recording procedures

3. To replace a milieu therapy program with a behaviorally oriented program

4. To collect behavioral data that could be used for program evaluation

5. To experimentally evaluate the effects of behavior modification treatment program for individual patients

6. To use a Goal Attainment Scaling method to compare the outcome of patients receiving behavioral treatment with patients receiving traditional treatment at another day treatment center.

7. To use behavior technology in the community consultation services of the clinic

8. To evaluate the effects of behavioral treatment on Mexican-American patients who comprise 30% of the population of Oxnard

9. To actively disseminate the results obtained from the BAM Project to other *clinical* treatment centers and personnel

The intensive training of staff proceeded along four levels. First, there was formal training in behavioral principles and techniques at a 3-hour seminar held once weekly. Second, the staff of the Day Treatment Center received individual supervision from the BAM staff on their caseloads. Third, the BAM staff conducted individual and group sessions with patients using various behavior modification techniques, while the clinical staff observed and participated. Fourth, the clinical staff engaged in their own self-management projects at the beginning of the year as a way of learning experientially behavior modification principles and procedures.

From the beginning of the training, it was understood that the BAM Project staff would be fading themselves out, and the behavioral treatment of the patients would be taken over more and more by the Day Treatment Center staff. In the last 3 months of the year, there was very reduced contact between the Day Treatment Center and the BAM Project staff. At the end of the year, the clinical staff were using behavioral methods autonomously with the supervision of a half-time behavioral consultant. A more complete description of the content and the methods by which the staff were trained is given in a technical report by King (1973b).

Before describing the programs instigated by the BAM Project, the authors will outline the necessary groundwork for a research team to obtain entry into a community mental health center. Although the entry problem must be solved before clinical research can be initiated, very few procedural suggestions are available to the interested reader (Frazier, 1972; Guyett, 1972; Ball,

1969). We devote a sizable portion of this chapter to a discussion of the preparation of the applied setting because of this deficiency in the literature. In reflecting back on our activities, we found that Alinsky (1972), a successful organizer, had many useful insights into the tangible problems and methods of innovation. Frequent reference is made to his work, which we fully recommended to any person about to embark in the murky waters of clinical research or innovation.

ESTABLISHING BEHAVIORAL MEASUREMENT

If we take seriously the dictum that the most important contribution of behavioral technology to clinical psychology and psychiatry lies in its emphasis on specification and measurement of behavior, then the influence of behavior modifiers in community mental health must be felt in record keeping and program evaluation. The clinical record as a point of entry for behavioral innovation looms even more critical when it is realized that most clinicians in community, institutional, or private practice characteristically keep very meager records of any kind. Unless behavioral specification and recording of clinically meaningful problems and goals become an everyday reality in mental health centers, the "behavioral revolution" will be just another clinical fad, a potpourri of techniques used, abused, and then finally placed in the pantheon of "eclectic" procedures such as hydrotherapy, lobotomy, insulin shock, and psychoanalysis. What then can be done to introduce behavioral recordkeeping into community mental health centers?

It is important to start this discussion by distinguishing the records kept by well-trained professionals coming from academic and research traditions in behaviorism from those kept by clinicians who lack skills and adherence to systematic methods in their work. The literature is overflowing with reports on the effective implementation

of behavioral technology with phobias, compulsions, social inadequacy, sexual problems, classroom management, and training parents in child management. In almost all of these published cases, however, the intervention is spearheaded by a behavioral therapist with an anchor in academia and a crew of students or research assistants. Once the demonstration of behavior control is completed, the therapist and his team leave the scene with little or no effort to implant the technology for others to continue.

In considering the reorganization of a community mental health center's record system, helpful guidelines for action can be obtained by a reading of Alinsky (1972), who has achieved considerable success in producing organizational change on the political scene. Alinsky advises the organizer "to recognize the world as it is. We must work with it on its terms if we are to change it to the kind of world we would like it to be. We must see the world, as all political realists have, in terms of what men do and not what they ought to do [p. 12]." Likewise for the behavioral innovator, the first step is to recognize the existing methods of record keeping and to make a preliminary judgment on "what" and "how much" to measure based on the current practice.

Getting a reliable assessment of the staff's recording baseline requires asking the right questions and making some careful observations. Clinical line staff tend to be very suspicious of outsiders who show interest in their record keeping. An outsider's interest smacks of an investigation, audit, program evaluation, or at least the potential for additional record keeping in the near future. Anyone who has worked closely with the therapists will appreciate that additional requirements for keeping records are viewed as odious and unreasonable demands by bureaucrats not familiar with clinicians' scarce time.

An innovator can increase his impact by becoming a clinician, helping with everyday clinical problems, and doing tasks that are difficult or undesirable. This amounts to an initiation into the "fraternity" of clinicians, a process that involves getting your feet wet and your hands dirty but that pays off in handsome dividends later when you begin asking the staff to change.

For the academic researcher, applied settings are a fertile field for sowing ideas and reaping reinforcers such as publications, grants, and invitations to consult and lecture. The clinician without academic roots, lacking incentives to pinpoint, record, and consequate, is not likely to maintain systematic record keeping since it does entail a response cost beyond ordinary and acceptable practice. It is very difficult to convince line clinicians of the utility of frequent measurement. As any researcher and his assistant know, data collection is laborious and tedious. The reinforcers for the clinician are fees or salaries, attention from colleagues for interesting (but not necessarily successful) clinical anecdotes, and the satisfactions emanating from the therapeutic changes and relationships developed with clients. Faced with the demand for service, the clinician must cope and intervene in some way with a wide variety of unselected cases, in contrast to the academic behavior modifier who generally plans his strategy in advance, conjures up an experimental design, and selects his case material carefully. These distinctions are important to grasp for anyone seriously intent on bringing about lasting changes in a community mental health center and its staff. If the distinctions are ignored, we may encounter a parade of convincing demonstrations of behavior modification that are as fleeting in their impact on the fields of psychology, psychiatry, counseling, and social work as they are elegant in their experimental analysis of behavior (Weiner, 1972; Liberman, 1972a). Without the involvement of the line clinical staff in the daily collection of data, actualization of ideal mental health settings in which measurement is a routine part of treatment (Risley, 1972) seems very far off indeed.

A fruitful way of planning behavioral innovation in a community mental health center is to ask three basic questions:

1. What kinds of behaviors can a clinical staff measure?
    a. Which behaviors, if measured, will be of interest to the clinician and helpful to him or her in the therapeutic endeavor?
    b. How much specification, recording, and monitoring can the clinician be expected reasonably to maintain?
    c. How fast a pace should be used to introduce successive increments of specification and recording methods into the various service elements of a community mental health center?

2. What reinforcers, especially natural reinforcers, can be mobilized to start the clinician on the road to measurement and then keep him or her on the road after the novelty wears off and the daily efforts seem increasingly to demand a dogged and plodding commitment to an ideal with questionable payoff?

3. What are the limitations of behavioral interventions when balanced against time, cost, and environmental constraints?

DEVELOPING BEHAVIORAL RECORDS

When the senior author first arrived at the Oxnard Community Mental Health Center, only occasional narrative notes were being written by the staff. These were done primarily at the time of intake and termination. A shaping approach was taken that aimed at ultimately developing staff competence in carrying out various kinds of recording behavior—event, duration, latency, interval, and time sampling. The first approximation was to have the staff of the Day Treatment Center fill out a simple, one-page Patient Review Form (see Table 16–2 for sample) at the time of intake. This form focused the clinician on specifying deficits and excesses of behaviors, setting specific goals, delineating a treatment program to meet the goals, and a measurement system to monitor progress. The staff were urged to substitute this form for more lengthy narrative notes, although they were offered the option of doing both.

TABLE 16-2   Patient review form

NAME—Jane Jones   DATE: 3/8/71

PROBLEMS:

Deficits or lacks of Adaptive Behavior
1. Boredom
2. Lack of constructive pursuits weekends and nights
3. Lack of achievement in school

Excesses or Surplusses of Maladaptive Behavior
1. Anxiety when bored
2. Drug taking
3. Truancy

GOALS:

Behavior to Shape or Build Up
1. Constructive activities
2. Increased social performance

Behavior to Extinguish or Decrease
1. Anxiety
2. Boredom

PLANS: TREATMENT PROGRAM
1. Contingency contract with her mother and tutor

MEASUREMENT OR RECORDING SYSTEM
(TO MONITOR PROGRESS)
1. Record sheet kept by patient

THERAPIST:
Gayle McDowell, R.N.

After one year of using this more specific, problem- and goal-oriented form, the next innovation was a weekly Behavioral Progress Record (see Table 16–3 for sample). All information necessary to a patient's program for the current week was displayed on a single page on a clipboard placed in an accessible location within the nurses' station. The conventional but unwieldy manila folder that previously had served as the patient's clinical chart was relegated to supplementary importance and kept "buried" in the file cabinet. Weekly goals were set and reviewed by patient, significant others, therapist, and the therapist's supervisor from the BAM Project.

Daily data on the frequency of behavior and the achievement of goals were placed on the Progress Board. The Progress Board cued the staff to set realistic and specific goals with the patients and to make behavioral observations that provided feed-back on patients' progress. Concurrently, the BAM project's training seminars taught recording techniques, and the staff began to use time sampling, event, duration, and latency recording on their weekly Behavioral Progress Records. At the beginning of the BAM Project, no staff members were graphing their patients' behavior. Six months after the project began, a research assistant made an unannounced survey of the clinical charts and found 62% of the patients with behavioral graphs. These graphs were posted on a large bulletin board and, for a time, the patient with the most impressive behavioral change graphed was awarded bonus coupons in the Day Treatment Center's token economy.

As time passed, however, and the BAM Project began fading its staff members out of frequent, supportive supervision of the day treatment team, two phenomena crystallized. The staff decreased its use of graphs to about 10% of the patients (a "reversal effect"), and they specified relatively trivial goals on their weekly Behavioral Progress Records. For example, punctual attendance at the center and earning coupons became overused goals instead of behaviors like finding friends and jobs that could be performed in the patient's natural environment outside the clinic. The BAM research staff decided that detailed, daily data on every patient were not necessarily the most valid or reliable indication of progress. Focusing on daily events preoccupied the staff's attention and misguided the staff into working toward daily attainment of discrete goals on the site of the center at the expense of achieving more functional goals in the community.

The research and clinical staffs discarded the weekly form for a monthly Behavioral Progress Record, which is shown in Table 16–4. The monthly form has been used regularly for 8 months by the clinical staff with limited supervision by the half-time behavioral consultant. The Progress Record requires the therapist to specify one to four goals on a weekly basis and to connect a

TABLE 16–3   Weekly behavioral progress report

WEEKLY BEHAVIORAL PROGRESS RECORD

TOTAL THERAPY SESSIONS THIS WEEK: _____

NAME: _____   INDIVIDUAL: _____

THERAPIST: _____   FAMILY: _____

WEEK ENDING: _____   COLLATERAL: _____

BEHAVIORAL GOALS (Countable)	Mon.	Tues.	Wed.	Thurs.	Fri.	Sat.	Sun.
1.							
2.							
3.							
4.							
5.							

MEDICATION: _____   NOTES: _____

TABLE 16–4   Behavioral goal record

BEHAVIORAL GOAL RECORD

NAME _____   THERAPIST _____

ENTRY DATE _____

4–WEEK GOALS

BE SPECIFIC				

WEEKLY SUBGOALS (SPECIFIC & OBSERVABLE)

	Goal:				
Week of	Method:				
	√				
	Goal:				
Week of	Method:				
	√				
	Goal:				
Week of	Method:				
	√				
	Goal:				
Week of	Method:				
	√				

MEDS

NOTES

specific intervention with each goal. For example, if the goal is to fill out three job applications in a particular week, the therapist might note "prompt and reinforce" as the method to help the client reach the goal. Each weekly goal is an approximation to the monthly goal. At the end of each week, the therapist checks those goals that were attained. Some patients are still observed for the frequency of behaviors on a daily basis; for instance, number of greetings initiated or duration of rational speech in 15-minute conversations. Graphs are made for approximately 10% of the patients. But the focus now is on functional goals that will enable the day treatment patients to learn new behaviors, extending their repertoires to facilitate their reentry into independent, community living.

In the process of evolving a workable recording system, we have learned that the pacing of innovations comes out of "the free flow of action and reaction, and requires on the part of the organizer an easy acceptance of apparent disorganization [Alinsky, 1972, p. 165]." This was not easy to grasp or understand since, as academic researchers and behavior modifiers, we were trained in logic, well-formulated designs for action, and structured, ordered experimentation.

MAINTAINING RECORD KEEPING

While the behavior therapist who enters a community mental health center with hopes of introducing behavioral technology to the clinical staff does not have to sacrifice such professional reinforcers as publications and scientific meetings, he must add to his reinforcement hierarchy the production of competence, recognition, and job satisfaction in the paraprofessional staff.

As noted above, Turner (1972) has built salary contingencies in a community mental health center in which clinical staff are paid in proportion to the amount of data collected. While this may be a possible strategy to pursue in private or independent, non-profit mental health centers where empiricism and behavior modification is regarded highly at the top echelons (Turner, 1972), it is not realistic for most existing centers, which are imbedded in inflexible service pay regulations. The BAM Project explored other avenues for reinforcers to sustain specification, measurement, and behavioral interventions in the clinical staff of the mental health center.

One source of reinforcers for the staff was college credits that were arranged through local junior colleges and universities. The credits were given to the staff contingent on their completing reading assignments and demonstrating mastery on performance measures. For example, towards the end of the year's training of the day treatment team, staff members obtained college credit if they wrote and verbally presented a synopsis of a clinical case, complete with descriptions of the patient, the methods and interventions used, reliability assessments, results graphed, and discussion of implications for generalization.

The Ventura County Mental Health Department, which administers and supports the Oxnard Mental Health Center, requires annual performance reviews and semiannual listings of performance objectives for each staff member. Some of the staff members included the obtaining of college credits and the mastery of a behavioral technique in their personal objectives, thereby further strengthening the reward value of the behavior modification training.

Wherever possible, the staff of the Day Treatment Center was also involved in the receipt of the usual reinforcers for doing research. Staff members have been junior authors on publications of work they have been involved with, they have been consultants to other mental health organizations, and they have conducted tours of the Day Treatment Center for the university and clinical personnel who have heard of the program and have come to visit. Students in psychology, nursing, social work, and residents in psychiatry regularly rotate through the center for training. Since the program will retain its uniqueness and its model features for many years, the staff will continue to be sought after as teachers, demonstrators, and consultants.

Just as instructions are powerful in modifying the clinical behavior of clients, the staff's behavior, too, is governed by the instructions and cues embedded in the program structure and schedule. The data reported below on staff contact with patients reflect the importance of scheduling events in a systematic manner to ensure that meaningful interactions occur between staff and clients throughout the day. These findings replicate those of Risley and his colleagues (Doke & Risley, 1972; Cataldo & Risley, 1973; Risley & Cataldo, 1973), which were carried out in day care centers for children and geriatric patients.

The most important natural consequences for maintaining and expanding innovation is the social attention given by the professional consultant who is viewed as an available and effective resource person. At the Oxnard Mental Health Center, the professional attends all supervision sessions and case reviews with staff members focusing on the Behavioral Progress Records. Support and encouragement is provided for ingenious, creative interventions with clients; for example, interventions in the homes using relatives as mediators. The staff are praised for setting realistic, functional, and specific goals. The professional is available for consultation on difficult problems and can be called in by the paraprofessional staff to assist in an intervention or demonstrate a new technique. The professional attends all the staff members' performance reviews and encourages the staff to set specific objectives for the future that will expand their competence in behavior analysis and modification. For example, some staff members have taken university-sponsored workshops in sexual counseling, assertion training, interventions with children, and family and couple therapy.

Others have set performance goals to develop a new workshop for the center or participate in an experimental study with the BAM Project. In short, the innovator's role in a community treatment program must be as a model and reinforcer for the staff performing the direct services. To be effective as a model and reinforcer, he or she must be available, down-to-earth, assertive, and competent as an organizer and clinician.

With this background on the process of gaining entry into a community mental health center, some of the behavioral programs being developed by the BAM Project will next be described.

Behavioral Programs at the Oxnard Community Mental Health Center

TOKEN ECONOMY IN THE DAY TREATMENT CENTER

The first behavioral intervention at the Day Treatment Center was the introduction of a coupon incentive, or token economy, system to the daily operation. One of the first requests of the staff was for help in simply getting the daily chores of the center completed. To achieve this goal the coupon incentive system was begun.

Coupons that resemble money are used as the medium of exchange. The back-up reinforcers are lunch, snacks, trips to the bowling alleys, individual time with the staff, and admission to group activities. There is also a weekly auction at which the patients bid their excess coupons for bonuses such as two free dinners at a local restaurant.

Behavioral requirements in the coupon system are prompt arrival at the center and the various maintenance tasks that have to be done in a day care situation; for example, cooking lunch, washing dishes, emptying ash trays, dusting furniture, and stacking magazines. With some patients, treatment goals are translated as targeted behaviors that are reinforced or fined with the coupons. The

TABLE 16–5   Contingencies of the credit (coupon) incentive system at the Oxnard Day Treatment Center

Earn Credits (Coupons) By:		Spend Credits (Coupons) For:	
Attend workshop	5	Coffee	5
Participate in workshop	5	Lunch	10
Complete workshop assignment	10	Weekly banquet	15
Credit system monitor (daily)	15	Bowling	8
Menu-planning chairman (weekly)	50	Bus trip	5
Cook or prepare lunch	5	Private therapy (15 min.)	5
Wipe off kitchen tables	3	Time off (per hour)	5
Wash dishes	5–10	Day off	20
Dry and put away dishes	5	Review with psychiatrist	10
Make coffee and clean urn	15	Prescription from doctor	10
Clean refrigerator	20	Being late (per 10 min.)	1
Complete O.T. project	5	Entry into O.T. shop	3
Assist Staff	5	Doing your own thing	5–10

contingencies of the system are shown in Table 16–5.

The coupon system has been largely run by the patients. There is a weekly meeting at which the patients decide if any prices need adjustment. At this meeting, a coupon system monitor is also elected by the patients. The patient who is elected monitor has the responsibility of dispensing, collecting, and recording coupons.

Although the patient-monitored system is not as systematically managed as a staff-monitored system, there are advantages to the former system. It provides a diagnostic tool to determine if a patient has improved to the point of adequately completing this rather complex task. If the patient is successful in the task, this offers another opportunity for the staff to dispense social reinforcers to him or her. Delegating responsibility and authority to the patients also promotes self-management, as the system is a simulated exercise in earning and budgeting money. Cohesiveness is enhanced because the patients view the coupon system as their own.

The role of social reinforcers in the coupon incentive system deserves special mention. While contingencies of behavior-to-coupon-to-backups are not strictly observed, when coupons are given out they are usually accompanied with social reinforcers from the monitor, staff, or other patients. In an open setting such as a day treatment center, the liberal use of social reinforcement more closely approximates the natural environment of the patients than strict and absolute reliance on a rigid, tangible quid pro quo system.

After 2 years of operation, a consensus developed that the coupon system should be somewhat tightened without sacrificing the voluntary participation by the patients or the use of uncontrived, natural reinforcers. It is a reflection of the clinical staff's training and "behavioral consciousness" that they were first to suggest that the patients' behavior be more consistently monitored and consequated. To accomplish this the current credit system was introduced.

Instead of coupons mediating contingencies of reinforcement in the Day Treatment Center, a credit card now serves that function. Each patient receives a credit card that is functional for 1 week. The card, displayed in Figure 16–1, has numbers equivalent to credits that are punched twice by staff and by patient monitors. A number is punched initially by a die with a small, special symbol (heart or diamond) when the patient has earned credits by performing ther-

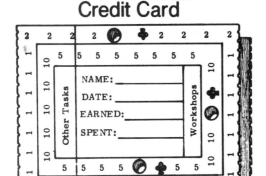

FIGURE 16–1   Credit card used in the token economy system at the Oxnard Day Treatment Center.

apeutic or maintenance behaviors. The same
number is overpunched by a large circular
die when the patient pays for a reinforcer,
such as lunch or coffee. The system using
punched cards (Aitchison, 1972) utilizes the
same contingencies of the coupon system
but enables the staff and the patient monitor
to more reliably dispense and collect
credits. Separate record keeping on a data
sheet is obviated since the credit cards themselves serve as permanent products of earnings and payments. The center's secretarial
crew computes the totals of credits earned
and spent by each patient on a weekly basis
and graphs the results on cumulative records. These totals and graphs are then used
to give feedback to the patients at the
weekly planning meeting.

The training of the clinical staff in behavior theory and experimental designs has
produced a readiness for research and experimental manipulations of the credit
economy. One BAB design has been completed showing that a 2-week withdrawal
of the credits produces a marked decline
in performance of chores. A second study is
underway that will withdraw the back-up
reinforcers with the credit-dispensing procedures remaining in operation. This BAB
experiment will shed light on the relative

importance of back-up reward versus the
symbolic rewards of contingent attention
and praise.

EDUCATIONAL WORKSHOPS AS DAY TREATMENT

Despite the implementation of a goal-
oriented method of patient management and
the coupon incentive system in the Day
Treatment Center, the participation by
patients in activities was still not at an acceptable level. Casual observations indicated that patients spent much of the day
sitting, drinking coffee, smoking, and remaining isolated from staff and one another.
This did not seem to be true during structured activities such as training in Personal
Effectiveness (a special form of group assertion training) during which patients participated frequently and animatedly. To
determine more objectively the level of
social interaction in the milieu of the Day
Treatment Center, client and staff behaviors
were time sampled by independent observers using the Behavior Observation Instrument (Liberman, DeRisi, King, Eckman,
& Wood, 1974). This instrument is a coding
system derived from Schaefer and Martin's
(1969) apathy scale. All behavior exhibited
by a person is coded into mutually exclusive and concomitant classes each time the
subject is observed. Components of general
categories of the Behavior Observation
Instrument (BOI) are shown in Table
16–6.

A randomly chosen sample of 10 patients
from the average daily census of 20 was
observed each day at the Oxnard Day Treatment Center and at a comparison Day
Treatment Center II in an adjoining city.
Four observations were made each day. Each
patient was observed for 5 seconds during
each observation. Reliability was calculated
by comparing the observational records of
two raters on an act-by-act basis. Mean
agreement across all observations was
94.9%.

The results of these systematic observa-

TABLE 16–6   Components of general categories of the Behavior Observation
Instrument

SOCIAL PARTICIPATION
Grooming—with or by another person
Recreation—group activities
Conversation with another student (speaking)
Conversation with another student (gestural indication of listening)
Conversation with a staff member (speaking)
Conversation with a staff member (gestural indication of listening)
Individual therapy (speaking or gestural indication of listening)
Group meeting—active participation in role-playing, discussion
Group meeting—alert, listening, eyes open, body seated toward focus of group

NONSOCIAL BEHAVIORS
Drinking
Smoking
Eating other than meals
Chewing
Grooming self
Reading, writing, looking through magazine or newspaper
Recreation—solitary
Group meeting—apparent inattention: eyes closed, looking away from focus of group

WORK
Cleaning or tidying up
Preparing, planning, shopping for Day Treatment Center meals
Working on occupational-therapy project

OTHER
Eating meals
Away on field trips
Absent from center after being present on this day

TABLE 16–7   Distribution of patient activity as time-sampled by the Behavior
Observation Instrument at the Oxnard Day Treatment Center (DTC) and Day
Treatment Center II (DTC II).

	Percent of Observations	
BOI General Categories	*DTC II*	*Oxnard DTC*
Pre-intervention		
Social participation	37.5	29.2*
Nonsocial	32.6	61.5*
Work	8.1	9.3
Other	21.8	0.0*
Post-intervention		
Social participation	52.5	67.7*
Nonsocial	36.8	17.2*
Work	.8	7.0*
Other	9.9	8.1

Note.—The intervention was the introduction of an educational workshop format
into the Oxnard Day Treatment Center.

* $P < .01$, DTC II vs. Oxnard DTC.

tions are shown in Table 16–7. Patients were socially isolated a majority of the time. Less than 30% of the behaviors observed involved social participation, while over 60% were nonsocial. Even given the operational coupon incentive system, under 10% of the patients' behaviors involved work. Comparable figures for the same classes of behavior observed at the other day treatment center showed that patients socialized more frequently than when they were in isolation from one another and the staff. A marked difference between the two centers was revealed in the "Other" class of behaviors, reflecting the fact that clients at Day Treatment Center II left and returned to the center often during the day. This was not the case at Oxnard, where clients tended to remain in the building. This interesting difference may be a result of the differences in architectural design. Day Treatment Center II has a modern floorplan that was designed to allow free and open access to the outside, whereas Oxnard Day Treatment Center, on the second floor of a traditional building, discourages convenient in-and-out transit.

The results of this program evaluation prompted a revamping of the Oxnard Day Treatment Center program. During the initial observations, only 47.6% of the Day Treatment Center's available hours were structured with some activity designed to evoke adaptive behaviors from clients. In considering alternative models that would build in social participation, the BAM staff drew upon two sources—the designs for rehabilitation settings by Cataldo and Risley (1973) and Spiegler (1972) and the fortuitous development of a workshop model for the Oxnard evening treatment program. In the evening program, workshops to meet the functional needs of clients striving for greater independence were being constructed—job-seeking skills, Personal Effectiveness (Assertion) Training, and living alone successfully. Clients remarked that coming to the evening program was like "going back to school."

The research staff and the clinical staff together decided that this "school" model might be attempted in the Day Treatment Center program. Staff reviewed their clients, past and present, to identify the subject matter that would serve their needs. Workshops were selected in subjects such as conversational skills, dealing with public agencies, consumer awareness, personal finances, grooming, vocational preparedness, anxiety and depression management, weight control, and R.E.S.T. (recreational-educational-social-transportation).

A planning period of 4 weeks then ensued. Behavioral objectives were written for each workshop. Lists of terminal behaviors that patients should be able to perform at the end of the workshop were drawn up. Lesson plans for the leaders specified the content, format, and homework assignments for the eight weekly sessions of the "semester." Leaders and coleaders were assigned to teach each workshop. A system of rotating staff members through the leadership position in each workshop was developed to avoid boredom and to generate overall competence in each staff member. A 2-week intersemester break was built into the schedule so that leaders could evaluate their methods, materials, objectives, and results. Patients were to be called "students," a change that also was aimed at reducing the stigma of coming to a mental health center. Class cards having each student's schedule were used in the manner similar to most colleges.

The contingencies of the credit system (token economy) were reordered to fit the higher priority being placed on participation in the workshops. Work behaviors, especially housekeeping chores, were deemphasized, and fewer credits could be earned for these tasks. Instead, the highest paying behaviors were those relating to participation in the workshop sessions. Attendance, verbal participation, and completion of homework assignments in the natural environment were richly consequated with credits.

Observations, using the BOI, were taken during the last 2 weeks of the first semester of the educational workshop program. The same number of observations were taken at Day Treatment Center II, which had not made a major problem change. The results of the direct behavioral observations are shown in Table 16–7. Following the introduction of the workshop format at Oxnard, social participation of patients rose by almost 40% over the initial period, while nonsocial behaviors decreased by 44%. A substantial increase in social participation also occurred at Day Treatment Center II. Interviews with observers indicated that this may have been the result of the reactivity of the BOI. Observations were done with the full knowledge and consent of patients and staff at Day Treatment Center II, who realized that they were being compared with the Oxnard Day Treatment Center. Observers at Day Treatment Center II overheard comments by staff that indicated a desire to "look good" even though the exact nature of the experimental variables was not disclosed.

The results of this program evaluation suggest a positive relationship between the amount of structured activities scheduled in a center and the amount of social participation observed. The implementation of an educational workshop format effectively increased the level of social interaction among staff and patients in the milieu. This finding supports the findings of Doke and Risley (1972), who performed similar interventions in a day care center for children. Before the workshop program was instituted at Oxnard, 47.6% of the Day Treatment Center time was filled by scheduled activities; after the workshops were begun, scheduled activities rose to fill 83.9% of the time.

It should be pointed out that the operational definition of "social participation" subsumed by the relevant BOI categories required more than mere physical presence at a structured activity. Clients had to be either talking, motorically participating, or attending by means of head and body

orientation toward the leader or a group member who was the focus of activity. Hence, the statistically significant rise in social participation was not an artifact of the particular measurement instrument used.

This experimental intervention demonstrates the usefulness of direct observation in program evaluation and effectiveness of the particular behavioral-educational program that served as the experimental program at the Oxnard Day Treatment Center. In the course of this study, it was demonstrated that direct observation is inexpensive (Eckman, 1973), reliable and valid (Alevizos, 1973; Callahan, 1973), and ethically defensible (DeRisi, 1973). The BOI is described in greater detail together with examples of its use in program evaluation in a series of articles (DeRisi, Eckman, Alevizos, Callahan, & Liberman, 1975; Alevizos, Callahan, DeRisi, Eckman, Berck, & Liberman, 1975; Liberman, DeRisi, Alevizos, Callahan, & Eckman, 1975).

TRAINING IN PERSONAL EFFECTIVENESS—A SAMPLE WORKSHOP. One of the cornerstones of the educational workshop model is training in Personal Effectiveness, a variant of assertive training. The format of assertive training—including goal setting, behavioral rehearsal, modeling, feedback, outside-of-clinic assignments, and reporting back to the therapist—is useful with the socially and emotionally deficient patients seen at the Day Treatment Center. However, the types of problems presented by these patients are much wider than the ones seen in a typical outpatient assertive-training session. The patients' problems were not so much a lack of assertion as they were incompetency in a wide range of verbal and social behaviors. Many of these patients did not have basic conversational skills. Others did not know how to conduct themselves at job interviews or when negotiating with social agencies. In Personal Effectiveness, instead of concentrating on assertion, the groups focus on interpersonal skills at whatever level is appropriate for the individual patients.

Because the daily census of patients at the Day Treatment Center ranges between 20 and 30, training in Personal Effectiveness is done in groups. A more complete version of how training in Personal Effectiveness is done at the Oxnard Day Treatment Center is given in a manual for group leaders (Liberman, King, DeRisi, & McCann, 1976; Liberman, 1972).

An evaluation of the Personal Effectiveness groups has been done (King, Liberman, & Roberts, 1974). The evaluation was concerned with the transfer of training from the Personal Effectiveness groups. Patients were asked if they completed their assignments and were also directly observed in their attempts to complete the assignments given them in the groups. Self-report data were collected on 50 consecutive assignments, and direct observations were made on another 50 consecutive assignments. The results show that on the self-report measure, 78% of the assignments were reported as completed. Of the directly observed assignments, 80% were actually performed.

While there are many methodological limitations in interpreting this evaluation, the results indicate that training in Personal Effectiveness does generalize to the patient's natural environment. More recent research has experimentally evaluated training in Personal Effectiveness through the use of multiple-baseline experimental designs and nonobtrusive measures. This research, conducted during the second year of the BAM project when the focus was on the outpatient clinic, demonstrated the training "package" to be causally linked to changes in patient's behaviors.

EXPERIMENTAL ANALYSIS OF UNSELECTED CASES

Although the BOI assessed the level of social participation in the Day Treatment Center, it did not provide outcome measures of individual treatment programs for the patients attending the center. To examine what effects behavioral interventions were having on the patient's problems, within-subject experimental designs were used. As a rigorous test of both the treatment effects and the within-subject designs, it was decided to designate every sixth patient who entered the Day Treatment Center as one whose treatment program would be experimentally analyzed.

The purpose of the experimental analyses were to evaluate:

1. Unselected cases as they came into the center

2. The feasibility of subjecting presenting complaints to behavior analysis

3. The effects of prescribed interventions on the targeted behaviors of the patients

4. Reliability of measuring targeted behaviors

5. Generalization of treatment effects, either across time, settings, or behaviors

This method of assessing treatment effects avoids a redundant demonstration of impressive short-term improvements in "selected" cases carried out in a special setting and with no report of generalization. A separate report (King, Levine, Liberman, DeRisi, & Austin, in progress) will give a thorough description of each patient in the experimental sample, an account of the treatment and measurement procedures, and the results obtained. For the purpose of this chapter, only a summary of the experimental studies will be presented.

A total of 15 patients was included in the sample. The age range of the patients was from 17 to 60. All but two of the patients had been hospitalized prior to coming to the Day Treatment Center. Most had multiple hospitalizations. All but three of the patients were diagnosed as psychotic. The diagnoses were made on the basis of prior hospital records, admission evaluations at the Day Treatment Center, and concurrence by a board-certified psychiatrist who reviewed each case. The years of formal education for the patients ranged from 6 to 15 years. The ethnic backgrounds of the sample included Anglos, Blacks, and Chicanos.

Behavioral goals for the patients were targeted for intervention after a 1–2 week period of assessment by the Day Treatment Center and BAM staff. Significant others in the patient's life also contributed to the choice of goals. An additional outcome measure was Goal Attainment Scaling (Kiresuk & Sherman, 1968) performed during the initial assessment period with followups at 3 and 6 months posttreament (Austin, Liberman, King, & DeRisi, 1975).

Table 16–8 presents a descriptive overview of the patients, including their ages, problems, targeted behavioral goals, interventions used, and results. Reliability measures were taken in 11 of the 15 cases. The percentage of observations across all cases in which reliability measures were taken ranged from 7 to 100%, with the mean being 51%. The range of agreement between observers was 75 to 100% with the mean being 93%.

The letters under Results in Table 16–8 refer to the procedures completed with each patient. For example, ABAB refers to a completed design: baseline, intervention, return to baseline, reinstatement of intervention. In some cases, only baseline (A) or intervention (B) data were collected. In other cases, multiple interventions were used. This is designated by ABCD.

Withdrawal, reversal, or multiple-baseline designs were completed in 5 of the 15 cases (Carol, Bob, Harold, JoAnne, and Marilyn). For these cases it was evident that the interventions produced a desirable change in the patient's targeted behavior. Partial reversal or withdrawal designs (ABA or BAB) were completed in two other cases (Joan and Juan). Although a desirable change in the patient's behavior was shown, it is not certain that the intervention produced this change. In five other cases, substantial improvement in the targeted behavior from baseline performance was shown, but no reversal or withdrawal procedures could be completed (AB or BA designs) (Donna, Steve, Peggy, Alfred, and Diane). In the three remaining cases, no improve-

ment was noted, or measures could be taken only in one or none of the conditions (Manuel—no improvement, Mary, and Ricardo).

Of the 12 cases in which improvement was shown following the introduction of the intervention, generalization measures across either time, settings, or responses were taken for 9 of the cases. Evidence for generalization was shown in 7 of the 9 cases.

The above results are informative in the light of their being the first obtained on unselected cases. Perhaps these figures should best be viewed as a baseline against which future attempts at experimental analysis in community mental health centers could be judged. When experimental research is conducted in a community mental health center, it is important to take into account such factors as the "openness" of the setting, the pressure to provide service, the mobility of patients with resultant high turnover, the independence of the adult patients from the treatment center, and the center's relative lack of control over social and material rewards for the voluntary patients. This combination of factors is not well represented in the behavior modification literature. Therefore, it is difficult to interpret the significance of the results of the experimental analyses on the 15 cases. It is recommended, however, that future reports of the use of behavior modification include the overall effectiveness of the interventions with groups of unselected patients. Only in such a manner will the field move toward a more mature and self-critical evaluation of its efforts.

INDIRECT COMMUNITY SERVICES

Indirect community services are provided at the center utilizing a variety of behavioral procedures. For almost 3 years, educational workshops have been held for small groups of parents who request assistance in managing their children's behavior. In fact, little or no conventional "child therapy" is carried out at the center: parents of deviant

TABLE 16–8   Description of experimental cases

Patient	Age	Problems	Targeted Behavioral Goals	Reliability % of total observations	Reliability % rater agreement	Interventions	Results	Generalization Measures taken	Generalization Evidence of Generalization
Donna	28	Provocative delusional comments to husband and staff members of clinic	Increase amount of appropriate conversation	0	—	Contingent staff attention	AB	Setting	Yes
Joan	48	(1) Attempted suicide, (2) depressed, (3) no task oriented activity or social contacts	Bring in newspaper articles to discuss with therapist	100	100	Instructions	BAB	Time	Yes
Carol	39	(1) Delusions, manic-related, (2) tangential speech, (3) separated from her family because of her problems	Increasing appropriate speech	20	82	Contingent staff attention	ABAB	Setting Time	Yes Yes
Steve	17	(1) Confusion and ambivalence about social and vocational goals, (2) truancy and failure at school	Attendance at community mental health center	13	100	Instructions and contingent money	ABCD	None	—
Bob	27	(1) Extreme seclusiveness and social withdrawal, (2) no friends or job, (3) totally dependent upon parents	(1) Located in designated social areas, (2) eyes open up (3) body oriented to people	29	1)100 2) 80 3) 88	Earned and lost time away from clinic	ABCDCD and multiple baseline	Time	1) No 2) No 3) Yes
Manuel	50	(1) Somatic complaints, (2) fears of going to hell, criticism, and dying	Reducing somatic complaints and fears	0	—	Placebo (Curanderismo)-Instructions	Multiple baseline	Response	No

Name	Age	Problem behaviors	Target behavior			Intervention	Design	Generalization	
Mary	36	(1) Suicide threats, (2) hostile, destruction of property, and temper tantrums, (3) high rate of sick-role talk	Decrease sick-role talk	7	100	Contingent staff attention	B	None	—
Ricardo	33	(1) Mute, (2) socially withdrawn, (3) uncooperative and apathetic at home and clinic	None	—	—	—	—	—	—
Harold	33	(1) Aggressiveness toward others, (2) lack of social contacts, (3) unstable work history	Attendance at community mental health center	75	100	Instructions re: implied contingency on VA pension	ABAB	Time	No
JoAnne	22	(1) Delusions of receiving radio messages, (2) hostile and uncooperative	(1) Increase initiated conversations, (2) increase greetings	11	80	Prompts	ABCDAD	None	—
Peggy	23	(1) Depressed, (2) almost mute, (3) inactive and lethargic	Increase chores performed at home and clinic	0	—	Contingencies (attention, food, etc.)	AB	Setting	Yes
Juan	20	(1) Depressed and anxious, (2) fearful of people and job, (3) unemployed	Bring in employment want-ads	100	100	Contingent access to rock music	ABA	None	—
Alfred	54	(1) Stopped working, (2) began writing nonsense phrases on walls of home and clinic	Decrease "psychotic" writing	100	85	Contingent cigarettes plus instructions	AB	Setting Time	Yes Yes
Diane	23	(1) Postpartum depression, (2) provocative attempts to gain attention	Complete household chores	100	75	Contingent staff attention	BA	None	—
Marilyn	18	(1) Standing rigidly in one place for long periods of time with a blank expression on face, (2) no initiated speech	(1) Latency of asking for coupons, (2) latency of sitting down, (3) increased greetings	8	1)100 2)100 3)100	Prompts and contingent staff attention	Multiple baseline	Time	1) Yes 2) Yes 3) No

children referred from schools, social agencies, and individual homes are offered the "Parent Workshop" as a first line of service. In these workshops, the parents, as consultees, learn to become therapists for their own children. These workshops, consisting of nine 1-hour weekly meetings, are led by paraprofessionals under the supervision of a psychologist. The curriculum (Liberman, 1971b; Aitchison & Liberman, 1973b) includes training in basic behavioral principles, graphing, pinpointing and consequating behaviors, token economy, and contingency contracting. Modeling sequences on videotapes and role-playing as in Personal Effectiveness have recently been added to the workshop to aid the parents in discriminating and improving their responses to their children. Evaluations of the workshops showed that 58% of the participating parents carried out at least one intervention that led to a change in their child's behavior. Followup at 2 months to 1 year after the completion of the workshop indicated that 65% of the parents reported using behavioral principles, but only 25% continued to keep behavioral records (Aitchison & Liberman, 1973a). An experiment comparing groups of parents trained in social learning principles using didactic versus role-playing techniques revealed the marked and statistically significant superiority of the role-playing format.

Another application of behavioral technology to the consultation services of the Oxnard Mental Health Center lies in the area of schools. One program is "Achievement Class," a special classroom on the site of a junior high school where students with behavioral and academic problems receive remedial programming in the context of a token economy; individualized, programmed instruction; and contingency contracting (Brown & Liberman, 1973). A second program, "Project Friendship," is underway with students from the third to sixth grades who are from multiple-problem families. The students are selected by their teachers and principals because of failing grades and poor social adjustments. The targeted students are assigned to volunteer college students or housewives who receive training and supervision in behavioral principles and relationship building from the project staff. Each volunteer works on an individual basis with one or two grade-school students and serves as a model, a reinforcer for adaptive behavior, an advocate for the child's needs, and an active consultant with the child's parents and teacher. An evaluation of the training of the volunteers showed statistically significant acquisition of skills in using behavioral principles and in benefits accruing to the grade-school children (Aitchison & Merrill, 1974).

Another effort to apply behavioral technology to the indirect services of the mental health center has been a workshop for operators of residential care facilities. Formerly hospitalized individuals, primarily those diagnosed as retarded or schizophrenic, have been released from the state hospitals and live in family-care and board-and-care homes, each of which contains 4 to 40 such expatients. While many of the operators of these homes are concerned and interested in providing more than simple custodial care, they do not have any training or know-how. An educational workshop, similar in structure to the workshop for parents, was constructed with a curriculum centered around behavior modification and practical psychopharmacology (DeRisi, Myron, & Goding, 1975). The 10 sessions of the workshop had over 90% attendance, and over 50% of the students completed at least one behavior-change experiment. The workshop is now being offered for credit at a local community college. One operator of a family-care home who attended the workshop developed a recreational program for chronic expatients held evenings in a school gymnasium. Another operator is consulting with BAM Project staff to introduce a token economy into his 65-bed residential care facility.

One final illustration of how behavior

technology is being disseminated via the indirect services of the community mental health center is a group home for delinquent boys. "Welcome Home" is a family-style facility, sponsored by citizens of the small city of Santa Paula and the County Probation Department. The home is run by an indigenous, nonprofessional Chicago couple who have been trained to use behavior modification methods in a replication of the Achievement Place model (Phillips, 1968; Phillips, Phillips, Fixsen, & Wolf, 1971). The staff from the Oxnard Mental Health Center provided training and consultation for the houseparents in developing the contingency management procedures, including methods for training parents and assertion training for the boys. An empirical evaluation has been conducted of the effects of the procedures and their generalized outcomes in school and community (Liberman, Ferris, Salgado, & Salgado, 1975). While initially established as a demonstration project, the home has gotten through its birth pangs and has generated enough favorable community response for its conversion into a permanent program.

OUTPATIENT, EMERGENCY, AND AFTERCARE SERVICES

The second and third years of the BAM Project were devoted to utilizing behavior principles to innovate models for outpatient, emergency, and aftercare services. The outpatient programs included group workshops centered around commonly encountered problem areas. For example, structured therapy groups are being offered for couples having marital conflict and distress (Turner, 1973a; Weiss, Hops, & Patterson, 1973). The coleaders of the married-couples group use problem specification, goal setting, and "homework assignments" during eight 2-hour sessions that are scheduled on a weekly basis. A follow-up session is held to assess and promote generalization 1 month after the eighth meeting. Each couple engages in behavior rehearsals, using

the Personal Effectiveness model described above, that aim at teaching them more effective communication skills. During the eight sessions, each couple develops negotiation skills that lead in a structured format to a contingency contract. This model for marriage counseling was given an empirical, experimental evaluation during 1974. Results indicate that a group based on behavioral-learning methods showed greater change in their communication skills than a comparison group that discussed their problems and received advice but did no behavioral rehearsal or contingency contracting.

Other problem areas for outpatients that were being programmed for behavioral innovation are anxiety-depression, emotional, and interpersonal expressiveness, chronic headaches (using biofeedback), vocational preparedness, crisis situations, and adolescent behavior disorders. In each of these areas, a behavioral approach has been experimentally or evaluatively demonstrated to be effective in producing therapeutic involvement.

Limitations and Challenges of Behavior Modification

The BAM Project was begun with favorable assumptions about the relevance and applicability of behavior analysis and modification to the range of problems managed by a typical community mental health center. Some of our assumptions have proven correct.

1. Clinical staff with no professional education or background in behavioral technology were successfully trained to specify, record, and intervene with a wide variety of clients. Basic behavioral principle were digested.

2. Staff members having digested basic behavioral principles, can now develop their own interventions or empirically monitor their effectiveness.

3. Many problems of clients—from delusional

speech to social withdrawal—have been proven to be amenable to behavioral intervention.

4. These interventions have been evaluated by within-subject and between-group experimental designs.

On the other hand, it may be more helpful to the young field of behavior modification to point out some limitations of the behavioral model in a community setting. Self-criticism goes hand in hand with an empirical philosophy. Fresh solutions and advances in technology can come about only if we openly and honestly share our problems and failures.

The optimistic, zealous ethos of behavior modification researchers has prompted them to attack unusually resistant problems, such as chronic mental patients and recidivistic criminals. It is now time that we critically evaluate the results of our techniques with various unselected populations of therapists and clients. For example, reevaluations of programs for training parents in child management indicate that methods previously published as successful interventions were not effectively replicated across unselected populations (Herbert, Pinkston, Hayden, Sajwaj, Pinkston, Cordua, & Jackson, 1973; Sajwaj, 1973).

PROBLEMS WITH SINGLE-SUBJECT DESIGNS

A question deserving serious discussion is the suitability of the within-subject experimental design for evaluating treatment effects in an open setting such as a day treatment center. Sidman (1960) has explicated the merits and uses of the within-subject design. Chief among these is the achievement of experimental control without resorting to statistical comparisons. When experimental control is achieved, it is possible to isolate the effects of the intervention or independent variable. Indeed, the task of the experimenter is to eliminate any extraneous sources of influence on the dependent variable so that the effects of the independent variable may be properly

evaluated. By such procedures, one does not have to be concerned with large numbers of subjects, control groups, and averaging of data. Effects are replicated both within subjects and across subjects, thus lending credence to the generalizability or external validity of the findings. These procedures have proved very useful in the laboratory and in applied settings in which control over the contingencies of reinforcement can be attained. When one moves into a setting in which total control is not exercised, however, problems appear.

The within-subject experimental design calls for many repeated measurements in order to assess experimental effects. This is easily done in a laboratory or tightly controlled applied setting in which the admission and discharge of subjects are controlled. What happens, however, in settings in which such control is not present, and the patient either decides to leave against the wishes of the staff or the staff decides that the patient has made satisfactory progress and can be discharged? Time constraints inhibited some of our efforts to demonstrate experimental control of the interventions. For instance, just as a reversal condition was attempted for Alfredo, he got his old job back and left the clinic in order to support himself and his family. It would appear extremely unethical to do anything to interfere with the patient's return to a productive life in order to satisfy experimental design requirements.

In other cases, the problem targeted for experimental control met preconditions for specification and reliability of measurement, but was not isomorphic with other behaviors that were more functionally related to the individual's adjustment to community living. For example, one patient (Peggy) showed very little improvement in carrying out chores at home and at the clinic under a reward condition but left the clinic to take a job with her father. We received reports that she functioned adequately in the work setting despite her lack of consistent performance with chores. The obvious relevance of stimulus control across different settings and differential reinforcement of work versus "sick" roles could not be sufficiently evaluated with Peggy given the time and cost constraints operating in the community mental health center.

Another problem with the single-subject experimental design comes from the need to establish a stable baseline before interventions are introduced (Sidman, 1960). This is a very real limitation in settings such as a community mental health center, where people enter in crisis situations and are very sensitive to environmental contingencies. Even in cases where problems and goals can be specified and measured, stable baselines are difficult to obtain. Behavioral baseline may be affected by favorable elements in the treatment milieu, physiological matrix, and/or fortuitous developments outside of the clinic. Collecting baseline data on targeted behaviors becomes an exercise in frustration because improvement occurs before stability is achieved and the planned intervention can begin. The opposite development also can occur, as in the case of Ricardo, who quickly regressed in his grooming and became anorexic and mute before a behavior could even be targeted and measured. Although he initially presented as a depressed person with apathy, later observations during hospitalization indicated that he was schizophrenic and very responsive to phenothiazine medication.

In a milieu such as the Oxnard Day Treatment Center, where the program is purposely structured to evoke and reinforce prosocial and instrumental task behaviors, it is often impossible and even ethically contraindicated to manipulate staff and patients' involvement in therapeutic activities to generate stable baseline measurements. To ensure more stable baselines and retention of patients for the duration of time-consuming experimental studies, control would have to be established over three major domains of variables—clients, change agents, and time (Paul, 1972). Even if control could be established over the domain

of time within a community facility that restricted the mobility of persons, controlling the other variables would be a massive undertaking. Up to now, behavior modifiers have worked in settings where these variables could be controlled (sometimes artificialy supporting dysfunctional behavior) or have ignored them by reporting only selected cases and outcomes. The time has come to admit to the shortcomings of our currently used designs so that we may make headway in research in community settings (Hartmann & Atkinson, 1973; Kazdin, 1973).

BEHAVIORAL EFFECTS OF MEDICATION

A major variable influencing behavior, the biochemical and neurophysiological status of an individual, has received scant attention from behavior therapists. There is an impressive body of evidence that indicates that schizophrenia has a genetic component (Wender, 1969; Reiss, 1974) and that drugs affect behavior (Brady, 1968; Liberman & Davis, 1974; Klein & Davis, 1969). While there is a wealth of data showing the effects of various psychotropic drugs on the behavior of animals subjected to schedules of reinforcement, behavioral pharmacologists have barely begun to use the experimental analysis of behavior to assess the effects of drugs on clinically significant behaviors in man (Liberman, Davis, Moore, & Moon, 1973; Sulzbacher, 1972). There is no doubt that phenothiazine drugs beneficially alter the deviant behaviors of schizophrenics and that lithium reduces the excessive motor and verbal behaviors of manic patients. It is the contention of the authors that withholding psychotropic drugs whose need is clearly indicated by behavioral disturbance is tantamount to unethical clinical practice. Correspondingly, the psychotic patients in the experimental study described above received appropriate medications during their time at the Oxnard Day Treatment Center. Efforts were made to keep the dosage and type of medication constant throughout the various conditions of the experimental designs, but there were obviously interactions between the effects of drugs and environmental interventions (Spohn, 1973). The analysis of such interactions is complicated by the fact that drug effects are not a linear function of dosage and have a latency after administration is started or dropped.

With clear evidence showing the profound therapeutic effectiveness of phenothiazines and lithium on psychotic behaviors, there should be research and demonstration projects mounted by behaviorists to increase the taking of medications by chronic mental patients. The failure of chronic psychotics to regularly ingest their medications is a major contribution to the high rate of readmission to psychiatric hospitals (Crane, 1973; Mason, 1973; Goldberg, DiMascio, & Chaudhary, 1970). The wasted resources and human misery produced by the revolving-door, discharge-readmission phenomenon in mental hospitals present a public health problem of great magnitude. Patients enter the hospital in a psychotic state and are rapidly medicated. Within a few weeks to a month they are sufficiently compensated behaviorally to be able to return to their homes and families in the community. They are discharged with a supply of medication or a prescription and strong urgings by nurses and doctors to "take your medicine." For a variety of reasons, the expatient soon stops taking his medication—it labels him as "crazy" or weak, it produces distressing side effects, it is a bothersome routine, and it costs a significant amount of money. For a while the person continues to feel well since the antipsychotic effects are longer lasting than the side effects: this honeymoon period only serves to reinforce the cessation of the medication. Within 1 to 12 months, the psychotic behavior returns as the medication is slowly metabolized and excreted. Once again the patient requires hospitalization, and the revolving door keeps turning.

An array of behavioral interventions could be studied for their effects on medication taking. Azrin and Powell (1969) showed how a simple mechanical time alarm could be used to prompt psychotics to take their medication. Their device was never submitted to a systematic evaluation, however. Turner (1972) has described a community-based reinforcement program that aims at increasing the reliability of medication taking among former mental patients. Thirty expatients were visited on a regular, time-interval schedule by rehabilitation workers who tested the patients' urine for the presence of phenothiazine metabolites. Positive urine tests resulted in the receipt of credits that could be used immediately or saved toward the purchase of desirable items from a reinforcement menu. After the individual is "hooked" on the reinforcers, the visits are faded to a variable-interval schedule with greater and greater durations between visits. Stretching out the schedule of reinforcement produces more reliable and durable taking of medication and a decrease in rehospitalization. After 1 year of evaluation, Turner (1973b) has reported a saving of 15,000 dollars based on a cost-effectiveness study comparing the community incentive program with a more conventional medical check by a physician.

At the Oxnard Mental Health Center, plans are being made to develop and evaluate a demonstration program for delivering medication services to the approximately 500 chronic psychotics living in the center's catchment area. The program will include a means of supplying medication and prescriptions other than by conventional medical check ups. A registry of all chronic psychotics will prompt the mental health center staff and volunteers to regularly monitor the social and vocational status of these individuals. A community-based reinforcement system similar to the one suggested by Turner (1972) will also be used. Prescriptions will be dispensed by a physician at a sumptuous banquet provided by the mental health department in a local social hall. The psychiatrist can observe the patient's "mental status" in a naturalistic setting where cues for sick-role behavior are not present. In addition, the receipt of a prescription and it is hoped, the subsequent use of medication will become paired with a pleasant, nonstressful social event replete with primary reinforcers.

The next 10 years should see the implementation of a variety of behavioral interventions aimed at increasing the medication-taking behavior of chronic psychotics as well as strengthening their use of birth-control methods (Duncan, Hilton, Kraeger, & Lumsdaine, 1973). Interventions such as therapeutic instructions, fading of prompts, classical conditioning, covert conditioning, self-monitoring, and community-based reinforcement systems will make major contribution to primary and secondary prevention in public health.

ANTECEDENTS OF BEHAVIOR

One finding from the BAM Project that diverges from the major emphasis and trend of the behavior modification literature concerns the relative importance of antecedents versus consequences of behavior. Most behavior modification studies have focused on consequences to change behavior. Research has shown, however, that antecedents, such as instructions, can exert control over behavior (Wincze, Leitenberg, & Agras, 1972; Ayllon & Azrin, 1964; Leitenberg, Agras, Barlow, & Oliveau, 1969; Geller, Farris, & Post, 1973). In our sample, many patients were found to respond quickly and durably to instructions. In fact, the within-subject experimental designs indicated that instructions were the controlling variables in the behavioral changes of four of the patients. If this finding is replicated by other investigators, it would have considerable import for the field of behavior modification. It would emphasize that people do have verbal repertoires that can be used to gain instructional control over socially significant behaviors. Mental health programs might fruitfully concentrate on establishing prompt structures, such as a systematic

orientation for patients at the very start of treatment. Careful scheduling of activities with an emphasis on instructions for carrying out behavioral assignments in the community should promote generalization. It should be noted that an empirical evaluation of the Oxnard Day Treatment Center program (see BOI data above) led to the introduction of an educational workshop format that relies heavily upon instructional control of staff and patient behaviors. Changing clinical behaviors may not always require elaborate contingency management but simply instruction in the desired behavior, a principle derived not from "modern learning theory" but from elementary communication theory.

PROBLEMS WITH GENERALIZATION AND PERSISTENCE OF BEHAVIOR

While the majority of patients exposed to the behavioral approach at the Oxnard Day Treatment Center showed a modicum of functional improvement, some did not. In many cases, the degree of improvement and its generalization into natural environments were disappointing. While the experimental patient Bob showed reliable improvement in his social behavior as a function of the treatment interventions, he still remained severely impaired, with limited generalization of social-approach behavior outside of the clinic and his home. While he carried out errands for his mother and held a menial, part-time job, he did not attempt to initiate social contact with peers and remained financially dependent upon his parents. Follow-up contacts indicated that he slipped back into isolated and withdrawn patterns of behavior when contingencies or frequent prompts were not in effect. Limited gains were accomplished, then, despite an intensive, costly, and 1-year investment of treatment.

Harold's attendance came under the control of instructions requiring that he attend the Day Treatment Center so that an evaluation might be properly made, with recommendations sent to the Veteran's Administration regarding his continuing need for a full-disability pension. However, he ceased coming to the mental health center as soon as the experimental design was completed on his attendance. Little impact was made on his presenting complaint of uninvolvement with people or vocational rehabilitation. While Marilyn responded to prompts in a highly reliable manner, her social behavior deteriorated as soon as attempts were made to fade the prompts. It appears that she and Bob, both poor-premorbid, "process"-type schizophrenics, would require prosthetic environments for the remainder of their lives if the treatment gains were to be consolidated.

It is our view that behavior modifiers, faced with cost accountability in community mental health centers, will have to temper their characteristic optimistic and idealistic strategy of trying to produce functional and generalized behavior change in severely deficient, chronic, and relapsing psychotic individuals. It will be necessary for behavioral engineers to limit their treatment goals and, concomitantly, to develop prosthetic, artificial, and supportive environments in the community to maintain marginally functioning individuals such as psychotics and retardates (Atthowe, 1973). Social clubs, sheltered workshops, and sheltered living residences must be increased in number and improved in quality (Wilder & Caulfield, 1972; McDonough, 1969; Morrison, 1972; Henderson, 1970; Fairweather, Sanders, Crissler, & Maynard, 1969). This realignment of goals for community mental health, away from "cures" and toward maximum feasible function, will stimulate the development of specialized services with documented cost effectiveness.

A day treatment program cannot provide comprehensive services and be an alternative to hospitalization as long as the staff tries to promote unrealistic behavior change in each client. The community mental health center must take its place alongside other agencies and facilities that provide supportive and remedial services to behaviorally deficient individuals. The day treatment program in a community mental health center can serve as an alternative to hospitalization or as a transitional setting for reentry into the community; however, these functions will succeed only for people having an *acute* behavioral decompensation who have a history of functioning on the job and in a family. Day treatment programs can evaluate chronically impaired individuals for their suitability for a variety of habilitation services. The community mental health center can initiate these services via brief interventions and appropriate referrals but cannot fully implement them. Otherwise, the staff may fall into a morass of spending all its resources and energy on lifelong problems and creating a crisis in staff morale. Time-limited services and a crisis-intervention philosophy require that the goals of a community mental health center be limited in scope and interlocked with other care-givers in the community.

If we aim to rehabilitate individuals and maintain their functional behaviors over time, then we must include in our treatment programs the goal of modifying natural environments. Depending upon professional consultation, these natural milieux can maintain or extinguish the social and vocational behaviors of a rehabilitated individual.

CONTINGENCY MANAGEMENT OF COMMUNITY SERVICES

While many problems posed by clients coming for help to a community mental health center can be alleviated or eliminated by treatment procedures instituted solely at the center, there are a significant number of individuals whose treatment must include the coordinated application of contingencies among several social agencies. The so-called "multiple-problem" family of the chronic alcoholic who encounters the welfare department, the police department, Alcoholics Anonymous, and the general-hospital emergency room as well as the mental health center is an example of cases that will not respond to a simple treatment approach directed from one site. Thus, a challenge to behavior modifiers will be to harness the spectrum of contingencies from different directions that concurrently have an impact on the patient's behaviors.

Of necessity this systems approach requires more skills of us than the straightforward "cookbook" application of behavior therapy. We must become sophisticated in community organization and in the development of mechanisms for interagency communication and consensus. This systems approach can be illuminted by a case study from the Oxnard Mental Health Center. A nurse-therapist was wrestling with the challenge of coordinating over a dozen social agencies and professionals who had provided services to a chronic alcoholic woman during the past 10 years. The basis of our contingency program was to use her welfare allotments as a reinforcer of sobriety and functional behaviors in her home. Her welfare caseworker made biweekly home visits to assess her housekeeping and cooking efforts and her therapist at the Day Treatment Center assessed her sobriety and her earnings of credits in the center's token economy. The woman's attendance at Alcoholics Anonymous meetings was monitored by the use of transmittal slips that were filled out and signed by the AA leader and returned to the therapist. The various physicians and hospitals that had treated her in the past were notified of changes in her program and were urged to withhold services unless her therapist, who coordinated the program, was first notified and given authorization. The payoffs for the patient came from social reinforcement she received from her caseworker and her therapist, informational feedback from viewing her cumulative record of sobriety, an opportunity to "earn" back the custody of her child, who was then in a foster home, and the receipt of cash instead of vendor payment slips for her monthly welfare support.

While the initial responses of this and other chronic patients and the associated community agencies have been modestly encouraging, it should be noted that relapses are frequent and progress must be measured over the course of many months or even years. This type of behavior therapy does not produce quick and easy improvements; furthermore, it is expensive and exhausting to the care-givers.

As pointed out by Atthowe (1973), "the process of modifying the behavior of marginal and submarginal men is a continual shaping and fading of all the relevant behaviors in the complicated rehabilitation chain from its initiation to its stabilization. For many individuals, the rehabilitative process may never end." In community mental health, the care-giver "cures" few of those who seek help. In other terms, generalization of behavior change over time (durability), responses, and settings is limited. The behaviors targeted for intervention in community settings are also changed in limited ways. Impressive changes in frequency, duration or latency that can be "eyeballed" on a graph may be of interest to researchers, but truly functional behavior change that is meaningful to the patient's life comes only occasionally in a community mental health center. Patients, clients, and consultees—whether successes or failures of behavioral intervention—come back to haunt the community mental health worker. There is no neat compartmentalization of terminated versus open cases. Yesterday's successfully terminated case becomes tomorrow's open case in crisis. Behavioral problems of individuals, especially chronic psychotics, alcoholics, and drug addicts, are lifelong with the vicissitudes determined by ecological, economic, biological, and therapeutic factors. The role of the specialist in community mental health will include a preoccupation with developing and coordinating the wide variety of social, economic, and political systems as well as dispensing direct psychological or biological services. Reviewing the field of social and community interventions, Cowen (1973) echoes this challenge to behavior modifiers for a systems approach to community mental health.

A key component of community interventions is an *active* approach to the analysis and modification of social systems, including engineering environments that maximize adaptation. The social and community approach turns us away from a fixed-entities view of disordered behavior and leaves open the possibility that many adverse "end states" can be averted by effective environmental engineering.

Summary

Taking its place as the third "revolution" in psychiatry, the community mental health movement is a challenge for citizens, government officials, administrators, and human service workers to actualize the ideal mental health service. This consists of accessible and comprehensive treatment programs for a wide range of people and problems, continuity of care, and prevention through education and consultation. The community mental health concept must now justify its continued support by demonstrating results and program effectiveness both in the delivery of direct treatment services to individuals and in changing social conditions and institutions that produce or maintain behavioral disabilities.

Behavioral approaches offer a viable model for the operation of a community mental health center (CMHC). Many behavioral techniques have been successfully used in the direct services offered by CMHC's. Behavioral and environmental engineering contribute to a three-level conceptualization of the role of the professional in the CMHC—as a therapist, as a consultant and educator, and as a change agent with social systems. The literature reveals a relative paucity of studies that report the effects of behavioral treatments on unselected cases or of generalization of im-

provement over time, settings, and responses. Behavior modifiers must go beyond the stage of demonstrating control over behavioral problems in special settings, with highly selected cases, using academically trained staff, and with little followup over time.

The Behavior Analysis and Modification (BAM) Project, located at the Oxnard (California) Mental Health Center, is a demonstration and clinical research effort designed to adapt behavior analysis and therapy to the problems, patients, staff, and setting of a typical, comprehensive CMHC. The BAM Project's objectives and accomplishments are:

1. *Train the clinical staff in behavior analysis and modification.* The training program uses didactic and experiential methods, weekly seminars, individual staff supervision, modeling with fading, and staff self-management projects.

2. *Adoption of behavioral assessment and recording procedures by the staff.* Behavioral records, responsive to the CMHC staff's demanding schedules and crisis orientation, were developed using specificity and goal attainment as models. Behavioral record keeping by the professional and paraprofessional staff is maintained through personal feedback from the program leaders, peer modeling, and status obtained from verbal presentations and coauthorship on articles developed from data collected on patients. The regular use of simple, convenient, and behaviorally specific records that provide feedback to staff, administrators, and patients regarding progress toward goals is the most important single innovation that can be brought about in mental health settings.

3. *Develop a range of behavior therapy services that would be relevant to the needs of the patients and to the skills of the staff.* The first behavioral intervention was the introduction of a token economy system into the operation of the Day Treatment Center. This served to cue staff and patients to attend and respond to constructive, positive behaviors. Prompted by data from direct behavioral observation, researchers and clinical staff replaced the relatively unstructured "milieu therapy" in the Day Treatment Center with an educational workshop format. Work-

shops are led and periodically reevaluated by the staff in such areas as Personal Effectiveness Training (assertion training), conversation skills, personal finances, consumerism, grooming, and vocational preparedness. Contingencies within the token economy were reordered to give higher payoffs for participation and progress in workshops. Outpatient services were also modified into the group workshop model including marriage counseling, anxiety-depression management, crisis intervention (goal setting and training in Personal Effectiveness), parent training in child management, and contracting with adolescents.

4. *Evaluate a mental health program using direct behavioral observation.* A randomly selected sample of patients was observed each day at two day treatment centers, using a reliable behavior-coding system. Observations yielded information about the patients' social participation, work, and social isolation in the neutral milieu of the mental health centers. Results indicated that the introduction of educational workshops for the Oxnard Day Treatment Center doubled the patients' social participation rate from its baseline level and increased it beyond the level at the comparison center to a statistically significant degree.

5. *Evaluate the effects of behavior modification for individual patients.* Fifteen unselected cases were experimentally and unreliably analyzed using single-subject designs. Of 15 cases, 5 showed marked improvement following introduction of the behaviorally targeted intervention, with definite control demonstrated over the response measure and generalization across time, settings, or responses. Goal Attainment Scaling, a predictive, goal-oriented system, was used for every third patient who came into the Oxnard Day Treatment Center and a com-

parison day treatment center. Outcome at 6 months followup indicated that patients at Oxnard receiving behaviorally oriented treatment attained their treatment goals to a higher degree than patients who received more traditional treatment.

6. *Use behavioral technology in community consultation.* The center provides indirect community services utilizing a variety of behavioral procedures. Services are offered to parents in child management; to schools for students with behavioral and academic problems; to operators of residential care facilities who are taught how to develop behavioral programs for chronic psychotics living in the community; and to a group home for delinquent boys based on the Achievement Place model.

Critical self-evaluation should also be an integral part of behavioral approaches to mental health services if fresh solutions and advances are to come about. Limitations and challenges of behavior modification in community mental health lie in the areas of the suitability of the single-subject experimental design for evaluating treatment effects; controlling variables in an open setting; assessing the behavioral effects of medication; emphasizing antecedents of behavior as well as consequences; developing supportive environments in the community to maintain marginally functioning individuals; promoting limited and realistic behavior change in clients; and coordinating application of contingencies among several social agencies, as part of an active approach to the analysis and modification of social systems.

References

Aitchison, R. A. A low-cost, rapid delivery point system with "automatic" recording. *Journal of Applied Behavior Analysis*, 1972, 5 (4), 527–528.

Aitchison, R. A., & Liberman, R. P. Evaluating groups for training parents in child management. Paper presented at the meeting of the American Psychological Association, Montreal, 1973. (a)

Aitchison, R. A., & Liberman, R. P. Leader's guide to parent workshops in child management. Unpublished manuscript, Oxnard Mental Health Center, 1973. (b)

Aitchison, R. A., & Merrill, J. Emphasis on environment: The partnership between home, mental health services, and school. *Exchange*, 1974, 2, 13–19.

Alevizos, P. The reliability of data sampling in direct patient observation. In L. W. King (Chm.), Resolving methodological issues in direct behavioral observation in applied settings.

Symposium presented at the meeting of the American Psychological Association, Montreal, 1973.

ALEVIZOS, P. N., CALLAHAN, E., DeRISI, W., ECKMAN, T., BERCK, P., & LIBERMAN, R. P. The behavior observation instrument: II. Psychometric issues in direct observational measurement. Submitted to *Journal of Applied Behavior Analysis,* 1975.

ALINSKY, S. *Rules for radicals: A pragmatic primer for realistic radicals.* New York: Vintage Books, 1972.

ATTHOWE, J. M. Behavior innovation and persistence. *American Psychologist,* 1973, **28**, 34–41.

AUSTIN, N. K., LIBERMAN, R. P., KING, L. W., & DeRISI, W. J. Comparative evaluation of two-day treatment programs: Goal Attainment Scaling in behavior therapy vs. milieu therapy. Submitted to *Archives of General Psychiatry,* 1975.

AYLLON, T. & AZRIN, N. H. Reinforcement and instructions with mental patients. *Journal of the Experimental Analysis of Behavior,* 1964, **7**, 327–331.

AYLLON, T., & MICHAEL, J. The psychiatric nurse as a behavioral engineer. *Journal of the Experimental Analysis of Behavior,* 1959, **2**, 323–334.

AZRIN, N. H., & POWELL, J. Behavioral engineering: The use of response priming to improve prescribed self-medication. *Journal of Applied Behavior Analysis,* 1969, **2**, 39–42.

BALL, T. N. S. The establishment and administration of operant conditioning programs in a state hospital for the retarded. California Mental Health Research Symposium No. 4. Sacramento: California Department of Mental Hygiene, 1969.

BEIGEL, A., & LEVENSON, A. I. (Eds.) *The community mental health center.* New York: Basic Books, 1972.

BRADY, J. P. Drugs in behavior therapy. In D. H. Efron (Ed.), *Psychopharmacology: A review of progress 1957–1967.* Washington, D.C.: U.S. Government Printing Office, 1968.

BROWN, J. M., & LIBERMAN, R. P. Partnership for prevention. *exChange,* 1973, **1** (7), 24–27.

BURGESS, R. L., CLARK, R. N., & HENDEE, J. C. An experimental analysis of anti-litter procedures. *Journal of Applied Behavior Analysis,* 1971, 4 (2), 71–76.

CALLAHAN, E. Reactive effects of direct observation on patient behaviors. In L. W. King (Chm.), Resolving methodological issues in direct behav-

ioral observations in applied settings. Symposium presented at the meeting of the American Psychological Association, Montreal, 1973.

CANTRELL, R. P., CANTRELL, M. L., HUDDLESTON, C. M., & WOOLRIDGE, R. L. Contingency contracting with school problems. *Journal of Applied Behavior Analysis,* 1969, **2** (3), 215–220.

CATALDO, M., & RISLEY, T. R. The development of a general evaluation program for residential institutions. Paper presented at the Fifth Banff International Conference on Behavior Modification, Banff, Canada, 1973.

CHU, F. D., & TROTTER, S. *The mental health complex. Part I: Community mental health centers.* Washington, D.C.: Center for Study of Responsive Law, 1972.

COWEN, E. L. Social and community interventions. *Annual Review of Psychology,* 1973, **24**, 423–472.

CRANE, G. E. Clinical psychopharmacology in its 20th year. *Science,* 1973, **181**, 124–128.

DeRISI, W. J. Ethics and the research imperative in the applied setting. In L. W. King (Chm.), Resolving methodological issues in direct behavioral observation in applied settings. Symposium presented at the meeting of the American Psychological Association, Montreal, 1973.

DeRISI, W. J., ECKMAN, T., ALEVIZOS, P., CALLAHAN, E., & LIBERMAN, R. P. The behavior observation instrument: I. Direct observation for program evaluation in applied settings. Submitted to *Journal of Applied Behavior Analysis,* 1975.

DeRISI, W. J., MYRON, M., & GODING, M. Extending the behavioral bridge toward continuity of care: Training the staff of community care facilities. *Hospital and Community Psychiatry,* in press, 1975.

DOKE, L. A., & RISLEY, T. R. The organization of day-care environments: Required vs. optional activities. *Journal of Applied Behavior Analysis,* 1972, 5, 405–420.

DUNCAN, G. W., HILTON, E. J., KRAEGER, P., & LUMSDAINE, A. A. (Eds.) *Fertility control methods: Strategies for introduction.* New York: Academic Press, 1973.

ECKMAN, T. Reducing the cost of obtaining reliability data in applied settings. In L. W. King (Chm.), Resolving methodological issues in direct behavioral observation in applied settings. Symposium presented at the meeting of the American Psychological Association, Montreal, 1973.

FAIRWEATHER, G. W., SANDERS, D. H., CRISSLER, D. L., & MAYNARD, H. *Community life for the mentally ill*. Chicago: Aldine, 1969.

FRAZIER, W. W. Training institutional staff in behavior modification principles and techniques. In R. Rubin, H. Fensterheim, J. D. Henderson, & L. P. Ullmann (Eds.), *Advances in behavior therapy*. New York: Academic Press, 1972.

GELLER, E. S., FARRIS, J. C., & POST, D. S. Prompting a consumer behavior for pollution control. *Journal of Applied Behavior Analysis*, 1973, 6, 367–376.

GOLDBERG, H. C., DiMASCIO, A., & CHAUDHARY, B. A clinical evaluation of prolixin enanthate. *Psychosomatics*, 1970, 11, 173–177.

GUYETT, I. P. R. Some strategies for shaping the acceptance of behavior modification programs. In R. Rubin, H. Fensterheim, J. D. Henderson, & L. P. Ullmann (Eds.), *Advances in behavior therapy*. New York: Academic Press, 1972.

HARTMANN, D. P., & ATKINSON, C. Having your cake and eating it, too: A note on some apparent contradictions between therapeutic achievements and design requirements in N=1 studies. *Behavior Therapy*, 1973, 4, 589–591.

HENDERSON, J. D. A community-based, operant learning environment—I: Overview. In R. Rubin, H. Fensterheim, A. A. Lazarus, & C. Franks (Eds.), *Advances in behavior therapy*. New York: Academic Press, 1971.

HERBERT, E. W., PINKSTON, E. M., HAYDEN, M. L., SAJWAJ, T. E., PINKSTON, S., CORDUA, G., & JACKSON, C. Adverse effects of differential parental attention. *Journal of Applied Behavior Analysis*, 1973, 6 (1), 15–30.

HERMAN, S. H., & TRAMONTANA, J. Instructions and group versus individual reinforcement in modifying disruptive group behavior. *Journal of Applied Behavior Analysis*, 1971, 4 (2), 113–120.

JOHNSON, S. M., & BOLSTEAD, O. D. Methodological issues in naturalistic observation: Some problems and solutions for field research. In L. A. Hamerlynck, L. C. Handy, & E. J. Mash (Eds.), *Behavior change—Methodology, concepts and practice; Proceedings of the Fourth Banff International Conference on Behavior Modification*. Champaign, Ill.: Research Press, 1973.

KAZDIN, A. E. Methodological and assessment considerations in evaluating reinforcement programs in applied settings. *Journal of Applied Behavior Analysis*, 6, 517–531.

KING, L. W. (Chm.) Resolving methodological issues in direct behavioral observations in applied settings. Symposium presented at the meeting of the American Psychological Association, Montreal, 1973. (a)

KING, L. W. Training staff of a community mental health center in behavior modification. Technical Report No. 1. Oxnard, Calif.: Oxnard Mental Health Center, 1973. Available from the author. (b)

KING, L. W., LEVINE, J. C., LIBERMAN, R. P., DeRISI, W. J., & AUSTIN, N. K. Experimental analysis of treatment effects of 15 unselected cases in a community mental health center. Manuscript in preparation, Oxnard Mental Health Center, 1975.

KING, L. W., LIBERMAN, R. P., & ROBERTS, J. An evaluation of Personal Effectiveness Training (assertive training): A behavioral group therapy. Paper presented at the Annual Conference of the American Group Psychotherapy Association, New York, 1974.

KIRESUK, T., & SHERMAN, R. Goal Attainment Scaling: A general method for evaluating comprehensive mental health programs. *Community Mental Health Journal*, 1968, 4 (6), 443–453.

KLEIN, D. F., & DAVIS, J. M. *Diagnosis and drug treatment of psychiatric disorders*. Baltimore: Williams & Wilkins, 1969.

KUHR, B. M. Partial hospitalization and the general hospital. In A. Beigel & A. I. Levenson (Eds.), *The community mental health center*. New York: Basic Books, 1972.

LEITENBERG, H., AGRAS, W. S., BARLOW, D. H., & OLIVEAU, D. C. Contribution of selective positive reinforcement and therapeutic instructions to systematic desensitization therapy. *Journal of Abnormal Psychology*, 1969, 74, 113–118.

LeLAURIN, K., & RISLEY, T. R. The organization of day-care environments: "Zone" versus "man-to-man" staff assignments. *Journal of Applied Behavior Analysis*, 1972, 5 (3), 225–232.

LIBERMAN, R. P. Coupon-incentive system at a community mental health center. Film presented at the meeting of the American Psychiatric Association, Washington, D.C., 1971. Available from California Behavioral Research Institute, PO. Box 5523, Oxnard, California 93030. (a)

LIBERMAN, R. P. Parents as therapists. Paper presented at the meeting of the American Association of Psychiatric Services to Children, Beverly Hills, California, 1971. (b)

LIBERMAN, R. P. Behavioral measurement in clinical settings or how to keep the charts dry in rough seas. In R. Rubin, H. Fensterheim, J. D. Henderson, & L. P. Ullmann (Eds.), *Advances in behavior therapy.* Vol. 3. New York: Academic Press, 1972. (a)

LIBERMAN, R. P. Behavioral methods in group and family therapy. *Seminars in Psychiatry,* 1972, 4, 145–156. (b)

LIBERMAN, R. P. Applying behavioral techniques in a community mental health center. In R. Rubin, J. P. Brady, & J. Henderson (Eds.), *Advances in behavior therapy.* Vol. 4. New York: Academic Press, 1973.

LIBERMAN, R. P., & DAVIS, J. Drugs and behavior analysis. In M. Hersen, R. M. Eisler, & P. M. Miller (Eds.), *Progress in behavior modification.* New York: Academic Press, 1974.

LIBERMAN, R. P., DAVIS, J., MOORE, J., & MOON, W. Research design for analyzing drug-environment-behavior interactions. *Journal of Nervous and Mental Disease,* 1973, 156, 432–439.

LIBERMAN, R. P., DERISI, W. J., ALEVIZOS, P. N., CALLAHAN, E., & ECKMAN, T. The behavior observation instrument: III. Evaluating psychiatric treatment settings. Submitted to *Journal of Applied Behavior Analysis,* 1975.

LIBERMAN, R. P., KING, L. W., DERISI, W. J., & McCANN, M. J. *Personal Effectiveness: Guiding People to Assert Their Feelings and Improve Their Social Skills.* Champaign, Ill.: Research Press, 1976.

LIBERMAN, R. P., DERISI, W. J., KING, L. W., ECKMAN, T., & WOOD, D. Behavioral measurement in a community mental health center. In P. Davidson, E. Mash, & W. Handy (Eds.), *Evaluating social programs in community settings: Proceedings of the Fifth International Banff Conference on Behavior Modification.* Champaign, Ill.: Research Press, 1974.

LIBERMAN, R. P., FERRIS, C., SALGADO, P., & SALGADO, J. Replication of the Achievement Place model in California. *Journal of Applied Behavior Analysis,* in press, 1975.

MACDONALD, K., HEDBERG, A., & CAMPBELL, L. M. A behavioral revolution in community mental health. Paper presented at the Fifth Annual Meeting of the Association for the Advancement of Behavior Therapy, Washington, D.C., 1971.

MASON, A. S. Basic principles in the use of antipsychotic agents. *Hospital and Community Psychiatry,* 1973, 24, 825–828.

McDONOUGH, J. M. The Veterans Administration and community mental health: New approaches in psychiatric rehabilitation. *Community Mental Health Journal,* 1969, 5, 275–279.

MILLER, L. K., & MILLER, O. L. Reinforcing self-help group activities of welfare recipients. *Journal of Applied Behavior Analysis,* 1970, 3 (1), 57–64.

MILLER, L. K., & SCHNIEDER, R. The use of a token system in project Head Start. *Journal of Applied Behavior Analysis,* 1970, 3 (3), 213–222.

MORRISON, D. J. Partial hospitalization programs in rural mental health centers. In A. Beigel & A. I. Levenson (Eds.), *The community mental health center.* New York: Basic Books, 1972.

NAGLER, S., & COOPER, S. Influencing social change in community mental health. *Canada's Mental Health,* 1969, 17, 6–12.

PAUL, G. L. Experimental-behavioral approaches to schizophrenia. Paper presented to a conference, "Newer Strategies for Intervention in Schizophrenia," sponsored by the Joint Commission on Schizophrenia and the New York State District Branches of the American Psychiatric Association, New York, 1972.

PHILLIPS, E. L. Achievement Place: Token reinforcement procedures in a home-style rehabilitation setting for predelinquent boys. *Journal of Applied Behavior Analysis,* 1968, 1, 213–223.

PHILLIPS, E. L., PHILLIPS, E. A., FIXSEN, D. L., & WOLF, M. M. Achievement Place: Modification of the behaviors of predelinquent boys within a token economy. *Journal of Applied Behavior Analysis,* 1971, 4, 45–50.

REISS, D. Competing hypotheses and warring factions: Applying knowledge of schizophrenia. *Schizophrenia Bulletin* (National Institute of Mental Health), 1974 (8), 7–12.

RISLEY, T. R. Behavior modification as an experimental-therapeutic endeavor. In R. Rubin, H. Fensterheim, J. D. Henderson, & L. Ullman (Eds.), *Advances in behavior therapy.* Vol. 3. New York: Academic Press, 1972.

RISLEY, T. R., & CATALDO, M. Program evaluation techniques for classroom settings. Paper presented at the Fifth Banff International Conference on Behavior Modification, Banff, Canada, 1973.

SAJWAJ, T. Difficulties in the use of behavioral techniques by parents in changing child behavior: Guides to success. *Journal of Nervous and Mental Disease,* 1973, 156, 395–403.

SCHAEFER, H. H., & MARTIN, P. *Behavioral Therapy.* New York: McGraw-Hill, 1969.

SCHWARTZ, D. A. Community mental health in 1972: An assessment. In H. H. Barten & L. Bellak (Eds.), *Progress in community mental health.* Vol. II. New York: Grune & Stratton, 1972.

SIDMAN, M. *Tactics of scientific research.* New York: Basic Books, 1960.

SPIEGLER, M. School days—Creditable treatment. Paper presented at the meeting of the Association for the Advancement of Behavior Therapy, New York, 1972.

SPOHN, H. E. The case for reporting the drug status of patient subjects in experimental studies of schizophrenic psychopathology. *Journal of Abnormal Psychology,* 1973, **82,** 102–106.

SULZBACHER, S. I. Behavior analysis of drug effects in the classroom. In G. Semb (Ed.), *Behavior analysis and education—1972.* Lawrence, Kans.: University of Kansas Development Center, 1972.

TURNER, A. J. Programs and evaluations. Annual report of the Huntsville-Madison County Community Mental Health Center, 1971. Available from the author.

TURNER, A. J. Shaping a community: The bird in the box approach to community mental health. Paper presented at the Sixth Annual Meeting of the Association for the Advancement of Behavior Therapy, New York, 1972.

TURNER, A. J. Couple and group treatment of marital discord: An experiment. Unpublished manuscript, Huntsville-Madison Community Mental Health Center, 1973. Available from the author. (a)

TURNER, A. J. Programs and evaluations. Annual report of the Huntsville-Madison County Community Mental Health Center, 1973. Available from the author. (b)

WAHLER, R. G. Setting generality: Some specific and general effects of child behavior therapy. *Journal of Applied Behavior Analysis,* 1969, **2** (4), 239–246. (a)

WAHLER, R. G. Oppositional children: A quest for parental reinforcement control. *Journal of Applied Behavior Analysis,* 1969, **2** (3), 159–170. (b)

WAHLER, R. G., & ERICKSON, M. Child behavior therapy: A community program in Appalachia. *Journal of Behaviour Research and Therapy,* 1969, **7** (1), 71–78.

WEINER, H. Discussion of Dr. Risley's paper. In R. Rubin, H. Fensterheim, J. D. Henderson, & L. Ullmann (Eds.), *Advances in behavior therapy.* Vol. 3. New York: Academic Press, 1972.

WEISS, R. L., HOPS, H., & PATTERSON, G. R. A framework for conceptualizing marital conflict, a technology for altering it, some data for evaluating it. In L. A. Hamerlynck, L. C. Handy, & E. J. Mash (Eds.), *Behavior change: Methodology, concepts, and practice.* Champaign, Ill.: Research Press, 1973.

WENDER, P. H. The role of genetics in the etiology of the schizophrenias. *American Journal of Orthopsychiatry,* 1969, **39,** 447–458.

WILDER, J. F., & CAULFIELD, S. C. Rehabilitation workshops in a partial hospitalization program. In A. Beigel & A. I. Levenson (Eds.), *The Community mental health center.* New York: Basic Books, 1972.

WINCZE, J. P., LEITENBERG, H., & AGRAS, W. S. The effects of token reinforcement and feedback on the delusional verbal behavior of chronic paranoid schizophrenics. *Journal of Applied Behavior Analysis,* 1972, **5,** 247–262.

ZEILBERGER, J., SAMPEN, S. E., & SLOANE, H. N. Modification of a child's problem behaviors in the home with the mother as therapist. *Journal of Applied Behavior Analysis,* 1968, **1** (1), 47–54.

Behavioral Technology

17   **ROBERT L. SCHWITZGEBEL**

"Wanted: A Good Cookbook"

In a paper with the above title, Paul Meehl (1956) argued that personality description should be based upon an automatic and mechanical interpretation of test data that would follow explicit rules in cookbook form. "I am quite aware," he admitted, "that the mere prospect of such a method will horrify some of you; in my weaker moments it horrifies me [p. 264]." But Meehl concluded that our responsibility to patients obliges us to accept or reject psychodiagnostic methods on the basis of empirically demonstrated efficiency rather than tradition, amount of excitement or "fun," and so forth.

A similar case can be made today for behavior technology. Designing instruments for behavior change is a practical endeavor. It would be appropriate, therefore, to present a "cookbook" in the form of an engineering guide, repair manual, or an instruction sheet for a do-it-yourself project. However, at present only the rudiments exist for such an endeavor, and it is necessary to present here more a programmatic essay than a completed cookbook.

Crafts, such as creative writing or jewelry making, have rules. So do societies (e.g., "the rule of law") and languages (e.g., rules of grammar). A *rule* prescribes a course of action by providing verbal S^{Ds} in a response chain required to achieve a desired goal— viz., "Do this, to get that." In medical treatment, such rules are termed "praxiological statements." An important characteristic of the experimental analysis of behavior is the particular manner in which rules of intervention are generated. The *method* of generating prescriptions for changing behavior is a critical programmatic step in the transition of psychotherapeutic practice from an intuitive art to an empirical craft and eventually perhaps to technology.

Rules are *not* scientific "laws" in the sense of theoretical or interpretive formulas that state universal relationships. A typical scientific prediction has the form: "If x occurs at time t, then y will occur at time t' with probability p." By contrast, a typical technological forecast is of the form: "If y

Preparation of this paper was supported in part by research grant MH20315 from the Mental Health Services Development Branch, NIMH. A note of thanks is owed my colleagues, Valerie Ackerland and John Rugh, for their comments on early drafts.

is to be achieved at time t' with probability p, then x should be done at time t." (Bunge, 1966, p. 342). This distinction between theoretical knowledge and practical knowledge permits apparent inconsistencies to exist such as science without corresponding technology (e.g., Greek science) or a technology without a science (e.g., intelligence testing). A theoretician is reinforced for "truth," a technician for results.

The goal of a cookbook is to present a series of precise praxiological statements rather than logically induced explanatory constructs. A good cookbook is not expected, for example, to spell out the nature of chemical reactions. Such is unnecessary for the intended purpose. Similarly, a street map is a useful visual tool when wishing to go to an unfamiliar location, but it does not give us reasons for the streets being laid out as they are, or how this particular town compares to some theoretically ideal town, and so forth. Chemists are not necessarily superior cooks, nor are theorists necessarily effective therapists.

Certainly some interplay between science and technology can occur. Certain scientific theories may be used as the basis for formulating sophisticated technical rules. However, the fact that a fairly complex and successful series of rules can sometimes be generated *prior to* scientific theory is important to defining opportunities for behavior technologists.

Critics, such as Breger and McGaugh (1965), who claim that behavior modification has little justification in learning theory, may be essentially correct. But this is no hindrance to the present development of behavior technology. Kranzberg (1968) and others (e.g., Brooks, 1965; Finch, 1960; Rabi, 1965) have argued that historical evidence does not always sustain the usual metaphorical assumption that technology "grows out of" or "flows from" science. The existence of an applicable scientific theory prior to its technological exploitation does not constitute proof that technologists drew upon it. For example, the caloric theory of

heat preceded but was probably not used by Watt in designing the steam engine. Price (1965) analyzed the frequency of author citations in scientific periodicals and concluded that "in general, new technology will flow from old technology rather than from any interaction there might be between the analogous but separate cumulating structures of science and technology [p. 561]."

If we can divest ourselves of enough explanatory fictions and verbal labels to agree upon tasks and an orderly description of procedure, interesting new combinations of practical knowledge might emerge. Parties who disagree *in theory* often find that they agree when they outline *specific operations*. For example, Skinner and Guthrie clearly disagree on the function of reinforcement in learning, yet each might employ very similar procedures in training an animal. In fact Guthrie (1952) noted at one point that "the practical difference between his [Skinners's] system and the systematic stand taken in this book is not always discernible [p. 241]." Being without theory is no virtue, but we might as well make the best of the situation. As applied psychology moves from prescriptive rules based on analogy and metaphor to rules based on empirical demonstration, the most crucial controversy will be about the *method* one should use to *judge effectiveness of treatment* and to *introduce procedural innovations*.

So where do we go from here? London (1972) concluded a cogent and feisty critique of behavior modification with the following suggestion: "It is time now, I think, for the remedial branch of this business [professional psychology] to stop worrying about its scientific pretensions, in the theoretical sense, as long as it keeps its functional nose clean, and to devise a kind of engineering subsidiary, or more precisely, a systems analysis approach to its own operations. We have gotten about as much mileage as we are going to out of old principles, even correct ones, but we have barely begun to work the new technology [p. 919]."

A Machine Taxonomy

"Technology" [Gr. *tékhnē*—craft + *logiā*—discourse] refers to the study of practical arts. "Technique" refers to the specific and formal procedure by which an artistic, scientific, or mechanical endeavor is accomplished. A method for modifying behavior such as desensitization or discrimination training is a technique, but it does not necessarily involve any apparatus. In contrast, "engineering" [L. *ingenium*—talent, ingenious device] refers to the designing of engines and machines (or more generally to other physical artifacts such as bridges, television sets, or plastic products). Hence, "behavioral engineering" (Azrin, Rubin, O'Brien, Ayllon, & Roll, 1968; Homme, C' de Baca, Cottingham, & Homme, 1968) would imply the purposeful use of a device or product to modify behavior. An "engineer" was originally, and to some extent still is, a designer of "military machines" (cf. *Oxford Dictionary of English Etymology*, 1966, p. 314). Though contemporary behavior modification apparatus certainly includes weaponry, the long tradition of making devices for punishment and negative reinforcement is not an attractive model for future development. Thus, the present writer prefers "psychotechnology" (broadly defined as the study of the interaction of electrical/mechanical/chemical technology and human conscious experience), but no term is completely adequate. The issue of primary concern here is the purposeful design apparatus for modifying human behavior and consciousness in accord with principles of operant conditioning.

If one is interested in exploiting functional relationships between man and his technological artifacts, then a useful beginning might well be the development of a descriptive taxonomy. A taxonomy is a way of simplifying complex events on the basis of some salient structural and/or functional characteristics associated with items in the particular genus. It is merely a systematic way of making discriminations.

Rather obviously, the nature of a classification scheme depends in part upon the goals of the users. At the present time, man-machine interactions cannot be usefully described by conventional prose, statistical statements, or mathematical formulas that might be appropriate in other psychological specialities. Conventional prose tends to describe behavior technology in terms of Rube Goldberg mechanical contraptions or esoteric brain implants—neither of which is very practical or representative. Statistical statements, based on group means, have been strongly criticized by some researchers (Sidman, 1960; Skinner, 1953) as an inappropriate method of operant analysis. And finally, mathematical formulas seem at present based upon conceptual models too abstract for practical application.

A simple taxonomy of artifacts of behavioral technology is suggested here with the hope that the operant nature of certain man-machine interactions will become more explicit and that new interactions will be synthesized. This taxonomy is tentative, heuristic, and nonrigorous. (A rigorous taxonomy, such as the periodic table in chemistry, based on a *count* of discrete items, is not feasible because a common, practical, and unidimensional element of all behavioral artifacts has not yet been conceptualized, or at least is not apparent to this writer.) Table 17-1 has been condensed and adapted from several sources (Boulding, 1956; Jones, 1967; Parkman, 1972) and particularly Rapoport (1963) who suggested a developmental sequence of four technological phyla: tools, clockworks, heat machines, and information machines.

Frameworks refer here to man-made static structures such as buildings, roadways, and ramp-ways, cables and conduits, physical partitions to restrict sound or sight, and so forth. Jeremy Bentham (1789, 1961) applied his hedonistic calculus to the design of a never-constructed five-story prison/factory, called the "Panopticon," wherein he claimed "morals [would be] reformed, health preserved, industry invigorated, and instruction diffused [p. 196]." Much more modest but feasible arrangements have been

TABLE 17–1   Classification of behavior modification devices[a]

Phylum	Major characteristic	Examples
Frameworks	Static structure with passive control of space, light, sound, and/or temperature variables. Large elements or units may be moveable or changeable.	Experimental chambers and isolated rooms (Finley, 1966; Stollack & Guerney, 1964); mobile lab (Bijou & Baer, 1966); prosthetic environments (Lindsley, 1964); "Aircrib" enclosure (Skinner, 1945); "Automated playroom" (L'Abate, 1968).
Hand tools	Simple implement with inert or rigidly related parts powered and operated by human.	Nasal support to inhibit snoring (Naso-Vent, 1972); plastic "speech mask" to reflect voice for articulation correction (Developmental Learning Materials, 1972); "musical toothbrush," cigarette holder with adjustable air/smoke ratio (cf. Schwitzgebel & Schwitzgebel, 1973).
Reactive apparatus	Assembly of moveable parts powered by human operator with fixed mechanical output, often of informational value.	Golf counters (Lindsley, 1968); counter in exercise jump rope; scales used in weight control programs.
Mechanical energy devices	Spring-driven apparatus that may or may not include escapement mechanism used to release tension in equal units.	Timers (Azrin & Powell, 1969); spring-driven metronome to pace speech (Barber, 1940; Beech & Fransella, 1968); certain teaching machines for behavior modification (Brown & L'Abate, 1969).
Electromechanical/chemical devices	Electronic or electromechanical apparatus with a fixed or analog output. Power supplied by battery or line current; little or no control by human.	Electronic ear metronome for stutterers (Brady, 1971; Silverman & Trotter, 1972; Wohl, 1968); sleep-inducing apparatus (Lewis, 1966; Singh, 1967); vibrotactile belt for constipation (Quarti & Renaud, 1964); audible timer (Worthy, 1968); motion telemetry (Stattelman & Cook, 1966); "brain polarization" by low voltage (Crow, 1968; Lippold & Redfern, 1964) .
Interdependent man-machine systems	Array of interrelated human and electronic components with some human control of apparatus output.	Manipulanda for conditioning movement (Friedlander, 1966); voice-activated masking tone for stutterers (Dallons Instruments, 1972); shock device for writer's cramp (Liversedge & Sylvester, 1955).
Information devices	Mechanical and electronic apparatus and displays producing signals for "informational" rather than "work" purposes.	Parking meters, audio- and videotape for therapy (Berger, 1970); "matching-to-sample" musical teaching device (Skinner, 1968); enuretic devices (Morgan, 1938; Morgan & Witmer, 1939; Mowrer & Mowrer, 1938; Seiger, 1936, 1952).
Interactive information systems	Assemblage in which apparatus (usually electronic) and human each act as subsystems with feedback-control loop. Often involves relatively complex subsystem processing.	Automated desensitization (Lang, 1969); TV communication loop (Nathan, Bull, & Rossi, 1968); biofeedback apparatus (Budzynski & Stoyva, 1969; Lang, Sroufo, & Hastings, 1967); teaching machines with branching programs (Clark, 1968).

[a] References cited were generally selected for historic value, thoroughness of report, novelty, or breadth of apparatus type within a particular phylum or class. This listing,therefore, is not comprehensive or systematically representative of current developments in behavioral instrumentation.

suggested by Lindsley (1964) for the design of "prosthetic environments" for handicapped persons. In addition to auditory traffic lights and arm-operated doorknobs, Lindsley urged the use of primitive discriminatory stimuli such as odors to mark paths to toilets for regressed, retarded individuals.

Many common social environments are still haphazardly designed with respect to the behaviors that occur within the space. For example, many classrooms have the clock in the front of the room where everyone except the lecturer, whose verbal behavior the device is intended to control, can see it.[1] A useful framework for behavior control is the flexible arrangement of metal stands and ropes that prompt persons to line up in a certain area for service at a bank, restaurant, theater, etc. "Take-a-number" systems have a similar effect in assuring that service is contingent on arrival time, but they permit more physical movement of patrons. As an interesting exercise, one might catalog relatively unobtrusive architectural and environmental arrangements that are used for behavior control in common social circumstances.

A "hand tool" is a physical object, usually of simple structure using inert and rigidly related parts, designed for a specific task (Hetzler, 1969). The most primitive form is the instrument designed to concentrate manual energy at a given point (e.g., hammers, paddles), but other devices such as stockades or "whirling beds," used as behavior-change devices in times past, can also be considered tools.

Contemporary examples would include handcuffs, restraint jackets, various prosthodontic devices for speech correction, cigarette holders with variable filters for

reducing smoking, plastic nasal inserts for inhibiting snoring, and so forth. The effectiveness of some of these devices is suspect, but they have the virtue of simplicity and, like the clockworks that follow, have no fuel energy requirements. Each machine phylum permits, in principle, the design of similar items within that category. For example, a simple "hand tool" might consist of a plastic vial of noxious odors opened by the person (when appropriate for self-conditioning) or of a rubber band with sharp prongs worn around the wrist that becomes aversive when snapped.

Reactive apparatus is characterized by movable mechanical parts so patterned that a fixed output occurs when activated. An early and interesting example of this class of devices is a self-recording map maker devised by a Dutch physician, Boetin de Broot, sometime before 1609 (Hoff & Geddes, 1962). Inside a small box attached to a person's waist were gears that moved by a cord tied below the knee and that drove a sheet of paper. Every 100 paces, a cam caused a compass needle to rise up and puncture the paper in the direction of movement.

Seventeenth- and eighteenth-century mechanistic explanations of human physiology (e.g., Descartes, 1649; La Mettrie, 1784) were certainly influenced by automata of the time, which included animal and human figures placed in gardens that would jump up and frighten visitors who stepped on a hidden platform. Descartes argued that the "ability to reason" and the "power of speech" were uniquely human. However, mechanicians soon began fabricating intellectual and speech-producing devices in the form of mechanical calculators (generally credited to Blaise Pascal circa 1642 and Gottfried Wilhelm Leibniz circa 1662) and manually operated bagpipelike machines capable of vocalizing simple words and phrases (Wolfgang Kempelen, circa 1778, as cited in Cohen, 1967).

Contemporary apparatus of this genus includes slide rules, pedometers, and counters (Fargo, 1969; Lindsley, 1968). A

---

[1] A "simple" solution to smog caused by auto emissions suggests itself: Because immediate consequences are more powerful than delayed ones, the exhaust pipe should be put at the *front* of the car rather than the rear! (A more realistic arrangement might be to have some indicator light or dial on the dashboard indicating the quality of emissions.)

widely used reactive device to decrease the stealing of a generalized reinforcer is the cash register. Its invention is credited to a restaurant owner, Jake Ritty, who in 1878 devised what he termed the "Incorruptible Cashier," which would ring a bell and prominently display deposits on a large clock-like dial easily seen by supervisory personnel. The principle of mechanical display counters is so simple yet useful in operant conditioning that one can imagine a variety of possible applications (e.g., counters on jumpropes used for exercise, word counters on typewriters).

Mechanical energy devices mark a significant development because these devices store mechanical energy that can be released at a later time. This separate energy source, which can give the appearance of autonomous activity, inspired mechanicians of the eighteenth and nineteenth centuries to build spring-operated automatons (cf. Burnham, 1968; Cohen, 1967). The "Alouette" was an early clockwork therapy device reportedly constructed by a Parisian inventor, Mathieu (cf. Moyer, 1903). It consisted of a mahogany box with rotating mirror panels powered by a clock spring. A ray of light was reflected from the mirrors for the purpose of inducing eye fatigue and sleep in persons with insomnia.

A recent example of a clockwork device is a portable apparatus for dispensing pills (Azrin & Powell, 1969). A study by Hare and Willcox (1967) showed that, on the evidence of urine tests, 37% of 120 psychiatric inpatients failed to take prescribed medication. The pill-dispensing apparatus by Azrin and Powell was designed to sound a tone at the time a pill was to be taken. The tone could be terminated by turning a knob that ejected the pill into the user's hand. Another clockwork apparatus reported by Azrin and Powell (1968) is a time-locked cigarette case designed to reduce the frequency of smoking by limiting access to cigarettes. Because chemical power, rather than mechanical power, was used for some components of these devices, they also have

characteristics of the next phylum, heat machines.

Illustrative future clockwork developments might include "bonus parking meters" or "talking sticks" with timers. Parking meters placed in areas of low traffic congestion could have, in addition to the usual red flag, which is an S^D for an aversive consequence, a variably timed green flag as an S^D for a positive consequence (e.g., free state-lottery tickets). The "talking stick" might control verbal behavior in groups if a rule were adopted whereby a person "has the floor" only when holding the talking stick, which has built into it an adjustable fixed-interval timer and an alarm.

A new operational principle is involved in *electromechanical/chemical devices*. Whereas energy used in earlier devices was in the form of mechanical stress associated in some direct way with our own muscular effort, heat machines use fuel. At this point, an apparatus can be "fed" rather than merely "pushed." Following the invention of the steam engine, one might say that machine evolution followed more the principle of the "carrot" than the "stick."

It is still common to picture man-machine relationships as involving devices with numerous gears when in fact electrical and electronic arrangements are much more typical of modern technology. Present-day "heat machines" in applied operant conditioning are line- or battery-operated devices with internally regulated stimulus output. One example of this class of machines is an apparatus that delivers low-voltage current to the forehead, eyes, scalp, and neck region by surface electrodes for the purpose of inducing mood change or sleep. Although a few researchers (Crow, 1968; Lippold & Redfearn, 1964; Ramsay & Schlagenhauf, 1966; Shagass, 1968) have reported mood changes such as increased talkativeness or tearfulness by this alleged "brain polarization," the results of the procedure seem even more variable or suspect than electrosleep, which has been reported for decades (Gwathemy, 1914; Knutson, 1954; Kubie & Margolin,

1944; Lewis, 1966), and which has generated some limited commercial interest (Electrosone, 1972; Singh, 1967; Wing, 1966).

Another example of contemporary electronic apparatus with preset output is a hearing-aid metronome used in the treatment of stuttering (Berman & Brady, 1973; Brady, 1968, 1971; Greenberg, 1970, Wohl, 1968). A portable apparatus using a rhythmic tactile, rather than auditory, stimulus for a similar purpose has been reported by Azrin, Jones, and Flye (1968).

The term *interdependent system* is used to designate the next, more complex interaction between an electromechanical apparatus and a human. In this arrangement, the human influences apparatus output. The main purpose of the system is "work" in the sense of directly causing physical movement or alteration of material goods (e.g., manufacturing) or of people (e.g., traveling, surgery). The most common example in behavior technology is avoidance conditioning wherein the subject controls the frequency or duration of an aversive stimulus (e.g., Liversedge & Sylvester, 1955; Powell & Azrin, 1968).

An interdependent man-machine system is clearly illustrated by a "tic chair" reported by Barrett (1962). An induction coil suspended within a large U-shaped magnet on the back of a tilt chair caused a patient's spasmodic movements to activate a tape recorder that then played aversive noise into the patient's earphones. Differential reinforcement of low rates (drl) of tics was accomplished by a timing circuit that also activated music as a positive consequence for sitting quietly. Recently, dog collars have been marketed that house a sound-activated shock device to inhibit barking. Another device now marketed uses an earphone alarm with a mercury switch to warn an automobile driver when (s)he becomes sleepy. The writer is presently working on a less significant device to get a sleepy person out of bed. It consists of a pressure-sensitive pad that will not permit an attached alarm clock to be turned off while the weight of the person is still on the pad.

Information machines characterize the next phylum. These devices are designed primarily to systematize operations rather than provide energy. "The 'power' of these machines," wrote Rapoport (1963, p. 32), "is not 'muscular' but 'mental.' " He illustrated this difference as follows:

> Consider the automobile traffic in a large city. . . . Suppose that all the traffic lights fail. Certainly the speed of the cars, thus the rate of flow of the traffic, would be reduced. Suppose [a visitor from Mars] stuck to his conceptualization in terms of energetics. He would then have to ascribe the reduced flow (or speed) to some failure of the automobile engines, and he would be wrong. The failure is not of the engines but of the traffic lights. True, it takes energy to activate the traffic lights, but it is negligible compared with the energy it takes to move the cars. Energy has therefore little to do with the traffic problem under consideration. The key concept is not that of energy but of *directions for the utilization of energy* (commands "stop" and "go" properly patterned, i.e., a matter of *information*). . . . Examples can be multiplied at will. Children well-trained in fire drills leave a burning building in a surprisingly short time, while a disorganized mob may never leave it.

The output of information machines does not directly prompt a response (e.g., pacing speech with metronome) or provide a reinforcing or punishing consequence (e.g., music or electric shock). The output signal is primarily informational and is more likely to be a discriminative stimulus or a secondary reinforcer.

Probably the most widely used and professionally tested behavior-change apparatus belongs in this phylum—signal devices for enuretics. Mowrer and Mowrer (1938) are generally credited with publishing the first systematic experimental account of such use, but a number of other clinicians had also used an alarm device (e.g., Morgan, 1938; Morgan & Witmer, 1939; Pfaundler, 1904;

Seiger, 1936, 1946). A bibliography on enuresis that includes references to studies using conditioning apparatus has been compiled by Franzini (1973) and his colleagues.

At least six organizations in the United States now sell or rent signal devices. All units give an auditory (and sometimes also a light) signal when the person voids. The devices vary greatly in sensitivity to moisture, which is an important variable when attempting to "backward" condition an inhibitory response. An alternative strategy is to place a signal device at the toilet and use the signal as an S^D for a positive consequence (Azrin & Foxx, 1971; Cheney, 1968).

Another type of device that is informational in nature includes systems for monitoring social behavior and sending contingent signals. A well-known study by Patterson, Jones, Whitter, and Wright (1965) described the use of an earphone radio device in a classroom to deliver conditioned positive reinforcers to a hyperactive 10-year-old. A two-way telemetry system for monitoring and reinforcing social behaviors of adolescent delinquents in natural environments has also been reported (Schwitzgebel & Bird, 1970). Thomas, Walter, and O'Flaherty (1972) arranged a computer-assisted communication system whereby light signals from a client or from the therapist/computer could be used as a reinforcer or punishment for verbal behavior during marital counseling. The original system (Thomas, Carter, Gambrill, & Butterfield, 1970), however, did not use a computer to store information and transmit light signals. Such upgrading of information systems by adding computer functions is a trend that emphasizes the need to make some cost/benefit assessment. There is no virtue in instrumentation per se. And clearly the effect is negative if there is only increased cost for equivalent service. Nonetheless, the complexity of human behavior, the large amount of clinical and research data, and the number of allegedly successful routines that comprise the artful practice

of behavior therapy are likely to force practitioners to rely on some type of electronic data processing.

The last phylum listed in the proposed taxonomy is *interactive information systems* in which the human receives input stimuli from the apparatus and, after processing (often with reference to a specific target behavior or "goal state"), responds to the apparatus. This feedback loop may be designed to maintain a steady state in the human while systematically changing stimulus input (e.g., automated desensitization —Lang, 1969) or, conversely, to induce a *new* behavior or state (e.g., branch-programmed teaching machines—Clark, 1968).

Despite Skinner's (1969, p. 83) caution regarding the use of metaphors such as "encode," "read out from storage," and "overload channels," interactive information systems will very likely prompt therapists to consider alternative paradigms (e.g., Powers, 1973; Newbold, 1972) which will, in turn, encourage new hardware. At one time, the "reflex" was a useful metaphor for the description of behavior (Dewey, 1896; Efron, 1966; Skinner, 1931), but "good technology always undermines bad theory [London, 1972, p. 918]." The history of operant conditioning properly includes Skinner's own interest, from childhood through his professional career, in mechanical innovation:

> I was always building things. I built roller-skate scooters, steerable wagons, sleds, and rafts to be poled about on shallow ponds. I made seesaws, merry-go-rounds, and slides. I made slingshots, bows and arrows, blow guns and water pistols from lengths of bamboo, and from a discarded water boiler a steam cannon with which I could shoot plugs of potato and carrot over the houses of our neighbors. I made tops, diabolos, model airplanes driven by twisted rubber bands, box kites, and tin propellers which could be sent high into the air with a spool-and-string spinner. I tried again and again to make a glider in which I myself might fly.
>
> I invented things, some of them in the

spirit of the outrageous contraptions in the cartoons which Rube Goldberg was publishing in the *Philadelphia Inquirer* (to which, as a good Republican, my father subscribed). For example, a friend and I used to gather elderberries and sell them from door to door; and I built a flotation system which separated ripe from green berries. I worked for years on the designs of a perpetual motion machine. (It did not work). [Skinner, 1967, p. 388; see also Skinner, 1959, pp. 70–100.]

The most popular interactive information systems involve biofeedback arrangements. Budzynski and Stoyva (1969) described, for example, an analog information feedback system with visual and audio outputs used for deep muscle relaxation, and Lang (1969) developed a computer-assisted desensitization routine permitting random access to 12 prerecorded messages triggered by a subject's voluntary hand signal and (potentially) by his autonomic responses. Interactive systems could also include "teaching machines" that shape discriminations or that provide role models for therapeutic purposes. A computer-generated visual drama on a cathode-ray tube, with client-paced episodes controlled by voluntary and automatic inputs, might be programmed in a manner similar to cityscape explorations now used by some urban planners (Negroponte, 1970).

There is, of course, no guarantee that the evolution of man and his artifacts will increase the probability of our survival. A high-energy technology may not be ultimately most adaptive. Complex apparatus is usually more costly to create and maintain and therefore suffers in its long-term cost/effectiveness. Old patents and some museum exhibits testify to the fact that the electromechanical world has been populated with its own forms of white elephants, dinosaurs, and dodo birds. A technical craft values more the *practical functions* of a system than apparent similarities to real-life situations. Thus, applied operant conditioners would not likely be impressed by life-size alley mazes to explore the "cogni-tive maps" of children (Davis & Batalla, 1932) or of small linoleum-floored rooms into which children are locked with a toy, book, and lever in order to investigate extinction rates (Warren & Brown, 1943). Today's technology is more flexible, "softer," less visible, and more functional.

Apparatus Design Procedure

Many matters to be mentioned in this section may seem rather obvious. This is due in part to necessary generality when dealing with instruments that range from simple plastic echo chambers for the purpose of correcting speech to sophisticated electronic apparatus for operant conditioning of blood flow. The following outline may, however, serve as a preliminary checklist for behavioral psychologists who are not familiar with design procedures.

SPECIFICATION OF APPARATUS FUNCTION

The first task of the designer is to describe accurately the behavioral problems for which the proposed apparatus is to be used. This is no simple matter, but the procedures will be familiar to persons who have previously conducted applied operant studies. Preliminary information should include: the rate and duration (and perhaps physical force) of the target behavior; topographic characteristics of the behavior; the places and times of its occurrence; and the age, sex, and socioeconomic status of persons known to have the problem.

Eventually this information is transformed into physically measurable quantities (e.g., centimeters, grams, decibels, frequencies) that constitute input to the proposed apparatus. The output of the apparatus requires similar specification. Precise information on input and output characteristics is essential in order to adequately construct a duplicate apparatus and to replicate a study. Apparatus specifications should also include the range of tolerance allowable for the input and output variables.

A useful example of instrument design was reported by Azrin, Rubin, O'Brien, Ayllon, and Roll (1968) for the operant conditioning of postural control. The target behavior, "slouching," was operationally defined for each subject by the amount of tension placed on an elastic strap that closed a microswitch and activated a 500-Hz 55-dB tone from a subject-worn speaker. This output, preceded by a warning click, was demonstrated to be an effective aversive stimulus. Of particular interest from a design standpoint, however, was the manner in which the parameters of input stimuli from the subjects to the apparatus had to be adjusted. For example, a 3-second delay function had to be built in to permit brief intervals of tension on the strap when a subject would look over his/her shoulder. Similarly, current to the speaker was cut off by means of a mercury tilt switch for extreme angles of movement such as bending over to pick up an object from the floor. This and other studies by Azrin and colleagues (e.g., Azrin, Bugle, & O'Brien, 1971) are noteworthy for their specification of apparatus function.

SELECTION OF OPTIMAL COMPONENTS

A second necessary step of apparatus designing involves decisions about the specific operations to be performed by the apparatus after the input and output parameters have been specified. These decisions will be followed by the selection of components and the fabrication of the apparatus. Fortunately, most behavior modification devices are relatively simple electronically, but this does not eliminate the need for consideration of, and compromise on, a number of variables.

SIZE.   Apparatus currently ranges in size from hearing-aid metronomes to computers with teletype and tape-punch. Obviously, in some applications, size is of little impor-

tance; in others it is critical. Each variable in the design formula can be ranked or assigned a weight according to external requirements. Physical discomfort of carrying or wearing a device is often a primary factor in estimating response costs for subjects. Car safety belts are worn less often than designers hoped because the immediate aversiveness of restrained movements apparently competed with a more remote low-probability accident.

WEIGHT.   (As with size)

FINANCIAL COSTS.   The initial expenditure for devices that presumably have similar function may vary widely without apparent reason. Bed pads for the treatment of enuresis range from 10 dollars for a do-it-yourself model to 300 dollars for rental of a commercial model. Portable brainwave feedback devices range from 50 to 350 dollars. Again the cost factor must be weighed against other variables. If, for example, response generalization of subjects outside the treatment situation is a critical matter, then the cost of a radio telemetry system, which would likely be twice that of a hardwire lab system, might be justified (Schwitzgebel & Bird, 1970). Long-term costs are even more elusive to estimate than initial costs. Long-term costs include energy requirements, maintenance, and downtime due to instrument failure. Costs per unit time of use may be reduced by devices that have versatility of function or multiuse, such as a cumulative recorder.

STATE-OF-THE-ART.   A person considering the purchase or fabrication of a device should have some knowledge of available design options. No comprehensive or widely recognized source of apparatus information presently exists for applied researchers and practitioners. Furthermore, many published studies fail to report sufficient technical detail to permit easy replication, and the principal investigator may not have obtained such information. Job contracts with electronic engineers or technicians should routinely require that a detailed schematic, wiring diagram, and a parts list accompany "home-made" apparatus. The parties should also come to some understanding in advance regarding publication rights.

The majority of published reports of devices appear in the form of clinical case studies of a specific disorder (and are abstracted under that topic) or are scattered among journal apparatus notes. The periodicals most relevant for applied operant conditioning are *Behavior Research Methods and Instrumentation, Behavior Therapy, Behavioral Science, Behaviour Research and Therapy, Educational Technology, Electronic Products, Journal of Applied Behavior Analysis, Popular Electronics,* and *Psychophysiology.* Another source of information includes published patents, which are available in 10 geographically dispersed depositories in the United States.

VALIDITY, RELIABILITY, DURABILITY. These factors are often difficult to assess in advance because they involve "hidden" technical aspects of componentry as well as packaging. An illustration of the difficulty of valid and reliable instrumentation involves a device to record movement known as the "actometer." Schulman and Reisman (1959) published a report describing a modified self-winding watch that reportedly was capable of automatically measuring activity of subjects in an "objective manner." A subsequent series of standardized tests by Johnson (1971), however, indicated that the actometer had very poor reliability and suspect validity. The report by Johnson is recommended as a model of practical clinical testing of instrument utility.

The longevity or durability of components in mass-produced items has well-established probability curves that are considered in the product design. Ideally, everything "falls apart at once." In prototype devices or those manufactured on a small scale, no such reliable curves exist.

The designer must also try to estimate the effects of potential misuse, abuse, or vandalism to which the device will be subjected. Published technical notes should indicate, at least generally, the expected frequency and type of repair under specified conditions of use.

EASE OF OPERATION AND RESPONSE COST. Because the proper operation of even relatively simple devices such as audio tape recorders is seldom self-apparent, instructions are necessary. It has been claimed that a 900,000-dollar failure in the *Gemini 9* spacecraft was due to insufficiently detailed written instructions to technicians installing certain lanyards (Wilford, 1966). In most operant studies, instructions are simply given orally by the technicians or researcher. If the operating procedure is elaborate or the device is sold commercially, written instructions should be provided. Desirable characteristics of such instructions include: (1) all physical features of the apparatus described in one place, (2) operational statements made in the order in which the user's movements are to be made, (3) actions of the user should be directly related to specific visual or auditory stimuli generated by the device that will serve as S^{D}s in a response chain, (4) some indication of how the device will respond when mistakes are made by the user.

EFFICIENCY OF OPERATION. In very simple devices, the efficiency of operation is seldom an important factor. Battery replacement, for example, might be little more than an inconvenience. However, more sophisticated circuitry usually requires more power and therefore more expense and/or inconvenience. For larger line-operated apparatus, efficiency can be a significant consideration.

SAFETY. A professional standard of care is required in the construction and use of all devices, but special precaution is necessary when using electrical or electronic apparatus. The amount of current that flows in a circuit is a function of the force (voltage or potential) and the resistance (or impedance) of the path. Body fluids are a good conductor due to low resistance; dry skin is a poor conductor. The greatest potential danger is triggering ventricular fibrillation (rapid, uncoordinated contractions of heart muscle) by a current flow between 60 milliamperes and 3 amperes through intact skin and a transthoracic pathway. With the possible exception of galvanic skin response or other autonomic response measurement, the most frequent direct application of electric current in operant conditioning is as a negative reinforcer or a punishment. A summary of recommendations by several investigators (Fried, 1967; Kushnor, 1968; Pfeiffer & Stevens, 1971; Tursky & Watson, 1964) with respect to aversive conditioning suggests the use of relatively high voltages (85–150 volts) at low amperage (3–6 milliamperes), direct or alternating sine wave current having a frequency between 50 and 150 hertz from an isolated source. Whenever a subject is attached to a device operated by line current, a three-wire ground in both the electrical system and the device is strongly advised in order to provide an alternate pathway for current leaks.

SOCIAL ACCEPTABILITY. Apparatus used in treatment conducted outside the lab or clinic will in most cases have to meet peer group standards of acceptability. For example, it is not likely that one could convince a subject to go about his normal activities with an antenna projecting above his head, although that would be the best technical configuration for radio telemetry. Obviously, instrument design should minimize aversive social consequences and, if possible, increase positive consequences received by a subject. If a device or system proves to be "technically recalcitrant," the designer's usual options are: plan more modest objectives, purchase more sophisticated technical help or materials, increase subject fees, or postpone the endeavor.

AESTHETICS. A "black box" does not have to be black, and a machine need not be "machine gray." Traditionally, aesthetic considerations have had a low priority. In behavioral applications, however, the reinforcing or aversive characteristics of apparatus may be important enough to justify even reduced electromechanical efficiency (e.g., a color or covering that reduces dissipation of internal heat).

One of the most unusual attempts to beautify a psychological device was undertaken by a small firm that sold alpha feedback devices as "functional sculpture" (cf. Figure 17–1). The components were housed in chicken wire and a collage of paper maché, ceramics, and electronic scraps. This form of packaging was later discontinued and replaced by more conventional black metal boxes due allegedly to a lack of customer interest. A sculptured unit purchased by this author had functional problems, perhaps aggravated by such unorthodox packaging, but the manufacturer's effort seems praiseworthy. As with some other products, however, the aesthetic appeal of tools and machines may also lie in elegant simplicity and careful craftsmanship.

DETERMINATION OF DISTRIBUTION POTENTIAL

A number of parameters of apparatus design are external to the componentry itself. These matters generally involve legal and economic considerations related to potential use and distribution of the device.

LEGAL CONSIDERATIONS. There is considerable agreement that all unnecessary, harmful effects of experimentation are to be avoided. Risks that may be intrinsically associated with a device should be eliminated; or, if this is not possible, these risks should be minimized as much as possible with the subject knowingly and voluntarily assuming the residual risk (R. K. Schwitzgebel, 1973, 1975). Most behavioral devices do not currently seem to fall within the jurisdiction of the FDA or the Federal

Biofeedback device, "Autogen 120," Autogenic Systems, Incorporated, Berkeley, California 94710.

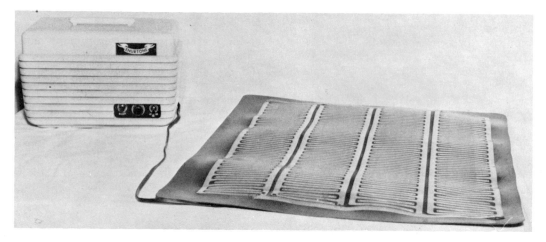

Auditory alarm device for treatment of enuresis, the "Enurtone" without flood lamp—Enurtone Company, Minneapolis, Minnesota 55435.

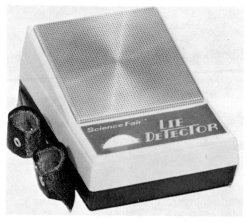

Audio GSR assembled kit, "Science Fair Lie Detector," Radio Shack, a Tandy Corporation Company, Fort Worth, Texas 76107.

FIGURE 17–1

"Snore Suppressor," Crossley Electronics, Corpus Christi, Texas 78412.

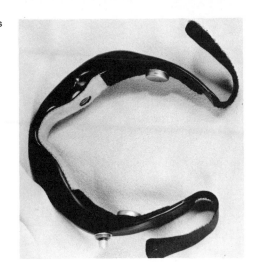

Alpha feedback device, special "functional sculpture" model, Psionics, Boulder, Colorado 80302.

Musical toilet training apparatus, "Startinkle," Nursery Training Devices, Incorporated, Van Nuys, California 91406.

Food, Drug, and Cosmetic Act (cf. generally sections 21 *U.S. Code Annotated* 321, 331–337, 351–357, 371–392), but the criteria for classification are not clear and new legislation is likely. Hearing aids and phonograph records for the treatment of insomnia are considered medical devices and therefore within FDA jurisdiction. The usual teaching machine would not be covered, but a teaching machine programmed to hypnotize a subject (Clark, 1968) might be. Some administrative action by the FDA has attempted to regulate the labeling and sale of brainwave and other feedback devices. In questionable situations, it would be desirable to obtain an opinion from the FDA prior to marketing a device.

The manufacturer and seller of a device may be liable for injuries caused under various theories of product liability *independent of*, or in addition to, FDA regulation. The traditional doctrines of breach of warranty and negligence are apparently merging into a theory of "strict liability." Under this theory, a seller is liable for harm caused by any device in a defective condition that is unreasonably dangerous to the user, as long as the harm is reasonably foreseeable.

POTENTIAL PATENTS. Securing a patent may or may not afford some eventual economic advantages to the inventor or designer. It is, however, evidence of a certain creativity and persistence. The questionable economic gain stems from the fact that a patent only gives the patentee *access* to federal courts to sue for infringements, but few inventors are financially able to go into a court to defend their rights against individuals or corporations with large financial resources who, in good or bad faith, commit such infringements.

Any new or useful machine, mechanism, device, or article potentially constitutes a "mechanical patent." The invention must be able to perform a novel and utilitarian function and not merely perform the same operation in a more efficient or practical manner than a preceding device.[2] The device must NOT have been known, in use, on public sale, or *described in any printed publication* for 2 years prior to filing the application.

A more creditable form of evidence as to the date of an invention than the popular practice of mailing oneself a registered letter is the U.S. Patent Office's "Disclosure Document Program." For a 10-dollar fee, the office will retain a description on file for 2 years, during which time the inventor is expected to file a patent application. Patent applications are quite complicated, and the advice of a patent attorney is almost essential. A "Directory of Attorneys and Agents Registered to Practice before the U.S. Patent Office" is available for one dollar from the U.S. Government Printing Office. Processing a very simple patent will cost at least 200 dollars; the rate of acceptance of completed applications has been running at approximately 60%.

MARKETING POSSIBILITIES. Hetzler (1969) has estimated that less than 2% of registered patents are ever successfully marketed.[3] An invention need have only a small relative advantage over a competing product, but this advantage must be perceived by potential users. Hence, the more tangible and reinforcing the invention, the more likely its adoption.

[2] Applications to patent perpetual-motion machines are routinely rejected by Patent Office examiners on the ground of "being inoperative for any useful purpose." A number of such applications are received each year, and it has also been the tradition to send a form letter and a refund of the application fee.

[3] Unlike old books, which are routinely stored in libraries, machines are often carelessly lost. A small but notable effort to preserve apparatus is that of Popplestone and McPherson (1971) at the Archives of the History of American Psychology, University of Akron (Ohio), which now houses approximately 600 "manufacts," including a "verbal summator" (Skinner, 1953). Researchers may wish to contact the archives regarding possible donations.

The following considerations are routinely involved in assessing potential markets: demonstrated user preferences, relation to competitors' products, costs and selling price, availability of sources of supply, company resources, legal requirements, selling methods (e.g., direct mail), packaging and shipping. As a rule of thumb, the selling price of hardware is figured by doubling twice the actual production costs (i.e., a pocket timer costing 1 dollar to manufacture would retail for 4 dollars). Because the large majority of behavior modification devices are sold by direct mailing, a substantial portion of the retail cost will involve individual client correspondence, shipping, billing and accounting, service and warranty matters, as well as initial mail advertising (a 1% response is considered acceptable). Direct-mail selling is *not* the method of choice for product distribution unless, as is the case in applied psychology, the potential users are relatively small in number and geographically scattered.

A study by the Battelle Columbus Laboratories reported that the time lag between ideas and marketable product for large and significant technological innovations averages 19 years (*Science News,* 1973). Three such innovations—commercial photocopy machines, videotape, and heart pacemakers—were strongly backed by one person, a "technical entrepreneur," who persisted despite an unfavorable market analysis. In summary, the results of a market analysis can be ignored *if* the inventor is lucky enough to find a technical entrepreneur; but because entrepreneurs are rarer than ideas, a systematic market analysis is the expected course of action.

EXAMINATION OF SELECTED DESIGN

The final step in apparatus design procedures is to determine whether the desired performance is achieved within stated restrictions. Generally, the evaluation phase should have three goals: (1) documentation

of subject safety, (2) solid experimental data supporting therapeutic claims, and (3) evidence that the device falls within an acceptable risk-to-benefit ratio (Edwards, 1970). Behavior therapists can be expected to be particularly competent and comfortable in carrying through procedures appropriately to demonstrate therapeutic efficiency, but items (1) and (3) may require a less familiar parametric-type research and evaluation. Relevant parameters include the physical, economic, and social factors previously listed as well as any additional idiosyncratic requirements that a particular practitioner or researcher may set.

It is impossible to make absolute judgments regarding the efficiency of a device in a particular application. Even an electrically nonfunctional apparatus may have a desirable "placebo effect" (R. K. Schwitzgebel & Traugott, 1968). Nonetheless, potential purchasers ought to be able to make their investment on some objective, though perhaps limited, basis. There is no equivalent to the Underwriters Laboratory, the Emergency Care Research Institute, or the Consumer's Union in the area of behavior technology, but some investigations have been conducted comparing the effectiveness of several types of bed pads for enuretics (Lovibond, 1963), electroconvulsive therapy instruments (Davies, Detre, Egger, Tucker, & Wyman, 1971), brainwave feedback devices (Wanderer, 1973), and of cost/safety/frequency-of-use of toys (Quilitch, 1973; Swartz, 1971).

A popular commercial device in recent years has been the brainwave feedback unit. Although a conservative behavioristic approach (e.g., Grossberg, 1972) might question Stoyva and Kamiya's (1968) working assumption that discriminable mental events associated with measurable physiological events can be reinforced, the brainwave became, for better or for worse, a commercially valuable operant. In 1974 more than 25 different manufacturers were selling brainwave feedback devices. Due to their popularity, potential user exploitation, and the complexity of evaluation, a substantial number of these devices were subjected to a series of standard tests (Schwitzgebel & Rugh, 1974). The purpose was not to determine the psychological effects of feedback but simply to evaluate the adequacy of apparatus design on the basis of specific, functional criteria (Table 17–2). More complex devices, as constructed by researchers or practitioners, would require more elaborate technical evaluation and would be subject to a demonstration of subject safety and therapeutic benefit as previously noted.

One effort toward the quantification of cost/benefit ratios for man-machine interactions has been reported by Starr (1969). Obviously, "cost" and "benefit" should be specified in relatively precise terms if possible. A reliable index of *cost* might be, for example, accidental deaths arising from a technical innovation. The *benefit* might be measured by a traditional socioeconomic variable such as health, education, or income. An urban dweller may move to the suburbs because of a lower crime rate and better schools but spend more time traveling with a higher probability of accidents. If traffic density subsequently increases, the response cost may be too great, and (s)he may move back to the city. Though (s)he might not be able to verbalize the contingencies, his/her behavior represents the outcome of a cost/benefit tradeoff. Similarly, one may estimate the reinforcing value of more hedonistic optional activities, such as skiing, by computing fatalities per exposure hour: e.g., 1 fatality, 17 days of skiing, 16,500 skiers per day, and 5 hours of skiing per skier per day (based on data provided by the National Ski Patrol for the 1967–68 Southern California ski season; Starr, 1969, p. 227). On the basis of analysis of motor vehicle travel, skiing, air travel, hunting, smoking, the Vietnam War, and so forth, Starr concluded that:

1. The public is willing to accept "voluntary" risks roughly 1,000 times greater than "involuntary" risks.

TABLE 17–2   Outline of standard lab tests for EEG apparatus

1. DC tests
   Battery drain with and without output signal

2. Amplifier characteristics
   Differential gain as measured by voltage in and out of amplifier checked for:
   a. Sensitivity
   b. Band-pass characteristics

3. Rejection characteristics
   a. Common mode
   b. Differential mode

4. Feedback characteristics
   a. Feedback stimulus (type of auditory and/or visual output)
   b. Time delay as measured by latency input and output signals

5. Mechanical aspects
   a. Strength of case and internal packaging techniques
   b. Quality of electrodes

6. Written instructions
   Accuracy and ease of following instructions assessed by user panel

7. Aesthetics rating
   a. Physical appearance
   b. Trade name appeal, honesty, and appeal of descriptive literature

2. The statistical risk of "death from disease" appears to be a psychological yardstick for establishing the level of acceptability of other risks.

3. The acceptability of risks appears to be crudely proportional to the third power of the benefits (real or imagined).

Again, we can cite automobile travel as an example of potential technological injury: in 1967, approximately 23,100 people died in traffic accidents. As a death prevention measure, Etzioni (1969) claimed that mechanical devices "were found to be much more economical, relative to their effectiveness, than the non-mechanical ones [p. 44]." He estimated the following costs per automobile death averted.

Seat belts—$87

Restraining devices—$100

Motorcyclists' helmets—$3,000

Driver education—$88,000

Even assuming considerable error in these costs, it seems evident that the technological approaches are much more feasible than the educational approach. Perhaps this is simply another illustration of the folly of trying to change *people*—by education, logic, friendly (or unfriendly) persuasion— rather than changing their *environment*.

It is interesting to note that Thorndike (1943) cited, as a particularly poor example of social management, an exceedingly long city ordinance requiring the registration of bicycles in order to reduce the rate of theft. He concluded, "It would surely have been more effective, and also much cheaper, for this city to have provided bicycle locks for all bicycles [p. 145]." It is this kind of social instrumentation that Weinberg (1966) has referred to as a "technological fix." Contemporary examples of technological fixes or short cuts to social change might include methadone, antabuse, instructional television, breath analyzers, intrauterine devices, and nonlethal weapons (Etzioni & Remp, 1972).

A Technology of Private Events

The development of an appropriate technology may be especially important for the accurate recording of so-called "private events" such as "sensations," "images," and "emotions." A single external stimulus event can result in quite different overt and covert responses depending upon the reinforcement history of the organism and its morphology (e.g., pain receptors). Very idiosyncratic *overt* responses may be recorded by audio- or videotape, and such events do not interfere with an objective analysis of behavior. In principle, "freaky" overt phenomena are susceptible to the same instrumentation and analysis procedures as more commonly observed events. Even poltergeists might be subject to instrumentation (Tart, 1965)!

Covert responses may be recorded by implements that amplify or make public such responses. "The line between public and private is not fixed. The boundary shifts with every discovery of a technique for making private events public [Skinner, 1953, p. 282]." A person who "thinks to himself" by scribbling notes on a piece of paper creates a public artifact. One novel attempt to translate and amplify covert responses was an "experiential typewriter" reported by Leary (1966). A typewriter keyboard, coded into feeling and topic categories, was attached to a 20-pen Easterline-Angus recorder. Pretrained subjects were then asked to punch appropriate keys during experimental drug sessions. Operantly oriented studies involving response rate measures of affect include work by Hefferline and Bruno (1971), Lindsley (1962), and Nathan, Bull, and Rossi (1968).

A technology capable of dealing with sensation perception must ultimately deal *not* with statics but with time derivatives and velocities. If we assume that the base rate of events is the speed of light (rather than accept the notion of an outdated physics that things tend to "stay at rest"), then the fluidity of mental events in contrast to the relative stability of our body surface becomes an exciting possibility rather than a bothersome problem. The question is how congruent velocities come to exist, how energy is exchanged to create matter (and then back again) how high-energy metastable systems such as athletes, pregnant women, live orchestra performances, cities, and perhaps even low-probability covert events of "trance" or "rapture" can be sustained or controlled. How is it that energy assemblages moving at different speeds become organized and then disorganized? Physicists and chemists can study this question at one level; sociologists and politicians at another; psychologists and psychiatrists at still another.

A very simple demonstration of electronically aided and publicly verifiable emotional integration of a small group consists of attaching one electrode of an audio galvanic skin response to one member of the group and the other electrode to another member. The circuit is completed by all members of the group holding hands. In this way a functional unit is formed at the autonomic level with auditory feedback based on the composite skin resistance.

A primary goal of behavior technology is to expand our individual and collective capacity for self-programmable psychological adventures. Such an enterprise necessarily involves risks. But it is neither tawdry nor trivial, and it promises to impassion and delight at least a few people of the future.

References

Azrin, N. H., Bugle, C., & O'Brien, F. Behavioral engineering: Two apparatuses for toilet training retarded children. *Journal of Applied Behavior Analysis,* 1971, 41, 249–253.

Azrin, N. H., & Foxx, R. M. A rapid method of toilet training the institutionalized retarded. *Journal of Applied Behavior Analysis,* 1971, 4, 53–63.

Azrin, N. H., Jones, R. J., & Flye, B. A synchronization effect and its application to stuttering by a portable apparatus. *Journal of Applied Behavior Analysis,* 1968, 1, 283–295.

Azrin, N. H., & Powell, J. Behavioral engineering: The reduction of smoking behavior by a conditioning apparatus and procedure. *Journal of Applied Behavior Analysis,* 1968, 1, 193–200.

Azrin, N. H., & Powell, J. Behavioral engineering: The use of response priming to improve prescribed self-medication. *Journal of Applied Behavior Analysis,* 1969, 2, 39–42.

Azrin, N. H., Rubin, H., O'Brien, F., Ayllon, T., & Roll, D. Behavioral engineering: Postural control by a portable operant apparatus. *Journal of Applied Behavior Analysis,* 1968, 1, 99–108.

Barrett, B. Reduction in rate of multiple tics by free-operant conditioning methods. *Journal of Nervous and Mental Diseases,* 1962, 135, 187–195.

Bentham, J. An introduction to the principles of morals and legislation (1789). In J. Bowditch & C. Ramsland (Eds.), *Voices of the industrial revolution.* Ann Arbor: The University of Michigan Press, 1961, pp. 35–47.

Berman, P. A., & Brady, J. P. Miniaturized metronomes in the treatment of stuttering: A survey of clinicians' experience. *Journal of Behavior Therapy and Experimental Psychiatry,* 1973, 4, 117–119.

Boulding, K. E. General systems theory—The skeleton of science. *Management of Science,* 1956, 13, 197–209.

Brady, J. P. Metronome-conditioned speech retraining for stuttering. *Behavior Therapy,* 1971, 2, 129–150.

Breger, L., & McGaugh, J. L. Critique and reformulation of "learning-theory" approaches to psychotherapy and neurosis. *Psychological Bulletin,* 1965, 63, 338–358.

Brooks, H. The interaction of science and technology: Another view. In A. W. Warner, D. Morse, & A. S. Eichner (Eds.), *The impact of science on technology.* New York: Columbia University Press, 1965.

BUDZYNSKI, T. H., & STOYVA, J. M. An instrument for producing deep muscle relaxation by means of analogue information feedback. *Journal of Applied Behavior Analysis,* 1969, 2, 231–237.

BUNGE, M. Technology as applied science. *Technology and Culture,* 1966, 7, 329–347.

BURNHAM, J. *Beyond modern sculpture.* New York: Braziller, 1968.

CHENEY, C. D. "Mechanically augmented human toilet-training, or the electric pottie chair." Mimeographed. Logan, Utah: Utah State University, College of Education, Department of Psychology, 1968.

CLARK, J. H. "The simulation of the human hypnotist by a teaching machine." Mimeographed. Manchester, England: Manchester University, Department of Psychology, 1968.

COHEN, J. *Human robots in myth and science.* South Brunswick & New York: A. S. Barnes & Co., 1967.

CROW, H. J. Electronic devices in psychiatry. In N. S. Kline & E. Laska (Eds.), *Computers and electronic devices in psychiatry.* New York: Grune & Stratton, 1968, pp. 158–168.

DAVIS, F., & BATALLA, M. A life-size alley maze for children. *Journal of Genetic Psychology,* 1932, 41, 235–239.

DAVIES, R. K., DETRO, R. P., EGGER, M. D., TUCKER, F. J., & WYMAN, R. J. Electroconvulsive therapy instruments. *Archives of General Psychiatry,* 1971, 25, 97–99.

DESCARTES, R. *Discourse on a method for the well guiding of reason, and the discovery of truth in the sciences.* London: Thomas Newcombe, 1649.

DEWEY, J. The reflex arch concept in psychology. *Psychological Review,* 1896, 3, 357–370.

EDWARDS, C. C. Medical devices and their regulation. *Medical Research Engineering,* 1970, 9, 3–4.

EFRON, R. The conditioned reflex: A meaningful concept. *Perspectives in Biology and Medicine,* 1966, 4, 488–514.

"ELECTROSONE 50." Electrosone Corporation, 375 Park Avenue, New York, N.Y. 10022.

ETZIONI, A. Agency for technological development for domestic programs. *Science,* 1969, 164, 43–50.

ETZIONI, A., & REMP, R. Technological "shortcuts" to social change. *Science,* 1972, 175, 31–38.

FARGO, G. A. Rapid computation and pupil self-recording of performance data. *Journal of Applied Behavior Analysis,* 1969, 2, 264.

FINCH, J. K. *The story of engineering.* New York: Doubleday, 1960.

FRANZINI, L. R. "Enuresis: A comprehensive bibliography." Mimeographed. San Diego: San Diego State University, Department of Psychology, 1973. Update of previous edition with co-authors N. F. Rocklin & H. A. Tilker.

FRIED, R. Essentials of electroshock and electroshock devices. *Newsletter of the Association for the Advancement of Behavior Therapies,* 1967, 1, 3–4.

GREENBERG, J. B. The effect of a metronome on the speech of young stutterers. *Behavior Therapy,* 1970, 1, 240–244.

GROSSBERG, J. M. Brainwave feedback experiments and the concept of mental mechanisms. *Journal of Behavior Therapy and Experimental Psychiatry,* 1972, 3, 1–7.

GUTHRIE, E. R. *The psychology of learning.* New York: Harper, 1952.

GWATHEMY, J. T. *Anesthesia.* New York: Appleton, 1914.

HARE, E. H., & WILCOX, D. R. Do psychiatric inpatients take their pills? *British Journal of Psychiatry,* 1967, 113, 1435–1439.

HEFFERLING, R. F., & BRUNO, L. J. The psychophysiology of private events. In A. Jacobs & L. B. Sachs (Eds.), *The psychology of private events.* New York: Academic Press, 1971.

HETZLER, S. A. *Technological growth and social change.* New York: Praeger Press, 1969.

HOFF, H. E., & GEDDES, L. A. The beginnings of graphic recording. *Isis,* 1962, 53, 287–324.

HOMME, L., C' DE BACA, P., COTTINGHAM, L., & HOMME, A. What behavioral engineering is. *Psychological Record,* 1968, 18, 425–434.

JOHNSON, C. F. Hyperactivity and the machine: The actometer. *Child Development,* 1971, 42, 2105–2110.

JONES, J. C. The designing of man-machine systems. In W. T. Singleton, R. S. Easterby, & D. C. Whitfield (Eds.), *The human operator in complex systems.* London: Taylor & Francis, 1967, pp. 1–11.

KNUTSON, R. C. Experiments in electronarcosis:

A preliminary study. *Anesthesiology,* 1954, **15,** 551–559.

KRANZBERG, M. The disunity of science-technology. *American Scientist,* 1968, **56,** 21–34.

KUBIE, L. S., & MARGOLIN, S. An apparatus for the use of breath sounds as a hypnogogic stimulus. *American Journal of Psychiatry,* 1944, **100,** 610.

KUSHNER, M. "Aversive conditioning: Parameter sand conditions." Mimeographed. Miami, Fla.: V. A. Hospital, Psychology Section, 1968.

LA METTRIE, J. O. *Man, a machine.* An English translation of the original French 1784 edition. La Salle, Ill.: Open Court Publishing Co., 1953.

LANG, P. J. The on-line computer in behavior therapy research. *American Psychologist,* 1969, **24,** 236–239.

LEARY, T. The experiential typewriter. *Psychedelic Review,* 1966, **2,** 70–85.

LEWIS, J. A. Electrosleep. In R. L. Williams & W. B. Webb (Eds.), *Sleep therapy.* Springfield, Ill.: Charles C Thomas, 1966.

LINDSLEY, O. R. Direct behavioral analysis of psychotherapy sessions by conjugately programmed closed circuit television. Paper presented at the meeting of the American Psychological Association, St. Louis, 1962.

LINDSLEY, O. R. Direct measurement and prosthesis of retarded behavior. *Journal of Education* (Boston University), 1964, **147,** 62–81.

LINDSLEY, O. R. A reliable wrist counter for recording behavior rates. *Journal of Applied Behavior Analysis,* 1968, **1,** 77–78.

LIPPOLD, O. C. J., & REDFEARN, J. W. T. Mental changes resulting from the passage of small direct currents through the human brain. *British Journal of Psychiatry,* 1964, **110,** 768–772.

LIVERSEDGE, L. A., & SYLVESTER, J. D. Conditioning techniques in the treatment of writer's cramp. *Lancet,* 1955, **5,** 1145–1149.

LONDON, P. The end of ideology in behavior modification. *American Psychologist,* 1972, **27,** 913–920.

LOVIBOND, S. H. The mechanism of conditioning treatment of enuresis. *Behaviour Research and Therapy,* 1963, **1,** 17–21.

MEEHL, P. E. Wanted: A good cookbook. *American Psychologist,* 1956, **11,** 263–272.

MORGAN, J. J. B. Treatment of enuresis by the conditioned reaction technique. *Psychological Bulletin,* 1938, **35,** 632–633. (Abstract)

MORGAN, J. J. B., & WITMER, F. J. The treatment of enuresis by the conditioned reaction technique. *The Journal of Genetic Psychology,* 1939, **55,** 59–65.

MOWRER, O. H., & MOWRER, W. M. Enuresis: A method for its study and treatment. *American Journal of Orthopsychiatry,* 1938, **8,** 436–459.

MOYER, W. *The witchery of sleep.* New York: Ostermoor & Co., 1903.

NATHAN, P. E., BULL, T. A., & ROSSI, A. M. Operant range and variability during psychotherapy: Description of possible communication signatures. *The Journal of Nervous and Mental Disease,* 1968, **146,** 41–49.

NEGROPONTE, N. *The architecture machine.* Cambridge, Mass.: M.I.T. Press, 1970.

NEWBOLD, H. L. *The psychiatric programming of people: Neo-behavioral orthomolecular psychiatry.* New York: Pergamon, 1972.

PARKMAN, R. *The cybernetic society.* New York: Pergamon, 1972.

PATTERSON, G. R., JONES, R., WHITTIER, J., & WRIGHT, M. A. A behavior-modification technique for the hyperactive child. *Behaviour Research and Therapy,* 1965, **2,** 217–226.

PFAUDLER, M. *Verhandlungen Gesellschaft Kinderheilkunde,* 1904, **21,** 219. Cited in I. G. Wickes, Treatment of persistent enuresis with electric buzzer. In R. Ulrich, T. Stachnik, & J. Mabry (Eds.), *Control of human behavior.* Glenview, Ill.: Scott, Foresman, 1966.

PFEIFFER, E. A., & STEVENS, D. A. Problems of electro-aversive shock in behavior therapy. In D. V. Reynolds & A. C. Sjoberg (Eds.), *Neuroelectric research: Electroneuroprosthesis, electroanesthesia and nonconvulsive electrotherapy.* Springfield, Ill.: Charles C Thomas, 1971, pp. 331–336.

POPPLESTONE, J. A., & McPHERSON, M. W. Prolegomenon to the study of apparatus in early psychological laboratories circa 1875–1915. *American Psychologist,* 1971, **26,** 656–657.

POWELL, J., & AZRIN, N. The effects of shock as a punisher for cigarette smoking. *Journal of Applied Behavior Analysis,* 1968, **1,** 63–71.

POWERS, W. T. Feedback: Beyond behaviorism. *Science,* January 26, 1973, **179,** 351–356.

PRICE, D. J. DES. Is technology historically independent of science? A study in statistical historiography. *Technology and Culture,* 1965, **6,** 533–567.

QUILITCH, H. R., & RISLEY, T. R. The effects of play materials on social play. *Journal of Applied Behavior Analysis,* 1973, **6**, 573–578.

RABI, I. I. The interaction of science and technology. In A. W. Warner, D. Morse, & A. S. Eichner (Eds.), *The impact of science on technology.* New York: Columbia University Press, 1965.

RAMSAY, J. C., & SCHLAGENHAUF, G. Treatment of depression with low voltage direct current. *Southern Medical Journal,* 1966, **59**, 932–934.

RAPOPORT, A. Technological models of the nervous system. In K. M. Sayre & F. J. Crosson (Eds.), *The modeling of the mind: Computers and intelligence.* Notre Dame, Ind.: University of Notre Dame Press, 1963, pp. 25–40.

SCHULMAN, J. L., & REISMAN, J. M. An objective measure of hyperactivity. *American Journal of Mental Deficiency,* 1959, **64**, 455–456.

SCHWITZGEBEL, R. K. Ethical and legal aspects of behavioral instrumentation. In R. L. Schwitzgebel & R. K. Schwitzgebel (Eds.), *Psychotechnology: Electronic control of mind and behavior.* New York: Holt, Rinehart & Winston, 1973, pp. 267–283.

SCHWITZGEBEL, R. K. Use and regulation of psychological devices. *Behavioral Engineering,* 1975, **2**, 44–46.

SCHWITZGEBEL, R. K., & TRAUGOTT, W. Initial note on the placebo effect of machines. *Behavioral Science,* 1968, **13**, 267–273.

SCHWITZGEBEL, R. L., & BIRD, R. M. Sociotechnical design factors in remote instrumentation with humans in natural environments. *Behavior Research Methods and Instrumentation,* 1970, **2**, 99–105.

SCHWITZGEBEL, R. L., & RUGH, J. D. Of bread, circuses, and alpha machines. *American Psychologist,* 1975, **30**, 363–370.

SCHWITZGEBEL, R. L., & SCHWITZGEBEL, R. K. *Psychotechnology: Electronic control of mind and behavior.* New York: Holt, Rinehart & Winston, 1973.

SEIGER, H. W. Practical urine or wet diaper signal. *Journal of Pediatrics,* 1946, **28**, 733–736. (This author also holds a 1936 U.S. patent on a line-operated pad.)

SHAGASS, C. "On responses to transcranial polarization." Mimeographed. Ames, Iowa: Iowa State University, Department of Physiology, 1968.

SIDMAN, M. *Tactics of scientific research.* New York: Basic Books, 1960.

SINGH, D. Sleep-inducing devices: A clinical trial with a Russian machine. *International Journal of Neuropsychiatry,* 1967, **3**, 311–318.

SKINNER, B. F. The concept of the reflex in the description of behavior. *Journal of General Psychology,* 1931, **5**, 427–458. Reprinted in *Cumulative record.* New York: Appleton-Century-Crofts, 1959, pp. 321–346.

SKINNER, B. F. Baby in a box. *Ladies Home Journal,* October 1945. Reprinted in *Cumulative record.* New York: Appleton-Century-Crofts, 1959, pp. 419–427.

SKINNER, B. F. *Science and human behavior.* New York: Macmillan, 1953.

SKINNER, B. F. Autobiography. In E. G. Boring & G. Lindsey (Eds.), *History of psychology in autobiography.* Vol. 5. New York: Appleton-Century-Crofts, 1967.

SKINNER, B. F. *Contingencies of reinforcement: A theoretical analysis.* New York: Appleton-Century-Crofts, 1969.

STARR, C. Social benefit vs. technological risk. *Science,* 1969, **165**, 1232–1238.

STOYVA, J., & KAMIYA, J. Electrophysiological studies of dreaming as the prototype of a new strategy in the study of consciousness. *Psychological Review,* 1968, **75**, 192–205.

SWARTZ, E. M. *Toys that don't care.* Boston: Gambit, 1971.

TART, C. P. Applications of instrumentation in the investigation of haunting and poltergeist cases. *Journal of the American Society for Psychical Research,* 1965, **59**, 190–201.

THOMAS, E J., CARTER, R. D., GAMBRILL, E. D., & BUTTERFIELD, W. H. A signal system for the assessment and modification of behavior (SAM). *Behavior Therapy,* 1970, **1**, 252–259.

THOMAS, E. J., WALTER, C. L., & O'FLAHERTY, K. Assessment and modification of marital verbal behavior using a computer-assisted signal system (CASAM). Paper presented at the meeting of the Association for the Advancement of Behavior Therapy, New York, October 1972.

THORNDIKE, E. L. *Man and his works.* Cambridge, Mass.: Harvard University Press, 1943.

TURSKY, B., & WATSON, P. D. Controlled physical and subjective intensities of electric shock. *Psychophysiology,* 1964, **1**, 151–162.

WANDERER, A. (Ed.) Biofeedback evaluation.

Newsbriefs, January 1973, 3–4, published by the Center for Behavior Therapy, Beverly Hills, Calif.

WARREN, A. B., & BROWN, R. H. Conditioned operant response phenomena in children. *Journal of General Psychology,* 1943, **28,** 181–207.

WEINBERG, A. M. Can technology replace social engineering science and public affairs. *The Bulletin of the Atomic Scientists,* 1966, **22,** 4–8.

WILFORD, J. N. Error blocked Gemini docking. *The New York Times,* June 8, 1966, 29.

WING, O. Electrical sleep machine and sleep inducing method. U.S. Patent No. 3,255,753 (assigned to National Patent Development Corporation, New York), 1966.

WOHL, H. T. The electronic metronome—An evaluative study. *British Journal of Disorders of Communication,* 1968, **3,** 89–94.

Behavioral Modification: Ethical Issues and Future Trends

18

LEONARD KRASNER

Overview

The intent of this chapter is to present an overview of the materials, ideas, and investigations that should be taken into consideration in the development of a system of ethics and values for those professionally identified with the process of behavior modification. The present author's view is that the model of conceptualizing and influencing human behavior subsumed under the rubric of behavior modification is intricately interwoven within a social, economic, and historical context and a social ethic and value system. Prognostication of future developments must take into consideration these contexts. If this chapter is to make any contribution to the already voluminous verbiage in this area, it will be to delineate the *issues* in the various controversies that touch upon ethics and behavior modification. To do even this much is not easy since complexities, paradoxes, and myths abound.

The issues involved in this field involve concepts of freedom, justice, the nature of man and science, human rights, and other abstract but "real" ideas and ideals. Thus we should seek our resources from many astute observers of man such as novelists, poets, utopiasts, social reformers, and social, biological, and physical scientists. Having duly pointed out the scope of the topic, we can proceed to narrow our focus to those observers identifying their work (research and application) within the scope of "behavior modification," which in itself represents a voluminous literature (e.g., Barrish, 1974; Begelman, 1973).

Problems of ethics are not unique to or caused by behavior modification, but it is believed by friends and foes alike that the development of human behavior modification brought with it certain issues and concerns that did not exist before. I once expressed the theme that since behavior modification had arrived on the scene, we must *do something* (unspecified as to what) *before it's too late*:

> Does this mean that we, as psychologists, researchers, or even therapists, *at this point* could modify somebody's behavior in any way we wanted? The answer is no, primarily because research into the techniques of control thus far is at the elementary stage. Science moves at a very rapid pace, however, and now is the time to concern ourselves with this problem before basic knowledge

about the techniques overwhelms us. [Krasner, 1962b, p. 201].

Others have, of course, expressed the same notion that at long last the complete manipulation and control of behavior is a possibility, and behavior modification is to receive the credit (blame). There may even be some who still believe that we are close to that state of nirvana (or catastrophe). Fortunately, the usage of any set of procedures, even behavior modification, in the ultimate control of our society (even for our own "good") is still a thing of the indefinite future. But the fact that the atom bomb of behavior control is not yet in sight does not exonerate the "behavior modifier" from the socially responsible task of continuing to investigate the multiplicity of social influences on behavior.

It is obviously difficult to discuss the future and the ethical problems associated with "behavior modification" unless one starts with a clear and concise definition of the term. This is a task that is ever growing more difficult. As this chapter is being prepared in the mid-1970s, the term has taken on such a surplus of meaning because of political, social, and scientific factors that it is impossible and even undesirable to divorce it from its social usage (and misusage), to take it out of its political and social context. A careful analysis of previous definitions used in this book may show some important differences. Since this is the last chapter, by this point what behavior modification is should speak for itself, but probably doesn't.

It is doubtful if there is any satisfactory current definition of the model of human behavior called "behavior modification." Unfortunately, many of the developments of the past decade have been on the assumption that behavior modification does indeed "exist" (as if there was a reality to it, separate from the behavior of the individuals endorsing it or condemning it).

When a generally careful and thoughtful reporter such as Tom Wicker of The New York Times criticizes "behavior modification," it is difficult to dismiss him as another example of a misunderstanding and hostile critic. Wicker contends that,

> nothing arouses the fears of prison inmates more than so-called "behavior modification" programs, and no wonder. Behavior modification is a catch-all term that can mean anything from brain surgery to a kind of "Clockwork Orange" mental conditioning. It usually includes drug experimentation and in all too many cases, it is aimed more nearly at producing docile prisoners than upright citizens [New York Times, February 8, 1974, p. 31].

In effect, then, Wicker accepts and enhances a growing usage of the term "behavior modification" that equates it with all methods of *controlling* and *manipulating* human behavior, including psychosurgery and the use of drugs. To investigators who have been identifying their work as belonging within behavior modification, this is, and should be, a disturbing development. There had been a tendency to dismiss such broad criticisms as misinterpretation that could be clarified once the true facts were brought forth. More recently the trend has been for the behavior modifiers to respond to charges immediately and even to take the initiative in contacts with the public and other professionals.

Wicker's comments appeared the day after another article in The New York Times described the termination of a "behavior modification" project as follows:

> In a significant victory for prison reformers, the Federal Bureau of Prisons had decided to dismantle its behavior modification project in Springfield, Missouri. In the project, prison guards and doctors tried to alter the conduct of troublesome inmates by first locking them in cells for hours and depriving them of all their privileges, then rewarding them if they behaved properly by restoring their privileges. The project known as START had become an object of fear and

hatred to inmates in Federal prisons across the country. Some inmates, hearing of START in the prison grapevine, staged hunger strikes against the program. Inmates and former inmates wrote letters and articles describing START—an acronym for Special Treatment and Rehabilitation Training—as "Pavlovian" and "Clockwork Orange" [*New York Times*, February 7, 1974, p. 12].

Thus "behavior modification" and procedures such as "token economy" have degenerated to the point where they have become symbols of and synonymous with the evils of our society both to the mass media and among some mental health professionals. How did we arrive at this point?

Historical Perspective of Behavior Modification

To understand the process of the development of behavior modification, it would be necessary to go into a detailed historical analysis including a functional analysis of the professional behavior of those identified with the behavioral model and a description of the social influence process as the beliefs and the research of the "behaviorist" interacted with the broader social influences of American society in the 1960s. However, such a history is beyond the scope of this chapter. Rather I will present a brief, limited, and biased view involving some of my own experiences, particularly with the definition of the term "behavior modification." The usage of the term as traced here offers a guideline to the elusive relationship between the value system of the investigator and his procedures.

In 1965 Leonard Ullmann and I co-edited two volumes of collected papers on research and case studies in "behavior modification" (Krasner & Ullmann, 1965; Ullmann & Krasner, 1965), which probably represented the first use of the term in a book title. We introduced the "research" collection by placing the work of the investigators involved (e.g., Ferster, Staats, Bijou,

Salzinger, Goldiamond, Patterson, Krasner, Sarason, Kanfer, Hastorf, Saslow, Colby, Bandura, & Sarbin) within the context of that segment of the broader field of "behavior influence" (Krasner & Ullmann, 1973; Krasner, 1962) that aimed

> to demonstrate the uniformities involved in the application of social reinforcement concepts to increasingly complex behavior. This area is germane and useful to the practicing clinical psychologist. If a single label had to be given to this subject, it would be *behavior modification* [Krasner & Ullmann, 1965, p. 1].

Thus we viewed behavior modification research within a broader category, that of *behavior influence* (Krasner & Ullmann, 1973) which included

> investigations of the ways in which human behavior is modified, changed, or influenced. It includes research on operant conditioning, psychotherapy, placebo, attitude change, hypnosis, sensory deprivation, brainwashing, drugs, modeling, and education. We conceive of a broad psychology of behavior influence that concerns itself with the basic variables determining the alteration of human behavior in both laboratory and "real life" situations. On the other hand, the term *behavior modification* refers to a very specific type of *behavior influence* [Krasner & Ullmann, 1965, pp. 1–2].

We then adopted the description of behavior modification offered by Watson (1962). (It should be noted that this reference is to Robert I. Watson, the historian of psychology, and not John B. Watson, the behaviorist.) In presenting an historical introduction to Bachrach's (1962) collection of research on the "experimental foundations" of clinical psychology, Watson used the term "behavior modification" to cover a multitude of approaches.

> It includes behavior modification as shown in the structured interview, in verbal conditioning, in the production of experimental neuroses, and in patient-doctor relationships.

In a broader sense, the topic of behavior modification is related to the whole field of learning. Studies of behavior modification are studies of learning with a particular intent—the goal of treatment [p. 19].

Watson included among the historical forbears of behavior modification those investigators who were doing systematic research into the process of psychotherapy. "It was a psychologist, Carl Rogers, who in 1942, through a book . . . and an article . . . launched the research approach in behavioral modification through psychotherapy [pp. 20–21]."

Having put our presentation of behavior modification within the context of "the clinical goal of treatment," we then sought the commonalities and general principles that characterized the work of these behavior modifiers.

A first commonality is the role identification of the investigators themselves. While all of them are interested in basic research they see socially important applications for their work. They conceive of themselves as behavioral scientists investigating the processes of changing human behavior.

Second, they investigate clinical phenomena through operationally defined and experimentally manipulated variables.

Third, all the investigators emphasize the effect of environmental stimulation in directing the individual's behavior. They virtually eliminate hypothetical concepts such as the unconscious, ego, and internal dynamics. For purposes of their present researches, even such concepts as heredity and maturation are de-emphasized.

A fourth commonality is the approach to maladaptive behavior through a psychological rather than a medical model. Behavior modification deals directly with behavior rather than with "underlying" or disease factors that "cause" symptoms. . . .

The psychological model used is that of social reinforcement. In the present volume, the term *social reinforcement* is used to emphasize the fact that other human beings are a source of meaningful stimuli that alter,

direct, or maintain the individual's behavior [Krasner and Ullmann, 1965, p. 3].

Approximately 50 illustrations of "behavior modification" (including the work of many of the authors in this present volume) were included within the same Watsonian context of "clinical treatment" (Ullmann & Krasner, 1965). The commonalities in these works were seen as "the insistence that the basis of treatment stems from learning theory, which deals with the effect of experience on behavior. . . . The basis of behavior modification is a body of experimental work dealing with the relationship between changes in the environment and changes in the subject's responses [p. 1]."

The terms behavior modification and behavior therapy were used interchangeably "to denote the modification of clinical or maladaptive behavior."

A major element in understanding behavior modification at that point was its focus on behavior that was *observable* and *definable*. The concern of the therapist started with the question, "What do we wish to accomplish through our application of learning theory?" Finally, behavior modification was linked to the broader issue of a *model* of behavior in which both adjustive and maladjustive behavior could be understood through learning theory concepts.

For purposes of looking at ethics and behavior modification, there are five major aspects of the above approach to conceptualizing behavior modification. These are: the clinical context in which it developed; the interaction of an individual with his environment; the role of environmental cues and stimulation; the use of a social reinforcement model and the social role identification of the investigators.

At this point, a decade later, these characteristics to a large extent still define the professional efforts that belong within behavior modification and, by exclusion, the techniques and procedures that do not (e.g., drugs, electroshock, psychosurgery, or coercion).

Ethics, Values, and the Social Consequences of Behavior

As for the term "ethics," we offer the following dictionary definition:

> The study of the general nature of morals and of the specific moral choices to be made by the individual in his relationship with others. . . . The rules or standard governing the conduct of the members of the profession. . . . Any set of moral principles or values. . . . The moral quality of a course of action; fitness; propriety [*American Heritage Dictionary*, p. 450].

To follow through on this definition it is necessary to see how the dictionary interprets the word "moral." For this term, the dictionary specifies, "Of or concern with the judgment of the goodness or badness of human action and character; pertaining to the discernment of good and evil. . . . Designed to teach goodness or correctness of character and behavior; instructive of what is good or bad [p. 852]."

Ethics then involves decisions on the part of the behavior modifier as to what is "good" or "bad" behavior for a specific individual. Ideally, a more "open" behavior modifier views his goals as helping an individual make these decisions himself. Some behavior modifiers would argue that their major contribution is to reinterpret or operationalize this decision-making process as involving the assessment of the consequences of a given behavior: that which leads to positive reinforcement for the individual is good; that which leads to aversive consequences is bad. Some would argue for the criterion of "survival" as an alternative or as a supplement to these goals. The issue of what is desirable behavior (and who determines it) will be returned to since it may well be the most crucial issue of all.

We have previously argued that many investigators are prone to hide behind a concept of "science" as a justification for avoiding the full consequences of their research (Krasner, 1965). A large segment of those involved in behavior modification continue to see a separation between their scientific activity and their value decisions. This view is succinctly expressed by Madsen (1973): "Who decides what values/behaviors should be taught to whom has nothing to do with behavior modification." We disagree. Our hypothesis is that who decides the values to be taught is the very heart of behavior modification.

Science is not a sacred cow, nor does it have an independent existence. Behavior modification as a scientific discipline represents a social product in a time and place (Ullmann, 1969). The social responsibility of behavior modification includes the placing of one's own contributions in the social context of the times. The behavior modifier is an influencer and is continually being influenced.

Virtually all the early investigators in behavior modification considered that there was a very close linkage between their research investigations and social and ethical applications and implications. This view was clearly influenced and led by Skinner's own writings, particularly *Walden Two*. Published in 1948, *Walden Two* anticipated many of the social and ethical issues arising from behavior modification that were to become a focus of concerns in the 1970s. Other investigators also pointed out the relationship between their research and social applications (e.g., Bragg & Wagner, 1968; Lucero, Vail, & Scherber, 1968; Kanfer, 1965; Myron, 1968).

Krasner and Ullmann (1965) linked behavior modification with concerns of social value as follows:

> The very effectiveness of behavior modification, the use of terms such as *manipulation*, *influence*, and *control of the environment*, and the concept that the therapist has the responsibility to determine the treatment program, all lead to concern with social values. Behavior modification, as an area of social influence, shares this problem with advertising, public relations, and education. These areas have in common individuals who

have the interest and the ability to alter the behavior of other people, that is, one person determining what is desirable behavior for another. There are circumstances in which this is beneficial for the individual and society and circumstances in which this is not the case. The ethical problem is not whether behavior influence is proper or improper, but a specification of the circumstances under which behavior influence is appropriate. This view reduces the problem from a general one to a more specific operational one. While a crucial variable is the behavior to be modified, other circumstances that must be taken into account are the methods of influence used and the impact on society of the individual's changed behavior [pp. 362–363].

Bandura (1969), in a most influential book, placed "the principles of behavior modification" within the "conceptual framework of social learning."

By requiring clear specification of treatment conditions and objective assessment of outcomes, the social-learning approach . . . contains a self-corrective feature that distinguishes it from change enterprises in which interventions remain ill-defined and their psychological effects are seldom objectively evaluated [p. v].

Bandura integrated the greatly expanded investigations derived from the influences of Skinner, Wolpe, and the British group and placed particular emphasis on the research on vicarious, symbolic, and self-regulatory processes.

Bandura devoted an entire chapter to the discussion of value issues in the modification of behavior. He argued for the *specification of goals* as the major value feature of behavior modification.

The selection of goals involves value choices. To the extent that people assume major responsibility for deciding the direction in which their behavior ought to be modified, the frequently voiced concerns about human manipulation become essentially pseudo

issues. The exchange agent's role in the decision process should be primarily to explore alternative courses of action available, and their probable consequences, on the basis of which clients can make informed choices. However, a change agent's value commitments will inevitably intrude to some degree on the goal selection process. These biases are not necessarily detrimental, provided clients and change agents subscribe to similar values and the change agent identifies his judgments as personal preferences rather than purported scientific prescriptions. Much more serious from an ethical standpoint is the unilateral redefinition of goals by which psychotherapists often impose insight objectives (which mainly involve subtle belief conversions) upon persons desiring changes in their behavioral functioning.

Behavioral problems of vast proportions can never be adequately eliminated on an individual basis but require treatment and prevention at the social systems level. As behavioral science makes further progress toward the development of efficacious principles of change, man's capacity to create the type of social environments he wants will be substantially increased. The decision processes by which cultural priorities are established must, therefore, be made more explicit to ensure that "social engineering" is utilized to produce living conditions that enrich life and behavioral freedom rather than aversive human effects. Control over value choices at the societal level can be increased by devising new systems of collective decision-making which enable members to participate more directly in the formulation of group objectives.

In discussions of the ethical implications of different modes of achieving personality changes, commentators often mistakenly ascribe a negative morality to behavioral approaches, as though this were inherent in the procedures. Social-learning theory is not a system of ethics; it is a system of scientific principles that can be successfully applied to the attainment of any moral outcome. In actuality, because of their relative efficacy, behavioral approaches hold much greater promise than traditional methods for the advancement of self-determination and the fulfillment of human capabilities. If applied toward the proper ends, social-learning methods can quite effectively support a humanistic morality [Bandura, 1969, p. 112].

These issues were also discussed by Kanfer (1965), who argued that the ethical dilemma of the then emerging behavior modification procedures consisted in

> justifying use of subtle influencing techniques in clinical procedures in the face of the popular assumption of the integrity, dignity and rights to freedom of the patient. The first step in the resolution of this dilemma is the recognition that a therapeutic effort *by necessity* influences the patient's value system as well as his specific symptoms. (P. 188)

The above statements clearly link the behavior of those identifying their professional efforts within behavior modification with a deep concern for the social and ethical implications of their work (see also Carrera & Adams, 1970; Lovibond, 1971; Stuart, 1973).

Currently, the growing concern on the part of both the professional and the public is "behavior mod for what?" *What* is desirable behavior on the part of a human being in a given set of circumstances and *who* is to decide? This has been the concern since the beginning of behavior modification. This issue involves philosophical, social, political, and religious values as to the meaning and purpose of scientific inquiry and of life itself. It just so happens that human beings have been debating, arguing, discussing, fighting, and even killing each other about such issues as far back as when man descended from the apes.

The only thing new at this point is that suddenly (or gradually, depending on how you perceive time) a group of individuals, self-identified as behaviorists, contend that they have the secret to changing, controlling, influencing, manipulating human behavior. The magic potion lies in our *learning theory* and the "techniques" that it has spawned. Fear, panic, concern, indignation —what if they are right and indeed human

behavior can be changed predictably and efficiently? We must then face the next, more awesome, and thus far never resolved issue of "What is good behavior?"

The fact that behavior modification presented a challenge to "society" because of its *avowed* effectiveness was but one factor in arousing the concern and discomfort that we have noted. A second factor lies in the subtle implications of the model that the behaviorists have been espousing. Under a "medical" or disease model, the role of the professional therapist is justified by the goal of *the restoration of health*. The ethical rationale of the therapist is to restore the individual to a hypothesized state of previous health, or "normality." Thus the therapist works within a clearly sanctioned societal role.

Health is defined as "the state of an organism with respect to functioning, disease, and abnormality at any given time. The state of an organism functioning normally without disease or abnormality. [*American Heritage Dictionary*, p. 607]." Health then implies an absence of abnormality.

This concept of health has usefulness and meaning insofar as body function is concerned. Restoration to physical health is clearly definable in terms of physiological measurements such as blood pressure, blood count, weight, X-ray, etc. It has little meaning in terms of human behavior.

The behavior modifier, on the other hand, to the extent that he eschews this model is faced with the problem of what social institution sanctions his role as a behavior changer. Who determines the goals and purposes of change? The behavior modifier should not continue to hide behind the myth of health restoration. But if the health-illness model with its justification of treatment procedures such as psychotherapy can no longer serve as an excuse, from what social institution should the behavior modifier seek his legitimacy? The answer to this question, which will become increasingly vexatious, may lie within the social institution of education. Before returning to this issue in the last section, some further issues of social consequences of professional behavior will be discussed.

VALUES AND EARLY TOKEN ECONOMY

Some personal experiences and observations are cited to illustrate the point that issues of values are implicitly and explicitly with us in our decisions as behavior modifiers. I was involved with the planning and carrying out of one of the early token economy programs in a mental hospital (Atthowe & Krasner, 1965). I had earlier visited Ted Ayllon and Nate Azrin at Anna State Hospital to view their program, the first such program in a mental hospital. What impressed me about the ward I visited, a tour of which was conducted in an exciting manner by a patient, was the way in which the staff related to or interacted with the patients and the way in which patients were relating to each other. The patients were viewed as human beings who were responsive to their environment. Influenced by what I had seen on this visit and by my own experiences as a participant-observer of hospital wards, I worked with Jack Atthowe in developing a program based on the same model at the VA Hospital in Palo Alto. The goal was the development of techniques to facilitate the likelihood of staff and patients behaving toward the individual patient as if he were a human being with rights and dignity (which he is). At that time, the kind of token economy developed by Ayllon and Azrin (1965) seemed most promising, and we adopted it with some variations.

In September 1963 a research program in behavior modification was begun which was intimately woven into the hospital's ongoing service and training programs. The objective was to create and maintain a systematic ward program within the ongoing social system of the hospital. The program reported here involves the life of the entire ward, patients, and staff, plus others who come in contact with the patients. The purpose of the program was to change the chronic patients' aberrant behavior, especially the behavior judged to be apathetic, overly dependent, detrimental, or annoying to others. The goal was to foster more responsible, active, and interested individuals who would be able to perform the routine activities associated with self-care, to make responsible decisions, and to delay immediate reinforcement in order to plan for the future [Atthowe & Krasner, 1965, p. 37].

Thus our goals involved value decisions as to what we would consider "good" behavior, with emphasis on fostering responsibility and activities. We felt that the most important way to do this was to *influence the training program of the staff*. The tokens served the purpose of assisting the staff in learning *how to observe* fellow human beings and learning *how to use their own behavior* to affect the patient in a positive manner.

In 1973, Wexler published a comprehensive critique of token economies insofar as they appeared to conflict with the emerging legal notion of the "rights of patients." Wexler was particularly critical of the apparent deprivation procedures utilized by Ayllon and Azrin and by ourselves in these early token programs. However, it must be noted that the notion of the importance of the value of "patients' rights" (e.g., to a bed, to food, to clothing, to respect from others) developed subsequent to these studies. In large part, this concern was a reflection of the larger social movements for people's rights (i.e., black, "third world," women). Both professional and lay people began to look upon the mental patient more as a *human being*, as a *victim*, as a *minority*, and less as a *sick* person. In effect, then, it was the development of behavior modification in general (and of token economies in mental hospitals specifically) that helped foster the movement for patients' rights by focusing on the question of what is appropriate behavior for any human being.

My own experience with token economies continued by developing a program involving systematic economic planning in a state hospital (Winkler & Krasner, 1971). One observation that Winkler and I made was that to the extent that we were successful in developing a token economy program on a hospital ward, we were helping maintain a social institution, the mental hospital, that in its current form, was no longer desirable in our society. We decided that based on our own value system, we would not develop further token economy programs in mental hospitals. We feel that value decisions, rightly or wrongly, have influenced our behavior as behavior modifiers, and this is true of all who are involved in behavior modification or, in fact, in any professional situation involving assistance to other people.

One area in which the ethical and value system of the professional may have important consequences on his work involves the collection of data in the systematic procedure called "research." The issues and problems insofar as behavior modification or token economy are concerned are similar to those in all other research on human behavior.

ON ETHICS IN RESEARCH

Stolz (1975) helps put the ethical issues of *research* in behavior modification and behavior therapy in broader context by drawing on data from review committees of the National Institute of Mental Health (NIMH). She poses a number of issues that are relevant for all research but that arose out of specific applications for research grants in some aspects of "behavior therapy."

First and foremost of these issues is the *definition of deviance.*

> Who decides that the client's behavior should be modified and in what direction it should be modified, is one general ethical issue. This decision can be made by society's representatives, teachers or policemen, by the researcher, or by the client or his agent. I mention this problem first to emphasize that

the most basic decision made by the behavior therapy researcher—which response to modify—involves a value judgement [p. 244].

A second issue involves the *justification of the intervention* and frequently is expressed (and criticized) on the basis of the proposal to "control the behavior of the child." "It seems to me that it is pertinent to ask who will benefit from the 'control' that results from the intervention."

"In some research studies in behavior therapy, investigators have been criticized for proposing to conduct the research without first obtaining the permission of the persons whose behavior is to be modified or that of the persons responsible for them [p. 6]." This is the issue of *informed consent,* which pervades almost all research with human beings. Various governmental agencies have developed guidelines for defining informed consent. Stolz interprets these guidelines, as applied to research in behavior therapy, to mean that

> the clients or their representatives should be told that the clients will be getting therapy; what the therapeutic procedures will involve; what problems might arise, if any; what the goal of the therapy is; and that the clients should be free to drop out the study at any time. Not mentioned in the guidelines, but in my opinion, essential whenever possible, is that the client should cooperate in specifying the way in which he wishes to be changed [p. 247].

The use of *unobtrusive measures* (measures taken of a subject's behavior without his awareness) does not simplify the problem since these in themselves create new and more complex ethical issues. Even in research terms it is clear that the very presence of an observer has an impact on the behavior being observed. (It is in recognition of this fact that we have become interested in developing and exploiting the social consequences of the role of "participant observer.")

The other issues that Stolz covers as they

relate to behavior therapy research studies are: *reversal designs*; the *treatment* of the *control group* (of particular concern with biofeedback studies utilizing subjects with serious physical diseases); *the use of new therapeutic procedures; unjustified risks* (e.g., using behavioral methods to develop socially inappropriate behavior); and the use of *aversive therapy procedures.*

The listing of these issues is of significance in that it should alert all investigators and therapists as to the complexities involved in ethical and value considerations. It should be again emphasized that the Stolz review was based on research grant applications written by individuals identifying their work within the behavior modification framework. We do not get an indication from the review as to the percentages of applications that cause concern. We would hope, however, that feedback to investigators such as in the Stolz report and other papers raising these issues will help minimize reasons for these concerns in subsequent studies.

Would there be greater protection for the rights of individuals and less concern if a systematic code of ethics were to be developed for investigators and practitioners of behavior modification?

CODE OF ETHICS

Is a code of ethics specific to the use of behavior modification possible, or even desirable? My own feeling here is that codes of ethics are highly necessary for the various professional disciplines but would be meaningless for "behavior modification" as such since we are stressing a philosophy and set of procedures that cut across a variety of disciplines but that should not be developed as a unique individual "discipline."

I would, however, advocate that the process of self-expression that has already begun in behavior modification be continued and enhanced by the process of developing general sets of ethical principles. More important than the publication or promulgation

of a set of guiding principles is the *process* of developing such principles. This involves an implicit agreement among those identifying themselves as belonging within this field to put ethical concerns in the foreground of their work. The process then includes discussion, contacts between investigators, suggestions from the consumers of behavior modification, be they clients, parents, children, teachers, or administrators, and feedback from students and from critics. In effect, we are arguing that there is no finished ultimate set of ethical principles but rather a process of change that should have input and participation from all involved.

New issues will arise; old ones will be seen in a different perspective. For example, the current concern with the deprivation of the rights of patients or prisoners in token economy programs grew out of, in part, the success of earlier programs in modifying behavior. The issue of "rights" developed because it is now clear that the clientele are human beings and not "abnormal" or "sick," and, as human beings, they have rights like anyone else. An ethical code developed in the early 1960s, if indeed the behavior modifiers would have seen the need for it at that point, would probably look very different than one developed currently. Conversely, a code developed 10 years from now will have to take into consideration items that none of us can now anticipate.

On the question of developing a basis for an ethical or value system, Goldiamond (1974) offers one of the most thoughtful and provocative suggestions. He argues that the Constitution of the United States should serve as a

> guide for a discussion of ethical and legal issues raised by applied behavior analysis. The arguments that will be developed are that its safeguards provide an excellent guide for program development of an effective application of behavior analysis to problems of social concern and that the violation of these rights can be counterproductive to the patient, to the aims of institutional agents whose incentives are therapeutic, and to the

therapeutic aim of the society which sponsors the patient-therapist (programmer, teacher, etc.) relation [p. 4].

Based on this strong civil libertarian and legal position, Goldiamond offers an orientation to the changing of behavior that he terms "constructional."

This is defined as an orientation whose solution to problems is the construction of repertoires (or their reinstatement or transfer to new situations) rather than the elimination of repertoires. Help is often sought because of the distress or suffering that certain repertoires, or their absence, entail. The prevalent approach at present focuses on the alleviation or the *elimination* of the distress through a variety of means which can include chemotherapy, psychotherapy, or behavior therapy. I shall designate these approaches as *pathologically* oriented (*pathos*, Greek, *suffering, feeling*). Such approaches often consider the problem in terms of a pathology which—regardless of how it was established, or developed, or is maintained—is to be eliminated. Presented with the same problem of distress and suffering, one can orient in a different direction. The focus here is on the production of desirables through means which *directly* increase available options or extend social repertoires, rather than *indirectly* doing so as a by-product of an eliminative procedure. Such approaches are *constructionally* oriented; they build repertoires [p. 14].

Goldiamond has thus expressed clearly and succinctly the major implication of the differences between the "disease" and the "behavioral" model. It is the crux of the difference in the value implications. It follows from this model that in Goldiamond's terms, "we can view the therapist not as a reinforcement machine, but as a program consultant, namely, a teacher or guide who tries to be explicit." As I will later state, the intent of the "social reinforcement machine" metaphor was to convey the role of the "teacher," and thus we are in agreement with this formulation.

The concept of "social contract" as the basis of value decisions can be combined with the concepts of "learning environments" (e.g., Ferster & Culbertson, 1974) to provide a set of procedures and a structure within which the individual can learn to formulate his own goals as related to his interests and to contract accordingly. The individual's options are increased by these procedures as are his spheres of responsibility. Goldiamond points out a link between these procedures and other operations of clinics: "The self-control procedures being developed in clinics using the same rationale also effectively increase options and spheres of responsibility of the patient." Much of this ethical philosophy is consistent with the rationale behind the development of behavior modification into the broader concept of "environmental design" (Krasner & Hutchison, 1974).

Despite the positive developments in the growing sensitivity to ethical and value implications, we cannot avoid consideration of potential and actual misuses of behavior modification.

The Misuse of Behavior Modification

One approach to the misuse of behavior modification would be to boldly state that the instances in which individual clients or patients have been abused or hurt or have had their rights violated represent a *misunderstanding* of behavior modification and hence are not really behavior modification at all. But many instances of misuse cannot be condoned as merely a misunderstanding.

A prototype example of the potential misuses or misunderstanding of behavior modification comes from a report by Cotter (1967) on the application of "operant conditioning" in a Vietnamese mental hospital. We have selected this particular paper to focus on because the broader ethical issues it raises are still current despite the fact that the study took place nearly a decade ago, in a distant land. Cotter, an American psychiatrist, had viewed a demonstration of operant conditioning by Lovaas, read some of Skinner's work, and had talked with ward personnel who were using operant conditioning.

With this training, Cotter then applied "operant conditioning" to patients on the chronic wards of a Vietnamese hospital, "most of whom were schizophrenics." The program took place on a ward of 130 male patients. The patients were asked, "Who wants to go home?" About 30 patients indicated their desire to do so. It was explained to these patients that they would have to work for 3 months to prove that they were capable of living outside the hospital. Ten of the patients indicated a willingness to work. The other 20 refused to work. These patients were given "120 unmodified electro-convulsive treatments (ECT)" that were given on a three-times-a-week schedule. Apparently most of the patients decided that work was preferable to ECT. "Our objective of motivating them to work was achieved."

These procedures were then taken to the women's ward in the same hospital. The women were expected to be more "pliable." Surprisingly, most of the women were still not working after 20 ECT treatments.

The next procedure used was to indicate to the women that if "you don't work, you don't eat." By the end of 3 days without food, all the patients volunteered for work. Cotter cited as justification for this kind of use of food as "positive reinforcement" the early work of Ayllon and Houghton (1962). Further justification was offered on the basis that not to use these procedures would result in greater damage than to use such apparently "cruel techniques." "Inflicting a little discomfort to provide motivation to move patients out of their zombie-like state of inactivity, apathy, and withdrawal was in our opinion well justified."

After this treatment procedure was successful and the patients were working regularly, the patients were paid one piastre (approximately one cent) for each day's work. With this money they could purchase articles in the patients' store. This program was extended to over 500 patients. In order to obtain funds to pay the piastre a day, Cotter had the patients begin manufacturing bows and arrows for the American soldiers as souvenirs. The next problem faced in this program was finding jobs outside the hospital for the discharged patients. An arrangement was made whereby patients were hired to work at growing crops at Green Beret camps. As to whether there was concern about ex-mental patients being under the stress of potential or actual Viet Cong attacks, Cotter felt that the experience of Londoners under wartime attack was analogous. "The stress of the danger from the bomb was more than neutralized by the enhanced feelings of worthwhileness. The good pay these expatients would receive plus the ego-expanding effects of being part of an elite with high esprit de corps should function as a fourth positive operant reinforcer."

Having completed the stint of duty in Vietnam and "impressed by the effectiveness of operant conditioning techniques for the motivation of difficult to activate patients" Cotter then visited mental hospitals in Asia and Europe and shared his experience with fellow psychiatrists. He concluded that operant conditioning is indicated for longterm patients. "The use of effective reinforcements should not be neglected due to a misguided idea of what constitutes kindness."

This study was cited extensively because of its importance in understanding the potential misuse of behavior modification. Not only does the distance of time and place allow for perspective, but also a number of the current concerns about behavior modification in prisons are about procedures that seem similar to those in the Cotter study. A major issue is whether the specific procedure described, the giving of shock to those who do not work, meets the technical requirements of using systematic environmental consequences contingent upon certain specified behaviors in carefully arranged schedules of reinforcement. My own impression is that it does not and that this study is not a "real" example of operant conditioning. In fact, Cotter's program, rather than being operant conditioning, clearly belongs within the rubric of "coercion" or "being controlled for *the explicit benefit of someone else* [Krasner & Ullmann, 1973, p. 416]."

Whether or not this particular study represents operant conditioning in a technical sense may be moot. But the issues the Cotter study stimulates are representative of many of the studies identified as behavior modification that are still with us. These issues include the lack of appropriate training by the planner of the program, a use of aversive and denigrating procedures, ignoring the "rights" of the patients to at least basic subsistence, and, most important of all, the "bad" social consequences of the changed behavior. It is this last that is of greatest concern. My own bias is that coercing patients to work in a field to support a war effort is "bad" behavior. Clearly, at the time of the study the investigator Cotter felt that this was "good" behavior. Thus from one biased observer, the patients were abused not only by the denigrating procedures but by being led without their consent to behaviors that were socially undesirable, whereas from another biased observer *in a position of power,* the outcome behavior was of benefit to the patients and to society.

Is my value system (or yours) better than Cotter's? By what behavioral decision does my value system (or yours) take precedence over anyone else's? Of course we are evoking the old dispute of "Who controls the controllers?" That this is a point of discussion in a set of circumstances such as described in the Cotter paper would seem to be quite clear. But the issue is the same albeit subtler in virtually every behavior modification study in institutional settings such as the schoolroom, the hospital, the prison, and the home. (Winett and Winkler, 1973, discuss these issues as they relate to the classroom.) The present author's contention is that the abusers of behavior modification are those who utilize the behavior-influence process for the "good of others" without involving those concerned, be they "sick," "retarded," or "too young," in the decision-making process.

A related issue of abuse involves the question of deprivation (Schaefer, 1968). It has been one of the clearest observations of human behavior that when an individual is deprived of a basic need such as water, shelter, air, he becomes highly "motivated" to do the things that will increase the likelihood of obtaining that that he has been deprived of. This was not a discovery unique to the first token economy. Like everything else, the issue of deprivation is highly complex.

A change in the model by which individual behavior is conceptualized is not a panacea. Yet an important element in avoiding subsequent abuses is to reconceptualize the individuals dealt with by professional helpers, from passive "patients" who must be protected "for their own good," to active human beings whose major "right" is to participate in the decision-making processes that influence their lives.

The Use and Misuse of Terminology

One area in which even behavior modifiers have great difficulty is language and terminology. Word usage has consequences, and, not infrequently, the consequences are aversive. We have seen earlier how the term "behavior modification" was born, developed, and may soon die because of misunderstanding and misuse by both its protagonists and its opponents. At this point we would like to develop a new slogan term. We have found ourselves utilizing the term "environmental design" more frequently. In this instance the term is not intended to be synonymous with behavior modification but rather represents an extension of behavior modification that we will discuss in a later section.

As another example, Skinner's use of the phrasing "beyond freedom and dignity" as a book title has had aversive impact, both among professionals and the general public. People have reacted to the title in many instances without having read the book and have cited the title as an illustration of the antihumanism of the behavior modifiers, particularly those influenced by Skinner.

My own experience of having to live with the consequences of a title goes back to a paper presented at the Second Conference of Research in Psychotherapy (Krasner, 1962a). This conference took place in 1962 in the ancient days of the behavior modification movement. The paper represented one of the first presentations of a social learning–behavioral viewpoint at a "psychotherapy" conference. To be dramatic and to emphasize the difference in viewpoint and model from traditional psychotherapy, I entitled the paper, "The Therapist as a Social Reinforcement Machine." In the paper, I very carefully qualified what was meant by the word "machine," but that did not undo the reaction to the title. In fact, in a number of subsequent critiques of behavior therapy, the title was cited as illustrating the mechanical nature and inhumanity of the behavioral position. Thus some of the points of the paper were misunderstood because of the sloganomic nature of the title. In retrospect, a title such as "The Therapist as a Warm, Humane, and Loving Social Reinforcer" would have been preferable and no less inaccurate than the original title. All of this points to the need for a much greater awareness and concern on the part of behavior therapists as to the social consequences of their theories and their slogans.

Concerns and critiques of behavior modification are linked conceptually (in both popular and professional views) with the broader field of behavior "control" (Begelman, 1971; Halleck, 1974). The latter term has generally encompassed a wide variety of pharmacological and surgical procedures as well as "psychological" procedures. In an early (1950) symposium at Berkeley on the "control of the mind," the emphasis was on the impact of the then developing array of new drugs including tranquilizers. London's (1969) book did much to facilitate the linkage of the behavior modification procedures of the period with the coercive drug and surgical procedures under the general rubric of "behavior control." Skinner has contributed to the terminological confusion by his insistence on continuing to use "control" to describe situations that could just as easily be given milder and less "flag waving" terms such as "influence."

PSYCHOSURGERY

The controversy about the use of psychosurgery warrants mention in this chapter primarily because of the continuing confusion of terminology. Brown, Wienckowski, and Bivens (1973) placed their discussion of psychosurgery within the context of "the control of human behavior." The November 1973 issue of *Civil Liberties* (the ACLU newspaper) had an article on behavior modification that included material on psychosurgery.

> "Behavior modification" has taken several forms. At the one extreme it is an almost purely medical model. Their methods are totally different, but they are based on the same false premise: that there is a short-cut to dealing with social, political, and psychological problems. By dealing directly and only with behavior, they begin at the end. . . . At the other end of the spectrum of behavior modification techniques is psychosurgery [p. 4–4].

This and similar categorizations of psychosurgery within the behavior modification category are disturbing and misleading and demonstrate a lack of understanding of both the behavioral and the medical approach. But, unfortunately, this linkage is becoming institutionalized. For example, in

February 1973, a Senate Subcommittee on Health, chaired by Senator Kennedy, met to look into biomedical research, with particular emphasis on psychosurgery. Among the witnesses on the first day of the hearing was a group of investigators including Peter Breggin, a physician on a virtual crusade against psychosurgery, Dr. Orlando Andy, a proponent of psychosurgery, and Dr. B. F. Skinner. Although his presentation stressed positive rather than aversive procedures, the very fact of Skinner's appearance before a congressional committee studying psychosurgery demonstrated the linkage between behavior modification and psychosurgery—even among sophisticated laymen.

Another example of this kind of misinterpretation of behavior modification through linkage with surgical and chemical procedures comes from an article written in a popular magazine, *Harpers.*

The most blatant behavior modification procedures—and technologically the most sophisticated—involve direct physical or chemical intervention into central nervous system functions. . . . The structure of the brain is becoming more understandable and transmitters the size of quarters can be inserted into the brain to pattern in or out "desirable" or "undesirable" behavior. This year's anxieties centered on psychosurgery, and while people may not know how the difference between a cingulectomy and a thalomotomy, they know enough to be frightened by both.

While conditioning is a less dramatic form of behavior modification than, for example, psychosurgery, it should concern us no less, especially when the federal government is preparing programs along Skinnerian lines [Gaylin, 1973, p. 48].

It should be noted that many of the individual writers we have been citing in the linkage of procedures "should know better." That is, if sophisticated professional investigators are unable to, and do not desire to, discriminate "Skinnerian" behavior modification, as we have conceived of it

thus far in this chapter, from surgical and chemical procedures, then there has been a failure to communicate on the part of behavior modifiers or distortion by these writers for whatever reasons of their own, or both.

The ethical issues involved in the control of psychosurgery illustrates the problem involved in the social control of other dangerous medical procedures (Schwitzgebel, 1970; Schwitzgebel, 1970). One approach is to urge the complete banning of psychosurgery by legal or any other means possible, such as breaking up meetings by the threat of violence, or labeling the investigator as "fascist," "racist," or whatever. We have had far too many illustrations of the use of coercive procedures (against behavior modification and in other situations in which professionals have expressed unpopular views) to in any way advocate such procedures. Opponents of psychosurgery should work not to make it an illegal procedure, which wouldn't work, but to influence the proponents of the model. The argument against lobotomy is that lobotomy is a manifestation or "symptom" of an outmoded model that simply has not been of assistance for the betterment of the individual patient receiving it and, in fact, may do irreversible damage. It is the conceptual model that links certain forms of aberrant behavior with functions of specific loci of the brain that is at fault. If there is strong evidence that demonstrates the direct relationship between the individual's behavior (e.g., epileptoid outbursts) with a specific malfunction in the neuroanatomy of that individual, then we see no reason to avoid a surgical procedure just because it is a surgical procedure. Just what constitutes "strong evidence" of such a relationship and who decides can be approached in the same way as other clearly medical problems. The impression one gets from reading the psychosurgery literature, however, is that *most* instances of psychosurgery probably do not fall into the strictly medical category.

In this section we have discussed some of

the negative aspects of terminology both within behavior modification and in areas tangential to it. We now turn to more positive terminology.

Behavior Modification and "Good" Slogans

ON HUMANISM

One of the major myths that has obfuscated the behavior modification–ethics issue is that behaviorism and humanism are antithetical. Both words have become slogans in a game of choose-up-sides, with good and bad meanings attached to both depending on one's predilections (e.g., behaviorist—scientific, mechanical; humanist—warm, kookie).

As Thoresen (1973) points out, "definitions of what constitutes humanism are as diverse as the individuals offering the definitions. Interestingly, many contemporary 'behaviorists,' i.e., behavior therapists, behavioral counselors, and operant psychologists or social learning psychologists, consider themselves humanists [p. 386]." The particular behaviorists described by Thoresen as self-considered humanists are Day, Hosford, Kanfer, Phillips, Lazarus, MacCorquodale, Skinner, Staats, Thoresen, Mahoney, Ullmann, and Krasner. (Many other self-identified behaviorists could be added to this list as self-confessed humanists.)

> Several reasons explain why behavior-oriented professionals see themselves this way. First of all, they focus on what the individual person *does* in the present life and not on who he *is* in terms of vague social labels or obscure descriptions. Secondly, they emphasize human problems as primarily learning situations where the person is seen as capable of changing. Thirdly, they examine how environments can be altered to reduce and prevent human problems, and, finally they use scientific procedures to improve techniques for helping individuals [Thoresen, 1973, p. 387].

Thoresen is using as the above definition of a humanist the criteria offered by Kurtz (1969). Clearly not all self-proclaimed humanists would accept these criteria. However, it is difficult enough to resolve definitions of behaviorism without tackling an even more controversial concept of humanism (Scriven, 1973).

That there is a distinction between behaviorists and humanists is arbitrary and artificially maintained by believers in labels and organizations and by those who receive their reinforcements for writing profound "anti the other side" papers (Hosford & Zimmer, 1972; Smith, 1973).

One final point about the artificiality of behaviorist-humanist dichotomy is that both sides contain a wide range of diversity of views and beliefs. Reviews of the behaviorist position (Bandura, 1969; Krasner, 1971) emphasize the range of diversity among behaviorists. The similar situation among humanists is typified by an incident that occurred when this writer was having dinner with a leading "humanist" after both had participated in an early (and unwise) behaviorist-versus-humanist panel. The humanist said words to the effect that, "I may have some difficulty in communicating with behaviorists like you, but that is nothing compared with the problems I have with the kooks who are supposedly on my side!"

ON FREEDOM

We cannot avoid a discussion of the concept of freedom as it relates to a goal of behavior modification. A term such as freedom has evoked controversy since man has been able to use words to express his thoughts and feelings. One expression of freedom and its relationship to social planners has been offered by Gardner Murphy (1958), one of the most influential and exciting psychologists of our generation:

> Another answer to the question about planning: Are planners such as ourselves trying to take away the free decision of future generations? My feeling is that man today is

very far from free and that it will take him a very long time to become free. Man is unfree not only because of his imperfect biological nature and the conflict between impulses and judgment but even more because of his cultural nature and, above all, by virtue of the blind assumptions he makes about his own limitations, especially his assumption that he can find no freedom essentially greater than that which he envies in the man nearby who has a little more freedom than he. . . . Freedom, in the sense of autonomy from social control, the sense that one's life is one's own, without any impairment of the power of individual decision (provided only that no damage is done to others), is an idea which has been with us only a few centuries, and with us more as an ideal than as a consummated reality. . . . we may be buying such freedom as we have in a market in which we are bargain-conscious, making the most of those precious freedoms which are genuinely ours and inclined to belittle or deny the vast and coercive restrictions on freedom of act and of thought which still prevail. . . . The question of freedom to choose is fundamental in all our thinking about the future. How can we speak of choices among future possibilities unless we define the kinds and degrees of freedom the individual or the race possesses [Murphy, 1958, pp. 277–289]?

Skinner (1971) approaches freedom as follows:

Two features of autonomous man are particularly troublesome. In the traditional view, a person is free. He is autonomous in the sense that his behavior is uncaused. He can therefore be held responsible for what he does and justly punished if he offends. We must reexamine the view together with its associated practices, when a scientific analysis reveals unsuspected controlling relations between behavior and the environment (p. 19–20).

In another section, Skinner expresses his view of freedom as involving the avoiding of aversive stimuli:

Man's struggle for freedom is not due to the will to be free, but to certain behavioral processes characteristic of the human organism, the chief effect of which is the avoidance of

or escape from so-called "aversive" features of the environment. Physical and biological technologies have been mainly concerned with natural aversive stimuli; the struggle for freedom is concerned with stimuli intentionally arranged by other people. The literature of freedom has identified the other people and has proposed ways of escaping from them or weakening or destroying their power. It has been successful in reducing the aversive stimuli used in intentional control, but it has made the mistake of defining freedom in terms of states of mind or feelings, and it has therefore not been able to deal effectively with techniques of control which do not breed escape or revolt but nevertheless have aversive consequences. It has been forced to brand all control as wrong and to misrepresent many of the advantages to be gained from a social environment. It is unprepared for the next step, which is not to free men from control but to analyze and change the kinds of control to which they are exposed [pp. 42–43].

Krasner (1968), using token economy as an illustration, has argued that planning and individual choice are not antithetical:

Token economy programs are far from deterministic or mechanistic. Systematization does not mean mechanization. In fact the major element in these programs is flexibility. Unless the program continually changes by incorporating new behaviors, changing values, and bringing in new "good things," it becomes as static as any traditional program. When a token program begins it is impossible to predict contingencies that may be available within a year. This is perhaps the most valid criticism against Utopias which try to offer solutions on an eternal basis. Even Walden Two represents a fixed society in which all human problems have been worked out. Change itself must be programmed into the design. The goal of the program is for an individual to be enabled to make choices in his life. If he has more than one behavior in his repertoire, an individual is obviously freer than if he has no alternatives [p. 170].

Patients may be reinforced, i.e., paid tokens for revising the token economy, for solving new problems for themselves, because this is what they must do for themselves when they are released from the hospital. There is every reason to make independence, creativity, and decision making reinforced behaviors (Lefcourt, 1973; Nolan, 1974).

This second aspect of freedom, that of having choice available, does not mean that free will, in the sense of an autonomous inner person, is free of outside influence directing the individual's behavior. It does mean we are comfortable with a concept of man that relies upon the availability of acceptable alternative learned behaviors as the major element in freedom. The saving grace of viewing man's behavior in the context of behavior influence is that influence or control is never absolute. At best, the converging of influences on man makes one behavior or another more likely to occur. There is a paradox when we say that despite the multitude of influences upon him, man is able to make decisions and select which one of a number of alternative behaviors is most likely to lead to positive consequences for himself. Man is influenced; man influences his environment. Can we have our proverbial cake and eat it too? The *belief* that man does have choice is necessary to increase the likelihood of man's being able to choose. If we believe this as parents, teachers, and therapists, we will design programs to make possible such behaviors on the part of our students.

ON OPENNESS

One of the major attractions of behavior modification is that by its very nature, the therapist or researcher can be "open" and honest with his client or subject. Associating openness with behavior modification may seem incongruous to both critics and proponents alike. To paraphrase one of the slogans of our time, the issue of the relationship between influencer and influencee can be summarized by saying "What is he (the subject) to know and when is he to know it?" Can the behavior modifier afford to

answer, "Everything that I know and as soon as possible?" Our view is that this answer has to be "yes" and that helping the individual become "aware" of the contingencies affecting his behavior is an integral part of the process of influencing behavior and, in fact, enhances the process.

Menges (1973) reviewed 1,000 studies published in APA journals on the dimension of "openness and honesty versus coercion and deception" in research. He concluded that: there was great difficulty in ensuring voluntary informed consent (over 60% of the subjects participated under some kind of external requirements); chances were about one in five that a study involved a deception condition: chances for debriefing after a deception experiment were about one in two and considerably less after other experiments; these findings were consistent with those reported in other studies of the same kinds of materials. The author found no evidence to indicate that the use of nonvolunteer subjects or the use of deception will decline, even though coercion and deception seem incompatible with the call for "openness and honesty" by APA (1973) as the essential relationship between the investigator and the research participant.

Thus a considerable number of psychological studies depend upon some elements of deception. Can we document that behavior modification does not, and that it can and should be "open"? That becomes an urgent task for the behavior modification investigator as well as an expression of values. Openness and honesty are valued, or good, behavior. They are also very influencing behaviors and are highly likely to enhance the role of the environmental designer.

ON ACCEPTABILITY

One of the most important distinctions that has to be made among behavior modifiers is between effectiveness and acceptability. The fact that a particular procedure may be effective in influencing a behavior does not necessarily mean that the procedure should be used. The name of the game is not change per se; rather it is change that has a good purpose (Ulrich, 1967). Risley and Twardosz (1974) make this key point in offering proposals for guidelines for the humane management of the behavior problems of the retarded. The investigators point out that there have been a number of procedures derived from operant principles that have been empirically demonstrated to reduce or eliminate a wide range of behavior problems in numerous populations and settings. These procedures include extinction, response cost, overcorrection, and the use of painful stimuli.

> When procedures for dealing with behavior problems are recommended for use in public settings such as institutions for the retarded, more than their effectiveness is at issue. The procedures must be acceptable to the general public. They must be able to be described in terms of common experiences and common practice. They must sound familiar and allow people to feel comfortable about their use. Furthermore, institutional staff must be able to understand and describe what they do and the resulting benefits to the residents so they can convey this information to the general public in a way which will avoid misunderstanding.
>
> Effectiveness and acceptability are not necessarily correlated. Time-out in a bare, locked closet, and electric shock, for example, are effective but rarely publicly acceptable. People cannot relate them to their own experiences or familiar methods of child-rearing and may confuse them with child abuse.

However, there are situations in certain areas, particularly in institutions for retardates, in which all procedures involving positive, educational techniques do not work (Ross, 1972). There are situations in which residents in institutions for retardates are so dangerous to themselves in terms of self-mutilation or aggressiveness to others that they are usually kept under heavy sedation, in physical restraints, and in isolated and locked rooms. In such instances,

the behavior modifiers are apt to point out that applications of aversive procedures (Azrin & Holz, 1966) such as electric shock are effective in eliminating the undesirable behavior (Bucher, 1969).

Risley and Twardosz point out that since aversive procedures are effective but unacceptable, a different set of guidelines must be established for their usage:

> Guidelines for the use of painful stimulation include the establishment of a department and treatment unit within an institution for its administration; the staffing of that department by a team of therapists supervised by an individual trained and recommended by an expert in the use of painful stimulation; and the provision that the use of painful stimulation outside of the treatment unit should only be a member of that treatment team, and that its use be thoroughly rationalized to other institutional staff. The department should be closely monitored by a public committee heavily composed of representatives of community organizations and parents of the retarded, who would consult on the admission of residents for treatment, and who would periodically observe the procedures and be able to interpret them to the concerned public [p. 6].

On the Future

Making calculated guesses about the future of any field, as with the prediction of any human behavior, is at best a risky and fun business. The prediction of the behavior of behavior modifiers is especially foolhardy. The following represents developments that are happening or should be happening (and are value laden):

We should continue to move more sharply away from a disease-oriented psychopathological model of man, with its emphasis on treatment, remediation, and adjustment, to a social learning-educational model with its emphasis on designing environments so that individuals can have impact upon the social and economic influences on their behavior.

We should continue the process of training a great variety and number of people (teachers, psychologists, nonprofessionals, parents, children, nurses, etc.) in environmental design principles and in the implicit value system that accompanies them.

We should continue research involving functional analyses of social systems such as the schoolroom, the hospital ward, the prison, the university, and the home.

We should continue to link conceptually in research and in applications to those investigators within economics, sociology, political science, education, law, and architecture, fields that also involve systematic observation of the impact of environmental influences on human behavior. It would be desirable to be less involved in links with conceptual models that are antithetical to the social learning model (Levis, 1970; Lovaas, 1971; London, 1972). Let each model push to the limits its own applications. Kuhn's (1970) view of the function of alternative paradigms in science is useful in that it puts in perspective the possibility of living comfortably with and with some respect for other models.

Professional behavior modifiers will continue involvement in social and political and other community organizations as well as in professional organizations. They will continue the process of involving many people in developing a better society. We are increasingly aware that there are no easy answers or cookbooks.

The collection of research data on human behavior will continue, but efforts will be concentrated on the observation of behavior in "natural" settings.

Serious consideration should continue to be given to the greater involvement of all individuals concerned with specific remediational situations in the decision making as to target behaviors and techniques to be utilized. The sharp demarcation between the therapist as giver of "medication" and the patient as passive recipient of what is "good for him" (the trademark of the disease model) is fast fading. Many ethical issues such as informed consent or the use of aversive procedures may be resolved to some extent by the greater involvement and awareness of significant figures in decision making.

A major point that derives from the social learning model is that the goal of helping individuals is to enable them to learn how to control, influence, or design their own environment. Implicit in this is a value judgment that individual freedom is a desirable goal and that the more an individual is able to affect his environment, the greater is his freedom. It should be clear that what we mean by "environment" is both the people and physical objects in one's life.

In dealing with people, we are involved in an influence process that is ubiquitous, not a process of curing or helping unfortunates. With this model, everyone is involved in designing environments: the individual who seeks help, the therapist, the researcher, the school teacher, the parent, the student, the warden, the ward chief, the architect. The question of how to train the experimental designer could be interpreted to mean "how to train people to live in our society." The reader can and should contribute to this process by asking, "What kind of a world do I want to live in, and what can I do to help move society (by influencing the behavior of individuals in my environment) at least a bit in that direction?"

If there is any one point we wish to emphasize in this chapter, it is that behavior modification is not a fixed entity but rather an historical process operationalized in the behavior of individual investigators. There is in process a resurgence of concern about ethical issues, the definition of the limits of "behavior modification," and the future of this approach. There are a number of national and regional meetings scheduled, avid preparations for these meetings, activity on the part of various professional organizations involved, and other activities —all related to the topic of this chapter. If we are correct in taking an historical and philosophical approach to behavior modification, then we are dealing with a phenomenon that is *in process*. As such, there is no ending but an ongoing stream of development.

Some years ago the author concluded a review of the status of the behavior modification field with the following epilogue:

The decade of the 1960s covered the childhood and adolescence of behavior therapy (its birth was in the 1950s). The 1970s should see its development into adulthood and perhaps even maturity. Ahead will almost certainly lie old age and senility in the 1980s, but by that time it will have given birth to a newer and at this point (at least by this observer) unpredictable paradigm [Krasner, 1971, p. 519].

At this point, about 5 years later, "traditional behavior modification" is indeed merging into a broader conceptualization of human behavior with exciting potentialities. Indeed, we are at the beginning.

References

ATTHOWE, J. M., Jr., & KRASNER, L. A preliminary report on the application of contingent reinforcement procedures (token economy) on a "chronic" psychiatric ward. *Journal of Abnormal Psychology*, 1968, **73**, 37–43.

AYLLON, T., & AZRIN, N. H. The measurement and reinforcement of behavior of psychotics. *Journal of the Experimental Analysis of Behavior*, 1965, **8**, 357–383.

AYLLON, T., & HAUGHTON, E. Control of the behavior of schizophrenic patients by food. *Journal of the Experimental Analysis of Behavior*, 1962, **5**, 343–352.

AZRIN, N. H., & HOLZ, W. C. Punishment. In W. K. Honig (Ed.), *Operant behavior*. New York: Appleton-Century-Crofts, 1966, pp. 380–447.

BACHRACH, A. J. (Ed.) *Experimental foundations of clinical psychology*. New York: Basic Books, 1962.

BANDURA, A. *Principles in behavior modification*. New York: Holt, Rinehart & Winston, 1969.

BARRISH, I. J. Ethical issues and answers to behavior modification. *Corrective and Social Psychiatry and Journal of Applied Behavior Therapy*, 1974, **20**, 30–37.

BARTZ, W. R. While psychologists doze on. *American Psychologist*, 1970, **25**, 500–503.

BEGELMAN, D. A. The ethics of behavioral control and a new mythology. *Psychotherapy: Theory, Research and Practice*, 1971, **8**, 165–169.

BEGELMAN, D. A. Ethical issues in behavioral control. *Journal of Nervous and Mental Disease*, 1973, **156**, 412–419.

BRAGG, R. A., & WAGNER, M. K. Can deprivation be justified? *Hospital and Community Psychiatry*, 1968, **19**, 229–230.

BROWN, B. S., WIENCKOWSKI, L. A., & BIVENS, L. W. Psychosurgery: Perspective on a current issue. Technical Report No. 73-9119. Baltimore Md.: National Institutes of Mental Health, 1973.

BUCHER, B. Some ethical issues in the therapeutic use of punishment. In R. D. Rubin & C. M. Franks (Eds.), *Advances in behavior therapy*. New York: Academic Press, 1969, pp. 59–72.

CARRERA, F., & ADAMS, P. L. An ethical perspective on operant conditioning. *Journal of the American Academy of Child Psychiatry*, 1970, **9**, 607–623.

COTTER, L. H. Operant conditioning in a Vietnamese mental hospital. *American Journal of Psychiatry*, 1967, **124**, 23–28.

FERSTER, C., & CULBERTSON, S. A psychology learning center. *The Psychological Record*, 1974, **24**, 33–46.

GAYLON, W. Skinner redux. In *Harper's Magazine*, October 1973, 48–56.

GOLDIAMOND, I. Toward a constitutional approach to social problems: Ethical and constitutional issues raised by applied behavior analysis. *Behaviorism*, 1974, **2**, 1–79.

HALLECK, S. L. Legal and ethical aspects of behavior control. *The American Journal of Psychiatry*, 1974, **131**, 381–385.

HOSFORD, R. E., & ZIMMER, J. M. Humanism through behaviorism. *Counseling and Values*, 1972, **16**, 162–168.

KANFER, F. H. Issues and ethics in behavior manipulation. *Psychological Reports*, 1965, **16**, 187–196.

KRASNER, L. The therapist as a social reinforcement machine. In H. H. Strupp & L. Luborsky (Eds.), *Research in psychotherapy*. Vol. 2. Washington, D.C.: American Psychological Association, 1962. (a)

KRASNER, L. Behavior control and social responsibility. *American Psychologist*, 1962, **17**, 199–204. (b)

KRASNER, L. The behavioral scientist and social responsibility: No place to hide. *Journal of social issues*, 1965, **21**, 9–30.

KRASNER, L. Assessment of token economy programmes in psychiatric hospitals. In R. Porter (Ed.), *Learning theory and psychotherapy*. London: Churchill, 1968.

KRASNER, L. Behavior therapy. In P. H. Mussen (Ed.), *Annual review of psychology*. Vol. 22. Palo Alto: Annual Reviews, 1971, pp. 483–532.

KRASNER, L., & HUTCHISON, W. Helping people change by designing environments. Unpublished manuscript, Environmental Design Center, Stony Brook, N.Y., 1974.

KRASNER, L., & ULLMANN, L. P. (Eds.) *Research in behavior modification*. New York: Holt, Rinehart & Winston, 1965.

KRASNER, L., & ULLMANN, L. P. *Behavior influence and personality: The social matrix of human action*. New York: Holt, Rinehart & Winston, 1973.

KRAUSE, M. S. Use of social situations for research purposes. *American Psychologist*, 1970, **25**, 748–753.

KUHN, T. S. *The structure of scientific revolutions* (2nd ed.). Chicago: University of Chicago Press, 1970.

KURTZ, P. "What is humanism?" In P. Kurtz (Ed.), *Moral problems in contemporary society*. Englewood Cliffs, N.J.: Prentice-Hall, 1969.

LEFCOURT, H. The function of the illusions of control and freedom. *American Psychologist*, 1973, **28**, 417–425.

LEVIS, D. J. Integration of behavior therapy and dynamic psychiatric techniques: A marriage with a high probability of ending in divorce. *Behavior Therapy*, 1970, **1**, 531–537.

LINDSEY, B., & CUNNINGHAM, J. Behavior modification: Some doubts and dangers. *Phi Delta Kappan*, 1973, 54, 596–597.

LONDON, P. *Behavior control*. New York: Harper, 1969.

LONDON, P. The end of ideology in behavior modification. *American Psychologist*, 1972, **27**, 913–920.

LOVAAS, O. I. Certain comparisons between psychodynamic and behavioristic approaches to treatment. *Psychotherapy: Theory, Research and Practice*, 1971, **8**, 175–178.

LOVIBOND, S. H. The ethics of behaviour modification. *Australian Psychologist*, 1971, **6**, 172–180.

LUCERO, R. J., VAIL, D. J., & SCHERBER, J. Regulating operant conditioning program. *Hospital and Community Psychiatry*, 1968, **19**, 53–54.

MADSEN, C. Values versus techniques: An analysis of behavior modification. *Phi Delta Kappan*, 1973, **54**, 598.

MENGES, R. J. Openness and honesty versus coercion and deception in psychological research. *American Psychologist*, 1973, **28**, 1030–1034.

MIRON, N. B. The primary ethical consideration. *Hospital and Community Psychiatry*, 1968, **19**, 226–228.

MURPHY, G. *Human potentialities*. New York: Basic Books, 1958.

NOLAN, J. D. Freedom and dignity: A "functional" analysis. *American Psychologist*, 1974, **29**, 157–160.

RISLEY, T. R., & TWARDOSZ, S. Suggesting guidelines for the humane management of the behavior problems of the retarded. Unpublished manuscript, Johnny Cake Child Study Center, January 1974.

ROOS, P. Mentally retarded citizens: Challenge for the 1970's. *Syracuse Law Review*, 1972, **23**, 1059–1074.

SCHAEFER, H. H. The ethics of deprivation. In R. D. Rubin & C. M. Franks (Eds.), *Advances in behaviour therapy*. New York: Academic Press, 1968.

SCRIVEN, M. The philosophy of behavioral modification. *The yearbook of the National Society for the Study of Education*, 1973, **72**, 422–445.

SCHWITZGEBEL, R. L. Ethical and legal aspects of behavioral instrumentation. *Behavior Therapy*, 1970, **1**, 498–509.

SCHWITZGEBEL, R. L. Behavior instrumentation and social technology. *American Psychologist*, 1970, **25**, 491–499.

SKINNER, B. F. *Walden two*. New York: Macmillan, 1948.

Skinner, B. F. *Beyond freedom and dignity.* New York: Knopf, 1971.

Smith, A. B. Humanism and behavior modification: Is there a conflict? *Elementary School Journal,* 1973, **74,** 59–67.

Stolz, S. B. Ethical issues in research on behavior therapy. In W. S. Wood (Ed.), *Evaluating behavior modification.* Champaign, Ill.: Research Press, 1975.

Stuart, R. B. Notes on the ethics of behavior research and intervention. In L. A. Hamerlynck, L. C. Handy, & E. J. Mash (Eds.), *Behavioral change: Methodology, concepts, and practice.* Champaign, Ill.: Research Press, 1973.

Thoresen, C. W. Behavioral humanism. In C. E. Thoresen (Ed.), *Behavior modification in education.* The 72nd Yearbook of the National Society for the Study of Education. Chicago: University of Chicago Press, 1973, pp. 385–421.

Ullmann, L. P. Behavior therapy as social movement. In C. M. Franks (Ed.), *Behavior therapy: Appraisal and status.* New York: McGraw-Hill, 1969, pp. 495–523.

Ullmann, L. P., & Krasner, L. (Eds.) *Case studies in behavior modification.* New York: Holt, Rinehart & Winston, 1965.

Ulrich, R. Behavior control and public concern. *Psychological Record,* 1967, **17,** 229–234.

Walker, E. L. Experimental psychology and social responsibility. *American Psychologist,* 1969, **23,** 862–868.

Wexler, D. B. Token and taboo: Behavior modification, token economies, and the law. *California Law Review,* 1973, **61,** 81–109.

Watson, R. I. The experimental tradition and clinical psychology. In A. J. Bachrach (Ed.), *Experimental foundations of clinical psychology.* New York: Basic Books, 1962.

Winett, R. A., & Winkler, R. C. Current behavior modification in the classroom: Be still, be quiet, be docile. *Journal of Applied Behavior Analysis,* 1972, **5,** 499–504.

Winkler, R. C., & Krasner, L. The contribution of economics to token economies. Paper presented at the meeting of the Eastern Psychological Association, New York: April 15, 1971.

Author Index

Subject Index